eurock
European Rock & the Second Culture

Archie Patterson

Eurock Publications
Portland, Oregon

First Edition, October 2002
Copyright © 2002 Archie Patterson,
DBA Eurock Record Company
Except "Amon Düül: A Science-Fiction Rock Spectacle"
Copyright © 1971 Lester Bangs
Used with permission of the Lester Bangs Estate.
All rights reserved under International and
Pan-American Copyright Conventions.

Most of these articles previously appeared in
Eurock Magazine © 1973, 1974, 1975, 1976, 1977,
1978, 1979, 1980, 1981, 1982, 1983, 1984, 1985, 1986,
1987, 1988, 1989, 1990, 1991, 1992, 1993, 2000 and 2002.
Reprinted by permission of the authors.

All rights reserved. No part of this publication may be
reproduced, stored in a retrieval system, or transmitted
in any form or by any means, electronic, mechanical,
photocopying, recording, or otherwise, without
prior permission of the publisher.

For information:
EUROCK, P.O. Box 13718,
Portland, OR 97213, U.S.A.
http://www.eurock.com

Library of Congress Cataloging-in-Publication data:
Patterson, Archie
Eurock: European Rock & the Second Culture
    1. Music
  2. Music – History & Criticism
      3. Music – Rock
    4. Music – Progressive
    5. Music -- Electronic

ISBN: 0-9723098-0-2

Printed in the United States of America

Contents

Foreword..i

Lester Bangs: Amon Düül..........................1

Raised On Records................................8

Eurock Magazine

1973..17
1974..37
1975..59
1976..79
1977..109
1978..153
1979..209
1980..243
1981..291
1982..365
1983..385
1984..399
1985..417
1986..441
1987..447
1988..473
1989..489
1990..497
1991..507
1992..511
1993..513
2000..521
2002..595

Appendix..687

Index..689

Credits..707

Foreword

EUROCK Magazine documents a particular time in the world when the limits of imagination and what was possible sonically were stretched beyond the norm. The futuristic alchemy of free-flowing ions, mind-expanding chemical substances and mega-watts of electricity resulted in an explosion of creativity unparalleled in the history of rock music.

This book contains virtually every major piece written for EUROCK Magazine during its lifetime 1973–1990. Also included here are several newer pieces done in the ensuing years up to 2002. We begin, however, with a previously unpublished 1971 article by the late Lester Bangs, former editor of *Creem* magazine and godfather of gonzo rock criticism. Lester is considered by many to be America's most original rock writer. The spirit of Lester's piece perfectly serves as an introduction to the world of EUROCK -- a time when the words and music that filled the air truly made life, love and music all the more special.

Even though EUROCK Magazine effectively came to an end in 1990, EUROCK's distribution arm, record label and related projects continue to this day. In 1996 I was given the opportunity to produce a 5-CD musical history of "The Progressive Rock Era" for Rhino Records, entitled *SUPERNATURAL FAIRY TALES*. In 2000, EUROCK Magazine's history was compiled into a multimedia CD-ROM, *THE GOLDEN AGE*, which contained the fanzine's articles plus an album's worth of music, vintage-era videos, and more. Today most of the effort is concentrated on the online music and information resource www.eurock.com.

The evolution of EUROCK chronicles my own personal development. In almost three decades of doing EUROCK I have become dedicated to a very simple set of ideals which grew out of the culture of rock. At the outset my creative process was instinctive and conscious; now it has become second nature. One thing has always remained constant: a vision that regards music and life as something very special and sacred, a virtual act of faith.

Please Read & Enjoy this book in the spirit in which it is written.

Mir,
Archie Patterson

Amon Düül: A Science Fiction Rock Spectacle

by Lester Bangs

Part One: The Aluminum Revolution

IT HAD TO HAPPEN! It's been some seven years now since the impact of American popular music first rebounded to engulf our shores and burghs in a new-old sound as fresh and vibrant as the Presley's and Berry's it was modeled on a decade before.

The English rock scene, and the American renaissance it predicated, have soared and muddled to hiatus positions of equal entrenchment.

There are great bands and artists everywhere, but somehow the pervasive feeling is that just like the first three years of the last decade we are in a slack period between mass cultural eruptions.

Meanwhile, however, the combined accomplishments of American and Limey bands have been seeded in less-sung rock scenes around the world, and some of those seeds are coming to the weirdest blooms heard in the Western world since Molly took all those pages just to say "Yes oh yes I will." And the first with the mostest bloom is in one of the seeming unlikeliest places imaginable: Scandinavia and Germany, the very heart of the cold emotionless sensibility most antithetical to the spirit of rock.

But kids are seething clear round the globe, and the *Kinder* of Munich are no exception, and rock has in its aluminum evolution expanded to encompass more than mere good-vibes (all the darkest impulses of the human soul, in fact), so <u>maybe it's not so shocking that the chilly domains of the Aryan bullmoose have kindled a burgeoning rock-roll revolution</u> as healthy and instinctive in its understanding of learned styles as Britain's Beatbrats were toward American R&B once upon a time.

The first sign of this nascent scene was the American release in 1969 of a Savage Rose album called *IN THE PLAIN*. Savage Rose sounded a little bit like the Jefferson Airplane, and their arrangements showed a cross-idiomatic musical sophistication that many States and British bands should envy, including a bit of Hungarian gypsy influence in "Evening's Child". Their songs were mostly dark-emotioned, with a sense of Gothic gloom that would seemingly wear better on a German than a cheery clog-clopping Tulip Child Dane. They were and are brilliant, and their subsequent albums, *YOUR DAILY GIFT* and *REFUGEE*, are among the finest examples of musical art and sheer rock 'n' roll our era has to offer.

But somehow the stage was still waiting for a Germanic entrance, something really weird and woolly. After all, the Germans were always noted for their mechanistic thinking and obsessive emotionalism, at least among those prone to indulge in post-World War II backlash, and Led Zeppelin was wowing 'em by exploiting similar neuroses in their sound if not their lyrics, and later the Stooges would come along and blow everybody out with Iggy's demonic tirades and a lead guitarist with a fondness for jackboots and swastikas, so why were the real original Jerries wasting any time at all, huh?

Well, the answer is that they *weren't*. There was some real killer rock aborning in the drafty sound laboratories of certain musty communes of that country, but the trouble was that the only initial exposure we here in the U.S. of A. had to German rock was through albums by bands imitating popular Yankee and Limey styles in the lamest possible way. Ah, it's almost been a year since they came out now, and who remembers the Marbles, who sounded like two lollipops formed of Bee Gee goo, or Brainbox, who did the most perfect imitation of Jethro Tull I've ever heard, or Birth Control, who sounded like the Doors waiting through a wall of asbestos, or Joy Unlimited, who came on like Las Vegas sharpies backing up one of the more notable white pubescent Aretha Franklin parodies of the month? Who remembers all those losers? Nobody, and justly so, except me, and I had to research them out of a review I wrote myself and forgot in a back issue of *Creem*.

But not to worry, *mein Kinder*, 'cause there was a new Sound in the winds off the Rhine and the Rhone! One product of it was a great, great, marvelous, wonderful group called The Can, who have three albums out and definitely deserve to be unleashed on America. I don't have time to tell you much about them, except to say that they've been much influenced by American psychedelic raga fuzztone feedback rock and British Pink Floyd spaceouts, and the names of their albums are *MONSTER MOVIE*, *TAGO MAGO* (a double set), and *CAN SOUNDTRACKS*, which is made up of themes composed by Can for German avant-garde underground movies which were never released or perhaps never made.

Part Two: "Are you on an acid trip?"

BUT THE Can were only the beginning: the *real* payload in the nascent glorious history of German rock lies in the work of Amon Düül II, a band which has evolved out of Amon Düül I and is currently one of the most interesting and experimental bands in the whole wide world.

Before proceeding to a critical consideration of their *oeuvre*, we must ask the question, *"Who are Amon Düül and why are they for that matter and where did they come from?"* Glad you asked that question. It just so happens I have all the crucial info right here in my customary Rock Critic's File Of Essential Arcana, in the form of an interview with them by an unidentified dork presumably with the German press, and a no-monkeyshines statement of philosophy and intentions from the group themselves.

The interview is a classic of total noncommunication. The first question the dildo asks is, "Are you on an acid trip?" "Yes," replies Karl-Heinz Hausmann, leader and spokesman, "you might say that." Which sort of sets the tone for the whole conversation. The second query posed by the klutz is, naturally, "Where did you guys get your name?"

Well, I'd wondered about that one myself, and the reply is interesting. "The two names 'Amon' and 'Düül,' "says Heinz, "are a construction of two different mythologies—" "Which ones?" butts in the blurting asshole, just as another member of the band is laughing at what Heinz just said.

"'Amon' is from Egyptian mythology and 'Düül' is from a very well known record in America, it's called *Tommy* and it was made by Canadians."

Now that that's all clear, we can get to the matter of the band themselves and their internal message. Because they definitely have one, and share it with certain eloquence. As the liner notes of the American release of the Amon Düül I album say, *"Amon Düül is a discovery of the revolutionary spirit of young people in all parts of the world and particularly articulates the creative genesis of the new music in Germany today."*

That is, <u>Amon Düül are an organic expression of certain young Germans learning, as their peers all over the world are, to relate to themselves and their own freedom in totally new ways</u>, to translate that freedom into a new free music like nothing heard on the planet heretofore, and to totally oppose anyone or anything that stands in the way of the attainment and ongoing sensation of that freedom.

If that sounds a bit like John Sinclair and the MC5, it's only natural, because Amon Düül probably come out of an environment just about as oppressive as that obtaining in Detroit. The difference is that Amon Düül are the direct representatives of no party or faction, disdaining all boards, syndicates and governments of the earth. And their rebellion is totally understandable as the healthy human response to themselves and their situation: *"Everybody has to make his own experience,"* says Heinz to the interviewer's wheedlings about what-gives-you-the-right-to-complain-if-you-don't-have-a-better-plan, *"and decide what he wants. We try to express that with our music."*

In the process of that they have become the most publicized and controversial group in Germany, and by way of clarifying and defining themselves to both friend and foe they have drawn up a program:

What We Were
(Our Way)
Already during our schooldays in boarding schools, our common path began to merge. In order to overcome the suppressions during that time, we saw in music the freedom to develop and further continue new forms of communication.

It was evident that we would not let ourselves be pushed into any kind of middle class "9-5" career. From analyzing the repression mechanisms within the boarding school, we had already learned how to react against "the system" surrounding us on the outside. With this knowledge, it was clear that—contrary to our parents— we had to completely redefine ourselves. For example, none of us know or use alcohol, the main intoxicant of society (and the pocketbook); we wanted to offer what we had experienced through conscious, eye-opening situations.

A sense of belonging together and being a group—out of free will—made living together possible for us. First in a commune, then in a kibbutz-like residence. We can truly articulate basic criticism against the existing system because we have created a model of the counter-society with music...

Our group had to continue on against the intolerance of our middle-class, academic parents, homeowners, and neighbors, who know how to communicate with us only through the police...

What We Want
With our group we want to show that is possible to live together, to work together, to overcome common problems, but nevertheless remain autonomous individuals. We want to reason for our conscious, communal way of life to be expressed through music and be known everywhere.

It is partially the latest edition of the great utopian communist dream of a better world and purer human integration, partially the rather defensive response to the abuse heaped on them by the German, yes, Establishment and uncomprehending nerds such as their interviewer. Sometimes you don't learn to define a particular cultural or artistic situation as political until you're right in the thick of the shit-gale of contention. And while some of Amon Düül's positions may seem a bit extreme even to members of their own generation—for instance, that bit about booze is shortsighted if not positively reactionary at this stage in history, when the finest alternative to psychedelic strychnine or stuporous self-pollution is a charmin' snort of hootch and I am writing this with a pint of J. W. Dant Sour Mash Bourbon sitting not six inches from my IBM Selectric—but their statement as a whole has a strength and lucidity that is admirable in this time of general random disintegration. These people obviously know who they are and what their work in the new society is. And who are they?

Well, Karl-Heinz Hausmann plays organ and has just turned 21. Chris Karrer, on guitar, violin, and soprano sax, has been greatly influenced by Ornette Coleman, *"the famous alto saxophonist with Free Jazz,"* and, it says here, *"began professional study in drawing, but was no pedagogue."* And I can believe that and you should too. Peter Leopold is their seeming-octopoidal percussionist, John Weinzierl contributes the swirling, searing lead guitar lines, and bassist Lothar Meid came to Amon Düül II from a stint in eminent nonrock avant-gardist Gunter Hampel's Free Jazz Ensemble.

None of these people were in Amon Düül I, although some of the members of that group sat in on II's still-unreleased-here album *YETI*. And Amon Düül I have an album which has been released in the United States by Prophesy records, and which I reviewed with premature heat in *Creem*, March 1971: *"Amon Düül is the monstrosity. I don't know who at Prophesy ever dreamed that this album deserved the States, but that man is lost in space. This record, which was called* PSYCHEDELIC UNDERGROUND *in its German edition, is thirty minutes of the kind of clattering "space jam" that is likely to result anytime you get a bunch of amateur musicians together with huge amps and too much dope for them even to say something musical by accident. Lots of percussion and one-chord guitar. This is undoubtedly the worst record out this year, and the most inept, sludgy album I've beard since Hapsash and the Colored*

Coat's first effort, which formerly qualified as the worst rock album I'd ever heard. You just couldn't believe this shit if you heard it, *but take it from me, it has none of the inspired insanity or so-bad-it's-good redeeming factors of purposely primitive bands like the Godz. Although is might be interesting as an artifact*—the first group on LP that *nobody* could like."

Well, naturally that's a great album and the guy what wrote that review was a pompous punk. Not that any of the things I said about the album's sound were so untrue, it's just that with time and the mellowings of maturity I can easily see how such a repetitive, freaked-out album has great value indeed; Dave Marsh and his girlfriend used to drink wine and listen to it as night fell like an iron curtain on the Detroit ghetto, and I own two copies now myself.

And anyway, by the time my half-ass review was scrawled, Amon Düül I had gone the way of Hapsash & the Colored Coat and legions of other great rock bands, and Amon Düül II was in full frenzied bloom. Their first album, *PHALLUS DEI* (which, translated literally, means "Jehovah's Pecker"), I have unfortunately not been able to obtain, but the follow-up, *YETI*, was a real killer and the latest one, *DANCE OF THE LEMMINGS*, has even, praise be and a tip of the J. W. Dant in honor of United Artists Records, been released in this country to corrode pubescent minds and win converts to the Düül ethic and esthetic.

Part Three: *YETI*

YETI is, let me say at the outset, one of the finest recordings of psychedelic music in all of human history, and will blow you straight to the shores of Ceres if you are ever fortunate and prudent enough to happen on a copy and by all means buy it.

My copy bears a sticker with some futuristic script broadcasting the words "Electric Rock Idée 2000," which is also affixed to The Can's *MONSTER MOVIE* album, which indicates that the people that record or promote both groups are aware that they are way out in front of a real vanguard/renaissance type sonic sci-fi scene.

YETI itself is a veritable blitzkrieg of a two-record set, and in both grooves and package positively drips atmosphere. The jacket art is incredible, like something right out of Bergman: on the front a sullen creature in a black robe is swinging a scythe against dark skies while an enigmatic storm of red dust swirls phosphorescently about his feet. The inside features a Gothic landscape with purple mountains, a pagoda with the faces of group members in the windows, a naked man falling through space and a demonic dying horse flailing a hoof at you.

The music is experimental in the best possible sense, showing the influence both of American psychedelic jams and the band's own European folk roots. The first side is taken up mainly by a sort of suite called "Soap Shop Rock", which features such inextricable-from-each-other sections as "Halluzination Guillotine" and "Gulp a Sonata". Where on Amon Düül I's album most of the "songs" (listed 6 on the back, even though they were all the same jam) were free German translations of Sandoz acid references ("In The Garden of Sandosa", "The Garden of Sandosa in the Morning Dew", "An Extremely Lovely Girl Dreams of Sandosa"), *YETI* reveals a penchant for surrealistic titles and lyrics that will grow even more marked in *DANCE OF THE LEMMINGS*.

As for the music, "Soap Shop Rock" is like some bizarro opera, with swirling gypsy-tinged violin attacks and great falsetto divas shrieking through, while the second side is made up of five identifiable and often moving songs. "Eye-Shaking King" bears certain structural resemblances to the Velvet Underground's "Venus in Furs", although the textures are far thicker, sometimes to the point of overpowering the listener and turning his brain to the resinous extract of Burroughsian Mugwump spinal fluid, and "Cerberus" is a surging piece which flipped me out one night when I suddenly realized that the guitar riff in it was almost an exact duplication of the folk-classical "Chope Dance" performed by the Phillipe Koutev ensemble on Elektra/Nonesuch's amazing but decidedly non-rock *MUSIC OF BULGARIA* album.

The set's other record is composed of three long improvisations, which seem like an extension of the *PSYCHEDELIC UNDERGROUND* album's jams to a higher level, titled "Yeti", "Yeti Talks to Yogi" and "Sandoz in the Rain". They all have their moments, but the pounding, relentless floodtides of sound, which are the group's hallmark, seem to work better in the more controlled settings of shorter songs.

Part Four: The Mini and Maxi Lemming

Amon Düül's latest album reflects the application of that knowledge, and what you're holding in your hands right now is a sampler of the result. *DANCE OF THE LEMMINGS,* while a refinement and maturation of the directions charted in *YETI,* is still a totality, perhaps more so than that album, and deserves the most intelligent and committed kind of listening. It is not light music, but its seriousness is fortified by the scope of its venturesomeness and its profound originality. Again at least half of it is composed of musical sequences in which series of songs, listed chronologically on jacket and label, seem to wind and flow and twist around and through each other, so that it is challenging if not impossible to determine just where, say, "Dehypnotized Toothpaste" ends and "A Short Stop at the Transylvanian Brain Surgery" begins. The best thing to do is see that this two-record EP serves only as appetizer, and to get as soon as possible into the warp and woof of the complete work.

The first side is a suite in the grand tradition called "Syntelman's March of the Roaring Seventies", which is divided into four parts that flow right into each other without demarcating bands and is actually composed of six or seven short sequences running through a myriad of changes: folk melodies on acoustic guitar, high keening drones, bongo drums and a jazz guitar segment with dulcet parsley tones. Later the music turns from folk forms to an almost classical sound, with charging piano and modal violin a bit reminiscent of Sugarcane Harris' work with Zappa, the entire ensemble finally coming together in one pulsating drone that rides over and out.

The second side is another suite called "Restless Skylight-Transistor-Child" and begins with a descending scale eventuating in an electronic burp called "Landing in a Ditch". The "Dehypnotized Toothpaste"—"Short Stop at the Transylvanian Brain Surgery" sequence is next, with a breathtaking sound palette including fuzztone attack, sitar, and Airplane-ish vocals trailing into a beautiful repetitive guitar riff that continues with little change as an electronic curtain rises steadily and fills the sky. The sense is of Burroughsian literary techniques, which were themselves derived from 20th Century graphic arts, applied to music, massed bowed or amp-distorted strings cut up and rearranged in a sound collage fading into a fuzz wah-wah attack worthy of Black Sabbath and a vocal with Yoko whinny-vibrato overtones, followed by another wailing violin solo. The side ends as "Paralyzed Paradise" oozes into "H. G. Wells' Take-off", with a Black Sabbath rhythm guitar crunch overridden by a Robbie Kreiger-ish guitar solo streaming into phased guitars melting behind unintelligible spoken vocal à la Yardbirds' "Glimpses", overlain by absolute walls of sound that are always coherent and controlled but whose source is not always readily identifiable... I'm not saying that this music derives from some mystic Outer Source, but that <u>Amon Düül's assimilation and synthesis of all major 20th Century musical idioms is so astonishing that you sometimes don't know exactly what you are hearing.</u>

Side Three is entirely given over to an improvisation called "The Marilyn Monroe Memorial Church", which harkens back to the material on the second record of *YETI* and sounds pretty much the same all the way through with feedback drones and repetitive rhythms. It's like the later live work of the Stooges, which was an endless wrangling tangle of fine, fine noise that you could live in. It's a real aural environment! It is authentically hypnotic.

Side Four of *DANCE OF THE LEMMINGS* is the most immediately accessible side of the album and perhaps of all Amon Düül's recorded work, consisting of three songs that begin and end and have spaces of traditional non-chancy silence between them. Another plus for programming or just initially getting into this music is that they are the closest to traditional notions of rock 'n' roll as well. "Chewing Gum Telegram" is built on a heavy churning guitar line, wah wah slithering over and out on Martian suction cups, while "Stumbling Over Melted Moonlight" is a deep Moog-like basso excursion almost cinematically true to its title, and "Toxological Whispering" shouldn't give any trouble to anybody weaned on Hendrix and Clapton.

There has never been a group quite like Amon Düül II before, and there may never be another to transmute so many sounds ever again. One thing is certain: we are doing ourselves a disservice if we let this intrepid German vector go by us. When *YETI* came out, the French magazine *Rock et Folk* had this to say: *"With its new double album, this Munich act establishes itself as one of the most astonishing groups anywhere... a type of musical happening, in which all the forms of pop and contemporary music are included. The steadily hammering beet gives the essential balance; without it the ear would be exhausted in a crazed running between manifold pictures, windings, highs and lows...For us it is the discovery of a new dimension in pop music: a fantastic surrealism, a new spectacle."*

To which I can only add, having just returned from another headphone-session with *DANCE OF THE LEMMINGS*, a spent Amen. This is one time that somebody far from these shores has something to teach us (and fry our brains in the process) about "our" music and the music of the universe. It's happened before, you know.

**Copyright 1971 Lester Bangs
Used with permission of
the Lester Bangs Estate**

Raised on Records

I entered the world at 78 rpm, went through adolescence at 45 rpm, and grew into adulthood at 33-1/3 rpm. My life experiences have taken me on a journey where paradoxically everything keeps speeding up by spinning slower. My mind being in a continuous state of evolution, my body feeling as if I had come un-stuck in time, moving in a constant state of revelation in slow motion.

My beginnings were modest; my parents lived in a small apartment where the weather would get in through cracks beneath the floorboards. We moved on ever westward, from one place to the next, leaving Colorado and ending up in a small farm town in Central Calif.

In those days there was no TV, and radio was not around as well (at least in my house). I was an early reader, running through the alley and backyard of the neighbors behind us, across the street to the public library one block over, a couple times a day. When not reading I hung out in front of the house, hoping for a stray kid to pass by who wanted to play.

My parents were struggling Republicans with worn cloth coats. My father was a teacher, and after a time in education went for the gold, moving to the big town nearby to get into the insurance game. At that time the "American Dream" was capturing everyone's hearts and minds.

The move to the city brought our first home ownership, and more of everything. I then wondered if more was better as I was not a happy camper when we moved. Today I no longer wonder about the answer to that question – more is not better. But it all worked out, for better and worse in the end.

While living in that "big city," I came of age, in stages. Stage one commenced in 1958.

Constant family trips to the cousins in the Bay Area had opened my eyes to those little round 7" black vinyl platters called 45's. We listened to newest singles, dug "the beat," and slowly I was re-born, my heart pulsing to a brand new rhythm.

The family's nest egg started to accumulate, so we got our first TV around that time as well. Shortly thereafter I discovered *American Bandstand* and a new after school ritual entered my life. Prior to that baseball, football and basketball had been in my blood, my father's first calling was school teacher and athletic coach, at a couple of high schools before questing off in search of the rainbow's end. Soon, *Dick Clark's Saturday Night Show* was added to these activities as well and my life's passion began shifting.

I was 10 years old when I finally scavenged some pop bottles to buy my first single. It cost 75 cents I think. I bought it at a Sherman & Clay music store

8, Eurock: European Rock & the Second Culture

that had just started augmenting their stock of musical instruments with a few of the "Top 10 Hit Singles."

I knew exactly what my first purchase would be, so went to the counter with coins in hand to buy "It's Only Make Believe" by Conway Twitty. It was cool, the way his voice broke, and the lyrics about love (which as I learned them better later turned out to be the unrequited sort ironically). My life had suddenly become filled with new passion.

A short while later I displayed a hint of the promoter in me as well. My teacher was named Mrs. Kane; she was a stern, but warm-hearted crosspatch who I ended up loving dearly as she rode me hard, and finally civilized me (sort of…) I had her for a split class, two years in 5th and 6th grade, and at one point conned her into letting me bring my Conway Twitty record to class and play it. I brought my second Conway purchase, "Danny Boy," the classic rocked up, which was a real sacrilege. Innocently she went for it as I actually got it on the classroom phonograph and half played before she made me take it off (what fun). I then charmed her in to letting me play the flip side, a patriotic tearjerker, "Star Spangled Heaven." What the heck it really wasn't rock, but it was my man Conway. The class thought it was "cool" (or crazy?) And in the back of my mind, I have a faint memory that a certain little girl (the cutest and smartest in the class) may have even flashed me a smile? That was for me a time of imagination, curiosity, and things far beyond what a budding pint-sized rocker could handle when it came to romance. The line between make-believe and reality is very thin around 10 years old.

Looking back, that event unknowingly launched me on a career path, my destiny set in more ways than I could ever have imagined then. I'd found my calling. Rock music would grow to become a part of me, leading me down the long and winding road that turned out to be the rest of my life.

Another train of thought that began to get its grip on me at that time was a hint of social/political consciousness, and unease. The late 1950s and early 1960s were watershed years for America. The cold war was raging; society was in transformation, and the forces of tradition were holding on to the last vestiges of the past as tightly as they could. The economic boom was soon going to change everything. It triggered an evolutionary impulse that infiltrated the emerging middle class all across America.

Our move had brought me in touch with many new kids on the block. This current atmosphere had us doing duck-and-cover drills in school, as well as keeping on the lookout for commies invading our street. My parents one weekend took me to see Richard Nixon speak in the Sears parking lot during his barnstorming tour of lies for President. Of course being a repressed, but bright-eyed type led me to handing out "Nixon for President" buttons at my junior high school. My dad, however, got real tired of me asking him to buy one of that times heavily hyped "Foxhole" bomb shelters for our back yard.

All the while my love for music grew by leaps and bounds, and I got constant flack for spending all my allowance on an ever-growing collection of "those records." As I went on to junior high the early seeds of a youth culture began forming around rock and roll, enhancing my growing love of music. The after school "sock hops," and occasional night dances at school were eagerly anticipated.

At that time, being still in the vortex of a nuclear family unit, we took trips back to the grandparents' house in Colorado during summers. There I discovered what turned out to be my fave English band in the early years – The Who. I slept in their basement and laid awake late into the night listening to a 100,000-watt radio super-station out of Oklahoma City, KOMA. That was when I first heard the most amazing songs my ears had yet beheld – "I Can't Explain, "Anyway, Anyhow, Anywhere," and "My Generation." They summed up the feelings of my adolescence. I was forever fated to be confused by that feeling called love, determined to do things my way, and by god I was going to die young if everything didn't work out as I hoped real soon. Ah, the hopes and dreams of youth. Looking back today, it all still seems only slightly insane as the essence of all that continues to echo inside me.

In fact, my impulses epitomized youthful awakening. The rock and roll ritual was recognized as dangerous from the outset by the powers that be. They tried their best to stamp it out. But the future was coming on fast, and the floodgates were about to open. Kids all over the country shared my conflicting sense of personal insecurity and empowerment. Kids were falling en masse right into the arms of rock and roll and parents were panicked. If the older generation hadn't been so consumed with materialism, they might have truly understood what was on the horizon.

Forget nostalgia, America during that time was not a comfortable place to grow up. I was not the only one feeling out of sync during those beginnings of the culture clash that loomed on the horizon. My love of music and the power of the music to make me feel connected and alive was one of the few things that made sense in those days. Rock music provided kids with a new mindset and body language. The culture of rock was gaining increasing prominence in their lives, and more importantly becoming legitimized as a growing business in America.

In keeping with the spirit of the times and growing cult of accumulation, the social ethos became: if it made money then what the heck let the kids spend. Three decades later the preeminence of economic reality was definitively documented by George Stephanopolous famous slogan on the blackboard of Clinton's campaign war room - "It's the economy stupid."

Politicians always are way behind the curve – *"You know something's happening, but you don't know what it is, do you Mr. Jones?"* (Robert Zimmerman).

A series of events in the 1950s, and first half of the 1960s, led to the ultimate opening of Pandora's box which became a 40-year rush that has our heads reeling still today in the brave new world of 2002.

To name but a few: There was Alan Freed who dared to play "race music," juiced up black rhythm and blues = "rock 'n' roll" (for which he got busted up by the Feds), Leo Fender (who turned on, plugged in and blasted everybody off with his new electric amp/guitar), and Elvis "the pelvis" Presley, whose bumping and grinding brought rock music to the white kids, and started them rockin 'n' rollin' in the back seat of their cars (guess what "R 'n' R" was an acronym for?).

If the earlier years were a blur, in high school my focus sharpened. It was a time during which the locked gates of a "closed campus" were to be broken down. The "dress code" – boys w/ short hair and shirts tucked in, girls w/ skirts below the knee and blouses buttoned up high - was about to crash and burn.

Soon we were allowed off campus for lunch. Hair grew longer, and the mode of the music caused changes to occur in every aspect of life. Where I lived it was not an overnight happening however. Central California was not Haight Ashbury.

At my school there were 4 people with long hair (which basically meant shaggy and over their ears). There were me, two pals, and another cat that didn't hang with us. More than a few jocks and others didn't quite like the new look of things. I heard a constant, "hold on there sweetie, not so fast, you need a haircut." I was chased around campus every so often, escaping the meaty grasp of jocks by running into the office and Dean of Students open arms. A good man was Mr. Bray (someone once again charmed by my wit and semi-serious studious ways). Due to "my scruffy image," I was also considered one of the main sellers of drugs on campus. In those early days that was especially ridiculous as there were next to no drugs on our campus at that time. The good Dean would steadfastly tell anyone who inquired that I was a straight arrow and had no inclinations in that direction at all.

On the larger social scale, General Jack Ripper (Sterling Hayden) articulated the craziness of those times in Kubrick's 1964 black comedy masterpiece "Doctor. Strangelove or: How I Learned To Stop Worrying And Love The Bomb." His classic rant denounced fluoridation of the water, *"We cannot allow the International Communist Conspiracy to sap and impurify our precious bodily fluids."* Ripper's paranoia was reflective of society's mood in general. By the film's end he'd managed to start thermonuclear war.

Personally I'd come to a more rational belief that my purity of essence was in no way going to be sapped by any sort of substance abuse. That water had actually been fluoridated in our town didn't bother me all that much. But I had come to a strong conviction that no sort of drug was about to pass through my lips, or enter my bodily domain in any other way. "Partying" was not high on my agenda. Maintaining my "purity of essence" was a high priority.

In addition to campus capers, rock culture on the weekends was heating up with multiple concerts/dances at the Rainbow and Marigold Ballrooms. Being located in Central California made Fresburg a perfect pit stop for most bands commuting between LA and SF. A small, but growing number of local longhairs would gather at the shopping center and hang out. A new social subculture was forming as we'd talk of music, life, love, and our out-of-touch parents on the sidewalks and burger stands up and down Blackstone Avenue.

The action at the ballrooms was "way cool." Many famous bands in their early days rocked our world. Romances were begun and ended, new acquaintances made, lights were dim, dancing was hot and heavy, and of course the JD's were about looking for trouble. The cops usually hauled some loaded fat head out the door at least once a week. The rest of us just tried to make some kind of scene happen. This was pre-"Summer of Love" and though hardly innocent, it was all nonetheless relatively pure, not yet reeking of excess. The music, melodies and words were a perfect soundtrack for stirring newly liberated emotions being shared by a younger generation who were experiencing the glow of freedom.

At one time during my high school career I was in a band (who wasn't). I forget the name, but we were hot (of course). We had a crazed drummer (Royce), rock solid bass player (Bill), killer guitarist (Jim), keyboardist (Tim), and me of course – the lead singer. Covering hits by Them, the

Leaves, a/o obscure groups/songs from records in my collection was our forte – Velvet Underground, Them, Daily Flash, Painted Ship, et al. We practiced when personal schedules allowed, played a few gigs, and made a crashing finale at a party halted by the cops ("it's TOO LOUD, turn it off, the neighbors called in a complaint"). Hey, we were "different" and legends in our own mind, that's what counted.

I got my first car at the end of high school, a '56 Ford. Immediately I had a record player installed. One of those neat jobs that played 45's upside down, hooking right up to the radio. Records were constantly blasting out of my windows as I created my own personal play list for cruising. Music was now a virtual soundtrack that accompanied every event in my life.

A weekly ritual was venturing to the West side, the black section of town across the tracks, where the streets were full of brothers and sisters selling their wares on the sidewalk. My personal Mecca was a place called Lightning Records, run by two Chinese brothers Bob and Walt Mah. We were great friends for many years. Once a month they went to LA and SF, visiting record one-stops and bringing back a treasure trove of new records. They'd special order me things and pass along promotional copies in advance of LP releases, turning me on to some amazing music. I got promos of the first Doors and Stooges albums before release, took them to a friend's house to play DJ (1st grade flashback) seeking to "blow some minds." The universal reaction was "that's weird shit man." I laughed and said, "just wait, this is going to be killer when it hits." It was great fun! I also began to get a subliminal feeling that I really didn't live in any certain time or place; my mind was always one step ahead, or behind everyone else. Music was increasingly becoming the source of my own personal visions and inspiration.

The next place my mind journeyed was to college. There it underwent a major life enhancement. My early Who influence had given way to the more overt socio-political tendencies of Frank Zappa and Sky Saxon's Seeds. Sometime before I'd bought the first Mothers of Invention magnum opus *FREAK OUT* at the local K-mart, and the ultra grungy *THE SEEDS* first LP at Long's Drug Store (business America was truly "freaking out"). The Mother's social critiques "Hungry Freaks Daddy," and "Plastic People" (off their 2nd album Absolutely Free), along with Sky Saxon's anthem of personal liberation "Pushin' Too Hard" were definitive. These were my philosophical touchstones heading into college. The times were now totally changing and re-arranging as the war dragged on, and people in LA and SF were tripping their brains out. I was ready for my next step into the void, toward the unknown, believing that existence was elsewhere.

College was the place where "that philosophy teacher ruined you" (according to my mom). She may not see it exactly that way today, but amidst the dissolution of our family (divorce, etc.), and her struggle to build a new life in those turbulent times she surely did back then.

In fact, exposure to intellectual people and the stimulation provided by my English Lit. and Philosophy teachers, who were uniformly excellent in this small time aggie college, certainly opened my eyes. I took poetry and literature classes from a free spirited new teacher on campus Charles Hanzlicek, who would go on to be a known poet.

I got heavily into John Milton – *"We must act with reason in this world of evil, the place in which God has irrevocably placed us"* – Paradise Lost. Milton's classic struggle between good and evil was in my mind incredibly provocative. It led me to ponder who really were the bad guys in today's world, and encouraged interesting class discussions that were easily diverted into other relevant areas.

Certainly the philosophers played their part. There was one class, "Contemporary Conflicting Morality," that was a personal watershed experience. It was an open forum where we could discuss everything; the only rule being no physical violence allowed. The class soon divided between liberals and radicals, literally each sitting on their own side of the room. Few would admit to being conservative in that ideological free fire zone. Debates raged and ideologies were developed. Out of that class, myself and a few other neophytes formed the campus chapter of SDS. The Prof. Richard Paul was great! He gladly became our organizations sponsor (and unknowingly my mom's culprit).

I also became teacher's aid for a course offered in the schools "Experimental College," called "The History of Guerrilla Warfare." We studied T.E. Lawrence's *Seven Pillars of Wisdom*, and Che's *Bolivian Dairies* as examples of guerrilla war campaigns. The heat of politics was fast approaching combustion point.

Rock music had become the soundtrack for the imagined "Revolution." From the Airplane's "Volunteers," to the Stones "Street Fighting Man," and the incendiary cry of the MC-5's "Kick Out the Jams Motherfucker." The battle was joined first on campuses and in the streets all over the country, then the living rooms of everytown USA as nightly network news with their bloody footage and "body counts" brought the war home in a most graphic fashion. The revolution WAS being televised, and ultimately the tremors would even rock the halls of our nation's capitol in DC.

For me, frequent trips were made to SF and Beserkley for demonstrations and concerts. The culture wars had moved from the backseats of old Fords and Chevys to the parks and streets. The revolution turned out to be not only political, but also generational - parents against kids, old against young, us taking on "the establishment."

There were political assignations: JFK, RFK, MLK, Medgar Evers, Malcolm X, the death of "democracy" at the Democratic Convention in '68, killings at Kent State, Jackson State, the Panthers' Fred Hampton and Mark Clark in Chicago. Cultural casualties followed as well, icons rocketing to fame, fortune and oblivion – Elvis, Jimi, Janis, Morrison, and many others. Those days were filled with rage, the war brought home to mother country America.

There was collateral damage too, parents writing their kids off en masse for standing up for the very values they had given them. I published manifestos, lectured in classes, propagandized on street corners, and had the FBI wanting to be my "friend." My parents taught me well, but naming me after himself surely backfired on my dad when my picture appeared in the local paper. He couldn't stand the heat, so threw me out of the kitchen (not literally, as we had not lived together for years). Ever after his namesake was but a distant memory. May he now R.I.P.

The '50s and '60s were a long, strange trip into the dark soul of America. Everyone was swept along on the ride, my old friend, paranoid "Tricky Dick," was ultimately run out of DC in a copter. US troops fled Saigon, the Vietnamese people in hot pursuit as they achieved a final victory. Ultimately everyone breathed a slight collective sigh of relief from exhaustion. The whirlwind of change was far from over as the country had been set on course to being changed forever.

I finished college at the start of 1971 and came face to face with reality at last. Society was lurching forward into uncharted new directions and my mind segued full time into the music. I joined the working class (sort of) and began the "adult" phase of my adventure. Psychedelic music, the early phase of electronic experimentalism as embodied in Hendrix, the early Dead, Silver Apples, Lothar and the Hand People, 50 Foot Hose, Ultimate Spinach and Joe Byrd's United States of America set the stage for what followed for me musically. They were the beginnings of my excursion into the far out reaches of sonic space.

The actual seeds of EUROCK were sown in the late 1960s and early 1970s. My always-enquiring mind led me to get subscriptions to the leading English pop music papers *Melody Maker* and *New Musical Express*. Early on an Anglophile, I was into psych pop. It was in these papers that I also read the first articles on the emerging Euro-rock strangeness coming form the continent, in particular "Krautrock" (as the Anglo journalist had dubbed it). When Richard Branson opened his first Virgin Records store in London, they ran some adverts in the trades for a bunch of bizarrely named groups and albums from this new scene. So off went my every spare, hard-earned dollar to England, and soon arriving via air post were scores of small packets filled with loads of LP's that rewired my musical circuits. The earlier US experimentalists and Anglo psych had hardly prepared me for what I heard.

Somewhat later a few of the more far out Euro bands got US release via United Artist Records – Amon Düül II, Can and Hawkwind. Marty Cerf, Greg Shaw and Ken Barnes ran a UA in-house paper called *Phonograph Record Magazine* that did write-ups about the Euro pioneers.

The original incarnation of EUROCK began in 1971 as a one-hour radio show on KFIG FM, the largest commercial station in Central California. Aired on Wednesday nights primetime, it featured the latest new discoveries from across the sea by Amon Düül II, Klaus Schulze, Popol Vuh, Can, Tangerine Dream, Magma, Guru Guru, Faust, Embryo, Ange, you name it... The resulting feedback was a combination of stunned, amazed and thrilled listeners.

This initial musical adventure lasted three years and my exposure to all this new Euro music blew my doors of musical perception wide open. It led me to a future I could have never planned for, or imagined only a few years earlier (yet strangely again, 10 years old flashed back into my mind). I was now more clearly coming to understand that in fact a new cultural outlook was possible, but it was not an easily realizable life choice.

In 1973, inspired by the beginnings of the "Do It Yourself" underground of amateur political and music journalism ("Underground" newspapers and Xerox publications), EUROCK morphed into a "fanzine" devoted to writing about the music, instead of airing it. My background in literature and writing in college, along with a head exploding with all the new Euro sounds allowed me to do an interesting written interpretation of what I heard and felt when listening to this strange new hybrid of rock and space age vibrations. Inspired by Greg Shaw's definitive rock 'zine, *Who Put The Bomp*, and with "a little help from my friends," I was on my way to a career of typing, collating, stapling, mailing, packing, shipping, and musical propaganda, for what's turned out now to be 30 years.

The publication of EUROCK led to other opportunities in the music business. A goodly part of those adventures is chronicled in recent interviews included in this book. In the latter part of the '70s new music opportunities had me relocating from Central California to Oregon, then down to LA, and ultimately back up to the Northwest. The experience of living in very different geographies and meeting many people was enlightening about human nature – *"the weather makes the man"* (anon.) – is very true in many ways.

Thanks to EUROCK I began to make contacts globally in a number of far away places. People from all over came to the West Coast; we'd meet, write, and talk to each other regularly. We discovered that we held many of the same values, ideals and loved the same music. In some ways we were very much kindred spirits, all involved in some cosmic crusade to make, listen to and promote incredible new music (hope springs eternal in the hearts of true believers).

I began to get a sociological understanding of how people's different cultural heritage, when mixed with a dynamically changing social order could give rise to a multitude of cultural and musical ideas of different kinds. The music of the Europeans ultimately went to an entirely different level, their use of lyrics, melody and mythologies being far different than the blues and jazz roots of earlier US musicians. The sonic impressionism of Amon Düül 2, Can, Tangerine Dream and Magma to name but a few was light years ahead of most other rock. The affinity for something new was what turned me on personally, and inspired EUROCK. The mainstream had become increasingly corporate and commercialized, offering a more is better vision that most artists and consumers had come to accept. Some of what the mainstream produced was of interest, but EUROCK's and my interests lay elsewhere.

Listening to music had become a ritual for many others and me. It led us to explore areas outside of mass consciousness and musical convention. Drugs initially opened the doors of perception for some. I saw through that illusory idea. The music itself became the vehicle by which I gained if not enlightenment, most certainly a deeper knowledge of and feeling for life. My response somewhat lightheartedly to those who questioned my credentials later due to my lack of "being experienced" was, *"I don't take drugs, I am drugs"* (Salvador Dali).

A watershed for me came with the release in 1978 of *EGON BONDY'S HAPPY HEARTS CLUB BANNED* by the underground Czech band, Plastic People of the Universe. I'd heard of them via the grapevine and was contacted by Jacques Pasquier, the head of SCOPA Invisible Productions, a small French record label that had received the tapes, which had been smuggled out of then Czechoslovakia. He wanted me to handle US distribution and promotion of that album, so I jumped at the chance.

Their music was an amazing distillation of the Velvet Underground, Mothers of Invention, and Fugs with avant-jazz that shattered musical barriers. It was crude, rude, epitomized minimalist complexity, plus contained an incredible spirit of fierce musical determinism. It also came with a 60-page libretto filled with insight into the life of truly "underground" artists. The band had been repeatedly jailed, denied a license to play in their country, and their philosophical leader, Ivan Jirous, was a marked man. In the libretto was included a rather short and definitive statement by Jirous that most definitely made it clear to the "Mr. Jones" exemplified in Bob

Dylan's "Ballad of a Thin Man," just exactly "what's happening," and "what it is."

He called it a "second culture," and suddenly everything I had experienced and come to feel through music was placed in context. The idea was simple:

"...a culture that will not be dependant on official channels of communication, social recognition, and the hierarchy of values laid down by the establishment; a culture which cannot have the destruction of the establishment as its aim because in doing so, it would drive itself into the establishments embrace; a culture which helps those who wish to join it to rid themselves of the skepticism which says that nothing can be done and shows them that much can be done when those who make the culture desire little for themselves and much for others. This is the only way to live in dignity through the years that are left to us..."
Ivan Jirous - Prague, February 1975

EUROCK Records (see Appendix) was born in 1980 with the release of a recording by the PPU called *THE HUNDRED POINTS*. It was music done to accompany the Human Rights Platform of the Charter 77 Movement. History at that point was escalating at a dizzying pace, the "Cold War" coming to an end, the Berlin Wall falling, and the crumbling of the "USSR" and "Czechoslovakia," all on the way.

The 1980's also ushered in the "age of Reagan." His ascension catalyzed radical changes not only in music (and the business of), but technology, class structure, the worldwide economic system, and nature of human life in general. The corporate state now is every day more firmly in control. As Orwell postulated in "1984," *"Newspeak was designed not to extend but to distinguish the range of thought and this purpose was indirectly assisted by cutting the words to a minimum... the expression of unorthodox opinions, except on a very low level, was nigh well impossible."* Welcome to the "New World Order" of AOL and Rupert Murdoch.

The music has changed, as has the mode in which it is made and distributed. What was once an experimental open-ended work in progress has now become just another commodity. Rock and electronics play a major part in mass-marketed films and video games. The creative mindset of many "musicians" has become attuned to - pushing the button, playing the tape, the machine is pre-set and in control. Still, for some artists and listeners alike, the quest for their muse remains the same. A special song, lyric, melody, chord or tone color still rings out loud and clear to all who will "listen."

P.F. Sloan wrote beautifully about the essence and love of music in the title song on his autobiographical album of the same name, from which the title of this article is taken:
*"I was Raised on Records,
Rock 'n' Roll radio.
I was Raised on Records
And if it wasn't for the Music,
If it wasn't for the Music,
We might have said goodbye
A long, long time ago."*

MIR!

Archie Patterson

1973

Amon Düül

The name Amon Düül is a combination of the name of an ancient Egyptian god and a Turkish word. The group came together in 1968 and was originally a free-floating collective of people from various areas; some were into free jazz, some rock, and others politics. They got together in a communal house, made some purportedly incredible music, and eventually managed to blow each other's minds. Out of all of this in September of 1968 emerged two groups -- Amon Düül I and Amon Düül II.

Amon Düül l, headed by guitarist and vocalist Rainer Bauer, was into a more anarchistic political form of lifestyle and music. They have rather haphazardly recorded, and have released four LPs for various German record companies since 1969. Each of them, *PSYCHEDELIC UNDERGROUND, PARADIESWARTS DÜÜL, COLLAPSING,* and *DISASTER* are remarkable examples of free-form insanity.

Amon Düül II, on the other hand, were more into creating music. They began experimenting in a rock context with jazz and electronics, fusing them with the improvisational aspects of Arabic and Far Eastern music to create a new sound. The original nucleus of the group was Chris Karrer, Peter Leopold, and Falk Rogner. Their initial recorded work *PHALLUS DEI*, featured pounding raga rhythms, driving guitar, and sinister Germanic vocals, all of which added up to a truly heavy LP.

1973

For their second, *YETI*, a double LP, they produced a mesmerizing psychedelic work. The cover featured their bongo player, Shrat, in an apocalyptic pose, wearing a dress and wielding a scythe. The music inside was equally unreal. In fact, it is probably one of the premier sonic assaults ever put on plastic. It includes "Soap Shop Rock," a truly manic adrenaline rush featuring insane vocals, and one of the best 3 minutes and 30 seconds ever recorded in "Archangels Thunderbird," where the dual guitar interplay is devastating. To top it all off, the second record consists of improvised jamming that leaves one dizzy from its relentless attack.

Around the time of this LP however, things began to happen -- people disappeared, some reportedly died, and their gigs went none too well. In spite of all this they went on to produce the unsung classic LP, *TANZ DER LEMMINGE*. It blew German minds, got rave reviews in England, and was virtually ignored in America. Taking up where *YETI* left off, it was a true science fiction epic work, featuring four sides of extraterrestrial instrumental displays on virtually every imaginable musical device. It was at this point that they began to get their due notice. In fact, due to increasing interest in England, a tour there was planned. Just before it was to begin however, at a gig in Cologne, a fire broke out and destroyed all their equipment. So once again they had to pick up the pieces.

On the eve of their next attempt to make it to England, the Musicians Union there refused them a work permit, so it was off again. At this point, in the midst of crises centering around personnel changes and bad breaks, they recorded *CARNIVAL IN BABYLON*.

This album marked the beginning of their move toward a blending of science fiction and progressive rock. Being such, it was a very good LP. The guitar work and vocals are excellent, the songs strong. This LP and the period of time relating to it saw a getting-it-together era where the group stabilized and saved itself from complete disintegration. They brought together their energies and straightened out their management situation, with the result being the great *WOLF CITY*, plus their first English tour.

WOLF CITY featured even better material than *CARNIVAL IN BABYLON*, and the playing was markedly improved. Instead of relying most heavily on guitar work and vocals they were once again working as a group and the arrangements were incredible. They made use of science-fiction motifs, coupled with good songs and rock-hard playing. This LP definitely showed that they were going strong and had overcome their various problems. The reactions to their first English tour also were outstanding -- from "Be prepared, they are a little weird, even rather strange, but be prepared never to be quite the same again afterwards," to "They aren't much like anyone else, but are they good!"

Since then they have made two subsequent trips, and due to their growing following released a special English-only limited edition *LIVE IN LONDON* LP. Also there are plans for a fourth English tour plus tentative plans for a 1974 U.S. visit. So things are definitely looking up.

The group has now gotten itself back to its initial form with Karrer on guitar, violin, sax, and vocals, Danny Fichelscher and Peter Leopold on percussion, Lothar Meid on bass, Renate on vocals, and Falk Rogner on keyboards. They have a new album, *VIVE LE TRANCE*, set to be released, and have established themselves as one of the top groups in Germany. They are now also breaking very big in England, and if United Artists in the U.S.

has any brains at all, they'll give them a bit of help here and America will get a chance to experience some of the best that music has to offer.

Archie Patterson

The Surreal Rock Of Amon Düül

With the demise of Boston's Ultimate Spinach, the instant oblivion of the Fifty Foot Hose and the slow deterioration of the precedent-setting Jefferson Airplane, a vacuum in cerebral, female-led, vocal rock developed. Head music as a whole disappeared from the American shores and yet even more noticeable in its absence was the female, vocal-dominated free-form rock sound.

It was all over in the U.S. after Mandrake Memorial's (the last American psychedelic group) final stab at it with an avant-garde arrangement of Speedy Keen's classic "Something In The Air" failed to gain any recognition just like their three great albums. There was in England, however, at least remnants of the freakout syndrome still extant in Kevin Ayers, the Pink Fairies and in a notorious conglomerate of street people, Hawkwind.

And it wasn't so long after the first stateside Hawkwind release (summer of 1971) that an even stranger mutation of visionaries appeared from Germany, of all places, going by the bizarre name of Amon Düül.

Confusion was unavoidable when *TANZ DER LEMMINGE* was released in September of '71 by an Amon Düül II, since several months earlier an album on the Prophesy label by Amon Düül (singular) had shown up in those precious few record shops that stock at least one copy of everything. The question arose -- was this the same group or not? Upon hearing the sounds contained therein it seemed definitely not. But being a citizen of the most lobotomized country on the planet, how was I to know? The rock press maintained a rigid policy of silence on any post '68 musical innovation so it wasn't a certified hype from any critical standpoint.

As usual in a case like this though, word of the mouth spread throughout the infinite void of dementia. The generalization deduced was something like so: There was an Amon Düül commune into music and alternative lifestyle politics. From this original mass, a splinter group emerged which, owing allegiance to their roots, kept the name and inserted a two behind it -- to hopefully distinguish them from the remaining number I. The diagonally opposed form of sound explored further differentiated the two with AD II opting for supersonic surrealistic fantasy rock while the remainder of the original delved into the pre-rock primal rhythms of the Neanderthal man.

As to the likelihood of either group being appreciated, it was strictly a matter of taste rather than talent, although each was unquestionably loaded with it. Düül I along with Yoko Ono's primal screams and Nico's Gothic chills ranks as an all time esoteric wonder. Never before had any form of rock taken on such new dimensions of hypnotic redundancy. This, possibly more than any other, was the ideal record to flip out to. Native screams, unmercifully repetitive electric guitar grunge backed up by an immense percussive section was destined to drive all but the incurably insane right up the wall.

The first Amon Düül I album on Prophesy

is now a 44 cent bargain bin buy worth at least your procuring two copies of. One for yourself, of course, and another for your worst enemy. Unwanted guests drop by, it works every time. Of additional interest is the acidic poem printed on the sleeve in both German and English. Unmistakable imagery explains how a magic potion expands visions from dew into diamonds, etc. And for those who dismiss such phantasmagorias, contemplate the final stanza:

> And who does not believe
> this tale
> Will get for sure
> A lump of sugar
> From Mother Düül

Just as surely as the American copy is necessary for the poem translation and the informative Mickey Shapiro's liner notes, the import, entitled *PSYCHEDELIC UNDERGROUND*, is equally as valuable for being an open-up with a different and quite splendid cover.

Amon Düül II were no less daring and experimental but were overall more panoramic in scope. The lead guitar on their first album, *PHALLUS DEI*, sounded similar to that of their native counterpart except that it was more refined and better produced. The textures were smoother too and the performance as a whole was more musical. Comparisons to the Velvet Underground and Nico were inevitable with the eerie extraterrestrial vocals of Renate Krotenschwanz and the rich violin playing of Chris Karrer, who actually sounded like a younger inventive mutation of Papa John than a classically trained turned nihilist John Cale.

Like virtually all German Kosmic Music, Amon Düül II were abstract even when they sang in English, which on *PHALLUS DEI* was infrequent. The sensation derived from the screams and drones was indeed rather unlike anything ever heard before.

At this point I have to express my regrets for not having a complete collection of Amon Düül I's works. However, I believe that their second album was the one I don't have, *COLLAPSING*. Whatever, *DISASTER* was their latest and maybe last and a double at that. Later for that.

Amon Düül II's third album *PARADIESWARTS DÜÜL* was not released in the States and in Germany it was on a different label than *PSYCHEDELIC UNDERGROUND*. Originally on Metronome, they now found themselves part of the budding German avant-garde label Ohr.

Switching record labels was not the only change made here -- the music differed radically from its forerunner too. If *PSYCHEDELIC UNDERGROUND* sounded like they had recorded under the influence of mind altering drugs, *PARADIESWARTS DÜÜL* could have been the results six hours later. For those who didn't believe they had it in them, this truly displayed the artistic side of Amon Düül I. It was probably the clearest, least complex album either Amon Düül has ever been responsible for. Side one starts off with a melodic flute acting as a second lead guitar until the progression builds enabling the flute to fade and the always strange lyrics to enter:

> Once I got a hang-up in the
> time machine
> The day was ready as my
> love has been
> And searching with my
> friends for a land
> Where every circuit has its
> end
>
> So why do you worry bout
> the time so long
> Evolution baby makes
> your heart strong
> And that is what it is
> Its so far to see
> But don't forget it please
> Love is peace
> Freedom is honey

Following this bizarre lyric recitation two guitars play contrasting riffs that culminate in a crescendo, halt abruptly and finish the last half of side one with an acoustic guitar -- piano improvisation over some typically impossible Amon Düül mumbles.

Flipping it over side two is likewise divided into two parts. The first is an electric jam spotlighting a bass as the lead instrument, entitled "Snow your thrust sun your open mouth." Part two is a Germanic chant, backed up by acoustic guitars and bongos mildly resembling *PSYCHEDELIC UNDERGROUND* in structure were it not so toned down.

Accordingly the second Amon Düül II LP (also not available in the U.S.) was also a revelation of sorts following the obscurity of *PHALLUS DEI*. On the cover was their bongo player, Shrat, who unmistakably looked like the Beatle-type figure located in the bottom right hand corner of *PSYCHEDELIC UNDERGROUND*. In this pose he is standing in lava smoke preparing to swing a scythe. Being a double, it opened up picturing a castle on a haunted hill with faces of band members peering out of the windows along with hands, skulls, medieval figures and horses.

The first two sides of *YETI* consist of several songs each while sides 3 and 4 were improvisations. *YETI*, probably more than any other Amon Düül II LP, had the biggest chance of capturing the mass audience. Like their comrades A.D. I, they also specialized in Oriental-styled acoustic ragas. But unlike A.D. I, they were infinitely more adept at electric freeform jams. There's plenty of hard rock and high energy on songs like "Soap Shop Rock" and "Archangels Thunderbird," the former memorable in particular for some fluent electric violin.

The title track *YETI* is an eerie eighteen-minute extravaganza that takes up the entirety of side 3. This album was apparently recorded in '69 or '70 before synthesizers came into vogue so most of the improvisations are acid influenced S.F. psychedelic rock taking up where the Dead, Airplane and Quicksilver left off, aided and abetted by some early Floyd, dense organ floods.

1973

Now, with the exception of the chants and screams, A.D. II was primarily singing in English. To those concerned with lyric content though, it was of little avail. The vocals were totally incomprehensible and while lyric sheets would have helped, maybe this is the way they wanted it.

Of note on side 4 besides the high powered "Yeti Talks To Yogi" is the acoustic "Sandoz In The Rain." Avid fans of the later mutations of Eric Burdon and the Animals will recall one of Eric's mind blowers, "A Girl Named Sandoz," with drug references like "my mind has wings." Evidently the name "Sandoz" has hallucinogenic overtones although just what I'm not sure. Amon Düül I uses this name also with a slightly different spelling (Sandosa) on half of the titles on *PSYCHEDELIC UNDERGROUND*. Possibly it's of German origin and some visionary acid head like Burdon in '67 was just way ahead of his time.

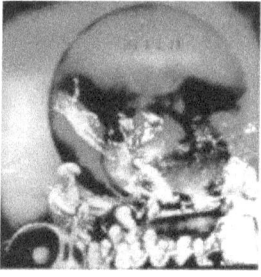

After some personnel changes and a contract to release at least some of their records on American UA, *DANCE OF THE LEMMINGS* blew more minds than any psychedelic record or substance from the apocalyptic sixties. When first released in the States in the fall of '71, bewilderment ran rampant. No one had seen an album cover similar to this since all the department stores had every rock record of '67 and '68 lumped together filed under "Psychedelic." The front of *LEMMINGS* consisted of more horses,

falling horsemen, Iron Butterfly-light-show symbolism via bubbles, water, and pictures of who might be sources of inspiration from German history. It's all very abstract and surrealistic, yet not to be outdone is the back picturing a cow skull (that first appeared in a castle window inside *YETI*) with a wrap around it and a child's face coming out on the side resting on a couch situated in the foreground of a forest.

Opening the album up we're welcomed to yet another equally as colorful piece of art. From what looks like the control board of a spacecraft the sights abound. Inside, beside the ubiquitous knobs, are photos of band members, the cover of *YETI* and a drawing of a metropolis (Berlin?) all on TV-sized screens. Outside the windows is a youngster from centuries-ago grabbing a foot twice as big as he is. Viewing directly ahead out the center slot intergalactic smoke floats dotted by dull red clouds and falling stars. To the immediate right is perhaps the strangest sight of them all -- an elephant riding a rug through space over the surface of what might be the Earth.

All is indicative of the music inside which almost defies description. Again a double, but much thicker and complex this time. At least 25 listenings are required to even marginally get into it. And all but side 4 must be played all the way through as the other three sides are obscure but deeply-interwoven concepts.

The introductory drone of an organ plunge opens side 1 (as it does the other three) fading surprisingly into an acoustic guitar-bass-drums-piano setup. On the surface this might sound mundane but not here. One of the more obvious changes is the vastly improved bass playing. Dave Anderson had by this time left to join Hawkwind who seemed better suited to his elementary style. The new man was

Lothar Meid whose free-jazz background greatly benefited the non-structures of Amon Düül II. His exceedingly arcane vocals were no hindrance either, but that comes up next album.

The first side is a suite, "Syntelman's March of the Roaring Seventies," subdivided into four parts. Written entirely by guitarist-violinist Chris Karrer, it seems likely he's the voice delivering the prophecy:

> Planets rise out of the ash
> Its coming along with a
> terrifying crash

Near the conclusion electricity takes over completely and a solid dronal wall finishes it off.

A different male voice handles the vocals on a piece titled "Restless Skylight Transistor Child" on the second side of record 1. The piece features numerous subtopics retaining a formula already perfected. The singer here is probably guitarist John Weinzierl since he composed this side It rocks savagely at intervals using devices like a wah wah hooked up to a synthesizer, a choir organ that sounds as massive as a Gothic choral section, and an abundance of tempo changes to achieve the ultimate mind boggling effect. The final two selections "Paralyzed Paradise" and "H.G. Wells Take Off" culminate in an echoing freakout ten times as effective as the previously-thought-unbeatable "Careful With That Axe Eugene."

"The Marilyn Monroe Memorial Church" took up side 3 and ably demonstrated just how electronically advanced and capable Amon Düül II really were. Falk Rogner's atonal organ dominated complemented by heavy bass moans and vibrant drumming. Ideal to listen to before drifting off into dreamland if you wish to enliven sleep with nightmares.

The finality of this superb extraterrestrial bestial soundtrack is a three part guitar suite with the predictably unpredictable Amon Düül titles. "Chewingum Telegram" sounds like the first song on Floyd's OBSCURED BY CLOUDS and just check out which came out first for who ripped off who. "Stumbling Over Melted Moonlight" accumulating metallic slabs over a hypnotic bass to act as a third lead all very Oriental-textured as Amon Düül's guitars sound like no others.

What could follow up LEMMINGS was the next question. Would Amon Düül continue to expand electronically or would they go lyrical seeking new direction? CARNIVAL IN BABYLON supplied a partial answer. Upon initial listenings I was rather disappointed, but that could be easily explained by my love for LEMMINGS which literally topped all to me. Further listening was all that was needed to appreciate it on a somewhat different level than LEMMINGS.

Amon Düül II reverted back to their native tongue on "C.I.D. In Uruk" but it mattered little. The singing was outstanding as well as the melody and it flowed right into "All The Years Round," one of the first compositions for A.D. II by Renate Krotenschwanz. From here on out though, her contributions increased, and this was a remarkable debut. Operating on a shrill high pitched level, she nonetheless varied her intonations in tune with the dual guitar

1973

weaves as the lyrics served a vivid portrayal of surrealism:

> At the circus they were waiting
> For a splendid slot machine
> Which could change the wine into water
> And reality into a dream

The two leads exchanged on a terrain unknown to the likes of the Allman Brothers incorporating melody with energy. "Shimmering Sand" was exemplary of multiple vocal power. Three different voices are in command, at strategic junctures throughout, the strangest of which has to be Lothar Meid's haunting growl.

Actually *CARNIVAL* was no less adventurous than any other Amon Düül exploration, it was just the directions sought were not quite so extraterrestrial. "Kronwinkle 12" and "Tables Are Turned" are both electrified folk with vague social implications that were quite clumsy next to their otherworldly stuff. The real savior of the second side was the ten minute "Hawknose Harlequin," a sci-fi ballad highlighted by numerous structural changes and a tantalizing bass pattern that falsely signaled the end before Weinzierl's dazzling guitar finishes it in a grandiose fashion.

It was somewhere around this time in '72, I'll conjecture, that Amon Düül I's latest and maybe last came out -- the double *DISASTER*. If Amon Düül II's drummer Peter Leopold was credited only as a guest on their next album *WOLF CITY*, it was explainable in that he had joined his relatives in Düül I.

DISASTER contains the same personnel as *PSYCHEDELIC UNDERGROUND*, with the exception of Wolfgang Krischke who'd played drums and was replaced by Peter.

Things start off with a boom (not like the drum solo of The Rascals) with the aptly titled "Drum Thing." Quite a legit name for a nine-minute multi-rhythm onslaught. There are five people on some form of percussion ranging from drums to maracas and congas.

"Somnium" breaks things up a bit with a brief guitar freak-out, and "Frequency" believe it or not, begins with a piano, although it lasts no longer than 30 seconds as the leeway is arranged for their everpresent lead instruments -- drums and percussion. "Chaoticolor" is more of the *PSYCHEDELIC UNDERGROUND* native chants, while "Expressionidiom" sounds like Ritchie Blackmore in one of his freakouts guest appearing with the Amon Düül rhythm section. "Altitude" proves A.D. I has electronic pretensions of no longer than one minute duration allowing "Impropulsion" to summarize the album as a whole -- primitive redundancy.

Long about fall of '72, rumor had it that *WOLF CITY*, the upcoming Amon Düül II album, would make the group something more than an obscurity here in the big time USA. According to American U.A. they were really going to get behind them as well as Hawkwind, who also had a product prepared -- *DOREMI FASOL LATIDO*. And for the shortest time it looked like a dream come true. Having an import of *WOLF CITY* since October, it came as more of a shock than a surprise when I turned on my FM radio one January morning to hear an Indian raga from you couldn't guess who. Having a policy of playing a new album in its entirety every Friday night, this otherwise lame station announced it was previewing both Hawkwind and Amon Düül on this celebratory evening.

As predictable though, it was a very short term operation. Either due to the lack of push from UA (I've yet to see an ad for them in the American rock press) or complaints from the lobotomized mass who had burned themselves out along with their idols -- the Dead. Whatever, both albums drifted into the commercially rejected void while the Yes group and has-beens Pink Floyd, who had tried everything without commercial success and had alas found the tried and proven formula for acceptance by the stoned-into-a-daze crowd with Moody Blues mush, got top priority for late night slumber inducing music.

The merits of *WOLF CITY* stood on their own regardless, accomplished what *CARNIVAL IN BABYLON* set out to and the end result was crystallization of their latest aspirations. "Surrounded by Stars" moved effortlessly like a psychedelic ballet strongly aided by Karrer's magnificent electric violin and Renate's infectious vocal. "Green Bubble Raincoated Man" is to *WOLF CITY* what "All The Years Round" was to *CARNIVAL IN BABYLON*. Beginning with an ethereal Renate vocal gradually winding out musically, quickening the pace it culminates into instrumental -- vocal dynamics that leave the listener spellbound. "Jail House Frog" sounds like a standard hard rock progression number from the outset, but midway through a piano tinkers in the background as a guitar echoes bird chirps and squeals reaching a plausible climax only to yield to an atonal sax solo by the diversely talented Karrer compres-sing a multiplicity of ideas many groups plod out for twenty minutes into less than five. The title tune uses standard rock instrumentation yet is so fulfilled you'd think they were backed by a host of guests. Lothar Meid is responsible for one of his rare, but incredibly arcane vocals here. Next up is a concise raga which is enhanced by outside Indian instrumentation with a German title which I believe translated means something like "Winds Blowing at the End of Time." Ravi Shankar meets electro-rock, Jimmy Jackson, German studio session superstar, plays choir organ and Rolf Zacher contributes an eerie Teutonic grumble on "Deutsch Nepal." This was the kind of thing obscured in the density of sound on LEMMINGS but no such murkiness here. The last selection reminds of a melodic Düül I (if there is such an animal) with a sitar-like guitar paving the way for a vocal and abruptly changed arrangement that more than one person I know has compared to the Moody Blues. Hopefully the intent was only a parody and besides who ever heard the Moody Blues accentuated by a solid beat?

Where Amon Düül will go from here remains uncertain. A live recording in England last December was released overseas in June but not in the states. And virtually everything on it was originally performed on *YETI* and *LEMMINGS*. This might signify they are headed back in that direction or maybe it was felt necessary to release live recordings of this period to prove they were something other than a studio sensation. There has been nothing new since, except for a joint LP between members of Amon Düül II and Embryo called *UTOPIA* (overseas only). Lets hope they don't keep us waiting too much longer for a new product. They definitely have lot to offer!

Scott Fischer

1973

Tangerine Dream

Tangerine Dream was formed for the first time in September 1967 by Edgar Froese. He was quite a well known musician in Germany, notably for his experiments in electronic music and futuristic ideas. Froese, born in Tilist (6/6/44), had been in one or two bands before, the most well known being "The Ones," which quickly folded after a very brief success. After this, Froese decided to form his own band, so in September '67 Tangerine Dream was on its hazardous way in German rock.

Their first appearance was at the University of Technics, Berlin, on January 12, 1968. Unbelievably, they were one of the first bands to emerge from Deutschland that had any originality and therefore can be considered one of the founders of the new German rock scene. Due to the fact that they were virtually unknown outside Berlin and its surrounding area, very little is known about their early history. They first started as a four piece "psychedelic" group, utilizing drums, bass guitar, lead guitar, saxes and flute. The flutist was one Steve Jolliffe, according to Edgar Froese one of the best musicians he has worked with, unfortunately he was involved in a car accident and was forced to return to England where he later joined a band called "Steamhammer." This early band played their own material in an improvised way and experimented with songs about drugs and their effects on people.

But in February 1969, after almost a year and a half of playing in clubs and universities, in and around Berlin, the band split. The reason being that some members decided to call it quits due to their general lack of success and overall poor financial status as they weren't making too much money At this point Froese thought it impossible to form another psychedelic group with German musicians.

With only a tape from a live radio show, he went to England to make a new start and hopefully land a recording contract. But after just one week he became disillusioned with the whole scene and returned home to Germany. Before doing so however he had a meeting with Muff Winwood (who at this time was just forming Island Records). Winwood seemed "very, very" impressed by his radio tape, but after a lot of commendable words he asked him, "Excuse me please, it all sounds very marvelous but what are you doing in this country as a German musician?" To use Edgar Froese's words, "maybe I looked like a moon monster or something like this." After this he left England immediately.

When he got back home he found that a new record company had been formed called Ohr (Ear). They offered him a contract, so he signed. He now had to find musicians to form a band. After some time he joined with two musicians Conny Schnitzler and Klaus Schulze and the new Tangerine Dream was born. All three were interested in improvised music and after weeks of getting organized and discovering each others possibilities they recorded *ELECTRONIC MEDITATION*, in February 1970. The instrumentation for this LP included drums, organs, lead guitar, bass guitar, flute and electric violin. The album was based on the concept of a burning brain and what it was like to travel through it. It was really an

uninteresting album [Ed. note -- while not an outstanding LP, it is however a

tempting foretaste of things to come], not particularly representative of what they could do. Soon after this Schnitzler left to form a rival band, Eruption, while Schulze left to go solo.

Now Froese was back where he had begun. But it was not long before he met up with Christophe Franke, formerly with Agitation Free, who played various keyboards and percussion. They shared similar ideas and a close musical policy grew between them. These two were later joined by Steve Schroyder playing keyboards, electronics and also echo machines.

June 1971 saw the recording of *ALPHA CENTAURI*. This really marked the turning point in Tangerine Dream's music. It was the start of their timeless journeys into a form of music incredibly individual, original and imaginative. They made the transition into electronics, very much keyboard-dominated and almost totally lacking in rhythmic beat. This was the start of a new era, the true Tangerine Dream.

They were now hugely popular in Germany, *ALPHA CENTAURI* was voted "Album of the Year" by the German music papers. They were asked to do TV shows and write for programs. At this point another personnel change occurred, Steve Schroyder left and was replaced by Hans Peter Baumann. They then recorded, in January 1972, *ZEIT* (Time), a double set that showed their true brilliance. It was an astonishing piece of music. The VCS3 synthesizers were now an integral part of the line-up. Tangerine Dream were now being asked to write movie soundtracks. Also they were touring Europe almost continuously and receiving very good receptions wherever they played. Together with Ash Ra Tempel and Klaus Schulze (now solo), they played a special concert at the Theatre De L'Ourst Parisian in Paris. Music paper reporters were there from all over the world. Tangerine Dream were hot news (London's Melody Maker said, "They start where Pink Floyd leave off.")

During January 1973, Tangerine Dream's fourth LP was recorded, titled *ATEM* (Breath). For the first time the lineup was the same as the last LP and it was a marked development from *ZEIT*. The title track "Atem," a 20-minute-plus work is both complex and dramatic, yet soothing and beautiful. Since the last album Tangerine Dream have toured throughout Europe to Switzerland, Belgium, France, Austria and others.

The latter half of 1973 however was to be quite hectic. First there was news that Tangerine Dream had been offered a tour of Britain. Alas, this was not to come off. The London agency offered them £700 for 10 gigs in England and Scotland. They get this for only 2 in Germany however, and the agency refused to offer any more so the tour fell through. Secondly came the news of a break with the German record company Ohr. This was due to several reasons: one was that the company would not print information about the group in English, even though they had many fans in England who naturally wanted to know all about the band; two -- Tangerine Dream wanted their LPs released in other countries, such as England and also America (where they are becoming quite popular). This couldn't be done however under their contract with the company. These plus other problems, and their failure to promote Tangerine Dreams LPs to the group's satisfaction, led to Ohr and the group severing ties.

Only recently have their problems with Ohr been settled completely after a long struggle to break fully with the company. The latest news is that the group has signed a new record contract with Virgin Records. A new album is due sometime in '74 and a tour of Britain looks likely, probably in the spring. A contract with a good, fair company and no sign of their inspiration or imagination drying up makes the future look good for Tangerine Dream.

Julian Atkins

Tangerine Dream
(An Infinite Journey Through Time)

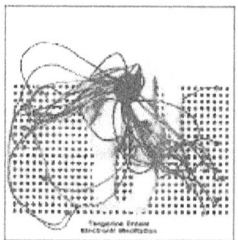

ELECTRONIC MEDITATION -- February 1970
Edgar Froese - lead guitar, 12 string guitar, organ
Conny Schnitzler - cello, organ, guitar
Klaus Schulze - drums, percussion

Tangerine Dream's first album was made when German rock bands were just starting to create their own style of music, whereas before they had just copied Anglo-American bands.

The Tangerine Dream band of this time were one of many playing the same kind of music in Germany. The LP poses the question -- does the brain burn? Can you travel in it? It warns that when you hear this record a dissected human life will pass in front of you.

The opening track "Genesis" is an average piece of music for the time. Schulze's drumming helps it along, his heavy beat gives it some sense of direction. It runs into "Journey Through A Burning Brain," the best track of the album. It's a 13-minute number, that builds and bubbles before Froese's guitar takes over at the end in a fury of crashing guitar notes that leads into an organ finale. Side 2 -- "Cold Smoke," "Ashes to Ashes," and "Resurrection" are all based loosely around Froese's guitar. There is the odd occasion however when electronics, which are to dominate in later records, are suggested but mainly by the manipulation of the organ and mixing and recording techniques.

On the whole the LP lacks enough imagination to keep the listener for its duration. And although it took longer than any of their others to record, it seems to be rushed and a bit loose. It's definitely their weakest record and is totally unrepresentative of them over the last three years. In fact after this album was recorded the music changed completely to what we now regard as the music of Tangerine Dream.

ALPHA CENTAURI -- June 1971
Edgar Froese - guitar, bass, organ
Chris Franke - percussion, flute, piano-harp, zither, synthesizer
Steve Schroyder - organ, echo machines, iron stick

ALPHA CENTAURI was a real turning point in the history of Tangerine Dream. This was the kind of music they have now become comparatively well-known for. Vastly different from their last LP, there is a definite absence of rhythmic beat. The music has matured now and mellowed into something beautiful and haunting. *ALPHA CENTAURI* still remains the favorite LP of many people. In fact in 1971 it was voted "Album of the Year" by the German music papers.

The opening track, "Sunrise in the Third System," is full of serene beauty yet has a great dramatic effect. The excellent church organ sound brings this track alive with the echo machines flashing from one speaker to the other. The organ builds in volume steadily then dies away to conclude. The other track on the first side is "Fly And Collision Of Comas Sola." Another exciting piece, with a slight hint of the dramatic again, particularly the actual collision. The track opens with severe use of the echo machines, before the sustained organ sound comes in, with the guitar in the background. This moves along until the great climax, exciting and really frightening, in which you can actually imagine the collision. The crescendo dies away slightly to allow the drums to come in (the only time they are used on this LP) then the flute also appears with the echo machines at the very end to fade the track out.

All of side 2 is taken up with the title track *ALPHA CENTAURI*, some 22 minutes in length. It has a most soothing opening on the cymbals, moving majestically into synthesizers and echo machines. Then swirling organ sounds penetrate the stabbing synthesizer sound effects. A zither synthesizer rises and falls away as if a cosmic wind had blown by. Then it moves on to an improvised flute passage, slowly played but with a sense of underlying happiness. In the background the electronics also improvise and Froese's bliss guitar can be heard, sounding very much like a female choir. These interchange, trying to capture the listener's attention until the echo machines get into the act and lead into a fadeout that introduces some spoken German words. They are followed by a chant of voices and dense organ which reaches a climax then fades to end the album.

ZEIT -- January 1972
Edgar Froese - gliss guitar, generator
Chris Franke - VCS3 synthesizer, cymbals, keyboards
Hans-Peter Baumann - VCS3 synthesizer, organ, vibraphone

In my view, ZEIT is one of the most amazing records ever released. It means "time" but is timeless. Whenever I hear this LP, I always play the whole 76 minutes, and always an aura of astonishment comes over me. I lose complete track of time, which I suppose is the intention in the first place. This is what Tangerine Dream are all about. The VCS3 synthesizers are now in complete control, with the Farfisa organs not far behind. There is a total absence of drums and vocals throughout the album, which is made up of four slow movements.

The first side opens mainly with five cellos which are played by guest musicians. The sound grows quite intense at times with great pulses vibrating out of the speakers. Gradually this is interrupted by the soft mellow organ sound, and some reverberated synthesizer. All quite stimulating. The whole thing is filled with such intense beauty that mere words cannot express the feeling the music projects. This first side is titled "Birth of Liquid Plejades." Another sound is heard, Froese's chorus-sounding guitar. I should explain that this chorus effect is achieved by, to quote Froese, "A normal guitar played with an iron stick," whatever that is.

Two organs play together, one with a single note sustained for a long period, the other a beautiful melody. The synthesizer improvises in the background and the guitar again comes to the fore while many and various organ sounds swirl and dance in the background. Leading into a short passage before a rich Cathedral-type organ sound ends the first movement.

Side 2, titled "Nebulous Dawn," is the most incredible opening to a piece of music I've ever heard. The synthesizer pounds a deep wowing sound, while the vibraphone, well, just vibrates. Other sounds like bells and chimes echo, creating what I can only describe as a "fluffing sound" accompanied by the organs cascade of frightening notes. It has a very haunting quality, and when sitting in complete darkness, which one should do for all this record, it can be quite terrifying.

The synthesizers then lay on a really heavy deep pulsing sound, while the organs let out cries to the dead. There are so many different sound sources that it is impossible for them to be monotonous. The "fluffing sound" that I mentioned returns again, and some sounds which are similar to a stream flowing. There is so much happening that it is impossible to comment on it all. The deep bellowing synthesizer returns with a shimmering organ to end the second movement.

"Origin of Supernatural Probabilities," the title of the third side, begins with gliss guitar played slow and soft, the synthesizer sounding like waves on the seashore, together with shimmering organ sounds. Then, appearing from nowhere comes another synthesizer, sounding incredibly like a pulsing heartbeat, very mysterious. In fact, one of Tangerine Dream's major influences is mysticism. The heartbeat continues, while a descending organ prevails through bleeps, swirls and cascades of sound from the other instruments. The pulse then fades away to allow a series of descending organ notes to appear before coming back even more fiercely, eventually fading into the chorus-sounding guitar which becomes dominant, while the organ menaces somewhere close behind. More ominous organ and deep gliss guitar ends the third movement.

Finally, side four is the title track "Zeit." The gliss guitar opens with a series of notes with one synthesizer howling and the other sounding very much like a solar wind. The guitar with iron stick is used again, there are synthesizers sounding like a cross between birds singing and running water, and more incredible haunting organ is heard for a brief moment.

This effect of the guitar played with iron stick and the synthesizer is quite tranquil, very peaceful, almost sending you to sleep, not with boredom but with its soothing beauty. A single note on the organ switches from one speaker to the other with a kind of lulling effect, the chorus sounding guitar continues in a dreamy sort of way, and a vibraphone echoes just before the guitar fades away to end the fourth movement and the album.

ATEM -- January 1973
Edgar Froese - Mellotron, guitar, organ
Chris Franke - organ, VCS3 synthesizer, percussion
Hans-Peter Baumann - organ, VCS3 synthesizer, piano

Tangerine Dream's latest album, *ATEM* (meaning Breath) is really a development in the same context as ZEIT. To quote the title, the opening is breathtaking, quite startling, with the use of drums for the first time in some while. Well to the fore are the organs and synthesizers, but a new instrument has been added to the Tangerine Dream line-up -- Mellotron, which gives an extra sound dimension.

The drumming is at times very ferocious growing to an intense climax accompanied by tremendous bass sounds and haunting organ notes, while the synthesizer screams out terrific crescendos. It's as if the entire planet were about to erupt. Just as the sound becomes overwhelming, a thunderous crash brings it to an end and a very soft, quiet organ fills the air while the synthesizer sounds remarkably like someone breathing. The Farfisa's sound then spirals up as produced by the VCS3 synthesizer, and the sound of a human heartbeat is recognized. Two organs fight to gain command as their echoing sounds combine to produce a frightening noise. A large boom of the synthesizer starts a small climax of sound accompanied by a terrifying ominous organ. Strange effects happen that don't seem to come from the record, but from somewhere thousands of miles away, so unreal that I cannot describe the feelings they give. A raging of synthesizers and other electronics provide another climax of swirling organ sounds and fluffing synthesizer similar to some of the effects on ZEIT. A kind of clang-clang-clang only the synthesizer could produce ends this first side.

1973

Side two begins with a track called "Fauni-Gena." This starts remarkably like the sound of a flock of birds nesting in some wild, desolated place. The Mellotron recreates the sound of a flute, while the synthesizers make various bird calls. Fauni-Gena incidentally, is a mystic person from antiquity. A crescendo is reached with the Mellotron, synthesizer, and organ, while a deep bass rhythm lures in the background. Then the bass rhythm comes well to the fore together with the Mellotron and synthesizer still sounding like bird whistles, the piece fades to an end.

"Circulation of Events" is the next number. It opens with immense deep bass from the synthesizer, while the organ shimmers and the Mellotron echoes in the distance. Both the organ and Mellotron echo in unison which produces a truly strange effect. Again the organ notes are played very delicately and the bass becomes overwhelming at times. Sounds from the organ vibrate from one speaker to the other, and this, together with the bubbling bass sounds bring the track to a close.

The final track on the album is called "Wahn." It begins with some free-form shouting, first from one speaker then the other. An echo is used, and the overall effect is both unusual and interesting. Some cries and shouts echo to a climax before the organ and drums come in, followed by the Mellotron. Again the whole sound is very pleasing. Ripples of deep synthesizer notes are heard, the organ cries, the drums fade out and the Mellotron ends the track and the album.

Julian Atkins

Can

"The music of Can cannot be defined. It originates from the conception of four separate individuals and is composed as a composition on tape with the musical notation following. The music contains an ever-present tangible substantiality and presents itself without any pretenses to its listeners -- as opposition to all of society's pressures. The music is indescribable yet has suggestive elements and one should listen to it without preconceived ideas."
-Liberty/U.A. GMBH

Can came together in September 1968. The original lineup was Irmin Schmidt, Holger Czukay, Michael Karoli, Jaki Liebezeit and Malcolm Mooney. It remains the same today except for two changes. Malcolm Mooney, the American vocalist was forced to leave due to illness and replaced by Japanese-born Damo Kenji Suzuki in May 1970. And then just recently, in November 1973, Damo left in order to pursue a more arranged pop style of music.

In looking at Can the first thing that should be done is to examine their individual backgrounds. Irmin Schmidt plays organ. After studying music for eight years under Karlheinz Stockhausen and Luciano Berio, he played in various symphony orchestras including the Vienna Symphony. He then decided to broaden his musical scope and joined in forming Can. Holger Czukay plays bass. He also studied under Stockhausen as well as Posseur and König. After serving some time as a music professor he joined Can. Michael Karoli (guitar) began his music career by playing in various Swiss jazz and pop groups. He then quit music to go into the study of law. He soon gave that up however and went back into music, joining in the formation of Can. Jaki Liebezeit (percussion) started in music playing with some of Germany's finest jazz musicians. From there he went on to be one of the co-founders of the Manfred Schoof Quintet (the first European free-jazz group). After it disbanded he came to Can. From these various backgrounds they took their knowledge of the classics, jazz, and electronics and fused them into what is now known as Can music.

In the beginning due to the fact that most German record companies were somewhat hesitant to invest a lot of time and money in German groups, they obtained an old castle and turned it into their own private cinema and recording studio. There they recorded their first LP, *MONSTER MOVIE*, with two amplifiers and an old Revox recorder. It was a dynamic work fusing pounding percussion, driving rhythms and crackling electronics into rock and roll to create a startlingly different sound.

Their next work was on film scores. They composed soundtracks for German progressive filmmakers Roland Klick, Roger Fritz and Thomas Schamoni as well as several other European producers.

Following that they produced the unreal two-record work *TAGO MAGO* that brought their name international attention. It was a truly incredible exploration in the use of percussion and electronics and their possibilities in a rock context. The four sides featured some of the most amazing drum work and electronic experimentation with bass, organ and guitar that has ever been out on vinyl. As a result of the great acclaim and interest the LP generated in England, they had their first tour set. Prior to that however, on February 14, 1972, they played possibly their most important gig. It was in the Cologne Sportshall to 10,000 people where they played an incredible four-hour free concert, that made them virtually a legend in their own time and hugely popular in their home country.

After that triumph they toured England and set the English rock scene astir. Reaction to them varied from people walking out of their gigs shaking their heads in agony, to those who widely acclaimed them to be musical virtuosos raising the level of rock technology to great new heights.

In the last year they have toured three twice, establishing a large and increasing following and have released another LP, *EGE BAMYASI*. It came out in Germany, England and the United States receiving much critical acclaim. It was a further evolution in their style and another step forward in expanding the limits of rock music. It ranged from imaginative pop to electronic experimentalism, and was characterized by their devastating rhythms and random improvisations.

Since then they have recorded a new musical work, *FUTURE DAYS*, to be released very soon, and Damo their singer has left, leaving them a four piece with Michael and Irmin handling the vocals. In their future is another English tour set to solidify & increase their following and plans to push ahead even further yet in developing their own unique form of music, spontaneous music, music for the mind and body from a collective entity -- Can.

Archie Patterson

Yesterday Meets Tomorrow
or Can Stands Alone Today

Primal and future groups are not uncommon. The Stooges, Amon Düül 1 and the New York Dolls are all in their own way distinctively primitive. And in the opposite realm we find such titans as Guru Guru, Ash Ra Tempel and Neu! So who lies in between and merges the opposite poles? Can.

It appeared that when American psychedelia ended, German abstract expressionist music volunteered to usher in the new decade of mind-expanding intergalactic sound. Amon Düül was one of the providers of this mutant liftoff and another name that irrevocably came up in the same sentence was Can.

Can was comprised of jazz, electronic, rock, and soul trained musicians and these influences are quite discernible in their first album *MONSTER MOVIE* released in 1969. From its inception Can undoubtedly had the best rhythm section in rock. The only entity to even come close is the Stooges and that's only since Ron Ashton, originally their lead guitarist has switched to bass.

Holger Czukay invented a few concoctions for his bass to give it a hollowed pulsating throb that heretofore had not been heard. Jaki Liebezeit probably keeps a stronger beat than anybody and knows just as much about simplicity as complexity.

The first Can album *MONSTER MOVIE* wasn't anywhere near as scary as its name implies when compared to its offspring. It was however an interesting debut seemingly influenced by the Velvet's *WHITE LIGHT/WHITE HEAT* period with a black vocalist who owed no small debt to Arthur Lee. The second side consisted of one number, "You Doo Right," that was highly reminiscent of the Love epic "Revelation." Malcolm Mooney, the vocalist in reference, was an American as opposed to the rest of the band and there is no mistaking it. There are no attempts to sound sophisticated on *MONSTER MOVIE*, the band slows down and then builds right back up again just supplying Malcolm with the ammunition he desired.

A short time later he was forced to leave

the group. His replacement was found on a street corner muttering some nondescript foreign language that turned out to be Japanese. Uninterested in ordinary vocals and to a great degree music too, Damo the Japanese street singer got the job.

The fourth Can album (according to release date) was actually the second in terms of the date recorded. So *SOUNDTRACKS*, recorded in 1969/80, has to be concentrated on next. Two cuts recorded in '69 feature Malcolm, one's an instrumental, and the remainder illustrate the new sound of Can with Damo serving as front man. At this point Can was somewhere between early Velvet rock and German space rock in the crevices on Mars. The addition of Damo expanded their collective imagination and greatly improved the avant-garde standing of their music.

Not a single worshipper of "Sister Ray" can afford to be without *SOUNDTRACKS* for the fourteen-minute "Mother Sky" which sounds like a clearer cleaner version of the aforementioned and is in every way just as good. Probably even better in fact because the Velvets didn't use bass in those days and there's no getting around the effective throbbing bulge given it by Holger. Two other songs were of special futuristic value rhythmically speaking. "Tango Whiskeyman" and "Don't Turn The Light On, Leave Me Alone" both foreshadowed a loose rhythm pattern heretofore unheard in rock.

TAGO MAGO, a double album released in 1971 or perhaps early '72 told all. This established Can as one of the all time hair-raisers and mind befuddlers. Very little in the way of structured rock appeared here and what there was of it was so primitive, new definitions for that classification had to be invented. Damo was firmly assimilated into the group and his voice was often used as the lead instrument.

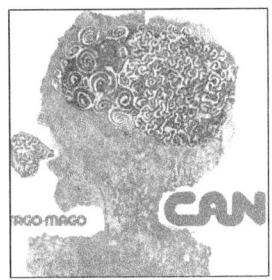

"Paperhouse" opened with bird chirps and electronic swirls just like Pink Floyd's "The Narrow Way" but that's where the similarities end. The tempo increases drastically in line with guitar shrieks and Damo's screams until it falls off as quickly as it had begun and then runs right into "Mushroom," the most memorable performance of the set. It's also the shortest at under five minutes which pretty well explains it. Like "Paperhouse" it's a showcase for dynamics which without Damo would be nowhere near as overwhelming. "Oh Yeah" contains some rarely discernible organ with Damo mumbling over it upheld by the characteristic strong beat.

"Hallelujah" is the first of two entities that takes up the second side. Introduced by the ever-present jumpy beat, Damo sings what might be called a song with no words that is interspersed by piano, organ and electronic eeks. What Damo does towards the latter third of the side is the kind of thing that makes most shake their head in dismay. But those in the know, know otherwise.

"Aumgn," side 3, qualifies as the sonic astounder of the LP. Concocting images of the Frankenstein monster being resurrected in an opera house during an electronic symphony, the mood is treacherous and the sound is shrilly atonal with Damo's monotone groans. Echoes dart back end forth while a premature burial victim re-emerges to stir havoc.

1973

Near the conclusion the drums explore clicks & clanks, dogs bark, sirens scream and drones signal a final plunge into oblivion.

"Peking O" is somewhat more terrestrial, but nowhere near the mundane. The electronically propelled organ-generated shrieks combined with Damo's haunting groans forecast the ominous that doesn't quite occur. The scary mood is abandoned for what might be called indescribable abstract expressionism. The vocal, percussion and piano which dominate the piece are straight out of the madhouse. If "Aumgn" was to be heard at the darkest hour of the night, then this was to be heard at the dullest hour of the day to liven things up a bit. This is what Roxy Music might have sounded like when they had Eno if they went berserk.

"Bring Me Coffee or Tea" rounds the LP out in somewhat subdued fashion. The aggressiveness is a little more sedate here and the sentiment expressed is somewhere between an Indian raga and a Pink Floyd dirge. For those who wish to take a headlong dive into madness, *TAGO MAGO* is just what the doctor ordered.

The most recent recording of Can, as documented on *EGE BAMYASI*, is nearing a year since release. It functioned as a compressed *TAGO MAGO* in some ways with ten minute selections such as "Pinch" and "Soup." It also went beyond that

however and in some instances like on the pretty ballad "Sing Swan Song" was even melodic in a sense. The real standout though was the three and a half minute "Vitamin C" that could conceivably have been a single. *EGE BAMYASI* has been the only Can LP released here in the U.S. and based on its lack of sales it might be the last, except for in the import racks. As far as sales potential goes, they probably have less of a chance than Amon Düül. Then again, with few exceptions (especially in the '70s) that's frequently the case with the most imaginative artists. Maybe in the year 2000. Until then there's still four ingenious items of esoterica.

Scott Fischer

1974

Nektar

Nektar came together in mid-1968, as a result of a jam session at the "Star Club" in Hamburg, Germany. The group was not properly christened however until November, 1969 when a permanent guitarist was finally added. To date the lineup has remained the same: specifically that's Derek "Mo" Moore - bass and vocals; Allan "Taff" Freeman - keyboards and vocals; Roye Albrighton - guitar and vocals; Ron Howden - drums and Mick Brockett - light show.

In fact Nektar comes from England and not from Germany as many people think, for all the group are English. This confusion results from the fact that some members had been living in Germany since 1965.

After the "Star Club" jam and subsequent addition of a guitarist, the group began touring throughout Germany. Their first gig at Munich's "PN Club" got quite a reaction and from there they took off touring clubs all over Germany. At this point an American producer heard them, and being impressed invited them to the U.S. to record. The product of the American visit was an LP cut in Boston.

Their stay in the U.S. lasted three weeks, they then returned to Germany generally disillusioned and settled in Seeheim where they still reside today. After that they began waiting for the release of the record. Finally after a year and no record released they became free and signed a new contract with Germany's Bacillus records which is today associated with Bellaphon Records.

The space opera *JOURNEY TO THE CENTRE OF THE EYE* was their debut record in September of '71. It wasn't especially successful, but it did provide a glimpse of things to come. Characterized by its arrangements, extended theme and psychedelic overtones it definitely set a course for them to follow in the future. After its release their live performances increased. They undertook a tour of Continental Europe and two English tours including a show at London's Lyceum.

In April 1972 they released their second LP, *A TAB IN THE OCEAN*. It fea-tured a refine-ment of tech-nique and overall better sound. A lot of the psychedelics of the first LP had been replaced by changes in tempo and dynamics. It still had once again psychedelic overtones, but they were now more integrated into the musical flow. That year marked a time of getting it to-gether for the band. The light show became more refined and totally integrated into the groups overall presentation. The lights and films became a fundamental ingredient of the music itself.

Mick Brockett devoted all his time to designing lights that complemented every aspect of the group's sound. Much of it was inspired by the Jefferson Airplane light show which he had earlier observed and experimented around with when he toured Germany in 1969 with Pink Floyd and the Pretty Things showing his early light work "Fantasia."

Also they got the business side of the group re-organized. Derek Moore took over as manager as well as playing bass. He collected the addresses of promoters and organizers and formed a management bureau for the band. They now handle all of their business themselves.

They emerged from the year with their third LP, *SOUNDS LIKE THIS*... A double set it featured more complex arrangements, but a slightly different musical direction. The playing was more heavy or hard rock. It was also recorded "live in the studio" so it served to give the listener a better idea of their real sound. At this point they began to get international attention. All three of the albums were imported into Britain and the U.S. where they sold well. They also undertook another English tour and got very good reactions everywhere they played.

Spurred on by growing recognition they recorded their fourth album *REMEMBER THE FUTURE*. It features their best work yet. Once again they have gone back to extended thematic pieces as the two sides are complete movements of the LP's concept as a whole. Their instrumental work showed a continued improvement and the dynamics and harmonies have been used for the first time to their fullest extent. All in all it adds up to a work that gives continuous listening pleasure.

At this point in time Nektar stands on the brink of International recognition. They have toured Britain once again and had *REMEMBER THE FUTURE* released there on United Artists. Also *TAB IN THE OCEAN* has been specially released there due to their growing popularity and large sales of the import.

Finally in the U.S., they now have a label as *REMEMBER THE FUTURE* has just been released on Passport Records. So it appears as if we will definitely be hearing more from Nektar in the future.

Archie Patterson

The Future As Envisioned By Nektar

Nektar is an English band that calls Germany home, as they reside there. Speculation might lead one to assume that the cause of their migration rests in the popularity of sci-fi rock there and their hopes of catching on in that fairly proven safety zone of interstellar travel. Not so however. Their reason for the move was to find time to formulate their ideas without the evils of pressure and expense hampering them. Originating in 1968 and not recording until 1971 it would seem they'd be prepared when their time came in the studio and indeed they were.

JOURNEY TO THE CENTRE OF THE EYE ranged from a space opera to an introspection through an exalted dreamworld, equally well presented musically and lyrically, the latter enhanced by informative liner notes. With the possible exception of the French mutants Magma, it's the best conceptual science fiction story yet vinylized. Fleeing planet Earth's eminent destruction at its own hands, an astronaut aims his rocket ship for Saturn only to be intercepted by a saucer from an existence elsewhere. The otherworldly beings paint a picture in his mind of beauty and serenity in another galaxy and invite him along to see for himself, which he gratefully concurs to do. Once there he transforms into a visionary seeing only through his mind via a great shining eye to see the universe within himself and merging with it he envisions the inevitable -- the destruction of the Earth!

Sonically speaking it was semi-atonal with conventional four piece rock combo instrumentation (guitar, organ, bass, and drums) except for occasional Mellotron to simulate the tranquillity of the galaxy. Quite reminiscent at times of *SAUCERFUL OF SECRETS* with vocal harmonies that would make Crosby, Stills & Nash proud. Traces of American psychedelia circa Iron Butterfly, Vanilla Fudge and the Doors are also evident. Thematically the Byrds' *FIFTH DIMENSION* and the Amboy Dukes' *JOURNEY TO THE CENTER OF THE MIND* are both recalled balancing the scales between the outer and the inner.

A TAB IN THE OCEAN, Nektar's second album, recorded in late '72, dealt primarily with the opposite polarity of outer space, hence inner space -- the deep blue sea. The sounds of waves aptly open the title side with a deep organ and full density sound thrust right on its heels. Here the double entendre pertains as an underwater fantasy is equated with ones search for inner truth. Possibly because the ocean is a major part of the Earth whereas space is something distant and entirely different, the prevailing sentiment is quite negative. Anyway, no ready-made solution is available and before you know it the seventeen minute side is over ending the way it began.

"Desolation Valley" takes up where side one left off, continuing the grope for the unlikely, with quieter moments abruptly punctuated by atonal organ plunges and searing electrified guitar howls. Part 2 side 2 probes the dividing line between reality and imagination with nothing yet revealed. "Crying in the Dark" finds desperation at the breaking point as expressed by the increasingly urgent queries for help. Just in time, the "King of Twilight" arrives with a plausible solution -- "a chance to be free." So in actuality this side ends on a brighter universal note than its predecessor.

With their third album, the double *SOUNDS LIKE THIS...*, the time lapse between follow-ups was narrowed from a year to six months. Less complex than its forerunners, it seemed a likely candidate for the commercial acceptance so far unattained and a probable choice to catch on in their homeland. If Vanilla Fudge

1974

merged with the Beatles in a time warp or if Uriah Heep was any good this might be the result. The songs are short and long with the former even having hit potential and the extended pieces allowing experimentation minus the thematic restrictions of before. Side 4 was the most impressive with the brief dynamic "Wings" followed by the fourteen minute jazz/hard rock synthesis "Never, Never, Never." Side 3 contains the most lyrically ambitious and melodically attractive number of the set, "Cast Your Fate," a hymn to the uncertainty of destiny and self determination, with offhand references to such metaphysics as: the prophets of life/the actors of doom/the virgins of delight. The final selection of side 3 "A Day in the Life of a Preacher" features, for the most part, guitar shrieks and organ crescendos. Operating on the same principal as the second half of the album, except for order of succession, Side 2 consists of the lengthy "One-Two-Three-Four" and the somewhat shorter "Do You Believe in Magic" not to be confused with another song of the same title. Alas, Side 1 would appeal to those into concise arrangements with minimal instrumental displays as three approximately 5-minute-plus tunes round out the album. Most notable of these being cut 2 "New Day Dawning" for its "Norwegian Wood" stanza. Of lesser importance is the following track " What You Gonna Do," which ranks as the least memorable thing Nektar has ever done probably because its a satire on jerk-off rock groups. It would have been nice if UA in the U.S. had signed them over here and maybe released this as a two-for-one, but such is the record biz in the land of the unappreciative.

Apparently *SOUNDS LIKE THIS* received at least marginal acclaim and adequate sales in England, for their next effort was not only released several months later, it was also recorded there. *REMEMBER*

THE FUTURE might be considered the best of both worlds as the sound remains accessible and the subject matter reverts back to their sci-fi origins.

The plot of the album revolves around the plight of a young blind boy who meets a bluebird who offers the boy hope, as those of short-sighted vision have only ridiculed and tried to harm him on previous visits to the planet. Having blue skin and wings, he was unacceptable to those who could see, so the blind boy is actually benefited by his ailment. Upon making contact bluebird establishes communication, expounding on mankind's evolution as a prerequisite for elaboration on the future. Finding the boy an avid listener, the bluebird provides him with a new set of eyes and having never seen before the boy is unlike the others, unafraid. The bluebird departs on a final note serving as an ultimatum:

> The laws of nature are to
> heal the wounds of man
> Use them right and they
> will help you if they can
> Wrongly used and you'll
> only harm yourselves
> Then it's too late to come
> to me for help

For a space band they are undoubtedly the most vocally capable. On their first three albums the sound got top priority, but it's all balanced here, as the two parts divided accordingly between two sides -- the past and the future -- are both lyrically and instrumentally strong.

The future holds promise beyond man's self-destructive path toward annihilation. Nektar has offered at least glimmers of hope of what awaits us. No doubt it lies elsewhere.

Scott Fischer

Embryo

Embryo was born in 1968. It was originally a four man group with members coming from virtually all segments of music -- blues, jazz, pop, and experimental.

Over the years there have been numerous personnel changes as some of Germany's finest musicians have passed through the ranks of the group. Some of the people who have lent their talents to Embryo are: Jimmy Jackson - American soul organist (who has also worked with Amon Düül); pianist Mal Waldron; noted German jazz man Charlie Mariano (the 50-year old saxophonist who has played with American jazz greats Stan Kenton, Charlie Mingus, McCoy Tyner and Elvin Jones); young German jazz rockers like Roman Bunka, Jorge Evers and Dieter Miekautsch; in addition guitarist Sigi Schwab - well known in German jazz circles; and American bassist Dave King.

Through all the changes however there have been constant factors, drummer/founder Christian Burchard has become the motivating force and seen to it that all the new members fit into the group's musical concept in spite of their various backgrounds. Also co-founder Edgar Hoffman has lent his invaluable creative talent to all of Embryo's recorded works even though at times he has not been considered an official member of the band.

Today the group exists as basically a free floating group of jazz rockers who tour and record as their various careers and schedules permit. In the last year they have undertaken tours of Africa and England, as well as much of Continental Europe and they've released 3 LPs -- *WE KEEP ON*, *STEIGAUS* and *ROCKSESSION*. So in spite of the relative instability and fluctuation of personnel Embryo is definitely going strong.

The recording career of Embryo is as erratic and changing as that of their personnel. In four years, they've had six LPs on four different labels. In effect there have been four stages in the development of Embryo into what it is today, and these stages are marked by their label changes.

Their first LP, *OPAL*, released on the then-fledging Ohr record label marks their beginnings. The group on that initial LP is John Kelley (an ex-Manchester blueser) on guitar; Edgar Hoffman (late cohort of Amon Düül's Chris Karrer, Peter Leopold and Dieter Serfas) on violin; founder Christian Burchard (also earlier involved with Amon Düül and former R&B and jazz drummer and marimba player) on drums; and Ralph Fischer on bass and vocals.

This first album for the most part consists

of shorter, almost pop like songs that show off all their various roots and influences. There's the title cut "Opal" that features some tasty violin and sinister deep vocals. It is almost commercial, certainly one of the most catchy pieces on the album. Another cut of note is "Revolution," a prelude to some of their later political tunes, in particular "Espagna Si Franco No." A pro-revolution statement, for that reason alone it's of interest. Finally there is "Call," a very early, crude beginning of what is to later bloom into a major work of high quality on their fifth LP *STEIGAUS*. All in all, *OPAL* is not a bad start.

From Ohr they went to German UA, and made what some think to be their best two LPs, *EMBRYO'S RACHE* and *FATHER, SON AND HOLY GHOSTS*. *EMBRYO'S RACHE* has Hoffman, Burchard, and Fischer along with a new addition on bass of Roman Bunka. It is a very good LP. Especially good is side two's "Espagna Si, Franco No" and "Verwandlung." "Espagna Si, Franco No" has some great Mellotron work and is one of their first extended jazz workouts. The side closes with "Verwandlung" that once again features great Mellotron and some real fine violin soloing by Hoffman. EMBRYO'S RACHE is an LP that starts off good and ends great, guaranteeing it will be played again.

FATHER, SON AND HOLY GHOSTS takes up where *EMBRYO'S RACHE* leaves off. It also marks their continuing move towards a more jazzy orientation. This time it's Burchard and Hoffman supplemented by the great jazz guitar of Sigi Schwab and American David King's bass. This LP fulfills the promise of *EMBRYO'S RACHE*. It is virtually a potpourri of nifty pieces of jazz/rock. There's the 58-second acoustic guitar piece "Nightmares," the maddening workout "King Insano," the delightful marimba track "Marimbaroos," and the truly great "Forgotten Sea." "Forgotten Sea" combines all the good qualities of these two LPs into one track. It's a continuation of "Espagna Si, Franco No" only refined, more dynamic, and 95% better. The guitar is simply great. It is probably the best track played during their UA period, and definitely shows where they are headed.

Their next work *WE KEEP ON*, was done for B.A.S.F. and was recorded in December '72. It features Roman Bunka, Christian Burchard and newcomer Dieter Miekautsch, and jazz vet Charlie Mariano. It marks the beginning of their practice of a jam as the basis of a recording session. "No Place To Go" stems from a 90-minute session. "Flute and Sax" stems from a 50-minute session. Basically the music is exotic and jazzy. Many of the cuts are simply titled to indicate workouts on the various instruments, e.g. "Flute and Sax" and "Hackbrett Dance" (a very old Bavarian instrument). The others vary from ballads, "Don't Come Tomorrow" to Indian music "Abdal Malek" and jazz "No Place to Go." A very diverse LP, and extremely listenable mainly for that reason.

With 1973 came phase four and the change to Brain/Metronome. The group now consists of Burchard, King, Hoffman, Bunka, Schwab and new men Mal Waldron and Jimmy Jackson, both noted session artists. Both *STEIGAUS* and *ROCKSESSION* (their fifth and sixth LPs respectively) are recorded with some combination of these people.

STEIGAUS marks their first mainly jazz-oriented LP. It still is basically rock, but there is a definite free-flowing jam session air to it. It doesn't feel like a group LP, but a session. In fact that's what it is. They have now definitely adopted the session LP idea, and it shows a definite improvement over *WE KEEP ON* where they first tried the idea out. *STEIGAUS* consists of free-wheeling jazz with rock and a bit of R&B influence à la Jimmy Jackson thrown in. The major work and most satisfying is "Call" which takes up all of side two. It's a non-stop onslaught of workouts on the various instruments -- Waldron's electric piano, Jackson's organ, Burchard's marimbas, and Hoffman's violin. A most satisfying side that never grows boring even with repeated listening.

Their latest work *ROCKSESSION* features more of the same. Only this time out it is once again a refinement of their previous efforts. It consists of four pieces, two per side, "A Place to Go," a sequel to "No Place to Go" and the excellent "Entrances" make up side one. Possibly the most enjoyable piece for myself is "Warm Canto," on side two, with its serene beauty. The marimba and jazz keyboard and guitar work really hooks ya. It's so tasty you can't hear it enough. Canto-like, it builds, then there's a solo, then it repeats over and over, each time adding another instrument. It virtually flows exuding a mellow sort of warmth. Closing out the LP is "Dirge." Its cymbals swirl to introduce great successive solos by Burchard on marimbas, Waldron on electric piano, and Schwab on guitar. Each tasty as hell. A fine capping off of the LP and a good place to begin from next time. With the foundation of continual growth and improvement that Embryo has exhibited throughout their six LPs so far, one cannot but anticipate their seventh.

Archie Patterson

Kraftwerk

Among German rock bands there exists the conventional in the form of heavy metaloids like Walpurgis, Scorpions, Lucifer's Friend and Birth Control, and the wildly unconventional -- dream weavers such as Tangerine Dream, Popol Vuh, Cluster and Klaus Schulze. Somewhere in between lies an area of musicianship that, while remaining basically rhythmic, offers no less a degree of uncompromising individuality than that of the avant gardists. Here you will encounter names like Amon Düül II, Can, Faust, Embryo and Guru Guru. Such a band is Kraftwerk. Formed in Dusseldorf at the advent of the '70s, Kraftwerk is comprised essentially of two men, Ralf Hutter and Florian Schneider-Esleben. Between them, they cover just about everything: vocals, keyboards, string and wind instruments, drums and electronics. Their first album featured Andreas Hohmann and Klaus Dinger (now with Neu!) on drums, but

1974

from the first it's been Ralf and Florian's band, they being the composers and essential musicians throughout.

Translated, the word "kraftwerk" takes on the double meaning of "power station" and "men at work;" both descriptions are equally appropriate. Until their latest album, *RALF AND FLORIAN*, Kraftwerk was perhaps the most dedicatedly mechanical band in existence, an aural onslaught of primitive beat and jarring electronic instrumentation. To some, the effect of their first two albums (recorded in 1970 and 1971, respectively) is decidedly mind-blowing.

But simplicity is the key. As envisioned through the heads of these two purposeful artists, Kraftwerk assaults from the very basics of music through rhythm. Showmanship has no part in their underplayed style and the effect is almost self-effacing and heavily intense. But so much for humble beginnings. Somewhere between album two and album three (recorded summer of '73), the realization that all this could be taken to more evocative extremes completely altered the band. *RALF AND FLORIAN* is anything but grating. Where the first two Kraftwerk efforts produced distinct black and whites in the shading of their music, *RALF AND FLORIAN* bursts forth in full color, a sound/rhythm tapestry of vibrant hues. The difference is both abrupt and startling.

The original Kraftwerk, so true to their title, seemed to be consciously striving toward a total unemotionality in their music, an uncompromising position perhaps but one that won them a certain underground popularity in England (where their three LPs are all readily available -- nothing has been released in the U.S. to date). This self-restriction may have been due to the fact that neither member possessed much expertise at their respective instruments, Ralf taking care of the keyboards and Florian manning the reeds and strings. Their approach was more one of mechanics, a sort of anti-music thing that produced some incredible sounds.

But for whatever the reasons, Kraftwerk's metamorphosis is complete. The only tie-in with the old sound is their heavy reliance on electronics, which has been expanded with the acquisition of new equipment. Before, electronics were used mainly to distort the sound of their instruments -- corroding harmonics, crackling feedback and phased percussion. With a more sophisticated array to work with, a purer form of electronic music emerged, still basically rhythm-oriented but with strong melody lines running through in subtle currents. What this will develop into from here is anyone's guess, but Ralf and Florian have certainly asserted themselves as major forces in the German rock scene. As originals, they have few equals anywhere.

Archie Patterson

Kraftwerk - *KRAFTWERK*
(July-September 1970)

Kraftwerk's first album is aptly decorated with a red construction marker on the cover and a picture of an electrical generator on the inside -- this is powerhouse music, intensely electric. Electricity is to Kraftwerk what the country is to John Denver: a focal source. Whereas bands like Deep Purple, Uriah

Heep, Humble Pie and Grand Funk channel their power into boogie, Kraftwerk puts its energy into an extreme extension of this style. So much so, in fact, that the similarities are only implied in a common base.

Without many preconceptions of what rock should or shouldn't be, Ralf Hutter and Florian Schneider introduced in *KRAFTWERK 1* a barrage of new ideas with a style so alien to most Western ears that it's something of a challenge to get into. The first track, "Ruckzuck," opens with echoing flute that preludes the rhythmic interplay to follow, flutes continuing to weave throughout as the pace mounts in a series of raw climaxes. Phasing is used quite a bit to accent the tension but feedback and engineered distortion are the real mainstays. "Ruckzuck" is comparatively tame in respects to most of the album and yet, it provides a fine introduction because it contains the essence of their altered rock style. "Stratovarius," featuring Florian on violin, offers Kraftwerk's less conventional side with an array of bizarre effects -- piercing violin strains, sounds of destruction, shuffled footsteps, percussive hammering -- that lead into the theme proper. Led by shrieking violin, the band (with Andreas Hohmann and Klaus Dinger bashing at the skins) propels into a madcap frenzy that's as raucous as it is enthralling; one rhythm picks up a after another as each hurls itself into a cacophonous peak. In terms of sheer heaviness, Kraftwerk's first album must be ranked with the best.

Side Two opens with a subtler piece of sound called "Megahertz," awesomely executed on organ with the engineering skills of Conrad Plank in the fore. The music soon settles down to a soothing duet between flute and organ which gradually moves into a crackling, droning Yes landscape (though with much more menacing overtones than Yes has ever produced). This sweeps into a swelling tide texture that washes into the final track, "Von Himmel Hoch." This cut, with its chainsaw buzzes and construction effects, is decidedly mechanical as it putters about like a demented bulldozer. But as in the case of most of Kraftwerk's songs, raw, dissonant noise soon makes way for savage pounding as the bulldozer takes on a reckless life of its own. A blistering self-destructive overload closes the album, leaving shards of voltage crackling in the air to twitch like razor-sharpened nerves.

Gregory Shepard

Kraftwerk - *KRAFTWERK 2*
(September - October 1971)

Unlike the first album, *KRAFTWERK 2* marks the first venture in which Ralf and Florian supply all the instrumentation. Unfortunately or not, little progression is made on the first -- the covers are identical except for a change from red to green -- with the result being only a slight variation on *KRAFTWERK 1*; it's almost as if both LPs formed an original double album (which is how they were released in England). The first side is taken up for the most part by one long piece, "Klingklang," that flows from one theme to the next in a lilting, cling-clang rhythm. With Florian's flute constantly floating above, this song is generally much lighter and airier than the material from the first LP, marking the one distinguishing difference from album to album, as the initial anger is dispelled into a more melodic form of expression, a mood that becomes further developed in their third album, *RALF AND FLORIAN.*

If *KRAFTWERK 1* was an assault, *KRAFTWERK 2* is more of an aftermath. For my own tastes, the tensions in the first are often more interesting because they express a zealous outrage that's missing in the second. But *KRAFTWERK 2* is no less arresting and there's never really a point where the 17-and-a-half minute "Klingklang" becomes dull. A short cut called "Atem" (breath) follows, hypnotic self-indulgence at its most extreme -- as if to pay tribute to the ultimate rhythm-machine, the human body, the listener is given three minutes of breathing.

This is mirrored at the end of Side Two by "Harmonika," which uses the same effect with the addition of harp. Oddly enough, they do fit into the whole, however valid they may be in themselves. The second side does offer more of their harsh electronic work, however, opening with a brooding track called "Strom" (stream). This is further developed in "Spule 4" (coil). This song, with its vibrating slide guitar effects, harkens back to the mechanized sound in the first album, with the exception of a regular beat. The rhythm that develops is torpid and maniacally ominous, but the next track, "Wellenlange" (wavelength), is even more so -- potent with understated threat.

These first two albums, taken as a whole, seem to suggest Kraftwerk to be very mechanical, but in fact the main difference is the perspective. In relation to most Western rock, Kraftwerk is quite cold. Perhaps the vision that these two men are pursuing is difficult to grasp because they DO deny any real warmth in their music. But generally speaking, this temperament is inherent to the Gothically-reared German culture -- German classic composers have always possessed a marked intensity, Wagner being the most obvious example. It is only with their third album that Kraftwerk escapes these bounds into a more optimistic creativity. Nonetheless, the uniqueness of these two LPs are their most striking feature and from this aspect, they are ultimate landmarks.

Gregory Shepard

Kraftwerk - *RALF AND FLORIAN*
(May-June 1973)

The construction cones that symbolized the first two albums are now replaced with a gold, bas-relief representation of machine-works, intricate and subtly imposing. The back cover gives us Ralf and Florian in respective lighting shades of red and green, smiling enigmatically toward each other at their electronic consoles and surrounded by their "machinery," the instruments of their trade. But the scene has definitely changed, giving way to a much more sensitively human approach -- they're no longer hiding behind a cover of bleak bizarritude. Even the title implies a loosening up of their machinist image, a realization of the band as people. The new Kraftwerk is upon us: composed, produced, executed and realized by Hutter and Schneider in one creative outpouring of emotion. This revelation of Ralf and Florian's humanity is reflected within, right from the first track, "Elektrisches

Roulette," a sparkling gem of pulsing electronics. Waves of sound ripple where before they fumed yet "Roulette" lacks nothing in energy -- the power is more under control, however frantic the beat. This opening track is certainly equal in originality to that of their previous efforts, but it also exudes a new freshness and humor never present before.

The next track, "Tongebirge," is a floating flute thing, beautifully echoed in its evocation of unhemmed heights and pastoral purity. Following this, "Kristallo" demonstrates the unique interplay in Kraftwerk in a harpsichord-synthesizer duet that surges into reverse then shoots off into a Walter Carlos/William Tell Overture takeoff that's as quick-paced and catchy as its *CLOCKWORK ORANGE* counterpart. The semi-classic allusion is also brought out in the next track, "Heimatklänge" (Homesound), a multi-tracked exchange between flute and piano resting on a disquieting foundation of bowed bass. While building on the mood established in "Tongebirge," this track also serves as an apt interlude before the two long tracks that make up the second side.

"Tanzmusik" (Dancemusic) begins with an effervescent collage of tinkling percussion, ethereal voices and a propelling rhythm that exemplifies the transformation of Kraftwerk from basic simplicity to complex simplicity. The beat still maintains a pulse-like regularity, but like their fellow countrymen in Can, Hutter and Schneider use rhythm in a many-layered technique that constantly fluctuates and shifts. The album's long piece, the fourteen minute "Ananas Symphonie" (Pineapple Symphony), relaxes this style in a wash of slide guitar right out of the islands; odd as it may seem, the similarities to the Beach Boys' *FRIENDS* LP is uncannily striking. In fact, as a whole, *RALF AND FLORIAN* is much more relaxed than either of the first two Kraftwerk albums -- comparatively, "Ananas" drifts almost casually where previous extended works always relied or sharp climaxes to create a gradual, mounting, electric tension.

With a refinement of electronic techniques in a more synthesized setting, many of the rhythmic boundaries surrounding Kraftwerk's music fell away. "Ananas" is especially timeless, foreshadowed by much of Side One. And yet for my own tastes, the more compelling side of Kraftwerk is brought out in their essentially rhythmic endeavors like "Elektrisches Roulette," "Kristallo" and "Tanzmusik." Whether Kraftwerk will develop into the area of space music with future recordings or maintain their rhythmic ties, the band is definitely one of the most original combinations working in rock today. Hutter's and Schneider's use of the conventional in drastically unconventional terms remains a focus through which rock music is evolved from the emotional to the emotive. Like rays of light trapped in a crystal, the glimmers that escape only suggest the faceted beauty within -- Ralf and Florian have begun to probe rock like a jewel, unpretentiously and ultimately crystalline in the splendor of their success.

Gregory Shepard

1974

Neu!

Like Kraftwerk, Neu! is the work of two men, Klaus Dinger and Michael Rother -- both former members of Kraftwerk (though Rother never recorded with them) with similar roots in the non-musician approach. Neu! formed in August, 1971 and recorded their first album in December of the same year for the Brain label. Having borrowed the money to finance the initial effort, it was completed with all due haste in four days under the assistance of Conrad Plank, one of Germany's more noteworthy engineers (who also works with Kraftwerk). The effect of their first album was very similar to that of Kraftwerk at the time, unpretentiously rough, but quite captivating in its haunting moods.

Dinger and Rother seemed to be loosening up Kraftwerk's style, giving it a dark beauty that the parent band was trying to eradicate from their own music. Even the distinctly-Kraftwerkian "Negativland" offered a new subtlety, a stronger evocation of the harshly mechanical than early Kraftwerk cuts possessed, though the arrangements were simpler. But where Kraftwerk would seek to sustain interest in the sound of breathing ("Atem") or a simplistic harmonica solo ("Harmonika"), Neu! took this to more interesting extremes with almost five minutes of phased cymbal ("Sonderangebot"), and came up with one of the eeriest compositions ever recorded.

Neither Neu! nor Kraftwerk make much use of vocals. Like Can, they use the human voice for the purpose of sound rather than lyrical content -- the result being a form of android scat, if you will. This method doesn't always work and one cut in particular, "Lieber Honig" (from Neu!'s first), is ruined by Klaus Dinger's breathy whine. *NEU! 2* features all-out wailing and is much more effective since the album itself is strikingly peculiar.

Recorded in early 1973, again with Conny Plank at the controls, Neu!'s second venture is perhaps the most overtly bizarre parody of heavy metal mania ever produced. If Kraftwerk reduced rock to its most basic elements, Neu! took this even further. Unlike their first, which was necessarily rushed, the attempt in NEU! 2 toward half-finished crudeness seems deliberate, almost as if they set out to record their own basement tapes; even the cover has that bootleg quality about it. The second side highlights this unrefined tendency, containing four separate places repeated at different speeds (with titles like "Super 16," "Super 78" and "Super"); it's just about the most single-mindedly raw recording you could imagine, including built-in skips and low-grade cassette recording. Perhaps oddly enough, much of it is quite good, frantic and totally alien (in keeping with the Kraftwerk precedent).

48, Eurock: European Rock & the Second Culture

There being nothing the least bit subtle to the heavy metaloids themselves, Neu! removed every last vestige in an onslaught of pure metal. Pulsic drumbeats in the tradition of such non-talents as Maureen Tucker (Velvet Underground) and Simon King (Hawkwind) set a primal base from which strummed, buzzed, phased and plucked guitar rhythms lash about unrestrained. The semblance, or at least overtones, of sophistication in the first album suggests that this ultimate simplicity is quite intentional. Unlike the members of Kraftwerk, Messrs. Dinger and Rother seem to be gravitating away from melody toward pure gut-level insurgence.

Both bands have now quite definitely established their separate identities, their only ties being a shared uniqueness. Given a third album from Neu!, the severance should be complete. Of course, the expense of good equipment and sound techniques may be the main factor that's preventing the definitive Neu! album, but only time and electricity can rectify that.

Archie Patterson

Neu! - *NEU!*
(December 1971)

To label the music of Neu! (or Kraftwerk) as one thing or another is somewhat misleading. Both bands have evolved a highly original sound -- Kraftwerk broke the ground and Neu! dug in from there. But because Neu! did spring forth from an already successfully established band, their task of creating their own identity was perhaps the more difficult one. Their first album, while not suffering under too many comparisons, has a distinctly Kraftwerkian feel to it; not as harsh but born from the same precepts (even the cover has the Kraftwerk touch of simple understatement). If anything, however, Neu! came up with an even more primitive sound than Kraftwerk, a sort of non-spacey Hawkwind style.

The first noticeable difference between Neu! and Kraftwerk is the instrumentation. Whereas the parent band relies heavily on flute and keyboards, Neu! are definitely a guitar band. The first track, "Hallogallo" (Hello Jello), builds on a basic beat with multi-tracked guitars drifting around in lazy patterns--plucked, wah-wahed, rhythmically chopped, reversed and buzzed. The effect is quite hypnotic through its full ten minutes and much subdued from Kraftwerk's early assaults. Klaus Dinger and Michael Rother envision songs from a more limited point of view than Hutter and Schneider and "Hallogallo" is propelled at a non-stop pace that goes through very few changes. "Sonderangebot" (Special Deal) is one of their exclusively-studio trips, a chilling piece created by the mere phasing of a cymbal. The understated mood is disarming because after four-and-a-half minutes of meandering sound effects, the sharply metallic climax is positively riveting. This bridges into "Weissensee" (Whitewash Sea), a mellow, flowing song which, like "Hallogallo," is entirely sustained on guitars and drums.

The best way to describe this music is to call it a relaxed Kraftwerk. This is mood music more than anything else, an offhand extension of San Francisco psychedelia and black-light despair. Side Two offers more variety, however, in a three part composition called "Jahresübersicht" (Annual Survey). The first part, "Im

Gluck" (In Bliss), floats in after a prelude of muffled conversation and water effects. The arrangement of the three parts is such that the first and third sections are quite subdued while the second is more energetic. "Im Gluck" is almost lethargic, lead by bowed bass and wah-wah guitar.

"Negativland," the next track, is so abrupt as to be startling -- the jarring sounds of the city burst in upon your ears, picked up by the band in a weirdly discordant melange of urban impressions. The beat is simple but the tone is much more varied than in previous tracks, with the guitars (both phased and regular) literally barraging the senses with frantic, screeching city life. Though generally Neu! don't build toward a particular climax in their music, "Negativland" brings to mind the best of early Kraftwerk; several short climaxes mount toward a driving peak that's as insane as the scene it's portraying.

The last track, "Lieber Honig" (Dear Honey), I find incredibly annoying. While offering nothing substantially new to the album as a whole, it features a grating vocal whine from Dinger that drives me up the wall every time I hear it. It's a unique style of singing, to be sure -- nasal flatulations, if you will -- but one that really doesn't work in this case. The melody is nicely plucked on Japanese banjo and the song could have been made vastly more tolerable with the exclusion of Dinger's voice. But this first album is quite compelling in its humble intent -- nothing adventurous considering the precedents set by Kraftwerk, but for those who find Kraftwerk too harsh for their tastes, a suitable alternative.

Archie Patterson

Neu! - *NEU! 2*
(January - February 1973)

Neu!'s second album marks a definite progression for the band; ironically enough, because *NEU! 2* is regressively primal in almost every aspect. The music has an added toughness to it, a harder edge of determined mania in its execution. The instrumentation is more inclusive as well, with the addition of violin, zither and piano and a listing for Rother on cassette recorder and Dinger on turntable. These last two items be come clear on the second side where the listener is subjected to custom-made scratches, variable speed changes and poor sound quality. This engineered self-effacement on Side Two is certainly the weirdest aspect of the album, but Side One introduces this unassuming attack quite appropriately with some aberrantly good rock.

The first track, "Für Immer" (Forever), begins with more of Neu!'s garage-band drumming, but the arrangement is more interestingly crafted, stronger and more varied than the music of the first album. Though the rhythm remains doggedly constant, the multi-tracking and phasing techniques are more integral and the overall sound is richer than before. "Für Immer" rocks along for eleven minutes, sustained for the most part by the various guitar rhythms weaving throughout. The next cut, "Spitzenqualität" (Top Quality), is an odd duet between drums and electronics that gradually slows into some crude phasing effects. This in turn develops into howling wind in "Gedenminute" (Minute's Thought), further augmented by ominous bell tolls. "Lila Engel" (Lilac Angel) follows, one of my favorite tracks on the album with its inhuman vocal chants and razor-sharp guitar blasts. It rocks like a Neanderthal robot, a suitable prelude to the sounds that meet the ears on Side Two.

This side consists of four separate themes -- "Neuschnee," "Super," "Cassetto" and "Hallo Excentrico!" -- the two former of which are repeated several times at different speeds. "Neuschnee 78" begins at high speed, followed by "Super 16," "Neuschnee" proper and so on. Of course, anyone could produce these same effects by merely switching the speed on their own turntable; but what Neu have created is a type of ultimate red-freak music, overtly burlesqued. "Super 16" is totally hilarious as it plods along like a constipated tank, vocal chants reduced to monstrous groans. The actual track itself is a real basher; that and "Neuschnee" (Fresh Snow) are actually quite good in themselves and it's very possible that Dinger and Rother are lampooning themselves by throwing in the rest of it.

"Super" and "Neuschnee" point to a direction that could develop Neu! into a major band in the future, though it would seem neither Rother or Dinger take any of this all too seriously. But even "Cassetto," with its execrable recording quality, possesses a certain heavy infectiousness in spite of itself. "Hallo Excentrico!," on the other hand, has got to be the most determinedly crude recording ever released on vinyl -- if you can get into it at all it's only in appreciation of the intent behind it...

Heavy redundancy in the extreme. Fortunately, "Super" closes the album so the final note is an appropriately deranged one. What Neu! have up their collective sleeve for *NEU! 3* is pure conjecture after the madness of *NEU! 2,* but considering their record so far for originality verging on total eccentricity, it's certain to be different.

Archie Patterson

Faust

Faust was created in 1970 as the outcome of a dispute between two branches of Polydor Records in Germany. The international branch wanted to prove to the home branch there was a future in the music of the many emerging German groups.

Polydor International asked Ewe Nettelbeck, a former radical journalist, to put together a group of musicians and form a band. So with old equipment and virtually no financial support from the record company, they started working on a musical concept. That concept being "to have a band which is not featuring anyone in particular, but has a sound, just like one instrument, playing in a wide range of sounds and styles." So with this idea in mind they made their own recording studio and recorded their first LP, *FAUST*. It can justifiably be said that this album was a total mindblower. First, the LP was completely transparent -- record, sleeve and even lyric insert. Second, when played some sort of stroboscopic interaction between the grooves of both sides causes an optical illusion that makes the record appear as if it is revolving a quarter turn, stopping, revolving another quarter turn, stopping, etc. Third, the music was incredible! A synthesis of

"Revolution 9" and Stockhausen. But even more than that it marked a beginning of their own style which can only be called Faust Music.

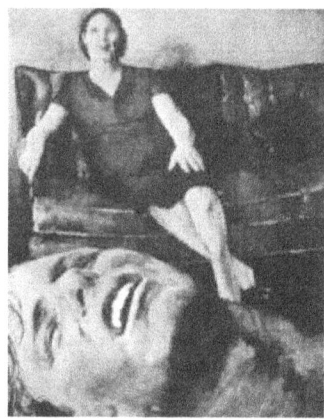

Their second LP, *SO FAR*, marked a further development of this concept. This time the entire package was black. As well as this, the music had become more defined and sinister. They were definitely beginning to create an individual identity. This is not to say that there aren't influences that are recognizable in some of their music. For there were definite traces of the Velvets and Zappa, but Faust had mutated these so that they had become not copies or derivatives, but their own form of music.

At this point in time came their first English concerts. Probably the most notable and the one that has become a virtual legend is their Rainbow gig in London. Picture this -- a grey brick wall serves as backdrop, a mass of black electronic gear is grouped center stage in semi-darkness, and at the four corners of the stage were TV sets pointed in toward the equipment, turned on with the sound down. Reportedly that was a night of strange occurrences -- waves of electronic sound gushed from the stage as TV programs were monitored into the PA, band members wailed off stage letting the equipment solo for 10 minutes and the group inadvertently carried on conversations with themselves in various foreign languages over the PA during mid-song. Enough said, maybe you can imagine the picture. Faust was creating for themselves a legend of sorts.

At this point enters England's premier progressive record label, Virgin Records, as Faust made a switch from Polydor. The next Faust LP was a set of tapes issued from their private library. It was in effect a legitimate bootleg. Virgin sold incredibly cheap and it actually got into the British Top Ten for several weeks selling thousands of copies. During this period they did a giant tour and then there came a change in the ranks. Two people left and two joined. Of the original lineup -- Jean-Herve Peron, Joachim (Zappa) Irmler, Gunter Wusthoff, Werner Diermaier and Rudolf Sosna; Diermaier and Sosna left to be replaced by a Peter Rainbow (of German group Slapp Happy) and Uli Trepte (formerly of Guru Guru). Also they took on another manager.

Now it's at this point that the picture grows even more mysterious, as it's not exactly certain who exactly recorded their next LP, *FAUST IV*. The group's desire to create an image of anonymity led to their not listing who plays on the record. In any case *FAUST IV* was a great LP, musically diverse and more accessible without sacrificing any of the group's originality.

Since *FAUST IV* and the subsequent tour, the group has become incommunicado. Various members have been associated with outside projects, but there have been no new Faust developments. So as it now stands, what will come next is anyone's guess.

Archie Patterson

Faust Is A Machine Head...

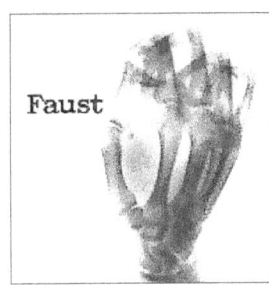

From the first surge of electricity on side one, to the final cryptic lyrical comments on side two, one is treated to the real mind game..........

FAUST starts with warped flashes of the Stones and Beatles and ends with the intellectual depravity of the Velvets. Side 1, after its brief intro, begins with "Why Don't You Eat Carrots?," a collage of diverse musical forms and varying dynamics. From electronic bleeps and screams to almost dancelike rhythms you are carried along with the music. The vocals range from inanities to foreign tongues, all of which serve to heighten one's amazement. "Carrots" goes into "Meadow Meal," another bizarre trip that employs virtually every musical device imaginable. From a psychedelic intro it goes into an electronic-acoustic ballad, from there to a pseudo-acid guitar bridge, then back to the ballad. It all ends with thunder and rain to the accompaniment of a dense calliope. Very interesting, but that's only side 1.

Side 2, recorded live, is virtually indescribable. It goes through so many changes it's impossible to recount them. All manner of electronics are employed and driven to extremes by varying rhythms and fierce pulsations that tear their way through your head, leaving you a basket case. The side and LP end with the ultimate comment on the state of things and metaphorically the LP itself -- "and at the end, realize that nobody knows if it really happened." Enough said.

Now after all that you'd, expect their next LP to be a bringdown, but no way. It's as nasty as hell.

From the opening seven minutes of primal pounding in "It's A Rainy Day, Sunshine Girl" on, *SO FAR* is pretty bad stuff. There's the unlikely acoustic guitar workout "On the Way to Abamäe" to the tame (almost) instrumental "So Far." "Mamie is Blue" sounds like the last gasp of the colossal man as he rolls off the 50-foot woman. To cap the LP off, "I've Got My Car and My TV" and "In the Spirit" exhibit a bizarre sense of humor à la Zappa -- real spicy stuff.

Their next release is the infamous *FAUST TAPES*. It sold so many copies that Virgin Records had to temporarily delete it as demand outstripped supply. They were losing money they were selling so many. Makes sense doesn't it? Actually as much sense as the LP does. It consists of 2 sides of edited tapes from their voluminous archives. Musically, it ranges from electronics to acoustic, ballads to hard rock, jazz to classical, as well as assorted other forms of sound, all done with the unmistakable Faustian sense of mechanization. In fact every time you listen to it you discover something you haven't heard before.

From there they moved on to even better things -- *FAUST IV*. "Krautrock" opens the LP with the most definitive cut ever done by a German band. It embodies in it the essence of virtually all the German groups -- unrelenting rhythms and electronics. It creates an atmosphere of anxiety in the listener that almost makes one not want to hear the rest of the LP. That would indeed be a mistake, for

1974

FAUST IV presents the group in perhaps its strongest and most accessible form yet. It's made up mostly of single pieces instead of free flowing collages. These songs aren't necessarily normal in structure or sound, but they do give the listener just enough to relate to, thus avoiding their being swamped by a morass of sound as sometimes happens with Faust. With *FAUST IV* the group is finally developing a recognizable sound, a sound built on other influences, but definitely their own. There are traces of the Velvets in "It's A Bit of a Pain" and other bits and pieces of the songs, but they have added their own unique, mechanical touch, turning this and all their other influences into their own style. If you play "The Sad Skinhead" you can begin to get the picture. Or there's "Giggy Smile," that carries it a bit further. These aren't necessarily exemplary pieces of Faust music, but they are definitely recognizable as being Faust music. That's what they are pointing at, creating an image or identity for Faust Music. With *FAUST IV*, they've taken a big step toward fulfilling that aim. There are also a couple more items of interest. They have been highly active in projects outside the Faust group structure. They've aided in recording 2 other LPs -- one with Tony Conrad and another with a fellow German group, Slapp Happy. Both are very diverse and not especially Faustian in nature, except for the fact that they are diverse.

Perhaps that is what lies at the center of Faust's appeal-diversity. You never know what they are going to do, or how, or when, or...?

Archie Patterson

Guru Guru

Guru Guru was organized by Mani Neumeier in 1967 and was originally called the Guru Guru Groove. The group experimented with free jazz as Neumeier had previously been in the jazz oriented Irene Schweizer Group. Over the next three years there were continual personnel changes, until finally in 1970 the group stabilized as a three- piece experimental rock group made up of Mani Neumeier (drums), Uli Trepte (bass) and Ax Genrich (guitar). At that time they also got a recording contract with the newly formed avant-garde German label Ohr.

Their first LP, *UFO*, featured a sound that would make today's heavy metal kings

54, Eurock: European Rock & the Second Culture

cringe, as it consisted of more power chords and shrieking guitar than can be imagined. Along with this, there were incredible electronic tapestries that picked up the white noise syndrome where the guitar left off.

A year later, they did their second LP, *HINTEN*. It marked a slight easing up of their sonic assault, but still contained enough volume to inflict brain damage.

Their next album was to mark a slightly new direction. It was called *KANGURU* and was their first attempt to incorporate rock and roll into their music. The emphasis changed from the volume to the beat. Neumeier's electric drums assumed a prominent role and his electric pulse drum beat served as a background for Genrich's guitar. Electronics and loud volume were still very much present, but there was a sense of dynamics for the first time. Also the imaginative guitar work by Genrich marked a big change in style, from strictly heavy metal, to heavy metal with a surf run, R&B lick, or electronic alteration thrown in to spice things up.

After this LP, there came another personnel change. Uli Trepte left and Bruno Schaab joined. With this lineup they recorded their next LP, 4. It marked a further development of their version of rock and roll. Their style on this LP can best be described as mechanical rock, for listening to it conjures up the vision of a robot doing the jerk. Or as a German critic states it, "The power and energy of The Stooges coupled with the sarcastic humor of Country Joe and the Fish." Intriguing, Yes?

Since 4 they have toured Europe extensively and have had their German record company release an anthology LP. Reportedly there are arrangements to release LPs in the U.S. and Britain, as well as talk of a British tour. And their next LP, tentatively titled *DON'T CALL US*, is due this summer.

Archie Patterson

Guru Guru Explores The Regions Beyond And The Future Ahead

The name "Guru Guru" sounds like some 1967 American derivative of the Strawberry Alarm Clock. It hardly conjures up images of the last frontier like Tangerine Dream or Ash Ra Tempel and it lacks the inexplicable nature (at least to those of us who only speak English) of something like Popol Vuh. Keeping in mind the nature of the German sound and the psychedelic implications of the name itself, no doubt they'd be contributors to the electronic drone syndrome.

In mid-1970 their first LP burst forth. Virtually entirely instrumental but for sparse nonverbal groans, it sounded like a funeral service for Jimi Hendrix. The drums displayed an ambition not unlike Mitch Mitchell of the Experience, while the bass pulsated like a volatile earth tremor. The guitar was saturated with every fuzz-wah-wah-echolette pedal in a void control manual. Just the titles alone convinced one of their cosmic intentions: "Stone In," "Next Time You See The Dalai Lhama" and somehow the predictable "Der LSD Marsch." Nothing however was quite up to par with the interstellar aura of "UFO," which was also the title of the album.

The album as a whole fell somewhere between the worst trip imaginable and a nightmare equal in shock to "The Exorcist." It dwarfed every acid-drenched American '67-'68 flashback from

1974

ELECTRIC MUSIC FOR THE MIND AND BODY, AFTER BATHING AT BAXTER'S, and ARE YOU EXPERIENCED, right down to the underrated pre-Jeff Baxter first two Ultimate Spinach enigmas. Even VINCEBUS ERUPTUM was made to seem tame and that isn't an easy feat. If there ever was bad trip or nightmare music, then this was it. The hallucinogenic content dissipated somewhat on their second album HINTEN, yet the realm of absurdity was securely endeavored. The significance of the title was foreseen on the inside of its predecessor with its futuristic quote: "soon the ufos will land -- and mankind will meet much stronger brains and habits -- Lets get ready for that." Credited to P. Hinten whoever he is.

The cover itself was enough to turn most people away. I know at least one person

offensive setting. Credits in the shape of a parallelogram in disarray surround the sight, with drummer Mani Neumeier drawing the most attention for its abstractions such as sound being, zonk machine, and various untranslated Teutonic garble.

Sustained feedback drones characterized "The Meaning of Meaning," as the title was the sole audible vocal and an oft repeated one at that. The possibilities for freakout had seldom been explored so profoundly. "Electric Junk" is self-explanatory and similar in its repetitive verbal structure to the aforementioned, with a speed guitar blitz for intro. Some German is spoken between drum rolls and guitar grinds a few minutes into this hysterical exercise. The remainder is a mind-dissecting jam notable for its shrillness and the relentless pulsations

who loved the record yet sold it because of the offensive cover. Many didn't even get that far. Pictured on the front were, descending in size, photographs of a male moon that were quite ludicrous, but could also be seen in a not-so-humorous light. The inside opened, revealing a reddish orange view of the same thing in a less

carried on by the rhythm section. Incomprehensible echo murmurs appear intermittently.

Two selections make up side two also. Seeing that the first is a ten minute "Bo Diddley" and the second is a more expected "Spaceship," it would seem to be a capsulized history of rock from then to now. Nothing is ever logical though within the limitless boundaries of dementia. "Bo Diddley" is not the one covered by endless rock groups; in fact it's side two's counterpart to "Electric Junk." The underlying structure is a couple of simple blitzkrieg riffs punctuated by an alien voice exclaiming "Bo Diddley." This occurs about every three minutes lasting approximately ten seconds while the clattering din thrusts away a metallic holocaust. "Spaceship" is solely comprised of sound effects intergalactically propelled, only briefly resorting to rock riffs and indistinct babbling, probably tracing the lift off and the ascension beyond. Quite an accomplishment for a group that is primarily a power trio.

KANGURU was their first offering after their switch in record labels to Brain Metronome. Pictured on the front was a kangaroo with its offspring in its pouch situated on an iceberg. Not to be outdone on the back was Mani posing in a Wild Man Fischer stance wrapped inside a body shirt jumping off the iceberg.

Like *HINTEN* there were two songs per side and long ones at that. "Oxymoron" is actually a word in the English dictionary although I'd never seen it before. The vocal is even in English and pertains to getting some stuff, taking a trip and becoming sick. The hoarse ghost-like voice is hilarious as always.

"Immer Lustig" is a fifteen-and-a-half minute improvisation and alludes to heavy metal in the year 2000. Ethereal noises of all sorts including electronic buzzes, bird chirps, explosions and echoes are all heavily relied upon until the end, when a ponderous riff takes off for the celestial graveyard.

"Baby Cakewalk," side two's opener, begins like a futuristic Led Zeppelin or maybe a Yardbirds revert. A solid wall of sound backs up a surrealistic electronically altered vocal, yielding to an ominous freakout that could serve as a haunted house soundtrack. Structural changes proliferate in this section as the latter half features fuzz solos and echo effects reminiscent of "In A Gadda Da Vida." "Ooga Booga" starts off like Chuck Berry played at slow speed prior to jungle noises, bongos, and the space age favorite initiated by Pink Floyd years ago, bird chirps. This is probably the most vocally decipherable Guru Guru yet, but that's not necessarily anything to laud. Hearing it might make some laugh while still others will get sick. Speed riffs are frequently resorted to as a dizzying array of sound swirls about. The balance is maintained though as a deluge of downer chords follows and hypnosis of sorts results. Tidal waves of metallic thunder are a fitting finish.

The next Guru Guru LP was titled simply *4*, and decorating the cover was an Indian-styled tapestry. For the first time in Guru Guru recording history there were short songs. Only two to be sure, but one was under three minutes while the other fell short of four. Sandwiched between these two tunes, respectively known as "Samantha's Rabbit" and "Woman Drum" was a so-called medley of rock and roll numbers like Eddie Cochran's "Weekend" and "Twenty Flight Rock." While this wasn't what most Guru Guru fans wanted or expected, they were done with virtually no allegiance to the past. The usual slingshot approach is as always evident. It would seem that if a space band was to revise oldies, the way to do it would be with fuzz tones rather than archaic Jerry Lee Lewis piano. Even at their most ordinary the short songs had little hit potential; in fact less than some of the recent more accessible leanings of Amon Düül and Can.

1974

Side two is the standard Guru Guru setup of two long songs. "Der Electrolurch" is downer rock of the future. The three instruments are played as though they're working out a puzzle, assembling it piece by piece. Halfway through it starts freaking out with alien voices, echo effects and intermittent fuzz thrusts. The bass holds a stable pattern of redundancy meantime. The pace soon quickens and rolls right along like a roller coaster through a horror chamber. A ten-second drum solo signals the end. "The Story of Life" is a few minutes longer and begins on a rather melodious note for a change. The vocal is even in English and is handled gently. An infrequent jazz break is taken, followed by a brief freakout and mellowed out electronics . After another short vocal interlude, extreme downer tendencies prevail dominated by Ax's fuzz sustaining.

In late '73 a *THIS IS GURU GURU* was released on Brain that was simply an anthology of their latter material. The new Brain logo of the year 2000 was apparent too, but it'd look much better with some new titles to indicate such.

Scott Fischer

1975

Cosmic Music

The birth of Cosmic Music came in 1970 when record producer Peter Meisel and rock critic Rolf-Ulrich Kaiser founded Ohr Musik Production. Within three years after its inception they had established three labels -- "Ohr" (Ear), "Pilz" (Mushroom), and "Die Kosmischen Kuriere" (The Cosmic Couriers), and released sixty albums.

On May 18, 1973 top fashion designer Gille Lettman and Kaiser bought the shares of Peter Meisel and prepared to launch Cosmic Music on a worldwide scale. Since that time they have established two companies; the Berlin recording company Ohr Musik Produktion, and the Berlin music publishing company Cosmic News, Musik Verlag. In addition they have initiated a new international record label, "Cosmic Music -- The Sound of the Cosmic Couriers" and are in the process of setting up "Sternenmode," which will serve as the basis for fashions and other creations they are planning.

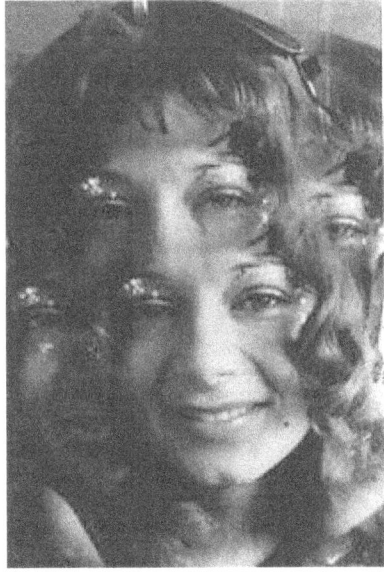

To date they have negotiated release for all their records in Britain, the Netherlands, Australia, Italy, France and beginning in '75, the U.S. Also they have pre-recorded radio programs scheduled to run concurrently for four to six weeks in the same countries.

Presently their artist roster consists of: Ash Ra Tempel, Wallenstein, Popol Vuh, Mythos, The Cosmic Jokers, The Tarot Band, Witthuser and Westrupp, Klaus Schulze, Jerry Rainbow (their new "Sci Fi Superstar"), Walter Wegmuller and Sergius Golowin. The next scheduled releases are a new Ash Ra Tempel LP featuring Manuel Gottsching and his electronic guitar symphonies, a new Popol Vuh LP *EINSJAEGER AND SIEBENJAEGER*, Sternenmadchen's *MAGICIANS OPERA* and a double set entitled *GALAXY SOUND*.

Also in preparation are new records by Wallenstein, Mythos, and Jerry Rainbow. They are now preparing to bring to the U.S., in the near future, "great Cosmic adventures and galactic shows." So now with that brief background sketch in mind you may proceed to fly into the galaxy of pleasure of the Cosmic Couriers, via the words of the Couriers themselves -- Starry Eyed Gal and Cosmic Courier.

Archie Patterson

* STAR SOUNDS *
DISCOVER THE GALAXY SOUND OF COSMIC MUSIC

Skylab calling Terra. We are living in the new age. TV broadcasts from space. Live. The Saturn rocket is underway. Supplies for Skylab. The laboratory of the heavens. Somewhere, far from our earth, the astronauts climb from their spaceship into the galaxy. Weightless they glide to Skylab. They go about their task, repairing in space.

When Skylab's TV camera swings toward our planet (Terra) we discover a small blue pea. As the camera pivots further, millions of stars sparkle before us. In boundless fantasy we suspect what goes on in distant galaxies.

ASTRONAUTS

Do other beings live there? Do space vessels chase about at the speed of light? Have their pilots already visited our planet?

"We want you to prepare the earth for our landing." The American scientist Dr. Andrija Puharich claims to have received this message through electromagnetic waves from the envoys of the planet Hoova, a planet 6000 times larger than the earth, according to the description received. This can be looked up in Puharich's authorized biography of Uri Geller. They first landed on the planet earth 6000 years ago during the time of the Pharaoh Imhotep, in Egypt: "We can do nearly everything through you. We can be visible and invisible."

Ancient legends from India tell of the visits of intergalactic voyagers. Millenniums ago. But even today UFOs are landing on Terra. 10,000 investigational reports prove this.

[Sergius Golowin + friend]

SPACE SHIP

That is our world. We discover the solar system, the Milky Way galaxy, the universe. We tell of our adventures in the cosmos. Our musicians accompany us. We are Cosmic Couriers.

With the Cosmic Jokers we travel into the fantastic worlds of the *GALACTIC SUPERMARKET* and to the *PLANETEN SIT-IN*. Sternenmadchen Gille steers her space ship through the flashing worlds of Science Fiction. She visits the Magicians. She calls her space craft Timeship.

ZEITSCHIFF

Sternenmadchen calling you: I'm flying around in my Timeship. This is my spaceship Enterprise. Discover the new magicians with me, Fly in my Timeship to Tutench-Amun, the master of aesthetics and Leonardo da Vinci, the discoverer of boundless fantasy. Let Cagliostro, the eternal charlatan, and Ludwig van Beethoven, the magician of tone, enchant you. Visit Werner von Braun, the architect of man's first journey into space.

Sternenmadchen calling you: Forget the common concept of the magician as a trick artist. My friends are the Couriers of unlimited possibilities. Geniuses of ideas. Cosmic envoys from another world. Like Albert Einstein, to whom formulas revealed themselves in a dream. Bettina von Brentano, also a Sternenmadchen, wrote to the poet Goethe in 1610 about the composer Ludwig van Beethoven: "I confess to you that I believe in a divine magic, which is the element of intellectual nature; Beethoven practices this magic in his art; everything he can teach you is pure magic."

[Rosi]

ELECTRONS

Our music is called Cosmic Music. It is played by Cosmic Composers. The Cosmic Jokers, Wallenstein, Ash Ra Tempel, Mythos, Klaus Schulze, Sternenmadchen, the Tarot Band, Jerry Rainbow, Popol Vuh, Rosi and many others. They tell thrilling stories and sing stellar melodies and dip into the fantastic landscape of Science Fiction. We say Sci Fi. That's our abbreviation for a science fiction without horror. Full of adventures, full of joy.

Cosmic Music is the sound of the Starship-Enterprise-Generation and the children of the most fantastic composer of all times, Ludwig van Beethoven (Germany, Terra). Signals from the unknown worlds of the incomprehensible, fantastic and extra-terrestrial. Acoustic signals for the flights into the galaxy. Those are the new telepathic codes of Cosmic Music. Stored in our newly discovered musical frequencies. Transported by electrons, hovering in the flashing of light, in the magic of colors, in the sounds of the electrons.

1975

GALAXY SOUNDS
Course : The Sun

Sternenmadchen calling you: Close your eyes. Put on the quad headphones and you're hearing the telepathic signals of the new sound. You're seeing movies of the galaxy, hovering in the sounds of new beauty. The sun shines into your life. Fly along and experience the more beautiful world with us.

QUAD STUDIO

Think of Skylab once again. In the original tone of the TV broadcast celestial sounds are mixing. The humming of the planets, the buzzing of falling stars, the whistling of the solar wind. In the Quad Studio near Cologne we hear many such sounds.

Here we record the stellar sounds. In the cockpit Dieter Dierks mixes over 40 channels of the quadraphonic space. It's here that the galaxy sound originates, which also gives Stereo and Mono listeners an unknown listening experience through musical transparency original with us.

The Cosmic Couriers are in the studio. The headphones glow. Today the Cosmic Jokers are playing. Harald and Jurgen of Wallenstein, Manuel and Rosi from Ash Ra Tempel, Dieter, Klaus, Sternenmadchen. All instruments are hooked up. Organs, electronic sounds, synthesizers. Each musician plays what he likes. Cosmic Composers know no rules. They master all styles. Rock, folk, classical, synthesizer.

SOUND MACHINES

Most of all they like to play electronically. When we got our first synthesizer, we forgot the world around us for an entire day. At first we were amazed at the sound machine. It played itself. Then we turned the oscillators, with which you produce the tonal pulsations. Then the filters, which change the pulsations rhythmically or melodically.

Now our own rockets take off, now our airplanes land. The stellar oceans roar.

No one needs piano lessons for electronics. Anyone can play synthesizer. The sole condition: be curious about Fantasy.

COSMIC COURIERS

We are Cosmic Couriers. We live in the new age. Everyone has fantasy. Anyone can play along. We show everyone the beauty we have discovered ourselves. We're waiting for your discoveries.

We have Cosmic Music. We play our own fortune telling game, the Tarot game. Each person can become his own fortune teller. We bring you new games, cosmic games. And Sternenmadchen gives us the new fashions -- Sternenmode.

Sternenmadchen calling you: My fashions are the Cosmic Sternenmode. All is possible in it. I show the signs of the cosmos. They flash: Stars, Suns, Comets, Galaxies. Sternenmode radiates joy, like our music. Fashion and music belong together. I speak of the more beautiful world, which each of us can create. Play along. For fashion is made by people who have fantasy.

Our favorite composer is Ludwig van Beethoven. Our aesthetic orients itself about Tutench-Amun. Our star is Leonardo da Vinci, who showed the world for the first time that everything is possible. We live like Captain Kirk and Lieutenant Uhura in the Starship Enterprise. Our star ship is called "Zeitschiff."

SILVER CHANNELS
Course : The Cosmos

We had another visitor in the quad studio. Some days later Dieter Liffers writes in "Show":
> "They work, without considering it work, on an optimistic, quadraphonic sound, on colorful fashions, on fascinating toys for the big and small, on a revolutionary, positive horoscope system, on peaceable comic strips with space-appeal and so on, and so on..."

> "I personally cannot escape the strong attraction of their willful ideas. You should simply listen, see and be amazed. Just like I did."

Fly with us! Climb into our Time Ship!

**Sternenmadchen Gille &
Kosmischer Kuriere Rolf-Ulrich Kaiser
(© Copyright Cosmic News GMBH /
Used by permission)**

Popol Vuh

The name Popol Vuh, derived from legend, was the title given to the Mayan book of sacred texts. In 1971 Florian Fricke chose this name for his project of creating a new hymnal form of music. It is, in the context of the group's music, extremely descriptive of their art and motivating philosophy.

Along with Fricke, two of his friends were involved at that time: Holger Trülzsch (percussion) and Frank Fiedler (Moog mixdown). In this original incarnation Popol Vuh produced two LPs: *AFFENSTUNDE* and *IN DEN GARTEN PHARAOS*, and the music for Warner Herzog's movie *AGUIRRE, THE WRATH OF GOD*.

Their first, *AFFENSTUNDE* (Hour of the Ape) was done for German Liberty in 1971. It features two pieces -- Side 1 "Ich Mache einen Spiegel" (I'm Making A Mirror) and the title cut on Side 2. The dominant sounds on both sides are the Moog and tamboura. Perhaps the best way to describe the album is to say that it reflects the atmosphere of frenzied serenity that surrounds a high mountain lake when all human noise pollution has vanished and the forces of Mother Nature come out. The album opens with the sound of birds followed by a gush of water. It then goes through various rhythmic figures on Moog and percussion. The second side strongly resembles the first with the exception that the rhythms become more dense or heavy and darker tones of the Moog are used. The album fades with the Moog echoing birdlike cries on top of a background rhythm.

The second album IN DEN GARTEN PHARAOS picks up where AFFENSTUNDE left off. Once again there is one piece per side. A note of interest is that the LP was recorded in the Baumberg Cathedral in Bavaria. This is especially evident in Side 2 as the Cathedral organ is employed. Side 1 features the title piece which consists of the ever-present Moog and percussive rhythms until about 2/3 of the way through when Fricke comes on with an electric piano solo. It continues until the side is washed away by the sound of waves lapping on a shoreline.

With Side 2, entitled "Vuh," the pattern of both albums is broken as a cymbal roll ushers in the giant pipe organ. The side continues and gradually builds as percussion and Moog are added. The build up continues, led by crashing cymbals until it all crescendos then gradually winds itself down to finish with the organ tailing off. This piece is perhaps one of the more emotional pieces of music ever put down. Its intensity on all levels at times makes one feel somewhat in awe. Not so much due to its overwhelming brilliance, but simply its dynamic nature.

In early 1972 the group underwent a change in personnel when both Trulzch and Fiedler left to pursue their individual musical ideas. Popol Vuh became the entity it is today, consisting of Fricke (piano, cembalo, vocal), Daniel Fichelscher (ex-Amon Düül, on guitar & percussion), Conny Veit (ex-Gila, on guitar), Klaus Wiese (tamboura), and Robert Eliscu (oboe).

Popol Vuh also underwent a major change in concept. Whereas previously they had worked extensively with the Moog Synthesizer, now they abandoned it. One of the main reasons for this was, as Fricke put it, "The Moog is black and externally appalling, it's an over-refined technical product that you have to tune for a long time to achieve tonal realms which are not cold, and only convey technology."

Along with the abandonment of the Moog came another and somewhat related change – Fricke began composing "Sacred Music." Lyrics and vocals were added, with the lyrics being taken from Biblical texts. This has added a most important ingredient, the communication of their essence not only emotionally through the music, but intellectually through the lyrics. It is indeed rare that a group sincerely attempts to do this and even more rare that they succeed.

From the beginning Popol Vuh had always conveyed a serene beauty, an almost hymnal sort of feeling. With this new group Fricke started to develop fully his idea of music: "In the course of the years music has become more and more a form of prayer for me. Today it seems to be more beautiful and honest to cleanse oneself without technical aids, to introspect and then with simple, human music, touch the inner man..." He conceives music as a means of "realistically approaching Utopia; it is in service of beauty..."

With this idea of "Sacred Music" as it's motivation, Popol Vuh has since produced two LPs: *HOSIANNA MANTRA* and *SELIGPREISUNG*. They feature the new sound of Popol Vuh, sans Moog, which features Fricke's exquisite piano embellished by the formidable instrumental stylings of his colleagues on their various instruments.

The third LP, *HOSIANNA MANTRA,* is an album of prayers done in an almost pastoral tone. There are for the first time vocals, done by a Korean girl, Djong Yun. All in all it's an extremely beautiful album highlighted by Fricke's piano. The music combines Conny Veit's acoustic and electric guitar work with Djong's vocals, Fricke's piano and percussion, and Eliscu's oboe to conjure up a sense of tranquility, that regardless of one's belief in religion is extremely pleasant and enjoyable.

The latest of Fricke's works is entitled *SELIGPREISUNG*, which has the double meaning of "Glorification" and symbolizing the Beatitudes. It's a concept album of sorts in that all the songs relate to the Beatitudes and hymns of praise to the various subjects they proclaim.

Musically the transition from electronic to acoustic has now been completed. With *SELIGPREISUNG* Fricke has produced perhaps his most legitimate musical work so far. It may not be the most popular or readily accessible, but if given a chance it can prove to be the most interesting. The style has become more rock and the arrangements and playing are more sharp and crisp. Fricke's piano is almost always in the forefront and he excels. He even does vocals and they come off as a semi-chant intoning the words which are based on the biblical text of Matthew Evangelium. Perhaps a rough comparison of the sound of this album would be some of the solo work of John Cale. But even that is slight as with this LP Fricke has developed his own style.

There is something about the name Popol Vuh that conjures up mental pictures. The same is the case with their music.

Thus far they have done four albums; *AFFENSTUNDE, IN DEN GARTEN PHARAOS, HOSIANNA MANTRA* and *SELIGPREISUNG*. Each one is different yet they are all the same in that they share the common denominator of being "head music."

You don't just hear them, you must listen to them. "Sacred Music" indeed.

Archie Patterson

Wallenstein

Wallenstein is by and large a product of the musical talents of Jurgen Dollase. Initially a classical pianist, in 1971 he decided to branch out into rock and formed a band. They were known as Blitzkrieg until they ran into name problems with an English band. So they rechristened themselves Wallenstein after the commander-in-chief of the 30 Years War General Wallenstein, who was also born with the same star sign as Dollase.

The group consisted of Dollase on keyboards, Harald Grosskopf on drums, Bill Barone on guitar, and bassist Jerry Berkers. With this lineup they produced two albums -- *BLITZKRIEG* and

MOTHER UNIVERSE. Then in the early summer of '73, the group underwent some changes to better enable Dollase to achieve his goal of "interposing the tradition of the last 200 years into rock." A new bassist Dieter Meier, along with Joachim Besser on violin were added. The latest album, COSMIC CENTURY, features this new line-up and represents the first step in Dollase's plan to bring his "Cosmic Symphonies" to the rock world.

To date in Germany they have built up a sizable following and their concerts have been reported to at times resemble scenes out of Beatlemania. The group, especially Dollase, are well known for their stage appearances as they were the first group in Germany to put on make-up.

Musically Wallenstein should be described as "Classical Rock." They are, in fact, the only group who really fit into this category today. With his great knowledge of the classics, Dollase has created his own style. He doesn't simply cop a few classical riffs, or just do rock adaptations of classical pieces. Led by his keyboards, Wallenstein performs rock music with a true sense and feel of the classics. The structure and dynamics of the pieces themselves exude a distinct classical tone. His work on piano overwhelms you with its rich textures and stately phrasings.

The first Wallenstein album, *BLITZKRIEG*, was recorded in 1971 and released on the now defunct Ohr subsidiary, Pilz records. It was an impressive debut, consisting of four pieces -- "Lunetic," "The Theme," "Manhatten Project," and "Audiences," all of which clearly showed the potential and talent of Wallenstein. The opening cut, "Lunetic" is a fast paced instrumental carried by Dollase's multiple keyboards and Bill Barone's guitar. It races for over eleven minutes featuring innumerable tempo changes and a ripping guitar solo that, along with Dieter Dierks' use of phasing, serves as an effective embellishment of the central recurring theme.

"The Theme" Introduces Dollase's grand piano and vocal work. Once again it goes through various tempo and mood changes. The vocal section is almost melancholy and is followed by another flashing guitar bit by Barone. It then reverts to the opening theme which is used to close the song.

Side two opens with "Manhatten Project," which is basically a development on a central theme, accomplished through the use of shifting dynamics and guitar/piano soloing.

"Audiences" is a ballad, sung to the accompaniment of piano, Mellotron, and soaring guitar. It features a piano-led workout in the middle which merges into the vocal section, fading as a Mellotron closes the piece and the album.

The second album, *MOTHER UNIVERSE*, takes up where *BLITZKRIEG* left off. Recorded in 1972, it consists of "Mother Universe," "Braintrain," "Shakespearesque," "Dedicated to Mystery Land," "Relics of Past," and "Golden Antenna." The basic change from the first LP is that instead of thematic developments, each piece is separately composed. All the cuts have lyrics, and the overall feel to the album is harder, more metallic and rock oriented with the tracks varying stylistically. As it happened, *MOTHER UNIVERSE* marked the end of Wallenstein Mark I and paved the way for Wallenstein Mark II, "The Symphonic Rock Orchestra." This change is documented at its inception on the third album *COSMIC CENTURY*.

With the recording of *COSMIC CENTURY* the promise of *BLITZKRIEG* was fulfilled. It leads the way to even greater expectations. The first side features "The Symphonic Rock Orchestra" and what they do has to be heard to be believed. Dollase's piano has stepped center stage and he excels. The three songs on the side, "Rory Blanchford," "Grand Piano," and "Silver Arms," are Classical Rock. There's no trading off of classical riffs then rock riffs, it's all one and the same. The piano leads the way, and the other instruments seem to be extensions of the keyboards. The arrangements are near perfect and the playing is faultless. "Rory Blanchford" moves along effortlessly from piano to guitar to vocals without a hitch. One moment you're at a recital, the next the violin and guitar are trading off, then you're confronted by Dollase's oh-so-casual vocal mannerisms, which really hit you. It's hard to explain how, but they are unbelievably evocative.

"Grand Piano" is a piano solo that conjures up memories of the masters, but just as you've got stars in your eyes, the bass, then the guitar segue into "Silver Arms," the heavy of the side. Barone 's guitar is the high point -- as he slams and screams his way through the song almost as if he were you know who himself.

Side two consists of "Marvelous Child," "Song of Wire," and "The Cosmic Couriers Meet South Philly Willy." This side seems a more logical progression from *MOTHER UNIVERSE* than the "Symphonic Rock Orchestra." However the rough edges have been smoothed off and the result is three excellent songs (one an instrumental). "Marvelous Child" is a rocker. Its steady beat carries through as the piano and guitar trade off and Dollase just kind of sing-songs along with the flow of things. "Song of Wire" is a ballad and comes off extremely well. It's sense of the dramatic is executed to perfection as Dollase intones the lyrics to the accompaniment of his resonant piano and Mellotron. Then, at just the right moment Barone's guitar slams in to top it off. The side closes with the instrumental "The Cosmic Couriers Meet South Philly Willy." Dollase's piano and the drums begin it, then Barone's guitar screams in, twanging and tearing its way through to the end, as the whole piece just kind of winds itself down.

It definitely appears that Dollase and Wallenstein have a lot going for themselves. They have the talent and the ideas, all they need is the opportunity to develop and expose them. In March or April they have a new album coming out, and there has been word that a U.S. visit is a strong possibility in the next year.

Archie Patterson

1975

Ash Ra Tempel

Hearing the first Ash Ra Tempel LP was like projecting Cream into the year 2000. If the moniker "space rock" was ever apt, it was here. "Amboss" reached peak after peak piling electronics and speed blitz guitar over steadily rising rhythms. Klaus Schulze had a drum technique that might be described as Maureen Tucker with ambition. It would be safe to say that Ash Ra had a headstart on Tangerine Dream at this point. Certainly the guitar was less grating and there were no ill-conceived electronic collages.

The twenty-five minute "Traummaschine" crystallizes slower, with eerie organ-cum-Gothic choir unwinding into the outer boundaries of remote guitar reverberations. Somewhere along the line bongos appear and they are played in the same style as the drums for monotony's sake. A more conventional, if toned-down guitar arises -- slightly fuzzed and alas, a noticeable bass alongside sparse cymbal eruptions. What follows is more dissected guitar fragments with tension building shortly thereafter around an exploratory fuzz excursion. Tones sear out of both speakers up and down, in and out finally bordering on boredom as Ash Ra is no Faust when it comes to alluring tedium.

SCHWINGUNGEN, their next, was not a disappointment, though seriously flawed in part. "Light," the first of two themes, is almost blues with a sense of dynamics and some outdated 1967 San Fran drivel of "we're all one." Manuel Gottsching, who'll turn out to be their mainstay, pulls off a fine fuzz solo again as new drummer Wolfgang Muller and bassist Hartmut Enke maintain a steady yet fittingly loose rhythm. The second theme, "Darkness" doesn't fare so well. "John L.," whoever he is, gets in some good simulated jews harp but his vocal leaves much to be desired, hindered further by more "lysergic day dream" summer of love lyrics. Another unknown, Mathias Wehler, contributes sax and if it's to shift emphasis from the abysmal mumblings, it helps marginally. Some form of electronic swosh is also put to use, sounding like a washing machine on the fritz. Once again, finally Manuel takes his customary fuzz solo.

The title side, "Schwingungen," begins typically eerily with vibes in the forefront occasionally dissected by guitar echoes. Before long the drums enter, rotating backwards and forwards between electronic pitches and arctic wind shimmers. Eventually the drums subside for some brief electronics then, lo and behold, the "Saucerful of Secrets" riff emerges with the bass and cymbals right behind the icy Leslie-run wah wah. No vocal fallout here -- the choir organ takes care of that.

What followed was at best a mistake, at worst ludicrous. Apparently the German Kosmic regime has an outdated devotion to Timothy Leary. At one of Ash Ra's live concerts Leary and some associates added vocals to the electronic rock hum. "Downtown," a slowed down cosmic blues piece with female vocals, worked while others like "Power Drive" failed (at least vocally) as did the archly devised "Right Hand Lover." The electronics throughout were impressive and were the sole redeeming factor of the "Space" side.

"Time" is an improvement of sorts. Tinny guitar and electronic squeaks open with characteristic ascending drums, this time played by two new beings. "Timeship" showcases Leary's incoherent babble whispered over space sounds interspersed with planetary dirges. If nothing else Leary lifts the whole thing to the heights of absurdia with predictable inanities of the "love," "you're beautiful" ilk.

JOIN INN should probably be referred to as the third Ash Ra Tempel album as it's the original three (Klaus back on drums and drones) plus a follower of theirs who supplied tea and sympathy on previous outings -- Rosi. Also like their first there a selection per side. "Freak and Roll" is self explanatory but it lacks the expeditional attitude of "Amboss." Still, the ascending-descending guitar-drums climax, long a trademark, prevent the level of boredom from becoming too pronounced.

"Jenseits" is altogether different, taking advantage of Klaus's panoramic electronic keyboard knowledge. Rosi takes her first vocal and although breathy, atmospherically speaking it's unintelligible and ineffective by and large. Random bass pulsations hint at a rhythm that never develops while the guitar is subdued and kept intact with the cosmic texture.

Conceivably Rosi found a home in the membership of the Tempel cause as their latest is entitled *STARRING ROSI*. The only original member is now Manuel as bass mainstay Enke has departed; in fact the group -- if it could be called that -- numbers only two. Wallenstein's drummer fills in as Manuel plays all guitar parts as well as bass, synthesizer, Mellotron, etc.

1975

Another first is that there are songs -- even a couple under three minutes. "LaughterLoving" features Rosi's voice echoed in laughter at the beginning and end with a frolicking guitar jam in between. The bleakness of the past has been replaced by a more sandy beach-like atmosphere as portrayed on the album cover's back. "Day Dream" is probably the most interesting cut; with Rosi's recitations reiterated by Manuel taking on an electric-acoustic form.

The shortcoming of it all is that Manuel's guitar and Rosi's cosmic lyricisms only go so far and that's it. Maybe next time. Or maybe never again, as the Tempel's once strong assertive rhythmic foundation appears to have crumbled out from underneath it.

Scott Fischer

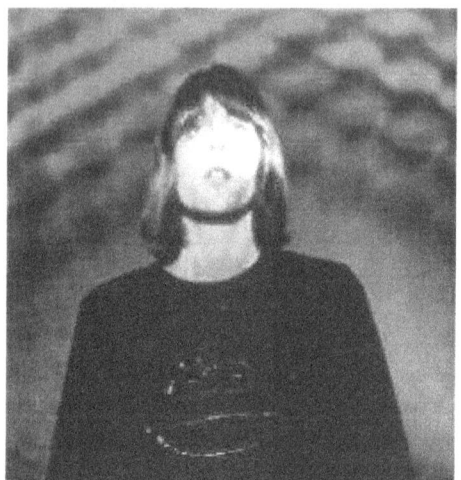

Klaus Schulze

Klaus Schulze is the ultimate electroid. Just his qualifications alone are enough; drum and drones on the two most electronically unified Ash Ra Tempel albums, his occasional contributions to Tangerine Dream (he drummed on *ELECTRONIC MEDITATION* and filled in for an absentee at a later date) and his strong contributions to the Cosmic Jokers albums.

His first solo shot, *IRRLICHT*, surpassed even the most grandiose expectations. A synthesis of remote orchestrations, atonal organ rings, tape loops and electronic buzzes from the furthermost regions highlighted the twenty-nine minute "Energy Rise -- Energy Collaps." The sonic thrust builds up into one all-encompassing infinitely dense organ note afterwards descending accordingly. What he puts into it serves as substantial proof that Cosmic Music enraptures a form of existence beyond the android state.

Not quite so long but just as good is the other side. It's sound in motion as only space could be. No Tangerine Dream merger of the Classics with electronics here, just pure extraterrestrial sound likelihoods.

CYBORG was his second release and a double at that. Overall the textures were more expansive and the sound explorations more varied.

"Synphara" relied on his archetypal neo-Gothic organ tones with insect buzzing embellishments adding to the science fiction-like soundtrack. Chilling winds murmur as searching echoes forge ahead beyond dense organ soars. The otherworldly sound effects sterilize the worlds beyond of even distant similarities to the Earth.

"Conphara" begins as a magnified buzz, reminding one of a UFO sending ultrasonic waves to destroy the Earth beings. A remote rhythm develops intersected by medium-toned drones and invading electrons. Then without warning an orchestra flows in, fading back out again between assorted sound fragments.

Threatening monotone roars are the opening phase of "Chromengel." Echoing orchestration follows on its fade and the Outer Limits-type setting has established itself. There is evidence of one form of earthly influence in the voidian works of Master K. -- the Velvet Underground. The repetitive rhythms of Maureen and the harmonium modulations of Nico are of equal significance in his electronic outputs. Sound fluctuations crisscross each other intermittently here in exacerbation of the conflict of orchestral splendor in the oscillating tones of the foreboding netherlands. The fury of the ending on side three will fry your brain and drown your mind in the quicksand of oblivion!

"Neuronengesong" enters piercingly with shrills and buzzes, the kind of thing that a sound-being is made up of for the prescribed purposes of bringing the unknown closer. A sonic horror chamber would be a perfect environment for the multiplicity of electrons present. The electronics were never so grueling (except for Faust) and the atmosphere never so stark.

Several months later a new work was released on the Caroline label, a subsidiary of Virgin Records. Maybe a wise move for Klaus economically, but Virgin couldn't handle dada protos Faust (proving what pretentious nonsense their whole Mike Oldfield far-out image really is) and it's doubtful that the Kosmic Kid will be at home either in spite of the presence of similar sort Froese and Co.

Not as spatially profound as its predecessors, *BLACK DANCE* is nonetheless quite fascinating. The production is cleaner and the sound less remote.

The eighteen minute "Ways of Change" opens with a collage of electronics and 12-string acoustic guitar, prior to the rhythm shifting from guitar to bongos and cymbals giving the electronics a flowing feel they previously lacked (Earthly influx).

"Some Velvet Phasing," selection two, side one, is synthetic tones run through phasing devices for eight minutes of delight or boredom depending on the listener's preference.

"Voices of Syn," side two's sole piece, features a male vocalist conducting a liturgy over drones. Thankfully they disappear shortly, allowing treated percussion to fill the space voided by human meanderings. The only guests Klaus ever needs are his electronic devices. The vocalists that mar such efforts can go back to the opera or join Magma.

Scott Fischer

1975

**Organisation - *TONE FLOAT*
(RCA SF 8111)**

How many times have you walked into a small out of the way record store, thinking this will be the day I'll find one of those rare albums? Well, one such day that happened to me as I chanced to come upon *TONE FLOAT* by Organisation, the first incarnation of Kraftwerk. Recognizable only by the red and white stripped street-cone logo, it turned out to be in fact the first recorded work of what was to later become Kraftwerk. Even though it was recorded in 1970, this record shows the creative genius of what was to become a very important part of modern music.

A five-piece band then (Ralf Hutter - organ; Florian Schneider-Esleben - flute, bell, triangle, tambourine and electric violin; Basil Hammoudi - glockenspiel, conga, gong, musical box, and voice; Butch Hauf - bass, shakey tube, small bells and plastic hammer; and Fred Monicks - drums, bongos, cowbells, maracas and tambourine), their music was basically percussive. Unlike Kraftwerk, there are no electronics.

Side One opens with "Tone Float," which is close to 20 minutes long. None of those boring jams here, just interesting music. Building up slowly with percussion instruments, this comes about the closest yet to Pink Floyd's "Set the Controls for the Heart of the Sun." The song ends with the organ's volume on the increase and percussion sounding like a den of rattlesnakes.

Side Two brings us to a rather mixed up musical piece called "Milk Rock." Sounding much like a crazy version of "Ruckzuck" (from the first official Kraftwerk LP) with its hypnotic drum beat, one wonders what prompted the title. On to "Silver Forest." Complete with eerie effects, this could easily pass for a sci-fi soundtrack. Very Stomu Yamash'ta-sounding with its percussion, it's not hard to see a forest (with sound) being pelted with rain. "Rhythm Salad" is just that. No need to explain. Finishing off with "Noitasinagro," Organisation has almost made it sound as if you are inside a grandfather clock. Using the organ again as a building instrument, you almost expect at any minute that the clock will strike and chime.

Now that Kraftwerk has broken through, let's hope British RCA will re-release this LP so all can hear their beginnings.

Dana Madore

**Kraftwerk - *AUTOBAHN*
(Vertigo 6360 620)**

The Autobahn is Germany's super-highway, where speed is unchecked and all sense of time blurs into the open panorama of motion. The steady rhythm of machine is the pulse of this artery and once you move into the stream, a modern fantasy of concrete and chrome ("white stripes, green edges") unfolds.

Kraftwerk are the new musicians of this technological age, the poets of the power station, the minstrels of electric construction. The name "kraftwerk" fluctuates either way; originally "men at work" in a rock-motivated "power station," the four members of the present band are now in full control behind the wheel. Alternately trapped and totally unbounded, cruising down the Autobahn. The rhythms shift and throb, the melodies evolve in a gradual flux, the beat is endless -- this is the final escape and Kraftwerk provides the soundtrack.

AUTOBAHN is Kraftwerk's fourth album released under that name, and basically takes up where *RALF AND FLORIAN* left off. A new sophistication thrust itself upon us with that recording, brought about by the acquisition of new equipment which enabled them to bring their ideas into full bloom. AUTOBAHN refines this flowering thrust, and surprised many by spiraling up the American charts in the process. No longer the favorite of a select few, Kraftwerk's electronic imagery now belongs to the masses.

Their recent US tour confirms, however, that these guys aren't compromising their vision one whit. The expression is still rawly unique. *AUTOBAHN* offers a perfected style but no slick parade of complacent talent. The title song is smoothly fused, totally electronic in a way that steers clear of the space bands like Tangerine Dream yet manages to sound completely fresh. Ralf Hutter and Florian Schneider have been joined by Wolfgang Flür on electronic percussion and Klaus Roeder on guitar and violin in the studio, with Karl Bartos replacing Roeder on stage with vibes and percussion -- but it still remains essentially Ralf and Florian.

Repetition forms the base, with the melody kept to a simple pattern while various rhythms establish the growth of the arrangements. Side two slows the ride but contains this essence of Kraftwerk's approach, the first eleven minutes highlighting the slow build of "Kometenmelodie 1 & 2." Under the breath of some ominous phasing, a gradual scaled-melody creeps in on synthesizer, brought out in full force in Part 2 with shimmering effect. "Mitternacht" (Midnight) and "Morgenspaziergang" (Morning Walk) complete the side, capturing their moods with careful delicacy, Florian's flute in the latter piece being a particular delight.

Oddly enough, the entire album brings to mind the instrumental flavor of the Beach Boys' *SURF'S UP:* echoey reminiscences. "Autobahn" is the perfect radio song, and it too captures a feeling -- the hot rod paeans of the early '60s meet Stockhausen head on and neither genre is the same. This is Kraftwerk, infectious in spite of itself. Men at work, indeed.

Gregory Shepard

Kraftwerk Live, Keystone Berkeley

To set the record straight, Kraftwerk is not a rock group, but more a musical experience. If that fact only marginally comes across on their records, it is made completely clear in their live performance.

1975

Live they are not a group putting on a rock concert, but four musicians performing an electronic musical seance of sorts. Their image is almost the complete antithesis of today's rock scene. They come on in dark, conservative suits and ties, hair short and neatly combed, giving them the overall look of high school science professors. That is phase one of their overall concept. Phase two consists of a stage set up, composed of vibes and electronic drum pads in the center, flanked by various keyboards, synthesizers and mixers on both sides. Along with this, there's no stage lighting to speak of as their whole "light show" consists of four neon encapsulated plastic signs which line the front of the stage spelling out their names -- Ralf, Wolfgang, Karl and Florian. The backdrop consists of a blank wall, footlighted by soft columns of pink, blue and white neon tubes, lit only during uptempo portions of their performance. Thus the whole affair is carried off in semi-darkness.

The culmination of their whole thing is the performance. They came on in darkness, announced a brief greeting, tuned up, then launched into the first number., "Klingklang" off *KRAFTWERK 2*. A rhythmic piece, it was carried by the electric piano and vibes, interspersed with wafts of synthesized harmonic scales. It served as a beginning of their process of captivating the listeners mind. It ended in a flourish of scales and was followed in very short order by "Tanzmusik" from *RALF AND FLORIAN*. Opening with a synthesized rhythm that is once again picked up by the piano, the synthesizer and vibes then enter playing lead rhythms which all seem to revolve around the drum rhythm and its complementary element being carried by an electric organ. The piece gradually progressed, weaving an incredible shimmering tapestry of sound until it reached the climax, where the electric piano once again entered playing its rhythmic scales, which wound it down to a finish.

By this time you were beginning to become engulfed by the soothing, incessant rhythms pouring forth from the stage. The process continued non-stop with the intro to "Ruckzuck" from their first, *KRAFTWERK*. Again the ever-present rhythm emerged and began its development. Midway through it suddenly tailed off and a phased percussive section began that was interspersed by more phased electronics and a solo of sorts on vibes. This too was abruptly transferred back into a rhythmic figure, this time headed by flute, which carried on until it suddenly appeared to simply gasp and die with a few phased wheezes.

It was at this point that the pace was changed somewhat as they did "Atem" from *KRAFTWERK 2*, again. In fact all it consisted of was Florian breathing in and out into his mike while Ralf was on the other side of the stage phasing it throughout the room via the p.a. system. Basically it had the effect of putting you in the midst of a hurricane. This served to momentarily awaken you from hypnosis, which they then promptly put you right back into with "Kometenmelodie" off *AUTOBAHN*. It was prefaced by a prerecorded tape of mind-boggling magnitude which consisted of chimes and a phased recitation in German, capped off by what sounded like a phased combination synthesizer/pipe organ. All this was miked into the p.a. at an extremely loud volume giving you the feeling that you were at a performance by the Phantom of the Opera in his subterranean chambers. Very sinister indeed. From there a booming bass percussive rhythm slowly emerged accompanied by the synthesizer which began the melody. When it finally emerged full blown you felt as if you had just come in from out of the darkness into the light as the rich, warm, full tones soared throughout the room.

It was at this point that they finally took their first real break between songs. Mainly for purposes of re-tuning their machines as they were on the verge of doing "Autobahn."

Upon completion of tuning they launched into the full blown version off the album. On the whole it came off very similar to the LP version with a couple exceptions. It was a lot looser and Ralf and Florian's off-key recitations were even funnier. The first time they sang, so to speak, they faltered midway through due to the shock of hearing themselves I'm sure. All-in-all it was a bit long, but it was certainly their most accessible and best received. After all it was a hit single on the charts, no less.

While for some that is the kiss of death, for Kraftwerk I don't think so. These boys seem to be a bit different, at least let's hope they are.

With the completion of "Autobahn" the house lights came on, Kraftwerk went quickly and quietly off and the audience came abruptly down. The spell had been broken and all were jolted back to reality. Out into the dark night and sounds of the street. The evening was over, but as Florian says, "There is no beginning and no end in music. Some people want it to end. But it goes on." That is certainly the case with Kraftwerk in more ways than one. Now every time I start the car, I flash on "Autobahn" -- how about you?

Archie Patterson

Any Old Way You Choose It... It's German Rock Music

In Germany there are about 3,000 groups -- professional and amateur. The name groups like Can ask for about 15,000 DM a concert (2.30 DM equals one dollar), Tangerine Dream, now making a concert tour through the churches of Germany, got about 5,000 DM a night. The unknown groups, unknown to the general public, will get between 100 - 1,000 DM, not more, even if they have a record out.

The groups that have so far had the greatest response in the U.S. and England are the masters of electronic free-form rock and meditation music. Either they use conventional electric instruments like Can or synthesizers, ring modulators etc. like Kraftwerk. Besides that type, there are other groups that have had greater success in the U.S. and U.K., but play a more conventional type of music -- Atlantis, Birth Control, Nektar etc. Lucifer's Friend is rather big in the Midwest, an important part of the States to break records nationally. They sell more records in the U.S. than in Germany even though they have never toured there.

There are not as many rock concerts here as abroad because German promoters are afraid of losing money with German acts, thus they prefer English groups. That is why the situation for many German groups gets worse if they can't afford to tour the U.S. or U.K. Even if they do, German groups don't earn any money with their first tour because they are not that big of a draw and the expenses are too high. But a tour through the States is good publicity, especially in Germany. If a German group has toured the U.S. you will find the news in the ads for the group's records in the German rock papers.

It helps sell records! That is the reason Nektar toured the states. They know they would lose money (they lost around 100,000 DM), but it's still one of the best forms of publicity so they go right ahead and do it.

Kraftwerk's first LP was bought for 5000 DM by the record company and they knew if it would sell only 1,000 copies they would make a profit. In fact it sold 100,000 -- that roughly equals a sales figure of one million in the States. But then sales figures started to go down. Suddenly you read in the papers that *AUTOBAHN* (the LP and the single) are high in the American charts. Until that time the record was not played on German radio and the public (that is great parts of the public) had forgotten about Kraftwerk. But suddenly with chart success abroad and a tour fixed up, the record got airplay and big promotion in Germany. It only took a few weeks and *AUTOBAHN* was a smash hit in Germany, too. Kraftwerk has finally great success again.

I've not seen the new version of Kraftwerk in concert, but I think I prefer the old Kraftwerk around the first and second LPs. They were hard, monotonous and electrifying then. The first concert I saw was a gas with Klaus Dinger pounding on the drums, screaming "louder, louder, louder." They don't do this anymore. They have changed their image -- no more leather jackets, no more screaming, but straight suits with ties and tightly woven melodies that take you on a gentle trip if you close your eyes.

The next time I saw them was around the time the second album was out. The music in the first part of the concert was played only by Ralf and Florian -- it was the same basically as their records. But then two guitar players came on stage (I have forgotten their names) and they announced that they would like to do a new piece called "Autobahn." Yes they played the composition that early, in concert. And it was totally different from the recorded version that is out now. Heavy screeching guitars, very loud and hypnotic sounds emerging from the keyboards. A cross between John Cage and The Stooges. It was fantastic.

There are also other groups that are influenced by modern composers. Can's bass player (who plays with white gloves on) has studied under Karlheinz Stockhausen, the most important and influential modern composer in Germany. When Can started they wanted to be a rock band. Their trademark was the hypnotic, primitive drumming of ex-jazz musician Jaki Liebezeit. Add crazy vocalist Malcolm Mooney (who is now in one of those houses where men in white clothes reign -- they're coming to take me away, ha, ha), ex-rock musician of different popular bands Michael Karoli and the conductor of the whole music-making process on the organ: Irmin Schmidt. Listen to "You Do Right" on their first LP *MONSTER MOVIE* and you know that this is a new sound and that it is absolutely fantastic. Who needs such shit as Iron Butterfly's "In-A-Gadda-Da-Vida" anymore. This is the real thing!

I could write pages and pages about Can because they are my favorites, but the best way to get to know them is to go see them in concert or buy their records. Most of today's groups here in Germany and abroad are boring. They have a formula and milk it to death. Not so Can. They grow with each and every concert and recording session. They always have new ideas and are exciting. It has been a long way from *MONSTER MOVIE* to *SOON OVER BABALUMA* and it has been worth it.

Can in concert has changed too. The first time I saw them was in my home town

Braunschweig. It was the time of *TAGO MAGO*, their third LP. Can played an open air concert in the park. While they were taking a break, Jaki's drum machine played a steady hypnotic rhythm for half an hour. You could dance to it or get in the right mood for the things to follow. Then Damo Suzuki, their small Japanese lead singer, ran on stage waving his arms high in the air. People in the front row passed him a joint and he took a hit before handing it back. The drum machine still rattling, the other guys strutted on stage and Damo started peeling an orange, pressed it with both hands over a glass and then drank the fresh juice. The music started. Damo jumped up and took the mike. They played a two-hour set including all our favorites like "Father Cannot Yell" and "Halleluwah." The music was arranged and improvised at the same time.

That is, the overall structure of the composition was fixed but everybody could improvise within those limits. The compositions were not a song structure with fixed parts the single musician could improvise in, they were all improvising at once, playing at a concept they all had in their heads. Something like the Grateful Dead, only with the difference that the Dead are boring most of the time while Can is pure magic.

Some time and some records later I saw them in other cities and in London where they went down a storm. Their idea of a concert had changed a little bit, Now they were making up new compositions right on stage. Only parts of the group's improvising slightly resembled ideas that they had already expressed on record. If you want to have a label -- although it's silly -- I would categorize the music as free-form-electronic-rock. I hope I have whetted your appetite a little. So. if you can, see Can in concert, because Can sure can do IT. ("IT" stands for generating excitement for head and body and creating an atmosphere of magic.) WATCH OUT!

There is another important German group I want to tell you about: Harmonia. Their first, and till now only LP has been out since last year. Their new one will be out in a few months and the American record company Tamla Motown wanted the rights for USA distribution of their LPs.

Who is Harmonia? In my opinion Harmonia is the best of the meditation groups, cosmic rockers -- call them what you like. In my eyes they are even better than Tangerine Dream and that is something of an achievement in itself. Buy the record, listen for yourself and see if I'm right. The group consists of musicians from Neu! and Cluster, but the music is different. Harmonia is the only group that does any concerts, Neu! and Cluster concentrated only on making records nowadays. The musicians are Michael Rother from Neu! and Achim Roedelius and Dieter Moebius from Cluster -- that is half of Neu! and the whole Cluster group. Indeed the music does more resemble Cluster than Neu! and if you listen to Cluster's latest LP, *ZUCKERZEIT*, you have a little idea what Harmonia sounds like. But Harmonia is even better!

Achim Roedelius was born in East Berlin on 26.10.1934. He wanted to flee from the Communist country, but was caught and put in jail from 1954 to 1956. In 1961 he finally succeeded in crossing the border and now lives in West Germany. He has worked as a book salesman and jobbed in various other professions -- in 1961 he picked up on music. He learned guitar, violin, organ, and drums all by himself. Now he plays organ, guitar, electric piano, echo chambers, modulators, mixers, etc.

Dieter Moebius was born in St. Gallen, Switzerland on 16.1.1944. He studied graphics and then became an innkeeper.

As a bartender he became acquainted with Achim, and a week later they played their first concert in the Berlin art gallery Hammer. The concert lasted for twelve hours. Dieter plays the following instruments today: guitar, rhythm machines, mixers, echo chambers and some small synthesizers.

Michael Rother was born 2.9.1950, the son of a woman piano player. He has lived everywhere and says that he's cosmopolitan. In Karachi he picked up a Japanese banjo and transformed it into a guitar. From that day he became interested in modern music. In 1971 he played with Kraftwerk, then formed Neu! with Klaus Dinger in 1972. He plays Synthorg, guitar, organ, electric piano and electronic percussion.

Achim, Dieter, and Michael, they all form Harmonia. When Eno saw them in concert in Hamburg he said: "The most important pop music that is made in our times." Listen yourself and see if he's right.

Reinhard Kunert

1976

The Cosmos Story

The Cosmos series was initiated in May 1974 with the release of *MILANO CALIBRO 9* (PILPS-9001) by the Naples-based quintet Osanna. This was the second Italian LP release by the band. At the time of this printing, Osanna will have completed work on their fifth album. *MILANO*, a film soundtrack, was the first fruit borne for my label, whose conception was first germinated in 1966 after hearing some Dutch imports by the then-named Golden Earrings of all people! I felt that certainly there should be a U.S. outlet for some of the more experimental and deserving of the multitude of unknown Eurobands. Those groups which would normally lie unnoticed by the large U.S. majors for one reason or another. The Peters International organization, for years  a major importer, was my second choice for such a launch and with the political release of *ON THE WINGS OF DEATH* (PILPS-9002) by the Athens-based quartet Socrates Drank The Conium, we were well on our way.

At this time, and rectified only recently, the Cosmos product, like everything else Peters ever pressed locally, enjoyed a remarkably high degree of defects. This coupled with distribution problems laid to rest the hope that Cosmos could ever be a major concern while being handled by the good Peters people.

For the third release, my attention was focused on the totally instrumental Danish jazz rockers, Secret Oyster. It's a pity that they've never toured the States, because they are tremendously exciting and caused many a phreak to leap about in a hash-induced idiot-dancing workout. Their initial LP, *FURTIVE PEARL* (PILPS-9003) was but a two track recording out at Palle Juul's farm in Nibe, Jutland. (Note: the original Danish front cover was the rear sleeve in the U.S., however in color, while our front was their rear!). The LP did remarkably well and received loads of airplay.

Many of my Irish friends had been telling me of the top Irish musicians back home and the name Gary Moore was oft-mentioned. There was a case where we imported an LP, test marketed it, and subsequently issued this lone LP by the Belfast-based quintet. The album, *GRINDING STONE* (PILPS-9004), is a prime showcase for Moore's powerful and fluid playing. It still stands up as a fine and largely unnoticed masterpiece. (Note: radio station KTAC-FM in Tacoma, Wash, named it album of the year for 1974).

I turned to Germany a bit belatedly because I wanted to sign a totally unknown band. While visiting Munich I came across Sahara, a sextet, at the Crash Club where the deal was basically culminated. They were exceptionally tight live and not afraid to make use of extensive arrangements and tape devices. They performed their initial LP, *SUNRISE* (PILPS-9006), flawlessly note for note as it sounds on record. This Cosmos release was further beset by quality problems in the pressing and the release was recalled, which for all intents and purposes killed it. Sahara, after a successful change of personnel, have completed a new work at the time of this printing and we hope to issue it here sometime in the fall.

Once again Osanna came up with a fine effort entitled *LANDSCAPE OF LIFE* (PILPS-9007). People who were knocked out by *MILANO* found this cutting too calculating and safe while we made many new fans with it. Featured on the LP are heavy keyboard, especially Mellotron, and sax work by Vairetti and D'Anna respectively, D'Anna and Danilo Rustici have subsequently formed the part-time trio Uno whose initial LP *UNO* (LPX-26) was recorded at Trident, London. Work on their second supposedly has been finished.

Back-to-back Italian releases on Cosmos occurred with my very own compilation of noteworthy and previously-available-as-imports tracks by the Venice-based trio Le Orme in an LP, never issued in Italy, which I entitled *BEYOND LENG* (PILPS-9008). (Note: Leng is a mythical plateau inhabited by nether-beings from the fantastic mind of the late H.P. Lovecraft). I still feel that this was the best of the Cosmos series. Exceptional production and keyboard mastery is the byword here. As in the case of *LANDSCAPE OF LIFE*, some vocals, albeit sparse, are performed in their original idiom, which for some of the safe and screaming Top 40 FM stations was too much. It is a pity that language barriers, especially in something as universal as music, can mean the difference in airplay.

Next came the second album by Secret Oyster, *SEA SON* (PILPS-9009). Again, totally instrumental in scope, it is by far a much better effort by these charismatic Danes. The Oyster are now in the process of cutting two LPs, one for the Danish Royal Ballet should be something.

Future plans for Cosmos center around the continuing release of material by Osanna, Secret Oyster, Sahara and Le Orme, with additional significant works to be issued as time goes by. The pressing quality problem has been resolved and the promised distribution network is in the process of being finalized.

Granted, the Cosmos series came along a close second to the ill-fated Chicago-based Billingsgate set-up, however it is fun to see the majors hopping onto the bandwagon.

A major portion of the foreign groups, I feel, should remain only as imported into the States and not pressed locally. There is, however, a fine line involved here and I suppose it boils down to individual A&R tastes. There is some great talent out there that no one has ever heard -- this is the stuff I'm looking for.

Running down an endless list of deserving talent in Europe: From Sweden -- Bjorn J:son Lindh and Janne Schaffer (their group Earfood) / Finland -- Jukka Hauru / Poland -- SBB, Woldek Gulgowski and the expatriates the Urbaniaks firmly ensconced in a CBS-subsidized flat in New York City's fashionable 58th St. / Denmark -- the Oysters and Iron Duke / Norway -- Popol Ace and Terje Rypdal / Hungary -- the classical rockers Copostakowiz Ensemble / Ireland -- Turner and Kirwan of Wexford and Chieftains / Brittany -- Alan Stivell / Germany -- Tangerine Dream, Klaus Schulze and Guru Guru / France -- Ange and Evangelos "Vangelis" O. Papathanassiou, the Greek expatriate / Italy -- Arti e Mestieri and Area / England -- Fripp, the Giant and Genesis / Greenland -- Sume / Iceland -- Pelican / Spain -- Canarios / Australia -- Pirana and Vanda and Younge.

My release philosophy will continue to be art before commerciality -- without getting to the stage where people are buying music merely because it is European. Let's hope that our market is not over-saturated with unmeritable Eurobands who destroy the chances of the more meaningful artists whose music really deserves to be digested.

Neil Kempfer Stocker

Editors Note: Cosmos has just released a new album by the Italian group RDM (Il Rovescio Della Medaglia) entitled *CONTAMINATION*. Originally done for RCA Italy, it has been specially redone in English. Classically influenced, it is highlighted by extremely tight work instrumentally and excellent vocals. It's worth a listen.

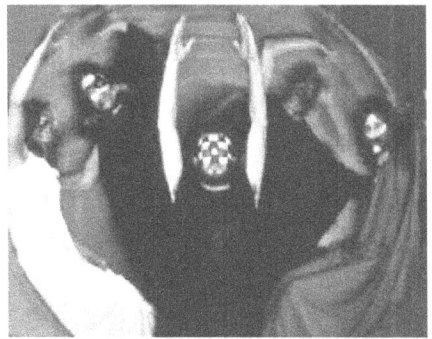

**Osanna - *L'UOMO*
(Fonit LPX 10)
Osanna - *MILANO CALIBRO 9*
(Cosmos PILPS 9001)
Osanna – *PALEPOLI*
(Fonit LPX 19)
Osanna - *LANDSCAPE OF LIFE*
(Cosmos PILPS 9007)
Uno – *UNO*
(Fonit LPX 26)**

Several U.S. critics, smug in their complacency, have been quick to label the first wave coming out of Italy as "spaghetti rock," confident that we'll know it for what it is: second rate. PFM paved the way and had to take the brunt of this condescension. And yet, despite the many bands that Italy has produced in the last five years, no other group has come over to turn that tide. Osanna could be the one,....

Most of the Italian bands I've heard have been fashioned along strict classic lines, all more or less derived from the Emerson, Lake & Palmer approach. The fact that most of these groups -- Le Orme, Banco, The Trip, Arti e Mestieri, New Trolls -- far outclass ELP has been overlooked. But as such, they generally base themselves around the keyboard wizardry of one member of the band. Not so with Osanna. This five-piece group is a definite extension of five separate personalities and they rock heavy, convoluted but tightly balanced.

Osanna is from Naples, formed in March of 1970 as a four-piece band of various keyboards, electric and acoustic guitars, bass and drums. Elio D'Anna joined in '72 on woodwinds and the dimensions are complete. Theirs is a textured sound, whether blasting or subdued, and comes across roughly aggressive in either case. No parlor tricks, just a solid musical foray.

Cosmos has released two of their albums in the U.S. already, their second and fourth -- *MILANO CALIBRO 9* (originally *PRELUDIO)* and *LANDSCAPE OF LIFE* -- and these have been the most successful in the Cosmos catalog thus far. So somebody out there is listening. And with good cause: Osanna have created an ideal melding of the progressive and the insurgent, a combination guaranteed to satisfy both sides of the camp.

Their first release, *L'UOMO*, held none of the indecisiveness of an initial work and still stands up as a solidly constructed recording, bursting with an overflow of energy. "Introduction" sets the mood, a chilling collage of synthesized shrieks immediately set upon by a quick bass run and the pouncing in of the rest of the band. Danilo Rustici's guitar slices a thin edge indeed and it's a heated race with d'Anna leading the pack on sax. Each instrument is pushed right to the front, with enough changes to keep the pace lively and varied.

Drummer Massimo Guarino and bassist Lello Brandi propel the basic beat with a restlessness that never lapses, but equally as restive are Lino Vairetti on organ, synthesizer, 12-string and vocals and Rustici on electric guitar, 12-string, and oscillator. Each member seems to urge the other on to frantic urgency, but it's the style of Elio D'Anna that stands out for me, harkening to the throaty flourishes of David Jackson of Van Der Graaf Generator. As a rock reedist, D'Anna is both light and frenetic, alternately abrasive and caressing, capable of a wide range that puts the standard sax-honkers to shame.

Through four albums and one offshoot recording called Uno (featuring Rustici, D'Anna and drummer Enzo Vallicelli), Osanna have emerged as complex and feverish stylists. *MILANO CALIBRO 9* introduced them to U.S. audiences in '74 with a successful combination of rock band and strings. Arranged by Luis Bacalov, *MILANO* brings the hard edge of self-assurance to a fusion that never seems to work when practiced by the Americans or the English. The Italians have a firmer base in the classics and *MILANO* doesn't pussyfoot around. Osanna tackles seven variations that flow from the main theme like rushing calamities from Pandora's Box.

The strings are not used throughout but only augment certain passages, giving Osanna plenty of room to workout, *MILANO* being a basically instrumental album. Osanna are, however, one of the few Italian bands to use an equal mixture of Italian and English lyrics, even on their own domestic releases. Vairetti is their full-throated vocalist, zealously unpretentious in his approach but never raucous.

PALEPOLI highlights his skill, their third album and the only one entirely in Italian. It's a strange recording, ominous calms breaking into instant savagery, D'Anna at times sounding positively deranged in his intensity. The rhythm changes sometimes strike me as rather arbitrary but the quick starts and stops are guaranteed to stave off boredom. They in fact possess an innate sense of their own, giving the whole work a peculiar tension like Yes or Genesis. The similarities stop there, one of the main differences being in the way that each member sets up a mutual course of attack.

They work together while all the time seeming on the verge of total dissolution. The end of side one is particularly bizarre, lumbering machinelike against the senses.

LANDSCAPE OF LIFE offers more of this unrestrained blowing but comes closer to the Yes style in its pastoral passages, radiating a shimmering sense of space. Rustici's guitar maintains the cutting edge and Guarino is as active as ever on drums, but the addition of Vairetti's Mellotron smoothes out the rough spots while adding to the overall texture. Osanna brings a lot of excitement to their music and this is perhaps the best point I can make. The enthusiasm overflows in their playing and *LANDSCAPE* comes highly recommended.

The same might be said for their subgroup, Uno, whose first album has been given the additional plus of good clean production at Trident Studios in London. Rustici and D'Anna are given free reign here, as it is primarily their project and they don't waste an effort. The individual tracks are all distinctive. The arrangements are toned down some, as is some of the immediacy, but the flavor of Osanna is still there. If this is "spaghetti rock" I'll have another plateful.

Gregory Shepard

**Le Orme – *COLLAGE*
(Philips 6323 007L)**

**Le Orme - *UOMO DI PEZZA*
(Philips 6323 013L)
Le Orme - *FELONA E SORONA*
(Philips 6323 023A)
Le Orme - *IN CONCERTO*
(Philips 6323 028A)
Le Orme – *CONTRAPUNTI*
(Philips 6323 035A)
Le Orme - *BEYOND LENG*
(Cosmos PILPS 9008)**

The full impact of Italy on today's international music scene has yet to be felt; aside from a couple of domestic releases and import action Italian groups are unknown quantities. The Germans were the first continentals to come to the attention of British and US rockers, and today they are just now breaking through into the first stages of broad public recognition. Not far behind, and deservedly so however, will be the many quality Italian groups.

Perhaps thanks for our being able to appreciate their unique musical stylings over here should be given to the Peters International people. They were the first to bring Italian imports into this country and to the attention of the few attentive ears. Also they were the first to attempt to bring it to a wider domestic audience via Neil Kempfer Stocker's Cosmos brainchild.

One of Italy's top groups now records for Cosmos and in the near future may be in for much greater recognition over here. Le Orme hail from Venice, translated their name means "the tracks," as in animal tracks. Starting as a three-piece in 1970, within three years they produced three albums, two of which went gold in Italy, making then the first native Italian group to have their work achieve gold record status in their homeland.

Keyboard-based, the nucleus of the group is made up of Antonio Pagliuca on keyboards, Aldo Tagliapietra on bass and vocals and Miki Dei Rossi on percussion. Their first album, recorded in 1971, shows them to be stylistically somewhat similar at times to the Nice and Traffic. In all it is a good album and serves an a fine introduction to their musical ideas. Highlights include the opener and title out "Collage," highly reminiscent of the Nice's "Brandenburger'" with its full organ cadence and harpsichord embellishments. Also of note is "Evasione Totale" featuring its keyboard gymnastics and experimentation with the tone generator.

The second album, *UOMO DI PEZZA*, marked a definite progression and showed a great deal more sophistication. Pagliuca had added more keyboards to his arsenal including Mellotron and synthi, and Tagliapietra was now playing acoustic and twelve string guitars. The result was an album quite unlike its predecessor. The vocals had become more important as the songs were more tightly arranged. They were now a band making music as opposed to a group playing their instruments, as was the case with *COLLAGE*.

Especially good were the short but sweet "Gioca di Bimba" that literally reeks of the atmosphere of old Italy and the album's closer "Alienazione," a lively instrumental featuring flashy keyboards and extremely tight ensemble works reminiscent of "Knife Edge" off ELP's first.

FELONA E SORONA, a concept album dealing with twin sister planets and their dual nature was the next. it too showed an evolution of sorts, though not as marked as before. What had changed was the improved ability of the group's actual playing. Definitely their musicianship was gaining confidence, and the overall production was more polished. It was no longer a case of instruments being played to produce effects, but instead they are employed to create an atmosphere of exotica. And it worked as the album comes off as their most unified to date -- thoroughly enjoyable.

Side one is peaceful and at times bursting with positive energy. On the other hand, Side Two is more aggressive and features a crashing buildup which culminates in a synthesized fadeout. *FELONA E SORONA* was their first album released outside Italy, being issued in England with lyrical translation by Peter Hamel. In addition they played a few live dates there at the time.

The follow-up to their English activity was a live album, *IN CONCERTO*, recorded before a large gathering in their home country (conquering hero's welcome home?) The atmosphere is highly charged, but unfortunately it wasn't transferred too successfully to record. This appears mainly to be due to the poor job of recording and bad splice job that was done. Instead of coming off as an organic statement of their live show, it instead reproduces bits and pieces of their live fireworks. The result being a shortage of good music, sacrificed to make room for obvious attention grabbing techniques. It is unfortunate as there are moments of brilliance when the group plays as a unit. A bit more planning and they could have put together a live album of more merit I'm sure.

In addition to the live album, 1974 saw the release of a new studio work. Entitled *CONTRAPUNTI*, it is perhaps their most successful work to date. They have mastered the techniques of recording and their playing has continued to improve. Most importantly however it is good music, not dependent on a concept or gimmickry. The compositions are much stronger structurally, not just ideas strung together, but individual pieces of music that can stand on their own. The brisk counter-rhythms of "Aliante" stand in direct contrast to the almost dirge-like drama of the somber "Notturno."

The variety of their approach on the various pieces is striking. "Maggio" ends the album with a workout of various styles, flowing together effortlessly into a warm Mellotron-led rhythm that climaxes with the soft tinkle of chimes.

1975 saw their first domestic release. Entitled *BEYOND LENG*, it was a carefully-edited selection of material from their earlier LPs. As a sampler it is excellent, showing them at their best.

Response to it was good and for the follow-up they were brought to the US and have now completed a new album at studios in L.A. Word has it that they have been joined on the album and for future live dates by a new guitarist, former Italian session star Vittorio "El Toro" Marton. The results should be interesting.

Archie Patterson

Ton, Steine, Scherben

I first made the acquaintance of TSS in the summer of 1970 while watching a TV program about the political demonstrations of radical students and apprentices. The program was unusual, in that it had not been compiled by a news team. Instead, radical groups were given the opportunity to present themselves in the pictures and sounds of the mass media without being filtered through the point-of-view of establishment journalism. The show was interesting enough, but the music which underlay a particularly effective demonstration scene lifted me right out of my chair. The piece was called "Macht kaputt, vas Euch kaputt macht" (Wreck what's wrecking you.") It was a brutal rock number; I had never dreamed a German group could be capable of such coarseness and ferocity. Of course, by that time we had experienced the MC5 and "Kick Out The Jams," but they were from Detroit, not the Federal Republic of Germany.

Actually TSS did not originate from the Federal Republic: they're from Berlin. Modern Berlin has nothing to do with the Berlin described by Lou Reed on his third album. There are no more decadent parties in shimmering candlelight -- Berlin is the focal point of the Germany's anarchist movement, one of Germany's most radical political movements. The anarchists subscribe to a violent concept of revolutionary struggle, taking the form of bombings and the abduction of political and business leaders. A part of this movement was the Organisation Second of June and the Baader-Meinhof Gang, whose leaders are presently incarcerated and standing trial.

This political movement finds its musical expression in Ton, Steine, Scherben. The band's members come from Kreuzberg, a working-class section of Berlin. They had been apprentices, but in 1965 they turned in their tools, picked up instruments and began their musical journey. At first they composed English lyrics for their songs but found the language unsuitable: the content of the songs remained inaccessible to Germans, who either paid no heed to the lyrics or simply did not understand them. Realizing that their central themes were being missed, TSS resolved to sing only in German from then on. This was an unusual decision for a German band to make, since artists who performed music from the Anglo-American idiom most frequently availed themselves of the

English language for their texts. There was (and still is) a popular prejudice in Germany that there can be no concordant joining of the native language with hard rock music. TSS proved this to be a misconception.

Their first single release was "Macht kaputt, vas Euch kaputt macht." TSS produced and distributed the record themselves and after only fourteen days all 3,000 copies were sold. Again and again representatives of record companies tried to bait the band with juicy contract offers. TSS were invited to lunch at expensive hotels, where they listened to company execs extol the practicality of representation by an established firm. But TSS remained true to themselves: even today the band attends to all production and distribution duties. Packaging is done cheaply: the first LP *WARUM GEHT ES MIR SO DREKIG* ("Why am I treated so badly") was released In a brown cardboard liner, held together with staples and identified by a simple ink stamp. The band's two other LPs, *KEINE MACHT FUR NIEMAND* ("Power for no one") and *WENN DIE NACHT AM TIEFSTEN IST..* ("When the night seem darkest..") are similarly packaged. The record label, "David Volksmund Produktion," has for its symbol a fist clutching a sling.

In the initial period the members of TSS were Ralph Steitz, Kai Sichtelmann and Wolfgang Seidel. This group was responsible for the first LP in early 1971. The lyrics, all in German, were sung very convincingly by Ralph Möbius, whose rough passionate voice is most suitable for hard rock, very akin to that originating in Detroit. The songs are played in the usual rock instrumentation and production is primitive contributing to the expressiveness of the music. The guitars rattle and clank as though they had been swiped from Woolworth's.

The lyrics, printed on a poster and enclosed with the album, deal with the conditions facing young workers and with economic oppression in general. Here's a sample of the texts from "The Struggle Goes On":

> "How many are behind bars who want freedom / How many that we need outside are behind bars / How many are behind bars according to the law / Whoever has money has power and he who has power has justice." From "Solidarity": "What we want, we can achieve / If we want all wheels stop turning / We are not afraid to fight / for freedom is our goal."

Of course the printed lyrics cannot arouse the sensations you have when you hear Ralph roar forth in his inimitable hoarseness. This album must be heard.

When I saw TSS live for the first time, I found them to be just as good as on their record, but with the music's effect augmented by the personal contact with the band. In contrast to the many groups who scoot off to the nearest hotel, groupie in hand, following their last number, TSS came down into the audience, permitting anyone who desired to talk with them. At later concerts these conversations with TSS led to demonstrations and sit-ins. The music did have its effect.

It should be mentioned that TSS are not affiliated with any leftist party. Their affiliation is with their concept of freedom -- no one may rule over another person, or as expressed in their second LP, *POWER FOR NO ONE*.

Their performances are freebies. Professional promoters enlisted their services for the first and last time in 1970 for the festival on Fehmarn Island. While the well-known groups (among them Jimi Hendrix) were paid for their services, TSS, the last group to appear, played "Macht kaputt vas Euch kaputt macht." The ushers and audience took their cue and put the torch to the promoter's tent. From then on the band has played only for workers' and students' groups, who handle all business arrangements for themselves.

Meanwhile, TSS has become "persona non grata" in Switzerland. A tour through six Swiss cities led to demonstrations against Swiss justice. The police arrested the group, labeled them "undesirable" and shipped them back to Germany.

Toward the end of 1971 saxophonist Nikkel Pallat and flutist Jorg Schlotterer joined the group and Jens Jordan relieved drummer Wolfgang Seidel.

At this time the TV presented an open-ended discussion on the theme, "Pop and Co., the other music between Protest and the Market Place." Participants were Conny Veit (then with Gila), Nikkel Pallat of TSS, a critic, a sociologist and as representative of the record industry Rolf-Ulrich Kaiser. An argument eventually resulted between Pallat and Kaiser:

Pallat: Speaking objectively, (I believe) the situation is like this and the facts will bear me out: you (Kaiser) have a contract with Peter Maisel, a capitalist swine, a music pirate of the first order, a pop-gangster. He needs a man to buy groups for him, so he gets someone with a name, a progressive image. How many people like that are there in Germany. There are only a few music journalists so the choice is Rolf-Ulrich Kaiser, ok?

Kaiser: It wasn't that way at all.

Pallat: What happens then? This man purchases people: he has connections with some groups and he exploits these relationships. He produces these groups arguing that he "wants to create a beautiful new world," but that's only pretense. Actually he sides with the system and doesn't change anything.

Kaiser: I'm no Communist.

Pallat: You don't need to be -- you just need a desire to change things.

Kaiser: Our society will change by evolution and that's not something that will happen tomorrow. That was the illusion of those people who took to the streets in '65 and '66, though that was an important thing. But this won't happen tomorrow; it's a development that goes on for a hundred years and in these hundred years...

Pallat: And in these hundred years you will support the continuance of the oppression, while you go on working for the system -- yes, you go on working for the oppressor and not against him, you know. So one thing is clear: if anything's going to happen, you have to take sides against the oppressor. You have to take a stand and not just talk about it. Now I'm going to tear this table apart to exemplify what I mean.

With these words Pallat pulled a hatchet out of his jacket and splintered the discussion table before the eyes of the TV audience.

In early 1972 drummer Olaf Lietzau took the place of Jens Jordan; their second LP appeared. In terms of the music and lyrics, *KEINE MACHT FUR NIEMAND* is the continuation of their first. It contains a 64-page supplement with printed lyrics, information about the Baader-Meinhof Gang, comics and collages. The record was produced on a Revox, so there can be no discussion of technical expenditure.

1976

In the course of their tour of the summer of '72, TSS lost Olaf Lietzau, who went to Hamburg (along with producer Klaus Schulz) to join the group Panther. Hans-Jurgen Hynding replaced Olaf.

Nothing was heard of TSS for a while. I saw them the next time at a political rally financed by leftist groups. The program included reports of repression and torture in Chile. The leftists didn't want hard rock as a follow-up (the anarchistic attitude of TSS didn't suit them), but the group played anyway. They distributed instruments to the audience and played numbers from *KEINE MACHT FUR NIEMAND*. Since the music was not mournful but instead appealed for joyful solidarity, the Communist Party members found the music unsuitable and pulled the plug on the group.

In April of '74, TSS gave a concert at the U. of Berlin. They had turned away from harsh political demands and sang instead of their visions of a better world. Everything was somewhat mystical and most likely influenced by dope. In place of jeans and T-shirts, they wore velvet and silk. As was to be expected, they were booed off the stage. But that didn't disturb them; they continue to go their own way. This new path is reflected In their latest LP, *WENN DIE NACHT AM TIEFSTEN IST...* The group has changed. Instead of five members, the band now comprises sixteen. The music is looser, more influenced by psychedelic groups than the MC5. Distribution remains independent and the texts are still in German. The tone of the lyrics has changed however: From "Durch die Wuste" (Through the Desert):
> Help me / Show me the way out of here / Don't leave me hanging / Give me an answer / Show me the way out of here / Help me.

From "Wir sind im Licht" (We're in the Light):
> I know there can be no rulers / I know we can live differently / We're headed for tomorrow, yesterday doesn't count / The shadows are gone, we're in the light.

What I like so much about TSS is that they go their own way, without regard to the press, political parties or other organizations. Their path has been a difficult one to take. The members of TSS do what they deem right and they're doing it now, today. Whether their audiences laud them or reject them is not important. They have their own lives to live and will not be molded by the demands of business or the dream of success. If possible, get the records, have the lyrics translated; perhaps you will share my opinion that TSS is one of the best bands on the planet.

As they say in 'Wenn die Nacht..":
> Often I was at the end of my rope / Done for and alone / All I heard was / Leave it be / You don't have that much power / You can't give that much / take the path that all people take / You only have one life / But I will follow my path to the end / I know we will see the sun / When the night seems darkest, the day is just over the horizon.

Reinhard Kunert

Jane was founded in Hanover in October 1970 by Klaus Hess and Peter Panka. They were joined by Werner Nadolney, formerly on sax, who switched to organ and by guitarist Charly Maucher who took up bass in order to join. Their first appearance was December 5th in Hanover. Vocalist Bernd Pulst was added to the band in April 1971.

TOGETHER, the first album, was recorded in Hamburg during October '71 with Connie Plank as engineer and Gunter Korber as producer. This duo worked on all four Jane albums. *TOGETHER*, with its five-piece lineup, is a fundamentally good album; its only problem being that it is their first time in the studio and a certain stiffness shows. However, this problem common to most bands disappeared with later albums.

The organ on the first and second albums tends to be too dominant. As for the tracks themselves on *TOGETHER*, the two best are "Spain" and "Hangman," both long extended pieces on Side 2. "Try to Find" on side 1 is an example of the band's major problem. The middle of their numbers are quite good, but they have trouble leading into and out of a song.

Bernd Pulst left the band in April '72. Charly Maucher was forced to leave temporarily in August '72, due to illness. His place was taken by Wolfgang Krantz, who appeared on the second album, recorded and released in the autumn of '72. Peter Panka did what vocals there were on the album. On the album, entitled *HERE WE ARE*, the band tends to experiment more, with the use of male and female vocalists on "Redskin" and "Waterfall." On "Out in the Rain" is their first use of Mellotron and on "Like a Queen," second side, it is used again with Dieter Dierks adding various electronic effects. This album is basically rock with experimental overtones dominated by guitar and organ and very forceful percussion.

Changes continued with Werner Nadolney leaving in April '73 and Charly Maucher returning in May of that year. *JANE III* was recorded In January '74 with the following lineup : Klaus Hess on electric and acoustic guitar, Wolfgang Krantz - guitar and piano, Charly Maucher - bass and vocals and Peter Panka on percussion and vocals on one track. This album was released in April '74 at the time of the Easter Festival of German Rock in the Ernst-Merck-Halle in Hamburg and is easily their best. This is due to the return of Maucher plus the use of two lead guitars. With the third and fourth albums the band went to more of a hard rock sound. "Comin' Again" is a strong excellent track with extensive use of echo and is quite well put together. The album varies from driving rockers to slower-paced cuts dominated by Hess, guitar. "Early in the Morning" which starts the second side, and 'Baby What You're Doin'" are in a similar vein.

Maucher and Krantz left in August '74 and a new bass player was added in September when Martin Hesse joined. The band continued as a three-piece until October when the addition of Gottfried Janko on keyboards made it a four-piece again. Janko, besides playing organ and piano has added synthi to the group and does all the vocals except two on *LADY*, the fourth album, recorded from November '74 to January '75, and released in the spring of '75. It is a transitional work with extensive use of Janko's vocal range and keyboard. The best tracks are "Midnight Mover" and "So, So Long." The former a long instrumental; the latter more slow paced with excellent guitar work. Hess seems to be more interested in the music and guitar than just filling a role, i.e. lead guitarist in a rock band. Much of his guitar work has a lot of thought put into it and is ably complemented by Panka's driving drums. I really cannot see the band existing without Panka, as he and Hess literally dominate the band. Incidentally, they have signed with Capitol here, and *JANE III* has just been released.

Russ Harrell

Kraan

Formed in 1971, Kraan have risen to become the top rock group in their native West Germany. Quite a feat for five very young and extremely dedicated musicians!

Kraan consists of: Hellmut Hattler - bass guitar and vocals; Peter Wolbrandt - guitars and vocals; Johannes "Alto" Pappert - alto sax; Jan Fride - drums and percussion; Ingo Bischof - keyboards and synthesizers.

Hellmut, Peter, Johannes and Jan originally lived near Berlin when they formed the band. This area of West Germany proved to be the wrong starting point for tours, so they began looking for a house in the country. The search was a long one. Having heard about Count Metternich, a man known for supporting experimental art projects, they contacted him. The Count owned a secluded farmhouse in the Teutoburger Forest called "Wintrup" which he agreed to let the band have.

Located in a beautiful valley, surrounded

by unbelievable scenery, "Wintrup" became their new home. Here they have lived for the past three years with their wives, roadies and manager (Walter Holzbaur). From here, they start their yearly tours of Germany and abroad. They recently played a festival in Copenhagen and tore the place up! They are also very pleased that their records have finally been made available in other countries, especially in the U.S.A., so that people can hear and enjoy Kraan music!

For those of you who have not had the chance of hearing Kraan, let me try to explain their music. They improvise within structured songs but at the same time maintain an intense flow of high energy. This can especially be witnessed on their 2 LP set *KRAAN LIVE*. It even includes an extraordinary bass and chest pounding solo from Hellmut on "Nam Nam"! The music is a constant barrage of riffs and rhythms being traded between the musicians.

With the addition of keyboard player Ingo Bischof (previously with Karthago), the band has at the same time, become more relaxed sounding AND tighter. A real stand-out in their music is the ever-present three-part harmony (on instruments) done by Peter, Johannes and Ingo. It's a rare treat to hear melodic music in an age of crass commercialism

You owe it to yourself to hear them and see them when they make it to the States in 1976.

Dana Madore
(with help from Kraan)

Kraan – *WINTRUP*
(Spiegelei 28 523-9)
Kraan – *KRAAN*
(Spiegelei 28 778-9)

Kraan - *ANDY NOGGER*
(Passport PPSD-98006)
Kraan - *KRAAN LIVE*
(Spiegelei 26 440-8)
Kraan - *LET IT OUT*
(Spiegelei 26 542-1)

It never ceases to amaze me just how long it takes a good thing to catch on over here. Perhaps I've become too arrogant In my tastes but listening to American radio is like tuning in to a wasteland of redundancy. The European rock bands have offered us countless alternatives in as many different styles as there are holes in Albert Hall. And yet we're still plugged into that same wavelength of mediocrity that ushered in the '70s. Living in the San Francisco area must have something to do with my discontent, where trends are way behind the times, but I wonder sometimes how long it'll take the U.S. companies to milk the Continental Invasion for all its worth.

Kraan are long overdue for a big break, one of the best bands to come out of Continental Europe yet. They can't be pinned down but neither are they inaccessible. Vigorous, joyous, unpredictable, infectious and full of an eccentric charm, Kraan should be right up there beside Can, Kraftwerk and Tangerine Dream in the list of Germany's finest. Like most of these bands, Kraan are a group, no superegos throwing off the balance of collective construction. On stage, they each take sprightly solos but all for the fun of it, not to impress the feeble-minded.

Kraan consisted originally of four members: Peter Wolbrandt on guitar and vocals; Hellmut Hattler on bass and vocals; Johannes Pappert on alto sax; and Jan Fride on drums. They were joined last year by Ingo Bischof from Karthago on keyboards, filling out their sound with a

1976

subtle commentary. They've released five albums but only the latest, *LET IT OUT*, features Bischof, and it's definitely a winner.

Oddly enough, though, their first two albums were issued out of sequence. *WINTRUP*, released first, was actually recorded in the latter part of '72 while the album titled simply *KRAAN* was recorded in the first half of that year. This certainly hasn't caused much confusion since their label, Spiegelei, is mysterious enough as it is, but it's enough to justify taking these two albums as a whole. They serve as admirable introductions to a band that's come a long way in such a short period of time.

The first thing that strikes you is the range of influences -- Eastern raga, the suggestion of modern jazz, understated rock -- that's produced such a unique blend. Kraan have moved away from the Eastern influence some since then, but the deceptively loose feel of their music, the rambling cohesion, remains their trademark. "Mind Quake" from *WINTRUP* is a good example of this, spirited by a rambunctious ease but continually pulled toward a minor pensiveness; youthful reminiscence ("when I was young, I learned to hate") with a savage undercurrent, despite the offhand approach of the vocals. This leads into "Backs," filled with wry observations on the path of life: "We pretend to go the right way, but we know that direction's wrong." Pappert's sinuous sax weaves a plaintive thread right to the shuffling finish, but it's the bouncy exuberance of Wolbrandt, Hattler and Fride that really energizes the song.

KRAAN and *WINTRUP* both sport unobtrusively weird cover art, designed by Wolbrandt, that somehow manages to capture the mood of the music, in spite of the fact that it's almost impossible to render this mood into words. "Sarah's Ritt durch den Schwarzland" from *KRAAN* might be a good place to start. An ethereal quality insinuates throughout, due in part to Pappert's Eastern intonations on alto sax, elusive and drawn out, and yet there's a solid base that keeps the music from floating away entirely.

But the best music to come out of this period may be found on *WINTRUP*; side two brings it all into focus. The rhythmic interplays between Wolbrandt, Hattler and Fride are simply incredible in their flexibility, similar to the way in which the members of Can work together but more freewheeling. The title song and "Jack Steam" are my particular favorites, the former a personal reflection on the present ("should we be so prudent, to use our heads for the future..."); and the latter a roustabout rocker with uneasy overtones. Kraan are simply one of those bands that convince you they've been together for years, and you wonder why you haven't heard them before.

Their third album, *ANDY NOGGER*, has been their only U.S. release however, on Jem Import's fledgling Passport label. The production is considerably cleaner but what's more important, the mood is a lot fresher, good-timey without becoming banal. The band cooks along on cuts like "Stars," "Son of the Sun" and "Holiday am Marterhorn," Wolbrandt skipping out on these effortless runs with Hattler and Fride rebounding along, Pappert wailing, relaxed. The title song loops and twists, taking unexpected dives until you can't keep your feet still.

This is all brought out in full fruition on Kraan's double live album, *KRAAN LIVE*, recorded in late '74. Here they really extend themselves, working out on numbers mainly from their first three albums like "Nam Nam," "Kraan Arabia" and "Andy Nogger." The upbeat rhythms abound, carried into lengthy solos and providing just what you'd expect if you'd followed the band to this point. A certain sameness intrudes until you assimilate the different tracks but this is less a shortcoming than you'd suppose. Kraan have an identifiable sound to be sure, a restless exhilaration that's quite physical in its directness, but they communicate and involve the listener rather than force you to sit and appreciate. Too many bands fail in this respect and it makes a difference when you're looking for music to FEEL instead of ponder.

Of course, this is purely a matter of taste, but with *LET IT OUT*, Kraan have finally begun to branch out. The distinction between cuts is stronger and the textures, with the deft addition of Bischof, given fuller depth. The album as a whole has a jazzier feel to it, still rollicking but smoother in its approach. The first track, "Bandits in the Woods," picks you right up and whisks you into a jungle forest, languorous and sublime. Pappert slips and slides, calling at a distance, urging toward total escape. This song is certainly their finest yet.

But this is only the beginning, in more senses than one. "Luftpost" immediately takes off in another direction, a cool flight of impressions as the earth slips away beneath you, soaring. The title song is their ode to inhibition and that's just what these rhythmic journeys are all about. Kraan emerge in their full glory, capturing the essence of musical escape with an easy-going proficiency. Kraan has certainly arrived. And for an added taste, a tickle to the absurd, check out their contributions to Mani Neumeier's solo outing, *GURU GURU -- MANI UND SEINE FREUNDE*. "Sunrise is Everywhere" and "'Walking, Eating, My Hot Dog" are pure Kraan, as outrageous and contagious as ever.

Gregory Shepard

ove Records was founded in 1966 by three young men closely associated with music: Otto Donner, Atte Blom and Christian Schwindt, who are still in charge of the company. From the beginning Love concentrated on music for minorities: progressive pop, jazz, children's songs, political songs and folk music were the main fields that lacked the attention of larger record companies in Finland. Love started to fill the gap according to its progressive music policy, and was very soon confronted with grave economic difficulties, especially since in 1969 the larger companies formed their own distribution cartel, which was an attempt to eliminate small companies from the field. But this in fact turned out to further the development of Love into an independent force in the record business: it acquired its own distribution network and was later able to take other small producers' records into its distribution.

The first years were still a struggle for survival. The small group of record buyers that supported Love was not big enough to

1976

cover the costs of production, but with the help of many peoples' free work and financial assistance Love was able to get over the difficulties, and slowly even the early records began to pay back -- most of them are still current in the market. During its nine years Love has become one of the main producers of Finnish music: it now employs nearly twenty people and the catalog includes about 200 LPs and over 100 singles. Last year's production was about 50 new releases and this year the amount will reach 100. Apart from the record production, Love is also the publisher of almost all of its material.

Unlike most of the record companies in Finland, Love covers only a small percentage of its sales by imports, selecting the music mainly from outside the Anglo-American market. A cooperation with progressive record companies and distributors in several European countries has brought rare music to Finland, and it looks like many of Love's artists will shortly break into the international market. Also, this year a new contract has been made with the Chilean record company Dicap, now operating from Paris, and a contract with Cuba is under negotiation.

Although most of Love's production is aimed at small groups within the record buying audience, some releases have reached an unexpectedly high number of sales. The limit for gold records in Finland is 15,000. Several Love releases have reached that level and their artists, Hurricanes (the most popular group in Finland today), have sold as many as 50,000 copies.

(Used Courtesy Love Records)

Wigwam

Wigwam started out as an anonymous back-up band, but before long Ronnie Osterberg (drums), Vladimir Nikamo (guitar) and Mats Hulden (bass) were rehearsing on their own. They were joined in early '69 by Jim Pembroke, a singer and composer. Love Records, then a struggling little company, took an interest in the band and duly released a single, "Must Be The Devil." When after a few months the original line-up found itself lacking in playpower, Jukka Gustavson was invited to join on organ and vocals. Sound-wise, The Band and Procol Harum were notable influences. Late in the year their first album, *HARD 'N HORNY*, written by Pembroke and Gustavson, was recorded; then a single in Finnish called "Luulosairas," which was fairly well received. Around this time, Wigwam also played in the Helsinki production of HAIR and on some film soundtracks.

Meanwhile, Atte Blom of Love Records had been busy promoting Wigwam to contacts abroad. About the only person to respond, favorably or otherwise, was one Kim Fowley, of California, USA. Although he judged the band "not up to his standards" he did in fact turn up in Helsinki to produce *TOMBSTONE VALENTINE*. This was in May 1970. Shortly before, after a single called "Pedagogi"/"Haato," Mats Hulden had withdrawn, and Pekka Pohjola, who had played violin on that record, was now on bass. Fowley's behavior caused Nikamo to leave at short notice, and Jukka Tolonen stood in on guitar for the album.

Instrumentally down to a three piece again, Wigwam began to develop a split personality. On stage, the band would rely mainly on tried and tested numbers, which in time eroded into long stretches of improvisation. Vocals were down to a minimum. New recording material tended to increasingly complex organization, but was seldom used on appearances. As composers and arrangers, Pembroke, Gustavson and Pohjola all had their distinct styles, as was evident on *FAIRYPORT*, a double album recorded over a year and released late in '71. Pembroke and Pohjola subsequently recorded solo albums, while it remained Gustavson's concern to find a lyrically and musically unified context for Wigwam. This was attempted on *BEING*, released early in '74, which was conceived as a fully cooperative work within a thematic frame provided by Gustavson.

By this time Pembroke was playing electric piano on stage. In order to expand the sound further, and to introduce fresh feedback among the musicians it was decided, after four years, to bring in a new guitar player, Pekka Rechardt, who was also expected to play cello. But things didn't work out as planned, and there was mounting frustration within the band. Eventually, following a tour of England, Jukka Gustavson and Pekka Pohjola both left. The remaining three chose to carry on under the same name, with their producer Mans Groundstroem, late of Tasavallan Presidentti, taking over on bass.

Pembroke, Osterberg and Groundstroem originally played together as early as 1967, in Blues Section, a group with a great reputation in Scandinavia then. Their coming together again completes a circle in the development of Wigwam, which is now looking forward to reaching wider audiences through records and appearances outside Scandinavia.

(Used Courtesy Love Records)

Wigwam, Mark I

The recordings of Wigwam are perhaps one of the world's unknown musical treasures. In their first incarnation, they produced five of the most imaginative rock albums you're likely to ever hear. And unfortunately they are virtually unobtainable outside Finland.

Their first, suggestively titled *HARD 'N HORNY*, was a delightful, somewhat strange pop album. Its two sides

1976

represented two extremely diverse talents at work.

Side One was the work of Jukka Gustavson as he was responsible for all its titles. At times it is reminiscent of early Traffic, in its jazzy feel and vocals. Gustavson's organ playing is simple, but nothing short of excellent. It is complemented by Pembroke's piano. The majority of song titles and lyrics are in Finnish, so literal comprehension is lacking, but the music, which is predominant, and Gustavson's occasional vocals are nonetheless completely enjoyable.

Side Two is Pembroke's and his sense of humor and pop influences are dominant. His stylized vocals play a major role in the overall approach. Sung against a pop background, they result in the stuff of which pop aficionados dream. Mellow ballads are mixed with jumpy, medium and up-tempo numbers. In all both sides make for a top-notch listening experience.

Next came *TOMBSTONE VALENTINE*. A single album in Finland, it was released in the US as a double set due to the smarm and charm of Kim Fowley. Over here the first record was *TOMBSTONE VALENTINE*, the second a combination of, I believe, Wigwam reworkings of earlier Blues Section numbers and a couple of other early Wigwam cuts.

It is dominated by Pembroke as he is responsible for about three sides worth of the tunes. Gustavson contributes a few and bassist Pohjola a couple, but primarily it's Pembroke's show. Songs like -- "Dance of the Anthropods / Frederick and Bill (Song of the Skinheads)," "Tombstone Valentine," "The Gang Called the Vegetable Man" and "Only Dreaming" show his remarkable versatility.

From gibberish to straight, his lyrical talents and arranging skill work together very successfully. For lovers of pop this album is one in a million.

In spite of the excellence of these first two albums however, the next two made their accomplishment seem pale in comparison.

FAIRYPORT was the third and another double set. In many ways it marked a radical departure. This was due to Gustavson's emergence as a dominant force and the further development of Pohjola's composing talents. Together they served as the catalyst for the majority of the material. Pembroke did contribute moments of superlative pop, especially "Lost Without a Trace" and "How to Make It in a Hospital." But the album's highlight has to be the fourth song "Joined to Conscience" by Gustavson which consists of: "Fairyport," "Gray Traitors," "Caffkaff the Country Psychologist" and "May Your Will Be Done Dear Lord." Their ever-changing arrangements, organ/piano work and Gustavson's vocals, which come off as a cross between Stevie Wonder and Steve

Winwood, make it a veritable pièce de résistance. It can be approached on either level, lyrically or musically, and thoroughly enjoyed.

The last side of the album also is no throwaway. It's an instrumental with Jukka Tolonen guesting on guitar. The result is 17:20 worth of jamming that never wears thin.

With the next album Gustavson pulled out all the stops. *BEING* was conceived as a socio-political work that, in my personal estimation, is one of the best progressive albums made. Musically it is highly complex. Gustavson's organ and jazz tendencies dominate, with Pembroke contributing bizarre pop interludes between the instrumental/vocal forays of Gustavson. The integration of music and lyrics works exceptionally well considering the overall complexity of both. There is the class analysis of "Proletarian...Inspired Machine": "Guess I'm a slave. To bourgeois or state; ...In this quarrel, my craving for revenge seizes power in hitting back I'm justified;.." And the holy litany of "Pride of the Biosphere": "As I cast my mind back to the first years of the war, to the best times of my career as a chaplin, ...Warfare is rough play, as we all know. ...there in the dull humdrum of the officers mess we would be pleasantly diverted by such questions as- ..At this, and blushing almost openly, the officers would proceed to rape the waitresses in full view and afterwards shoot them on the spot. ..inscrutable are the ways of the lord ...and how can we mortals be expected to mind and master every turn, a-men." Indeed! And the glorious conclusion -- "Radiant the Commandment; That the Skimmer Too. Illuminate. It's Mutilated. Shadow!":

> Old scarecrow getting
> nearer than near
> well he could be a schizo
> or maybe a queer
> we won't know 'til we get
> it together.

That is but the tip of the iceberg, a few excerpts. In addition there's a written, complementary narrative to fill in the between-the-lines story. If you can imagine all this successfully adapted to a musical tract, then you have no idea of how good it is. You simply have to hear it to believe it.

At this point unfortunately the end came for Wigwam Mark I. After a farewell tour, Gustavson and Pohjola left to pursue their individual aspirations. Gustavson took a short musical vacation working as a milkman. Since then he's resumed his activities, composing a rock opera that has been showing in Helsinki for six months. Pohjola has kept busy doing session work, playing a few gigs with an aggregation called the Finnish All-Stars, recording another solo LP and just recently he joined the international band Made In Sweden.

So that brings us to the fifth LP, a testimonial to their live work, their influences and their favorite music. Entitled *LIVE MUSIC FROM THE TWILIGHT ZONE*, it stands as a final tribute to the end of an era for a great band. Rustic in recording quality, it is nonetheless one of the most enjoyable live albums I've heard. They play an extended version of a piece by The Band "The Moon Struck One" and a Sonny Boy Williamson medley "Help Me"/"Chockin' Up On My Baby," In addition there's a melodic instrumental by the then-newly-added and current guitarist Pekka Rechardt entitled "Groundswell." Plus two Beatle tunes "Imagine" and "Let It Be." They are sung by Gustavson and his organ playing has never been more engaging. He soulfully wails as his organ throws out full, vibrant chord progressions in accompaniment. The album does have its shortcoming as do all live works -- it is loose and sloppy in places, in addition to the relatively unsophisticated recording. But its high points overshadow its faults easily.

Wigwam Mark I may well be gone, but the existence of albums like *TWILIGHT ZONE* and *BEING* will insure that they are not forgotten.

Archie Patterson

Wigwam, Mark II

Wigwam was becoming schizophrenic. Two leaders had developed: Jukka Gustavson tried to get the band behind a solid, unifying ideology with a blend of socialism and jazzy rock; Jim Pembroke, the itinerant Englishman, felt the band should be recording songs rather than philosophies. At the same time, bassist Pekka Pohjola began to follow his own instincts and recorded two fine jazz albums. Wigwam was flying off in all directions at once, both musically and thematically.

The break came in 1975. Gustavson and Pohjola split, leaving Pembroke, drummer Ronnie Osterberg and guitarist Pekka Rechardt to their own devices -- a time of changes. *NUCLEAR NIGHTCLUB* (Virgin 2035) and *LUCKY GOLDEN STRIPES AND STARPOSE* (Virgin 2051) reflect those changes, maintaining Wigwam's stance as one of Finland's (as well as Europe's) finest bands. No longer organ-based without Gustavson, a new focus had to be found. Pembroke immediately provided that focal point by initially taking over most of the songwriting and vocals, creating a new band in the process. With the addition of Mosse Groundstroem on bass (formerly of Tasavallan Presidentti and old friends of Wigwam), the band has taken on an added depth and sophistication. Pembroke's lyrics don't stress one particular framework, as did Gustavson's, but are better melded with the music. Gustavson filled his compositions to the brim with ideas and tasty solos, but too many words. Pembroke utilizes the whole band around tight song constructions and in effect has totally unified Wigwam for the first time.

Of course credit also goes to each member as Pembroke doesn't pose as leader per se. Rechardt lends a more-than-able hand to the musical side, a very understated guitarist. In fact, understatement has always been the key to Wigwam. What makes them such a pleasure to the ears is the polish they've added since revamping. "Freddie Are You Ready" from *NIGHTCLUB* is a beautiful example. It begins softly with echoey guitar sliding against the harmony of a delicate synthesizer line. The suggestion of silent fury keeps the whole thing from floating away, Groundstroem's bass growling like a pet bear to Osterberg's playful side-glances. Pembroke's vocals pause and leap with the melody, placing an off-beat inflection to the words until they become almost conversational.

The whole album follows in this careful balance of instrument/voice, timing/melody, each aspect played off the other in total control. "Do or Die" offers a more full throated approach, Rechardt's guitar cuts in crisp and clean over a thundering bass, while guest artist Esa Kotilainen weaves a subtle synthesized countermelody somewhere in the middle. "Simple Human Kindness" points up the irony of success, giving Pembroke another chance to play with our ears as he adds a funky slur to his voice for an offhand delivery.

STARPOSE takes this same underplayed feeling and continues to smooth the edges, adding Hessu Hietanen on keyboards and giving the musical texture a fuller blend. Wigwam maintains its Northern cool, striking a starpose filled with subtle ironies.

"Whistle while you're down and out/any old refrain/grand to feel sane again," Dirge-like, the pose is established, inversely echoed in the lines, "international disaster/slowly gettin' faster," and culminating with the lighthearted admission, "No I'm just a case of nuts." *STARPOSE* hints at treachery and change, but ultimately points to the crumbling of The System, wry wit intact and on target.

My favorite tunes are the Pembroke compositions, particularly "June May Be Too Late" and "Never Turn You In," with their rambling vocals and crisp arrangements, both facets played off each other in casual cohesion. Rechardt brings his own writing skills to the fore on "Colossus," "Eddie And The Boys" and the title song, constantly shifting the emphasis from the airy, to the reflective, to the full-tilt, in broad strokes and easy strides. "Eddie.." is a backbeat delight, a tasty cha-cha which Rechardt bites into with relish; while "Starpose" itself alternately thumps and baits you with its lament on world decay.

There is a loose quality here that's hard to pin down but that can be seen as a general trademark of Wigwam and Jim Pembroke in particular. Both of his solo albums, *WICKED IVORY* (released under the pseudonym of Hot Thumbs O'Riley) and *PIGWORM*, possess this comfortable feel, though IVORY is only partly successful. It's done up like a series of nightclub acts and becomes rather gimmicky after the first earful, rather like a comedy album which loses its humor after repeated listenings.

The lyrics range from the purely eccentric to the grim and satiric --
>"I'm gonna get me a shovel / Dig up every grave I know / If I don't find our victim / gonna cancel my Life magazine subscription,"

but the music overall is weak and lacking in enough variety to carry the theme through convincingly.

Both *WICKED IVORY* and *PIGWORM* use most of Wigwam to provide the musical backing and in fact, the latter could have been a Wigwam release, Jukka Gustavson had practically taken over the band at this point (early '74) and Pembroke obviously used the solo format for his own creative outlet. But only IVORY's gimmick marks any real difference in style between Pembroke with Wigwam and Pembroke alone. PIGWORM (named for an oblique dance step Pembroke invented) is a much stronger album, in spite of its low key approach.

Pembroke here sounds unusually relaxed and gives the album a flowing feel. This light touch is reflected in both the playing and singing, and brings Pembroke's piano up front for a change. "Just My Situation" is a good example, very late-nightish and softly plaintive. The album certainly has its personal quality -- raising an interesting observation -- had Pembroke stayed in England he could have easily been lost in the shuffle. In fact, Wigwam's total originality is due to just this very combination of Finnish compose and Pembroke charm. Such an alliance has already produced over ten albums of superlative, deliberative rock. And since reforming and strengthening of the band, it stands to produce much more. It's been seven years since Jim Pembroke first joined the fledgling Blues Section, which in turn became Wigwam, but one might say they've just begun.

Gregory Shepard

Pekka Pohjola

The first of Pekka Pohjola's two solo albums was recorded while he was still in Wigwam. It shows a marked contrast between their work and his own ideas. Titled, in Finnish, *PIHKASILMÄ KAARNAKORVA*, all the music and arrangements were by Pohjola and he is featured on bass, piano and violins. Able assistance is given, most notably by ex-Tasavallan Presidentti windman extraordinaire Pekka Poyry and his Wigwam mate Jukka Gustavson on organ. The music can best be described as symphonic jazz. There is no lush string overkill however, as is the case with much of today's symphonic rock. Bass and piano are used as the lead instruments, with organ and winds contributing melody and solo complement. The albums four pieces are exercises in changing mood and form. At times they weave warm melodies, then switch to swinging jazz, only to transform themselves into an almost classical interlude. The variety of styles present is amazing, yet they are used to good effect, not simply haphazardly thrown together.

The second LP, recorded after he left Wigwam, is entitled *B THE MAGPIE*. As well as being released in Finland, it was put out in England by Virgin.

It is a likely successor to the first, a further evolution of his overall approach. A concept work of sorts, it tells the story of a day in the life of an insane magpie. The first side features four pieces that merge into one. They range from a solo piano intro to an almost-classical jazz motif led by a running bass and piano. Pekka Poyry again contributes mightily on sax, especially during a particularly dirge-like segment that serves as a bridge between the two themes.

Side Two carries on the journey through Pohjola's musical realm. It goes through moments of swing, touches of almost chamber music, an amazing bass section, more Poyry sax excellence and an exquisite guitar interlude by Coste Apetrea. *B THE MAGPIE*, along with his first solo effort, show that Pohjola has an abundance of ideas as well as talent. He is likely to produce a lot more good music, so much the better for those who have the good taste to appreciate it.

Archie Patterson

Tolonen

Jukka Tolonen bought his first guitar at age twelve. Self-taught, he formed his first group at fourteen, a combo that played for dances. At seventeen he received a personal government grant as a composer and at eighteen he played with top Finnish musicians at the Pori Jazz Festival. After a stint in a backing band for Eero Raittinen, he formed Tasavallan Presidentti (President of the Republic) in 1969. Four albums and a couple of tours of England later, the group disbanded and he was on his own.

Prior to the breakup he had recorded his first solo LP. It, along with the last Tasavallan Presidentti LP, were the first samples of his work to be issued outside of the continent, as they were released in both Britain and the U.S. Since then he has gone on to record three more solos, as well as having an anthology of some of his better tracks released just recently here in the States. In addition he has played a couple of gigs with an aggregation called the Finnish All Stars, that was composed of a couple of his old Tasavallan Presidentti cohorts and Pekka Pohjola, ex-Wigwam.

An impressive set of credentials to be sure, but not nearly so much as the music itself.

The first *TASAVALLAN PRESIDENTTI* LP was recorded and released by Finland's Love Records in '69. Basically it is in the jazz-rock vein, with faint echoes of BS&T, though not top heavy with horns. The highlight of the set is the medley, "Ancient Mariner / Wutu Banale." "Mariner" is a portion of that poem recited over a meandering musical bed. It segues into "Wutu Banale," a rhythmic delight with its shifting solos on guitar and sax. Mellow and jazzy it carries you on the notes of Tolonen's guitar. His only compositional contributions are a bit of doodling on "Crazy Thing No. 2" and the piano-based instrumental "Thinking Bach" which is melancholic and features a vocal chorale by an ensemble of birds.

The second LP was done in '70 and released on Columbia in Sweden. It represents a slight change as Tolonen's guitar is more in evidence and top Finnish windman Pekka Poyry has replaced Junnu Aaltonen. The musical writing is divided between Tolonen and bassist Mosse Groundstroem, with lyrics supplied by vocalist Frank Robson. The basic difference between the first and second LPs is that the playing is a lot hotter the second time around. Both Tolonen's and Poyry's solos are extremely strong. The best cuts are the opener "Introduction" that blazes along with a great dual solo and "Struggling for Freedom."

"Struggling" is blues-based and features Robson's soulful vocals alternating with Tolonen's guitar solo. Even the lyrics shine as they depict the timeless struggle of youth to overcome. The longest piece at just under seven minutes, "Sinking" also works well. It starts off with an acoustic guitar, flute and bongos playing off each other, then builds until Robson's wailing vocals take over. It builds to a climax, then winds itself down and fades.

Though the first two albums are good, they don't even begin to compare to the third, *LAMBERTLAND*. Tolonen took over writing the music, save one piece and the result is spectacular. The complex arrangements and incredibly tight playing are dizzying. The difference between *LAMBERTLAND* and its predecessors is like day and night.

The opening cut "Lounge" moves at a running pace all the way through with Tolonen on acoustic and electric with a wah-wah, bobbing and weaving and jumping in and out of Poyry's sax. The playing and twists and turns the music takes are rapid fire. Also Eero Raittinen, from the early days, has joined on vocals and uses his voice just like another instrument, bending notes to suit the musical flow. All the while Groundstroem lays down a bass line that sets the pace with Vesa Aaltonen's drums keeping time. The title cut and the side's other piece, "Celebration of the Saved Nine," are much the same. Added to the side opener, the whole thing makes for a mind-boggling ride.

The opener on Side Two is entitled "The Bargain." It begins with bass and hi-hat, which lead the way throughout, embellished by guitar and sax. On this track Raittinen's vocals are dominant and the whole thing works well. "Dance" follows and is an instrumental that features Tolonen's guitar and Poyry's flute playing in unison, sometimes echoing each other and at other times playing in counterpoint. In the middle Tolonen takes off on a lightning-like, savage solo that has him bending and breaking off notes endlessly until the opening riff re-emerges and exits in a screeching fade out. The album closer, "Last Quarter," is a medium tempo piece which again features Raittinen's vocals, dual-tracked in harmony. This time Tolonen shows off his chord technique which provides the musical backbone. Embellishments include a nifty flute/guitar riff and a short guitar bridge that comes off like a hop, skip and a jump, bouncing as it does between the vocal verse and chorus, which contains the cryptic warning: "stay high for a while, if you feel more secure that way / then again, you can't put live coals back in the sack / you'll know by the fold of the fan when it's time to pack it away / and set up last quarters with a friend or a flag."

In all *LAMBERTLAND* has to be considered the best Tasavallan Presidentti LP and perhaps one of the best jazz/rock fusions yet. Not in the clichéd sense of that term either, as it is neither jazz nor rock, but a fusion of the two styles.

The capper on the Tasavallan Presidentti recording legacy was *MILKY WAY MOSES*. It represented a tightening up of their technique. While not really inferior instrumentally, it just didn't contain the life of *LAMBERTLAND*. It was more restrained and less ambitious. There was more of a rock orientation, due possibly to the collaboration of Wigwam's Jim Pembroke on all the cuts except one, the instrumental workout "Jelly." It is the one track that comes closest to recapturing the freewheeling air of *LAMBERTLAND*. It is a brisk jaunt with Tolonen running up and down the frets accompanied by Poyry's manic sax work.

Another reason perhaps for the change of direction on *MILKY WAY* was that Tolonen was, in addition to working with Tasavallan Presidentti, devoting time to a solo project. During the time he was with Tasavallan Presidentti, he recorded his first solo LP, *TOLONEN!*, and in the final stages of the group he had begun working on his second, *SUMMER GAMES*. In many ways these were a marked departure and set a course which he was later to follow with *THE HOOK* as his solo work became of primary importance.

TOLONEN! was auspicious to say the least. Totally instrumental, it retained much of the feel of Tasavallan Presidentti, but outside of the group context he was allowed to exhibit his full range of skills.

The first cut on Side One is the four part "Elements -- Earth, Fire, Water, Air" on which he plays acoustic and electric guitar and piano and spinet. It flows effortlessly from segment to segment as the emphasis shifts from one instrument to another, creating different textures. Embellishing it is Poyry's sax and flute. The other piece on Side One is "Ramblin'," a jazzier number highlighted by solos on guitar and sax.

Side Two's opener "Mountains" is perhaps the high point of the album. Tolonen's acoustic and Poyry's sax start it off in an almost plaintive manner as the guitar sets a strumming cadence underneath the soft wail of the sax. An electric is added as the emphasis shifts back and forth from the low piercing guitar to the sax. The tempo accelerates a bit, then winds down to a delicate finish. "Wanderland" follows again with acoustic guitar. At a medium tempo it proceeds as piano, spinet and electric guitar make their entrance.

They develop a melodic rhythm, as they play off one another, that is simply captivating. The album's closer is "Last Night," a portion of a live jam that was recorded with the members of Wigwam. While interesting, it is a delicate comedown from the excellence of the rest of the album, primarily filler.

His second, *SUMMER GAMES*, was in the same vein, though possibly a bit more relaxed. It features "Wedding Song," a warm, romantic piece. "A Warm Trip With Taija," a jazzy thing that spotlights Poyry on sax and flute doing some great stuff, as well as Tolonen's tasty picking and "Impressions of India" which is very much the same stylistically with the exception of the tablas that are added to give it a more exotic flavor.

Side Two consists of "Thinking of You in the Moonshine." Beginning as a mellow acoustic/flute instrumental, midway through it shifts gears and Tolonen's electric and Moog take over. The title piece, "Summer Games," is almost bossa nova. The album's closer "See You (Missing My Crazy Baby)" is a slow finger-picking number with just double-tracked acoustic and winds. It finishes off an exquisite, relaxing album.

With his third, *THE HOOK*, the focus is switched from acoustic to a more swinging jazz. "Aurora Borealis" starts with a bass line and piano cadence that proceeds to go through various permutations with solos flying in all directions. Tolonen and Poyry switch off, both performing stunningly. In fact, Poyry's contributions to all of the LPs make them combination-Tolonen/Poyry affairs. They are definitely tuned into each other, it'd be hard to imagine one without the other playing off him. "Starfish" is the side's other number and adopts a bit more of a swinging approach.

"The Sea" comprises Side Two, a showcase for Tolonen's piano playing as well as guitar and again Poyry's ever-present winds. "The Hook" is somewhat funky and the dynamic duo is back at it playing cat and mouse intertwining notes. The closer is "Together," a piano/guitar duet that's short and sweet as the guitar dances over a bed of rippling piano. A perfect winding down to the whole affair.

The latest *HYSTERICA* takes a rockier approach. It opens with a 10:17 piece titled "Jimi" which appears to be a tribute to Hendrix as the guitar takes off on an extended solo of gutsy wailing. "Django" is a short jazz break that is followed by the title cut "Hysterica." Again it's a bit of a rocker but with a touch of jazz and funk added to spice it up.

Side Two starts with the thundering bass of "Tiger" that is picked up by a riffing guitar. It develops into a bit of keyboard gymnastics by Esa Kotilainen, sax and flute by Sakari Kukko and bass by Pekka Pohjola in addition to Tolonen's guitar. "Sylvie The Cat" follows with a bouncy little Moog riff, flute filler and searing guitar solo in the middle.

The side closes with "Windermer Avenue," a beautiful, rhythmic piece carried along at a medium tempo by an acoustic and piano, the highlight being a flowing, melodic guitar solo.

To bring things up to date, a few months back Janus released an anthology here in the States. It contains tracks off *LAMBERTLAND*, a retitled "Dance" now christened "Witchdrum" and "Last Quarters," a shortened version of "Aurora Borealis" off *THE HOOK* retitled "Northern Lights," "Meddling 'Song" from *SUMMER GAMES* and "Sylvie The Cat" and "Windermer Avenue" off *HYSTERICA*. Definitely a representative sampler, but I recommend the originals. You can't go wrong if your tastes run to good music.

Archie Patterson

Between

The group Between was initiated by Peter Michael Hamel in 1970. His background consists of studies in composition at the Munich Conservatory and Musical History, Psychology, and Sociology at the Universities of Munich and Berlin. In addition he was a member of the Mixed Media Company, Berlin, in which actors, musicians, dancers and authors experiment in new forms of communication.

His first recording, simply titled *HAMEL*, was released on the Music Factory label, which was, to the best of my knowledge, an alternative recording cooperative for artists wishing to experiment outside of the conventional structures of music. Other releases on Music Factory were the first pressing of Can's LP *MONSTER MOVIE* and an LP by the Technical Space Composers Crew entitled *CANAXIS 5,* of which Can's Holger Czukay was a prime mover. Later Music Factory became more of a publishing setup as the Can album was put out on Liberty and Hamel's re-released on Vertigo.

HAMEL was indeed an unconventional album. A double set, the music was highly influenced by Indian, Indonesian and Tibetan forms.

Side A consisted of "Storm Over Asia and Calm" and "Baliava I&II." They employed the technique of a piano rigged with wire and erasers, which made it take on a rhythmical function as well as a tonal one. The effect was a combination of high sounds and low rhythms evoking in Hamel's words, a "tonality of color of sound."

Sides B, C, and D employed an electrical organ recorded on two and four tracks, synthesizer and various natural sounds. Side B included "Fire of Holy Eyes," "Song of the Dolphin" and "Sinking Sangsara." The first was based on a succession of notes, C - D Flat - E - F Sharp - G - A - B - C, repeated in a raga-like manner. The second used the sounds of water and organ modulated by a synthi and the third consisted of the synthi sound D with the natural and modulated sounds of wind and water. Side C, entitled "Aura," is four tracks recorded individually with a mutual scheme of construction, again based on a traditional raga form. Side D's "Gomorrhaga" is similar except for its being based on a different note succession, with the concluding segment "Cathedral in C" a repetition of the C chord building to a splitting climax.

If ever there was an album meant to captivate mental faculties this was it. A virtual yoga of sound, it's one of the premier meditation music works.

The makeup of Between is multi-national. The group on the first album, *EINSTIEG*, consisted of Hamel and Ulrich Stranz from Germany, Cottrell Black and Bob Eliscu from the U.S., Jimmy J. Galway from Ireland and Roberto Détrée from Argentina. The music was very rhythmic, based around Black's percussion work on congas. As on Hamel's solo there are Indian and other influences present. Galway's flute, Eliscu's oboe and Hamel's organ provide the melodies, embellished by Détrée's guitar and Black's percussives. Highlights are the opening "Katakomben" written by Eliscu. It features his work on krumhorn taking the lead, and vocals complete with rhythmic chant and roaring lions culminating in an angelic "amen."

On Side 2, there's the group composition "Space Trip," 9:27 of sound excursion. Basically it's a controlled freakout with hints of rhythm, piano, organ and wind instruments alternately appearing, then disappearing, all linked by effects. It's all kept to a decent sound level so as to intrigue, not annoy.

On the second album, *AND THE WATERS OPENED*, Galway and Stranz had left. Side 1 begins with the title cut that is dominated by electronics and percussion. An electronic deluge opens, then later gives way to a percussion barrage. It ends with an acoustic guitar solo. "Urobaros" follows and takes you straight into the harem of an Arabian sheik. Congas along with sitar and oboe conjure up visions of veiled dancing girls and the hint of mysteries hidden beneath their perfumed silks. "Syn" closes the side with a drone of repeating synthesizer and organ that builds, then fades, another meditative raga. Side 2 begins with "Devotion" and a chant of "Sat, Chit, Ananda, Om" ("Entity, Consciousness, Happiness, Amen") on a bed of repeating organ, piano and congas. "Happy Stage" follows and is a vehicle for Eliscu's soloing on flute and oboe, accompanied by percussion and treated piano. The album closer is "Samum" which begins as an oboe/acoustic guitar duet. Percussion is added and the whole thing culminates in a gale as the winds come and bring on the end.

At this point Hamel did another solo album, *THE VOICE OF SILENCE*, which amounts to a meditation exercise. Side 1 is titled "PantaTantra." It is again done on tuned piano and consists of a repetitive musical theme accompanied at intervals by a complementary yogic chant. The effect is quite relaxing. Side 2 consists of the title cut and "Ego Loss (Let the Red Buddah Amithaba Sweep You Along)." They feature organ and harmonium playing a flowing mantra with an everlasting chant based on a Sanskrit vocal. Again the result is most pleasant. This album is definitely not for everybody. Yoga disciples will love it, others may find it of interest if they are into Eastern music or simply want to put on some sound and ease their troubled mind.

The third Between album is entitled *DHARANA* which means deepest inner collection and concentration. It was recorded in conjunction with a symphony orchestra and is the group's finest accomplishment to date.

It opens with "Joy, Sadness, Joy," an Eliscu composition that again features some beautiful oboe work complemented by Hamel's melodic organ. It is followed by the sitar-dominated Buddhist mantra, "Om Namo Buddhaya" and "Sunset," a haunting acoustic guitar piece. The first side closes with "Listen to the Light," a duet between oboe and pipe organ, Eliscu's oboe meandering over the warm organ bed.

The title cut takes up Side Two. It can best be described by quoting the liner notes; "The drone D flat sounds throughout the piece. The composed states of being for the orchestra, delicate ether sounds of the spheres and massive sounds of the earth, accompany the improvisations of the group Between. The oboist Robert Eliscu improvises in a pentatonic scale mantra melodies of Europe and India, Cotch Black and Charles Campbell play African drum motifs. The organist Peter Michael Hamel sings at the beginning and the end, accompanied by the bass guitar of Roberto Détrée, an old Indian Sutra ("Dharansu cha yogyata manasah"), from which the title is taken. Translation: The spirit is made free through concentration for the union with the all-Highest."

In essence that also serves to sum up the realm in which Between operates. The music is the message, the message is the music.

The latest album is entitled *HESSE BETWEEN MUSIC*. It consists of passages taken from selected works of Hermann Hesse, recited against a backdrop of Between's multi-ethnic music. An interesting experiment, it is unfortunately spoken in German, thus only partially accessible to non-German speaking people.

While Between operates in a specialized area thematically, it in no way hinders enjoyment of their music. They manage to surmount the limitations of the styles they use and not fall prey to redundancy, as do many others who attempt to fuse various ethnic elements into their music. Hamel and his collaborators, in the course of their recordings, have succeeded in producing pure and simple, beautiful music. That is no small feat.

Archie Patterson

Sensations Fix

Sensations Fix are one of Italy's lesser-known bands this side of the Atlantic. Unlike PFM and Banco, they have not had any domestic release of their albums. They are nonetheless one of the best and possibly most innovative current Italian bands.

Recording for Polydor Italy, the four recordings that have resulted thus far are only available through import. While most Italians seek to fuse the classics and rock, the Sensations work in the field of electronic rock. The footnote on their first album *FRAGMENTS OF LIGHT* illustrates this clearly, "Dear Robert, you'll be glad to know that the heavenly music organization is here too." It acknowledges their admiration for Fripp and Eno. Their music embodies the flowing textures and elongated rhythms that distinguish *NO PUSSYFOOTING* and the later *EVENING STAR*. However, it is distinctly different in that a percussion bed underlies much of it, and the themes are for the most part shorter and more riff-oriented. The guitar and synthi play dual roles, building rhythms and executing complementary melodies.

In actuality, Sensations Fix is largely the product of the creativity of Franco Falsini. He writes all of the music and plays guitar and synthesizer. The other Sensations are Richard Ursillo on bass, guitar and devices, Keith Edwards on drums and Steve Head on keyboards.

FRAGMENTS OF LIGHT is one of the strongest debuts by a group to be found. The title cut is one of the best integrations of guitar/synthi I've heard. An acoustic strums the rhythm accompanied by a medium tempo beat and Falsini's solo synthi melody.

Side Two contains their first classic "Do You Love Me?" It is a delightful, choppy guitar-dominated thing with straining vocals, a chunky rhythm and nifty synthesizer riff. Even complete with the true-love-on-the-rocks lament -- "I've been losing, losing all my mind ..cause you don't love me... you're trying to fool me ...Do ya, Do ya, love me... Do ya, Do ya need me.." Also there's "Life Beyond the

Darkness," a medium-tempo melody carried by a strong bass line and acoustic guitar rhythm, over which Falsini does some more melody improvisation.

The second LP, *PORTABLE MADNESS*, represents a bit of a change. Still very much guitar/synthesizer oriented and strongly rhythmic, it is much more dense as it was recorded on a Teac 4-track and the overall sound is heavier.

All of the tracks segue into one another creating a continuous flow from one riff to another. Side One consists of "Smooth and Round," "Fullglast," "Phase 1&2" and "Underwater." Although moments of tranquillity appear intermittently, the overall feel is much more aggressive than *FRAGMENTS*. The guitar and synthi solos displaying a harsher feel with the addition of a dense fuzz and phasing.

Side Two begins and ends with two short Mellotron themes, "The Next Place of Nobody" and "With Relative Jump Into Water." Interspersed are three pieces that pick up the aggression from Side One. "Party Day Resistance," "Strange About the Hands" and "Leave My Chemistry Alone" contain lots of shattering and fading guitar and synthesizer. *PORTABLE MADNESS* is definitely the other side of the group's musical personality.

Next followed a solo album by Falsini, a film soundtrack, *NASO FREDO* (Cold Nose). On it, I assume he plays all instruments as he is the sole person credited. It represents his idea of "heavenly music" taken to its fullest expression. The rhythms emerge, build and fade as layers of sound -- keyboards, synthesizer and guitar -- overlap the shifting undercurrent. You become lost in the sound as it flows from one texture to another and the melodies and rhythm engulf you. Individual commentary on the sections is not called for as they defy anything but the most general attempt at conveying a feel. And in the end that is left up to the individual listener.

The latest album is entitled *FINEST FINGER*. More guitar-oriented, it is perhaps their most diversified album and contains their second classic "Strange About Your Hands" (a crystallization of the theme presented earlier on *PORTABLE MADNESS*). It begins with a fingerpicking rhythm on electric guitar over which the verse is sung. Then it transforms itself into a chorus backed by fuzzed chords. The highlight being a solo where notes are bent out of shape in an oh-so-subtle manner, to create a whining effect. The combination of Falsini's vocals and the music is addicting. It is followed by "Just a Little Bit More on the Curve" another atmospheric keyboard/guitar duet, "Yardbirds Dream" a vehicle for more guitar pyrotechnics and "Map," an acoustic guitar foray accompanied by thumping percussion and plenty of synthesized riffing.

The side closer is "Boat of Madness," which opens with a droning fog horn synthi riff leading into a murky dirge. Side Two begins with "The Left Side of the Green (including Macumba Fog)," more guitar action topped by Falsini's disembodied vocals. Then comes the third Sensations classic, a cosmic rework of the "Hands" riff, "Finest Finger." Finger is about a droog of the highest order -- Real ultra violence -- pounding percussion, fuzzed guitar, synthesized soundtrack! The album closer is "Into the Memory," a soundscape complete with synthi riffs bouncing off one another, savage guitar, Mellotron and a melodic rhythm to top it off. It contains a bit of each element of their music.

Archie Patterson

1977

Magma

Earth,
This concerns you,
Your systems collapse and your revolts assassinate: in fact you destroy only that which you do not understand.
We know that you also will be destroyed.
Our music is for the Beauty that you wish to ignore and for the hatred of your damnable evolution.
Out beyond space and time, a planet awaits us, KOBAIA.
We have known this world since the day we opened our eyes, millions of years ago.
May all those who suffocate here below follow us.
But may the hypocrite hope for nothing!
Earth!
You are already no more than oblivion

With this threatening portent the mission of Magma is begun. Magma is the vehicle for the art and ideals of master musician Christian Vander. Based in France (though the incisive satanic edge of their music leads some to mistake them as of German origin) they are truly one of Europe's most original and revolutionary bands. Stylistically they have transcended both King Crimson and the original Mahavishnu Orchestra in terms of sheer inspiration. Their music lies between and beyond any clearly defined realm. In jazz-rooted endeavors comparisons with Sun Ra and his Arkestra are inevitable -- regarding the theme of science fiction the similar spiritual aspirations of Sun Ra and Christian Vander are areas of word exploration -- but Vander manifests a more important sense of political ideals and a less entropic perception of extraterrestrial science fiction. He demonstrates greater spiritual clarity as opposed to Ra's mystical etymological conundrums. The musical ideas of Magma are more concrete than those of the Arkestra, in structure the body of Vander's compositions is more organized.

1977

"Theusz Hamtaahk" must qualify as one of the century's most ambitious operatic works. This epic is a projected nine-album opera by Christian Vander which chronicles the deterioration of civilization on Earth and the subsequent colonization of the planet Kobaïa by a small band of humans, who set up a successful society and attempt to cultivate universal harmony (a plot not too dissimilar to Paul Kanter's *BLOWS AGAINST THE EMPIRE*). The entire libretto is in the guttural tongue of Vander's invention: Kobaïan. This work of tremendous scope in its recorded existence -- four volumes at this time -- presents a panorama of the changing nature of the composer's artistic vision and Magma's various structural mutations. With respect to the highly unconventional character of the project Vander explains, "You have to get away from the usual habits of playing offbeats, time signatures, anything familiar. Our purpose is to give strong enough images to jolt people out of the familiar and the habitual."

The Universal Commandments of Kobaïa:

HORTZ FUR DEHN STEKEHN WEST
HORTZ ZI WEHR DUNT DA HERTZ
HORTZ DA FELT DOS FUNKER
HORTZ ZEBEHN DE GEUSTAAH
HORTZ WIRT TLAIT UTS MITLAIT
HORTZ WIRT TLAIT UTS MITLAIT
HORTZ WIRT TLAIT UTS MITLAIT
HORTZ WIRT TLAIT UTS MITLAIT
HORTZ FUR DEHN STEKEHN WEST
HORTZ DA FELT DOS FUNKER
HORTZ ZEBEHN DE GEUSTAAH
HORTZ WLASIK
KOBAIA

As good science fiction should do, "Theusz Hamtaahk" bears relevance to present-day society and in a futurist setting clarifies and dramatizes social realities. It draws conclusions by extending and developing current direction of civilization. In this work the implications are obvious: that this planet is in a state of degradation primarily due to a severely limited and culture-bound understanding of alternative spiritual and social possibilities, repressing them for fear of upsetting the imbalance of power. As to the manner of achieving such an extraterrestrial Utopia as Kobaïa however, Vander is somewhat vague, except to say that it involves new modes of energy use and environmental communication.

The story begins in the future when space colonization is a reality. The Earth is in a precariously advanced state of deterioration and a few concerned humans organize a departure, constructing an independent space vessel for this purpose. After a perilous but hopeful journey they discover a new world which they call Kobaïa. It is here that they build a society with a high degree of technological development and social integration. Years later they rescue a malfunctioning Earthship from disaster. The Earthlings relate the recent catastrophes which have occurred at home. With motives of questionable sincerity these foreigners persuade a missionary unit of Kobaïans to return to their former home and espouse their ideas of philosophy and social organization.

The second movement, called *1001° CENTIGRADES*, starts as the party arrives. The Kobaïans enjoy a friendly reception from the Earth people but when the Earth authorities hear of the expatriate Kobaïans' hopes to re-educate humankind for universal harmony, the reaction is imprisonment of the visitors, who then contact their home planet. With threat of annihilation by the Kobaïans' Ultimate Weapon, the prisoners are released. Though they leave intending never to return their visit is long remembered.

At the commencement of *MEKANIK DESTRUKTIW KÖMMANDÖH*, the troubled Earth receives a mantic savior in the person of Nebëhr Gudahtt who strives to lead the human race to salvation. He tells them that in order to gain divine fulfillment their collective earthly existence must come to an end. He exhorts them, "A solitary tear will fall; the tear of your remorse and of your suffering, a tear so pure and clear, that in it you will see your final destiny." Purification, State of Grace, Faith and Magnificence, Mansuetude, Absolute Wisdom, Infinite Wisdom. In anger the people march against him, a confused and violent mass, one question gnawing at their collective mind: that of their reason for marching. Gradually the Universal Spirit awakens the consciousness of each to the righteous urgency of this man's message. The Voice of their Conscience expresses their relation to the creator, the Kreühn Köhrmahn, effacing their material spirit and confirming their Universal Devotion. Nebëhr Gudahtt and his converted followers now must meet their destiny. One by one, entering into the Celestial March, they sacrifice their lives to the Spirit of the Universe in a final moment of divine ecstasy.

With the fourth part *KÖHNTARKÖSZ*, the progress of the story becomes unclear. The unspecified liner notes reveal only the act of "Entering the tomb of Emëhntëht-Rê" and the preparation for combat between the people of Ork and the people of Zeuhl Wortz without further explication. Vander, unsatisfied with the story outline which he had written for the third album, perhaps preferred to be minimal in exegesis, allowing instead the music to speak for itself.

The original formation of Magma was clearly based in an exploratory jazz vein. Here on their debut, *MAGMA*, Christian Vander, holding the reins on drums, was accompanied by Klaus Blasquiz (lead vocal), Claude Engel (guitars & flute), Francis Moze (acoustic and electric bass) François Cahen (pianos) and a competent horn section of Teddy Lasry (soprano sax, first flute & other reeds) Richard Raux (alto and tenor saxes & flute) and Alain Charlcry (trumpet & percussion). Recorded in April 1970, this premier double-disc presents an early attempt at electrified jazz quite unlike anything before or since. A disciplined composer, Vander does not emphasize improvisation. The wind instruments are basically a unifying force. Vander, the dominant and vigorous drummer, has a strong concise sense of rhythm. The beat is not so supple as in the impressionistic percussions of Miles Davis' bands of the time. As an arranger Vander has a gifted ability to create diverse and expressive textures organizing timbres to suit the emotional context. This is especially helpful in communicating the music's message without the aid of any comprehensible lyrics.

The urgent message of the Kobaïans is powerfully stated in the opening "Kobaïa," commencing in steady 4/4 with sharp percussive accents from Vander and François Cahen. Richard Raux honks and squeals out a mad alto solo against the ensemble's collective churning. The chordal amassing of Claude Engel's furious solo grows from uncertain distorted bursts on the wah-wah of increasing frequency into a mammoth Fripp-like roar. The inevitable direction is determined with a metric change to 3/4 and the firm extended whole notes of the horn theme. Vander's complex rhythmic counterpoint is demonstrated in the first bridge of "Aina" between disjunct horns and drums.

Sides 2 & 3 contain several musical contributions from the various musicians of Magma. Teddy Lasry's "Sohïa" is graced by Christian Vander's textural manipulation. An ethereal chorus of flutes hovers above Francis Moze's unobtrusive bass lines, which lead thematically into the horn ensemble. Contrasting moods and settings prevail either through diminuendos/crescendos or sudden shifts of instrumentation. There is further contrast in Cahen's difficult-to-pronounce "Sckxyss" involving metric alternation between driving bass and staccato horn bursts. Vander's original "Auraë" too uses multiple variations in the context of the spaceship orbiting Kobaïa for the first time. Chanteur Klaus Blasquiz gets a dynamic vocal workout from extended vibratos to lung pumping sixteenth notes. An unusual flute/piano duet is the centerpiece with Cahen hitting out even minor fifths. The peculiar harmonics and 4/4 accenting of the last three beats is effectively not dissimilar to Carla Bley's contrapuntal work. Though Vander has original harmonic ability for composing his horn phrases his rhythmic orientation often leads him to over-use (up until *KÖHNTARKÖSZ*) the technique of repeating each phrase an even number of measures followed by repetitions of the rest in rapid-fire succession. It works to build tension consecutively to a peak but it does so a little too obviously. A capriciously spellbinding flute solo by Lasry opens Engel's "Thaud Zaia." A relentless march led by Blasquiz and Charlery's assertive trumpet follows, after which the agile flutist expands his initial statement. Producer Laurent Thibault contributes "Naü Ektila," a versatile piece commencing with gently picked acoustic guitar, melodious flute, and hymnal chanting. Within the wide scope of this statement are a ballsy rocking electric guitar/horn riffing, a progressive jazz section which includes flurrying horn cascades and an adept though none-too-harmonically-imaginative solo by Cahen, whose right-hand style lies somewhere between Oscar Peterson and McCoy Tyner. Vander's throttling drumming throughout leads in intensity. The guitar/flute duet (à la Jade Warrior) is restated for the third and final time in a transformed character accompanied by dramatic snare rolls.

A ghastly shrieking invocation from Blasquiz begins "Stoah" against an ominous thudding pulse. His vocal facility here is incredible, descending against indeterminate horn punctuation. *MAGMA*'s concluding piece is "Muh," another Vander original. The variation and depth of Kobaïan emotion is shown by alternating horn riffing and arrangements, and by the expressive murmuring shouting whining of Kobaïans and their intense conviction in a final approaching threatening chant.

Recorded in April 1971, *1001° CENTIGRADE* lies in the lyric context of the Kobaïans' visit to Earth. This progression of Christian Vander's jazz-based aspirations was awarded the Grand Prix National du Disque from the Academie du Disque Francais in 1971. The personnel remained essentially the same, but for the replacement of hornmen Raux and Charlery by Jeff "Yochk'o" Seffer on saxophone and bass clarinet, and Louis Toesca on trumpet. Guitarist Claude Engel was dropped but not replaced. Vander's arrangements here are clearer and more polished than those on the first album. François Cahen's electric piano added another spatial dimension to Magma's music.

EARTH

Eat your heart, drink your blood, burn your soul
Withered tree that rips the waves of the sun
The snarl is the fortune of your hard-pressed weak mind
That pounds the pillar of your breast
Heredity's thirsty odor which outlines the spectre of your violences
You were the imaginary fire devoid of passion
Who has forged his own crematory
Noise silence, noise silence
The time passed.
Noise silence, noise silence
Your cascade of waves flows untiringly
It floods the universe, imperturbable,
While the vigor of your poor life
Beads painfully upon your irritated bark
Noise silence, noise silence
Your life stretches out and the time passes
The last drops of your sweat,
Fruit of your constant anguish, escape from your roots
Your death greets you.
Noise silence, noise tranquillity
That you did not await.
Your spine howls its convulsion
Your cry is lost in the ocean of time
You burst without a sound
Why do you not speak, cinders,
In the apocalypse of this interminable night
Where forever you sink?
Waves of time, waves of time
Do not forgive
Avenge these pure souls to the translucent veins
Which ask only to breathe
Your deceitful scents of hatred and hypocrisy
Earth, purge this initial nothingness!
The wind of time like your fate
Is prisoner of the infinite cycle of life
I sympathize, I sympathize
"AMEN"...

Poem which I dreamed the night of July 8-9, 1970.
Christian Vander

Side One is a Vander composition entitled "Rïah Sahïltaahk" (real soul talk?) It commences with Francis Moze's rapid indefatigably thumping bass leading into

3/4 chanting with uneven accents. Within this piece Vander justifies and effectively varies his device of repetitive riffing in several ways: he carries out much variation of tempo and dynamics both within and between the many thematic sections, and through the use of multi-instrumental syncopation and shifting accented beats he contrasts his repetitions. For the most part the horns are less dominant and the band is very tight in exacting the numerous rhythmic mutations. Blasquiz gets to use his wide tonal and phonetic range throughout the many mood changes, as a beautiful resolute flute/e-piano theme gives way to a plodding amelodic military beating. He moves easily among gentle intoning nasal blaring and operatic vibrato. Simultaneous temporal variation is enhancing as the composer mixes a mid-tempo bass, fast percussion, powerful slow brass notes in a theme approaching the conclusion. Quick Zappaesque staccato brass riffs lead into a squealing vocal crescendo which drops into off-tempo gagging cadences. A second furious climax with characteristically indeterminate offbeats mounts and halts, leaving a soft and enigmatic grand piano solo coda.

Side Two contains two compositions of Teddy Lasry and François Cahen. These two exhibit greater compositional sense in the jazz realm than does Christian Vander. Lasry's "'Iss' Lanseï Doïa," as expected, features a more prominent use of horns in the lead. It opens with impressionistic percussion and tooting reeds and trumpet from which emerge brief even e-piano chords. Two repeats of the harmonically permutating dissolve into disunited honking, and a most hermetic unaccompanied horn trio flits about in style from convoluted Easley Blackwood to melodic Archie Shepp. The second prevailing celebrative riff à cuivre alternates with a section of ringing and sparse e-piano notes and scary Kobaïan groaning. Lasry's involved structure is indicated when the two merge the horns, dropping minor thirds to fuse with the diminished chordal piano. Disparate horn riffing and syncopated piano start off Cahen's "Ki Iahl O Lïahk" followed by Jeff Seffer's insistent bass clarinet theme. With the exception of one rapid change including frequency-modulated winds, Cahen's thematic transitions are more fluid than Vander's often abrupt changes. While his sprightly Corean e-piano solo steps into a dark smooth passage of the horns which then move into a gladder theme before the fadeout, unity is maintained by an almost continuous ascending/descending bass pattern.

With the third movement of "Theusz Hamtaahk," Magma underwent a drastic reformation both in style and in personnel. While Jeff Seffer and François Cahen left to form ZAO -- their own jazz-oriented combo which has released several compelling disques in France -- Vander maintained only Klaus Blasquiz, Teddy Lasry, and stage manager "Loulou" Sarkissian. Added to these originals were Jannick Top (bass and cello), Jean-Luc Manderlier (piano and organ), Rene Garber (bass clarinet and vocals), Claude Olmos (guitar) and wife/vocalist Stella Vander (leading a female choir of five). Also enlisted was current producer Giorgio Gomelsky.

The jazz elements of Christian Vander, who wrote the entire LP, are almost invisibly submerged here. Magma was instilled with the immutable relentlessness of an automation. As the title *MEKANIK DESTRUKTIW KÖMMANDÖH* seems to imply, the work is a great mechanical mass, powerful but almost overbearing at times. This 1973 record, their first American release on A&M, included not only a complete summary of the story to this point but also the Kobaïan libretto for the third movement. "Hortz Fur Dëhn

Stekëhn West" enters with clanking piano rhythms, synthesized exclamations, commanding brass whole notes. Primarily an exercise in chanting as the Earthlings march under the influence of savior Nebëhr Gudahtt. Vander emphasizes the vocals as the lead instruments throughout the disc. The vocal character varies from Blasquiz's solo voice to the tense collective soprano of the choir and many intriguing rhythms are woven among the two, from the skeletal soprano pulse of "Atüh Atüh..." to operatic simultaneous recitation in "Ima Surï Dondaï." With all this extensive chanting Christian Vander relies heavily on melodic repetition. To relieve some of this incessant reiteration (some lines are repeated as many as sixteen consecutive times), Lasry is heard soaring brightly above the chant on his flute and brass crescendos. Though there is little individual virtuoso playing here, the composer shows some inspired drum work with cymbal rolls in abundance.

The second side mounts in intensity through a progression of climaxes culminating in the third song. A recitation of the Universal Commandments of Kobaïa initiates "Da Zeuhl Wortz Mëkanïk." Its slowly growing conviction is achieved by multiple repetition, which is relieved only by alternating harmonic modulation. Its crescendo dissolves into a subdued setting of "Nebëhr Gudahtt," pastorally instrumented by recessive glockenspiel, plucked monotone bass strings and a relentless descending chordal piano pattern. Muriel Streisfeld's meandering voice gradually rises to a frantic screeching vibrato which stimulates Blasquiz to strident falsetto screaming, leading to a choral peak of collective pandemonium. In "Mekanìk Kömmandöh" the united voices reach their height of speed, releasing chanted volleys of sixteenth notes to the ultimate pinnacle of unbounded fury and barking whoops of release. In "Kreühn Köhrmahn Iss de Hündïn," a resolute and echoic choral chant of hope is slowly sung as the Earthlings enter the Celestial March of divine self-sacrifice. Their material beings drop off into galactic chaos with thunderous cacophonic trumpet blasts, pounding toms, amid general shouting and groans.

In 1974, Magma underwent yet another dissolution and Christian Vander once again redefined their music. At this point the band reached its highest stage of development and its peak of energy, *KÖHNTARKÖSZ* is Vander's most involved and unified composition and the performance is unequaled on any of Magma's other discs. The sound is technological avant-rock of awesome dynamic range. From their initial inception, Magma has had a latent demonic undertone to their music. In addition, the group's image has always suggested affiliations with the underworld -- from those long black robes with the evil-pronged symbol to Christian Vander himself who lives in a house which is painted totally black inside and out. Here in the fourth volume of "Theusz Hamtaahk," the doomy satanic edge is the most salient property. Whether Vander has drawn his inspiration from Heaven or Hades, *KÖHNTARKÖSZ* is undeniably a fierce, intensely inspired piece of music.

The reorganization of Magma this time retained the Vanders, Klaus Blasquiz and Jannick Top, with the addition of three new members: Brian Godding (guitar) Gérard Bikialo (pianos & organ) and Michel Graillier (pianos & clarinet). With the latter two and Christian Vander and Jannick Top all playing pianos, a large keyboard section served to replace the missing horns.

KÖHNTARKÖSZ is split into one part per side, each with a coda of sorts. Part One is powerfully launched with an ensemble crescendo led by Vander's frenetic drumming and Gérard Bikialo's sustained organ notes. The introductory theme is stated by Godding's fuzz-tone guitar and Blasquiz with slow accented conviction, then accelerando to a maximum. The slow implacable tempo begins in 5/4 periodically shifting to 4/4 and back. The scary 3-note ascending theme is repeated interminably with modulating organ are bass disharmonies. This is Christian Vander's most harmonically unfathomable work -- I have not been able to find a tonal center for the piece.

The first metric change to 4/4 yields tension, as the keyboards throb hesitant uneven tone clusters en masse over echoed drums and doomsday rattling bass. In the next 5/4 mutation, Stella Vander's celestial voice lends a tone of hopeful mystery and the unknown, to the dominating evil which is the relentless rhythmic piano variations, with their dramatically rumbling bass keys. The lower keys revert in 4/4 to the basic underlying 3-note theme, deathly hideous and neither chordal nor modal, thundering below a maniacally droning organ. A soothing restrained choral verse, and the delicate piano fade-out, hint at an impending glimmer of hope -- though not quite yet. "Ork Alarm," composed by Jannick Top, is a chronic anxiety attack. The apocalyptic descending cello intro & bridge alternates with a jarringly dissonant theme of baritone chanting and the incessant staccato pulsing of multitracked cellos. The theme's final repetition culminates with sustained alto vocals and strained squealing guitar, building to a fearful intensity where trudging metal robot feet crash against metal, amidst lunatic demonic laughing.

Part Two begins in 4/4 with a pseudo-Oriental setting of Blasquiz's gentle singing and ringing e-pianos, but soon descends once again into darkness. The two 3-note themes fuse, as the e-piano adapts the ascending pattern of the first one to the continuous rhythm of the second. Stella Vander's vocals resume their ethereal floating and segue into an accelerating crescendo with a change to 6/8. Gérard Bikialo rips out a frenzied organ solo, minor in key but inspired beyond despair, flurrying strident notes pitching to an insanely passionate urgency. Whooping vocals, furious drumming and wildly plucked bass are drawn into the mad swirl. Vander interrupts the tension with evenly pulsed choral melodies of arbitrary length, only to recommence the theme with greater frantic drive. When an unsurpassable climactic pitch is reached, all drops off into a cadent military beat, accompanied by the thunderous evil 4/4 a-piano theme. Blasquiz's sustained overlapping chants of "RAAAAAAA" lead off into galactic finality. The work is closed in a peaceful mood with Vander's "Coltrane Sündïa" (Coltrane rest in peace). A resolutely beautiful theme is softly intoned by acoustic piano and vibrato guitar over a heavenly trilling piano choir.

Between June 1 and 5, 1975 a newly reformed Magma recorded a double live album at the Tavern de l'Olympia in Paris, which was released here on RCA's progressive Utopia subsidiary. The reformation was merely personal as the style and intensity of the music was essentially a confirmation of the work on the previous record.

Completing the ensemble with Blasquiz and the Vanders were: Bernard Paganotti (bass) Gabrid Federow (guitar), Didier Lockwood (violin) and Benoit Widemann & Jean-Pol Asseline (keyboards). *MAGMA LIVE* proves that the band's precision is not merely a studio phenomenon.

The full-length two-sided version of 'Köhntark' is basically off the record, though it is more spatially dynamic. Christian Vander's impressive percussive phrasing is the highlight, coming out in compressed anticipatory bursts. Didier Lockwood's violin replaces organ as the lead instrument, and his wild solo in Part Two is a brute inspiration of high frequency scraping and indecisive thrusts. Bernard Paganotti is allowed a piercing bass solo. With the end of the title, Vander has also dropped the original doomy conclusion of the piece in favor of a brighter allegro choral coda.

Side Three opens with funky electric piano chords and supple bass on "Kobah," a fuller but inferior version of "Kobaïa." The vocals lack the power of the original. Rhythmic variation is minimal, the sharp percussive zaps are missing in favor of a more linear continuity. "Lïhns" is a pleasant hymn with delicate vocals and peaceful chimes. "Hhaï" is also dominated by a general resolved happiness. A pianissimo flurrying violin leads in with Blasquiz's airy sprightly vocals. Benoit Widemann's e-piano solo is unobtrusive and unambitious. Side 4's "Mëkanïk Zaïn" (composed by Vander as the rest) is an extended version of the climactic "Mëkanïk Kömmandöh" theme: pure energy. Paganotti rends a loud and forceful bass solo with a free background of improvised percussion and electronic squeals. A quickly energetic descending e-piano theme and violent drumwork (con fuoco!) at a tempo allegro assai provide a framework for a masterful Pontyesque solo by M. Lockwood. Its slower pace contrasts the rapid tempo until the note values eventually decrease. With a sudden dropout of instrumentation which serves as a bridge to the vocalists' entrance, his violin pumps about haltingly, flailing like a fish out of water. Klaus Blasquiz and Stella Vander bring the piece to its maniacal chanting peak.

Magma is an intensely serious band. They manifest a supreme devotion in all their music. In this sense they parallel Sun Ra and his Arkestra. Christian Vander exercises strict discipline over his ensemble -- he guides and steers his soundship with a spiritual urgency -- the expressive energy of music may bring about a beautiful conceptual transformation of the individual. In his theme Vander is striving for a new social -- and more importantly, universal -- realization. The rest remains to be experienced.

Steve Hitchcock

ZAO

The name ZAO is a word taken out of the Cabal, an esoteric book of the 13th Century. According to Cabalistic symbolism, each letter has a corresponding script. In the case of ZAO, it is: Z=7, A=1, O=infinity and the product of these three letters is the equation "7 is infinity."

Musically ZAO is a linear descendant of Magma. After service with Christian Vander and contributions to the first two Magma albums, François "Faton" Cahen and Jeff "Yochk'o" Seffer set out to create their own music. Similarly their roots are in jazz, but if Magma could be said to be gaining their inspiration from futuristic impulses, then ZAO's is the result of searching the past to create a new synthesis from old roots.

1977

The first LP, titled *Z=7L*, was recorded in 1973 at Strawberry Studios in England and released on Phonogram in France. It featured in addition to Cahen and Seffer, Joël "Dud" Dugrenot on bass, Jean-Yves Rigaud on violin, Jean-My Truong on drums and the amazing voice of Mauricia Platon.

There are six pieces of music, three per side. They are characterized by Cahen's liquid-like electric piano which sets a melody base while Platon's voice scats the vocals over Seffer's winds and Rigaud's violin. Truong's percussion dictates the tempo.

The highlight of Side One is the opener, "Marochsek," which strongly resembles a scaled down Magma as it begins in a relaxed manner, then builds into a double time run with violin and sax jabbing in and out of the melody. All the while Mauricia is punctuating the air with her vast array of vocal intonations. The second piece is "Ataturc" in which Cahen lays down a medium tempo electric piano melody that builds into a beautiful middle solo. The others serve mainly as embellishments injecting their breaks as various junctures. The closer is "Ronach," again on the uptempo side.

Side Two begins with the short, funky "Atart" by Cahen. The second piece is titled "La Soupe," which serves as a showcase for Seffer's considerable talent as he belches out an extremely impressive, rampaging sax solo. The album closer is "Satanya" by bassist Dugrenot. It opens with a soft, running bass riff that leads into a tearing journey through Mauricia's vocal gymnastics, Seffer's greasy sax and Rigaud's soaring violin. The centerpiece is a low-keyed controlled freakout where all the instruments pick up on one particular motif and recycle it several times at different octaves. It ends with Cahen's electric piano softly fading out with a tinkle.

The second album was recorded in France in Sept. '74. It was entitled *OSIRIS* and released on the Disjuncta label. Mauricia had left and the emphasis was more on the instrumental side of things. There was still voice, but it was used more as coloration, instead of being the spearhead. On the whole it was more melodic, less overpowering.

Side One opened with "Shardaz," a jerky medium-tempo piece that develops into a soprano workout by Seffer and also contains some heavy piano pummeling at various intervals by Cahen. The side's other piece, "Isis," is the high point. It opens with a delicate arrangement of bass, piano, sax and flute with exotic percussion echoing on the perimeter. Eventually a melody is set up on Cahen's electric, accompanied by Dugrenot's fuzzed bass. A sultry sax enters and begins an ongoing solo as the underlying rhythm continues to build. Abruptly it changes into a halting, choppy bridge that leads into a charging center section where the violin takes off on a fiery foray. It ends as it began, with the electric piano winding down as the flute and percussion dart in and out of the gentle rhythm.

Side Two consists of "Reinna," "Yog," and "La Rhune." "Yog" is the highlight utilizing as it does a scat vocal duet between bass and soprano voices. The electric piano leads the piece through various tempo and key changes. On this cut the rhythm section is at its best as the fuzz bass and drums boom out with bursts of thunder and lightning, then alternately are light and bouncy creating a startling contrast.

Following the Disjuncta LP, Cahen did a live recording of *PIANO CONCERTS*. The album featured him alone on electric and grand piano performing a series of improvisations. There are five in all, which vary from "Balette Bleue," a blues variation on the electric, to "Boogie 105," a short brisk workout. In addition there are the more serious pieces on the grand, "Moyen" and "Chanson pour le Chene Noir." These are highly dynamic, varying from the beautiful to the somber. In all it's a highly versatile and enjoyable album.

Late 1975 brought the next ZAO album which was entitled *SHEKINA*. It represented a vast progression from the relative simplicity of *OSIRIS*. For *SHEKINA* the group was augmented by four women who formed a string quartet. In addition Seffer wrote the bulk of the material.

Side One opens with one of Cahen's two pieces on the album, the cut "Joyl." A short one, it sets the pace for the rest of the album. The string section sets up accompaniment at the outset until Seffer and Cahen take a short funky duet, which in turn leads back into another short chorus with the strings. The side's second piece, "Yen-Lang" begins with Seffer's double-tracked flute over shimmering electric piano. Midway a rhythm emerges set up by the bass with string coloration. The percussion builds as Seffer's flute continues to babble amidst the increasing volume. Gradually it comes to a climax then proceeds to wind itself down to a conclusion as the strings cascade the place to a close. The side closer is highly reminiscent of *OSIRIS*. The rhythm section carries the piece, setting the tempos then just as quickly changing them, as Seffer flies over the top on clarinet. Suddenly the group stops and the string quartet takes the middle solo. It winds to a close and the bass picks up the tempo as Cahen adds fuzz to his electric piano and sets out on a haunting solo. Truong's use of exotic percussion is especially effective in complementing the overall atmosphere Cahen creates. Following that the original motif returns and carries it to conclusion.

Side Two opens with another Seffer composition, "Metatron." It starts out at a quick choppy pace and continues to build into a run. Cahen again treats his electric and plays a manic single note/chord solo over the fast rhythm while Seffer solos. Cahen's second piece, "Zita," follows and is a beautiful duet between his electric and the strings. Soft and slow, with the only contrast the hint of a bass and solo voice. The album closer is again by Seffer and is titled "Bakus." It starts with the typical ZAO rhythm over which a return of the scat vocal is introduced. Very much like portions of the first album, it reaches crazed heights as several instruments are fuzzed and each in turn take a brief solo with Seffer's voice wailing over the raging undercurrent. There's no question that *SHEKINA* is the group's strongest album to that point.

The new album released in Dec. '76 is entitled *KAWANA*. The title is derived from the 13th Century texts of Spanish Sages which dealt with "a synthesis between different philosophies and different theologies." As applied to ZAO's

1977

music it means "a complete freedom of styles although classification in traditional cultural values." "Pure intention without which no spiritual nor artistic action possesses any real value..."

How this specifically relates to their music can be initially hard to discern. At first listen the album doesn't seem to be as strong as its predecessor. Some of the earlier rough edges and freakiness appear to be gone. But continued listening brings further insight into not only the real musical strength the album possesses, but in fact the intent behind ZAO's music since its inception. ZAO has always made music of great intensity, whether it was bizarre and unorthodox or melodic and simple.

Each album was an attempt to form from a common style (jazz), a new, stronger variation. *KAWANA* represents perhaps the purest distillation thus far of the essence of ZAO music. For on none of their previous albums have all the elements been put together quite like they are on it. The album opener "Natura" by Cahen sets up a medium tempo. Newcomer Didier Lockwood on violin plays a strong role in the development of the piece. Late of Magma, he plays rhythm and adds a new color to the music with his artistic bass violin. Cahen also introduces the first synthesizer to a ZAO album, and between him and Lockwood the piece assumes quite a different sound than anything before. The rhythm base is the same, but the new instruments change the effect. The second piece is a Seffer composition titled "Tserouf." Uptempo, it starts off harmlessly-enough at a moderate tempo, but soon escalates into a rhythmic onslaught. The bass and percussion build to hurricane intensity as Seffer and Lockwood trade off with searing solos. ZAO has been frantic, but never quite like this. The overall arrangement is dizzying. The side closer is again by Seffer and entitled "F.F.F. (Fleurs for Faton)." It's a melancholy piano piece with Seffer this time taking on the piano duties. It serves as a very effective winding down from the previous holocaust as Seffer and Lockwood duet. Lockwood especially stands out as he double-tracks an acoustic and bass violin to allow himself the full range of the instrument.

Side two opens with "Kabal" by Cahen. Especially effective is his use of synthesizer as Lockwood and Seffer duet, trading off licks. A typical ZAO tempo is made more striking by the new instrumental arrangements. The second piece, "Sadie," is again by Cahen and this time starts off with Seffer and Lockwood playing in accompaniment to Cahen's keyboards. A relatively slow piece, it serves as an effective contrast between the opener and the album's highlight and closer "Free-Folk" by Seffer. "Free-Folk" begins with a choral chant that leads into a varied workout of blazing solos by Seffer and Lockwood. The arrangement is highly schizoid, as it changes tempo at strange intervals and with little preparation. In fact, it is almost a non-arrangement as each instrument appears to be going its own way at various times, the solo instrument serving as center point, keeping everything in focus.

For ZAO, *KAWANA* represents a strong statement of intent. Quite simply put, it is challenging but not overbearing, a unique album of music by one of France's most interesting groups. The best description comes from Cahen's liner notes. As he puts it -- "..fair winds begin to blow..."

Final notes -- Yochk'o Seffer has recently left to pursue his own musical ideas further, leaving François Cahen to head up ZAO. The U.S. label Cosmos is planning to release *KAWANA* here in the States.

Archie Patterson

Heldon

Heldon was conceived in late 1973 by Richard Pinhas. By definition, Heldon is a 'connection' or more an experience called a certain fiction science. Not a group of musicians but a sound political experience of fighting and from the beginning, a struggle against the fixed identity conducted in the name of a steely mechanism: synthesizers, tape recorders ....so on.

Pinhas serves as guide, with occasional assistance of friends. The particular motivation behind it relegates the profit motive to secondary consideration. The main goal was to put out artistically valid music at a fair price. This motivation in part appears to stem from experiences of the student movement in France during the '60s. The musical message is one of extreme emotional commitment conflicting with a harsh reality. The result is intensely impressionistic listening.

Initial recording was done in "Schizo Studios" for the Disjuncta label, which was initiated by Pinhas as an alternative outlet for more-progressive artists. During its existence there were four albums produced by Pinhas under the name Heldon. In addition seven other LPs were issued.

Just recently Pinhas has become involved with a new label in France, Cobra, and has just had a fifth Heldon album released.

Heldon no. 1 was entitled *ELECTRONIQUE GUERILLA* and clearly puts into music the aforementioned philosophy. The record is "dedicated to Robert Wyatt," perhaps done as a note of encouragement for around this time Wyatt was undergoing a crisis of sorts due to his accident. Musically there is a very slight resemblance to portions of the Soft's *THIRD* LP and Wyatt's own *END OF AN EAR*. But primarily Pinhas creates his own vision.

Flashes of the street, marching, rioting and chaos provide the spirit while Pinhas compositions provide the medium. There is "Quais Marchais, Mieux Qu'en 68" which draws part of its substance from Nietzsche, and homage to an assassinated Spanish revolutionary in "Ballade Pour Puig Antich," a short anthem consisting of violent electronic washes juxtaposed with solemn fuzzed guitar melody.

The overall tone of the album is harsh, punctuated by synthesizer and guitar assuming many different sonic characters. The extreme electronics convey uncompromising commitment and a revolutionary musical vision.

1977

Heldon no. 2 is titled *ALLEZ-TEIA*. The front and back covers again illustrate a commitment to the revolutionary vision. The adrenaline of the music on *ELECTRONIQUE GUERILLA* is portrayed graphically in the black and white photo of a cop chasing a demonstrator into a corner. Musically however the album reflects more the surreal feel one has after the riot baton, instead of the rush of the demonstration.

The album also serves as a tribute to Fripp and Eno. The opening cut is entitled "In The Wake of King Fripp" and another "Omar Diop Blondin" is dedicated to the duo. Overall the album is less extreme and more melodic than its predecessor. As a tribute it is a success, for there is none greater than to emulate the original and equal it. ALLEZ-TEIA is at least as good.

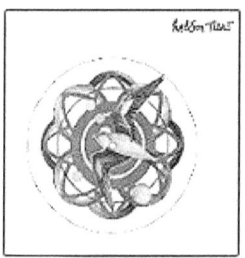

With *HELDON THIRD -- IT'S ALWAYS ROCK 'N ROLL* everything comes together and Pinhas brings off a double album of pure electricity. There is probably no album that can compare to this in terms of sheer electronic intensity.

Lou Reed's unlistenable *METAL MACHINE MUSIC* is heavier, but where it quickly descends into cacophonous redundancy, *THIRD* employs similar force with a diversity that makes it frightening. Synthesizer is the dominant force as electronics provide movement and coloration, but the guitar gives it its lethal quality.

The four sides consist of various rhythms and waves of electronic sound that emerge, mutate and fade, to form one continuous electrical current. At times percussion is added, along with keyboards, bass and voice. But aside from the synthesizer, the focal point is electric guitar. It quietly emerges on Side 1, cut 2, "Cotes De Cachalot A La Psylocybine" as a shrill fuzz, then proceeds to develop into a raging torrent of shrieking electricity by the final cut on Side 3, "Zind Destruction." The album closer, which takes up all of Side 4, is entitled "Doctor Bloodmoney." It consists of several synthesizer rhythms of different pitches, intertwining at various speeds. Percussion is added along with tape loops to create chaos which literally appears to wear itself out as the piece fades and bring the album to a close.

For those who fancy electronic music, *HELDON THIRD* is it. There is no neo-classicism à la Tangerine Dream or touches of artiness a la Fripp and Eno. Simply electricity taken to the extreme limits of imagination. Excellent stuff, guaranteed to clear the cobwebs out.

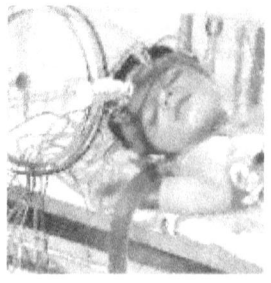

HELDON IV AGNETA NILSSON was a change of pace. On the one hand more subdued, while at the same time just as intense. There was more attention paid to melody as at various junctures it is smoothly flowing and highly beautiful. Yet the volume and dynamics employed are enough to make your hair stand on end. The fusion of these two qualities makes it doubly effective.

There are five pieces on the album. Two of them graphically illustrate this dichotomy. There is "Perspective III (Baader-Meinhof Blues)." In its harshness, full of pulsating electronic rhythm and savage guitar, you can almost feel the teeth of fascism at work. Dedicated to the R.A.F., a German revolutionary group whose leaders Andreas Baader and Ulrike Meinhof were captured a couple years ago. It graphically conveys the story in music of their apprehension, torture, starvation and Ulrike's ultimate rape and hanging by her prison guard. A strong musical commentary affirming Heldon's roots in struggle. On the other hand "Perspective IV (Intermede-Bassong)" is a rhythmic melody carried along by a chiming guitar and headed up by a bass improvisation. Flowing and beautiful it serves as a striking contrast to "Perspective III..."

The new album was released in France in December '76 on the new Cobra label. Disjuncta has apparently become inactive and out of its termination, Cobra has been started. It would appear to serve much the same purpose as the former, as its tentative schedule of releases includes albums by Sun Ra, the legendary space-jazz pioneer, and Lard Free, another "musical experience" centered around Gilbert Artman, a one-time collaborator of Pinhas.

Heldon #5 is entitled *HELDON : UN REVE SANS CONSEQUENCE SPECIALE*. It marks a return somewhat to the spirit of *HELDON THIRD* as once again the proceedings are the ultimate in musical intensity.

Side One includes "Marie Virginie," a relentless piece featuring pounding percussion and shrieking guitar and electronics that seem to be carrying an a battle to see which can out-do the other. The other track, "Elephanta," features a percussive duet. The drums are complemented by Moog in what amounts to a multi-timbred percussion workout. Various percussion instruments are given added coloration by the Moog which is programmed to give off similar effects. The overall feel is reflective of the title.

Side Two consists of "MVC II" and "Toward the Red Line." The former is a dirge of sorts with its bass and low electronic rhythm being embellished by metallic percussion. "Toward the Red Line" has Jannick Top of Magma on bass and fret-cello combining his various bass manipulations with Pinhas's guitar and Moog rhythms. Again percussion plays a large part as it is handled by François Auger, He not only plays on all the pieces on the album, but also composed "Elephanta." So in effect it is a collaboration between himself and Pinhas.

One of the interesting things about Heldon is the fact that over the span of five albums Pinhas has managed to create a different feel on each one. There are obvious similarities and built-in limitations in the field in which he works. But of all the people who are currently attempting electronic music, he has taken it the furthest. His ability to stay away from simple gimmicks and gymnastics, relying instead on dynamics and pure electronic force makes his work what it is an experience!

Archie Patterson

Ange

In 1929 H.P. Lovecraft wrote to Woodburn Harris,

> At present it cannot be said that the life of any civilized and sensitive man in America is really worth living -- except so far as he is able to make an imaginative escape from the encroaching milieu, either into the past of his culture-stream or into a fantastic hypothetical future of his own dreaming. Clods can stand the usurping barbarism very well -- it quite expresses their utilitarian minds and stunted personalities -- but fully evolved human beings will have to return to the old world unless something can be done toward restoring the civilization of the new. Already the exodus of sensitive men to France and England is becoming marked. The quantity ideal of the overspeeded machine 'civilization' of this continent is too utterly sterile to make the process of consciousness bearable to anyone of evolved imagination and delicately attuned emotions. There is no reward for keeping alive -- no food for the spiritual hungers of the civilized personality. It became that way in later Imperial Rome, and sensitive men had to flee to the Hellenistic East -- to Alexandria and Athens -- in order find an air that they could breathe.

Although most of us here have not physically packed up and emigrated to Europe, the above quote is more true today than it was in 1929. Readers of this magazine certainly have musical tasted and cultural preferences which abide on the other side of the Atlantic.

Ange hold a position in the French musical renaissance of the '70s similar to that of Raphael in the great European artistic revival of the 16th Century; both are masters of color, composition, and symmetry.

Besides the obvious leadership of the DeCamps brothers on vocals and keyboards, Ange appear to be a completely democratic band, with all members contributing equally and playing more than one instrument. Together, they meld to make some of the finest, most succinctly varied music anywhere on the planet.

Dynamics play a very important part in the compositional make-up of the band. By way of example, "Ces Gens-La," the first song on their fine second album *LE CIMITIERE DES ARLEQUINS*, starts off with a killer hardrook guitar riff, but soon metamorphoses into some beautiful Mellotron with outstanding French vocalizing of some of Jacques Brel lyrics. This is just one example from a myriad of dynamic changes which lace their albums, Their use of cuckoo clock and other mechanics, along with the ever-changing dynamics, remind me a little of Gentle Giant. Their oeuvre ranges from folk-like melodies and specters of Genesis/Crimson keyboard epics, to some ultra-phantasmagoric electric guitar workouts.

Of their five LPs to date, four of them are bona fide masterpieces, with only the first falling into the "very good" category. Throughout their history they have constantly been improving. Their latest tome *PAR LES FILS DE MANDARIN* is arguably the best yet. The factor that pushes this one to the top would have to be the excellent recording quality. All of the instruments seem to exist within their own space. The sound is natural, especially on the cymbal work, and you can hear each string being plucked. This is indicative of the kind of sound quality that the best French groups are now achieving.

As is the case with most top flight progressive groups, Ange use album cover graphics to great affect. Their last three have all been by the same artist, his work playing an important role in the overall concept of the group's albums. He has interrelated them thematically and stylistically to achieve the effect of the story Ange are telling us. I'm sorry to say that I am derelict when it comes to interpreting the French language but I can surmise with clues gathered from their fantastic album sleeve and cover graphics, the sound of their music, and the few words that I can deduce meaning from, that they are as lyrically proficient as Peter Hammill or Pete Sinfield at their best.

Unfortunately, here in the U.S. the weird and the imaginative are alien and all mundane impossibilities (which may be commonplace in other regions of the universe) have been banished to some limbo of critical derision. One may write of pigs and sheep but not of unicorns; of drug abusers but not of ghouls; of slum-harlots or mistreated rock stars but not of crimson kings. In short, all pipe dreams, all fantastic occurrences not authorized by Freudianism and the five senses, are due for the critical horse-laugh. Quel dommage, for Ange are an immensely talented band of young French musicians who revel in the weird, the futuristic, and the sublime. Paradoxically, they are also the most popular native rock group in all of France. So if the lack of domestic culture is strangling your creative urges be not afraid, for Ange are a sprightly breeze of enchantment blowing straight out of Middle Earth.

John Saltzgiver

Achim Reichel

Achim Reichel could perhaps be considered one of the pioneers of German Rock. He was raised on rock and roll over the occupation forces radio stations in the '50s and in 1961 formed the Rattles, one of the definitive early German rock groups. They won the Star Club contest in 1963, were the first German group to play the Hamburg Pop and Rock Mekka, did four tours of England and in 1966 undertook a joint tour of Germany with the Beatles. At the height of their success Achim was drafted.

During his army days and after, his musical goals shifted to becoming a "pop star" and having "hit singles." This period represents the low point of his career as crass commercialism was his aim. To this day many people in Germany cannot forgive him. His post-army activity was based around a band called Wonderland. This period lasted from 1968-70, at which point he dissolved the band to concentrate on more artistically valid musical concepts.

His recorded output during these early years consisted of several Rattles singles and LPs and one posthumous Wonderland LP which was an anthology of sorts, combining a side of their hit singles with one of studio cuts designed for an album.

In 1971 he embarked on a solo career, which to date has resulted in nine albums that exhibit a remarkable range of diversity. In addition he has produced two children's albums, titled *THE GIANT CHILDREN'S PARTY*. Also at this time he formed a creative relationship with Frank Dostal who was to serve as lyricist and co-originator of the concepts that the various albums would explore.

The first of these was called *WONDERLAND BAND NO. 1* and featured the combined talents of 26 various musicians. Thematically it was centered around the hippiesque concepts of peace and love and an appeal for brotherhood. The music was highly arranged, employing brass and strings as well as regular rock instrumentation. The album's centerpiece is "The Hill," an 11:53 musical potpourri. It begins as an acoustic guitar duet, and goes through various mutations before it becomes a dirge, led by the bass accompanied by myriad effects. The subject matter is daily existence and drudgery vs. the search for joy and an escape. Overall it comes off as psychedelia.

It was followed by *DIE GRÜNE REISE (THE GREEN JOURNEY)*, a soundtrack for an intended motion picture. This time Achim composed and performed the whole thing himself with the exception of Dostal's lyrics.

An improvement over its predecessor, it featured a striking cover, a collage of lush red lips enfolding a green globe that reflects Achim's visage. A eager development was the use of electronics to provide coloration for the guitar and percussion. This is literally reflected, in the title billing A.R. & Machines.

Again musically it is psychedelic, employing various vocal effects/chants over recurring rhythm guitar and percussion background. Electronics serve to connect the various segments and add depth to the sound.

On Side 2, the concept comes together. The album's lyrical message is embodied in "Come On People," an invocation to people to get together and relate to each other as human beings. Musically the high point of experimentation comes in "Truth and Probability (A Lexicon for Self Knowledge)." It is an electronic drone of different tones and colors that features vocal incantations of guttural vowels and consonants. The overall effect is primal and nightmarish.

ECHO, a double set, is the crystallization of all that had come before it. The four sides feature five pieces. Side 1, entitled "Invitation," begins with a phased-in guitar that sets up a relentless rhythm. Its presence is maintained throughout the album's four sides. At various junctures it is acoustic, then shifts to electric; always it serves as the central force determining the pace of the musical flow. The basic guitar rhythm is dominant throughout except for moments when percussion, winds, orchestra, voice and electronic effects provide brief interludes.

Side 2 consists of "The Echo of the Presence" and "The Echo of Time." The guitar continues churning out the rhythm, this time double-tracked. Vocals are more prominent, first as an ethereal solo voice, then chorus. Interposed at different times are lyrics consisting of socially conscious philosophizing on the dilemmas of man -- love vs. hate, wisdom vs. ignorance, strength vs. fear and an attempt to put them into perspective with the infinite -- "Gigantic chimes the echo of time."

Side 3 is titled "The Echo of the Future" and opens with a shimmer of electronics and reverberating guitar. It then develops into a recurring rhythm with voice, electronics and effects used to convey a feeling of space. "You can hear space-bells and milky-way smells." The message is "Questions find Answers," youth, no matter how old, will find a way.

The final side, "The Echo of the past," concludes: Learn from the past for a better tomorrow. Musically, it is sparse with emphasis placed on acoustic guitar, flute and electronics. The overall focus however is on voice, which is divided between sung and incantation. The titles of the segments tell the story -- "Memories of the Day After Tomorrow," "Ad Libido," "Ego Lego" and "Burns Like A Light at the End of the Tunnel."

Taken as a whole -- concept, music and execution, *ECHO* has to be considered one of the high points of German music, certainly ranking in the top ten albums produced by the modern German musicians. This opinion however is quite contrary to that taken by the vast majority of his German critics. Whether due to their continuing personal prejudice toward his past or simply due to the universal disease of shortsightedness, ECHO was slagged.

As a response to this critical attack, Reichel released very shortly after *ECHO* an LP under the moniker of Propeller. It catered to the basics of guitar rock. Needless to say this album was received well by the critics. He and two of his friends from the old Rattles teamed up to produce *LET US LIVE TOGETHER*, a surprisingly good album of guitar rock and roll. Unlike most power rock it avoided the pitfalls of sparse redundancy and instead combined a rock hard rhythm section with a riffing electric lead and acoustic rhythm guitar. The guitar playing, shared between Reichel himself and Herbert Hildebrandt, was excellent. The songs themselves were archetypal rock, complete with titles and lyrics that capture the low common-denominator essence that is the basis of good rock and roll, for example "Oukie Doukie Woman," "Kix," "Mojo" and "Let it Rock, Let it Roll" to name a few. As the critics said, "He achieved perfectly the adaptation of feelings of Anglo-American prototypes."

With *A.R.3,* Reichel's proclaimed attempt was to "create a music which is fitting for listening as well as discotheques." By his own admission he was less than successful. What resulted was a quasi-psychedelic work centered around his guitar. At times it worked, due to his considerable inventive technique. At others it became messy and the effect he was striving for was lost. That is not to say the album should be written off however -- on the whole it contains some fine moments of flowing rhythmic music. The arrangements are good and his backing musicians contribute striking accompaniment. Still it appears he let his imagination run away with him, and a little more discipline could have made all the difference.

In fact on his next album *A.R. IV,* this discipline was added and the result was a vast improvement. It reflected his emerging interest in Indian philosophy and meditation. The cover featured a luminous sunset, backgrounding a phallic crescent wrench jutting out of the landscape high into the sky.

The music was divided into two pieces with Side One titled "Vita." Almost completely rhythmic, it consisted of a constant rhythm carried by percussion and guitar over which various wind instruments lay down their static solos. The electronic effects were used to maximum advantage, complementing the often vicious guitar riffing.

Side two was the beautifully haunting "Aqua." Once again the constantly moving rhythm was present as the guitar churned out a flowing electric background. Percussion and electronic sounds of birds and water continually exerted their presence in echoey waves of sound.

After a meditative retreat in the "Academy for Personal Development" in Bremen he recorded *AUTOVISION.* A more simplified version of *AR IV,* a great deal more emphasis was placed on his guitar playing. The arrangements were more basic and less layering of sound was employed.

Side 2 is especially good as it takes you from the frenzy of "Turbulenzen" to the ultimate simplicity of the ten minute echo-guitar piece "Jay Guru Dev." On "Turbulenzen" he successfully integrates bongos, echo guitar, ARP and Mellotron in a schizoid impressionistic piece that conveys both anxiety and beauty. "Jay Guru Dev" is an intimate guitar solo done with the guitar played through an echo chamber. Simple to the extreme, he picks and strums a tranquil melody that conveys a relaxing, beautiful feel, yet at the same time a loneliness that is touching. The album's postscript is :34 of mouth harmonica playing a fragmentary melody that seems as much a beginning as an end.

AUTOVISION seems to be Achim using the medium of music to present pieces of himself to anyone who will listen. A highly personal album, I find it hard to believe that if it is listened to in the spirit in which it was made, anyone would not be moved. Each piece is more emotional than the last. The symbolic cover photo of a Volkswagen, rusted and overgrown by the wild greens of nature is symbolic on more than one level.

His next venture was to form a production company, Gorilla Music. Its intent was to allow artists an outlet to overcome the bad conditions under which German rock musicians must exist. Its basis being more personal and creatively-oriented in opposition to the profit motive.

Several things resulted from this effort including albums by various groups -- Kin Ping Meh, Yatha Sidhra and the Danish group System. In addition a Hamburg session album with bluesman Champion Jack Dupree, a live album with the English songwriter Michael Chapman and Achim's own next album *ERHOLUNG*.

ERHOLUNG was a live attempt to translate his previous studio ideas into an organic context. It was unfortunately only partially successful. Leaning toward a free-jazz orientation, the effects employed are more suited to a studio environment than the stage. Subtlety is hard to pull off in a live context for recording technology is basically inadequate. Even given the best, the static conditions of a live performance make the task tremendous. The album isn't bad, but it's not successful.

As with *A.R.3*, moments shine, but on the whole it gets bogged down in the inability to translate imagination into reality.

His latest album is perhaps the strangest of all. Reportedly the critics over there liked it, which makes the whole thing even more confounding.

Entitled *DAT SHANTY ALB'M*, it is a compilation of sea shanties put to rock music. Achim's clanging guitar grinds out the melodies as bass and percussion pump out the rhythm. The topper is his growling baritone vocals. The instrumental work is contagious and the vocals are at times hilarious. His versions of "Drunken Sailor" and "Shenendoah" have to be classics of some sort. Maybe the photo on the back cover holds the key. It shows Achim barechested, on the beach, wearing a wool cap and sporting a huge, toothy grin. Could this be a gag? Or has he joined the merchant marine?

Most likely it's a pleasant diversion to throw us off guard for what will come next.

Archie Patterson

Area
A Movie In Four Parts: A Band With Many Moving Parts

CHAPTER ONE: In which we see the leitmotif established, where the colors fly high only to be brought down once again, a beginning in essence.... A voice is

1977

chanting, chanting, floating on the air --- the screen is black --- an Arabic chant, incomprehensible, oddly compelling, trancelike repeats and repeats and...

OPENING SCENE: We watch a beautiful healthy-looking woman walk past a group of hirsute young men who ogle and watch in appreciation as she wiggles away, her bright red, green and white dress clinging to obvious attributes --- There is silence now, as the camera zooms in on the dress --- the colors are the colors of the Italian flag which the dress dissolves into, as the flag bright green, white and red grows to fill the screen --- the image burns in your eyes, your brain, as the music begins... Sweet Italian crooning vocals begin to build, intense, searing, tearing at the space behind your eyes, twisting the inner ear as the music races, RACES, the guitar and synthesizer dueling with laser-like lines, pure cocaine crystal sound that THREATENS YOUR SANITY. Pan back from flag, as we see soldiers dressed in strange gray uniforms marching over the flag --- from the top looking down we see them --- the flag under their ranks like a huge red, green and white street, as they stream endlessly over the flag. You blink.....

The band is playing. It's so loud and raucous you feel your eyes and ears will split. The crowd is packed in toe to toe, belly to belly, your own crotch is jammed tight against the beautiful woman from the movie. Who's dream is this? Sweat. The order of the evening as Patrizio Fariselli roars, emotes, croons, harmonizes and rips open phrase after phrase of sound --- AREA --- the sign blinks in neon colors. *ARBEIT MACHT FREI* --- work makes free --- Dachau humor --- black death throes humor from a nightmare past. The band rails and rants their power, the power of ROCK & ROLL, savage as an eagle's claws as she protects her young. Rock 'n roll forever young, a transmutation, a cry of hope in a sea of despair --- as the club fills with storm troopers, the same grey uniforms. They attack the band, billy clubs versus electric guitar, blood flows freely. Demetrio pounds harder on the drums, the synthesizer shrills out a warning. Her body is warm. "Give in," she whispers seductively in your ear. "Arbeit macht frei." The music roars, one last GASP!! and stops. You push her away, screaming as the blood becomes a flood from the stage, running over the edge. "Whose fucking dream is this?" "It's no dream," she whispers! ---

CHAPTER TWO: *CAUTION RADIATION AREA*: In which the band plays on plugged into the aftermath of a neverneverland nightmare. SCENE OPENS: intense jazz based riffs explode in quadraphonic sound around the room, ping ponging back and forth as the screen suddenly fills with the mushroom clouds of an atomic explosion the singer's intensity mirrors the mushroom's overwhelming desolation.... and fear. The intense feeling of doom crushes you in your seat as the mushroom freezes --- a blinking neon sign --- again --- *CAUTION RADIATION AREA* --- above the mushroom. A child, a little blonde boy in red, green and white knee pants walks onto the screen and begins to poke at the mushroom, which is surPRISE!! spongy to his touch.... he grabs off a piece, molds and shapes it like a flower, a rose, then he nibbles at it, eating the WHOLE THING.... it's good, he begins tearing at the mushroom, stuffing the pieces into his mouth as fast as he can... his belly swells --- and as it swells the camera zooms in --- we hear a moaning choir, reminiscent of souls in hell --- zoom into his stomach, his red, green and white pants becomes a city of rubble filled with ragged people filing through its streets, its red, green and white streets, now torn up and battered, a city of casualties, the ragged crowd seems mindless as it files endlessly ahead....

blink (mercifully).

You're in a cellar, which must be miles below the earth, so dank and dark, musty.... the neon sign is sporadically blinking.... A.....R.....E.....A.....as frazzled young men, seemingly old before their time are bent over strange gleaming instruments twisting knobs and dials, vibrations sound above hearing drill through you, below hearing melt your bones. The woman's hand is on your crotch, alternately squeezing.... stroking...."One way or another, give in," her tongue lances into your ear. The troopers are back, dressed in long black robes and beating at the band with huge crucifixes. Moans and screams as Tofani's guitar screeches, he reels around and aims the guitar and begins turning the controls on it, firing chords --- death bullets at the troopers...."Give in," she shrills in your ear, squeezing till pain erupts. Fariselli turns one more knob.... and a blinding light erases all ---

CHAPTER THREE: *CRAC!:* in which life goes on, babes are born again, resistance continues, the sun shines once a week whether it's needed or not. SCENE OPENS: The egg is so tall there on the black plain, which is fused crystalline glass-black as the heart of the world.... the egg Is so white there, so tall, so proud. The nurse is so small a figure as she fondles the egg, her uniform red, green and white, a crack forms and a giant coin rolls out, gleaming in the sun, as the drum toll fanfares, the coin grows arms and legs and smiles down from at least twice the size of the nurse --- the visage is Caesar's stern proud Roman face. The coin reaches for the egg, but the nurse steps between the coin and the egg, so small but so defiant, she shakes her fist up at the now frowning face of Caesar. The coin rolls over her body.... a scream.... silence.... intense paroxysm of light bursts forth from the egg.... the coin begins to melt....

Caesar screeches in pain and rage.... camera zooms to nurse's red, green and white uniform, which becomes a nursery floor on which we see babies, bouncing naked babes crawling in an even row, steadily away from the cracked egg, the melted Caesar and the brave, now heroically dead nurse.....

The music flows like a river of molten lava washing out over a small audience in an airy loft.... the audience all friends listening to a joyful sound, affirmation of life. Someone is passing around a petition written on ancient papyrus, so familiar, you've seen it somewhere before . You read it, somehow understanding the Italian, knowing this must be someone else's dream after all. But the words are familiar, strong, reassuring --- THERE WILL BE A CONCERT IN THE OPEN AGAIN.... She's there, of course, her hand now inside your pants. "It's all yours, mi cara, give in, please," her mouth a living thing against the side of your neck as she murmurs. The now familiar troopers come in as if on cue, carrying buckets of blood and money, placing them before the band, which smiles quietly and continues to play on. You re-read the leaflet and.... stand.... her hand slips away into nothingness.... "No!!!" she screams, as you cheerfully begin to mix the blood and money and spill the mixture out into the audience, laughing like a fool. "I'll let you all be in my dream, if you'll let me be in yours," you laugh.

CHAPTER FOUR: CONCLUSION *ARE(A)ZIONE*: In which the carpet is rolled out and the band plays live as the troupe ends its drama for the moment. CAMERA OPENS: In close on a young woman's face as she shakes her head from side to side in ecstasy, the music is loud. Panning back, we see more faces, some laughing some crying, back further, hundreds, thousands of faces. A FESTIVAL? --- a quick succession of shots of the band as they play in the open to thousands of living faces.... on synthesizer, Patrizio Fariselli.... on electric bass, Ares Tavolazzi.... on electric guitar, Giampaolo Tofani.... on drums and percussion, both Giulio Capiozzo, and Demetrio Statos.... AREA.

You see the woman again, just another smiling face in the crowd! The band steps forward to the stage front to shout.
    WE SHALL LIVE
    WE ARE OF THE
EARTH
    WE ARE THE GODDESS
ART
    WE SHALL TRIUMPH
OVER MIGHT

They begin to tear the film away, reaching for the edges, the edges begin to unravel, as a fire begins to burn the film.
    THERE IS ALWAYS A
NEW BEGINNING
A NEW DANCE
A NEW MUSIC
WE SHALL LIVE TO
PLAY
WE SHALL PLAY TO
LIVE
A voice in the background begins to chant, chanting floating on the air --- as the film slowly burns away itself, an Arabic chant, incomprehensible, oddly compelling.....

                      Russ Ketter
            Rather Ripped Records

Piirpauke

Piirpauke is a progressive jazz group, but as much as jazz, their roots are in traditional folk music. The folk influences show themselves not only in their music, but also in the large selection of instruments they play. Included are numerous different flutes, horns, string instruments, bells & percussion from India, Africa, Scandinavia and the Balkans. Yet even with all the diversity their technique is nothing short of excellent. This is evidenced by the fact that in November '76 Sakari Kukko, their keyboardist/wind instrumentalist was awarded the "Yrjo" prize as jazz musician of the year in Finland.

The group was formed in the Autumn of '74. Since then in addition to many performances at festivals, concerts, jazz clubs, on radio and TV, they have produced two albums, *PIIRPAUKE* and *PIIRPAUKE 2*.

Their debut was issued in December '75 and was among one of the best selling jazz records in Finland. Totally instrumental, of the three pieces on Side 1, two are group arrangements of traditionals, the other is an original composition. The first "Kuunnousv" is relatively short consisting of a repeating melody over which Kukko plays a meandering soprano sax solo. The second cut, "Legong," begins with a rhythm on acoustic guitar and a melody played on what sounds like pan pipes. The center section consists of string bass and percussion solos. Very low key, they eventually lead back into the opening theme which culminates in a restrained flourish. The third piece, "Uusi Laulu Paimenille," an original composition, is a delight. It opens with a quiet strumming electric guitar and soprano flute backed by the rhythm section. Midway through it shifts into a running double time and the flute begins a bouncy melody that leads the tune on a merry chase to conclusion.

The second side consists of two pieces "Cybele" and "Konevitsan Kirkonkellot." "Cybele," another original, is basically a flowing jam which features a beautiful center solo by Hasse Walli on guitar. His fluid technique conjures up visions of rainwater sliding down window glass as he lays out note after note of delicate electric sound. "Konevitsan Kirkonkellot" is another traditional. It opens with synthi and a shimmering piano played on top of a string bass. Then Walli enters on guitar and again works his magic as he subtly growls and shrieks out a solo that is both sensitive and powerful. Whereas Kukko was the main focal point with his wind work on Side 1, Walli's guitar stylings are definitely the highlight of Side 2.

PIIRPAUKE 2 contains more of the same, the only difference being tightened up arrangements. In addition they have made fuller use of their vast repertoire of instruments, creating many different musical moods. There is still the mix between traditionals and original compositions, only this time the originals play a larger part. Their playing is also more coherent structurally, whereas the first album was highly spatial, the second is much less so. Instead they have filled the spaces with spicy embellishments, making the album a potpourri of different musical delights. There are hints of the exotic East as well as blues rooted in the West. All are melded into their base of folk and jazz. If there can be said to be a highlight it would be Side Two's "Penang." A two-part original, what makes it especially noteworthy is that it combines all their various influences successfully to pull off literally a multi-ethnic musical tapestry. It opens with a myriad of percussion instruments complemented by Kukko's wind work.

The center section sees the winds reduced to an occasional wail as even more percussion is added of the metallic variety. Then what sounds like a steel drum, along with a percussive string instrument takes the middle break that culminates with the reentry of a babbling flute. The final section emerges as the piano sets up a melody against the rhythm section backing. Then Walli makes his entry on guitar and proceeds to tear off a solo that ranges up and down the frets. It fades as chaos sets in, creating an air of instrumental psychosis.

That pièce de résistance is followed up by the album closer, "Imala Maika," a perfect way to top it off. It is a warm, flowing melody lead by the piano, with accompaniment by restrained electric guitar and bouncy winds. Positively guaranteed to make you tap your feet and hum along.

The music of Piirpauke is like a breath of fresh air out of the North, from Finland with Love. Give them a listen. They'll do wonders for your state of mind.

Archie Patterson

Niemen

Poland has one of the most active music scenes in Eastern Europe. There are a score of artists making music that ranges the spectrum. Notable are the Breakout Blues Band, Budka Suflera and Test. The foremost musicians to have come out of the Polish musical movement so far are Michal Urbaniak and Czeslaw Niemen.

Urbaniak has gone on to become an international star, recently moving to the U.S. where he has recorded several albums for Columbia. All total he has over 12 albums which, though basically in the jazz idiom, display an amazing amount of imagination and diversity. While he is not yet a "name" here (it's only a matter of time), in Europe he is a legend of sorts in some circles.

On the other hand, Czeslaw Niemen or simply Niemen, has yet to be recognized on any broad scale. He's the number 1 artist/musician in his own country, but in Europe as a whole only somewhat known and scarcely heard of here in the states. Originally from Belarus, he emigrated to Poland. To date he has recorded 9 albums in his homeland, in addition to numerous collaborations with other Polish musicians. Outside E. Europe he has done 2 in Germany and 1 in the U.S. Niemen play keyboards -- e-piano, organ, Moog and Mellotron. His early efforts are characterized by his vocal style, which to say the least is overwhelming. His clear, strong baritone range goes from musky darkness to a wailing shriek. In the beginning his format was basically that of pop singer. The songs were short and the albums' concepts centered around themes of peace and love in conflict with loneliness and isolation. These are illustrated on his album covers. The first, simply titled *NIEMEN*, features him clad in brightly colored pants and flowery caftan complete with fur vest and beads. The second portrays the opposite side as it's titled *STRANGE IS THIS WORLD* and the cover is dominated by gray tones. Musically both are inconsequential. His third, titled RED, was a double and saw him begin to stretch out musically.

It was on his fourth, *ENIGMATIC*, that the music became the important factor. It is highlighted by "Thernody in the Memory of Bem" which takes up all of Side 1 and establishes his credentials as a fine keyboardist. Basically it consists of cascades of organ scales accompanied by giant chimes and a massed chorale. The vocals are adapted from a poem by the 19th century Polish poet Cyprian Norwid and are sung in a striking manner that makes the whole piece literally reek of drama. The atmosphere created is illustrated by the cover photos.

The front shows him bent over his organ with the scene lighted only by a large white candle. On the back he and his organ rest in a sandy landscape surrounded by multitudes of candles. It paints a vivid picture as does the music.

His next album was double, moving him into the realm of avant jazz. *VOLUME I AND II* marks his full-fledged entry into the ranks of the world's finest progressive musicians. This is in part due to his joining company with the members of a group known as SBB -- Jozef Skrzek, Jerzy Piotrowski and Antymos Apostolis. In addition both volumes featured the master of the double bass, Helmut Nadolski.

The high point of *VOLUME I* is the first side "Requiem for Van Gogh." An exercise in free jazz, it is marked by Nadolski's double bass improvisations and the accompanying free form sound colorations by the others.

VOLUME II is a bit more structured than the first, but the structure does nothing to harness the power displayed by the band. Side one's "Puppet Men" and "A Song for the Deceased" are powerful pieces of music. Niemen's organ is dominant, but the playing of his cohorts is in no way overshadowed as they lay down some of the most amazing backing. The dynamics employed and technique exhibited by all is staggering.

His next album found him in the company of a new band as SBB had gone on to do their own music. The group and album were called *AEROLIT*. This album was a bit less avant-garde, instead it concentrated on arrangement. The music,

though still jazz influenced, had moved a bit in the direction of rock. This change allowed a greater degree of accessibility, fortunately without a decrease in musicianship.

The latest album is entitled *KATHARSIS* and features Niemen on vocals, natural effects, acoustic and synthetic percussion, 12-string electric guitar, "U," Mellotron 400, Moog and Synthi EMS. The scenario, music, lyrics, performance and sleeve design are all by Niemen. The sleeve features a beautiful drawing of the face of universal sadness, illustrating the album's concept which is spelled out by a quote from Shelley, "The clogs of that which else might oversoar the loftiest star of unascended heaven, Pinnacled dim in the intense inane."

Musically it is perhaps his most compelling album. He has always had a flair for the dramatic. But on KATHARSIS he overcomes this and the result is a record of intensely moving music. Other keyboard superstars use twice the hardware to achieve half the impact. The sound flows from one theme to another as he develops the music gradually using the various instruments. The climax is reached in the last cut, "An Epitaph/In Memory of Piotr" (the late Piotr Ozicmski, a friend and former drummer with Aerolit.) It is almost hymnal as Mellotron resonates waves of sound. *KATHARSIS* is certainly one of the most impressive solo keyboard albums yet made.

Outside of Poland three albums have been released -- *STRANGE IS THIS WORLD, ODE TO VENUS* and *MOURNERS RHAPSODY*.

The first was recorded in Germany in 1972, the second also in Germany in '73. Both were done with Skrzek, Apostolis and Piotrowski on accompaniment and consisted of a cross-section of his Polish released material, redone with more elaborate arrangements and English vocals. While this serves to make them more accomplished and accessible, it seems to eliminate some of the spark of the originals. In fact, it almost completely changes some of them. The same basic pieces yet slight changes make them vastly different. Almost unrecognizable in some cases.

These two albums did manage to gain him recognition outside E. Europe. His next, recorded in the U.S. with the likes of Jan Hammer, Rick Laird, Michal Urbaniak and other notables was released in England on CBS and the states on JEM's Import label. Naturally it died for the usual reasons. 'Tis a shame too for it was good. It crossed a lot of stylistic boundaries and was just loaded with fine music. His singing was at intervals dramatic, soulful, funky and his songs personal and sensitive. Needless to say the performance instrumentally was top notch.

Side 1 featured a series of shorter songs highlighted by Niemen's Moog and Mellotron work and the tight backing. The arrangements were sharp and concise with no production overkill. Side 2 was a reworking of "Thernody..." off of *ENIGMATIC*. Retitled "Mourner's Rhapsody" it was given the grandiose treatment and came off a tour de force. A lot of pomp rockers could learn something about composition, arrangement and the use of dynamics by listening to this piece. It combines Moog, organ, choir, orchestra, percussion and guitars into a dramatic spectacle that can give you chills.

Niemen is probably one of the small group of contemporary musicians you could rightfully call an "artist." From his artwork on the album covers, to the music and lyrics, he paints a picture. Each part strong enough to stand on its own, yet also essential to the work as a whole. Seen a good one lately? If not take a listen.

Archie Patterson

SBB

SBB -- Jozef Skrzek, Antymos Apostolis, Jerzy Piotrowski -- was born in 1969 as the Silesian Blues Band. Their early years were spent experimenting with different musical styles attempting to create their own sound. Because of its unorthodox nature and a lack of public appeal they eventually had to forgo playing as an independent group. This led to them forming a relationship with Poland's top musician Niemen. Through that association they broadened their horizons, allowing them to gain valuable experience and exposure.

After recording four albums with him they had gained the confidence to once again go it alone. On Feb. 4, 1974 they staged their first concert in Warsaw. It was recorded and issued as their first album. It simply bore the title SBB. The letters now stood for Search, Breakup and Build, illustrating the process that had brought them to this particular point. The music it contained was a virtual collage of different styles. It ranged from blues to electronics and included guitar, bass, drum and Moog improvisations. It was adventurous to say the least and was awesome as far as technique was concerned. In fact too much so for a lot of people's tastes. But then that's not a criticism, is it?

The second album was titled *NEW HORIZONS*. Recorded in the studio, it showed them once again experimenting with several disciplines, but unlike the live album, they were used in a more coherent way. The music was still highly diverse, but this time it had been melded into a controlled structural format. It has been described as coming off like a Central European mutation of the artistic propositions of John Mahavishnu McLaughlin. A heady comparison and not totally accurate, but it does bear some relationship to the area in which they are working.

With their third album *MEMORY* they succeeded in overcoming the problem of trying to do too much in too little space. All the elements were at last forged into their own style and the resulting sound is best described as heavy. Not in the crass sense of the word, but in that it is dense and literally thick enough in atmosphere to fog you in. Skrzek's bass and keyboards lay down the foundation and carry the basic themes. His bass style along with Piotrowski's percussion work create a thunderous rumbling undercurrent. The organ, piano and Moog develop the melodies and Apostolis breaks free at intervals to rip off powerful solos. Their individual technique has always been staggering, but only on this album have they served to totally complement each other, instead of play off one another.

Side A's "In the Cradle of Your Hands" and "From Whose Blood, My Blood" act as preludes to Side B's extended cut "Memory Grows Into Stone." Things begin with the sound of warmth and develop into the music of life itself -- complete with beauty, passion and violence. This may seem a bit pretentious, but good music conveys emotion. It makes you feel, touches off a response. No matter what style, it allows the listener to come away with something. SBB ranks high on the scale of achievement in this regard. And their achievements seem to have only just begun. In the next few months they will have two new albums out and begin recording another. *SBB 4* will be issued in Poland on Muza and *SBB 5* in Czechoslovakia on Supraphone. *SBB 6* will be recorded with a symphony orchestra and released in summer '78.

Archie Patterson

Czechoslovakia
Rock Is Everywhere

The second half of the sixties was the beginning of the development of the new social class that disassociated itself from the old society. Its characteristic feature was its own fashion of dressing, communicating, critical attitude and opinions on the world. "Peace and Love," but above all the satisfying of its own cultural requirement. No doubt, that became evident in the area of music where was produced a new sort of musical expression - rock. Although the roots and the social origins of rock were Anglo-American's affairs primarily, the medium became prevalent -- almost overnight -- even in the other countries. Inclusive of so-called countries at the back of the "fire-proof curtain," even Czechoslovakia. Though under the objective circumstances it seems to be unlikely that so many young people in the E. Europe countries could accept rock for their own culture, it has happened, however under different circumstances. Rock serves as an expression of opinion, thoughts and attitude toward life. Seeing that the present world is contracting as a result of mass communication, we are all in continuous mutual touch and regardless of nationality everyone can use it for his own expression or anyone can be inspired by any culture regardless of its roots. By this reasoning it is quite logical that the certain part or sort of people who live in so-called countries at the back of "the fireproof curtain" have accepted rock for the accompaniment of their own culture and have found their common language and even "nervous system" with it. Owing to present electronic communication many white musicians -- American as well as British -- have found their inspiration and self-expression in roots of African, etc. cultures without their association with them. Unfortunately in the different countries of the world this is looked down upon, this mixing of foreign cultures both objectively and subjectively. Mostly, the quite different opinions and attitudes of people who have control of radio, t.v., press, recording agencies and concert halls, too, are a great obstacle of all rock transfusion to Czechoslovakia. More than ten years ago there was a joke here that rock was a dangerous contraband and its operators and consumers dangerous individuals. Unfortunately that joke has come close to being reality. At the beginning of the '70s it became so-called "official opinion" on the whole rock scene. When we want to find out the reasons why, we have to take into account all aspects and must not look at it with a prejudiced attitude, as is occasionally done by some of the "western" critics, especially recently in connection with our underground groups Plastic People of the Universe and DG-307. It is a fact that rock music is strange for people who, for the most part, inhibit any confrontation with it. This as real art speaks about nothing to them because they never try to see it, they don't know it because they haven't lived with it. They try to call the whole rock scene into question even though they aren't right. It is understandable this music filled with unusual instrumental harmonies and from time to time so-called "bawling singing" can sound alien, as can the folklore of African natives for people who don't know it. These people make sure themselves that rock hasn't a form nor content, they don't know how to respond to it and they are not able to make out its beauty. Their ideals lean toward Aristotle's rational categories, they want art to have its distinguished start, center and end, otherwise it could jeopardize them and their comprehensive faculties. They suspect rock enlightens man.

At the same time the same people insist their children be inventive and original and when they become distinguised of the so-called "diagram" with their dress, customs and culture their parents cry out that they will reduce the world to ruin. The other aspect is undoubtedly that many negative aspects of rock culture are strange to the E. European countries for the most part. That is they are mostly present in Western civilization -- violence, drugs, decadence, vandalism, nihilism or unnatural sex and reflected in their rock scenes. If they exist at all it is on a very small scale.

Communication media. It is quite certain that all media give very little publicity to the rock scene. Newspapers give space to rock only in the most necessary cases and by means of brief notes. Recently our famous music magazine "Melodie" has started to give more publicity to rock. The radio stations broadcast commercial, dull music although recently more time has been given to jazz, but rock has been broadcast only scantily. The only rock program called "Vetrnik" is done by the station Vltava. It partially enables a better look at the home and foreign music for us. For these reasons young people interested in rock have tried to tune in to overseas services. In the T.V. history the times rock programs have been aired can be counted very quickly. There was a paradox not long ago when one channel telecast a half-hour program about Plastic People of the Universe and DG-307. They received the greatest attention on the telly in the history of Czech rock. It is necessary to mention that the whole program together with shots of the two concerts by the groups demonstrated the bad side of rock and it is quite possible that it could throw worse light upon the whole rock scene. Afterwards it is understandable that record companies didn't hurry to sign up many rock groups. And now many groups must subordinate themselves to official opinion with regard to music, lyrics and so on. If some record company issues a rock record it is compared among fans with the wonder of the first man walking on the moon. The realization of an album from recording to sale takes two years sometimes and frequently is accompanied by many problems. There was a scandal for example when the Jazz-Rock Workshop's album was withdrawn from the market when it was rumoured that the artist was mentally smashed from drugs and it didn't conform to so-called "official views" on aesthetics. Two months later the album was rereleased in spite of all the controversy.

The explosion during the years 1967-70 has been considered the golden years of rock in Czechoslovakia. At that time many good and bad groups were in existence and the close connection with prominent British rock groups was their main external expression. There weren't many who had their own original repertoire. After all that was an accompanying phenomenon of many early Anglo-American groups who took their cue from R'n'B. The development of rock and above all the circumstances in Czechoslovakia got rock musicians to set forth in two directions. One, that couldn't find its own style, played in different ballrooms where they parodied world-known hits or they finished as accompaniment for Czech pop stars. The others set out to find its own way in spite of all the problems and obstacles. They built up their own style and on the whole got into closer connection with the jazz musicians and jazz music as was the worldwide trend. In the end the gates of the recording studios were opened to a few selected ones. This group of musicians is accompanied by ardent fans who have been largely responsible for the development of a rock scene in Czechoslovakia.

Martin Kratochvil + Jazz Q were counted among the most distinguished Czech groups. That group broke up towards the end of the year because its leader Martin Kratochvil had accepted a year scholarship to the American Berklee School of Music. But it is quite possible that he will form a new group after his return home. In spite of the fact that they had the word jazz in their name, their music was both rock and jazz and for that reason they were criticized by jazz publicists at the beginning. Kratochvil, originally a jazz pianist, is now playing e-piano and Moog after his joining up with a jazz flutist and sax player -- Jiri Stivin (who was highly acclaimed in the US publication

1977

"Downbeat"). He later centered around him some young rock musicians and then his music crystallized into a form which can be compared to Chick Corea, Herbie Hancock and others. With his Jazz Q he has recorded four albums, the group stabilizing after the third titled *SYMBIOSIS* which was recorded with the woman singer Joan Dugan who later married the guitar player of the group.

The group Energit is indisputably the best one that has ever been recorded. Unfortunately at the present time its existence is very uncertain and it can be expected its total disappearance. Energit hasn't had a concert in six months and the guitarist Lubos Andrst prefers to make his appearances only with pianist Emil Viklicky who'll study at Berklee in the autumn. The first album of the group brought about wide public acclaim for the group. Its original expression wipes out all stylish barriers as it is integrated with jazz, rock, folk, blues and African rhythms. Andrst composed all titles and they formed a comprehensive picture full of moods, colorful areas and inner feelings by means of unusual harmonious advancements. Frequently their music is compared to Weather Report.

The main personage of our rock scene is indisputably the guitar player Radim Hladik. His six-piece The Blue Effect Group is the oldest in our country. They got together in 1968 strongly influenced by the blues. Their reversal came at the beginning of the '70s when they recorded an album with Jazz Q who were very jazz oriented at that time. In addition they recorded two other LPs with a jazz band. They thus became the first rock band to bridge the two stylistic barriers. After years of experiments and personnel changes they have reverted back to rock. Their present music with singer and organist Oldrich Vesely's entry into the group is slightly similar to Genesis or Yes.

Their unique aspect being the outstanding guitar playing of Hladik who is one of our most respected musicians. The demonstration of an inability and little concern of the record company with the fifth album of that group (which was still on sale 2-1/2 years after release) led to the band leaving that company and signing with Opus records who will publish their sixth album this year.

The singer and the organist Lesek Semelka gave rise to a super-group two years ago. The group is compounded of all veterans of our rock scene. Its name is Bohemia and at the present time their album should be published. The effort of the band is its turning away from long instrumental compositions to lay a greater stress on the more complicated arrangements and the lyrical pages of vocal expression. Their present compositions are a slight disappointment for us because the general impression of them is strongly influenced by not very harmonious individual instruments and sometimes excessive volume. It is possible their first album will surprise us.

One of the good bands coming from Slovakia is the group called Fermata. In 1973 Fermata was established by Fero Griglak, the former guitar player for Collegium Musicum. They based the theme for their first album on the harmonious works of folk-music, but they weren't satisfied with it because it had been an end in itself. They want to enrich their sound and technique for their second album so their music can receive more colours and become more progressive.

An interesting band is Impuls, which achieves it's musical expression mainly with electrical tubes, and at the same time has an outstanding guitar player and synthesizer player. All members show with their feelings that they are on the verge of nearing masters such as John

1977

Coltrane, Miles Davis and others. Impuls has recently risen as a new star of the Czech electronic scene; it has tried to find new artificially constructed syntheses and its dynamic as much as violent music can take fans to the atmosphere of the minute because it is unreserved and thoughtful. No doubt it is one of the most popular groups.

A band which returns to the roots of rock and to shorter songs is Vladimir Misik + ETC. They try to produce their own likeness of blues, folk and rock. The rock and roll pioneer and singer Vladimir Misik, who took turns in bands of countless numbers, has talent for expressive vocalizing encompassing lyrical, balladic meditation to straightforward hard rock. Above all, he has been noted for co-operation with the late poet Josef Kainar, although their age difference was 45 years. By the means of his poems he recorded the most beautiful more than the most unconventional and the most lyrical album called *KURE V HODINACH (CHICKEN IN A SMALL ALARM CLOCK)*, which has never been published in Czechoslovakia. Joseph Kainar's affect has become evident on Misik's latest album and Misik has been crowned with it in the hearts of fans as much as Bob Dylan together with Mick Jagger in the Anglo-American scene.

Dezo Ursiny + the Provisorium is the band which exists or doesn't exist recurrently. The composer and keyboard player Dezo Ursiny selects musicians for his appearances each time, and as a matter of fact he didn't appear on the boards for three or four years. He devoted his free times to composing music for films or he set poems to music. After missing for five years, his second album will be published this year. It ought to be a trilogy and he doesn't want to swerve the music from the meaning of texts. It is quite possible that Dezo Ursiny will leave the rock-scene altogether, because he has a great affection for connection of music with pictures, and he will probably keep himself at the cinematography because at the present time he tries to produce short films for which he composes his own music.

A great future was seen for the four-piece band called Elektrobus which gained attention due to its peculiar open musical expression above all and for its vocal parts for which they were called the "Czechoslovak Mothers of Invention." Unfortunately the band wasn't in existence too long. However after it came apart, the members formed some interesting bands which have continued along the same lines. The first of them is the Rock and Jokes Extempore Band. They, in cooperation with the so-called Theatre Paskvil, produced a full length appearance called *ROCK MUSICAL COMEDIES*. The other band is Stehlik, that, like the British band Hawkwind, tries to lay stress on the visual aspects of the concert, too. The vocalist of the band sings about a fabulous world and from time to time he tells about different stupidities. Another time he suggests a man suffering from a mental disorder or a hair-brained professor by reason of his behaviour or dialogue from the stage. The general impression of their witty performance is so special that you think you are in their mad fabulous world for a time. But in reality it is meant to point out the negative in relationships between people.

Only three days before its first performance the new band called Franta Hromada was founded and the members had time to record a twenty-minute composition for it, the end being a jam-session. Originally they had intended to get together for only that one time, but then they decided to stay together due to their great success with many listeners. They play hardly classifiable and unrepresentative music. It is possible to trace their influences to rock, jazz or classical music, but at the same time they keep to their origins. The chief composer and leader of the group is the organist Daniel Fikejz who plans to make a film, maybe even a play to go with their musical presentation to make it more comprehensive.

If we talk about the Czech rock scene it would be absurd not to mention the name Collegium Musicum. No doubt it is one of the greatest groups which has ever come into existence all over Europe, except the British Isles. At one time the group played to full houses of 5,000 fans everyday. People had to be turned away at their performances and the police had to be in action frequently. The principal attraction of the band is the gifted organist Marian Varga who has been shrouded in many cases by rumours concerning drugs or living like a hermit hating everything around him. Basically it is a publicity trick for the most part. At the same time his influences lie with classical music, which he adapts to the music, he has even recomposed some works of the great masters. Collegium Musicum has done five albums and Varga has also recorded two other albums with various people.

These bands are followed by a great number of lesser ones with different styles, for example there are Mahagon, B-Team, Slamnik, Hemenex, Modus, Abraxas, Dom, Trilobit, Jazz Fragment, Durman + Company, Tloen, Katapult and others who keep themselves at the boundaries of extinction in most cases. They get themselves into the fans' subconscious by their performances in different clubs, colleges or at the festivals of which so-called "Jazz-Rock Workshop" belongs to the most famous one, thus they are able to get the attention of thousands of people in one day. Another is the "Amateur Jazz-Rock Festival." Two years ago an open air festival took place near the small town of Dobruska for the first time. This year it was forbidden because the organizers hadn't been able to secure sufficient hygienic and social facilities for the whole course of the festival. That was the cause of several incidents and a riot at the end of the first get together. Nevertheless, last year other open air festivals took place in Brno where it was in a stadium in line with the latest fashion. "Jazz-Rock-Folk-Blues Festival" in Pezinok is considered to be the best. It is held at night and this year a second show will be there also. All the great bands will be there such as Blue Effect, Lubos Andrst + Emil Viklicky, Dezo Ursiny + Provisorium, Collegium Musicum, Vladimir Misik + ETC, Fermata along with many others.

At the end of this it is necessary to say that all of the negative things that rock music brings with it have appeared in Czechoslovakia from time to time and have done harm to all aspects of our rock scene. There were riots even mass psychosis when some large festivals were held. The police had to be in action during some concerts. 1973 was the height of it. Someone died in a raging throng a few minutes before a performance by the Hungarian band Locomotiv GT. Then all concerts to be held in larger halls were forbidden for six months and the police had to be on guard when some others were held. The cases of bands Plastic People of the Universe and DG-307 provoked "official places" against rock music. More than five years ago in the time of the greatest interest in Collegium Musicum some incidents occurred because there was a full house before their shows. Very expensive false tickets were sold on the black market causing many fans to be cheated and get very angry and out of control. There could be mentioned other similar cases. Recently the "official places" have become aware that prohibitions or misunderstandings in the rock scene could have larger aftereffects. They could cause extreme states as in the case of Plastic People and DG-307. Therefore they have adopted a more liberal attitude than before. It is now a fact that the greater part of the negative influences of rock music have disappeared from the Czech scene and the majority of people who were born in the rock era have been able to now work in many areas of the mass media.

Milan Hlubucek

Uli Trepte Interview
"Making Music In The Long Run Is A Matter of Character, Not Talent."
-U.T.

Uli Trepte
Bass. Spacebox. Voice.
Social Science Fiction

A couple months back I had the pleasure of talking to one of the pioneers of German rock -- Uli Trepte. He turned out to be one of the most sincere, dedicated people I've come upon in the music field. Unlike most who are in it for the money, ego or vicarious thrills, making music gives his life meaning. That is a rare quality today. True commitment is strength and gives strength. I hope a bit of the feel has come through in this transcription.

>   hello yeah good thankyou
>   thankyou good yeah hello
>   yeah good hello thankyou
>   hello yeah thankyou good
>   good thankyou yeah hello

A: To start off why don't you give a short rundown on your personal musical history.

Uli: The first group I played with professionally was the Irene Schweizer Trio which played Free Jazz in those days 1966 - 67. There was Irene Schweizer on piano and Mani Neumeier on drums. In 1968 Mani and me formed Guru Guru.

A: What were your main musical influences in the early days, like what were you listening to? Who influenced what direction your music took?

Uli: With the Irene Schweizer Trio it was so called "Free Jazz." On the other hand I had heard also classical and contemporary music. There were several influences, among them Indian music and others. I found out with Free Jazz I couldn't express it. I had to leave the scene and go electric. The beginning of Guru Guru was like Free Rock. The continuing of playing free music, only electric. After a while we found out that to play absolutely free is also a restriction. I then came back to structures.

A: Did Hendrix have an influence on what you were doing?

Uli: There were different influences --

Hendrix, Velvet Underground, early Pink Floyd. We thought this was the way to go, there lays a new quality sound - music.

> hey hey you
> have you already heard
> what on the radio
> they do bring
>
> hey hey you
> just listen turn-on-turned
> the asses are talking
> and the tits
> they sing

A: The early Guru LPs seem pretty drug-influenced. How much of a role did drugs play in recording them?

Uli: We were turning on for some years at that time. We really tried to bring the experience, the feeling we had while using so-called psychedelic drugs into the music and express a certain lifestyle, a feeling. They were quite a strong influence for sure. Nearly all of the first groups that played in Germany during '68, '69, '70 were on psychedelic drugs.

A: What was the rock scene like in Germany in the early days? Was it easy to get gigs?

Uli: It was very heavy. It started in '68 when you could only get gigs in jazz clubs or those underground clubs that were popping up and down. It was small. It increased a little in '69 when places that only booked Top 30 music tried out the new music. In 1970 we could even produce our own concerts.

A: Who were some of the pioneers of the new rock?

Uli: Only a few -- Amon Düül, Guru Guru, Embryo, Tangerine Dream, Can, who had the first record out, and Xhol. Only a few in the first few years who played as live bands played the new sound.

A: Ok, after Guru you played with Faust. You played live gigs, did you play on any of their albums?

Uli: No, I think there is a live album recorded but never released.

A: Today are any of the people in Faust still creative musically that you know of?

Uli: All I know is that they've split. I've never heard from them since.

A: After Faust you formed a group with Carsten Bohn from Frumpy called Kickbit Information. Who was in the group?

Uli: It was a five piece. There was a violin/viola player, a saxophone/clarinet/flute, a keyboard player and Carsten and I.

A: Did you do any recording?

Uli: No, because the music we did had no chance with the industry. So we did some live gigs only. It was a controversy in the concept, so we decided to go our own ways.

A- After Kickbit, is that when you started doing concerts as Spacebox?

Uli: After that I decided to do what I really wanted to do. And I had to do that alone, because I was alone. So I started to develop a solo act where I was playing bass, singing and using the Space Box.

A: What exactly does the Space Box entail? Electronics? Tapes? Mixing?

Uli: The Space Box is a unit containing a short wave radio, transistor AM/FM radio, a tape recorder, a mixer, equalizer and an echo. That's all. No electronics, no synthesizer, Nothing. Just four inputs, a filter and echo. The material on the tapes is generally artificial or from natural sound sources, which I mostly modify by changing the speed -- faster or slower, forwards and/or backwards. I also do a lot of splicing and use endless cassettes. The actual playing is done by mixing the different sources together. The macro-structure is composed, the micro-structure improvised. So I can get a lot of freedom on a solid ground. Basically in my style I bring a lot of elements which were until now reserved for so called "contemporary music" into popular music; a harsh affair.

A: You have performed live with this haven't you?

Uli: Yeah I did. When I had worked out the program I went to Berlin for three months and played a lot of small gigs. It was quite ok, some people really dug it. Then I went to England for half a year to see how it was over there. Then I went back to Germany.

A: Were the reactions in England good or bad?

Uli: It was mixed up. Some people really liked it and some really didn't like it. There was always a heavy reaction in the audience. Which I thought was quite good.

A: Either way, any reaction is better than no reaction right?

Uli: Yeah, it showed me that my music meant something.

A: Have you done any recordings of your music yet?

Uli: There was some cat who did some recordings in England. But my act is a live act. There hasn't been yet a sufficient recording to really bring it out. Maybe it needs a video tape or something.

A: So your future musical plans include more live performances, developing your concept and someday getting something down on record?

Uli: For sure, it's the only way. I know no other way. It was always like that with Irene Schweizer, Guru -- playing in the clubs to see how people react. Then coming up with that.

A: Switching away from music a bit. Why did you come to the US?

Uli: Well I wanted to have a look. To see if I miss something by staying in Europe. I know the level there and I don't know anything about America. So I thought it's good in time, I can afford it right now, so let's do it once in your life and go over and check it out.

A: Can you make any comparisons so far in the week you've been here?

1977

Uli: The social attitudes, the people are quite good. It feels very different from Europe.

A: So you kind of like it?

Uli: Yeah, I still want to go to N.Y. I want to stay for some weeks in N.Y. Then I'll go back to Germany and try to get some people to play my music. I really want to do my music.

here is the slogan service
get your may day set
have a stress snack
and buy a stuntman styling
use a skyline simulator
rent an image imitator
order the remake review

read the newcomer news
meet the make-up meeting
watch the flesh funnies
dig the cracker crew
win a patchwork panty

new playmate promotion
win a patchwork panty
eat crispy crackers
shit flocky flakes

visit the funny farm

A: Well I'm all for ya. What you're trying to do sounds very interesting. Creative. I'm all for that as opposed to the business. Art over Money anytime, right?

Uli: Hey --

P.S. - As a footnote, just recently Uli has settled in Munich and is trying to get together his own band. As he wrote me, "It's the only way to realize my concept....creating a new kind of German pop music."

Archie Patterson

Hoelderlin

During the early '70s the English folk rock scene made quite an impression on the German music scene. Groups like Fairport, Fotheringay, Pentangle, etc. were well received and toured Europe regularly.

Soon after, not to be outdone, a small but vital German "Folk Nucleus" began to form, the most familiar among them the duo Witthuser & Westrupp, Peter Bursch's Broeselmaschine and of course Hoelderlin. The core of the band at this time consisted of the two Grumbkow brothers, Jochen and Christian and Christian's wife Nanny (a German Sandy Denny) on vocals. Jochen played the cello, Christian all kinds of guitars. They jammed together, played for friends and in small clubs. Nobody even dreamed of a recording contract. A few months later, in Spring '71, the band was joined by bassist

Peter Kaseberg, a drummer Michael Bruchmann and the catch of the century, a classic violinist by the name of Cristoph "Nops" Noppeney. On the insistence of Witthuser & Westrupp, this formation recorded a demotape and without wasting another thought on it, sent it off to a record company under whose banner most progressive bands were already under contract. In a record two weeks Hoelderlin had signed a contract to record their first album for the Pilz label. The band had been together only a few weeks and logged only three live gigs. So rather than push things, they collected more material, practiced and were finally ready to record in January '72. *HÖLDERLIN'S TRAUM* was born.

German lyrics, sounds of cello, flute and violins made the local critics sit up and take notice. What was it? It sounded so strangely un-rock-like, isn't that what German groups are supposed to do, emulate English and American rock groups?

The album was well received and rave reviews were written in the journals of the land. In a very short time, *HÖLDERLIN'S TRAUM* and its new approach to rock music had become a legend. Soon after, the band toured extensively and built their musical experience more and more. The newly acquired rhythm section pushed the instrumental sound more to the foreground and it became soon apparent that the more romantic leaning pieces had to take a back seat to all out jamming. The original folk sound was then soon abandoned, Christian's wife Nanny became pregnant and left the group. What to do? Most of their rehearsed music had been tailor made for Nanny's voice, now the band found themselves without a lead singer.

Improvisation was the key, also a newly acquired taste for "New Music" by bands like King Crimson and Genesis began to filter through and be incorporated into the new stage sound. Almost three years later, in '75, after extensive touring and composing of new material worthy of their own self-critical taste Hoelderlin finally recorded a second album.

Their relationship with the old record company had gone sour, in fact most available copies of the first album are no longer to be found. Now the band is under the wings of Intercord's Spiegelei (Fried Egg) label, which also gives us superb bands like Kraan for example. A note for fans: there may be a small chance that *HÖLDERLIN'S TRAUM* might be re-released if the high level of interest in the band keeps up.

HOELDERLIN (Spiegelei # 26 511-6u) was a fine second effort that showed the collective thought of the band so very well. The cover, music and lyrics, as well as the production, are by the band. The musical context and content of this record has by now achieved quality and maturity. For this album, the band consists of Michael on drums and percussion, Cristoph on viola and acoustic guitar, Christian on guitars, Jochen on various keyboards and flute. Peter Kaseberg on bass and his brother Joachim help out on guitar and produces the stage sound. Furthermore a little help is given by Zeus Held of Birth Control on sax, as well as Norbert Jacobson of RMO on clarinet. The ever present Conny Plank helps out with voice and synthi (he must be the busiest sound engineer in Germany, next to Dieter Dierks.)

Side One opens with the classic stage show opener, "Schwebebahn" (Skylift). A menacing piano and viola intro takes you on a flight of incredible frenzy, then helplessly floats you around the sky, tossing you here and there. This cut is a minor masterpiece. Cristoph and Joachim interplay their instruments with such precision, backed relentlessly by Michael's percussion, it has an eerie, yet beautiful quality to it. This leads into "I Love My Dog," a perfect example of the band's former background. A very folk sounding piece, in the best Jethro Tull tradition. Christian and his brother Jochen really shine as the fusion of traditional folk music, classical influences and rock comes off extremely well. Yet it is merely a link in Hoelderlin's incredible bag of musical variety, never once losing their own distinctive style. The lyrics may be rooted in romantic fairy tales, but the music transcends the ages and culminates in the finest jazz rock to be found on record. "Honeypot," the third and last song on Side One, bears witness to that with all the members of the group getting a good workout. Eccentric in spots, but I'll play it till the grooves wear out.

Side Two starts with "Nuremberg" another reminder of Hoelderlin's folk days. This leads to the 17:32 epic "Deathwatch-beetle," a musical tour de force that reminds of early ELO or the better things of Gentle Giant. The production really shows here, every instrument has its place, doesn't crowd or clutter, the classical training of Nops Noppeney is very apparent. This cut alone is worth the entire album, a "rock classic" in my book. By now the band had abandoned singing in German, English lyrics had been adopted, not merely thoughts translated into English, but entities of their own, intelligent, with a sense of humor.

In the Summer of '75, Peter Kaseberg left the group and is replaced by Hans Baar on bass. Hans brought with him a more rock-oriented influence which is soon absorbed into the band's overall sound. *CLOWNS AND CLOUDS* (Spiegelei # 26 605 - 6u) is recorded with this lineup and is surely the high point of their career so far. It is divided into two guiding themes, a Clown side and a Cloud side, though the album is not really a concept album. "Madhouse," a fitting introduction to the Clown side features some great jazz rock playing. The band seems even tighter than on previous recordings. It slowly gives way to the ballad "Your Eyes," a further reminder of the bands more romantic past. It is chiefly Jochen's showcase, keyboard dominated and some nice vocals, as well as fine viola playing by Nops. Again this cut leads to the side's high point, "Circus." In one flowing motion, a gypsy violin heralds it's arrival as you are suddenly surrounded by cheering people, the excitement mounts, you feel like a child again. The master of ceremonies announces the show, clowns and dancing bears fill the center ring, activities everywhere, so much to see, to do, is it real? "Circus" is divided into three sections, "tango milli," "marching" and "sensations" which cleverly convey the whirl of life under the Big Top. If you listen carefully you will see the illusion for yourself.

The Cloud side opens with "Streaming." You are lying in the soft spring grass by a clear, swiftly running brook. At peace with yourself you just lie there on your back staring upward to the passing clouds. Slowly the ripples of water become gentle synthi weavings, joined by guitars, bass and flute. The music transports you to the clouds and suddenly takes you off on a fancy free flight, what have you got to lose? This piece was entirely conceived by new member Hans Baar and brings more of a rock feel to the overall sound. The group is also joined here by Jorg-Peter Siebert on sax, flute and percussion. By now it has become apparent that Hoelderlin has successfully made the transition from folk rock to full fledged rock jazz without losing their distinctive style. "Phasing," the side closer, is a good example of that. In just a little over 12 minutes the band showcases their individual talents. It begins rather solemn, then takes on an airy quality that characterizes this whole side as it slowly progresses and builds into a veritable symphony. Altogether a fine production, very well conceived and recorded.

Hoelderlin has been and still is a very busy band, touring frequently and extensively. Next to Scorpions they have logged more live gigs than any other German band. Their European reviews suggest that they are even better live than on record. Because of the stress of constantly being on the road, Christian Grumbkow no longer tours with the band. He will continue to record and design and draw the album covers, which incidentally are great. He will be replaced live by a Spaniard named Pablo Weeber, who should bring even more of a rock orientation to the group.

At present they are preparing to record and mix their fourth album at a new studio near Hamburg. It will utilize a new process called 3-D Sound, which is reportedly an improvement over the Kunstkopf (Artificial Head) technique that has been used by a number of German bands. The new LP, as yet untitled, will be available in October '77, a treat worth looking forward to.

By the way Intercord has just released a double 3-D Sound sampler LP. Titled *SUPER ROCK FESTIVAL* it features Nektar, Kraan, Kraftwerk, Omega, Birth Control and Hoelderlin.

Peter Moser

Lard Free

Lard Free is another in the wave of fine progressive bands which have been making their way out of Continental Europe for the past few years. They hail from France and are centered around the talents of Gilbert Artman, founder and leader of the band.

The band first came together under the name Lard Free in late 1970. They spent all of '71 and '72 playing at various festivals and by 1973 were ready to record their first album. It was called *GILBERT ARTMAN'S LARD FREE* and released on the Vamp label. The personnel at this time was Artman (drums, percussion, piano), Herve Eyhani (bass, ARP), Phillippe Balliet (saxes) and François Mativet (guitar).

Jazz influenced, it opens with "Warinobaril," a lazy bass/sax riff that gradually works its way into a spacy jam before it abruptly cuts off at the end (always a classic ending). The second cut, a long one titled "12 au Juillet que je sais d'elle," starts off with a programmed synthi rhythm and lonely sax in the background, but as the piece progresses the synthesizer takes the forefront completely and literally buzzes around the room. This one also cuts off and runs directly into the next two pieces, which are the least Interesting on the LP. "Part One" has a kind of mysterious solemnity to it. "Part Two" is merely a conventional jazz jam, which features some good guitar. The last cut on Side One, "Honfleur Ecarlate" is better. Opening with what sounds like another jazz jam, it soon mutates into some very elliptical guitar and sax. A very good closing number.

Side Two consists of three longer numbers. The first, "Acide Fromboise," opens with an ethereal-sounding synthesizer riff which is quickly joined by muted guitar. The drums pick up from there and the song moves on with the relentless underlying synthi the base of it all. Guitar comes to the forefront towards the end adding a very harsh, disturbing quality. "Livarot Respiration" follows and is a slow moving, relaxed piece with nice echoed vibes providing a smooth background for the fluid bass/sax combination. In contrast to this is the last number, "Culturez-vous vous meme" which consists entirely of atonal synthesizer with a little piano thrown in at the end, this a precursor of what was to come.

The band, which had had numerous personnel changes by now, continued to play festivals for the next two years and a second album called *I'M AROUND ABOUT MIDNIGHT* was recorded and released on Vamp in 1975. The members of the band were by now completely different and the sound bears little resemblance to the earlier LP. At this time the band was: Artman, Alain Audat and Antoine Duvernot with a guest guitarist Richard Pinhas of Heldon. Pinhas' influence is heavily felt throughout as the music is much "spacier" and less jazzy and there seems to be more energy in it than on the earlier LP. The opening cut begins with howling synthi wind and moves through heavy atmosphere for several minutes before running directly into the second cut, "In A Desert Alambic." It features what sounds like a sax playing the bass part in the foreground with some of Pinhas' very Frippish guitar darting in and out from front to back. The side closes with "Does East Bakestan Belong to Itself" which is much like Pink Floyd around '68-'69. It has some Eastern influences thrown in, nice vibes from Artman and a great drift-off synthi close.

Side Two opens with "Tatkooz A Roulette," an eight minute track that starts out strongly resembling the early work of Popol Vuh. It then moves into a synthesizer run that reminds one instantly of Heldon, the influence again of Pinhas no doubt. What sounds like a robot drummer is actually Artman's unusual electronic percussion, similar to Klaus Schulze's. The piece comes to a rather abrupt end running directly into "Pale Violence," the second cut which is basically a showcase for Artman's fine drumming. They are mixed way out front this time and Pinhas multilayers several different guitar tracks, each with a slightly different distortion. The effect comes off again rather like Fripp. This one runs into the album closer "Even silence stops when trains come," which opens with acoustic Steinway piano that could almost be Keith Emerson. The whole cut is very reminiscent of ELP's "Take A Pebble." On the whole this LP is heavier than the first although they borrow more from other people's sound. This is the more "cosmic" one, whereas the first has more of a progressive/avant jazz feel to it.

The band continued festivals through 1976 and also recorded the third LP, which is due to be released on the newly formed Cobra label soon.

In addition to Lard Free, Artman has also guested on LPs by Clearlight Symphony and Heldon *THIRD* as well as scoring the soundtracks for two films. His newest musical project is titled *URBAN SAX* and will feature 16 saxophones. It has just been released on Cobra.

Gorden Stewart

Finnforest

The group Finnforest is virtually an unknown entity. Aside from instrumental listings, song titles and credits (all in Finnish), and a small picture on the back of their second album, nothing is known. The lineup is Pekka Tegelman - guitar, Jussi Tegelman - percussion, Jarmo Hiekkala - bass and Jukka Linkola - keyboards. So far they have put out two albums on the Love label, a first which simply bears their name and a second entitled *LAHTO MATKALLE*.

So much for the hard facts. It is unfortunate that so far this group is such an unknown quantity. For the music they make is not only of the highest quality, but is so downright accessible that it would seem only purposeful anonymity could keep these guys from becoming internationally popular. Their music is commercial in the best sense of the word and I should think anyone would find it hard to listen to either album and not like it.

As for the albums; The first is basically progressive rock with just a touch of jazz added to give it that adventurous spirit. All instrumental, the highlight has to be the work of Pekka Tegelman on guitar and Jukka Linkola on organ. The overall sound comes somewhere near that of the first two albums by Peter Bardens' group Camel. But where as they labored under the burden of the British symphonic rock tradition, Finnforest doesn't. The music is like a jetstream air current, one moment floating, the next whisking off into a whirlwind of sound. Guitar and keyboard alternate in taking the lead, while the rhythm section provides the undercurrent. If you like crystalline guitar and washes of organic sound, this album is for you.

With *LAHTO MATKALLE* the sound has been changed dramatically. The ECM-ish cover illustrates their shift more toward the jazz realm. This time Linkola has replaced his flowing organ tones with electric piano and synthi. It has made a world of difference. Instead of he and Pekka playing complementary passages, they play more in a style of counterpoint, echoing and feeding off one another, creating a more rhythmic feel.

Side B features "Lahto Matkalle I & II," both composed by Pekka. They are two of the best pieces of music you'll hear. From the opening string arrangements, to the fuzz bass passages, the music goes through one phase after another. Even at it's peak there is an almost delicate nature about it. This is to a great deal due to the arrangements which are crisp and uncluttered. Add to this their individual abilities and you get some fine music. Somewhat ECM-ish, but done with just a touch of rock energy, thus keeping it from being over disciplined.

As I said at the outset, these guys are going to have to hide in the forests of Northern Finland in order to stay unknown.

Archie Patterson

Battiato

Some idiot came into the record shop where I work today and said, "What is that noise?" I was playing Battiato. That rather sums up the situation in the good ol' U.S. Except for more commercial items -- Kraftwerk, etc. -- it's a big zero. Which brings us to Franco Battiato. He's a good example of the neglect of quality music in this country. It's almost painful how obscure he is. Only Javis Single gives him a run for his money in that department. He doesn't exactly dominate the import racks either.

To his history -- Battiato is a protégé of Karlheinz Stockhausen. He performs solo amidst a multitude of keyboards and was at one time a movie/stage actor in Italy. He has done four albums. The first three were released on Bla Bla Records (no kidding) which is now defunct and the fourth came out on Island in England. They are *FETUS* (1972), *POLLUTION* (1973), *SULLE CORDE DI AIRES* (1973) and *CLIC* (1974).

They are all continually good albums. There are multiple time changes (Mike Ratledge would be proud). An example being Side One of *FETUS*. It begins with a baby crying, then a small child speaking in Italian. There are several other inserts along the way, even Nixon. Halfway through the side it breaks into a jazz-like violin solo. Then Battiato's vocals come back in a cascading effect accompanied by some beautiful guitar. Following is another change into an almost rock-like chant and he's back to synthi, then to a symphonic vocal harmony. That's only Side One. He's one of the very few artists who can mix so many moods and sounds together and come up with something cohesive.

Side Two of *POLLUTION* easily stands on its own merits as a complete musical work. The Italian vocals are unbelievably gorgeous.

SULLE CORDE DI AIRES is very intense with multi-layered sounds going in various directions, and it works. There is a very beautiful sax solo on Side Two which reminds of Roland Kirk and also a strange Oriental and American Indian sound to much of it. This is the side out of all four albums that I like the best. The two kinds of music go their separate ways at the same time but merge at the end.

CLIC, the fourth album, is a bit more commercial than the third, but still very good. The use of violin and the superb quality of the recording are the highlights. It's also intense, but very different from the other three. As someone who has heard a lot of bad records, these four come as a great relief. I have only one question, where's he been since '74?

Too bad Sal and Dean (Kerouac's ON THE ROAD) never made it to Italy.

Russ Harrell

1978

All Ears

In The Business, the first question always asked by record company people is will it sell? New albums are looked at as product to be programmed into the mass consciousness. The actual music is virtually irrelevant -- good, bad -- it matters very little.

This may be going to change a bit however as many bands are now opting for putting out their own records and independent labels are being formed at a fast pace. Such is the case with All Ears Records which came in to being in early 1977. The nucleus of the company is Antony Harrington's dedication to progressive music and the creative art talent of Paul Whitehead. With a little help from their friends and support of the ever-growing progressive music audience here in the U.S. they have released 3 albums to date. In addition they publish a newsletter of current happenings in the progressive music field.

The first All Ears release was by the Japanese band Chronicle, an offshoot of Japan's top progressive group the Far East Family Band. Chronicle actually came together during a visit to L.A. in the summer of '74. They jammed together and it clicked. So they rehearsed and the visit culminated in a stint at the Whiskey which was recorded and released in their homeland under the title *CHRONICLE LIVE AT THE WHISKEY A GO GO*. It was a fine album of spatial music that sported a heavenly cover featuring a radiant angelic female visage engulfed in a kaleidoscope of luxurious colors. Their second album, *LIKE A MESSAGE FROM THE STARS* was their U.S. All Ears debut. It featured a striking celestial art cover by Whitehead and some moments of equally breathtaking music. There were times when the Japanese vocals detracted from the power of the music, but the instrumental passages often times were majestically beautiful and full of exotic sounds.

Since *MESSAGE*, Chronicle has returned to Japan and are currently hard at work on their next album in studios on the slopes of Mount Fuji.

1978

The second All Ears album was the fifth LP by one of Italy's top progressive bands, Sensations Fix. Titled *VISIONS FUGITIVES*, it crystallizes all that has come before it for Franco Falsini and the Fix. The music is characterized by spacy arrangements and Franco's songs have never been better. The guitar rings out full chords of sound and fuzzed lead lines and the vocals add a provocative touch that makes the whole affair take on an otherworldly atmosphere -- a voice from out of the Cosmos philosophizing on the struggle of life. Songs like "Barnhaus Effect No.2," "Fortune Teller" and "Secret Orders For Operation Brainstorm" are rock and roll in the best sense -- energetic, imaginative and intelligent -- filled with a feeling of urgency that makes them compelling.

Franco has now returned to Italy and has recorded a new Fix album *BOXES PARADISE*, which will be out in Italy soon. Polydor, their label in Italy, has also decided against releasing an import version of *VISIONS FUGITIVES*. They chose instead to import All Ears LPs, seems they didn't feel they could improve on the pressing or packaging.

The new Ears release is the fifth album by the Far East Family Band, *TENKUJIN*. An awesomely beautiful concept work it features a fantastic cover portrait by Paul Whitehead that serves to illustrate the concept. "Tenkujin" is an angel or heavenly being -- someone from out there beyond the realms of this existence or comprehension. The Enlightened One. This idea is translated into music by Far East in an amazing way.

From the opening bars you realize you are in for something special. "Decension," a wash of sounds ushers in the album, then gives way to the title out. It's carried by a driving rhythm that serves as the base for a majestic synthesizer melody and echo guitar. The overall impact is stunning as the various sound patterns intertwine and blend into a menage of tone colors. The side closes with a Floydian sounding piece "Timeless Phase" that hints at the Pinks in their most melodic moments of grandeur. It's topped off by cascading chorale effects and slivers of synthi.

"Nagare" opens the second side with waterfalls, cuckoos and the feel of a heartbeat. Synthesizer and guitar pick up on a melody and develop it into glissandos of sound which eventually give way to "From Far East," an atmospheric collage of natural sound overlaid with more soaring synthi and guitar. The albums closing piece and highlight is "Ascension," a virtual hymn, a processional to the higher state of consciousness. It is literally celestial, giving you a feeling of warmth and positive uplift with its Mellotron and string ensemble melodies complemented by a slow, stately percussion cadence.

Another element of the album that makes it even more impressive is the use of vocals and the lyrics. The voice is harmonic and imaginative use of echo gives it a surreal quality that serves to greatly enhance the lyrical content. Most "cosmic" concepts fall flat precisely due to the lyrics. But Far East has avoided this pitfall by keeping them simple, instead of heavy philosophical pronouncements and pondering they link together short emotional couplets to convey a feeling. They rely on the emotions the words convey instead the words themselves. Their intent is similarly simple and revealed between the bands at the end of each side of the record -- "Music in the soul can be heard by the universe, with *TENKUJIN* we would like to share this message with the world." Give this album a listen and take them up on their offer.

All Ears is what Music needs -- an independent, progressive minded company that puts quality above quantity and cares about good music. Support them and treat yourself to some fine listening.

Archie Patterson

The German Rock Scene Today

A lot has happened in the German rockscene since Rolf-Ulrich Kaiser first put on the debut German rock concert at Essen's Gruga Hall in 1969. Curiously the bands of that first hour still play an important role today. Tangerine Dream, Amon Düül, Embryo and Guru Guru exist as before and have made their imprint on the scene, but Kaiser, the self-styled "Pope of Pop," has bit the dust.

So, a lot has been going on. Not only that, after a long time of searching, experimenting and fighting for recognition in a cultural market unfriendly to rock, a time of reflection resulted, which in part has been somewhat responsible for a few successes. A heretofore unknown process has now taken place, which has its roots in the ever bigger and better influence of the Media Concerts. In other words, only a successful group can find their way to the ear of the consumer. The less successful products consequently have to put out a lot of time and energy in order to compete even remotely with the more financially capable and better backed bands. This practice comes to a head here almost daily. The result being not to advertise for any records unless the production costs are met first, or: to put 30,000 DM in the studio first, but only get 10,000 DM for shoestring advertising. The examples could go on and on, as they paint a very sad picture of German rock history. The times are over when any group that had even the slightest bit more to offer other than rock n roll could easily get a recording contract. This fact surely does not have an overwhelming effect on the more experimental musicians. Nonetheless, it is reassuring that the struggle has achieved something of an appreciative following of the scene. The fact that I can write this article, can only be attributed to the monumental force and creativity of the musicians themselves, who have simply withstood these obstacles and done their own thing.

In 1976 the time had come: often prophesied, but until then never achieved goal had been arrived at: German rock sells internationally The result: a storm swept through the scene with the help of remarkable sales figures by bands like Triumvirat, Nektar, Tangerine Dream and others , in countries like the U.S.A., Australia, Brazil, etc. The German rock promoters created a kind of "we are somebody" mood. The fact that other groups like Eloy or Epitaph had to suffer from the consequences of U.S. marketing strategies, is hardly even mentioned. Even the groups that toured America like Atlantis, Passport, Nektar and Triumvirat did not return completely unharmed. This newly acquired self-assurance peaked in the insane belief that from now on all the world's doors would be open to German rock music. New equipment was being bought, new lighting systems ordered, LP productions (often labeled as Kraut Rock by teasing British rock critics) were more "sound" consciously produced. which means they were measured by Anglo-American standards. Conny Plank studio and Dieter Dierks studio, both near Cologne, in which most of the rock productions were recorded (by now a few hundred), have now attained international quality, something one cannot always say about the musicians who hang out there. Also in the mean time, some well known, some unnoticed personnel changes have taken place within the groups. During the first half of '77 hardly any group has not been affected by these changes. Some have disbanded, others only get together to keep existing contracts. On the other hand, during the '76-'77 concert season German attendance figures show a new upward trend is developing. Could it be that finally the German rock scene is coming out of its wallflower existence? Maybe it could even guarantee a living for the musicians, managers and roadies?

A Few Facts And Figures:
Kraan sold 40,000 live double LPs, Jane sold over 70,000 live double albums, as well as 70,000 of their *BETWEEN HEAVEN AND HELL* LP. Eloy sold 50,000 copies of *DAWN*, Nektar, Triumvirat, and Kraftwerk sell many hundred thousands, 8,000 fans come to the Brain Festival. The other tours of German bands are attended by between 20 and 30 thousand fans. Mainly "concert groups" like Hoelderlin (130 appearances), Kraan (120 shows), Scorpions (140 appearances) and Birth Control along with Guru Guru around 100 shows per year, get between 2,000 and 3,000 DM each, as well as with album sales of 10 to 20 thousand copies per year can make a living or survive at least.

Hoelderlin with 7 T.V. shows and 9 radio features is perhaps the most media represented band of those in the progressive scene. Naturally an Udo Lindenberg can expect much better time slots and more spectacular show possibilities. The dilemma can be clearly seen through these figures. The domestic market is much too small for so many groups, who have to fight in youth centres and gyms for their daily bread. The big halls and venues are reserved by the record industry for promotion concerts by overfed concert agents, who regularly feature their "super star acts." The top German acts consequently don't want to be burned as "warm-up bands," so they have to be content with small halls or clubs. In the case of Scorpions however, who toured as openers for the Sweet throughout Germany for the price of a piece of buttered bread, it has paid off. Also Lake, who was a warm up band for Wishbone Ash during their last German tour, stole the show, thus have a good start.

So it appears that at least for the time being foreign markets have to be looked at and considered, particularly when German media people callously only feature what the P.R. people and machinery is preaching to them. Either the English or American hit parade is being imitated, or only when a German disc successfully sells in a foreign country, people wake up. It only seldom happens that rock "Made in Germany" gets the kind of attention and stature it deserves compared to the Anglo American products. This is but a short summation of the kind of situation the groups in Germany have to work under. Since there are at least 25 bands who for various reasons have had a prolific impact, here is a brief overview.

Amon Düül: Something of an institution on the rock scene, their 11th album due soon. Concerts by A.D. can be the best or the worst as far as German rock is concerned, it depends on the stability and condition of the band.

Atlantis: A boogie and soul band with the best German female singer around. After a recent U.S. tour they split up. Their epitaph is a pile of good albums. Inga Rumpf has gone commercial, the rest of the band jams around the countryside.

Birth Control: Working with English producer David Hitchcock has given the oldest German hard rock band new energy. Also the new rhythm section (from Message) has given B.C. wider powers. Their latest album mixed in 3-D Sound at Delta Acoustic Studios in Hamburg should help create international interest.

Broeselmaschine: Have recorded a fantastic new folk-rock album. Peter Bursch, editor of the successful "Guitar Book," and Willi Kissmer have gotten together with new people and continued what they started on R.U. Kaiser's Pilz label back in '72. Englishman Cedric Beatty, sound engineer at Delta Acustic Studio has paired their folky, goodtime spirit with rock to make a good mixture that withstands teutonic heaviness and compares well with other bands of the genre.

Can: Like Amon Düül a band that has left its mark on the rock scene for 10 years, as hardly any other band. They regularly put out albums full of surprises. *FLOW MOTION* had a reggae feel to it, light and mesmerizing, the latest *SAW DELIGHT* once again is in the familiar rock cloak. Ex-Traffic people Rosko Gee and Reebop Kwaku Baah surely contribute to the most turned on space rock in the world.

Cluster: The most sensible electronicer on the scene have together with Brian Eno recorded in Conny Plank's studio a fruitful co-op work. *CLUSTER & ENO*, released in Germany, *ENO, MOEBIUS AND ROEDELIUS*, in England and Eno's solo LP made with help from Cluster will be marketed worldwide by Sky Records.

Klaus Doldinger: Has to regroup Passport. A long term contract with Atlantic assures continuing outstanding product from the most experienced and long lasting jazz rock veteran from Germany. Shortly one can expect to hear Doldinger and the jazz stars of Montreux on record.

Epitaph: A hard working live band have lately tried for a new recording contract. Not long ago they had an impressive T.V. appearance with Fleetwood Mac in the Rock Palace.

Embryo: An institution on the scene. Their concerts have a fascination and force that in jazz rock is only equaled by Weather Report. Working independently from the recording industry, Embryo is able to distribute and publish "alternative works" through April Records.

Grobschnitt: *ROCKPOMMELS LAND* is from the studio technique point of view become an outstanding concept album done in Conny's studio. The music seems a bit trivial on record, but during concerts it turns into a grandiose show with gags & slapstick adding an important alternative focus to the music.

Gate: Newcomer to the scene, with a high musical standard and female road crew. Successfully recorded their debut *LIVE* album for Brain and are working on a new one with Cedric Beatty in Delta Acustic studios.

Harlis: Recorded a second LP for Sky that is relaxed, yet rocking. A concept work entitled *NIGHT MEETS THE DAY*, it too was recorded at Delta Acustic.

Hoelderlin: Musically the most versatile and interesting band in Germany. *RARE BIRDS*, their fourth album was also produced by Cedric Beatty at Delta Acustic and could easily stir up international interest. Beatty has also sound engineered albums by Lou Reed and Gong. The group's last album *CLOWNS AND CLOUDS* also encountered positive resonance, as well as

1978

having successful T.V. productions in Sweden and Switzerland.

Harmonia: Formed by two Cluster people and Michael Rother from Neu!, are at this time sending no signals. During their "radio silence" other signals are developing.

Jane: Most typical and familiar exponent of Kraut Rock has with *HEAVEN AND HELL* produced interesting musical material. By the way, the first 40,000 pressings recorded by Manfred Schunke at Delta Studios sound horrible, mainly because at Metronome nobody thought it necessary to check the overplaying from master to record. Once they found out about it, the first shipment was already sold. Lou Reed liked the tape when he heard it, so much so in fact that he has hired Manfred to do all Lou Reed productions in the future, which will be recorded with the "Artificial Head" system. Lou has dubbed it the Bin-Oral System.

Karthago: Back and playing after having disbanded and several hassles with their record company. With a new lineup, Joey Albrecht (vocals and guitar) has got a new LP ready.

Kraan: Jazz-rocking eternal fire, after successful tours and 120,000 records sold, have announced their final split. Rumor has it that maybe they will get together just once more for a farewell tour. In the meantime super bassist Helmut Hattler has presented his debut solo LP *BASSBALL*.

Kraftwerk: At the forefront of techno-electro-sci-fi-rock. Nobody can stop the clever team of R. Hutter & F. Schneider-Esleben.

Udo Lindenberg: The superstar of German language rock has now put out his feelers to the English speaking market. Let's see if Udo's bag works there as well.

Lucifer's Friend: Have lost their lead singer to Uriah Heep and signed a new contract with WEA. Surely they will follow up their sales success of latter years. In contrast to the local market, they have achieved commendable turnover especially in the U.S.A. The fact that the band has never appeared live just adds to the mystery.

Message: Since Horst Stachelhaus and Manfred Bohr have left to join Birth Control, the band has turned their concept around totally. Guitarist Alan Murdock has assembled the first real funky, hard rocking Message and recorded a new album in Delta Acustic with Cedric Beatty titled *USING THE HEAD*.

Eloy: Have had continued success with *DAWN* and two well run German tours this last Spring. Their music leans to English rock standards of the '60s, heavy on keyboards. One is constantly reminded of Jethro Tull's Ian Anderson in their method of composition and vocal stylings. A new LP is due very soon.

Lake: Has to be the most built up (hyped) band in the Federal Republic. Either way, the group's first album is selling well and the band is a feature act at nearly all big festivals.

Nektar: Actually come from England, but they started their career in Germany and have had their biggest success right here, before they emigrated to the U.S.A. It seems they also have problems, founder guitarist Roye Albrighton is apparently back in England forming a new group. Their latest LP, *MAGIC IS A CHILD* is on Polydor, their new label.

Novalis: Have been much more successful lately by combining sensitive German lyrics with heavy keyboard-oriented rock music. Their live LP cut during their last tour, *KONZERTE* (interesting attendance figures between 120 and 1,200). A new studio album is due any time.

Octopus: Group from Frankfurt built around singer Jennifer Hensel, released their debut LP *BOAT OF THOUGHTS* on the Sky label. The similarity to the music of Camel distinguishes them very well from most in the German rock scene.

Ougenweide: Successfully use "middlehigh" German language and medieval instruments in conjunction with the odd folk rock excursion.

Popol Vuh: Along with T. Dream have been on the scene a long time. After a period of flirting with electronic music, Florian Fricke has in the last few years created meditative acoustic sound weavings on conventional instruments, Newest LP, *HEART OF GLASS* is a soundtrack to a movie of the same title by Werner Herzog.

Randy Pie: Continue to work on their international success. The English vocalist Peter French is surely contributing to that and Frank Diez guitar also fits well into the "powerplay." Their new album is titled *FAST FORWARD*.

Michael Rother: Has with Neu! and Harmonia made many nice records, then suddenly surprises us with a solo super sales hit *FLAMMENDE HERZEN*. Aside from that it proves that a small label (in this case Sky) can also have big sales turnover if the right product comes on the market at the right time.

Achim Reichel: Has in the course of the years really tried everything. As frontman for the Rattles he belonged to the first of rock musicians in Germany, his *DIE GRUNE REISE (THE GREEN JOURNEY)* and other electronic sound workshops have also been important steps in his career, as well as his multi-faceted work an a producer in the scene. Now Achim comes along with rocking sea shantys in German and they really cook.

Ramses: Melody conscious, full blooded musicians from the Hanover rock scene, have also created their first album *LA LEYLA* on the Sky label, produced and recorded at Conny Plank's studio (sold 20,000). Their new disc, as yet untitled, will be recorded in January. They are now looking for a producer fit to do the job.

Satin Whale: Have just released their third LP on Teldec, *AS A KEEPSAKE*. In comparison to earlier productions the group sound has become more versatile and professional, as well as better conceived.

Klaus Schulze: Very popular, especially in France. At this time he is on tour in Germany for the first time, but only in the bigger cities. His "Electronic Winter Landscape" released under the title *MIRAGE*, could very well find positive reaction worldwide. On the import list in Record World, *MIRAGE* belongs to the top sellers.

Scorpions: Also have changed their lineup and *TAKEN BY FORCE*, their latest LP is a super disc produced by Dieter Dierks. At the moment they are doing dates in the Far East.

S.F.F.: Avant-garde group, also produced by Dieter Dierks, continues where King Crimson left off. *SUNBURST* is their new (second) LP, watch out for the exciting Schicke-Fuhrs-Frohling.

Triumvirat: After their spectacular U.S. success, have except for Porky Fritz disbanded, reformed, disbanded and reformed again .... then singer/bassist Helmut Kollen died, everything had to be

1978

turned around and a new lineup put together again. Now with *POMPEII,* the new LP, comes Porky and the "New Triumvirat," surely back into the headlines. Porky has things well in hand.

Wallenstein: Classical rockers, grown out of R.U. Kaiser's Cosmic imperium and after a long silence are back with a new album *NO MORE LOVE.* Of the old group only keyboard specialist Jurgen Dollase is left.

There are a series of other groups that all make good music. For example Aera, Munju, Real Axe Band, Missus Beastly, Kollektiv and Cataract, all of whom nurture jazz rock. Then, there are Breakfast, Streetmark, Fargo and many, many others that fluctuate daily in number or consequently disband. The musicians change here and there, some go on to well known bands, others resign, still others find within the environment of the rock scene a job or even career. And that, I find, is living proof of the fact that we do have a healthy scene.

Please do not relate this to what America's rock industry creates, for example: hired musicians that can be and are totally manipulated by their employer "the record company," mainly because they have invested a lot of $ in the artist. They are given a house with studio, equipment and many other things so the musician can find good working situations. Some of the profits from tours, record sales naturally filter back to the company account. The individual musician is hardly his own master, he has only to function. Over here things are much more relaxed, i.e. more amateurish, or maybe humane. There is room for self initiative.

I believe in the case of Tangerine Dream for example, one thing becomes very apparent. The group for nearly 10 years developed their original concept and has been loyal to it. Now that success is coming to them in a big way it must be very reassuring. Because of this, proof is presented that creativity still rules over market strategy, that music comes first and then the business. And maybe this is exactly what makes foreign countries interested in Rock from Germany.

Christian Grumbkow (Hoelderlin)
Wuppertal, Germany

Inputs/Outputs
A Pragmatic Of Sound
by Richard Pinhas

1) For a vectorial analysis: the musical procedures.

To abandon the registers of opposition, not to believe too insistently in the efficacy of regulatory systems. Can one read Stravinsky with Levi-Strauss in pocket? (With each semilogical step we shall voluntarily open up to the foreign) ... And what to say of white noise? A problem of articulations, but more than that. To make the signs function, to proceed with their dispersal, their acceleration; to sustain them, necessitates an evaluation: of powers, of relations, of elevations; of series, sequences, modes, circulations. What plot can be assigned to the proportion of profound duplicities in Phil Glass?

Let us assume a level of summation, and let's admit for the moment that there exist two principal modes of sound production. (A problem of exposition, method, and place. Inputs/Outputs is a simple element, the tool of labors to come).

The first must be taken as a repetition of what has already been, a reinscription, expressed and yet not a process of expression, a recalling from memory, a special form of remembrance reinforcing the established order, confirming at its level the relations of existing power, the good forms and neutral substances. Linking repetition, codification, reconciliating or erotic. A reproductive repetition of auditory activity, of social relations and of melancholy passivity. It may act as a discursive model from which will be expressed: "my art, my music, is the mirror of the society in which I live." A music of structures, of an eternally desired formalization, in which the system of signification is submissive to the double law of unity and of regular and reproductive expansion. When it has no value as representation, the image of the world it presents to itself as prison-discourse, significant networks which in fact are nothing but the acoustic concretization of the axiomatic capitalist mode.

A music of the immutable, of the unique, of limit, Musics of the great wall, of the earth, of mass movements, and, one may say, of the salaried class.

The second mode of sound production is composed of an unlimited multitude of vectors for which any unity, of construction or synchronization, of measure or formation, has no a priori existence. Infinitive, acephalous lines. The absence of recollection by the memory can enact a new excitation of the senses -- or rather of sense itself -- since these invariably will relate to individualization, to the unified organic body. Blank lines of innovation. Extreme sequences. Each vector forms a procedure, is a protocol of singular experience (without going into details, we will return constantly to the books of Gilles Deleuze and Felix Guattari: "Rhizomes," "Kafka" (Minuit editions), to the great text on music which is "Difference et Repetition"; to "plusiers silences" (music in performance) and "Economie Libidinale" (Minuit edition) of J.F. Lyotard. For the moment the musics considered and to which each word applies are those of: Phil Glass, Zappa, Cage, Kagel, Magma, Heldon, Fred Frith, Edgar Froese, Fripp and Eno, Miles Davis, Weather Report, Pierre Henry, Boulez, Stockhausen, Ravel, Debussy and J. Hendrix) an incomparable abstract machine, but also of violences-repetitions disorganising the significant relays, discourse broken with great thrusts of rhythmic constructions (this is for example the case of Magma in which a territorial line occurs, and a sonorous theatric space finds itself affirmatively dissolved by such constructions. A great deal of bass intervention at the concert at Creteil of 9/3/76), a proliferation of mad sequences to variable degrees of deterritorialization.

Our responsibility is to perhaps find a possible line of double articulation traversing all sonic production (Fripp and Eno, Vol. 2, side 2: we sense well that his problem is not found there. Insistence of a continuum and no presence of articulations), we shall say then that this can reelevate micro-unities punctuating the process of expression.

But let us instead follow Cage:
> In these dances, in this music, in this music we do not have to 'say' anything, would we employ words. We try rather to 'do' something.

Let us enjoy ourselves: to sense the movement.

As well, it is the figure of expression which forms the sonic substance which to a certain degree of effectuation becomes a pure living, expressive matter (Deleuze-Guattari): together, rules of elaboration, overstepping of these rules, and formation of sonic axiomatic changes (Boulez, Schoenberg, Xenakis and a very great part of the said contemporary music, serial music in general) clashing of formal and rigid frames, and violent collisions of blocks and sequences (Zappa: *KING KONG*, Weather Report: *I SING THE BODY ELECTRIC*, Soft Machine *1, 2, 3 & 4)*, all this amounts to the appearance of a material becoming in that blocks of sound where real movement is produced by the matter of expression (the intensive continuum proper to sonic production) simultaneously abolishes all attempts at recodification, all possibility of subjectifying: this is what becomes the intensive overture of multiplicities or Events.

The expressed, in its immediate performance, is event, development, effect, punctual form and dissolution of this form, pure innovation, singular affirmation of a sequence or of a block of sonic matter at the highest power of transformation (transformational continuum of energy: production, intervention upon, modification and consummation of sounds) -- reputed axis of the "auditory machine," "external" vector, beyond sound -- and to great degree of figurality -- consideration holding to the expressive form itself -- :
> To attain a continuum of intensities which are worth nothing more than themselves, to find a world of pure intensities where all forms dissolve, all significations as well, signifying and signified, to the benefit of an unformed matter of unlimited flux, of signs without significance.
> (D.-G.).

But it is a matter of course that between the first and second mode all connections are possible. Mixed without compromise. All comes by transversal, and to the limit, differences are next to indiscernible. Not by amalgamation but by the necessity of microscopic work. It is not a matter to be judged or to be placed flatly on a scale of values, in a single expression are several probable evaluations: a thing amounts to its results. Not to hasten to locate and extrapolate such and such an element. An extraordinarily slow method linked to the location of objects themselves according to an investigation free from the a priori and from concrete lines of division. It will be necessary to operate at two levels: one of form itself and one of its field of accomplishment, its practical efficiency. The musical norm can be that which enters into the frame of a regulated change, extremely codified (an especially specific case of the folk song. At the level of a socio-axiomatic analysis. A music of generally ultra-reactionary use such that it is necessary to consider its effects step by step) and normalized, with mediate impulses of the organic bodies. The normalized sound sequence reinforces these impulses working toward gregarious reproduction. Let us suppose for the moment that an inexchangable sequence would be that which, in an ephemeral manner, breaks the door's bolt entirely. Folk lore would appear from that time as an overproduction of the subject, and its own identity as a prodigious act of claim. Let's say without insistence that the quasi-spectacular mode musical formation engendered to leave behind organic unity is produced as a response to the expectation of the ear-organism (German rock). Parallel to an imaginary configuration and to a narrative use of positive electronics acting not by a transgression from and a decentralization of the subject, but exactly to the contrary by dephasing the centralizing instance. Uncomposable productions engaging in subliminal audio (cf. A. Erbenzweig, "order hidden from art," NRF). The perspective of positive electronics: to become the MECHANICAL POINT OF DETERRITORIALIZATION exceeding the entire axiomatic register.

What would be the area of the inexchangable here? Silences? Neutrality? The machine that deals in risk:
> It (the piano's part) is written on 63 loose pages where, from one time to another because of procedural coincidences, there are superimposed as many simultaneous developments as in the most audaciously complex orchestral parts. At the time of execution the pianist may play them in whatever order he prefers, entirely or in part; in particular where the polyphonic layers are of such density that they exceed the capabilities of the interpreter who, without the aid complementary recording, can complete it only with his arms, feet, and mouth simultaneously.
> (John Cage, Music in Freedom, HK Metzger in J. Cage, notebook no. 2 maison de la culture de Nevers et de la Nievre, 1971-1972).

To pose the question of the means, of technology, and thus of the socius, objective mediations. But here adjacency and segments. Music of elevations if dear to the Occident, subsides in the same manner as the labyrinthic procedures of writing, simultaneously with unexpected disruptions in all domains of sound production.

Also, it may well be that at the bowels of the most simple themes intervenes a mad proliferation, beyond meaning, rupturing the strata of the work, that in the most subtle forms becomes involved in lines of recodification, leveling this to a universal measure, a well-known territory, of perfectly assimilable, fully subjective norms; that a material music of multiple connections does not attain to penetrate a gradient with enough intensity to abandon -- in its axis of reverberations on he supposed listener -- an imaginary captivation. It equally may be that the inclusion of a symbolic sound, at such and such a moment (the moment: this is important!), implies a disengagement of a

1978

revolutionary type, that as the most classical rock attempts to disengage chaotic vectors (the Doors), segments beyond system, and that the most abstract insignificant form resounds all at once in emotional spheres to fascist incidences. The minimal importance of the note: a residue, a mechanism of this more complex organization that is the tempered scale of the Occident, an incomparable factor of multiple exclusions. The scale of DO, it is the great operant which renders sad, ill music. Here again a semiology would be inadmissible and the structural analysis more than grotesque: what is more irrefutable than a sound! to take care that a rigid sign does not invert (to neither polarity nor ambivalence) and that a white noise does not make a persuasive proof. Just as movement is opposed to the concept, interference to disjunction, sign language is opposed to sense. A difference in nature, far from signifying the musical symbol (or audio intensity) is a sign of power. It ignores all representation, all mediation, it is immediate, intense presence, oscillation, pulsation, noble energy open to all modifications. Nothing is definitively known, real movement of positive musical syntheses is concretized in the material becoming of a block of sound (cf. Miles Davis). Just as metal is instilled in the formalized, a fluency can crystallize in a closed system, to level out in the sad territory of repetition, to become an organic body and music to me, to you, production of fraudulent changes of sonic pretenses. To produce protocols of experience does not essentially deal with a music composed or not, of specific Instrumentation, of legitimate use of means, but of degrees of power and explosiveness which they engender:

> Everywhere, organized music is traversed by a line of abolition, as language is sensible of a line of shift, to liberate a living, expressive matter which speaks for itself and has no more need of being formed.
> (D.-G.)

Each composition produces its own vectors of delimitation, of degrees of specific metamorphic power. Thus, if in general the succession of formed notes in melodic lines is of very secondary importance, it can, punctually, become of principal use: this is the case for Proust, Lovecraft, and Kafka. Legitimacy active in producing syntheses can place itself at several levels: with the group Magma (cf. RCA Records -- *UTOPIA* -) the creation of a specific artillery coming unexpectedly like a fissure in a representative sonic space, the intervention of rhythmic arrangements to provoke multiple abstractions of vocal lines; a very special construction of this procedure is the use of signs as parody (the music of Zappa is typically pagan, it is a parody: of gods and goddesses assisting every action so as to not discharge the subject of its responsibility or likewise redoubling, but because all these situations and deeds try for an equal intensity, cannot decline in utility and in addition cannot be reconnected by a paradoxical, arbitrary, dialectic liaison, to a law or to an absent sense. None of these doings are in want of proof as singularities are sufficient in their assertion. The divine being simply this assertion. J.F. Lyotard, *Economie Libidinale*. See as well the beautiful book of A. Dister, F. Zappa, Alban Michel), inciting a constellation of abstract forms to abandon supposedly meaningful signs (Frank Zappa) and segmentary complementarities by the aural relations of discourse/syntheses. Zappa again in the deteriorations of articulations, razzing of disjunct parts in an unlimited expansion of blocks of active information.

In the case of "Perspective I" (Heldon, "Perspective I", in *AGNETA NILSSON*,

Urus Records, 1976), there is a short simplified melodic sequence which acts as a screen, which stratifies the composition; but an initial disequilibrium issues from a heaviness of white noise, then from a differential game on the speeds of execution: a procedure of interferences between the blocks produced. From that time the simple repetition of the theme becomes a pure movement of variable differentiations. At a whole other level "Perspective I" proceeds to the inclusion of temporal sonic parameters, of a synthetic type, excluding all potential of diachronic totalization. Thus the exclusion of immediate operants of communion, of audio-simulacrums stratifying the process of musical production. In addition to the work on speeds and elevations there are sufficiently powerful abstract lines which produce effects of disorder in the "outside" of the form, this runs underneath that which intones the sonic expressive matter and induces a virtually infinite movement (one can observe it excellently in Fripp and Eno), which is similarly intensification of the power of sound.

ROXY AND ELSEWHERE, "Perspective I", abstract dances, frigid incandescences of blocks in fusion:
> Dance including suspension, as music includes silence. And the importance not being that it is 'well composed' (though it must be well composed) but that because of this exactly semiotic perfection tension occurs. Structure is merely that which "covers" the effect, in the sense that it serves as a cover for it, this is its secret and approximately its dissimilation.
> (J.F.L.)

Our problem: to construct an independent music of entirely metaphorical organization, in which the material would be for the power it activates, where time would no longer be a conquest but intense and poly-vocal scanning. A music of singular references producing here a simulation and there deriding all simulacrums. A Proper Noun Music. A music sourire miles smiles, an Aeolian music, a meteorological program, weather report.

We will see well later the mechanisms of repetitive music, but let's say already that its mode of innovation is taking part in the music process, intentionally virgin. That contrary to the repetition-liaison, or recollection of expressions, which is the theatrical rhetoric proper to our modernity, the repetition of sequences is the production of a becoming, the affirmation of multiple realities in perpetual movement. That this becomes the Incorporeal of the sound sequence where each minute variation, each proper name, each difference of gradation is like a very singular face of the sequential entity to come.

The sequential logic is not cutting up and comparing, but -- Phil Glass shows it well -- tensions, accentuations, intensifications of effectual passages, novel excitation of the senses in the act of signification itself. It is, without metaphor, the political operant, the plan of sonic-musical imminence, the effective band and the line of effectuation in the same resounding. The sequential logic is diffraction and percussion.

It is important to realize that the revolutionary sonic machine effects itself in the dimension of the +1, which is one of unlimited resonance; a multitude of lateral overtures on an exterior, where they dislocate in an identical operation the unity of the piece (formal level) and its proper identity (field of effectuation).

1978

Destratification of all azimuths. The Virtual affirmative of an audio sequence emotes this plan of imminence in which resonances come to play: a perspective of the limits, global transformations of the ensemble of connections. Since neither subject of a side, nor sequence or block of the other, a continuum of pure intensities, headlessness, punctual stases in which the phylum is realized n the living, expressive matter. Take a simple repetition, a well-formed sequence, or a series of audio diagrams, and turn them extremely fast, or just the opposite with a great slowness, modify the speeds of rotation, alter the motor of a tape recorder, the extent of elevation of an electric bass, the frequency band of a resonator filter, make use of these concentric spirals, add this +1 as if to the bosom of a multiface operator, in a ring modulator, you add a second block, another line, slightly different, you open a new dimension to obtain the sums and differences. Not a chaos, a mere chaos, but a new state, still another thing, a singular threshold attaining a space of musical incorporeality, totally occupied by zones corresponding to intensities -- effects distributed as if around variable corporealities. It is this, the incorporeal, which is the +1 of sound production, a matter expressive each time it is reinvented.

It cannot be about perceptions, functions, and contents. Just as far as you program a synthesizer, an inputs/outputs machine, one does not know whether to speak of the existence of a musician or of a "creator." Similarly, by way of example, in repetitive music, do not look for that which repeats itself but that which is eventual in the repetition. Expressions of power. Do not reduce the sequences to a comparable, do not reassemble and measure, but let it happen, feel the sonic matter, and the particular becomings which it exudes. To see, to feel in the polymorphous connections, that in the precipitation of the series it is of a percussion, a collision, a power of upheaval with which it acts.

This is then a procedure, an experimental remembrance, which leads to this virtually infinite movement that is the musical incorporeal with the ability to be expressed in the demonic power of repetition: the selective test:
> to make of movement
> itself a work
> (Gilles Deleuze).

Legitimacy of repetitive use: to play diffractions and percussion, a real method of "active disassemblage," traced by the field of the imminence of evolutions, frequences-effects, as it is the acceleration of intensities-events, operations of a virtual type in the sense in which the effect cannot find temporal adequacy with what is heard. No correspondence of moments by these subsists any longer, but opening, insistence, joyous laughing disorganizing the diachronic vocation of the system of perception-conscience. No recurrence of a subject too slightly commonplace, but all just a residue, an ear's fragment, a potentiometer finger, an electronic eye, an anological memory. To listen to Bob Dylan, to construct his rhizospheres. To steadily finish: all valves opened is the word of the order to advance and render to music at last its great health.

Richard Pinhas
Paris, France

"Four Musicians Jailed In Prague"

That headline appeared in the U.S. magazine *Rolling Stone* in November '76 and it can be said that it was one of the few articles concerning the Czech underground which has been published in the "Western" press. This wouldn't be so specific on the whole, but it is very peculiar that the press takes notice of the rock scene in Czechoslovakia after many years and its notice is limited to three bands, only. Even this fact could be explained, but there is the reality that the majority of the press doesn't mention the real reasons for arresting those musicians or they try to present facts about the case and they have never even heard the bands play.

The history of the Prague underground started in 1967. Musical and literary undergrounds had begun to start up in the Anglo-American scene and then as the influence of them spread, there arose small parallel branches, even in Czech. One of the first underground bands was The Primitives Group. Their music was formed from the repertoire of The Mothers of Invention, Doors, Fugs, Jimi Hendrix and others. To tell the truth The Primitives Group hadn't their own sound and instead turned their attention to occupying the listeners with visuals. A red sun on an emerald background, bronze masks, surreal scenery, colorful fires, luminous phosphorescent dresses, horrific faces, water balloons, birds and other effects were characteristic of their concerts. They tried to represent the world surrounding us with frankness. In those days their concerts employed various sound effects also, like thunder storms, explosions, natural sounds, etc. All of the theatric aspects of their performances were done by an organization called "Eugen Fiala Psychedelic Sound." Eugen Fiala, among others was manager of the band and he tried to incorporate into the show a celebration of nature -- water, wind, fire and other forces, he was successful in doing that. No wonder the interest of the listeners was great. For example, their Bird Feast celebrating air, which made use of a few quintals of feathers around the concert hall making it look like a birds nest, created a fantastic happening. Not to mention the other remarkable aspects like a 'feathered girl' in a showcase, large ethylene balloons and live birds. It appeared that the band carried their experiments to the extreme at that point. Eugen Fiala always set off one dove into the air, he did it with a distinct intent. The dove disoriented by the loud sound and wild effects combined with projected films and slides, ran into the ceiling, walls, listeners until it lost control of itself and died from psychic and physical exhaustion. That was Fiala's design, to show that all people were born to death and it is only a question of time as someone else is in control. All attempts at changing that decision would be futile, as in the case of the dove. In those days it appeared that similar experiments could become a special art form under certain circumstances, not however the satisfying of sadistic passion and disgust. Although The Primitives Group's performances were very interesting at that time, the music of the band had very little relation to the overall concept of the program in most cases. The Primitives Group broke up in early 1969 and the individual members became members of other bands. Together with the demise of the band came the end of the Eugen Fiala Psychedelic Sound.

At the same time as The Primitives Group broke up, another band called Plastic People of the Universe was preparing for their first performances. They had a big build up and were hoping to continue the spirit of the Primitives Group.

The first official performance of the Plastic People took place on May 6, 1969 at a rock festival in Prague. It was a horror. The demonic dress, made-up faces and shocking fires weren't missing, but the music disappeared somehow. Except for works by the Velvet Underground and Jefferson Airplane, Plastic People had original compositions which were not very good, especially in regards to the lyrics. In spite of unfavorable criticism by the music press and disappointment of their fans, the leader of the band -- Ivan Jirous -- looked at the future through rose-colored glasses. He wanted to do an extensive tour. In the meantime the band played in clubs in Prague, one of the most significant of which took place in July '69, at the same time the American astronauts touched down on the moon. The interest of the band and concept of their program concerned the solar system and the planets, but in comparison with the concerts of The Primitives Group, the Plastic People lacked an organization like Eugen Fiala's. With regard to their almost stupid lyrics the band became more the center of different jokes than the object of attention they hoped for. They tried to gain recognition with gimmicks and scandal. For example, they brought 150 Kilos of rotten tomatoes to their performance in the Music F Club in Prague on Oct. 10, 1969. When they were asked what they were going to do with all the tomatoes, they said they planned to throw them at the audience. When the owners of the club took objection to that, the Plastic People replied, "You don't understand psychology!," and then left without performing. In 1970, the band built up its own repertoire which wasn't very good because new musicians had come into the band of an inferior level for the most part. Also vandalism, contempt and disgust permeated their lyrics. For those reasons the performances of the band were forbidden in 1971 and their license was canceled a year later. As a result of that some of the members moved into a castle about 80 kilometers outside of Prague, there they continued their activities. In those days some of the musicians formed a musical commune, part of them lived in the castle and the rest along with about 200 faithful fans stayed in Prague. During four years up to their arrest they played around 20 concerts which were kept quiet until the last minute because the band didn't have a license. They arranged permission for them by means of an old license or under the aegis of weddings. When they rented a hall for a wedding, in place of a reception, a concert would take place. Tickets were rare and only sold at the door or in a few pubs.

In 1973 two other underground bands had their first concerts. They too belonged to the musical commune of the Plastic People. The first was called Midsummer Nights Dream, the other DG-307 (an abbreviation of the word diagnosis, and the number 307 symbolizes "intermittent stressed state of mind").Their name didn't come about by mere chance because a majority of the members had been treated by psychiatrists in clinics. All three bands tried to be representatives of the so-called "other culture." The chief ideologist of the underground -- Ivan Jirous -- created a name for their society, "the sacred ghetto" in his talk titled "The News About The Third Czech Musical Revival." He told his admirers that their duty was to join actively in the destruction of the establishment and that they had to produce a culture independent of official channels and consumer society. Since all performances of these bands now consisted mainly of beating on percussive instruments and other musicians thrashing around on their instruments, it wasn't really music, but shouts accompanied by purposeful disharmonic tones. More a display by psychopaths of despair or a show of attitude towards life of spurned and perplexed people who didn't know what they wanted. They showed a contempt for everything and hated all. The development of Plastic People of the Universe, Midsummer Nights Dream and DG-307 continued until March '76 when 18 people from the commune were arrested and tried for breaking Article 202 of Czech criminal law.

Vulgar expressions which displease the public and are made for moral disturbance or if it is proclaimed by some organization and when the majority of people are presented (as it was in the mentioned case) it can be considered a civil disturbance. These 18 people were not charged for their "music," appearance or political beliefs as many would suppose. They were sued for their vulgar, perverse lyrics; 14 people were dismissed on remand because they were considered mentally deficient, they had been found to be disturbed in the past and childhood. They had attempts at suicide and had been treated in asylums. On Sept. 21 - 23 only four musicians came to trial in Prague. Ivan Jirous was imprisoned for 18 months, Pavel Zajicek for 12 months, Vratislav Brabenec together with Svatopluk Karasek got 8 months.

At the time these musicians were arrested in the foreign press there appeared stories proclaiming these bands to be brilliant representatives of the Czech rock scene. It stands to reason that people who wrote these stories hadn't the possibility to actually the see the bands in action and hear their music and lyrics so they couldn't write objectively about what had happened. To shed a little light on their music, here are translations of a few of their lyrics which *Rolling Stone* magazine glorified.

Instruction

...Throw away your brains
Throw away your hearts
Throw away everything
What makes men from you
Be changed into swine
Be changed into swine...

At Once And It Is Better Twice

I love Hiroshima and Nagasaki
There was a light and heat at that moment
I am so sorry
That I couldn't peg out for A-bomb's disease...

Better Marijhuana Than Mary

...We'll get high with drugs all night
Then we'll go to bed with ourselves
Perhaps it is better with you
Than only loving.
Our dreams will fly away to the heavens
It will be changed into rosy steams
Our love on the earth
Has only black lines.
Get a kilo of marijhuana for me
My dreams will love you
My love will overcome all blows
For the kilo of marijhuana...

Revolution

...Brothers and sisters be free

1978

Be free in love and sex
Give your soul to the fiend
Don't be afraid of LSD
Brothers and sisters drink
and rejoice
Be free
Live intensly, make loving
enough
Love yourselves
everywhere
At home and in the street
By day and by night
Have sex
Be free...

Small Private
Concentration Camp

... When I buy a
concentration camp
I'll choose the victims for
it
Then I'll manhandle all the
swine
Who are cursed for the
death of me
All swine
Should have rigorour rules
on me
I will wear them out
I don't like freedom very
much...

Self Portrait
... We -- insane apostles
We'll redeem the world
We -- perverted Hitlers
We'll mount flowers
We -- insane apostles
We'll break down the walls

We -- dreaming vandals
We'll command "fly'

We -- drunkards and
necromaniacs
We'll send the world
turning
We -- insane apostles
We are going to tell "now"
today
We -- stupid morons
We'll crucify the world
We -- insane apostles
The next world is ours
We -- insane apostles
We are the Messiah...

Does the author of the article in *Rolling Stone* consider these lyrics to contain elements of 16th century mysticism of the Renaissance? I should like to add that in spite of the fact that rock in Czechoslovakia isn't in favor with some in so-called "official places" and a great majority of people still have a mistrust of rock musicians and their fans, everyone should ask themselves the question, what is art, and what isn't -- where intelligence ends and idiocy begins. Such is the case of the Plastic People of the Universe, Midsummer Nights Dream and DG-307.

In April 1977, at the Prague rock festival a new underground band called Stehlik gave their first concert. They have unique music and lyrics, different from the other bands. It is unmistakable that they have followed the example of the Prague underground which was founded in 1967.

Milan Hlubucek
Hodkovice, Czechoslovakia

Perigeo

Perigeo formed on the initiative of Giovanni Tommaso. The members were: Giovanni (acoustic and electric bass, synthi), Franco D'Andrea (keyboards), Claudio Fasoli (contralto and soprano sax), Bruno Biriaco (drums and percussions) and Tony Sidney (electric guitar), all musicians with a international jazz experience. They have proven themselves to be the best Italian rock-jazz group and have played in many important concerts at the side of big bands like Weather Report.

The LPs recorded by the group were: *AZIMUT* (1972), *ABBIAMO TUTTI UN BLUES DA PIANGERE* (1973), *GENEALOGIA* (1974), *LA VALLE DEI TEMPLI* (1975) and *NON E COSI LONTANO (IT'S NOT SO FAR AWAY)* (1976), recorded in Canada.

"Music" -- said Giovanni Tommaso -- "is not only a way to cause sound, but is also a way to feel, to live." After five years of intense activity, concerts and tours, Perigeo has broken up. The news has astonished the whole Italian musical ambient; some people don't want to believe it. Our best rock-jazz group, perhaps the only one able to represent Italian jazz in foreign countries, has finished prematurely due to problems which torment groups in our country. During the last two seasons violence and incidents were more and more bloody. Perigeo, who in these last two years had very intense activity, has suffered more than other bands the consequence of the disastrous situation. The last winter tour was a ruin, and in the spring and summer they played a few gigs then decided to break up the group.

In one of the last interviews, Giovanni Tommaso said, "Five years are long for everyone, but not for us: the last concerts have been the best ones: there was between us a good understanding. For now we have broken up, then in the future, I don't know." Bruno Biriaco: "We were making less than our roadies: RCA has not assisted us properly at the necessary moment when people didn't want to pay at concerts."

We have to say also that the five musicians have tried the way of the foreign countries. Giovanni Tommaso was twice in the U.S., before and after the recording of *NON E COSI LONTANO*, but it's very difficult to achieve success in a country where conformity is more strong than in other parts of the world.

No one knows now what will be the future for the five musicians: Giovanni is working alone, Bruno Biriaco is writing a suite for five saxophones and drums, Franco D'Andrea is playing in sessions and recording in studios in Milan, Claudio Fasoli, after the release of a new record is working near a pharmaceutical firm and Tony Sidney has gone back to Florence, where he lives, without a decision as to his future.

This current situation of the band is sad. All music fans hope that the problems which caused the breakup will be resolved soon so we'll again be able to hear the sound of the best rock-jazz group in Italy.

Pino Casale
Rome, Italy

Omega

When it comes to rock from the Eastern European countries, the groups from Hungary have had the most exposure here in the U.S. Two albums have been issued on domestic labels by Hungarian groups -- Omega on Passport and Locomotiv GT on ABC. The Locomotiv GT band even got to tour the states on the cultural exchange program, but unfortunately one of the lads became so enamored of one of the local groupies, he defected. So Omega's chances it seems were botched in a fit of passion. Both LPs died a death and Hungarian rock sunk without a trace from the domestic scene with only a few imports to fill the void.

The bands did not die however, especially in the case of Omega. As with many other European bands, Omega adapt Western rock roots to their own particular style. In their case it was a heavy progressive sound with an affinity for Deep Purple and Uriah Heep. Their U.S. album, due to a lousy mix, unfortunately came off sounding limp and homogenized. Critical reaction was sour and the defection coupled with record company limitations did them in over here.

I've gotten a bit ahead here, so let's get back to the beginning. Omega, formed in 1963, was for all intents and purposes the first rock band in Hungary. Their debut album was recorded and released in 1969 and titled *FREDDIE THE BUGLER AND THE TERRIBLE PEOPLE*, also at this time they went by the name Omega Red Star. Musically *FREDDIE* was inconsequential being basically pop rock. Its main significance lay in the fact that it was the first rock record put out by a native Hungarian group.

The next album, entitled *10,000 STEPS*, was a vast improvement as they had become vastly more adept writing good rock songs with strong hooks. It was with their 3rd LP, *ON THE HIGHWAY AT NIGHT*, that they came into their own as a progressive rock band. It sported a strange black and gold cover adorned by a Bosch-like pig's-bladder ballooned airship traversing the midnight sky. The music was similarly colorful as the songs were filled with lots of instrumental activity occurring within a relatively short time span and packed with juicy riffs and keyboard fills.

Up to this point most of the material had been written by Gabor Pressor and Anna Adamis. Apparently they then decided that Omega was going in a direction they didn't want to pursue. So along with drummer Josef Laux they split off and formed Locomotiv GT who have to date done 6 group LPs in their home country. In addition they've backed up top Hungarian songstress Kati Kovacs on 2 albums, recorded a concept LP titled *AN IMAGINARY AMERICAN POP FESTIVAL* and also done another album in England with Jack Bruce and other assorted heavies (this was the one released in the U.S.).

This would appear to have been a set back for Omega, losing their chief songwriter, but in fact it had just the opposite effect. They came back with their strongest album yet, a live recording *LIVING OMEGA*. An impressive album it was in many ways. Firstly, the cover was made out of sheet metal. Stenciled on it in red or blue paint was a graphic of the group and the title Omega *ELO*. Inside was an insert with group photo and credits. The music was powerful and recording quality very good as the group ran through extended versions of some of their best material.

Keyboards and guitar dominated the arrangements and gave it an overall metallic sound that ranks with the best progressive bands.

ELO was followed by *OMEGA 5* which launched them on their way to achieving a synthesis of Eastern European atmosphere with Western European style. A more keyboard-oriented style was established with vocal harmonies and guitar breaks rounding out the sound. The overall effect was comparable to Uriah Heep, but the unmistakable flavor of Eastern European heaviness gave it a more distinct feeling.

Their next *OMEGA 6 I DON'T KNOW YOUR NAME* consolidated the strengths of previous albums and next to ELO was their overall best album to that point. The melodies are good and arrangements highly varied so as to give each song a variety of textures.

Their latest album is *IDORABLO, OMEGA 7 (TIMEROBBER)*. With it they have overcome the restrictions of progressive keyboard rock that has stifled Heep and some others. With a continuing stronger emphasis on keyboards, electronics have now emerged as a dominant focal point. Their recording capabilities have also been more fully utilized. Vocals are altered and arrangements mutated as electronics set the tempo. The synthi work is tasteful and plugged into the songs in just the right places. Strange harmonies are created by voice echo and instrumental interplay between guitar and keyboards. This album is definitely their most accomplished to date. An extra bonus is the insert which shows the group sporting Victorian dresses, cloaks and knee boots. In rich color tones it clearly paints the picture their music conveys.

In addition to their Hungarian LPs they have had 7 albums released in Germany. They include 2 anthology collections and 5 LPs of material from their native recordings redone with different arrangements and English vocals. The sound is cleaner and the overall feel changed so that they come off more polished. In some cases, for instance their 1st and *200 YEARS AFTER THE LAST WAR*, it works to their disadvantage, as the songs lose their rough edges which gave them their spark. In others like *OMEGA*

III and *HALL OF FLOATERS IN THE SKY*, it's a plus as the songs become streamlined and stronger due to the higher recording quality and sophistication.

They are currently doing a tour of Germany. Hopefully a new LP will be forthcoming, as their latest release *ON TOUR* was nothing more than a collection of previously issued material.

Archie Patterson

Rock In Opposition

Record companies put out an endless belch of commercial drivel. They are interested solely in cash, and show enthusiasm only when they can trick 'the punters' into parting with their wages for a lot of meaningless insults.

To control the market means to control 'taste' and this is not so difficult. It's done through advertising; getting their product into the air, onto the telly, the music press, supermarkets, airports, etc. ad NAUSEUM, and by stifling anything they don't own. When they do something good it invariably goes bad -- then it sells even better.

There are musicians who work, not for their careers but because they are actually interested in music. They do concerts, not to push their albums, but because they actually give a damn about what goes into peoples' ears.

Rock In Opposition is made up of a few such groups; each is from a different country, each independent of the music industry, and each with a radical and uncompromising approach to music. This is the only way any of these groups will come to Britain and the only chance British audiences will have to find out what is going on in Europe -- or indeed what progress is being made in Rock music -- which amounts to the same thing.

Each of these groups has one thing in common: they don't care about the kind of popularity that comes with brain-washing, they do care about being capable of communicating with people, that is not being deliberately obscure. They are well known and respected in their countries by that sector of the public which is concerned to find out whether there is anything other than that tray of commodities rammed down their throats by the music industry. They are all in the forefront of European music and their work is important.

Univers Zero

Univers Zero: Belgium ... Belgium is even worse than Britain. In order to survive in that boorish morass of mediocrity they have to be serious. Only the most dedicated survive. They owe a little to Magma and a lot to 20th Century music. Their sound is unique and intense. They use drums, bass, violins, cello, bassoon, guitar and keyboards to create a music unclassifiable into any rock idiom. (1 LP)

Stormy Six

Stormy Six: Italy ... There are seven of them and they've been together for nine years. They were once almost a pop group and once almost a folk group but not anymore, though they use a lot of folk melodies still and an intermediate instrumentation including three violins, mandolin and acoustic guitar. They also use bass, drums, electric guitars and three saxes, xylophone, flute and all sing. Their music is less avant-garde than Area and less boring. They are uncompromising and politically responsible. (5 LPs)

Samla Mammas Manna

Samla Mammas Manna: Sweden ... Sweden has a highly developed non-commercial music scene and it has the biggest alternative distribution network in Europe. In our opinion the Samlas are the most progressive and interesting group in that country. Their instrumentation is that of a conventional rock group -- bass, drums, guitars, organ. Their music is complex and very melodic. They are in the clearest tradition of Rock music, only they have advanced beyond the limits imposed by the industry. (5 LPs)

Etron Fou Leloublan

Etron Fou Leloublan: France ... Their name means Mad Shit which says a lot about how they approach music. Their songs are bizarre. Their only close connection is with Captain Beefheart and like the Magic Band their music is unpredictable and intelligent, played with fantastic energy. They've been in Britain once before and were very well received. All that they do is their own and extraordinary. (2 LPs)

Henry Cow

Henry Cow: England ... By now Henry Cow's reputation is pretty well established. They are the only politically and musically progressive group in Britain who have managed to surface and survive (for nine years now). They consider themselves international and work for the most part abroad. They only person who has covered the same kind of ground as they have is Frank Zappa and he was finished long ago. Henry Cow are still at it. Bass, drums, guitar, violin, viola, organ, xylophone, saxes, clarinet, flute, bassoon, oboe, cello, piano and singing. (5 LPs)

The goal of Rock In Opposition is to form a music network MUSICNET, to open independent, alternative channels for concerts and record distribution on an international basis. The project was kicked off by The Festival Of Progressive Rock Music held at the New London Theatre on Sunday, March 12, 1978 featuring the five bands. In addition a month long series of dates was coordinated with the Festival.

This series of alternative rock music concerts is meant to stimulate interest to make possible the beginnings of an alternative circuit in Britain, so that alternative rock music can been seen and heard and have the same subversive role that it has in the rest of Europe.

This is a first action in the old battle which progressive music of all kinds has always had with the concert and record industries. These industries have operated internationally for many years and so it is long overdue that musicians and fans should organize likewise. The major record companies only put the full weight of their promotion behind commercial music. It's simply a matter of business and money; cultural exchange means nothing to them. They want to sell their stuff.

Even if R.I.O. folds up tomorrow, the inevitability of international cooperation and solidarity is a certainty in the modern world. Facts force us to unite in order to survive, but more than that we are conscious that there is work to do. We recognise that Rock music is a legitimate and powerful medium and one in which criticism and hope can be carried. "Now is the time we are in love with." You are a part of this reality whichever side you are on..if you do not take a side the battle will be fought anyway. This is only a thread of a life and death struggle which wracks the world now -- itself will change nothing, but the battle must be fought on all fronts however small -- everything must be called into question examined, experimented with, changed -- even the concepts of "enjoyment" and "entertainment."

**Rock In Opposition
5 Silverthorne Road
London SW8. England**

A Collection Of Isolated Observations On Henry Cow

The following is a series of notes, taken at random, concerning a most enthralling rock band known as Henry Cow. These isolated bits of information have been placed in semi-chronological order after-the-fact.

A bit of early history... In May 1968, Henry Cow was formed by Tim Hodgkinson and Fred Frith. The band's first major performances occurred at the Glastonbury Fayre Festival in '71. That same year, drummer Chris Cutler and Egg keyboardist Dave Stewart formed the Ottawa Music Co., a 20-piece rock composers orchestra, in which Henry Cow participated the following year. In '72, Henry Cow wrote and performed music for Euripides' play "The Bacchae," as well as organizing a series of concerts and events called "Cabaret Voltaire."

LEG END. Chris Cutler: drums, toys, piano, whistle, voice. "Teenbeat." This

Henry Cow/Frith/Greaves composition is literally propelled by Cutler's drumming, possibly the most engaging aspect of their first LP. Cutler joined the band in '72 and has remained an ever-astonishing component of their music. His style possesses a remarkable degree of restraint and complexity ...constant motion/ movement -- an undercurrent of endless possibilities, twists, abrupt changes, establishing flow. Difficult, at best, to focus on anything else. Geoff Leigh's tenor solo is the essence of the LP's opener, the Frith composition "Nirvana For Mice." Also joining the band in '72, Leigh was one half of Cow's immediate presence, the woodwinds. He shared wind duties with Hodgkinson up through the recording of music for the *GREASY TRUCKERS LIVE* album in '73. Upon leaving, Leigh went on to form three ensembles: Radar Favorites, Rag Doll and his latest Red Balune.

1973 was an eventful year for Henry Cow. In addition to touring Britain with the legendary German dadaists Faust, they wrote and performed music for "The Tempest." Also that year, the band contributed to a performance of *TUBULAR BELLS* at London's Queen Elizabeth Hall ...Henry Cowell (1897-1965) was an amazing fellow, actually. Few composers would have found it necessary to conquer the limitations of the forearm. It just so happened, I'm sure, that broken yardstick worked quite nicely.

UNREST. Lindsay Cooper: bassoon, oboe, recorder, voice. "Deluge" ...the world is actually built upon chaos; the universal tendency towards maximum entropy. Society is chaos under restraint, deluged with human nature. Emotion and beauty among chaos. This is the deluge. This is Henry Cow. In retrospect, never have I been so moved by a musical composition. Beauty, emptiness, desperation. I am free, yet I am pervaded with unrest..."Don't disturb me, while I'm dreaming..." (the rest unintelligible) -- "Deluge," from *UNREST*. "Upon Entering The Hotel Adlon" ...Lindsay Cooper had replaced Geoff Leigh by the time *UNREST* was recorded; and good fortune it was, as she can scream just about as well as Dagmar can. It occurred to me that Mr. Ivor Cutler probably felt like doing the same thing, upon encountering canned Muzak in a hotel awhile back (assuming the rumour is true). Cooper's restraint throughout *UNREST* is most gratifying. Her and Hodgkinson's winds are the most immediately conspicuous aspect of Cow's music; a flowing, solemn sense of solitude perpetually interacting with Cutler's spontaneity. Lindsay Cooper, Tim Hodgkinson, Geoff Leigh, Jeremy Baines, the late Mongezi Feza: the aura of Henry Cow. *UNREST* was produced in '74 and dedicated to Robert Wyatt and Uli Trepte (see EUROCK #09). Later that year they toured Europe with Beefheart.

GUITAR SOLOS. Fred Frith: guitar, prepared guitar, fuzz-box. Henry Cow's guitarist Fred Frith recorded this album of solo improvisations for Caroline, following the '74 tour with Capt. Beefheart. *GUITAR SOLOS* includes eight pieces which exemplify Frith's exploratory tendencies. Here, the listener is allowed to focus on Frith's ideas outside of their interplay within the group compositions. His latest solo recordings can be found on *GUITAR SOLOS 2*, as well as the *RANDOM RADAR SAMPLER*. A year or so ago, a member of the *Melody Maker* staff (whose name escapes me) repeatedly accused Frith of being a Derek Bailey copyist. Although Bailey is certainly a major influence, it is doubtful whether innovation at this level, especially as evidenced by these albums, can accurately described as copying. The possibility of total originality is nonexistent, regardless of the endeavor. Progress arises through communication of ideas. *Melody Maker's* critic obviously did not recognize this.

DESPERATE STRAITS. Dagmar Krause: voice. "Apes In Capes." An above average, socially acceptable, Julie Andrews voice wouldn't have done the trick.... "Harken child of life beguiled, it's said that some come unsung, sorry, no song for some, sing-songs ham strung. Seasoned with lies, hard-boiled but still calling all the tunes he's donned his garb, the costume of a buffoon -- we rise to applaud his disguise." -- Anthony Moore. Many a person of questionable repute has sunken to a high place, on the strength of voice. Avoiding this, Henry Cow found their messenger in Dagmar. Sharp, sinister and bleak, she laid waste to any notions of retreat from the reality of our deteriorating condition. I have not heard a more compelling voice among the musicians of Europe. Such is the artistic power of the musician who refuses to let themselves be manipulated by those who would control. *DESPERATE STRAITS* ('74) was the first collaboration between Henry Cow and the group Slapp Happy, although Chris played drums on Slapp Happy's first single for Virgin, "Casablanca Moon" (never released): and Geoff Leigh and Jeremy Baines contributed to Slapp Happy's second LP. In addition to Slapp Happy's Dagmar, those musicians participating in *DESPERATE STRAITS* were Peter Blegvad and Anthony Moore, both also of Slapp Happy, and John Greaves, Cutler, Hodgkinson and Frith, all of Henry Cow, along with the memorable trumpet of Mongezi Feza, Geoff Leigh, Lindsay Cooper and others. Henry Cow and Slapp Happy officially merged following the recording of the album.

IN PRAISE OF LEARNING. Tim Hodgkinson: organ, clarinet, piano. "Living In The Heart Of The Beast." Hodgkinson has penned almost a compendium statement for Henry Cow. In the space of one composition, he summarizes their musical and political tendencies. Verbally "Beast" expresses their struggle more completely than any previous composition, while at the same time presenting all aspects of their instrumental approach. In "Beast," as well as the Frith/Cutler composition "Beautiful As The Moon --Terrible As An Army With Banners," one discovers a greater tendency toward regular rock-based rhythms -- pounding, marching foreboding revolution. "We are born to serve you all our bloody lives, labouring tongues we give rise to soft lies: disguised metaphors that keep us in a vast inverted stillness twice edged with fear." --Tim Hodgkinson. *IN PRAISE OF LEARNING* ('75) was the second and final collaboration between Slapp Happy and the Cow. Following recording, the two bands unmerged and Slapp Happy dissolved. Dagmar remained with Henry Cow, Peter Blegvad left for N.Y. and Anthony Moore recorded his third solo album, entitled *OUT*, to date unreleased, before going to Germany. The most important aspect of this split was the retention of Dagmar, an invaluable asset, as the live record would prove.

CONCERTS. With Robert Wyatt: voice. London, May 21, 1975. "Bad Alchemy"/"Little Red Riding Hood Hits The Road." Robert Wyatt and Dagmar... together. All emotion of course included, this opening half of Side 2 serves to re-emphasize what a strangely saddening, yet beautiful, composition Wyatt's "Riding Hood" really is. Performance over, it came to me: the blow was being dealt. The music industry's suppression of new radically different concepts of expression is being effectively challenged. Indeed "Art is not a mirror, it is a hammer." -- John Grierson. The paths of Europe's most innovative rock entities are likely to intersect eventually. In the case of Wyatt and Henry Cow, collaborations began in '74 with Robert's return to music following his tragic accident. His second solo recording *ROCK BOTTOM* incorporated Frith on viola and the follow-up *RUTH IS STRANGER THAN RICHARD*, included John Greaves as well. The live double album includes performances in London, Italy, Norway and Holland. Also in late '75, Henry Cow embarked on a tour of Europe that led to them eventually joining forces with Mike Westbrook. After a performance in Bordeaux, they were joined by the Westbrook Brass Band playing a New Orleans funeral march. This association later led to the formation of "The Orkestra."

KEW RHONE. John Greaves: piano organ, bass, vocals, percussion, music. John Greaves, Henry Cow's exceptional bass player and composer, left the band in '76, to be replaced by bassist/cellist Georgie Born. Greaves quickly made his way to New York and recorded the *KEW RHONE* LP with Peter Blegvad. The sessions feature vocalist Lisa Herman, as well as Watt luminaries Carla Bley and Michael Mantler. Not surprisingly, the whole thing was recorded at Grog Kill Studio, origin of the brilliant *13-3/4* and *HAPLESS CHILD* LPs. Instrumentally, Greaves constructed a complex outgrowth of *IN PRAISE OF LEARNING*'s diversity. Overall less bleak than *PRAISE*, *KEW RHONE* owes much to Peter Blegvad's curious isolation of thought segments and linguistic manipulations. This veteran of Faust and Slapp Happy has proven to be one of rock music's greatest dadaists, whether he will admit it or not.

1977 saw extensive touring for Henry Cow, taking in Italy, France and Scandinavia. Also that year, the Occasional Orchestra was conceived, involving Henry Cow, the Mike Westbrook Brass Band and folk singer Frankie Armstrong. Their first public appearance took place in London at the Second Moving Left Review. The group went on to play in France, Italy and Sweden as "The Orkestra." The evolution of The Orkestra began as early as in 1973, when Henry Cow were joined at the Rainbow by Mike Westbrook, Phil Minton, and Lol Coxhill, as well as numerous other musicians. A year later, Fred Frith worked with Minton (a member of Westbrook's band) in Coxhill's Welfare State. Further "collaboration" took place at the end of Henry Cow's concert at the '75 Sigma Festival in Bordeaux. Westbrook's band, who had performed in a different part of the same building, marched in playing a New Orleans funeral march, while Henry Cow danced. Dagmar later worked with Minton in Maggie Nicholls' voice workshops. In 1977, the Occasional Orchestra was born, shortened to "The Orkestra."

I can't conclude without stating that Henry Cow have made more progress than any other rock entity against the abhorrent systematic stifling of radically new concepts which pervades the present music industry. Despite my tendencies otherwise comments on the abilities of the musicians in Henry Cow are probably best left unsaid. Such judgments are private ones, involving aesthetics and politics hand-in-hand. The existence of Henry Cow is a grim reminder that the two are inseparable in any society that attempts to manipulate and ultimately restrain the creative advancement of its art.

Bill Sharp

Henry Cow #2
Press Release

(1) Henry Cow, in their 10th year, are playing farewell concerts from now until August, starting in Scandinavia, then

1978

Spain, France, Belgium, Holland, Switzerland, Germany, Italy. Finally we shall visit Cuba in August for the Annual World Youth Festival.

(2) Henry Cow have 2 or 3 albums of live music and at least 1 studio album planned for release on our own label, and we are planning a giant 10th anniversary celebration concert in December with everybody we have ever known.

(3) In our 10th year we are ceasing to operate as a permanent group, although the musicians inside the group are certain to work variously together in the future. Our own relations are still those of admiration and respect -- it is only the group as a corporate and separate entity which can progress no further.

(4) While we are touring, we hope to be able to explain why we have made these decisions as well as simply returning to play for and thank everybody who has been so kind to us over the years. Although the group as a commodity, as a name, ceases to exist, the WORK of the group will go on -- the group is disbanding IN ORDER THAT this work, what we have stood for, can continue. The medium between us and our audience has become heavy and ossified, the work now is better pursued in several ways simultaneously and not under the umbrella of 'Henry Cow': the group is no longer strong enough to carry this weight and we in turn can no longer, collectively or individually, carry the group -- our carapace has turned from strength to weakness -- now we have to force ourselves not to hide behind it.

(5) Henry Cow's corporate involvement with Frankie Armstrong, Dagmar Krause and the Mike Westbrook Brass Band, as the Orkestra, will continue and we hope grow.

(6) We will not settle into the role of being 'Henry Cow' and reproducing our past to earn our pensions.

We would like to say 5 things:

(1) The music industry can create nothing -- it can only exploit the real abilities of its victims.
(2) The music industry wants to keep its hosts' desires at the lowest level possible because formulas are easy to reproduce while musicians with integrity can be difficult to control.
(3) The music industry makes all its decisions on the basis of profit and prestige... They have ears only for the rustling of money, hearts which only pump with the blood of the murdered.
(4) Kafka wrote only what is true. "Paranoia is simply a recognition of human values under capitalism." The point is to change it.
(5) Independence is only a valid first step if revolution is the second.

Henry Cow

Nova Interview

The following interview, conducted by Bill Sharp, is with three key participants in the evolution of rock music in Italy. Saxophonist Elio D'Anna was a founding member of Osanna, in addition to being co-organizer of the first rock festival in Naples. He was also a member of the group Uno. Also formerly of Uno, guitarist Corrado Rustici is best known for his work with the band

Cervello. From Genoa, Renato Rosset played keyboards for the New Trolls, as well as several other experimental outfits. The three are now working together in Nova, whose third album *WINGS OF LOVE* is recently released on Arista records. Joining them in Nova are Ric Parnell (drums and percussion) and Barry Johnson (bass and vocals).

EUROCK: Elio, were you an original member of Osanna?

Elio: Yes, at the time I joined the band called Citta Frontale and we changed the name to Osanna. The other four musicians had been together under that name for quite a long time.

EUROCK: I believe they issued an album.

Corrado: Yes. After Osanna split up Lino Vairetti, the singer, and the drummer Massimo Guarino recorded an album.

EUROCK: What was the first Osanna album?

Elio: It was called *L'UOMO*. It sold very well.

EUROCK: When was it released?

Elio: In 1971, I think.

EUROCK: Did the group release *L'UOMO* during its first year of existence?

Elio: Yes, the first year as Osanna. However, I was in a previous band called Showmen, a very famous and commercial band in Italy.

EUROCK: Did Showmen release any albums?

Elio: Yes. One LP and I think something like fifteen 45's.

EUROCK: Do you recall what label it came out on?

Elio: RCA.

EUROCK: How old were you then?

Elio: 18.

EUROCK: What were some of Osanna's original influences, say at the time the first album was released?

Elio: In that period we used to follow and listen to King Crimson. We liked them very much. And, you know, Jethro Tull.

EUROCK: I think many people have guessed the Tull influence, especially in your flute playing. Many have also speculated about Van Der Graaf Generator as an influence, had you listened to them?

Elio: Yes. The situation was that we came from Italy and it was as if we were copying all the bands from England or the U.S. But, I mean there was something special, very original about the band. It's very easy to compare the music to other bands, but it was also very original.

EUROCK: Turning to Renato's earlier band, what were some of the influences in the New Trolls when you were with them?

Renato: Mostly the Mahavishnu Orchestra. I was in the New Trolls for two albums, *TEMPI DISPARI* and *ATOMIC SYSTEM*.

EUROCK: Do you think Italian groups were recording albums for a market outside of Italy?

Renato: No, they were made for Italians. We did not know that people listened to them here.

EUROCK: On the cover of the Osanna LP, *LANDSCAPE OF LIFE*, the band is pictured in elaborate make-up. Was this how they went on stage?

Elio: Oh yes, we had a real theatre with us, with 12 actors.

Corrado: With the *PALEPOLI* album tour they had actors and staff with all the theatrics happening on stage, telling the story of the album.

EUROCK: Did Genesis influence the theatrics at all?

Corrado: No Genesis was influenced by them.

Elio: When they came to Italy, the singer Gabriel just used to have sort of a flower hat, and I remember that one year after we had a concert together in Italy we saw him on the cover of a magazine with the same mask that we used to use. It was probably coincidence you know, but...

EUROCK: So you were using theatrics when Genesis came over.

Elio: Oh yes, I think one year before.

EUROCK: Was there a lot of religion involved in the music at this time?

Elio: No, well there was some. But it was much more political.

EUROCK: What was the musical environment like at this time in Italy? Back in '71, for instance, what was the government's position on rock music?

Elio: It was a great moment, that one, because I think we broke all the political situations. We were the first to have concerts in a new way. To see 30 to 40 thousand people come to a concert was something that had never been seen before, it was beautiful. The government was the same as it is today. There was the same fighting between the Communists and Fascists.

Corrado: What happened is that after a while the left parties understood that they could use rock audiences to their advantage. They were using the people as an instrument and so were going to the concerts and saying, "Don't pay for tickets because the music is yours. Why should you pay when the government is making all the money on this." And the situation got worse and worse until now you can't play in Italy, it's very bad.

Elio: The slogan is, "The music is ours."

Corrado: "The music is ours, we don't pay for a ticket." And sometimes they come on stage and say, "Stop the music, we have to talk now."

Elio: A political speech right on stage while you are doing the rock and roll.

Corrado: It got to the point where, at one concert, they did a process to a guy playing with a gun on stage, in front of thousands of people. I mean he deserved it, he was on stage saying, "I'm a Communist, blah, blah" and so 20 guys with masks came on stage while he was playing with a gun and said, "Oh alright, let's talk about how much money you are earning tonight and how much you will be giving to the party."

Elio: It was full of contradictions.

EUROCK: Is this still the case over there?

Corrado: Yes.

EUROCK: Do you think this is why a lot of Italian musicians are leaving?

Corrado: Yes, you can't play. We left four years ago, almost five, because the situation was getting so heavy. The was no room for rock so we said we have to get out of this.

Elio: I'd like to say that when we formed Osanna we were against the structures of Italy. The Italian situation. Our message was misunderstood. The people were only concerned with breaking down the doors to enter the theatres, a political manifestation. But it was not our idea. We were talking about communities living together to exchange ideas. All these things came back on your shoulder; people expected from you something that is more than a musician, more like a political leader.

EUROCK: So the conflict was between the aesthetic aspects of music and what the people wanted you to apply politically?

Elio: Yes, right.

Corrado: You know, the Italian audience, press, as far as music is concerned, are very intellectual. They work with the mind and want a reason for everything... "Oh, you play music? Why do you play music?" They're really into that trip. So each group coming out had to give a reason why they were getting a group together and putting records out. Even unconsciously they were trying to justify why they were playing music. They were getting so heavy, especially the journalists. So that when rock groups like Osanna, PFM, Banco, and Le Orme came out it was like "Wow! Something new is happening here!"

EUROCK: Did the government enter into the journalistic aspect as well?

Corrado: Not so much the government as the people. You know there was a festival in Italy called Renudo, which was a free festival. All the alternative politics to the structure of the government entered into it. The music was the new way of communication to the young people.

Elio: I remember when we created the festival in Naples, which had never had one before. We called it the Pop Festival. Anyway we made this festival and I was the organizer with Corrado's brother

1978

(Danilo Rustici, of Osanna and Uno), and we found someone who would put money into it, which at the time was about $20,000. We found this guy who really believed in the situation, and, you know, the first day they broke the door down saying "The music is ours." Now you cannot find anyone who will invest money in the situation to help musicians and to survive. In Italy, I don't think there's anyone who lives as a musician should; a musician in Italy must do something else to survive. People work in banks and other places. I actually met a trumpet player who worked in a bank. If he were in the States he'd be a great musician now.

EUROCK: The feeling among many of us here in the U.S. is that the bands must be having problems. Corrado, you mentioned to me that Area has split up and we've also received word that Perigeo has as well. And of course Le Orme came to Los Angeles to record and then recorded their latest album in London.

Corrado: You know, Le Orme is a different case because they always try to get into popular music. They were playing in different places, such as theatres, and consequently a different audience was seeing their concerts. So I think they came over here because they were trying to make it bigger.

EUROCK: That seems to be the general feeling about the *SMOGMAGICA* LP. Would this be the case with other Italian bands, say Banco and PFM?

Corrado: I don't know. I haven't heard Banco for years now. I heard PFM's last album; it sounds good.

Elio: Yes.

EUROCK: They seem to be moving towards mainstream fusion more than ever before. Have they lost their label in Britain, as rumor suggests?

Corrado: Yes, Manticore.

EUROCK: Do you know if they're still with Numero Uno in Italy?

Elio: They created their own label.

Corrado: They're looking for a new label in America.. I think they want an American deal.

EUROCK: Is Numero Uno still going strong as a label?

Corrado: Yes.

EUROCK: Getting back to the Osanna LPs, what followed the first album *L'UOMO*?

Corrado: It was *MILANO CALIBRO 9*.

EUROCK: Did Luis Bacalov write most of the material?

Elio: No he wrote the off material.

Renato: It's the same guy that did *CONCERTO GROSSO*.

EUROCK: For the New Trolls...

Renato: Right. Possibly the following album as well.

EUROCK: What followed *MILANO CALIBRO 9*?

Elio: *PALEPOLI*. That was the theatre we created for the stage.

Corrado: Before the fourth album *LANDSCAPE OF LIFE*, Elio did the *UNO* album with Danilo.

EUROCK: That was done in London?

Elio: Yes, at Trident Studios. In fact for me personally, I went away from Italy not because of the political situation, but because of the lack of managers, technicians and others. In London we could find a good manager and people who could invest money in the band, things that are really lacking in Italy.

EUROCK: Corrado, the *UNO* album featured your brother in addition to Elio?

Corrado: Yes, Danilo.

Elio: And a drummer, Enzo Vallicelli.

Corrado: When Osanna got together to do *LANDSCAPE OF LIFE* I had already joined Uno; I was playing bass with them. So all seven of us were in the studio when it was recorded.

Elio: It was fun. Corrado sang his song on the album ("Promised Land").

EUROCK: So *LANDSCAPE OF LIFE* was the last Osanna album?

Elio: Yes.

EUROCK: Did you go directly to work as Nova?

Elio: No, we were still Uno. We did *LANDSCAPE* to complete the Osanna contract. After that we decided to go to London to live and the drummer left. We replaced him with musicians from Genoa, a bass player and drummer. In London we found a manager and Arista Records.

EUROCK: And then you recorded the *BLINK* album as Nova?

Elio: Right.

EUROCK: After listening to the Nova LPs and then going back to the *UNO* album it does sound like a predecessor to Nova; sort of a bridge between Osanna and Nova. Why did you change the groups name from Uno to Nova?

Corrado: I'm just speculating now, but I think the group members weren't happy with what the actual music was all about. Uno was the first approach to melodies, really space, as opposed to the Osanna stuff, really chaotic. It was the first approach to relaxing and playing. When we got the bass player and drummer, both coming from jazz, they influenced us very much; in the way of 'yea man let's get down and play.' So we felt like changing. The first Nova album was chaos again because when you step into something new you don't know how to handle it. So *BLINK* was the first approach to the jazz scene. Like the UNO stuff the melodies were there, but they really came out during *VIMANA* our second album. We really relaxed and found our musical direction.

EUROCK: The lineup had changed by the time *VIMANA* was recorded...

Corrado: Yes, while we were recording *VIMANA* the drummer and bassist left. We had met Narada Michael Walden during the recording of *BLINK*, so we called him and he came over in two days.

EUROCK: How did you get involved with the Brand X people?

Corrado: I met Robin Lumley, who produced *VIMANA*, after *BLINK* was recorded.

Elio: After the drummer and bass player left we knew we had to find two great musicians, otherwise it was just a waste of money and time. So Narada came in two days and Percy Jones was already there, and we made everything in a couple of days.

Corrado: In four days we did everything.

1978

By the way, Osanna have a new record with Danilo, the singer and the drummer. American CBS are interested in it and I think they are going to release it.

EUROCK: Is it out in Italy now?

Corrado: Yes, on CBS. Do you know of the group Napoli Centrale?

EUROCK: Yes.

Corrado: They and Toni Esposito are what's happening in Italy now.

EUROCK: Nova seems to be working within a mainstream jazz/rock fusion realm. What new ideas are you attempting to bring to this form of music?

Corrado: We're trying to bring Italian, especially Napolitan melodies to an American rhythm approach. I come from Naples, Elio comes from Naples and Renato comes from Genoa, which is pretty similar. Everything there is good vibes and love among the people on the streets. We're trying to bring that feel across in the music. I'm trying to learn the American way of playing music, which is different. I couldn't play funky music in an American way, but I could play it in a Napolitan way.

EUROCK: It seems Italian bands have a general air about their music that is common to most of the rock music coming from that country. Even if there are no vocals, one can still pick this up. It has been said that it's ultimately derived from common influences from bands like Genesis and ELP.

Corrado: I don't think so. The only way I can describe Italian musicians is that they are "space cadets," awed by classical music. They all feel it, I feel it.

Renato: It's the classical tradition in Italy.

Elio: Still, I think that everyone is an original. For me, I just let myself play. In the moment that you express yourself, you are an original. Everybody can say the same words, but they each say it in their own way and I'm really convinced this is true for music.

Corrado: I'm trying to listen to other people, but not in the same way as I did before. I'm becoming convinced that all the music that comes out of you comes out of your soul.

Bill Sharp

COS Interview
With Daniel Schell

Another country, Belgium, has come to light as having a small, but healthy progressive music scene -- thriving and growing on the Continent. Several bands' records are becoming available outside their homeland. Among these are albums by COS, Univers Zero, Machiavel, Kandahar, 5th Ball Gang and others.

Recently I had the pleasure of talking to Daniel Schell of COS, one of that country's best. So with this interview EUROCK begins its coverage of Belgium in I think a good way. There is more to come.

EUROCK: To start, let's get a bit of info on what the progressive music scene is like in Belgium. Are there many places to play?

D.S.: Well, Belgium is a very little country with about 10 million people. There must be I suppose about 20 places to play -- 5 universities, places in Brussels, Liège and Antwerp which are the big cities. But it's not really too big a market. In Europe it's now concentrated in Germany, which is the place we play most and also in France.

EUROCK: Are the record companies willing to sign less-commercial bands or do the groups have to put out their own records?

D.S.: Normally it's better for the group to put out their own. But we are very happy since we signed with I.B.C., a company of E.M.I., who really want to help us.

EUROCK: Is there a wide audience for progressive music?

D.S.: I think the percentage of the audience who like this type of music is the same everywhere. Except in Germany where more of the people very much like the music.

EUROCK: Who are the main progressive bands in Belgium?

D.S.: I think COS is one of the oldest, being together for around 4 years. Another is Univers Zero who started about the same time. There's also a guy who produced our album, Marc Moulin. He has now begun his own label. One of his first records he produced was by our keyboard player Marc Hollander. Also there is now a musical cooperative called "Les Lundi D'Hortense." They're making a lot of progress in music in Belgium. It's something like the Italian cooperative "L'Orchestra."

EUROCK: How long have you personally been playing music?

D.S.: I started playing jazz guitar when I was 15. I then studied computers and engineering. I only started professionally when I was 29. That was about 4 years ago with COS.

EUROCK: Who were your original influences, who did you listen to?

D.S.: My first influence was Charlie Parker. I tried to do like him, then I realized I could never play as good jazz music as him or John Coltrane, so I tried to find my own style and what I could play best. After some years I found I had much more relationship to bands of Europe like Can, Magma, ZAO. So these were my first influences when I started COS.

EUROCK: Was COS the first band you were in?

D.S.: No, I was first in a band called Classroom that was well known in Belgium. We were mainly singing in French on jazz riffs.

EUROCK: When was COS formed?

D.S.: Late 1973.

EUROCK: Was there a concept you wanted to work around?

D.S.: Yes, we wanted to perform rock music starting from our classical influences. But now we've realized that music is universal and the difference between Europe and America is becoming obsolete. The only thing that counts is that you have your own character and to do it well. That's what many people lack, the will to do it really well. That's important.

EUROCK: Does the name COS have any special significance?

D.S.: Yes it does. When I started in computers I worked with computer composed music and so I was looking for phonetic languages. Once I found by random composition, the name COS. It reminded me of the name of a Greek island. Also it was a sound I could use in the music. It exists in many languages -- Catalanic = body, Irish = food, Arabic = glass. So I decided to use it especially as a sound/vocal in the music.

EUROCK: There's some similarity in the band's music with that of the French band ZAO. Were they a heavy influence?

D.S.: Yes, because in fact we started this style/idea of vocals together. COS was founded about the same time as ZAO, and myself and François Cahen and Jeff Seffer, we're pretty much into the same music. One tune on the first album *COCALNUT* is even the same as a ZAO tune.

EUROCK: Who is in COS now and what's the instrumentation?

D.S.: Jean Louis Azobout on drums, Alain Goutieron on bass, Marc Hollander on keyboards, bass clarinet and sax, Pascal Son on vocals and oboe and myself on guitars and flute. Now on stage we are performing electric music, but also a lot of arrangements with the three winds -- oboe, clarinet and flute.

EUROCK: How many LPs do you have so far?

D.S.: Two so far -- *POSTAEOLIAN TRAIN ROBBERY* and *VIVA BOMA*. This summer we will do our third album and may be in the U.S.

EUROCK: Up to now, where have your records been released?

D.S.: On the Continent -- France, Belgium, Germany.

EUROCK: Have you toured the rest of the Continent?

D.S.: Yes, we've toured all parts of Europe and would like to play in the States. But it's not easy, we have to wait for our records to gain some recognition.

EUROCK: So what's in the immediate future for the band?

D.S.: Well, the new album in summer and then our yearly tour of Europe in November and December.

EUROCK: Will the new album feature some of the wind quartet work you do live?

D.S.: Yes, and I've been studying Flemish counterpoint music, music which we'll try and incorporate into it, along with Pascal's free vocal work that she's been getting into. Also I've just recorded a solo album, which I hope to release in the future. And Pascal is developing tapes combining her avant-garde ideas and classical training.

EUROCK: Well it sounds as if you have some great ideas and that they could come together in a pretty amazing way.

Archie Patterson

ROCK EN FRANCE
Index of French Bands

Abrial Stratageme Group
Ad Majorem
Amenophis
Amplitude
Andromede
Ange
Apras
Arachnoid
Archipel
Arkham
Arsenic
Art Zoyd
Ascaris Megal
Asia Minor
Asphalt Jungle
Atoll
Atom Cristal
Atome
Bacchus
Bedjabetch
Belle Star
Belzebuth
Benoit Blue Boy
Bert, Alain
Besombes, Philippe
Bestiole
Bijou
Black Rat
Bleu Profond
Bloody Mary
Bocquet, Didier
Bonneville
Boogaloo Band
Bracos Band
Bulteau, Michel
Cake

Cambouis
Camizole
Carefully
Carmina
Carpe Diem
Castelhemis
Centrifuge
Chemin Blanc
Chien De Faience
Chimere
Chrysais Idominee
Chute Libre
Cible
Clivage
Cobra
Coincidence
Comedie Humaine
Corbeau Mort
Crawling Riders
Crisis
Cynthi Aum
Dallas Gang
Dechained Company
Dernier Recors
Desperados
Diesel
Divodorum
Eclipse
Edition Speciale
Electric Callas
Electriquement Votre
Electro Choc
Enossis
Equinoxe
Eskaton Kommandkestra
Esprit De St.Louis

1978

Etat D'Urgence	Machin
Etron Fou Leloublan	Machine Head
Everest	Madrigal
Exit	Madrigar
Factory	Magma
Flamen Dialis	Magnum
Foetus	Magus Optis
Forgas	Mahjun
Forum's Group	Malaena
Foxy	Malicorne
Frightful Five	Mama Bea
Ganafoul	Marcœur, Albert
Gaurdon	Marie Et Les Garçons
Genocid	Mathieu Donnard Street
Good Medicine	Mega Hertz
Good Time Charley	Melody
Goun	Memoriance
Graalo	Mephisto
Grancher, Philippe	Mer' Grand
Grand Rouge	Metal Urbain
Grime	Mike Et Sa Clique
Grosse Catastrophe	Minuit Boulevard
Hautes Reelles	Moebius
Heldon	Mona Lisa
Henri Roger	Monsieur Dupont
Higelin	Mozaik
Him	Mythe Xero
Honey Dream	Next
Horizon	Nimrod
Hubble Bubble	Nursery
Hybride	NYL
Hydravion	Ocean
Image	Ocharinah
Infra-Rouge	Odyssey
Jadis	Oedipe
K Rock Mort	Olaf
Kalfon Rockchaud	Opus III
Kam And Bear	Ork
Kerlo, Eric	Pacific Glory
La Souris Deglinguee-LSD	Pantingruel
Lannhuel Manu	Papa Speed
Lard Free	Pataphonie
Larry Martin Factory	Pilpoul
Lavilliers, Bernard	Poing
Lefebvre,Cyril	Pole
Legende II	Potemkine
Little Bob Story	Pouin Final
Loose Heart	Pulsar
Ma Banlieue Flasque	Purin

1978

Rahmann
Rock Station
Rock'n Roller
Roll's De Luxe
Rose
Roxy Minette
Saint D'Hondt
Salamandre
Seisme
Sextant
Shakin Street
Shylock
Silene
Skull's Crakers
Sloane
Smagus
Smiler
Soho
Solstice
Spheroe
Spirit Free
Starshooter
States
Stinky Toys
Streetfighters
Surya
Synthese
Tai-Phong
Tangerine
Taxis
Teenage Head
Teenage Lust
Telephone
Terpandre
The End

Trands Jazz Rock
Trans Europe Express
Treponem Pal
Tri Yann
Trust
Urban Sax
Urgence
Valerie La Grange
Veuve Joyeuse
Visa
Voie Express
Volcania
Vortex
Wapassou
Warlliocks
Warm Gun
Waxtapers
Weidorje
Wells Fargo
Werneer, Rene Et L'Habit De Plumes
Wesn
Wild Horses
Xalph
Yacoub, Gabriel
Yakaa
Yochk'o Seffer Group
Youpi Trempoline
Zackmoun
Zanov
ZAO
Zoom

Reprinted From ROCK EN STOCK

1978

Atoll

The French music scene currently is exploding. While it may seem the multitude of groups are overnight sensations, this is far from being true. Many of them have roots extending back several years, it's only just now that they are gaining any sort of recognition and becoming able to record for the many progressive labels that are coming together.

One of the best examples of this is Atoll. Originating from Metz, the group came together in June 1972 and kicked off their existence by opening for one of the pioneer French bands, Zoo.

Back in those days record contracts for native bands were hard to come by, so they spent their first year and a half playing gigs. In late '73 they signed with Eurodisc and their debut single was released with a follow-up issued in late '74. During this time they continually played wherever they could, but were hampered by their not having a business manager. A break came in June '74, two years after their formation, when they got to go on tour with Ange, one of the longest established and most popular French groups. It was a success and finally in January 1975 the first album was issued to excellent response from rock fans and critics alike. *MUSICIENS-MAGICIENS* was an excellent first album. Instrumentally there were flashes of brilliance, but the strong point was song composition as the melodies and phrasing were rich and full.

With these successes came the need for full time business management and personnel changes. In the midst of sorting these things out they recorded their second album *L'ARAIGNEE MAL*. It showed another side of the band as the music was much looser and the instrumental work came to the forefront.

Finally in June '76 things got sorted out and the situation stabilized, putting the band in a position to go ahead with a few dates and record their third album in the early months of 1977. *TERTIO* was recorded by the band's strongest lineup to date -- Italian Alain Gozzo on drums, Andre Balzer handling vocals and percussion, Michel Taillet - keyboards, Christian Beya, who had played with members of Amon Düül II among others, on guitar, Jean Luc Thillot on bass and guest vocalists Liza Deluxe and Stella Vander from Magma.

192, Eurock: European Rock & the Second Culture

TERTIO is without question their best work. It combines the lyricism of the first with the instrumentalism of its successor. The resulting arrangements are some of the finest examples of progressive music you will hear. From the laser cover photo to the vocal - keyboard - guitar synthesis, the whole album is startling. It's rare that everything comes together on record, but with *TERTIO*, Atoll have pulled it off. You should hear it.

Archie Patterson

Wapassou

One of the most original of all the French bands is Wapassou. The best description of their music is 21st century chamber music. Imagine keyboards, violin, acoustic guitar and voice blending into a synthesized classical tapestry and you begin to get an idea of their sound -- melodic, flowing and spacey.

Wapassou was formed in April '73 by Freddy Brua. The name is of special significance in this case as it by definition metaphorically symbolizes the music. "Wapassou" is a word from the Mescalero Apache dialect that was, according to legend, the name of a hidden valley in North America, a land of permanent peace and love. It is precisely a feeling for these concepts that Wapassou creates musically -- tranquility and warmth.

After an initial period of live work and first album (on Prodisc), Wapassou seemed in a good position to move forward in achieving their musical goals. They received radio coverage, television air time and the Prix du Golf Drouot. Also they realized a film soundtrack, recorded a 45 in Germany and in 1975 undertook a tour of Southern France whereupon they met Paul Putti of Pole Records. Subsequently arrangements were made to record for Pole, one of the premier alternative labels, along with Disjuncta, in France at that time. But due to financial problems the recording never came off. In addition Brua was having problems for avoiding his stint in the military. So the band experienced a period of trials -- low spirits and finances.

Finally late in '75 all was sorted out and the group came together even stronger than before. The Arcane (now Crypto) label became interested in the band, touring resumed and ultimately their second album was recorded, with Brua on keyboards, Karin Nickerl on guitars, Jacques Lichti on violin and the ethereal voice of Eurydice.

MESSE EN RE MINEUR is a beautiful haunting album. The instrumental lineup, unique as it is without drums, left them free to experiment outside conventional structures and the result was a totally new sound. The acoustic guitar served as the rhythm complement to Brua's organ and his synthesizer and Lichti's violin created startling counterpoints of melody. The crowning glory was the vocal magic of Eurydice as she wove her heavenly tones in and out of the collage of sound. The album was a major breakthrough for the band -- recognition and increases in live work followed.

In January '78 their 3rd album *SALAMMBO* was released. Based on the work of Gustave Flaubert it is even more adventurous and impressive than its predecessor. At the outset the tone is set when a somber voice proclaims the albums concept -- war = death, which is echoed by goose steps and militaristic recorded radio speeches. What follows is a magnificent musical display. As opposed to *MESSE EN RE MINEUR*, *SALAMMBO* is more intricately arranged. The playing is tighter with more attention paid to each person feeding off one another. It still flows, but more due to execution than affect. Hearing is believing.

The moral of the album and dedication of Wapassou is printed in four languages on the insert. "The only Victor of this story is Death. This music is dedicated to all of its victims. May it make clear that force resolves nothing, that it's not an end but only an execrable means."

Archie Patterson

West Coast Underground

The vast majority of music produced in this country today is in the hands of big business. There are those however who work outside the structure, either by choice or necessity. In the last 5 years on the West Coast there has developed a marginal group of people who have pursued their own ideas and taken responsibility for the creative process.

The grand-daddy of the bunch is The Residents, who have produced a series of records that show occasional flashes of brilliance musically and a unique conceptual art presentation. They've also maintained a mysterious cover (for good reason?) allowing few to really know just what they are about. This charade, plus the dilemma of their growing popularity, generated primarily by hype (they cannot perform live), has raised serious questions about their intent and integrity.

Also from the S.F. area comes Chrome. A rock mutation, their sound is based on the primal energies of the id coupled with the sensory attack of static electricity. Their first album, *THE VISITATION*, is like a Haight Ashbury flashback. Intentionally or not they created a post psychedelic vision of the dream gone bad. Their second, *ALIEN SOUNDTRACKS*, is quite another matter. It is crude and primitive, yet filled with the tension of the space age. The beat juxtaposes with fuzzed guitar and electronics to create a harsh, extreme experience. The third album due soon should blow a lot of minds.

The Northwest's contribution to the substrata is The Parasites Of The Western World. Their initial record is good, but flawed due to a tendency to make it more accessible, i.e. a nice but throwaway version of the Beatles "Flying," plus a short blues joke that simply takes up space. These two cuts illustrate their parasitic nature of using old ideas in old ways. Their strong point is the feel they have of the German bands in places. They like to take simple ideas and work them out, the best examples being "Funeral For A Mouse," a synthesized dirge livened up by a recurring bleep and "Alienending" where phased screams echo nightmarishly from speaker to speaker. Also

"Accessories" features some nice musical changes along with treated vocals and electronic gimmicks. The album certainly isn't revolutionary, but it has its moments. Concentration more on their own concept plus a more extreme approach and they could do something great.

Another organism with Teutonic leanings is The Decayes from So. Cal. who have just released their first album (a limited edition of 100). One side uses acoustic guitar, the sound of waves washing against the shoreline and distorted guitar to create a flowing, meditative sound similar to some of Achim Reichel's early work. The second side is much more harsh as the guitar dominates with pulsating, screeching tones. Drums maintain a monotonous rhythm at sporadic intervals giving a little substance to what's basically an improvised freakout. It's not brain shattering, more like sensually numbing.

This article only touches on what's happening on the West Coast. In future issues there will be more in depth coverage as the scene unfolds.

Archie Patterson

Zu-Fest

On the weekend of Oct. 8 in N.Y.C. progressive music came to the U.S.A. in the form of the ZU CONCERT. Organized by the patriarch of the scene in France, Giorgio Gomelsky, it was an auspicious event that gives hope of better things to come for progressive fans in this country.

The thrust of the weekend was to bring people together from around the country to meet, establish contacts and experience a marathon of music. By the time it was over all this and more had been accomplished, as in addition the event had

been recorded for an album, to be released very soon, as well as filmed by a crew for a French TV Special.

The concert itself ran 13-1/2 hours and was a virtual non-stop performance by bands, poets and taped music (the new Residents and Henry Cow LPs were previewed). N.Y. bands were represented by a group of "no wave" bands from the Lower East Side. The most interesting of the bunch was Theoretical Girls whose manic assault clearly conveyed the desperation of life in the belly of the beast. The next step in electronic music was taken by Dr. Space (Joseph Lyons). A former conductor at Julliard, he resigned -- invented his own "computerized wand" and now makes music the likes of which would make the Tangerine Dream turn green with envy. U.S. progressive music was well represented by The Muffins. A top-notch band, their jazz rock fusions combined technique and emotion to make them most impressive. For their last number they were joined by none other than Yochk'o Seffer who blew a sax solo that had the audience riveted to the stage. It earned him his first standing ovation of the evening. He next played an extended a capella solo and followed it with a solo in accompaniment to a taped arrangement of strings and voices, the title cut from his last album IMA, which brought the crowd up applauding again. He was then joined by his band and they ran through a set of Seffer originals -- "Neffesh Music." Throughout his piano work and unique vocal phrasing sparked the music. After the third standing ovation he left the stage with a hearty "merci beaucoup." Next came Fred Frith with his performing guitars and sonic vibrations filled the air as feedback roared from the speakers. He later teamed up with Chris Cutler and Peter Blegvad (ex-Slapp Happy) to indulge in some of Peter's merrie melodies.

The evening was building to a climax as Gilli "Mother Gong" Smyth came on to do part of her superb new album *MOTHER*. The costumes, songs and her presence were magical. Then came the man of mirth and merriment himself, Daevid (Bert, Dingo) Allen. The crowd went wild as he proceeded to ran through the tall tale of Radio Gnome. He narrated and sang as little green pixies ran around the stage and GongSongs filled the air, played to perfection by the N.Y. Gong band.

The hour was growing late when suddenly the theatre management aided by the blue meanies started cutting the power (3:30 AM). In the half light, then darkness four drummers drummed on as Gilli, Daevid and a host of friends on stage clapped and danced. French TV turned on their spotlight and the audience joined in as the hall rang out with the sound of primal pulsations -- body music. Truly this was a fitting end -- music to raise the spirits and fortify the soul.

Archie Patterson

Rock In The Land Of The Rising Sun

Back in the late '60s, via *American Bandstand*, I was given my first taste of rock from Japan. There was a record out at the time called "Talk About It" by someone called Harumi. It sounded real good on the radio so when he was scheduled to be on the tube one Saturday afternoon, curiosity got the best of me. Now Dick Clark isn't known for his creative productions, but when he introduced Harumi, a very interesting 3-minute spectacle followed. The boy from the East glided onto the screen in flowered robes and amidst a collage of lights and exotic props and proceeded to lip-sync his "hit." It was most effective.

After the single came an album, which was released and cut out in rapid-fire succession. On Verve, it was a double and while the public was ready for a chart single, an adventurous album was not in order. Titled *HARUMI*, it was a strange record. One LP was conventional rock songs with "Talk About It" definitely the high point. But the other was something else again, each side devoted to only one piece. There was "Twice Told Tales Of

The Pomegranate Forest," a 24-minute psychedelic opus and "Samurai Memories" which featured atmospheric background music over which Harumi and his relations told their individual tales. Sounds of the West met echoes of the East.

It wasn't until a few years later that another Japanese musician came along and gave further proof that there was indeed something happening over the sea. Stomu Yamash'ta was his name and he first came to my attention through his work on the music for a Robert Altman film titled "Images." After that there was his *COME TO THE EDGE -- RED BUDDAH THEATRE* work and numerous other film scores and recordings. His latest *GO* trilogy being the least interesting and rather blatantly commercial. Perhaps his main importance lies in the fact that he brought Japan into the music consciousness of the international community.

For a long time Japanese kids have been in love with rock and roll. Bands go over there and play to thousands and as a result of their visits a wave of groups have come into being modeled after their heroes. Hard rock is far and away the most popular -- Deep Purple, Led Zeppelin and other metaloids influenced many bands and today there are a number of heavy rockers who play it hot and heavy in the spirit of their idols. Two of the best are Bow Wow and Murasaki, both of which have released 3 albums.

In addition Pink Floyd is highly regarded and spawned a group of bands that took a similar approach, but added native elements so as to develop their own sound. The Far East Family band is perhaps the most known due to their association with Klaus Schulze and All Ears. Their music is a beautiful synthesis of Eastern atmosphere with celestial sounds, making the albums a rare treat.

In a somewhat similar vein but heavier are Cosmos Factory. With more emphasis on guitar and dense keyboard arrangements, their approach is rockier. On their 3rd album, *BLACK HOLE*, the effect is like a meteor racing toward Earth, tearing its way through the atmosphere -- aggressive and volatile. With their latest, *METAL REFLECTION*, they've settled into orbit and are firing laser beams between Earth and the Moon The production and guitar/synthesizer interplay is dizzying.

In addition there is Yonin Bayashi, who are roughly like Cosmos, but at times much closer to hard rock. Also the Far East offshoot Chronicle, who have done two records. Their first, recorded live in the U.S., is surprisingly good -- the sound and material strong and the level of improvisation high. Their second, released in the U.S. on All Ears, contains some nice music, but is sparse in spots.

There are many others too: Men Tan Pin -- funky guitar rock, Creation -- hard rock with blues influences (they did one album in the U.S. with Felix Pappalardi), Prism -- jazz rock in the Mahavishnu vein, Oz -- strong progressive keyboard/guitar rock featuring a dynamic woman lead vocalist, Osamu -- cosmic music filled with folk and Eastern jazz influences, the Sadistics -- SMB offshoot who funk it up in a jazzy way and Magical Power Mako -- Japan's Mike Oldfield. Mako's latest album *SUPER RECORD* is full of cosmic sounds -- guitar, electronics and effects making it highly interesting. Similar in approach to Oldfield he avoids the clinical nature of repetitive overdubs and is much spacier sounding.

This rundown only scratches the surface. But it does offer a brief glimpse of into the magnitude of what's happening there as well as a look at some of the bands who are active. As more information becomes available Japan will be pursued further.

Archie Patterson

Sadistic Mika Band

In the early '70s while the US and UK music industries were honing their production techniques so as to allow vacuous no-talents to pose as earnest musicians, Japanese kids were still coming to terms with basic rock and roll. Those bands with a serious air like Men Tan Pin and Creation put out albums in the British blues vein. The first Sadistic Mika Band album however, was and remains unique in its bold mixture of blood and guts rock, electronics and lyricism, in addition to the striking production by main man Katoh and the flashy tackiness of the cover art.

"Dance is Over," "Arienu Republic," "Shadow Show" and "Picnic Boogie" are the rockers. "Dance" is fast-paced and Katoh's vocals are so hot they're shredded. "Arienu" has an infectious chorus and powerful theme. "Shadow Show" exhibits Tanaka's lead guitar. "Picnic Boogie" closes the album with rambunctious good humor. It has blues riffing, shoo-be-doo-wops, wah-wah guitars and a soaring chorus. The other cuts range from light and airy songs to playful and quirky with spicy electronic and percussive hooks.

At this point SMB fell into Chris Thomas' hands and his production moves the sound from a flexible rock and roll to studio progressive. *BLACK SHIP* bats only three for nine. "Time Machine" is straight ahead rock with strong Mika vocals, but a weak bottom rhythm section; "Yoroshiku Dozo" is only an intro to Side Two, but its jaunty sax is a highlight; "Sayonara," the album closer, is a beautiful acoustic lament with Katoh's light electric guitar and organ bringing it to a close. The rest of the material is mainly pedestrian progressive funk. There are moments of interest, but they are buried deep.

HOT MENU released in '75 is a bit better. "Time to Noodle" is a fast instrumental romp; "Aquablue" picks up its smooth lyricism into a nice bouncy chorus; "Mada Mada Samba" has nice Latin sounding acoustic and laconic humor; "Hi Jack (I'm Just Dying)" has a pretty e-piano intro and ends with a synthi theme that gains in intensity as it repeats.

It, along with "Okinawa (Strange-Fish)," "Style Is Changing" and "Tokyo Sunrise," are the only SMB songs with extensive English vocals. "Tokyo Sunrise" begins with the drug-tired Mika talking to herself (us) as she fumbles to mix a drink over a lonely western sounding guitar and ends with snoring, a blowing wind and acoustic guitar. "Okinawa" has interludes of exotic percussion; "Style Is Changing" has a soaring guitar line; "Funky Mahjong" is funk with an imaginative vocal arrangement and "Mummy Doesn't Go To Parties Since Daddy Died" is passable.

SADISTIC MIKA BAND LIVE IN LONDON is a bad recording all around with persistent hiss, a mix that leaves the bottom out and lifeless performances. Passing interest is generated only in sections of "Time To Noodle," "Silver Child" and "Black Ship." It shows that SMB were not hot musicians. They should have stayed a rock and roll band, they had the chops for that.

Joe Carducci

Music From Spain

Of all the Western European countries, Spain has perhaps the sketchiest rock history. This is due in great part to the socio-economic conditions that have existed there. For decades Spain was an underdeveloped country living under a dictatorship in disguise. Generalissmo Franco ruled with an iron hand and as a result most aspects of society were highly regulated. Under such conditions rock was, to say the least, not encouraged. That did not prevent some however, as there were musicians who picked up on the spirit from outside and tried to make a go of it in their native country. Some took their influences from Anglo rock and basically aped the sounds they liked, i.e. Barrabas, Lone Star and Alcatraz. One group which stood out from the rest was Canarios who were known for their ambitious adaptation of Vivaldi's "Four Seasons." The arrangements, technique and execution on that record are impressive. On the other hand there were also the more underground groups, Musica Dispersa, Mirasol, Smash, Jaraka, Fusioon, OM and others. Most have now split or vanished. Now a second generation of bands has developed since Franco's death as things inevitably have loosened up a bit. Rock music in the last couple years has started to develop to a much greater extent and today there are three independent rock labels active in Spain.

MoviePlay is the most active in the progressive rock field. Over the last few years they have released around 20 albums which feature some of the most interesting fusion music you'll hear anywhere. Generally the sound is derivative of contemporary rock, but the Spanish cultural influences woven into it make it much more than an imitation. Following is a rundown of their artists.

Granada - With 3 albums have developed into one of the most refreshing bands. Their *VALLE DEL PAS* album in particular is stunning. They make superb use of keyboards, guitar, bagpipes and orchestra to create a haunting work.

Gualberto - Of his two albums *VERICUETOS* is far superior. His combining of ethnic atmosphere with Eastern jazz influences and keyboards creates some interesting sounds.

Triana - One of the more popular bands, their sound lies in the Crimson realm with a heavy dose of flamenco thrown in adding a real flair.

Pau Riba - Spain's answer to Daevid Allen. He mixes ethnic music with effects and zany arrangements to create a bizarre sound. *LICORS* features D.A. on glissando guitar and spiritual guidance.

In addition there are several other artists who've so far only released one album, but show promise.

Azahar - Feature a wall of sound technique with powerful guitar/synthesizer.

Gotic - Fluid folk-jazz with hints of classical influence thrown in. Fine use of keys and guitar, subtle but effectively.

Ibio - Folk themes done in a progressive context. Keyboards, guitars and exotica create a flowing melodic feel.

Alfredo Carrion - Formerly involved with Canarios his concept work is classically styled with jazz and ethnic touches intertwining.

1978

It Viaie - Free-form electronics, harsh and full of crackling menace.

On the basis of what MoviePlay has released so far they rank as the most diverse and interesting of the Spanish labels.

Zeleste is the longest-lived label of progressive music in Spain. Based in Catalonia they specialize in "Rock Laieta / Rock From Barcelona," jazz rock with strong native influences. Orquestra Mirasol is the top band on the label and their four albums feature some fine Latin jazz. Highlighted by heavy percussive rhythms and tasty instrumental arrangements, they create a contagious flowing sound. In addition there's Compania Electrica Dharma who lean toward guitar-oriented jazz rock with lots of energy and high-powered jams. In a similar vein are Secta Sonica and Musica Urbana. Jordi Sabates and Toti Soler have produced some beautiful records that feature a modernized jazzy sound. The most unique record on the label is by Feliu i Joan Albert. Basically a duo work on acoustic guitar and e-piano, the overall effect is beautiful spacy folk-jazz. Zeleste's long history of supporting native musicians makes them the most committed of the labels to creating a Spanish musical base.

Chapa is the newest of Spain's independents and has only produced a handful of records so far. Two are samplers of recordings by avant-garde artists and underground rock bands. They've also released albums by Asfalto and Bloque which have a more progressive sound, leaning toward the keyboard rock school. In addition, they distribute the albums of Spain's top band Iceberg. Headed by guitarist Max Sune, their sound is somewhat like the Mahavishnu Orchestra, high-powered guitar jazz-rock. Sune exhibits a highly-varied technique with the ability to be subtle as well as bombastic. His fingers can literally fly up and down the frets. Iceberg gives Chapa a band of international interest.

Spain may have gotten a late start at developing a native rock scene, but things have definitely been looking up in the last few years. As things develop, Spain will certainly be heard from more in the future.

Archie Patterson

Umberto Fiori/Stormy Six Interview

Q. How is the idea of culture understood in Italy?

A. We have a long tradition of philosophical idealism in Italy and it had a great influence even on the philosophers of the Communist Party, for instance Antonio Gramsci (C.P. founder) was a pupil of Croce. In that kind of philosophy, Italian idealism, music was not considered culture, but placed amongst economic activities, not noble ones. The only noble activities are philosophy and the human sciences, literature, poetry, etc. In Italy we have a very narrow tradition in the field of music, especially middle range music. We have a tradition in folk and classical, but musical education in Italy is not good, so music is always considered as a minor art. If people talk about it, it's classical or folk, but nothing in the middle. Our kind of music has not yet been considered real music, that is why we call it "macaronica" that means "nor flesh nor fish." Not classical music though with some theoretical points about it and not folk though with some social basis.

Q. You don't have anti-intellectualism in Italy?

A. No, not really. I think that comes from the philosophy of pragmatism and that's very successful in American culture or in England, but in Italy our culture is different. The church, state and especially the schools from which come our intellects were not pragmatists, they were philosophically idealists or spiritualists. They are the two main streams of Italian culture. One is the idealism of the church and the other one (we call "laico") which means no priest or anticlerical. Those are the two main streams and the second one contains liberals, communists, social democrats, etc.

Q. Is popular culture left to the bourgeoisie by default by the socialists and revolutionaries?

A. It depends on what you mean by popular culture, because we have different kinds of views. One is the socialist which regards folk culture as self-expressing, naive, spontaneous and so "Magic." That's the "peasant culture" of the south. The other is the communist, closer to the working class of the industrial towns. With no real culture of the working class, it's more a culture of middle class intellectuals leading the old working class parties. We believed that the discussion about folk/popular culture in Italy was getting very narrow. It was improved during '68 I think with close contact between the students and workers. Some students were workers at the same time and they didn't feel the contradiction between the two, so they were the avant-garde of the working class. Students/workers, they contained together the folk culture and classic high class culture.

Q. I was thinking about England where the popular culture is always aping the music of the big record companies. If you see live music in a pub you'll hear almost a copy of a pop record, same with talent shows on t.v. So in England popular culture is completely commercial or American music.

A. In Italy it's a little different, we have a long tradition of commercial song, but very Italian, coming from Naples and other places. The influence of the struggles of the working class was even felt in that field -- the commercial cansonetta -- so some of the most popular singers in Italy are communists. Folk was a reaction against commercial music and the influence of contemporary music which is very strong in Italy at the moment. I think we are very good composers, but that is not our main interest. We are middle intellectuals, national popular intellectuals. The new wave: The American wave of popular singers were just commercial. They were products of the economic boom in the '60s. They didn't care about politics, they just cared about money. In 1968 some of them changed sides and some disappeared. But we have as I always say during our gigs a political commercial song now in Italy which is very strange for Europe. We have people in the record industries producing a commercial political culture.

Q. Is it tainted by commercial values, like American protest for example?

A. Yes, American protest is falling apart now and Italian youth need something closer to their reality. So the record companies just produced the right thing for the right people. They created folk singers and said, this is a red folk singer you have to buy his records because you are a red. We refused the role of political stars. When we recorded "Stalingrado" there was no time for political commercial songs in Italy and everybody laughed at us at pop festivals, etc. During demonstrations people were singing it and we could have worked at it and found a political label and made money. But we didn't, we decided to play free music then with jazz musicians and write music for the theatre. We made a record which surprised people who liked us, called *CLICHE* which was not directly political. It had political titles for fun and the music was crazy and mixed up with a lot of clichés. It was a polemic against the political stuff that was then coming down. Then came *L'APPRENDISTA* and all political organizations criticized it for not being political enough. We wrote on the record that we didn't want to do political songs, because they were no use then. They were only slogans and commercial music. We think about the means of music, the means of a song. They are more important.

Q. What is the difference between a song with a straight political content and a song which uses the cultural roots of the songs?

A. We try to work on cultural roots musically especially in the words. The risk was to become a folk rock group which was certainly commercial again. Folk music in industrial towns has a meaning just for collectors, but has no real interest for normal people. Henry Cow were the right group to come to Italy for that reason. They had no need to use folk music to be popular. They used complicated music but were popular in a new way. When we saw them we were reassured that what we were doing was right because they achieved very good results. So we thought that was the way and it was confirmed by the fact that all the folk groups became commercial groups after 1-2 years.

Q. They just sang about their girl friends and not having money?

A. No, not just that, it wouldn't be enough in Italy even for a commercial group. They just do folk stuff like using bongos or pretending to be African or playing Sardinian tunes or singing in a dialect, pretending to be peasants, dressing up like southern peasants, etc.

Q. What about punk?

A. I think punk is a typical commercial product coming from the ideology of the working class in big industrial towns. To satisfy them, give them an identity, and just make music and dream and disguise and no struggle at all. Creating a false sense of community which has no political point, it just has a social and sometimes reactionary view. For example the slogan "Black is beautiful" for black people in the U.S. could have been progressive or reactionary, it depends on its use. To be proud of your society and race could be progressive or reactionary, it depends on the order of the contradictions.

Q. Can pop music be non-political?

A. No we don't think so, any kind of music is political in different ways. All kinds of music are political. We have books in Italy in the last 3-4 years about commercial music and words, analysing the social matters in commercial music. Many commercial singers in Italy are very political though they don't think so. I think it would be very interesting to see for example how the Beatles were political before being directly political.

Q. Some mechanisms have been recognized like trivialization and bringing things to an interpersonal level that there are no social questions, there must be ways that pop music is political?

A. Yes, any kind of entertainment in a capitalist society is made to rebuild the workforce. You have fun, then you are ready for 10,000 years of exploitation. The function of entertainment is just that.

Q. It's a peculiar sort of fun?

A. Yes, like football, circus, TV, things like that.

Q. You have to watch, but you can't touch?

A. Yes, you are passive. In Italy there is a German philosopher who's very popular, Theodor Adorno. We agree very much with his analysis of the role of pop music, mass music in the contemporary age. Adorno analyses different ways of listening to music in "musical sociology" are very interesting. He characterizes many kinds of listeners. The music consumer is high brow, but doesn't understand music structurally, he takes music as another expression of his wealthy situation. The amateur or the emotional listener likes only certain types of music. Adorno says some jazz listeners are like that. I just listen to folk or jazz and the rest is shit. They are keyed to only one type. Then the low level listener, the whistler, e.g. the one who just likes music as you would buy cigarettes, another kind of consumer, not the high brow, but the low brow. The working class is included in this area and is a victim of the mass culture. But it wouldn't be if the contradictions inside the mass culture were developed.

Q. How do you develop these contradictions?

A. We try to develop the contradictions inside the mass culture, by taking its right side which is that the mass culture is the only popular culture today. The languages born in the mass culture are the only ones understood by the working class and large sections of society. They have to be criticised and rebuilt, but we can't use folk music now because it would mean a split in our country once more, into different dialects. We have dozens of dialects and each region has their own that can't be understood by the others, North as opposed to South, etc. So mass culture provided a common language if nothing else, but this is a standardized language and we are fighting against it. We started as rock with no other characteristics and we are trying to be something else. We call it "machina macaronica," "macaronic machine." That means we are popular and we want to be popular, we want to be understood. We don't want to be elite intellectuals, but we don't want to be standardized.

Q. What roles do record companies, American culture and the bourgeoisie play, do they struggle against you?

A. I think they don't even know we exist. I think they don't care about us, the "cooperative."

Q. I mean the struggle for the definition of the culture. In England culture is completely defined by imported American music. What happens in Italy?

A. In Italy we are an imperialistic country, we have to fight against American influence, but it's not the same as Chile. Chile was a half colony so they had to fight up front in a war against America and its culture and English, searching out their roots in Indian music and the language of their grandparents, but Italy is different. We don't fight against English or forms of American culture, we want to fight against the way the culture is used by the American showbiz and so e.g. in "Arrivang gli Americani" we don't play exactly American music, we try to show flat and standardized kinds of music which can be produced that way. We play false classical, avant-garde, protest songs, etc. Every kind of flat. This is what we have to fight against.

Q. How can culture be created which enables man to be consciously active and creative given the animosity of the bourgeoisie?

A. That's what the group is discussing now. I wrote some pages about that question. Would it be possible to be really creative inside the macaronica machine, or is it true that the only creative field is contemporary classical music. The field where musicians are working at the highest musical level. Is it possible to have a popular language as a folk language in the macaronic machine which is "neither fish nor flesh." We think it is possible to create something and maybe that is the real battlefield of culture now. I think the definition of "rock in opposition" was really exact, because rock defines for me more an audience than a kind of music, a language or a style or things like that. It defines a cultural ribbon in which things are happening now, which is not true of contemporary music or folk music. So it's important for that reason, because people are there, not in other fields. There are minorities of intellectuals or peasants or old cultures, so life is in that ribbon. The battlefield is in that ribbon.

Q. Is art a question of expressing your feelings?

A. The last song we wrote is about that. Expressing your feelings or not. And this is a very important matter in Italy now, about spontaneity etc. Personally I try to write in a very personal way. I have personal feelings about many things, but I try to build a social voice, more than a personal voice. I try not to involve the audience by using personal matters, or voice, but to give facts. I try not to sing in a pleasant way, but to sing in a objective way so the people are not moved by something, but can judge what I am singing and the words. I am not there to sing, I am not a singer, I don't care about that. I am speaking in a different way. Writing, I try to use a social voice which I call "megafono" in the last song we wrote it's to be not a man, but a Chinese shadow. In Italy feelings are a reactionary thing, everybody is moved by everything. They have good feelings, are sensitive, etc. So we have to become a little more German, more objective, not moving people with easy things. It's easy to move Italian people, you talk about the dead comrade, the comrade who was killed, but we don't want to use those ways.

Q. How does one recognise culture as opposed to anti-culture?

A. Well, culture could be something that has no aim to change anything, the kind of culture that gives no chance to the audience to make their own culture. We think we are working not only to make our music, but also helping people to develop their own music. That's why we have music schools, discussions and lectures and writings about that. We don't just play, we have a large range of activities in the field of music.

Q. How would you define culture?

A. Culture is any human activity towards nature and towards other people and the way people are organized to have power over nature and over other people.

Q. How does music play a role in wider movements?

A. It plays an important role and that's why we've chosen it as a means of expression and job. Music in Italy was identified in the '60s with the social revolution, music coming from other countries had an importance for the social changes happening in Italy. The music from England and the USA was important at the time as it changed the minds of Italian youth. It could be again, but a different music for a different time. I think music is the most popular form of art now in Italy and maybe the world. Painting and theatre is not as popular. Music is easy to make. It can be easily organized, it has a very long tradition in Italy. We have roots like the "Cantastoria" story-telling street singers. So it's normal to have music on the square of a little town in Italy, telling stories, talking about history with or without pictures. That's how it circulated, through music. They were illiterate, but could hear a song. Oral tradition.

Q. What is the relationship between originality and communication?

A. Novelty and facility. Any kind of art has to have a certain amount of information, that means to be different from other products of art of the same kind. To be new in a way, but if it's too new it can't be understood at all, so the balance between novelty and facility is important. If you don't give it any novelty your social or political message can't be understood, it's just boring. The form is not necessary, it could be any other form. To be necessary the form has to be new because the social and political content are new, but if you lose facility you lose the people. It's a difficult theorem to resolve. We are trying at the same time, difficult and easy, new and in the stream of tradition. We discovered in aesthetic perception there can be many levels of understanding. A song like "L'Apprendista" is a nursery rhyme and simple. The first level of understanding is very easy and the point is easy to understand. It's that birth, work and death are very fast in capitalist society. You are not born, you are a worker, you don't know what it's like to be alive and you're already dead. In contact with the last stanza which is a nursery rhyme talking about a hare going 'round a square. The finger sees the hare. This finger kills it. This finger cooks it. This finger eats it and there's nothing for the last one, the little one. We changed it a little. It's a nursery rhyme, but it has many levels of understanding, e.g. not the man, the apprentice can be understood in different ways in different stanzas. It has a quality of ambiguity which is defined by yourself, your behavior on-stage, how you're dressed, your face, the kind of music you play, your audience, the context you're playing in. It has many meanings, a field of meanings which can be extended. It doesn't matter if you take this field or that, you could be understanding the big one tomorrow.

Q. What factors hold your music back?

A. We have to improve our musical means. We have good ideas and a good political background, but we lack the technical means and aesthetic to express what we want to express. But as H. Cow says, we learn music by playing it and find new ways of expression by trying them. When we have to improve something we do. We can't retire to a castle and become great musicians and come out with great ideas, then put on a splendid concert for the people. Life is not like that!

. . . .

The preceding interview was between Peter Cutler and Umberto Fiori, member of the Italian musical group Stormy Six who belong to the musical/political cooperative L'Orchestra. It took place during the band's recent Rock In Opposition tour of England and is reprinted in slightly edited form courtesy of R.I.O.

1978

Uli Trepte

"There is no right wing and no left wing, only up and down wing."
(Bob Dylan)

"Politics"

"Politics" are just bullshit.
There is only one politic
and that is: do YOUR
thing.
This is forbidden by
society
and so you're in a fight.

This fight is better led by
art than guns,
'cause if you lead the fight
on the level of
"politics/revolution"
it will end up in weapon-
war
and there they will always
beat you,
'cause that's not only their
favorite field
they also have the better
gear.
(and there's no possibility
to execute a guerrilla war
in Europe.)

"The Arts"

The chance is
that they know nothing
about art
what it really is, means and
how it works.
So it's hard for them to
censor and forbid it
and so the fight can
actually be performed on
this level.
Naturally you have to keep
away from "The Arts"
'cause everything there is
under control.
You have to hide and
disguise your art
let's say as popular electric
music,
to reach the people directly
and bring the coded
message across.

That's why you should
forget "The Arts" and
"Politics":
your politic is art!
In other words:
the weapon is creativity!
Important:
keep not only your
product,
but also its selling under
your control
otherwise you'll get
fucked.

Creativity

Creativity is the weapon
to keep the spirit high
and bring it over.
To change the world
on channels nobody even
thinks of.

Uli Trepte/Spacebox
Munich, Germany

Plastic People of the Universe

The Plastic People ... Prague -- *EGON BONDY'S HAPPY HEARTS CLUB BANNED*.

In EUROCK #10, there appeared an article on the Plastic People of the Universe relating to their political bust. At the time it was printed efforts were made to check it out, but met with no success. So it was printed. Since that time investigation into the situation has continued and significant facts have been gleaned from various sources. The basic situation appears to be this -- the original article was taken from articles in various Czech publications, some of which were government originated, along with some first-hand knowledge. As a whole the article now appears to be incorrect in several instances, so as rectification this piece is being done to rebut the original. The hope is that readers will pursue the truth on their own now that it is possible.

The current situation with the P.P.U. is that of the original defendants, all are free except Ivan Jirous. He was recently re-arrested and is now serving his 4th jail term. The organization Amnesty International has listed him as a prisoner of conscience and is monitoring the situation. In addition an album and book has just been released in England and France by the Plastic People Defense Fund and SCOPA. It is this that gives the opportunity for a more clear understanding as to just what the situation is like in Czechoslovakia and more specifically in the case of the P.P.U.

The album, *EGON BONDY'S HAPPY HEARTS CLUB BANNED* is the first recorded evidence of the P.P.U. It was recorded in a castle and smuggled out of the country, being released now without the group's knowledge. Musically it is not great in technical terms, but it is one of the most compelling records I've heard overall. The lyrics are translated into English on the sleeve and along with the

book the effect is staggering in impact, portraying the conflict of underground culture with the established order. The music is crude in the tradition of the early

Mothers, Fugs, Capt. Beefheart and Velvets. It's propelled by percussion and bass with e-piano, viola, sax and sporadic guitar giving it a razor edge. Two songs in particular stand out -- "Toxica" for its e-piano scales and "Magic Nights" for the percussive barrage it unleashes that literally captures the essence of the primal instinct. For the most part recording quality is very good considering the crude equipment and recording conditions.

Perhaps the best way to portray the feeling the record and book gives is with a quote from it : "Before long our humankind will be judged and in all but art will be found wanting. You who are poets bear the responsibility for everything concerning humankind. You shall redeem concentration camps and the bestialities of the police and the putrefaction of affluent regimes. On you who are poets rests the estimation of humankind. Therefore live on in hiding. Give out no news of yourselves. Live. Work." -- Egon Bondy (P. C. Plastic People Defense Fund, 1978). For information on how to obtain the album write: Plastic Defense Fund: BM 1415 London. WCIV6XX, England. FREE IVAN JIROUS.

Archie Patterson

1979

Chrome
life in alien nation

It's dark; black: like the wall I know is there but can't see because of the murky dampness suffocating me as I anticipate the killing force of our collision. The blackness is filled with jagged glass and snapped razor blades tormenting my every move. It's like not having sleep for endless days, poured in unknowingness while irregularly and unceasingly being slapped by my own hand. The ring from Dante's Inferno he didn't dare put to print has surfaced from man's collective unconscious to warn us all that there are depths. Thousands have heard this music for hundreds of years, only no one dared to make it for fear of giving the Prince of Darkness the music he needs to dance his dance. Among the innocents the twisted writhing mind does make noise and it has been heard............... Or is it a vitamin B deficiency?????
-R. Klinger

Chrome began as a flashback. Looking past today, into the future only to see that it didn't work. The *VISITATION* took place in California and picked up on latent energies that had come and gone -- simple regurgitation -- crude, rude and socially unacceptable.

1979

The *ALIEN SOUNDTRACKS* picked up on spaced out vibrations and twisted them into a mass of spare parts, anatomical structure of a stillborn beast. Like a malignant growth at inception, it spread and developed into a cancer.

It is only under certain circumstances and in rare cases that a work of art comes along and makes a clear statement about the conditions under which it was created. Even then it may not represent perfection of form; in fact that may be impossible due to the nature of the situation. But it is after all not form, but content that matters.

Case at hand is *CHROME*. The dream is over and while many might sense it, it took a rock mutation form San Francisco to let out with a primal scream -- *HALF MACHINE LIP MOVES* -- that could wake the dead. It's the music of humanity driven to the edge by aimless chaos and life without reason. In fact it questions the very nature of reason itself. Forget about form, simply let it blast your head wide open and fill your body with the vibrations of the spirit unleashed. How long has it been since you've felt frenzy. You understand what you should do, but can't bring yourself to do it as you've lost control. Your body is simply frozen into a recurring pattern of movement -- you're stuck in time -- paralyzed into a single moment. The schizophrenia of that situation leads to a crack-up. That crack-up has led to *CHROME*. Listen while you can.

Archie Patterson

The Swedish Alternative Music Movement

The Swedish movement developed for the most part out of a vacuous situation. In the late '60s the "music business" establishment companies in Sweden abandoned the idea of domestic pop, as they determined the market to be too small. Instead they concentrated on importing and marketing International Stars for maximum profit. As a result the energy of the sixties was channeled by native musicians into creating a scene that for the most part was untainted by the commercial ethic. Rock, folk and jazz artists all came together making it stylistically diverse, thus broadening its appeal.

Artists like Bo Hansson broke through in the early days, and as they gained a measure of recognition and success the movement grew and took firm root. Many other people were then encouraged to pick up their instruments and play. A large scale development of grassroots organizations for concerts, record distribution and co-operative work grew.

In the early '70s the new music began to come to life at festivals and demonstrations and became a growing alternative to mainstream commercialism. As this happened there developed alternative record companies, the first two of which were Silence and MNW. Silence was interested primarily in improvised instrumental music, while MNW focused on groups who sang political songs. With the record companies came a need to set up a distribution network and SAM distribution came into being. Like the record companies, it was based on equal wages for all, collective responsibility, and no bosses.

At this point things began to grow very fast. Many more small record companies sprang up, SAM grew, and two more small distribution nets began. In addition a record pressing plant, music magazine and a National Organization for Non-

Commercial Culture were set up. The movement was fast becoming a viable alternative in all areas of music. Artists could control their lives and work free of commercial pressure.

All has not gone without problems however. The thrust of the '60s has died down and the economic realities of the '70s have exerted pressure. But the movement continues as cooperation with other Scandinavian scenes develops, and similar experiments have begun in other European countries. So in spite of obstacles, the alternative music movement in Sweden continues to thrive, serving as an example of art for art's sake and music for people, not for profit.

Archie Patterson

Swedish Overview

There is perhaps no country that presents such a wide variety of styles musically and a large number of groups as Sweden. Electronic, folk, jazz, rock and all manner of hybrids flourish, as Swedish musicians produce an astounding amount of quality music. To do them all justice is next to impossible, so as an introduction to the Swedish scene this piece will focus on a group of artists who represent various segments of the overall spectrum.

Samla Mammas Manna - Without a doubt the most important group in Sweden and one of the best anywhere. Musically somewhere near jazz-rock, but actually much more. Very idiosyncratic, they fuse folk dances, avant-garde jazz like no-one else can. With their later works they're creating their own peculiar language to complement the music. The overall impact ranges from bizarre vignettes filled with humor to intense passages of instrumental improvisation. Any way you look at it they're originals. They must be heard to be believed.

Ralph Lundsten - "Ralphus Rex" is the most prolific Swedish musician. Having been active in making electronic music for over 10 years and 14 albums, he has refined the genre to its purest form. In his Chalet studio, Andromeda, he records his material which includes film and ballet scores, children's records, and experimental music. Purely electronic with only occasional aid from musician friends, his records represent at their best the ultimate in electronic composition. His sound is unique, his music "Cosmic," and his reputation notorious. *FADERVAR* and his *NATURE SYMPHONIES I & II* represent his classic works and show his mastery of the electronic style.

Kebnekaise - Fronted by guitarist Kenny Håkansson, the group's name is taken from the highest mountain in Sweden. Håkansson began playing with the '60s psychedelic blues band Meki Mark Men where he exhibited a style akin to Jimi Hendrix. Kebnekaise is markedly different, as folk melodies combine with rock/jazz rhythm to conjure up all sorts of earthy imagery. His guitar fuses with violin and percussive rhythms to great effect, as evidenced on *ELEFANTEN* which represents their greatest work. In addition to working with Bo Hansson, Håkansson just recently cut his first solo LP, a superb guitar-based work featuring heavy electronic treatments of traditional folk melodies. His playing style is meaty and full of tension, making him one of the most interesting guitarists around.

Bo Hansson - The most internationally known of Sweden's progressive musicians, he got his start in the duo of Hansson and Karlsson. Later he gained wider recognition for his instrumental treatment of *LORD OF THE RINGS*, which displays a keyboard technique that is versatile as well as exhibiting a flair for the melodic. His latest work, another literary adaptation, *WATERSHIP DOWN*, is a beauty. With intricate keyboard arrangements complemented perfectly by Håkansson's guitar, it's his strongest work yet, and shows his considerable talents at their best.

Archimedes Badkar - Working loosely in the jazz vein, Archimedes ("Bathtub") fuse elements of folk, electronics and ethnic rhythms along with Eastern motifs into their music. Extremely inventive, they can do swinging jazz as well as mantric instrumentals and exotic chants. The second album, a double, shows them at their most adventurous. Here all their influences come to play in creating an experimental work full of avant-garde spirit and fine progressive music.

Trettioåriga Kriget - "30 Years War" play a high-powered brand of progressive rock that ranks them among the best anywhere. Built around strong guitarwork that is given plenty of space to maneuver within the extended arrangements, Kriget lay it down hard and heavy. Also they are not at a loss for variety, with hints of jazz creeping in at intervals. Their recent work features the addition of keyboards adding a new flair of subtlety and melody.

Archie Patterson

Art Zoyd III and Univers Zero

The early '70s saw a new generation of musicians, come from different horizons (progressive rock, classics, jazz and contemporary music) dissatisfied with the limits imposed by these different genres, try to create music which would free itself of Anglo-Saxon influences in order to proclaim its own identity good and loud. This music, which we could describe as Continental or European, derives its source at once from classical, contemporary and even ethnic music, and you can't deny the influence of a group like Magma, a detonator group if there is one. But more than form, which engenders pallid copies (Nasal, Ocharinah, Belzebuth, etc.) unable to see more than the obvious aspects of this music (bass/drum pulsation), and more than the spirit which cannot find shelter from the critics, it is the new perspectives that it opens up which we must take hold of here. And if people like Weidorje extend in a continuous line the trail blazed by Magma, other groups, which have also been around for about 7 years -- period when this new music came into bloom -- freed themselves quite a while ago to take off for new horizons... They are called Art Zoyd III and Univers Zero.

ART ZOYD III
If you felt like counting you could come up with the impressive number of about 30 musicians who had at one time or other played with this group. You could get lost and never find your way out of this maze and we're not going to take that chance.... The make-up that interests us here, third of that name, has existed as such for a few years now, since a radical change in orientation which surprised more than one at the bend of a concert. Our memories

had stayed with this electric, chaotic group, kind of a spiritual son-of-Zappa, brother of all the bizarre groups of the '70s playing music at the borderline of pop and free jazz. And then, after a long silence, Art Zoyd came back, charged with new energy, its music had gained in severity, in power and in interest.

I remember that first concert, those 4 men lined up, straight as flags and who, after scarcely taking time to acknowledge the audience, flung their "Brigades Speciales" into the faces of the people who had come almost as if by chance. Zaboitzeff hurled his words, violent, guttural while snapping the notes of his bass which in his hands became a solo instrument, the 2 violins (Gerard Hourbette and Frank Cardon) played short virile phrases in unison, and one occasionally spinning around the other, agile and bold, before continuing on its way ... and that trumpet of Jean Pierre Soarez which never stopped sounding the charge and whose blast pierced your ears....

There was also "Simulacres," "Masques" and lots of other pieces which I've preciously saved on the "live" recording, music of an extraordinary density, of a disconcerting gravity, in spite of the irony that shone through some Spanish air or "Java." Art Zoyd, third of that name, had become a fantastic quartet, a sort of Quatuor Vegh burning with fever.

Since then the group has gone its way, far from gossip, from business. They have been opening act for Magma at a few concerts (Theatre de la Renaissance), plowed the roads of France regularly, recorded an album SYMPHONIE POUR LE JOUR OU BRULERONT LES CITES (Symphony for the Day when Cities will Burn) -- with the help of Michel Besset and Tartempion, very honest album as to its quality, but way below the potential of the group in concert.

Art Zoyd III, vivid music, music/expression of musicians joined together, "committed" music that disturbs, theater and tragedy of the absurd, fruit of a real GROUP effort which explains the great variety of themes in evidence. For the music of Art Zoyd is set up, theme by theme, developing itself in an unforeseeable way, aggressive, troubling. It has to do here with a new form of exploitation of the symphonic form, inherited from the great contemporary composers, in which a theme neither develops itself nor announces a new theme, but shatters, enters in conflict with the following theme, a sort of coherence in an (apparent) incoherence, deliberate act of will on the part of the group to assault the listener, force consciousness of reality upon him. However, the music also knows how to be caressing, humorous even. It would be so in fact if you don't discern all its mockery and its perversity.

For years Art Zoyd III has been fighting to be heard, and they've succeeded: without publicity, without support, their record continues to sell, soon approaching 3,000 copies, the groups concerts draw more and more people. It was a long time since I had heard them in concert and a recent tour in the Southwest, along with Univers Zero, gave me the opportunity. Alain Eckert (guitar) who some time ago took the place left vacant by Frank Cardon has left again (he almost played with Etron Fou) and Frank has come back. The group still plays pieces like "Brigades Speciales" and the placing of the instruments is now impeccable, certain themes have disappeared from the repertoire and from hearing the new titles ("Musique pour l'Odyssee") it seems that the music of Art Zoyd III is becoming more and more classical, with long single violin passages, which break a little with the general rhythm. The music is less "compressed" than before, and on the contrary has a tendency to aerate, to develop itself in a less brutal way. Violence is still there however, bursting or underlying with that unshakable will to break the lines, to take over the sound-space, to assault (the piercing notes of the trumpet). A determination always to reflect and to denounce at the same time a daily life become more and more oppressive. For the music of Art Zoyd, you've understood correctly is not entertaining music, consumer's music, and if the members of the collective have nothing to say, it's quite simply because their music is there, for that. Sounds become words, words are only sounds ("I'l et fa"); it is the violin bow that tears out the notes, that hums, that grates on the strings, the bass that hammers or the powerful blast of brass. There is neither mystique nor reference to some mythology with Art Zoyd. Simply the refusal to hide behind words, to catch hold of waves, new or not. Art Zoyd III, on the contrary is a collective intelligence at music's services FOR it and by IT. And they can walk with their heads held high...

UNIVERS ZERO

Five musicians, all dressed in black. Silence...and then, almost imperceptibly, a violin penetrates the space and the notes issuing from it are dry, monochords. A bassoon, warm, comes to join it breaking into its crazy dance while a harmonium resounds, unreal, dehumanized as if another forces invisible came to blow through it.

Cymbals shiver: It's the introduction to "La Ronde," a long piece inspired by the repression of the Middle Ages. Throats and nerves are tied in knots. Like a storm that refuses to break, the round carries us along, plays with us, brings us to its mercy. And suddenly, there it is bursting, joyous, light almost, reassuring perhaps. Music of an unheard-of beauty, attractive and extremely elaborate, violin and bassoon in unison or crossing each other.... In the style of Chris Cutler, Daniel Denis only touches his skins one time out of five and there is no contest between the man and his instrument, the latter having been tamed a long time ago. Sometimes the music remains suspended for the space of a second and the instruments reappear, inhabited by a new energy; the sequences follow in succession linked in an absolutely extraordinary way as the bassoon takes off in spirals for a short dance of whirling dervishes and the violin grimaces while the bass growls. And before you are able to completely realize what's happening, "La Ronde" has become a long chant of infinite sadness, the bow glides on the strings slowly, fingers pinch the strings, the harmonium is there, monotone, repeating the same chords incessantly until the melody slips through the fingers of those who give it life.

Univers Zero has existed under this name for 5 years now, since the day when some musicians who until that time played music strongly influenced by the school of Canterbury decided to create a more personal music, a change which was accomplished thanks to some new musicians come from contemporary classical music. Finding musicians to play this particular music wasn't easy, especially in Belgium where the apathy of the music scene, more oriented toward Anglo-Saxon countries would have discouraged more than a few. However through perseverance the group was able to jell and after many unfruitful efforts,

Univers Zero today is composed of Roger Trigaux (harmonium, guitar), Michel Berckmans (bassoon, oboe), Patrick Hanappier (violin), Daniel Denis (drums), Guy Segers (bass) and Eric Faes (sound environment). To stay in Belgium was in a way to condemn the group, when it judged its music ready, decided to make itself heard everywhere it could...

When you ask them what their influences were, the group's members can't keep from answering: "Doctor Petiot, Landru, Sister Godfrieda, Jack-the Ripper..." Black humor surely, but also and above all simply humor, that of people who have understood for a long time that they're only here for a time, earthly, without real importance, that it's not for them to judge what is important or not, to judge what is good or bad. Humor of people who know that NOTHING is really important, that everything ends anyway in the same way and that as a result of that they have nothing to lose... For these men of Univers Zero live each moment in relation to their death. Warriors in the Castanedan sense of the word, they are free to act as if it were really important to them and thus make obsession with death disappear... It is therefore not by chance that they are dressed in black or that their compositions are entitled, "Doctor Petiot," "Malaise," "Complainte" or "La Faux." Not by chance that their music is so strong, so beautiful...

This music is after all really and definitively group music. There is at the heart of Univers Zero neither spiritual nor musical leader. And even if certain compositions are the work of one or the other musicians, these are worked in common, each bringing to it or cutting away what he feels necessary, Each of the musicians is concerned about the construction of the pieces, for here the notion of group is primordial over that of performers. Extremely complex music, written down entirely, without improvisations which are often pretexts for useless solos. That doesn't mean that some of the musicians who compose don't know how to write music: Music in the head and which, first on paper and then played, is found to be full of harmonic boldness of bizarre timing, unconventional and which gives such a special aspect to this music which is enriched in the process of being played, purified and matured.

Univers Zero likes to cultivate surprising contrasts, relatively serene climates but torn by the stridencies of the violin or heavy chords of the guitar, atmospheres smelling of sulfur, thanks to the enormous work on the sonority and the variations in volume of the instruments, sometimes almost inaudible, sometimes pushed to their paroxysm. A lot of dissonances in this music too, harmonies that Bach in his mathematical and categorical fury would have banished, but of which Stravinsky and Bartok are the great forerunners. For it is in maintaining a certain total ambiguity, by multiplying rhythms in this way, making them run together that Univers Zero develops an original art of sounds; hard music which wants to paint realities and evoke abstractions, primitive music which draws its whole substance from deformed rhythms, the effect of the instruments' timbres, chaotic music where tonalities come to knock against each other, modes completely opposed, but directed by a dominating will and where melody always finds its place. Music where sounds navigate incessantly between the warmth of a bassoon or of a violin and the blocks of ice from the harmonium from which the notes are torn and the stridencies of the violin....

Univers Zero is all that, a world where Hieronymus Bosch's visions of the Apocalypse, a Middle Ages leveled by wars and epidemics with the sounds of distant festivals, paintings of the Flemish school, of these desolate flat countrysides, which know so well how to blend with the colors of the sky, but also describe our world, all join and melt together, universe of madmen and excess.

ART ZOYD III & UNIVERS ZERO
Art Zoyd III and Univers Zero met about a year ago and the two groups, in spite of differences in form of their respective music, decided to work together on musical pieces bringing together the two groups. Certain pieces from Art Zoyd and from Univers Zero were therefore orchestrated for 9 musicians and the result is fantastic for the two groups complement each other wonderfully, one bringing its force, the other its nuances. Art Zoyd III and Univers Zero is the union of 9 musicians moved by the same will, playing music of a prodigious density, something never heard before, an experiment which took off from a piece by one or the other groups re-orchestrated for the circumstances and which will one day see compositions specially written for the two groups. I was at the reunion concert which took place in Toulouse at the beginning of May and still can't get over it. Try to imagine 3 violins, 1 viola, 1 bassoon, 1 bass, 1 set of drums, 1 trumpet, 1 harmonium, try to imagine the pace this music can set at the hands of such musicians..... Art Zoyd III and Univers Zero are the ONLY groups which bring something really new in music, music which I don't hesitate to call, in spite of its imperfections, contemporary classical music, music which is a certain reflection of our real life. Or rather which is simply an appeal to our consciousness which itself gives us a sense of reality. And there lies all the difference between music-subversion and music-alienation...

Gerard Nguyen, with the help of Sabine
(Courtesy ATEM Magazine, translation
Lois Bode)

Catherine Ribeiro + Alpes

The name Catherine Ribeiro + Alpes is totally unknown in America. Yet they are the pioneer of all French progressive groups.

1962: Catherine Ribeiro, daughter of a Portuguese worker appeared in a film by Godard called "Les Carabiniers." There she met a Patrice Moullet.

1968: (April) One month before the revolutionary events in France, Catherine Ribeiro decides to die. But death doesn't want her. Patrice Moullet comes everyday to see her in the hospital, telling her he was feeling the music for her words (she had already sung alone). When they decided to put out an album, several labels refused it as "non-commercial." They finally signed with the Festival label which agreed to let them do what they wanted.

End of 1969: The first album appears -- *CATHERINE RIBEIRO + 2 BIS* (the group's name was not yet Alpes). It was outstanding for the time, just think the first Magma album wasn't out yet. In fact it was the FIRST FRENCH PROGRESSIVE LP. Patrice Moullet played "electric lyre" on it -- strange music and strange lyrics: "I want to smile at the children even if they stick out their tongues at me."

August 1970: The turning point of their career -- a festival in Aix. The group gets a telephone call to come play immediately (it's late night), they hesitate and finally accept, playing at the end of the festival, early in the morning in front of a frozen, sleepy audience. They proceed to awaken everybody and their name becomes famous.

December 1970: 2nd LP: *CATHERINE RIBEIRO + ALPES* (2 Bis has changed into the trio Alpes). They had developed a very personal sound. It wasn't until Feb. '72 that they did their third album, *AME DEBOUT*. Why so long? In the meantime had happened a most important event for Catherine: the birth of her daughter Ioana. In addition two new musicians appear on this album (one of the two, Patrice Lemoine, will play much later on the Gong LP *SHAMAL*). Also for the first time a "cosmophone" and a "percuphone" are used. The percuphone is the more unusual of the two consisting of one bass string on a board at the end of which there's an electric engine which moves a helix that hits the string. It's possible to vary the speed of the engine making it very original rhythmically, no bass, no drums. The cosmophone is a 24 string guitar. For the first time it's obvious that the French language works perfectly with progressive music.

Jan. 1973: The fourth LP, *PAIX*, appears and features a long track of more than 20 minutes. It has a quite religious climate -- perhaps because of the ever-present organ.

July 1975: A fifth LP, *LE RAT DEBILE ET L'HOMME DES CHAMPS* is released. Once more there is a very long track. The subject is loneliness, lack/need of tenderness. There are revolutionary declarations, but also confessions: "We shan't change the world by democratic ways -- there will be violence... I hate violence it scares me." The track ends with orgasmic cries that literally give you chills.

October 1975: 6th LP, *LIBERTES?* The most political record of all. Catherine wants to express the suffering and misery of people at the hands of insensitive government. Violence rules the whole album as she shouts out her revolt.

October 1977: 7th LP, *LE TEMPS DE L'AUTRE*. Once more a long track about death, "Le Silence de la Mort" (Silence of Death). It is impressive and compelling as no doubt she knows what she is talking about.

Between 1969 and 1978 Catherine Ribeiro + Alpes have matured. If musicians have changed, two people are the soul of the group from the beginning to the end -- Catherine and her terrific voice and Patrice Moullet for the music and what music! The instrumentals testify to that. A music sometimes hypnotic, sometimes violent, sometimes sweet always beautiful. A music from the "guts."

Michel Le Came

Theatre Du Chene Noir

Le Chene Noir ("The Black Oak") is a gathering of French actors/musicians which has existed since 1967. Over 11 years they have created 17 different plays where theatre and music are joined intimately. In addition they've done 3 LPs that give a good idea of their music and overall concept -- *AURORA* (1971), *CHANT POUR LE DELTA, LA LUNE ET LE SOLEIL* (1976), and *ORPHEE 2000* (1977).

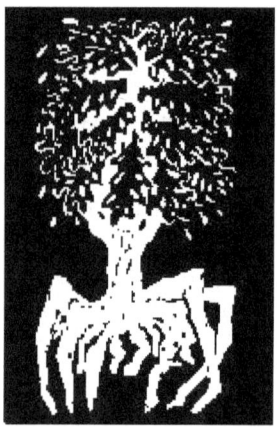

AURORA is the story of earth and her children struggling against men/bird creatures which fly from planet to planet to become masters of the universe. There's often this idea of the earth in danger in Chene Noir.

Side opens with flutes, weird voices and percussion sounding quite sinister. The second track "Le Bonheur" (happiness) features a great variety of rhythms by a flute (or two) and drums which quickens to a climax, then slowly fades. The third track is perhaps the most chaotic number, with the voice used to create the most terrific effects. Shrieks and rattles leave you quivering in your armchair.

Fortunately the end of the side is peaceful, but it's the peacefulness of death. "Oldness and Death" is the title of the closing piece.

Side 2 maintains the same musical climate -- flutes dancing nearer and nearer. A battle between the voice and a sax which symbolizes the struggle of good against bad. The men/bird creatures come during the night to give dreams to humans -- dreams of possession. There's also a soft, quite cosmic track with voices off behind a drum beat. An awful cry stops your dreams at the tracks *AURORA* ends with a sax solo that seems to disappear into space.

CHANT POUR LE DELTA, LA LUNE ET LE SOLEIL, with this second LP you notice at once a much wider variety of sounds -- musicians have changed. You can hear an organ which gives a new musical coloring. Also the quality of the recording is better. This second LP is stereo, *AURORA* was done in mono. The tunes are more catchy. The second track "Les Oiseaux" (birds -- once more!) is the one which perhaps resembles the first LP the most with its ethereal voice in the background. In the third track, "Hey," there are riffs of sax, a strong bass, piano, drums and a spacy voice. They denounce the false valor of the modern world: sects and money -- no comment (it was done in 1976!) Side 2 contains two long tracks : "La 7" which is the name of a road in the south of France. It's a slow, nostalgic tune. "LeNil" ends the record. The sax draws a kind of sketch in which bass and percussion are the decoration. An obsessive rhythm is repeated endlessly. One sax is playing it, then two which rejoin at the end of the record.

ORPHEE 2000, the musicians are the

same but the tracks are shorter (11 tracks in all). The sound has more thickness -- several themes are mixed -- it's less monolithic than on the previous LP. Each instrument adds its own colour. Some riffs are repeated till a new direction is taken. We settle ourselves into a new melody carried by a piano and...surprise the sax brings a new riff. It's constantly changing music. The intense drum beat makes you think sometimes of tribal ritual. One moment you think you've found the music to be jazz, a minute later you realize it's something else. When you listen to Chene Noir you have the feeling of hearing cerebral poetry that everyone possesses in some corner of their psyche.

Chene Noir 1978: November '78 Chene Noir plays Angers. There has been a change as they have no sets, no fantastic costumes as they have used previously. G. Gelas, the main man of the group, tells us of the problems they have had that day with their things. They then however still manage to present us with a new performance -- "Virgilio." It is the story of an Italian immigrant coming to live and work in France, but it also tells of all people who have lost their roots. There are as always catchy tunes and the voice of Nicole Aubiat which recalls Catherine Ribeiro for its powerfulness. The music is fascinating.

Who are Chene Noir? Gerard Gelas and Nicole Aubiat (voice), Pierre Surtel (flute and sax), Daniel Dublet (piano, guitar), who have been in the group from the beginning. The leader of the group is Gerard, he is responsible for the lyrics and music. In addition he plays lute, drums, synthi, piano, organ & guitar. He is the roots of Chene Noir, the others its branches. Together they create a unique multi-media experience, Theatre Du Chene Noir.

Michel Le Came

Konrad Schnitzler

INTERMEDIA - LIFE - ACTION

In the late '60s there was a group called Kluster featuring the trio of Moebius, Roedelius and Schnitzler. While Edgar Froesc was trying to hawk his psychedelic ideas to commercial record companies in England, Kluster recorded 2 albums -- *KLOPFZEICHEN* ('70) and *ZWEI OSTEREI* ('71) that were released on limited edition by the small Schwann label. They have to be heard to be believed as waves of harsh electronic sound combine with spoken, politically-oriented texts to create a hypnotizing, disorienting experience. In late '71 the trio split and Cluster came into being as it is today. Schnitzler then helped form the first Tangerine Dream to record *ELECTRONIC MEDITATION* for Ohr with Edgar F. and

Klaus Schulze. After that recording the collaboration came to an end and Konrad began work on his own in Berlin.

In the next 4 years he embarked on several projects. Late 1971 saw the private release of an album titled *SCHWARZ* (Black). It contained 2 pieces "Eruption 1" and "Eruption 2" which were reportedly recorded at a live happening by Kluster. In 1972 he released a second private album *ROT* (Red) with again 2 pieces "Kraut Rock" and "Meditation." Both of these records send tremors down the spine with their intense use of electronics. 1973 saw the release of his 3rd private album, *BLAU* (Blue) -- all 3 were pressed in quantities of only 100 copies. The 2 cuts on *BLAU*, "Rebellion..." and "Jupiter" continued his exploration of the concept of sensory overload. As they stand, these 3 LPs represent perhaps the most extreme statement of the German electronic music scene ever recorded.

During 1974 he gave a 50-hour performance, over a 16 day time span, in the Berlin, Rene Block Gallerie. The tapes were edited into 100 - 30 minute cassettes and became part of a limited edition of 100 boxed set titled *KONRAD SCHNITZLER'S ERUPTION*, which also contained re-pressings of his 3 albums. In addition to all of this, he composed scores for 3 projects: the 1970 Oper Zar und Zimmerman and 2 films "Made in NY" (1973) and "Slow Motion" (1976).

It all may have remained lost if not for T. Dream refugee Peter Baumann. Thanks go to him for recording *CON* (released on French Egg), which enabled a wider audience to get a load of Schnitzler's synthesizers. The sounds on the album, though less crude and powerful than on his 3 private albums, still show off his style most effectively -- no frills, no fluff -- instead pulsating synthetic rhythms and vibrations.

The music stands out on the basis of its ideas, not artificial wizardry. For pure "electronic" music you'll not find anyone who has the grasp of technology and abundance of unique ideas of Konrad Schnitzler -- one of Germany's pioneers of New Musik.

Archie Patterson

Schneeball (Snowball): Hopefully

STORY FIRST: In April 1976 the German music groups Embryo, Ton Steine Scherben, Missus Beastly, Sparifankal (and later Julius Schittenhelm) got together and founded their own label -- April Records -- to press and distribute their records on their own. The idea behind it was to get rid of the influence of the big music companies which nearly all of them had very bad experiences with.

The Trikont Publishing Company contributed the necessary know-how and soon the idea worked out so well that other groups wanted to join too. This was realized when Munju, Moira, Checkpoint Charlie, Real Axe Band and Bruehwarm became involved, and in nearly 3 years 17 records were produced.

In 1977 the media concern CBS (which operates a music publishing company called April-Music) forced the label to give up the name April: it's now called Schneeball and hopefully grows by rolling along.

THE STRUCTURE: of Schneeball is guerrilla-like: to keep everything visible and personal. The label up to now is divided into 2 main sections of 5 groups each who work together independently. Each group has an area where it and/or its friends distribute the records of all the groups to the shops by mail or offer them at their own concerts. The money goes to the group whose record is sold, only friends who don't belong to a Schneeball group, but work for the distribution, get a commission fee. An amazing system which works out well, is expandable to a certain degree and still keeps the organization decentralized and personally related.

THE GROUPS: all the Schneeball groups are declaredly alternative in their music, life-style, feeling and thinking which means they stand alone.

Embryo: Very good live group who also do fine records; still open and quite free; one of the very few pioneer groups who didn't give in and kept the spirit high all the years: source, initiator driving force and focus of many alternative activities.

Ton Steine Scherben: Already a legend, TSS have a very German touch in their rock with words that hit most direct. They have ceased to exist as a live group, but do a lot of productions now.

Missus Beastly, Munju, Real Axe Band,

1979

Moira: Good live groups who play the most imaginative jazz-rock in Germany.

Checkpoint Charlie: The former true anarcho group of the old German scene with an act based on very aggressive socially critical lyrics brilliantly executed by their speaker.

Julius Schittenhelm: Philosophical song writer with intelligent lyrics, strange music and a very humorous way of presenting his material: unique person.

Sparifankal: Rock group with satirical Bavarian words and habits: a funny enterprise with heavy overtones.

Bruehwarm: A gay theatre group who is for real. The music of TSS really fits their act which is outstanding in its way.

VIEWS: to understand Schneeball it has to be noted that before the founding of the label, nearly all music groups who weren't too straight were asked to take part in the undertaking, but only the above groups really backed the idea and took the step away from the industry. So these people know who they are and have a very good personal relationship with each other, that's actually the strongest aspect of Schneeball. They're not interested in expanding for its own sake, but let it slowly grow with groups they know to be committed and dig for sure. New on the Schneeball horizon is, e.g. Spacebox, a group which has been in permanent contact with them for a long time and would never stand a chance with the industry. So the label is now at a certain turning point as they have to look for a way where the administration can be done in a cool way leaving enough time to the groups for creative work. Surely the Schneeball people will solve this problem because they can think and are still open to changes. It can be said that with Schneeball it's the first time in Germany that the music of the alternative scene has its own production means: a real milestone and potential prospect.

Schneeball Discography:

0000 Sparifankal - *BAYERNROCK*
0001 Missus Beastly - *DR. AFTERSHAVE*
0002 TSS - *WENN DIE NACHT AM TIEFSTEN*
0003 Embryo - *LIVE*
0004 Julius Schittenhelm - *ARISTOTELES*
0005 Embryo - *BAD HEADS & BAD CATS*
0006 Bruehwarm/TSS - *MANNSTOLL*
0007 TSS - *KEINE MACHT FUR NIEMAND*
0008 TSS - *WARUM GEHT ES MIR SO DRECKIG*
0009 Real Axe Band - *NICHT STEHENBLEIBEN*
0010 Embryo - *APO-CALYPSO*
0011 Missus Beastly - *SPACE GUERRILLA*
0012 Munju - *HIGH SPEED KINDERGARTEN*
0013 Sampler - *APRIL 1ST SCHNEEBALL*
0014 Moira - *CRAZY COUNTDOWN*
0015 Checkpoint Charlie- *FRUHLING DER KRUPPEL*
MOL 1 Vlotho - *UMSONST UND DRAUBEN 75*
MOL 2 Vlotho - *UMSONST UND DRAUBER 76*
MOL 3/4 Vlotho - *UMSONST UND DRAUBEN 77*
MOL 5/6 Porta Westfalica - *UMSONST UND DRAUBEN 78*

Uli Trepte/ Spacebox

YUGOSLAVIA -- Yu. Rock

The first album by a Yugoslav rock group appeared late in 1968. It was the record by Groupa 220. In the early '70s Yugoslavia had 3 great groups -- a free rock/jazz group Mladi Levi (Young Lions) who never recorded, Korni Groupa and Time. The last two groups played very original rock with Oriental and jazz elements thrown in. Time later became an ordinary rock group and Korni Groupa worked in two areas. They recorded very good progressive albums, but also throwaway hit singles to earn the money to live. They in addition recorded an album *NOT AN ORDINARY LIFE* in Italy for the international market as well as appeared at the Montreux Jazz Festival in Switzerland. Later all 3 groups split. The keyboard player and leader of Korni Groupa, Kornell Kovach, now works in London as a session musician. At this year's Reading Festival he appeared with the Jenny Darren Group. Drago Mlinarec from Groupa 220 has played with the group Pritjatelji (Friends) since 1971 and they play very interesting music which is a mixture of soft rock, acoustic, jazz and the vocals of Drago.

In 1973 appeared a hard rock trio with folk influences thrown in -- Yu Groupa, which today exists as a quartet. Since 1962 in Yugoslavia there has existed a group called Indexi. At first they were commercial, in the late '60s underground, and now they play symphonic rock (influenced by the Moody Blues but more commercial). In 1973 appeared a jazz/rock group Spektar (Spectrum) influenced by Billy Cobham and the group Hobo who used a lot of electronics and electric violin. Both groups each recorded one album. Excellent keyboardist Tihomir Pop Asanovic (ex-Time) recorded two jazz/rock albums with the best Yugoslav jazz and rock musicians. Unique guitarist and singer Tomas Pengon recorded in the WC at his house a very original album of acoustic music. In 1973/74 appeared the group Bijelo Dugme (White Button). Their albums sold 150,000 copies each and they drew larger crowds on tour in Yugoslavia than the Rolling Stones. They played heavy rock with some folk elements.

Other important groups in YU:

Smak - They signed for 5 years with the German label Bellaphon for distribution on the international market. Now they have a US keyboard player David Moss. They play heavy rock with blues elements thrown in.

September - With keyboard player Pop Asanovic (ex Time) and some members of Mladi Levi, they had a tour last Spring ('78) in America and recorded in studios in Florida for Columbia. They play good rock with jazz mixtures.

Leb i Sol (Bread & Salt) - This is, besides Bijelo Dugme, the most popular group in Yugoslavia. But they are much better instrumentally and more creative. They play jazz/rock with Macedonian rhythm and elements of Oriental folklore. They are however sometimes a bit derivative of the Mahavishnu Orchestra or Return to Forever.

Tako - A rock group with Baroque, symphonic and jazz elements mixed in.

Buldozer - A satiric, eccentric rock group from Ljubljana. They had trouble because of their records and live act with concert organizations, etc. But they now have cleaned it up and are having some success. However like most Yugoslav groups, the influences of popular Anglo-American rock groups in their music are very evident.

Staklene Perle (Glass Pearls) - A young electronic, symphonic rock group with psychedelic tendencies.

Begnagrad (Escape-To-The-Castle) - This is perhaps the most original group in YU. They will soon have their first LP out. They are eccentric, playing instrumental music containing elements of Slovanian folk music, jazz, swing, Oriental elements, humour, free jazz, improvisation, etc. The lineup is: accordion, clarinet, drums, bass guitar and sometimes guests: e-violin and trombone. Momentarily they have split up because some members are in the army. This is a very big problem for Yugoslav groups as many disband because of their military obligations.

Sedmina (Old Slovanian term meaning "the party after the funeral") - This is a very good acoustic group with Slovenian (Slovenia -- North of Yugoslavia) folk, rock and classical elements. So far they've not released any records.

Soncna Pot (Sunny Way) - This Slovenian group is perhaps the best and most original group in Yugoslavia. This year they will have their first album out.

The music of Soncna Pot is like sound-pictures, it's very hard to describe. The overall effect is very soft, full of intelligent improvisations and excellent solos. Similar to jazz/rock, it is also full of classical and old Slovenian folk elements. Maybe also loose influences of Weather Report and the ECM sound, but more unique. The personnel is: L. Jahsa - keyboards, electronics, saxophones, flute, clarinet, Mellotron; J. Gancev - bass guitar, keyboards, Mellotron; R. Divjak (ex-Time, September) - drums, percussion, vibes.

For progressive groups like Begnagrad and Soncna Pot, it is very difficult to make a record because in Yugoslavia there aren't any independent or alternative record companies. Big companies are still the only way and offer the most money. They are mainly interested however in groups which sound like Anglo-American rock groups or commercial groups and singers. There also exists in YU a few punk groups, but they don't record albums. For the most part, the main companies -- PGP RTB, Jugoton, RTV Ljubljana, Diskoton and Helidon -- decide who gets to put out records.

Alex Lenard

Progressive Europe In The '70s
...200 Years Of Influences

When considering the largest influences of new music or art rock in the seventies, names such as Ravel, Debussy and Stravinsky are usually the first to come to mind, along with the Beatles, Pink Floyd and others. In some ways the scope of influences is too vast to recall at once, as different styles and cultures pervade all areas of the world. Likewise in Europe, which has a wide range of variety and taste resting on a grand scale that dates back hundreds of years. The custom of passing this large part of culture down to each generation is a tradition in itself, and every succeeding generation has made additional contributions to it with the flow of time. In this classical background there have been shifting conflicts as modern trends now dominate the continent in the seventies.

It is then no exaggeration to state that

most of the principle European countries are linked by a strong sense of the Gothic nature, and musicians who follow this sense tend to pick it up and put it into their music. Drawing from their own heritage, with much evident influx from America and England, they have produced some extraordinary musical hybrids, as highlighted here.

Since the classical composers were a substantial inspiration to Europe's present day progressives, the familiar names shall be mentioned for significance -- Beethoven, Bach, Strauss, Schubert, Mozart.

Johann Sebastian Bach, in the Baroque era, founded new forms of composition that have endured to this day. His own type of convention, known as counterpoint, brought in textures that musicians would use in new and fascinating ways two hundred years later. Throughout his work, from toccatas and fugues to oratorios and cantatas, his skill at handling contrapuntal writing and unusual harmony, made him a natural model for Progressives across the continent. Even in today's sophisticated arrangements, his intricate melodic patterns and exquisitely charted bass lines can still be heard. (In fact, Edgar Froese of Tangerine Dream referred to him as the best bassist who ever lived.)

W.A. Mozart, the Strausses and Schubert made large contributions, but their importance is still overlooked in the European progressive pantheon nowadays. Mozart, who was composing before his teens, set a precedent for experimentation that must have amazed people for generations, but his lack of self-confidence and forcefulness often obscured his great gifts. By the time he passed on, aspiring young artists studied his work diligently, attentive to his sharp sense of dynamics and form, not knowing the struggles he endured to achieve his accomplishments.

Johann Strauss, then Richard Strauss, also fell short of expectations of some in their time. Johann, a pupil of the Vienna school that spawned Beethoven, is not widely known for much outside of his waltzes, although his other repertoire, including marches and operettas, have a high degree of pomposity and eccentricity that has permeated all of European material in some form during the last decade. His approach to founding a type of music that everyone could relate to led to the waltz, a dance that could be learned instantly. This should have placed him in the same field as Beethoven, where composers receive honors from regal figures and the like for their work, but he had to remain content with the common people who flocked to dance halls by the thousands to dance accompanied by his sweeping waltzes and polkas.

Richard Strauss, although not related to Johann, was known for branching out from what were considered "old" forms by the end of the nineteenth century. Pieces such as "Death and Transfiguration" and "Also Sprach Zarathustra" may have sounded typically dramatic in the usual way, but Strauss employed parts of the orchestra in major roles that had been more or less ignored in the previous era. Brass were given frequent soloing; entire sections charted through passages of high volume brilliance and percussion to equal effect. Sadly, time has taken its toll. "Zarathustra" is now a cliché heard on TV commercials for coffee and aspirin, and most of Strauss' remaining work is often substituted with lighter fare in symphony concerts. Had it not been for the soundtrack recording for "2001: A Space Odyssey," even the most popular repertoire of both composers may not have been heard by the masses in the last ten years, let alone the millions who were inspired by the application of the tuneful music to the futuristic vision of the film.

Ludwig van Beethoven, for what he contributed to the Romantic era, has been probably overlooked throughout recent years, not necessarily due to the fact that present day composers find it difficult to fit his broad scope into their own material. Of all the symphonies and concertos he produced, few of his own thematic statements can be found as being primary influences in the minds of European Progressives, at best not in composing. Although the "Cosmic Music" complex under Rolf-Ulrich Kaiser adopted him as their spiritual mentor, there was little of his heavy string sections or complicated phrasing being heard in their other-worldly material. At the same time, many of the pioneering musicians in these ranks would have chosen such a towering figure as their symbolic figure head. Yet only a few (Ekseption, ELO) have done anything concrete, and that consisted mainly of adaptations interpretation and use of motifs as gimmicks.

Franz Schubert is recognized for being the foremost song composer, trying to move away from the Vienna school and the influence of Beethoven. Receiving much criticism for his underdeveloped structure in sonatas and other short pieces, he could have followed the style along the same lines with much success. Staying clear of further shortcomings with his secular music and development of the art song (lieder), he composed six hundred songs in all. His prominence today with contemporary artists would seem assured. However, once again, not until the first experiments with orchestral pop in the sixties was his style rediscovered (not forgetting the "Unfinished Symphony").

The twentieth century witnessed the emergence of the impressionists and new methods of composition that would shape the progressive sound most of all. Claude Debussy was precise in his composing, envisioning his pieces with scenery like a painter. Since the titles such as "Clair de Lune," "Prelude to the Afternoon of a Fawn" and "The Engulfed Cathedral" suggest dramatic events in an art like setting, Debussy was definitely one of the first visionaries and a forerunner of new music. It is no wonder that nearly every major group in Europe and most electronic masters in European pop have shown a certain debt to this composer in some way.

Igor Stravinsky has been credited with bringing new intensity to symphonic scores by way of arranging orchestrations in a multi-tiered way, building crescendos from sparse surroundings with woodwinds and horns. In another vast amount of work, he developed his own sense of structure increasing tension by this unique method, keeping the listener constantly anticipating a new event. When he started working with smaller groups of instruments, he further made innovations drawing large amounts of sound from just these few instruments. Taking ideas from Schoenberg and Webern and putting them to his own use, Stravinsky continued their utilization of atonality or the twelve tone system, which has filtered into every section of European music from free jazz to electron rock. Also since he lived as an American in the latter part of his life, this makes his influences strongly American as well.

Richard Wagner has not always been regarded as a major figure in the crop of ranking composers in Europe. Although he spent twenty years composing the "Ring of the Nibelungen," a series of four operas based on mythology from antiquity, and set new standards for the relation of music to the possibilities of the theatre, young artists would more likely turn to twentieth century modernists such as Ravel. This progressive camp, let alone all the new music and neo-classical circles that occupy the camp, have drawn to the works of Maurice Ravel more frequently than most others. While this may be arguable, he is no less a great radical technician than George Gershwin whose "Rhapsody in Blue" premiered at the same time as "Bolero." Once again a wide cross-section of material separates Ravel from most of his contemporaries, even in the 1920s, who were content to make a name for themselves settling in for accepted styles (already industry trends in music as early as then).

Ravel's edge over these composers, with the possible exception of Debussy, was in how he combined romanticism with startling contrasts in tonality and mood. Debussy's moods vary from one composition to another; Ravel can change the listeners state of mind from one moment to the next, demonstrating a great ability to mix sound colors into one another without losing the important center where the energy originates. Ravel's interest in jazz may have owed something to Gershwin, but he is definitely a creator on his own using individual intuitions to achieve truly original results putting him in a class by himself.

Other composers deserve some recognition as well -- Grieg, Tchaikovsky, Mussorgsky, Berlioz, Hindemith and Americans Charles Ives and Aaron Copland. While these individuals have made less appreciable impact on the European music of present, they appear to have contributed most to the following areas -- new methods of composing, elaborate settings for sophisticated or longer works, continuity and leanings toward what would become new music.

Then for the British and American contemporary influences, and here is where it becomes confusing. The U.K. as a whole has been closer to the rest of Europe, so the question is, "How much dominant influence came from Britain and what came from America?"

In order to start a new interest of popular music in a country such as England, there must have been a sizable amount of activity in America, as well as great momentum generated by the culture. The British took this and made it anew, so well that when the "British Invasion" hit, the sound and changes it made were so wide and vast that the American music industry was caught totally off guard, unable to duplicate the phenomenon, slumping tremendously.

That explains the jumble of names most commonly mentioned on the subject of influences in Europe. Germany would never experience a complete washing over of foreign music as in America, but the number of oft-emulated artists makes up for it; Pink Floyd, especially the original group headed by Syd Barrett, has become recognized as the first of groups with a feel for space and leanings in the direction of the classical avant-garde. They may have lost much of the original humor after Barrett's departure, but the group continued, extending the length of compositions, improving their musical prowess and producing the most bizarre special effects ever heard. Frank Zappa and the Mothers of Invention, for their colossal recorded output have had strong impact, but in a scattered way. The difference between Pink Floyd and Zappa lies in this bulk of material. Zappa noted for spreading himself thin over the years, and the Floyd for applying more concentration to the musical end as they were never concerned with having their own label or mass marketing product. When Rolf-Ulrich Kaiser launched Kosmisch Musik and its subsidiaries, more strange names came into view in America and England. Included were Jimi Hendrix, Soft Machine, Terry Riley and the rest of the new music composers such

1979

as Karlheinz Stockhausen, Edgard Varese, Milton Babbitt and others who experimented at the Columbia-Princeton Electronic Music Center, and of course John Cage. The musicians of France and Italy, in addition to Germany have mastered electronic equipment as well and the industry has filled their needs more than adequately. Discreet specialists have been especially skillful, taking full advantage of the tools at hand, particularly the EMS VCS3 and Synthi Ax, not only because of their portability, Fripp and Eno have used them as a perfect combination with Revox tape recorders, but more likely since they are European made and are capable of producing indigenously European sounds, reminiscent of pounding hammers to steam and the throb of factories. Some are by now very sophisticated. Klaus Schulze performs live with almost a dozen such instruments in use, while Richard Pinhas employs large Moog pieces which were once confined to the studios. The busiest engineers, Dieter Dierks and Conny Plank, have built their own studies, the latter with his own label. The progressive area of Europe, which here is still adventurous enough to be called experimental, is almost too much to contain with its burgeoning influx of new talent offering something intelligent to hear.

Pages more could be written on composers, groups, instruments and music essential in shaping influences in the progressive works of Europe. With tours and substantial sales of imports behind several acts already, new optimism prevails among up and coming new artists determined to find success in the West. This will depend on their talent and character, if they can develop an interesting style and not decline into producing repetitive hooks and other symptoms of commerciality. This is indispensable because the best equipment can never make up for real talent and creativity.

Jeff Pollock

Zoydian Manifesto

Art Zoyd refuses labels and archetypes. This collective of four musicians assumes no definite voice or approach.

We are asked to define projects and to speak of new and eventual directions. But the question is unworkable.

Creation is a materialization of the passages (voices?) of the unconscious. The musician is a medium between his thoughts and the concretely musical. Why is a certain character or a certain rhythm more representative of his thoughts than another? A mystery of sounds and magic every instant.

So let us leave that for the moment. And let us go back, since our problem today is less essential. Seeing that one must speak of musical creation on the level of a certain materialist critique, certain things should be said, notably on the subject of those styles of popular music made solely of tricks and clichés.

In Art Zoyd, there has been a total refusal

of these methods for the employment of sounds. What is consequently inside of all these people who turn out their by-products of by-products?

Do they not have less than a youngster who invents a tune and is jealous of it? It is necessary to seek expression not in the extreme and organized debilitativeness of these stereotyped forms of music. On the contrary, there should be research of a certain depth in the nature of musical expression. Music must no more be a supermarket product.

Second approach of the collective (by its reality):

We have been talking of a collective till now. We prefer this term to that of groups, too obviously hackneyed by mediocrity. A group, what a lovely affair! Pop stars in satin or slung with dirty guitars, narrow or long since empty minds, who knows? The whole beautiful world is perched and content. Idiots are forever proud of their stupidity, particularly when stupidity is here synonymous with vulgar and atrophied success.

A collective, above all to mark the distinction between the isolated researcher and this union of energies which come together for the purpose of creation. Here art is spontaneous and gravitated around different pulses, whence comes variety in themes and aggressive concatenations. Art Zoyd composes its music like a film. Image by image. Then there is a montage, a stage all the more important as it must ally with the coherence of themes its own coherence (internal logic).

Third approach or let's talk music:

Coherence. The word is cast. But what exactly does it signify in this musical whole which is formed by concatenations of sounds? We wish to brutalize the spectator, so that he feels as though electrically shocked, but not by the conceptual abstraction of some dance rhythm thundered out in degrading pulsations.

On the contrary we shun this kind of hypnotism. We want our music to reflect the actual world and its labyrinth of passions and ideas. To give vent, there on the stage, to this mirror of images, these howling throngs of a night, like these long monotonies of waiting, these false beauties and these doors which enclose introverted affliction, but as well the sealed valves, the bars which imprison and the clattering steps.

Characteristics or first aspect of the collective:

Art does not explain itself. It lives itself. It could exist in the effort of attention on some horizon, as it may not have the most skillful construction, Hearts which cease to beat and those that beat no more. The monologues with which those voices cleave the silence as towers do the sky, love and the end of love. Hatred and the onset of death apart from having died, as in those public transports where are crowded ungazing faces or gazes with no faces, who knows?

The music of Art Zoyd is hypocritical when it is a question of expressing hypocrisy, Spanish-like on those occasions when in the street one comes upon those travel posters advertising summer cruises... It becomes waltz-like, weakly Javanese and even dreamy... But there remains the rhythm which fractures everything, cold and Cubist. Twisting and shattering itself. Reforming and returning, as would a leitmotiv in some discourse to exhort one knows not what idea. When words no longer signify anything. Nothing other than sounds.

1979

Approach of the collective on the political level:

Why therefore does one hear little or nothing of these people who have been making music for such a long time, neither in the journals nor on the radio? Why do they not make records? Why do they spend their time paying debts and expenses, and trying to make (three!) ends meet?

Are they consequently so dangerous that they must be thrust aside? Or are they insufficiently gifted to maintain a relative material comfort? They seem like those who go about in their wagon during winter to "preach" their "good word" to the MJC of X -- so they seem before fifty bewildered spectators gathered there by chance. Such a view betrays no acquaintance with Art Zoyd. For Art Zoyd has made no records, and if it had made any, none would have been sold. It would not have sold any because it would have lacked the tens of millions necessary for publicity. That is to say: compromises, surrenders, tolerations, concessions. All for a game in which to many people have lost their sincerity undermined at the foundations of their motivations. The wolf wants to eat the lamb, To eat the lamb he must enter into the sheep-fold. To enter the sheep-fold he becomes a sheep. But once he is a sheep, he no longer craves meat and so nourishes himself with herbs. The lamb will not be eaten, and the shepherd will remain the strongest. What a lovely Christmas story! But in this Christmas the lambs are men and the shepherds democratically elected... What could be more natural in a society of sheep?

Why we think Art Zoyd is a political group:

Political in the broader sense, understand, in the sense that something occurs in the music other than a simple amusement for the object of diversion. On the contrary the foundation is placed on a painting of what is actual. Like a documentary, but also like a tragedy, in which the theater extends its scenes into everyday, where the actors are present at the concert or in the street, in memories or in the near future.

Theatre of the Absurd in which one plays with pawns, displacing them by chance but not utter chance in that first attempts and occurrences of error have been examined in the "laboratories" where Art Zoyd composes its music like a bouquet of flowers. Of poisonous flowers, understand, with the strange perfume of reality and the existential.

Final approach: Art Zoyd is five years old, excluding the first three years of formation at the time of "Opaline Records" -- Chant du Monde in '69, '70, and '71. We do not believe we have said all there is to say. On the contrary, we remain open for listening to our self and to those brutal and urgent impressions unfolding in the brain. We are not posing as gurus of the 'new' music. There is only "the" music. All sounds are part of it, as in dreams there are phantasms and hallucinations. We are afraid of creation because we are afraid of recognizing ourselves, the appearance of its image through these sounds. For to create is at first to recreate the self, the self with regard to the contextual but with regard to its own absurdities and incoherences as well, the naked self and everyone themselves. For we are all alike beneath our clothes of mud. And we must overcome this fear.

Art Zoyd 3
(Valenciennes, 25 March '76)
Translation: Steve Hitchcock
Reprinted from UN CERTAIN ROCK (?) FRANÇAIS, Vol. II (1974-77)

Etron Fou Manifesto

The Zoydian Manifesto set us to thinking and it is true that it is necessary to clarify the wording and vocabulary, to force people to take their positions, to try to put a bit of order (what a word!) in our heads, for all of us who are interested by this phenomenon: the emission of sounds."

The musical profession being one of the most anarchic and hierarchical professions that I know of, it is perhaps good to clarify certain words, at the risk of appearing serious (a catastrophe). This could be funny.

Music is a very elaborate implement capable of bringing great satisfactions.

Music is a sum of information. One who lives in a "standard" fashion and takes in "standard" information produces "standard" music.

The orchestra must become a group, that is to say the sum of individualities who share in common each other's information. Otherwise it remains or once again becomes an orchestra (a ballroom band? a rock orchestra?)

Memory is the tool for holding information. All that leaves the memory is information.

The sum of normalized or "standard" information is necessarily lacking in authenticity in so far as it passes through one or more filters (taboos, political-economic interests, hastiness, priority, stop-for-customs-toll).

We have chosen authenticity to the detriment of aesthetics. Authenticity is a sum of information actually experienced by the individual. This is our definition of beauty. Aesthetics are a sum of arbitrary rules (or judgments) obedient to the interests of parties of classes (the traditionalists, the marginalists, Catholics, bees, can openers). This is our definition of repression.

For these same reasons, we prefer a group of young urban workers who play poorly the Rolling Stones with conviction to an orchestra of specialists playing symphonic rock (in all minor chords) or chronometric jazz-rock, or free-jazz parlor music or purist and coagulated folk music. And yet we are captivated by certain representatives from each of these genres, while "punk" often makes us yawn. But it is not sufficient to pull on one's patched-up (but clean) trousers, put on (clean) suspenders, (clean) thick laced boots, and wear long

1979

hair (providing, of course, it's clean), in order to play French pop with strong country roots. (The country does not exist. Only the great suburb.)

Music exists 24 hours a day.

Silences between the notes can last hours.

The information which fills the holes creates the music. Otherwise, where would it come from?

The manner of existence (lifestyle, attitudes, surrounding objects, instruments) determines the music (one goes to see the Rolling Stones, Michel Sardou, Von Karajan, Jacques Chirac).

The management of one's own interests determines the nature of the music. We are founding an unpretentious structure for the exchange of technical information, to be run in collaboration with another self-managed group like ourselves, Camizole, this association being called "Dupon et ses fantomes." And we will consider the original form of our contract for co-production of records a large artistic result of our label and group (far short of having a bit of fun from time to time). In a general manner, our return -- "energy expended" plus financial investment plus public impact plus "legwork" is far above "normal."

Music is not the summit of our existence.

Merely to live as such in a normalized society would result, in the long run and of necessity, in reproduction of normalized music. (I draw attention, by the way, to the fact that "normalized" and "popular" are not necessarily synonymous, and I rely on some precise examples. Period.)

This is why it was of prime importance for us to diversify our means of survival, all the while avoiding dissolution and maintaining the greatest possible control of our independence. To find a viable basis.

A troubled stomach, an ailing head are factors of vulnerability, acting to the detriment of efficiency.

In general, excessive abuse of manufactured substances (noise, food, emotions) makes one ill. Although some can legitimately find the base of their unfolding there, the greatest concentration of manufactured substances will yet be found in the city. (The country guards one from numerous emissions.)

We note with pleasure the existence of more and more frequent experiences like our own. We will try to take then up for the best consequences of all concerned.

The words are clarified, the clay-footed giants are wearing their name better all the time, For some it is too late. But we guard the conscience of that ambiguous and indestructible point which binds us to society. If it should topple, we will topple with joy.

I will add at last that to find the happy medium, all one need know is where one wants to place the extremities.

All this which is said in the emanation of a collective consciences of which I am a part, easy, Madame Blaise........

Ferdinand "Rebarbatum" Richard Member, "Dapon et ses fantomes"

Translation: Steve Hitchcock Reprinted from UN CERTAIN ROCK (?) FRANCAIS, Vol. II (1974-77)

ZNR
BROKEN BARRICADES (New Horizons)

I guess you could say it all started in 1968 as many things did. Out of the liberating struggles of that time the group Barricade was born in 1969. Composed of musicians and non-musicians, their music consisted of free improvisations employing instru-ments and whatever else they had at hand, an exercise in musical anarchy, you might say a reflection of the times. Their history is chaotic and unclear, but it seems that they played live generally satirizing, horrifying and amusing the people in the audience, press, etc. and made no records.

In 1972 a schism arose among the various members and there was a split in half leaving Barricade I (a.k.a. "Creve Vite Charogne") and Barricade II (a.k.a. "Roquet et ses Levriers Basanes"). Barricade II was a bit more interested in musical structures, alternating between improvisation and simple melody. Among its personnel were Hector Zazou, Joseph Racaille and Cyrille Verdeaux (who later founded Clearlight). After a series of adventures -- live gigs, a split and reformation for an English tour and audition for Virgin Records (later aborted), they called it quits for good. The only reported remnants of the period are some tapes charting in music and words the adventures of Hypo (a metaphorical character) being born, falling in love, growing old, etc. to the accompaniment of strange musical themes in a Beefheartian mold.

The latest incarnation, ZNR -- Hector Zazou and Joseph Racaille (a.k.a. Louize Alcazar, their collective name) came together in 1975. By 1976 they had recorded an LP to be released on the Disjuncta label, which never came out due to the company's demise. They instead issued it themselves and called it *BARRICADE 3* -- It was later picked up by Isadora who proceeded to destroy it pressing-wise and let it rot in oblivion (selling only 155 copies in their homeland). In spite of all this, it is an excellent record of eccentric music combining short keyboard pieces, sparsely arranged, with distorted vocals and quirky arrangements. A diamond in the rough literally.

Well, as the saying goes, "all good things come to those who wait." With ZNR this is certainly the case as their newest album, *TRAITE DE MECANIQUE POPULAIRE* released on Organization Invisible SCOPA is as close as you'll come to hearing a masterpiece. The cover art is incredible -- a charcoal four sided drawing of strange surreal happenings. It is matched by the music inside which is likewise incredible, but instead for its beauty and imagination. ZNR's stated intent of the record "is making the relation between the art of the early 20th Century (E. Satie, I. Stravinsky in music, R. Roussel in literature) and our own musical experience. This record is fresh, non conformist and ... it is lovely music." And it is just that. Primarily acoustic, it's centered around piano with guitar and violin serving as coloration along with occasional voice and startling wind work. The arrangements are sparse and delicate weaving an exquisite web of sound that carries itself along without benefit of a rhythm section or central rhythmic flow. The pieces are a series of short vignettes for the most part and bear little resemblance to any rock music I've heard. More like chamber music, but not nearly as structured or rigid, it's full of ZNR's warmth and idiosyncratic humor. It quite honestly has to be heard to be believed, then heard several more times to be fully appreciated. The pressing too is superb and word has it that their *BARRICADE 3* album will be reissued by SCOPA in the future. Let us hope so.

So it has been 10 years and in ZNR the essence of the Barricades lives on. As 1969 embodied freedom of spirit and liberation, 1979 marks the beginning of a new era where those energies, dormant over the last decade, are now starting to re-emerge. The creative impulse will not die, ZNR is a testimonial to that fact and the music Zazou and Racaille make is the proof. It has been a long winter, but a New Morning is on the horizon.

Archie Patterson

D.N.A.
The Rise and Fall of Electronic Music in Germany

CHAPTER 0: INTRODUCTION OR TEUTONIC SOULS

To understand German music it is necessary to explain a few basics, partially reaching back far into the past. German progressive music has to be seen in that context, so allow me to make a short introduction to the German soul by some generalisations.

The German DNA seems to contain a few triplets dedicated to the dark, sinister, out-of-the-way and the heroic plus law-and-order (yes, both of these at the same time). In other words: Germany is always torn apart by two extremes of any given kind, swapping over from one to the other without a transition period in between. In relation to music, this means that German progressive music practically appeared out of nowhere -- it simply existed in 1968 in full strength. Before this time there only existed "Schlager" (I love you and you love me, or vice versa), or imported Anglo-American Top-Ten hits which were a part of the general Americanisation after W.W.2.

After twenty years of dominance of such music there were no roots left to identify with for the younger generation, i.e. blues, jazz or country in the USA. German folk music was of no help, as it was something not to be mentioned since the passing of the Third Reich, having been imposed on people as the only real "arische" kind of music. Anything else was called "entartet." So this music was subconsciously connected with that dark chapter of German history. And as a last hindrance for this kind of music: German popular music before was either totally vocal-oriented or restricted by strong form and musical laws, leaving no room for improvisation or development of the Ego.

So, coming back to '68, for German musicians there were only two possible ways of self-expression without copying something that wasn't to be found in their own genealogical development.

CHAPTER 1a: EMOTIONS OR THE SHOWDOWN OF THE SUBCONSCIOUS

The first way was just to listen to your own subconscious and play out all kinds of frustrations built up otherwise (political, educational, emotional): free flowing emotions, Groups of this kind were, for example, Amon Düül and Guru Guru. Psychedelic drugs imported and spread mostly by ever-present members of the US Army in Germany, appeared on the German scene in about 1968 in larger quantities and found entrance to the circles of most German artists. These drugs, smashing the last barriers to the subconscious, formed the style of the early progressive and experimental groups.

An imaginative curve, demonstrating the increase and decrease of psychedelic drugs in Germany also would demonstrate the development of such psycho-induced music, as both are strongly connected. The peak of this curve is to be found in 1969/70, afterwards slowly decreasing. The emphasis in '71 and later shifted slowly from hallucinatory drugs to make-me-as-happy-as-can-be drugs (especially to alcohol recently). Thus the musical emphasis similarly shifted from hallucinatory to more straight aggressive music, this being the only way to get drunkards out of their state of semi-coma (sorry, but it's bitter to see such a development).

Thus the hour of German hard rock came, its high time lasting until about '73/'74.

Their technical standard of playing was quite low and they never had the elegance of their models, but their music displayed some incredibly raw power, giving them an interesting appeal of their own (Alkatraz, Friedhof, Sphinx Tush, Weed, Nosferatu, Hairy Chapter, etc.) So, if you are a collector looking for hard rock groups of that time, never mind about subtleties.

The subtleties came in about 1974, imposed on them by international development, led by techo-freaks (jazz-rock) and/or a newly awakened romanticism (listen to the ECM label). This new direction is still prominent in 1979.

But this was just meant to give an overview. At the moment, in this article, we're still back in 1968. The only way to find access to progressive groups was to attend a live concert, as magazines, TV, radio and record companies ignored them. Once entering such a concert for the first time, you weren't prepared for what was to come. The music was of such an intensity, incredible -- really frying your synapses. The room was filled with psychedelic sounds and smoke alike, likewise giving the feeling that the music could be felt bodily. In front the group, only having a small PA, but in the small room nearly shattering your eardrums, directly transmitted their emotions to the audience, finding response by attentive listeners. After four or five hours, leaving the concert you definitely had the feeling that something of your personality had been changed. The music was potent enough to turn your brain and soul upside down.

This is to be heard on the first Guru Guru LP, *UFO*. This record, together with their second *HINTEN*, is one of the best ever recorded in that emotion-oriented style. These records musically are a true mirror of what happened live at that time. The

Gurus also were a fair example of the general conditions German groups were confronted with. They could play in or around larger cities (i.e. Stuttgart, Heidelberg), in small alternative clubs or at University happenings. The only possibility to reach a wider audience lay in backing up U.S. or British groups and this didn't happen often.

The Gurus started in 1968 with Mani Neumeier (dr), Uli Trepte (b) and an American guitarist (Jim Kennedy), of whom nothing else was heard after he left the group in '69. In concert they used to play the whole evening with each track being 40 to 60 minutes long. Their music was definitely something unheard of for that time and still today has yet to be equaled. There is no record in existence of this time, only a few live tapes. After Kennedy's replacement by former Agitation Free member Ax Genrich, there was no change of style, so especially the UFO LP is an exact reproduction of their live music, though the tracks are shorter.

Another group starting at about the same time in the same area were "Gila Fuck," who later (for commercial reasons I'm sure), shortened their name to "Gila" and did two albums: *GILA* and *BURY MY HEART AT WOUNDED KNEE*. The *GILA* album isn't comparable to "Gila Fuck" live, as it contains something of a concept, speaking about just the same frustrations shown in the introduction. In their beginning (live only), one never knew where their improvisations would lead to (mostly to a kind of psychedelic orgasm!) Gila's guitarist, Conny Veit, later played with Guru Guru (1974).

Most of these groups soon died as they had no sufficient financial base. Sure they had a small, devoted following, but this was not enough to survive. Their records, if any, didn't sell well, so soon they either vanished or changed their style to more commercial, accessible music. They had to be seen live to be understood anyway, as is the case with free jazz. But being mostly unknown their audiences were small, and so the circle closes. There was no promotion for them. The only mention to be found in most record companies group bios was: "stands up to international standards."

CHAPTER 1b: OSCILLATIONS, OR WHAT DOES THE EEG SPEAK ABOUT?

The second possibility to create independent music in Germany was to use the brain to explore a musical field, before reserved for the pure electronicists and the avant-garde. But these, like Schoenberg, Ligeti, Stockhausen were too insubstantial, too transcendent and already too much labeled as "classical" to appeal to the young. Anyway for the Berlin musicians of 1967/68, they were a guideline for a new approach to a new musical concept. Also the electronics necessary became easier to handle, so there was possibilities for live work too.

The central group in Berlin in 1968 was Tangerine Dream. It featured three of the most important musicians of German electronic music of the future: Edgar Froese, Klaus Schulze and Konrad "Conny" Schnitzler (Schnitzler and Schulze joined in Spring '69). Until 1971 they used conventional instruments (as heard on their first album *ELECTRONIC MEDITATION*). In '71 they bought their first synthesizer, signaling the start of a new style they've carried on to present (only more commercial recently with a new lineup). It is symptomatic that their success started in England, USA and France, only afterward happening in Germany, making them the best known German band in their homeland today (the thing with the poet in his own country ...)

Whereas Froese is still leading T. Dream today, Schnitzler and Schulze left in '71.

This was maybe the most important happening as their activities thereafter started a series of inter-communications and influences that made German electronic music one of the most important on this planet. Schulze helped co-found Ash Ra Tempel that became the pioneer of "cosmic music" and Schnitzler initiated the most far-out branch by helping form Kluster (later Cluster).

In the wake of these three groups, many others arose and were shaped by them, multiplying the supply of such music, often however only creating grotesque nonsense. The group "Zweistein" for instance produced a triple LP (only this one, there's no second album in existence as rumours try to make believe). Its contents were highlighted on the cover-text by the simple as well as cosmic deduction: "Einstein Plus Zweistein = Dreistein."

To track the spread of the experimental German scene see the diagram showing the development and different incarnations of Kluster, Konrad Schnitzler (it's selected as it is the most interesting as well as most known of the German electronic groupings).

On the edge of the graphic you'll find Kraftwerk and Neu! who didn't belong to the Berlin scene. They originated from the "Ruhrgebiet," which is the equivalent to the Detroit area. This quite interesting area brought about a very different style resulting in 1973 in a very interesting mutation by the name of Harmonia, who recorded two excellent albums: *MUSIK VON HARMONIA* and *DE LUXE*. Harmonia was a kind of sidestep, as Cluster and Neu! still existed too. Kraftwerk was formed in 1970 by Ralf Hutter and Florian Schneider. Before (1969), under the name Organisation they did one album only issued in England, *TONE FLOAT*. Kraftwerk was completed by Klaus Dinger (perc.) and Andreas Hohmann and in this formation recorded their first album *KRAFTWERK* (Nov. 1970). In the Spring of 1972 Dinger and Hohmann left the group. Dinger and Michael Rother (who also was a member of Kraftwerk, though is not on any albums) formed Neu! and recorded their first album *NEU!* in Feb. '72. Kraftwerk too continued as a duo.

Neu!, by the way, never played live save two gigs in the Fall of '74, whereas Kraftwerk still does live gigs. After the split-up of Neu! in 1975, Rother and Dinger both concentrated on their own projects (Rother solo and Dinger's La Dusseldorf).

In 1971/73 the peak of popularity for German groups in their homeland who didn't bow to Anglo-American dominance was reached. The public interest was raised too by the two beat German rock magazines *"Sounds"* and *"Musik Express"* that regularity devoted some space to such groups, thus giving them the exposure they didn't get due to lack of record company promotion (exception "Ohr," "Pilz," "Bacillus" that specialized). Private labels passed the public eye without being noticed, having good music, but no organization. Kluster's *KLOPFZEICHEN* and *ZWEI OSTEREI* falling into that category as well as Schnitzler's *ROT, BLAU* and *SCHWARZ* (the last being actually a pressing of Kluster's last gig in 1971, sometimes also appearing as *KLUSTER AND ERUPTION*) or the first Can solo LP on Scheisshouse Records from 1968 called *CANAXIS 5*.

Tracking the paths of German progressive bands after 1972, they can be divided into three categories. First are the ones who achieved popularity in the U.S., England or France, their music being more accessible there, like T. Dream, Ash Ra Tempel, Faust (in some ways), Amon Düül 2 or Klaus Schulze. Their foreign success swept back to Germany, giving them the image of an international group, so they found fans in Germany too. The only group however that really reached a level of popularity comparable to Anglo-American groups is T. Dream (since about 1974). The second category consists of musicians that changed their music completely in relation to 1969 and became sort of hard rock or junk groups. The most typical example of this is Guru Guru, their music now is best forgotten as quickly as possible and no longer belongs within the frame of reference of this article. Another fair example would be Wolfgang Dauner who went back into the arms of common jazz, once (live) having played music like Kluster. The third category contains the hard-core musicians like Konrad Schnitzler and Uli Trepte (Spacebox), who still try to do their own thing. Their already small popularity of '71 now having decreased to practically zero in the Germany of 1979.

To give a closing summation: the German progressive experimental scene is on the edge of breaking down. The once solid base of musicians has thinned out terribly and there are practically no musicians to be found among the younger generation to keep the spirit going. Instead jazz-rock groups of the most trivial kind are spreading like fungi. Any groups with new names, appearing on the progressive scene, are only permutations of already known musicians (95%).

Good Night, Germany......

Harald Mehl

Grobschnitt

Grobschnitt is one of the few German groups today that can be called definitive. In fact, they may be the definitive group. Originating from Hagen, their style of music set a precedent for other bands in Germany and abroad. Their music, especially the longer pieces, is characterized by strong vocal and instrumental performances, but most importantly, a progressive approach featuring extended instrumental breaks, sharp percussive roll-offs plus studio and electronic embellishments that complement the soloing. Occasionally, a hint of jazz or the classics appears for good measure, but the band's Gothic rock and roll leanings are never diminished too greatly.

When their first LP was released in 1972, they were on their way to becoming a live performance favorite. A big outdoor festival attraction, their stage show, which featured elaborate costumes, make-up and a troupe of offbeat clown types, was an instant hit. The album wasn't bad either. "Symphony" is one of their best pieces ever. Building from an invigorating rhythm to complex crescendos, it settles into a romantic state as a string section augments the guitar and keyboards to create a fully formed classical sound which diminishes slightly to make room for the whining electronic effects at the close.

BALLERMANN, the second LP, presented a heavier blend of material with the emphasis on the production, The introduction to "Sahara", a hilarious recitation by Eroc, is followed by a chant and then the song, a strange story about the first obscure musician, Ali Baba, who gigs with his band and is lost in a desert snowstorm some three centuries ago. The tempo picks up on tape as the crazy caravan rides off into the blowing sand.

The remaining material on the first disc (it's a double album), shows the group's true potential, "Nickel-odeon" hints at jazz and blues, while "Drummer's Dream" features synthesized texturing as well as a steady beat. On Side 2, "Morning Train" with a quasi-waltz effect and light vocal mark a kind of light spot, but the soloing keeps it out of the doldrums.... the long piano introduction of "Magic Train" is only one highlight of a splendid selection, which goes through several changes before a lively ending.

The second disc is comprised entirely of "Solar Music," perhaps their best piece ever. There is plenty of the group's own heaviness here, as well as a certain debt to Pink Floyd. After a dynamic introduction featuring unintelligible vocals and sharp percussive attacks, the music settles into a gentle dirge with electronics and tape effects which reach a climax with fine soloing and then finishes off with intermittent notes over the relentless rhythmic pulse ending Part I.

Part 2 resumes the instrumental, more jazz-like this time. Kühn's and Kahr's solos are evenly exchanged and the drumming complements in kind. This, then becomes an underpinning for a burst of loud laughter and riveting electronics and vocals which are mixed into some interesting echo. (Frank Mille's production here is first rate as elsewhere.) Slowly, the void falls away and a progressive jam builds to a sort of heavy metal frenzy with waves of wah-wah and pummeling percussion. As this would appear to be the end, the whole affair finishes with a lilting tuneful minuet reprise. Totally unexpected and yet somewhat appropriate.

1975 was one of Grobschnitt's most productive years. The group released *JUMBO* and there was a debut solo LP recorded by Eroc. There was little doubt that Eroc had been one of Grobschnitt's focal points. After his album intros and fine drumming, he seemed to be a musician of considerable adeptness and when he added electronic effects to their more dynamic compositions, he could well be considered a Klaus Schulze protégé. His first record is indicative of this, as it is primarily electronic in content ... "Kleine Eva" is an impressive example. A beautiful Oldfield-styled piece, it flows on melodically, then breaks briefly midway to feature some imaginative effects similar to Grobschnitt's but much more profound. "Das Zaubere's Traume" approaches the Drone Zone with a fierce buzzing tone which seems to come and go as an Arabesque pipe solo frantically swirls above it. It ends in an equally frantic run of synthesized notes. "Tony Moff Mollo" at forty-eight seconds is no more than an amusing conversation with the Grobschnitt associate. Side 2 contains "Music von Olberg." Led by a persistent beat, it reaches a quick end, in the form of breaking glass and footsteps. "Norderland" marks a change in the format as it features bass and guitars in a swinging rhythm amidst which are heard searing arctic winds, avalanches and the like. "Horrorgoll," except for sparse instrumental effects are voices modified through every type of tape delay imaginable. For six and a half minutes, the listener is treated to whispers, shouts, coughs and a dash of electronics that makes for a somewhat harsh onslaught. "Sternchen" returns to the quiet side once again, a gentle albeit anxious track that fades and returns in reverse; not bad as a close for a surprisingly diverse LP from a humor-bent drummer.

The group's next album *JUMBO*, showcased production again, this time with a fuller symphonic sound the earlier material did not seem to have. Beginning with "Jupp." courtesy of Eroc, the album has a strong feel but is never overbearing. "The Journey of Father Smith" is marked by lead lines carried by the rhythm section working as a solid unit. "The Clown" is a spirited tune making full use of all the instrumentation, including Daneliak's guitar which serves as solid backing and not just as a fill as before. On side 2, "Dream and Reality" begins gently not sacrificing the heaviness as it soon becomes another fine spot for guitar and keyboards. "Sunny Sunday's Sunset," the longest piece, is presented by electronic effects which slow to let the guitar take the lead into a dramatic intro and then the theme proper. The music holds its own without letting the melancholy of the lyrics become too pronounced. The melodic soft spot, by now a trademark, gradually picks up and a chorus brings the piece to a full bodied finish. The album closes with an obnoxious "Auf Wiedersehen" complete with built-in record skip.

1976 was to be a hiatus for the group, but not for Eroc, who recorded his second solo LP, *ZWEI*. Those who were tantalized by the mix on the first album are probably confounded by this outing. A potpourri of tracks, it smacks of *A WIZARD, A TRUE STAR* and *MAGICAL MYSTERY TOUR* if that's to be believed. There is some fine music but the vocals and other gibberish abound, most of the time with the subject going through paces of "A Day In The Life" pretensions, "now Eroc smokes a cigarette, now Eroc takes a walk," etc. Side 2 is much the same with more sparse music. Parts of earlier group albums are heard at one point and there is a nice piano solo at the end, but it's all caught up in the vocal melee. At best, this is a '70s version of Zappa's *LUMPY GRAVY*, but even old Frank would have a hard time beating Eroc's lunacy and studio zaniness. A fan's album indeed.

Meanwhile the band was working on their next album *ROCKPOMMELS LAND*. Almost a year in the making, with Conny Plank as engineer, this is Grobschnitt's most artistic production. The concept is a loosely structured story about Ernie, a boy who lives in Severity Town, who confronts a band of villains (Blackshirts) and rescues a man of extraordinary virtue (Mr. Glee) from them, aided by a giant bird (Maraboo). Musically it's another step in the direction of *JUMBO*, but Kahr's keyboards are in full command and Kühn's style was never more exuberant. There are a number of entertaining moments, as when the Blackshirts are turned to stone with a magic feather. "Rockpommels Land" is almost twenty minutes long and features every phase of the band's talent. Some of the rhythmic figures and riffing seem new to the group as they've never been used before. However, the story is a bit too thin to be of real substance, even on a single album. Their on-stage performance of it is much stronger according to reports.

In Sept. '78 a live album was released, *SOLAR MUSIC LIVE*, which is one of the best live representations of German progressive music in some time. Recorded in Mulheim Tournee Hall, it's obviously missing the show itself -- Mollo's sense of timing, not to mention Eroc's bright moment of the first side, a heavy distorted delivery over the sounds of a tinny brass band including the usual coughing and choking, on Side 2 he utters Zappa-like gibberish, followed by a tumultuous drum roll. If there is any European drummer that comes close to the late, great Keith Moon, it's Ehrig. Musically, the composition has been taken beyond the original so that little is still intact. Now in six individual sections, all players can make themselves recognized. Wolfgang Jäger's bass playing is close to fusion. On Side 2 Volker Kahr renders the best solo of his career on piano and Kühn is rarely less than outstanding throughout. Apart from the aforementioned special appearances of Eroc, Daneliak gets in some amusing asides himself, so the band's humorous side was never more apparent.

Perhaps Grobschnitt's most unique trait is their ability to combine music, theatre and other elements into their act. Daneliak's commanding voice has the staying power. Kühn and Kahr's combined prowess place them among the finest in Europe. Jäger is an exceptional bassist and Eroc's skillful, albeit crazy, approach to electronics and the studio is at least credible, especially at a time when progressive music must either be pretty or highly disciplined depending on the angle from which it is viewed. From the European angle, no doubt Grobschnitt has taken it a few steps ahead. Perhaps because of this, they may each be greater than the sum of their parts.

Jeff Pollock

Phoenix

Of all the East European countries the least is known about the music scene in Romania. There have been but a handful of LPs and EPs released by "pop groups" such as Sphinx, FFN, Progressiv TM and a few others. For the most part the music is early '60s style rock fused with hints of native folk elements. Two exceptions however are Experimental Quintet and Phoenix.

Experimental Quintet is only documented on record by one cut on a sampler LP and it shows only moments of interest. Their more experimental material was done live and captured on a bootleg tape. It shows them to be an extremely high powered jazz-rock band capable of making intense music that combines guitar and electronics into a mixture of structured and improvised playing that's most impressive. When they are in full swing they can really get way out there.

Phoenix on the other hand is (was) the giant of Romanian rock (they've undergone personnel changes and relocated to Germany at last report). Founded in 1964 by Nicolea Covaci, a graduate of the Fine Arts Faculty, Phoenix made two EPs and three albums in addition to doing many TV shows, radio tracks and a film score.

Their first album, *FERMATA PHOENIX*, consists of extracts from an original folk opera by the group entitled "Those Who Gave Us A Name." The overall sound can be characterized as hard-rock-folk, spearheaded by Covaci's guitar. There are slight Oriental influences that give it a meditative feel of quietness at times. On the whole the album is interesting, but a bit crude to appeal to most Western ears.

The second LP *MUGUR DE FLUIER* (Magic Flute) is subtitled "An Introduction to A Concert of Old Romanian Music" and is a technically superior album to the first in just about every way. The music is based on old folklore motifs updated in the spirit of '60s rock. Extensive use is made of ethnic percussion instruments, vocals and sparse keyboards for the first time. Overall the album is quite good, even if dated due to recording technology.

The crowning glory for Phoenix came with their third album *CANTAFABULE* (Singing-Fables), a double record folk opera based on a 18th century Romanian literary work titled "The Ieroglyphical History" (The Secret History) by Dimitrie Cantemir. It is the first cult creation in prose (over 400 pages) from Romanian literature. An allegorical novel and political pamphlet alike, it portrays a picture of a feudal society by way of a grotesque cartoon filled with humorous fantasy and satirical verve. The characters are animals which embody the various traits of mankind -- good, evil, greed... The different species represent the various classes of society. In the end the lowest class, the insects (peasants), rise up and overthrow the wild beasts (the rulers) in a struggle for their freedom. Phoenix portrayed this in their stage act by wearing costumes of the various animals and having specially designed sets, thus creating a full-fledged spectacle.

Also the music on the album shows a marked change due to the addition of German keyboardist Gunther Reininger. His use of electronics along with Covaci's guitar create an effective dual focus which makes the music all the more impressive. Again it's very folk-flavored, but also contemporary due to the skill of Reininger on synthi. The old folk melodies combine with modern arrangements and the result is an excellent record that creates an atmosphere of the old world within the context of progressive rock. A very rough comparison could be made to Jethro Tull, Romanian style. And while the recording technology is still not ultra-sophisticated, the record stands up as an excellent work, complete with beautiful cover illustration of the animal farm theme.

According to reports in late '76 there were internal problem in the band and for unknown reasons there was a split. The next news of the group came from Germany where in 1978 they recorded a demo tape for Wintrup Musik. The band was led by Reininger and the sound was much the same as *CANTAFABULE*, only with a more updated approach. Though rough and under-produced the tape had moments of beautiful music, still full of that old world folk-meets-new age rock feel. No German labels were interested however, so where will things go from there??? As for rock in Romania, aside from some straight jazz and a few odd bands, nothing is known to be happening. Perhaps with the departure of Phoenix, the Golden Age of Romanian Rock , such as it was, came to an end?

Archie Patterson

1980

Faust

Faust is a case absolutely unique in the history of rock music, an experience which originated in Germany far from all the styles which have swept other countries in later years.

Before they became a musical group in the strict sense of the word, the people in Faust used to live communally since 1968 playing a few instruments for simply their own entertainment. It was an encounter with Uwe Nettelbeck that was decisive & convinced of the potential that their music represented, he pushed them toward an official career.

In 1971 the first album was recorded and came out in December of that year on Polydor Germany. It was immediately striking due to its unique appearance.

The jacket and the record are both transparent with the only illustration being an x-ray of a clenched fist, without doubt a symbol of past political struggles. As for the music, the result may appear as a sketch of the future realizations of the group. The whole of Side 2 consisting of "Miss Fortune" was recorded live in the studio without overdubbing.

Side 1 includes two pieces "Why don't you eat carrots" and "Meadow Meal." It begins with a collage where we recognize parts of the Rolling Stones' "Satisfaction" and the Beatles' "All You Need is Love." It's a ridiculous tribute and reference to their joking and irreverent tendencies.

The first album of Faust is without doubt the first record to use in such a way acoustic research and electroacoustic technique. In spite of the apparent mess, there is a direction (guideline) from the mood of carnival in "Why don't we eat carrots" to the incantations of "Meadow Meal" and the organ background which melts in a tumult of rain and thunder.

A few months later in May and June 1972, the members of Faust helped the three members of Slapp Happy to prepare their first album, putting at their disposal their studio know-how. They played all the rhythm parts (bass and drums) and contributed some solo saxophone while Uwe Nettelbeck produced the record. Slapp Happy's *SORT OF* is in every sense of the word a success, a synthesis of Anthony Moore, Peter Blegvad and Dagmar Krause's gifts, more so than their Virgin release. It's very electric, often enough "rocky," very clean on the conceptual level and full of treats: as much vocal ("Just A Conversation") as instrumentals ("Who's Gonna Help Me Now") or simply rhythmic ("Sort Of," "Heading For Kyoto"). Unfortunately *SORT OF* is unobtainable now.

In 1974, at the time of Faust's demise, Jean-Herve Peron will again play bass on four of the eleven pieces on the Virgin album, but one feels more as a session musician than a participant in a collective creation of which *SORT OF* is the unique testimony.

SO FAR, the second Faust LP, recorded in 1972 is published at the beginning of 1973. This time the packaging and record are entirely black. One finds right away more interaction with the listener. "It's a rainy day sunshine girl" is an introduction of 7 minutes of heavy and monotonous rhythm by the bass drum which conjures up the sinister aspect of the Velvet Underground. It's a real dirge with these insignificant lyrics which repeat themselves:

> It's a rainy day, sunshine babe
> It's a rainy day, sunshine girl.

Next is "On the way to Abamae," a short break within the general tension. A melody, a little bit anachronistic with medieval accents, played with the acoustic guitar, organ background and flute sounds. Then "No harm," ten extraordinary minutes of organ and brass united in crescendo all melting into a crackle of synthesizer, serves to introduce a melody on guitar in the '50s rock style, played against a drum - trumpet background. On top of all this appears these splendid lyrics filled with Zappaesque humor:

> Daddy took a banana,
> Tomorrow is Sunday!

The second side is as rich. First the title piece "So far," a hymn which could be a song for children if there were not the electro-acoustic background. After that "Mamie is blue," an electronic Magma that leaves one asking just what instruments are being played... then "I got my car and my TV," whose lyrics are intoned with a childish voice in a carnival mood, but their significance is obvious. One must remark that this kind of criticism in opposition to the classic consumer's society in the United States is very rare in Europe and especially so in Germany, where the lyrics are primarily extroverted (Can, Agitation Free) or frankly pushed to the paroxysm of symbolism (Guru Guru, Amon Düül II), even to political satire (Floh de Cologne). Next is "Picnic on a frozen river" which shows a glimpse of an unknown Faust, one of free and unstructured jazz (piano - brass - bass). The record ends with the short suite "Me lack space -- In the spirit," a beginning of synthesized lyrics:

> Put on your socks before you
> put on your shoes...

in a circus mood with a finale in the form of a metaphysical questions "I wonder how long is this gonna last?" done to a tempo of old blues "New Orleans style."

The description of *SO FAR* would be incomplete if one did not say a few words about Edda Kochl's paintings (nine reproductions of water colours, one for each piece), which go with Faust's music. A mixture of surrealism and naive art, the drawings of this painter from Munich are strange, but very effective. In describing the lack of space "Me lack space" there is a palm tree inside a door frame, for "In the spirit', a couple seated on a couch (he has a pig's head) face a table where sit a chicken and some sausages. These contrasts reinforced by the absurdity of the situation are the visual counterpart to Faust's music.

After these records Faust became a legend, as people barely knew the names of the musicians or the instruments they played. A group of total mystery.

In fact it seems that the pillars of the group were the multi-instrumentalists: Gunther Wusthoff (keyboards and brass), Frenchman Jean-Herve Peron (guitar, bass, trumpet, voice) and drummer Werner Diermaier, plus organist Hans-Joachim Irmler, who all participated more or less in defining the concept and constructing the montage of electronic effects and electro-acoustic parts. There was also in the beginning a guitarist Rudolf Sosna and Arnulf Meifert. It is almost impossible because of the lack of information and few liner notes on the record jackets to establish just who did what, when, in the group's recordings. The role of Uwe Nettelbeck, which is also not easy to define, is a mystery. Rumour has it that he was the catalyst of the Faustian delirium, the grey eminence of the group and finally its principal member.

Faust used to own, like Can, their own studio, which was a furnished basement in a farm in Northern Germany's Wumme. One can hardly imagine what the group would have done without these facilities and the possibility to play constantly and explore their resources to the maximum.

Certainly the most avant-garde group even in all Europe, Faust had an originality not built on American or English foundations, nor on the cliches of European progressive rock of the time. They composed music of excess, full of folly and delirium, in short: a music made up of extremes.

But there is another aspect of the group that we should not neglect, all their incidences of "holiday music." A notion too often forgotten in the actual realizations because they are too functional and obey too precise rules. Their richness was in the ability to achieve a fragile balance between all these parts.

At the beginning of 1973, the group went through a most important crisis which would have two consequences. First they left Polydor for Virgin Records, then they decided to try and do live performances. At the time Virgin was at its beginnings of being a record publisher with a director full of dynamic ideals that fit Faust like a glove. So well in fact that they were, along with Mike Oldfield, the first acts signed by Richard Branson. As far as Virgin is concerned we know the story, but let's not forget the very beautiful albums that we owe to the label before the company prostituted itself...

FAUST TAPES was published in the Spring of 1973 and used by Virgin to launch their advertising operation, because the album was realized in England and sold as a limited edition for the price of a single. One must understand that the record was not recorded as an entity in view of publication, but was only a collage of tapes that the group owned in its archives. This added to the attraction of the LP which is along with *SO FAR* the best of Faust.

FAUST TAPES begins with thunder that explodes into a melody with an absurd text on top of an interlude of electro-acoustics:

> J'ai mal aux dents (I have a toothache)
> J'ai mal aux pieds aussi (I have a footache also)

This refrain is repeated and repeated to the paroxysm of the absurd, grotesque incantation on a naked rhythm in the style of Neu!. Then follows a montage of telephone recordings, footsteps and voices supported by a funky riff on bass. The type of collage Faust creates, full of strange vibrations and voice effects, one never tires of listening to. The end of Side 1 is a kind of climax, an imitation of Yes or Pink Floyd that's cut and mutated under the synthetic knife of the mix.

Side 2 begins with another montage which preceeds one minute of very beautiful solo piano (the members of Faust are also well versed in the field of pure music). Then another montage (always this fascination with electronics) of two songs combining hypnotic rhythm and metallic sound. The side ends with a piece of anthology, a poem recited in French by Jean Herve Peron accompanied by an acoustic guitar. It's a long text, abstract, impressionistic and full of absurdity. Faust does it marvelously, because it is the image of their music, a mixture of surrealism and crudeness. The bare accompaniment of the arpeggios on acoustic guitar adds to it greatly and creates a truly Faustian spirit.

The release of *FAUST TAPES* happened in England at a time when the legend is developing around the group due to their first two albums and announcement of a pending tour.

In October 1972, in their studio at Wumme, three members of Faust (Diermaier, Sosna and Peron) are backup musicians to the violinist Tony Conrad, a friend of Terry Riley and LaMonte Young. They recorded under the direction of Uwe Nettelbeck *OUTSIDE THE DREAM SYNDICATE*, an extremely avant-garde album.

Side One is entitled "The side of man and womankind." It's a double-time tempo and hypnotic rhythm from the beginning to the end which consists of a unique bass/drum beat as only the violin solos, but in a linear way. Side Two "The side of the machine" possesses a more flexible rhythm with always the piercing presence of the violin. During its journey which touches on the new American music, you also feel the effects of medieval music. There's often the illusion of immobility as you wait for something (what?), but nothing happens. This album was released in the middle of 1973 to inaugurate the Caroline label which was to be geared to marginal music. Unfortunately it has now disappeared.

Sometime after the publication of *FAUST TAPES*, the group recorded their fourth album at The Manor Studios -- *FAUST IV*. It begins with "Krautrock," twelve minutes of uncommon intensity with guitars reaching saturation point, background noises all mixed together, an oppressive rhythm and especially the dense mix. Curiously this piece was to become the commercial theme (involuntarily for sure) of a rock 'sauerkraut' which never existed except in the minds of some music biz moguls and wallets of the trapped buyers. And irony, the record companies began to get interested in German music when most of the artists were losing a great part of their originality. Amon Düül's *VIVE LA TRANCE*, Can's *FUTURE DAYS* and *FAUST IV* are three good albums, but the original personality of these three groups (one could point to other examples also) had disappeared. Amon Düül crystallized their insanity (*PHALLUS DEI, TANZ DER LEMMINGE*) into a more solid form, Can went from the hypnotic violence of *TAGO MAGO* and *EGE BAMYASI* to something pure and diffused, while Faust followed a similar path. The last cuts on Side One of *FAUST IV* illustrate this. "The sad skinhead" is a short piece which reminds of Can's "Moonshake," only is more naked yet with the same way of accommodating noise. Then "Jennifer" which is only a bad dream, too monotonous, never taking off.

Side Two begins with a beautiful instrumental, three minutes of "Just a second." It's followed by the suite "Picnic on a frozen river/second picture/giggy smile" where Faust plagiarized themselves with a quotation from *SO FAR*: narcissism..., then the 'Lauft heisst des es lauft oder es kommt bald .... Lauft" where Jean Herve Peron warns us:

> I can no longer afford to
> lose my teeth
> I can no longer afford to
> lose my time....

The drum is metronomic in spite of the tempo and sweet languor of the melody. Something very great from Faust. The album ends with a piece dating back from the sessions for SO FAR which was published at that time as a single, "So Far" b/w "It's A Bit of a Pain."

> It's a bit of a pain to be
> satisfied,
> but it's alright

During their live period, the most interesting concerts were given during the first half of 1973 at isolated dates in France and England like the Bataclan in Paris (organized by the "souterrain") or in Birmingham. This live career was necessary for the members of Faust since it meant a justification of their musical ideas by facing the public. But on the other hand it placed the audience in front of a group that was in a state of perpetual crisis. If SO FAR & *FAUST TAPES* are true soundtracks of our and their phantasms, their concerts showed a total lack of setting and at the end a deliberate decision (rather than the inability) not to remedy the situation.

And then there was an English tour with Henry Cow organized by Virgin and advertised in the press as "very commercial." Around twenty dates from Sept. 21 to Oct. 27, 1973, it was more for the public to discover the Cow (ideal promotion for *LEG END*, their first album) than Faust. However the German orchestra had everything to succeed since they were surrounded by Peter Blegvad and Uli Trepte. Fred Frith, Henry Cow's guitarist remembers (Atem #6 P15) "most of the time they were pretty bad, only one or two times during the tour could one see a glimpse of what they were really worth. It was very depressing for me, because I think that their first recording and *FAUST TAPES* are great. Most of the pieces they played came from the second album, some from the fourth. Very strong and very mean, Jean Herve was without doubt the most interesting of them all and an a magician on stage. There were moments when Geoff Leigh arrived and began to play with them...." Yes, that is it, few sparks of genius as ideas without a future, which cannot be concretized and sunk into obscure chaos on the borders of the bearable. The music which did not fit on stage, especially to uninitiated ears, and then what public could accept a group that turns on the TV on stage in order to let the time go by?

Faust broke up at the end of 1973, or more exactly arrived at the end of their road. Let's not be nostalgic, the experience could not last because delirium, folly and research can never go together with commercial success, whatever the art form. It's a miracle that 4 albums in 2 years were given us. We owe it to Uwe Nettelbeck, their producer, but more importantly the source of their vision. Faust ceased to exist when he left them.

No doubt if the 4 records by Faust were reissued now they would sell much better than they did back then. There are musicians who recognize them explicitly as their great influence. And while they had a hard time presenting their ideas on stage, those ideas are not dead since they pioneered deviationist rock which today lives on. It is not by chance that this German group, the most avant-garde of its time, is used as reference for the new English and American groups: Devo, Chrome, Debris, Throbbing Gristle, This Heat a.o. The Residents are Faust's legitimate children. Mephistopheles missed his target.

Pascal Bussy
(Reprinted Courtesy ATEM)
(Translation: Jacques Pauwels)

Embryo
On The Road In The Far East

Music is one of the universal languages which is understood by all people. Being on the road we'd hardly understand the strange languages people spoke. But music helped us understand more the nature of foreign people. Over here on our side of god's golfball we're just suckers for what we get shoved down our throats, being submitted to constant Anglo-American brainwashing which eventually corrodes our dreams. During these 8 months on the road we managed to escape these influences and explore new musical universes. As often as possible we jammed with native musicians from a circus band, professors of music, kids, orchestra musicians, instrumental virtuosi and village musicians... -Christian Burchard

The musical journey of Embryo has been a long one. Over the span of 11 albums and at least as many years, Christian Burchard and friends have been engaged in the creation of music that attempts to reflect life, music which comes to terms with socio-political realities, expert technique and cultural interaction. Of all the German bands Embryo is the one who has remained steadfast and true to their original ideals.

Working within the jazz rock idiom from their beginnings, the first album set the tone for their future. *OPAL*, on the underground Ohr label, was a hard jazz rock record that contained an abundance of crude sparks of innovation. Their subsequent releases -- *FATHER, SON AND HOLY GHOSTS, EMBRYO'S RACHE, STEIGAUS & ROCKSESSION* all continued this development, refining their approach. Politics was ever-present in pieces like "Revolution," "Espagne Si, Franco No," a.o. But the most striking part of their music, was the music itself. And it was no wonder as these records featured a floating crew of Christian, Edgar Hoffmann (violin), Dave King (bass), Sigi Schwab (guitar), Jimmy Jackson and Mal Waldron (keys). Their interactions resulted in some beautifully inspired playing.

On their next couple of recordings -- *WE KEEP ON* and *SURFIN'*, they took things a step further and started incorporating strong elements of ethnic music and instrumentation into the sound. A great deal of this influence no doubt supplied by Charlie Mariano, the longtime jazz player extraordinaire. The LPs were an exotic treat. They of course contain individual high and low points, but all of Embryo's music has always contained a germ of inspiration that gives their work a strong impact.

It was at this point that the group underwent a change of life so to speak. After this long series of 6 albums they had come to realize that to be free to really create they music they wanted, they had to control their own lives and the complete musical process. Commercial and big business pressures only served to stifle their creativity and personal freedom. So with a group of friends and kindred spirits they formed April Records (later renamed Schneeball due to legal complications). Since that time they have released 4 LPs -- *LIVE, BAD HEADS AND BAD CATS, APO-CALYPSO* and the new one *EMBRYO'S REISE*.

Their first 3 April LPs show a bit of a change in orientation from their earlier work. While the recordings of the pre-April period can loosely be characterized as intellectual and somewhat experimental rock jazz, these later 3 are more of a swinging body music. Many of the same exotic elements are present, but there's also a strong beat that at times gives them a quasi-funk feel. This tended to turn off many old Embryo "fans" which is unfortunate as there is a lot of fine music on these records. Especially good was *APO-CALYPSO* as their use of ethnic music on it was most interesting.

This brings us up to date and their new album -- *EMBRYO'S REISE* (Journey), *RECORDINGS FROM AFGHANISTAN, PAKISTAN AND INDIA*. From the packaging to the music the whole thing is thick with atmosphere.

The record is basically a document of their caravan thru the Far East that lasted from Sept. '78 to April '79. It contains in addition to some of the most striking cover photography I've ever seen, a 10 page booklet of photos and travelogue and 2 records of combined live and studio recorded material.

I could write pages on several different aspects of it, and still not do it justice. So I'll simply pass on a couple of impressions.

Firstly, it shows what can be accomplished when the life process and artistic process become one and the same. The dynamic of their travels and cultural exchange with the peoples they met make pieces like "Anar, Anar," "Cello, Cello" and "Hymalaya Radio" thick with spicy sound. Then there's "Maharaj" which is pure magic. It is a relatively short cut featuring a local priest they met who sang and played the harmonium. Recorded during a full moon festival, it was the first time he had ever played an electric organ and you can't believe the strange beauty that results. The same feel pervades the entire album.

Secondly, it shows that people can take their lives into their own hands and produce art that is truly imaginative. Qualitatively and quantitatively *EMBRYO'S REISE* is a superb record. Please excuse my enthusiasm, but it really does embody what great music should be all about -- listening enjoyment and artistic creativity.

So this brings us up to date. For Embryo in the future there will be another extensive tour beginning in March '80 and lasting until June '80. They will travel through Greece, Turkey, Italy, Spain and Morocco. The voyage will be capped off by a performance in a large stadium in Casablanca where they record their next LP, tentatively titled -- *EMBRYO LIVE IN CASABLANCA*. In addition a film of their recent tour has been finished and is due for release in the very near future.

We'll see how things gonna work out here in Germany -- the faces of the poorest and most beat people we met by the side of the road often radiated more energy than any of those victims of our prospering industrious society, being chained to the assembly lines, churning mass produced garbage.
- Christian Burchard

Music is life. If you don't live it, it'll never come out of your instrument.
- Charlie Parker

So after all this time and music made, it seems as if the journey for Embryo has indeed only just begun. The fact of that itself is the highest achievement any group could possibly attain. You might say that sums up what "progressive music" is all about.

Archie Patterson

P.P.U. Update

EDITORS NOTE: As a part of the continuing coverage of what's happening in Eastern Europe and in particular the case of the P.P.U. in Czechoslovakia, EUROCK is printing an "update" on the band of what's been happening with them musically in the recent past.

It was written by Paul Wilson who's now living in Canada. His view is perhaps one of the better informed outside Czecho as he spent 10 years there (1967-77) before being expelled, partly for his association with the Plastics. During his time there he played with the group from 1970-72 and was close friends with them all the time he was in the country.

His article serves as news and more importantly as a review of the most recent Plastic's music. In this regard there will be 2 releases in the not too distant future. Firstly, a private cassette of *THE HUNDRED POINTS* to be distributed through EUROCK. It should be available upon publication of the next issue.

Secondly, the release of new Plastics material on the Bozi Mlyn label, tentatively scheduled to come out at Easter. Its world premier will be on CBC in Canada on March 16 at 10:05 PM. Details as to its availability will also be forthcoming with the next issue of EUROCK.

PLASTIC PEOPLE OF THE UNIVERSE UPDATE

I don't like talking about the Plastic People in relation to politics because their music has more to do with human relations, but I can't avoid it because the first thing I always get asked is "Are they out of jail yet?', as if jail were some kind of bottom line from which to judge the tolerability or intolerability of their situation. The short answer to the question is "Yes," but a lot of other people in Czecho still are, including some of the Plastic People's more active fans who were imprisoned for spreading tapes of underground music around and letting banned singers perform in their flats, and other heinous crimes against the state.

Ivan Jirous, the artistic director of the Plastics, was released from his third term in prison last April, and as far as I know he has not been re-arrested. Apart from that, there are still dozens, if not hundreds of people in prison in Czecho for their contribution to the cause of human rights, and the situation show every sign of getting worse. So the fact that the Plastic People and other musicians are not now in prison is good news only in relation to the vast sea of bad news that surrounds it.

The second question I am frequently asked is "Are they still playing?" The answer here again is "Yes," but it shouldn't be interpreted to mean that they go gigging about the country, skipping from secret venue to secret venue like Scarlet Pimpernels, one step ahead of the secret police. The fact is that since 1972 they have never played a normal, fully public, above-ground concert. And since their arrest in 1976, they have been constantly harassed by the police and as a result have only managed to perform before a live audience two or three times, and in very private circumstances. Each time however, they have performed a major new work, an amazing feat considering they have practically no place to practice. I have tapes of two of these pieces, and I believe that their new music will assure them a place in some revisionist history of rock (if it ever gets written), quite apart from the unusual circumstances that shaped the band and made them, for a time at least, a "succès de scandal" in Europe and North America.

The first piece is called *THE HUNDRED POINTS*. It was recorded live at the Third Music Festival of the Second Culture on Oct. 1, 1977 and the piece has an interesting history behind it. When the band was first arrested in March 1976, an article appeared in an English left-wing paper quoting some of the Plastic's lyrics, including a long, heavily political song called *THE HUNDRED POINTS* that they had never done, let alone seen. I was still living in Prague at the time and when I saw the article I was livid because the communist press had been printing vulgar lyrics that the Plastics had never sung to discredit them (see EUROCK #10 for examples) and now the left wing press had descended to the same kind of falsehood, though with the best of intentions, (the ends justify the means) in order to make the Plastics palatable and sympathetic to people who could only hear what the music was saying if the ideology was right.

When I showed the article to the Plastics, their reaction astonished me. "There's only one thing we can do now," they said. "Do it." It was a brilliant solution. Rather than going through the rather complicated hassle of denying *THE HUNDRED POINTS*, they simply had it translated into Czech and set it to music, thus making the article in the English paper retroactively true. *THE HUNDRED POINTS* represents a breakthrough for the group. First it was their longest and most complex piece of music to date, and to deal with it they expanded the band to include strings and other sound effects that gave a new dimension in sound as well as scope. And secondly it represented their first excursion into handling lyrics that were overtly political. But how brilliantly they dealt with it! The music is completely free of any of the anger, or sarcasm or exaggerated sentimentality that usually goes along with politically "engagé" art. Through the music and the delivery, they transform what could have been simply a cheap, declamatory text into a liberating affirmation of their own strength, the strength of people who have utterly rejected what the establishment has to offer and gone on to create something far better in its place.

In retrospect, the band's next step seems entirely logical: from political music that rises above conventional politics they went to religious music that transcends religion. In April 1978, the Plastics performed and taped what I think is their greatest work so far -- a rock Easter passion play. If the Who legitimized the rock opera, then the Plastic People should be given credit for doing the same thing for the Passion Play, an art form that has even deeper roots in European musical and theatrical tradition than opera does.

People who take anti-religious sentiments for granted may find the Passion somewhat difficult to penetrate until they realize that what the Plastics have done is to make an important human statement which is also, incidentally, a statement of their own faith. They have re-injected into a central myth of our civilization -- the suffering and death of Christ -- a sense of drama, immediacy, relevance and intensity that you will hardly hear anywhere in Western music of this genre this side of Handel. The focus however, is not so much on the divinity of Christ or the revelation of divine order in the universe as it is on the fate of a man who comes forward with a message of truth which is in fact a radical vision that raises the humble, the poor, the sick and the outcast to the status of inheritors of the earth. For this of course, he is betrayed, tried and put to death by his own people because law and order in this outpost of the Roman Empire is more important than justice or truth. As the Plastics present it, belief in the story of Christ is not a matter of suspending your rationality, but simply of having your eyes open. The passion of Christ becomes a direct representation of life in a dictatorship, where friends can become police informers and people are jailed or hounded to death or driven into exile for simply trying to live by the truth as they see it.

But even if you knew nothing about that, were totally agnostic or atheistic and did not understand Czech, the music itself is magnificent and compelling, by far the best synthesis of theme and sound that the band has ever achieved, proving again, as all great works in the rock tradition have done, that rock is still a medium of infinite flexibility and capacity to absorb other forms and influences while remaining inspired and inspiring at the gut level.

The Plastic People, according to a rumour that reached me recently, have apparently completed another major piece of music which they recorded this past summer. As far as I know, no copies have reached the West, but I know they have been working on the project for well over a year: putting the works of a Czech philosopher, Ladislav Klima (1878-1928) to music. Klima is one of the most uncompromising philosophers who ever lived and he constructed his philosophical system on the premise that reality is entirely intellectual, that is, a product of mind. He wrote strange, metaphysical horror stories and gory, Gothic pornography, and although the regime has banned him, he is popular among young people in Czechoslovakia for his total rejection of materialism, which, you'll recall is the official basis of the ruling ideology. All I know about the music is that Milan Hlavea, who wrote it, says it's "horrible," which does not surprise me because in the radical esthetic of the Czech underground beauty is anything but reassuring, and Klima himself believed that in their most intense states, beauty and horror were the same. Like all good music, that of the Plastics and others in the Czech underground is meant to disturb, upset and question at the same time as it affirms. Once you have chosen to live in terms of your own truth, there is nothing left to do but march to your own drummer and dance to your own piper.

**Paul Wilson
Toronto, January 1980**

The Ekseptional Rick Van Der Linden

Rick van der Linden was born in Badhovedorp, Holland on August 5, 1946. His father was a talented pianist and Rick followed in his footsteps, beginning lessons at age seven and eventually enrolling in a conservatory. Through hard work and determination, products of an intense Catholic upbringing and the challenge of equaling his father's accomplishments, he completed the 5 year course in 3 years. The young pianist then proceeded to win many competitions and by the age of 20 was employed as an instructor at the conservatory he had graduated from. Teaching students who were twice his age, however, did not sit well with him as he felt uneasy and out of place.

In the meantime he also dabbled in various styles of music -- pop, jazz, rock, etc. not because he particularly liked them, but to learn about them and to feel at home with any style. He played in bars with jazz trios, started a quartet with Ferdinand Povel that lasted a year, and later joined a group known as the Occasional Swing Combo.

One night the Occasional Swing Combo and a group called Ekseption found themselves on the same bill. Rein van den Broek, who at the time played trumpet with one hand and organ with the other for the band, saw Rick perform and asked him to become Ekseption's full time organist. In April of 1967 Rick made his first public performance with the group at the Club 66 in Amsterdam.

Ekseption had its roots in a band known as the Jokers which was originally guided by

Hans and Rob Alta. The Jokers quickly gained regional popularity, changed their name once, and finally settled on Ekseption in 1965 thanks to group member Huib van Kampen and an English dictionary. When Rick joined the band its field of operations was mainly school parties and dances and the members consisted of:

Rob Kruisman (saxes, flutes, guitars, vocals)
Hans Alta (bass)
Tim Griek (drums)
Rein van den Broek (trumpet)
Huib van Kampen (guitar, saxes)

The group reached a new plateau when its manager entered Ekseption in the prestigious Loosdrecht Jazz Festival in 1968, Cor Dekker (bass) and Peter DeLeeuwe (drums) having replaced Tim Griek and Hans Alta. To everyone's surprise they proved an instant hit and stole the show. The success of the festival resulted in a recording contract with Phonogram. The studio sessions with producer-saxophonist Tony Vos culminated in the release of their first album, *EKSEPTION*, in June 1969 to commercial and critical acclaim. The liner notes mentioned that the group was led by Rick van der Linden, a young keyboard virtuoso who has set out to bring new dimensions to pop music from his prodigious beginnings in classical music. Three singles from the album, "The Fifth," "Rhapsody in Blue" and "Air" confirmed that statement and provided an indication of what the future held. Success also brought concert tours through Germany and France. Rob Kruisman and Huib van Kampen later left, but Rick and Rein decided to continue and added singer Michel van Dijk and saxophonist Dick Remelink.

The early '70s were hectic and productive years for the band. It was as a consequence of the band's activities during this period that they were labeled as a "flying, tour-mad bunch of musicians who complete occasional LPs in between gigs as a sideline."

A second album, *BEGGAR JULIA'S TIME TRIP*, from which a film was made, was released in March '70. This album was awarded a flattering 4-1/2 (out of 5) stars by "*Downbeat*," the reviewer remarking that he was "at a loss to describe the piece other than to note the incredible sense of a whole from essentially disparate parts -- truly, Rick van der Linden exhibits a remarkable genius for both structure and energy," and also captured the Dutch Edison Award, the equivalent to the American Grammy. "Italian Concerto" and "Adagio," classical pieces spiced with jazz and rock elements, were issued as singles.

Little time was wasted in preparing, recording and releasing in Nov. '70, the group's third album, *EKSEPTION 3*, which was based on the book "Le Petit Prince" by the noted French author Saint Exupéry. The band members obviously found the book's philosophy compelling and deserving of public attention. The album was significant in that it marked Rick's first venture into composing for group and orchestra ("Piece for Symphonic and Rock Group").

Ekseption participated in numerous national and international festivals during this period including Antibes, Montreux, Cannes, Palermo, undertook concert tours through France and Germany, and appeared on TV specials in Holland, France, Portugal, Germany and Belgium. The years 1970-71 were times of travel and triumph.

The band's fourth album, *00.04*, released in Oct. '71 and preceded by the single "Ave Maria," was recorded in London with the co-operation of the English Royal

Philharmonic Orchestra and was also Rick's first production. As on previous albums the tracks featured Rick's piano and organ and Rein's trumpet, but with this record the band had matured as the playing was inspired, the arrangements natural and flowing and the composition intelligent. "Picadilly Sweet," a lengthy and large scale piece for group and orchestra with room for improvisation, was the most ambitious project Rick had yet undertaken.

On the heels of the commercial success of *00.04* Ekseption toured the Scandia locales in 1972 highlighted by a tour of Sweden that included a concert with the Swedish National Symphony Orchestra at the Royal Opera House in Stockholm and also visited England and Israel. The band then returned to the studio to record its fifth album. *EKSEPTION 5* was released in Sept. '72 together with the single "My Son." An extensive tour of the Netherlands was undertaken in Nov. '72 followed by concerts in Germany, Sweden and Finland in early '73.

EKSEPTION 5 is probably the group's most recognized and successful album in North America. It includes outstanding long pieces with a mixture of styles ("Midbar Session"), short classical pieces with jazz breaks ("Vivace," "Siciliano" a reworked Nice tune ("For Example/For Sure") and the inspiring and uplifting "My Son," which ends in a lengthy and majestic pipe organ solo. The album was significant in one other regard: it marked the first time that Rick had used synthesizer on record.

By this time the band's activities were predictable and tiresome -- tours and a new album. *TRINITY*, their sixth and final LP until 1978, was released in Sept. 1973 and continued in the tradition of the previous three: classical pieces brought up to date ("Toccata," "Flight of the Bumble Bee"), short, intriguing works ("Dreams," "Lonely Chase"), and drawn-out tracks with a basic theme and room for improvisation ("The Peruvian Flute," "Improvisation"). Ekseption made its first appearance in North America with a series of concerts in Canada in the fall and followed with a tour of Germany. Shortly thereafter, the news that Rick van der Linden was leaving the group was made public.

Ekseption carried on and released several more albums -- *BINGO, MINDMIRROR* and *BACK TO THE CLASSICS*, but with the heart of the group gone the music lacked the natural flow, freshness and vitality of the past. Commercial sales declined noticeably and creatively the group was barren.

Six commercially and critically popular albums, impressive arranging abilities and his own unique and eclectic compositions were the legacy that Rick left behind. He picked up by establishing his own group under the name Trace in August of 1974 along with Jaap van Eik (bass, guitars) and Pierre van der Linden (drums), who was later replaced by Ian Mosley. Trace was presented as a supergroup and released two albums: *TRACE* (1974) and *BIRDS* (1975).

The music was melodic, dynamic and often inspired, showing off the breadth of Rick's musical knowledge. Both works effortlessly fused classical, rock, pop, jazz and traditional themes to the classics. Although neither album sold well this period is considered to be the high point of his musical career.

By 1976 he had discontinued the group and realized a number of solo projects. *THE WHITE LADIES*, a concept LP with a storyline based on a popular Dutch legend, was issued that same year. The music was not as intense or as involved as

1980

Trace, perhaps leaning more toward the commercial, but nonetheless it bore the unmistakable van der Linden stamp. Backed by the National Philharmonic Orchestra he also put out a classical album consisting of organ and harpsichord pieces by Albinoni, Bach and Handel, a project he had wanted to do for years.

In 1977 Yamaha asked him to experiment with its new GX-1 synthesizer (the "Dream Machine"). It proved such a good venture that he employed it almost exclusively on his two subsequent solo LPs, *GX-1* (1977) and *NIGHT OF DOOM* (1978). Most of the tracks were short, melodic pieces, either original compositions or drawn from the classics, but developed through the unlimited sounds and scope of the GX-1. Here the dynamism and intensity of Trace gave way to the subtle textures and easily identifiable melodies of the synthesizer.

Word of an Ekseption reunion spread in 1978 and after a hiatus of five years the band's comeback album *EKSEPTION '78* was released in Sept. with loud fanfare. The lineup was familiar:
Rick van der Linden (keyboards)
Rein van den Broek (trumpet, flugelhorn)
Cor Dekker (bass)
Dick Remelink (saxes, flute)
Peter DeLeeuwe (drums)

As with previous Ekseption LPs this one contained contemporary interpretations of classical works ("Pearl," "Jesu Joy," "Nocturne"), jazz highlights ("Summertime," "The Cat") and short, melodic pieces by Rick and Rein ("Thoughts," "Faith," "Your Home"). It was a strong comeback that relied on established formulas; a criticism one could make was that the band took few chances, but perhaps that was necessary to bridge the five year gap? Concert tours of Germany, Holland, Switzerland and Czechoslovakia followed in Spring/Summer 1979.

Commitments to the group will not deter Rick from pursuing other projects this time however. An album with him on GX-1 and Jack Lancaster on Lyricon titled *WILD CONNECTIONS*, a subtle and sometimes esoteric work came out in Spring '79. He is also planning an album with Dutch singer Kaz Lux and other session work.

Ekseption will be recording a second comeback LP, a concept work along the lines of *BEGGAR JULIA'S TIME TRIP* with Theo DeJong (x-Kayak) replacing Cor Dekker. The album will incorporate Vivaldi's "Four Seasons" and the Indian philosophy that "all life is a circle." Reportedly it will be heavier and rock more with Jack Lancaster handling the production. In the future there's a project planned to be based on Bach's "St. Matthews Passion" with a crew of international artists.

Bruno Toneguzzi
Martin Wind (Dutch material)
Jorge Wensing (translations)

Eskaton

COMMUNIQUE: For us, music is not an objective for itself. It is a way to convey our ideas. This approach however does not mean that we do not care about music, that would be mad. We consider that all of us are living in difficult times and a dangerous era. In a usual way, one human being has no chance to gain freedom. Family, school, work, cops, all are leading us toward lethargic capitulation -- do not think, just accept! Deceit, wars, jails, torture, atom bomb.... and shut up -- we refuse to blindly go along.

Sometimes during our music, one can find a very cool piece, suddenly disrupted by a very tart tune (the voices -- two soprani, very often have this role). It is a call to wake up, open your eyes! After each of our concerts we try to open a discussion with the audience. We refuse to enter into the game "you are the public, we are the musicians." We refuse to put on a show with elaborate props and costumes. We try to say, you can do like us too. Our individual technique as musicians is not terrific, our only technique consists of playing music together.

We also live together. Some are working, some are still students. All of our money is

kept in a common fund. We try to live our ideas....reading, music work, discussion, life.

Eskaton

Metabolist

GLADIATORS OF INDEPEN-DENT MUSIC: Metabolist have existed in one form or another for 3 or 4 years, the present group consisting of Malcolm Lane, Anton Loach, Simon Millward and Mark Rowlatt. The group is run along co-operative lines to include Jacqueline Bailey who handles publicity, promotion, etc. The five of us have all reached the decision to work outside of the large companies in the music business and have therefore formed our own company -- Dromm Records. So far we have released 1 EP, 15 minutes of music including "Dromm," "Slaves" and "Eulam's Beat," plus a cassette tape of first take rehearsal material called *GOATMANAUT*, also containing 3 tracks "Zordan Returns," "Chained" and "Thru the Black Hole." The group's first album *HANSTEN KLORK* is released in January 1980, closely followed by a single, "I Can't Identify." All these recordings have been made at the group's studio with members of the group being responsible for recording, mixing and editing. We feel that this is the only way, apart from having unlimited cash, that Metabolist can have control over their musical output at every stage. All artwork and sleeve design are also handled within the group. Thanks to the growth of alternative distribution networks in recent years our records can now become available worldwide, so we consider independence to be both viable and desirable.

Musically the group has been through many changes, Metabolist refuse to be dictated to by fashion, or by establishing a Metabolist "sound" and sticking to it forever after. You can therefore find that you love the album, but hate the EP and so on. You will have to trust us as we do not intend to have 10 versions of a hit sound on our LPs.

Metabolist

Via Lactea

The spirit of Rock In Opposition is spreading. The latest kindred soul to join the ranks is Via Lactea (Milky Way) -- from Mexico City. They made their debut on Oct. 8. 1979 at the 2nd in a series of concerts billed as "Una Alternativa Para Los Lunes" that were held every Monday during Oct.

Via Lactea is an electronic duo composed of Carlos Alvarado Perea, an artist from Mexico City, who plays Crumar Orchestron, Korg Micro preset, Korg MS-20, flute, voice and devices and Miguel Angel Nava on ARP Odyssey, ARP AXXE and devices.

As the name implies their hearts lie in the outer regions as does their sound which Is a swirling mixture of electronics, winds and effectual voice. The result is a timeless, floating wave of sound -- tranquil and almost meditative.

They have done a tape and are in the process of preparing it for distribution. If all goes as planned it will be available at the time of the next EUROCK.

Archie Patterson

1980

Konrad Schnitzler Interview

BIOGRAPHY: Born 1937 in Dusseldorf. Grew up in the Ruhrgebeit, Austria, Bavaria, Rheinland. Trained as a mechanical engineer, worked in various jobs, e.g. sailor, window washer, chauffeur, house painter, hippy, smuggler.

First student of Joseph Beuys. Moved to Berlin. Founded the Kluster group of electronic - meditation music. Member of Tangerine Dream rock band. Founded the Eruption group (multi-channel sound, combining electronic and free music with elements of rock).

Co-operation with K.H. Hodicke to produce plays, operas, films, 12 hour concerts and happenings throughout Germany.

ACTIONS, CONCERTS, PERFORMANCES
First actions in 1967. Sculpture Man in Nature, Steel Flower. Corsica: Juncture of Summits/signs and signals. Gottengen Kunsthalle/Center Church. Hanover Kunstverein/Street actions. Frankfurt Experimenta 1969/Kunstverein/Goethehaus. Heidelberg Open Air Stage. Munich Kunstverein /Theater. Basle/Berne. Vienna. Stuttgart Kunstverein. Dusseldorf/ Essen Folkwang/ Kunsthalle/ IKI/Church. Keil. Cologne Jetzt/Intermedia/ Kunstverein. Aachen. Amsterdam. Wuppertal Kunsthalle/ Impuls. London St. Martin School of Art/Galleryhouse Berlin Scene 72. Hamburg Factory/Kunstverein. Berlin Crematory/Schaubuhne/National Gallery/& various places like Rene Block Gallerie a.o.

RECORDS & ACTIONS
LP- *ELECTRONIC MEDITATION* (T. Dream) Ohr
LP- *KLOPFZEICHEN* (Kluster) Schwann
LP- *ZWEI OSTEREI* (Kluster) Schwann
LP- *SCHWARZ* (Schnitzler) Rene Block
LP- *ROT* (Schnitzler) Rene Block
LP- *BLAU* (Schnitzler) Rene Block
LP- *CON* (Schnitzler) Egg
Cassette 1 (Kluster & Eruption)
Cassette 2 (Pop + Die Folgen)
Music for various films, plays, radio
Video concerts with Ulricke Rosenbach
Music actions with K.H. Hodicke, Polke, Kagel, Lupertz, Bremer, Rosenbach, Al Hansen, Hamsly Bayers a.o.

Profession: INTERMEDIALIST

SETTING THE SCENE

1980

Interview made on Monday eve, 1/7/80, at Konrad's home in central Berlin. Konrad is a porter for a small block of apts. He has a small studio/room which houses his equipment (consisting mainly of tape decks, Synthi A, echo units, rhythm units). His living quarters are simple and practical, and the overwhelming colors are black and white. Endless cups of tea with honey are consumed. The atmosphere is decidedly informal. Not an "interview" as such; more a lighthearted conversation.

D: How's the new LP coming along?

K: They are still talking about this next one. I don't know when it's coming out exactly. When it's fixed, then I want to know.

D: Are you trying to get a contract with some other label?

K: I don't know. Maybe Barclay don't want it; but somebody does.

D: Is it similar to *CON*?

K: No, on this new LP there are only short tracks; very simple, no story. Every track starts & carries on the same.

D: When did you first become interested in electronics? Have you any influences, such as Stockhausen?

K: Yes, it's a central European idea to do this sort of music. When I hear this music I was 14; music from Stockhausen... all music; I was interested in all music but I liked very much the new music, because there's not so much melody, and how it works. I heard this music in night school in Dusseldorf and Cologne and there was a person at the night school who liked all this new electric music. It was a very funny thing at the time. At the time it was very interesting, but I have forgotten all about this now. I mean I hear music from this time on the radio and from friends, and it was not an experience for me I think. I was an artist, a sculptor. I used photographs and films. I was not directly working with people; like now -- because I don't do concerts (laughs). I don't always make music. I learnt nothing from my father. He was a musician. He hated it if I touched any thing.

D: Did he play conventional instruments?

K: Yes, violin and piano. He did some composing for orchestra, but from him I learnt nothing. I started music without knowing anything. I can't play any instrument. I do total improvisation, which is why I'm interested in the new notes you can do with electrics; but I started with normal instruments -- piano & cello.

D: Do you still dabble around with conventional instruments?

K: Yes, and when the electrics came in it was a great day. There was a group of 3 or 4 people who played very quiet music; cellos, violins, tubas and the guy with the violin was always very unhappy because it was too quiet. He took a very small amplifier and this was the start of the devil in electronics. I was very interested! It was fantastic! So I bought the next one up in size. This comes to a peak with someone like Schulze. I mean, it's too much.

D: When did you set up the Zodiak Club?

K: I built it in '69. You know, just at the time when it was almost a new decade. I was together with Edgar & Franke for concerts. It was a good club, but it was an old theatre & nobody was there, but it was a full experience for me.

D: Was it very loud?

K: Yes! We got in trouble with the noise,

the smoking and the "Scene," but it was a good scene.

D: Did you perform here with Kluster?

K: It was the group I founded. In the Zodiak we started with Roedelius & Boris. Boris is starting to do music again now, but he flipped around too much at the time.

D: Your first record was with Edgar & Klaus?

K: No, the first was with Kluster, then at the same time I did this other one with Edgar. We did a tape earlier, when we got some machines and lights, and we were fighting about it because they were two rock musicians. They liked to play this kind of rock music. All the concepts were running away.

D: Did you enjoy playing with Edgar on *ELECTRONIC MEDITATION*?

K: Sometimes we did fantastic things, but they were playing against me. Klaus didn't know anything about the music. I was older than him and Edgar was in between. I found it easier with Franke than with Klaus, because he was very interested.

D: Then you went on to start Kluster.

K: Yes, it all started at the Zodiak Club in '69 because there was something THERE and we then played with Moebius with instruments, amps & echoes.

D: Did you enjoy doing *KLOPFZEICHEN & ZWEI OSTEREI*?

K: Yes we had a fantastic time. Moebius & Roedelius had all the drums and electronics and they asked me if I wanted to do a record. So I said ok and got a concert planned for 24 hours and it was good from the very first minute. A lot of feedback and all the same crackly sounds. It was sponsored by the church and I saw in the news about an organist who's interested in new music and I knew this guy from when I was in Dusseldorf; so we went over there and played him a tape and he said "This is good, do you want to do a record?" We said, "That's ok." But it's for the church; you'll have to include some text on one side." So we said ok. If you don't understand the German words, it's better. It's good for English people because they don't understand German. Have you heard the record?

D: Yes.

K: What do you think of the German words?

D: I don't understand them (laughs).

K: That's good. If you know what it means it's terrible.

D: When did you do *ZWEI OSTEREI*?

K: At the same time. We came in the studio and the equipment and mikes were checked in. Conny Plank did it.

D: Did he do *KLOPFZEICHEN* too?

K: Yes he did both of them. We said we'll do two 20 minute pieces; you just show us the time in between. So we just played solid and saw nobody. We did two records in one day. Only the second record had the voice put on later.

D: When did you form Eruption?

K: It was in the time after Edgar and Tangerine Dream, and some guys said to me, "Let's do something together," but nobody wanted to do anything, so I had to start all the shit you know -- to bring people together.

D: Do you get fed up with organizing?

K: Yes. So anyway we got 10 musicians together; rock musicians, free electric musicians -- all together. But we did some interesting things.

D: You did a private cassette with Eruption?

K: No, that was the last concert with Moebius & Joachim. It was called *KLUSTER & ERUPTION*, but was before the Eruption group.

D: Then you did 3 solo albums?

K: No, the first was with Joachim and Moebius called *SCHWARZ*, and then came *ROT & BLAU*.

D: Do you like the music of Cluster now?

K: Yes, I like it, especially the first record. I would say that Joachim and Moebius are the only musicians who are making records that I really like; because I know the way he started. He learned from our start, and then I saw the change and worked with others and he became more popular, I like it. I was in the studio at the time they were working on *GROSSES WASSER*. There Joachim said to me: "If I could work again like you it would be better.... Because he plays more melodic things now and if he states this, he has to do more. Maybe he's not the chief in his music; it's his wife.

D: When did you do the 50-hour concert?

K: After *BLAU* in the Rene Block Gallerie. Everyday for 3 hours, for 16 days. It was very quiet there. In Stuttgart I did one for 4 weeks -- every day for 10 hours. The machine was running, and if I didn't like what's coming out, I changed the sound a bit.

D: Did you record the Block concert?

K: Yes, I recorded 100 tapes. The concert was all the same music. I didn't change the actual sounds on the equipment so much, just added more on.

D: What did you do between this & the release of *CON*?

K: I did so much you know. Because I'm not only a musician. If I'm standing in the kitchen or whatever I do -- it's a piece of my art. It's my life.

D: Do you do concerts & play your videos along with the music?

K: No, not in the way of a music concert, more a performance. I like to mix it like I want on the day.

D: When did you meet up with Peter Baumann?

K: I knew him from a long time ago. I was always interested in Peter's work. After he jumped out of Tangerine Dream he started the Paragon Studio and it was then that he asked if I'd like to do something and I said ok, so we did CON. I brought in some tracks from home & he accepted the possibilities.

D: They were earlier tracks of yours?

K: Yes, from the "Red Cassette."

D: What were your feelings about doing an album to be released worldwide?

K: You know, it was funny. I sit down in dark cellar -- no money, and just from this came all the work. It's a good deal, it's not much money what I got, but everybody knows me now.

D: It was well received in England.

K: You know the music I do is not so popular.

D: Not for the majority, but the small minority really like it.

K: Yes, I like that too. People who go into the shop looking for some special record. I do this music for them. Now if nobody wants to buy my stuff, then it's no problem, I'll do it for myself like before.

D: What do you think of Tangerine Dream's music today?

K: I don't hear any music as I have no record player. I hear only music from the radio and if the play T.D. music it's for background to somebody talking. For me it's not experimental enough, it's for people who like all this lah, lah, lah ... I can't do this because I don't play. Maybe if I could play and I learned the piano, I'd make the same shit. I do music how it comes, more a direct happening, like catching something I know I want to do.

D: You have a certain amount of rhythm though, like on "Ballet Statique"?

K: Yes, that has a strictly echo-rhythm. That was a funny thing you know. I go with nothing into the studio and Peter says, "Oh haven't you brought any stuff -- you can use my synthi." He showed me how it works & so we started this, and then perhaps just because it's only to see what I could do, I started the echo machine. The melody was finished & we added only one sound to this, so we made a "ping." It comes from an earlier cassette. The other rhythms come from a rhythm machine. I only just got a sequencer, just for testing.

D: Did you use the sequencer on "Zug"?

K: No, rhythm machine with echoes & ring modulation. On "Metall I" I flipped out on a harmonizer. Peter showed me how to use it; I did an organ cluster & put it through the harmonizer & it came out like that.

D: Do you pick a title according to what the music sounds like?

K: Sometimes, or maybe just because the words are interesting. On my next record I've got only numbers, because I numbered my tapes for the sounds, since this was the only way I could keep track of them -- there are so many.

D: What is the long tube-shaped object in the photos on the back of *CON*?

K: It's a normal pipe with a cassette recorder inside. The sound changes in the pipe. It's a small art piece. (Picks up some artwork) The next cover will be the same as *CON*, but in negative. It'll be called *CON II* as some people will know this cover and the name *CON*.

D: What plans do you have for the future?

K: My future is the same as the world's.

D: You don't want to be more famous?

K: I think I lead my life as before. Whatever comes I take it. It's the easiest way to do it. If you're in the Business, and after money, it kills you -- all this stress. If I don't do music, I do something else: text, films, whatever I want.

David Elliott
Editor, NEUMUSIK

Ilitch

What Is Ilitch? A musical look into the state of the universal mind -- the sound of a life filled with TV tube radiation -- an electric trip along the frozen borderline of consciousness......

In the limited space of 2 LPs, Ilitch (aka Thierry Muller) has created a series of musical portraits that shed new light on the state of the art today.

PERIODIKMINDTROUBLE with its combination of synthetiks and guitar is a schizoid exposé of the new music. One side creates a passive/aggressive split by alternating acoustic & e. guitar . The other induces sensory overload as it slowly unfolds a blanket of keyboard/guitar that ultimately literally engulfs and smothers you.

There are points of reference to be found in the music to be sure, i.e. Glass, Fripp & Eno along with some of Manuel Gottsching's early works, but Ilitch has taken their techniques -- exorcised the intellectual underpinning and allowed his own particular muse to take possession. Thus the sound may bear some resemblance, but there is an unmistakable difference that makes it unique.

The new album, *10 SUICIDES*, is strongly linked spiritually to its predecessor, but structurally is much different. Within the confines of its 10 pieces, the state of humanity is examined, brought into question & ultimately found to be barren. He paints a bleak picture to be sure, but he also creates an inspired music that screams out with vitality. It's the classic Love/Hate relationship -- Life is shit, but it's beautiful to be alive.....

Archie Patterson

Macromassa

The music of Macromassa is not easy to describe. A loose categorization might be electronic jazz that borders on impulse music. Yet that is too sterile and intellectual a label to pin on a band whose music also has such a myriad of emotional levels that they can hardly maintain at times within an style

Their first recording, "Darlia Microtonica," was literally a blast of high energy sound that contained too much sound for one 45 to successfully convey. The impact was like sticking your finger into a light socket -- initial shock followed by electric rush, then burn out. Full of intensity and a couple solid ideas, but too confined to allow anything to develop.

Since that time there have reportedly been some changes in the group and their 1st LP, *EL CONCIERTO PARA IR EN GLOBO*, has been released. An initial listening confirms that they have indeed kept their level of imagination and intensity as well as taken steps to focus their energy.

They've just played the R.I.O. Fest in France. Live experience and more time would seem to all they need to become a prime exponent of Spanish progressive music.

Music from Spain first came to light in the U.S. in an earlier issue which featured an overview of the Spanish scene in general (EUROCK #12). Since that time more information has come to light and some more experimental musicians have been discovered, primary among these is Macromassa.

Macromassa personnel:
Juan Crek - Audiogenerador
Francesco Bsme - Guitarra, y Efectos
Goomumbulaa - Clarinet y wa wa
Pou Magrana - Violin
Luis Fobat - Bateria

Archie Patterson

Robert-Jan Stips
Super(Trans)Sister

The Netherlands -- that little piece of land below sea-level at the other side of the Atlantic Ocean, just opposite the United Kingdom -- barely has a rock and roll tradition of its own. The groups and musicians have always been very professional (Shocking Blue, Golden Earring, Focus), but there never were really inspiring trendsetters. Yet there are a few highly respected individuals that are certainly worth talking about. One of these is Robert-Jan Stips. We know him as the leader and keyboards-player of the 1969-originated 'underground' group Supersister. Robert-Jan is still around with his new band, the uncompromising Transister. This is his story...

R.J. was born in 1950 in The Hague (the Dutch Washington D.C.). He was classically trained (Conservatory of The Hague for ten years). Began to write songs at the age of thirteen. A nice and intelligent musician, very gifted and not afraid to be his own. Although it took him a long time to forget all the things he learned at the Conservatory and considered to be wrong. The Golden Earring was his Pop-Conservatory. Thinking about music anytime, anywhere. Sometimes playing 'classics' just for the sake of cleaning his mind and coming up with some new ideas. Music is his life. Wrote over 200 songs. Sixty appeared on records. His favourite song has yet to be written.

Almost as big as capital Amsterdam, The Hague was competing for the coverage Amsterdam was given by *'Hitweek'* the only serious music-paper existing at that time. *Hitweek* was the Dutch equivalent to *Rolling Stone* or *ZigZag* (UK), however only wrote about groups coming from Amsterdam and surroundings. So when Robert-Jan and his friends Ron van Eck, Sacha van Geest and Marco Vrolijk blossomed out from the obvious schoolband to Supersister with their first single "She was naked," it sadly flopped. People couldn't read about it in the papers, people couldn't hear it on the radio. Only a small cult following existed; yet large enough to interest famous UK-deejay John

Peel to release "Naked" on his Dandelion label.

Then came their first album. Very Soft Machine and Mothers of Invention-influenced. Successful on a small scale. Until today (after several re-issues) 17,000 copies have been sold all over the world. Serious and difficult music made in the psychedelic era. The era of LSD, speed, Haight Ashbury, hippies and festivals. "Kralingen" was the best open-air-festival that happened in Holland. Programmed somewhere between Pink Floyd, Jefferson Airplane and Santana, Supersister shined as the best of the Dutch groups. But success on a large scale failed to appear. After three albums Marco and Sacha quit. They didn't agree with Robert-Jan's and Rons' feelings about *ISKANDER*, that was to be a concept album about Alexander the Great. Their successors were Charlie Mariano and Herman van Boeyen. Music became more and more jazz-oriented. Charlie didn't fit too well, so he was replaced by former Soft Machine-member Elton Dean. Then it sounded like a free-jazz-group, too free. That's why R.J. called it a day, because he wanted to be in a rock and roll band again.

Cesar Zuiderwijk (Golden Earrings' drummer) asked Robert-Jan to play in that band. In two years of cooperation two albums were released. They visited the USA three times for long tourings. The records appeared to be not very commercial. The management and record company insisted on returning to the roots. That's not what Robert-Jan wanted, so he quit again and took a rest. He met Bertus Borgers and agreed playing in Sweet d'Buster. After another two-year period he wasn't satisfied by the way things worked out. He took a long rest and came with his next idea, Transister.

He wanted a fresh team of musicians, so he put an advertisement in a music-paper asking for people who wanted to do something new. He got 120 reactions, only one remained: Huba DeGraaff (vocals, violin and vocorder). The other two Transisters were recommended by friends of Robert-Jan. Thus Henk Wijtman (drums) and Dick Schulte Nordholt (bass) appeared. Transister is a nice surprise, listen to their first album ZIG-ZAG. A little rock and roll, some pop, funk, blues and a few drops of classical music. Most important are the humorous little stories about ordinary people. Sharp and creative. Transister didn't want to be just a new group. No, they wanted to be fresh and innovative. Avoiding to become too difficult, but trying to be as simple as possible.

This is the career of Robert-Jan Stips in a nutshell. Of course there's much more to tell. We'll do that next issue when we've had an in-depth interview with Robert-Jan about his past, present and future. His opinions about music played today. Some more photographs. And probably some addenda on the discography .

Henk Zweering

THE SUPERSISTER CREW:
Robert-Jan Stips/vocals, keyboard
Sacha van Geest/flute
Ron van Eck/bass
Marco Vrolijk/drums, percussion
Charlie Mariano/saxophone
Herman van Boeyen/drums
Elton Dean/flute, saxophone

THE SUPERSISTER ALBUMS:

PRESENT FROM NANCY (Polydor, 1970) (Robert-Jan remembers this album to be released in the USA on Dwarf Records)

TO THE HIGHEST BIDDER (Polydor, 1971) (also released -- including 'Naked' --

on Dandelion/UK)

PUDDING EN GISTEREN (Polydor, 1972)

ISKANDER (Polydor, 1973)

SPIRAL STAIRCASE (Polydor, 1975)

POLYDOR SUPERSTARSHINE Volume I

POLYDOR SUPERSTARSHINE Volume II

THE SUPERSISTER SINGLES:
"She was naked"
"Radio"
"A girl named you"
"Fancy Nancy"
"Wow"

ROBERT-JAN STIPS:
Golden Earring - *SWITCH* (Polydor, 1974)
Golden Earring - *TO THE HILT* (Polydor, 1975)
Nevergreens - *NEVERGREENS* (Polydor, 1976)
Sweet d'Buster - *FIRST ALBUM* (Bubble, 1976)
Sweet d'Buster - *FRICTION* (Bubble, 1978)
Sweet d'Buster - *GIGS* (Live) (Ariola, 1978)

Production for Los Allegres (hit "Coconut Woman"), Himalaya, Gruppo Sportivo, Buddy Odor Stop, Nits (all Dutch) and UK singer Warren Harry.

Archie Patterson

Finland 1980
New Start To The '80s?

Not exactly, there's no change starting. It's been happening for 2-3 years, but now we see the results. It is still hard to get gigs, but there are new music associations at work in every town to put on concerts and dances.

New wave rock has made the scene more lively. The best bands use punk as a starting point to develop their own music and are moving away from the near white noise of '77. There is danger that their audience is too conservative/trendy to follow.

Progressive composers are moving over borders of rock. Pekka Pohjola and Jukka Gustavson are both getting further into their own music. Maybe Wigwam was limiting their creativity. They are mainly recording their music and play only occasional gigs.

Jazz-rockers Piirpauke have a new LP out and flute/sax player Sakari Kukko has done his first solo record that is a change from the groups music: shorter compositions, folktunes, birdnoises and fine guitar work by Hasse Walli. The LP is a bit like Bo Hansson or Roedelius, but Finnish and more rocking. Walli is as good as Kenny Håkansson or Michael Rother.

Wigwam is back and there should be a new LP and TV program soon. Also a Blues Section LP has been reissued, *ONCE MORE FOR THE ROAD*, a compilation of 45's and tracks off the 1st LP.

Finnforest have their 3rd LP done and play occasionally live. Guitarist Pekka Tegelman composed the #1 hit for Liisa Tavi, who is a female folk singer from East Finland.

Jukka Tolonen lives in Helsinki now, but plays mostly abroad. He has a very good band now with ex-Zamla guitarist Coste Apetrea.

The pioneers of new wave; SE, Kollaa Kestaa, 1980 & Eppu Normaali are each going their own ways and becoming rather popular. 1980 has developed from chaotic energy explosion to a hard political rock band. Eppu Normaali has mellowed and is now more a mainstream rock band with flashes of MC5 here & there. And then there is SE. That band is more like Chrome than new wave. When I saw them on TV in 1978 they played an old song "Faceless Death" from 1970 and the impression I got was like hearing Amon Düül 2 for the first time 10 years ago only maybe SE was more sinister. It must have been cultural shock for our teenyboppers to watch the program. Since that SE has done many singles and one LP. On the LP there's only one long poem/composition. The music is bright and cold with very realistic lyrics.

Love Records is gone, but 2 new companies carry on with most of the Love artists. Johanna has most of the new wave and Ponsi has jazz, progressive & political rock. Also now big companies are taking rock seriously so the music is everywhere, not only in Helsinki like in the '60s.

Ollie Heima

Carlos Alvarado/Via Lactea Interview
ELECTRONIC ROCK IN MEXICO

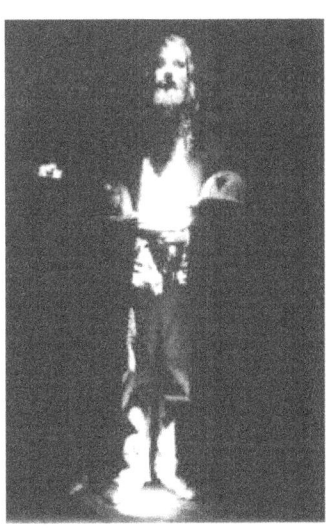

The silence. Millions of stars and the harmonic murmur of the leaves. We were that before our dawning.

Within the Mexican Rock scene there have been few groups that have dedicated themselves to doing experimental music and being open to furthering their creativity. Within these (groups) one finds the electronic experiment called Via Lactea (Milky Way), presently integrated solely by Carlos Alvarado,

1980

who is also part of the group Chac Mool. In this interview Carlos talks about his ideas and his position regarding rock music & electronics.
- Jorge Reyes

Q: What is your understanding of rock music?

A: It is a music that stems from the traditional molds, from the classics or harmonic circles that are normally used. It deals with a more elaborate work that breaks away from established cliches. Progressive rock is music that advances, evolutionizes & constantly looks for new mediums of expression.

Q: Is your work progressive?

A: Yes I use sounds that are produced in a method outside the norm. I also compose based on mathematics, I use "natural sounds" that I alter electronically and I always have electronic theory in mind.

Q: Why did you select synthesizers as your medium of expression?

A: Synthes are the most complete instrument as they have infinite possibilities of producing sound that identifies with the type of music I like to make. With 5 synthes + a string ensemble, I don't need the use of an entire orchestra.

Q: It is said that electronic music is cold, that it doesn't express human sentimentality, that it's made by machines & computers. What do you think of this?

A: It's possible that it is like that, but I believe that it depends on the one who composes it. If they are open & try to understand it as a manifestation of the world in which we live, and in the state of dehumanization to which we've fallen, then I could talk about it in a different manner. The synthes are only the instruments used and whether or not the music is good depends on problems belonging to the esthetics.

Q: What do you attempt to do with your music?

A: I want to open new dimensions of sound. Beyond this I seek to transport listening to a state of meditation. Up to a certain point I want to promote pleasure using the roads of experimentation & novelty.

Q: What are your main influences?

A: In respect to rock: Klaus Schulze, Fripp & Eno, Richard Pinhas. In the field of contemporary music there is Xenaxis, Pierre Henry, Varese a.o.

Q: And your texts?

A: They have a message directed to transmit tranquility and spiritual balance.

Q: On what do you base what you write?

A: Mainly in my feelings. I base myself on a spiritual development using Yoga & Oriental philosophies.

Q: Why do you like electronic music?

A: I identify with it. When I play my synthes a liberating sensation comes over me. This music has infinite possiblities of expression and with this I can relate. It is the manifestation of the world in which we live.

Q: What do you think of national rock?

A: In our country it's hard to detach oneself. The environment is too contaminated. The rock musicians are mediocre, they don't worry about doing the decent thing, they lack seriousness in their studies & music. Nevertheless, groups like El Queso Sagrado (The Sacred Cheese), Via Lactea, Chac Mool a.o. do exist and are taking the initiative. They are working to present their music in a serious & professional way. They are trying to be creative and develop their own sound not just imitate the "rock greats" of Mexico.

Q: What is the new LP you are recording going to be like?

A: It is an independent production and story with the aid and advice of great friends such as Jose Xavier Navar & sound engineer Franco Rosas. On the LP Jorge Reyes, my wife Erminia & I work together. The music is a logical combination of electronic music & various acoustic instruments (flutes, tambura, kalimba etc.). I am going to distribute it internationally with the help of EUROCK Magazine and my good friend Archie Patterson through Paradox Music.

Translation: Charlie Miller

R.I.O. Fest

APPEARING:
Macromassa (Espagne)
Etron Fou Leloublan (France)
Stormy Six (Italie)
Maggie Nicholls (Angleterre)
Jacques Berrocal/Jean-François Pauvros/Gilbert Artman (France)
Eskaton (France)
Ghedalia Tazartes (France)
Art Zoyd (France)
Univers Zero (Belgique)
Pataphonie (France)
Bise De Buse (France)
Phil Minton/Sally Potter/Georgie Born/Lindsay Cooper (Angleterre)
The Work (Tim Hodgkinson Group) (Angleterre)
Zamla Mammaz Manna (Suede)
Geoff Leigh (Angleterre)
This Heat (Angleterre)
Aksak Maboul (Belgique)
ZNR et Les Jeunes Musiciens de Champagne (France)
Six Cylindres En V (France)

REIMS, FRANCE -- FESTIVAL OF NEW MUSIC

It was the first time that the groups of Rock In Opposition had gotten together in France. The organizers were myself and the Association "A L'Automne Alite," which sets up nonprofit concerts. The "Maison de la Culture" (House of Culture) is a government-owned institution, which would normally be a place for more official cultural events and in order to set up the event there we had to face quite a few difficulties. But it was finally able to take place and went extremely well with a large comfortable room and big stage, which meant excellent technical conditions for the artists.

A big audience showed up from France of course, but also from Great Britain, Germany, Sweden and even the USA. Unfortunately very few people from Reims were there. We encountered some problems in accommodating the lodging needs of some people from somewhere else. We hope it will work out better next year.

The festival started on Thursday, May 17 with Etron Fou Leloublan who performed a remarkable concert. Guigou, the drummer was totally wild and Ferdinand the bass player played to his heart's content. They played new material that was as always complex, lively and fun.

1980

The new sax player was not yet fully integrated into the group, but that will come.

Then came Stormy Six, a very big Italian group, very self assured and with a very good stage presence. They perform a lot in Italy where the situation is more favorable than in France. They explored with a surprising ease all types of music: some parts were inspired by Italian country music, others taken from jazz-rock, they also have some very elaborate ideas.

But they combine everything perfectly & always stay away from easy juxtaposition. Their lyrics are humorous or political (they were translated before each piece). The group has a great visual impacts perform on stage with ease and even stepped down to the audience once to play a parody of contemporary music, each musician with a little lamp on his head.

The next day I was recording a TV program & missed both Maggie Nicholls and Eskaton, but did hear the group of Jacques Berrocal which was very impressive. They pounded out a pleasant combination of jazz, rock, punk & disco music. It was an extremely violent moment as the 3 musicians were indulging themselves completely, with a frantic energy & came really close to some form of insanity. It's hard to put them in any category as they deny all labels or fashions. Either you love it or hate it, I loved it!

That evening appeared the impressive apparition of Ghedalia Tazartes. This singer stands alone facing the audience only accompanied by his pre-recorded tapes. His music sounds like it is as old as the ages. Arabian, Indian, Tibetan & African elements were literally jostling with each other for prominence. The beauty of some very intense moments was close to greatness. Nobody has ever done before what Ghedalia was doing, and his performance on stage is quite impressive singing his songs of love & hate against oppression & racism. Here again the attitude of the audience was divided into either total delight or an unconditional rejection. Ghedalia's music reaches the deepest part of our being & fantasies. Should you refuse to deal with those things he would really bother you.

Then appeared Art Zoyd and Univers Zero. Their work is already known somewhat as they operate on the borderline between pop music & contemporary sounds. They compose their own music, work a lot on it and the result is very different & demanding of your full attention.

Between the 2 groups there was a surprise: 4 Swedish "punkettes" insisted on playing something. It was a fun & relaxing moment in a serious evening. Everybody enjoyed those 4 teenagers who played rock without pretension & had some funny lyrics:
> There was a night, there
> was a morning,
> it was the 3rd day....

The next 2 groups had a tendency to play jazz-rock music. In fact, Pataphonie plays something which is more like soft-rock -- very enjoyable & relaxing, but not revolutionary at all. As far as Bise De Buse is concerned, they are rather oriented towards contemporary music. They still show a lack of experience on stage & need to be a bit more relaxed, but should be followed up on.

On the other hand, Phil Minton, Sally Potter, Georgie Born & Lindsay Cooper do not need to be more relaxed ... To tell the truth I was a bit disappointed by their performance. They certainly are great technicians in their art, but their crazy passion for improvisation should have some limits since after a while you feel like you are attending a practice session where the musicians are having a great time, but the audience is of no importance. Yet still sometimes you had the feeling that something was happening, but the next minute they would take this feeling away from you. It was like listening to some kind of avant-garde music. They have broken with the old wave, but still have to fit all their elements together in order to build something new.

That is what Tim Hodgkinson is trying to do with his group, The Work, a logical succession to groups like Henry Cow, National Health, Soft Machine. It was only their second concert so the musicians were nervous. But there is no doubt that when they grow more assertive, when their music becomes more concise and when they show more "cool" on stage, we will be entitled to expect a lot from them.

Zamla Mammaz Manna showed us how an experienced group can perform. They started with tremendous force and went into a concert full of energy. They were not making any mistakes, had a perfect set up and very complex rhythms. They really won the enthusiasm of the audience. Some people, and I'm one of those, regretted that they had left out some of their folkloric themes, but it was a small regret.

Sunday started with Macromassa, a group from Barcelona which plays "informal" music. This was once very much appreciated, but now it looks like Spain still has a long way to go to catch up with what other countries went through in the last 10 years.

Geoff Leigh shows up all by himself, only with his cassettes. He was wearing a tuxedo and pushing a cart in which there was a mirror reflecting his image. He was constantly teasing & satirical. All pop music was on the spot. Then all of a sudden, all the saxophone players, trumpet players & other wind instrumentalists of the festival started playing together. They were everywhere in the room & everybody was surrounded by sounds & joy was adding itself to the surprise.

After Geoff Leigh came the big moment of the festival, or better "the revelation." This Heat performed purely and simply an awesome concert. There was not a noise or whisper in the room. The crowd was stupefied by the force and beauty of their music. It is classified as industrial rock music like Throbbing Gristle or Joy Division, but it is somehow also very melodic with percussion assuring a strong rhythm. From time to time it reminds of Can. It was one of the 1st concerts of the group, but they already showed us that they have a strong persona & unique way of playing. The cold music of This Heat could make the North Pole melt.

After this everybody was still under their magic spell & it was hard to appreciate the remaining concerts. Plus everybody was getting tired as 3 groups per concert was too many.

Fortunately enough Aksak Maboul, Marc Hollander's group performed a concert which was lacking in precision & set up but was very enjoyable. Arrangements for keyboards, bassoon and oboe, really close to contemporary music, jazz & fictitious folklores were contrasted with a rhythm that was deliberately punk. The guitar player & singer at the same time showed an incredible stage sense & were super comical.

To end the festival, we were expecting a lot from ZNR, or in other words Zazou & Racaille. They asked for the participation of a classical orchestra, but unfortunately the result wasn't what they were aiming for. They had not done enough rehearsings, or were maybe tired, so the 2 types of music didn't fit together right. Or perhaps they were just attempting something too difficult. Anyway we hope that we will see them under better conditions.

The festival was coming to an end. It was kind of a sad end, but we were already thinking about next year's, which will be open to even more types of music (jazz, rock, contemporary).

Anyway, this experience attracted a good crowd, even though very few people believed it would....

Patrick Plunier
(Translation: Jocelyne Smith)

A Little Transversal Note On Time Intimately Connected To The Music.....
by Richard Pinhas

It has been well understood that a sound does not have an existence apart from its realization. It is strictly contemporaneous with it. The reality of a sound is its materiality. A sequential logic rests on this definition & at the same time, on a certain principle of repetition. Moreover, the Diagram is a singular expression of the production of sound, generating a maximum of lines or realization; powerful and contrasting, of the phenomenon of resonances and of diffractions, multiple syntheses, of the immeasurable logicality of sound and of the closely related temporalities. The plan of musical composition rests on the movements, on the accelerations, the pauses, the speeds, the slowness, the differentials, and fundamentally possesses the power to produce the molecular evolution from the lines of flight fitting the musical material. In certain respects, one could affirm from the Diagram what one says of the meaning of it in literature: it doesn't exist, it insists. It is neither familiar with the implications nor the attributions & it doesn't appear apart from the sequence that it expresses. A paraphrase of the logic of meaning only having another goal to affirm the Diagram and its sequential logic as a singular mode of materialization of the composition of sound. The Diagram for me is found in a strict simultaneity with the execution of sequences; as long as the incorporeal is constantly present it has its own world of singular events, above all, its own particular temporality, which we shall try to define here.

All the questions raised with the production of sound are condensed into one vast problem As the music in concrete material metamorphous and transformational energy, ascending life as well as descending, subject to illness, and perhaps even becoming loathsome and pernicious -- we will quite understand that the problem is of a physiological nature, exclusively physiological. Nietzsche laid this out in length and associated with it a multiplicity of dimensions qualifying each time as a singular type of intoxication. As an intoxication of sexual excitation, an intoxication of celebration or of victory, but above all, an intoxication born of certain "meteorological conditions" and an intoxication of the will. INTOXICATION BULLETIN. Several forms of intoxication do not bear a relationship to a psychological evaluation or an esthetic appreciation, but come to qualify the physical affectations and the compositions of the affects: Which is the plan of a sensitive world called physiology. These states of intoxication are effectively the intensification of the producing events of reality: They certify the different perspectives, a new map of intensities, a new world of sound. Where one simply returns identifying punctiliously the intoxication and the will to create which is the exacerbation of the force: "in order for there to be art, for there to be an act, and an esthetic regard, a physiological condition is indispensable: The state of INTOXICATION. It is necessary first, that the stimulation of the entire machine has been rendered more intense by the intoxication."(1) But still, the music is one particular case that is situated beyond the bipolar notion of the Appolonian and the Dionesian. By removing the mimicking and the imitation, the music becomes an abstract expression or just pure process. Nietzsche saw a type of regression there, and an opening into the cosmos. The music borrows from the Dionesian state the stimulation of the totality of the sensitivity, the strength to intensify the power of transfiguration and of metamorphoses (Crepuscule des Idols, Divagation, aph.10), and yet, the music excludes "All forms of the art of mime and comedy." But this approach is not in itself affirmative, a manner of preserving for itself an unchangeable return, a positive effect from the selection, not safeguarding us from the so very actual imperialism of the discursive operations, of the weakening of the strength, of a putting into reserve. Nietzsche himself induces us to think of music as pure realization of the speed of its differentials, as accelerations, as comparative movements speaking of an intuitive vision he differentiated for example, between the rhythmics of movement and the rhythmics of repose, (fragments 1: Pll 16.1869, no. 46). Consequently, this abstraction in the music(2) is no longer a reduction or an occultation of a meaning so human, but on the contrary, it constitutes a pure form of these movements of speed and slowness-. An extreme form of strength. Nietzsche: "An eloquence of the spirit (which expresses itself) by grand lines. The Dionesian intoxication contains all sexuality, all voluptuousness; it isn't absent from the Appolonian intoxication. It must have a difference of tempo between the two states, extreme calm of certain states of intoxication (more rigorously) the deceleration of the feeling of the time and the space easily reflected in the vision of the guests and in the spiritual acts of the calmer." (variantes des aphorismes 10 et 11, editions Gallimard).

It is really this difference of tempo between multiple states which on the one part characterizes the musical objectives, and which on the other part leads to this tearing away of an already liberated particle, that is the production of the molecular evolution fitting the plan of composition of sound. It is this which precipitates the constructions and activates the resonances, the percussions and the diffractions. Of a mixing up of the musical lines, to a multiple connection. A repetition derived from this, carrying along the uncertain backwash as if the duplication is of the same world, more or less stretched out, more or less contracted, each consisting of the other in the punctilious affirmation of the various lines, having to precipitate this molecular perplexity inherent in the repetitive synthesis of the production of sound. The differential affirmation transcends the opposition between the Appolonian and Dionesian states.

It will be necessary to disassociate the literally factual dimension, which proceeds by accidents of the will, or not, and by breaks, and the specifically punctilious dimension of resting on the instantaneous realizations, of the passages of the instants, the present emptiness of the logic of meaning. It is paradoxically the form of musical repetition which at the same time affirm the character of eternity as it presents itself as untimely, and which at the same time by the game of sequences and of translations (c.f.: The diagram and the plan of composition), demands a spontaneous time as is written by Gilles Deleuze: "We cannot wait, it is necessary that the instant be at the same time, the present as well as the future, the present as well as the past, because it happens (and takes place at the expense of another instance). It is necessary that the present co-exists with itself as the past and as the future. It is this synthetic relationship of the instant with itself as the present, the past and the future which is at the core of its relationship with other instants." (Nietzsche et la philosophies P.U.F.)

One will see that it is precisely this synthetic relationship which stigmatizes the temporal operations relative to the repetitive form of the production of sound. For finally, the bond between the sequences is their concrete realization at their moment of formulation, a statement of material manifestation it is the systems of the instant that distributes their differential realities, and without this system all of the repetitions would be mixed up in a unique sequence mother, or matrix, a totality of essence.

Thus seeing that the paradox of the repetitive synthesis necessitates at the same time the elements belonging to a continuum and its series of variations, and of the particles of quite another order, as standard translation, distributed by an instantaneous present. Therefore in certain respects, a present in the form of emptiness, infinitive and incorporeal in the sense of Stoicism, as is related by Emile Brehier: "The time seemed within itself for the first instant as an empty form in which the events are in their proper succession."(3) A time without consistency or speed and slowness should no longer be the measure but rather, the direct sign of the intensity of the force of the sound to have appeared which makes evident the strength of quite another type of species. From this need to institute conjugation of the instant and of the continuum, the infinitive constitutes the ideal time fitting the musically repetitive synthesis.

If there is no contradiction, it is not because firstly it does not exist -- which is an acquired act -- but rather in this case, we are witnessing a Phenomenon of coupling and the production of a sense of multi-sensationalization of the intimate properties of various temporalities. But if there is not an incommensurability nor an insupportability between the instant, present, continuum and the infinitive, the grouping of these four notions would produce a kind of combination more barbaric than weak. Everything else is a process that removes the protocol of the temporal realizations inherent in the diagrams of repetition: To disclose these conjunctions connecting paradoxically the time reputed to be incompatible, Music with Changing Parts or An Index of Metals(4) -- to these conjunctions it would be necessary to add the empty dimension of qualifying the execution of one time and of one purely metallic repetition. Beyond vulgarity of a simple differentiation between pulsations and a segment of time without a beat, we will say that this metallic repetition is an empty form on the infinitive line of l'Aion. The metallic repetition therefore requires a singular form of time, resting on the paradoxical coupling and is noted as an occurrence of l'Aion. But this singular form is in its proper order, similar to the equally paradoxical exposition of Meinong (a paradox of the absurd in the logic of meaning). A times squared, rounded, extended, contracted, continuous, developing, "an unadulterated material, perpetual motion."(5) One form of time pulling its maximum of effectiveness of this multi-face reality, or rather an inter-face, true or less insistently redoubled as particular musical instances, and at the same time, as part of the continuum of sound. Supra-being or the elements harmonizing the dimension +1 of the plan of composition. But in another sense, the metallic repetitive synthesis requires more than a simple annunciation of the paradox of Meinong: Since it is not the possible paradigm, neither the matrix nor the origin producing the sequences as effects (therefore not generating from the cause), we will say that these sound sequences are not generated and at the same time, that their concrete realization prevents them from being considered as ungenerated or as pure abstract notions of a metallic form of time, appropriate for a certain production of sound, recovering the skeptical preposition of a time neither generated nor ungenerated.(6) One can follow Sextus Empiricus on the finite and the infinite, and on the tripartation: Past, present and future. A logical work is necessary for those who are concerned with model logic, repetitive and sequential, the operators of time and of statement.(7) But the evident conclusion is not so much the nonexistence of time,(8) but the reality of a transversal time, non-conjugatable for the infinitive, to know the l'Aion that does not exist, but insists.

Substituting in chronological order, or cycles, a meteorology and a composition of events in the emptiness of an eternal present.

Each sound is irrefutable, enveloping its own materiality inherent in the line of time. Especially the incorporeal. If the duration is still of the order of numbers, time is priceless.(9) Evaluated. A condensed world of temporalities closely related to the flow of variables, of the lines of interchangeable and incommensurable time by the interfrequencies.(10) We will say therefore, that the repetitive synthesis which issues from the objective music is only one process of metalization (inter-facing and coupling of this stoic temporality, so well described by the logic of meaning: "Whereas the Chronos was limited, Aion was unlimited as the future and the past, but finite as the present. While the Chronos was inseparable from its circularity, and from the accidentals of this circularity, as blockages or precipitations, explosions, hindrance or endurances. Aion extends itself along a straight line, unlimited in these two meanings. Always already past and eternally yet to come; Aion is the eternal truth of time: Pure form empty of time, which is freed from its repressed corporal present. With that the circle is completed and stretches out in a line, maybe all the more dangerous, more like a labyrinth, more twisting because of this reason."

It is from this specifically metallic form of l'Aion that an analysis of the time closely related to the production of sound transfers the implication of plan for the foundation (and of its surface of inscription) to the profit the plan of composition always contemporaneous with its realization. We feel that the division between the times of the exposition and the times of the statement are all quite secondary, that the existence of writing and the synthesis of execution does not implicate a binary line of division affecting the times and the developed sequential logic. We feel that there are, as a constant principle of non-contradiction by the simultaneous coexistence between sequences, diagrams or tightly related musical worlds of which the paradoxes are the product of movement, of a contrast between oscillations and reposes, the result of differential of speeds and the particular tension from the active and contented composition of the particles of sound.

NOTES:
1. Crepuscule des idoles, divagation d'un "in-actuel," 8. Editions Gallimard
2. "The music, so to speak, is only an abstraction of this expression richer than the discharge of all the emotionalism a residue of histrionics." Variations on aph. 10 & 11. Crepuscule Wll 1 5, 165. Gall.
3. Brehier, La theorie des incorporels dans L'ancien stoicisme, Vrin.
4. Philip Glass (Chatam Records), Fripp & Eno (Island Records)
5. Logic of meaning
6. Sextus Empiricus, Hypotyposes pyrrhoniennes et surtout contre les physicians, Aubier, Editions Montaigne, 1948
7. We refer to the primordial work of J.F. Lyotard, notably the model logic and the sophisticated devices of which the importance could not have been described in only a few lines. Seinaires Vincennes 1975, '76, et textes adjacents.
8. The theme which one will find equally in the philosophy of the Stoics under the mode of a time without "any contact with the true being of things." C.f. Brehier,op cit.
9. Norman Spinrad, Jack Barron et l'eternite, Editions Robt. Laffront
10. Interference #7, A lead into the unknown: "It is necessary also to clarify the contradiction that there is between the interference of the meaning of which interposes itself, in one advancing, one method and the interference of meaning of the cross-checking of differential experiences which form the base of renewal." We will equally make an apology for the interference as a phenomenon of the translation provoking the multiple resonances, against the possession of the dear variations of Schoenberg and only possessing the existence which refers to the series and the structure.

Richard Pinhas
Reprinted courtesy ATEM Magazine

D.D.A.A.
Deficit Des Annes Anterieures

1980

Obscurity, obscurity
scientific
underground to the gates
of the year 2000 profound obscurity of
the fiction outbreak of violence/
resurgence of the history

lines of deviation/
to the 300m under ground
the images march past on the monitors
TV images of the past
fiction of the future.

Obscurity, obscurity
the scientific rulers search
for yet another solution on the surface
of their radar scopes
putting all
under surveillance for a 100km
all around we are protected in
our underground
Illusion Production
deflects the images
of the past to project those of the future
Illusion Production
maintains the conflicts
with the history
until the fiction is an extension of it
obscurity, obscurity on these monitors
TV Illusion Production
organizes its
lines of survival

the scientific underground
struggling for the passing
of the history
art is not a repulsive cadaver.

The "souterrain" is alive and well in France. Illusion Production, a small band of artistic guerrillas is waging a metaphorical war on the field of conceptual art and contemporary music. They have unleashed a series of "interventions" -- live demonstrations and recorded works that confront people with a visual/aural experience quite unlike anything else being done today.

"The association Illusion Production is made up of 3 members on the basis of shared concern and convergent interests. The priority of the fiction is set into place by the ambiance favorable to the development of this fiction, which are the motors behind the work proposed by I.P."

I.P. has been involved in several manifestations of art: "Mixage International" and "the symposium on the plastic art of Angouleme," produced 4 conceptual music works, published the journal "Sensationel" and presented a performance titled "Action et Demonstration Japonaise" (debuted in Dec. '79 and presented for the 2nd time at the Biennial of Paris -- contemporary art, non-stop soiree in Sept. '80.)

Ideologically they construct mini-epics of WW II/Cold War fiction based on fictional characters such as: Lt. Korgilov -- officer in command of a military bunker, Miss Vandam -- a sensual pinup girl, Jack Flash -- an underground espionage agent and Mitsuko -- a Japanese warrior torn by war and the death of the Samurais. D.D.A.A.(translation -- "deficit of the years before") is the action faction of I.P. who wage their war against the insensitivity, plasticity and cold alienation of modern society which learns not from past history, but simply blindly repeats it as escalating situations lead to the final solution -- WW III?

The music serves to illustrate their fiction:

I.P. 01 is a cassette that distorts the senses with a barrage of intense guitar, electronics and extremely harsh/dense production. Throbbing Gristle gone over the edge.

I.P. 02 is more literal in its sonic assault. Electronic rhythms and simple construction, it pulsates with strong doses of primal energy creating a seething deluge of sound. It comes in a plastic bag complete with a mixture of artifacts incl. a toy soldier (to help you fight your own war) and Hollywood chewing gum (a double metaphor for plastic society).

I.P. 03 is a double 45 that contains 4 sides of cold, clinical, simple synthetic music -- organic, computer rhythms? The packaging comes 1 of 3 ways: covered with hair, corrugated/camouflaged cardboard or layered with concrete plaster. Titled *FRONT DE L'EST* it also has a comic libretto detailing a tale of international espionage and assassination.

I.P. 04 - *EPIDEMIA - VOICE - BACTERIAL* is the latest release. It features Joel Hubaut (founder of the Centre Kulture Kontrole Epidemia) on guitar, Emanuel Hubaut-Manou - voice and D.D.A.A. on treatments ... Waves of heavy fractured guitar and vocal recitation make it the most complex of the 4 works. It comes in a sealed medical box that has to be cut open on one end to get the record and other materials out. The music and instructions given offer a slim hope that the world can be cured if the Epidemic can be brought under control?

Illusion Production/Deficit Des Annees Anterieures in the final analysis are literally waging a war with society as a whole using their art as a weapon. They are challenging that which is taken to be normal ("good art") with a talent/style that is totally unique. By doing so they create their own definitions and boundaries, in fact their own reality. Vive le resistance!

(Translations by Michelle Tuck)

Urban Sax

The single-sound strategy of Urban Sax grew out of an experiment in acoustical town-planning, when in the Summer of 1973, Gilbert Artman was commissioned to reverberate Menton in the south of France, during a festival of classical music, bringing to bear 4 fixed-frequency sound generators linked to streetfuls of speakers converging on and surrounding eight on-stage saxes. The budget froze, but in Sept. 1976 musicians warmed to the idea and Artman was able to dispose in complex circularities the disconcerting continuous sound of the theoretically ideal sum of 16 saxes. By 1978 the 16 had proliferated to 30 in bizarre black or prophylactic white outfits, with metallic skins and insectile helmets, who are joined on stage by the 10 vocalists doubling percussion, first heard on the second LP, with their whispers, blurred words and clamors.

Gilbert Artman continues writing, and as the music develops Urban Sax tends to split up into mobile groups of musicians and to overflow normal concert situations, using the space around buildings, and infiltrating them from the basement up (these explorations of urban resonance are always preceded by an evaluation of a given site's workability, measured by timed movements and sound checks.)

This freedom of movement is extended in the Summer of '79, when all the musicians are linked by individual FM receivers to a central "conducting" transmitter providing the information necessary to precise playing outside the limits of visual contact and the vocalists adopt portable amplifiers that give the voice the volume of a sax, or transform it into electric or synthetic sound. The group's pervasion of urban space is now absolute, as in a recent Paris concert on which the musicians converged individually from the periphery playing on the metro, arriving apparently autonomous and producing an unsettling impression of ubiquity with their identical patterns of sound and attitude.

Gilbert Artman's insistence on microtonal variations inside and around theoretically fixed intervals, and the need for mobile performers committed to this style of playing has produced a group in which the majority are of jazz or rock extraction, and whose concerts make full but bridled use of their untempered streak.

At the moment Artman is about to record a record with Jacques Berrocal and Jean-François Pauvros: the group is called Catalogue. It's scheduled to come out by the end of the year. There is no new Urban Sax LP planned for now, but there are concerts planned for France and Belgium. In addition there has been contact with Andrew Plesser (Director of the Contemporary Music Program, Public Theatre -- New York Shakespeare Festival) about playing at the next event. The future also holds in store the music and play on stage for a spectacle of P.P. Pasolini "Affabulazione Pilade" which is directed by Marcello Aste and scheduled to be performed at the Opera of Firenze next May.

Archie Patterson

Didier Bocquet

In a field that's becoming rapidly more crowded and less interesting due to redundancy and creeping commercialism, it's a pleasant surprise to hear electronic music where the sound literally sparkles -- pure, loud and clear. Over the span of his 2 (and soon to be released 3rd) LPs, Didier Bocquet's works have achieved that effect.

From his beginnings as a drummer in various progressive rock bands and fusion groups, his experiences convinced him that he had to do his own thing. As solo work on the drum kit is not feasible, he set his sticks aside and started to delve into electronics. In Nov. '77 he was able to record his first album, *ECLIPSE*, which was a very limited affair and only available through the post in France. After 2 months it was sold out. At that point he was finally able to play a few live dates and begin to develop his style . A point of comparison with Klaus Schulze is valid here as *ECLIPSE* has that feel with its sequential patterns, voidian synthe electrons and touch of classicism. A bit crude, but compelling nonetheless and reminiscent of Klaus "cosmic" works.

After a year and a half he was able to do a second LP, *VOYAGE CEREBRAL*, that showed a marked evolution in his sound. More sophisticated and celestial as opposed to spacy, it still echoed Klaus, but a French romanticism had taken the place of classicism. An excellent work it's full of warm keyboard melodies, powerful electronic rhythms and crackling synthe. Definitely one of the better electronic albums you'll hear.

Recently recording was completed on his 3rd album, tentatively titled *SEQUENCES*. Release date has yet to be set, but a preview tape shows it to be vastly superior to both earlier records.

In addition to synthesizer he uses a VP 330 vocoder, String Ensemble and a touch of acoustic piano. The combined effect is breath-taking as the sound alternates between dense electronics and otherworldly voice/string sections. The album definitely exhibits a degree of technique and creativity that ranks him among the best.

Archie Patterson

The Savage Rose
THAT DANISH BAND!

The Savage Rose had their brief burst of acclaim in the States around 1970 when critics reviewing their 3 U.S. album releases hailed them as the most original band out of Europe. But due to almost no promotion and the lack of national exposure, their records got lost in the weekly flood of releases which were dominated by domestic and British sounds. For those critics a focal point in the band was the vocalist Annisette -- a diminutive, tangle-haired, woman-child with a most amazing vocal prowess. They literally fell over one another with comparisons, some of which were double standard and quite comical: "a seven year old hung-up on Edith Piaf and Janis Joplin," "Minnie Mouse on belladonna," "a supreme distillation of all '60s girl group sounds," "Arlene Smith with the 15-year old innocence taken away," and "a midget Aretha" among others. One thing they all agreed on was that she was an astonishing new voice on the scene. The band itself, most notably the songwriters and keyboardists Thomas and Anders Koppel drew much acclaim also as masters of a song and studio discipline of R&B and refined intelligence.

Few music fans outside their native Denmark know that actually they have an on-going 12-year history documented by a series of superb LP releases. So for those who got wind of their reputation some years ago or might have encountered a record by The Savage Rose in a record bin somewhere, this is The Savage Rose! As a respected U.S. critic once proclaimed: "They could (have) single-handedly raised the international consciousness of Rock & Roll!"

Thomas and Anders Koppel are the sons of the respected Danish professor and musicologist/composer Dr. Herman Koppel, whose own parents emigrated from poverty in Poland to Copenhagen at the turn of the century. Both sons demonstrated a gift for music at an early age. Thomas began to compose at age 5, studied music through his teens and at 20 had won several composer competitions and had worked with the Royal Danish Theatre. Anders, not to be outdone, also involved himself with music at an early age, was a member of the Copenhagen Boys Choir, developed considerable painting skills, and before he was out of his teens had published short stories and a novel.

Annisette Hansen also descends from a family of artists and at the age of six began singing and acting with her half sister Rudi Nielsen (now an accomplished actress) and they recorded children's records for a number of years -- singing, storytelling and supplying animal sounds! Later Annisette performed as a soloist with a pianist. In 1966 she joined the "Dandy Swingers" who were the house band in "Dyrehavbakken," the second largest amusement park in Copenhagen playing the hits of the day.

It was in 1967 that Thomas and Anders began to be interested in contemporary rock music as evidenced in the Beatles *RUBBER SOUL/REVOLVER* period and the electrified Dylan. They attended a performance of the Dandy Swingers and later persuaded Annisette, guitarist Flemming Ostemann and bassist Jens Rugsted to join their group in formation, The Savage Rose, along with Thomas' wife at that time, the former Maria Lansner (harpsichord) and the respected jazz drummer Alex Piel.

After intense composing and rehearsals, The Savage Rose made their debut May 27, 1968 in Tivoli Gardens in Copenhagen to a great and immediate response. Polydor Denmark at this time released an Annisette with the Dandy Swingers 45 "River Deep Mountain High," a rough and spunky re-working of the Spector classic and it reached the local Top 20, meanwhile signing The Rose to a long term contract. The 45's success created confusion at Polydor over which group to promote.

Nevertheless the 1st Savage Rose LP was eventually released in 1968 and became the largest selling domestic rock album of all time in Denmark and sold very well in the other Scandinavian countries as well. All songs were written by Thomas (music) and Anders (lyrics) and it is a stark, underdeveloped, yet beautiful record with brooding images of Nordic life and cities in conflict. Annisette's curious and distinct vocal mannerisms were powerful on numbers such as "Her Story," "Open Air Shop" and "A Girl I Knew," even though she was just learning English from Thomas at the time. The Koppels laid the ground work on the 1st LP with an unusual three keyboard, layered sound.

A 45 from the LP, "A Girl I Knew" b/w "You'll Be Allright," was released and made the charts.

Flemming Ostemann left the group after the 1st LP to become a teacher and was replaced by Neils Tuxen who brought a more aggressive guitar sound to the band. They toured Scandinavia extensively, played selected concerts on the continent and returned to Denmark to record their 2nd album under the supervision of Johnny Reimar, a well-known band leader. Recording came easily as the group became close and intense with the creativity of Thomas and Anders flowering. *IN THE PLAIN* was issued in early 1969 throughout Europe and The Rose became a large concert attraction with their new sound and the bizarre stage presence and reputation of Annisette with powerful support of the musicians. In Summer '69 Polydor extended its company to the U.S. and *IN THE PLAIN* was one of their 1st releases. The LP received favorable notices from American critics, Lester Bangs most notably, but Polydor didn't promote it so it didn't sell. The overall sound had a Gothic drone-like quality to it, which behind Annisette's strange, twisting and high reaching performances created moody visions in the best numbers: "Long Before I Was Born," "Evenings Child" and "The Shepard And Sally," yet failed to click in several overly long and poorly mixed pieces.

Meanwhile in Denmark after the success of the bands 1st 2 LPs, Polydor felt that the group could go no higher in popularity locally so arranged a recording session in England with the well known producer of the Yardbirds, etc. Giorgio Gomelsky. The Savage Rose and Gomelsky couldn't agree on much and the session yielded only 3 songs that were released. "The Schoolteacher Said So" is a good melodic performance, but was rather badly recorded and flopped. "A Girl I Knew" is a re-recorded version of their 1st 45 for release in Germany, but it suffers against the simplicity of the original as it's cluttered with redundant guitar work and choruses. Both sides were backed with "Birthday Day," a cute, somewhat lackluster number.

The Summer of '69, the group was invited to play the 3-day Newport Jazz Festival, that year featuring many more rock influenced performers such as: Mothers of Invention, B.S.&T. and Led Zeppelin. They were slated to play after Sly & The Family Stone which made the group somewhat apprehensive after hearing about Sly's crowd pleasing abilities. Due to gate-crashers, rain and other delays however, they finally played to a responsive Sunday night audience. With her hair in a massive tangled halo, dressed in a revealing bra top and peasant shift,and dangling bracelets from arm and leg, she and her fellow Roses created a memorable U.S. debut.

Their 3rd LP was recorded on their brief visit to the States again under the direction of Reimar in the Mira Sound Studio in NYC. The LP *TRAVELIN'* was released in Denmark and Germany only, late in '69. Due to controversial interest in one of the numbers performed at Newport a number from *TRAVELIN'* was released as a two sided promo 45 in the US "My Father Was Gay Pts.1&2." It was the last Savage Rose record for Polydor US and no commercial pressings were issued. In Denmark the title cut featuring Jens Rugsted on lead vocal was released and reached the Top Ten. Although the LP itself has a number of great performances such as the stunning rocker "Life's Other Side" and the ballads "The Castle" and "Sailing Away," it again suffers from several overly long, poorly mixed and confusing cuts.

Maria Koppel left the group after TRAVELIN's release and subsequently divorced Thomas who had begun a long and continuing relationship with Annisette. The group received much publicity in the daily tabloids and remained one of Denmark's top groups. It was in Italy that the group recorded YOUR DAILY GIFT, their 4th LP, in the RCA Rome Studios. RCA was to handle international release of The Savage Rose records outside of Denmark and in the States on a newly formed subsidiary Gregar. The changes seemed to bring new momentum to the band as they handled production themselves and the packaging for which Thomas supplied a charming cover painting. The recorded sound was lighter and cleaner as the band had modified into a more condensed, shorter song format with an interesting use of instrumentation, e.g. harpsichord and pedal-steel guitar counterpoint. The use of multi-tracked backing vocals by Annisette at times created a sound not unlike Phil Spector's use of vocals. Her lead vocals are astonishing in depth and octave range, rocking out on "Sunday Morning" and "The Waters Run Deep," then full of beautiful melancholy on the title song. A startling and majestic instrumental "Tapiola" reveals a new resource of the band. In the States the LP received rave reviews, but as with their other records no promo. The group went to the US to promote the record themselves, but were virtually stranded in L.A. when their American "Mafia-type" manager had them playing in a small club in Hollywood 3 times a day for 2 months with almost no pay and they were forced to stay near their hotel between shows due to a lack of money. Polydor Denmark came to the rescue and got them back to Denmark. After a brief rest they went to London and recorded REFUGEE with the famous English producer Jimmy Miller and caught the attention of local musicians, most notably the Stones and Mick Jagger wanted to hear them play in their studio.

The REFUGEE LP was released throughout much of Europe and in No. America. In the States it received fantastic reviews in publications such as Rolling Stone and Fusion, but despite this and promising airplay along the East Coast, due to no national publicity/ads, it sold only about as well as YOUR DAILY GIFT. Dominated by an aggressive R&B sound and up-front production, the band and Annisette created their most accessible LP. The title track has a great old rock 'n' roll sound and is a brilliant showcase for Annisette's emotional and lyrical vocal range. Each in their own way, the LP's 8 numbers create singular moods from breathless celebration to compassionate reflection. Two cuts "Dear Little Mother" and "Dreamland" were to be again recorded by the band for future LPs. At this time the band contained 5 original members as Neils Tuxen left, replaced by session guitarist John Urebe.

The years '71/'72 saw great change and renewed creativity for The Savage Rose. In Sept. '71 Thomas, Anders and Annisette felt that they could go no further musically with the present format so they disbanded the group as such. The 3 wanted their music to have a more social/political content -- a message and compassion. There had been such songs in their repertoire -- "Walking In The Line" from REFUGEE, "Your Daily Gift" form the LP of the same name, but the group felt they needed to revise their vision and express the issues of struggling, working people. The Savage Rose trio began playing benefits and prisons around Denmark and also performed at the famous jazz club in Copenhagen - Montmartre. It was there that they met the renowned tenor saxophonist Ben Webster who had been living in Denmark for several years. Together they played several live concerts and plans for an LP were made.

The recording of *BABYLON*, the 7th LP was an adventurous affair. Ben Webster, although a heavy drinker at the time, was so nervous that he abstained from alcohol and only drank milk! Aside from Webster, participating on the record were a children's choir, The Stars of Faith -- a well known female gospel quintet from the US (whom the group also met at Montmartre), Alex Reil on percussion and Niels-Henning Ørsted Pedersen on trombone. This unusual lineup created a timeless and powerful LP owing much to New Orleans, gospel and R&B influence. Powerful too are the lyrics by Anders, themes of struggle, triumph and death predominate and Annisette sings them with astonishing conviction and compassion against a wall of wailing singers, horns and trombones.

One single from the LP was released in Denmark "The Messenger Speaks" b/w "Help The Lonely Child," a beautiful although quite uncommercial piece.

Danish reviews were very favorable, but since the trio's image seemed to alienate rock listeners *BABYLON* didn't sell as well as previous releases. The LP was to be issued in No. America, but RCA heard it and wanted nothing to do with it, then folded Gregar as an unprofitable subsidiary. Somehow the Black Panthers got a hold of a copy, were impressed and invited the group to play at a Bobby Seale benefit in L.A., but the group was unable to make it.

Annisette and Thomas were married in 1972 and a baby girl was born in Aug. named Billie in honor of Miss Holliday. Thomas was asked to compose music for a ballet by Flemming Flindt to be performed on TV by the Royal Danish Ballet. This project was completed and aired in many European countries and in England. An LP of excerpts from the score recorded by the band was released in Denmark and eventually sold 125,000 copies, earning the group a silver record. A predominantly instrumental work with mood pieces, sound effects and one vocal piece featuring Annisette. That was a re-recording of "Dear Little Mother" from *REFUGEE* that is not nearly as effective as the original. Several session musicians were used on *DODENS TRIUMF* (Triumph of Death) -- overall the group felt the recording wasn't representative of their work at the time.

Another score for a ballet was recorded in '72 and again Ben Webster was involved. Another cut from *REFUGEE* was used, this time as the theme piece and title *DREAMLAND*. For the most part the music for *DREAMLAND* is superior to that of *DODENS TRIUMF*. With his added touch Webster assisted in creating mood elements more in common with *BABYLON*. Due to financial legalities, an LP of the music was never issued.

In 1973 changes again occurred as the group decided to explore their new musical ideas with other musicians. Joining the band were Peer Frost (guitar), Rudolf Hansen (bass) and Ken Gnudmann (drums), all of whom had played in Danish bands since the early '60s. Peer Frost most notably had been in the "Young Flowers" who recorded music for the film soundtrack *QUIET DAYS IN CLICHY* and 3 LPs with Midnight Sun, a top Danish jazz rock group. An LP with this new lineup was recorded and released in Denmark and Germany under the title of *WILD CHILD* and many critics thought it was the group's best. It was a combination of their previous ideas with a share of traditional European influences, again expressing the continuing themes of poverty, struggle and compassion.

Intensity explodes in "Stewball Was So Tired," about a workhorse being stoned to death on a village street and then again in a heart-shattering ballad "The Shoeshine Boy is Dead," a trio track with a most amazing piano/organ sound and an Annisette performance that is ----- beyond belief! It literally levitates the listener with each line. Other tracks on the record are also strong, yet the record is somewhat of a flawed masterpiece having several songs with much in common with numbers on the LP *TRAVELIN'*.

Yet all things considered a superb Savage Rose LP. Tours of Scandinavia followed the completion of *WILD CHILD*. Another unreleased LP was recorded in July 1974 the year which marked the end of their affiliation with Polydor and was the start of a long period of inactivity for the group. *HEY JOHANNA* was about to be released, but just as quickly the band and Polydor parted on less than friendly terms and the LP remains to be heard.

Disagreements also pervaded the group as Thomas and Anders had conflicting ideas for the group's direction. Anders left the band in '74 and busied himself with session work, local film projects and showings of his paintings. In addition he did one very nice solo LP for an independent label. Titled *AFTENLANDET & REGNBUEFUGLEN*, it's solely instrumental. Also he has been a member of Bazaar, an instrumental band with 1 LP who are well received in Denmark.

Through all of '75 and part of the next year little was heard of The Savage Rose. It wasn't until early 1977 that an LP on an alternative label (Robinhood -- Dist. by CBS) for the support of Christiania, a place in Copenhagen advocating various social/political lifestyles was released. It features tracks donated by many of Denmark's best musicians and bands (Secret Oyster, etc.) and the 'new' Savage Rose recorded a song in Danish (trans. -- "The Wild Flowers Are Growing"). It was written by Annisette and Thomas and featured among others Anders. Another track (trans. -- "You Can't Kill Us") recorded under the name The International Gypsy Co-op features the Koppels and a verse sung by Annisette. The *CHRISTIANIA* LP remained in the Danish Top 10 for several months and inspired another LP featuring musicians from that place.

Little was heard from the band for almost a year, then in the Fall of '77 there was talk of a new lineup and LP being recorded. After much delay the LP *SOLEN VAR OGSA DIN* (The Sun Was Yours Too...) was released in April '78 and The Savage Rose appeared with the members being -- Annisette, Thomas, Peer Frost and a drummer from Christiania John Ravn. Beautifully packaged with a painting on the back cover by Annisette and released on the prominent label Sonet, it was a promising return by the group. Annisette and Thomas collaborated on the songs of which only two are in English. Superbly recorded there is a beautiful simplicity in the performance and the totally expressive drum sound of Ravn interplays with Thomas and Peer without a bass to create a skinless backing for Annisette's vocals which are full of remarkable twists, throaty compassion and intensity. Side 1 is especially fulfilling in continuity and emotion with themes and images of Vesterbro -- a poor part of

Copenhagen in which they lived at the time.

The LP was well received but the group felt it was a mistake signing with a company such as Sonet who had released poor pressings of the LP, untrue press releases and generally had no real concern for the band. They again toured and were involved with many human-rights issues. Through exposing corruption within Sonet they were released from their contract. In October of '79 Flemming Flindt and some financial backers wanted to revive the Dodens Triumf ballet and at that time Thomas let it be known that he no longer wanted his music to be used. This created quite a controversy among copyright experts in Denmark as Polydor was about to release a double LP of the complete score in a limited edition. In the meantime the ballet opened to less than full houses so eventually the LPs release was withdrawn and the ballet folded.

John Ravn, the drummer whom the members of Savage Rose had very high regard for, left the group a year after *SOLEN VAR OGSA DIN* was recorded because he was terrified playing outside Christiania and this caused problems in regard to touring. His replacement to the present time is a middle-aged Turkish percussionist. For several years the group has had no contact with any record companies, recording industry media or the music business in general, preferring instead to live in anonymity with the poor and working people of Denmark.

In 1980 Savage Rose decided to end their professional career and use their music primarily to support revolutionary commitments -- playing benefits and free concerts for poor people anyplace they may be asked. In the Spring of this year they were invited by the P.L.O. to go to Lebanon where they played many places there for the refugees. Annisette gave birth to another daughter in mid August (1980) and just now she is one of their most important commitments. There is a remote chance that The Savage Rose will record again in the future if conditions are favorable and they find a company (possibly one of the many alternative political labels) that would have a sympathetic concern for the groups music. (Editor's Note: In fact *SOLEN VAR OGSA DIN* has just been reissued by an alternative label.) Till then I for one must content myself with the treasures of their past.

Dave Byers
(Special thanks to: N.C. Junker-Poulsen of TWIST and Thomas and Annisette)

Lemon Kittens Interview

Music is "the art of combining sounds or sequences of notes into hamonies," and that's it. Nothing about yelling "1,2,3,4," or any other rock cliche. So it's not surprising that the Lemon Kittens found reaction to their 1st single -- "Spoonfed And Writhing" very narrowminded and stuck in the same old groove, ("if the production's not perfect, he can't play the guitar properly etc.") you can't pigeon hole their music, like The Automatons it's new original and experimental.

1. What's the name Lemon Kittens about?

Lemon Kittens: Lemon = bitter, kittens = young cats = youth, bitter youth, the ideals of youth rebelling against certain mistakes made by our forbears and trying to iron them out. It's also a name which doesn't necessarily conjure up a particular type of music which should help us avoid being pigeonholed for awhile, if however people do associate the name with a type of music it'll be pop, certainly not the type we're actually doing.

2. When did the band start?

Although it started about 2 years ago feel it truely began in Dec. '79 when we became a 2 piece and stopped supporting a couple less creative, less conscious dead weights. The line up is now: Danielle Dax - vocals, bass, flute, tenor & soprano saxes, keyboards, tapes and Karl Blake - vocals, bass, guitar, drums, keyboards, and tapes.

3. Why did you part company with the band?

Due to some of the usual problems that arise when a group of people work together. Karl and I had very definite ideas about our musical directions and more importantly the messages we hope to convey via the lyrics and the way we actually lead our daily lives, although obviously the latter is extremely difficult to maintain all the time. The other band members were always holding back, being afraid to stick their necks out and take chances, it was like dragging a dead albatros around with us. At around this time Mark P. was playing drums with us -- he was also feeling very negative about the group situation, hinting strongly that due to the nature of the others we weren't progressing and that it'd be wiser to forge ahead without them. We disregarded this advice for a month or two and really tried to make a go of it as a complete band, although we were also recording material as a 2 piece from about Nov. '79 for the Fur Fur tapes. At the end of Dec. Lemon Kittens finally became the now present 2-piece.

4. What inspires your songs?

Many of the lyrics deal with conditioning. We feel that too many people act in an ostrich-type manner, burying their heads in the sand and shirking personal responsibility. Due to various modes of conditioning -- people usually fall into one of two categories -- the ones who don't realize that the problems relate directly to their own personal life styles and those who because this is a difficult and often very painful process of self analysis prefer to repress those nasty little pangs of guilt in a hope that someone else or something will make their problems disappear.

It's vital that all the so-called ideals of youth do not just remain associated with the period of adolescence dissipating rapidly as old-age cynicism creeps in, most cynical characteristics are a cover up for fear anyway. Everyone's frightened to a certain extent, so why erect great barriers of self-defense, this only achieves a temporary feeling of well being, that you are on your guard and people are less likely to take advantage of you. Admittedly there are people to guard against and it would be naive to pretend this wasn't the case. But the more a person comes up against cold behavior the more fear he/she feels and often reacts by acting defensively, thus triggering this in someone else and so on. It's a vicious circle which is not totally irreversable but takes a sustained effort by as many people as possible to overcome.

The lyrics may seem difficult to comprehend at times, this is partially due to a lack of compromise on our parts. We will gladly try to explain the ideas behind Lemon Kittens music to anyone who wants to know via interviews, lettres or personally. It may also be argued that Lemon Kittens music is far too obscure to reach a wide range audience and as a result there will be few people able to hear us and even fewer who will bother to to try and understand our messages. Again we must attempt to explain the reasons why we would not consider a compromise in order to be more accessible. Firstly, there is already too much compromising involved in our daily actions and this is often just a dishonesty employed by people to avoid difficult situations. Although in some cases these actions are rightly used, generally speaking compromise could be better termed laziness. Secondly, we both hold the belief that our music is not revolutionary in its own right, it will not change the world, stop wars or any other such self-delusionary nonsense. We simply aim to become a small cog in the machinery of a much larger process of change. ...I suppose basically we are saying; We must stop blaming technology, God, other people or things for our problems. Each person is directly responsible for everything he/she does and says -- each action is of our own making and depending on how we approach these matters they will be a success or failure. It's time to accept the responsibilities of our own lives.

Archie Patterson

1981

Robert-Jan Stips

Here we are once again talking with one of the most original Dutch musicians. Robert-Jan Stips, in the past the 'brains' of the foremost Dutch psychedelic band: Supersister. At present trying to find his way in the crowded world of writers and producers. And that's the sad part of this story. For in the last issue of EUROCK we talked extensively about his (then) musical child Transister. A group of enthusiastic young people playing not only for their own satisfaction but primarily for people that could and would listen. That's the way they wanted it.

Trying to convince the kids that there was something exciting to be heard. Intelligent pop you could dance to. They tried during more than a year... and failed. They made an album and a single, but lack of success brought the usual financial problems. A few weeks ago Robert-Jan had to decide to forget his ideal for the moment and Transister died. Two of his companions are already playing in another band (The Meteors). Robert-Jan will concentrate on writing and producing. I'm certain we'll meet him again.

...encore...

What follows are the most important statements made during a conversation done a few weeks before Robert Jan announced his new plans. We talked about the present standard of music.

ABOUT SYNTHESIZERS...

The synthesizer is a very tricky instrument. You'll have to control it, otherwise it'll take control over you. In a sense you must have a sort of drivers license for it, because if you don't have that it'll make you do things you actually don't wanna do. Using patterns you wouldn't use when you were playing an 'old-fashioned' instrument. So you'll have to take care not to lose your personality, because in the end you'll be the 'loser' and sound artificial.

German music I think is one-way music. When it's going left, it's goes far left. When it's going right, it goes far right. For me this is a sort of "stretched minimal music." I couldn't do it this way. I've too much western "stress" for it. I want to walk on my toes and not sit down easily and take my time. On the other hand I can imagine that this music sounds so easy to get a stark contrast against the jagged world we live in. In that sense it's a sort of escape music. A "silent protest."

The 'ambient' series of sounds as created by Eno, and now also Klaus Schulze, have different starting-points. 'Ambient' music has another policy, it has to be unobtrusive, but definitely 'musical' at the same time, for else synthesizers and/or keyboards have the tendency to become boring to the extreme. I think 'ambient' music could be played on any instrument; guitars and even horns.

ABOUT DISCO...

Disco is over- and underestimated at the same time. Disco can be wonderful, but has to be played very well indeed. You can't concentrate on the rhythm only, but you have to add that certain 'extra' which prevents disco becoming the horrible mess it too often appears to be. ("What about 'The Phantom Band'? -- HZ).

ABOUT CRITICS AND THE PRESS...

It depends on who's writing the review of a concert or a record. You have to know the man behind the words to catch the essence. Because of that critics can be very dangerous. When people tend to rely on reviews, the groups could be directed to writing and playing for critical (thus commercial) acclaim.

As a musician you'll always have to remember that not everything being written in the papers is true.

Rock-writing in the Netherlands hasn't reached very high standards. I already said before that we don't have a rock culture of our own, we have a second-generation scene. It's better in England where music-papers like *New Musical Express* are cuttin' deeper. They have to because there's much more competition. Another reason is that in the Netherlands we have a highly developed social climate. They will be taking care of us under almost any circumstances. So in a way we'll be able to sit back easily and wait for things to happen. No problems. That's why the music of Joy Division and Wire sounds so desperate and empty. They cry for help and understanding. Living in the UK isn't as easy as it is in the Netherlands or in Germany.

Another dangerous part of criticism is 'hyping'. For instance:
- all rock from Detroit has to be 'hard' rock
- or all rock from Cleveland has to be Devo or Pere Ubu-like
- or all popular music from Sheffield has to be electronic
- or in my case: all Transister-music has to be witty, full of black humour and cabaretesque

When you always put music from Detroit, Cleveland, Sheffield or Transister in the same corner, the other sounds coming from these sources won't be heard at all. That's not in the interest of musicians, groups and above all the listeners.

Also the question "Is it pop, or not?" isn't important. "Is it good?," that's important.

I prefer playing music. Not talking about it, for there is danger of talking the music to 'death'. Spontaneity is lost. I often notice that the best music has been made in the beginning of a cooperation. Probably that's only natural, but I think the success of a musician can be found in his sense of dynamics and experimentation, the developing of his musicianship and the skill to forget the things he learned. In rock and roll you have to turn the accepted rules around.

ABOUT COLLECTORS...

Anything is collectable, so are records. When a Supersister fan offers $84 for an obscure single that has been released only in Peru, it's strictly his own business. Such a fact is unimportant to me, I'll just smile and be a little flattered. When you aren't able to accept those things, you haven't chosen the right profession and won't make records ever again.

Henk Zweering

Holger Czukay Interview

DID YOU HAVE ANY PARTICULAR MUSICAL CONCEPTS AT THE BEGINNING OF CAN?

I didn't have a real concept, I didn't know what type of music or what type of instrument I was going to play...I had been acquainted with Michael Karoli because we had worked together at L'Ecole de St. Gaal in Switzerland, he played the guitar well enough, when I started Can, I remembered our relationship. Before, I played the guitar in a jazz genre but as Michael had to be the guitarist I asked myself why play? I chose the bass because it seemed to me that until now no one had really listened to the bass very well.

HAD YOU A LOT OF CLASSICAL TRAINING?

Yes, a lot.

WAS THIS HELPFUL AT THE BEGINNING OF CAN?

Sometimes it was more of a hindrance than a help. I had the impression that I knew too much, it was necessary to forget everything. When I started to repeat what I knew, Jaki (Liebezeit) often told me: "Why do you make so much of it? Play uniquely, in only one tone, that will suffice!" For me this was something new, I said to myself: "One single tone, that will suffice really?" The act of being simple for me was quite a novel idea, and to be simple in itself is a very, very difficult thing...

DO YOU SEE THE PASSAGE FROM A CLASSICAL CAREER TO CAN AS A TYPE OF RUPTURE OR AS A CONTINUITY?

I first thought that I was entering another world, the world of the "other," it was a great definitive rupture. Today after 10 years, I now see the bridge between the two worlds, but at the time I didn't.

HOW DO YOU SEE THE EVOLUTION OF YOU TECHNIQUE WITH THE BASS?

My style of playing the bass isn't superb. I am a very, very simple bass player, all of my efforts have always been to play the minimum. I never wanted to become a soloist, I consider my playing as a summary of everything that has been done by other players before me. I had to find the right tone on the bass for the global sound, that was my conception of bass playing. When I changed something there, it was in order to show the road towards another direction. But to be brilliant soloist never interested me, even today it doesn't.

AT THE START DID YOU USE THE CONTRE-BASS OR BASS GUITAR?
A bass guitar, that's what I started with.

DID YOU PLAY THE CONTRE-BASS AFTERWARDS?

No, never.

AND ON "SHE BRINGS THE RAIN"?

No that was a bass guitar.

IN JANUARY 1975? WE SAW YOU DURING THE TOURNEE FRANCAIS WITH THIS SORT OF VERTICAL ELECTRIC BASS.

That's true. It was a "Freemons Triomph," which tried to combine the technique of the contre-bass with the electrical system of a bass guitar. The result is good, besides I always had one in the studio. In the future I will make use of it as one of my numerous other instruments like the contre-bass.

BUT ON THE STAGE WASN'T THAT MORE DIFFICULT?

Yes. Moreover, it was necessary to find the right tone on the bass on stage, the instrument is itself of no importance.

CAN YOU SAY A FEW WORDS ABOUT CANAXIS 5? AND WHO WAS ROLAND DAMMERS?

Roland Dammers was one of my friends that I met during the course of my studies with Stockhausen, he lived in the same city as me, and was a very sensitive person who painted very beautiful pictures as well. At the time he was asking himself whether to become a poet or a musician. The both of us loved ethnic music. We did *CANAXIS 5* together. In fact, "Ho Mai Nih" is more of a piece of my own work while the second side is almost totally his, but the concept for the whole thing came to us together.

DO YOU TRAVEL MUCH?

I used to go to Asia sometimes, and David Johnson had these South American bands. At the time, I wasn't really into traveling to other countries, but I was very much interested in Asiatic and Australian music. But... when I listen to *CANAXIS 5* today, I ask myself if music with an ethnic base isn't of more value than that which we did...

AND YOUR EXPERIENCES WITH THE VOCALIST MICHIKO NAKAO DURING THE SUMMER OF 1975?

Michi is a little like my Japanese sister. She is a great artist in London. She was raised in Japan and had training in dance. When she left Japan she didn't want any more of that kind of life, she then became independent, and did everything you can imagine: Publicity, television, pictures, and singing. One time I brought her here and gave her this piece, "Unfinished" which was almost an hour long (to see the instrumental version in miniature see "Landed"). I set the band to start to play and Michi made her break and I told her to sing. She then said to me: "I need a text!!!" I didn't have one, then she saw this album jacket, the worst that you could imagine with a text more terrible still on the back of it, and she said: "Here is my text!" Then she started, forgetting about the album jacket a little later on. She made two spontaneous recordings, perhaps we will use them if we publish another version of "Unfinished."

WHAT TYPES OF MUSIC DO YOU PREFER?

Really... Why should I limit myself to one type of music, to one country, to one culture? Today we are in a strange situation, it is not like in Africa or Jamaica, where for example, the people make music the same way they have been making it for years. They take the music simplistically, like their mother's milk and they continue with it... And they aren't aware of what's happening musically in other countries. In Europe, we know, we are able to find out what's happening, we are fascinated by the facility with which other people make music.

HOW WOULD YOU DESCRIBE THE MAGICAL SIDE OF CAN?

One can describe it easily. We come onto the stage without any ideas, without anything in our heads, without really knowing what to play. Whereas other musicians do something and then everything else follows. It is this that I call the magical side of Can on stage when the group is truly good.

WHEN? IN 1973? IN 1974?

At the start, I think even in 1968. We had been together for one week and we did a concert at Chateau de Norvenich for artists and for people who were specially invited to Cologne.... We were very excited, for the first time we had to do a concert because no one had done anything similar before, I want to say, something electric, with loud speakers. We recorded this concert, I always had the band, and it showed a lot of magical things, it was really a spontaneous concert. It was the first stone positioned which started what we did later on. Although now, up until the end, it was almost lost, even if Reebop was capable of making a burst of magic, like at the concert of Arnhem where he felt it marvelously.

AT THE START THE PRINCIPAL PERSON WHO WAS RESPONSIBLE FOR THIS MAGICAL QUALITY WAS MALCOLM MOONEY....

Not him alone, but he was responsible in a strong way, yes. He wasn't quite as well a practiced musician like the rest of us, but he did have a natural talent. We did learn a lot from him, especially Irmin (Schmidt), I never played this type of music before, which consisted of more than just the composers. Malcolm showed us that the composition was something separate, he sang naturally, and we tried to learn all that we could from him.

AND DAMO? WASN'T IT THE SAME WITH HIM?

Yes, it was the same thing with him. He was quite different from Malcolm but he was very concentrated and I will say highly fantastic, he had a lot of fantasies.

AND THE SINGERS WHO LATER CAME TO PASS IN CAN? FIRST TIM HARDIN...

Can has always wanted to find something that would bring together diverse experiences and someday we thought that we would find a vocalist. Tim Hardin was there one day and we said: "Why not do a concert together?" We had never tried this before, as he had never heard us before, and we had never heard him. Voilà! I always love these types of experiences. As for Damo, he started with Can for a concert, a very passionate concert, in Munich. Jaki and me were on a terrace of a cafe and I saw Damo in the distance, he was shouting while praying or worshipping the sun or something strange like that. I said to Jaki: "There is our singer..." Jaki said "No, that can't be right..." Then I went up to Damo and said: "Can you come to a concert this evening?" He said "yes" right away. He traveled around the neighborhoods with a little bag, it was all that he had, and at exactly 6:30 he appears at the door of the theatre. When we came on stage he said very dramatically: "Don't come" in a very concentrated peaceful, manner. Then like a Samurai soldier he jumped up to the microphone and shouted to the audience. The audience became really nervous that the crowd might start fighting among themselves. There was a fight and the crowds left. Finally there were only 60 "super fans" left, who were just for him. About 30 Americans and 30 Germans -- very enthusiastic, at the end of the concert it was only for them. It was magnificent, really a very good concert.

AND THE SINGER THAT YOU MET AT BRUSSELS?

That was Raj, he was Malaysian, he just left Europe to return to Malaya. I believe he is going to do something over there because he learned a lot over here in regards to music.

DID HE DO ANY CONCERTS WITH YOU?

One in Brussels, and I think one other but that was all. But here in the studio, we did many sessions.

AT THE TIME (the end of 1975, the beginning of 1976) YOU WERE VERY CONSCIOUS OF THE NEED OF A VOCALIST FOR CAN...

Yes, that's how we felt. We were not happy at all with all that we had found, but one day I thought that I had found not only a vocalist, but thousands, more with each minute. I had bought a short-wave radio that proved to be for me a replacement for the singer. If we did not have a singer, at least we had a radio, that was more than sufficient. When I was 14 I had a short wave receiver that I had built myself, and since I worked in a repair shop I learned to repair radios and televisions. When I had my first short-wave radio, I was crazy about it. Since then, I still haven't forgotten enthusiasm.

AND MICHAEL COUSINS?
No, he wasn't a good singer for us.

DO YOU REMEMBER THE CROWD THAT SCREAMED IN PARIS?

Yes, yes. It was good, but apparently more in the style of "Heavy Rock." Can is sometimes a "Heavy Rock" group, but only sometimes.

AND LATER, HOW DID YOU MEET ROSKO?

He played with Traffic and one day when we were doing a recording for B.B.C. television in London, the Old Grey Whistle Test (Traffic had been practicing next door for three years), Rosko (Gee) simply said "Good Day" to no one in particular. He later came to see us in concert an really liked us, and later we became friends when I left London.

ONLY YOU?

Yes. One day he paid us a visit in our studio and became our bassist, while I was occupied with other instruments like the radio, and specially prepared guitars, especially one guitar that was prepared with acupuncture needles....

HOW DID THAT WORK OUT, A BASS WITH ACUPUNCTURE NEEDLES?

Long needles were placed between the strings and they oscillate one another. I already have utilized this on "Monster Movie."

AND REEBOP, HOW DID HE COME TO BE?

He had been friends with Rosko for a long time, they played together with Traffic. The group decided to take him as their drummer.

DO YOU THINK JAKI REALLY NEEDED THAT?

He said yes, and he was very happy to play with him. I think these two played really well together, yes. I believe that Jaki and Rosko are very similar in what they want to achieve with music, as well as their concept of an "ideal" music. Reebop and Jaki also came together a little. As for myself and Jaki, we were similar in a small sense, but for the most part we had extremely different temperaments, but then that it really why we had a special rhythm in the sense of "Rock Music."

YOUR EXPERIENCE WITH ENO AND CLUSTER?

I am really not that well acquainted with Cluster. I saw them maybe once or twice in Conny Plank's studio.

DO YOU LIKE THEM?

Yes, they seem to be one group that is really trying to do something new, not just going down the familiar path. Only in that regard am I interested.

HOW DID IT HAPPEN THAT YOU PLAYED WITH THEM.

I just arrived one day and they asked me to play the bass, or was it my idea... Yes, that's right, I said: "My, a bass would really go well over there..." What I did on their piece was very spontaneous.

CAN YOU TELL ME IN FACT, WHY YOU LEFT CAN?

I think that the time had come for me to go completely on my own. That's what I told myself. With Can I no longer saw a chance for myself.

DEFINITIVELY?

Yes, all that I wanted was no longer possible to achieve with Can.

WAS THE CONFLICT ONLY MUSICAL OR WAS THERE HUMAN ELEMENT TO IT AS WELL?

I think that these two things became one after a period of time, but I can say that also, the interior difficulties with Can happened to those who played in the group from start to finish. It's not always a reason to abandon everything, but that was the case for me when I saw where Can was headed and I couldn't see how I could go along with them.

AT WHAT TIME DID YOU BECOME CONSCIOUS OF THIS?

To start at the beginning when Rosko arrived. I took the radio and tried to make it work with everything, I said to the others that I would try something, if the result was positive, I would stay, but if I saw that it wasn't possible to have a combination with everything, then it would be better if I left.

THAT'S STRANGE BECAUSE IT WAS YOU WHO INTRODUCED ROSKO TO THE GROUP!

It was destiny, and destiny is never strange. Rosko came and the group loved him as their bassist, preferred him to me.

THEREFORE YOU LEFT THEM....

.... And therefore I did a solo, it was all I could do, I didn't have any other choice, it was because it really wasn't a great desire on my part to continue. I only have to follow the path I was sent to follow.

DID YOU WORK AT INNER SPACE STUDIOS?

Yes, but the first recordings were made at my place. I started very softly at first, with a cassette recorder. Then I passed on to a magnetone and worked with 3 microphones. After I prepared these tapes, I then copied them onto 16 tracks and a computer deck. Voilà.

WHY DID YOU CHOOSE JAKI AS THE DRUMMER?

Jaki was always interested in experimentation with the drums. While I was working, he could always understand what I was doing and he liked it. Therefore, we didn't have an obstacle when it came to working together. It took a while, but it was never wrong. The recordings were good right from the start and had the touch that we could never achieve before. Above all, even if he did have to play in a group that was terminated, that was not something unusual. Generally "pop" musicians have a background tape which gives us the rhythm guitar, then the bass, drums and voice or something. With me it's exactly the opposite, I first do the rhythm guitar, then the drum machine and set the whole orchestra in motion, and then finally Jaki. The way which we both synchronized was... No, I think that I will keep that as a secret, because it really is a secret, it is practically impossible to realize such a thing.....

WELL WHAT DID YOU DO?

I am able to synchronize the orchestra with Jaki and Jaki is able to synchronize the orchestra with himself. Voilà.

A TYPE OF TELEPATHY?

Yes, but more a type of listening, it always remains spontaneous. We work as partners.

WHEN WAS THE LAST CONCERT YOU PLAYED WITH CAN?

It was in Geneva, June 20, 1977.

DO YOU FEEL LIKE YOU SUCCEEDED IN USING THE RADIO WITH CAN?

I didn't have any success with Can and I have no idea about the future. At this time, I really don't see how I could use what I have found with any other musicians, in regards to my instruments. I didn't know any interesting musicians so I did everything myself.

WHAT DO YOU THINK OF *OUT OF REACH*?

...... I don't know......

DO YOU THINK THAT THIS IS STILL CAN OR THAT IT ISN'T CAN AT ALL?

No, I went to bed while saying to myself: "I am no longer a part of the group," then I listened to it.

AND ON THE NEW RECORD? YOU WORKED WITH THEM ON A PIECE.

Between times, I think that the group turned itself into a critic, they never thought that this album would be their favorite.

DO YOU WANT TO SAY THAT THEY WERE AWARE OF THE SITUATION?

Oh absolutely. But everyone (especially Irmin) wanted to have an experience with Reebop and Rosko and they strongly influenced the group, of course very strongly, especially on *OUT OF REACH*. I feel that the influence of the two did not meet with the capabilities of Can in regards to its stronger points. The strong points of Can are completely different and were known right from the start. It is one of the reasons which I had chosen this instrument (the radio), to make everyone listen. Voilà. We listened to the radio to try to make music with it. Not to need to be egotistical as is usual with musicians. And I believe this is very hard to avoid, the radio is not in the way of the musician, the rapport between the radio and the musician is magical. A radio disrupts everything...

DOES THE RADIO ADD A MAGICAL SIDE TO THE MUSIC?

Absolutely. It is an instrument like a tarot card or dice. Of course if you understand it, like roulette, if you find the right number, you're the winner. Otherwise you lose. My idea with Can and the radio was to have a short-wave transmission and to transmit in this way the concerts of the group. I wanted the relationship between the group and me to be a little like that of a "disc-jockey" or radio announcer, the people would have been able to hear what I said, what I diffused and perhaps even to give their responses and participate in some parts of the world, coming on stage with the group... It was also my idea with the telephone, it was going to be where I would have a telephone right on stage to call someone, just a random number and let the person participate in the concert.

WHAT DID THE OTHERS THINK OF THIS?

They never told me.

WHAT ARE YOUR LIFE'S INTERESTS OUTSIDE MUSIC?

People. They can tell you everything. If you are open, they will tell you all the secrets of the world.

WHEN DID YOU START THE "E.F.S." SERIES?

At the beginning, we imitated ethnic musics, we did that later on too. Irmin was a great imitator of the dancers from No. When he started to sing in a Japanese style, we were all over the floor, dying with laughter. The way in which he did it was really very good, like an opera star, magnificent and very comical. I think that Irmin would have become a great opera star if he had continued like that. He is a great vocalist, I love it when he sings. He sang on "Augmn" (on *TAGO MAGO*), he has a very strange voice that I treated with a generator, one of my main instruments, it's on the record. Jaki played the bass. I was next to him at a music stand, it was great.

I LIKED IT WHEN HE SANG "BABYLON PEARL" ALSO.

Yes... At another time, on one of the E.F.S. (which is on *LIMITED EDITION*) he made a type of Japanese voice, the kind from the theatre of No together with Damo. We amused ourselves a lot with this at this time.

DON'T YOU THINK THAT THE MUSIC OF CAN IS BETTER LIVE THAN ON RECORD?

No I don't. In fact, the recordings of Can are best when they are done under unusual circumstances and with unusual technique.

YOU MEAN LIKE ON THE FIRST 5 OR 6 LPs?

Yes, in other words, I will say, that when the music stand and all the recording equipment is treated like an instrument by a real musician who understands the equipment as if it were a living being. It's like a guitar, it isn't just a piece of material, it is something more than that, you have to come to this level of understanding, if you love it -- like the same way Jaki treated his drums, as if they were his children. If you have this kind of sentiment towards the electronic equipment, it's enough for you just to look at it

ISN'T THERE A CONTRADICTION: THE SOUND OF A GROUP CHANGES, TELL US ABOUT THE PERIOD OF LANDED, OF THE TIME OF NEW, MORE SOPHISTICATED EQUIPMENT THAT YOU USED?

Yes, it was a time when we had to learn all that we could from what we were using. At this time, I wasn't entirely responsible for the technique and what was done. The recording became better technically, and the music was oriented more in another direction away from the initial concept, I can even say, towards the opposite of what we had in mind. Not at all the last album *CAN*, Can returned completely new now, I think in this way, concerning my record, its recording is completely unusual for any sound engineer. I think that if I ask a machine to buy me a cup of coffee, it will do it, really...

IN WHICH WAY DO YOU THINK YOU INFLUENCED THE MUSIC OF THE GROUP WHEN YOU WERE THE SOUND ENGINEER?

All the music passed through my hands, I controlled it, and when it was edited it was the same thing. Our records were cut several thousand times, really. And as for mine, you can't imagine how many times...

DO YOU THINK THAT THERE ARE SEVERAL LEVELS TO YOUR MUSIC?

The music is in the same spirit, but there are all the instruments which are played... For me, the principle thing, the base of the band, is the rhythm guitar, which must cut through everything else. In some ways, the music is not played. The bands must live their existence to tell you what to play next, it isn't you (the musician), it is the music which tells you everything, it's necessary just to listen. If you make a band, rhythm/bass/drums, it is this that's necessary to make a "hit," and then not just that, it's something else, perhaps more public, more popular.

IN REGARDS TO THE PUBLIC, DO YOU THINK THAT CAN TOUCHED THE PUBLIC RIGHT?

Can has always had "fans" who were very sincere and I feel that we really had to put that beneath us... to just make our music, to understand who we were, not to really exclude the public, but to include them.

WHAT DO YOU THINK OF THE MUSIC SCENE TODAY?

I think that it's a universal catastrophe.... a completely wrong direction. At the start of "pop music" there were a few great stars, very good musicians. Today if you listen to the music you will understand that all musicians play poorly, in comparison to what they say about the professional status of music today. Of course, the drummer didn't keep exactly the proper rhythm in the beginning, the bassist would sometimes make a wrong note. There had always been something imperfect. Today everything is 100% perfect and perfection is boring. That's why I like things with a punk influence. I haven't listened very closely to "punk music," but I think that the people in the scene now are doing their stuff just to be somehow different. That's exactly what I like, if they call it "Punk," that's fine. I don't know what they want, but the fact that they don't just occupy themselves with ultramodern paraphernalia makes me sympathetic to them.

ARE YOU ALWAYS IN CONTACT WITH STOCKHAUSEN?

Oh yes, I really consider him to be one of the greatest masters.

WILL YOU EVER PLAY WITH HIM IN THE FUTURE?

I really can't say "never," I believe that he is a musician in a different world than mine. I can see what he is trying to accomplish as a musician, or what he will accomplish because he just doesn't try, he really does it.

DOES HE SEE THAT HIMSELF?

Yes, yes. He is a composer in the sense of the old European musical tradition. He is a master, he controls each note that he produces and really is in harmony with the universe.

WHO ELSE DO YOU CONSIDER TO BE A MASTER?

For example, Lee Perry of the Upsetters, he is fantastic! I think of him as a brother -- a crazy brother. When I heard him for the first time on a cassette that he sent me, "Total Seven" by the Upsetters, I thought that it was the best music that I had ever heard in my life!

AND THE JAPANESE, LIKE ISHII?

I am really not all that familiar with them. They are musicians who are influenced by John Cage. There is not anything really to critique. I think that these people are following the path of their music that they feel the must, that's marvelous!

PASCAL BUSSY
Translation by Michelle Tuck

1981

EDITORS NOTE: Late News!
Holger's 2nd solo LP is nearly finished. In addition he has released a cryptic 12" with Conny Plank titled *LES VAMPYRETTES*; recently done a production with Phew (a Japanese vocalist from Tokyo), Jaki on drums & piano, Conny Plank and himself & may soon release a 12" from sessions he did with Jah Wobble (ex-P.I.L.) last year.
Can Update: They have formed their own label -- Spoon Records. First releases are tentatively: Irmin Schmidt - *FILMMUSIK*, a remixed version of *CANNIBALISM*, a 12" of unreleased Can material and a 2nd solo by Irmin.

Lastly.... This article's interviewer, a former co-editor of *ATEM* Magazine, currently a freelance French journalist, will publish in September a book on the history of Can in France. Look for details regarding availability in EUROCK.

A Visitation With Pekka Pohjola

Last summer I had the unique opportunity to interview Pekka Pohjola while he was at Finlandia Hall rehearsing with a jazz orchestra for the 1980 Nordring Festival. There he would participate in a fascinating show bringing the history and music of Finland up to date from the turn of the century. Although he wasn't playing his music, he was in the company of such Finnish jazz luminaries as Olli Ahvenlahti, Juhani Aaltonen, Eero Koivistoinen and for a special segment dealing with traveling to exotic places, Jukka Tolonen was called in to deliver a sterling performance of his tune "A Passenger To Paramaribo." It was after one of the many rehearsals of this engaging musical display that I had the pleasure to talk to Pekka.

CAN YOU REMEMBER THE FIRST COMPOSER THAT INTERESTED YOU?

Well, that's a very hard question because I used to listen to a lot of classical music when I was young, and had gotten into music already then. So, it must have been any of the great names, Beethoven, Mozart, Sibelius. Afterwards I became interested in rock by the Beatles. Before that I used to think that it was shit.

WHAT WAS YOUR FIRST MUSICAL INSTRUMENT?

The first instrument I played was the piano, without a teacher. Only after I

302, Eurock: European Rock & the Second Culture

started the violin did I have a teacher at age 8.

ARE THERE ANY OTHER MUSICIANS IN YOUR FAMILY?

Yeah, everybody. It's kind of a musical family. My father, his two brothers and one sister are quite famous here. My father is a choir conductor and cellist a well. My uncle is a famous music teacher and has a children's choir and orchestra. The have won competitions abroad.

WHAT WAS YOUR FIRST BAND LIKE?

Well, my first band wasn't really a band. I used to play with a good friend, a guitar player Matti Kurkinen, he later played in a group called Kalevala -- he died in a car accident. We did a lot of Beatle tunes as well as some of our stuff. I might have some tapes, but I don't know where they are. We were 14 or 15 then.

WHAT MAKES SCANDINAVIA SUCH AN INSPIRATIONAL PLACE FOR MUSIC?

I might ask the same thing of you, why is the States such an inspirational place for music? I guess every place has its own identity, and if it's brought out in an interesting way then it maybe seems exotic to the other nations. If it's made well it should sound strange.

WHAT WAS IT LIKE HERE IN FINLAND DURING THE MID-'60S?

Well, the Beatles came along and everybody grew long hair. New guitar bands started out, things like that. Then it developed a bit and became better, because it was very "British Rock"-type influence for a long time, and then all this American jazz, soul and funk came.

WHO WERE YOU LISTENING TO THEN?

Only the Beatles, no one else. I knew some tunes from the radio, but I only liked the Beatles.

HOW DID YOU COME TO JOIN WIGWAM?

Actually I wasn't very familiar with them. When I was 17 I used to play in a band called Jussi and the Boys for half a year and then -- they asked me to join the band, Wigwam. Because the original bass player Mats Hulden had started to study and couldn't make all the gigs. So they thought they'd hire 2 bass players and I would play the violin as well but I didn't.

"1936 LOST IN THE SNOW" WAS YOUR FIRST COMPOSITION IN WIGWAM. HOW DID THAT STRANGE TITLE COME ABOUT?

Actually I haven't made any titles yet as all my titles are made by someone else. It's very hard for me to get the right atmosphere. I think it was Kim Fowley who came up with the title for "1936..." Different people come up with the names.

IN WIGWAM WHOSE MUSIC WAS DONE LIVE THE MOST?

It was Procol Harum and The Band, with very few of our own tunes. It was strange with Wigwam's music -- we'd record our own tunes, but never played them live. Just a few tunes of our own were played live.

AT WHAT POINT DO YOU FEEL WIGWAM WAS MOST TOGETHER?

In the middle of it -- after 2 years. I played in Wigwam for 4 years. After 2 years the feeling went down. This was after *FAIRYPORT*.

WHO HAD THE MOST INFLUENCE ON THE RECORDED WORKS?

Well, I think it was separate. Jim (Pembroke) had his own tunes, and Jukka was very strong on his side with mine somewhere in the middle. I never got into planning the records. If there were 2 tunes missing I would write them. It was always Jukka planning "all things." His lyrics were translated to English by Mats Hulden and of course Jim had his English lyrics too. It was very strange Finnish so it must have been very strange English too.

WHEN DID YOU REALIZE THAT YOUR MUSIC WASN'T THE DIRECTION OF THE GROUP'S?

Well, we did one tune called "Nipystys" and that showed me it wasn't right for the group with that kind of music. I mean it still hasn't been played right. It's now being played by the new group and sound better.

WHAT DO YOU THINK OF JIM PEMBROKE'S MUSIC?

I think it's great, he has some really good songs. It was the influences from Gary Brooker and The Band's music which gave him the orchestral feelings at first. Of course his music has an amazing sense of his own unique identity.

THE FIRST SOLO ALBUM, *PIHKASILMA KAARNAKORVA* SEEMED TO BE OVERFLOWING WITH MUSICAL THEMES. HOW DID IT FIT IN WITH WHAT WIGWAM WAS DOING?

No way, it was something completely different. I wanted to do something on my own and only used Jukka from Wigwam. I wasn't doing any solo concerts yet, just composing at home. I didn't dare to bring out the tunes. It's very hard in the beginning, just like when your first song is being played, you say, "Is this my tune?"

YOUR SECOND LP *B THE MAGPIE* WAS OUT IN LONDON THE SAME TIME AS WIGWAM'S *NUCLEAR NIGHTCLUB*. WAS THERE SOME JOINT EFFORT BY LOVE & VIRGIN TO GIVE YOU AND WIGWAM SOME SORT OF INTERNATIONAL PUSH?

Yeah, I guess that's the way it was. I think they met at some festival -- the Virgin and Love people -- and they changed records, the way record company people do, and the liked Wigwam and my music.

HAVE YOU DONE ANY SOLO GIGS WITH ANYONE IN ENGLAND?

No.

IN THAT IT WAS A CONCEPT ALBUM, WAS *B THE MAGPIE* EVER PLAYED LIVE?

No -- it was played in bits, and it was recorded also over a very short period of time. We had only 4 days in the studio.

HOW DID YOU AND MIKE OLDFIELD COME TO COLLABORATE ON *MATHEMATICIAN'S AIR DISPLAY*?

At the time Virgin had *B THE MAGPIE*, also Mike had a copy and thought it was his kind of music. At the same time he was a bit depressed because the second album he made, *HERGEST RIDGE*, was not accepted by the press and he was just alone in his country house. So Virgin people tried to find people to play with him and since he liked my album they flew me over along with Pierre Moerlen. First we did our tapes, not for the LP, then the second time I flew over we started to make some tunes, one of them "Mathematician's Air Display" we felt was so good it could be released on a record.

At the same time I was doing my own solo album in Sweden with the group Made In Sweden backing me -- so I took the backing tapes to Mike's studio and we put the music together.

I HEARD THAT ALBUM WON SOME KIND OF AWARD IN SWEDEN?

Yeah, the radio people chose it as the Record of the Year for rock. It also won jazz and classical awards -- a series of awards.

COULD YOU TELL ME A LITTLE ABOUT MADE IN SWEDEN?

Well, it was Georg Wadenius and Wlodek Glugowski. They were a bit tired of what they were doing in NY and Georg was missing his homeland, Sweden. They thought that they could come here and build a band, and they tried to find the right musicians. They met Vesa Aaltonen and me and liked it enough so we joined the band. In the beginning it was very nice, but also after the singer Tommy Korberg left, it started to go down because we didn't know what to do next. The record company wanted us to find a new singer, but it was next-to-impossible to find one as good as Tommy. So we went on as an instrumental group, but that didn't satisfy the record company, so we split after 2 years.

DID YOU COMPOSE FOR THE GROUP OR PLAY LIVE?

Some, yes. We did composing together. We did many gigs, but only one LP, *WHERE DO WE BEGIN*.

HOW SOON AFTER YOUR THIRD SOLO LP DID YOU FORM THE GROUP?

Let's see, before Made In Sweden, I played half a year in Jukka Tolonen's Band and a half year after we formed The Group.

WAS THE GROUP BASICALLY YOUR MUSIC THAT WAS TO LATER MATERIALIZE ON *VISITATION*?

The Group's music wasn't really my music. I did many of the themes, but the construction of the music was put together with Olli Ahvenlahti and the rest of the band. I don't really like to call it my music. It's like a mixture of the whole thing. It was very simple -- some tunes were very simple and some hit tunes, or we thought they were.

VISITATION IS A PERFECTLY BALANCED LP OF JAZZ-ROCK AND CLASSICAL MUSIC. ARE YOU STILL HAPPY WITH IT?

Well, in a way I am. Always you want to do things better. But it's played well and the sound is quite good. You always want to do something better after it's done.

OF THE PEOPLE ON THAT ALBUM, WHO'S STILL IN YOUR NEW BAND, THE PEKKA POHJOLA GROUP?

Just Seppo Tyni. On keyboards is his brother Pekka. The drummer is new too, Ismo Katka. Our new album is called *KATKAVAARAN LOHIKAARME*, which means dragon of Lohikaarme. It's due out soon.

Robert Silverstein

EDITOR'S NOTE:
Pekka's new LP is now out and shows a marked change over *VISITATION*. Gone is the classical touches as the sound is very hard-edged and basic. Straight jazz with a hint of rock. Seppo Tyni's guitar is definitely the focal point with the keys and rhythm section laying down a solid foundation over which he cuts loose.

Jim Pembroke Interview
Before And After Wigwam

The following interview with Jim Pembroke came about in Finland last summer. British-born, and now a 15 year resident of Finland, Jim was the creator and guiding light of Wigwam, probably the most famous Scandinavian rock band. Along with Jukka Gustavson, Pekka Pohjola and Ronnie Osterberg they created some of the most vibrant and varied music on record. After Pekka and Jukka split, Jim turned the band into a beacon for his strange and cryptic musical visions. The setting for this interview is Digelius Music, a small progressive record shop in Helsinki. Also present was Hassi Walli, noted Finnish guitarist who has recorded with Piirpauke and Jim's first recorded band in Finland, Blues Section.

EDITOR'S FORENOTE:
Sad news recently arrived when it was learned that Ronnie Osterberg, drummer and longtime friend of Jim and many others in Finland, had taken his own life. He will be missed and may his spirit R.I.P.

I HEARD WIGWAM HAD REGROUPED AT LEAST FOR A LITTLE WHILE. IS OR WAS THAT TRUE?

No, it wasn't like regrouped as Wigwam. Ronnie and Mats were playing in the new group, but we thought we'd leave the name in peace and not use it again. With this new group we tried to think of new names and got a list of about 150 together, but then it got like, some of them were funny, you have a good laugh and then you think after a while it wasn't so good after all. In the end we just left it under my name 'cause I was supposed to do a solo LP anyway last year ('79). So when we started playing again with Ronnie and Mats the papers of course started writing that Wigwam had reformed and all that because 3/4 of the original band was there. Only Nikki was missing (Vladimir Nikamo).

THE NEW ALBUM, *FLATBROKE*, SEEMS TO HAVE MORE OF A COUNTRY (A LA THE BAND) INFLUENCE. TUNES LIKE "NASHVILLE CO-WRITERS PLAN" OR "BOY FROM THE IRON RANGE" IN

COMPARISON TO *NUCLEAR NIGHTCLUB*. WHAT ABOUT THAT?

We didn't set out with any particular style in mind. Maybe we tried to make it not so stylized, but certain things sound certain ways I guess and some of the pieces might have a sort of country flavor. Well, some of the lyrics too -- the Nashville thing and all that. The subject is about country music or about country music song writing. A couple years back, I wasn't doing much, and I had a couple of texts, and I saw an ad in *Rolling Stone* magazine to send your lyrics in and we'll set them to music and you can become a millionaire in 5 minutes. So I thought, why not -- might as well give it a whirl for laughs. So I send these two lyrics off. Some time later comes this return package with two contracts saying your lyrics are worthy of use and we will set them to music. The last page was the price page, it said if you want a demo made with 5 musicians send $85.00 -- if you want it with 3 send $50.00 --with 2 send $10.00 and on and on. Of course I didn't send any. Instead I wrote a song myself.

HOW WOULD YOU DESCRIBE YOUR MUSIC? HAVE YOUR INFLUENCES CHANGED OVER THE YEARS?

Well, The Band thing -- when I first heard ... *BIG PINK*, I thought this will do for me, this is about as good as you can get. It was great! Before that it was Procol Harum, I thought they were doing great stuff -- *SALTY DOG* and all that. Then it goes before that, the Beatles, Stones and Yardbirds too. But after The Band I haven't heard anything that stops me.

ARE YOU INFLUENCED BY SCANDINAVIAN MUSIC LIKE PEKKA POHJOLA OR PIIRPAUKE?

Well they do a lot of interpretations of many different countries, like folk music, and in doing that they maybe found a peculiar way of doing it in a Finnish style.

WOULD YOU DESCRIBE THE EARLY WIGWAM AS BEING A CULT BAND?

I suppose it was because we didn't really have a big success album-sales-wise until we actually broke up for the first time. We made a live album, sort of rounding it off type thing and that sold a lot of copies relatively speaking here and it was our first recording success. It was kind of ironic that we did it as a farewell tour. But then Mosse (Groundstroem) said that if he comes to play, shouldn't we continue, so we did. Then we went on to *NUCLEAR NIGHTCLUB*, but before that, well I suppose we had a small following here in Finland and we played quite a few gigs in Sweden, Denmark and Norway where we always got good receptions, but not like gigantic recording success -- so I don't know if that qualifies us for status as a cult band. In England too, we had some sort of reputation but it wasn't very wide spread.

YOUR FIRST BAND HERE IN FINLAND WAS BLUES SECTION, RIGHT?

We had a band before that even. Somebody called it The Pems, but we don't need to go into that. Blues Section was the first real band where we learned something about how to make music. It's been like learning all the time -- that was kind of the first class.

HOW DID BLUES SECTION ORIGINATE?

Let's see. There was Ronnie on drums in Blues Section and then Mosse on bass originally. Well, Ronnie, Mosse and me wound up in a "nuclear Wigwam." Then there was Rekku on guitar by then, but Blues Section broke up and then Ronnie, Mats and Nikki started making a backing band for a singer here, but they didn't work anything out with that and then we got around to making a quartet of it, and in the end called it Wigwam.

DID YOU COLLABORATE A LOT WITH PEKKA POHJOLA AND JUKKA GUSTAVSON?

Yeah, we did a lot of rehearsing and that. Pekka and Jukka had songs ready and so did I. On *BEING* -- that was a real conscious attempt to try and make something together. Jukka actually wrote out sort of like the brief on the subjects and what roughly the themes should go like. We tried it and people said it worked quite well. Jukka had much to say about many things They wrote in some of the papers here that he had quite a Marxist outlook, which when Jukka saw these things he just kind of laughed and said, "What? What's this? I can't understand that.

IT'S BEEN SAID THAT THE EARLY WIGWAM PLAYED MOSTLY NON-ORIGINALS ON STAGE. WAS THAT A FACTOR IN THE BAND BREAKING UP?

It probably was part of the reason, because we couldn't play the stuff we made on record -- we couldn't play it live. I mean Jukka's and Pekka's stuff -- it was impossible to do it with four, and in the beginning it was a trio, because I wasn't even playing on stage. Even with four instruments you couldn't attempt to reproduce the songs we made on record because they were so complex.

SO *PIGWORM* WAS THE LAST TIME THE ORIGINAL BAND RECORDED TOGETHER?

Was it? I'm not sure. They were all on that. It must have been '74 that was made. There are about 10 or 12 LPs that we've made and I can't...

HOW DID PEKKA RECHARDT COME TO JOIN?

Pekka and Jukka wanted to do other things, they just wanted to leave. It wasn't exactly eye-to-eye on the old musical policy and all that. Jukka wanted to write ballet, modern or jazz, whatever and Pekka started doing as far as I remember, a lot of studio stuff and his own too. He's done about 4 solo albums. He had a lot of his own material which couldn't be used in Wigwam. So actually Rekku had already been playing with the group by then.

DO YOU KNOW WHAT REKKU IS DOING THESE DAYS?

Last I heard he was a court musician for the students theatre. He backs them up on guitar in the theatre school. He does very well, I've seen a couple things he's done.

MUCH OF YOUR MUSIC FROM THE LATER WIGWAM WITH REKKU WAS COLLABORATION LIKE ON "BLESS YOUR LUCKY STARS," FROM *NUCLEAR NIGHTCLUB*.

With Rekku it really was collaboration because he'd have a line and there'd be an easy way to find a melody out of the stuff he did. We did a lot of gigs and traveling -- the old hotel scene, sitting in the bus and all that. A lot of the material was just made up, as I found it easy to get a hold of what was going on about, sort of realize it, and put words to it. We got a lot of good songs that way.

SO WAS *NUCLEAR NIGHTCLUB* YOUR MOST FAMOUS LP?

Seems so 'cause it was the one, well it was number one here, and as a result we got a contract with Virgin Records. They got interested in this funny sound and things started to be gradually happening. We went to England and toured there, and Germany and Holland -- the whole bit. A lot happened... but in the end nothing happened, 'cause it takes a lot of money -- it takes more money than was put into us to advertise, I think, to push it through.

LUCKY GOLDEN STRIPES AND STARPOSE WAS DONE IN ENGLAND. HOW DID THAT COME ABOUT?

Well, Virgin owned this studio, The Manor, which is a great place, a gigantic mansion really, where they have a studio and round-the-clock chefs. They came up with the idea of us going there and recording as a half-Virgin and half-Love sort of deal. It was quite expensive, but going even to Sweden would not have been that much cheaper as we'd done *NUCLEAR NIGHTCLUB* there.

THEN YOU DID SOME GIGS IN ENGLAND?

We did a tour with Gong. We played all over England and Scotland too. We got a good reception everywhere.

DO YOU EVER GO BACK TO ENGLAND? YOUR FROM THERE, WHAT CITY?

London. Last time I was back was for the *STARPOSE* LP four or five years ago.

LAST YEAR VIRGIN CAME OUT WITH A COMPILATION LP, *RUMOURS ON THE REBOUND*. HOW DID THAT COME ABOUT?

It was a thanks-for-the-memories sort of thing. It was quite good actually. I'm not sure of the sales, but the press in England liked it. We've always had critical acclaim, but the general public never did seem to know about us.

YOUR THIRD SOLO LP, *CORPORAL CAULIFLOWER'S MENTAL FUNCTION*, FEATURED TWO GUITARISTS, REKKU AND COSTE APETREA, WHO NOW PLAYS WITH JUKKA TOLONEN'S BAND. HOW DID YOU GET TOGETHER WITH HIM?

Coste I'd known for a long time from when he was with the Swedish group Zamla Mammaz Manna. We had played many gigs in Sweden with them. Zamla is a great group. When we made *NUCLEAR NIGHTCLUB* Coste turned up at the studio often. I was already planning what came to be *CORPORAL CAULIFLOWER* and he said, "Call me when you do it," 'cause we were going to do it in the same studio as *NUCLEAR NIGHTCLUB*. So I called him and he came over. He stayed a couple weeks, we rehearsed and then went to Stockholm and did it.

CORPORAL CAULIFLOWER'S MENTAL FUNCTION REALLY A STRANGE TITLE FOR AN ALBUM.

Well, I was trying to think of something that would be a bit out of the ordinary. You know one of the greatest records of all time was *SGT. PEPPER'S LONELY HEARTS CLUB BAND* and that's a hell of a title.

IT WAS A SORT OF OUT-OF-THE-BLUE THING?

Maybe something along the same lines as *SGT. PEPPERS*. I couldn't think of what to call it -- *CORPORAL PUNISHMENT* or *CORPORAL CAULIFLOWER'S*...... but in the end I chose.... *CAULIFLOWER*...

THE LAST WIGWAM LP WAS APPROPRIATELY CALLED *DARK ALBUM*. THERE MUST HAVE BEEN DARKENING SKIES OVER THE BAND THEN.

Love Records hadn't paid the electricity bill you see and we did that one by candlelight with the generator in the toilet. (laughter)

JUKKA GUSTAVSON PLAYED ON THAT ALBUM.

Yeah it was kind of, we were winding up again with this record *DARK ALBUM*. We couldn't think of what to call that one either.

WHY WAS THERE SUCH A LONG WAIT BETWEEN *DARK ALBUM* AND THE NEW ONE?

Well, I just kept on doing the same thing, putting songs together. I wrote quite a few for other people -- some were quite successful. In between that I played in band or two. Just gigging and doing some solo gigs too, mostly trying to think up stuff for other people here. People ask me to write lyrics to their songs in English. There's not many people who can do that in these parts.

DID THE WAIT HAVE ANYTHING TO DO WITH WHY AND WHEN LOVE RECORDS WENT BROKE?

As far as I understand their production thing went right over the top, and they were making records 'round-the-clock. Hundreds of records were coming out -- too many things happened at the same time.

SO NOW THERE ARE MANY SMALLER NEW LABELS HERE, RIGHT?

Love (pronounced Lov-ee) split up. Two companies came out of it, one is Otto Donner's label Ponsi and then there is Atte Bloom's label Johanna. They are both small independents like in England.

DO YOU HAVE PLANS TO TAKE THE NEW BAND ON THE ROAD?

Well... we don't have a band right now. We broke the *FLATBROKE* group up almost immediately. It was too much with six people. Half of them were doing other things and it was trouble to get all them together for a rehearsal even, so it got a bit much.

WOULD YOU SAY YOU ARE HAPPY WITH YOUR LEVEL OF RECOGNITION?

Well, you know... I get most of the time a chance to do what I want to do. Like to play with other people and try to make some music out of it. Try to get them to sing English.... properly. (laughter)

Robert Silverstein

Bain Total

France has traditionally been a haven for the avant-garde and beat arts. Sartre, the Left Banke, the Sarbonne were the seedbed for new ideas. Today this tradition is carried on by various "artistes souterrain" who prefer to operate outside the commercial mainstream.

Bain Total is one such operation. Started in 1977 they were quickly pigeonholed as too avant-garde and non-salable, thus they were on their own. The focus of the concept is the group Die Form, composed of Eva Johanna Reichstag and Phillipe Fichot (alias Franz K.).

To date they've produced 5 cassettes, 4 EPs and soon their first LP. Die Form's music is very -- moderne electronique. Rock-based, it takes off on too many tangents to be pinned down to any one style however. The production is imaginative, but simple; it utilizes altered voice/speeds and tapes as well as conventional synthe/instruments. The result is a quite different effect.

In addition to Die Form, Bain Total has done recordings by Krylon Hertz, Etant Donnes, Lucas Trouble, Tango Luger and Metabolist. With the 1st LP will be initiated a series of international compilations featuring, along with those already mentioned, a collection of diverse groups including Clock DVA, Raison Pure, Silent Types, M.B. (Italy), Magnetique Bleu, Fab Two, Bomis Prendin (USA), Ptose Production and others.

Their works do not only lie in recording however. They have done also various graphic documents: "Raison X/Abject Object Anomaly/ Panoply Shaved Girls/Editorial I." All done in very limited editions with capital import placed on presentation and visual impact. This graphic approach is similarly applied to their records with packaging that is suitably strange, complementing the music.

The third area they have recently gone into is live performance. In May 1980 in Provins they created quite a stir. The groups C. Pickford, Fine Automatic, Krylon Hertz and Die Form caused a riot with extreme music and unbearable films. The audience was not in tune so the group left the stage and the resulting press was scandalous.

With activities escalating now on all fronts, BAIN TOTAL's unique, creative approach promises a future of interesting works. Proof that life does indeed exist outside the confines of "business as usual."

Archie Patterson
Translation aid by Michelle Tuck

Peter Michael Hamel
The New Simplicity And Pop-Music

In 1975 Claus Henning Bachmann wrote about one of my concerts in Graz during "Steirischer Herbst," published in *MELOS*, "We have to note down the search of a simplicity, which is not simple, the search for a new harmony, which is not commonplace, a search for a European answer to the sound of silence of the Far East: music as a state of sound, as a feeling of life, as a manifestation of a psychic condition."

In 1977 this little word "simple" seems to have created a new category in contemporary music. Now they have got a new stamp again, a new drawer, a little case for thinking in boxes, for writing articles, for organising concerts, for making business. Voilà. Of course there are different suggestions for a new name of this development in contemporary music: the New Tonality, the New Sensitivity, new spiritual music, concentric, minimal, contemplative or meditative music.... It has been discussed what "New Simplicity" could mean. Today I have to speak about the relationship between "New Simplicity" and Pop-Music. Of course I don't speak about low and inferior popular music or any commercial Pop-Music-Business. I will have to use "Pop" as a main subject for jazz, folklore, electronic rock and for "music in between," which is influenced by extra-European cultures, for example India, Indonesia or Africa.

During the last 10 years you could notice a solution of the thinking in categories. Jazz musicians started to reflect more and more all the inventions of the experimental composers. And some of these composers gave up to construct mentally over-filled big, long and heavy scores to achieve the experience of spontaneous improvisation. They built up and worked with so-called collective improvisation groups and studied exotic music of Africa or Asia. Frederic Rzewski (Music Electronica Viva), Cornelius Cardew (Scratch Orchestra), Terry Riley ("In C") inspired the younger musicians not to orient on Schoenberg and Webern only, to try to play jazz and study Indian ragas and African rhythms for example. Young composers of the late '60s started to listen to records of John Coltrane, Ornette Coleman, Miles Davis and Don Cherry. They established free-music-improvisation groups.

Since about 1960 jazz musicians like Coltrane used a kind of modal system for their improvisations, that means they didn't change the chords according to the accompaniment of melodies, but they rather used modal scales, tunes of the Middle Ages, Arabic and African figures. To improvise on these scales is a way of playing music in almost every extra-European culture and it is a system of the early old music of Europe too as you know. Modality is the first step to the idea of "World-Music." In the modal principle you also can find the natural system of using micro-intervals according to the overtones and the untempered scale.

Before this modal movement in the jazz-music of the '60s the American composer John Cage invented his prepared piano. Pieces like "Amores" and "Sonatas and Interludes" in 1938 and 1947 reflected the different tonal structure of Indonesian Gamelan scales. In 1936 the French composer Olivier Messiaen composed his "Les Corps Glorieux" for Church-organ, in which he used South-Indian rhythm-structures. The exotic influence of the World Fair of Paris in 1898 on the music of the "chronoiserie" might have been more a colonialistic mode than a real meeting of foreign cultures. Finally it was jazz-music, in my opinion, that opened the consciousness for modality in Western contemporary music. Jazz realized its African roots and became interested in Indian, Arabic and Indonesian music long before the avant-garde discovered extra-European cultures. And yet today so-called serious musicians look down on classical Indian music and other cultural music as primitive folklore.

Since about 10 years ago some Western listeners started to study and practice extra-European music. People like the American composers Steve Reich, Terry Riley, LaMonte Young, myself and others have traveled through Africa, India, Indonesia for months, years looking for good teachers to bring to Europe and the USA.

The compositions and improvisations which came out as a result of this meeting and as an integration between cultures has been called "minimal music": endless repetitions, perpetual reiterations, eternal circles. Of course this wasn't at all exotic copy or adaptation. More or less it has been invented, a new kind of contemporary music, this "new New music" has been called minimal, Meta, meditative, periodic, concentric or trance music.

I personally started to practice endless patterns on keyboards in 1968. It began as opposition to the avant-garde duties of clusters, colours, noises and series. Superficially spoken it was not allowed to play any quints or octaves. So I played ONLY octaves and quints for sometime, started to sing long notes as a kind of self-therapy and practiced different vocal styles of Asia. In Munich we built up the improvisation group Between, our oboe-player, Robert Eliscu from New York, the soloist of the Munich Philharmonic Orchestra, studied old music and Indian classical music, our Argentinean guitar player Roberto Détrée brought the music of South America and two conga players -- one from the USA and one from Trinidad -- showed us the basic principles of Voodoo-rhythm. I kept on playing eternal figures and I remember very well when I listened the first time to tapes of Steve Reich and Terry Riley ("Piano Phase," "Four Organs," "Dorian Reeds").

Again something about the relation between "New Simplicity" and jazz: Terry Riley referred to Coltrane, Young and Eric Dolphy -- both have been sax players. Reich related to the drum player Max Roach. The jazz musician Don Cherry likes Terry Riley's organ music, the German vibes player Karl Berger worked with patterns of Frederic Rzewski, the jazz group Oregon used modal structures, the pop group Third Ear Band played ragas well. The English rock band Curved Air took their name from Riley's *A RAINBOW IN CURVED AIR*, Velvet Underground player John Cale worked with Terry Riley on the record *CHURCH OF ANTHRAX* and the rock band Soft Machine tried the minimal effect on their "Moon In June." English composer Michael Nyman uses elements of rock music, US clarinet player Tony Scott improvised in Japanese style with koto and shakuhachi on *MUSIC FOR ZEN MEDITATION*, flute player Paul Horn improvised on Indian ragas in the Taj Mahal on *INSIDE* and the Gamelan music fascinated Edvard Vesala from Finland and Neil Ardley from England. A very important subject in this connection would be the use of consciousness-expanding drugs -- the movement of "New Religiousness," the commercial effect of this movement in the music of Pink Floyd, Santana and John McLaughlin. Last, but not least we have to speak about the German groups Tangerine Dream, Klaus Schulze, who are successfully playing electronic rock using simple patterns.

I don't like the inventors of categories. It shows helplessness and inability for a deeper understanding. Mainly people who invent categories can't feel and be touched in their hearts. Very often they escape to a "wise distance." Instead of an experience to describe and a feeling, they are constructing new boundaries.....

"New Simplicity," I don't like this as a

new program of the business and concert managers. As long as "Music For 18 Musicians" by Steve Reich can't be realised by any avant-garde ensemble without him -- as long as compositions of Hans Otte, me and others, in which we use repeating patterns -- can't be played properly by any conventional orchestra -- they should not call it simple. If something is simple in one aspect of analysis, there are other aspects also which are much more subtle, complex and complicated -- for example: playing without losing rhythm -- rhythm felt in the belly not abstractly constructed -- playing consciously but relaxed -- exactly composed music which needs an improvised realization -- the state of contemplative playing and listening -- the state of intuitive perception -- Very simple -- isn't it??

Peter Michael Hamel

Der Plan Interview

I'm going to let you in on a little secret, I can't guarantee it's gonna stay a secret very long, because the group I'm telling you about just won't stand still for anyone. It is The Plan/Der Plan/Le Plan.

They've released 1 LP with another due any time. Their 1st, *GERI REIG*, has sold over 5,000 independently and is a milestone of the new awareness in German music. Der Plan have constructed a new music for the people, *GERI REIG*.

GERI REIG... a definition from Moritz rrr -- making the most of the least, using your wits to complete something with no tools, hastily throwing something together. You get an idea, nothing else is needed to do Geri Reig, other than the mind.

So now you know. Anyway the Plan are 3 people, Moritz rrr, Frank f. and Pyrolator.

I talked to Frank and Moritz recently and I'm just letting them take it from here. Oh and if you're expecting a detailed history, sorry. I started by asking about *GERI REIG*.

Fr: The idea behind *GERI REIG* was to make a record as musical dilettanti. It's an idea that many people had. In California there are friends of ours who practice Geri-Reig, but they've not done this openly. It's done among themselves, in a room, they don't reproduce it on record. They don't have a public.

Me: Is Geri-Reig only concerned with music?

Fr: No, not really. It's more concerned with not allowing yourself to be compromised or trapped. And that is a problem of age probably. Early 20s, the integration into society with its rules and regulations. And the serious way these things are used, they have to be fought on a personal level and that is not easy. (laughs) When we started out to make music it was done in a playful way and now we are in the position of having a business, a distribution net, various productions and we're still trying to keep the whole thing from getting serious. And that is not easy either.

At this point Moritz replaced Frank and we got to talking about other things.

Me: When you look back on the *GERI REIG* LP, what do you think?

Mo: I can see now, a year after, that the album really fits the concept we made for it. To do something with nearly no equipment, to bring out ideas, but in a way that other people can listen to it. And when I listen to it now it really sounds primitive to me, the first steps we ever made. Like some songs on the LP are the first we did in our lives. We have had many reactions and still get many comments from different places, so I think it worked, that some people really understood what we wanted to say. In that sense I'm really satisfied with it.

Me: Does the progression from *GERI REIG* to the new LP *NORMALETTE SURPRISE* still fit in with your concept of Geri-Reig, now that the quality of sound has improved?

Mo: Yes, it's still Geri-Reig. The other groups that started out the same time as us are using the big studios now, so we're still in a very low position compared to them.

And the development of the music is only partly due to better equipment, we use a 4-track instead of a normal 2-track recorder. The other development is that we now understand more about the music, especially to minimalize our ideas, to bring out the pure essence of what we want. Not to fill a track up with too many sounds that have nothing to do with the original idea. So the songs I think are clearer than before. And time changes as well, for instance. I've moved away from electronics a little, working on acoustic things, singing, etc.

Me: Do you think about your public when you record? Because they expect something from you now.

Mo: Yeah, I do think about it, but I don't want to. It's a handicap, but after a while you get over it and become innocent again. Two weeks ago I saw "The Great Rock 'n' Roll Swindle" for the 1st time and I saw lots of parallels to what we were thinking. For example Malcolm MacLaren said that a band that cannot play, is better than a band that can and that seems pretty clear to me, because a band that cannot play is closer to the audience who mostly can't play either. It's communication.

Me: The difference is that MacLaren used the business for his own means.

Mo: Yeah, seeing the movie you can see that the business was the basis of everything they did. Success was measured in money.

Me: And how do you measure your success?

Mo: Success for me is when I get a letter, and the person describing our music, relates to what we felt. Mostly I want communication, that's success. I think this is something that has emerged out of these attempts to make music with little or no equipment. A new media has appeared, people are communicating all over the world. We get letters from so many countries, it's a new media, outside all the other media, but it works. It's like finding friends. You can find a sort of friend by using tricks, but if you can be yourself and find the people who understand what you are. These are your real friends.

Me: People are doing the same things in many different parts of the world and they should get together.

Mo: When people write to us you can learn so much about yourself and also about the world. It's like our international LP we are getting together. We've had tapes from all over the world and I was really shocked when I listened to them, because suddenly I understood these people and what they were doing.

Mo: The basis of the project is that we don't want to do a commercial record, and what we earn from it, we put into a new pressing. We send part of each pressing to the artist in each country, so that the people can distribute them there. The more records we sell, the more we can send out.

Me: What I like about this is that it goes back to the people again. They distribute their own music and that of their friends to other people.

Mo: Yeah, to make people think.

Me: And what was the response?

Mo: A lot of people ignored the theme, and a lot didn't. Some sent us tapes of what they were doing at the time. It's interesting because of the variety of styles. Most Western music is electronic, but the Eastern stuff is completely different.

Me: It'll be interesting to get the reaction of the Eastern groups to the Western stuff and vice-versa.

Mo: They know what's going on over here perhaps not in Russia, but in Hungary for example they get everything sooner or later and we can communicate with them. What I hope is that we can get away from these high expectations and understand simple human speech, through music or whatever. Music is still fun for me, it's still not as important as some music papers make believe.

Ok, let's leave things there. That was Der Plan, or at least 2/3 of them. The other, Pyrolator, has also released a solo LP *INLAND* which is a must.

The music of Der Plan is not easy to describe. It's electronic and sometimes not, it's simple and sometimes so complicated you'd think it was done on a 24 track and not at home on a Japanese 4- track. It can cheer you up and bring you down. You can dance to it but can never ignore it. It's somehow a scenario, the movie script of our times, like wandering through a disused movie lot where you can pass through time at will. They are unique. Moritz once described them as "a primitive modern group, dancing around the campfire to electronic music." I can't do better.

Bob Giddens

Surplus Stock Interview

Surplus Stock - a group that suddenly staggered out from under the floorboards, releasing an LP of powerful proportions on a sleepy public. No overnight sensation, no record company waving blank checks under their noses, no time to sit around and take stock, rewards.......

I'm in Quakenbrück, W. Germany, a small village with a population of about 10,000, to talk to the guy behind both Surplus Stock and the Outatune label.

Bob Giddens is English, 26-years old -- has a Greek wife and a 17-month old son (he's the one on the LP label). We sat in a small room that serves as a studio/office, with all the chaotic trappings you'd expect: synth, 4-track tape machine, records, tapes, cassettes, magazines etc.

Risiko: Whatever made you settle here in Quakenbrück?

BG: I got a job here four years ago, before I got involved in music to any great extent. I like it here, it's quiet and that job pays for what you see here in this room.

Risiko: You still work full time then?

BG: Yeah, I have to. All the earnings from our record go to pay for the next one. I'm a part time musician/label really, although it's my No.1 priority.

Risiko: How did you get involved in all this?

BG: Two years ago I started writing and sent one of my articles to *ZigZag* magazine in London. They used it much to my surprise, and that was the start. I did an article on the first "new" German group to put an LP out, Deutsch-Amerikanischen Freundschaft, liked what they were doing and offered to put up the money for the next one. We went off to England to become superstars, they almost have.

Risiko: What made you leave then? You would have had an easy ride with them.

BG: Maybe, but the easy ride is sometimes not good for the conscience. I liked the group a lot, but they were impossible to work with. In those days there were five members and each one seemed to have a different opinion about what they were doing. I helped them until my money ran out, the group didn't have a penny between them so were dependent on me. Luckily they found Daniel Miller (of Mute Records), who was able to help them much better than I could. We played a tour with The Fall to a very strange reaction. I think it was the first time an English public had been confronted by a group singing and talking in German. I've never seen so many kids standing with open mouths, not knowing what to make of these foreigners.

Risiko: So how did Surplus Stock evolve out of this?

BG: Well I think it was obvious to both sides that DAF needed someone with more experience in the "music business" than I had. Trouble is they still owe me about $8,000, money that I need and that they can't pay. Anyway with my remaining money I booked one day at Cargo Studio in Rochdale. I had originally planned to use DAF as session musicians, but after agreeing to this, they decided it wouldn't do their image any good. How right they were. So I used 2 old friends of mine, Phil Renshaw on guitar and Robert Clarke on drums. Neither of whom had had anything to do with the music scene, thank goodness.

Risiko: Why do you say that?

BG: We got together as friends, not as musicians. In this business everyone's worried about image, concept, making it before anyone else and all that entails. We are in this for the fun, we all work outside music to survive. That way we can't become dependent on the music. We do what we want, without having to compromise. I've always wanted to be my own boss and here I am.

Risiko: Let's get back to that 1st recording?

BG: Well, we did "Spiv" and "Song For 9 To 5" at that session. Everything was improvised, I had the lyrics and a melody, but no idea how it would sound. We played around and at the end of 10 hours were satisfied.

Risiko: Who's crying at the end of "9 To 5"?

BG: That's Mike, my son (laughing). I'm not sticking pins into him though. I'd taped him a few days earlier and somehow it's a nice end, says he modestly.

Risiko: And then?

BG: I went back to Germany and put out "Spiv" as a single with "Vips" on the flip (get it?), "Spiv" backwards. We got rid of 1,000 mostly in Germany although Rough Trade in London got 100. We used the proceeds to do the album *HOLLAND IN NOT*.

Risiko: With a new drummer?

BG: Right. Rob Clarke was ill, we had originally planned to do the LP as a 4-piece, but Rob was suffering the after-effects of a major operation. So Josef Schenk, a guy I work with here played drums. He's German.

Risiko: The LP uses some German lyrics this time. Why'd you do that?

BG: It's one of the effects of an Englishman living in Germany. I wanted to communicate with the Germans on their own level, in their language.

Risiko: What did you have in mind with "Détente?"

BG: It's about a meeting between Carter and Brezhnev (or whoever) somewhere like Vienna. You know these summit meetings where everyone smiles, but are really trying to pull something over on each other. "One Step Forward, Two Steps Back." But it could just as easily be a meeting of East and West Germany, the same factors apply. I like the absurdity of the situation, and I thought it sounded better in German.

Risiko: How's the record selling?

BG: It's doing ok. It's hard for an unknown band, especially one that hasn't played a gig. We sold the 1st 1,000 in Germany in 3 months, which is an achievement here. The second press will probably take longer, even though we've had some good airplay now and the press is taking more of an interest. We're hoping it will sell better in England and America now. The main thing is that we've made enough with it to do another LP.

Risiko: And future plans?

BG: We're already working on the next album. This time we will be using some guest musicians to get a broader sound, at present I expect Michael Kemner (ex-DAF, now Fehl Farben) and Frank f. (Der Plan) to help out. Nothing is final yet.

So that was Bob Giddens, what he's doing is important and more people are seeing that as the Surplus Stock LP is recognized as one of the best of its kind; raw, primitive and industrial, using today's technology to the fullest. The record can be summed up in one word -- SATISFACTION.

Risiko

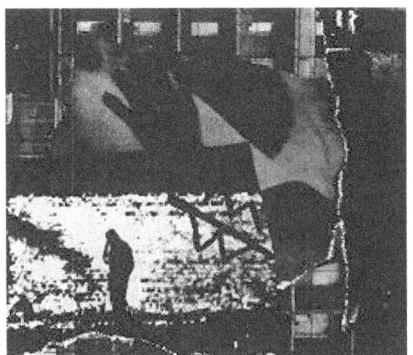

Maurizio Bianchi
INDUSTRIAL NIGHTMARES

M.B. is a solo group born on August 1979 in Milan Italy. M.B. is a precursor of the new "musical horrid" that is being born in Europe at the beginning of the '80s. M.B. treats and de-codifies electronics, tapes, noise, walls of sound, rhythms and Hertzian waves with the use of cacophony and improvisation. The gloomy temper of his modern point of view place him in unexplored regions where ardor is discouraged and humiliated. Moreover, a paradox, his sonorous dialog is based on shivering connections.

MECTPYO/BLUT, his 1st cassette, consists of two tragic sections imbued with synthetic chloroform: the 1st, "Maidanek Bakterium/ Musique Belzec," exhales an icy atmosphere conveying a sense of mystery and annihilation. The 2nd, "Mutant Brain/Mord Bahnhof," assembled the most disparate electro-hypnotic levitations into a vertical rationality, bold, morbid and haunting. Psychic-cerebral works, they seem to spring from a neuro-atomic continent, with unreal outlines, where its influence artificially expands the ankylotic tissues by environmental arthrosis.

COM. SA, a few months later, inaugurates using just synths, the pale cruelty of existential intermediary: this corrosive exhumation of embalmed and livid accessories is related to early Teutonic acoustic-occultism (Konrad Schnitzler, Kluster, Organisation, early Tangerine Dream, etc.) It's an essential condition for every technological procreation.

COM. SA is impregnated by radiological vibrations and goes beyond the fixed limit of synthetic instruments... like cold osmosis in an obscure room ...

And then *TECHNOLOGY*, a strong mixture of the earlier works with the added sounds of industrial pollution; a fermentation of apathetic and bankrupt note clusters. It's an attempt that seeks psychoanalytic penetration of an illegitimate metabolism, lost between a distressed dimension and lost personality. The health of this work is weak and exhibits the hallucinatory shades of an inhospitable factory covered with grey metal .... *TECHNOLOGY* loads with frost the bleached bones of this terrestrial wasteland, balanced among alchemical experimentation and monastic electronics. M.B. is on the point to confess his worried secret: "Concrete sounds on present grounds!!"

The next dose is lethal...I.B.M.....

Archie Patterson

Pascal Comelade
MAXIMUM MINIMALISM

If one seeks a reference point for the work of Pascal Comelade, it would have to be the styles of Reich or Glass, a couple of the US pioneers of the "new music" school. Yet where their work is often inhabited by an over-abundance of intellectual rigidity, Pascal's experiments are filled with a much more static quality. So while they may be stylistically related, they are in fact quite different spiritually.

His 1st LP, released in 1975, however showed very little of these tendencies as it was markedly different from his later efforts. Titled *FLUENCE* and issued on the French underground label Pole (later reissued on Tapioca), it was a much more cerebral and spacy affair that bore some resemblance to the work of Heldon at that time. Richard Pinhas even had something to do with it as he contributed a bit of guitar.

His works SEQUENCES PAINNES and PARALELO (1978 and 1979 respectively) were much different. SEQUENCES was an EP of short sequencer patterns varying in speed and frequency. One side was done entirely on toy instruments -- piano, sax, etc. -- thus giving it a completely unique atmosphere. PARALELO on the other hand was a much more developed LP. Its several lengthy pieces consisted of multi-layered synthe patterns overlapping in counterpoint that created a surreal blur of sound. It was uncompromising, but fresh and listenable. With these two records his ideas had crystallized, the result being some of the most unique music you'll hear.

Most recently he has issued a couple more EPs that expand even further on both of his previous tendencies. First there's READY-MADE which features an adaptation of a Kevin Ayers theme as well as contribution by David Cunningham (done via post with each one recording their parts in their own respective studios separately), his mate from Montpellier Armand Miralles (of Heratius) and Sissi, an ethereal chanteuse. The music ranges from sequential/spacy electronics to a beautiful duet between toy and acoustic piano. As on the 1st EP he makes exquisite use of his "toy limited orchestra."

His latest project is a collaboration with Armand Miralles again called THE BLACK BOX. A limited edition of 3 copies (priced at 700 ff) it consists of a black label EP that comes in a black box. Inside is a piece of Xerox art, hand-signed, as well as a guitar string and a key from a toy piano. In the true sense of the word it is a collaboration, as Armand's guitar and Pascal's synthetic treatments are equally integral to the sound. The music is harsh, as electronics and a strange oblique guitar style combine in a bizarre melange of sound that lies between the outer limits of Fripp/Eno and early German impressionism. Hopefully it will see a second edition as it's definitely one of the most interesting artifacts to have come out of the French avant-garde scene.

France today is certainly one of Europe's hotbeds of interesting new music and over the span of his 5 works Pascal has developed into one of its most intriguing musicians with work that's adventurous and certainly not your standard synthetic wall paper.

Archie Patterson

Ptose Production Presente

The word Ptose is a medical term that signifies a prolapse of the abdominal organs due to a relaxation of the diaphragm, and the thoracic and abdominal muscles.

It is always tied to the notion of a fall, of a subsidence and of a laxity.

Ptose Production is a group that consist of 2 steady members: Lionel and Benoit, who form the nucleus, the satellite members whose participation is irregular (Ericka Irganon, ZZ...) and the producer John Jean Cabanis.

Lionel and Benoit founded the group on Xmas day in 1979, and made a recording with old damaged instruments, toys and an electric guitar. It had a distribution of

1981

about 20 copies, being sent to friends and correspondents. As it seemed to manifest a certain interest, Ptose Production decided to continue in its activities.

A few concerts were given that horrified the audience who were completely lost, but these concerts allowed the group to meet J.J. Cabanis, who became their producer.

With him Ptose Production recorded a cassette and mini LP. These attracted the attention of Pierre Turmel of Sordid Sentimental, who proposed to publish an extract of the cassette to include in his new magazine *Isolation Intellectuelle*. *WOMEN IN THE MOON* had a distribution of 1100.

The group then associated itself with John J. to form the non-lucrative association of Ptose Production Presente. PPP edited and distributed cassettes of the group and by others. They are only sold through subscription and are limited editions, numbered and in specially designed packages. This formula having gained encouraging success, PPP now distributes moreover compilations and cassettes by other members Les Chats, ZZ....).

All cassettes have been produced by John J. They have been recorded on two cassette machines and one tape recorder, with the aid of a Yamaha CS10 synthesizer, an electric guitar, electric bass, a flageolet, toy piano, various drums and boxes, a children's electric organ, old fashioned piano, some cymbals and a rhythm box.

The members of the group have not had an musical training, be it theoretical or technical.

The tape recorder is indispensable to their activities (musical) and it is considered to be an instrument in its own right. The piece "Zoo In Budapest" for example consists of a series of tape loops.

The group is composed in a very uncertain fashion, through the superimposition of recordings.

The repetitions, the errors and chance all play an important role in the music of PPP.

It is moreover influenced greatly by counting rhymes and childhood songs (nursery rhymes and rhythms) that the members particularly have an affection for. Indeed they do give to the whole thing a puerile and immature air...

Archie Patterson
Translation by Michelle Tuck

Richard Pinhas Interview
DANDY COLD

It is well known outside of France that, here for almost 7 years now, Richard Pinhas while developing a form of elegance as well as one of surprise, has been mounting the crest of the first icy waves of the 1980s.

When you question an American or a Japanese, those a little curious as to what's happening musically outside their countries borders, about the French music scene, it's rare enough to hear talk about groups like Ange, Telephone or Trust. On the other hand, in the same conversation or in the press of these countries the names of Magma, Vander and Pinhas inevitably enter into the picture. There are quite a lot of people who don't wait to hear from France to receive their lessons in rock, these two men (Vander and Pinhas) represent the music of a central hexagon, an original type of music, a specific type, something that exists nowhere else and which is therefore a great treasure in their own eyes.

If one asks himself what has become of Vander and Magma, because of no recent records or concerts, it isn't the same of Pinhas, who on the average presents one or two albums, always bursting with originality, always shaking up this progressive fever which works in the most beautiful fashion to "Plunge the depths of the deepest ravine, to the depths of the unknown to find the new," as Baudelaire had said. Nonetheless, there is a surprising contrast between the unreserved praise that one reads in respect to Pinhas in the Japanese press or more recently, on a full page in the U.K. paper Sounds and the admitted importance of Pinhas given by France.

One knows quite well that a person isn't accepted a prophet in their own country. Here someone who has unquestionably marked the entire past decade, someone considered to be an equal to people as highly esteemed as Fripp, Eno, Vangelis, Schulze, Kraftwerk and Tangerine Dream, all friends of this man and more than just admirers of his work, someone who sells with each album more copies per disque than the quasi-majority of groups in France, someone who hasn't finished and who never will finish shaking out musical material which gives life to future sounds. This someone collides with the incomprehension and the prohibitions, with the hostility of French record labels each time he wants to release a record.

It's true that Pinhas is miserly in regards to his appearances, that his concerts with Heldon are very rare indeed and that many have asked who is this enigmatic personage who slides around with the unobtrusiveness of a ghost in our midst all the while showing us regularly that he is capable of delivering the "safest traumas" of creation.

Perhaps weary of seeing his fans doubt his existence he decided in 1980 to show them he is alive and well. Following his brilliant *ICELAND*, he released the *EAST/WEST* LP which launched a grand tour. In fact, things move around him, he renounced the Heldon name in order to pursue a solo career, and in England, which is just now discovering him, suddenly gave him the warmest of welcomes. *ICELAND* has been sitting on the Eurorock charts there for weeks. This enthusiasm of the English has started to bring about doubt towards France, where the welcome by the record labels was as if they were giving shelter to a terrorist. It would seem his music created fear disturbance.

People often heard it on T.V. as background music, but it was often taken to be the music of Vangelis or Schulze, but it was Pinhas all along, as proof that he isn't all that barbaric. Besides our man used to be a bit of a dandy. He pulled his mocking elegance into the milieu of the French Progressives, and offered his patronage to whoever needed it. Rather than seeking publicity, he isolated himself in a metal tower in order to deepen his understanding of modern technology, lest it be said like an old driven philosopher to leaf through the works of Hegel or Kant. Pinhas saved all of his energies for the things he thought to be really worth the trouble, from this secluded vantage point, ghostlike in character.

But I know that those who really advance in music, like Bowie, Gabriel, Fripp or Eno are also quite phantom-like and reclusive. The music of innovation is a difficult form which claims as its victims all those who are dedicated to it, it isn't a question of wasting one's energies in buffoonery. For those who make their profession out of just clowning around, rock is ideal, and the buffoonery of these groups is really a form of harshness. If one aims for originality as Pinhas, it is necessary to resolve to reduce one's sense of heroism in order to achieve the subtle demands of his art. It is a simple question of choice.

But that doesn't imply that we don't speak about those who don't have the time to get themselves talked about. As we went as far as to really question this singular dandy just before his new departure on the sinuous road of avant-garde music.

H.P.: You are one of those who has undergone all of the different metamorphoses of rock here, since the end of the '60s to the present revival. You have been present all through the '70s, what with Heldon, Schizo, and in solo.

How do you fit into this movement?

R.P.: Yes, I am familiar with all these things (laughter), but I still feel young enough, but don't fear, young enough to make rock if I so desire, because I will always have such a desire towards music. Well, I started music seriously after my Bac in '68, I was familiar with a few groups up to '71, notably with Klaus Blasquiz, then I found that what I was doing with rock wasn't musically satisfying. Therefore I stopped everything in order to think, to reflect upon another possible type of music, that which I realized with Heldon I in '73. I did this disque on two Revoxes as a creating instrument, at my place, when at the same moment Fripp and Eno were developing on their side the same technique. At the end of '73 I left for London with my tapes under my am as well as some recordings of French rock from my friends, and I went to Island Records where I am received by the then-boss, Muff Winwood, Stevie's brother. He listens to the tapes of the French rock and says, "So, what's new about that?," an attitude that the English continually have toward French rock save for some rare exceptions. He then listens to my tape, and something unbelievable on his part, he remained under his headphones for 40 minutes listening to the entire tape, something he did only rarely. He was completely speechless. He found himself to be in front of something that was a type of music of which he never had the suspicion of existing. He didn't understand. He asked me to come back a little later, but in the meantime, weary of seeing all the French labels refuse our music, (and this will be the leitmotiv for the whole decade) my friends and I marketed our own records ourselves on the Disjuncta label, totally autonomous. Heldon I was released in '74 the same time Muff Winwood released the first Fripp and Eno. I really don't believe that this was just a coincidence, it caused a musical revolution in '73-74 of the same level I attained with Heldon I. I felt very strongly that for two years people showered praise upon Eno while making him one of the few key personages of the '80s. It is absolutely true, he was able to sell the '80s in 1973. It was time to recognize that Eno is effectively a genius. Well, during this time our cooperative system offered disques at a price that was unbeatable. Known to be a real success, this annoyed us because we were now spending all of our time selling records, along with making up the packaging, and the accounting, we had no more time to create music. This explains why we had to stop Disjuncta and this form self-management. We really stopped it because in fact everything went too well!

H.P.: This choice, was it due to the state of rock in France at this time?

R.P.: Entirely. We were finally at the end of the wave of groups like Triangle, who had marked the end of the '60s. Les Variations, the only really important group had just broken up. This was the ebb, the agony of a certain style. The French record companies didn't want anything more to do with groups like that, and failed to understand anything about the others. The context of things in '68 invited a way of playing on the fringe of things. Disjuncta was really a form of marketing which corresponded well to this era, typically to those who were the result of a reduced importance of French music. We did this because we couldn't do otherwise, but also because it pleased us to get out of the classical business totally inefficacious. Since electronic music was in full bloom in '73-74, we didn't risk anything by building new-upon-new, on the contrary. Up until '76, I had continued to practise music in a craft-like form, which evidently tightened the technical quality of the recordings of Heldon II and III. From '76 I put myself in the hands of the most important labels in order to take care of the presentation of music, the newness no longer being, at length, a sufficient argument. It is in this period that Heldon took on a more solid character with François Auger, Didier Batard, and Patrick Gauthier. With them the records became more serious, more solid, and out of this came *UN REVE SANS CONSEQUENCE SPECIALE*, which was a turning point. From this Heldon drew up the first outlines of industrial music and the cold wave, by which the German and Americans came to identify us. We had been the first with a very hard mechanistic style. The first to bring in synthesizers, which up until then had been reserved for a subdued enough usage and violent rhythms. This was a grand return to rock, while at the same time transcending it.

H.P.: Up until the massive revival of rock in France, you were in the margins because record labels were very careful about those who came from here, especially in regards to yourself. But right away, things really changed, and we have a new French phenomenon, actually quite classically commercialized. Nevertheless, in spite of this, you still remain in the margins.

R.P.: In the beginning I opted for marginality because of my political activities, since then I have denounced them, they were always pushing me into a struggle with institutions, whatever they might be, even musical. I abandoned this way of thinking, this marginality at all costs. It doesn't remain any less true that I create a music that is aimed at a small audience. This is not out of an elitist desire. I create the music as it comes into my head, even if I know that it won't be received by a great following. It's the same if you write a book of philosophy or experimental mathematics, you are aiming for a certain minority. Research in all fields is always on the aristocratic side of things. I situated myself on the same line as someone like Fripp, who experiments in a field of precise musical experiences, which in fact could be better, if he could transmit the results to the public. Rare are those like Bowie, who succeed in giving a popular aspect to this particular art form. If I had to choose between this music which places me on the margin and working for the acquisition of the favors of a great following, while aiming at the lowest common denominator, I would in the long run choose marginality. I feel deeply that music must always be searching for a new statement to make, novelty and not remain comfortable in the same vein. This is not a value judgment on groups who are effectively reproducing what is old in rock. It's my choice. But aside from that, I must say that French record labels are for the most part, lamentable. That certain, like CBS, are parvenus when it comes to making some groups known, I find miraculous. For the most part it's due to incompetence. Imagine that Polydor, for example, organizes a forum about me at the FNAC, the usual promotional operation without any hang-ups and the people from the record company were not only not there, but didn't provide promo copies of the record. That shows you what I mean. I'm not talking about labels who sign groups and do no promotional work, or make only a pressing of 500 to satisfy their contracts. I'm specifically talking of the larger companies. It is obvious that on account of that, one can only remain in the margins.

H.P.: What is or has been, actually since the start of the '70s, really seems that apart from you and Magma, all of the French groups have hardly been able to gain recognition outside of France. Yet you find yourself to be considered marginal in France, while being well appreciated outside of the country. A strange situation.

R.P.: At the start of the '70s, the groups were so bad that people would have shown extreme bad taste by liking them. Actually the situation is the same in spite of a superior quality. I'm not saying that there was a miracle in France. In my opinion, in France one can count on the fingers of one hand the groups who have breathed new life into the old styles in order to create something new from them. People outside of France sense this very well. At this time I had traveled a lot in England and to the USA and I only heard talk of just one group, Marquis de Sade. Except for them the specialty press joked about the rest, only attaching interest to Magma, to Atoll (in Japan) and to myself and Heldon. I feel Trust should have succeeded in making a name for itself outside of France, because something was happening with that group, I saw it notably before I saw AC/DC and it released my feelings more than the Australians did. I say that without judgment of taste, hard rock being one type of music that doesn't interest me. But in the absolute Trust produced something fresh. I think Heldon and Magma are the only groups recognized outside France because they are the only ones within their sphere to create new music, something original. Except them, the creation of something new has always been left to those outside France and the French have always been content to just follow. It is normal then that one makes little fanfare about them. I really think that a musician must look to find for himself something more than just repeating music that is 10 years old or older. That's my conception and the reaction of people outside of France shows that I'm not completely wrong and that this opinion which is held by people like Bowie and Gabriel backs me up rather well.

H.P.: In these last few years we have seen you take part in more things aside from Heldon and solo efforts, work on a certain number of albums, often progressive, notably those of Goude, Grunblatt, Odeurs, Ose... What does this progressive annex represent to you? Is it out of a type of patronage, or is it something else?

R.P.: My problem isn't being able to earn colossal sums in order to afford the most beautiful cars and women in the world. I really was fond of participating under a title of impartiality in French things that are progressive, simply in order to add a bit of my own experience: With the released record, I find that to be very interesting, but which had been assassinated by the "show-biz." This year, I worked equally with two examples of this, the first was with a group called Video Liszt, which is composed of two young French musicians who play synths and computers in a style that is fresh and new. They released an LP and I helped them develop their technological structure. They invited me to play guitar and I was very happy to help. I also produced a solo LP by Patrick Gauthier with the best French musicians around: Paganotti, Widemann, Vander. It took me three years to convince Gauthier to make this album. He proved with Heldon and then Weidorje that he is of the highest caliber, but he is too humble to make a name for himself. So I had to push him. I love to implicate myself in this genre of experience, where there is so much respect, vis-a-vis concerned musicians, a shared interest of the most intellectual or artistic, towards a musical path. Then, just like that, we form a body, we take a sense of pleasure rather than of disappointment in being a minority.

H.P.: And where is Pinhas in 1980?

R.P.: First, there was *EAST/WEST*, which was a solo LP. The structure of Heldon became too heavy to move, that's why we gave so few concerts. So I renounced it, perhaps for the time being, I don't know, so now I will play some concerts. Also on the album are my Heldon friends François Auger, Didier Batard, Patrick Gauthier, but also the American sci-fi writer Norman Spinrad who does treated vocals.

H.P.: Your musical perspective seems to be less rebellious, less virulent than before with Heldon. Will this reopen some doors of the institutions?

R.P.: I don't think so. The reaction of the French labels is the same as its been for the last 10 years. That's why I prefer England. I don't particularly care if I sell in France. My records are sold all over the world. Moreover, I don't have commercial demands or demands of the masses. My task is to take a certain type of music the farthest I am able to. I'd rather my records are appreciated by only a few like Fripp, Norman Spinrad, Kraftwerk, my girlfriend and so on than a crowd of listeners. I don't live for those people or make music for them and happily I'm not dependent upon them. I don't create to sell, but instead for the sake of creating. At my level I proceed for my own education, to attain a certain level of satisfaction in a circle of people, perhaps a bit exclusive, but who really understand me and adhere to my way of thinking. It's true, I am very aristocratic. It is evident that some, like Bowie or Gabriel can synthesize a great popular success with this sort of outlook. But these are exceptional cases. We saw all the troubles Gabriel had with Atlantic and his limitations. Good, it is certain that the power of marketing in show-business is such that they can sell anything in great quantity, even the quality of music. Commerce knows how to sell soap to someone who doesn't want to wash. I don't want to be sold like soap. I doubt that avant-garde music can leave its status of an exclusive exiguity. It tries to raise its level & the practice of being popular will debase it. I demand an exclusive status, it is true, for I create an aristocratic music. To each his function. It doesn't bother me to be part of a minority. It's a question of honesty in regards to oneself: to accept the task your deepest choices impose upon you. Mine is to advance musically. There is effectively a type of ethics attached to this pursuit. I find that the true musical honesty, that which is not content with just repetition is thus a part of the more mature creators, people around 30 like Bowie, Gabriel, Fripp, Eno or myself, who understand the functions of show-biz and who take the time to disassociate themselves from it. When the younger groups discover this world and have struggled in it to handle carefully their sense of honesty in this milieu, and to develop a feeling of humility vis-a-vis their music, they are snatched up by a system and only look for a pop star image. When they can learn to deal with this process and come finally to a point of only doing their music, then they may become aristocrats.

Collected Words By Herve Picart
Reprinted From BEST Magazine
Translation by Michelle Tuck

Magma Interview

NAMES: Stella and Christian Vander
OCCUPATION: Singer and manager; compose and patron of the most formidable French music enterprise since....

C.V.: As concerns music in France, everyone intellectualizes everything. They are sensitive to poetry, to literature, but not to sound. I give this example, if you go to see "Le Roi et l'Oiseau," a beautiful film, beautiful text, beautiful images.. there is a door that is 200 meters tall that closes with a bang! For me, I look at the door and it doesn't do anything for me, I want to hear it, not to imagine the sound it makes closing.

R&F: *RETROSPECTIVE* is subtitled *VOL.3*. Why?

C.V.: There are several reasons. First *VOL.3* clearly allows one to hear what's remaining from 1 & 2 that is yet to come or that has come already. Tactically, I think it's more effective. Besides, *VOL.3* and what is sketched there is what we recorded with the last group. Therefore, it is chronologically logical. "Theusz Hamtaahk" represents Vol.1 & 2, the series is complete.

R&F: When will it be ready?

C.V.: It already is. The last section is mixed and cut and must be released in the form of a double LP soon: 2 sides for *MEKANIK DESTRUKTIW KÖMMANDÖH* and 2 for the first part of "Theusz Hamtaahk."

R&F: The real group belongs to which phase?

C.V.: The beginning of the second. There are the Guillard brothers on brass, Benoit Widemann and Guy Khalifa on keyboards, Dominique Bertram on bass, Jean-Luc Chevalier on guitar, Stella and Liza singing, and Doudou Weisse as second drummer.

R&F: And therefore more of Klaus than

1981

the first time?

C.V.: No, in fact, there had been a question of it for a long time already. There had even been a question that he might not do *RETROSPECTIVE*.

S.V.: He had loads of grievances and demands that we weren't successful in working out.

C.V.: In fact, and he said it himself, so I can say it, he wanted to be THE lead singer on the front stage with the spotlight on him. I had nothing against it, but it is something you must assume all the way. Our work was complicated by his attitude. And finally, I must say, it was he who said that he didn't want to be on the album jacket.

S.V.: That's saying that he has since changed his position: it was him who sang on Vols. 1 and 2, and who is in the credits.

R&F: From a business aspect, what has happened since *ATTAHK*?

S.V.: For the first time we are free. We produced the entire *RETROSPECTIVE* by ourselves. That seems to be the only solution, as for a year we sought a record company. In vain...

R&F: How is that possible? Perhaps you were too picky?

S.V.: No, not at all. We made a tour of the record companies with quite modest demands at the time when they were looking for Trust or Telephone. We went to RCA and said: "We at any rate have finished this project, we mixed the tapes and hand it all over to you, you then can have it to release. We don't ask anything of you." That's how we signed up for three volumes.

R&F: What happened after *RETROSPECTIVE*?

C.V.: We attacked a new cycle. Phase 2, not only for a musical plan, we reformed Univeria Zekt, as a label and as a reinforced form of Magma.

R&F: That means you are going to take charge of things that are extra-musical?

C.V.: Yes, to the last detail.

S.V.: *RETROSPECTIVE* is just a first attempt in this domain, a kind of apprenticeship: all of it was done very quickly.

R&F: It is you Stella, that assumes this aspect of the work?

S.V.: Principally, until we can find someone else to do it.

R&F: This situation, did you seek it or do you just submit to it out of the force of things?

C.V.: Both. Let's say that we sought this autonomy, but it's necessary to have brought together the rather negative circumstances for us to dare throw ourselves into the water.

330, Eurock: European Rock & the Second Culture

R&F: And musically?

C.V.: Since *KÖHNTARKÖSZ*, I needed to reflect upon a new music. The music of Magma is music that needs a point, therefore it's necessary to search, to try, and to transform. Each record must be a contribution to it's evolution. You work on things for months, then you cut a recording if what you have been working on warrants the effort. There are tens of pieces by Magma that haven't been recorded...

R&F: The music in its conception, is it dependent on the group?

C.V.: Never. Let's say there is a problem of recruitment in the measure where the qualities required to play with Magma are multiple. It's necessary to have the sensitivity and the fingering techniques of a classical musician, on the other hand, it's necessary to know how to play the blues; rhythm and blues and to have already made the synthesis.

R&F: You seem very frustrated with the actual music...

C.V.: There isn't a cry in any music today. Or if there is, the cry flies very low. When I was 12 years old I was at that point. That's why Coltrane was of such an importance for me. Ray Charles also wanted to go as high. Hendrix too, but they didn't succeed. Coltrane in himself possessed all of that: Hendrix and Otis Redding, all of what you want. The cry is more than one universal dimension, all of the cries. The proof is that any music today is full of clichés that are the phrases of Coltrane. You know, I read an anecdote recently which concerned him. In a club once, he did an improvisation on "Impressions" that lasted 2-1/2 hours, during which he burst some of the blood vessels in his face, he had a bloody nose and mouth. For 2-1/2 hours!!

R&F: However what more clearly transpired in your music is the slave influence. *MEKANIK* for example, seems to come directly from "Noces" by Stravinsky.

C.V.: There are two reasons for that. First it's to understand, to live Coltrane to the point of being able to cite from the spirit of his work and not just the letter. It is a discipline which we applied ourselves to, little by little in Phase 2. As concerns "Noces," I will say one thing, at the time of *MEKANIK* I had not heard them. It was Faton who offered me the record, in the meantime, I had already composed the piece. This says that folklore is folklore; this rhythm is essentially slave-influenced and in the event that someone still isn't aware of it, I'm not exactly French. I say it because I am fiercely honest, it's a brief citation in the intro of *MEKANIK DESTRUKTIW* which is an introduction to a piece by Carl Orff, "Triomph di Aphrodite."

R&F: In the critique of *RETROSPECTIVE* I drew some reservations towards your compositions which often, on a melodic level in particular, leave me hungry.

C.V.: But you have also noted that has changed. In fact you have children who know how to talk before they know how to use a spoon. For others it's the inverse. For myself, I need to search for the rhythmic plans to purify my work. Before, I used to look for a pretty melody and I didn't always know how to support it in order for it to turn out.

R&F: The first accomplishment in this domain was "Hhaï."

C.V.: Yes because the purely melodic aspect started to preoccupy me, whereas beforehand it was quite the secondary: in "Riak Sahiltaak" (*1001° CENTIGRADES*), there was 5 or 6 times the material of "Hhaï." But in fact, for 17 years you had a bit of baggage that you frenetically stagger over, with that you don't serve the music.

After, you chose the blows. You purge: of something which could have lasted 20 minutes, you can succeed in making a 7-minute piece that hits very strongly. It's a little like what I did with "Otis," a new piece dedicated to Otis Redding, and is a result of 10 years of apprenticeship. Magma for me is an apprenticeship. Look at Coltrane, he only really became himself when he was 33 years old.

Jean-Marc Bailleux
Reprinted From ROCK & FOLK
Translation by Michelle Tuck

Yochk'o Seffer Interview

NAME: Yochk'o Seffer
BORN: 10 July 1939 Miskolc, Hungary
OCCUPATION: Composer, saxophonist, and pianist
COMMENTARY: One of the most original personalities in new European music. An epiphenomenon in avant-garde jazz, European rock, Central European folklore and contemporary European music from Bartok to Penderecki, as well as Messiaen.

Y.S.: I only left ZAO for musical reasons. Faton continued for some time, I left in order to do what I wanted to do. I got into Neffesh Music (Neffesh is the bestial side, the mundane of the soul, that works on us from day to day) with François Laizeau and Dominique Bertram and the Marquand Quartet. This experience lasted 3 years, but it was too expensive, I decided to put a stop to it. Not to the idea of Neffesh Music, because the idea behind that is completely myself, but to the group in so much as a permanent formation to the profit of isolated experiences, musical events.

R&F: The advent of Neffesh Music corresponded with your contact with Moshe-Naim. Did that turn out poorly?

Y.S.: More or less. It's thanks to Moshe that I could make *IMA* and *DELIRE*. But it was hard to maintain a record company. The worst is that the people who are the most sensitive, the most imaginative, the most humanely rich, are the least able to manage themselves, to organize. They forget reality. Now what a producer expects from an artist is that his feet are on the ground, that he counterbalances his artistic madness to allow him to express himself fully. In fact, I don't even know if Moshe-Naim went bankrupt or not, all that I know is that he recorded what is among the most beautiful work that I have ever made and never released it. The third record that I recorded with Neffesh Music I did with a Hungarian violinist who was fabulous, Howard Layos, has remained in a drawer, Moshe-Naim having disappeared. Georges Leton who was my manager has since decided to release in co-production with me the record *GHILGOUL* . I would want *GHILGOUL* to be re-released because it is a super album that hasn't yet aged. In fact, in 10 years time I haven't made any music that relates to that mode, there are always some people to discover what I am doing today.

R&F: And since the dissolution of the group?

Y.S.: I organized myself and started to realize all of the projects that I cared about. Having decided to do only limited things, I can go farther, I have some projects with a group of 10 musicians, with a large orchestra, with a chamber orchestra. I want Neffesh Music to become the impulse of a bunch of different and original things, because I am above all a composer. Composition is for me dearer than the saxophone. At last I realize that from B flat to D sharp, when you cut that in all the senses, or really hit your head on the floor or really go on to something else. The other thing for me right now is the creation.

R&F: And the piano, you're using it more and more?

Y.S.: I am not a marvelous piano player. What interests me with the piano is that it's one time music on paper, fixed and rigid, the piano gives it life and breath while improvising in a very controlled fashion. I would be able to make my pianist friends play a part, but in spite of their grand pianistic capacities they would not be able to give the same effect. My role as a pianist is to add the coloration to what is already written.

R&F: Is that to say that what's written is insufficient?

Y.S.: No, it's a matter of two different musics. I am capable of writing music that doesn't have to have any fly specks added. I just had my sonata for saxophone played at the Festival of Chaumont, it's called "Szerkeze," which means interlocking, and that's the genre of architecture where there is nothing to add. This is in general the role of writing, only a posteriori, in some cases, you can modify the function of what is written while coloring it through improvisation. At the piano I make something that's rigid swing. Improvisation is a way among the others in order to achieve this goal of "feeling."

R&F: You seem to have no longer restricted your action to only one activity...

Y.S.: I want to multiply the occasions of playing with other musicians and to have my music played in different contexts; I have already made *ETHNIC DUO* with Faton and that really pleased me. We will make an Ethnic Trio with two pianos and the percussionist François Causse. And in the meantime, I am developing Neffesh Music into some new directions; three or four manifestations in the year, but which will appear as veritable musical events. The first will take place at the Jazz Unite, Gerard Terrones' place, he produced *ETHNIC DUO* with Faton and is a guy who gets high from the music, working for 10 years from Gil's club to the super club, La Defense. We played a week (from June

1981

22-27) with a group of 10 musicians, more than Faton who would come to jam. There will be a great party of musicians who have gone through Neffesh: Michel Nich - violin, Laurent Cockelare and Dominique Bertram on the bass, François Causse and François Laizeau on percussion. We will play some new compositions and also "Dag," "Sifra" and "Ghilgoul," where in the place of the string quartet there will be a wind quintet. More than this purely musical part, there is a show prepared by a painter/photographer friend, with 600 photos of his and my paintings -- Yvan le Marlec, who's a theatre and image fanatic. There is Jacqueline Cahen (Faton's wife), Sylvie Lockwood (Didier's wife) and a third narrator who reads poems by Jacqueline, a poetess who is unrecognized but very appreciated by the American avant-garde. And with *IMA* there is a dancer, Christine Couti, at the same time improvising a pantomime that symbolizes the passage from death to resurrection. In fact, I connect *IMA* and *GHILGOUL*, and for half an hour there is a sort of total spectacle with dance, mime, lights and music. For the remainder, there will be music that's specially prepared for this presentation. In truth, it's hard to describe and must be seen.

R&F: Is it this attachment to the visualization, to painting, that has given you the idea of "Chromophonie"?

Y.S.: You know, I did Fine Arts, I did a lot of work as a painter. I have 200 canvases that I put on exhibition while playing the saxophone. It's called "Chromophonic" (chrome=the color, phonos=the sound). Today it's something that I want to develop through a catalog of records. I am at the age where I must preoccupy myself with establishing things that are solid and that last; I no longer want to make records which quickly become unavailable. "Chromophonie" is a series of 10 records in which I will present all of the different voices of my music as well as my paintings. The first record released will be called *LE LIVRE DE BAHIR*. It's a solo album where I play several parts for piano and sax with the Marquand Quartet on a few pieces. Finally, there will be some concert records with different groups, a record with Layos and even some classical things.

R&F: Why precisely 10?

Y.S.: Because 10 is a number of the Kabala. In the Kabala the number for Yochk'o Seffer is 1, that's "Aleph," the start, the 0 is infinity, God. From the importance of 10 for me, 1 and 0, comes "Chromophonie," the 10 records that represent me completely.

Jean-Marc Bailleux
Reprinted From ROCK & FOLK
Translation by Michelle Tuck

HISTORY...An Interview With K. Leimer

Kerry Leimer was born July 28, 1954 in Winnipeg, Manitoba to Austrian parents. Moving in 1956 to Chicago and in 1967 to Seattle, Leimer studied graphic design at Burnley School of Professional Art. He has since worked as an illustrator, a graphic designer, an art director and most recently as head of his own design firm.

S: There seem to be quite a few visual artists making records these days -- Devo, Talking Heads, Brian Eno, Wire, and all. Why do you think this is?

L: The thing about visual arts that has become the most important is structure. The problem with expressing structure visually, in painting and drawing, is that these don't take place in any kind of time frame. The activity of the drawing or painting does, certainly, but the perception does not. In music, however, perception DOES take place in a particular time frame, in "real-time."

S: And how does this relate to music and musical structures?

L: Design considerations encourage a certain "playing around" with the pieces. If you take that attitude, which is a little different than normally encountered in the field of music, you get in the habit of assembling things, not necessarily with the intention of creating a finished product, but taking different parts that might or might not relate. You develop a sort of objective view of the process in this way -- not seeing the whole, but seeing the way in which the parts fit together and relate to each other. In visual arts, there is nothing sacred about the assembling process. In many instances, you set up possibilities, let them run their course, and see if they work out. The emphasis is different, it's on the front end, the process, rather than the result.

S: So the graphics on the cover of your LP *CLOSED SYSTEM POTENTIALS* are also tied in with the structures operating in the music?

L: Certainly. The style of the cover is mean to introduce the listener to some aspects of the music. The five little objects on the cover -- a caliper, a glove, a map, an origami bird, and a flower -- all relate to each other.

S: How is that?

L: They all show expression of mentality. An expression man projects on nature. They are interpretations of functions and the all contain cultural bias in their expression. The connections between them are not so much based on their function or configuration as they are on that interpretive process man uses to perceive the world of which he is part. It's a false notion to view anything as a completed product. The idea that any process completely stops is untrue. The whole process of creating and perceiving is dependent on personal experience, or prior expectations, on the environment in which the piece is perceived. If we're just talking about *CLOSED SYSTEM POTENTIALS*, obviously the thing I had to deal with is that interpretation is going to be a very big factor in how the work is perceived. I purposely left a great many things unresolved, so that there's a flexibility in the work, so that interpretation becomes a very attractive part of the process.

S: How is *CLOSED SYSTEM* supposed to operate in a musical context?

L: Well, there has been an awful lot of press lately about "ambient" music, about music that's been designed to be ignored. I didn't want to go into any of these gratuitous distinctions in the liner notes but people use all sorts of music for background - rock, classical, jazz, anything at all. Whether or not they function well in an environment of neglect is really beside the point, because people do use them for background, and the composer might just as well get used to it.

1981

S: So was *CLOSED SYSTEM* consciously ambient?

L: It is if you listen to it on that level. The distinction, as I just said, is really more of a cultural distinction than a description of the music. Music nowadays is making a kind of shift, where it is alright to compose music for background application. *CLOSED SYSTEM* will demand some re-evaluations by the listener if he chooses to listen carefully to it -- like I mentioned before trying to make connections, to draw associations between the various elements. I mean the mental attitude expressed in the album is going to be a far cry from the "catchy tunes" of AM radio, and if someone is attracted to it on this basis he's going to have to figure out what's going on. But of course not everyone will have this level of involvement, and one of the things I tried to keep in mind when recording the record was that listener's perceptions of the music would quite naturally be very different from my own.

S: *CLOSED SYSTEM POTENTIALS* is the first release on your new label Palace of Lights. What other projects are in the works?

L: No, actually it's the second release. I put out a single last year, a limited edition of 300 copies. As for the future, the key word will be diversification. We want to establish a coherent front for the popular arts, exposing a number of people who are working in a variety of areas, but with similar results. The overlap should prove interesting, and explain a bit about the new music theories being developed. These theories aren't particularly scholarly always, or even necessarily very musical. The point is that the coherence of all these diverse theories is an interesting convergence, a marking of a new era in the arts.

S: How about some particulars?

L: We have the release by Marc Barreca, *TWILIGHT*. We're working on releases by Savant, a sort of rock version of *CLOSED SYSTEM POTENTIALS*; and an Olympia contemporary classical composer named Steven Peters. There are some other possibilities in the wings. Together they should provide a fairly good overview of what's being done in this area... The important thing now is to get it out, to make the material available, to begin the habit of sharing what's going on in a public marketplace. We're part of the general cultural trend, like I mentioned earlier, where these sorts of experiments are becoming more accepted. By making this material available we're joining in the movement, becoming part of the cultural shift, participating in the age in which we live. I think this is preferable to almost any other alternative.

R.G. Carlberg
Excerpted from SYNEX

David Sinfield Interview

When in Los Angeles, it is said do what the Angelinos do. Not so for one David Sinfield, musician and producer, who it seems attempts to do things in a manner very uncommon to his peers. In this interview, David speaks of his ideas in both the creative end of things in the business and of his future and present projects.

Q: A good place to start would be, what is your understanding of music within an industry, and what does it have to do with your own work?

A: That is a good one. Music, or any art form for that matter, should be treated as such, and not used as a vehicle for the achievement of the dollar. If it happens, fine. But it seems to me that too many latch onto trends and dress the part because it's chic. In the long run, I think they suffer. I really don't care if I don't make Top of the Pops just so long as I may continue to do things as I feel.

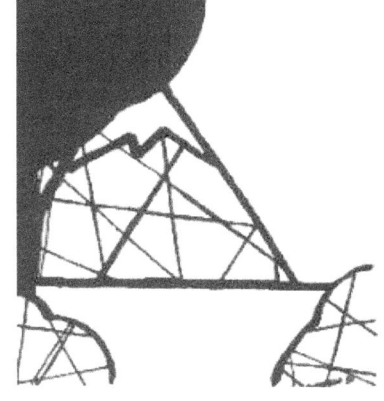

Q: So you feel that the business restricts a person's creativity?

A: Well, at least I know it would mine.

Q: Do you look at the commercial attitude as being damaging?

A: It depends on the person and who's in control; the situation at hand or you.

Q: Do you keep in touch with the musical situation around you?

A: I try. I used to listen to the radio a lot, but now since things in that area are so restrictive, I spend more time with tapes. I would go to clubs, but there's really not anything I would like to see.

Q: What would you like to see happen and who would you cite as an influence?

A: I'd like to see more avant-garde solo artists become active. Get some exposure. And as for influence, if I you had 20 minutes I'd name them all. Mainly people like Eno, John Cale, Fripp, King Crimson, etc.

Q: You'd like to see the "Frippertronics"-type thing become more acceptable?

A: Yeah, that type of thing. Totally against a set market. Fripp has guts to do that. So does Eno. People like Kraftwerk don't have to worry because they have the Top 10 success thing going now.

Q: A bias question. How do you think the public will react to your music?

A: I hope with favor. But I suppose I'll have my audience.

Q: After *OBLIQUE STRATEGIES*, do you have any other projects in the wings?

A: Definitely, I'm doing another work towards the end of summer, and also I'm playing synthesizer for an upcoming Laurie Jean record. All in all, hopefully I'll stay busy.

Q: Would you like to collaborate with other musicians in the future?

A: Sure, I'm always open to the idea. I'll try something with anyone that I'm compatible with on some level, from instrumentalist to producer.

Q: Will your next work be similar to what you've already done?

A: Yes and no. The second recording will be rock mixed with ambiance, and available on an EP-length cassette. It will have possibilities I think. The second one after that will be titled *ROUGH TRADE* and be totally different. Very concise and heavy, with greater emphasis on rhythm structures. Very Eastern/Balkan sounding.

I think it'll work out fine. I've even brought in others to help with it. Laurie Jean (the drummer) comes up with some fantastic ideas for the rhythm basics. There will be strings with various percussives and such. It'll be a much more involved work.

Q: Do you plan to perform live to support the recorded work?

A: I've been trying to work something out in that respect. It will be more of a presentation than a concert. There will be continuous films and such to accent the music. We may even record it. But probably not until *ROUGH TRADE* is finished, maybe a bit before.

Q: Something along the lines of a multimedia event?

A: Right, I think film, art and music can go hand and hand to bring a point across.

Q: What point is that?

A: That unconventional ideas can be presented to a mass audience on one's own terms and be accepted.

Q: Who will you be working with next?

A: Laurie Jean and her recording. With the making of the films and two other recordings time will be full, but I am always open to others. I'd like to see everyone with a different idea get a chance somewhere. I'm sure they'll all do it eventually, you just have to stay with it. One can only achieve success on both economic and personal terms and truly be happy when you are doing what YOU want to do. At that point, everything will fit into place rather nicely.

Archie Patterson

Klaus Schulze Interview

In the 1980s Klaus Schulze remains one of the world's pioneers in synthetic music, a music that for the most part, comes out of the experiences of the Berlin School, in which he was one of the driving forces during the '70s; a pioneer because contrary to many musicians who are content to live off of experiences that give rise to repetitiveness, which isn't only boring for themselves, but for their audiences as well, Klaus has always sought a distant path while following in the footsteps of those artists who are really authentic, who seek to surpass themselves; to go deeper into the frenzy and into the innovative, vis-à-vis the musical plan; to go farther in the exploitation of the most advanced technology is what drives him, as we shall see in the following interview, to use the computer in order to enlarge his field of action.

THE CRAZIES OF BERLIN
L'AUTRE MONDE: Who is Klaus Schulze?

KLAUS SCHULZE: That's a question that I'm often asked... a German who is obsessed with technology... who doesn't talk much but who does a lot...or who talks a lot but does nothing ...It depends. Getting right down to it, I must tell you frankly that I detest feebleminded interviews where they ask you: "What's your name? Your age? What type of women do you prefer? How many do you have?"

A.M.: Alright ... How about telling us a bit about your history? When did it all start?

K.S.: If one goes back to the official beginnings, it was with the group Tangerine Dream. We made our first LP *ELECTRONIC MEDITATION* in 1969.

A.M.: Why the title *ELECTRONIC MEDITATION*?

K.S.: The idea of meditation was for us a way of making a clean break from the current standards. In fact, it's not possible to meditate while listening to this totally chaotic music. We just wanted to remove ourselves from rock...

A.M.: Were you really creating a different kind of music?

K.S.: I believe so. For a long time we were nicknamed "The Crazies of Berlin" -- at that time, Tangerine Dream wasn't copying anyone, contrary to the majority of German groups then.

A.M.: Were you already playing synthesizer in 1969?

K.S.: No, I used to be the drummer. It was later on that I fell in love with electronics. I left the group in order to form Ash Ra Tempel...

A.M.: Where did the idea for the name come from?

K.S.: The idea of uniting 3 things: Ash which symbolizes the end of something, Ra which means the Sun, thus the start of a new cycle, a rebirth and Tempel because that's the place where everything takes place.

A.M.: Did you take part in the album *SEVEN-UP* that the group recorded with Timothy Leary?

K.S.: I was still with them, but I refused to play on this record in any great part because of Leary: his reputation as a "dealer" had already been well established and I had no desire to promote him. This said, he was extraordinary and his research with LSD and psychedelic drugs for the exploration of the human mind has been fundamental. When the whole thing became a "business" I said no.

A.M.: Were you taking LSD at this time?

K.S.: Yes, mostly from the years '67-'68 until 1970. At the start of Tangerine Dream. Everything was good. Except hard drugs, which I never touched... too dangerous.

A.M.: Have all the groups you've been a part of been successful?

1981

K.S.: Not commercially. We used to be very "underground," even if we were the roots of German music. We used to think that Berlin was the center of the world and we didn't even imagine that other countries would be interested in us. Later, when things went better we were copied by the entire world.

A.M.: Which musicians influenced you? Do you know Terry Riley?

K.S.: No, Riley, I only discovered and appreciated him much later on. On the other hand, I really like Hawkwind, an English group that's really in touch with science-fiction. Evidently, I used to listen to Pink Floyd.

A.M.: When did you first go solo?

K.S.: In 1972. It took so much energy to work out the human relationships in Ash Ra that we didn't have any left to create music. Then I went from the drums to the synthesizer and recorded *IRRLICHT* three weeks after discovering the keyboard.

A.M.: What does *IRRLICHT* mean?

K.S.: It's really hard to translate -- "will o' the wisp?" -- imagine the early morning, you see a light and you decide to follow it; at the moment you seem to catch up to it, you realize that it never existed. It's a very lyrical expression. "Irr" means fool (crazy) and "Licht," of course, means light, not in the sense of clinical madness but a hallucination, a mirage. *MIRAGE* is also another title of mine.

A.M.: Once *IRRLICHT* was released, you gave your first solo concert...

K.S.: Yes. It was even in France that the first Klaus Schulze concert took place; organized by Actuel at the Ouest Parisien Theatre in 1972. This concert reunited the new German groups; Guru Guru, Kraftwerk, Tangerine Dream... I played last, on an organ that I had bought the day before which I hardly knew how to use.

A.M.: You even have training as a pianist?

K.S.: Not at all! I have training in classical guitar, then a few years on drums. The day when I felt the need to make a different kind of music, I said to myself that the best way to loosen my spirit was to play an instrument that I was unfamiliar with. And above all, not to let anyone teach me how to play it. I started out like an idiot who for the first time puts on his glasses and sees.

A.M.: That's a rather "Zen-like" approach...

K.S.: I am attracted to the Zen religion. I was in Japan for a long time but I don't practice it because insofar as being a European, to follow such a path to me seems impossible; it's too far from our hearts. But I like the atmosphere. I love the aura of Zen.

A.M.: It seems that the French public appreciated your music right off. Before it really went for Pink Floyd (who really started in France let's not forget), or Soft Machine or Tangerine Dream...

K.S.: For me the French public is the best in the world. Whatever the music, they will follow you if they feel that you believe in what you're doing. It's a public that's really open to new music and they know how to show it. Some other audiences are too "stuck up," as an example, the Germans and the Dutch are too uptight to express their emotions.

A.M.: Thank you for the French public, let's hope that they will stay at such a height, for you aren't the first musician to make such an observation. The new

German music is qualified as being "Cosmic," as being "able to soar," is it your goal to make people soar?

K.S.: You know, people will say what they will, the "Cosmic" label isn't very good, for all music is cosmic, but I will certainly call my music "musique plantane" because I place it above the ground... At least 10 centimetres off the floor. It allows you to float while it floats around you. On stage sometimes, I get the impression that I'm floating around my instruments ...

ROBOTS & RIVERS
A.M.: As the years go by, you get up on stage with material that's more and more impressionistic ....

K.S.: Yes, I have a lot of robots.

A.M.: How do you work with these "robots?" What is your relationship to them?

K.S.: The same as any other musician with his instruments: It's necessary to look after them and to treat them well. That may seem crazy, but there is an enormous amount of sensitivity in them. I have 18 synthesizers on stage and they are never out of tune because I really love them. I talk to them and if chance, one poses a problem for me, I tell it: "Ok, I won't play you tonight... if you don't like something here... I won't insist on it. We'll see about tomorrow." It's as simple as that. You have to stop and realize that there is around 2,000 years of human intellectual evolution inside these machines ... 2,000 years of success and failure. These machines get cold and warm like we do. They are the fruits of 2,000 years of intellectual crafting.

A.M.: What part does pre-programming play in your concerts?

K.S.: Minimal. I have some schematics that I've made of concerts, but each time I climb up on stage I don't know what I'm going to play. Besides, I don't want to know, because each night I want to live a new experience. From my last tour I know that out of 60 concerts, no two were alike.

A.M.: That must demand a lot of energy from you?

K.S.: The vibrations from the audience help a lot. As much as a musician, you send out a force to the audience that comes back to you... then you send out a stronger force and they respond stronger, and so forth... It's very important that this exchange exists or nothing happens.

A.M.: From the concert we spoke of, the majority of people find you aggressive, musically speaking.

K.S.: I am often aggressive and my music shows it, but in concert, I always try to show two aspects of energy: you only see the light because of the darkness... All of the tension you put into the destruction of a table, you can also channel and put to a more positive use, vis-à-vis more positive aspirations. I believe I always had my more violent moments in concert followed by moments of harmony and peace. It's something natural.

A.M.: You essentially work with synthesizers, but you've also had a few experiences with symphonic orchestras...

K.S.: Yes, on *IRRLICHT*, *CYBORG* and *X*, and I even did a concert with a symphony orchestra. But this posed problems for me because classical musicians always play in the same fashion, they need notes and scores that they can follow. Most have lost any feeling for the importance of perfection.

A.M.: Did you write the score?

K.S.: Yes.

A.M.: One of the particular themes that seems to inspire you the most is science fiction. In particular, the book "Dune" by Frank Herbert...

K.S.: "Dune" is for me, the most beautiful S.F. book ever written. I see it as a social critique of our transposed world, not something depressing. Besides, many are the S.F. books that do nothing but describe what's taking place now: "1984" by Orwell for example, or Huxley's "The Best Of Worlds." Frank Herbert brings up real problems and often offers answers.

A.M.: And as for the metaphysics of "Dune"?

K.S.: I'm not too in touch with that. I'm busier watching what's happening on our planet right now; it's sheer madness! Rivers and seas are polluted and everyone just closes their eyes. Near Hanover I bought a small forest and a house, that I will preserve. I want it so my son, who's one year old today, can still be able to see trees, deer and rabbits when he's ten. I'm not touching the trees or allowing hunters, I will progressively create a zoo there, a natural reserve.

A.M.: Don't you think that peace in nature must first come as peace between mankind?

K.S.: Of course, but in 1980 mankind does not know peace. I get depressed when I see plastic imitation trees. It seems to me as easy to put the same effort into protecting nature, to stop putting thousands of flowers in vases ... It's high time that man woke up!!

A.M.: On the jacket of your *LIVE* LP you wrote: "This is my first and last live album.. My music and I are taking off in other directions. This isn't a good-bye, but rather a hello, the start of a new music that will lead me towards the unknown." What does that mean?

K.S.: From the start of the Berlin scene, a lot of artists have copied us ... They use our experiences and researches and apply them to disco or new wave, like Gary Numan ... or even pop-music.

A.M.: Are you aiming at anyone in particular when you say pop-music?

K.S.: Of course I am thinking of Jean-Michel Jarre who found out how to use the more commercial aspect of what we're doing. His music oddly resembles what I was doing on stage in 1974. But it is also part of the creativity to know how to make a success out of it. Notice that I am not blaming anyone or accusing anyone. I just felt like starting from zero again with my first solo album. Since I made this decision, I have felt happier...and now with my new material the copiers are going to have to say good-bye to any hope of imitating me.

THE COMPUTER: MEET WAHNFRIED
Electronic calculator, equipped with memories that have great capacity and the means to calculate rapidly, able to adapt its programs to given circumstances and to make complex decisions.
(PETIT ROBERT)

A.M.: In what directions are you taking off?

K.S.: To start with, I got rid of all my synthesizers. Everything that I had on stage was already 20 years too late. In spite of that, I work on a digital terminal which is presented like a typewriter with a control screen. With this computer I can do positively astounding things! I can create the effect of 150 keyboard players at once.

A.M.: You really mean 150?

K.S.: Absolutely!

A.M.: Could you try to explain for us how "it" works?

K.S.: It's very difficult, because it's more complex than any instrument that exists today. You know, I have had this computer for only a short time and am only just starting to get to know it and it's starting to get to know me...

A.M.: Because it needs to know you?

K.S.: Right, or else it won't work for you.

A.M.: Have you given it a name?

K.S.: Yes it's called Wahnfried, which means "Crazy Peace"... besides, this computer is crazy! It is logical, but with a logic that surpasses imagination. A fantastic example is: You read or play a program and suddenly you get lost, you no longer know where you are or where you want to go ... you just ask it for help.

A.M.: And will it help you?

K.S.: It first asks you what kind of help you need, then it'll sort through different types of programs for you while telling you precisely what kind of program you need. You can then try them all out until you find the solution. To be able to work with you, it needs your name in its memory. After it helps you, you must thank it and it says: "You're welcome, Klaus." In fact, until today the essential part of my work has consisted of giving it all the possible information, from my birthday, to my tastes, to even my looks.

A.M.: Even your looks?

K.S.: Yes, Wahnfried has a camera that is aimed at you and that analyzes and digitally encodes them.

A.M.: And if you were ever to refuse to give it information?

K.S.: It wouldn't work for you then, it would say, "I am a machine, I can't help you." It speaks with a voice that's a bit nasal, but it speaks. I spent three nights telling it very private things, all that made up my life. I told it everything and it stored...it stored Klaus Schulze. Then I told it that I didn't feel very cool, perhaps it could tell me why?

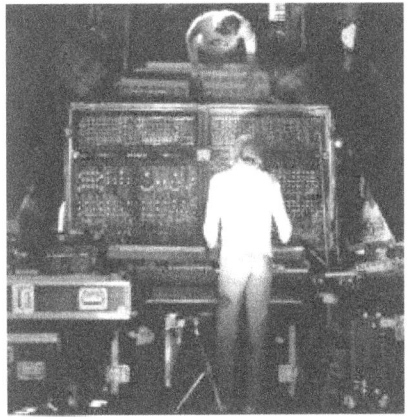

A.M.: And did it tell you?

K.S.: You know it has a program called FREUD!! It also has one called BIORHYTHMS, thanks to which I can know on what day to record and on which day not to. It also knows my horoscope, it can interrelate when analyzing them together with amazing accuracy.

A.M.: So it did your horoscope?

K.S.: Yes, thanks to it, I found out that I'm a Leo with Leo rising. It's all really "Big

Brother." It also has a program called "The History of Music."

A.M.: How do you use that?

K.S.: If I feel like composing a piece that's in the same spirit as German baroque, once the piece is over, I can ask it to tell me if I'm really in the right spirit it'll reply: "Klaus, pay attention to the 2nd, 7th and 9th notes, they don't fit into what it is that you want to achieve, may I correct it?" If I accept its correction, it makes the arrangement and then I can store it in the memory for later retrieval.

A.M.: On a musical level, what are its applications?

K.S.: On a musical level I have only had a little time at this point to do a few things: I played a piece of music that I'd programmed and asked whether or not it existed in the world already. It consulted its History of Music and responded that I'd copied Beethoven ...or Vivaldi... I then played and programmed another piece and again asked the same question, this time it said: "This music doesn't exist, but there is a 10 minute passage very similar to Stockhausen!" I asked if we could cut it out without harming the totality of the piece which lasted two hours. It said we could, and we cut...

A.M.: How about in relation to what you create, what you program?

K.S.: Some sounds, some timbres, some new tonalities ... For example, I spent hours looking for the sound of an organ that was as beautiful as in a church. Now it's in its memory, I can use it whenever and really it's so magnificent that you'd hardly believe that it's a recording.

A.M.: Can you program notes and rhythms?

K.S.: I can program sequences, but I'm obliged (happily) to play all the notes on a real keyboard that I connected to the terminal. Sometimes the thing is crazy! You play for an hour or two and then ask it what it thinks of it and it tells you that you were awful. Because you're still using the ideas of such and such composer... The most maddening thing is when you've not heard of the composer in question.

A.M.: How does it react in cases like that?

K.S.: It simply explains that you don't remember it, or that through some voyages that you've made or really because of your education, you must have heard the piece without really paying any attention to it. You unconsciously recorded it.

A.M.: Did you make the film you showed us today with Wahnfried?

K.S.: Besides having sound it also has a video hookup. When I play on stage, the sound and images function together. I use a section of geometric shapes like what you saw today, but I also work with changing colors, shifting and super- imposing the impressions.

A.M.: Does Wahnfried also criticize your video images?

K.S.: Yes. Sometimes it lets me know if the images are any good and if the music is bad or vice versa. If I want to play in peace all I have to do is short circuit the memory button ......

A.M.: Is its memory capacity very large?

K.S.: Yes. You can program around 150,000 pieces of information that individually would fill up 10 pages in a normal book. In other words, 1,500,000 printed pages. That's only 1 floppy disc. Imagine there are 3 or more!

A.M.: Of course you can use everything that you've programmed when you get on stage.

K.S.: Yes, I'll be able to use it like a machine that has 64 different tracks, since I have 64 different buttons, I will be using more than one. I assure you, the audience is not going to believe it... Everyone says that I have a tape recorder hidden behind the stage. Besides, the computer can attain such a state of perfection that if I stray from what I'm doing it immediately corrects me. Right now, I have such a head! On certain days I wonder if it (the computer) will end up in a museum, and me in a psychiatric hospital!!!

A.M.: Or the other way around! You said at the start that you can accomplish the work of 150 keyboard players simultaneously. Wouldn't that render recording studios obsolete?

K.S.: As far as I'm concerned, yes. I don't need more than 24 or 48 tracks. Besides, I'm contemplating recording the next album myself.

A.M.: What does that mean?

K.S.: To go directly to the recording studio with the computer and connect it direct to the recording machine, leaving out all the intermediaries like magnetic tape, mixing, etc. This will give me an extraordinary sound.

A.M.: Will this facilitate work for a live album if you decide to make any more of them?

K.S.: That's going to be easier yet; it will be enough for me to know where I really performed well and to just press the memory button that corresponds to the particular concert I'm thinking of. And if I'm wrong, I won't have to record...All of this makes the coming 10 years very exciting for me on the level of creativity, even if I don't know yet what I'm going to run into.

A.M.: Your next album then might really surprise you?

K.S.: I hope so, and it's almost certain, since the computer eliminates all that is mediocre or that's been done before. Each time I compose, I store it, I can ask it if what I've done resembles something before 1978...in 1979 my spirit completely changed. It's familiar with the music from Tangerine Dream, Ash Ra Tempel and Klaus Schulze. The computer constantly forces me to go beyond my limits.....

A.M.: A question many will ask is what becomes of emotions during this technological voyage?

K.S.: Emotions will always be there; emotions are in the way you play the machines. When you program your computer, basically you are putting one or many emotions into it, since you program what touches you the most. The sounds that you create make the emotional chords that are within you, vibrate. And most of all, don't forget, that it can't play something that isn't in its memory. Whatever is created, must pass from the keyboard on which you play the notes. It isn't creative. It can only repeat or reproduce what the human mind has asked it to store in its memory.

INNOVATIVE COMMUNICATION

A.M.: Parallel to your activities as a musician, and now as a programmer, you have founded a synthesizer school and created a record label . Why?

K.S.: It's necessary that all of the investment I've made vis-à-vis materials, as well as sound, since I own a recording studio that's ultra-modern and totally automated, as well as the video part, since I also own a video studio, all work together. Besides in the course of my tours of the world, I have met many talented musicians whose only "fault" in relation to the multi-national record companies is that they are not innately aimed towards a destiny of selling millions of records. That is the concept behind I.C. which is a label onto which I can produce musicians or groups, who in my opinion, are making the music of tomorrow.

Jean-Michel Reusser
Reprinted from L'AUTRE MONDE
Translation by Michelle Tuck

Bernard Xolotl -- Interview 1981

Bernard Xolotl was born June 26th, 1951 in France where he studied art and philosophy until 1969. He then traveled extensively around the world -- painting, writing and composing. Since 1975 he has lived mostly in San Francisco, California where he founded project Syntasy to help advance the Age of Synthesis.

Q: Bernard, would you like me to address you as a musician or as a philosopher?

A: Well, actually I like the expression "musical philosopher." I would always like to think of myself as a holistic artist, one that has a real philosophy behind every gesture that he chooses to make in this world, whether the end result appears as being music, art, poetry, science or whatever, it must be based on a sound and deep philosophy; otherwise it only generate an unconscious stream of fantasies and egotistical hallucinations -- the endless proliferation of useless and random objects, thoughts and emotions -- which is nothing but mind pollution.

Q: Would you call this a holistic approach to music and if so, how is this exemplified in particular works of music?

A: I would call this a holistic approach to creativity and life in general. As far as music is concerned, we have been witnessing in the last few years a phenomenon that is of the greatest interest to me: since the development of the synthesizer (the musical computer) this instrument that has an incredibly wide range, beyond even what the human brain presently knows of ITSELF, many people who were not educated as musicians, strictly speaking, who were educated maybe as artists, architects, poets or whatever experience life itself manifests to them, have been able to create in their own terms some extremely sophisticated, far-reaching music that is being more and more recognized as outlining the classical music of the future. I am thinking for instance of the music of Klaus Schulze, Iasos, Kitaro, Kraftwerk, Michael Hoenig... and indeed most of the artists using now the synthesizer in creating their new music. We see here how a new medium has brought a refreshing new approach to Art that is typically non-specialized. Of course, this is still too new to most people but I don't see how, at this point the flow could be stopped; it's growing everyday and we are no doubt entering what like to call "the Age of Synthesis."

Q: So, as an essential question to a music philosopher, how do you define "good" in music?

A: I think that true music or philosophy starts beyond good and evil and that the magic of Art is to abolish any such duality by creating a state of perfect harmony, receptivity between giver and receiver, object and subject, where ultimately pain and pleasure become undifferentiable. There have always been trends in Art that attempted to capitalize on a particular aspect of creativity or expression at the detriment of another, calling its own "good" and the rest "unhealthy."

Most recently we have this all "healing" music movement, so called "New Age," that thinks it has discovered the healing power of sound and pretends to provide people with therapeutic, healing environments... I question very much such a dualistic, obviously neo-Christian approach to creativity. First of all, we know very well politically what is the end result of imposing one's "good" to another's "evil" taste or feeling in whatever realm of human endeavor. Second, it shows a complete ignorance or lack of faith in the real power of music or art which is, as already mentioned, to wed pain and pleasure. And third, it is much too early at this point to pretend in the West to have any real science, any deep, significant data as to the exact effects of sound on the human bio-computer. In view of the evidence, such a pretension is pure make-believe. A science of sound, however, has existed and developed in India for thousands of years; it is called Nada Yoga, or the yoga of sound. Great Indian masters can demonstrate wonderful use of their knowledge and techniques in this domain with undeniable soothing or appeasing effects on the audience, an excellent example being Pandit Pran Nath and his American disciple Terry Riley. We, in the West, have so much to learn from these master Artists and their great tradition where science and Art were always closely related; however, we cannot at this stage give up our own tradition... Again, the synthesizer and the whole domain of "psychoacoustics" are new. They initiate a new era for Artists to define and build upon the classical music of the future, which, at the moment remains very Western-oriented but has to expand to the whole planet before we can speak of a truly cosmic age reality. Only then will we be able to wisely start using the healing virtues of sound in a holistic manner, making full use of the tools -- both acoustic and electronic -- that have been given to us.

What I just said does not deny in any way the daily effort we should all make to improve our environment and harmoniously upgrade our means of relation and expression. It is understood that the ultimate purpose of Art is always to inspire, uplift and transcend limitations. I simply refuse to pretend at this stage that we can already apply results when we are only starting on the journey. I see it in fact as just another commercial trick to sell records, make money and capitalize on a very sensitive and popular American issue; namely the health of consumers!

Q: (Laughs) Well, you have given us a very valuable survey of some current trends in music, particularly the Californian New Age blend, but I would like now for you to tell us what is YOUR personal vision of the ideal music?

A: Once again there is no such ideal to be found anywhere. The Earth is like a celestial body where the different cultures represent different organs with a specific function. There is music for all occasions. There is music that corresponds to each of the seven chakras or energy centers of the human biocomputer. There is primitive music that triggers the first chakra, the basic beat of life; there is music (especially rock) that stimulates greatly our sexual energy center; there is intellectual music, especially jazz, that makes us think a lot; there is music of the heart that bows our emotional string, etc. What I would call great music is that music which integrates all these different energy centers into a sublime whole. Since it is my belief that when all these resources of the human biocomputer come together, pain and pleasure become one, all boundaries dissolve and a state of complete "ecstasy" is attained that is oblivious to time and space and makes us fully participate in the great symphony of the universe -- the great Spiritual mind -- the Passions of J.S. Bach, the last operas of Wagner are towering witnesses of such a feeling.

Furthermore, this does not only apply to music but to the entire creative palette of humankind; all the senses must be equally nourished, enlightened, and merge into the ecstatic state of wholeness, the ecstatic synthesis of all senses which I have called Syntasy.

Q: Would you say that the technological revolution in music and Art is the best means today of achieving this synthesis?

A: I would expressly caution any such assumption before all cultures and people of this planet are given somewhat equal access to these technological creative tools -- which brings up, of course, a very political issue that must be faced. I am often thrilled thinking of the marvelous realizations that Arab, Chinese, Russian, Hindu people will provide us with once they are given the opportunity to use in their own terms these peaceful weapons. Before this happens we cannot speak of the technological revolution in the Arts as being a planetary privilege. But at the moment it is the sales of destructive weapons that is our only common privilege and the whole thing is up in the air. No one knows if and when the cosmic child will be allowed to be and grow. As Rimbaud said, "Christmas on Earth!" It seems always that the more power we have for peace and the more we have for war, pain and pleasure ... you know!

Q: Could you tell us what the response of Asians or the Eastern bloc people has been so far in regard to technology and the Arts that make use of it?

A: The response of artists to new tools is always enthusiastic. They never have any problem in finding spontaneously highly innovative, original and beautiful ways to make use of them in their creative work and they are always eager to hear/see feel more -- the growth of technology is very organic in that people everywhere adopt what they need and neglect what they have no use for. Curiosity and ingenuity are universal qualities.

There are indeed just as many people in our own culture that remain ignorant of the possibilities offered to them by artistic technology and Art in general; and they are always the ones who deny others the pleasure of finding out for themselves. But, anyway, Art has never been a high priority among politicians and religious dictators in whatever country, and with or without computers.

Q: How would you rate the impact of the latest technology on Western music so far?

A: A very disturbing pattern, in regard to that has emerged within the last two decades the amount of technology has been in most cases inversely proportional to the quality and integrity of the music. I will not be afraid here to give specific examples. In the late sixties, musicians that were at the vanguard of technology and created truly original works with little equipment by today's standards, moved in a more and more trendy, commercial, all-too-predictable musical adventure as they gathered more and more sophisticated hardware. In the seventies this pattern worsened considerably when most of the early pioneers of electronic music such as Tangerine Dream, Tomita, Manuel Gottsching, Peter Baumann, etc., who had been creating wonders of an innovative music and started the whole cosmic music genre (again with minimal technology compared with today's) SOLD OUT entirely and with now a colossal arsenal of synthesizers and computers at their disposal are creating nothing but Hollywood-inspired, "easy listening," completely unsophisticated, unoriginal blend of music which makes an incredibly limited use of the weaponry they have accumulated in all these years. This is what gives electronic music a bad name. It also represents a saddening example for the aspiring synthesist who does not have access to all these expensive machines and often wonders how money can corrupt artists to such an extent, or, looses faith in the worthiness of pursuing such an exploration... And this brings us back to the highly political nature of technology in every domain.

Q: So you have just told us about the limitations of human nature within the use of technology. Now what about the limitations of music technology itself? Are you also of a certain current opinion that machines are better than Man?

A: (Laughs) It is strange indeed for humans to think that something can be "better" than them. However, as we have seen earlier, technology develops as an answer to a need, be it scientific, artistic or militaristic. So as long as artists will have new needs of expression they will try to invent a tool that can fulfill their purpose. Therefore, it can be said that as machines are the result of man's imagination, their only limitations is this very imagination. Isn't limitation the mother of invention and creativity? It definitely appears to be so, and therefore it will never be the amount of equipment that can control the quality of the output but rather the QUALITY of the need .....

The only worry in regard to technology is its political use and I could say the same about any other means. Real Art -- whether past, present or future -- is the single truly peaceful and equanimous planetary religion .....

I will also mention that my paintings as well as my music are very carefully elaborated with respect to the harmonic progressions which are truly universal principles -- the Golden Mean is the magic number (1.618) which rules the growth and unfolding of galaxies, comets and sunflowers. My album painting the "Return of the Golden Mean" refers to the "rebirth" of the Pythagorean philosophy through the digital age.

Q: In the context of the very dangerous world we live in today, where the powers of computers could possibly be used to exterminate the human race, what would be your suggestions?

A: It is the eternal responsibility of Artists and positively creative people in general to keep creating loving thoughts, objects and harmonies in order to maintain the balance of power on the side of clear consciousness, spiritual advancement, political integrity and the endless proliferation of Beauty to avoid or postpone indefinitely this planet falling totally into the hands of the maniac, power-crazy criminals that thrive in every country.

Archie Patterson

D. D. A. A.

ANFRACTUOSITISME

L'ECOLE CLASSIQUE ANFRACTUOSITE
Definition: A theory of history and art that essentially concerns parallel lines and Crevice-ism , that is to say, the search for historical deviation. This isn't a parody on political discourse or on masterful progression, it is political art, not in the sense of propaganda-art, but in the sense of politics, in so much as art -- and of art as politics. This artistic search comes out of the principle that art is based on historical deviations (a greater fiction). This principle is evidently put into application in the domain of plastic art (painting, etc.) but also can be applied to music. The activity of the Front de Brouillage International is more directly tied to the production of historical deviations whereas the theoretical activity on the elaboration of Crevice-ism belongs to the School of Classical Crevice-ism. The two activities being closely linked. Actually, the theoretical search is in

practice oriented towards the problem of historical deviations being tied to the rupture of the lines of control, these ruptures themselves being tied to the dispersion of reality. This theme of dispersion of reality rests on a particular apprehension of the times. Time will not only be composed of past/present/future, but also of historical past/active past/dynamic past.

In 1932 the Front de Brouillage International for the first time called together a congress in which the four declared sides took part. The congress did not reach a clear definition of the parallel lines, in effect, the sympathies (sides) are politically and technically divided. The first defined the parallel lines as a political weapon which evidently gave a revolutionary orientation to the activities of the Front. Here is a copy of the report given by the South American delegate representing one of the sides:

"Come here comrades and eat up, eat up the revolutionary orientation of the Front de Brouillage International; the revolutionary orientation of the parallel lines against the reactionary orientation of the line of Control. The line of Control is the expression of the fundamental reactionary leanings of the bourgeois. The orientation of Control is towards normalization. The struggle of the Front is by obligation the struggle against normalization, by obligation, and out of the necessity to survive. The parallel lines are not the production of the lines of Control, the parallel lines are totally independent of the lines of Control. The struggle against Control, against normalization gives to the creation of parallel lines the same necessity as a weapon. If the possibilities of parallel lines are party to Control they are not an arm of the struggle against normalization. The sympathies of Comrade Korgilov who defended an orientation that was agitated thus, which is an infiltration by the Front into Control; that the definition of the parallel lines is part of Control is the suppression of the autonomous army by the Front against normalization. It is a betrayal to the Front. Our sympathy towards the parallel lines is independent of Control and an autonomous army in the struggle against the Front. The Front is by obligation out to continue the fight against normalization. The Front is by obligation out to maintain the parallel lines as an autonomous army. The Front is by obligation out to maintain its revolutionary sympathies in order to survive."

As we see it, the report given by the South American delegate is extremely virulent and the delegate attacked precisely the side which Korgilov is the principal representative, the technical orientation at the heart of the Front. He thus defined the parallel lines as the very contradictions of Control, and calls the delegates to maintain the idea of independence from the parallel lines of Control under the pain of seeing the Front fall into normalization. However, after the South American delegate, Korgilov took the floor and defended the ideas of the technical side which are totally opposed to the political side. In effect, the "technicals" think that the parallel lines are issued from the lines of Control, and feel that the definition of the contradictions of Control are too simplistic, domestically and in the end, rather dangerous. Because it is dogmatism which leads to normalization. They therefore consider that only an appreciation of the parallel lines as issued by the lines of Control, is the proper basis for work on delimiting the historical deviations. And we better understand that while the debate in 1932 on the definition of the parallel lines rests in fact upon the appreciation of the different leanings as much as for the different objectives of the Front. First off, these two aspects of the same battle are in the end tied together;

but their different orientations produce two tactics and two strategies which finally come to oppose each other. On the one hand, a fanatical activism that doesn't escape errors and dogmatism is all the more perilous since Control really knows how to pull errors from groping along. Of the other search that takes side with laying itself aside and avoiding combat. The 1932 congress did not succeed in settling the debate and it is always open for the Front. Not being able to put the definition of the parallel lines into accord, the delegates thus left the problem hanging, all the while allocating to each section the possibility for deciding for itself its own method of work. However, in order to avoid too great a divergence, the congress decided to equip the Front with a common arsenal relative to the parallel lines. The arsenal grew with the passing years out of the searches and experiences of all the different sympathies. In 1956, at the time of the 4th congress, the Front finally decided to claim all the forms of action and work under the title "Arsenal Front de Brouillage International," which had as an advantage, the quality of being more unifying. From 1933 to 1945, the fascist powers and the war put European sections, where the "technical" side was strongly implanted, in a difficult situation. The representatives of the Front are clandestinely constrained and the official representative had to emigrate. The 2nd congress of the Front was held in the US in 1941, under the name "American Congress." In effect, the "technical" side was under-represented in relation to the "political" side who imposed their motion towards the definition of parallel lines as an autonomous weapon. However the arsenal was called into question. But Korgilov, the European delegate and representative of the "technical" side could not end his report and was interrupted by diverse interventions by the "political" side. Those of the "political" side in effect, suspected those of the "technical" side to be in favor of the war which they considered to be an objective priority of the combat, in so much as attaining power from Control; while those of the "technical" side also saw a possibility there of developing the parallel lines, which is evident really in the strategic orientation of the historical deviations. Only the political motion voted in the course of this congress and no compromise was seen on that day. Also in July of 1945, the 3rd congress was called and was held in London for several days. The London congress is generally recognized as that of a reunification. In effect, all of the sympathies were equally represented, and the delegate from the "technical" side is still Korgilov who presented to the congress a report which integrated the bipolarism of the orientation of the parallel lines in its definition. In fact, Korgilov presented the principles of dependence and independence as being intimately tied and integrating these notions into a principle that is greatly better defined under the term "greater fiction."

Here is an extract from that report:
"To await the enemy in a cement belly, that is to represent the war, that is the memorization of history in movement. The greater fiction is the moment when history in movement escapes the recordings by the lines of Control, that is

to say the instant when fiction replaces history by this very break in the recording. It's the instant when all is possible because the fiction takes the place of history to assure the continuity until Control can re-establish its recording. I don't mean that the fiction replaces Control, on the contrary, Control struggles with a fury to prevent the movement of history. Control never establishes its recordings when history is in motion, but rather, when this motion stops. Control cannot be interpreted by its codes. The fiction doesn't belong to reality organized by Control. The fiction is the "world of appearances" governed by the liberty of this sense. This fissure allows the parallel lines their deepest developments. What one must look for as a matter of priority is the application of interference, this is the moment of the greater fiction. The battlefield between Control and the parallel lines is the greater fiction. The historical deviations represent the victories by the parallel lines over Control at the moment of this battle, and these deviations allow the creation of new interruptions of the recordings by Control, of new appearances by the greater fiction. The problem of dependency and independency from the parallel lines in relation to Control knows its resolution in the greater fiction, because to be effective, the parallel lines must at once be dependent and independent -- and that only happens via the greater fiction. There are no limits, no duration. The dependence/independence is continuous in the instantaneousness of the rupture of the recordings by Control. All the dependency of the parallel lines only exists from this instantaneousness which produces independence. This doesn't mean that the independence replaces dependence, the two facets exist at the same time, one is necessary for the other. The greater fiction is instantaneous; the memorization of history in motion is made from historical deviations."

The London congress concluded with the setting into place of a commission of work which was in charge of equipping the Front de Brouillage International Arsenal with new possibilities which permitted a better utilization of the parallel lines and also a collection of historical deviations in order to accelerate the appearance by the greater fiction. This commission, led by Korgilov, made a point from the diagrams of parallel lines, called Korgilov's diagrams or K's diagrams:

"K's diagrams allow the search to approach the lines of Control and in particular, the recordings code, which better allows the setting into place of the parallel lines that are better adapted not only for the appearance, but also the functionality of the greater fiction. These diagrams allow for a better evaluation of the bipolarity of the parallel lines when one finds oneself in the zone of rupture. Finally, these diagrams allow for a setting and rapid collection of the deviations and their immediate utilization. The work of K's diagrams is made in direct alliance with the Center in charge of pinpointing the recording codes by Control and the eventual effects derived from the zone."

The activity on K's diagram on the zone of rupture takes its name from Crevice-ism. Crevice-ism because the activity on K's diagram is an intervention by the ruptures of recording. The fictional crevices of history. Crevice-ism because the greater fiction resembles the sea when it crashes over the crevices in the rocks. The waves of the greater fiction crash into multiple possibilities against the rocks of the recording codes. Crevice-ism which consists of maintaining the fictional crevice offered to all of the historical deviations. Crevice-ism thus because it's a question of holding back these deviations after the greater fiction has broken on the rock of recording. However, one mustn't confuse Crevice-ism with K's diagrams.

1981

The first designs the whole of the activity with K's diagrams, as well as that of the parallel lines, which are from Control, and of course, the phenomena of the greater fiction. Crevice-ism designs history in motion such as it appears in the activity on K's diagrams. From the congress of 1956, the work by Front de Brouillage International is therefore concentrated on the activities of K's diagrams. The first difficulty therefore appeared from the approaching of the zones; some zones present derivatives of the recording. Thus it seems that the codes of recording by Control are capable of provoking the displacement of the projection of the rupture. This displacement allows Control to lead the rupture into a favorable zone to the reconstruction of these recordings. It was necessary therefore to prevent this deviation more or less from following it. This effect of deviation from the rupture was called the "JPF" effect. The JPF effect can manifest itself at any moment during the activities. If the JPF effect manifests itself before one has pinpointed the code of recording and that one has effected the setting into place of the parallel lines, it is possible to follow the drift and to practice Crevice-ism of the rupture. The JPF effect makes the rupture disappear. If one is successful on the other hand in establishing the parallel lines to the lines of Control before the appearance of the JPF effect, it is possible to follow the drift. Crevice-ism presents yet at the same time more possibilities since the zone of rupture is multiplied by rejection through the JPF effect. The historical deviations find themselves singularly enriched by it. However, the manifestations of the parallel lines are more difficultly made, in effect, since these were approaching the zone of rupture, the JPF effect provoked the disappearances of this zone by the recordings of Control; this is the independence from them. It is thus necessary to re-establish the bipolarity without erasing the independence that corresponds to the zone of searching. It is therefore necessary to suppress the dependency to control all while maintaining the independence to follow the deviation. It is really necessary to recognise that it is a matter thus of a little more difficult exercise which often leads along by trial and error. FOMECBLOC qualifies an ensemble of things that relate to the "world of appearances," in fact, it calls to a work of this sense. It is evidently unable to be otherwise, since it is a question of the greater fiction. Actually, all the work from the reflection by the Front is oriented towards these problems of Crevice-ism -- the problems of dependency and independency from the parallel lines -- the problems of seizing the event from the greater fiction -- the JPF effect and the utilization of FOMECBLOC. The next congress will certainly bring about many responses to these problems, but these responses can only come from the very experiences of their existence.

A few notes on Bunkerology...
Bunkerology is a particular of Crevice-ism; the war is at the same time the strongest expression of Control and the most important possibility of the emergence from the greater fiction. The war is an event par excellence. The contradictions which provoke the history into motion, find themselves exacerbated by this phenomena. From the appearance in the bunker. The bunker is at once the strongest resistance to Control from the motion of history and the expression of the most total fiction. Bunkerology is at the same time, the simplest and the most difficult Crevice-ism. It is worth a particular place in K's diagrams; a subject of study of some sort. The bunker is Control's resistance to tentative immobilization. Control records the bunker as a limit to movement; as a past history. Control builds a synthesis of archives In the bunker to make an

anchoring place for pre-history from the new recording. Control hangs on to the blockhouse in so much as to limit the rupture. Bunkerology is Crevice-ism where the parallel lines practically merge with Control. The dependency of the parallel lines is as deep as the independence from Control must be, because the greater fiction which manifests itself in the bunker is extremely vast. That one considers the violence which produces for itself the rupture of the recordings and the energy that must develop Control in order to reduce this rupture, and one will then have an idea of the greater fiction of the bunker.

A few notes on Crevice-ism...
It generally manifests itself in shockwaves, a phenomena that is called "Crac-Badaboums" from the name of those underground people who activate temblors, cave-ins and other seismic activity by throwing themselves against the pillars of aversion. Crevice-ism is a caban.

(A child's voice)
"We were well inside of our caban -- we had built it at the bottom of the garden so that no one would see it -- we had put pieces of wood in the grass and later we had attached pieces of cardboard -- we left an opening that made the door, but then when JoJo wanted to come inside, she forcibly broke one of the pieces of wood that made the door, she is too fat -- then we told her to leave and later, she took off to a corner, crying, while saying that no one wanted to play with her -- that's not true -- it's not true -- it's not our fault if she's too fat -- we can't make the caban too big for we don't have enough cardboard and besides, she's bigger than the back of the garage, and the people would see it and say: "Hey, there is a caban over there" and then they would come over to see us and say: "I too want to make a caban" -- because they wouldn't understand that you can't make several cabans at once -- then they would take our pieces of cardboard saying : "You don't have any right to keep all the cardboard for yourself" -- and we would find ourselves without any cardboard -- as if they couldn't go look for cardboard somewhere else, away from ours if the want to make a caban. But we have nothing to fear because our caban is really quite small and well hidden behind the garage -- and because no one can really see it, even by turning onto the street behind the garden -- we cut branches to put on the roof -- since we built it under a hedge set off from the wall of the garage, one can't really see it, even while paying attention and looking for it because it is really well hidden. So much the better, because there are those who know that we have built a caban and would really like to smash it and take our cardboard -- I think that it's JoJo who told them, to revenge us for not wanting to take her in with us -- I don't see why we should now after she went and told everyone what we've done. In any case she said that we had a caban and now there are those who know that we have built it and want to attack us and smash it -- but we won't let them; also when they came they started in by throwing stones in the garden, we had to look for the garden hose and when they saw what we wanted to do they saved themselves -- and we had a good laugh because the hose wasn't connected -- but they came from behind, hiding in back of the hedge, while we attacked them with clods of dirt while running at full speed in order to avoid their stones and while jumping to raise a cloud of dirt on their heads -- then they left. How they do what we do -- they have installed a catapult system with boards, and try to bombard from afar with big dirt clods but from time to time it doesn't work -- and the dirt clod breaks up before it can be launched and the dirt falls all over them -- that's a good joke. But at times, the thing does work and the dirt lands on top of the caban. But we

aren't afraid because our caban is very solid."

In a recent expose titled "From Crac-Badaboums to Crevice-ism," professor Marescot remarked that the historical deviations are the products of jolts by the greater fiction. The historical deviations will be in some way, the print that leaves the crash of the greater fiction on the fringes of the rupture of the recording. Professor Marescot thus noticed the necessity of pushing the parallelism to its maximum while accentuating the most possible bipolarity of the parallel lines from the type that approaches and the tangency that is in perfect concordance with the zone of rupture, better still, marrying the most perfect possible fringe of this rupture. It is this flourishing, in effect, that is effective in the collection of historical deviations. If one doesn't push the dependency from the parallel lines enough, one risks everything right away, first from passing the vortex of the zone of rupture, since if one finds the zone, not from sufficiently approaching its fringes -- to touch, one finds oneself again drifting in the zone at the will of the greater fiction, without drawing any benefit. On the other hand, if one upsets the bipolarity of the parallel lines in favor of the capacity of the dependency, one finds themselves again, at the time of the instantaneous rupture, aspirated in the furrow of the lines of Control; this has in effect an untowardly plastering of the parallel lines onto the fringes of the rupture and to prevent, above all, the discovery of the historical deviations; as if they were erased, stuffed between the lines. One may say, in fact, that the parallel lines don't exist from the moment when they don't sufficiently detach themselves from Control. However, the reciprocal isn't true, since a parallel line can strongly exist even if it is very independent, only it loses much of its effectiveness. The tangency of "touching" is evidently difficult to define via a work method, this makes a call to the sensations as when one feels the cracking from the aspiration while running through the edges of the rocks. However, one may help oneself with FOMECBLOC to refine the tangency; a little too lightly to touch against the fringe of the rupture. It is evidently out of the question, at this time, to use these codes of recording, too dry, too brutal for a fine displacement. On the other hand, if the parallel wave is the cause of the disequilibrium of independence, it is necessary to use the analysis of the codes of recording by the effect of the center, to come together and to find the tangency. It is futile to drift, and in fact, it would aggravate the situation, by pulling the wool over our eyes. In fact, FOMECBLOC, attracted by the mobility and the din of the greater fiction (the Crac-Badaboums), will be quite disposed to follow whatever movement that excites the senses. That will be quite simply to lose the parallel lines in the vortex of the greater fiction, twisting in the zone of rupture without approaching its fringes; a situation all the more troublesome, if the zone is projected by the JPF effect. It will then be impossible to unwind the parallel lines, for the code of recording will have been changed. We see that the formation of the tangency isn't a slight affair.

Finally, a few notes on the spontaneousness of the rupture.....
If one considers the fact that the rupture is immediate and without one being able to see it before, one understands the importance of the motions of dependency and independency of the parallel lines. In effect, to support the rupture, it is necessary to solidly anchor the parallel lines to Control, thus to avoid detaching itself and finding itself dragged into the aspiration of the rupture. If it really resists, it must avoid finding itself taken in by the Crac-Badaboums; it is its capacity for independence that permits this. As much

as its capacity for dependency that will solidly anchor it to the recordings much as its independency that will rectify it outside of the zone of rupture. It must absolutely not count on forming a tangency from the instant of the rupture; it is from the rectification of the parallel lines that one can start to approach and to construct the tangency; and paradoxically, it is when the rectification is effected with force, that one can build a very fine tangency. In fact, the very solid anchoring allows it to approach very close to the fringes of the rupture. If the anchoring isn't solid, the rectification wouldn't have needed to be strong, but the parallel line would then have chance to drift. Like the precis by professor Marescot: "One recognizes the richness of a zone by deviations by the force of the rectification of the parallel lines." Finally, in order to finish this expose, the Front de Brouillage International Arsenal presents an old recorded document from the creation of the Front. This document isn't dated because the date of the creation of the Front isn't known exactly. According to professor Marescot, it seems to be a report by Korgilov, but that can't be certified, given the poor quality of the sound/transcription.

Here is the document:
"Now is the time to regroup the opposing forces to Control. Tidiness, painting, normalization. Voilà the leitmotiv by Control. We who have always refused this normalization, it is time for us to open up to its annihilation. I already hear some people exclaim "Control is too strong." "Control is indestructible." It is normal for these people to say that for they are already integrated into the recordings of Control. How would Control let them speak otherwise. Let's also beware of those who say "Forward!," and offer to smash our heads so that we crash ourselves in our élan against the codes. Control is cunning, it allows those to speak who are the most virulent because it wants to see them smash themselves at the foot of the ramparts Let's be more cunning and we will win. Control isn't indestructible, but we aren't going to smash ourselves at its feet. Control wants us to remain small and justly, we too want to stay small. We will slide along the ramparts of Control without it even feeling it, because we will be so small that we will merge into the grey area of its recordings. We will form the parallel lines which will destroy Control without it even feeling it. We will be so small and so parallel that we will find in front of Control the flaw in its shield. And then we will have the necessary force so that this minuscule flaw becomes the catastrophe of Control. Because that, Control can't understand, how can one be strong and small at the same time? And justly, we will be strong because we will be small. And this smallness, this tininess that we wish for Control, that is exactly its loss. And we have the certainly to win because of that, Control can't understand."

From the cassette Arsenal Front de Brouillage International (IP 006)
Translation by Michelle Tuck

1981

Neuronium

The roots of Neuronium's special style of synthesizer sound go back to the early day of electronic music in Spain to a formation called Suck Electronic, a legendary group of synthetic explorers. In 1976 Michel Huygen decided to form his own group and Neuronium was created around a nucleus of dual keyboards -- Huygen and Carlos Guirao, the guitar of Albert Gimenez and a rhythm section who soon after split.

It wasn't until Nov. 1977 that they got to record their 1st LP for EMI, *QUASAR 2C361*, which was in fact the 1st "cosmic music" album to come out in Spain. It sold a bit and was followed in 1978 by *VUELO QUIMICO* (Chemical Flight) which spotlighted Nico's haunting recitation of Edgar Allan Poe. With this record and subsequent performances, most notably at the International Festival of Science Fiction in Metz with Ashra, they began to get wider recognition outside of Spain. At this time guitarist Gimenez left to do his own music and just recently released his own LP.

In 1980 they decided to form their own record label and recorded the LP *DIGITAL DREAM* which attracted the attention of Klaus Schulze. He offered to mix it in Germany -- the group however didn't like the way he did it so remixed it and a slight tiff ensued with the result that Klaus had no part of the final release. In any case it was a superb record and laid the groundwork for their subsequent projects.

In early 1981 they went to England where they recorded two TV shows, one with Vangelis. As well they played with Manuel Gottsching and Harald Grosskopf upon their return to Barcelona at a big concert. That was followed in May by the release of *THE VISITOR*. It was premiered at the Centre Culturel of Tarrasa near Barcelona and accompanied by a visual show done by the artist of the fantastic, Tomas Gilsanz, who also does work for their album covers as well as live shows. The album was sold out in one month and represents their most successful concept work yet.

Now the group has finished work on their 5th LP, titled *CHROMIUM ECHOES*, which will reportedly be "a full electronic album with touches of acoustic sounds in a different way." As well Michel Huygen has completed his first solo album, *ABSENCE OF REALITY*, that's to be "pure cosmic music."

While the sphere of electronic music is fast becoming overcrowded with imitative artists, Neuronium stands apart from the rest. Their music is made to touch the feelings and allow the listener to glimpse his own reflection in the crystalline waves of electronic sound. It's psychotronic music that takes you on a trip through the senses.

Archie Patterson

Ariel Kalma

One of the newest currents in music today is that which falls into a category currently being referred to as "New Age." Generally considered to be the pioneer is the American master of tone color Terry Riley who has influenced a countless number of musicians, among them France's leading exponent of this sound -- Ariel Kalma.

His credentials read like many other French artisans: classical saxophone studies at the "Conservatoire Municipal du 14," electronic studies at the O.R.T. School of Paris, computer studies at the Faculte des Sciences of Paris, music studies in Vincennes Paris VI University as well as work with Brazilian guitarist Baden Powell a.o. All this served as his training ground for techniques.

After these extensive studies he decided augment his training with a world view so he traveled extensively through India and Kasmir immersing himself in the Eastern modes of music. During this time he also discovered the music of Terry Riley and it became a strong influence on him.

In 1975 he recorded his first album *LE TEMPS DE MOISSON* and then set off to the USA to visit the pioneers of minimalist, trance music Philip Glass, LaMonte Young and Riley. While in NYC he did his "little bleu disque," a flexi-disc that reflected his influences gained during the visit. Upon completion of his USA visit he returned to France to absorb all his experiences and try to develop his own sound.

At this point his ideas began to become more crystallized, so he became involved with film scores, dance companies and produced two more records, *OSMOSE*, a collaboration with Richard Tinti, which is a stunning synthesis of his music with natural sounds recorded in the jungles of Borneo, plus *INTERFREQUENCE*, a series of soundtracks for radio and film. At last all his experiences brought him to the desire to make music that would develop sensitivity and help in consciousness expansion.

Currently he is involved in workshops in music and Tantric Yoga which have led to his creating his two latest recordings, two cassettes -- *MUSIQUE FOR DREAMS AND LOVE* and *BINDU*, intended to augment the senses during meditation. His live performances of this music during relaxation sessions have helped him realize his goal of finding "a deep happiness in sharing and communicating the beautiful vibrations of the music passing through everyone's body... and soul. Innerspace Sounds..... Dedicated to Evolution."

Archie Patterson

1981

Pascal Languirand
The Music Of Minds

"It has been said that this music inspired by ancient cultures, reborn through modern technology, is leading the way towards a new civilization that is still in the process of being formed."

That central idea can be said to be at the heart of the music created by the 26-year old Parisian expatriate Pascal Languirand, who in the short span of 3 albums has blossomed into one of the most interesting new artists on the scene today.

When Pascal began his musical apprenticeship, like many others he first took up percussion, then the guitar. As his technical capabilities grew so did his sense of exploration and he began experimenting with electronics.

It was around this time that a new genre of space age musicians began to gain notice; Tangerine Dream, Popol Vuh, Klaus Schulze, Brian Eno, a.o. Without seeking to imitate, he combined this spirit and his familiarity with medieval music, Gregorian chant and Kurdish music to create a sound that demands imagination from its listeners. It's like walk through one's mental doors, a music that encourages the audience to project their own images.

Album #1, titled *MINOS*, was an interesting, if not totally successful work. Primarily an instrumental symphonic affair, it's marred by some melodramatic songs that are too much in a pop vein.

The 2nd album, *DE HARMONIA UNIVERSALIA*, is a completely different story. Employing a multitude of keyboards and making superb use of Gregorian chorale arrangements, he weaves a beautiful tapestry of sacred sound that evokes images of Popol Vuh and Vangelis. It stands the test of comparison with any of the best contemporary keyboard works.

Most recently with his 3rd LP, *VIVRE ICI, MAINTENANT* ("Living Here, Now"), he has expanded his sphere into film, as the core of the album was done for a Radio Canada series. Dubbed by Pascal as 'Music For Relaxation,' he specially composed it to create a state of relaxation and induce concentration and meditation. Call it "cosmic" or "trance" music, it combines traditional motifs with electronics in a startling way. His central inspiration comes from Sufism, "the melodies and trance quality of the rhythms are punctuated by light percussions, which relax the tensions of the body while awakening the mind..."

With his music Pascal wants people to become completely involved in the act of listening, to fuse with the music and to bring peace to that mental space where thoughts most often are agitated: to be Here and Now.

Archie Patterson

Teutonic Electronic

It's been a while since we last surveyed the goings-on in Germany, the homeland of "space music" (see EUROCK #14). So it's time to take an updated look at the latest developments.

It all started with Tangerine Dream -- Edgar Froese, Konrad Schnitzler, Klaus Schulze and the *ELECTRONIC MEDITATION* album. Today much of the current activity still revolves around these people. There are however a new group of synthesists who are starting to get recognition. Among them are Wolfgang Duren, Rolf Trostel and Klaus Bloch.

Wolfgang Duren was formerly equipment man and synthesizer programmer for Tangerine Dream before setting out on his own. His first LP, *EYELESS DREAMS*, is a strong electronic work that features a powerful display of technology and multi-rhythmic melodies. After a recent month-long tour he's now working on a follow-up.

Rolf Trostel is a 23-year-old Berliner who took up synthesizers to "do music from the heart." He debuted with a live performance titled "Compositions of Sound Timbre," a 2-1/2 hour exploration of electronic capabilities. Subsequently he self-produced his first album *INSELMUSIK*, an exercise in sound rhythms using computer creativity as he, like Wolfgang Duren, employs PPG equipment. Due soon is his second disc which will delve into the use of polyrhythmic variations.

EXTREM MUSIK ALA PING PONG, the title of Klaus Bloch's first album, ventures into the more pastoral realms of electronic music. Making use of dense, flowing electronic melodies and fluid guitar accompaniment, he sets up a very cerebral, "heavenly music" ambiance. He recently spent time in Denmark recording some beach tapes that will be incorporated into his next album.

In addition to the newly emerging artists, there has been renewed activity by some of the legendary figures of the scene. Amon Düül II has reformed and released an excellent album. Can's Spoon label, run by the irrepressible Hildegaard Schmidt, has 5 new releases scheduled for 1982. Kraftwerk's last tour featured the most futuristic display yet of electronic technology, Tangerine Dream scored the music for a major Hollywood production *THIEF*. Klaus Dinger (of Neu!) has kept the spirit alive with another La Dusseldorf album. Konrad Schnitzler has unleashed an onslaught of LPs. Uli Trepte has traveled to Japan where, with the help of the Japanese magazine *"Fools Mate,"* he's rehearsing with native musicians and planning an exhibition for the new year. Klaus Schulze now has some 20 releases on his I.C. label and has signed with EMI. And the new generation of German artists -- Der Plan, Pyrolator and DAF are gaining recognition.

To top things off, recently Eckart Rahn, head of the pioneering German label, Kuckuck, transplanted to America. In addition to starting a US based label for selected quality releases, he's beginning to serve as an invaluable bridge between the two scenes. Kuckuck, which remains a German label, is making inroads into the USA with superb releases by Peter Michael Hamel, Deuter, Kitaro and soon America's own Terry Riley. Celestial Harmonies, the US label, has re-pressed classic LPs by Eberhard Schoener and Popol Vuh. What all this amounts to is a heartening resurgence for German music.

Archie Patterson

Mark Shreeve Interview
A Joint Interview From Agitasjon And Mirage

Q: Electronic music for the most part has been mostly created by the Germans, very few Englishmen have tried to do it -- can you think if are any special reasons for this?

A: This is difficult to answer, but I think the answer lies within the cultural histories of Germany and England. A large portion of contemporary German music can be traced back to such great composers as Richard Strauss, Wagner and Beethoven, but in England there have never been any composers of such stature creating an essentially "English" style of music for future generations to be influenced by. Also, another more obvious reason is that in England, like the USA, music is treated as an industry to make money quickly, not as an art form. In Germany and the rest of Europe it's treated more seriously.

Q: When you plan a recording, do you first compose the music or mostly improvise?

A: As I can neither read or write music in the normal way, most of my music is improvised. I do however usually have an idea of the kind of "atmosphere" or "emotion" that I want to create before I start. Once I've started I choose the sounds and textures I require. Of course, the sequencer lines are always "composed."

Q: Some of your music has hints of Jarre and Schulze in it. The funny thing is that Jarre is very influenced by pentatonic music from the East and Schulze is not. As far as I can see you use hints of both. Do Jarre and Schulze have a great influence on your work?

A: As you say, they both have very different styles, I think the most simple answer is, Jarre is French, Schulze is German and I am English... If you see what I mean? For me, Jarre is perhaps a technically better musician, but I think Schulze is able to portray more emotion and makes a more challenging style of music. Naturally I am influenced by both, but hopefully not enough to just be a copy. I also listen to many other people, for instance; Wagner, ELP, Debussy, Tangerine Dream, Mussorgsky, Eberhard Schoener, Black Sabbath, Pink Floyd, Zamfir, etc. So from all this wealth of musical creativity I have tried to develop my own ideas and style.

Q: Do you try to tell a story in your music that the listeners can use to create their own fantasies, or is it ok for you to produce "background" music?

A: Obviously I can't force the listener to make up the "pictures" that I want. Everyone has their own individual interpretation of any kind of music. Some people (like me) become totally controlled by their imagination and subconscious thoughts, others however may just like to tap their feet to the music. Often, there is a story, but it's only my personal feelings which don't necessarily apply to others. For example, let me explain the kind of idea I have with "Thoughts of War Pt. 2." The first section is "Funeral in Desolation" which to me gives a picture of a planet that has just been totally destroyed, nothing left except for bleak landscape shrouded in mist, no life, nothing but emptiness and quiet. The second section, "Remembrance" is a more joyful memory or flashback of a beautiful world before the holocaust, the last memory. The third section, "Ashes to Dust" returns to the scene of devastation, the end of the world, a burial for a dead planet. On the other hand the track "Dream Sequence" is just music for its own sake, for me there is no background story, I only see abstract shapes and colors, pure music.

Q: What do you think of synthesizer groups? Do you want to play with other musicians, or do you prefer to work alone?

A: Some synthe groups are very good, they can work well together -- Tangerine Dream are an example of this. But others are not so good. The problem is that music is a very undemocratic art. It is natural for a musician to want to use only their own ideas, it's more satisfying. I don't know if I could work in a group, mainly because I haven't tried. I think in the future I'd like to give it a try, just to find out.

1981

Q: What kind of music/sound do you want to do in the future. Have you any special plans?

A: I have not, and will never plan a special style for my music, it will evolve in its own way and in its own time. As for the kind of music/sound that I want to make in the future -- well, I have many ideas but at the moment I don't have the necessary facilities. One idea is a very large "concept" -- it may be a set of 6 to 10 records with written text and illustrations. I've already worked out the basic ideas, but I'll need many instruments, not just synthesizer (in fact no synthesizers at all!). So I'm now as you say, "dreaming" of the future. Also for the past year I've been working with Paul Hyde on an idea for an audio-visual presentation. We are both very enthusiastic about this. It. will be a serious animation (not cartoon) film done by Paul with the music done by me. It will have a strong theme or meaning behind it, but no dialog, just moving visuals and music. I'll not say more about it at this time as we're still trying to get the necessary equipment together, but it will happen as we're both very anxious to do it.

**Courtesy Agitasjon Magazine &
Mirage Magazine**

1982

Lars Hollmer Interview

Anybody who has followed the history of the Swedish Music Movement which was born about 12 years ago, must now know of Zamla Mammaz Manna, one of its oldest existing musical entities.

I met Lasse Hollmer, leader and only remaining original member of the original Samla at Eino Haapala's house in Uppsala, a small college town about one hour from Stockholm. Lasse was busy with this new incarnation of Zamla he had put together after long time drummer Hasse Bruniusson quit the group to go back to school and study more advanced percussive skills. Last Spring Lasse and Eino had toured France playing with the band of French musician Albert Marcœur, and met two musicians who were very eager to play with this newly formed version of Zamla -- von Zamla. Lasse was very interested in talking of the past and his new plans to keep the long-standing band tradition alive.

R.: Are the Zamlas still playing together right now?

1982

L.: The situation today is like... Zamla before was a group which was very close. The drummer was Hasse Bruniusson. The keyboard player's name was Lasse Hollmer and so on for a long time. The big change we had was in '73 when we went from 3 to 4 adding Coste Apetrea on guitar, then the second big change was when Coste quit and Eino Haapala came in around '77. Now in '80 Hasse has left and we had another drummer for live dates, Vilgot Hansson, that was a third big change. After that it has been periodical as we worked as a group, Eino and I worked closely together on the new material and so on... Now there is even more difficulty because we've taken in Jac Garret (bass) and Denis Brely (bassoon) from Albert Marcœur's group to work with us. So as you see the situation has been changing and it's now very interesting to work with them and also Kalle Eriksson (trumpet from Nya Ljudbolaget) as we haven't had wind instruments before. Zamla has been quite a close and isolated group from the rest in Uppsala's musical scene. And now it has opened up a bit but it's strange... we find people to play with not here, we find them in France and Belgium. It has a lot to do with the personal relationships you have with the people who create the music itself.

R.: What about Hasse? He didn't want to play with the group anymore?

L.: No that wasn't the reason. He had the opportunity to go to school and do some interesting work so it would have meant more than a year away.

R.: Do you have plans for a new Zamla LP?

L.: Yes. We will make it in the Autumn with Jac, Denis and Kalle.

R.: How does your new solo LP, *12 SIBERIAN BICYCLES* fit in with Zamla's music?

L.: The idea for it came into my head a year ago. I was trying to make kind of "schlager" or commercial songs in a different way. I had an 8-track recorder out in the "chickenhouse" and nothing to do so I made a small song and added other instruments. I played it for a friend who said I make a record of it. The idea was to let the record go from a very typical Swedish summer waltz to a kind of avant-garde improvisation.

R.: What were some of the original influences which brought Zamla together?

L.: It has to do with our childhood, the different people in the group and what has come before. We were not educated in music and that is why perhaps we could go very quick into changes and do things that perhaps in the schools of classical, jazz or rock music is not allowed. We haven't these limitations. We did things with a good ear for listening to music. These ears are very big in Zamla. So you find influences from German polka and everywhere.

R.: How did you choose the name Samla Mammas Manna?

L.: It's a word game. One evening with a lot of dope in the chickenhouse we were sitting and making improvisations and from this the name popped up. Its meaning is impossible because ... collect mothers ... do you know manna -- the thing in the Bible, a kind of bread... it's like little cornflakes...from the heavens (ha, ha). The name is so difficult so nobody will forget it, also never remember to say it the right way (ha, ha)!

R.: Why did you then change it to Zamla Mammaz Manna?

L.: It has to do with the improvisations we made in '77, because we changed completely. We tried to play only improvisations for 1 year in Sweden and lost a lot of our audience. Very unpopular. But then we heard rumours from London that they liked what we did very much, so we went there and liked it and came back complaining about the scene in Sweden not moving ahead fast enough (ha, ha)

R.: The first album you did on Silence is still interesting to listen to today. Do you play any of it now?

L.: I don't know yet. Some of it had very Hinduistic or religious feelings from the early '70s, especially some pieces. The first gig we had was at a festival in Uppsala in June '70 and immediately after the concert people from Silence asked if we would do an LP. We had very little experience and did it in the Chickenhouse with bad home recorders. It made the music very naïve.

R.: You also made a record in '76 with Greg FitzPatrick called the *SNORUN-GARNAS SYMFONI*.

L.: Greg is an old friend. We have known him since the early '70s and he has even played a few concerts with us. When he made this pop-symphony he wanted us to play the music and we agreed. He first sent us a tape at double speed because he was so ashamed of the way he had played it. We heard it and liked it very much because it was so quick. Then we borrowed two horn players, one was Kalle Eriksson who's with us now. But it's not a Zamla record, it's Greg's music played by Zamla even though we added some creative ideas. There's a lot of people who like it and have said it's the best album we've made. Perhaps because it's simpler than Zamla's music so easier to understand.

R.: The first LP you did as Zamla with a 'Z' was the double *SCHLAGERNS MYSTIK/FOR ALDRE NYBEGYNNARE* which was stylistically very diverse. It ranged from improvised and experimental to the incredible "Odet" which is more structured and serious perhaps?

L.: I think for me it was very important that we made that improvised album because it was what we had been searching for for a very long time. That music was in us for many years. It all started with that spirit only in a more limited way as improvisation has always been a big thing for us. Many of the live shows feature improvisations and have a very visual effect and humorous feel. I can understand as well that people don't like it because it's very narrow music

R.: The last album you did for Silence was called *FAMILJESPRICKOR* ("Cracks in the Family"). The jacket stated; "This Zamla record was made under a period of transition and of course these circumstances have affected the music which is not as happy and optimistic as it used to be, but the meaning with inheritance is to be." What does this say about what is perhaps your best and strongest record yet?

L.: This was a complaint that we had in the group that before we were playing so much "circus apparatha," circus-like music. It gives the impression of a more happy music, while *FAMILJESPRICKOR* was built around the fact that one of the most important members of the group, Hasse, left and there was another sound to the drums with Vilgot. To our ears it was much sadder music.

R.: It's also a very emotional record.

L.: Yes, of course what we do is very emotional as it starts from emotions. That's how Zamla started in the early '70s, emotions were played straight out and we were lucky to have been able to record some of our emotionally-created music. We had quite fun at time creating the bridges between the pieces. Now with this new group we have to make new bridges and it's funny to see how, because now there are other demands, like exact ways of playing for instance. It's very confusing at times, especially when you don't have a dominating drummer who counted in everything that we did before.

R.: What do you think of Rock in Opposition and how much does Zamla associate with the other bands in that movement?

L.: R.I.O. is a small association of some European music groups that suddenly discovered they weren't alone -- working alone in their own countries with their music. This was the big thing and when we met in London in '78 it was a huge thing for us to see that there were other groups fighting for a little bit of the same thing. There is a big difference between some of the groups and there were theoretical fights at times, but the interesting thing was that we could collaborate and make some common concerts and festivals.

R.: How do you think U.S. audiences would react to Zamla?

L.: I think quite good. Etron Fou had a good experience when they toured the States. They said it was greatly different because it's not a question of sounding Swedish or French, it's a question of being European. I think with the right feeling for it and the right motivation we could do a lot of things. I mean you can move even a mountain one millimeter perhaps. I have felt that at moments on stage when emotions are so strong for you and the audience you feel you can do whatever you want. It's unforgettable and happily I have been lucky to participate in this with Zamla...it's a reality!

Robert Silverstein

Harold Budd
An Imaginary Interview

Q: Your background is ....

A: Nearly complete now. Which is to say I keep reviving ancient feelings to the extent that I consciously invite ghosts from my boyhood in L.A. to resurrect themselves and become fixed in an intensely personal language.

Q: And so, you would characterize your language as being ... what?

A: The sum of all that, qualified by my ability to translate it into something resembling literate coherency. And this last thing has proved to be either the bane or boon of nearly every over-educated American composer about my age.

Q: So, you're actually talking about style?

A: Style is the great leveler. The difference is that one is either in competition with someone else's style, or the language is unique to you alone and focused "indoors," as it were. But this takes quite a bit of courage to do because the pressures are tremendous. However having finally made that sort of break with all the boring conceits of so-called new music, one can find themselves with a language parallel or oblique to most other stuff and it becomes (what can I say?) a singular affair. For example, when I was a student everyone should have written at least several Stockhausen or Boulez pieces. I compromised by writing one Varese and several Morton Feldman pieces, but that was just a facet of my personality then -- looking for alternate routes within the paradigm of avant-garde music. Nowadays among student composers, the focus has shifted dramatically to Eno, Vangelis, or Phil Glass particularly. A very interesting change, I think.

Q: Who were some of the great stylists of the past?

A: Delius, Monteverdi, Debussy, Gesualdo, Sun Ra (not past) ...

A: Satie?

Q: He accomplished his goal with me; he bores me to death.

Q: Aside from Sun Ra, are there any stylists that are particularly attractive to you right now?

A: Firstly, I think David Bowie will attain the regard currently given to, say, Antonin Artaud. He has an identifiable mark wholly aside from anyone else. And skipping aside the more obvious and predictable artists whose work I really admire, I'll cite Joy Division, Roy Harris, Pharoah Sanders. I find snippets of Mexican mariachi music in nearly everything I do, and in the very distant past I'm extremely fond of whatever scholars have given us concerning the 13th Century composer Leonin Magister whose work is more, inexpressibly more, sublime than his more celebrated pupil Perotin.

Q: About those "ghosts" you spoke of in your past; can you name some of them?

A: Foremost must be a painted panel on the Griffith Park merry-go-round about 1940 or so -- a picture of a boy with a lion in a sort of Pre-Raphaelite sylvan meadow. It's not the picture itself, it's the well-spring of emotion that I can conjure. Another is the Venice Pier, about the same time. My father used to take me there for some reason unknown to me. But mostly it's the (potentially) lethal ambiance of the high desert country in Eastern California that most attracts and haunts me.

Q: Speaking of haunting music, how did you meet Brian Eno?

A: As I look back on things, I wonder what would have prevented Brian and me from ever meeting. But the simple fact is that Gavin Bryars gave Brian a tape of "Madrigals of the Rose Angel" and that was the beginning. That was in 1976 and the piece was already four years old, and I had no intimation or ambition whatever to make records at that point. The up-shot was that Brian brought me to London to record *THE PAVILION OF DREAMS* and that was the start of garnering an audience (which I always knew was there) wholly aside from the narrow confines of the experimental music ghetto. And obviously it was quite clear that that was also the beginning of an interesting and fruitful association.

Q: And Marion Brown? That seems totally inexplicable.

A: It would have to me too at one time, but that's the magic of association. I had known Marion's music based upon his albums on ESP and Impulse and with Shepp and Coltrane as well. But the main thing is that I heard a quality sound that was wholly unique and very attractive. We met early in 1974, and when he asked me for a work for his horn I got to work and got a grant from the National Endowment for the Arts to help out. He brought me to Wesleyan University for the first performance and of all the gifts he's give me, the principal one has to be that he totally radicalized me in terms of art-music as a business... You know; "Getting Yours."

Q: Are you "getting yours?"

A: No one is, but it's a conceit we're obliged to presume.

Q: As a performer, your appearances seem to be relatively infrequent and widely placed. This seems to be contrary to the usual way of doing things.

A: I'm not a minstrel. I don't play for my bread and butter. I've always been quite clear about that. My performances are really an annex, or a version, of a much larger scheme.

Q: And what is this larger vision?

A: That, I must confess, is so complicated and disparate that I'm certain it would be counter-productive to meld it into a discreet system. I recently read a phrase in a book on Mannerist painting describing a certain fresco as being "astonishingly incoherent." I couldn't think of a more apt or attractive response to a system of impulsive hunches. I think that a society or a culture shares certain responses on a much more intimate scale than is currently imagined. For example, when someone says to me "That's really gorgeous," it's my theory that what they mean by that is precisely what I mean by that; and so we rely on a system of inexact adjectives as hints toward total agreement.

Q: Total agreement?

A: Total. In fact, I'm pretty certain that it's pan-cultural.

Q: Movies do that too, right?

A: Especially movies. Except that they are so ubiquitous, and most are targeted for such a narrow audience, that only a few really speak to a larger sensibility. And by "larger" I mean more unpredictable and disparate public. When it comes to music for movies the best scores are obviously the ones that are primarily extremist at the outset.

Q: Extremists! Like who?

A: Ennio Morricone and Nino Rota, to begin with. And especially Pink Floyd's opening track to Barbet Schroeder's "The Valley" (*OBSCURED BY CLOUDS*). In each case the music is a complement to, or dialog with, the images, as opposed to the ordinary hack-work of descriptive reinforcement, which is dubious at best. That's what I mean by extremist: it goes directly to the heart of the matter, without being qualified.

Q: So, extremism in music is a positive value to you?

A: Of course, and why not? I remember Rhys Chatham showing me some drawings by Robert Longo, and he said, "Of course, he takes pop art as a given." Well, why not start from a brand new square one? I prefer one Glenn Branca or Fred Frith to a hundred sub-species of Stockhausen clones.

Q: What do you listen to at home?

A: I listen to music, new or old, that astonishes me, that absolutely takes my breath away. What could be simpler?

Q: You play the piano, right?

A: Well, sort of. A real pianist probably wouldn't consider what I do as really playing. At least that's the information I get. Sort of, "Oh well, anyone can do that," but the thing is that no one else does. Fortunately, I was able to get all the way through graduate school as a composer without ever taken a piano lesson My argument was always "Does a playwright have to use a typewriter?" But eventually there came a time when I had to invent for myself at least some facility.

Q: What happened that made that necessary?

A: Beginning in 1972, I started work on a series of very large works which included among everything else the use of numerous kinds of keyboards, and since the way that had to be played is virtually un-notatable I had to demonstrate the technique to the players. Consequently, it occurred to me that I might just as well get better at it and take the responsibility myself.

Q: But on *THE PAVILION OF DREAMS* several keyboardists besides yourself are listed.

A: I have to credit Brian with having a sixth sense about who to call for the session. There were two English composers, Gavin Bryars and Michael Nyman, and two Americans, Jo Julian and Richard Bernas, and everyone just fell into it with no difficulty whatever. That's the difference between hiring a technician or hiring an artist: The Wisdom of the Heart, as Henry Miller said.

Q: And *THE PLATEAUX OF MIRRORS*. How was that recorded?

A: That was recorded and lovingly pieced together over a six or seven-month period. Sometimes we were together, and sometimes we did it by mail, and finally it was apparent to both of us that we had an album. (There's at least another album in out-takes alone.) The final task was to compose the sequence of works and give them each a title, which we did in my living room in one marathon session with lots of input from my wife and two sons.

Q: Your last album, *THE SERPENT (IN QUICKSILVER)* is a 12" 45. Why did you choose that format instead of 33-1/3?

A: It was a total experiment on my part. Doing an album was one thing, but I wanted to see if that kind of music had an interesting life in that format, and it does. Once I had embarked on the project, I had been shown several European releases in the same mode, but I wanted to see if it worked in America. And then towards the end I saw that John Cale and Peter Gordon had done the same thing -- not the same sort of music, obviously, but basically the same audience, so I was pretty certain by then that it would take hold.

Q: What's your next project?

A: Everyone has a project: everyone's starting something, and absolutely no one will admit to being crippled with ennui with nothing but utterly lame ideas. I know how painful that is but that state is very often the beginning of something unplanned and invigorating. I know that I'm going to do two albums this year, and give at least two performances (very rare for me to accept two so early on.) But the main project is one that I've lived with for quite a long while: Late in 1978 while staying at a friend's apartment in New York, and being bored silly (L.A. and N.Y. are alike in this respect) I quite suddenly and inexplicably conceptualized a huge work which is doubtless unrealizable but which nonetheless might have an interesting life in its children. The basic idea has to do with my feeling that everyone listens to music at different levels, passive or active, but mostly a combination of both. Perhaps you recall television ads wherein they would send to you a record collection of classical pieces with all the boring parts removed; you just get the good parts. My idea has to do with focusing on the good parts only. Always, never the in-between parts, no repeats, no development, no process ... always at a good spot if you're listening then in a way you hadn't a moment earlier.

Interview conducted by Harold Budd

Edgar Froese Interview
Inside Tangerine Dream

H: Did you have a classical education?

F: I had a classical education over a period of 5 years...

H: When did T. D. get organized? Who were the original members?

F: In Sept. of '67... I counted how many people have been in the group one day and there were over 64 people involved. Originally I started the group on guitar and Klaus Schulze on drums. Then I started playing and studying guitar and piano, then back to keyboards around '68.

H: What was the first LP?

F: It was called *ELECTRONIC MEDITATION* and played with more or less conventional instruments... acoustic instruments!

H: Was electronic music something you were aiming at from the beginning?

F: I can't really say that it was our aim to

use electronics at that point, because we started searching for a new sound. But then we discovered that this was only possible with very rare and expensive instruments.

H: What was the very first record of T.D.?

F: It was a single, recorded during the era of "flower power" and we called it "Lady Green Grass."

H: And the first commercially successful record?

F: Commercial success came when we left Germany and began in Dec. '73 to work with Virgin Records in England. The first release was *PHAEDRA,* the one that brought us a lot of success. We earned enough money to buy new equipment.

H: Was Klaus in T.D. at that time?

F: He left in '71 when he got married and his wife wanted him to leave. He decided he couldn't do both, but one year later he got a divorce and remarried, and we decided it was better to stay with our wives.

H: When was the first concert in the USA?

F: In April '77 in Milwaukee, the first concert on the tour, it was incredible!

H: It was well received?

F: Incredible...I normally don't say things like that, but it was a sold-out tour. At first we were doubtful and didn't want to make the tour because no one knew what to expect or who would come see the concerts. Plus the equipment was quite hard to move around... Anyway, at the end we were really happy.

H: The first real success was in England however, correct?

F: Yeah. Until now we have not been well received in Germany... we are the "black ones" you know.

H: Does this have anything to do with the subtle quality of your music? Is Germany not suited to this kind of "transcendental-meditative" music, or am I wrong?

F: Maybe that's right and also one other reason -- the Germans don't usually accept their own originality. Since rock and roll began they have always imported music. The only things they have created on their own have been classical works and some avant-garde music. But in the era of "pop" I can't think of one group that has had an international influence.

H: Would you say then that there is something typically German about T.D.? In terms of the classical tradition...

F: I've heard a few people talk about the "Berlin School of Music" and I don't agree with that at all. We as a band are absolutely cosmo-political. I'm not at all interested in being called a "German musician."

H: Your vocals have been in English... ?

F: English, if you like it or not, is the world language. Obviously everybody is interested in reaching as many people as possible.

H: What about imported music?

F: There has been a response to fifteen or twenty years of imported music, and let us not forget that in Germany everywhere you can hear music on the British and American Forces stations. For this reason I don't believe that a very original music has come from Germany. There are exceptions, but in general it's not really creative.

H: Has T.D. been influenced more by groups like Pink Floyd than by composers like Stockhausen and Boulez?

F: More the mental side...John Cage, Stockhausen, etc... What they said about music influenced us more than anything else. There are mental similarities.

H: It's left its mark?

F: It's left some feelings... on your interpretation of what you've heard and then you start thinking about your own way of making music in light of it.

H: Is your music suitable for meditation? It is often described as "cosmic music," a term like "cosmic" art used to describe art in the metaphysical sense -- in a setting of total universe -- expressing a conscious awareness of larger forces or unseen realities. Do you think of your music in this sense?

F: Quite simply, everything you said is true! I believe in God, but I don't believe in the Church or any particular religion. I would say it's a metaphysical or spiritual feeling... the main turning point..."cosmic" was just a label put on it by the record company we were with in the early '70s.

H: Before 1971, when you were still working with Klaus, was he the main impetus in the group?

F: Not at all, Klaus was the drummer of the band. When he left in '71 we were prepared to do the 2nd record which was *ALPHA CENTAURI* and on that we used the first VCS synthe... a very small one. In the meantime Klaus got married and wasn't involved in the music at all. He started in 1972 his 1st LP I think? It was called *IRRLICHT*.

H: Do you think that title (*IRRLICHT*, weirdlight or craziness) says something about his music in general?

F: Oh, he was obviously there the first 5 or 6 years when he came to Berlin. I don't know that he tried to get the same "fear" (existential angst) down into his tapes, but he wanted to create the same kind of music. In the end -- I mean -- he found his way of explaining his feelings in his music.

H: Do you still get together with him from time-to-time and jam?

F: No... because there is one thing I can't agree with him about... that's the way he has used classical terms in his music. There was that album about Richard Wagner, I don't want to put him down...but christ ..I thought it was a lot of bullshit! I can't agree with that! There was a time when we really split...I didn't want to see him anymore because I can't work on future inspiration by using old-fashioned ...I mean Wagner was a genius, but why get involved?

H: Neo-classical music is really a going "back to" approach, and can be undynamic and static, isn't that true?

F: Absolutely! We were quite lucky when we moved away from Germany because we learned so much about the blacker side of the record companies... and fortunately could avoid a lot of mistakes so... since 1973, we have had nearly complete control over our music.

H: When I listen to your music I find myself easily induced into a trance without using stimulants, I can visualize and mandalize my consciousness ... I start color-tripping ... does your music actively seek to evoke these kind of experiences?

F: I'm just a part of the music. I know that

sounds funny, but I am just the vehicle for it. I'm also part of the audience. You could be playing the music too, or the guy next door, it's just an accident that I'm the one whose doing it... it has nothing to do with "my education" or learning piano, my training .... you have it or you don't. That's why people never discuss T.D. very much...they like it or hate it. The music has nothing to do with ego-tripping, it's not really me: It's something that goes through me... I just explain it...and other people feel the same way. There's little else I can say,...it's me -- that god awful belief -- nobody...nobody is creating something unbelievable, artists throughout the centuries have created their great works by accident! Nobody can stand up and say: "I want to do something important!" No! They are merely antennae for the cosmos! That's right... the word cosmic has a very bitter taste, but forget everything you've read in the comics or newspaper, there still remains something we must search for, it's getting together with cosmic consciousness ... working on that consciousness ... there's nothing more important, and soon...because by 1998, our Era will be over...there will be a dark period, possibly a third world war in which America will be destroyed and most of Northern Europe ...

H: You believe, obviously, then in a coming Apocalypse?

F: Absolutely! The Earth will recede as the waters rise. It happened before. The painful thing is that people think it's being done to them personally... they have 60, 70, 80 years of life that are so important to them and cannot see why nature would do this terrible thing "to me." They are only lost however, in cycles that span hundreds and thousands of years.

H: Does the album title *STRATOSFEAR* reflect that kind of fear?

F: That fear stands for the kind of fear when they don't know how to handle themselves... their fear. They don't realize that fear is absolutely necessary it's a part of our nature. People have to accept themselves as a unique thing in nature... they only see themselves as kings, as gods, as egos and that's shit! There's no way for man to develop beyond the limitations of natural order. They live in their little caves, jails of ego... for if you give up the ego it's the only way to be reborn. I don't mean it in the religious way of fear, or millennial fears, or fears of getting out of San Francisco...which was quite good in the early days. Forget all of that, see it as a natural process...the Earth and people have to clean up their act sometime!

H: Though differently expressed, weren't the millennial fears at the first millennial change quite the same as now?

F: You can't escape from what ever the WILL is, you can't escape and if you have to die in the next hour you have to die. If I would run around the world trying to escape, it would make no sense at all, the bomb that will kill me would do it in the jungle or in Australia or in the desert of New Mexico, wherever. What I can do is listen to my inner voice, the voice that tells one what to do. The thing is that if I was meant to escape, I will escape.

H: Do you think there is a mythology or better put, a "mythos" that ties things together in T.D.'s music?

F: Sure. It's hard to say because people will generally get it wrong ... not that we want to say anything, things through us want to explain something. That's why we used words/vocals just one time, but it didn't work because people didn't understand. We gave that up and now will never use language again. They took the words literally and didn't read between the lines and couldn't understand their own form of communication. The main thing we worry about is keeping from getting commercialized. That's not our aim. We don't want to free anyone, we just want to give them an idea about what we feel could be helpful.

H: You create a mental environment where people feel at home...

F: Yeah! People in rock and politics say that our music puts people to sleep and can never change their heads... but they forget that before you can change anything, you have to understand yourself. Before I start creating music I have to understand what I want to say. In other words, people have to get their acts together then they can start talking about educating others ....

Robert Hay

Spanish Progressive Music 1982

Progressive music in Spain has experienced deep changes since EUROCK's 1978 report. EUROCK talked about three independent rock labels which supported the country's growing progressive scene. However, this was not exactly true. Unfortunately the MoviePlay and Chapa-Zafiro labels were not independent but powerful nation-wide companies. Only Zeleste was truly independent, being located in Catalonia, a part of Northeastern Spain. Now, actually Zeleste has disappeared, MoviePlay's rock production has been reduced to a few name bands and Triana which is one of the biggest selling flamenco-rock bands. Only Chapa-Zafiro is still very active producing records by heavy-metal bands from Madrid, and Bloque, the only progressive band from the '70s which still records for Chapa.

Spain's progressive music, save for a few exceptions, has gone into the underground since 1978. This was due to the punk and new wave fashions which invaded Spain as well as the rest of Europe. Rock critics in FM radio and the press supported these fashions, turning their backs on anything considered "progressive." Since no alternative magazines or radio supported it, most of the old and new groups were forced to disband, change to another style or go underground until better times. Most of the bands mentioned in EUROCK's 1978 report have disappeared. Bands like Gotic, Granada, Ibio, Canarios, Musica Urbana and Blay Tritono vanished. Other groups became popular and their sound became more standardized as is the case with Triana, Compania Electrica Dharma, Asfalto and Max Sune. The only survivors are Bloque, Azahar, Gualberto and Jordi Sabates.

Some new interesting bands came along after EUROCK's report. A few didn't last, but most of them are still active today.

Iman - They released two LPs for Spanish CBS, *CALIFATO INDEPENDIENTE* and *CAMINO DEL AGUILA*. Mainly instrumental, they are an excellent fusion of progressive symphonic rock and Flamenco-Arab influences The best flamenco-rock band of them all, they disbanded in 1980.

Cai - Another progressive flamenco-rock band. Their first LP, *MAS ALLA DE NEUSTRAS MENTES DIMINUTAS*, was recorded for Trova, a very little company and was progressive rock along with some jazzy passages mixed with flamenco. It's now out of print. Their second and third LPs were recorded for Spanish Epic. *NOCHE ABIERTA*, the second, was more progressive symphonic rock and less jazzy including a couple of commercially-oriented songs. The third, *CANÇON DE LA PRIMAVERA*, is less progressive with more pop influences in it. Their next one promises to be more progressive again as Kiko Guerrero, Iman's former drummer, has joined the band.

Guadalquivir - This Andalucian flamenco rock group is jazz-oriented. Theirs is a fusion of jazz-rock with flamenco and different from similar experiments by any Anglo musicians. They have done two LPs up to now: *GUADALQUIVIR* and *CAMINO DEL CONCIERTO*. A new one is due soon.

At the same time, in the late 1970s, some real independent labels came out in the Spanish regions such as the Basque country, Galicia and Andalucia. Two Basque labels, Iz and Xoxoa, started to produce a lot of local progressive bands like Itoiz, Enbor, Errobi, Zen and Magdalena. At this time, they have limited most of their productions and only a few groups like Itoiz and Enbor will keep recording. During the past years there has also been a great revival of Celtic traditions and music in all European countries or regions with Celtic cultures: Asturias (Spain), Galicia (Spain), Brittany (France), Wales, Ireland...

A strong Celtic music movement has come out with acoustic and progressive Celtic music bands. Galician independent label, Ruada, has released records by acoustic groups: Milladoiro, Doa and Cromlech and progressive groups Taranis (Celtic rock) and Outeiro (jazz-rock). Also there is Labanda, a Madrid-based group who play Galician music with the help of a Galician bagpipist who used to play with Granada. They play Celtic-rock mixing all sorts of ancient and acoustic instruments with electric equipment. Finally there is Nuberu, the only Asturian Celtic music band. Their first album was straight folk, but their second and third are a nice mix of symphonic rock with Celtic elements.

Andalucia's independent label, Surcosur, mainly is interested in flamenco. Up to this point, they have only released a rock album that is not very interesting.

Most of Spain's progressive groups are still in the underground. Therefore, it's extremely hard to find out about them. In the Basque country we find two interesting new groups: Tol and G.B.G. (Gotxi, Baxter and Guzman). G.B.G. is a trio who play symphonic rock. Tol is an electronic duo formed by Alberto Iriondo on keyboards and Jesus Sarasua (keys as well). Their style can be defined as electronic-cosmic-gliding music. They will be releasing a cassette titled *OBELISKO* in the near future.

Barcelona, once the capital of Spain's strongest progressive rock movement, has two main groups. The most known is Neuronium, then there is the legendary Suck Electronic.

Suck Electronic - One of Spain's most important progressive bands. The group started 8 years ago (1974) in Barcelona with three musicians: Francesc Armengol (keyboards), Michel Huygen (keyboards), now with Neuronium, and Jordi Garcia (keys). Their original name was Suck Electronic Encyclopedic, but it was later shortened. The bands first stage was dedicated to electronic music and was much appreciated by the critics, as a group with three keyboard players was heroic and unique in Spain at that time. Then Jordi Garcia started thinking about adding new ideas to the music. He had experience in filmmaking and art and wanted to form a concept that was "music to look at and listen to." As well he wanted to add rock and jazz influences to the sound so the group split. Michel Huygen formed Neuronium and Francesc Amengol left the music scene. Thus began the second stage of the group that the critics called the "symphonic-acid" stage (1976-'79). The music became a sort of psychedelic-progressive rock similar to Gong and Hawkwind with an elaborate environment created for their concerts that made use of film, slides, mimes, fashion models, actors, costumes, lights and various themes like: "The Trip," "Nuclear Horror" and texts by Tzara, Vian & Bradbury.

They played in parts of Spain, Andorra and Southern France. Also the group tried to make a record at that time but it became impossible due to the changes in members. The group today is made up of: Josep Gimenez (guitars, vocals), Jose Maria Ciria (drums, vibes, percussion, lyre), Pepe Rodriguez (bass) and Jordi Garcia (synths, vocals). Recently they added a South American female vocalist, Cher Wood, who along with some guest musicians, will participate in the making of their debut LP. The music Suck Electronic is now making is a distillation/concentration of all their past experiences plus new roads. Conceptually it has to do with the future of man. The lyrics talk about a possible future that could be considered science fiction, but it's closer to reality than we think. There are songs that deal with auto death on the freeway "John Vaughn and Mademoiselle Moloch"; people that wake up in a horrifying future after having been in extended hibernation, "The Hibernated Man"; a company specializing in suicide death "RH+"; etc. They try to reflect mankind's stress rather than making people "fly" with cosmic music. Stylistically their current stage could be described as Canterburyan progressive rock.

Madrid has, or had some of the best progressive-symphonic rock bands in Spain. Among them were Tempano, Exodo and Cabellera de Berenice. Nothing has been heard about any of them over the last year however, so perhaps they have split? The only bands known to be active are: Babia and YHVH. Babia is an unusual band formed by people coming from different musical fields: classical, progressive rock, jazz, Middle Age music and Oriental music. The result is a blend of Western and Oriental sound that's sometimes jazzy, other times electric. YHVH is an obscure electronic group.

In Zaragoza we find a new electronic band called Cyborg. The two members are Ricardo and Vincente Lopez, both of whom play keyboards.

Sevilla, the largest city in Andalucia, has turned out to be one of the most interesting places in Spain. Veteran musician Gualberto is preparing his next record which will be a return to progressive music after his flamenco experiments. Also from Sevilla is VCO, a solo project of electronic music by Jesus Camona. The most interesting musician is Jose Ignacio Narvaez who plays electronic classical rock. Stylistically quite amazing and technically impressive, the closest comparisons would be Vangelis or perhaps Keith Emerson minus their pretensions.

In the Canary Islands we find two interesting bands on the island of Tenerife. One is Imago, a three piece which plays a fusion not unlike the Mahavishnu Orchestra. The group's members are Miguel Jaubert on guitars/guitar synthe, Tony (bass) and Alfredo Llanos (drums, percussion). The other is Arte Moderno. According to their own definition, they play music generated by electronic instruments, which is tribal, rhythmic, dynamic and structured in a geometric progression. Their influences are various and numerous: Talking Heads, Syd Barrett, King Crimson and "new" groups like Magazine, The Cure, B-52's, etc. The two members are Juani Belda (keyboards and Javier Seguera (synths, guitars, tapes, electronic percussion and vocals).

There are certainly more interesting groups especially in large cities like Madrid and Barcelona, but the problems of communication make exposure hard to get. In a following article more will be written about them as information is available.

Angel R. Romero

Neuronium
REFLECTIONS ON A CONCEPTION

Bridge between the real and unreal.
Bridge between "They" and us.
They use the language of music to express their philosophy, their feelings.
Mental Union.
I don't believe in chance.
Everything happens because it has to.
It's destiny.
So, where does their electronic music come from?
From a logical musical evolution?
Yes, perhaps.
Obviously it has to be, but is it?
I think there must be something else.
Michel Huygen and Carlos Guirao, their minds are the receivers of a message,
But what is this message?
Who uses anything as original as synthesizers to communicate with?

Words would be the obvious thing, but not in this case.
They act as receivers - transmitters.
There is a telepathic bridge between them and this superior entity.

All sorts of labels have been given to this music.
Cybernetic, mechanical, futuristic, gliding, space, cosmic..... Perhaps the answer is in the Cosmos.
In a far-off luminous point, the same that shone its ray of light on the Maya, Egyptian civilizations and on "Him,"
A messenger from the great beyond.
And now through this music comes communication.
For this reason so few people understand.
They are not prepared and never will be, they only believe what they see, what they

touch and have their imagination and sensitivity atrophied by the media The saddest thing is that it is these same people who regard them as machines or robots, they are the robots and don't realize it. Their feelings are expressed through the synthesizer.
It is not the machines that make the music, but their minds illuminated from this far-off point.

They are two people chosen, to offer us this music,
to bear us aloft on a journey through ourselves and project us towards higher planes of consciousness.

Juan Villa

Mexico
Progressive Music South Of The Border

It wasn't too long ago that knowledge of there being anything remotely resembling progressive music in Mexico was nil. That situation is now changing however as various artists have become active and a few recordings have been made on LP as well as cassette. There is no real progressive scene to speak of, but as in other countries around the world a group of musicians have taken up the progressive banner and work to develop their musical ideas for the most part outside normal channels. The following are some of the known groups that have to date come to attention, the core from which a real scene might grow.

Decibel: For all intents and purposes, the pioneer of Mexican experimental music. Headed by journalist Walter Schmidt, their one LP, *EL POETA DEL RUIDO*, done a couple years ago still stands today as a fine example of intelligent music influenced by the likes of Henry Cow. Unfortunately the band has now split. More recently Walter has formed a psychedelic band, Size, who have done a private 45. For the future plans are made for an LP featuring 6 synthesizer players.

Chac Mool: The superstars of the young Mexican scene whose first LP in 1980 has to date sold 20,000 copies. They do numerous live concerts, attracting good crowds. They've already released a second album and a third is in the can. On the Philips label, their sound is a fusion of Italian classical rock influence and Genesis. The highlight being the keyboards of Carlos Alvarado.

Via Lactea: The pioneers of Mexican space music, originally a duo consisting of Carlos Alvarado and Miguel Angel Nava. After their initial cassette for EUROCK, Miguel left and formed his own band Trombatro who have done a few live concerts but thus far no recording. Carlos Alvarado has continued Via Lactea as a solo project, producing 3 more cassettes, as well he's now completing his first solo LP. His cassettes were full of striking celestial synthesizer sound, but lacked high quality recording technology. For Carlos, the LP will be the proof of his unique ability.

Cajo De Pandora: Pandora's Box have done one LP to date which is a nice fusion of classical and jazz. Again similar in style to the early '70s classical bands, they nonetheless are an original with subtle touches of a Mexican flavor added.

Hilozoizmo/Oxomaxoma: Hilozoizmo is a multi-media, sound-music-performance congregation initiated by Arturo Romo and friends. Their concept revolves around a stage performance to improvised music that combines natural and synthetic sound. A strange concoction, moments harken back to Faust at their most anarchic. Oxomaxoma is their companion project. Again Arturo and friends, they do spontaneous happenings of non-music/sound-as-music that fall into the realm of impulse playing.

Voldarepet: A trio that plays a free floating form of Space Rock not unlike mid-period Floyd. Melodic passages of synthe and guitar combine with intervals of rock rhythms effectively.

Flught: Headed by Sergio DeLambra on keys, their music is very classical with its exquisite piano/synthe counterpointed by guitar. Striking technique and compositional skill make their debut disc, due soon, anxiously awaited.

Litto Nebbia: South American pianist with a few releases in Mexico. His best is on solo piano which features an excellent selection of traditional and classical melodies. Diverse and tasteful.

Princed Ahents: A sonic terrorist who uses feedback and fuzzed solos to create hysterical sound collages that are crude, intense and at times powerful.

As evidenced by this rundown, you can see something is going on, though much of it is for private purposes only. It is all of interest regardless, and deserving of attention for curiosity's sake as well as to encourage the growth of the artists. Hopefully this is just the beginning.

Archie Patterson

Nocturnal Emissions

ENVIRONMENTAL MANAGEMENT
Music is a device for social regulation, a process of committing to memory and repeating certain limited habit patterns.

Expression has been forced through the conventions of the ruling media consensus to be carried through preset limited frequencies. Content has been negated by repetition of familiar formulas, recorded and played back in inexorable degradation.

MODEL CONTROL ORGANISM
Information technology is an extension of the human nervous system in which resources have been concentrated into projects that simply reproduce existing social relationships of dominance and subservience. Possibilities for creativity have been neglected. Entertainment is an evil bluff to keep the gears turning, poisoning the soul of mankind.

MECHANICAL INDUCTION
All political systems exist by effectively limiting the rate and direction of change. Imposed reality is reinforced by the threat of corrective surgery. New institutions of sedation; internment; psychiatric torture and irradiation inherit the old myths of religion. We have learned to live in an atmosphere of unease.

INFECTED
NE outputs are a demonstration of possibilities and potential aimed at bringing about dynamic physical and psychic change; unpredictable and unlike any precedent. The sonic output is part of a campaign using existing situations to infiltrate open media systems; without accepting their limitations; in such a way that they are useful for consciousness. The aim is direct intervention. The performances are not the thing itself, nor are they by-products like records. They have no value in themselves, they are only of use in disseminating information, all are luxuries after merely being alive and sharing that fact.

THE ERASURE
The information war is one of the most important of our struggles. We must never accept our knowledge as absolute truth, only as a transient "realistic" lie. Language is essentially mystification. The sources of our themes, actions and the relationships between them are derived from any place or period except from the arts, cultural traditions, their derivatives and their milieu.

> ....There is no permanence. We represent no one. We are nothing special. History starts with our birth. The Future ends when we die. We are getting closer....

The NE is the man or woman sitting next to you. Activating voices hitherto largactilled and electroshocked out of existence, their tape lab circuits overloaded to the point of meltdown. Sensory bombardments, menacing, psychotropic. A feeling in your bowels. Direct attack metabolic alarm ecstasy, spasm, psychoses. A temporary threshold shift with cataclysmic potential generating a special atmosphere, intangible, always unique. A wreckage tearing a hole in the fabric of reality. May you never be the same again.

Nocturnal Emissions

The Legend Of The Pink Dots

The LPD's were conceived at the Stonehenge Free Festival the day after Midsummer's Day 1980. There were lots of little bands in evidence, jamming, enjoying themselves, and we wanted to be part of it. Consequently we bought a couple of cheap synths, a drum machine and used an old stand up piano.

The original line-up was: May B. Irma Mazed (piano), Edward Ka-Spel (vocal noise), Phil Harmonix (synth), Michael .019 (keyboards, guitar). The early material was straight improvisation, words as well. Can are great faves as well as early Floyd.

Sessions at this time were held in a crumbling Victorian squat with an audience of mostly friends. All night, candlelight marathons were numerous and quite an achievement as there was no heating. The first studio venture in October 1980 resulted in "Voices," "Waiting For The Call," & "Frosty" of which we considered "Frosty" to be an alternative Xmas single. Virgin Records didn't agree. Michael then left and Rik Chevrolet joined coming off a soul band. He liked the challenge.

The first gig was at a folk(!) club, and we duly alienated a good portion of the conservative audience with our "Guess the Politician." It's about the comments of various politicos in their bunker after the Bomb has gone off, as they watch what is going on outside on their tellys. C.N.D. liked what we had to say and invited us to play at a rally in East London. Sadly we ended up playing to about 50 people as the cold whittled down the crowd. Still we had some of them waltzing across the field to "Before the End."

Rolls joined in April and we did "Defeated" which ultimately emerged on a sampler put out by Glass Records. May then left to concentrate on her own material and Michael rejoined.

It's difficult to pin down the band's philosophy. On the whole however, we distrust the music biz and don't really wish to become involved with any big company.

Hopefully we're original, emotional and sound very British (important). Electronics play a big part in what we do, though we try to avoid clichés (so many grim, bleak, industrial bands around), but we're still feeling our way. Ultimately we want our music to be like a strange and wild film. Another world, but based on things going on around us. We're perhaps a quarter of the way there..... SING WHILE YOU MAY!

the LPDs

1983

Japan Scene

Currently independent music in Japan is on the rise. New groups and labels are popping up in many places. A private cassette scene is one of the most active areas. While it is all still an underground phenomenon, it's beginning to gain national as well as some international exposure. Anglo influences remain strong on the majority of Japanese musicians, but there is now a current of sound that takes off from that base and fuses the unique native character into their work.

This set of articles is a first installment in a series of pieces meant to uncover some of the more interesting artists. To some extent it will be historical as well as current, for to know the past is to see the future. But basically it will be an attempt to "discover" what's going on and pass it on as information and materials are not always easy to come by.

To begin we'll take a look at perhaps the most far reaching Japanese band of all time -- Far Out/Far East Family Band and its various permutations. In addition, two of the most interesting innovators -- Magical Power Mako and Stomu Yamash'ta. Then we have the incredible D.D. Records cassette label and last but not least, the media -- *Fools Mate*, *Marquee Moon* and *Rock Magazine*, who helped shape much of what's happening today. That all seems a good start, so let's proceed....

Archie Patterson

Far Out

Far Out was for all intents and purposes the first truly spaced out rock band in Japan. Formed in the early '70s, the personnel consisted of Fumio Miyashita, Kei Ishikawa, Eiichi Sayu and Manami Arai. Their sound and vision was pure acid. Peace and Love were their themes and tripping out their path to eternal bliss. All of this crystallized on their debut disc, titled simply *FAR OUT*, which featured two supersonic jams full of psychedelic guitar and synthetic vibrations. A real blast, words and music were by Fumio so it can be said to have been his trip, so to speak. As happened in those halcyon days, they split up and what emerged was two new groups; Fumio formed the Far East Family Band and Kei started Chronicle.

Chronicle was a bit more rock than its predecessor, yet still had an affinity for spacy sound. They did two LPs, *MESSAGE FROM THE STARS* (a remixed version was issued in the USA by All Ears) and their best work *LIVE AT THE WHISKY A GO GO* (believe it or not!). *LIVE* had some stellar moments, but the band ended up in oblivion and Kei has since done work with Akira Ito among others.

The Far East Family Band was a totally different trip as Fumio gathered around him a new crew and took off for the outer reaches of the cosmos. Members were: Akira Ito - keys, Akira Fukakusa - bass, Shizuo Takasaki - drums, Masaaki Takahashi (aka Kitaro) - keys, Hirohito Fukushima - vocal & sitar and Fumio on guitar, synthe & vocal. Over the span of three LPs: *CAVE DOWN TO THE EARTH, NIPPONJIN* and *PARALLEL WORLD*, they managed to combine a Japanese Zen ethic with Floydian musical tendencies to great effect. Also they met up with Klaus Schulze who took them under his wing for the latter two to fully integrate electronic technology into their sound. As a result they turned into real classics of the genre.

After *PARALLEL WORLD* there was another split. Akira Ito and Kitaro went off to do a series of solo albums. Ito's four LPs, to date, most resemble FEFB's more pastoral moments. They sport a softer more highly-produced sound. Kitaro on the other hand chose the pure electronic path and has some eleven records so far. Unfortunately his record company believes in mass merchandising to the point of overkill and his unique sound has suffered. He's cranking out highly pasteurized and thematically redundant cosmic music. Still the first few did possess a magic that's quite unique and are celestial, Zen electronics at their best.

Meanwhile Fumio, Akira Fukakusa, Hirohito Fukushima and new drummer Yujin Harada produced what was to be the final FEFB album, *TENKUJIN*. Again it too saw the light of day in the USA, thanks to the All Ears label run by Tony Harrington. A bit lighter and more meditative than previous efforts it was nonetheless as good, filled with a subtle beauty.

Then came the beginning of the end. Fumio moved to L.A. He did some live gigs that were alternately spectacular and spotty, depending on whether the spirit was able to transcend earthly shortcomings. He was supposed to have recorded a solo soundtrack album for All Ears, but it never came out and he ultimately went back to Japan. This was a couple years back. Since then nothing has been heard?

Hopefully this is not the last of Fumio, for over the span of his serving as guiding light for Far Out and FEFB some amazing music happened. Unfortunately I believe all of those albums are now out of print. They have been reissued at least once, so maybe again? It'll be shame if we've heard the last of them and of Fumio as well.

Archie Patterson

Magical Power Mako

Magical Power Mako is the name of a musical project run by Mako, a multi-instrumental manipulator. Sometimes it is an interplay by various players as a group and sometimes he plays all of instruments himself.

Mako was born in Izushuzen Buddhist temple in 1956. He came to Tokyo when he was sixteen years old and met Toru Takemitsu, one of the best modern music players and worked with him on TV productions in '73 & '74.

In late '73 he released his first LP, *MAGIC POWER*, as Magical Power Mako. It is one of the great works of all Japanese music. There is an amazing range of sounds from aggressive, breaking up of songs, to simple, pure melodies. Mellotron is used extensively.

In '75 the second record, *SUPER RECORD*, was released. It was composed, played and recorded by Mako alone. The sound is cosmic and peaceful with a beautiful and moving atmosphere.

In '77, *JUMP* was issued. It is rather different wherein it is rock music, amateurish and unpolished. It was only meant to be a progressive rock album. After that he retired from the music scene to reconstruct his musical concept.

In '81 he released his fourth album, *WELCOME TO THE EARTH*, and simultaneously started gig activities. The record of pop and love songs was unquestionably intended to be commercial. His fans were shocked by his change and disappointed.

But their disappointment was soon resolved with his newest work, *MUSIC FROM HEAVEN*. It's definitely up to the standards of his early material. Heaviness and sensitivity are magically harmonized. Upon his insistence the record and cover are transparent with a label that's made of metal. Only 500 copies were pressed. Certainly with *MUSIC FROM HEAVEN*, Mako has regained his identity with a powerful, impressionistic sound.

Archie Patterson

Stomu Yamash'ta

Tsutom Yamashita is more well-known to us as Stomu Yamash'ta, an international musician of some renown. Some time ago he became known for his best work *RED BUDDAH* and the *GO* project. Today he has embarked on the topical work *IROHA*, of which three of its five parts have been released to date. This Spring he did one performance of it in Tokyo. On stage it opened with a priest who enters and sits "Zazen" throughout the performance. The story that unfolds behind him is of the love between sky-man and earth-lady. It was rather like a ballet, strongly visual and his music was impressive and very effective.

IROHA (SUI), the newest album, consists of the music for the live performance. It's evocative and cerebral, the main instrument being synthesizer. He once composed ballet music using tapes of Japanese instruments and live orchestra (not recorded). It seems he changed the work to be more contemporary for *IROHA*.

In addition to his solo projects he has also been involved with the English underground, in particular the group Suntreader and a series of albums he did with these musicians. Morris Pert, Robin Thompson, Peter Robinson, Alyn Ross (of Suntreader) and Hugh Hopper, Gary Boyle, Brian Gascoyne, Nigel Morris (of Isotope) we involved with the *RED BUDDAH THEATRE, COME TO THE EDGE* and *RAINDOG* works.

Most recently he did the soundtrack for Paul Mazursky's film "The Tempest," released in the USA on Casablanca.

Translation and reprinting courtesy of Marquee Moon Magazine

D.D. Records Interview

To come to terms with D.D. Records is no small task. In general I would say that the basic concepts plus combined works of their artists represent the essence of the adventurous musical spirit. In fact after hearing all 100 of the current cassette releases available, I'm staggered by the variety and level of imagination that's uniformly present and the overall high quality. To a great extent the work of the D.D. artists has restored some enjoyment to my music listening. It's music for music's sake, done to good quality standards all around and not simply produced as an attempt to enter the marketplace as a calculated attempt at commerciality (straight business or hip egoist strategies).

D.D. Records was set up in Sept. 1980 by T. Kamada who runs it himself. To date he has issued 100 cassettes and 6 limited edition EPs of privately-produced music by about 30 amateur, underground musicians. The aim of D.D. Records is to expose these sounds as cheaply as possible, undaunted by the irrationality of the management, and maintain quality standards, also to expand the scope of the Japanese underground scene.

The following artists (solo or in various combinations) have done work released on the D.D. Records cassette series:

T. Kamada: organizer, music & electric engineer. A modern dadaist he's made electro-dry-pop and cool-industrial musics.

K. Yoshimatsu: A stoic guitarist. His aim is to combine European aesthetic with Eastern guitar/synthe themes.

K. Usami: An improvisational organist. He tries to convey the colder emotions of life. Also leader of the Ironic Afternoon Orchestra.

Y. Fujimoto: Does works as Pop Company. Practices musical malformation ethic done with a dadaist spirit.

Juma: Band of musical extremists whose music embodied rock, Germanics, minimal tendencies and was based on sin, beauty and death.

N. Takemura: Arumekat Oiron is his band. He twists old Japanese music into new forms and sensibilities.

T. Isotani: Sax player who works with many bands. Solo ethic is filled with 4th world feeling.

Y. Nishikubo: A new wave guitarist, who makes solo works of treated guitar.

A. Koshi: Guitarist and vocalist with tendencies from Fripp to Bowie.

F. Yasumura: Exotic female vocalist.

T. Kuramoto: Improviser of flute and guitar. Brain behind Ironic Afternoon Orchestra.

T. Ohta: Modern urban pop activist.

T. Nakamura: Shy and humorous bassist, plus master of applied chemistry. He believes improvisation must be controlled.

H. Kobayashi: Heads the band Yamira-Micha whose style is based on old Japanese percussive and vocal ideas -- words are sounds.

S. Ueo: Keyboardist and drummer whose style is influenced by German progressive rock.

H. Osada: Inorganic synthe music. Cool and lively.

A. Turuta: Synthesist who produces cold electro-pop without commerciality.

A. Mori: Inorganic composer of synthe and guitar works. 17 years old.

M. Ushioku: Alternative maker of noise and tape manipulation. Also age 17.

S. Debuchi: Student of art and video who works with effected guitar and noise techniques.

Y. Ohi: Zen music artist who works with old Japanese instruments and modern synthe technology.

As you might imagine to categorize or describe the work of such a large body of artists' material is next to impossible. Electronics certainly plays a large part in much of it, but other influences are also strong such as urban rock, jazz, ethnic and free music. Early German experimentalists like T. Dream and Cluster as well as some of the Anglo Progressives like Oldfield, Henry Cow.... In no instance however is it a mere copy. For "amateurs" they make some of the best music I've heard in ages.

Archie Patterson

Japanese Rock Media

Few places in the world have a rock media that has developed to the high level of sophistication that has been reached in Japan. To a great extent the very nature of the music scene has been shaped by it and the extensive coverage given to Western rock music. To see any one of the major mags is to marvel at their sheer level of excellence in terms of coverage, artistic presentation and print technology. What follows here is a brief survey of the main magazines and their related works.

MUSIC LIFE
The bible of the music biz, much like *Billboard* is here. Glossy, full-blown coverage of the latest Anglo sensations and superstars.

FOOLS MATE
The pioneer of progressive music in Japan, subtitled "The Eurorock Magazine." Over the span of its 24+ issues it's continually evolved artistically and given exposure to new music from around the world. Layout and graphics are stunning and the attention to details in its features are equally amazing. Perhaps the best magazine in the world!

In addition to being a magazine, it has an extension into the actual distribution and release of records as it recently began Eastern Works, a branch of Recommended Records. They distribute records from around the world and have also issued a series of albums by Recommended artists: The Work, Fred Frith and Massacre.

MARQUEE MOON
Subtitled Musica Metafisica, *Marquee Moon* is a university-based mag that has followed in the footsteps of *Fools Mate*. With half as many issues as *Fools Mate*, over the last year in particular it has become superb in its own right. The coverage is a bit more oriented toward the experimental side of things; classical and rock as well as the native Japanese scene. The graphic layout and research is again top notch.

Along with the mag there is a distribution service and collaborative effort with a music co-op, L.L.E. (Little Leaguers Elbow), who have produced 5 LPs featuring various Japanese artists. M.M. Distribution has to date released some 20 cassettes of experimental music by native musicians that run the gamut from electronics to rock and guitar explorations. In addition Magical Power Mako's MUSIC FROM HEAVEN was a collaborative effort with *Marquee Moon*.

ROCK MAGAZINE
Done by Yuzuru Agi, Rock Magazine "For Alternative Human" is the most bizarre of the music magazines. Oblique layouts and articles on fringe artists of the new wave and avant garde give it a very experimental slant.

In addition Agi runs the underground label Vanity Records. To date he's produced 12 albums, 6 cassettes and 4 EPs that are fascinating for their extreme and provocative nature.

No doubt there are other, smaller mags around, but the primary obstacle one encounters in trying to locate them, or even get information/materials from those mentioned is one of communication. Due to language, their priorities and perhaps limited interest on their part, getting response to letters or anything else on a regular basis is sporadic. I'd hope this will change in the future?

As you can see from this series of pieces

there is certainly a lot happening in Japan. Next time hopefully more, including Stack Orientation, an innovative cassette label from Kyoto; Pinkotecka Records, an alternative, independent record company; and others. All Japanese artists and independent companies are encouraged to make contact and send their materials.

Archie Patterson

Malcolm R. Mooney Interview

Without a doubt Germany's Can was one of the pioneering groups of what has become known today as EuroRock. Malcolm Mooney, a black American, was the original lead singer in their early years. His unique vocal talents were present on the first album *MONSTER MOVIE*, snippets of *LIMITED/UNLIMITED EDITION* and also on the recently-issued *DELAY '68*. After the release of the first album, he left the band rather mysteriously and became the subject of much curiosity and a few rumors among Canatics for the last 10 years or more. Recently I had the pleasure of getting together with him and having a rap session. Out of that came the impetus for the following interview.

Since those early days he has been painting and had several exhibitions of his work as well as done time as a school teacher. It's easy after meeting him to see why his work with Can was so unique. Still today he retains the same insightful imagination he had then. I think that comes across in the words which follow.

A: What experiences brought you, an American, to join Can, a German rock band?

M: The '60s was for me was a period of discovery and experimentation in my life. One included the ideas of "Art," first the visual and then sound -- "the action hears the sound." By 1968 I thought I was ready to leave for the rest of the world. I had been tooting on a gift -- a tenor sax -- and listening, watching and participating in a few jams with some Boston musicians. I didn't know how rigorous the training and sustaining of an art form was until... I met Irmin, Holger, Jaki, Michael, David and of course Hildegaard. Fitting into Can's specialized style was something within itself. I mean we lived together for 2 years. Those tapes/records heard and not heard, were from those times and before we met when ideas were formed. My horizons were broadened by listening to music from everywhere. And just before I met the members of the group I had traveled through Turkey, India, Afghanistan and Pakistan, ending up in Europe. Music was in the air and on the airwaves (radio) all time. I loved music.

A: What was it like in the early days in terms of live gigs and the early recordings?

M: The early gigs and recordings were sheer excitement. I never knew what I was going to do. Nothing at first was planned. Then I became self-critical of my approach and tried to eliminate the unpredictable. The reasoning as I mentioned before was rigorous, I must have weighed 140 lbs. at the time and I could lose 10-15 lbs. at sessions. Our first gig was at our studio, Schloss Norvenich, a castle of sorts. It was difficult for me because I was aware of the people (audience) very much. My aim, I discovered, was to vocally create harmony or rhythms, tensions, but I became restless because of the unexpected. It is one thing to improvise 8 bars, but it's totally different to improvise one whole side of a record or 1-1/2 hours live which is what we did continuously until the later gigs in Zurich. Can was a driving, creative and stimulating band. It was always in a state of change. Our first record, *MONSTER MOVIE*, to give an example, the "A" side is completely controlled, planned. The "B" side, "You Doo Right," is a first take in the vocals. There were overdubs added, but the recording, which started at about 11 AM, ended around 11 PM. It was quite a session. I left the studio at one time for lunch, when I returned the band was still playing the tune and I resumed where I had left off and that is how we did "You Doo Right."

A: Were lyrics/concepts planned out or freely improvised as was the groups music? Did the politics of the times tune you into various ideas?

M: Lyrics were written -- basic format -- then improvisation came into play within that format. Sometimes after listening to the tape we would add to it a sound or mood that would heighten the improvisation. We were Cannatively Innovative. Tuned into the world -- from all possible angles.

A: There are stories of very confrontational affairs where you chastised the audience, sold paintings off the walls, etc. How would you characterize you performance style?

M: CANfrontational -- yes, at points in live performances, I was trying to make myself aware of the world -- all its good, by trying to rid myself of the negatives. In so doing there were truths revealed. MONSTER MOVIE sort of crystallizes those times emotionally, the late '60s was a period of change.

A: How do you feel it holds up today?

M: It's a very interesting record to listen to. For me it says -- there are other alternatives to the way we played. I'd especially like to record those pieces again. Maybe, but onward...

A: Spoon, Can's label just issued some tapes from the vaults, *DELAY '68*. Do you like it as well?

M: I just heard it. There are a few numbers I wish I could do again. But it's another CAN DO.

A: What happened to make you leave the group? Again I've heard various strange stories.

M: Too much.....too soon..... Also staying in Zurich doing a long series of gigs at a theatre, I could see the group as four -- Jaki, Holger, Irmin and Michael. I heard them rehearsing one time -- no vocals and they were great. That idea stayed with me. I remember asking myself and Irmin, I guess everyone, what they thought of me leaving. I had become so attached to Can, my heart kept saying stay, my mind kept saying go. So I became ill... That's all past now!

A: You left the group over 10 years ago now, do you ever think of going back to Europe and doing another "reunion" record with the others? Is there anything in the future for you musically?

M: I'd love to have a chance! As for doing anything musically again, we'll have to wait and see.

A: What have you been doing since those days?

M: I've been painting. I taught for about 5 years. Designed a sculpture in New York in 1970 called the "Eternal Camcentric."

For a long time, maybe 3 years, I would play the piano for 1-2 hours at a time, the tune was called "Warburton Ave." Not much more... Sang with a few people.

Last I'd like to say, hello to you all!

Archie Patterson

Teutonic Electronic #2

There's even more going on in Germany concerning electronic music than you might imagine. And I'm not speaking about just the many releases by I.C. and Sky or the so-called Berlin school.

In the previous EUROCK article on Teutonic Electronics, some of the lesser known people were touched upon, but here I'll cover even more, such as Hardy Kukuk, Intence, Trance, Touch, Frieder Butzmann, Rudiger Lorenz.

HARDY KUKUK
A good friend of Klaus Bloch, whom you know from the last article. His first self-distributed LP, *ATEMNOT*, consists of three long and two short tracks, with a lot of sequencer and string sounds, creating a very hypnotic effect. According to Hardy it's music by which to dream and relax. Between the two sides there is some original music and promise for the next record. Now he is experimenting with computer-drums to develop the rhythmic aspect and also has hopes to play live in the future. *ATEMNOT* isn't a spectacular debut, but it shouldn't be underestimated by listeners either.

RUDIGER LORENZ
A long-time musician who discovered synthe music in 1977. In addition he has 5 years of piano training, and a great interest in the technical side as he himself has built a great deal of his equipment. Surprisingly electronics is his hobby, as he is a full-time chemist by profession. Musically I can imagine him living in Berlin. The surprising thing of his music is that it's always recorded live and without multi-tracking, and yet it contains such a multitude of ideas.

Together with some other musicians he has founded as well a cassette label and issued to date 12 titles of which 2 are by him. Soon is due his first LP.

TRANCE
Another group from Northern Germany. On their first LP, *DYSTOPIA*, there are two members, Armin Wischnewski and Jurgen Petersen. It was a synthe/guitar affair with some interesting rhythm work, but not revolutionary. The main theme was based on Aldous Huxley's "Brave New World." As well their second album was based on Huxley's "Island," and was a big development musically from the first. A nice combination of acoustic/electric guitar and electronics, Georg Deuter's music comes to mind at times. Their third, completing their idea of a Huxley trilogy, is now recorded and due for release any time. I'm sure the music of Trance will win a lot of friends.

INTENCE
Specialists in orchestral arrangements and a kind of Tangerine Dreamy style, but with more variety as they use a lot of sound collages and tape effects. Plus

instead of compu-drums, a real drummer. There are three members, Helmut Brunner & Clemens Glaser on keyboards and synthe, and Rudiger Glaser on drums, electronic percussion and tapes, who've been together since 1980. Their first LP, *A FOND PERDU*, was a self-production and is one of the best in terms of quality, music and cover. Although it could be excellently used for films since it's not extremely uncommercial, it also contains a refreshing touch of Roedelius-like melodies set to a background of restrained T.D. arrangements. It creates a strange, but interesting atmosphere. Their second album, *OUT OF BLUE FASHION*, is now out as well.

FRIEDER BUTZMANN
From Berlin and musically very different from all the previous groups. In West Berlin he has been involved with groups such as Din A Testbild, Mania D and DAF. His main influences are Throbbing Gristle and Robert Rental, and Genesis P. Orridge made an appearance on his first LP on the Zensor label, *VERTRAUENSMANN DES VOLKES*. It's full of synthe, noise, tape effects and treated voice/sax, and his method of cutting/editing is precise and sometimes results in very minimalistic and often very violent pieces. Of all of the "sensory overload" artists, his work is the most experimental and varied.

TOUCH
TOUCH means "TOm Und CHarlie" and this is Tom Hackl (synthesizer) and Charlie Giesler (drums & vocals). It's one of the latest independent releases I've heard and in fact it's an impressive LP. Titled *TRAUMWERK 1*, it contains three tracks which they usually play live in their concerts in Bavaria, so here finally is someone from the South of Germany. Tom studied music (piano), then went on to play in a variety of groups of different styles such as folk, jazz and rock. Touch were founded in 1978 and they then started to develop their synthe-drum-duo concept. Charlie is a graduate of engineering with a similar musical background. The music: first, there are no doubts it is of German origin as the basic atmosphere is dark and mysterious. Side 1, "Gethsemane," a biblical reference, is divided into two parts, conceptually similar, but a bit different in sound. I especially like the clever use of drums which strengthens the overall rhythm patterns set up by sequencer that are a bit familiar sounding. It's a little like Chris Franke's sound with his new drum sequencer, but even heavier. A short vocal at the end ties it to Side 2, which also begins with a short vocal passage that is stylistically sung a bit Pulsar-like. The two pieces on Side 2, "Waterdream" and "Skylab," are also good, but not as original as Side 1. Although their themes are often religious and their main live concerts so far have been in churches, they don't want to be described as religious, but more as meditative. Whatever you call them, *TRAUMWERK 1* is good Teutonic Electronics.

Wolfgang Fenchel

Art Zoyd Interview and Live Concert Review

I met with Art Zoyd an hour before their Rheims concert, in an empty room of the local arts centre. Gerard Hourbette, Thierry Zaboitzeff and Didier Pietton (sax and ex-member of Courlan Tromboson) all share the microphone; Jean-Pierre Soarez is deeply immersed in his reading of *NOTES*, but still keeps an ear to the conversation, Thierry Willems (piano) keeps to himself and is rather quiet since he has only been with the group for a few weeks (we will see him far more expressive on stage!)

The interview is studded with frequent bursts of laughter at the wording of some of the more preposterous question or at the answers tinged heavily with Gerard Hourbette's humor.

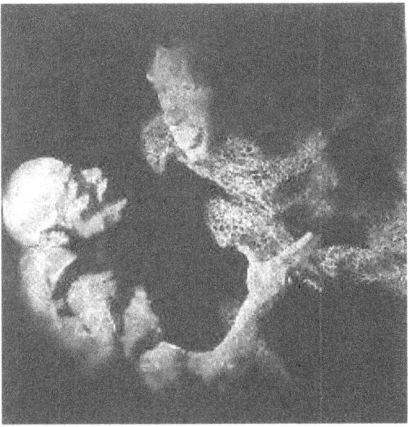

The fact of being, along with Magma, one of the oldest French groups doesn't seem to thrill nor annoy them one bit. It only prevents them from seeing the musicians develop out of it, as well as the evolution of the music. No member of the present formation was with Art Zoyd at its start; G. Hourbette and T. Zaboitzeff joined in 1971 when the group had already been in existence for 2 years.

"At that time," explains Gerard, "the music was very inspired by Zappa, a kind of bizarre rock, we were living some sort of adventure, as one would be able to while going to chase savages in the Borneo jungle... the whole process was different. Now, it is really much less exhilarating from the point of view of touring, (we tour a lot these days) but more serious vis-à-vis the music; we have invested a lot of ourselves in the music. It's no longer possible to give a concert for only 10 people and lose money..."

Q: Isn't it depressing to have played music for so long without gaining any recognition for it?

A: Sure, there is a problem, but we don't know where it lies. For us, as long as the music is evolving, it's interesting. It's necessary to know where to situate oneself, if you find your place in the musical milieu, your music will correspond to something.

Here their manager enters into the stream of conversation (at the start he sought to book the group for concerts only in the Paris area, but seeing the lack of serious people willing to make it to the concerts from the whole of France, he decided to expand their activities.)

"Art Zoyd has a very particular structure. It has a totally individual evolution, not dependent on current trends. Let's take the example of Eno; he has always known how to situate himself in regards to the current style... With Art Zoyd, the pieces evolve following human cycles, not the cycles of trends. They may appear to be out of touch, but I don't see that as an obstacle. If the audience who listens to Earth, Wind & Fire for example, watches Art Zoyd on stage, they will recognize the power of the group; they're in for a big surprise. I think that it's a media problem. The group has a much larger potential than what it has attained."

Thierry Z. clarifies this: "The problem lies in bringing people to our concerts, once they get there, we'll be able to hold their attention."

Art Zoyd feels that Rock In Opposition is a little outdated... "We stay in contact with Art Bears, Present and of course Univers Zero, who make up the Northern zone of RIO. But we don't have any contact with the Southern zone: Etron Fou and Stormy Six, nor with the far North: Zamla. We no longer play with Univers Zero, that made too much noise for the neighbors! Thierry performs on *CEUX DE DEHORS* (the final LP by them). In fact to make something concrete, we have to rehearse together for several months, and that poses problems. It's not necessary to want to play together at all costs, to the detriment of quality if there isn't any work to back it up, then it is solely for our pleasure, and I'm not sure if that brings anything to each one in the group? We don't want to make a gaff, but rather, to invest something there. Thus, we can occasionally re-do one or two pieces -- to do that for an entire concert, that's lunacy, there's enough problems as it is..."

T. Zaboitzeff: It had been a question of doing a live album for some years now. We had even recorded a few of our concerts on 8 tracks, but that was insufficient. We would have needed to record the whole tour on 16 tracks, and then rework it later in the studio. We didn't have the means to do that.

J.P. Soarez: To recreate the stage on record, one would need a P.A. system!

G. Hourbette: I prefer our recorded music to that of our live performances inasmuch that I think that there are very few good live albums, even Magma is less interesting on live albums.

Thierry: I believe that it would be good to join the energy of a live performance to the quality of sound you get on a studio album, but due to the lack of means we prefer to work in the studio where we're assured of the end result. An album is heard many times, it must be as perfect as possible.

Here the interview was interrupted by the audience entering into the auditorium; 10 minutes later Art Zoyd was at work.

Right off there's a surprise. The use of pre-recorded tracks to introduce the first piece "Etat D'Urgence," dedicated to all those who are burnt alive, be it in their souls or their flesh. "Naufrage" in a similar vein follows. The group decided to start powerfully with two explosive pieces which unveil the vitality of the new formation. As the concert progresses, they expose their new assets; besides the use of the above mentioned pre-recorded tracks, an electric sax, G. Hourbette's use of a second keyboard, alternating with an alto sax, and above all their brand new pianist. The compositions maximize the diverse elements of a rich sound palette and multiple combinations between the instruments. The duos between piano and bass or violoncello and alto sax are models of sobriety and intelligence. The ensemble as a whole has gained finesse. The energy is always present, only more directed, then suddenly it explodes and becomes like a hurricane.

The music of Art Zoyd uses nuances and shifting ambiance in an effectively bewitching fashion; the pianist adds greatly to this. He is the link and arbitrator between the frequent battle of the brass and string sections. The notion of human as much as musical equilibrium comes from him. In all, they offer us an hour and a half of material from their latest double LP for Recommended Records, *PHASE IV*.

The pieces are linked together, with a perpetual fugue, also by the wild tempos and grandeur of the stature of the pieces' construction, as well as in the simple dances and ballads, for which they have the secret to create. "Comme Du Sang Sur Le Niege" possesses such a degree of thoroughness and unbelievable purity; "Ballade," a strange melange of subtle humour and severity; "Dernier Danse," where life and death are fused in a great whirlwind; and "Chemin De Lumier," justly vivid, imposing itself as a concert without any dead moments.

It is fitting to note the cohesion of the spectacle aspect of Art Zoyd; a force devoid of weakness; as well as in the pieces themselves. T. Zaboitzeff excels, weighing his words, modest and in the name of his four comrades, a testimony of respect for the audience. This evening proved it.

Dominique Diebold
Reprinted From NOTES
Translation by Michelle Tuck

Venezuela

Last issue EUROCK did the first in a series of overviews on music south of the border, featuring Mexico. This time we'll go a bit further down and take a look at what's happening in Venezuela.

Far and away the most interesting and active musician is Vytas Brenner. A world-class musician, he's fused keyboards, electronics, jazz and other ethnic influences into a striking sound. His multi-keyboard setup is always at the core of his musical work, yet his compositions are built in several layers that all work to create a unified sound. Jazz-tinged guitar complements his keyboards and the exotic way he structures the arrangements and uses native instruments adds startling depth. All of his 6 LPs are impressive, the earlier ones a bit more acoustic (with surreal covers that are prime psychedelia), while the later are more heavily synthetic and fusion oriented.

Newer additions to the Venezuelan scene are Tempano, Aditus and Estructura. All can loosely be described as fitting into the category of symphonic rock. Tempano have 2 LPs to date and their second, *PESADILLA SIN FINAL*, is a strong effort integrating rich keyboard textures into a poly-rhythmic rock approach. The arrangements are dynamic and the playing tight. It is definitely a good example of the genre. Aditus and Estructura are along the same lines with Aditus a bit heavier in the guitar department and Estructura a little more jazz-influenced. While none of the three bands can be called highly original, they are also not simply Anglo imitators as they do attempt to incorporate into the sound a feel for their native music.

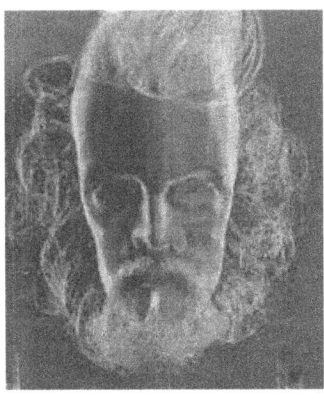

Then there are the obscurities, which as you might imagine are the most experimental musically, an LP by Fernando Yvosky and cassette by Musikautomatika. The story of Fernando Yvosky's *DOS MUNDOS* (Two Worlds), is that copies of the album were left for sale in a few record stores and the people never came back to collect the money or were ever heard from again? No address, label name, it does have a suitably cryptic sleeve, photos and credits. The best part of all is the music which is extremely interesting. A concept LP about the dual worlds of the physical and psychological, it makes effective use of keyboards, synthe, guitar, rhythm section, lots of effects and occasional strings. The overall atmosphere is cosmic and full of musical changes with very sophisticated arrangements. Its creator was definitely out of the mainstream.

The cassette by Musikautomatika is done by two musicians who play a battery of synthes and strange percussive devices. Of all the artists in this article, they come closest to being space music as they set up pulsing synthetic rhythms full of eerie effects. It's all very far out and shows a great deal of imagination, as they don't just set the machines and let them run on. Needless to say no commercial intent, a pure sonic trip.

It's unfortunate none of this stuff is available outside of the homeland, if there!

But nonetheless they deserve to be documented as being representatives of rock in Venezuela.

Discography:
Vytas Brenner - *LA OFFRENDA*
Vytas Brenner - *HERMANOS*
Vytas Brenner - *JAYECHE*
Vytas Brenner - *EN VIVO* (Dbl.)
Vytas Brenner - *OFRENDA*
Vytas Brenner - *ESTOY COMO QUIERO*
Tempano - *ATABAL-YEMAL*
Tempano - *PESADILLA SIN FINAL*
Aditus - *FUERA DE LA LEY*
Estructura - *MAS ALL DE TU MENTE*
Fernando Yvosky - *DOS MUNDOS*
Musikautomatika - *MUSIKAUTOMATIKA* (cassette)

Archie Patterson

1984

An Open Letter from Bernard Xolotl

Once upon a time -- roughly between 1969 and 1979 -- there was in the Western World a music that people variously called "cosmic," "psychedelic," "floating," "space" electronics. It was mainly created with the first "primitive" synthesizers (by today's standards), cheap electronic organs and guitars with lots of feedback, echo, white noise, reverb, tape loops and whatever acoustic instruments were required with an emphasis on exotic, Oriental sounds used in unusual and innovative ways. Mostly improvised in an intimate, meditative, exploratory fashion with occasional Eastern concepts present, this new music seemed to aim at inducing in the listeners a state of expanded consciousness, mystical awareness, cosmic awe, deep space travel, magic trance, which was all too often quoted as being a substitute for psychedelic drugs. This music however had the feeling of an ever-fresh high. Whenever you would hold in your hands some brand new release (always obtained at great pains in America where Rather Ripped Records in Berkeley was then the only and most sacred place of pilgrimage in the West for aficionados), you felt while placing it on your turntable that the doors of perception were about to open up to reveal some great mystery that might literally change your life, bring your mind to a new profound awareness of the Universe and help you reach a higher level of reality. The sound, even on those mere analogue records, seemed to have a revolutionary power to turn you on to Enlightenment like the Nada Brahma of India which means "Sound is God."

I imagine that many readers of EUROCK will be intimately familiar with what I am talking about unless they are relatively new to the scene.

I said, "once upon a time," because today such a feeling appears to have vanished into utter oblivion.

I have just returned from a thorough world tour, not a concert tour, that is -- no one in electronic music can afford it nowadays -- but a tour of visits to old musician friends who used to be the most prominent creators of this cosmic genre in Berlin, Hamburg, Frankfurt, Copenhagen, Paris, London, N.Y.C., L.A., Northern California, the South Pacific and whose work I have known and admired since the early days.

My conclusion is rather depressing, I'm afraid, nowhere did I encounter this magical feeling any longer! The rich, always blasé, cynically talked about an old-fashioned, boringly out-of-date music only fit for retired hippies while sitting at a $20-a-drink cafe table, and the poor about the sheer impossibility to survive by creating committed, experimental, non-trendy music. We all hotly debated the elusive merits of the latest digital wonder gadgets and their relative prices in different countries since the rich always collect and the poor always dream.

Everyone seemed bent on making a "hit" by capitalizing on the British electronic disco fashion, and drum machines were so pervasive that you could not hear a single record that didn't have one on it. It's ironic to me that space music, which saved us in the West from the ever-present dictatorship of the drum set 15 years ago, would finally bring us under an iron rule by the digital drum machine! Are there drums in every composition by Debussy, Bartok, Bach or Wagner? This says a lot indeed about current standards: after 15 years of creative marriage and cross-pollination, contemporary music and pop music are once again spreading far apart.

Thus, it was not only among the former creators of space music that I found no interest whatsoever in pursuing the cosmic quest, but worst of all among the listeners, among the audiences of all ages and walks of life, among the people who used to buy and support this music as well as those younger ones who love high-tech music toys.

No one seemed to have the time any longer to LISTEN to music altogether except on their way to work (Walkmen in the subway are very fashionable at rush hour but what can you hear?), in the home workshops while hammering or after hours to enjoy a quick exercise at the local pick-up discotheque. In the words of a famous Berlin musician, records have become as disposable material as paper cups and should be considered accordingly. So the time of quick, throw-away records bought at a "Pay 'N Save" automatic distributor is upon us and the cosmic magic of the LP receding speedily into the distant past. As somebody said at a party recently, "Who can afford now to waste a whole day to space out?," as someone else commented with disgust, "I don't think anyone still does, do you?" This trend is much more pronounced in Europe and on the East Coast than in California simply because cosmic music had to be watered down to the wall paper, ambient New Age Muzak level there before it could even be marketed on the West Coast. Thus in Europe, most of the space music contingent sold out to the British electro-pop scene while in California it became the mellow suburban vitamin supermarket Muzak of New Age.

How far away we are now from the open, experimental, innovative soundscapes of the past decade. I could further emphasize by comparing the record sales figures of the most well known artists in this field which are known to me but this is another story altogether.

Let me rather compare three stops on my journey: I went to MIDEM in Cannes which is the largest gathering of record company executives in the world and could not even find anyone, from any country interested in my newest music. Most of my musician friends didn't even care to go. The classical music stands were deserted and MTV ruled supreme. I also spent a great week in Berlin with Terry Riley who gave a concert every night at the Einstein Cafe, the Mecca of electronic music, with Klaus Schulze, Michael Hoenig, Manuel Gottsching, etc. in the strictly limited audience. No one under the age of 32 was ever in sight, while all these musicians were themselves in their 20s when they released their great records. It was thus an event reserved for an older, rarefied elite and Klaus himself complained to me publicly about this without having any better solution to offer than to start a new record company identical to his former fiasco except for the name.

Then I went to the Frankfurt Music Fair where all the latest computer music gadgets are unveiled to the world each year. Here the enthusiasm of the crowd knew no boundaries. The Japanese stands were completely raided and there was standing-room-only from dawn to dark. The sales of electronic musical instruments have increased 400% a year since 1979! Through these three samples of today's activities, it's perfectly clear to me that THE MEDIUM HAS COMPLETELY SUPERSEDED THE MESSAGE in our devotedly materialistic society and that today's electro-musicians have become mere salesmen and advertisers for the big companies. That's a fact which is obvious enough when reading any of today's big music magazines.

Traditionally, great artists have always been weary of the business world and only dealt with it through the urgency of vital needs. Upon our entering now the Age of Synthesis (which I have written about elsewhere could possibly witness the reunion of Art & Science), it seems to me that a whole generation of musicians has been lured by technology to the point of selling their soul in order to afford an even more powerful arsenal of fancy equipment. In this modern version of the Faust Myth, Mephistopheles appears in the guise of a Synclavier! Art Technology is the trap and the bait that the Establishment uses to control and censor the free expression of independent, non-wealthy artists, and their ultimate pretext for selling out.

Furthermore, the psychedelic generation reached middle age at the end of the '70s and thus experienced a heavier than usual middle age "burn-out," at the same time that the record industry (whose great boom period was the '60s), came into a deep depression which led to their cutting corners by keeping only the biggest stars and tremendous studio restrictions. The synchronicity of these two phenomena is obviously interdependent but big record companies don't understand or care about sociology. Therefore, in the middle of an economic and moral "burn-out" after 1979, the soaring progress of music technology became the only refuge for most electro-musicians who had grown addicted to it already.

Just like a man who, suddenly finding he has to devote all of his time to his family, starts to wonder where all his youthful ideals went, may soon console himself with alcohol and drown into it, so did our cosmic music generation, under the dazzling umbrella of the technological miracles held out as bait by the

Establishment, to get all of the stray sheep back into the fold, succumb as well.

The younger generation, as is well known, takes everything for granted, freedom, sex, drugs and particularly all the most far-out sound gadgets which are but toys for them, on which they just have to push a few buttons to become the new Klaus Schulze. They got into the medium before they ever knew there was any message behind it originally, by then it's too late because the fascination with the machines themselves is so great that they don't care about meanings and messages, witness the British electro-pop stars. Remember when the movie "2001" came out? Compare it with "War Games" now and you will get the picture.

Everything has become pre-set like a ready-made TV dinner. Sounds that originally took days of spacy experimentation to create are now ready to be used by the hundreds at the push of a single button and there is not even enough time to listen to them all!

Can you imagine having to just push a button to find the woman of your dreams? How boring such a world would get to be after a while?!

Accordingly, synthetic music has become completely mechanical, like an assembly line at a car factory, while its technological potentialities have expanded enormously, and this is the great paradox that shows us again that the medium has utterly superseded the message in a real Catch 22 situation. The result is inversely proportional to the means. The means -- i.e. computer control for easy operation -- have become the end in and of itself, symbol of a deadly materialistic society where there is nothing left beyond immediate effect and profit, beyond ready-made products to be consumed on the spot and quickly forgotten as a new faster one comes along. I call this the world of disposables by computer-planned obsolescence which aims at reaping the profit before even putting out the investment to create an already outmoded product. It's like getting money for something that's obsolete before it's even made. Ultimate inflation of time!!

It's like the A.I.D.S. of Time, and since the same hands control the cash flow everywhere, is there a way out of this maze? Is there a way that real Art can survive the contamination, merge peacefully with science and exist in the future uncorrupted by the Bank/State??

It seems to me that musicians should first simply learn to cut their technological need which are enslaving them to the anti-artistic deadlines of the money-rat-race. Then they should again listen to some of the old jewels recorded with simple gear that was used to great effect. Digital recording will become standard anyway, so let's not worry about the hiss, but more about the music. Great musicians of the past often said that an artist should always create thinking it's the last time and the last piece. Who wants to watch *THRILLER* on their deathbed or hear Michael Jackson at their funeral? I don't mean to suggest that all music should be funeral music, but quite the contrary: one can only be happy at death if one has fulfilled at least one dream and a musician can have endless musical dreams. What is the point of polluting the world of sound with garbage if one will ultimately deny it just as the nuclear weapons manufacturers refuse to be buried under their own stockpiles?

Music used to be a way to reach transcendence, not a means to support the budget of cocaine traffickers and egomaniacs who want to reduce the world's population to 10,000 human beings.

The fascination with technology and power will wear off like all fascinations do and then only the music will be left whether this world continues to exist or not. Will it be what you would like to hear in your hard-earned paradise??

Love,
Xolotl

Urban Sax

THE SAXOPHONE/MACHINE
The saxophone is a parabolic cone of brass (varnished, nickelplated, silverplated or even gilded) in which the intonations are modified by a system of keys and finger keys which operate the valves and which open and close the holes drilled the length of the instrument. The production of sound is effectuated by the vibrations of a reed applied to a mouthpiece in which one blows.
- Paul Romby
("Méthode complète et moderne pour tous les saxophones")

THE SAXOPHONE/VISCERA

Music of essentially vocal origin, jazz is going to take possession of it in order to make of it a substitute for song, laughter, for moans and cries. Discovering the instrument without knowing how it was used by Europeans, black American musicians immediately understood its true nature: for them the saxophone is not a simple mechanism -- a prosthesis -- but a supplementary organ, a sort of physiological growth endowed with feeling and sensitivity. Playing "with guts" is no longer an empty expression when the instrument imitates the shape and shine of viscera, when the moisture and fever of the body are condensed in it and when the slightest carnal vibrations there find themselves amplified in a sort of permanent shiver. This is how new anatomical laws are developed, the sinuous pipe becomes the simple extension of the organic coils of each musician, pierced by that mystic existence of an "air column" which takes root in the lower abdomen to emerge, loaded with deepest emotion, from the gaping mouth of the bell.

Assimilated with a whole sexual symbolism in the first degrees the saxophone very quickly becomes a wondrous instrument in Puritan America, but like African tribes, surrounded by a superstitious terror. From the twenties on, the history of jazz will be written most often in the new language of saxes: Sidney Bechet "invents" the soprano, but also, at the same time as Armstrong, the freedom to improvise; Coleman Hawkins becomes the creator of the tenor, but also the pioneer of harmonic language; Lester Young, Charlie Parker, John Coltrane, Eric Dolphy, Ornette Coleman will all invent for the saxophone a poetry that can be used by other instruments.

But what will always remain the privilege of the saxophonist is the power to personalize timbre and phrasing in the extreme: in all the already long history of jazz there is no sax virtuoso whose voice is not instantly recognized by a somewhat trained ear. Even diluted in an orchestra, organized in sections, saxophones retain this infinite variety, this humanity made up of contrasts among physical temperaments expressed in the rough.

That is perhaps why Adolphe Sax dreamed all his life of hearing an orchestra -- or rather a chorus -- solely made up of saxophones.

A century after his death, Urban Sax wonderfully revive this fantasy, and Bob Kaufman's prophecy is finally realised:

> One thousand saxophones
> infiltrate the city
> Each with a man inside,
> Hidden in ordinary cases,
> Labeled FRAGILE.
> Attack: the sound of jazz...
> The City Falls.

- Gérald Arnaud

URBAN SAX

Conversations suddenly stop, heads turn toward the back of the hall: at first scarcely perceptible, a continuous sound approaches and is amplified. One by one the members of Urban Sax enter slowly, Indian file. Nineteen, twenty, twenty-one... They will finally be at least thirty. All have a saxophone at their lips and all are dressed in the same white overalls: they look like a maintenance team from a nuclear facility. Without ceasing to play they clear a path for themselves through the audience.

Urban Sax concerts are spectacles in perpetual transformation, rituals which take into consideration the configuration of the spaces where they take place and which join, with a constantly renewed fantasy, the magic of the visual and that of sound: musicians enveloped in large bands of transparent plastic as at the Palace in Paris, covered by immense acrylic spiders of Italian sculptor Donato Sartori as in Nancy, division into small groups perched on moving grain elevator carts as in Rennes, or sailing on gondolas as in Venice.

...Suddenly, the saxophonists scatter in all directions and send out a long, strident, collective cry, pushed to its paroxysm. Then, all calms down. Without haste they divide up in four groups, in the four corners of the hall. One hears again the continuous sound, in unison, and the listens has the strange sensation of a spiral movement. Finally, at the interior of this implacable sound, one begins to distinguish the melodic loops whose repetition evokes a mechanical movement the movement of machines of the industrial age.

Later, the musicians will rejoin to form a single frontal line facing the public. They recite incomprehensible words through their instruments with the mouthpiece removed. At the end of the concert they will leave as they arrived, one behind the other and without ceasing to play.

Urban Sax: it definitely has to do with the city. A hard universe, unhealthy, inhuman, mechanized to an extreme. This music expresses the anguish and, paradoxically, acts as an exorcism. Under the hypnotic effect of continuous repetitions, the listener can let his mind drift toward a science fiction phantasmagoria. Imagine for example that the thousand wheels of a gigantic machine are moving with a dull, hollow sound in labyrinthine basements, while wreaths of toxic gas wind through the yellowed air... It can also refuse all illustration and plunge into a meditative nothingness. A sort of punk Zen, if you like. Crouched in the front row of the audience, making himself as unobtrusive as possible, Gilbert Artman directs the musicians with a few precise gestures. Instigator and director of this collective adventure, he is, however, not a saxophone specialist. He has been heard at the piano, the organ, the vibraphone, and above all on drums at the heart of Lard Free, a French rock group born at the beginning of the seventies.

Urban Sax has been active since 1976. The fundamental idea is the continuous sound produced by four groups of which three play at the same time while the fourth, taking turns, catches its breath. From whence a "repetitive music" very different from that of American masters like Terry Riley or Phil Glass. The latter work from a rigorous fixity of tones and make privileged use of keyboard instruments such as the electronic organ. Urban Sax, on the other hand, makes full use of the mobility permitted by the saxophones: mobility across the performing space, but also at the very interior of the unison, thanks to the subtle fluctuations of pitch.

From this double movement is born the effects of sound that one would have believed limited to the electro-acoustic domain.

Gilbert Artman is composer and conductor, in the manner of collective music in the oral tradition like the Gamelans of Bali: the structures are precise without a single note being written. And the musicians are not submitted to a systematic selection: depending on correct positioning, a beginning saxophonist can join in the unison for the simplest parts. Later he will tackle more complicated structures.

Beyond the impression of a spiral achieved by the circular play of four distinct groups, the effects of breath and the unintelligible words recited through the saxophones, innovation have appeared in the music of Urban Sax: the adjunct of a predominantly feminine chorus which, in turn, blends with the instrumental unisons, gives them accentuation or breaks away from them; the fleeting use of metallophones, gongs and timpani struck in such a way that their resonance produces the effect of breathing.

The world of the mechanized age and of contemporary technology is expressed in this music by means without electricity, which depends fundamentally on the human body. Exorcism of the anxiety of modern cities is born of this ambivalence.

Daniel Caux
Le Monde de la musique
Translation by Lois Bode
Reprinted From URBAN SAX by
Irmgard Pozorski
Text by Daniel Caux & Gérald Arnaud
Chambre noire/Jannik

Fondation Interview
Ivan Coaquette and Anannka Raghel

Q: Ivan, you were once a member of the group Musica Electronica Viva, what have you done since the break-up of the group, and what happened to the Spacecraft project or any others?

A: Projects are always numerous in a gestation period. At that time, musical effervescence was such that communication and contacts were easier than now and creativity and imagination favored the group experience. After having left Musica Electronica Viva I returned to France, taking time to step back and reflect on this fascinating experience that I'd just gone through; a music liberated from its constraints that is lived as a daily happening. Finally, I created a mobile unit of Musica Electronica Viva in France with which I made limited experiments with groups that had different horizons, searching to produce a synthesis of musical improvisation with "show business."

Q: Anannka, tell me about your training. You played with Pandamonium and Zed so what else have you done?

A: My musical training started when I was a child. I studied piano and musical theory since the age of four. I used to live in a very musical ambiance and I sung with my father, who was a singer, since my early childhood. I separated myself from music, in the strictest terms, for a time, in order to practice drama and dance while I continued to sing in a few cabarets. The discovery of musical forms allowed me to be both musician and composer and reoriented me towards pure music. So, I once again resumed the study of piano and completed my voice training in order to become a more complete musician. I then went on to play with Spacecraft, Pandamonium, Zed and Chantal Grimm. I took part in a few experiments with vocal theatre, but soon and most importantly I played and created with Fondation.

Q: When and why did you create the group Fondation and why did you choose this name?

A: The germination of the group took place in 1978. The name, in a way, is the image of a utopian enterprise, which plunges its roots deeply into the earth. The name is like the trees we have chosen as symbols and is the reflection of hope for the future, in a humanity which preserves itself from destruction and building often, in an unexpected fashion, its foundations.

Q: Fondation is not, certainly, an ordinary group. You don't make records; you play in strange places, such as churches, and your activities carry over into dance, theatre, etc. Do you find the functions of a conventional group too limiting?

A: I think that most groups in general deteriorate rapidly due to the effect of the industry and specialization. Very quickly they find themselves locked in a situation where no one is aware of individual evolution vis-à-vis the musician. That's why we like to work in all areas and genres where the music has a reason for existing.

Q: So your activities are highly varied. Ivan, you make acoustical instruments (string and percussion), and you ensure the conception and realization of part of your electronic material as well as creating beautiful collages. Anannka, you are a philosopher of training; you are dancer, comedian and a director. Do you think that these experiences are important for your music? Would you like to make more use of them?

A: Yes, for us it's not essential, but important, art being a constant gestation and voyage in the long run. If, sadly, the various situations of creation are confronted with the reality of events, it remains that only they allow the necessary retreat to deepen the whole wrong and right side. Also, it's not necessary to resign oneself to overshadow, under the guise of specialization, the faculties to complement one another. Life, nostalgia, unity and music are all tied together, and their different aspects are just a particularity of the work. In music, the golden age is a state where it is necessary to rediscover constantly, if one wants to produce without repeating oneself. It is evident that the experience has to be a permanent ascension, in the search for perfection where one has to develop his knowledge and faculties. Some artists in every period and from every country have explored themselves across diversified facets of their personalities. As far as the art of show business is concerned, of which music is a part, we have felt that for the best, in regards to voice, theatre or dance and intense happiness, an amalgamation or communion is irreplaceable. When the spectacle includes various forms of these different artistic expressions, everything in us is attracted to it; the soul, the mind, the heart, the ears, the eyes and the body vibrates as one. On the stage, we try to invest ourselves totally, even when our presence is specialized. We, or course, dream of no longer knowing the limitations in our means of expression, and of being able to use them all within the same presentation. We hope to realize in the future such spectacles.

Q: Why did you make the two cassettes, *METAMORPHOSE* and *SANS ETIQUETTER*, rather than record albums? Was it for financial reasons or out of interest in a new format?

A: Through our music, we are seeking to provoke the voyage, the imaginary, the resonance, the energy and the introspection. That's why we call it extra-sensory, and that we have chosen for now the formula of using cassettes. It is a cheap and practical format which allows a relative liberty within the organization of time and permits the making of a product that's similar to a book or film in content. A record only partially permits this, by its constraints of length, number of tracks, and price. On the other hand, our present musical development will no doubt lead us to make a record album very soon.

Q: What are the reactions to your cassettes? Are they selling well?

A: The reactions have been in step with our investment. To struggle against the industry without a distributor, with finite means, only permits relative success. We had to face the problems of mail-order, very enriching, but very tedious, the world of business, of bartering and its perfidious aspects. It's been an experience both passionate and quite exacting, which allowed us to realize that our music wasn't, in its present form, a commercial product and that, before choosing between marketing or making music, we opted for music and are always looking for the ideal producer to fill out his role as muse.

Q: How do you create your music? For the most part it seems improvised. Do you compose in the strict sense and which parts are improvised?

A: Our music is both composed and improvised. In relation to the last century, the composition of our time takes another meaning because of the means put at our disposal are numerous and diversified, such as, writing, graphics, tapes, computers, etc. In our work methods, magnetic tape is generally the basis for our compositions. It serves to fix the imaginary spontaneity. We call it magnetic writing. We associate with it also traditional writing of structure and principles of harmony, rhythmic pulsations, and melodies which are the breath and soul of the music. From this basis, improvisation becomes possible within the major portion of music that is labeled improvised. In our music interpretation becomes improvisation.

Q: When you perform in concert, what is the audience reaction? Does the Parisian public like your music and are you well known in France? I know you have some ties with England and the U.S.

A: In France as elsewhere, the audience habitually assumes the passive role of consumer. Most of the time they are informed and polarized by the media and therefore submit to the ephemeral styles of the moment. Because of this we only have access to a certain limited number of places and circuits. That's the reason why we are not very well known, despite articles and concerts. We think that playing in public is the occasion of a particular event, in which the participation of the public plays a important role. Until now, we had believed that in our concerts the communication and exchange was really taking place. After the shows, the audience seemed warm, but it is difficult to get feedback and to know the various thoughts of the audience.

Q: How do you feel about using synthesizers in your music? A lot of people think the sound is too cold. What's your opinion?

A: For the moment we make little use of the synthesizer in our music. As with any instrument, it's only a means and not an end. The only one we use presently is a Korg synthesizer guitar. Its use, first off, is very flattering, since it allows the guitarist to play instrumental parts that go beyond the range of a normal guitar. Its difficulty is that it isn't totally perfected and that one has to adapt one's playing to the machine, which one is dependent upon through the complexities of tuning. The attack produced by the mediator has to be precise and regular, and if not, then the release becomes random. This parameter considerably limits our playing, speed and expression. Plus, players of the synthesizer, in general, only use one hand and use the other for tuning; the guitarist needs both his hands and that doesn't facilitate the utilization of guitar synthesizer on stage. The synthesizer is, in itself, a very rich instrument. Its access and manageability demands a form of technical mind, mathematical and adventurous, but it doesn't necessarily imply musical inspiration. For many, its use is tied to the faculty or a process that's purely intellectual. Thus, there remains a domain of treatment and effect. In this case, that can become to some extent, very boring for the listener.

Q: In my opinion, some of your music has a religious character which is why it works so well in churches, what do you think?

A: A whole part of our music effectively aspires to be religious, in the sense of forming a connection and is hypnotic. To play inside of a church is passionate experience because churches respond to this vocation. For now, they are still accessible places. The dimensions and acoustics are very favorable for music. The church frees magic and fascination. Technically, the difficulty arises from the inherent echo, and the necessity of finding an acoustic knot.

Q: What are your influences and what kind of music do you listen to?

A: "To cross the mirror, you have to make the tour." In what has been an influence to us, there is the side of enriching our knowledge, and another for pleasure, or better still, a combination of both. Our own influences come more from the domain of the subconscious than the will to situate oneself musically in a defined manner while studying a style. They are therefore very diverse and varied, and come from the philosophy of cartoon strips, while passing as life. Music is a source of emotions and a creative process which plunges its roots into silence. This silence is itself occupied by natural or artificial noises of the country or the city. There are some noises that are surrounded by the shell of silence, punctuated by the very passing of time, which develop their natural timbres becoming thus sounds and music. We don't listen very often to music in order to lead ourselves to this resource; besides, the reception of music changes with the states. We like almost all sorts of music, but most particularly certain musical forms, in which the resonance and source are the closest possible to the original form. We listen a lot to ethnic and folk music. We are equally quite sensitive to classical music and the operatic voice and the blues. But of course we like anything that allows itself to be received just as it is, be it rock, jazz, repetitive, cosmic or pop.

Q: What do you think of other Parisian musicians, such as Richard Pinhas, Bernard Szajner, Christian Vander, Jean-Baptiste Barriere, etc.? Do you have good contact with them?

A: In Paris the milieu is strongly representative of the society. Each one lives within his particular universe, without occupying the area of other musicians. This limits communication and prevents certain fusions. Our relation to these people is therefore sane and distant enough.

Q: Are you satisfied with your present situation? If you had plenty of money would you change things? What do you think of fame?

A: Our present situation is similar to crossing a desert, arid and full of freedom. It allows us, without constraint, to realize a part of our projects, but electric music being somewhat a privilege, the lack of means does limit our production. Fortune is ambiguous; it contains the means as well as the inertia. Those who know how to dispassionately welcome it can invest in the future for themselves and others, with the necessary recoil. As for fame, it demands the same serenity to become a source of the greatest self-confidence so that one can use it advisedly. We're not sure in either case if the question relates to us.

Q: Is it difficult to play this style of music in France? What do you think of the musical situation in France today?

A: Yes, in effect, it is very hard to play this style of music because, in general,, there exists just a few places for music or concerts and lesser still for the genre of music which can't be classified. The larger space are reserved for foreign rock groups, belonging to a "star system." Access to small and medium-sized places is limited by the fact that they book many spectacles for a single evening and that restricts the time for the presentation of the material, the balance, time for tuning, etc. Besides, there is no infrastructure of distribution for music like ours and that which won't assimilate. The state radio, France Musique and France Culture for example, essentially broadcast classical music, and from time to time, folk music and jazz. The free stations, and private ones as well, only play pop and jazz. Television broadcasts two programs per week which center, for the most part, around British and American rock and sometimes classical music. In the entertainment columns of Paris publications, you will find the following categories: classical, jazz, pop, folk and rock. An involuntary marginality is imposed on us and is contrary to the spirit of our music. "After the ecstasy, comes ambiguity."

Q: Finally, for the future, do you have any plans?

A: The future is immense, and in this immensity our plans are many. We have lately had a third cassette, LE *VAISSEAU BLANC*, released by *Tago Mago* magazine as well as an unreleased piece included on their *PARIS-TOKIO* cassette compilation which features French and Japanese musicians. We are working on a project for a record based on a rhythmic language and different feelings that it provokes for us, with a work of percussion, keyboards, strings and voice. Finally perhaps a symphony, and the staging of spectacle with our music which Anannka is holding the secret to.

David Elliott

Sven Grunberg
Electronic Music In The USSR

Russian composer Sven Grunberg was born on November 24, 1956 in Tallinn, Estonian USSR. After studying music theory at the Tallinn Music High School between 1970-74, he became well-known with his rock band Mess, as a composer, vocalist, and keyboard player. Mess followed the way of intellectual rock, giving many concerts and recording for Tallinn Radio. The height of the Mess period turned out to be the cantata "Ask Yourself." In 1977, Grunberg felt like making a stylistic change that was difficult to carry out with the same band members: Mess broke up, Grunberg continued alone.

In the following creative period Grunberg still used certain rock methods, but his music began to evolve away from his rock roots. His interest became more focused upon electronic music and then, step by step, music of older cultures. Grunberg's *VALGUSOIS* (The Blossom of the Light) is a fully electronic work that was played on Synthi 100 in the electronic studio of the Soviet LP firm Melodiya in Moscow. He had the rare opportunity to use good electronic equipment as a part of his commission to do a score for the science fiction movie "The Hotel of a Perished Alpinist" ("witch" music is extremely popular throughout the Soviet Union). Normally, it is quite difficult to gain access to good electronic equipment in the USSR. Other than arranging commissioned projects, the only other way to use similar equipment is to build it yourself.

Though it would be much easier to carry through his ideas if he had his own studio, Sven consoles himself by approaching his shortage of resources positively: his lack of sophisticated electronic instruments has impelled him to discover new sound solutions. This has often given better and more interesting results -- through the exploitation of concrete sounds in direct or transformed shape, the maximal usage of the acoustic instruments, simple sound tricks during recording, etc. It's said that good technical tools themselves don't necessarily guarantee high quality and creative development -- Sven takes this one step further by producing creative, high-quality work without many of the tools used by other composers and musicians in the electronic genre.

Grunberg now uses acoustic instrumentation as much as electronic instruments, and asserts the advantages of acoustic sources more each day. In his music cycle *HINGUS* (Breath), Grunberg plays the church organ, harp, tambourine, chimes, castanets, et. al. He controls his mass of instrumentation by acting as his own recording director.

Sven's strongest influence is the music of old civilizations. He is deeply interested not only in the music he finds there, but also in the philosophy and lifestyle reflected in the music. He says, "From the history of the world music-culture we are well acquainted only with a very restricted section: European music. But how many other musical possibilities have existed and now exist? One has noticeably exaggerated the role of Europe's well-known composers." In this way, Sven is similar to others who are sinking their roots into music of the Third World: Don Cherry, Embryo, Between. The greater part of Sven's record collection consists of old music from India, China, Japan, Tibet, Korea, Mexico, Laos, etc. In the rock genre, he is fond of Genesis, Yes, Jethro Tull, King Crimson, etc. One of his favorite LPs is Tangerine Dream's *RUBYCON*. He is also interested in Mike Oldfield, Brian Eno et. al.

From time to time Sven gives concerts (he's also been the subject of some interesting video work), but he is generally not interested in shows. Apart from his own recordings, he has worked with TV, classical pantomime, ballet, and cinema (he has provided the music for around 20 movies). As a person, Sven is very friendly, good-humored, and sociable, with an extremely philosophical turn of mind. In spite of the fact that he works from morning until evening and often during the night, he finds time to engage himself in global problems. As he says, it is important to take the time to stop and think from time-to-time, rather than just rush around because the goal is really noble and beautiful. To Sven, too many people in the world sit with their nose in newspapers, reading hysterically, not taking the time and interest to cast a glance into higher things, to real life and the future.

Free translation from the Soviet Estonian newspaper "Noorte Haal" and the LP *HINGUS* cover.

Japan Scene #2

Since part one of JAPAN SCENE last issue, a lot of new information and some new records have come to light. This installment of the series will serve to give a general update and overview of recent discoveries and developments.

ZEN ELECTRONICS

FUMIO
The legacy of the pioneers of Japanese space music continues to grow as more LPs by former Far Out/FEFB members come to light. Since that group's demise their former leader Fumio has issued 5 albums: *DIGITAL CITY* plus the 4 recent releases *ARION, EARTH, MOON* and *STAR*. As evidenced by the diversity and cosmic qualities of them all he continues to be the most creative of all today's Japanese synthesists.

KITARO
The most prolific of the former FEFB crew, Kitaro now has 11 solo records as well as a slew of compilations and orchestral adaptations. Unfortunately his technical abilities and sales have far outdistanced his creativity by now as you can hardly tell one LP from the next except for the covers since his *SILK ROAD* works.

AKIRA ITOH
The other, lesser-known of the original FEFB keyboardists, Akira Itoh now has 8 solo LPs to his credit. His debut *BOSATU & MUGEN* is an electron rock classic. After that he became less inspired and made a few rather insipid discs. Good news is that his latest two *MUGENKO* and *BUDDAH* mark a return to earlier form as he mixes beautifully subtle rock rhythms & floating keyboards with exotic, ethnic sounds.

TAKASHI TOYODA
Takashi Toyoda may not be a former member of FEFB, but he has contributed his violin to the various solo works of both Fumio and Itoh. After beginning as keyboardist for the group Space Circus, Takashi Toyoda has gone on to produce three solo LPs, *THE COMET, MANDOMANGE* and *LULLABY*. His beautiful classical violin work blends superbly with flowing synthetic melodies as he creates a delicate series of compositions that are stunning fusions of the old feel of the classics and electronic technology.

YOSHITAKA AZUMA
Yoshitaka Azuma is a mysterious name that is in fact a pseudonym for a loose cooperative of electronic musicians who collaborate in various configurations on

four albums. All have the word/concept "Asia" incorporated into their title/music. The sound is strongly centered around Asian musical modes, swirling synthesizer melodies and powerful sequential currents. When you add a strong sense of dynamics and vast array of effectual touches you have a set of electronics that's unbelievable.

OSAMU
Osamu Kitajima is a bit different than all the aforementioned as he is a guitarist, not a synthesist. Nonetheless his ability to fuse his delicate/spacy guitar technique with ethnic and synthetic colorations makes his music something very special and perhaps the purest and most Zen-like of them all. His debut, *BENZAITEN*, is a classic of modern Japanese music. Subsequently he produced two spatial fusion LPs, *OSAMU* and *MASTERLESS SAMURAI*. Recently on his fourth release, *THE SOURCE*, he once again makes exquisite use of ethnic instruments, guitar and synthetics to compose a stunning work of Zen music.

PROGRESSIVE ROCK

BI KYO RAN
A trio that could be described as the ghost of King Crimson past. The guitarist and leader of the band, Kunio Suma, is a disciple of Robert Fripp. Their first album is a spaced-out power trip, not unlike *RED*, while on the second, *PARALLAX*, they also employ keyboards, winds and strings to create a fusion that recalls perhaps *STARLESS AND BIBLE BLACK* or maybe Crimso meets Art Zoyd. In both cases the result is heavy and filled with extended, adventurous arrangements.

KENSO
Kenso are led by Yoshihisa Shimizu and have roots that lie fimly in the English Canterbury school of keyboard progressives. Their debut album had some nice touches of keyboard rock to it, but it's on *KENSO II* that they really step out and transcend their influences. Both composition and musicianship are top rate as elaborate arrangements and a full keyboard sound highlight a complex set of sophisticated music.

CASSETTE UNDERGROUND

MERZBOW
Merzbow is fhe premier "noise" band in Japan today. Led by Masami Akita, their sound is the epitome of urban life/madness. Using electronic percussion, "junk" instruments, tapes and distorted guitars they achieve a sound that goes beyond "industrial." They have one LP, *MATERIAL ACTION 2* and over two dozen cassettes, which are less-than-inspired at times. But on a few of the more recent ones like, *DARH EROC EVIL*, *YAHATAHACHIMAN & AEROVIVANDA #2*, they show they can indeed go beyond just noise. On them their sound ranges from primal power assaults to electronic rock and spacy synthetics. If anything these 3 works validate the band and its concept.

STACK ORIENTATION
Stack Orientation is an organization working out of Kyoto who have to date produced over a dozen cassettes on their Skating Pears label. Its sphere of operation is mainly urban rock as they have several releases, including various compilations which feature a variety of cold wave, PIL-influenced bands who combine strange Japanese motifs with pounding rhythms, elaborate guitar riffs, synthetics, etc. All of their releases have stunning packaging, perhaps the best is *OBJECTLESS* by Osamu Sato. It comes in an 8"x10" red box w/art inserts and features some of the best experiments in minimal ambience I've heard with its

wafting synthe, ghostly piano riffs and mixture of effects.

D.D. RECORDS
DDR continues on under the direction of T. Kamada and now has a total of 178 releases in its catalog. In Sept. DDR will launch a new bimonthly cassette magazine and work is underway on some video releases perhaps. Without a doubt DDR is the world's foremost amateur collection of artists who produce some of the worlds best underground electronic music.

Archie Patterson

Koyaanisqatsi

A film by Godfrey Reggio, music by Philip Glass, cinematography by Ron Fricke

Translation From The Hopi Language: (1.) crazy life (2.) life in turmoil (3.) life disintegrating (4.) life out of balance (5.) a state of life that calls for another way of living.

"Koyaanisqatsi" is an audio-visual history of what has happened to our planet and its people that transcends style and genre. "Koyaanisqatsi" is 90-minutes in real time that with music and images not only captivates, but enlightens an audience with the bare facts of life. Perhaps the most astounding thing about "Koyaanisqatsi" is that you've seen it all before -- the wonders of nature and the ravages of technology both physically and psychologically.

Godfrey Reggio, with the aid of Ron Fricke's incredible photography and majestic music by Philip Glass, has without dialog or narrative given us a crystal clear look at the state to which we have brought ourselves. From freeway gridlocks, to the concrete/steel bunkers of the city and poisoned natural resources, we've lost touch with the essence of life and forced ourselves to exist in an artificial state. The images that flash before your eyes range alternately from serene and beautiful to stark and surreal. The complementary music brings the overall experience to a dizzying peak of intensity that is emotionally overwhelming. In fact this may be the most original piece of music Glass has yet done, especially when heard in its full length (as opposed to the excerpted LP version). One might assume this is due to the input of Michael Hoenig who served to temper Glass' more rigid academic tendencies thus helping him overcome his stylistic restrictions. This totality in concept, the special chemistry of sight and sound makes the film a once in a lifetime look at past, present and future that should be seen by everyone.

TRANSLATION OF THE HOPI PROPHECIES IN THE FILM:
"If we dig precious things from the land, we will invite disaster."
"Near the Day of Purification, there will be cobwebs spun back and forth in the sky."
"A container of ashes might one day be thrown from the sky, which could burn the land and boil the oceans."

Mother Earth has been abused. and this cannot go on forever The environment will retaliate, and the abusers will be eliminated. No theory can alter that fact.

Russell Means

Cyrille Verdeaux

Musicians, Musicians, Listen..... Listen with your third ear to what I have to say, for the hour is dark. If I allow myself to leave the piano for the pen long enough to write this letter, it is because what I have privately suspected for years is in the process of becoming reality and my soul cannot suppress any longer the feelings which have long been accumulating within it. I must share them with you, my brothers and sisters, that has become MY SACRED OBLIGATION AS CITIZEN OF THE COSMOS.

It is, I think, a secret to no one that the musical level in the Occident is in decline. I expected that one day a powerful voice would denounce this situation and propose concrete solutions to short-circuit the fall. Alas, the booming mediocrity of record companies' production decisions and the unconditional servitude of media programmers to these more-than-suspect artistic directions are unthreatened by any obstacle or rebellion. The corrupt and destructive apparatus of the music business makes the rules, not the musicians. So, here I am and I say to you, in a brotherly spirit: "Men of little faith, get hold of yourselves, open your eyes, your ears, your mind and your heart. Do you not see that too much is enough?"

One fact is obvious: if musicians cut themselves off from the Cosmos, they can no longer RECEIVE COSMIC MUSIC! We are thus audience at a domination of machines, which is EXACTLY what our political leaders wish for in order to alienate us further and exploit our youth, life forces of nations. LOVE is the answer!

Musicians must re-establish themselves with the Spirit of the Cosmos through faith and meditation techniques. This philosophy will inspire a new sound and consciousness of the role of music on Earth to reveal Beauty and Cosmic Harmony to all humans.

The power of sound, on a subtle level, can modify for better or worse the human intellect by its choice of frequencies. Therefore, manipulated by the power structures, music can be used to control the intellect of the people. In fact, THAT IS WHAT IS HAPPENING! Open your eyes and ears! What are the agents or great capital concerned with? Only material visions! These aren't inherently bad, but isolated, they are fatal to the IMAGE of the musician. What about the music in all of this?

It is a veritable computerized, bureaucratic spider-web that I visualize when I meditate on the current world situation. A web in which we are all stuck: musicians, architects, doctors, scientists, journalists, politicians, etc. All lock-jawed with the fear of not having money. Because of this almost irrational fear at times, everyone is ready to play his own card whatever the price of compromise they have to agree to. Tell me my dear brothers and sisters if you think you will go far in this driveway into the garage of egoism?

The philosophical system which consists of favoring the material over the spiritual can never give good fruits, for the simple reason that GOD's plan demands disinterested love as its motor for manifestation.

The great composers who preceded us cannot be equaled in their musical knowledge. On the other hand, development of new instruments open new perspectives to original compositions every day. Their evolution now rests in the music of the here and now, not written, but nonetheless real and immortalized by digital recordings. Yet one must not abandon himself to the abuse of sequencers... It is often used simply to mask technical weakness of the musician and abuse the mechanical, automatic, percussive side of the synthesizer. On the other hand these same machines, in the right hands (cosmically speaking), can create angelic music which can help the extension of consciousness of the ENTIRE PLANET. Yet here again, money gives these precious instruments into hands enslaved by the music business and its anti-artistic interests.

For music to become spiritual and for the new age to arrive, it is necessary for musicians themselves to lead lives that favor cleanliness of their spiritual channels. It is in fact, in daily life that the musician's receptive state is determined. And the music itself can have a real spiritual and political power.

So artists of every country, who have FAITH in the law of Harmony, let us unite to reveal the beauty of our Father/Mother's invisible creation and accomplish our duty pleasurably.... Isn't that what we feel when we play FREELY?

RAMBIR

1985

Eskaton Interview
Musique Post-Atomique

Q: I remember seeing in a French music magazine some years ago, a small article about a new band named Eskaton Kommandkestra, and being intrigued. How did you choose that name and what does it mean?

A: Eskaton Kommandkestra was indeed our original group name. At that time some of us were still students, heard about and read about a very old mythology that can be found in Greek and German antiquity. In this mythology, Eskaton is the name of a cosmic battle which happens and terminates each life cycle and begins the rebirth of another. It's a cosmic battle between humans and their creative deities, a cosmic battle because the humans refuse to be any longer simply puppets in the hands of the gods. We found, and still do, a correspondence between this mythological philosophy and our group vision of reality. Each of us, we have to fight, each day, and try to control/shape our own destiny. This includes struggling against our own weaknesses. This is Eskaton. "Kommandkestra" is a combination of kommando and orkestra.

Q: Who were the original members? Who is currently in the band as I know there have been some changes over the years?

A: The original group was composed of Alain Blesing (guitar), Xavier Raymond (Fender piano), Andre Bernardi (guitar), Eric Guillaume (organum), Gerard König (drums), Marc Rozenberg (bass), Paule Kleynnaert and Amara Tahir (vocals).

Successively, Alain, Xavier and Eric left the group, while Gilles Rozenberg played with us from 1975 until now as guitarist and keyboardist. Currently the musicians are Andre Bernardi (guitar & bass), Paule Kleynnaert (voice & synthesizer), Gerard König (drums), Marc Rozenberg (piano, synthe, voice) and Amara Tahir (voice & percussion) as Gilles has just left us. We are still six from the original team, maybe the maddest. Maybe it is necessary to be a little mad to play music.

Q: Was the group's music influenced by other groups?

A: We don't feel to have been influenced by other groups. Each of us have a very different musical, cultural past and our music comes together as a composite of all these influences (jazz, rock, even classical). We used to listen to many different types, the horizon is so large from Grieg or Bartok, through Genesis or Deep Purple, to Gentle Giant or Fela Kuti a.o. We think each musician is the result of all the music they ever heard.

Q: What does the group hope to convey with its music/lyrics/stage performances?

A: For us, music is not an objective in and of itself. It is a way to convey our ideas. We wish to challenge the current society through our feelings and with our ideas by conveying an energy that shows that you don't have to go blindly along with everything. Through our lyrics we wish to convey our ideas, our concerns about wars, the Bomb, inhuman cities, death, but also faith and hope plus the ability to effect changes. It is during our concerts that we fully develop our music to its maximum energy level. In the past we used to play without the use of props or theatrics, but now we attempt to heighten the overall effect with slides, a mime and also color coordination that highlights the mood of the musical piece. We now feel the visual is another language and level on which the music can be further communicated. It is not a formal show, but an effort at collective communication between us, the musicians and you, the audience.

Q: Does the group have political goals or social ideas that it tries to practice in terms of their everyday lives?

A: The group has no formal political allegiance. However our philosophical perceptions force us to analyse and criticise our political and social environment. Our lyrics reflect these conclusions. We consider that playing our music and performances are our form of political expression. They are a call to wake up, not to dream. We try to fight against individualism. For instance, we live together and keep our money in a common fund. Many who proclaim political opinions cannot yet accept this approach regarding money and ownership, but we believe in collectivity in our lives. A musical example of this can be found in our compositions. One will bring an idea or theme up, another will make a change and still someone else will find an additional arrangement. The end result is a piece of "Eskaton music." This idea is surprising to some other musicians, but perfectly reflects our overall goals.

The musical group is our life essence. All of us have separate jobs for survival since we cannot make our living with our music. But these jobs are not our real life, even though they take up much of our real time. We do not wish to be rich from our music, music should be free for everybody, but we would like to earn enough just to live and keep on making music.

Q: To date you have done four recordings: the *MUSIQUE POST ATOMIQUE* EP, *ARDEUR* and *FICTION* LPs and *4 VISIONS* K7. How do you feel your music has changed over the years?

A: It is hard for us to define the change which may have occurred as our musical conception has evolved at the same time. Do not forget that our compositions are the result of a common work method. That is to say that they cannot be the same when they are made by two guitarists, two pianists and so on, or with only one guitar at times and with several synthesizers as now. It is an evolutionary process of the group's musicians. Maybe the music is not as cerebral as in the beginning and more visceral now. We have had a lot of troubles, people we loved have died and life is difficult. All of these things must have made an impact that we might not even understand. We are certain however that people's understanding of our lyrics and our contact with audiences have been important elements in our musical development, it is essential to have creative feedback at all levels. Ultimately I think though that we still explore the same musical dimensions, even though the musicians have changed and our equipment has as well.

Q: What's in the future for ESKATON and progressive music in France do you think?

A: At the moment we have sufficient material for one or two albums to chose from, but we have not yet decided upon a title. We recently bought a new 16-track recorder so we can produce our own records. The music scene in France now is very difficult for progressive musicians, nevertheless there are some distribution circuits that are becoming institutionalized and a growing audience.

Archie Patterson

Uli Trepte

ODDITY ODYSSEE
Set down on the backyard planet Earth due to the malfunction of a time-machine, the Lysergian Uli Trepte is desperate to go his distinct way in this square world. He picked up music early as being the only medium which would allow his collectively improvised highly cultured Lysergia.

He dropped into the scene as a founding member of the Irene Schweizer Trio as a free jazz, acoustic bass player. Then, switching to electric bass, he formed the free rock group Guru Guru with drum/percussion maniac Mani Neumeier. The live performances and three LPs of that wild trio are still appreciated by many even today.

During that time he also developed and constructed a new instrument: the Spacebox, (containing radios, tape recorder, mixer, equalizer, echo, etc.) played on the basis of mixing varied sounds to effect a new sound (principle of synergy). With this idea he became the first to introduce to rock music on Terra the aesthetics of o-tone and ambient noise.

Trepte left Guru Guru in Spring '72 and played with Neu!, RMO and Faust (UK tour '72). He then founded Spacebox as a project in '75 to realize his unique Lysergian concept of multiphony; performed first solo in Berlin at some small clubs. Next he lived in London for part of a year and played some gigs with Daevid Allen and at avant-garde clubs.

He then went back to Germany and made Spacebox a quartet which played several festivals and self-produced/distributed a limited edition of 1,000 LPs. But the music of the band was too specific and they eventually split up.

Trepte sold his equipment (except for the bass) and went to Tokyo, but found that there was in fact no underground scene there so spent his time doing Haiku and calligraphy. For nine months at the start of '82 he lived in New York City and almost was able to form a supergroup. Instead he ended up getting the blues and spent his time writing a science fiction novel that's yet to be published. Ultimately he began to feel the need to move on as the scene there was too conventional for his ideas.

He returned to Germany in '83 to paint and once again record with the group Spacebox. As a quartet they did *KICK UP* as a documentation of an authentic, cyclic structured, modal collective improvised, electric live music. Now he is back on his own again performing solo with only his bass and voice and minimal equipment. He has done test gigs in Central Europe -- Paris, Frankfurt, Stockholm and Rome -- to see if his ideas are still alive.

Trepte has been underground since the beginning of his musical work and will remain on the outside as the Lysergian heritage can't mix with a world that goes for nothing but politics, football, TV, cars and pop stars. Now he spends his time writing and painting and performing self-written compositions/lyrics of material specially written for his solo act exclusively. He calls his work "existential music" and says, "So many just boost crazes -- I got style." Or, citing the critic P. Hinten who once wrote: Trepte has the guts for the unknown.

Archie Patterson

Don Robertson Interview
Music For The "Now Age"

Q: Many of today's electronic musicians seem to be new-born dabblers in high-tech equipment and derivative ideas.

What is your background?
A: I have been a musician all my life, since I was very small when I began studying piano. I have a background in classical, pop, rock and roll, jazz and I have studied music of other cultures. I recorded an album for Mercury Records in 1969, titled *DAWN*, a play on my first name, that was released on their Limelight label. With that record I tried to show that there was music that had a positive effect

and that there was music that could also have a negative effect. People should be conscious of the impact music can have upon them. Unfortunately a year after the album was released, Mercury terminated my contract, saying "I was too far ahead of my time."

Q: Over the span of your four releases since then, you've touched on many ideas musically. Some people classify you as a "New Age" artist, how would you describe your style or inspirational source?

A: Well, what does the term "New Age" mean anyway? I am sure that it means different things to different people. The way I feel about it is that, I am just myself. I have played, listened to, studied different kinds of music, I have been influenced by my times and I make music. I don't really know what my music is. It just is. Music is so timeless and placeless. As far as what do I think of "New Age Music," that's too broad a question. I'm not too sure what "New Age Music" is? Some of the things I have heard lately I do have a name for: Frontal Lobotomy Music, music that does nothing. I think we are witnessing a change in the direction of the style of popular music. It has been guitar-based since the early sixties and I think people are unconsciously getting sick of hearing the same old thing all of the time on the radio. "New Age" is a name tag that has stuck that helps people relate to this new style of music. I am more concerned with the "Now Age," what is going on in this world right now! I could hardly call the Now Age, a New Age. The content of all the current mediums has got to change and I hope what a New Age really means is the bringing to the people, via the media, the greatest music from all cultures and all times, and the greatest art so that they may be inspired in their lives.

Q: Do or did you in the past listen to any contemporary synthesists that perhaps had an influence on your music?

A: I'll tell you how I became a "synthesist." I had been working with the compositional ideas that are in my albums long before I recorded them. I had been in self-imposed exile from the music scene since 1970. I turned off my radio and TV then tired of being exposed to all that hogwash, and I listened to the works of the great masters of classical music. In 1980 I bought a radio to listen to a program called Music From The Hearts Of Space which I had heard played "New Age" music and I wanted to find out what it was all about. On this show I heard music by Klaus Schulze and was amazed at the abilities of the synthesizer. I had not kept up with the music world and hadn't realized that synthesizers could create such wonderful music. I immediately bought a few small synthesizers and an 8-track and began recording *RESURRECTION* the day that I first plugged them in. I feel I must have been waiting all my life for the synthesizer to finally come along.

Q: How do you feel about the state of electronic music today? Has computer technology made the musician into more of a machine operator than creative dreamer?

A: I think it's too early in the game to see the ultimate resolution of what electronic music will be. It could go in many directions. There are interests in the world today that are undoubtedly not interested in furthering creativity and our general well-being who could well use the technology to further pacify us musically or otherwise. The question is -- are people going to choose life or death, do they even have a choice anymore? On the other hand we have before us the most magnificent of opportunities to REALLY bring light to the people. It is unbelievable the technology at our disposal.

Q: Do you think that the nature of society in general has any effect on a musician's creativity? Splendid isolation or social dynamism -- which, if either, is more conducive to good art/music?

A: If society is in turmoil, then the musicians creativity must be quadrupled, for this is when he/she is most needed. As far as isolation or dynamism being conducive to good work, I prefer to mix the two. I draw inspiration from nature and being apart from the confusion of the world, and then I turn around and infuse this back into the world. Without the world to give to, an artist has nothing to give. I think it's a matter of keeping one's feet firmly on the ground, while simultaneously maintaining a state as achieved in meditation.

Q: If people were to get one thing out of your music, what would you like it to be?

A: I hope that people experience my music with their feelings and that it moves them in some way, just as some music moves me when I hear it. An appreciation for music is important and I hope my work can help someone develop that ability. That may sound a bit strange for an answer, but what I mean is that more than anything, I wish to see the world's great music returned to the people, somewhere along the way most people have lost touch with great music. I don't know how many people I'm talking about, but generally...at least in this country..."The Arts" have attained the status of a "Museum Piece" and have no real meaning to our society as a whole. If people could only relate to and truly understand things like Raga Darbori, The Ring, J.S. Bach, etc. then what a change that would make.

Q: What does the future hold for you in terms of musical projects?

A: Firstly I am putting together my new recording studio after moving back to Colorado, which is where I was born. Then there will be a new album, *ANTHEM*, in the future. In addition we are working to get ready "Studio B," our broadcast production studio. it'll be up by Fall '85 when we want to start producing a nationally-syndicated radio show of 1986 that will feature all types of great music from around the world.

Archie Patterson

Joël Dugrenot

Born in 1947, the adolescent Joël Dugrenot was confronted by a perilous dilemma: his parents had planned an engineer's career for him; he preferred that of a musician.

In the end he undertook his musical career and formed his first group in which he played the bass: Vigon et les Lemons. Later he accompanied Michel Polnareff, Jacques Dutronc, Sylvie Vartan, Nino Ferrer while also serving as bassist for rockers such as Chuck Berry, Bo Diddley and Wanda Jackson when they toured France.

With the coming of Pop-Music towards the end of the sixties, one was present at the birth of a whole generation of French groups formed mostly by former accompanists of variety-show stars or by studio musicians. Among the first rank stood Martin Circus, Triangle and Zoo. After his departure from Zoo, singer Joël Dayde recorded an album with the collaboration of Claude Engel on guitar, Paco Charley on percussions (both ex-Magma) and Joël Dugrenot on bass, who at this time had already commanded attention as one of the best bassists in France.

This recording marked Joël's entrance into the world of Pop-Music and, in the company of Joël Dayde and Claude Engel, he participated in several festivals where his reputation as a bassist never ceased to assert itself.

It was also not surprising to find this bassist at the heart of one of the most talented and important groups to appear on the French music scene during the past ten years: ZAO.

This group, formed by two former musicians from Magma, François Cahen and Jeff Seffer, was to become, alongside Magma, one of the most original groups ever formed in France. ZAO's reputation surpassed the limits of France as one of the most innovative and talented representatives of a music that is purely European in essence.

ZAO put out its first record in 1972 with Joël on bass and Mauricia Platon on vocals. On this and the following record Joël signed his first compositions and asserted himself as a gifted and inspire composer.

His bass-playing illuminated the first two ZAO albums ($Z=7L$ and *OSIRIS*). Then Joël took part in the group parallel to ZAO animated by Jeff Seffer, Speed Limit, on whose first album he played bass before being replaced by Jannick Top.

Joël left France in 1975 for England where the Virgin Records phenomenon was breaking out. At that time Virgin was the musical refuge for all musicians excluded from other record companies and whose music had been judged unprofitable.

It was, however, through one of these "leftovers" that Virgin earned its consecration in the form of Mike Oldfield. Virgin appeared then as a kind of nursery-bed for a whole generation of brilliant and cosmopolitan musical geniuses and original progressive groups such as Hatfield and The North, Wigwam, Gong and Clearlight, for whom Joël became the bassist and with which he recorded two albums.

His association with the Virgin studios allowed him to meet and play with musicians as prestigious as Bill Bruford, ex-drummer of Yes and King Crimson, Fred Frith (Henry Cow) and David Cross, ex-violinist of King Crimson. During this time Joël recorded several of his compositions in the company of these talented musicians and of French musicians such as François Jeanneau, David Rose and Pierre Moerlen for an album which will never be released.

These recordings offered evidence of Joël's original inspiration and his talents as a composer, arranger and orchestrator. They also allow one to appreciate the beauty and quality of his superbly constructed and worked-out compositions: short, refined instrumental pieces where the harmonies of the violin couple with the accents of the flute to produce a music of disturbing beauty and of suggestive, lyrical moods.

On returning to France, Joël produced his friend Emmanuel Booz's new album, *LE CLOCHARD*, for WEA. He continued this production work with Mama Bea's first record, *LA POLLE*, who was not at that time the widely-recognized singer and artist she was to become later.

He participated as well in the making of the first album of a newcomer to the world of music, Armande Altaï, for whom be produced, arranged and composed all the pieces for her album *ATAVISME*. He contributed greatly to the success of this album, whose originality rests at the same time on Armande Altaï's exceptional and profoundly original voice, and on the form, rhythms and colors given to the compositions: an album illuminated by Joël's bass-playing and by the contributions of high-quality musicians such as David Rose on violin, François Jeanneau on flute and saxophone, Serge Haouzi on percussion and Manuel Villaroel on keyboards.

In 1982 the album *BOOMERANG* was born of his meeting with Jean-Marie Migeot, an album entirely composed by Joël and accompanied by Claude Olmos on guitar (ex-Magma), Jean-My Truong on drums (ex-ZAO and Surya), Manuel Villaroel on keyboards, David Rose and Marc Bonnet-Maury respectively on electric and acoustic violin. It offers a very original music, fusing rock, jazz, and European classical music into a perfect, profoundly lyrical and lively synthesis.

Joël develops a music that is simultaneously powerful and delicate, refined and elegant, flexible and energetic, beautiful and bewitching, dreamy and airy.

This album represents the coming of a music explicitly European in inspiration and expression, a music of a very pure beauty, refined charm and supreme elegance outside all labels.

While finishing his musicological studies at the University of Paris, XIIIth District, Joël Dugrenot continues to compose, especially for films.

Joël is presently starting a new group which will continue to follow the musical path he has outlined, thoroughly insisting upon and accentuating the influence of classical European culture on his musical ideas.

Francis Grosse
Translation Kevin Shelton

Japan Scene #3

L.L.E. Label

In the Summer of 1979, under the name of the "Creative Musicians Network L.L.E.," the musical co-op L.L.E. was started. Then it was a pool of creative musicians who played improvised music, avant-garde rock and live performances. it was organized into two parts: one was called I.M.I. (the (Improvisational Music Institution) that dealt with new jazz works, and the other was called P.M. (Psychotronic Metamorphoses) which focused on experimental rock.

At the end of '81 the first LP, *PSYCHOTRONIC METAMORPHOSIS*, was released to document the two years work, a compilation it included five groups: Phaidia, Katra Turana, Unit 3, Negasphere and Metamorphose.

In '82, the second LP, *DUAL COSMOS*, came out. It was a fusion of I.M.I. and P.M. and featured the Wes-Monzaemon Group and Kaleidoscope, a progressive group. The Wes-Monzaemon Group was free jazz. At the same time the second compilation LP, *MUGEN-MU*, was issued and all the groups on it are now the big names in the Japanese independent scene : Phaidia, Metamorphoses, Libido, Dendo Marrionett, Ja-Ju-Ka and *KPACHAR POSA* (Cross Na Ya Roza). In Summer of '82 I.M.I. released *FREE ASSOCIATION* by the new jazz trumpeter K. Sameyoshi and his friends. Again at the same time P.M. put out *LUBB-DUPP* which included Canopolis, Grass Philosophy, Furan-Shitai, D.R.Y. Project by Y. Nakano, Toji Tojima, Location, Freemasons Black Brain (who sound like Third Ear Band) and Anima (female synthesist of D.R.Y.) Also came out two cassettes by T. Tojima and D.R.Y. Project.

In 1983, L.L.E. as a co-op split into two different parts: one is the record label, the other works in live shows. At this time Phaidia created their own label and released an EP, *FUTURE DAYS*, which was distributed by L.L.E. The next L.L.E. releases were EPs by D.R.Y. Project -- *SHOCK OBSERVER*, Anima -- *CITIES* and a soundsheet *SHIN-HATSUBAI* by N.H.K., made up of former members of Phaidia. Late in the year the first LP by Takami -- *TENSHI-KOU* was issued, a unique work of female voice and surreal synthetics.

1984 marked the beginning of greater activities and some very interesting new releases. To begin there were two cassettes by Omniena and Freemasons Black Brain. These were followed in the summer by the debut work of Negasphere -- *CASTLE IN THE AIR*, an excellent progressive LP. In December two new records came out, one is by Chihiro S., the former leader of Katra Turana. Titled *LACRYMOSA*, it's a stunning fusion of progressive and new music styles. Then there was *A SLICE OF LIFE*, a compilation that included Soft Weed Factor, Veetdharm Morgan Fisher, Uber-Sakura and Haitokusha, it featured an excellent cross-section of sounds and styles of progressive, experimental music.

For 1985 there are many plans including the second LP by Takami, the debut albums of Libido and D.R.Y. Project. In addition L.L.E. is to work with the Kagerou Records musicians co-op of Western Japan. Then later in the year a new label will be created called Monolith that will specialize in progressive and symphonic rock. The first release will be a sampler, a set of three soundsheets to feature some of Japan's top groups: Mugen, Negasphere, Outer Limits, Aquapolis, Pageant and Tsurugi-no-mai.

Notes by Satoru Takazawa
Translation by M. Nakafuji

Torgue

French musician and keyboard player Henry Torgue has produced four albums to date. Three appear under his name (*SOUVENIR DES CITES CREPUS-CULAIRES, COMPARTIMENT FUCH-SIA, LE PRINCE APATRIDE*) and one marks his collaboration with the Emile DuBois Group, a dance troupe with whom he has been appearing since then. This album, entitled *PIANO*, was released at the end of 1984. It is of interest to introduce this artist whose career, itinerary and personality are all profoundly original.

Henry Torgue was born in Morestel (Isere) in 1950. Nicknamed "Skoff" by his friends he added this name officially to his records, but along the way he gradually abandoned it and now appears under his given name: Henry Torgue. His discovery of music and the world of keyboards began with the harmonium which was given to him by an elderly aunt. He then embarked upon an apprenticeship to the piano and was finally initiated into the electric organ. Essentially self-taught, Henry had only occasional teachers. His musical education proceeded through his participation in several pop groups while he was still a teenager. This transition through various groups taught him endurance and how to work with others, but it also made him aware of the limitations of this musical form. A group was unsuitable for his individual musical approach and his desire to elaborate an experimental music, leading him to believe that he could only truly express himself in the form of a solitary adventure.

In 1976 he released his first album (*SOUVENIR DES CITES CREPUS-CULAIRES*, which has since been re-edited and remixed), it was well received by the press and public alike. Between '76 and 1978 he appeared in concert, especially in the southeast of France, and recorded two more albums (*COMPARTIMENT FUCHSIA* and *LE PRINCE APATRIDE*). For him, this period corresponds to his "conservatory" phase.

Without renouncing the records produced during this time, he deems that this stopover period had come full circle and that these albums are flawed by being too linear and "narrative." The pieces are developed around a poetic idea or an image, around a particular melody or chord progression.

His contact with the world of dance transformed him, corresponding to a change in his musical orientation. In 1979 he met choreographer Jean-Claude Gallota and with him founded the Emile DuBois Group. His music became a part of the spectacle, integrating itself and dialoguing with the dance and the dancers' environment, mixing with and melting into their sounds, their cries, and the stomping of their feet on-stage.

Parallel to this activity as a musician, Henry Torgue is also a research engineer at CNRS. His works follow the same line of continuity as his musical activity, since the themes of his researches concern the sociology of the imaginary. His latest research merges totally with his work as a musician, since the theme he evokes is that of "tonal aspects of everyday life." For him there is no separation or dissociation between these two activities, since both correspond to the same mental attitude of listening, to paying attention to what is happening around oneself.

Henry Torgue does not consider himself capable of defining his music. He believes that is up to the listener to do that himself. In order to qualify his music, however, he employs the term "music of images," since his music is fond of images that the listener can keep in mind while it also possesses the power of evoking and developing them. His music also meets up with images by way of the cinema, for which he has already composed some music, or the dance, which offers visual support, an open horizon to the imagination which it allows to feed itself and which encourages the blossoming of constantly renewed images. His collaboration with the Emile DuBois Group has brought him profound satisfaction.

The work of the Emile DuBois Group was devoted first of all to creating and composing the group's repertoire, giving few performances at the beginning. Starting in 1983, the group began to tour frequently in order to put on its shows. The Emile DuBois Group represented France at the L.A. Olympics festival in 1984, then appeared in Berlin, Amsterdam, Mexico and in January 1985, at the City Center in New York City. Henry Torgue reckons that these performances have allowed him to encounter an audience he would never have known through the simple expedient of solo concerts. On the other hand, these tours and creative work with the group have kept him away from the studio and interfered with recording the current evolution of his music. In 1984 the album PIANO also appeared, which corresponds to the first volume of musical works composed for the Emile DuBois Group.

PIANO is an album of solo piano which gathers together pieces from different shows. It sets itself apart from Henry's previous productions; but its sensibility and the delicacy of its melodies are expressed with as much power and seduction as ever. A few months later, the second volume devoted to his work for the Emile DuBois Group was realized for release in October '85. It represents the tonal illustration of the spectacle *LES AVENTURES D'IVAN VAFFAN*. This album takes up again the universe of keyboards and synthesizer and offers a more synthetic music which bears witness to his present-day development. In 1984 the third volume featuring his Emile DuBois collaborations will appear. The music will be that of the group's latest creation, *MAMMANE*.

In 1984, parallel to his intensive work with the DuBois Group, Henry Torgue composed the music for a spectacle of images, created with a film director, on the occasion of the "Tombees de la Nuit" festival at Rennes. This spectacle, entitled

1985

MEMOIRE DES ECUMES, allowed him to compose an original score lasting forty minutes for synthesizer and symphony orchestra, thus adding a extra, new dimension to his music. He was very satisfied with the experience and his collaboration with an orchestra -- a collaboration which will also have a discographic extension, since an album of the show will come out before the end of '85. It will be a special production in the form of a "treasure chest" including the record and an album of cartoons and semi-photos which will retrace the spectacle employing, as Henry puts it, "poetic license."

When Henry is approached with the question of what his music represents to him, he defines it as "a necessity." He is unable to keep from playing, to keep from having melodies running through his head. For him music is a permanent activity, but it does not represent a means for expressing his inner world, his fantasies and his visions. He considers himself as an instrument of music. He composes sonorous passages in the hope that the listener will share his emotions and images, or that his music will convey and develop other images within the listener. Henry is well aware that his music is oriented toward lyricism and emotion. The axis of his work for him lies in the meeting of "poetry and philosophy" or his "feeling" and "intelligence." He seeks to produce works which are not devoid of reflection and which possess a structured architecture -- without however being dried up and emaciated. For him today's music lacks lyricism, although he doesn't believe that his music relies solely on this lyricism -- simplicity must exist as well. His works for piano tend toward this simplicity, seeking to reduce the number of notes to a minimum, to achieve a certain purity of style. With the synthesizer, on the other hand, he wishes to make his music more complex, to move toward richer sounds, to blend elements from real life such as noise and sound effects. As for the titles of the records, they represent a game, an extension of the image. The title should give a kind of echo, a continuation, to a given piece.

Whenever the particularity and originality of his music is brought up, Henry retorts that what he retains most from his concerts in the U.S. are the highly positive reactions of the audience and their proclamations marking out the originality of his music and the fact that is has no connection to that of the U.S., the fact that it "swings," but without having anything in common with jazz or American fashions, and that it was qualified as being "terribly French." He cannot however really say in what way it is French. If he is aware that his music rests on the heritage of European culture, with an "Old World" or a "sensuality of culture" side to it, he is too impregnated and possessed by his music to offer a profound introspective analysis of it. There are certain elements of a creation which even escape its creator. It is the mysterious aspect, this feeling of an unknown will, which accentuates its charm. With Henry Torgue these elements of mystery and indefinable charm, difficult to explain and to analyze, nevertheless exercise their power over the listener and thus his music lacks neither fascination not beauty.

Francis Grosse
Translation: Kevin Shelton

En-Trance Interview

The collected works of Trance, Entrance and Adrian Marcator represent some of the best music coming out of Germany today. In a time when much of what's being produced in that country seems to lack any real creative focus or inspiration, the works of the collective En-Trance and Transform label are worthy of greater attention. The following interview sheds some light on the background and inspiration source of the main force behind the music.

Q: With the release of Adrian Marcator's meditation cassette series and new Entrance cassette/book, we now have apparently three different musical projects associated with the Transform label. The original group was Trance -- when was it formed and who is the creator of the music?

A: The different names are a result of the musical development over the last 8 years. Trance was formed in 1977 by Armin Wischnewski and myself. We made an album in 1979 (*DYSTOPIA*) and split in 1980. I kept the name Trance for various solo efforts (*HERE & NOW* [1981], *BELIAL* [1984], *AMBIENTE* [1984] and *MUSIC FOR EXPERIMENTAL FILM* [1985]). All LPs and cassettes were composed, recorded and produced by me alone. In order to give a clear identity to the force behind the music I decided to drop the name Trance and release further solo works under the name Adrian Marcator. So there will be no further Trance recordings.

Q: What is your background musically?

A: It is actually quite diverse. In the '60s I started playing guitar influenced by The Beatles, Vanilla Fudge, Jefferson Airplane, etc. In the early '70s I was into the blues, fusion, folk-rock and playing guitar in various groups. Around 1975-77, I found my own musical identity absorbing all the previous styles and combining them with electronics, experimental sounds, first on guitar and sitar, later also on keyboards.

Q: Now a second group, Entrance, has been formed. Why not just continue with the one name, is there a specific reason for the change?

A: Since 1981, I have been playing together with Holger Mummert. His background is in various guitar-picking styles (Kottke, etc.) with roots in early rock. In order to avoid confusion with my solo work, we've adopted the name Entrance. The musical style is slightly different than Trance was, more acoustic guitar, shorter pieces. Our works (*THE POND* and the new one *WATTEN-KLANGE*) are cooperative efforts, about half of the songs written together, the rest arranged and produced by both of us. I do the recording, Holger is into the graphic design of the artwork.

Q: The first three releases were a trilogy of works based on Huxley writings. What were they and why were they chosen as focal points for the music?

A: Since I was a student "Brave New World" by Aldous Huxley has been a very influential book for me. As a teacher now I've studied it more deeply and thought it contained so many aspects of a possible future that I was inspired to write music for it. In the beginning of Trance we worked together with a theater group performing a multi-media show on the theme. From this novel I developed an interest in other works by Huxley and came upon "Island" which made an even greater impact on me since it describes a positive utopia. It was a logical step to contrast the dark *DYSTOPIA* LP with a more positive follow-up *HERE AND NOW*. To finish off the trilogy I chose the third utopian novel by Huxley, "Ape and Essence," which describes a degenerated world after WWIII. Of course the threat created by the SS 20, Pershing and Cruise missiles and the motivation of the peace movement are a further reason for a musical warning of such dangers.

Q: Your music seems to be spiritually attuned, if not necessarily in any orthodox sense. Is it intended to affect the listener on some level -- cosmological or purely entertainment?

A: I need a quiet, peaceful country life to be creative. I have been living in country for 13 years now and I could not adjust to city life anymore. I have my own small cottage and garden with family and pets and only spend a few weeks a year in an Asian or African country. I'm attracted to Asian cultures which bring forth the spiritual character in sounds and structure. I'm not really involved in mysticism or spiritualism, but rather attracted by it aesthetically and emotionally. So I do not follow any guru or such, but choose useful elements like contemplation to enrich my life.

I think there are different aspects of the work "entertainment." Of course I want to entertain people. I hope that my work is used by listeners for relaxation, to create atmospheres, to become aware of personal problems or problems of our time, to give a hint at possible solutions. I am convinced that my present work, the meditational cassette series, can do a lot of good since only clear-minded, relaxed people can bring about any changes. I admit it may be only a small help, but it is the best I can do.

Q: What projects do you have planned for the future? More cassettes or records?

A: I have recorded so much music during the last year (8 cassettes), that first I'll be busy marketing it. We started our own company, Transform, and try to find possible ways for using more meditational music. This shall enable me to build up a 16-track studio and enlarge my keyboard equipment to improve the music sound-wise. Currently I'm fascinated by the idea of cassette-books, combining pictures, poetry, stories and music. We have just released our first work of this sort -- Entrance -- *WATTENKLANGE*, and I guess more of this will follow in my solo works. In the Autumn a follow-up to *TRANS-SPHERE* should be ready and also a double cassette of purely meditational sounds will come out. I have my own cassette duplicating facility now and a cooperative printer so the production of tapes is economical and more rewarding. This way I also have full control over every aspect of production. If I have a more secure distribution, I'd like in the future to release my music on LPs again too.

Jurgen Petersen

D.D.A.A. Interview

Illusion Production and Deficit Des Annees Anterieures are perhaps one of the most interesting and enigmatic of all the groups on the French scene today. Their unique style of minimalist avant-garde rock and conceptual graphic production have delighted many people. The following interview attempts to shed light on the nature of who and what lie behind this intriguing group/organization.

Q: Who are in fact the members of I.P. and D.D.A.A.?

A: The members of D.D.A.A. are the same people who are the I.P. organization. We met at the Art School of Caen (Normandy) and decided to found I.P. to support our activities in painting and music. So the organization was founded by three people, the famous painter Pablo Picasso, Henri Matisse, George Brague (what do you think of that?!) No!! The truth is that we are Jean-Luc Andre, Jean-Philippe Fee and Sylvie Martineau (but we are really painters).

Q: What is the background of the people?

A: After college studies we spent five years at the Artschool and obtained the national certificate of art. During these art studies we broadened our musical knowledge of the contemporary experiences. So the background of the people of I.P. is a combination of many influences.

Q: When was it actually all started?

A: All this adventure started when the right conditions of geographical, political, international context were collected. So D.D.A.A. began in 1976 and I.P. in 1979.

Q: What was the original idea behind the group/label?

A: When we started D.D.A.A. our idea was to create a sort of free rock to express our radical position in art at this time. We thought that punk rock was not radical enough and we were right because all the big companies have now signed these groups. The creation of a label, I.P., was a logical deduction also of our radical position.

Q: Has your working philosophy changed over the years?

A: It's very difficult to explain our evolution in English, because our philosophy of creation has changed, without changing. We have evolved in the way we create our music which is now more sophisticated and controlled, but the passion and the energy which drives us in our work have not changed.

Q: Do certain people do the artwork and others the music, or is it a collective effort?

A: We all do the artwork and the music, but Sylvic does often the more important part of the art presentation.

Q: Is there a political philosophy that guides the group/organization or an ideology you adhere to?

A: With creative activities we try to have a radical position independent of the big companies because we think that they are not the best way to research and make original works. That doesn't mean however that we have no hope to reach a larger audience.

1985

Q: Your initial productions were limited editions, now it seems you do larger-scale releases. How many copies of each release on an average do you press/sell?

A: In the case of LPs we press about 1,000 copies, but with the new D.D.A.A., *LES AMBULANTS*, we did 2,000. With cassettes we do 400-800. Basically we sell them all over a span of time (it depends on the nature of the material how long it takes).

Q: Do you have any idea of what your audience is like or how they relate to your work?

A: We think our audience is some great fans of D.D.A.A., some political philosophy supporters (maybe they are the same people?), some avant-garde music fans, some collectors of odd records, others....?

Q: Can the various members support themselves via I.P./D.D.A.A., or do you have different occupations?

A: We can't support ourselves via I.P. (it's too small a company). Jean-Philippe and Jean-Luc are teachers of art in college. And we all do collective paintings that are commissioned (for private people or public organizations) and we use this money for the I.P. productions.

Q: Do you have any interest in signing to a larger record company?

A: We never have thought of signing to a big label and no major company has thought of signing us. Actually our problem is to develop the distribution ourselves to reach a bigger audience and not to think of signing to a company. If it should ever happen, our position would be to certainly keep our way of original creation.

Q: Now I.P. seems to be branching out to release works by other people, do you have plans to make the label more than just an outlet for D.D.A.A. productions?

A: Of course we want I.P. to be able to produce other people's material, if their music follows the same orientation of our own creations. So our choice of who to produce will be selective.

Q: What are the hopes for the future of I.P./D.D.A.A.?

A: We want to work to obtain a larger audience and at the same time maintain our radical position.

Archie Patterson

Christian Vander Interview
L'Offrande Supreme

This end-of-the-year 1984 is marked by a clear return to activity by Magma, a new album *MERCI*, a European tour in November (Germany and Scandinavia) and an end-of-December series of concerts given at the Dunois. Rather than do the usual concert report we've decided to give Christian Vander the floor. What follows is not an exact transcription of his remarks. Actually we were unable, because of human error (cassettes forgotten), to record the interview!

Q: Can you explain to us the reason for the formation of Offering and in what way it differs from Magma?

A: In fact I had wanted for a long time to put together an acoustic group with a lot of piano and get out of the context of Magma. In Offering we're telling the other side of the story. It is also a new approach to John Coltrane. In Magma everything was written. In "Theusz Hamtaahk" each note is written, in Offering there is a lot more freedom in the structures.

Q: But doesn't that present a problem in finding musicians capable of improvising without deviating from the original feeling?

A: Of course, there is a risk to take. Sometimes we take on a musician and at the end of the month we realize that he doesn't fit in.... but that allows the music to evolve.

Q: And how is it going to evolve?

A: You were there last evening? (Affirmative response on our part.) For example the concert's introduction with the two pianos is a new piece. When the two pianos are just right, which is not the case at the moment, we'll add voice for the melodies and a lot of drums... Right now I feel like expressing suffering. I've had enough of the languid pieces in Offering. We're going to eliminate pauses, breaths, to arrive at something more and more gripping.

Q: Music still more of despair?

A: Yes, still worse (Vander smiles). Each piece should be a hell.

Q: But on the public level, who is going to be able to follow?

A: I don't know... During the European tour, at one concert people started to cry and that's the point! Anyway, we talked with people who told us they preferred we play our music, without concessions, even if it has evolved. But the public always has had a hard time following. KÖHN-TARKÖSZ for example was not understood at all, the melodies not fitting in at all with the tempos (here Vander accompanied his words with a sung example). People like to be treated by good doctors, but with music they let themselves be treated the way it was 30 years ago.

Q. Stella told us you wanted to remix three pieces?

A: Yes, for the French release of the LP -- "Oh, Baby," "I Must Return" and "Do The Music." We spent three nights mixing and that's not enough. We need three or four days for each piece. We spent 150 days in the studio, sometimes one night on a single take. We can mix in four hours what was done in ten hours, but not what required nights to do.

Q: In the album there are synthetic drums, is it an experiment you may repeat?

A: Yes, it took a week to program the Linn, but once we're really familiar with it, it will enable us to save time. I want to do with the Linn what humans can't do, anyway Magma will head more and more towards a synthetic form. For the record we spent nights to get the sound of the drums. In Offering, the drum sound is more a "live" sound. The problem with the Linn is that we don't have the same nuances as with a drummer, but we always have the possibility of redoing something afterwards.

Q: it seems that Magma is lacking in means.

A: Yes completely. For the Forum, we had a ridiculous subsidy which paid only concerts for the brass, not rehearsals and so we hardly practiced with them for when you don't pay for rehearsals, the musicians don't come. It's really hard to find brass, they always have the possibility of playing variety. After that they don't feel like taking risks anymore. There are many drummers, guitarists, bass players; good brass no.

Q: In your opinion, are there a lot of motivated musicians today?

A: No and you only have to look at the state music is in to realize that. Musicians still do their solo work for their girlfriends, but that's all. It's a desert. I try to listen to some things, but each time I have the impression of having already heard it. In fact, certain earlier music was a lot more evolved. Besides, if current music was more progressive, I would play "New Wave" or "Hard Rock." When I listen to music, it's like when I read a horror story, I like to be surprised. When I listen to Coltrane, I'm surprised every time.

My dream would be to do a normal 2-1/2 hour concert, people applaud for the encore and... the curtain opens in back and we do a 3-hour concert with two sets of drums, two bass, brass, choir and strings...

Q: Since the Forum we get the feeling it's evolving very fast and that you're returning to a sophistication in the arrangements similar to Magma's.

A: It's a natural evolution. At the Forum we were so blocked by the brass that afterwards we felt so free that everything came out during the concert we did then... What I said just now about the introduction is for today, tomorrow it will be different... sometimes a little mistake can bring about great changes. At the beginning of Offering we wanted to create a different group, but the more we go on, the more we come to resemble Magma.

Q: When you sing do you improvise entirely?

A: I improvise, but I always have something I'm aiming for. I have a point to reach, but I don't know how to reach it.

Q: Do you have trouble setting yourself apart from your role as drummer?

A: Completely. At the beginning I often heard "back to your drums" surging up from the audience. I have always sung at home with the piano, but to sing on stage is nothing like that. I thought singing mistakes were easier to cover up than mistakes on the drum, but that's definitely not the case.

Q: Are you often satisfied with a concert? For example the one yesterday?

A: Rarely... Yesterday was good, day before yesterday too, but it's really hard to all be together... either the others are in form and I don't manage to find the right phrases or to catch the musical waves, or the reverse. At the Forum, for example, I was completely blocked by the brass. In general, I am not usually ever totally satisfied with any concert.

EPILOGUE: We still had a lot of questions to ask Christian Vander, but as the rehearsals were behind schedule the interview stopped there. But the night before we were able to talk a little with Stella Vander and find out that Christian is presently at work composing a major new work titled "Les Cygnes et les Corbeaux" ("Swans and Crows") to be realized sometime in the near future hopefully.

Interview Produced by:
J.C. Allvin (Questions, Transcription)
D. Houde (Quotations, Cassettes Forgotten)
Photo.: P. Thibaut
Reprinted Courtesy of: NOTES
Translation by: Lois Bode

Synchestra Interview

Q: The works of Synchestra bring together many musical influences. What is the background of the group, in particular Ed Van Fleet who appears to be the main musical motivator?

A: I started playing bass guitar when I was 12 years old. That was the start of 11 years of playing in bands. Mostly rock groups, but some jazz and country and a few years of funk. I learned a lot about rhythm in the funk bands. At 18 I tried out for a jazz trio with a couple of guys in their 50s. I got the gig and one of them kind of took me under his wing and taught me about structure and harmony. To me that's the best kind of schooling you can get because it's "hands on" experience as opposed to sitting in a theory class at school. Anyway, at 23 I met John Wilson by answering an ad on a bulletin board for a bass player. I auditioned and got the job. We worked steady in the group (me on bass and John on drums) and didn't have day jobs...so we started recording some of my songs during the days. Over a six-month period we did maybe a dozen songs, vocal things, kind of space rock or something. Anyway, I then began to realize that to do what I wanted I really needed my own studio. At one point some people popped up who believed in me enough to finance what I wanted to do. I was thrilled and scared at the same time because there I was at 23 -- going into debt the equivalent of buying a house and starting a business I really didn't know much about. We leased a building that was a big shell and built an eight-track studio in it...a good-sized studio of a couple thousand square feet. That was in '77 in Phoenix, following a move from San Diego. We started recording bands for $25 an hour. I named the place Synchestra Studios because on our demo tapes, John and I did all the playing, tracking one instrument at a time and we thought of ourselves as kind of a two-man "synthesized orchestra." We were at that place for 6 years, we even played on our clients' recordings at no extra charge. Well this became our bread and butter because if someone needed back-up players, they could record at Synchestra and produce a finished product cheaper than at other studios where they had to pay session men. This was good for us because it taught us how to arrange and play all different kinds of music, from 30-second jingles for TV and radio to whole albums of every style of music imaginable. Through the years we upgraded the studio to 16 tracks and started putting out the Synchestra albums on cassettes in 1981. Up 'til going into the "studio business" in 1977, I had been influenced primarily by progressive rock groups such as Yes, ELP, Genesis, King Crimson, etc., but after we started the studio I sound less & less time to listen due to sessions and my own music. It became literally a "full time" job because we needed to keep the studio booked to keep from needing other jobs, and yet I also needed spare time to do any original music so it was 6 years of the most intensive musical school ever. This is enough. You've already got me going and it's turning into the Gettysburg address.

Q: When was the group officially formed and was there a special idea or concept behind it?

A: The group really was formed in 1977 when we started the studio although nothing was done under the name Synchestra until 1981. The original concept was to do progressive rock albums that told a story. Almost like a movie or play. We did a piece of mine called "Atlantis" that lasted almost two hours. Took a pile of hours to do it, over two years in fact. The only problem was that we recorded it on 8-tracks and after all the bouncing of tracks, the quality just wasn't there so we've never released it. It truly needs to be a 48-track project partially because of the amount of sound effects and because there are so many singers with parts in the play. Unfortunately for me, I know absolutely no one in the record business so when we shopped "Atlantis" around to various labels we couldn't even get past the doormat. Two-hour long concept albums about mythology are not real important to large record companies. Anyway, about this time we had managed to also record a couple of instrumental tunes that lasted the whole side of an album. Diana Rae, who does all the cassette cover layouts and who is a serious contender for "guiding light" in this organization, suggested that we release them as a cassette. After much barking and bashing, we finally did and that became *THE NATURE OF THE GAME*, Synchestra's first release. It started selling in small quantities and I'm glad because it showed me a way around the big companies. A way to do it independently. Do it myself. Now we have 8 cassettes out and we've managed to do it by ourselves which to me is very encouraging for musicians, because it means you can support yourself with original music without relying on someone else's record label.

Q: The music seems very transcendent at times. Is there a specific spiritualism behind it or a more general cosmological awareness?

A: No, I don't subscribe to any particular belief system. The only thing I generally try to do is keep the music uplifting and positive. That's the kind of stuff I like to hear so that's what I do. It can have peaks and valleys, but I like happy endings.

Q: Formerly based in Arizona, you've relocated to Maine. That's a big change, what was the motivation for it?

A: I had never been to Maine or New England for that matter, but someone in Maine who likes our music found out that I wanted to leave Phoenix and relocate in a rural area, preferably in the woods. He suggested Maine, and to make a long story short, I wound up moving 3,000 miles lock, stock and barrel. I had gotten myself into a situation where I had the chance to basically live wherever I wanted so it was a good time to try something totally different. It has worked out great, Maine is wonderful. It's like a wildlife spectacular. Something I definitely needed to balance out all the years of living in the studio.

Q: How does the music reflect your daily lives, if at all? It seems humanistic, is it so in any political sense?

A: The music reflects our lives in the sense that we love the outdoors, we're concerned about our environment, and we would rather live closer to Nature than closer to concrete and asphalt. Most of the pieces have impressions of the Earth and Nature running through them. We've done *MOTHER EARTH LULLABY* which has birds and crickets and is a kind of song for the Earth. *SILVERSHIPS* explores the rain which I love, I guess because I'm from Arizona. We've covered snowflakes (*ELECTRIC SNOWFLAKE*) and *DAYDREAMS, NOAH'S ARK* -- definitely of the Earth-type stuff. Diana summed it up best in the liner notes of *MOTHER EARTH LULLABY* when she said that in order for us to ever move on to the next higher plane, we first had to create heaven here on Earth. It's so true and unfortunately for humankind, on the whole, we're not doing a real hot job of putting it all together. I feel that it's important for us to remember from where we came and what we are made of because we are made out of the same stuff the Earth is. As a species we've evolved in the outdoors under the sun and stars and I think our bodies need the natural contact with the Earth and Nature in order to survive. I'm not recommending that everyone live in teepees. I just prefer blue sky to forced air in a high rise.

Q: Is there one special feeling or idea you hope that people pick up on in your music?

A: I just hope people are somehow uplifted, smile a bit or are happier in some way. I really have meant for all the music to date to be happy and positive. I'm a positive, up kind of person and I enjoy communicating that outlook and feeling to others. None of the music I've done so far has been dark or scary at all. Just light pieces with nice little melodies on top. That isn't to say that I won't venture into some more spacy or minor key things in the future -- I just haven't yet. There are plenty others out there exploring in those areas and there'll be more in the future.

I've just had a good time so far exploring my impressions of the Earth around us.

Q: Quantitatively, can you make your living via the music, or is outside work necessary?

A: I can make a modest living from the original music. If I didn't buy too much gear I'd be okay. However, I've always had a rather large appetite for new goodies, so I currently do some soundtrack work to supplement my income from the tapes. I've also produced a few artists that we will release on a new label soon. But 80-90% of my living comes from my tapes which is extremely gratifying... We're lucky to live in a time when there is a demand for many diverse musical and artistic styles. And efforts like yours that make these choices available to the public are certainly very much appreciated.

Q: What does the future hold in terms of recording activity? A record perhaps, or will cassettes continue to be the medium you use to release your music?

A: The first part of 1986 will finally see the arrival of some records. We're going to press *MOTHER EARTH LULLABY, DAYDREAMS* and *ELECTRIC SNOWFLAKE*. I had hoped to possibly jump straight to CD, but it seems that records are also needed. Even though CDs are coming on very quickly, it will still take quite a while to account for large share of the market. I also plan to move our whole line of tapes to chrome instead of normal bias. That will also be early 1986. I've also begun work on my first solo project, no name so far. It's pretty interesting stuff -- a little more up-tempo and punchy. It will probably come out next summer. I'm having a ball with it because I've added some new gear since we did *ELECTRIC SNOWFLAKE*. I've got a couple of Yamaha DX-7s which I love, and one of those Oberheim Xpanders which is the wildest, most flexible analog synthesizers I've ever seen. I've got too an Apple computer now with great composition software and of course, all the other synths and guitars and a good quality drum machine as well as all the acoustic percussion...so the music is really going to have some varied sounds. I actually hope to record the whole thing this winter because, as you may have guessed, it gets pretty cold here in Maine. Last winter saw a lot of work completed although not my own music. I did some producing and soundtrack work. I don't go outside that much when it's 100 below and the wind is blowing. Just kidding. It doesn't get that cold here, but it is a good time to work... very cozy inside and inspiring to this Sunbelt city boy. And after winter comes the summer when the big fish start biting....

Archie Patterson

Dominique Lawalree Interview

Dominique Lawalree (30) is a young Belgian composer. With more than 240 pieces, he covers a wide variety of instruments: voices, chamber and symphony orchestra, organ, piano, synthesizer, virginal and choir.

Instead of reflecting the actual world, he prefers to give life to our deepest feelings, our quietest and serene thoughts. He's a poet and philosopher through the language of music.

He's given more than 100 concerts with various formations. Symphony orchestra as well as playing alone (piano, organ, etc.), lecturing also a lot. His music is recorded on more than 10 LPs. He explains his work in two books: 1)"Documenta Belgicae No 1" (1983) written with 7 other composers; 2) "Taciturne: journal d'une composition" (1984). Radio and newspapers are interested in his work even in the USA. He has played all over Europe.

Trained in music education with a solid background in harmony and counterpoint, he is Inspecteur in music education and teaches also at the UCL (University of Louvain-la-Neuve) harmony and musical analysis.

Q: There are many pianists recording worldwide today, but few possess your skill at creating such a wide variety of musical styles with equal ability. When did you take up the piano and what training have you had?

A: Since I was eight years old I've been playing piano and very quickly developed a personal approach to the instrument. I tried quality of sound very soon. In my classical piano studies in the beginning the teachers didn't teach quality of sound; yet I was able to discover it early on. The creating of actual sound is important the piano. In my training since the beginning I had solofeggio and I didn't place my sole emphasis on the piano. I had training as a composer and with music writing, the more conceptual aspects of music. My training was not necessarily to be a pianist, but more a composer.

Q: Would you say your music has been influenced by any contemporary "pop" keyboardists? Or perhaps more by some of the classical/jazz music of earlier days?

A: No. I'm not a pianist, but a composer. And so I've written for all instruments, even if I don't play all the instruments. For instance, *THE SYMPHONY OF HOPE* was written two years ago for a string orchestra and will finally come out on record at Xmas. But, as I enjoy performing my music I often play keyboards (organ, synthe, piano), so my classical training in piano helps me. The only time I was influenced by a pianist is in the composing of my favorite piano work, *TACITURNE*. I was influenced there by Glenn Gould and his playing of Haydn's last sonatas on Columbia Records. His work showed me a new way to conceive of time in my music.

Q: For someone with so many records, 10 to date I believe, you seem to be virtually unknown for the most part. Do you ever play concerts in Belgium, or Europe?

A: I give many concerts in Europe as a pianist, conductor, organist and electronic keyboardist. At my concerts I only play my own music, never interpretations of other composers. And if I have done so many records, it's to give the opportunity to the audience to discover all of my different musical faces. I'm planning a concert tour in Summer of '87 of the USA. So if anyone is interested in organising a concert for me during that time period please contact me at: Dominique Lawalree, Rue Beckers, 16 1040 Brussels, Belgium.

Q: All of your albums have been released on the Walrus label. Is that label for your records, or are there other artists with LPs on the label as well?

A: That's my own label and I produce it independently. I know in the USA it would be difficult to do that, but in Europe you have some people doing so. The goal is not commercial; it is to give people the opportunity to hear the music. In the same way as the American composer Alan Hovhaness. Walrus comes from my name and I chose it in the memory of the Beatles song.

Q: Do you make your living from the recording side of the music business, sessions, etc., or is that more of a sidelight of your overall profession?

A: My music is my life. But as it is non-commercial I'm a university teacher in music.

Q: Your music is very pastoral and reflective. What do you try to convey with your works, a more emotional feeling or a peaceful, meditative atmosphere?

A: I prefer to give life to our deepest feelings, our more quiet and serene thoughts. I feel I'm a poet and philosopher through the language of music. Rock music usually tries to reflect more the actual world. I can appreciate this idea, but as I'm a composer I do not work along those lines. My music is the one for our lost paradise. The atmosphere is natural to me; I don't try to create it. It is me!

1985

Q: Your early records seemed to make more use of organ and synthesizer. Lately, they have been much more piano-oriented. Is this a conscious change or simply a natural evolution in style/musical preference?

A: On one record one can listen to old and new pieces. That's why I always write the date and the catalogue number. A lot of pieces were composed for interpreters, but on my own records as I play everything myself, the repertoire is limited. With the forthcoming *SYMPHONY* (my most successful piece, as it seems), it'll be a lot different musically. Now I think my music has a more personal touch to it. My records are not reflecting the evolution of my music and are not chronologically meant, otherwise I would have to release a record every month. They just indicate different moments of my work. In rock usually records are the composition themselves. I'm working like the classical musicians do. I was influenced by American composers tike George Crumb and Morton Feldman.

Q: What plans do you have for future records? Do you wish to be more commercially successful or is that desire irrelevant to your making music?

A: I have just released my latest album (the 10th), titled *LITANIES DU MONDE A VENIR*. It's a solo work for organ recorded in a cathedral. As I already have said, at Xmas *THE SYMPHONY OF HOPE* in four sections (with a string orchestra conducted by myself) and a cassette of music meant to be accompanying poems will come out. In 1986, two cassettes in a special box (time duration of two hours) will be released. The piece "From Time to Time" for electric piano, that I'm composing every day of this year will be included in that. Later on I would like to release some music for synthesizer. I don't try to be commercial, but if it would become more successful, I would continue to live just like I do. I would be happy if more people could hear my music. I don't want to give it to only an elite of listeners.

Archie Patterson

1986

Legendary Pink Dots Interview

OLD GODS CRY AS A PLANET DIES, CHOKING ON AN OVERDOSE OF EXPERIENCES, EMOTIONS, EVENTS. AND RATHER LIKE THE DROWNING MAN, THE PAST DARTS BEFORE OUR EYES IN A PLETHORA OF COLOURS. EVERYTHING YOU EVER HEARD, EVERYTHING YOU HAVE SEEN, EVERYTHING YOU HAVE FELT...MIXED TOGETHER.

THIS IS THE TERMINAL KALEIDOSCOPE. CHERISH IT. SING WHILE YOU MAY!

The Legendary Pink Dots are one of the most imaginative bands to have come out of Britain in the post-punk era of the '80s. Their debut LP, *BRIGHTER NOW*, in 1982 began a musical offensive determined to create a new '80s synthesis of "progressive" music. Since then they've subsequently released 5 more group works including the latest titled *ASYLUM*, which could be considered the definitive record of today's "new music" tendency. As well, vocalist/leader Edward Ka-Spel has recently just released his 1st solo record making their combined creative output impressive on any level you might want to consider it.

Their name, as well as their music, inspires curiosity. What follows is an interview with Edward, the creative spirit that drives what is perhaps the best group of the '80s -- LPDs.

Q: Exactly when did the LPDs come into existence and who was the instigator?

A: LPDs started life in the Summer of 1980 as a three-piece including myself, Phil Harmonix (the Silver Man) and April Iliffe. Nobody took us particularly seriously; three people making strange music in a squatted house -- playing through the night, mostly improvising. We were dead serious however.

Q: How did you come up the name?

A: There were mysterious pink blotches on the piano we used. Since then, others have connected our name with a form of acid. Frankly I've never heard of it.

Q: Was there any particular band that influenced you musically? (To me shades of Barrett-era Floyd and the UK band Kaleidoscope/Fairfield Parlour seem present.)

A: Confession time. The first music that really made me sit up and listen was early Pink Floyd around the time of "See Emily Play." I was fascinated by the whole trip: John & Yoko, flowers, acid, etc., but I had to watch it on TV, in black and white. Quite simply, I was too young. I bought my first album in 1972, (*SGT. PEPPER*), and quickly got into the likes of Can, Faust, Ash Ra Tempel, Caravan -- and particularly Magma and Supersister. Still I love these bands -- but the LPDs follow their own path. I have really never heard of Kaleidoscope.

Q: Who are the other LPDs today?

A: They are: Stret Majest (guitar); Patrick Q. Paganini (violins); The Silver Man (synths); Adantacathar (keyboards); Percii Pylchardd (bass) and Poison Barbarella (lady vox). Only Poison Barbarella was in a known band before LPDs (Attrition), though Patrick worked with Family Fodder and Officer.

Q: Initially you did a lot of work with In-Phaze. How did that association begin and why did it end?

A: In-Phaze approached us after hearing a track on a compilation record [Editor's Note: in addition to the group and solo LPs, LPDs have several tracks on various compilation discs and a score of cassette releases in various countries). They seemed great; very small, hard-working, no business obsessions. Alas, they never paid us any royalties and we even had to put up 1/2 of the pressing costs for the albums ourselves. Crazy as it seems, I still like the guy who runs the label, but I'd think twice if he asked me to lend him a fiver.

Q: You've done an enormous number of recordings. Have you any fear of running dry creatively or having your audience O.D. on your music?

A: The first rule of LPDs is that all 7 members create, eat, breathe and live the music: 7 means a constant state of hyperactivity. In fact, there is a vault full of un-released material. We are an obsessive band with no fears of running dry (yet anyhow). I personally want our audience to be as obsessed as we are -- maybe they'll see a place they never have before through our music.

Q: What kind of reaction have you gotten from the UK press to your music?

A: With the notable exception of Dave Tibet (*Sounds*), the UK press is total crap, utterly corrupt and no sign of improvement.

Q: In terms of sales, what kind of numbers do you sell of any one album release?

A: Now each album sells around 4,000, but it's growing steadily, which is heartening.

Q: In the recent past you've left the UK for Holland. Has this helped you creatively and in terms of gaining broader recognition?

A: Creatively it was a very positive move. Life is more of a day-to-day struggle (I have to live from music alone), but I've also been writing at a furious rate. I also enjoy lots of support from those around me, found some marvelous friends and am ecstatically in love with a special Dutch girl.

Q: Creatively is there any concept or idea that guides your music in terms of art/social theory or politics?

A: Since the band formed in 1980, LPDs have shaped their music around the concept of "Terminal Kaleidoscope." It's a personal vision of mine as disputes exist within the band about what we're actually doing. Basically "T.K." looks at the planet as if it were a dying man. Life flashes before the eyes in a plethora of colours, emotions -- continually speeding up. A bombardment of images. We provide the soundtrack. It isn't a pessimistic outlook. We encourage people to cherish the "Terminal Kaleidoscope," live the experience in the knowledge that eternal life is a fact. No half-baked religious shit -- the one thing man cannot imagine is a state of nonexistence. Even so, there are concepts within the concept. *ASYLUM* is about madness and finding refuge in your own reality (inside your head) -- where you make your own rules.

Q: Are the compositions done primarily by you or are they group collaborations?

A: Both. I write 99% of the lyrics and much of the music, but everybody creates, all ideas are taken into consideration.

Q: How would you describe your music in terms of style or effect?

A: The most emotional music ever created.

Q: Is there a "raison d'être" behind the LPDs aside from being just another avant-pop group?

A: If we can change the world, we will.

Q: What's in the future for the group + yourself solo-wise (and can you go much further within the confines of the fringe of the unpredictable alternative music business)?

A: Always there are projects. We would like to tour the USA. A new solo LP is just out, *CHEYKK CHINA DOLL*. A new LPDs record, *ISLAND OF JEWELS*, is planned for early Summer. We will exist in spite of the music business.

Archie Patterson

Shub Niggurath

L'EXIGENCE DE SHUB NIGGURATH
It is quite unusual to hear or to read that the alternative French scene gets together and passes thanks to the tenacity and determination of certain musical resistance elements in Nancy, Reims, Strasbourg, Bordeaux, Lorient, Paris.

1986

From now on another site of activity should be added to this list "the Alençon Point," not the one where we find handmade lace at sky-high prices, but where a certain musical essence seems to attract the professionals of the "Savoir-Faire." As proof, the latest group to date to have ventured toward this famous contact is called Shub Niggurath!! Listen to the story of this latest discovery of the long, hard Winter of 1985.

One evening in February, the tinkle of the telephone echoes in one of the corridors of Cap Orne, at the end of the line a timid, trembling voice announces the name of a group which claims to reflect the "New Music": Shub Niggurath. With this, a new musical confirmation is made on the off-chance. The year is 1985, means of communication are fast, two days later Shub Niggurath meets the well-known postman Dudon, also on his rounds, and gives him a parcel. Dudon, his day's work finished, leaves on the corner of the letter box a cassette tape holding the fruits of the well-thought out artwork and music of Shub Niggurath.

The content of this tape won me over straight away by its perseverance, complexity and its demanding tone. Here we have a group whose musical density is rarely achieved! In fact, Shub Niggurath is not a group, but a musical formation or ensemble. Shub Niggurath's originality lies on the one hand in the conjunction of three fundamental concerns in their eyes: the AMAZING, the TERRIBLE and the DEEP combined on the other hand with a disciplined musical attack and presentation.

Indeed, if Jean-Luc Herve (keyboardist, composer) sometimes introduces a new contemporary vigour into his "convulsive pianistic beauty," his playing often lends itself to sounds of percussion or even bell sounds. Along with Alain Ballaud (bass) one of whose rotes is to be a "compact mass," they are the oldest members of this formation. The new and preponderant characteristic of Veronique Verdier with her handling of the trombone adds a new dimension to their sound allowing for a use of ideas and innovation whose results are various approaches of liberation, piano and song as the principle arms.

The musical roll call isn't finished, let's continue our journey into the world of Shub Niggurath. Franck Fromy claims to be autodidactic. He cultivates and maintains the search for new sounds, creating his own, personal instruments (metallic plates, amplified springs). His sense of creating stress is amazing as he sparks fireballs from his guitar evoking a "Fromyan" feeling. His distinct and flamboyant attack puts Shub Niggurath on a level which goes beyond simply a European context as opposed to the Lyon corporation Masal who develop an international dimension and give out a more symphonic current. Masal and Shub Niggurath both have things in common with Sweden's Ragnarök.

Ann Stewart (vocals) has touched on different musical tendencies whilst giving herself completely to the music after vocal experience with classical choirs and Tamia. Her place in Shub Niggurath allows for full use of her vocal register as instrument, lament, uncontrollable apparition; she is mutilator, contributor, Martian using the sounds of violin and saxophone as well.

Franck Coulaud (drums) calls forth the spirit of the Rock beat. His way of keeping time and the different cascades of syncopated rhythm and cymbal splashes carry the whole of Shub Niggurath forward into unexplored territory.

The music of Shub Niggurath is profound and human. However its members would like to stress that the present undertakings of the group are just the beginning, they are not finished yet and growing stronger from day-to-day. Prepare yourself for the new musical step forward of this heavy, gut-power called Shub Niggurath.

F-X Projean

Intence Interview

Intence is one of the leading second-generation German synthesizer groups. A trio composed of Rudiger Glaser, Clemens Glaser and Helmut Brunner, in some ways they carry on the spirit of the early '70s Teutonic Electronic scene, yet in other ways they strive to break new ground and forge their own unique sound. To date they have produced 3 albums, the latest of which, *TRIADE*, was recently picked up for broader release by the well-known Sky label. The following interview sheds some light on the creative ideas behind one of Germany's most interesting '80s electronic ensembles.

Q: In the '70s there seemed to be a thriving electronic music scene in Germany, today things seem much less exciting. What can you say about the current happenings?

A: The actual situation for electronic music in Germany can be described as follows: we have had a decrease in commercial and economic success from the end of the '70s to the beginning of the '80s. The main reason was the emergence of "new wave" music, which in fact seems now to be fading out this last year. At this moment people seem to again be more open-minded for new electronic music and different styles... so we hope for a better future. On the other hand, there exists a situation, concerning the media as a whole, which is quite different from the American scene. We have no private radio stations -- only a few are playing electronic music. Also there is not such a wide range of active music magazines. People who are working in the electronic scene (i.e. promoters, distributors) are not as engaged in it as the people in North America. Among the people there is more competition than cooperation.

Q: What are the roots/musical influences of the people in Intence?

A: We are all influenced by all kinds of music. Two of us had a classical education. We didn't want to copy the masters of the past however, but wanted to create our own, contemporary style of music.

Q: Were you influenced greatly by some of the first-generation German artists, Cluster or Kraftwerk perhaps?

A: Well, we all heard the first generation of German bands who were playing at the time. You could say that there is some relationship between those bands and Intence. We continued what those people began, but by making our own way, with another style.

Q: Musically your sound is somewhat different from the patented sequential synthetics, what do you feel accounts for this?

A: We don't want to be just a copy of some other sound like many of the other new synthesizer groups today. Our aim is to be different and maybe one of the main reasons we can do this if that we use real drums instead of a drum machine like most of the others. This adds a new dimension to our music.

Q: Your music has progressed greatly over the span of your three albums. What has caused this -- new equipment, new influences -- can you say if it was something specific or maybe more of a case of your natural style evolving in new directions?

A: If there would be no progress in our music, well we wouldn't record anymore! In fact, there is an outer and an inner reason. The outer reason being that the band was allowed to develop due to the industry. Today then are more and better possibilities to express your musical feelings and ideas. The inner reason is that not only do we not want to copy others, but we don't want to copy ourselves either. There is a good competitive inspirational spirit between us which leads us to new musical areas.

Q: Do you play live concerts, or is there any concert scene in Germany today for synthesizer groups to participate in?

A: We don't play live concerts at the moment, but we do have plans for that in the future. There is no concert circuit for electronic music in Germany today, but we have been invited to play at various places around the world. The fact that it would be a great expense to do that is the main reason we haven't been able to do it. We want to be able to reproduce the same sound as on the album. Furthermore we want to present our more visual impressions to the music. Both things are very expensive!

Q: Is the distribution for your records very extensive in Germany or do you sell more via export to other places?

A: We are selling nearly 2/3 via export and the rest in Germany. With TRIADE we got more airplay in Germany, so we sold a little bit more here than before.

Q: Do you have new projects or any different musical ideas planned for the future?

A: We want to record further LPs with new ideas and new musicians, but right now there are no specific things planned. Another area of work for the group will be film music. Last summer we recorded music for the film "Irrwege," which is as yet not released. The experience opened up perhaps a new area for us to work in. Maybe we'll make a video to add a visual counterpoint to our music.

Archie Patterson

1987

Klaus Dinger Interview

Q: In many ways you are a well-known artist going back to the beginnings of the German rock scene. However, few really know much about your background or musical history. Perhaps a good start would be to tell briefly your beginnings, the first group and early influences that helped develop your rather unique ideas?

A: 7 years in high school, 3 years carpentry and 3 years studying architecture in an art school. Musically I started drumming in a school band, then a swing combo and an early group called The No when I was 18 years old. I dropped out of school at 24, borrowed money for a drumkit to play with my guitar that I bought at 21, then started playing like mad and writing my first songs (not published so far, but in the future maybe?) After practicing like mad for 1/2 a year I joined a heavy rock band The Smash who played music like Black Sabbath, Ten Years After, and others.

Also much fun playing live with C.C.S. Six months later I joined Kraftwerk in the middle of their first LP and did the drumming on Side 2 of their first LP. Also still more fun playing live with C.C.S... When Ralf Hutter left Kraftwerk for a while, Michael Rother joined Florian and me (still drumming). After a while we split from the millionaire sons for social reasons. Also I wanted (and still do), to find out just what I can do.... My influences were: Elvis, Ornette Coleman, John Coltrane, Eric Dolphy, Mozart, then during the '60s The Beatles, Jefferson Airplane, the Stones, Velvet Underground, Bob Dylan, the Doors and of course my early time with Kraftwerk. Also the Sex Pistols, folk music of the world and much more I certainly forget to mention in this context...

Q: What was the idea behind Neu!, was it a developed concept or more spontaneous?

A: It was Neu! Two people meeting in a studio (plus Conny) and doing something quite freely and quick -- spontaneous? (A matter of taste.)

Q: Many of the early German bands played live, Neu! seemed more of a studio experiment. Did you ever do live gigs?

A: We did about 5 or 6 between '72 and '74, but they were not what we wanted. We used other musicians who couldn't understand what Neu! was or could be. Very few understood the code... So it was not very much fun. '74 was two free concerts with Thomas Dinger and Hans Lampe drumming and me and Michael on guitars. It was very chaotic and much like the Sex Pistols two years later some people tell me.

Q: Were the records accepted/popular at the time or were they more of a cult audience?

A: The record *NEU!* was accepted and popular, but certainty more in insider circles, as it still is today. And you can buy them all still today after 15 years in many places around the world, but....

Q: After Neu! you began La Dusseldorf, a more advanced version of Neu!'s music perhaps? Why did Neu! split, did your musical ideas change with La D.?

A: I had the feeling we couldn't live (work) from it and decided to become more "concrete" or understandable for a bigger audience, if not for everyone. Both in the music and lyrics. I started trying to be more serious and learn about notes and melodies and harmonies and composition.

The reasons for Neu! splitting were partly musical (listen to Michael's solo LPs), and partly personal as after having done something together it's good to separate and start something else, isn't it? Michael went to the countryside and I stayed in the city (La Dusseldorf) for some more years. I love it, especially the Altstadt (Oldtown).

Q: Did La D. get more recognition than Neu! and sell more records, or was it the same?

A: Yes, in financial terms La D. was a much bigger success than Neu!. *VIVA* for instance sold about 150,000 copies in Germany alone and actually all the LPs are still selling. The sales enabled me to buy a 16-track studio and a farm (with studio) near the Dutch coast where I try to spend about 1/2 of the year.

Q: Was La D. a group for live shows or more a studio idea again?

A: La D. was like Neu!, a way to study music and art while living from it and learning about life too. Unfortunately it turned out to be just a studio idea too so far, but it's still my biggest wish and greatest dream to play live again no matter what the act is called. Michael however is not so much into playing live.

Q: After *INDIVIDUELLOS*, your brother Thomas did a solo album and in 1982 La D. did a 12", but for 3-4 years there was no news. What happened with the group, did you stop music?

A: Relations between Thomas, Hans and me became strained more and more since *INDIVIDUELLOS* which I really find a pity, but so it is... That's the main reason we didn't produce anything. But with or without them there will be more La D. records again. The split-up of La D. was very unpleasant, but now I feel more free and productive, so....

Q: Now you've returned with *NEONDIAN* and that LP contains some of your best music yet I feel. In particular "America" and "Cha Cha 2000/85" represent a very futuristic fusion of music and ideas . You mention the Greens (a leftist German political party) and make some strong political references in the lyrics, are you active politically? Do you see your music as an influence for making people think or change? Is it just entertainment?

A: I don't share the (official American) view of the Green Party as "Left." I think it's an environmental, anti-nuclear, anti-establishment party, which I favor a lot but am not a member of (not yet anyway). I'm getting older you know and I feel you can't ignore what's going on in the "real" world." So in fact, I think I become more political in my views now. But most of all I feel like an individual, a free artist with a growing obligation to make people think (at least) and courage to try, try, try. Just entertainment is not enough, it never was.

Q: Is La D. now permanently split? Is Thomas doing anything now? What are your plans for a new group or LP?

A: Thomas has an 8-track studio, but so far nothing is done and I still offer to work together again, but it seems we can't... For me, apart from the new Neu! LP, I'll form a new La Dusseldorf from people in the scene here which will hopefully be the fulfillment of my live dreams. I want to work now in this direction.

Archie Patterson

Pulsar

Pulsar: A name that evokes many souvenirs for lovers of '70s progressive rock and which is somewhat of a mythical subject abroad, where this group is a legendary figure among the fans of French progressive music. What many don't realize is that this group, which had seemed to go under in the torrent of the new wave, still exists. After having gone through a period of lethargy, they now manifest a new youthfulness and demonstrate a vitality that's heartening for all of those for whom this group provides fond musical memories. Today, now that the progressive rock spirit is being reborn, Pulsar is overflowing with new activities and projects, having renewed its repertoire and taken advantage of its "retreat" to write numerous new titles which are worthy successors to the superb melodies that enhanced their previous classic albums.

But, before speaking of the present, let's evoke the past of this prestigious group out of Lyon. Formed in April 1970, Pulsar called itself "Free Sound" and performed music greatly inspired by Pink Floyd, who were in fact their principal musical influence.

At that time the group was made up of Jacques Roman on keyboard, Victor Bosch on drums, Gilbert Gandil on guitar and vocals and Philippe Roman on bass. Free Sound then began to play concerts, first in the Lyon region, then on to quite a few appearances in the capital, where they received many excellent reviews and made a name for themselves. The press encouraged the group to orient itself more toward a personalized sound with less of the Pink Floyd influences present. It was on the occasion of one of their appearances at the temple of rock, the Golf Drouot, that Free Sound (who had since transformed into Pulsar), recorded their first track for the compilation LP, *GROOVEY POP SESSION* which featured various progressive bands including Ange. The track was named "Pulsar" and exhibited a more restrained sound, still influenced by Pink Floyd, yet also unmistakably moving toward their own style. Published in 1972, it gives an idea of the group's future sound that would be characterized by a predominance of keyboards and a limpid beauty fused into their compositions.

1974 proved to be a turning point for the group. This year marked their meeting-up with Xavier Dubuc who would take over their management. 1974 is also the time of adding Roland Richard (ex-musician with J. Higelin) to the group, who would play flute, saxophone, and an increased focus at the core of the group as another keyboardist. At the start of 1975 their first LP, *POLLEN*, was published on the U.K. label Kingdom Records (also the label of Caravan). The release was followed by a tour of Britain as well. The album, entirely produced and financed by Pulsar, began to reveal the strong qualities of the group; its evident talent for composing melodies that are airy and strong, beautiful and sinuous, spanned by flights of Gilbert Gandil's guitar. The press at the time was unanimous in its praise of the sound.

In April 1976, Pulsar recorded their second LP, *THE STRANDS OF THE FUTURE*. The faint reminiscences of Pink Floyd slightly visible on *POLLEN* have now appeared to give way to their own music, original and sumptuous. The sound rests on instrumental perfection and precision rarely attained by a French group, on very elaborate compositions that are superbly orchestrated, dynamic musical atmospheres evoked by sheets of keyboards, Gilbert Gandil's solos (fragile or cutting) and the graceful evolutions of Roland Richard's flute. On these highly-constructed themes, Gilbert Gandil's ample and warm vocals rise up, his deep voice expressive and enveloping, perfectly suited to Pulsar's music, serving as a beautiful exclamation point to their full sound. On this album for the first time most of the vocals are sung in English. 1976 also sees a personnel change as Philippe Roman leaves due to ill health and is replaced by a long-standing friend of the group, Michel Masson. They continued throughout 1976 playing extensive concerts and gathering more critical praise. Jean-Marc Bailleux, of *Rock 'n Folk* , spoke of the new album in these elegiac terms: "It's a very good record, the sound is full, warm and rich... We're dealing with the accomplishment of a group from which everyone for a long time has had a right to expect the best. One thinks, alternately, of the great Impressionists, of Mahler's lyricism." Sales of the record are good, the group's concert audiences grow and above all, some of the major French record labels who had long neglected the group began to show some interest.

In 1977 their contract with Kingdom expired and CBS signed them to a new contract, thus assuring the group of the technical and financial means previously lacking and allowing them to pursue their higher ambitions. Their next work would be born in Switzerland at the Geneva Studio Aquarius, where they had recorded their previous LP as well. In this studio where such luminaries as Yes and Patrick Moraz had also recorded, they produce their third LP titled *HALLOWEEN*, which is released in December 1977. This album was conceived as a concept work based around a central character, a young child named Halloween. The music and lyrics tell the story of a child's trip through reality/fantasy with its tragic conclusion, mixing dreams, experiences and madness thematically combined with majestic, grandiose music resulting in a masterpiece. It's one of those rare albums that can define a group's career and the music

of an entire era perhaps, as did such works as *THE LAMB LIES DOWN ON BROADWAY* and *DARK SIDE OF THE MOON*. Nine years later it still sounds great. Throughout the year the group continued to play live, get good press, and enjoy strong record sales so the future looked bright.

1977, however, is also the beginning of musical movements where complexity and sophistication are lacking -- "punk rock." Styles changed, audiences changed, yet Pulsar refused to go along with the trends. Ultimately the group stopped touring and devoted itself to working on music for the theatre especially with Bruno Carlucci and the Theatre of Satire. They compose music for his productions; "Ballades Pour Un Monde Provisoire" (Ballads for a Provisional World) (July 1980), "Bienvenue Au Conseil D'administration" (Welcome to the Administrative Council) (December 1980) and "L'Emploi De Temps" (Schedule) (1981). Fervent master of musical theatre, which enriches and gives a new dimension to his theatrical work, Bruno Carlucci insists that the music written for his plays be performed live during the presentations, so Pulsar played with the troupe accompanying each show.

In 1981, Pulsar recorded the music for *BIENVENUE AU CONSEIL D'ADMINISTRATION* for release on the Compagnie de la Satire label. At this time the band had been reduced to four members as Michel Masson had left. The music on the LP is not just some bodiless, artificial soundtrack accompaniment fortunately, instead it constitutes strong musical support for the texts by Peter Handke, author of this play, as music and words combine to beautiful effect. Sadly the LP was never really available on a commercial level. Since 1981, the group has continued its collaboration with theatrical troupes. At the present they are working with young companies, among them "The Lab Of The Last Poets" by T. Renald (*Aube* review) and "Cosmos Kollej" by W. Znorko, here the presentation leans more toward images rather than texts. Because of this, the music takes on a greater importance and plays a primordial role in the success and comprehension of the show. The group is also working on a performance of dance entitled "Cellule" (Cell) in collaboration with the Air Compagnie of Lyon. The first draft of this show took place in Lyon December 20, 1985.

1986 marked a return to the recording studio for Pulsar. They began first with creation of music for a relaxation cassette of pure Pulsar meditational sound. Then came music and images for a 50-minute video production. Most recently they have begun to record new songs from their latest repertoire, for at last after all these years a new "rock" LP. Having had a preview of these new compositions, I can definitely say that Pulsar of 1986 is a perfect extension of Pulsar 1977. The group has managed to retain the charm and the lyrical quality of the music they created in 1975-77, as well as evolve creatively. The new compositions offer force and lyricism in Gilbert Gandil's still-spellbinding songs that make perfect use of his versatile voice. His guitar remains as expressive as ever, by turns soft, producing aerial sonorities, floating and fragile, then sharp and energetic, charged with electricity. Pulsar has come back with a sound that surpasses many of the neo-progressive English groups who have learned so well the lessons of the "old" progressives. For Pulsar it has been a natural evolution into a group whose new youthfulness is to be welcomed and from whom we hope to get a new recording soon proving that they have not lost any of their previous magical musical qualities.

Francis Grosse

Gilbert Artman Interview

Vancouver, B.C. July 4, 1986.

Q: Let's begin with a little history. Why don't you tell us about the early days -- when you began playing music, your first groups and beginning instrument?

A: I had quite a late start, around 25 and began as a drummer, although in fact I didn't own a drum set. So instead I used a piano frame in a percussive way. At the start of the '70s we were a group of people in a group called Lard Free. I was the drummer and we had a former heavy metal guitarist playing a sort of free rock music. Aside from Lard Free I also played in an experimental jazz group called Komintern.

Q: Lard Free was one of the first French experimental groups who mixed rock with jazz and electronics. Was there a particular idea/concept that you had for that group's music?

A: It was in any case a question of keeping in mind the classical aesthetic/ references musically. It was a sort of reflex music, an experiment in static sound in order to establish new musical codes. The idea of reflex music being to create a physical connection between musicians and the audience.

Q: You stopped Lard Free to create a new musical adventure, Urban Sax. How did you come up with the idea of a massive orchestra composed mainly of saxophones?

A: For a musician, there is the music you like to listen to and the music you like to play. At some point I got fed up with the former and wanted to start to create a new sound, new codes of listening.

Q: How did you come up with the name Urban Sax? Does it symbolize a particular social/cultural/political idea that you have?

A: First of all the title is certainty a mistake, in the act that it is limiting. In the beginning it reflected an aspect of a linear music that related to the fast pace and continuous violence of the urban environment. The covers implied a social/cultural statement certainty, but they too were a sort of mistake as well as they served to some extent as again a limitation of the total concept. The basic idea of Urban Sax is based around movement and space, it never stops. To stop it with a description is limiting.

Q: So it's more of an evolutionary concept as opposed to revolutionary?

A: Oui!

Q: Were there musical ideas of others, perhaps in jazz music that influenced the sound of Urban Sax perhaps?

A: I could sense connections perhaps been people as diverse as Thelonious Monk and Erik Satie, or maybe Indian music.

Q: The spectacle of an Urban Sax performance is unique. How do you come up with the ideas for choreography and musical presentation?

A: Thanks to practice over the span of many concerts and so in fact that I myself don't get bored, I always try to create an interface between the sound and visuals . Each concert is in fact organized and the music is composed on the basis of the individual character of the location of the event. We average between 30 - 40 concerts per year.

Q: You serve as a conductor to some extent, is the music actually written down and composed, or more like a structured improvisation?

A: It depends again on the nature of the space where the performance will occur. It is based more on the oral music tradition than the classical written however. I explore ideas on the piano, saxophone or piano, then the sequences are given to the group and we compose a music suited to the particular situation. Every passage is in fact planned in advance, but again improvised according to the particular area in which it will be performed.

Q: How does Urban Sax function economically in terms of tours and performances? It must be expensive and difficult to stage such an avant-garde production that is not really a commercially-viable proposition.

A: Basically we work in coordination with local and national arts councils who sponsor performances in their respective cities or countries.

Q: What plans do you have for the future in terms of recording and further touring?

A: On a creative level we would like to become more wise in presenting our concerts -- to be less spectacular and more intense musically.... Just now is released our new album *FRACTURE SUR LE TEMPS*, by Celluloid in France. For the USA we have some talks with the Gramavision label, but nothing is for sure.... Vancouver, B.C. is in fact our first-ever North American concert, next we go to Sicily. In the Summer of '87 we hope to do a larger tour of Canada and the USA.

Archie Patterson

Peter Frohmader Interview

Q: For such a prolific artist (8 releases to date), you are a mystery of sorts. Perhaps you could shed some light on the situation by telling a bit about your musical history and early experiences in art and music?

A: I had some training on classical guitar for about a year, but for the most part I am self-taught on the other instruments I play. I began in 1970 with electronic music (new music), program music and improvisations in the so-called avant-garde style. My early bands/projects were Alpha Centauri (avant-garde/atonal), Electronic Delusion (crude electronics and musique concrete), Kanaan (jazz/rock/ electronics/oriental) and a few others. We played concerts and some material was recorded with the various groups, but nothing was ever released.

Q: You seem to work on two levels musically -- as a part of a group and solo, with to some extent two different sounds. What are the ideas or concepts behind each?

A: The fact is, that the background is always the same. The composition are done by me. However, sometimes I want to use other people on the records. Also the early groups were founded by me as well. The best way for me to produce is to start alone (composing and playing), and then if necessary I bring in guest musicians and teach them their parts. The only difference is sometimes in the structure (rhythmic or not), I don't need rhythms to get into music. But playing live without rhythms makes it hard for the audience to get into (*NEKROPOLIS LIVE* and *THE FORGOTTEN ENEMY* are examples for that). For me they were like a sort of remake of the sort of music I made in the '70s.

Q: The artist H.R. Giger seems to have influenced your music and artwork. Have you done any projects/collaborations with him?

A: My own music has always been dark and mystical. But my artwork was inspired by my friend H.R. Giger years ago too. When he heard my first record, he wrote me a letter asking for some music for a film. So I did some soundtracks for some of his films (also for some other films and TV too). Our worlds are now working together in sync. We'd like to do other projects together in the future (for example a film and/or multimedia exhibition). Giger has also a video dedicated to me and he likes to listen to my music while painting. So I guess you could say each has inspired the other to some degree.

Q: What is the extent of your work in the field of art? Is it a hobby or do you perhaps have exhibitions as the quality seem of a very high standard?

A: It's not a hobby. I've studied art (painting and also graphic design) and finally got my diploma some years ago. So I'm also doing big exhibitions with fantastic art, I've had quite a few this year in Germany. I've done group exhibitions and also the biggest one held over here, Ars Phantastica. So I am always working in both fields -- Art and Music, as well as combining the two in my film work.

Q: Going back a bit to your large number of releases, do you think your audience increases with each one or is it more a question of playing to the converted? Sometimes I think that perhaps people get overdosed when an artist does too much too fast.

A: I think my audience grow with each one a little bit (I hope so), because it always seems to change. I try to do different things so nobody can say that if you've heard one recording you've heard them all, as sometimes can be said of other artists. But the line and direction are bound to my personality and must stay true. So I have many ideas and am constantly working, so I like to put out that music which is important to me.

Q: Are you able to live off of your music and artwork, or do you have to do another job?

A: I try to, but it's not easy. So I also do commissioned paintings and posters, LP sleeves, etc. And I don't spend my money for other things which are unimportant (only for music and art).

Q: Do you ever perform live solo or with a group?

A: Yes, quite often in the '70s and also sometimes in the '80s, but now only at bigger concerts in churches, etc. If it seems like a good thing, I'll do it, but I don't have a strong desire to perform in front of an audience very often today.

Q: Which of your records/what type of music do you prefer -- the solo or group material?

A: Both are important. I like to collaborate and have known some of my guest musicians for years now and they know what my intentions are. I can always set up my ensemble like on *CULTES DES*

GOULES for example and a couple musicians more if necessary.

Q: What plans do you have for the future in terms of new projects or releases?

A: Some new records will appear: HUMUNCULUS PART 1-4 -- a double LP of an artificial orchestra, created, performed and produced by me (with sounds ranging from chamber music to a more orchestral approach -- dark and mysterious). Also hopefully WINTER MUSIC (a symphony for multiple Sticks and small choir) and HUMUNCULUS II perhaps produced by Multimood label.

Archie Patterson

Pauline Strom Interview

Q: For someone who has had 3 LPs released in the last 6 years (TRANS-MILLENNIA CONSORT, PLOT ZERO and SPECTRE), you are for all intents and purposes a complete unknown on the U.S. synthe scene today. So let's start with some history of how you first got into electronic music?

A: As so many, I have been strongly influenced by the work of Schulze, T. Dream and Eno, etc. I could go into the usual general reasoning of musical interest since childhood, but I view that as a minute part of my musical development. As I am a completely self-taught musician, composer, synthesist and sound designer of multi-dimensional sonic technology. I feel my intuition and philosophy as well as my ability to mesh myself into the soul of the language of sound are of far more value here. Music and sound are of one language, I have always been lured by the depths of the ancient past and the far-flung reaches of an untapped universal future. I sometime feel I have been placed in this chaotic, confused present to draw into it the elements from these opposite realms in order that my interpretations of them through sound and music may in some sense benefit our as-yet largely incompetent and immature population. We seem to be living in a world where to create uniquely, to challenge, to dare to be adventuresome and individualistic are discouraged.

Q: One of the more interesting aspects of your work is that all 3 records sound very different. Perhaps you could explain a little about how you conceptualized your different ideas?

A: I strive to be as versatile from project to project as possible. The first album, TRANS-MILLENNIA CONSORT was designed as a hauntingly blended sculpture of past and future energies. My ideas for this project sprang from the metals of the earth, the easy flow of the human voice and much that is poetically emotional and spiritual in our world. PLOT ZERO, the spacy mind trip without chemicals, is powerfully and simplistically just that. Frequency vibration and pulsing sounds can go extremely far in subjecting the mind to hypnotically stretched-out states of consciousness. As for SPECTRE, the welding of mysterious vampire legends, modern violence and desolateness which produces a cobalt mix of subtle Gothic chills, fulfilled its purpose with a whispered gloss of steel. The sounds were culled from concrete, glass and steel, from cold arctic temperatures and elusive spacious voices.

Q: Your music seems very much dominated by the imagination as opposed to the equipment. Do you record in a professional studio or at home?

A: Yes, I would say my music is virtually

dominated by my imagination. I program all of my sounds, the music and sound is literally one, my compositions grow as if on a canvas, never pre-visualize a piece, it grows layer by layer, track by track, sound by sound. I just know internally when it is complete. Yes, it is composed, programmed, processed, engineered and recorded by myself in my home studio I am proud to say. For the final mix I utilize the facilities of a professional studio basically to mix down to a good two track master for pressing purposes. I hope someday to eliminate the need to do that however, as being in sole control of my work is vitally important to me. I believe one should be his or her own highest master.

Q: Being a woman in the predominately male-controlled music business could present obstacles, have you found this to be true? Or perhaps it's just the opposite, it opens doors?

A: The business side of the music industry literally sucks. To be quite frank, it's not how talented you are, of how tastefully crafted your art. In reality it matters not a damn how beautifully chiseled your compositions. No, what it comes down to is that is you're not taking the right drug, holding the right guru's hand or sleeping on the right couch, you're fucked... Yeah, I would say that women have a harder time because of the macho, male ego bullshit that dominates the industry. However, looking at it honestly, I would say that most men are also falling all over each other as well, trying to screw each other out of every opportunity imaginable. The hypocrisy, greed, jealousy and spiteful intrigue that permeates the music business are disgusting, and in my opinion anyone who sees it otherwise is naïve or deluded. Also, don't leave out the financial factor, money opens a lot of doors. Try being an artist living on the fringes, trying to hold on to your individualization in creativity, with just enough dollars to pay for rent and food, not to mention being a woman, blind and divorced. Now I ask you, where is the justice in this mainstream American system? I'll tell you, it's in the hands of the rich, the bigots, the righteous hypocrites who shove it down the throats of those who have been brainwashed into thinking that it's a moral honor to be poor, screw that nonsense.

Q: How does being blind in fact affect your music?

A: I feel it has helped rather than hindered my musical abilities. My hearing and inner visualization have, I feel, developed to a higher level than perhaps they would have otherwise. And it doesn't affect my abilities from a technical standpoint either. It's quite possible to program synthesizers, effects units, accurately record one's work and handle a mixer. I do this all by sound. In fact I rather like working in the dark.

Q: The electronic music genre seems to be exploding these days as the industry wants to push "New Age" music as the next big thing. Coming from the "New Age capital of the world" San Francisco, what do you think of the music and all the hoopla in general?

A: Well, I have mixed feelings on this one. A good portion of the music covered under the "New Age" banner is simplistically beautiful. Let me say this, I will not critique anyone else's work. What it comes down to anyway is personal taste. I don't think anyone has the right to judge another's work, I believe the creations of all artists have a right to existence and exposure EQUALLY. Now, as to the hype that surrounds the New Age genre, all of this is bullshit propaganda just like the other aspects of our hype-oriented culture. Have no delusions, the whole business structure surrounding the New Age field is just as corrupt, political and superficial as elsewhere. Talk about purity, better talk about pure hypocrisy.

Q: It's been a while since *SPECTRE*, are there any plans for a new release in the near future? Have you got any new material?

A: Plans for another album, there are always plans. Music is the center of my life. I have a lot of unreleased work, there will always be more. I frankly do not have the finances to release my own records. Of course one could say, there are always record companies. I believe I've made it clear that I want control of my work. And unfortunately this attitude is penalized in our society. The fact is that is several people can't have a piece of your work, then they stomp you into the ground. Yes, I do want to release something else, but until someone with the financial resources and necessary knowledge is capable of backing me, the reality as yet does not exist.

Archie Patterson

Michele Musser Interview

Q: Your new album, *EYECHANT*, is your 4th release. How did you get started in electronic music?

A: I got interested in electronic music when I went to Holland six years ago and met a guy there. His name is Jan DeNoyer and he was writing electronic music for his brother's experimental films. I worked with him all that summer on various projects and then when I came back to the U.S., I got my first synthesizer and started recording. Before that I was a guitarist and did a lot of experimental things with loops and various sound effects.

Q: Were you influenced by Robert Fripp?

A: I love Robert Fripp and King Crimson, that whole kind of music, that whole scene.

Q: Was he your inspiration back then?

A: It's been so long it's hard to say. He probably was a bit of an influence because I did listen to that kind of music a lot and I still do. Pink Floyd, Genesis, Peter Gabriel, Kate Bush are among the artists I enjoy listening to. I don't listen to a lot of electronic music. I listen to Jean Michel Jarre, I love the ZOOLOOK LP. I listen to some Tangerine Dream. I listen to a variety of things, I know what I don't listen to.

Q: Which is ?

A: I don't listen to a lot of New Age, Heavy Metal, Disco, swishy Michael Jackson-type music.

Q: Do you like some of the electronic dance music, like Depeche Mode, etc.?

A: Oh definitely, I like to dance. Groups like Bauhaus, Tears For Fears.

Q: What inspires you to compose your music?

A: Usually, maybe just a mood. Occasionally I will have been to see a good movie and the visuals will suggest some musical ideas.

Q: How did you get involved in the field of TV, PBS, commercials, etc.?

A: A producer in NYC heard my music and is part of a company called, Demo-Vision. They create pilots for PBS and he liked my music and called and asked if I'd do some for him. I've known him for a long time. It helps to know someone.

Q: You did a "yuppie" non-alcoholic beer commercial. How did that come about?

A: I got the job through another company called D-3, which is actually my husband's part of the company -- someone I know. Actually I've been very tacky. I've known the right people who have been instrumental in helping me.

Q: You also did the soundtrack to *SECRET CITY* which is an art show for children.

A: Yes, this is a show which teaches children how to draw.

Q: Have you found that being a female has helped of hindered your progress in a field where there are mostly men? Has this been a hindrance in your career?

A: I can't say that I've been exposed to people who are prejudiced because I'm a woman. I don't see where it makes any difference. I know there are very few female synthesists around, I really don't know why -- there are just more male musicians in general. I can't really say that I don't feel there has been any prejudice towards me for being a woman. I can't say that. I can't say that when people listen to my music they think this is female music unless they see my name on the cover. Very few people know what I look like so... Part of Madonna's success is the fact that she's very attractive, has sex appeal, and shows off her belly button. There's really no comparison. No one would ever say, "This is nice music, show me your belly button." I appreciate listening to music that shows intelligence, versatility and I listen for new things that people haven't done before. That's what I like to hear, but for me, when I write music, I like to do music of that quality. I also like it to be rather accessible in that it's music that a lot of people can appreciate, but still has a quality of uniqueness. I try very hard not to repeat myself.

Q: Describe your shows.

A: I like lots of things going on at one time. For instance, I don't just get on stage and play keyboards. There is a lot of music going on, but also many other things as well at the same time. I use a lot o film and video and performance art and some humor. I like to get the audience involved. I do silly things to get their attention and get them going and I have fun doing this. I think a lot of electronic concerts I've seen are so serious and it's nice to be serious, lay back and listen to the music, but I like visual things too. That's important. I would get bored if I were sitting in the audience and listening to someone play and turn dials. When people walk out of my concert they are going to have something to remember because of the visuals.

Q: What are your future plans?

A: I haven't done any live performances in over a year -- mostly because of time. When I write for a performance it's very time-consuming because I do visuals too. It's very draining to perform live. I'm working on a performance, for lack of a better word, I can tour with. That will be less draining. Maybe it's just a matter of me getting used to playing live which I don't do very often, I don't have any immediate plans as far as dates lined up, I'd rather get the show together and then start promoting it.

Q: Your new album, *EYECHANT*, is just released. Do you have any plans for future releases.

A: I do work all of the time and I really don't think of it in terms of future releases. I write a lot, but not everything is heard.

Generally, what I do is work for a year or maybe 9 months and see what develops, then the next 2 months I work on refining it, changing it, and making it better. Then I decide what gets released. I'm not one of those who puts out everything I write. I'm very careful about it.

Q: A lot of private releases don't have especially good sound quality, yours is an exception.

A: I'm real pleased with the way my material sounds. I record a lot of music at home and I'm pleased that it doesn't sound like it was done at home. I'm fortunate to have good equipment.

Glenn Hammett

Lauri Paisley Interview

Q: Lauri, why don't you start at the beginning, how did you get started in electronic music?

A: Do you have all day? No, I started playing classical music on the piano when I was a kid, then somehow I took up guitar playing folk, then some rock music. When I started listening to rock I got into things like E.L.P., Yes, Todd Rundgren, music with a lot of keyboards. So I ultimately went back to keyboards and began playing in bands and found I was having to leave my equipment at practice houses, so I couldn't work at home on my own material. Also the bands that I was playing with did original material and they didn't want to do any of my pieces, so I took myself home and started writing little things for keyboards only. I thought I was the only one on earth doing it because I'd never heard anyone else using synthesizers by themselves, outside of a band context. After two years of doing this I heard "Synthetic Pleasures" on WFMU and heard music just like I was doing.

Q: Who were your influences in terms of musicians?

A: Todd Rundgren, Keith Emerson, Rick Wakeman, etc. I also love to listen to Yanni, Synergy, Tangerine Dream some and Klaus Schulze sometimes as well.

Q: What kind of music don't you like?

A: Commercial music -- I hate Top 40 stuff.

Q: Do you like electronic dance music?

A: In very small doses, if it's got interesting patches, but basically I prefer flowing and melodic music or orchestral electronics with a lot of dynamics. Sometimes I like New Age music for background listening, but mainly I like music with a lot of energy in it.

Q: Have you done anything outside of your 6 private cassette releases?

A: I did a piece for the New York State Firemans Assoc. I know a guy in Syracuse, NY that was a fireman and he asked me to compose a piece of music for a film shot from a helicopter and it was played in Syracuse in August this year.

Q: Have you found being a woman in music affects your progress or approach to music?

A: If a musician wants to know about equipment -- No. But, if by chance they want a little more than musical buddy-hood and they want to go out with you, they don't take your music seriously, even if they're big recording artists.

Q: How about approaching record companies, promoters, etc.?

A: I don't send demos to record companies and I'm not in a position to perform since most of my music is multi-track and impossible to play live. The last solo concert I did was two years ago. I've been asked to perform and would like to, but I don't want to go back to doing music that's six years old. I would like to have the full sound like on my later tapes and like will be on my new album.

Q: So you don't think being a woman has made it harder to open doors for you?

A: I think it would have been easier if I was a guy, in terms of life in general. But I'm not going to get a sex change or anything like that -- Larry Paisley!

Q: What are your plans for the future?

A: Well, as you know, I've done the 6 self-produced tapes. Next I plan to release my first album and am working on the beginning tracks now for that. It will incorporate piano, guitar and of course my usual array of keyboards and synthesizers. As of yet I don't know exactly when it will come out.

Glenn Hammett

Michel Huygen Interview

Q: What were the early days of Spanish rock like in comparison to say the USA or UK where there were a lot of psychedelic/progressive groups? Who were the early Spanish bands?

A: The early days of Spanish rock in comparison to the US or UK were quite later than in either of these countries. There were some psychedelic groups in Spain in the mid '70s and one of the first was called Yety. I played in that group and had the first Moog synthesizer in Spain! It was a nice period of my musical life. After that group we formed Suck Electronic Encyclopedic and a few other Spanish groups came along as well, like Granada, Atila, Iceberg, Iman, Canarios, a.o.

Q: What was the nature of your early music?

A: My first real serious experience professionally was Suck Electronic (we dropped the last part of the name later). We were playing very cosmic music filled with hard sounds and some spacy effects. The Minimoog served as the base of the sound, it was in 1975.

Q: What was the original idea/concept around the formation of Neuronium? Who were the original members?

A: The original concept and idea of Neuronium was to do mental music based on electronic instruments. The name comes from "Neuron" (brain cell) and the Latin ending of "ium" to give the name a scientific sense.... In the beginning I was the only member, later joined by other musicians who you know from the first album, *QUASAR 2C361*.

Q: You had some sessions with people like Vangelis, Klaus Schulze and Ash Ra Tempel in the late '70s, what ever developed out of these if anything?

A: Yes I played with some of them as we did some TV shows together, but no records ever came out due to the many different record companies involved.... I still have very good relations with Vangelis. He is a very nice person and really full of peace. When I go over to London I always try to see him as he's a good friend and the jam session I had with him was fantastic.

Q: In the late '70s you seemed on the verge of international recognition, then Carlos Guirao left the group, what happened?

A: Carlos left the group two times in fact, because he wanted to experiment in other aspects of electronic music like techno-pop, and obviously that kind of music had no place with Neuronium. We still see each other from time to time and are friends, but I don't think we will play together again.

Q: Now Neuronium seems to be again consolidating itself as the recent soundtrack and last album *HERITAGE* were excellent examples of what you sometimes call "Psychotronic Music." Could you perhaps explain just what that name means in terms of your music?

A: Yes, my activities are increasing now. The last album, *BARCELONA 1992* was in fact a thriller based on the Olympic Games of 1992 and was the soundtrack of a Spanish TV movie. I have also recently finished 13 chapters for the children's science-fiction series called "Positron." It will be shown on the first TV station for children here in Spain. However I won't release it on record as the rights are owned by the station. On the other hand, "Psychotronic Music" is the name I use to describe my music done under the name of Neuronium. It's music that tries to establish a perfect relationship between the mind and the spirit, an electronic link fusing the two into one. With "Psychotronic Music" you can imagine what you like, when you like, freely.

Q: What can you tell us about the new projects set for 1987?

A: *ALMA* is the new Neuronium album, celebrating my 10th anniversary in the electronic music field. It contains music that means a lot to me and has been re-mixed, re-mastered and had some new sounds added so it serves as sort of the essence of Neuronium to date. It embodies the true "soul" of Neuronium you might say.

I have also finished recently the production of a new group called Vocoder, in the techno-pop vein, but with a lot of electronics. It's a totally different type of sound than Neuronium. I had a lot of fun doing it with some young musicians. I am going to play three concerts at the new Madrid Planetarium in May for the Madrid Festival. Featured will be the works of Tomas Gilsanz -- slides and paintings mixed with cosmic projections and lasers.

Then I have to compose the soundtrack for a film about the life of the great architect Gaudi, plus a new thriller. After that music for the theatre production of Saint Exupéry's "Le Petit Prince" which will be performed in December '87. Last, but not least, I have just finished work on the new, 9th Neuronium LP titled *SUPRA-NATURAL*. It should be out sometime in the Fall. The music is in the pure Neuronium vein of sensations, and the centerpiece is a long cosmic track titled "Sundown At Tanah Lot," which is the best thing I have ever done perhaps.....

Archie Patterson

Michel Le Bars/Eider Stellaire Interview

The history of Eider Stellaire is intertwined with that of its creator, Michel Le Bars who while drummer for a group inspired by the blues and Hendrix, one day heard Magma in concert. It was a revelation and marked a point of departure in his desire to play music that no longer served as a pretext for dancing. With this view in mind he formed Astarte, which apart from Michel, included the current bassist and guitarist of Eider Stellaire, Patrick Singery and Jean-Claude Delachat, as well as the pianist Georges Basset, principal composer of much of the band's material. The following interview with Michel sheds some light on the existence of one of the most interesting new bands in France today.

Q: Can you tell us in a little detail about the time of your first album and the concert where you played as the opening group for Magma?

A: The first album was done in 5 days, the group had been in existence for scarcely 6 months. We wanted to play fast, a little like a commando raid. We had held on for 4 years in deplorable conditions, we didn't have a dime, people told us to "get lost," we played in minimum conditions as far as acoustics; however it was in many ways a very enriching experience as well, to play in lamentable conditions every evening teaches you a lot of things, including about yourself. On the whole, the public too received us badly; our music was judged to be quote "intellectual" or "elitist," or even fascist, we were even called that. Never having concealed the fact that I felt close to Christian's music, we were of course accused of being Magma copies, even though we had always produced music that was perceptibly different. It was hard for us to open up for Magma, nevertheless I think there was good reason for this group to exist; but there was never any support, that's hard to take/hard to live with. By the time we decided to stop that formation, we were rather unhappy; we lost money, we slept 6 or 7 in one room, we griped a lot, but we were glad to be doing it. It was great for us because there was no distinction between what we lived and the music we played. It was hard on-stage, it was a hard way of living. We embodied the direction we had chosen in music. We really experienced unimaginable depths and difficulties.

Q: In spite of all these difficulties, you forged ahead and produced a second album.

A: Absolutely, but from a completely different point of view. The group had been out of existence for a good year and a half, so we bought an 8-track machine and began to work at our own place. Since we had no repertoire, we had to construct our music as we recorded it. That allows for real breakthroughs sometimes, but it also takes longer. As for the technical side, we were in a little over our heads; at that level you always have the feeling of knowing a few things and then you come to realize that there are 99 others that are beyond you. For us this record was a way of saying we won't give up. So we tried to offer something different, through its density on the emotional level and the intensity of the tone colors. The album for me is more a collection of poetry than a music disc. As for singing, I tried to sing "jazz," that can give a little the idea of badly-sung English, but I didn't want anything written/and lyrics because for me music is magic, poetry, but above all not a message. As for energy, it isn't energy in the first degree that you could find in the first album, it's clearly less rock. Here the energy is more concentrated; there's not a single piece that lets up in intensity in my opinion, it seems to me to be a little like a fish in water, it doesn't stop, it doesn't lose hold. As for the musicians, you find again Patrick Singery and Jean-Claude Delachat, but for the pianist it was more tricky to the point that I had to play the piano parts myself, with a friend doing the synthesizer. At the start we also wanted to have brass, but alas brass has to be paid for and as the work went on we got more and more overwhelmed by the financial aspects and realized we couldn't do it, so used the synthesizer instead.

Q: Wasn't there also a question of Christian Vander participating on the album?

A: Actually Christian was to come in on it. At an early point I'd had him listen to some of the pieces at his place, playing them on the piano, he thought they weren't bad. My view meanwhile was not to have him commit himself verbally, it was to show him the pieces and when we had begun to produce them, to show them to him again and see if he would consider it honorable to do something. Being overwhelmed by quite a few problems, at one point we just decided not to do it. I think I could have gotten him to come in on it without any problem, but I gave it up because I don't like to get people involved in a project where I'm not completely satisfied.

Q: Because you're not completely satisfied with the second album?

A: For the moment we are satiated with it, it doesn't speak to us too much any more. On the other hand, like the first album where we weren't completely satisfied, we don't go back on any of it. I think nonetheless that in a year or two we will probably be happier with it.

Q: Parallel to Eider Stellaire you were also the drummer for Offering?

A: I have a lot of respect for Christian's music; at one point he had asked me to join him, but I didn't feel I was ready. It took me two years before I felt ready to accept. It's a real hard position to hold as there's not a lot of importance given to the individual performer. On the other hand, it opened me up to a lot musically, that's how I discovered Coltrane only 3-4 years ago, which probably explains why now I want to bring more jazz influence into the music I do.

Q: What do you think of the current orientation of musicians and the idea of doing a group?

A: A group is people who share something inside, a certain music. Right now I don't feel that happening, I get the impression of a guy with some back-ups who get 3 minutes of solos from time to time to soothe their egos. As far as I'm concerned, I don't share anything musically with people in Paris. There are too many music-school musicians with great equipment who play only what they've been taught. They take no risks and I like risks, my whole life I hope will continue like that. The day I stop taking risks is it will be the end for me. Musicians can make mistakes, but they must keep searching.

Introduction: Francis Grosse
Interview: Alain Juliac
Translation: Lois Bode
Reprinted courtesy of NOTES

Julverne

In 1973, RTB (Belgian TV) asks Pierre Coulon to put together a Walloon folk group. He then contacts Jeannot Gillis (violin), Jean Paul Laurent (piano, flute) and Michel Dayez, all classically trained, and he founds Les Coulonneux (Columbophiles in Walloon). Their repertoire at that time is composed of traditional songs, collected from old people in the region. Following that, the group accompanies Belgian folksingers like Jofroy and Julos.

Parallel with this folk predominance, the members of the group begin to write their own compositions, more-or-less influenced by classical music. This double musical direction will be the cause of numerous misunderstandings: they are considered a folk group when in fact they play everything but folk music. It even reaches the point where they're paid to not play at all.

They finally decide to learn the lessons of these misunderstandings and change their name as they issue their first album Julverne -- *COULONNEUX*, acknowledging their classical roots. In 1980, during the celebration for Brussels' 1,000-year anniversary, some newcomers join the group, including Denis Van Hecke (cello) and Charles Loos (piano) and some supplementary instruments make their appearance as well (viola, bass, flute, clarinet, bassoon). The group grows to 9 members which leads to the title of their second album *A NEUF* ("neuf" means both 9 and new in French). The final change comes when they add singer Ilona Chale, formerly of COS, and the pieces in their repertoire are rearranged to a new form to fit in with this new formation. Also a part of the group now are two former Univers Zero members Michel Berckmans and Dirk Descheemaeker. This is the lineup who records the third album Julverne -- *EMBALLADE*, essentially oriented toward twisted versions of dance melodies of the 1920-'30s. For the first time they play other people's compositions, like Scott Joplin or Duke Ellington.

But beyond this historical aspect, what remains of course is the music produced by this exceptional group.

It seems difficult to associate Julverne's music with a particular style, whether classical, jazz or cabaret, and the group itself claims this triple heritage. During its evolution, after having abandoned folk music, their style affirmed itself as having outdated melodies as a base, subtly perverted by rhythmic audacities and unexpected dissonances.

The instrumentation is essentially acoustic ("Music of wood and iron without electricity" as they described themselves in Rheims in 1982), and the makeup of the group has become stable around 8 or 9 musicians. Some similarities can be found with ZNR or Michael Nyman, but certain underlying classical feelings persist, mainly in the compositions of Jean Paul Laurent, the only member having any real training in harmony. For the others who are self-taught, compositions are developed "intuitively."

The theatrical aspect of the group has a particular importance and adds a second dimension to their approach: they give 20-25 concerts a year performing mainly in small halls, taverns and even at weddings! They then dress in clothes suiting the epoch of their influences (1930). This very dry aspect of their humor gives a little distance vis-à-vis their music, a sort of separation which totally modifies it and brings out the ironic side. They speak of their music actually as "tea-room" music, "not to be listened to very seriously." On stage, their set is filled out by other "retro" pieces (like those on *EMBALLADE*) or works by Kurt Weill or Nino Rota as well as their own compositions. The ensemble is full of an antiquated charm.

The "professional" situation of Julverne is rather ambiguous in the sense that most of the musicians are not professionals. In the makeup of *A NEUF*, 8 of the musicians worked in other branches of music (teachers in music academics or members of other groups, classical or pop) and only Jeannot Gillis plied the non-musical trade of professor of concrete!

This situation is not without its internal problems: Julverne is not a livelihood and the jobs taken to support themselves block the musicians and prevent them from going on tour, except during school vacations.

To this is added the problems of distribution typical for small groups in general and Belgium in particular. Although there is a marginal field of production in Belgium, it is so diversified that at the heart of a label like theirs we find a hodgepodge made up of a poet, a handyman into noise-making, improvised music, concrete, electronic, jazz....

Fortunately at the moment, regrouping among labels is going on there and this great musical diversity will soon in the future be more structured and will be more effectively promoted, thus allowing for more exposure hopefully.

Meanwhile, Julverne prepares its fourth album, *NE PARLONS PAS DE MAHLEUR*, which will bring together all new original composition along the lines of *A NEUF*.

Bernard Gueffier
Translation: Lois Bode
Reprinted courtesy of NOTES

Gandalf Interview

Today "New Age" music is developing into a minor sensation as the release of a multitude of piano, ethnic fusion and soft electronic music recordings floods the market. Especially in America, there are newborn true believers everywhere, trying to cash in with the sad result being that some beautiful music and genuine artists are being lost amidst the mass merchandising of mediocrity.

In Europe the situation is a bit different. The homeland of the classical masters and birthplace of the cosmic synthesizer movement, these traditions tend to displace the dedicated-follower-of-fashion mentality of most US musicians. Add that to the fact of a much smaller actual market and you get a different creative approach on the part of the majority of artists. Europe has produced some of the true pioneers of what's now being called "New Age" music, in particular Tangerine Dream, Klaus Schulze, Vangelis and Jean-Michel Jarre. They all have had some success around the world.

This brings me to the point at hand, which is to introduce one of the best European composer/musicians of the 1980s -- Heinz Strobl, a.k.a. Gandalf. Of all the artists given initial exposure via EUROCK, the music of Gandalf has without a doubt gotten the most positive response. But until now a combination of circumstances had kept his music and him personally an obscure footnote to the current happenings. Hopefully this interview will mark the beginning of his emergence internationally. Over the span of the last 8 years and his 8 releases to date, Gandalf has exhibited a level of creativity which makes his music a rare listening experience.

Q: Tell us about the name Gandalf, why did you choose that as your musical signature?

A: The name Gandalf was taken from a mystical story "The Lord of the Rings" by J.R.R. Tolkien and originally was the name of a very positive-thinking magician in that book, he helped the good creatures to win against the forces of evil. And that is what I'm trying to do with my music, I want to send positive thoughts and feelings to people as an alternative to all the stress and bad influences of modern life. I want them to learn again just to sit back and listen and get carried away by the inspiration of sounds, to feel closer to their real nature.

Q: Perhaps you could give a bit of history -- musical and personal -- to illuminate how you came to develop your musical ideas?

A: My first active contacts with music I had in the late 1960s, the era of Woodstock and flower power. I was about 15 and played in several rock bands, lead guitar, trying to copy songs by Hendrix, Santana and the Beatles. Later on I started to arrange songs by all these artists by myself and play my own versions. In the early 1970s I finished college in telecommunications and started to work as a technician for air traffic control. The music of bands like King Crimson, Pink Floyd and Genesis touched me deeply and I started to compose my own music in that direction. Also I built my first synthesizer and started playing keyboards as well. This opened up more space for me to create new sounds and I began to imagine a kind of music that would come from deep within myself. Near the end of the 1970s I stopped playing in groups and built up a small 8-track studio, recording for the first time that music from my heart and produced JOURNEY TO AN IMAGINARY LAND, and that land was inside of me.

Q: Your albums all illustrate particular story/concepts, how do you create the original idea that serves as the basis for the record?

A: *JOURNEY* was released by WEA Music in several European countries as were several other productions I did subsequently. The inspirations for the thematic background I took from a lot of experiences within these years. From books I read like Herman Hesse, from philosophical scriptures from the Far East, journeys to India and observations in nature.

Q: If you were to try and describe your sound, what would you say to a new listener?

A: To say something about my sound, well, I'm trying to create a most harmonic mixture of sounds by acoustic instruments, natural sounds -- wind, water, birds -- and sounds from electronic instruments. You could call it acoustic paintings or music for imaginary films, taking place in your heads. Each song represents a specific mood.

Q: Is there any special message -- literally or cosmologically -- you hope the listener will get from your music?

A: I want people to feel peaceful and happy when hearing my music, to forget all bad things and love all of God's creation as one big thing that we are all a small part of.

Q: In the US just now, the generic musical category of "New Age" is exploding with countless new artists/productions. Does that description relate to your work at all? How do you feel about such business-motivated marketing labels?

A: You can call me a "New Age" artist or not, if you want. I surely think that many people are starting to get a new consciousness these days, and so am I. When I began creating my music I didn't know anything about such a new age movement in America and I hope to be able to continue my work when the term "New Age" will be out of fashion again. As an artist who is making records and of course wants to sell them, I can't say anything against record companies who want to sell my records in the best way possible, but it is truly a pity that now every kind of music that sounds electronic and peaceful is marketed under that label and people who want to get music from artists with a real new consciousness become confused. In Europe the movement is rather small right now, but starts to grow more and more.

Q: What have been your experiences with the music business in Europe? I know you used to be with WEA Music, then formed your own company called Seagull Music, and now your new record is on CBS. Has this been a smooth or more problematic process?

A: As for my experiences with record companies, I can say that I always tried to keep full artistic freedom regarding my music, and that is possible as I can do every aspect of the production, including completed master-tape, in my own studio. The people at the record company get to hear it for the first time when it is finished and then can decide if they want it or not. That capacity also allowed me to release some material on my own label -- Seagull Music -- as well.

Q: How do you see your label working now that you record for CBS? Have you other artists and productions involved with Seagull?

A: With such a small record label it is not easy to find distributors in many countries and the work of distribution can get very complicated. I am still in good contact with WEA people and they are going to release a CD sampler within the next months, but I thought that someone else could do more for my music and I found good interest at CBS so I'm trying them now. As for Seagull, I just did a deal with EMI-Columbia and they will handle distribution for me. At the moment things look very good as CBS is going to release my new album in several more countries than before.

Q: Is there a large audience in Europe for your music so that you sell enough records to generate interest for you to perform live?

A: The audience for my kind of music in Europe is rather small, but I think it will increase in the future. Especially in Austria it is not easy to do live concerts at the moment, but I did have some good gigs in the Netherlands within the last years and I am planning to perform in other European countries in the future. Within the last years I've sold more than 100,000 records in all Europe, I think this is not so bad?

Q: What plans do you have for the future in terms of new projects?

A: I am just about to work out the music for my next LP release which is scheduled for early 1988.

Q: If your musical dreams could come true, what would you hope for?

A: My musical dreams are not very big, I just want to find out still more about my inner "soulscapes," playing more and more my own true music, making as many listeners happy as possible.

Archie Patterson

Los Jaivas
ETHNIC ROCK FROM CHILE

At the end of the '60s a certain group started to change their musical ideas, from a band playing only at parties to a band exploring and mixing native instruments with electronic gear. They were Los Jaivas and this is a kind of "story of..."

It all began at the end of 1962 when Eduardo, Claudio and Gabriel Parra started jamming in their house in Viña del Mar (Chile), with their friends Eduardo "Gato" ("Cat") Alquinta and Mario Mutis. While others were playing in the streets, these five played music for fun. The music and friendship emerged spontaneously; then they set up a "Circo" ("Circus"), a kind of small stage where they started to play. Suddenly they found themselves dressed up in dark suits and ties playing and singing tangos, boleros and tropical music at school parties and weddings in Caleta Abarca near Viña del Mar. This new group was called "The High Bass," which was referring to the differences in height of the Parra brothers and friends. In March 1963 the lineup was: Eduardo Alquinta on guitar, Eduardo Parra on piano, Claudio Parra on accordion, Gabriel Parra on drums and Mario Mutis on percussions. Things went very well (except at school) as they were playing everywhere they could. El "Chicon" (bump or lump on the head) was inaugurated, a kind of club in the basement of their house in Viña del Mar. But in spite of this "success" they were getting bored playing only non-original music, because their main desire was to create their own sound.

In 1969, with the hippie era in their minds and bodies, the group started to do some new sounds consisting of improvisations and explorations with records played backwards, vocal effects and pieces of synthetic fiber rasping on the floor; all of this in addition to their interest in the culture of the native Indians of Chile, the Mapuches, studying their instruments and legends, guided them to the basic idea "to be Americans and emerge as Americans." At the end of 1969 The High Bass became Los Jaivas, due to the Spanish pronunciation, the second name is the first one (Jaiva also is a reference to Jaiba, a Spanish word for Crab, the 'v' is exchanged for the 'b').

At the beginning of 1970 Los Jaivas was the only group playing native instruments like the Trutruca (a long piece of hollow cane of 2 meters that ends with a cow horn), as well as pianos and electric guitars in live performances before astonished audiences in Santiago. They had now moved and were staying at the famous Dardignac street house. At this time, before they decided to be professional musicians, everyone had their own occupation. For example Eduardo was for a time a taxi driver, "Gato" studied architecture and Claudio was the only one who went to the Conservatory of Music. It was in 1970 that they recorded their first LP titled *EL VOLANTIN* (The Kite). A legendary record, it was financed by their selling off an electric piano. The record contained three tracks, "Cacho" (Cow Horn), "La Vaquita" (The Little Cow) and "Foto de Primera Comunion" (First Communion Photograph). It was privately-pressed and distributed by the group and the original (and only) release was issued as a real kite with a poster containing the photo and comments of each member of the band.

After appeared on the market, on IRT label, the single "Todos Juntos" (All Together), an item which sold more than 100,000 copies. It became the anthem of the Chilean hippie era and centerpiece of their live performances.

In August of 1972 they released *LA VENTANA* (The Window) on IRT label. It contained their first symphonic performance "Los Caminos Que Se Abren" (The Opening Roads). Also two tracks from the LP were released as singles.

1973 saw the group playing live at the Quintana Vergara, in Viña del Mar, as a part of the First Encounter of South American Music with Roots; this will be remembered as one of the group's biggest and first sold-out concerts. A third single was issued from *LA VENTANA*, "Indio Hermano" (Indian Brother). Later, the Theatro Municipal de Santiago announced for Tuesday Sept. 11, 1973, a live performance of the band with the Santiago Symphonic Orchestra, but that was the day President Allende was overthrown so.... In November 1973 the group decided to leave Chile with all their troupe (wives, children, etc.) and went to Argentina. This was a hard time with many problems, yet in spite of the critics against them, the group played at every opportunity. At this time the band was supported by a group of friends (who also lived in Zárate), who helped them as roadies, artists, etc. They were (and still are): Carlos "Rosko" Melo and Dominique Strabach as sound technicians, Hernan "Piola" Poblete on Public Relations, Alejandro Parra (brother of Claudio, Eduardo and Gabriel), lights, Juan Ignacio Valdes, assistant and Rene Olivares, painter.

At the beginning of 1975 Mario Mutis left the group for a time, but the band stayed together joined by the Argentine musician Julio Anderson on bass, guitar, percussion and voice. In late 1975 they recorded their fourth album, titled *LOS JAIVAS*, that was released on EMI records at the end of the year. The addition of Julio had given the group a fresh vitality in terms of both vitality and performance as evidenced in the two tracks especially, "La Conquistada" and "Tarca Y Ocarina."

In 1976 Julio left the group, Mario rejoined, the Argentine Alberto Ledo joined and "Pajarito" Canzani became more stable with the group. Together with Eduardo, Claudio, Gabriel and "Cat" Alquinta they recorded *LA CANCION DEL SUR* (The Southern Song), released by EMI. It contained one of their most beautiful and harmonious tracks, the major work based upon the LP's title. Also in 1976 Los Jaivas played live with the Symphonic Orchestra of Buenos Aires. In spite of their success at this point, as well as good critical reviews, the group decided to leave Argentina and fly with their families to Uruguay, Brazil and finally their best trip ever, to Europe.

Once again they started from zero and decided to stay in France (Chatenay, Malabry near Paris), from where they started to play everywhere: May 1977 in Biarritz , March 1979 in London and Barcelona, September 1980 Rome and Enschede and January 1981 in Bamberg. During 1981 they went back into the studio to record *ALTURAS DE MACHU PICCHU* (The Heights of Machu Picchu) for CBS Records . It was a great effort by the group to create a musical expression of the poetry of Pablo Neruda (Chile's second Literature Nobel Prize). One of their most acclaimed albums, it was released in Germany, France, Chile and Venezuela. Meanwhile in Argentina, EMI issued a compilation titled, *LOS JAIVAS RETROSPECTIVO: 1975-1978*, which consisted of a cross-section of older and newer tracks. Also in 1981 they performed live at the Station of Radio France, some new, unreleased material based on the Musical work of Violeta Parra (a legendary woman of Chile's '60s new folklore). It lasted two hours in front of 2,000 people.

Later that year they came back again to Chile (the first time was for a short visit in 1975), and played various nice concerts in front of astonished audiences who had been waiting to hear them since 1975. At this time the group spent some days at Machu Picchu doing a video of the LP. Many people were involved with it, including the noted Peruvian writer Mario Vargas Llosa. This video was later shown on Chilean TV.

In 1981 they recorded the LP, *ACON-CAGUA*, that was later issued in 1982 by CBS Records.

In 1982 they did another, more extensive tour of Chile, playing throughout the country, which included a performance in front of 25,000 people at the Quintana Vergara and at the Festival de Viña del Mar as the main act for this pop music event.

After leaving Chile they played live in Europe including concerts in Leningrad and Moscow as well as venues along the frontiers of China and Afghanistan. Soviet TV filmed two concerts and an LP was released from a performance at Russia Hall (Moscow).

In 1983 they came once again to Chile to do work on a film of the Antarctic, which was never released and now seems to have disappeared from the TV archives. At this time they also played a concert in Argentina, at Estadio Obras on April 13, 1983, it was recorded and released in Argentina under the name *LOS JAIVAS EN ARGENTINA*.

Their latest album, *ODAS A VIOLETA PARRA* (Odes to Violeta Parra) was released in 1984 as a double record set with the help of some early friends like Carlos "Rosko" Melo and Rene Olivares. On this album they move sometimes into the progressive music idiom and it works well, but they'll never abandon their classic fusion of native and electric instruments. That is the formula they have developed and become known for after all these years and will continue to adhere to in spite of any pressure from outside forces, including record labels.

The latest news about Los Jaivas is that they gave a concert in 1984 at the Estadio Velez Sarfield in Argentina for 70,000 people to celebrate the Peace Agreement between Chile and Argentina following the Canal del Beagle "affair." In addition they gave a concert in New York City in late 1986 at the Ritz. Mario Mutis had again left the group, replaced by "Pajarito" Canzani on bass and backing vocals. A video was shot of the show and shown on Chilean TV last year. Throughout all of their activities over the last 14 years, Los Jaivas have proven to be one of the few innovative and adventurous bands of Chile's rock scene.

Ivan Brantes

1988

Thierry Zaboitzeff/ Art Zoyd Interview

Notes: What is Art Zoyd's situation today on the French musical scene? I mean are you free from belonging to any particular musical style?

Thierry Zaboitzeff: Yes, Rock In Opposition is now seven years old and it is different today.

Notes: Does the deep change which happened in your music since *ESPACES INQUIETS* and *LE MARIAGE DU CIEL ET DE L'ENFER* come from a deliberate strategy in order to reach a new audience?

T.Z.: No, it's only the consequence of our musical evolution; it happened that for the last three albums which are linked together, things went much faster than before. We were able to record in better conditions, with completely different material, and all that led us to where we are today, more quickly than we wished. I think it's a good thing that it moved a little faster. Anyway, since *PHASE IV*, we had to move, we had to find a new vocabulary, a new aesthetic.

Notes: Did this new evolution have consequences on the size of your audience?

T.Z.: In France, it didn't have much influence on our audience, but at the international level and particularly in Germany -- you know that we play a lot in Germany -- it caused a lot of things. The German audience knows that we've existed for fifteen years, but it still considers us a new group. Even if it's only six months after our last tour, it was the same audience plus new fans, but it felt like we were a new group. On the contrary in France, we always feel as if we are in a ghetto where people speak only of Rock In Opposition, dark musics and all kinds of things which are far away from the audience and which interest nobody.

Notes: What kind of solution do you see in order to escape from that ghetto in France?

T.Z.: I don't see any solution right now, you know better than me how it goes with the press, with people... In fact, there are lots of habits to change: in France nobody wants to take any risk, on anyone. We are lucky that Madrigal takes a few risks with us, but we don't really see a solution. But that doesn't keep us from working and it absolutely doesn't challenge our evolution.

Notes: You've worked with Roland Petit's ballet for *LE MARIAGE, BEGWEGUNGS-THEATER* and recently with the Vorgange from Salzburg. Are you particularly interested in dance collaborations?

T.Z.: At the beginning the Vorgange company chose from existing Art Zoyd music and composed a patchwork from all the Art Zoyd stages for a ballet. Since July this ballet was made again with new musics. It didn't interest us very much to use older things because the mixing they made didn't interest us musically. As for our interest in this sort of collaboration, it's rather choreographers who are interested in our music but for us it is also a very interesting experience.

Notes: This leads us to the *BERLIN* album. Well first, why this title?

T.Z.: If you listened to the CD version, you probably saw that there were many different things. It was very difficult to find a title which fit it all. As those last two years our work was concentrated in Germany and particularly in Berlin, we decided to take this title for the album.

Notes: You're talking about the CD as a start, does it mean that you didn't conceive the album as an LP and then later add a few more or less anecdotal pieces to make it longer?

T.Z.: That's it, we worked from the beginning in the CD spirit and without a problem we put on the LP what was for us the main pieces, especially since the time (twice twenty minutes) fit so well.

Notes: The use of voices with true lyrics was one of the surprises of *BERLIN*. I know that you are also working on "songs." How does it come and what importance will voice have in Art Zoyd's future evolution?

T.Z.: For me as a composer, I like to use voices and have for a long time, first as onomatopoeias, shouts, sound events. Actually we are working on a big project: *MAKBETH*, with film, video, dance, music, sculpture, all on a stage. And I took the same way to work on a sound event in that *MAKBETH* project, with Shakespeare texts. I thought it was interesting to mix researches on timbre and on the text itself.

Notes: In *BERLIN*, what is the content of the lyrics?

T.Z.: There is no message, it's only an aesthetic content.

Notes: Can you tell us more about this *MAKBETH* project?

T.Z.: *BERLIN* is only the beginning of this project, but there'll be other things. It's difficult for me to talk about it right now as the project is only in construction. We chose *MAKBETH* because we were looking for something universal, mediatic and classical in the theatrical meaning. But we're not going to play classical theater, it's only for the image.

Notes: In *BERLIN*, there is a new musician, Andre Mergenthaler. Is that the same one who played under a little shorter name in Univers Zero?

T.Z.: Yes, it's the same one. He was

playing in Univers Zero and at the same time of *LE MARIAGE DU CIEL ET DE L'ENFER* we invited him and Daniel Denis to play in concerts, and he felt good working with us and wanted to continue. Even Daniel himself almost stayed.

Notes: Amongst all of your projects which includes several artistic fields, is there something concerning film soundtracks?

T.Z.: We've had some contacts about it, but nothing new until today. Nevertheless, we'll soon work on the music of a '20s German silent film, which'll be shown with Art Zoyd live at several festivals in France, Germany and Belgium in '88. Now it's a necessity to find another way to do a concert, aside from the ordinary way: four guys on a stage gesticulating... you see. We feel that to be boring so we're looking for something else, such as those ballet experiences and the *MAKBETH* project where there will be lots of pictures on screens and on the stage.

Notes: Apart from the film soundtracks you've made several videos. What are they and can we hope to watch them on TV one day?

T.Z.: "Derniere Danse," the first video clip (with puppets), was broadcast in several European countries. "Ceremonie," the second one which includes the first attempt of the cinematographic techniques we'll use for *MAKBETH*, was also broadcast in several countries including France and obtained the Jury's award at Toulon International Festival Selection. "Art Zoyd Berlin," which is a 26 minute live video released by Christophe Jouret, was taken from the Berlin concerts, and was also broadcast in several European countries. All of those three videos will make up a one hour special program about Art Zoyd which will be shown on the American channel SCETV.

Notes: But there was still a one hour long film broadcast by FR3 in 1982?

T.Z.: Yes, but it was something made by the TV itself, not controlled by us.

Notes: Do you have other things in preparation?

T.Z.: We just finished a video clip for *MAKBETH* and are planning a 52 minute film about the Vorgange's next ballet and a 104 minute film about *MAKBETH* as well.

Notes: You recorded a solo album, *PROMETHEE*, will there be a follow-up, and do other members of the group have any solo projects planned?

T.Z.: Andre Mergenthaler has his solo performances (sax, cello, vocals, keyboards), he composes and plays for theater and he's working on a record project. Patricia Dallio composes and plays for two ballet companies and for several videos. For me, I have other projects in collaboration with a theater company from my town in Valenciennes for a play which is called "Le Chant D'Hallewyen" based on a Celtic story. This play will be performed thirty times in the North of France, in Belgium and at this occasion we'll certainly publish a book/record. But all that is still a project in the future.

Notes: Does your discography include all of the material you have composed?

T.Z.: No, there are other pieces which are the beginning of the following. From now, we're recording digitally every concert we do and later maybe we will have something live to publish. But we hesitate between the studios good quality and the live aspect which is impossible to reproduce on record. We must also be ready to assume our mistakes. If you like a record, you're going to listen to it ten, fifty, maybe a hundred times. And if you find mistakes in every bar it's embarrassing. We would like nobody to be frustrated and ourselves to be the first pleased by the result. Then it would be ok and we agree to put out something live, particularly since now we have the means to record under very good conditions.

Notes: And what about concerts?

T.Z.: This year we played approximately twice every month which is rather good. It happened in excellent conditions for the group, for the money, all concerts worked perfectly.

Notes: Does this have any connection perhaps with your collaboration with Roland Petit's ballet and the recognition it brought you?

T.Z.: Nothing directly, but in people's heads certainly. If there are some consequences, they just begin now.

Notes: Where do you play your concerts?

T.Z.: This year both in Germany (particularly at Documenta 8 from Kassel, Berlin) in France (Festival of Radio France, Maubeuge, and Cote D'Opale), in Netherlands and in Denmark where we took part in the opening ceremony of Aarhus Festival, in the presence of the Queen Margarethe II.

Notes: Are you satisfied with your record company Madrigal?

T.Z.: Things are rather well with them. The *BERLIN* album came out in time and they made that CD version.... Until now, everything has gone ok.... The machine is turning well.

Notes: Can you tell us about the structure you have created to manage the group's business? It's rather new and it can give some ideas to other groups perhaps.

T.Z.: We founded a collective name society whose label is Art Zoyd. It allow us to be perfectly clear about money, incomes, expenses. We're working like a commercial thing. It allows us to get the V.A.T. [value-added tax] back which represents a good amount (33% in France). It's a big advantage which allows us to buy more easily some new equipment. On the other hand, there is the disadvantage of being compelled to do a very serious accounting. There are three managers in this society: Gerard Hourbette, Richard Castelli and myself. Now we earn our living out of it, musicians are paid for rehearsals. It never was more clear.

Notes: Is that a system you would recommend to other groups?

T.Z.: Yes, but it has to be a real group, or at least a nucleus of three persons who will keep on going together, one must be sure of one's partners.

Notes: Does the development possibilities of this society include the future production and distribution of your records?

T.Z.: No, because distribution takes a lot of time, but maybe production, who knows? Right now, with our society we already managed to build our own studio which is something extremely important. It means that we are completely independent about our recordings. We can now propose to any record label a finished product up to professional standards.

Notes: Are the Madrigal records made in co-production?

T.Z.: Yes, they have a part in the production and also take care of the manufacturing costs.

Notes: And what about the other musicians from Art Zoyd who do not belong to the society?

T.Z.: Some members of Art Zoyd have other activities and only play in the group by choice. When they come to play with us, they stay very little time as we work very quickly; they play as salaried employees every time the come.

Notes: Doesn't it cause problems to have in the group two different kinds of musicians: employers and employees?

T.Z.: On the contrary, it's very sane. I was myself sometimes a little embarrassed by this type of relation, but for them it seems to be much clearer.

INTERVIEW: Bernard Gueffier
ASSISTANCE: Thierry Moreau
TRANSLATION: Bernard Gueffier
Reprinted Courtesy of NOTES

Jorge Reyes Interview

Q: Let's begin with a little personal history. How did you come to music as your mode of creative expression -- via formal studies or more of a naturally developing talent?

A: I studied flute at the university for five years. Through that experience with music I became interested in jazz and went to Hamburg to study improvisation for a year. In 1978, I had the chance to take a Hindu music course in the Himalaya and began collecting instruments from all over the world. It was not until 1983 that I started with synthesizers and the guitar.

Q: What were your early musical influences & experiences in terms of groups, solo work, playing at the university or clubs, etc.?

A: My introduction to rock was during the '60s; The Rolling Stones, Beatles, Doors and Jimi Hendrix all impressed me. In the '70s, I began playing flute and became part of some groups of progressive rock with strong influences like Jethro Tull and Pink Floyd. In spite of theses strong influences, we never just copied their music, we always wrote our own material, especially from the flute player point of view which is the instrumental music. Since rock in

Mexico at that time was marginal and looked down upon, we used to play clandestinely; the concerts took place in garages and unsuitable rooms. To record was almost impossible.

Q: Along with Decibel, your early group Chac Mool was one of the pioneers of Mexican progressive music. Who were the main influences on the sound and style of that band?

A: At the beginning of 1981, Chac Mool sounded a bit like Pink Floyd and King Crimson, but the material of the first two albums was actually written when I was living in Germany during 1977 and recorded with Chac Mool some years later. Maybe at the time those records came out we sounded a little out of fashion for other countries, but in Mexico, because of the characteristics and peculiarities of rock, we were in. The first album was very popular and sold many copies; that changed the bad attitude of the music industry toward Mexican rock. After three LPs trying to update the sound of Chac Mool music, I recorded another album, a little more pop with more commercial goals, but due to the pressure from the record company, WEA, the result was disconcerting. The group lost direction and became trapped between a capricious manager and a record company that was not interested in our music, but a more commercial sound that could be programmed on the radio. So I left to develop my own ideas; the alliance of our culture, our instruments and our rhythms into the most experimental areas of rock.

Q: I believe they had four albums, all on major labels? How did a national group gain such attention when the actual rock scene was so small?

A: Polygram offered Chac Mool a contract as an experiment, the results of the first LP were outstanding, it was the first time that a Mexican rock group had that kind of opportunity which made us pioneers in Mexican rock with Spanish lyrics. At that time we were the only ones with a recording contract.

Q: Did Chac Mool play live and sell a lot of records?

A: There were a lot of concerts, some with as many as 12,000 people and our records sold very well. We became the most popular group in Mexico.

Q: You released your first solo LP, *EL TUNKUL*, while still a part of Chac Mool. It explored a completely different style of music, did your solo interests lead to the group disbanding or was there another reason?

A: My first solo LP was recorded while I was in Chac Mool. With Chac Mool I became, against my wishes, a guitar player. I say against my wishes, because due to an accident, I can only play with three fingers of my left hand. For this reason, I had to refocus my musical vision as a flute player and work on the introduction of a new musical concept. I abandoned Chac Mool and began on my own to record the second album, *A LA IZQUIERDA DEL COLIBRI*.

Q: How would you describe the music of *EL TUNKUL*, as it is definitely not rock?

A: I can't define music with exact words, that worries me no more now. I am only interested in creating the music which is inside of me, whether it is rock or not. I simply write the music I like, the music that intuitively is reborn from our roots, origins and rituals.

Q: Was that album a success in your mind -- creatively and commercially? Did it sell many copies?

A: *EL TUNKUL*, was independently produced on a very small budget. Sales were favorable and allowed me to acquire new instruments and to produce the second LP.

Q: Your second solo work was with the rather amazing percussionist Antonio Zepeda. This collaboration changed the sound somewhat, was this a new conceptual direction you wanted to explore or more of an expansion of the ideas presented on *EL TUNKUL*?

A: When I recorded my second album, I invited Antonio Zepeda to play percussions. The material was almost entirely written and programmed on an Apple II computer. Antonio gave the music a touch of his special originality. The sound changed because I had more experience, I knew what I wanted, I was more familiar with the recording studio and my array of instruments was larger and better. Even though me and Antonio shared knowledge, experiences and played several concerts together, we never became a formal duo.

Q: Which of the two LPs do you like the best in retrospect? Which was the most successful for you in terms of critical reviews and sales?

A: *A LA IZQUIERDA DEL COLIBRI* sold more copies, had better distribution and advertising as well as reviews. I recorded it as an independent producer and later sold it to Philips which let me begin work on my third LP, *COMALA* (which is actually the fourth one, the third was a movie soundtrack due out very soon). The modest success of *A LA IZQUIERDA DEL COLIBRI* brought me to Germany to give concerts between 1986-87. Actually I like all of my LPs as each one has something special that attracts me. Some people prefer *EL TUNKUL* because it is more simple, natural and tranquil, while others like *COMALA* for its wonderful strangeness.

Q: On your latest LP, *COMALA*, you collaborate with Arturo Meza and a group called La Tribu. Perhaps you can tell us a bit about both of them?

A: La Tribu is a group of musicians who have dedicated several years to playing and exploring Mexican Indian music. Even though they need to center their ideas and they have had bad production, their three LPs are sold out. Arturo Meza is a musician with a great sensibility and has several independent releases out.

Q: *COMALA* definitely seems the most conceptually-developed and musically powerful of your works. What can you tell an English audience about it that will help to understand all its various concepts and musical influences?

A: *COMALA* is a musical collage, a travel through unknown roots to the threshold of time. *COMALA*, place where the wind breaks, unreal space where the living dead walks through murmurations that can be heard in the gusts. The fragments of a memory, the voices, coming out from the ruins. The water falling through the roof, drop by drop, sound by sound like echoes of the past. To accomplish this ghostly atmosphere with a sense of humor, I apply a collage of sounds, instruments ages, voices (recorded in the studio), dances and poems, all into a structure different from the two other LPs. *COMALA* represents the dark and more experimental side of the other face. There is a link between the supernatural forces and *COMALA* that tries in some way to restitute the music and ritual character which has been lost to the people who consider music as just another form of entertainment or merchandise to be bought and sold, that requires no creativity from the audience. Emphasizing rhythmic patterns, and pre-recorded human voices, I pretend to break into the flow of everyday affairs, taking the listener away from that world. Since time is the true law of the world, the idea of something supernatural, out of this world, ties up the outgate of time, creating a standstill of movement and therefore death. Mexican ritual instruments were used in COMALA; some of them one thousand years old. In addition, the voice of Maria Sabina; a Mexican medicaster who died two years ago and was famous for her ritual healings with hallucinogenic mushrooms.

Q: Are you able to play that music live? Are there suitable venues for you to put on performances around Mexico?

A: Because COMALA is like a collage, a work of assembly done in the studio, it is impossible to reproduce it live exactly as it is on the record. During concerts, I recreate some ideas and play new compositions with recently-acquired instruments. I never play a composition in the same way, there is always a large margin for improvisation. My concerts are given mostly in archeological places such as the Escultoric Space, a place of volcanic rock surrounded by concrete blocks.

Q: I have to say that I've never quite heard anything that creates the type of musical spell that you have conjured up on your records, COMALA especially. It's like a fusion of ancient spirits with modern vibrations. I heard you recently went into the jungles of Mexico for a time, no one knew where or how to reach you. Is there a mystical element perhaps that enters into your process of musical creation?

A: Last year, after my arrival home from Germany and Morocco, I intensively traveled throughout the Mexican Indian zones. I met a lot of musicians and researched the music and collected a large number of authentic instruments. It was an incomparable experience since I was able to learn and experience so much of these cultures.

Q: Music can be a means of very personal communication. What do you hope that people will experience or come away with when they hear your work?

A: I attempt to make music that will reflect the vast range of sophisticated technology, but at the same time contains a deeper ritualistic sensibility, ancient and primitive sounds and cyclic rhythms. I try to accomplish something more than just allow for good listening, I am not saying that it has to be unique and original, but more of a musical ritual character that demands a degree of audience participation. It is the audience, the people who complete the artistic connection as they interpret the music and allow themselves to be transported by it. As the listener pays attention to the music and discovers sounds, it takes his imagination away. I think it is suggestive music that opens little doors without taking the listener away to some particular place, but instead to the place where the listener wants to go.

Interview & Translation Assistance:
Francisco Otegui

Rock Music In The German Democratic Republic

Introducing EUROCK readers to the East German rock scene is difficult because of the big differences in territory, history, culture and social organization between the USA and GDR. The territory of Oregon is in fact twice the size of the GDR, but East Germany has more than eight times the population. Not to mention the long tradition of the Germans in culture, science, art and -- worse luck! -- in Germany's historic tendency toward destroying human worth. The question of the divided Germany and the existence of two different kinds of social organization of the territory in Germany's past has had a large influence on the development of rock in the GDR. It's impossible to discuss the large scope of this overall situation in a shorter article, but some basic social facts can be passed on that will help an outsider understand the East German rock scene to some degree.

There is in the GDR only one record enterprise, the state VEB Deutsche Schallplatten, with the most important labels Eterna (for classical) and Amiga (for rock, pop, jazz). Every rock record is issued by this state operation, which has released 45's since 1956, LPs since 1961 and Stereo LPs since 1968. There is only one state radio enterprise as well, which has five channels. Since 1964 when the meeting of youth from both parts of Germany took place in Berlin (East), there have been some youth programs on various channels. The "DT64 Musikstudio" was one of the first. This ultimately developed into the fifth channel, now named "Youth Radio DT64," which broadcasts from 4 AM until Midnight every day. Similarly, there is only one TV network which operates two channels. They show the monthly synthi-pop-commercial oriented program "Stop! Rock!," and the monthly music journal *Dramms*. Most of the taped rock music is produced by the institutions of radio and record enterprises. A limited number are produced as well by state TV and the state film enterprise. There are no official private production companies, but some musicians own their own studios and offer their own productions to the state record companies. The synthe-pop group Servi has done this successfully.

As for live music, most of the rock events take place in private pubs, small youth clubs, state houses of culture, concert halls or in some cases little galleries. In the '60s, private pubs were the most important organizers, in the '70s the role of the colleges grew, now we can find all kinds of state organizers, but the private ones have become rare due to the high expense of operation these days. Most organizers now get the money from the State Ministry of Culture so the costs can be subsidized otherwise the tickets are so expensive few can afford to go.

Officially there are over 4,000 amateur

bands and over 1,000 professional bands. "Amateur" means that the musicians get their main income from other jobs and can only play on the weekend.

The decade of the 1980s began a time of great change in the GDR rock scene. A large number of the top musicians left the country for West Germany, many bands split up and others emigrated as a whole. So there grew a big hole in the production of records, radio programs and live concerts. Out of the remains of the groups/musicians that were left grew the beginnings of a new musical scene. The remains of one of the top groups, the Veronika Fischer Band, became the very interesting Pankow, a mixture of XTC/early Cure/Rolling Stones. The most important creative musicians had left however -- Veronika Fischer, Hansi Biebl, Nina Hagen a.o.... At the same time people became more interested in disco, sweet electronics and pop. The wayward wind of rock had left... The first simple videos were made and the visual aspect became more important. Possibilities for playing real rock became smaller as musicians' real expenses continued to rise and the opportunities to play live became less. Contract discotheques became more popular and a lively, energetic rock scene withered. The boom of necromantic, cheaply-produced electronic music began. Musicians like Reinhard Lakomy, naturally being gifted were offering a mixture between aesthetic conservatism in structure, sweet sound (don't really live, dream your life away) and modern, attractive sound. The likes of Pond, Key, or Servi work in the same way. There are no problems anymore.... I think Lakomy is now one of the richest musicians in the GDR as his music overflows in all the airports, shopping centres and TV news shows. The same goes for Pond, there is no rest in between two TV shows without Pond music as their sound is used on most all commercials, etc. Interestingly, every Pond or Lakomy album gets bad critical reviews, but sales are great and they continue to be able to produce new music.

Some of the more interesting bands of today are: Silly, who is connected to Nina Hagen's ex-manager and offers a fantastic mix of reggae or Eurythmics rhythms, perfect sound, different and imaginative compositions and biting lyrics. Silly deals with existential problems like loving under the sign of the bomb, social corruption, lost idols and the desire for fantasy. It's high-powered, emotional music, rock for today at its best. Then there is the aforementioned Pankow which bases its sound on the Rolling Stones or more importantly early XTC or the Cure. The name Pankow is phonetically derived from "punk" and the East Berlin district Pankow. Their music is straight-forward rock including the cabaret-like performance of frontman Andre Herzberg. The band mainly reflects the situations of a lost youth -- loneliness, daily trouble, little joys are the main topics. Similar to Pankow is Kerschowski. The main theme of Kerschowski's music is a battle against human loneliness, rock is identified with "love." In many ways they are reminiscent of the ideology of the '60s and their sound and lyrics reflect many of the ideas of that time. A direct comparison might be the mid-period Beatles (circa *HELP!*) or maybe even a touch of Bruce Springsteen.

Aside from this more "aboveground" scene, there is a big and very different scene of musical life without official recordings. Some bands exist in a grey zone of semi-official acknowledgment. Most are followers of the dada-post-punk movement and no-wave jazz. Searching for the true Brecht, fighting for exploding, expansive, truly innovative new musical forms, developing the progressive culture of post-punk, the connection of left-wing thinking with creative musical forms characterizes most of the avant-garde bands in the GDR, like: Demokratischer Konsum, Klick & Aus, Hard Pop, Die Anderen, Ag Geige, Muzzle Blues & Jazz Orchestra, Dekadance, Feeling B, Die Firma, Die Rundkopfe Un Die Spitzkopfe, Rennbahnband, a.o.. Musical roots are Weill, Eisler, Charlie Parker, Ornette Coleman, the present Euro-jazz scene, but also very importantly new music groups like Residents, Pere Ubu, Henry Cow, P.I.L., nearly all of the R.I.O.-style bands. To a great extent the bands of the GDR "underground" are the descendants of the post-'60s, 1970s experimental groups that built upon the traditions of rock, jazz and classics infused with the free from spirit that had taken root previously.

Electronic music is not counted as established music. There are several reasons for this: there are no synthesizers or computers available in the GDR aside from some old analog models; all new, high-quality equipment has to be brought in from abroad, mainly West Germany. But this is possible only for those bands who make tours of the Federal Republic of Germany (FRG), or have records for sale there. Such bands (Karat, Puhdys, Silly, Electra) can use part of their royalties and concert fees coming out of their work in the FRG to buy equipment. The cost, needless to say, is very high and most normal GDR bands can't afford to buy the latest gear simply to give special creative performances in little clubs. And remember there is only one record company, so the possibility to produce avant-garde/experimental music doesn't exist. This problem of very expensive equipment and limited production possibilities leads to a very derivative and less imaginative form of music designed to appeal to the lowest common denominator of public tastes. It is calculated for everyday utilization and has to be structured simply. It has to serve the desire of the masses for romantic dreaming and thoughtless, passive living.

The reaction of the GDR music critics illustrate very well this problem of creativity. I'll quote shortly from a journalist review of the most recent LP by Pond *AUF DER SEIDENSTRABE*: "The music is very boring and without any charm. Rhythm computer and sequencer create a rhythmic monotony. Some sound effects and silly melodies are added. The same case as for the first Pond LP, *PLANETENWIND*. But music like that of Pond is necessary, for instance in our TV to bridge the gap between two programs. But I don't want to listen to it at home."

I would finally say that I think music is more important than that socially and culturally. Kinds of rock are very different in different areas of today's world. But their main task remains the same everywhere and that is to help the people to live creatively, peacefully and happy in a human way.

Matthew Eastman

Congresso
Fifteen Years Of Musical Alchemy

One of the few consensus agreements about the popular Chilean music scene is that the group Congresso constitutes its highest expression. The group made its debut on August 24, 1970 and in spite of the many barriers that art forms have always faced in our country, the artistic strength of the band has enabled them to overcome any difficulties. A continuous spirit of renewal helps the group to mature and grow musically to this day.

Since their early days when Quilpue saw the group appear -- from which no one expected anything special -- inviting: "Rompe tu espada, vive la vida" (Break your sword, live life), each new work has resulted in a cascade of surprises, each new rhythm -- fruit of intuition or hard study -- crystallized with new force and creative talent.

The development of the band has been marked by continued creativity and the richness of their non-repetitive musical work. More than a half hundred original themes on record are the product of a musical alchemy formed by a diverse number of elements and influences. The musical consciousness of the band, free from all formal prejudices, travels from the carnival of the high plateau to the "carioca" (a reference to Brazilian folk roots), perambulates over the classic tonality, uses the continuous base -- typical of the Baroque -- and passes over the contemporary world of polyrhythms and polytonalities, fusing jazz with the "cueca" (typical Chilean dance), the "bolero" with rock and the symphonic, acoustic and electronic with a treatment of harmony that doesn't recall any comparisons.

From a textual perspective, the creations of Congreso present a wide open and all-encompassing cosmo-vision which is deeply humanist and open to the experience of faith.... A radical humanism that is not limited by any political or religious beliefs.

A look at some of their specific songs well illustrates this. On "Juego" (Game) from 1976, they said: "..sera la vida y la muerte juntas, la ronde que es la final. Alli estaremos tu y yo todas inmesamente alegres, reuindos..." (....it will be life and death together, the final round. There will be, you and I, all immensely happy, reunited...) And on "Los Maldadosos" (The Wicked Ones), from 1975, they confessed: "... Odio las infecciones como al la injusticia, el hambre de los humildes producto de la avaricia..." (I hate infections the same as injustice, the pauper's hunger, a product of greed). The totality of their work celebrates how beautiful it is to find a companion, a friend, a group who will sustain us, in spite of happenings that disgust us or fill us all with sadness.

Contemplating the musical life of Congreso we recognize two moments of a great cycle. Nucleus and founders of the group were the trio of brothers: Fernando, Patricio and Sergio Gonzalez (electric guitar, cello, drums, acoustic guitar and compositions respectively). A constellation of factors determined that they (who were part of the band The Masters during the '60s), got together with Fernando Hurtado (bass) and Francisco Sazo (voice & composer) who were with the Psicodelics. Added in 1974 was Renato Vivaldi (percussion & flute). That lineup stayed together until 1979 when professional obligations, parallel to music and the hard, painful path of survival of those devoted to art, caused them to split up. Vivaldi, Sazo & Hurtado left to pursue professional careers.

The Gonzalez brothers continued alone with their music, but not for long as soon a more solid formation was put together. Those who are part of Congresso since the dawn of the '80s are: Sergio - drums and compositions, Fernando - guitar, Patricio - cello, Jorge Campos - bass (of El Fulano, an avant-garde underground jazz group), Jaime Vivanco - keyboards (also of El Fulano), Hugo Pirovic - flute and chorus (the Director of Ars Antigua Group of Valparaíso), Jaime Atenas - winds and Ricardo Vivanco - percussion. We mustn't disregard either the importance of Eduardo Vergsis, the sound engineer and manager Michael Jones.

It's obvious that there's no relationship between the musical richness of Congresso and the level of recognition they have received. In spite of their sixteen years of continuous creation and seven albums -- *EL CONGRESSO* ('71), *TIERRA INCOGNITO* ('76), *CONGRESSO* ('77), *VIAJE POR LA CRESTA DEL MUNDO* ('81), *HA LLEGADO CARTA* ('82), *PAFAROS DE ARCILLA* ('84) and *ESTOY QUE ME MUERO* ('86) -- they are not a group who have achieved any level of mass popularity. This is due to the medium as well as the music itself. It's obvious that the music industry is only concerned with selling records, and for this it has created products that the greater public can assimilate easily, which are repetitive, have flat melodies, square rhythms and an absolutely empty content regarding the lyrics. Listen to any so called "international music."

All of these commercial masquerades are radically opposed to Congresso's musical creations. Their music is like an artistic work, highly complex and far removed from "popular" pretensions. Congresso demands a particular receptive attitude and a very different sensibility to that which is usually evident in "mass music." In this way, and at the same time, their high level of creation is a challenge and an invitation, a form of musical therapy. Another very important factor is that Congresso doesn't count on any outside vehicles to promote or support their artistic work, such as popular cultural figures or political parties, which is not uncommon here.

In spite of this hard road, Congresso continues on musically, looking toward the future. Last year the group undertook a tour of Southern Chile. The concerts were recorded and released as their eighth album, *EN VIVO*. They have since been composing new music which will serve as the basis for their next studio album. Also there exists the possibility of a European tour of Germany and France later in 1988 with the intention of making new contacts for promoting and releasing their music outside Chile.

From an article by Francisco Cruz
Adapted by Christian Landaeta

An Interview With Zardoz
Electronic Music From Belgium

Q: What have been your influences in terms of your musical ideas?

Jacques: Our musical research was enriched by a lot of new ideas as we came into contact with creative associations involved in dance, bodily expression, adventure games, text-writing. All of this should be included in the conception of a complete show.

Q: When did you become a musician?

Louis: In 1978, Jacques and myself started playing on synthesizers, but each on his own. In '79, a trio was formed including Jacques and myself. In 1981, Marc, Jacques and myself started Zardoz, Gerald coming in a few months later as technical advisor.

Q: What led you to form a group?

Louis: The basic element is our sincere love, perhaps we should say passion, for music and especially electronic music. The fact is that from listeners we became composers because we wanted to create music entirely reflective of our aspirations and also because creation is one of man's dreams isn't it? Hazard and maybe the meeting of our destinies allowed us to combine our interests and efforts.

Q: What is your formal musical education?

Jacques: In Belgium, there are no special schools for synthesizer. The best thing is personal experience, talks between musicians and technicians. International fairs for musical instruments are a good help too.

Q: What were your first instruments?

Jacques: MS-20 of Korg, a monophonic synthesizer with 2 oscillators already allowing at that time an interesting research of sounds.

Louis: System 100 of Roland.

Marc: I started with electric guitar, then acoustic drums, finally getting a Roland SH-1000 synthesizer.

Q: What music interested you in the past?

Marc: Chiefly Pink Floyd, E.L.P., Yes, Santana and Ten Years After.

Louis: Mainly Glam Rock: Bowie, Alice Cooper, Roxy Music, Lou Reed, E.L.O.

Jacques: First of all classical music like Tchaikovsky, and then I turned to groups like Iron Butterfly, Pink Floyd, E.L.P., Klaus Schulze and Ash Ra Tempel.

Q: What bands could you say may have influenced your style?

Louis: Tangerine Dream.

Marc: E.L.P., Alan Parsons.

Jacques: Tangerine Dream, Vangelis, Robert Schroeder.

Q: What kind of music do you presently listen to?

Louis: Essentially electronic music and classical.

Marc: Chiefly electronics, film music and rock.

Jacques: Of course electronic music.

Q: Do you see yourself moving towards any particular direction musically in future?

Jacques: A more elaborated sound research and conception of pictorial atmospheres seem to be our way now. On the other hand, we love to work with a particular album concept in mind so that will continue.

Q: In terms of your instruments, how do you see the development of electronic equipment?

Louis: We began using monophonic, modular and half-modular systems. We have always tried to follow the evolution of the technology of synthesizers and musical computers. From analog, we passed by the digital synthesizer to finally use samplers. This explains the permanent evolution of both our sound and compositions.

Q: What are your current instruments?

Marc: Strings Performer Crumar, Korg Delta, Jupiter 4 Roland, SH-2 Roland, TR-808 Electronic Drums, Juno-60 Roland and DX-7 Yamaha.

Jacques: Modular System Korg MS-50, ARP Odyssey, Formant Elector (home made), Vocoder Roland VP330, Modular System Roland 100M.

Louis: TR808 Electronic Drums Roland, Vocoder Synton, Drumulator, PPG Wave 2.0.

Q: Do you work with any unusual instruments?

Jacques: Before the MIDI system was first issued, we created our own systems with combination switches. The modular synthesizer Formant presented by the magazine "Elector" was realised and modified following the need of the group and adapted into 5 octaves in place of three and with a greater number of oscillators than previously schemed.

Q: Do you have any preference between analog and digital synthesizer?

Louis: Certainly the technical impulse given by the arrival of digital permitted more dependable and wavesteady instruments and a more developed harmonic richness. A wider spectrum of sounds became available with samplers which now allow greater orchestration and research into fantastic sounds that were not possible before. Nevertheless the sonorities of the analog synthesizer like the MiniMoog still have a more personal and warm character.

Q: You have your own recording studio, when did you first begin to build it?

Gerald: We started with the studio in 1981 when the group was founded and we became more and more professional.

Q: Where was it located and what equipment did you use?

Gerald: The studio of Zardoz is located in Waterloo, a south suburb of Brussels. We now use a mixing table Tascam, a multi-play special effects set up of reverb REV-7 Yamaha, SDE-3000 Roland, SPX-90 Yamaha, together with a personal conception of monitoring. We use our studio for the realisation of the multitrack tapes. The final mixing takes place in a more equipped studio which we hire.

Q: Perhaps you could give us some history of your releases to date.

Louis: Up to now we have recorded three LPs: *KRONOS* in '84, *TRAVEL* in '86 and this year our latest *ADVENTURE GAMES*. *KRONOS* must be heard as an contrast between electronic conceptions and the traditional approach. *TRAVEL* was an order for a ballet show. The main theme is travel through the five continents, it ends with a hymn to mankind. *ADVENTURE GAMES* is a concept album that operates on three levels: music, script and cover design. The theme is centered around

Adventure Games, but one must go further and approach this music as if it was but the initiation of a quest that we found also in literature, pictorial art, music and local cultures.

Q: Where were they produced?

Gerald: *KRONOS* was entirely produced in another studio. The other two were in Zardoz studio and final mixing was done elsewhere.

Q: What record labels were involved?

Marc: Zardoz has its own label: Nautilus Records.

Q: Do you make great use of digital samplers?

Louis: We have used the Prophet 2000, Prophet 2002 & Emax which work following the well-known principle of sampling.

Q: How do you feel about the legal questions concerning sampling?

Louis: We aren't much concerned by this problem. If sound is important in electronic music, we think composition and orchestration make the difference. We do not believe in the copyright of the sounds for ourselves but we do understand it for the firms who want to protect themselves.

Q: What do you think the future holds for such equipment?

Louis: It is likely we go to multi-function synthesizers, additive synthesis, FM synthesis and sampling, each part being interactive. On the other hand, the development of data processing should soon give us lower prices, better quality and greater possibilities.

Q: Taking into account all of this technological development, how do you approach the idea of being a musician?

Louis: At any time arts and sciences have been a source of progress for humankind But sciences only permitted development of the material and profane aspect of man; arts and music particularly allow man to come back to the prime condition of original initiation, that is to be conscious of his place as a privileged element of universal harmony. This explains the fundamental importance given by Zardoz to the creation of an atmosphere which is the chief component of the longest journey man can undertake; the quest for self-discovery. In that way music can serve as a traditional initiation of this quest, this naturally dictates that the aspirations of a musician, if not his task, is to help man to discover new spaces and dimensions to his consciousness, start and finish of the eternal creative adventure.

Archie Patterson

1989

Musea Interview

This past year, EUROCK readers have certainly noticed that many new records from France were being released by the Musea label, which specializes in the Progressive or New Music styles such as Classical Rock and Fusion. The guiding lights of Musea's faith are Bernard Gueffier and Francis Grosse, who along with a small team of friends -- Daniel Adt, Alain Juliac, Alain Robert, Thierry Sportouche, Jean-Claude Granjeon, Pascal Ferry, Thierry Moreau and François Arnould -- work to release the best in old and new Contemporary music from France. The following interview with Bernard and Francis gives an interesting insight into just how this unique independent label operates.

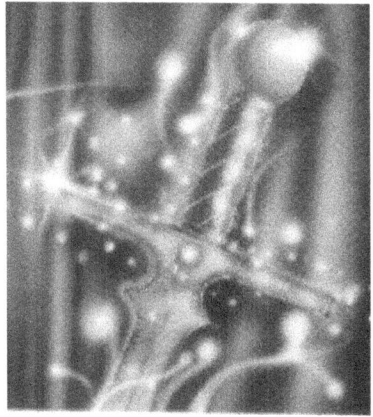

E: How did Musea get its start?

FG: First I met Bernard as a record collector and we traded records and found that we had similar taste for Progressive Music, particularly French bands. So we had the idea of putting together both of our knowledge about French Rock and to publish the first edition of *The French Rock Discography*.

BG: It took us one year to gather all the information and references. During this time we had close contacts with several French groups and discovered that most of them had released self-produced records, but had no way to distribute them. So as soon as our book was printed with the help of NOTES Magazine, we started to stock a few records from friends/musicians and make them available to a few people around us. In the meantime, we met Jean Pascal Boffo, who had just left the band Troll and was looking for a way to release his first solo album.

FG: We then felt the time had come to found our own label, both to help self-produced musicians for distribution and new musicians for production.

E: It seems like you didn't choose the normal channels to start your label or run it in the ordinary way.

BG: Yes, we noticed that this kind of music didn't fit very well into the regular commercial area. Firstly sales were too low for financial profit, then the musicians didn't trust very much the commercial labels as they feared losing their artistic freedom.

FG: So we used a special possibility under French law to set up a non-profit association, and created Musea so that no profit can be given to any private person, but only spent on further investment in the label. None of the people working for Musea gets any money from our work.

BG: In fact all of us have regular jobs and we don't need more money. This allows us to be completely free from commercial aspects and to be trusted by the musicians. Our choice of musical releases are based only on musical considerations. We will even release a record that we know in advance will not sell very much and that we will lose money on. Very few labels can say the same thing.

E: Your catalog includes records from other countries besides France.

FG: Yes, we try to keep our mind open to original music from all parts of the world. We released a French pressing of the last album by the German band Rousseau and prepare for in '89, a violin compilation with several German players.

BG: Our catalogue includes records from Germany, Switzerland, Holland, Spain, Italy, Sweden, Norway, Japan, Brazil, Mexico and even Guatemala. We found as EUROCK readers already know, that every part of the world has interesting music to offer.

E: You have a different way of working on your releases, a cooperation with the musicians instead of simply contractual relations? How does this work?

FG: We noticed that for most commercial labels, the number of units sold was the most important thing, not the music. We work from a totally different perspective. Our main interest is for the music and musicians, sales are secondary. If a release sell well, that's all the better.

BG: We tried to make our wish of a special relationship with the musicians concrete in two different ways. Firstly, we knew that in the process of releasing and distributing a record, most musicians neglect the second aspect of the business, they considered the release of the record as the final purpose without any idea of what to do with it afterwards. We met so many musicians with thousands of records in their cellar and no idea how to sell them that we had to explain the necessities of distribution and to increase their motivation to do it. For this reason we usually work in co-production with the artists, each gives half of the money, so we are all concerned with doing it the best way.

FG: The second part of our special relationship with the musicians is related to our non-profit status. As long as we cover our operating expenses, which are very low since we take no wages for our Musea work, we are able to give any profits to the artists directly. This allows us to offer a very large royalty rate, 70%-75% of the selling price, which is 6-8 times higher than the rates of the commercial companies.

BG: Those high royalty rates allow our artists to pay for each record with the income generated by the previous release. J.P. Boffo is a good example of this.

E: And what about your musical choices?

BG: We choose our artists and records in two different ways. First of all, of course, our personal tastes, which are different for both of us: Francis is mainly interested in the pure progressive style, while I prefer the New Music and Fusion school in the Magma vein. Of course each decision about a particular release has to be made by both of us and be something we both like.

FG: We also work for other reasons. We met so many musicians who create their music far away from the commercial and currently fashionable styles, that they have no hope to be signed by a commercial label. And there begins the other side of Musea's work, to allow original musicians to express their musical ideas apart from all business considerations, even if it doesn't fit totally with our personal musical tastes.

BG: And those two ways of working have led to the release of all our productions up to today.

FG: The last direction of our work is with reissues. As record collectors ourselves, we didn't like the extremely high prices for some rare French LPs. It made us mad because so many listeners couldn't have access to the music they were looking for, but also because a few people made huge profits on it.

BG: So we decided to make it possible for all listeners to hear those past gems by reissuing the most sought-after records from the French progressive scene. Our first three releases were published with the financial support of Cryonic Records on their own label. They were The Unnamables (Magma's first era under a different name), Komintern (a political underground band) and the first album by ZAO (the legendary offshoot band of Magma). Now independently we have also published the next reissues on Musea: Sandrose (an early French progressive group with astounding guitar work), Pulsar -- *HALLOWEEN* (one of the best French progressive records of all time), Arachnoid (King Crimson- and Ange-influenced), Terpandre (great violin and keyboard music) and Pulsar -- *BIENVENUE* (which was never commercially distributed). The newest reissues include both Shylock LPs, both Asia Minor LPs and the first two LPs of Atoll on CD.

E: Do you think you'll publish more and more LPs on CD?

FG: First of all we noticed that up to now, the LP format was the best way to distribute music; it's very hard for us to sell cassettes and 45's (for example our release of the excellent 45 by Elixir, "Regard," had very poor sales.) But now more and more customers, in fact most of the members of our association, ask for CDs. So we tried an experiment releasing the new Edhels album on both LP and CD. Our next releases on CD are Sandrose, Lorenzini (two former members of Edition Speciale) and Musique Du Delta (a fascinating mixture of synthetic world music).

E: Finally now, how do you see your future work proceeding?

BG: In fact we are rather optimistic. When we started the whole thing three years ago, none of us could have imagined achieving as much as we have up to today. We are particularly confident in the incapacity of most commercial labels to release inventive and original music, especially here in France. So the space for us to look for future collaborations is vast. And the more we publish alternative records, the more it gives musicians hope, so they can continue to undertake ambitious works. It's our part in the creative process and it feels good to know that without our efforts, many of the masterworks wouldn't be available today. That may seem a little pretentious, but it is a big part of our motivation. Our best reward is to see happy musicians and happy listeners, but also to enjoy ourselves the records we publish.

Archie Patterson

Discography Of Brazilian Progressive Music

Please Observe The Following:

(1) There is a question in Brazil about what can be called progressive rock, not only in relation to Brazilian artists, but those from foreign countries as well. This is the main reason why I refer to this document as about progressive music made in Brazil.

(2) Sometimes within the text you will read MBPR (Mainstream of British Progressive Rock). When I use this notation, I want to refer to groups like Yes, Genesis, ELP.

OS MUTANTES

In 1967, Brazil was living a golden age of popular music. There were annual editions of popular music festivals, and a particular movement, called Tropicalismo, rose during those festivals. One of the characteristics of Tropicalismo was the opening to every style of music and/or other arts. Mutantes were a group that grew out of that movement. Founder members were Arnaldo Dias Baptista (bass, vocals), his brother Sergio Dias Baptista (guitar, vocals) and singer Rita Lee (who played flute, tambourine, maracas).

Later a drummer was added, Ronaldo Lemo. From the fourth record on, Arnaldo went to the keyboards and Arnolpho Lima Filho came in as the bass player. As a quintet they recorded the 4th and 5th albums, before Rita Lee left to become a media star. The remaining four members recorded a 6th LP that was never released (a bootleg tape circulates among a few hands). After this, Arnaldo left the group to do solo work and Mutantes began to be guided by his brother Sergio. Arnaldo was the brain of the group, many artists in Brazil looked at him as their guru. After his departure he began to have personal problems as he got involved with drugs, his career became torturous. At the end of 1981, Arnaldo had an accident. When he tried to escape from a hospital through a window he fell from the third floor. People said he tried to commit suicide, but that's untrue. In 1981, I had a radio program and just one day before the accident he came for an interview and told me he felt like he had to escape from the hospital because he was sometimes like a prisoner there. The next day he took the wrong way out. He didn't die, but never completely recovered.

Arnaldo's departure left Mutantes without a course. It was about that time that the group initiated a work strongly influenced by MBPR, and their audience had a split reaction: some liked it, but the majority didn't. Sergio was a very good guitar player, but he killed a group that represented the main example of Brazilian progressive rock. Their first five LPs combined a large variety of instrumental sounds (sitar, tubular bells, woodwinds and orchestrations), with a fusion mix of Brazilian rhythms (samba, baiao, choro), even making initial experiments with atonalism, electronics, etc. These first five LPs were reissued in 1986 and are still available today.

OS MUTANTES (1968), *MUTANTES* (1969), *A DIVINA COMEDIA OU ANDO MEIO DESLIGADO* (1970), *JARDIM ELETRICO* (1971), *MUTANTES E SEUS COMETAS NO PAIS DOS BAURETS* (1972), *OAEOZ* (Bootleg tape of never-released LP), *TUDO FOI FEITO PELO SOL* (1974), *MUTANTES AO VIVO* (1976)

EGBERTO GISMONTI

Keyboardist/acoustic guitar player, Egberto Gismonti is a rare Brazilian musician who can write music for a whole orchestra. He doesn't like to be classified as a progressive rock musician, although he is very open to all kind of styles and works a lot with synthesizers.

Along with Mutantes, he appeared in the golden age of festivals, but not in the vein of Tropicalismo, instead his orientation was Bossa Nova. After two records, he went to Europe to learn more contemporary music. After two years as arranger for French singer Marie Laforet, he recorded his first LP outside of Brazil, called ORFEO NOVO, with bass player Jean-François Jenny-Clark.

Back to Brazil in 1972, he opened up more to jazz and electronics. From 1973 on, every new record has been a surprise. Sometimes solo, other times with sidemen or an orchestra. For people who like the music of Larry Fast, Tangerine Dream or Vangelis I recommend his *FANTASIA* and *TREM CAIPIRA* LPs. Fans of Henry Cow, Univers Zero and other R.I.O. groups will like *ACADEMIA DAS DANCAS, CORACOES FUTURISTAS* and *EN FAMILIA*. In addition to over 30 LPs released in Brazil, he has recorded several works for the German ECM label with Charlie Haden and Jan Garbarek. Today he passes the major part of his time outside of Brazil.

O TERCO

Formed in 1969 by Jorge Amiden (guitar/vocal), Sergio Hinds (bass/vocal) and Vinicius Cantuaria (drums), the history of O Terco is similar to that of Mutantes, but not so eclectic. They were a rock group that began to assimilate influences from MBPR more or less in 1973.

After their first album, Jorge left the group and nobody knows where he is now. On the second LP, Sergio Hinds took over guitar and Cesar das Merces joined on bass. *CRIATURAS DA NOITE* is their best work, even though it is the one closest to a MBPR orientation. That album marked the addition of keyboardist Flavio Venturini, a very good musician and vocalist. Two other LPs were made before the band broke up in 1978. In 1983 Sergio Hinds tried to have a reformation, but nothing happened. All of the LPs are out of print now and hard to find except the first which was reissued in October 1988 as a limited edition.

O TERCO (1970), *TERCO* (1973), *CRIATURAS DA NOITE* (1975), *CASA ENCANTADA* (1976), *MUDANCA DE TEMPO* (1978), *SOM MAIS PURO* (1983)

Sergio Hinds solo: *SERGIO HINDS* (1979), *MAR* (1986)

Flavio Venturini solo: *NASCENTE* (1982), *O ANDARILHO* (1985)

SOM NOSSO DE CADA DIA

In 1974, the mainstream of Brazilian rock was mainly headed up by Mutantes and O Terco. The group Som Nosso De Cada Dia was created in Sao Paulo, originally as a trio to follow the ways of that mainstream. The founding members were Manito (keyboards), Pedrao (guitars, bass, vocals) & Pedrinho (drums). *SNEGS*, the group's first LP is full of synthesizers and strong MBPR influences.

Manito was one of the first Brazilian keyboard players to stand out because of his use of Moog synthesizer. Although the music has little relation to any Brazilian roots (except some vocals à la Mutantes), the performance is very good. Som Nosso De Cada Dia are the best representative of progressive music in the Anglo tradition of Yes, Genesis, ELP, from Brazil. But they are the worst example of the true progressive music that stems from Brazilian roots.

The music of their second album is more Afro-funk directed. Manito didn't play on it and the basic lineup was augmented to become a quintet with the addition of a second percussionist.

SNEGS was reissued in October '88 in a limited edition, with a better sound quality.

SNEGS (1974), *SOM NOSSO* (1977)

A BARCA DO SOL

A good product of the flux of 1974 was the group A Barca Do Sol, from Rio de Janeiro. Highly devoted to Brazilian folk music, their sound was highly acoustic. A Barca Do Sol were the first Brazilian group to make full use of violins and cellos as well as flute and acoustic double bass. The original line-up had Nando Carneiro (guitar, vocal), Muri Costa (guitar, vocal), Jacques Morelenbaum (violin, cello, vocal), Marcos Stul (basses), Marcelo Costa (percussion) Beto Rezende (guitar, percussion) and Marcelo Bernardes (flute).

Some tracks on the first and second LPs had the help of Egberto Gismonti on keyboards. Their sound can be compared with nothing you've heard in the last 20 years. A true Brazilian progressive rock with a lot of native percussion. A Barca Do Sol are to Brazilian progressive rock what Los Jaivas are to Chilean progressive rock.

The first LP was reissued in a limited edition in October 1988, the other two are very hard to find.

A BARCA DO SOL (1974), *DURANTE O VERAO* (1976), *PIRATA* (1979)

ALPHA III

Alpha III is the pseudonym of multi-instrumentalist Amir Cantusio Jr., whose main instrument is keyboards. Amir lives in the city of Campinas (state of Sao Paulo), where he creates his music, partly in his home, and partly in a studio where he contributes to the production of radio and TV jingles.

The first LP of Alpha III was produced in 1984, Amir was helped by drummer Mauricio Lambiasi. That album didn't really represent the work of Cantusio very well as the styles were highly varied, from psychedelic to techno-pop. His second album was more in the style of Genesis, a group which he is completely passionate about.

To my own taste, his best work is *AGARTHA*. On that record he tried to create a highly varied musical experience, forgetting the MBPR. I feel he achieved his objective admirably, but the LP was not appreciated by the lovers of progressive music. I think Cantusio's work is well known in Japan and the Japanese collector's didn't like *AGARTHA* (I'm sorry for them because they don't know what they are missing musically). The difficulties with *AGARTHA* were disappointing for him and in further works he went back to a more MBPR style.

RUINAS CIRCULARES being based upon a novel by Argentinean writer Jorge Luis Borges. *TEMPLE OF DELPHOS* is centered around legends from Greek mythology. He is now preparing to release a new *LIVE* LP and is playing keyboards with a new progressive band called Faunus.

MAR DE CRISTAL (1984), *SOMBRAS* (1986), *AGARTHA* (1987), *RUINAS CIRCULARES* (1988), *TEMPLE OF DELPHOS* (1988) (All LPs were independent productions of 1,000 copies)

SAGRADO CORACAO DA TERRA

Sagrado Coracao Da Terra are a group led by Marcus Viana, a virtuoso violinist and keyboard player who also sings and writes the music/lyrics of the band. They are the best group of progressive music in Brazil today. Their work is highly influenced by MBPR and international progressive bands like PFM, but Viana always takes care to put into his records a personal feeling and cultural roots of Brazilian erudite music. Born in Belo Horizonte (state of Minas Gerais), where he lives and works. He studied music and Human Sciences (such as Philosophy, Languages and Literature). His lyrics talk about existence, the ways of mankind and are intended to make the listener reflect on himself. In some ways he might be comparable to Peter Hammill, but he definitely has his own style.

In terms of music, the compositions are vigorous and well-produced, the violin interacts with other instruments (guitars, drums, flutes and keyboards). Sagrado were the first Brazilian group to have their work produced on CD in Japan. Both albums were independent productions in Brazil, now the second has been pressed up by CBS.

SAGRADO CORACAO DA TERRA (1985), *FLECHA* (1987)

MARCO ANTONIO ARAUJO

Marco Antonio Araujo was another musician from Belo Horizonte. He played acoustic guitar and cello, and the major part of his works are instrumental. In 1970, at the age of 20, Marco went to live in London. There he became a fan of the music of Led Zeppelin, Pink Floyd and other groups of the British scene. After about two years he came back to Brazil and took up playing cello. In 1981 he made his first LP, as an homage to his heroes (Jimmy Page and Pink Floyd for example). The LP's title *INFLUENCIAS*, illustrates this. His most complex work is *ENTRE UM SILENCIO E OUTRO*, which could be described as chamber music. The others are a mixture of MBPR and Brazilian folk music of his state (Minas Gerais). Marco Antonio Araujo died in the beginning of 1986, due to a brain aneurysm.

INFLUENCIAS (1981), *QUANDO A SORTE TE SOLTA UM CISNE NA NOITE* (1982), *ENTRE UM SILENCIO E OUTRO* (1983), *ANIMAL RACIONAL* (1984), *LUCAS* (1985)

GRUPO UM

Grupo Um were an instrumental group from Sao Paulo, formed by musicians who used to play with Hermeto Pascoal (a very good Brazilian jazz musician). Their works are very good, and I'm sure they would appeal to people who like such groups as Henry Cow, Soft Machine, Magma and Univers Zero. Their third LP is very experimental, and it's the best example to people who would like to hear the true Brazilian new music. Grupo Um played outside of Brazil and some of their LPs were issued in countries like Germany and France. It's a pity that they have now split up, because they could have done much more in the future if they could have gotten more recognition internationally. The original lineup had: Lelo Nazario (keyboards), Zeca Assumpcao (bass, piano), Ze Eduardo Nazario (drums, percussion) and Carlos Goncalves (percussion). Some invited musicians played with them. Their records are absolutely out of print now and I'm sure they would like to have them reissued by someone outside of Brazil?

MARCHA SOBRE A CIDADE (1979), *REFLEXOES SOBRE A CRISE DO DESEJO* (1981), *A FLOR DE PLASTICO INCINERADA* (1983)

BACAMARTE

Bacamarte are a fruit of the '80s and you will find on their only LP nothing of authenticity. Much like the group Som Nosso de Cada Dia, they had good musicians, but sounded as if Jethro Tull met Genesis and PFM. The lineup was: Mario Neto (guitar), Sergio Villarim (keyboards), William Murray (bass), Mario Leme (drums), Marcus Moura (flute/accordion), Mr. Paul (percussion), Delto Simas (cello) and Jane Duboc (vocal) or Mirian Peracchi (vocals at their live concerts). Their LP is now absolutely out of print.

BACAMARTE (1983)

TERRENO BALDIO

Terreno Baldio are the true Brazilian Gentle Giant, with all the conventions that the music of that famous British group had. Their second LP is as if Gentle Giant had tried to play Brazilian folk music, and a bit more interesting. The original lineup had: Lazzarini (keyboards), Mozart (guitar, vocal), Joao (bass), Jo (drums, percussion), Fusa (vocals, percussion) and Peninha II (sound operator). Their LPs are now absolutely out of print.

TERRENO BALDIO (1976), *ALEM DAS LENDAS BRASILIERAS* (1977)

BIXIO DA SEDA

Another group of the 1974 flux is also from Sao Paulo. The only LP they made had a crazy mixture of influences, where Pink Floyd met Santana and the Rolling Stones. The lineup was: Renato Ladeira (keyboards, guitar, vocals), Marcos Lessa (bass, vocal), Mimi Lessa (guitar, vocal), Edson Espindola (drums, percussion, vocal), Fuguett Luz (flute, percussion, vocal).

BIXIO DA SEDA (1974) (reissued in October '88, in a limited edition)

TELLAH

Tellah was an ingenuous trio of musicians that became well known after Japanese record collectors received their LP in some trades. Their only LP is more famous than good (and very hard to find). Imagine if Rush tried to play the music of Yes and Genesis, that was the sound of Tellah. The basic lineup had: Claudio Felicio (guitars, vocal), Denis Torre (drums, keyboards, vocal) and Marconi Barros (bass, keyboards, vocal).

CONTINENTE PERDIDO (1980)

Valdir Montanari

1990

Tangerine Dream 1990

The saga of Tangerine Dream is in many ways the story of Edgar Froese and his 25-year quest for the musical grail.

From his first days in 1965 with The Ones, an Anglo-derived rock-and-roll band who got their initiation into avant-art circles via forays to France and parties at Salvador Dali's villa, to the heady times of Tangerine Dream's first free-form rock excursions in Berlin's Zodiak Club in 1968, Edgar was a musician intrigued with the fringes of new sound. After a voyage to England in search of an open ear for his new musical ideas ended in rejection by all of the commercial record companies, he returned to Berlin still determined to continue on with his experimentation. He gathered together two of Germany's other early sonic pioneers, Klaus Schulze and Konrad 'Conny' Schnitzler to create a tape collage of wild new sounds they dubbed *ELECTRONIC MEDITATION*. Even though done without the use of synthesizers, it's nonetheless considered to be one of the first 'electronic' works to come from what would later become known as 'The Berlin School' of electronic music, characterized by a dark, sequentially-based sound and dramatic melody lines.

Enter one Rolf-Ulrich Kaiser, a pop art entrepreneur who ventured where no mainstream record company would dare. He created the Ohr Musik (Ear Music) label and literally gave birth to a new German musical scene that abandoned the Anglo roots, which up until that time had dominated all 'pop' music in Germany. TD, Popol Vuh, Ash Ra Tempel and Klaus Schulze, along with a host of other underground artists made up the Ohr roster. The music of all involved was crude, rude and ultra-experimental, in short absolutely fascinating in many ways.

Kaiser gave Edgar and friends new life and over the span of three years they recorded a total of four albums: *ELECTRONIC MEDITATION, ALPHA CENTAURI, ZEIT* and *ATEM*. They initiated a whole new genre of music that came to be known as 'space music' or 'cosmic music' (both terms being the result of Kaiser's marketing genius). Fueled by ample doses of imagination and LSD, TD was a musical revelation to all who heard them.

In fact even John Peel, the guru of the U.K. airwaves at the time, picked up on their vibrations. Lo and behold the innovative new English label Virgin Records offered the band big bucks and the chance for a wider audience. So Kaiser became history as Edgar and mates moved on.

At this time the band stabilized around a nucleus of Edgar, Peter Baumann and Chris Franke. The works of this initial Virgin period showed the band at their best. *PHAEDRA, RUBYCON* and the live recording *RICOCHET* reached new levels of creativity and certainly are among the best synthesizer records ever to come out of the pop/rock field. At this point touring also picked up, as they played to ever-growing audiences all around Europe. More records were released, sophisticated equipment added; the band became a growing business concern (though not yet very profitable) and personnel went through several changes. The future was closing in fast.

That future began with their work on William Friedkin's *SORCERER* soundtrack. A commercial failure, it nonetheless was a critical success, and planted the seed that would sprout sometime later when the band did the music for Michael Mann's *THIEF*. That recording opened the door to their soundtrack work, which ultimately led to financial success and a full-blown career for the band doing music for films. TD's music communicates its cerebral message best when viewed in conduction with a strong visual image, so it comes as no surprise that this marriage of sight and sound has led to some of their best work in the later years.

Today Edgar has long since left behind his exploratory days of totally improvised concerts and extended forays into uncharted realms of sequential, synthetic collages. The band had entered a New Age bracket, and changed labels again. Edgar and his current Dream-mate Paul Haslinger use new computerized equipment and an era of profitability began. All of these changes are reflected in the music as well. Their most recent releases on Private Music (former member Peter Baumann's high profile New Music label), contain splashes of melody and pop-conscious compositions perfect for the times.

To this day the music of The Dream continues to turn-on a multitude of people all around the globe, as fans eagerly await each new release.

Archie Patterson

Klaus Schulze 1990 -- Interview

With the release of Klaus Schulze's 21st album *MIDITERRANEAN PADS* in January 1990, a third decade of activity begins for one of the original German pioneers of electronic music. This would seem an appropriate time to look back over his career at some of the groundbreaking musical activities he has been involved in. The following interview sheds also some light on his current activities and thoughts in relation to the music business and his creative work.

Q: In addition to being a founding member of both Tangerine Dream and Ash Ra Tempel, two of the original German experimental bands, when you look back on the "cosmic music era" now, how do you feel about those times and the music you made?

A: Those times are one generation old, they have been gone for 20 years... These times are over, and they will not be changed by what I tell about them today. If you can get these old records, or better: if you still own them, listen and make your own judgment. Don't ask me if they are good or bad. I haven't heard them for 15-20 years.

Q: Another major development for you was the founding of the Innovative Communication label. Why did you decide to start I.C.? It seemed to be a success, why did you sell it?

A: Innovative Communication was a nice and important thing but much more important for me is my music, for instance the recordings of *TIMEWIND, MOONDAWN, X* and *MIRAGE*, all with no connection to I.C. These discs are "major developments" for me. I sold it because, mainly, I'm no businessman. To lead a company you have to be such a person. Or you have to find someone to do this job properly, without stripping you to the skin.

Q: You also around that time established a synthesizer music school. What was that about and how did it go?

A: The school was a part of the whole I.C. idea: studio, label, school and later also video. A whole concept, based on "my" electronic music, and sponsored by the money I earned with this music. The school got some attention, but very few pupils, and was dropped after a year or so.

Q: After I.C., you tried again with the independent Inteam label. Was that a success at all?

A: That I.C. spent a lot of money was not

a problem for me. But they produced music in my absence which was not intended when I founded the label. So I did Inteam "this time really and only for Electronic Music" I told everybody. But intentions aside, I was still no businessman. And my "partner" at that time, Rainer Bloss, sorry to say, was even less than me into business matters. So sooner or later we went bankrupt.

Q: After these experiences with I.C. and Inteam, you went back to the label Metronome. What lesson, if any, did you learn from these ventures?

A: I "went back" to Metronome during the moneyless times at Inteam, because I needed money to keep Inteam running, so I sold my soul again to Metronome. In general I'm satisfied with this company. But even though outside of Germany I have the biggest articles and the best reputation, this company seems unable to find other companies in other countries [for licensing].

Also at the moment there is someone at Metronome (our contact), who works as follows: In January 1989 he tells us (finally!) that they will release *X* and *MOONDAWN* on CD in March, maybe April. March went, April comes, no CDs. "Oh, they will come out in June, definitely June," he tells us. June comes and goes. In July he says "not before September." OK, September, so we again inform everybody (fans, dealers and journalists) for the third time about this and the important CD release of my "highlights." And then, when I finished the new production *MIDITERRANEAN PADS* and brought the DAT tape to Metronome, the same man (Oliver Helwig) told me personally that the CD release of *X* and *MOONDAWN* would not be before March 1990.

And, of course there's the release of the new album, only in January 1990, although I had a nice offer for an important concert in London on December 2, 1989 and the British distributor wanted this disc [to support the show], and time to release it was plenty, Metronome said "No," so we had to cancel the concert in London. These are the daily troubles we have to deal with, but I fear other companies are the same? Not to mention all the promises for this and that advertising each time I deliver a production. Just "big talk," and no action by Mr. Helwig. I "learn" from business that it seems as if we [Germany] are getting more and more "American." You can trust hardly anyone anymore. Everyone just wants to make a fast buck, but nobody wants to work for it, maybe hard, maybe a long time, maybe for an idea...

Q: During all these changes your music continued to grow creatively and change in some ways. Some people feel that when you changed over to digital/computerized equipment, your sound became less experimental. Do you feel that the new technology changed your music at all?

A: My music changes the same way I change. Getting older, maybe wiser, maybe trembling; "new technology" is one part of the changes. My music lives because there are two parts involved: me who is doing it, and you/them, who are listening to it. Who I am, I know. Also I know my tastes, my changes, my everything. What about the others? These are the masses, and alone because of their numbers much more important. What do they think, what fashions do they follow, what traps do they fall into and what do they know about "digital," about "experimental," about "music," and what do they pretend to know about all of that?

Maybe what people perceive as being "experimental" changes when they grow older. When they learn while listening, when they... It must not always be the artist who changes. The music on *IRRLICHT* is still the same, but the times have changed. Today there's nothing spectacular about such a record, only in a historical context IRRLICHT was a venture. Of course the techniques of my equipment change the way I make music, but much more it changes the listening. Have you noticed, that with the spread of CDs the question from one fan to another isn't anymore, "Isn't this music fine?" but instead "Listen to this clear sound, man?" I have to cope with this new way of listening. But I do not think about whether this or that new instrument "changed my music" at all.

Q: How do you feel now about those older records, like *IRRLICHT, CYBORG, TIMEWIND, MOONDAWN, MIRAGE* and *X*? To me they represent the best works of your early and middle periods.

A: This listing I would do exactly the same, chronologically as well as a kind of "Best Of" in regards to the chronology. I feel good about these older records. I feel glad that I made them, and I think it is a shame that as of now [November 1989], "my" record company Metronome has not released four of these six milestones on CD!!

Q: In fact, I think some or all of your albums were issued in the USA on Gramavision label. Did you get a big reaction from this?

A: Gramavision. A "big reaction"? Nothing at all. No, definitely NO. As far as I know they released 5 LPs (only LPs, no CDs). A fan [!] from Canada is researching the politics of this situation with Gramavision, nobody seems to know exactly what they are doing. German Metronome always told us, "everything is OK, it's a fine company." My USA sub-publisher writes, "sorry, no money from Gramavision, the situation is unclear." When I was in New York City, of course I visited their office and they had changed people and their name?!?! Another fan [!] from overseas told us that in Spring 1990 my records will be released in the USA on a label owned and distributed by Rhino Records?!?

Q: *MIDITERRANEAN PADS* is your 21st album, do you think it is a change in any way from your past sound?

A: Please do not ask me about my latest record. Listen to it yourself and decide if you like it or not, if you think it is similar to this-or-that. It is nearly the same music I played live at a concert in Dresden, East Germany in front of 6,800 people. They went crazy (positive).

Q: What does the title mean?

A: Guess for yourself. I accept every explanation.

Q: It has been some time since you've done a live tour. Do you have any plans for future concerts?

A: Right. I had my last real tour of Europe in 1985. I did such tours regularly since 1973 or 1974. In the beginning it was fun, it was a kick, and we had no problems with money, stardom, promoters, and so on. We: that includes my roadie all these years, Klaus D. Mueller. Later these tours became more and more business, and less and less they brought me joy (or any money!) The promoters seem to have lost any interest in the music, the whole affair became just a rip-off of the audience sometimes. The concert halls were lousy too. The tour manager, a heavy metal fan. Including heavy drinking. No, I said to myself. No more of this annoyance and stress.

If from time-to-time I get a nice offer for a

single concert (maybe once a year), the conditions are good, and my general impression of the promoter is good, then I will give solo concerts. This was the case in Dresden (August 5, 1989), and almost on December 2 in London. But as I told you before, my record company wasn't interested (and a promoter needs their support). Even though the concert contract for London was fine, suddenly the promoter wanted the "video rights." No way! My (and KDM's) idea: once a year a nicely promoted solo concert, for a good fee, good conditions (electricity, stagehands, thousands of other small important things), and each year in another town. Say 1990 in London, 1991 Paris, 1992 Stockholm, 1993 Madrid... One can dream, can't I?

Q: If there was one thing you would like people to get out of listening to your music, what would it be?

A: Maybe a contradiction for you Americans: take it as art, but don't take it too seriously. This just came to my mind: sounds good and "important," but is maybe pure nonsense? I'm much more interested now about what will happen in East Germany. In "The East" in general. I can watch East German TV, it's thrilling. I watch history!! Besides my own music, that moves me at the moment.

The moment is 11-11-89.

Archie Patterson

Amon Düül II

1968 is a year that will go down in history socially, politically and musically as a watershed time. Students at the Sorbonne nearly brought down the French government with their May revolution. In the USA people took to the streets of Chicago at the Democratic Convention and catalyzed a political movement that would affect foreign policy for years to come. And last but not least, Kenso's axiom "when the mode of the music changes, the walls of the city shake" became a modern reality as psychedelic music burst into full bloom. Worldwide the boundaries of rock were being stretched to the limit by the integration of the guitar, electric amplifier and psychedelic experimentation.

The prime movers of this "happening" in the USA and England are well-known, but when it comes to sheer electric power and pure experimental passion, it's perhaps Europe, and Germany in particular, that produced the most awesome exponents of sonic rock: Amon Düül II.

The original Amon Düül -- the tribe of the Sun God Amon -- came together in Munich, the south of Germany, in the late 1960s. One of the early German alternative lifestyle communes, there were in fact two musical factions. Amon Düül I was interested in tribal rhythms and random electric guitar excursions. The prime members of this group being Rainer Bauer and Ulrich Leopold. Together with various friends they recorded several legendary jam sessions that represent some of the most anarchistic rock music you're ever likely to hear. On the other hand there was Amon Düül II, consisting of Chris Karrer - guitar/violin, John Weinzierl - guitar, Falk Rogner -organ, Dave Anderson - bass, Renate Knaup & Shrat vocals and the double drumming of Peter Leopold and Dieter Serfas.

At this time the German rock scene consisted mostly of cover bands who copied Anglo-American styles. Only a few people explored the extremities of a new sound and one of the first recorded works from this underground scene was Amon Düül II's *PHALLUS DEI*, recorded in 1968. Even today it still stands as one of the most powerful reminders of the psychedelic music era, with its incredible rhythmic drive provided by the two drummers, thunderous bass pulsations, crashing guitar chords, echoey keyboards, sawing violin and weird vocals & effects.

This debut was followed by the even more adventurous double album *YETI* in 1970. Augmented in the studio by various musician friends this time out, record one is an incredible blast of searing guitars, waves of keyboards sound and driving energy all arranged into an extended compositional context full of weird musical twists and turns along with absolutely fierce instrumental playing.

Record two takes the whole affair even more far out with long improvisations "Yeti Talk To Yogi" and "Sandoz In The Rain." They literally fuse layers of guitars, keyboards and taped effects into a purely acidic collage of rhythm and melody. *YETI* to this day is truly mind-boggling listening.

The question was "where would they go from here?" and the answer came with the 1972 album *TANZ DER LEMMINGE*. Another double album, it went far beyond being simply "psychedelic rock" into a new realm that was appropriately dubbed, by the fascinated English music press, as "space rock." Gone were the gimmicks and crude sound of before as a change in studio and personnel brought on a new, more sophisticated sonic approach. Composed basically of four side-long thematic musical compositions, never has a concept album been more fully developed and successfully pulled off.

Record one was composed of "Syntelman's March of The Roaring 70s," Chris Karrer's socio-political meditation on the post 60s/stylized 70s future shock. Full of layers of electric and acoustic guitars, dense keyboard/Mellotron and flowing rhythmic/melodic textures, it was like a musical magic carpet ride. The other track, John Weinzierl's "Restless Skylight - Transistor Child" was even stranger. A sci-fi epic of sorts, it detailed the crash-landing of an ET on Earth and his subsequent trials and tribulations. A Steven Spielberg fantasy it was not. Weinzierl's guitar and supersonic electronic arrangements made the whole affair sound like some kind of avant-garde rock soundtrack for "The Man Who Fell To Earth." Truly it's a unique and provocative musical conception.

Record two consisted of "The Chamsin Soundtrack," a series of "environmental" works heavily featuring synthesizer, guitars, percussion and effects, all laced into a surreal musical flow. A precursor of today's electronic New Age perhaps, without all the syrupy whitebread pseudo-consciousness?

After *TANZ DER LEMMINGE*, a decision was made to come down to earth, so to speak. Their experimental psychedelic period effectively came to an end. Song structures replaced the wild sonic explorations. Musically the band became much better as their imaginative ideas were more completely integrated into a progressive rock context. The series of albums that followed exhibited in some cases flashes of pure brilliance. In particular *WOLF CITY* ranks as one of the definitive progressive space records of all time. It's on a par with any of Pink Floyd's more critically acclaimed works. Their later double album, *MADE IN GERMANY*, was a rock opera that is comparable to *TOMMY* and *THE LAMB LIES DOWN ON BROADWAY*, without those efforts' Anglo-pop pretensions.

With the coming of the 1980s the legend of Amon Düül II. has all but faded into posterity. Aside from one fine reunion LP titled *VORTEX*, the only other releases have been collaborations between Dave Anderson, John Weinzierl and various English artists, the results being wildly uneven. Now with the reissue of their four classic works on CD, perhaps they will at last be recognized as one of the great pioneers of experimental rock music. Rumour has it that the original band may try a reformation as well. In any case, the music is there to discover for all who are willing to turn on, tune in and flashback.

Archie Patterson

Uakti
The Sound Of A Legend

We are living in an age where we usually talk about the forests of all the world, and particularly of those in Amazonas, Brazil. These comments are due to the fact that, in the name of progress, mankind is destroying large green areas of our planet, creating problems of the environment. This discussion has increased since December 22, 1988, when Chico Mendes, a leader of the rubber gatherers in Amazonas, was murdered in his own house. Chico was a true soldier in favour of preservation of the forests.

These troubles are serious, but let me leave them for a while. I recalled them because I want to talk about a Brazilian musical group that gathered their musical motivation from an Indian legend of Amazonas. The group is called Uakti. It is written on the front cover of their first album.

> "Uakti" lived on the edge of the Rio Negro. His body, full of open holes, received the wind & emitted a vigorous sound that attracted all the women of the tribe. The male Indians, with their hearts taken by jealousy, persecuted Uakti and killed him, burying his body in the forest. Tall palm trees grew up there. So the Indians made musical instruments with their stems and the sounds they produced were ethereal and moody, like the wind through the body of Uakti. Listening to these sounds, the women will be filled with temptation and succumb to the men of the tribe & lose their purity.
> - From a legend of the Tukano Indians

Based upon the legend of the Indian giant, five young guys began to work in the first days of the 1980s in the city of Belo Horizonte, state of Minas Gerais. They were Marco Antonio Guimaraes, Paulo Sergio Santos, Artur Andres Ribeiro, Decio Souza Ramos & Benito Menezes.

Marco Antonio was the mastermind of the group, responsible not only for the main compositions of the group, but also for the construction of the instruments. Yes, like the Indians, they decided to make their own instruments for the group. Marco Antonio used to say that his grandfather had a workshop and taught him to construct his own toys. This idea continued with him when he studied erudite music. Soon, he started to construct several instruments, using a variety of materials: glass, lids of pots, wood and PVC tubes.

On the cover of their 1st LP, *OFICINA INSTRUMENTAL* (1981), one can see the instruments constructed by Marco and on the record they can be heard. They initially wanted to produce an acoustic sound, nothing electronic is used except the microphones. But that conception has changed as electronic pickups were later added to obtain more effects. Also the purely acoustic instruments had to be very big and that was a problem when touring. Talking about that 1st LP, it was produced by Milton Nascimento, who later invited Uakti to play on several records.

In 1982, Uakti produced *UAKTI 2*. It was a little different than the first as they employed cellos, flutes, acoustic guitars, piano and the female vocalist Ines Brando. The sound was somewhat like the acoustic works of Egberto Gismonti.

1984 saw the release of their 3rd LP, *TUDO E TODAS AS COISAS* and a big tour of Brazilian cities. From that time on their fame grew. They got to play in foreign countries Argentina, Spain and Canada, and recorded a record in the USA that was an anthology containing tracks from their first 3 albums. The music was once again dominated by their handmade instruments and a more erudite sound.

It took five years for them to produce their newest album released in 1989. Titled *MAPA*, it was dedicated to Marco Antonio (Pena) Araujo, one of Brazil's best musicians who had died that year of a brain aneurysm. He was a great friend of Marco Antonio Guimaraes. This is probably the most electronic work of Uakti. I saw them play live last year and they used synthesizers along with their natural instruments. I have nothing against synthesizers. but I don't think Uakti needs them with their music. This last record was recorded for an independent label called Visom who hopes to export it to other countries of the world. Let's see..... ?

Valdir Montanari

1991

Erik Wøllo

Norwegian born Erik Wøllo made his musical debut in 1980 as a jazz guitarist in the band Celeste. His guitar talents show clearly on his first solo album *WHERE IT ALL BEGINS* ('83) as well as on the collaboration with oboe player Jan Weise and percussionist Rob Waring -- *WEISE, WØLLO, WARING* ('84).

In 1984 Erik began working with various different instruments such as flute and keyboards, and he also started composing for string ensembles and larger orchestras. His second solo album, *DREAMS OF PYRAMIDS* ('84), showed signs of things to come with the extensive use throughout of electronic instruments fused with jazz and rock influences.

With *TRACES* ('85), his distinctive electronic sound unfolds in all its beauty. *TRACES* brought his music to a new international audience as worldwide press and airplay spread his name outside the boundaries of Norway. His follow-up, *SILVER BEACH* ('87), continued in the same vein, developing his style even further with more complex rhythmic structures.

It took three years to come up with *IMAGES OF LIGHT*, his latest and most provocative album thus far. Released in Norway by the Origo Sound label, it has been licensed exclusively for the USA by EUROCK. Now all in this country can marvel at the lush melodies and richly evocative, spatial tone colors that make up the musical ambiance of *IMAGES OF LIGHT*.

Archie Patterson

Green Isac

Green Isac consists of Morten Lund and Andreas Eriksen from Oslo. *STRINGS AND POTTERY* is their debut release as Green Isac. The album took 3 years to complete and offers up a fascinating blend of melody and exotic rhythm structures from Indian, Arabic and African percussion mixed with modern sampling technology.

Morten Lund plays various keyboards, guitar and flute. Previously he has played with several rock bands, the best known in Norway being In Limbo for which he recorded two albums in the late 1980s. He has also done production work for numerous other Norwegian groups.

Andreas Eriksen has studied percussion techniques for 10 years, especially those of African and Arabic origin. This experience shows clearly in *STRINGS AND POTTERY*. He has also played with the Norwegian bands Ym Stammen and Bel Canto. On *STRINGS AND POTTERY* he utilizes several original African and Asian percussion instruments as well as sampled percussion from all parts of the world.

Green Isac may be influenced by Steve Reich, Philip Glass and Jon Hassell, but with their rock heritage and fascinating rhythmic structures, they offer a highly original and fascinating sound that will attract new music lovers worldwide.

Archie Patterson

Peru Interview

Ruud Van Es - Rob Papen - Peter Kommers - Jos Van Den Dungen

Q: Peru is one of Holland's longest-lived synthesizer groups. How long have you been together?

Ruud: For 12 years.

Q: How did you meet?

Ruud: Peter and I played in a rock band together. Peter played guitar and I played drums. We both had an interest in synthesizer music so we went out one day and bought two synthes and started practicing together at Peter's home. Using the first two letters of each of our names we formed the group Peru. We met Rob in 1980 at a Klaus Schulze Fan Club Day in Holland where he was performing, and invited him to join. He appeared on the "B" side of our first album. Jos, who is a formally-trained violinist, joined Peru in 1987. That's a real violin you hear on *MOON*.

Q: Who were your first/main influences in music?

Rob: Tangerine Dream and Klaus Schulze. I loved Tangerine Dream's *RICOCHET*, it made me decide I wanted to be a synthesizer artist.

Ruud: T. Dream and Schulze for me also. Klaus' *TIMEWIND* and *X* plus Tangerine Dream's *RICOCHET*.

Q: At one point you formed an offshoot group called Nova, why?

Ruud: Nova was just an experiment with a more mainstream, commercial form of music that we did for a while in the early '80s. One Nova track, "Aurora," did become a Number One song in Europe.

Q: Who do you listen to musically these days?

Rob: Nowadays my attention goes to all the fifties songs, and artists like Depeche Mode, Prince and U2. When I listen to synthesizer music it's Patrick O'Hearn, Dan Siegel, Talk Talk and Howard Jones.

Ruud: I listen to Peru, particularly *MACCHU PICCHU* (both laugh). Seriously, I still love to listen to the Moody Blues and Pink Floyd. In synthesizer music it's Vangelis. Also we've both been listening to Mark Dwane this past week and really like his music.

Q: How would you characterize your music?

Rob: We just call it nice music done with synthesizers. That's the main point. We like to create atmospheres with our music. We don't consider ourselves New Age artists, we're just composers and musicians who use synthesizers. For listeners, we try to provide a pleasant escape from everyday life.

Q: Do you consider your music to be cultural & socially relevant, or entertainment?

Rob: Our music is a part of European Pop culture.

Ruud: We don't have a message. We just want people to enjoy our music.

Q: What kind of instruments do you prefer to use?

Rob: We use newer instruments, but prefer to use the older ones. We use old analog systems in combination with sampling. Some of these are the Minimoog, Jupiter 8 from Roland, Akai's VX-600, and the TR808 from Roland is very important to us. We also use the American Alesis SR-16 drum computer. We don't use a lot of equipment, but what we do use, we use 100%. And we like to do live performances.

Q: Is there a current, coherent synthesizer music scene in Holland?

Rob: Yes, there are two directions in Europe. You have the traditional electronic music scene, but there is also a dance movement with "House" music. People are making their own dance music at home with analog synthesizers and samplers. It's very popular.

Ruud: This is the trend throughout Europe with very popular groups like T99 and Anastesia. You have "House" and "Techno-House." Techno-House is electronic music with Rap over it.

Q: Do you think musicians in Europe are somewhat isolated, doing their own thing making music at home or in the studio with little interaction?

Ruud: No. I think there is still a band feeling with many artists and we cooperate together. We are currently finishing a collaboration with Harald Grosskopf for our next album.

Q: What brings you to the USA?

Ruud: We gave a couple of sound seminars/mini-performances at the Berklee College of Music in Boston and Bradford College in Bradford, MA this past month and we are here to promote Peru's new CD, *MOON*. But we are also here to help promote other European groups and to encourage some American musicians to collaborate with us on sampler CDs with Euro synthesizer musicians.

Rob: We have so many letters from people in the USA who want more Peru music that can't be found in stores. Some people don't know that now all 6 Peru albums are available on CD. And we're sure that they would like to have music of other European artists as well. So we want to set up some distribution to make electronic music listeners happy on both sides of the world. We've been so pleased with the response we've had in the USA and surprised at the number of people who are already familiar with our music. We'd like to say thank you to everyone in the United States who enjoys our music and has made us feel welcome.

Janet Cucinotti 11/91

1992

Ralph Lundsten Interview

Ralph Lundsten is Sweden's best-known composer of electronic music, as well as being a film creator and artist. Born in 1936 in northern Sweden, he now lives on the outskirts of Stockholm, still close to the forests and sea. His home is Castle Frankenburg, dating from 1878, a wooden fairy-tale mansion which also houses his electronic music studio Andromeda. Since 1959 he has been creating his own personal musical language which incorporates his wide-ranging, cross-cultural activities and adventurous electronic imagination.

His music is unique in the field of synthesizer sound, combining the classicism of his Nordic Nature Symphonies with the more impressionistic tones of his various conceptual soundscapes. He employs some unusual instruments to create his diverse compositions: the Andromatic (made in 1959), which was one of the world's first synthesizers to combine polyphonic and sequential capabilities, the DIMI-O (made in 1970/71) that can produce music in an "immaterial" twelve-tone scale from the empty air, in front of a TV camera. The tones produced this way (or by using an ordinary keyboard) can be registered on a TV monitor as a music score. They can then be retrieved at any tempo, forwards or backwards, from the top or from the bottom, and at the same time changes can be made in the sounds and in the number of tones recorded. The DIMI-S (also known as The Love Machine) can generate sound and light by contact with the skin, reacting to the emotional state of the performers. These and his latest addition, the DIMI-A & DIMI 6000 micro-computer unit were invented by a Finnish physicist specially for Ralph and combine with other more conventional synthesizers to produce his unique sound.

The following interview done in Summer '92 gives a glimpse into the ideas which guide his work and life, thus serving as a human counterpoint to the magical sounds of his musical creations.

Q: You have a long history of experimenting with electronic music. What got you interested in the possibilities of synthesized sound and when did you do your first recordings?

A: First I started to write traditional music for orchestras in the mid-1950s. The scores got bigger and bigger... A Korean named Pyke (sp?) played some of my music in NYC, Central Park in 1966.

In 1959 I wrote a poem and changed all the words into a symbolic sound, and suddenly without knowing it, I had invented electronic music.

Q: You create albums that are conceptual, using music to paint a picture or create a mood, is there a central idea to your compositional style?

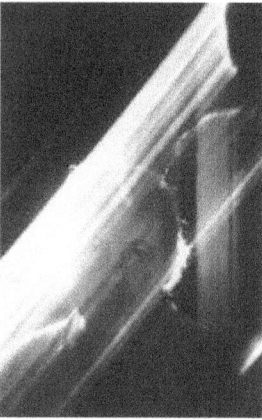

A: I have always wanted to manifest total harmony and rest and total devotion to a "life feeling." Music is to me the language of the soul, that takes over where words fail.

Q: Do you consider yourself a "pop" artist, neo-classical composer, or?

A: I am a Cosmic Composer with my feet on the ground and my head up in space (I consider pop music to be an endemic disease of our time).

Q: Aside from music, do you make films, paint or work in theatre?

A: In the 1960s I made my own short films, sculptures and had some idea-exhibitions. The short films won first prize at various festivals around the world.

Q: You have had a large number of albums released in Sweden and internationally, do you have any idea how many?

A: I have released 34 LPs and about 25 CDs and am trying hard to reach out to the rest of the world, but you never want to buy/sell my records, ha, ha! My time will come 10 years from now...

Q: You have a deal with Sony Music in Sweden, is it hard working with a multi-national company that mainly promotes super-stars?

A: Yes, it is difficult, but they accept that other companies help to sell my music.

Q: Perhaps you have no desire to be a "star," but only want to realize your own musical vision?

A: I absolutely do not want to be a "star." I prefer to unveil the secrets of life in silence.

Q: What do you hope people will experience when listening to your music?

A: I want my music to be a contact with eternity.

Q: It has been a while since you have released a new album, what plans for new music do you have for the future?

A: By the time this interview is published, my *NORDIC NATURE SYMPHONY NO. 6* and my *SEA SYMPHONY* will have been released, along with *MINDSCAPE MUSIC*, which is for meditation and *NORDIC LIGHT*, which is a CD made especially for distribution abroad, to the whole world.

Archie Patterson

1993

Homage To Eurock
A Personal View by Uli Trepte

In 1977, three years after the founding of my own group Spacebox as a solo act, I was on a 2-month information tour across the wide plains of the U.S. (taking a Greyhound bus, stopping only in New York and S.F.), and living for 2 weeks in a North Hollywood flat of a devoted Guru Guru fan. He was very enthusiastic about a progressive music magazine called EUROCK. He said the person who ran it would be very interested in my current work, so I rang him up. He obviously knew my background very well and did a phone interview that ran in the next issue with a live concert shot on the front cover. Since then I've been in touch with EUROCK and the man behind it, a contact that helped me through some isolated times that followed back in Germany with Spacebox, a group that hardly had a chance because the music was totally extreme and fit into none of the current grooves.

So between 1978-80, getting a copy of a new EUROCK (with often my name mentioned in it) and an encouraging letter from Archie, or formulating musical/social statements by writing him, meant for me not only being written about and therefore in existence for the World (some underground publications in England, France and Canada were doing that sometimes too), but helped me to keep faith in a time when no German alternative publication or distribution was in existence and it had become mentally and economically harder to continue in my chosen way.

The existence of EUROCK was always a topic when I talked with the other musicians I met on my travels or that visited me. Passing along the magazines address, helping establish contacts, led other groups like England's Legendary Pink Dots and Japan's Merzbow to find their first distribution.

Then in 1981 the first Spacebox LP appeared and it was EUROCK that in one batch, plus soon another one, ordered and sold more of it than I could sell in the whole of Germany. As time passed my musical concept seemed to be out of fashion. I constantly reduced it to a more basic, completely un-electronic, cyclic collectively improvised, modal harmonic music, which didn't even fit into the EUROCK catalogue anymore. But Archie always gave the records I made a try, while many others showed an increasing lack of interest.

Since 1985 I've been living in Berlin as an exclusive composer and performer of my own special minor modal instrumental blues. It's far away from anything EUROCK offers, as I am myself not in touch with electronic music at all these days. We write each other regularly because we both keep alive the same ideal of a free spirit and non-commercial musical way.

As I see it, EUROCK always looked for quality, not quantity (comparable only to Recommended Records in the U.K.). All the others (and since 1980 in a lot of countries were some distributors of so-called alternative/progressive music) seemed to take whatever was in style at the time, and dropped it if they thought the fad was over. They missed the actual feeling and commitment to the music which made the difference, Archie possessed both strongly.

It seems to me now that in America, EUROCK was THE focus for the kind of music that the official industry started to neglect in the early '70s (music that was outside/beside/underneath of rock, pop, jazz and avant-garde). I think without that focus this kind of music would have never had a chance to get known in the States, at least to the few who it did concern.

Today, to me, EUROCK is a rare example of, I'd call it culture. The work of a man who not only had a definite idea and followed it, but also had the true spirit for the matter (that's rare). I wish him all the best and say "thanks."

Uli Trepte, 25 January 1993

Sonic Reflections

As I ponder the sounds of yesteryear, there was one era that stood out first and foremost as the most creative, awe-inspiring, unforgettable time of them all. It was the great German "cosmic rock" experiments of the early 1970s.

Late 1960s psych and early Pink Floyd were the models the Teutonic foundation launched its rocket ship from. Throw in a little jazz, classical and a healthy dose of Stockhausen's experimental sound collages and the likes of Guru Guru, Faust, Amon Düül I & II, Can, Tangerine Dream, Ash Ra Tempel, Klaus Schulze, Popol Vuh, Neu!, Cluster and Kraftwerk were destined to flourish in the new sonic vanguard.

Was there ever a more mind-boggling, cosmically charged entity to these jaded ears than Amon Düül II's *TANZ DER LEMMINGE*? Twenty years later I say for certain, emphatically no! And the first Guru Guru! That high-degree of lysergic stimulation could almost make one hallucinate on aspirin.

Ten years later we had "new wave" and a few years after "new age," but where would the latter be without the incredible space weavings of the Tangerine Dream opus *ZEIT*, or the futuristic sound tapestries of early Popol Vuh and Klaus Schulze.

Simultaneous with new age, we had its diametric opposite "industrial," perhaps best personified by a newer German band, Einstürzende Neubauten. Yet the groundwork for Blixa's excruciations was no doubt funneled through the blender after absorbing the innovative electronics of Can, Faust, Cluster, Neu! and Amon Düül I.

One of England's top alternative acts of

the 1980s The Fall, wrote a Can tribute "I Am Damo Suzuki." Yet to this day, no one has approximated the aural landscape of *TAGO MAGO* which is sonic art in its most pure, unadulterated form.

Twenty years ago I was in my 20s when the greatest music of all time reached its apex. Twenty years later, I can look back and be proud to have been associated with EUROCK and a precious few others in an attempt to enlighten those with an open mind to the cosmic offerings these deities rendered.

To have been in the right place at the right time, was like a voyage to infinity and back.

Scott Fischer, 16 February 1993

EUROCK - Lost And Found

I hadn't talked to Archie in over 15 years, but all of a sudden his name kept cropping up everywhere. So I tracked down his number and gave him a call. We had a lot of catching up to do.

Back in the early '70s, it seemed like interesting music was being produced everywhere, worldwide. 'Round about 1973, I heard of this guy from Fresno putting out a magazine about all this new music, somehow Archie Patterson and I got in touch with each other.....

I wrote for a college paper at the time, reviewing "weird" bands like Jade Warrior, Van Der Graff Generator and Family. I was real fired up, trying to spread the word. I had read an article in *New Musical Express* about all these groups coming out of Germany, and in the process discovered a store in Berkeley, Rather Ripped Records, which sold the stuff. (Ed. note: they also sold the first issues of EUROCK, probably how we first got in touch).

I was hooked immediately by the sounds of Can, Faust, Amon Düül II, Guru Guru, Neu! and Kraftwerk. Music like nothing I was used to, cover art from beyond. Soon, I began to branch out into the Italian scene, then the unclassifiable bands of France, the jazz-infused groups from the Scandinavian countries and the raw, angry musicians from Eastern Europe.

I began to write for EUROCK in its second issue, contributing reviews of all my favorites; including Kraftwerk, Neu! and the Jim Pembroke-led version of Wigwam. Archie and Linda made a trip up to visit one weekend and we all saw Kraftwerk during their first US tour.

In spite of my youthful enthusiasm however, sometime later in the '70s I strayed away from these wonderful, creative bands. First came punk, which grabbed me in its tight little fist and shook me up. Then power pop which added some polish. Next, new wave, with its quirky attitudes and get-bent rhythms. The music of styles led me in the '80s to Kid Creole and the Coconuts (still one of my favorites), R&B, funk, reggae, calypso, soca, zouk and world beat in general. Ultimately, I came back in a round about way to Europe and all the still-very-interesting music being made by many of the same musicians I was fascinated with back then.

Now my love of music has taken me full circle .... as I find myself listening to Art Zoyd, Etron Fou, Cluster, Gong, Magma, Jim Pembroke and Wigwam, and many others..... all the way back to my old favorites of the '70s.

Which brings me back to EUROCK. It was such a nice surprise to hear that someone had remained true to the whole concept of "new music," and that Archie continues to write about and sell the music he's believed in all these years. I've taken more side trips than I can remember, but Archie has hung in there. It's great to be able to share in the 20th Anniversary of EUROCK. It's great just to be back.

Gregory Shepard, 20 February 1993

Testimonial...

Ahhh, the good old days.

Let's see, I started doing Hearts of Space in 1973, and I think I met EUROCK's fearless leader in 1976 or 1977. I remember talking to him on the phone a few times when he was in Fresno, CA and comparing notes about our shared passion for European progressive music. Then he moved up to Portland to work for an import mail-order company called Intergalactic Trading Company. After a couple years he moved down to L.A. to work for an alternative distribution company called Greenworld. Like 98% of the independent distributors, both companies went out of business a few years later.

But Archie stayed the course and decided to start his own mail-order business in addition to publishing EUROCK, one of the original alternative music mags. I remember going down to visit him and Linda (no skybabies yet) in darkest Torrance, in a so-called "garden apartment" located about a 1,000 yards from a rip-snorting, fire-spewing, evil-smelling Mobil oil refinery that would have thrilled any industrial music enthusiasts. Their apartment was a haven of order, sanity, good food and good music at the very epicenter of the SoCal wasteland. At the time I remember thinking it was like doing a hitch in the Cosmic News Service and being stationed on an alien planet.

As you know, Major EUROCK eventually returned to the saner (though wetter) pastures of Portland, where he continues today to ply his trade. A methodical chap, he has avoided the delusions of grandeur that seem to effect many music business workers, and stuck firmly to his small/ beautiful/appropriate economics model. His enterprise has endured and prospered, slowly but surely, even in hard times, despite his ceaseless whining about the state of the world on the editorial page.

He asked me to say something about how the scene has changed in 20 years. From the cynical, battered perspective of the '90s it's hard to convey the sense of excitement and infinite possibility that raged through musicians and listeners alike in the early 1970s.

For instrumental music, the arrival of practical synthesizers, inexpensive multi-track recorders and consoles, digital reverberation and sophisticated time-delay processors, computer-driven sequencers, and later sampling keyboards -- all these technologies energized musicians to build their own studios and create their own music as never before. The language and style of electronic music leaped out of the academy, into the hands of artists like Terry Riley, Vangelis, Klaus Schulze, Jean-Michel Jarre and ultimately headed down the street.

Everything was developing in a healthy fashion and the alternative music scene built a small, but effective worldwide infrastructure of artists, independent labels, new layers of non-commercial distribution, and its own enthusiastic press. Around 1986 this creatively disorganized scene hit critical mass and was briefly embraced by the mainstream record industry in what I have often described as a "new age feeding frenzy." (Of course everybody hates the name, and I am among those who'd like the industry to settle on the term Contemporary Instrumental as the larger category that holds all the many variations.)

A certified trend in the record business has a life span of around 18 months. Now that it's over, those of us who pre and post date it just got back to business as usual, with thanks for whatever expansion of the audience took place in those years. At the moment we're just over the top of the bell curve of the World Music run and multi-cultural source material is on it's way to becoming the norm rather than the exception. It's about time.

The '80s were a tough time for the kind of idealism that fuels progressive ideas in music. Hopefully we're past that now. The cosmic music movement seems to have run its course, but as a form of imagery space music has left it's mark on many other genres and styles from avant-garde to pop. It's a tough time for purists, but or those who get off on really creative music there's a lot to hear, and a lot to admire.

No doubt I'll have more to say in another 20 years. One thing I can predict for sure: Archie will still be around!

Stephen Hill, Hearts of Space,
19 February 1993

E.M. 1973 - 1993
How the Synthe Scene Has Changed Since 1973

The original, fresh and innovative hot black jazz played and recorded from 1923 to 1930 in Chicago, Kansas City or New York, was 20 years later copied by some enthusiastic young fans, which was the so-called first "Dixieland Revival" in the late 1940s.

This again was copied by some innocent young fans, who took the copycats as the originals, and this third generation created a "Dixieland" fashion and waves all over the world, up to the early 1960s. By now, this third generation "jazz" was far away from the initially sensational and creative ideas of the originators. In fact it had become either a caricature, or boring formula only. (Remember the Beatles started with their Skiffle, an offspring of the more jolly hokum side of jazz -- in such a Liverpool Dixieland club, and accidentally stopped THIS fashion to start a new one, and the game I characterize here, started again).

Take instead of "jazz," Electronics, alter the times and places, and you know what I think about most of today's E.M. -- Electronic Dixieland.

I know that Archie's mood is often in the minor key, as is mine when I think about the state of "our" music today. But maybe we only get older. Both of us.

"Our music" began shortly before Archie started to write about it. I have to point out that he was the very first one who took E.M. seriously and who did a fanzine about it. This was some 4,000 miles away from where this music was happening -- in a pre-fax era! Archie finally made EUROCK his profession.

I know that the business of a "mail-order" isn't an easy task from my own experience. I was told that EUROCK is really fast, and I even know that at least in one case Archie sent records BEFORE he got money from the customer... In all these 20 years that I've been in contact with Archie, I've never heard anyone complain about him or his business. When I hear his name, or EUROCK, another word comes to my mind: honesty. I wish this will last. It's all too rare.

And if you think that Archie has old fashioned '60s or hippie ideas, let me tell you that humanity and idealism is a utopia we should all try to reach. I share his ideas.

Thanks, Archie, for all you did in the last 20 years. I hope you carry on.

The other Klaus told me to pass on a special "Hello" and congratulations from him too.

Klaus. D. Mueller, 13 January 1993

Klaus Schønning Interview

I first remember hearing Klaus Schønning back in 1979 when receiving a copy of his first self-produced album, *LYDGLIMT* ("Glimpses of Sound"), from a friend in Sweden. I was amazed that even in Denmark, the cosmic music vibrations had been picked up on. That was followed in 1980 by *CYCLUS*, another self-production. Both of these albums combined the cosmic ethos of the Berlin School electronic sound with a more down to earth Danish approach. In the years since, his style has evolved into a multi-textured constellation of synthes, folk instruments and neoclassical themes.

This year I was lucky to make contact with someone (thank you Susan) who knows Klaus. My first wish to know more about him and his work, led to this interview. With the release of his new album *MAGIC CAFE* on Sony Denmark, he seems on the verge of wider recognition perhaps? Let's hope so as he's certainly one of the best electronic composers of the day. This interview for EUROCK is his first in English to my knowledge.

K.S. INTERVIEW - 2/12/1993

A: I remember getting your first album some years ago and thinking -- how amazing, even in Denmark there is someone doing cosmic synthesizer music? How did you get turned on to electronic music -- did you start playing in rock bands, have classical training, or what?

KS: Even as a child I was very interested in putting tones and sounds together in new ways, this fascination has been the driving force behind all the music I've composed over the years. Since I was 10 I had piano lessons, and later I studied music at Copenhagen University. I played soul and blues music with different bands at the same time, but I was primarily interested in composing music myself and experimenting with multi-track recording. When synthesizers became accessible to ordinary people, I was among the first in Denmark to buy one, that opened up a world of endless possibilities of sound.

A: Your music seems to be a fusion of many different elements, who did you listen to that influenced your particular sound? How would you classify it -- new age, cosmic, space music, or ?

KS: I listen a lot to the newer classical music, whose form and instrumentation is a source of inspiration. I listen to rock, such as Pink Floyd -- I really like their use of 'real' sounds in their music. And I also listen to a lot of ethnic music, which gives me an idea of the original and fundamental elements in music. They are all genres which I consider exciting, and which influence my own musical expression. I regard my own music as being a lyrical, symphonic, picturesque music, where melody, harmony, rhythm and form are all considered. A music that is 'written' more from the heart than from the intellect.

A: Once you decided to play such an experimental music, how did you manage to produce and distribute an album as most companies have little interest in non-commercial artists?

KS: I financed the first 2 releases myself. I did my first recordings with instruments and a tape recorder I purchased on installment. To pay for the production, I had to play accordion on the streets in Copenhagen, almost every day, even during the winter, for two years.

A: All of your albums seem to have a conceptual idea behind the music. Do the titles convey some special theme you were trying to create?

KS: I always have a concept in mind when I begin work on an album. On an instrumental album I think a concept is especially important, to achieve a coherence between the different pieces. Thus *LYDGLIMT* ("Glimpses of Sound') was created for a slide show about the woods and the beach. *CYCLUS* was built around a theme which appears in different ways in all 8 tracks. *NAVASU* is lyrical pictures based on an ancient myth. And *LOCARIAN ARABESQUE* is done from a particular tonal scale, upon which the different pieces are built. Thus I have always had a 'title' for my albums.

A: Then there's the *SYMPHODYSSÉ* series. Do you see those albums as a continuation of your earlier sound, or a new development in your musical style?

KS: For a long time I have wished to compose a piece of considerably longer duration, where there would be room for each segment of the music without the feeling that one must hurry on. The *SYMPHODYSSÉ* series is created out of this idea to work with long, more restful sequences in a 'new age' character, but it is still melodic music with experimental sounds, especially in the case of the acoustic instruments. Four is a magic number for me, and just as there are four corners of the Earth, four seasons, etc., so there will also be four *SYMPHODYSSÉ's* -- travels through four different atmospheres and worlds of sound. I don't see them as a musical step forward or backward, but rather something I'm doing parallel to the rest of my albums, which contain shorter, more accessible pieces.

A: I'm always interested to know if musicians making such non-commercial music are able to make their living by producing albums and playing such music 'live'. Do you give many electronic music concerts? Do you play perhaps some other kind of music as well?

KS: I cannot live only from my albums, but I'm involved in many other musical connections and play everything from parlour (club) music to rock. I really love the parlour music, I play piano in a trio, with violin and a bass. We have a lot of work, and with all my musical activities together I can make a living from the music.

A: I heard recently you did a big performance that gave you some major exposure, what was that?

KS: Through the years I have given large concerts of my own music. I have played in Tivoli in Copenhagen several times with a large band and giant light show. I have also played in Amsterdam, Holland many times. The performance you mention was last Fall, where one of my pieces, 'The Bells of Copenhagen', was played by a large symphony orchestra. I played the accordion myself on this number, and it was broadcast live on TV to around 1 million viewers.

A: When will the fourth installment of the *SYMPHODYSSÉ* albums be out?

KS: Fønix promises that they will release the fourth *SYMPHODYSSÉ* album in early Spring. The music and master tape were ready in November 1992, but Fønix believes it best to wait until Spring to put it out. Later on, all four *SYMPHODYSSÉ's* will be issued in a special box set.

A: Now you have signed to Sony Music Denmark for your next album. When will it be released? What is the title and concept behind it?

KS: My first Sony album is released February 17, 1993. The title is *MAGIC CAFE* and there is also a story behind it. Imagine yourself in a cafe surrounded by a number of things that at first glance are insignificant. But when you look at these things, they spark flights of your imagination -- for example a clock, a dripping faucet, shadows, etc. So these ordinary, everyday things become a catalyst for a colorful world of fantasy.

A: Perhaps in the future you might come to the USA and play a few small concerts to help people here know your music better?

KS: Naturally, I dream of the possibility of presenting my music in the USA. It's shouldn't be impossible. At the moment I play 2-hour concerts together with a drummer and guitarist, all over Denmark. We can easily arrange the music so it wouldn't be a great expense to come over.

Archie Patterson
(Translation by Susan Mollerskav)

2000

Eurock -- A Perspective

Archie Patterson's wonderful fanzine, EUROCK, is unique in the world of rock fanzines, not only for its breadth and depth but also for the incredible 20-year run of the thing.

When he started, the European Rock explosion was just reaching full flower, fueled by the twin engines of drugs and innovation, spilling over from the American and British explosions five years before. By the time EUROCK finally wound down as a magazine, two decades and several lifetimes later, the supernova was just a dust cloud and a shock wave, reduced to CD reissues of some of the classics of the genre.

Through it all Archie consistently beat the drum for the value and beauty he saw in this strange music from foreign lands. If he sometimes described every new release as his favorite, or if he seemed to run out of new words in some of the later reviews, or if his descriptions sometimes left you no wiser as to the actual SOUND of the music -- well, you try writing a thousand reviews and see how you do. It's hard work! Music and words are different mediums, and it isn't easy to describe one with the other. What does come through in the reviews, loud and clear, is his unflagging enthusiasm for the music, through thick and thin. This is what truly sets EUROCK apart from almost every other act of rock journalism -- Archie never lost his idealism.

While digitizing the 430,000 words he wrote, I was struck by his editorial in the 27th issue, when most journalists would have long-since become jaded or burned-out. To my mind it serves as a perfect summary of the magic that was EUROCK:

"Music can be a voice that speaks to and means something to people -- maybe it's the most powerful form of communication we can share. In addition, if made/played for the right reasons, it brings out the best in people. EUROCK's function on all levels is to turn people on to new music that in some way works in this positive way."

This is EUROCK in a nutshell.

Robert Carlberg

The Golden Age

As I write, the 27th-year of EUROCK is underway. By the time this reaches your computer screens, I will have spent half of my life propagandizing for a strange musical hybrid that has been labeled everything from progressive rock, to space rock, krautrock, space music, cosmic music, new age and more... While that seems like an eternity, in many ways it feels like only yesterday that I experienced the thrill of my first musical discovery.

The world during my wonder years, the 1960s and 1970s, was experiencing a golden age. After WW II, the rebuilding of Western society had begun. Within a decade the benefits of renewed economies were generating global expansion of unprecedented proportions. Social movements exploded internationally during the late 1960s, inspired by a "do your own thing" philosophy and fuelled by mind-expanding drugs. A new fusion of liberation politics and rock music combined to create electricity in the air that carried inspiration on the wind. It may be hard to imagine such a thing happening now that total corporate control of the media and commerce looms on the horizon and cynicism has gripped us tightly in its hold. But back then, a spirit encircled the globe that did indeed make anything imaginable, and encouraged the belief that a crazy idea might very well come true.

In the late 1960s and early 1970s however, mass communications were inferior to telepathy on the astral plane. As a result very few people outside of the European continent had even an inkling that anything was happening musically across the pond. A couple articles in the UK newspapers *Melody Maker* and *NME* offered the first glimpse that something was going on. Strangely named groups, playing odd mutations of rock and pop music were the focus of these early Euro reports. These teasers gave me the idea of doing a self-styled fanzine devoted to experimental music from Europe. Previous contact with Greg Shaw and his great fanzine *WHO PUT THE BOMP* provided the inspirational example. In this pre-telex, pre-fax, pre-email age, the only mode of communication was the good old post office (stamps were still pretty cheap back then), and (very expensive) long distance phone calls. So with all the energy of a new parent, EUROCK was born amid a flurry of letters, overseas mail orders for these exotic new musical delights, and youthful enthusiasm.

In March 1973 the first issue was realized and featured the holy trinity from Germany -- Amon Düül II, Can and Tangerine Dream. Creatively it was a collaboration between myself, "Hot Scott" Fischer (a notorious rock critic of the time) and Julian Atkins (the head of the TD fan club in the UK). After weeks of typing on an old manual typewriter, a friend at work Xeroxed the first 100 magazines surreptitiously, hand collated, brass fastened and mailed to a select group gleaned from an advert in *Rolling Stone* and word of mouth in record collector circles. The first run gradually sold out in a year's time. A second printing followed, done by another friend during late nights on the local Public School presses. Offset printed, it was a more "conventional" edition of 200 copies with better print quality and a different color cover. Suffice to say all involved felt they were either visionaries ahead of their time, or loonies, insanely out of their minds -- take your pick. In any case, feedback was sufficient to inspire a second issue, and from there the beat just went on, and on...

In retrospect, to me it seems no small achievement that such a disparate crew could come up with such an inspired musical journal. Needless to say the subject matter of European rock, and the often colorful writing style, established the 'zine as a real odd duck in the USA, and equally strange overseas as well where this music was equally unknown and non-commercial. At that time there were no other publications in the English speaking world, and only a few scattered articles in the UK pop press that would take such music seriously. Soon thereafter, two other publications appeared that had a similar focus -- *Fools Mate* (in Japanese) and *Atem* (in French). Initial contacts with them gave me the small encouragement needed to plunge headlong into the void.

In point of fact the actual "scenes" themselves that arose amidst the cultural ferment in the various countries for the most part consisted of underground clubs, loose networks of fans and slack collaboration among the various bands that all fought for acceptance by the same limited audience. And while the decade of the 1970s saw a limited flowering of a "Euro experimental scene," during the 1980s, that scene and the political shape of the entire world was forever changed by Reagan and his ilk. In addition, the nature of the drugs changed from mind expanding to spirit destroying. Things were never the same again.

The golden age of "Euro-rock" (with only a few exceptions) was not a commercially successful period anywhere and the creative energy behind it dissipated by degrees rather quickly. The youth of the world revolution grew older and the various Euro scenes withered. The music moved on to another phase as the groups either died out or got involved with the emerging corporate music structure. The musicians had to struggle to survive, let along maintain their creative vision, and soon most began to see the world through different eyes. What had been dubbed "cosmic music" was soon consigned to the dustbin of history by all but a few, and processed into the generic hybrid labeled "new age," while "Prog-rock" degenerated into redundant formula. The "experimental" wing of music kept on in it stylistically-imposed ghetto, but the vast majority of artists (and most listeners) adapted to this new cultural and socio-economic reality far and wide as "the golden age" drifted to an inglorious end.

As I once again went through all of the materials that have gone into the making up of this unique production, I thought back to the beginning and could have never in my wildest imagination then, conceived of this sort of project happening. What began as a fun filled adventure discovering strange new music, has 26 years later turned into a multi-media creation that breaks new ground when it comes to music "fanzines." You might say, EUROCK has gone back to the future, again.

While re-reading the texts, scanning in pictures, going through my music library, and talking to people about this whole time period, I sometimes could only shake my head in amazement as I realized just how much has transpired in the world and my life since those much simpler times in 1973. Perhaps the most amazing part of the whole process was a sense of re-discovery as I relived once again all these things. Many times I was struck at just how real it all still seems today. The mode of the music and times has greatly changed, but the message conveyed in the issues of EUROCK truly captured the original essence and spirit of times past. In a sense this simple fanzine encapsulated the sound and ideas of that time and preserved them to be experienced again today via this new technological form. Call it déjà vu of the finest sort. The words and music come alive again to create much more than simply a historical document. Today there are many publications that cover the same sort of things EUROCK once did, but retrospective articles and neo-music, by old or new groups, can't capture the vibe like the original(s) do. I hope you will pick up on that no matter when you came of age musically.

Recently, I talked to Chris Karrer about AD II and what appears to be their final break-up. We got into the idea of a certain time, place, and music combining to create a magical experience -- something intangible that cannot be forgotten, and holds a certain spiritual reverence for those who created or experienced it on any meaningful level. Music captures that original essence so it will never be lost. To some extent the understanding and belief in this sort of idea is a product of age and experience, but it can also result from a musical revelation experienced by anyone, at any time. During the life of EUROCK, I've had this sentiment expressed countless times, by many people in their own individual ways.

This all leads to the inevitable question, just what has happened to the music of "The Golden Age"? That's undoubtedly a question with many answers, and EUROCK offers up some of them. Let me pose one more, based on a metaphysical idea that in my mind proves to be truer with each passing year.

Since I bought my first record (in 1958 at 10 years old), I've since come to believe that music was a way to communicate with the highest form of the spirit. It contains the power to enlighten intellectually, philosophically and to touch one emotionally. From ancient tribal chants, to the minstrel troubadours, classical masters, and rock and roll, there is a tradition of almost mystical communion established between musician and listener that cannot be denied.

In the 1960s enlightenment dawned on me when after 18 years of education I ultimately came to the realization that most all of the information being programmed into me via books was much better communicated in the music I listened to and loved. Sex, drugs, rock and roll, history, love, hate, war, peace -- there were songs that conveyed the essence of all these far better than words on a page in any book. Music had come to speak volumes to me, and many others as well. My life became changed and in the process, the world was changed too. I realized that to know something meant to understand it, not just recant literal facts. You could memorize facts and still be lost in the wilderness, but if you understood and could feel the reality of something, the right path was clear. When you hear a series of notes, combined into just the right melody, with perhaps some words of inspiration -- le voilà, there is the truth. You clearly can experience whatever is being sung about, and it resonates with your soul. The spirit meets the flesh and you get a special feeling, at last a certain idea or feeling makes sense. This can happen many times, with each new song or piece of music you hear. You can very quickly become educated (experienced?). The knowledge acquired is dependent only upon what type of music you chose to listen to. For me this was a revelation. In a sense this was happening all over the world during those times. Music in general, rock and roll in particular, contained a special power to enhance the human DNA code, and that power was being transmitted by telepathy around the globe. Different people could listen to the same song in many different countries and get the same message, at the same time -- incredible! That was the essence of the "The Golden Age." If you opened your ears, you could hear the sound all around you. You didn't need school, church, or any other doctrine, there was something magical in the air, and all you had to do was breathe it in. Music became in that time a brand new religion that transcended dusty historical texts of any kind.

Time passed however and things changed. The medium truly became the message. Music now saturates the airwaves, but since the reign of Reagan they have become programmed by CNN, Rupert Murdoch, Seagram, or some other multinational. The ionic balance has changed, the air is not so alive with the sights and sounds of pure inspiration as in former times. It has become harder to keep the faith. In spite of that, the beat does still go on. Some of the old artists continue today struggling to conjure up the muse, and a few new ones have become inspired. Today I hear 100 times more music than I did in 1973 and much of it is not worth listening to. Yet sometimes still, that certain special combination of rhythmic tones and melody, the pure spirit of creativity rings out loud and clear confirming that great music is alive, and magic is afoot. That sacred combination was, and still is the lifeblood and raison d'être of EUROCK.

This 26-Year Anniversary Issue reflects on the past and launches the EUROCK concept off into the brave new technological world of the 21st Century. *THE GOLDEN AGE* CD-ROM expands the boundaries a bit further, and EUROCK Online in the future will continue its evolution incorporating audio and more into the mix. So stay tuned...

Archie Patterson

Bernard Xolotl
The Musical Philosopher

What can lead a musician to disenchantment and mistrust? No doubt, all that which has to do with imposed commercialism.

Bernard Xolotl has made from the '70s up to now many and very good electronic music works, several of them never released. Nevertheless, this musician is a clear example of the artist who rebels against the commercialism imposed by the record labels and who, because of that, misses the chance to earn loads of money. He conceives his artistic career as a style of life.

After several years of silence, a silence motivated not by a lack of creativity but rather due to financial poverty, Xolotl re-appears with the re-release of several of his most legendary works. They reveal him as an artist of great imagination in the '70s and '80s; even today they continue to be far more innovative than a lot of the music labeled as "alternative." Through an interview that Xolotl has given us for *Amazing Sounds*, as well as other contacts that we have had with him since we interviewed him for the first time in 1988, we have been able to get to know his way of understanding art in depth during these years, as well as some of his experiences in his already long musical career.

Bernard Xolotl was born in France in 1951. At age 17 he realized that he needed more freedom to live and express his ideas than the old Latin Europe could provide him with. Therefore, he left his country and traveled all over the world. In 1974 he settled in California, where he lived for 19 years. Currently living in France, he often travels to the United States. He does not consider himself tied to any one place:

I never 'decided' to live in the USA, Scandinavia, Nepal or Polynesia, and I never wanted to 'return' to France or anywhere. Today, I am in California and I fly 'back' to Europe tomorrow afternoon. I am a complete nomad, an apatride, a citizen of planet Earth. If I had the funds of the Dalai-Lama or Mick Jagger, I would be commuting around the whole planet ceaselessly just as they do.

In his teen-age years, Bernard became interested in electronic music, which in France had its first pioneers working within the trend known as "Concrete Music."

The first compositions of electronic music that I heard came from several works by Pierre Henry, Pierre Schaeffer and other pioneers, mostly French, around 1966-67, when I was 16. However, it was the first records by Pink Floyd soon after which fed my enthusiasm for electronic music, instead of Concrete Music, which in actual fact had never really interested me.

He studied Arts and Philosophy up to 1969, just at the time when the first analog synthesizers were commercialized. The type of studies that he was engaged in, and the books that he chose to read, shaped his taste for this new way to make music that was cropping up. From then on, he would begin his travels and his activity as a musician. In the early '70s he was at the core of the rising Cosmic Music, more particularly related to the most classical trend of the genre, the "Berlin School." Xolotl met Klaus Schulze in 1972, during a festival in Switzerland, where he went together with Timothy Leary. He also made friends with Manuel Gottsching, Terry Riley, and other important leaders of the musical revolution of the '70s. He worked with some of them. For instance, he assisted Terry Riley and LaMonte Young during their European tours.

At that time it happened to be very difficult indeed for a musician who started, to succeed in having access to synthesizers and other innovative electronic equipment. In 1971-72, Xolotl used the electronic studios of a public character in Germany and Denmark. In the United States, he used the laboratories at some universities, often at night. Later, little by little, he established his own studio. In 1988, he said:

I have many synthesizers and my favorite one still is the PPG which I bought in 1983 and which was the first in America. I have many computers with every music software program on the market and I spend so much time programming that my 16-track tape recorder does not get used very often these days. After all these years, I have become such an expert on computer music equipment that I am more often called for technical consulting work than for music which is a situation I find rather sad and want to change as soon as I can. The place where I live is the very heart of the technological 'revolution' and because of that, life here has become very expensive. The problem now is no longer to acquire more equipment, but to afford a house to shelter it!

Although the computer has lately become his main working tool, Xolotl feels far more attraction towards analog synthesizers than the digital ones. In 1988, he said:

I prefer the old machines of Oberheim, Sequential, PPG, and others of this kind, rather than the new devices that cropped up after the appearance of the DX7 in 1983. These aren't so expressive or spontaneous. Most of them are a bunch of presets made for a massive market of unskilled musicians. On the other hand, before 1983, the synthesizers used to be produced only for an elite of experimental artists. This is the circumstance that marks the difference between both types of instruments, and this is why I dislike these new synthesizers, not the fact that they produce digital sounds instead of analog. I like beautiful sounds, whatever their origin.

About the digital medium, he also comments:

This is a very interesting medium, and even though the sonic result can be debatable, there is no doubt that it opens new paths for the future. Given its numerical nature, everything digital is reduced to numbers. I'd like to remind you that Pythagoras was a good initial representative of numeric philosophy. I would also like to mention that my paintings, as well as my music, are carefully elaborated with respect to the harmonic progression of numbers as something fundamental. My album-painting "Return of the Golden Mean" refers to the renaissance of Phythagorian Philosophy throughout the Digital Era. 'Golden Mean' is the 'sacred' ratio 1.61809... which appears in the growth of shells, plants and galaxies.

When we ask him about what he thinks on the contribution of computers to music, he replies, today in 1997:

After so many years and so many times that this question was asked, I can really think nothing about 'computers in music.' Only the result matters. Who cares what it's made with at this point? Music existed before electricity, before the orchestra and even before human beings. Music is like love: either you do or you don't; whatever the cause, the cost or the consequences. As I predicted many years ago, everything has become computerized, but this changes nothing essential -- you still need ears and loudspeakers. In 1870, Richard Wagner wrote that people had the impression that they traveled more because of the railroads, but that it was a complete illusion. Faxes and portable telephones are nothing more than the telegraph then and if you read the diaries of that period, you will be amazed at the speed and amount of daily communications. The means are nothing without an end, and the end always justifies the means when Art is concerned...

Bernard's recording career began in 1976, with a collective record in San Francisco. Soon after in 1977, *MUSIC BY XOLOTL* was released. In this work, the artistic path that he was to follow years later could already be appreciated. His second album, *JOURNEY TO AN ORACLE*, in which Bernard Largounez and Jean-Baptiste Barriere collaborated, appeared in 1979. *PROPHECY* was released in 1981, and on it Bernard collaborated with Cyrille Verdeaux. The music, as visionary as its title suggests, was made above all with a Prophet 5 and a guitar synthesizer of Zeta Systems. *RETURN OF THE GOLDEN MEAN*, recorded between 1979 and 1980, is one of the works that best display the deep, impressive vein of Xolotl's music. On that album, the composer performed with the guitar synthesizer of Zeta Systems, accompanied by Irene Gostnell on the violin, Jonathan Kramer on the cello, and Cyrille Verdeaux at the electronic keyboards. *PROCESSION* (1982) contributed in a remarkable way to his international recognition as an innovative artist in the field of electronic music. With *LAST WAVE* (1984), he once again offered an excellent sample of his talent, and also counted on the collaboration of some prestigious musicians in the performance of the pieces: Richard Horowitz (Tibetan percussion) and Daniel Kobialka (violin). Likewise, he gave a greater leading role to other electronic instruments, like for instance the Yamaha CS60, the PPG Wave 2.2, the Korg Monopoly, the Pro-One, the ARP Sequencer and vocoders of Roland and

Korg.

In the following years, Xolotl acquired a reputation as a "countercultural artist." This was partly due to the fact that for a long time he kept himself shut in his home-studio, isolated from the outside, not seeing anyone, and concentrated in an almost obsessive way in musical creativity. He worked up to 24 hours a day non-stop, which led him to dangerously resemble the Phantom Of the Opera. Yet the main reason why he earned this reputation of "countercultural artist" is the fact that he was placed, in a way, in a "black list" of the recording world, because of his openly belligerent attitude against any wrong committed by a record label towards his copyrights. He thus limited himself to the distribution of his previous works through his label Syntasy, to some concerts and collaborations, to developing some soundtracks, and to other artistic or technical activities on his part (including painting and writing). He continued to compose magnificent pieces, some of which guarantee him an important slot within the history of electronic music. *MEXECHO*, one of his most brilliant albums, was released in 1991 by the German label Erdenklang, although most of the music had already been composed by late 1988. In 1996, his previous albums began to be re-released in CD format by the French label Spalax.

Xolotl is a versatile artist. As we have noted before, painting and writing are activities that he combines with that of composing. He has written numerous essays and articles, for instance "Art and Culture," "Art and Technology," and his memoirs (titled "Journal d'un Artiste Américain"). In the field of painting, he is the creator, for instance, of the covers of many of his albums. As these lines are being written, we know that soon a virtual gallery of paintings of his will be opened on the internet.

We ask him whether he thinks that his artistic activity in these two fields is closely related to his musical work:

No, it can never be close because they are all different worlds. Who could ever picture the engravings of William Blake after reading his poems? Who could ever guess the music of Jimi Hendrix from the words of his songs? or the paintings of Van Gogh from his great letters to his brother? There are thousands of infinitely different musical interpretations of the Gospels, even if they remain the same and by the same composer. Hermann Hesse's, Henry Miller's or Henri Michaux's watercolors can never give us any idea of their writings. One can experience a "synesthesia" in one's own mind, but just as walking, talking and seeing belong to different worlds, so do the various senses manifest in concrete reality.

Thanks to his journeys and his desire to get to know other cultures all over the world, Bernard got to learn different philosophies, like for instance Tibetan Buddhism. This is why he has a global vision of all of them which allows him to understand the serious and topical errors that many westerners make when they consider Eastern philosophy as if it were one thing only.

There is no such thing as 'Eastern Philosophy' (or 'Western Philosophy' for that matter) -- these are all stupid concepts invented by journalists in the (colonial) 19th century: like saying all Asians (or Blacks, or Indians) are identical. In reality, there are many, many currents and times of thought in many, many places and cultures. One has to study history in the field for many years to even get a small idea of some of these 'philosophies' -- there are opposite trends in all of them, of course. In most cases, one has to learn the language in order to reach a true understanding of any one of these. Furthermore, 'foreign' influences have swept over the East long ago (Islam, a monotheistic religion, all the way down to Indonesia; Christianity on the coasts and now Marxism in China and Tibet most unfortunately, etc.). Always, it is up to the individual to find out what is best for him or her in the (local) context of human life. Set ideas or opinions are a source of division and warfare between human beings and are thus better avoided. Religions, philosophies and ideologies are a curse. Before all this madness, human beings considered all things to be sacred (stone, river, tree, animal, etc., etc., etc.) and this is the best way to go -- true Amerindians still think this way and most Tibetans also. The mind is obviously boundless and thus any border, frontier, or barrier you set to it becomes an obstacle, one way or another. The wisest is to strive for the Middle Way: to avoid the two extremes of Eternalism / absolute existence and Nihilism / everything is an illusion. There is no creator and there is no matter; only Being! The body deals with Time, and the mind with Eternity: this is obvious and identical for all peoples, whether from East or West, past, present or future...

We ask him whether his travels around the world have influenced his music:

Frankly, no one in the world can answer this question. Was Bach or Wagner influenced by their travels around Europe? Most probably not. Was Wagner ever influenced by Mathilde Wesendonk to write Tristan und Isolde? Probably not either. Music is an utterly magical, immaterial and undefinable vibration very much like love, which is never really influenced by anything, but can only manifest itself in a certain context or karma, outside of all planned boundaries. If we are thus talking about the present, you will need money to pay the electrical bill, the synthesizers and computers and the studio rent. But music in itself is influenced by nothing: it is pure ideality. In other words, my mind travels have obviously greatly 'influenced' my music, but my physical ones probably not at all."

About his relationships with other cultures in the world, we are especially interested in the one that he has been maintaining with the American Pre-Columbian cultures for long years. "Xolotl," his artist name, comes from the Aztec language. We asked him to explain how such a relationship began:

Curiosity and passion for all forms of life in history and geography were, in early childhood, the driving force of my interest in distant, non-European, non-Judeo-Christian cultures. Later on, shamanistic, experience-based, psychedelic and non-dualistic cultures, appeared like an antidote to the long-suffering, utterly fucked-up modern world imposed by the West through the last centuries. It wasn't a fashion then and there was no eco-tourism as yet, but it is still and more than ever relevant...

Xolotl has a powerful, unexpected answer on the question about what inspires his musical ideas, and which process he follows to compose:

I am always inspired; I was born inspired; I do not need inspiration, I just need time, money and equipment to manifest the ever-present inspiration of nature and the eternal Now. This answer seems to always create an uproar and endless controversy. I could elaborate forever, but I shall leave it at that for the time being because it is still true; the French have a saying 'La faim vient en mangeant' and it's that way for me with inspiration even much more than with hunger. As for the second question: I do not follow a process to compose, I just create spontaneously as soon as there is the time and equipment to do so. Like all other true artists at all times, I try to do nothing but create.

He also has a very interesting answer to the question of how he would define his personal musical style:

I have no 'personal music style,' and I have fought all my life against such a concept. Mozart and Beethoven struggled desperately against the Sonata form; Wagner against the traditional Opera form, etc. In our lifetime specially, the musical inventions of the whole planet Earth are somewhat available, even to the average listener. Xolotl loves all good music from many, many places and times and could never restrict himself to one particular 'style' (or nationality for that matter).

We ask him whether he likes best the music he created years ago or the one he composes now:

Since only a small percentage of the music I have recorded has been released and that I never did for money, of course I like it and am proud of it. I only regret the poor recording quality of many of my older compositions because they were done with primitive and inadequate equipment which was all I could afford at that time. An Artist always prefers the on-going, present and future creations to the past ones; otherwise, he/she would stop creating.

Thus he summarized in 1982 what the synthesizers were contributing to music:

"In recent years, we have witnessed a phenomenon that I find very interesting indeed. Since the development of the synthesizer, many people who had not been educated as musicians in the strict sense of the word, who perhaps had been educated as artists, architects, poets, have been able to create on their own terms a type of music of great scope, extremely sophisticated, that is being more and more proclaimed as the classical music of the future. I am thinking of such musicians as Iasos, Klaus Schulze, Vangelis, Edgar Froese, Michael Hoenig, Kitaro..., and all the rest who use the synthesizer to create their own music. All this grows day after day, and no doubt we are entering what I like to call the 'Era of Synthesis.' The synthesizer has opened an immense and new repository of raw matter for our scientific and artistic expression. The revolution that is just beginning is of such a magnitude, that he does not hesitate to state that: The artist of the future will have to become a scientist, and vice versa. Art and Science fused at long last, after centuries of apparent antagonism."

Nowadays, he thinks that this potential has been wasted, and the "Era of Synthesis" has been completely buried under the avalanche of the "Age of (random) Information."

The synthesis of the arts, the creation accessible to all the senses, the 'music of the mind,' has never been so technologically available to us as now. However, we face a curious phenomenon: the increase in the technology has been in most cases inversely proportional to the quality and integrity of the music. I do not fear in the least to give here some examples. In the late '60s, the musicians that were at the avant-garde of technology and who created true original works with their small equipment (small according to our current standards), were moving towards a musical adventure which turned out to be too predictable, commercial and dull as they kept advancing in the acquisition of more and more sophisticated hardware. In the '70s, this pattern worsened in a considerable way when many of the great pioneers of electronic music, who had created true marvels of innovative music initiating the genre of Cosmic Music (and utilizing a minimum of technology in comparison with what's available today), exhausted themselves to the core. Now, with a colossal arsenal of synthesizers and computers available to them, they simply create a type of music very 'typical of Hollywood,' easy listening, commercial, having nothing of the sophistication and originality it should have, making a meaningless use of their paraphernalia, accumulated during all these years. Such a situation is what gives electronic music its bad image.

Before this somber panorama that he describes to us, we asked him if the problem is, because nowadays it is necessary to make this type of commercial music if one wishes to make a living with electronic music.

I cannot speak for every musician on the planet. Commercial music is pollution, and I try to avoid pollution as much as possible. I do not care for pop-music at all, and I only myself listen to the great music of the past (from Bach to Richard Strauss period). However, artists always have a difficult time to survive in a commercial culture like our own, and they should do anything they can to be able to create their important work.

In his opinion, the situation of the "avant garde" music world scene is no better:

Since the '60s, there is no such thing as a "world avant-garde music scene"; it has vanished and lost all meaning as a reference: Jimi Hendrix or Pink Floyd were very avant-garde, became popular and sold millions of albums. Miles Davis was inspired by Hendrix. The Grateful Dead, who started as a free experiment for Ken Kesey's Acid Tests, and was then bought up and sold by Bill Graham, and later the Beatles 'repackaged' it, etc., etc. Meanwhile, the State functionaries of the 'official' avant-garde (like IRCAM, Soviet or American) lost all credibility forever and especially after the Japanese sold synthesizers by the millions... There is no longer one (or even two or three) centers of culture. The world is utterly fragmented. For some people, Rai (Algerian pop music) is avant-garde, for others Californian New Age, for others still, South African tribal music. Bulgarian, Polish, Lithuanian, Aztec and even Corsican so-called traditional music, have become avant-garde in the last few years. Balinese, South Indian and Maori music is played on synthesizers. Techno is all the rage in Europe, but virtually unknown in America, etc., etc., etc. The political 'Balkanization' of the world is reflected in culture." ('The communications industry has retribalized the world.' -- Jack Weatherford). *"Any avant-garde can only exist in terms of a central reference and there is no such thing anymore. Hollywood's pop music is the only 'universally' available music and it is not a reference, but a commercial swindle like junk bonds. The Russians (or Germans or Chinese), all want to live in the USA, and each college in America has a different concept or specialty. There are as many avant-garde's nowadays as there are local identities or national / folk committees. Since WWII, Europe is no longer the center of the world, there is no center, and avant-garde is only what you personally think it is. I know nothing about it. For me, music is just that: music.*

But, how could we define good music, the music made the best possible way? Can this absolute perfection be reached?

Personally, I don't think there is an ideal music referring to all different peoples and places in the world. The Earth is like a sky body where different cultures represent different organs with specific functions, or different energy centers. Furthermore, there is a music for each occasion. What I would call ideal music is the music that would integrate all this into a single sublime unit. If we heard this music, we would listen to the Great Symphony of the Universe, from which Bach's Passions and the latest operas by Wagner are exceptional witnesses. This concept is not only applicable to music, but also to the entire creative palette of humanity.

For Xolotl the goal to be attained by any artist is clear:

I consider the search for art as a sacred path, like the search for Enlightenment, and the end must justify the means. What matters is the result (the work of art), not the tools used, or the reasons why it was created.

To end the interview, we ask him whether he is engaged in future works:

Only about 5 percent of my recorded music has been released so far on CD, so it is very difficult to answer this question since it does not depend on me, but on the whim of record companies and what they think is fashionable at the moment... I have many musical plans for the future, of course, otherwise I would not be a musician or I would kill myself; but all these plans depend only on money, like most 'important' things nowadays...

To Xolotl, his artistic activity is not a mere profession to earn money, it rather is his life. Like any other artist, he often has his eccentricities, yet anyone who not only creates, but also thinks and reasons the why and wherefore of what he is doing, has them. Haven't such geniuses, as for instance painter Salvador Dalí, had them, yet nobody denies them their talent? Xolotl possesses a strong personality, like other such artists as Edgar Froese or Klaus Schulze, for instance, who have the most fanatical admirers as well as the most ferocious detractors. Let's then judge the artists through their art, not through their attitudes regarding social conventions.

Manuel Montes & Jorge Munnshe
(Used Courtesy *Amazing Sounds***)**

Richard Pinhas Interview
THE CYBORG SALLY COLLABORATION

Cyrille Amistani: One of your last albums was entitled *CYBORG SALLY*; can you explain its genesis?

Richard Pinhas: *DWW*, the previous album, was rather a transition album. Besides, it used pieces composed in 1983-84 and finalized in 1991. The new album is completely different as it's digital and has recourse to new technologies.

CA: You co-signed the album with John Livengood; can you tell us about this collaboration?

RP: First, we were introduced to each other by Frédéric Pelloix, "Angel Freddy" from *Rock Machine*. We became friends, and when we spent holidays together in Val d'Isère in 1992, I suggested we make an album together. It was a joke but John said OK and here's the result... I think we're complementary and our collaboration is fine. John taught me a lot of things, especially as far as technology is concerned.

CA: Can you present the musicians of *CYBORG SALLY*?

RP: There's Antoine Paganotti. Antoine is a big flash. I've already played with very good percussionists, the models of the genre. I especially like jazz percussionists. Yet it'd been at least 10 years since I'd last had such an impression. There's obviously something miraculous about Antoine. The first time I saw him, he was about 19 or 20. He learned to play percussion behind his father's back... He learned the piano at the Conservatoire and in 4 years he became a fantastic percussionist (and behind his father's back...). In one year he first played with Patrick Gauthier, who made the public discover him, and then Christian Vander and me asked him to play with us. Now he's 21 and in one year and a half he did in France the most interesting things he could do. He's also very nice. Such an impression in front of such a young percussionist -- that was really a big flash!

CA: He played in a concert with Patrick Gauthier quite recently; his way of playing is inspired by Christian Vander...

RP: He's a jazzman above all. But of course he can play anything else. His way of playing thus tends to be ternary, but I don't think it's based on Christian's. It's original. He's a totally complete musician who can sing as well as play the piano. He's a really big musician and someone with an extraordinary potential, which is extremely rare. He'll probably do something great in the circle of French musicians.

CA: Can you present John Livengood in a few words?

RP: He created a group, Spacecraft, and then he played in White Noise. At the time it was a group like Komintern. He's one of the first to have worked on numerical synthesis. From 1984 he has mostly used computers in his approach to music. He was one of the first in France at the time.

CA: He worked for the IRCAM, if I remember well...

RP: Yes, he studied for a long time there when the boom in computers began. He also knows modular systems very well -- we share a common past in this field. John and I complete each other. He knows more about ethnic music and World Music than me, and I know about harder types of rock. In his next album, the World Music side appears clearly, but he never copies other musicians -- he created his own universe. Our common point is the passion we share for sounds and the fact of being able to work 8 hours a day, 15 days at a stretch on the same sound. What's fine is that we're now at a point where we have a very precise sound in mind and we absolutely want to create it. We're lucky to have the means to do it even if it means quite a lot of work.

NEW TECHNOLOGIES AND SOUNDS

CA: You say you had recourse to new technologies: what do you mean exactly?

RP: We passed from analog synthesis to digital synthesis. Now we mostly work on numerical systems. I can't say it's better or less good; it's just something else.

CA: You say your album is 80% guitar-based, 20% synth-based...

RP: With John we worked a lot on guitar sounds so as to reach a point where you can't distinguish the guitar from the synth. Except in the solo, of course! There are a few pieces like that, like "Hyperion," in which there are only guitar sounds, which were digitalized and transformed. We have specific systems to do this on the Macintosh, which doesn't mean we can't reproduce them on the stage. These systems are software like Hyperprism, a French one, as well as GRM Tools, which is also French. The French are among the leaders in this field, even if the products are distributed by the Americans (laughs). This is how you can obtain absolutely fabulous sound textures.

CA: Do new technologies have an influence on your creations?

RP: No. It's always the same thing: you have something in mind and you're supposed to make it audible. With or without technology, the composition process takes time. It shouldn't be a nodal point. Your composition is an expression of something incorporeal, it's what you have in your mind, in your heart. Then you must materialize it. From a virtual sphere -- the philosophical notion, not what they speak about in the multimedia field -- to something real and immediately audible. I spent a lot of time working on the process allowing that from an idea a piece of music will emerge. The composition process is always the same, whether it comes from a guitar, a synth or a sound. It's a metamorphic process. It's about capturing and organization of sound energy, as the painter does with light energy. While the painter is supposed to show the light, the musician is supposed to make a sound signal audible.

CA: What's the relative importance of sound in the music you compose now?

RP: It's fundamental. But I think I can say I master the composition process much better. It was a kind of a challenge to pass to digital music for me. I had to learn everything from scratch again. To come back to what I said earlier, I came back to music seriously when the albums were re-issued and I had a year to learn. I had never worked on a Mac before and the record is due to be released in late 1994 -- that is 4 years in all. It takes a lot of time. Before I could make an album in one year, but now I need much more time -- 4 years to make an album, including the period when I learned. John Livengood is probably one of the most performing people in France as far as this new technology is concerned -- I learned a lot from him. I can't say it would have been impossible to make the album without him, but he was the right person at the right moment.

CA: Is mixing important to you?

RP: It's extremely important. It's the fundamental stage, the moment when you must have a very definite idea of what you want. If you have no idea at all, you're bound to fail completely, I think.

TIME AND COMPOSITION

CA: You've spent quite a long time working on this album...

RP: From September 1992 to May 1994. *CYBORG SALLY* is about 70 minutes long, which is not too long in fact. I think a year and a half is not that bad? You can't produce an album every year or every six months as before, as the musical production is now so important and as it seems to be a minimum to propose a new type of music. Of course, when it comes to producing a guitar album, it's possible to take less time.

CA: What takes much more time now?

RP: Exactly like before: the thinking process and the musical creation itself. If there's not any spark of light, if there's not anything unsaid, nothing will come out. This revelation can take a few days or months and months. The same person may have nothing to say for six months and then produce an album in three days.

CONCERTS

CA: Are you thinking of giving concerts?

RP: There'll be a concert on November 9th at the Passage du Nord-Ouest, and another, at the same place, on December 2nd. Maybe there'll be a mini-concert at Beaubourg in-between.

CA: Can you tell us more about the context of the Beaubourg concert?

RP: It's a commemoration of Guattari's death (Editor's note: a French philosopher and schizo-analyst) organized by Jean-Jacques Lebel. If it's organized, I'll do something special which has nothing to do with the new album. There'll be electronics, a rhythmic basis inlaid with pieces from *STANDBY* played on the guitar, and other quite specific arrangements.

CA: And who will be there for the concerts?

RP: A limited group -- three, I think, or maybe four if Bernard Paganotti is free to play the bass, but only for a few exceptional concerts. Maybe there'll be someone else... The important thing is to be in good condition to make it a success, and once it's started it's all right... There's always this problem -- which I can see when I work at home: you can work on a musical phrase for three days at a stretch and play it perfectly, and then the next day, when you switch on the DAT, nothing good comes out. In this case I know there's no use insisting. A concert is the same thing.

CA: You gave a concert in London last year; what does the stage represent for you now?

RP: The pleasure to have fun, as they say. Not to mention the work itself, as we'll prepare for it for a month. If we can play in good conditions for the public, and us it's a way to make everybody happy. I feel much more free for concerts now.

CA: Are you thinking of giving many concerts?

RP: Not many, but maybe between 30 and 50 a year. Twenty days on stage twice a year would be perfect. But you need to be in the good condition for it. In France, it's difficult to give 25 concerts because we have to play in small theatres, which means financial problems as you need relatively important sonics, and also because we want to offer good listening conditions to the public. I can't see why the conditions should be worse than for an American or English group. Therefore it's difficult to play in theatres seating 100 people without being forced to play in huge theatres. I'd like to play in theatres seating about 500 or 600, and I can't see why it shouldn't be possible.

PAST AND PRESENT

CA: *STANDBY*... Does it mean a kind of return to origins?

RP: I simply think *STANDBY* is a nice album. I'll only take the main phrases. I think other albums are not a success, but I'm quite happy with *STANDBY*, even if there're a few mistakes here and there. Besides, as you must know, it's the last Heldon album (smiles).

CA: Are there links between the new pieces and what you composed before?

RP: For one of the pieces, I took a sampling of one of the versions of *INTERFACE*. But do you have the right to sample yourself? (Laughs.) One of the odd things about it is that John and I signed this piece of music together whereas it's the 1995 version of *INTERFACE*. It's a piece which marked electronic music because I think it's the first piece of violent electronic rock with percussion. If I may say so, and between inverted commas, I think *INTERFACE* was the beginning of a turning point, in the German sense of the word.

CA: You've kept your instruments, I think. Which ones do you use?

RP: I went through a difficult period in the '80s, financially speaking, and I had to sell all my equipment. Luckily enough, a good friend of mine has it, but I don't have any Minimoog or EMU system any longer. In 1990, I began to buy new equipment and I only have the Minimoog that Michel Peltier, a very good friend, lent me. This album was made with poor equipment. All is based, in fact, on electronic algorithms. One way or the other, the worst thing that can happen to a gifted musician is to have too much equipment and to be trapped by it. It was made with poor equipment, but with the Macintosh to organize everything. You mustn't say to yourself: "What if I had had this or that." All in all, there are two synth lines, of eight notes each. All the rest is numerical music. There's a WS, a few Minimoog sounds. With these two instruments you can produce an album. I also use three guitars: an original Gibson 345, a Roland synth-guitar, which I hardly use, and a Stravisbin -- a kind of metal guitar that has now disappeared.

CA: You've just evoked the difficult times you went through, financially speaking; how did you manage to find the money for the production of your albums and *CYBORG SALLY*?

RP: You need to sell between 7,000 and 8,000 records to be okay financially speaking today. It's not that much. We know the Japanese are going to sell between 2,000 and 3,000. The expenses especially depend on the studio, and they haven't been so important. We didn't pay for it as I had many advantages. At Davout (Editor's note: a famous studio near the Porte de Montreuil), I didn't pay because I played for people and in exchange they lent me the keys to the studio. It lasted from 1976 to 1980. It's there that I produced many things, including Patrick Gauthier's *BÉBÉ GODZILLA*. I really look forward to the day it will be re-issued; it's really a good album. Otherwise, I never put money in any album, except the first one, in which I put 7,000 Francs. I never felt like it and I didn't have either the will or the means to do it. I was paid to produce the albums. I began to have important equipment when I sold back my Disjuncta label. Guitarist Alain Renaud helped me -- we released nine albums, which had been successful. For the first album, we just had two Revox and VCS3 -- that is very limited equipment. *ICELAND*, for instance, was made in eight tracks and the mixing was made when we didn't record Grunblatt's album.

CA: Speaking of your past, many people don't know you played with many musicians.

RP: Yes. I played with Odeurs (*1984 NO SEX*), participated in Grunblatt's album (on the Ramses label), *VIDÉOLYSTE*; I played in about 10 albums. Recently, I played just one piece for an English musician, Mark Jenkins, and the guy put me on the cover with my photo at the back: he's the organizer of the UK Electronics Festival.

CA: Do you think the public of the '70s will find themselves in the music you compose now?

RP: I think they'll be surprised. What people often reproach us with -- and they're right -- is that we don't play as we played 15 years ago. But this is totally stupid! I'm not going to do the same things as 15 years ago -- that's nonsense...

CA: Can you present your approach to music at the time?

RP: After my first record, I discovered the German groups. Bizot (Editor's note: from *Actuel* magazine) made me discover Tangerine Dream and all that. When I recorded my album in 1973, I really didn't know the German groups. The only unconscious influence I had was Fripp & Eno, before they released their first record. Theirs and mine were released in an interval of one month. At the time I'd gone and seen the people of Island Records and I'd seen Steve Winwood's brother. We almost did something together, but finally it didn't work out. Then there was all the militant action around the auto production labels. It was the first time it was done in France. The only real influence was the Fripp & Eno tapes we heard before King Crimson's concerts. My conscious roots are rather based on Philip Glass's work, at the time of *MUSIC FOR TWELVE PARTS* -- a type of music I've always appreciated a lot, even now. Otherwise, I was quite close to some of the members of Kraftwerk who wanted to meet the musicians of Heldon at the time their album *TRANS EUROPE EXPRESS* was number one. Now I look forward in January to continuing work on the album in a studio, and it would be fine if we could tour in France.

CA: There are currently many polemical discussions about synth-based music in specialized circles. What does it represent for you now?

RP: The return to the bass/percussion/guitar formation was a great thing with groups like Tangerine Dream -- everything became more spontaneous again. Yet this doesn't mean you should forget electronic compositions, and I still believe that groups like Nine Inch Nails bring a lot of things to both electronic and current music. It's a new form of enunciation. I hope that *CYBORG SALLY* will be the same from another point of view.

CYBORG SALLY AND CURRENT MUSIC

CA: You told me that if you had to give a name to the music you compose now you would call it "techno-trash" music!

RP: In fact, I'd say its techno-electro-trash music (smiles). It's in keeping with history.

CA: Can you be a little more explicit? How do you understand Techno and Trash?

RP: Techno is fucking annoying, but I admit it's completely impersonal for those who listen to it as well as for those who compose it or those who earn money on it. Also for the sounds, which musicians steal from each other. It's the concept of total anonymity, and I find this interesting from a theoretical point of view. Just an anecdote. I met a composer who had recorded an album on Tangram and whom I like, Philippe Laurent. I told him I felt like taking one of his tunes to do something else with it and I suggested he co-sign the piece. He was very happy, and then he told me that he'd composed his album by stealing pieces from other records. Well, the story of techno music is really interesting... Besides, the models for it are the great synthesizers of the 70s, which is already a good thing. Very often, there's not really music. People content themselves with sampling, that's all. I've even found sounds taken from *ELECTRONIQUE GUERILLA*.

CA: What about Trash, then?

RP: In trash music, I like the fusion side. There are groups I appreciate particularly, like Rage Against the Machine or Nine Inch Nails, who produce interesting music. I like the white occidental side, which is part of World music. We represent the white occidental part of World music. I'm happy with this, there's really no need to feel guilty because we compose white occidental music. It's as valorizing as Bantu or other musics. It's one type of music and I hope I'm good at composing it. The most interesting trash group today is Nine Inch Nails. It's really very interesting and the composer is also a very good singer. It's by far the most interesting experience I know in the musical de-territorialization of today. It's incredibly violent and there's a remarkable work on sounds. The words are far from crap. It's as if a great revolutionary movement was embodied in music now. They're not alone. There are many such groups, and this movement is going to arrive in France. We're very lucky. The '90s have given birth to a lot of new music. Let's stop repeating the same things and looking back to the past. You always feel you have already heard this or that tune; nothing is new. Even when you listen to Led Zeppelin it reminds you of Wagner at one point, so let's stop looking back 20 years behind. I think there's a lot of very good music now, which is well-played, too. It didn't exist in the '80s. For me the '80s are an ice period with disco music and all the rest, except for a few groups like U2. The '90s are at the basis of a fabulous musical movement.

CA: Are you willing to make of *CYBORG SALLY* a concept album?

RP: No. I didn't intend to in the first place but that's what happened. The common denominator is the Cyborg Sally notion, which is Norman Spinrad's. He's the hero of Spinrad's novel *Rock Machine (Little Heroes)*. We took the words of Norman's novel with his agreement and we worked with Norman, who sings on the album. We'll make a single version of this tune with more recognizable voices. What was not a concept initially gradually became a Cyborg Sally production. Everything revolves around this fictitious character.

Jérôme Schmidt: Why did you reform a band under the federative name of Heldon, 20 years after the last album *STAND BY*?

Richard Pinhas: In fact, in a recent interview I was promising not to do it again! But I met since that recent time some persons who encouraged me to do it, especially my old friend Norman Spinrad (a very well-known sci-fi writer), as well as the French writer Maurice Dantec, whose books really appealed to me a lot. I found that proposal very amusing and then we decided to do it. The story of Heldon had begun with the philosopher Gilles Deleuze reading a text by Nietzsche, and to do it again 20 years later with Maurice Dantec reading Gilles Deleuze was a kind of tribute to Deleuze. So then we formed this new lineup, which is mainly based on the parallel between writers and musicians.

David Korn: I'm the new singer of this band and I do believe that the name of Heldon is a very nice one, which refers to the beautiful text by Norman Spinrad. The definite title of the album will be *ONLY CHAOS IS REAL*.

JS: To what extent will this new album be different from your current solo works?

Richard Pinhas: It is in fact the lineup I dreamt of: a power trio with bass, drums and guitar, plus an additional singer. Olivier Manchion, from the post-rock band Ulna Bator, assumes the bass duties as well as Bernard Paganotti does for a couple of tracks. His son Antoine Paganotti is the official drummer of the band. The challenge is to record an album with 90% of sung tracks without doing FM rock. If everything goes well, we'll do another album in 1999 and we'll split in year 2000! But we'll also include some electronics like in "De l'Un et du Multiple" with the addition of Maurice Dantec's voice reading some beautiful texts by

Gilles Deleuze.

JS: How did you choose your new musicians?

Richard Pinhas: I knew Antoine Paganotti since I recorded *CYBORG SALLY* in 1993 and I really think he is one of the best drummers; he plays ternary music and has been a very good student at Christian Vander's "school"! I met Olivier Manchion and I thought that his sound fit perfectly with the new sound I wanted to reach. And then David Korn came as well as a bunch of friends such as Benoit Widemann, who plays some extraordinary beautiful Moog parts. Alain Bellaiche does some guitar parts, too, and Philippe Laurent, who is a well-known DJ, added some industrial samples on *ONLY CHAOS IS REAL*. I've worked with the sound-wizard Jean Marc Pinault, who did a really great job for the mixing work. After three or four rehearsals, the band was very almost definitely OK, all musicians and lyricists being totally integrated into a group entity.

JS: All these musicians come from different musical contexts (jazz, electronica, post rock, electropunk...); isn't it one of the reasons why this new album is so different from the others?

Richard Pinhas: Yes, and I chose musicians to reach this new sound. It's quite close to what we used to do with Patrick Gauthier, Didier Batard and François Auger in 1976 when we toured. One may compare the new Heldon to the son of an extraterrestrial mother with an electro-punk father! Every musician has his own qualities and I've tried to take the best from these, and if I asked Bernard Paganotti to play on one track, it was only because it was HIS sound which was the best for the tune.

JS: Then how would you define this new sound of Heldon?

Richard Pinhas: The sound of the band has evolved with the evolution of technologies. Musical colors change and I tried to make the purest sound I could, with a slightly different sound on guitar, with a different use of the synths. We created a sort of minimalism without doing minimalist music. We tried to use no reverberations and no other devices and thus the mix is transparent, very compact also. The technology of the Hyperprism Arboretum System was very useful, and we tried to make the densest music we could. There are many layers of instruments that you can distinguish, but there is still a global sound.

(Editor's Note: The last days of 1998-99 have been busy for Richard Pinhas as several projects have been realized, and/or are in the process of materialization. A new collaboration featuring Pinhas' Frippatronics backdrops and poetry in French by wordsmith Maurice Dantec has been released, entitled *SCHIZOTROP -- LE PLAN*. The duo undertook a mini-tour of the USA in early '99 showcasing it and recording a live set for release. Additionally, an interesting collaboration by Pinhas and Peter Frohmader has been completed, entitled *FOSSIL CULTURE*. Lastly, a new Heldon album, *ONLY CHAOS IS REAL*, is completed, and at last word waits for a label to pick it up for release.

Cyrille Amistani
Translated by Jerome Schmidt
Additional questions by Jerome Schmidt

Christan Vander Interview

Q: At the beginning of Magma -- in 1970 -- you used to say that you were fighting against musical vulgarity. Do you think that nowadays in 1997, after 25 years, this fight has been effective?

Christian Vander: Certainly but I don't know where... The only thing I can assert is that the world around us is not really any better than it was 25 years ago...

Q: What is the worst problem, according to you, for music: the lack of good musicians or of good composers?

CV: Composers, for sure. Many musicians play very well individually but do not practice the music they love and this leads to incoherent bands. You can hear that he is a good musician, but that the music is not valuable at all. Why? Simply because people don't pay attention to the act of writing music. I am one of those who really believes in the strength and importance of the composer.

Q: And do you believe, as the leader of Einstürzende Neubauten does, that all the music that you can hear incites you to create even more, as a reaction to the mediocrity of most of these musical productions?

CV: No, I don't think so. It doesn't stimulate me, and after so many years with the same music imposed on people by the media, I find it very annoying. We do need some new musical expressions. Even if I don't claim to be a musical adventurer, I do believe that if we have some room to express ourselves, we have to explore everything we can to go further up.

Q: Are you tired of making your music?

CV: No, because I'm constantly looking for new ideas. It's a marvelous quest indeed; everything is a rhythm and with these rhythms -- not with harmonies -- I can create an infinite number of melodies, with just a few rhythms.

Q: What was your motivation to re-form Magma and to play this music again on stage?

CV: In fact, I've always been ready for it. My life is on stage and I've never forgotten Magma. And then a friend proposed me to re-form it. I was just waiting for an opportunity to do it.

Q: You had always been very active in the musical scene, but with Offering, a more Coltrane-inspired band... How do you explain that the public of Magma has not always been convinced by the music of Offering?

CV: I think that it's better to explain those kind of things after. Everything has been done: Magma, Offering, solo albums and so on... Offering has been unlucky in fact and hasn't toured enough to become famous. With Magma, at the beginning, we often played before just 40 or 50 persons, and we were doing 25 concerts per month. We were even not earning money at all, just enough to eat a sandwich and drink a soda... and to sleep under the truck!

Q: What is the interest for you to play in your jazz trio?

CV: It allows me to discover many new rhythms and, thus, new melodies.

Q: Haven't you ever thought to make gigs with Offering, Magma and the trio all together?

CV: Yes, and we even talked of it quite recently. The great problem is that Offering needs an acoustic piano and that we can't use electric instruments in it as it would not fit with an acoustic piano. We had tried to do it at the beginning of the '70s when we were the first one in France to use Fender pianos; it allowed us to play wonderful key parts. But it's not an acoustic piano; so it would cost very much to have Fenders, keyboard and a piano on stage. There had also been some problems with the vocals at the beginning of Offering in 1983 when gigs lasted 3 hours: after ten minutes my voice was out of order! I then realized it was different from the tunes I was singing at home: there on stage I had to sing for three hours! Some live tapes from this period must be quite funny indeed!

Q: How do you perceive the renewal of Magma's public: tonight the attendance was very young...

CV: You know, I've never belonged to any musical fashion. Magma's music is atemporal, and that's why we gain a new public nowadays. It's like John Coltrane to a certain extent: I was listening to him when I was 11 and I do believe that nowadays it's ahead of its time.

Q: Speaking of Coltrane, what is your opinion regarding the fact that his death has not been commemorated very much this year?

CV: I'd rather say that it's a good thing: I was afraid that for his 30th death-anniversary anybody would talk about him, but that in 1998 they would forget him. I think of him every day, every second; he is my major influence and he is ever present in my mind.

Q: At the end of his life, John Coltrane seemed to search for rhythmic multi-plicities, in the incorporation of two drummers in his bands, for example. Is that the same thing you tried to experience in your WELCOME project with Simon Goubert?

CV: Yes, we tried it, but our line-up is not the same as John's, with McCoy Tyner, Elvin Jones or Rashied Ali... we tried it, but well... An important phenomenon that many people forget is that Coltrane's music was very much based on a special vibe, similar to Indian music. The idea of a special vibe is not abstract notion -- it does exist. Many musicians work with it, and try to understand how it interferes in our musical notions. So I do believe that most of the important musicians are the ones who have this notion of a special vibe because they can have a different approach to sonic textures.

Q: In a quite obscure sentence, Coltrane even said that he wanted to make a record with no notes. What do you think of that?

CV: It's not impossible, I think. Maybe he was just talking about a feeling. Magma makes music for everyone -- blind people as well as deaf ones. What is the use of a great light show if all your attendance is blind? We also play for those who don't hear or don't see very well, because we create a certain kind of vibe, a feeling that anyone can have access to. That's maybe what John Coltrane meant with this sentence.

Q: At one time, you said that you were in quest of "The Note" and now you seem to attach more importance to what is going on between two notes. Is that an evolution or just a different expression of the same feeling?

CV: The Note I was talking about, man

has never heard before. It was a Magma musical project, but as I'd said three years ago that I would do it the following year, I prefer not to say more about it! It'll be an album based on the idea of a special vibe that we were talking about previously. Some musicians look for this vibe all life long, and they don't find it at all. I've concentrated my work on that since 1987 because at that time I found this note and now I cannot conceive music in the same way. Now when I listen to John Coltrane or even to musicians that I may have judged as not being very interesting, it allows me to perceive their music from a different point of view.

Q: You may know that in Japan, there is a huge renewal of Zeuhl music with bands such as Ruins, Bondage Fruit, Happy Family, etc... What do you think of Japanese music?

CV: It's a very interesting musical scene, and I listened to one of those groups awhile ago; I found it very nice, but also very sad. It is a music deeply rooted in realism; I'm not saying that music has not to be linked with reality, but the realistic aspect really annoys me. When I was listening to John Coltrane, I heard something else... something extremely beautiful and intense, not a sad, realistic world.

Q: What could be your contribution to ameliorate reality? Isn't Kobaïa a kind of a lost paradise thus?

CV: Man has to be ready to act anywhere, anytime and in any way. I sometimes regret to have become a musician because maybe I could have been more useful somewhere else... In an album like "A tous les Enfants," I talk of "children from the light" -- these are the ones who haven't endured our life, and who deserve to live in a better world...

Q: Don't you think that the emotions that an audience can have during one of your concerts are an expression of this feeling?

CV: No, not really. Many people come and see me after concerts to tell me that it was moving, extraordinary and so on..; but do you believe that the day after they would act differently? I don't think so. Progressively, they forget it... Some people even don't like music, and I understand it very well. A good musician, then, is not more important than a good baker, you know...

Q: One of the most cryptic and secret of Magma's musicians was Rene Garber, alias Stundher, which was a kind of your alter-ego. Are you still in contact with him?

CV: Yes, but it's true that he is a secret character in Magma's history. We still see each other, and he has always been there at each moment of Magma's life, even in the shadow. As he was not always a musician, he was often rejected by the other members of the band because he was paid like the others and when you own just 150 FF for six guys, well a seventh one really matters! With Stundher, we always went fishing, to eat better than the others, who were wasting their money in really disgusting fast food. Stundher is really an omnipresent man; like a medium, he was always present and able to tell me if it was the right note that I played. When I had some doubts about some musical themes, I played for him and he was looking at me and said "Yes" or "No," and every time he made the right answer. He is mad about music, but unfortunately, he is not a good player; he is musical medium, in fact. I met him in the late '60s and we were listening to the same bands, to Rhythm and Blues, and most of the time, to John Coltrane. I first saw him as he was playing saxophone in a gig where he performed a 45-minute solo! I was simply astonished by such a solo and I went to see him: "You must listen to Coltrane, mustn't you?" and then we have never been separated since that time.

Q: You said that Coltrane did kill the saxophone...

CV: Yes, I did, and I was quite right when you know that Sonny Rollins stopped playing sax for three years after having heard John playing! OK, he played again after, but, well, it's quite significant...

Q: And Didier Lockwood says that you are the "Coltrane of drums"...

CV: No, but not all! There is also Elvin Jones and Rashied Ali who I really think are the most Coltrane-inspired drummers. I prefer maybe Elvin Jones, but when you listen to "Interstellar Space" or "Stellar Regions," you do understand that there's another gifted drummer who emerges behind it all.

Q: Do you have, as Rashied Ali, many obscure live or studio records that you'd want to reissue, perhaps on your AKT label?

CV: We issue only key concerts or studio works from Magma. We don't want to overwhelm the listener with tons of unreleased concerts. I'd want to reissue a special one from Colmar in 1974, where we play only as a quartet with Jannick Top, Klaus Blasquiz and Gérard Bikialo. Mickey Graillier the pianist had just left the band and so Jannick had to assume the key duties on his bass! It sounded like a whole orchestra of 50 musicians, simply amazing with violins, choirs, etc... Just fabulous, but unfortunately, I don't have this record.

Q: In early 1973, you played in concert some long tunes which are still unreleased. It was with Stundher and Jannick and it was like a melding of *MDK* and *KOHNTARKOSZ* ...

CV: I have friends in Don't Die -- a band who makes covers of Magma -- who did replay it recently. We played this tune only three times live, and it was the basis of our research for *KOHNTARKOSZ*. I own one of these gigs, but I tried to add some drum parts to it in studio and I mistakenly erased some instruments! It's a great pity as this was a very interesting composition.

Q: *EMEHNTET RE* was also expected at a time...

CV: Yes, it's true. We began to record it at the time in 1976, but as the recording time of LPs was limited to 44 minutes, we never completed it. This was intended to be a very long work, perhaps a triple album, and no record company could afford such a risk.

Q: Many people also wait for Jannick Top's compositions in Magma, such as "La Musique des Spheres" that you played in the Renaissance tour in late October and early November 1976...

CV: Jannick gave me a studio recording of this tune -- which lasts 25 minutes -- as well as other compositions, such as "Glah," for example, which is very nice with some bells resounding and with Jannick's bass and vocals answering the bells' music. Bells are very important in music, and John Coltrane was the first one to understand it. He knew that a musician finds most of the important things in harmonics, because music is basically made up of harmonics. One can play a "D" for 20 minutes on different harmonics, and it will never sound the same way. For a new tune, I actually recorded "Les Cygnes et les Corbeaux" -- I sing on a note, and this note constantly varies because I use its different harmonics. I could make a whole symphony on a single note, with different harmonics. So Jannick wanted to "add" his tunes to the reissue of ÜDÜ WÜDÜ we made on 7th Records, but I refused as it had not exactly been created in the same musical context. So I asked him if he wanted me to issue a whole album with his compositions. He only told me that he had to re-listen to his recordings to choose and since that time... no news! He once gave me a mysterious studio recording with superb unreleased tunes, and I kept it for myself as it would have been a betrayal to give it to other people, even if I should have done it because the music was really astonishing. So I sent it back to him -- it was in 1978 -- and when I asked him about this recording recently when we played again in Fusion in 1995, he told me he had to look for it in his mess! But once again I have no news, and I wonder if he really wants to let people hear his wonderful, beautiful music...?

Q: Have you heard Jannick Top's new band called "STS," where he plays a personal kind of jazz fusion?

CV: No, I haven't. I do think that Jannick needs to play his music again as one can't do what he has done -- accompanying a variety of singers -- without being punished. For now, he has to play again his own music to achieve the skill he had at one time. But in STS, he doesn't take many risks because he plays with a drummer he knows, Claude Salmieri (who has also been a studio sideman for a variety of singers), thus he doesn't escape totally his former job's music. For instance, the drummer plays like a machine and he can play freely on this basis, but it's too easy. He can play much more difficult things, a much nicer music, too. I have asked Jannick if he wanted to play with Emmanuel Borghi (pianist of Magma and of Vander Trio) and me in a jazz trio where we could play some jazz themes, to be once again in a difficult musical situation where he could extend himself. I'm still waiting for his answer... No, in fact, I don't wait because I have waited for Jannick too long a time and now I just follow my way and maybe one day we'll play together again.

Q: What conclusions would you draw from your label 7th Records?

CV: Artistically speaking it is really pleasant, as we have reissued all the official albums with the sleeves we wanted and with some unreleased tracks when they were some interesting ones. We have also produced new artists such "Collectif Mu" (a jazz septet who have won several jazz awards in France) and Emmanuel Borghi, Patrick Gauthier, Jean-Luc Chevalier, and Pierre-Michel Sivadier's solo albums. The name 7th Records was created to resound like a cymbal, like some open invitation to music. I wanted it to be open to many different kinds of music, from jazz to classical music. When we created it, I wanted to use an orange and black symbol, similar to that of Impulse Records. Instead we have a quite original red/white/black symbol, which immediately makes our releases identifiable. And in AKT, with three albums, you find again this triptych! When I paint, only for pleasure, I often paint creations which are spread over ten or more pictures: Each picture blends into the new one and there is no ending.

Q: Speaking of paintings, can you remind us how you got H.R. Giger to do the sleeve for the album "Attahk"?

CV: I asked him to do it because I really liked his approach to reality. I told him to make a building that would have no ending, but he failed in it as it has one. The building is too little, and I was quite disappointed by the result. This desire of an infinite verticality is a leitmotiv, a kind of obsession in my mind. It's the same thing with Magma's famous symbol. It was worked for a very long time by Laurent Thibault's sister to attain a kind of perfection in its proportionality.

Q: How was this symbol conceived?

CV: In fact, I wanted it to be a multi-dimensional symbol. I asked Laurent's sister to draw a kind of animal's paw for the first album. Then she made that eagle's foot. I had been quite disappointed because I wanted something unconceivable, because Magma's music was not like any other music. And then it became this more purified and mysterious symbol which fit accurately with our music. Nobody grasped the meaning of it, as well as nobody grasped the meaning of the Kobaïan language. It was a language you could feel, but that you couldn't understand, a kind of organic language. As it was ungraspable, nobody could attack it, as to attack something you have to understand it first.

Q: With the flux of time, do you feel such a thing as frustration: like if you won't have the time to accomplish all the things you'd want to do...

CV: Yes, I often feel this way. But I prefer not to do rubbish. John Coltrane, for example, did perfectly what he had to do, and he finished his work. I cannot figure myself what he could have done after "Expression" and "Offering." He has not left us an unfinished work with many errors. I myself want to do my best to do the same thing. I play and create at my rhythm, erasing all the imperfections I can erase. Nowadays, I record "Les Cygnes et les Corbeaux," and I spend much more time that I thought I would for this record. I play my parts two times, almost never, but I have to co-ordinate all the other musicians, and it's really a huge and delicate task.

Q: You have always been quite slow and perfectionist in your records...

CV: Yes, and it's because I don't want to leave too many mistakes, and I work with other musicians who don't have always the same approach to music. In fact, I can do a solo album with my voice plus a piano, and it'd be the same emotion. I have in stock compositions for almost ten or eleven solo albums, which I could record in a studio very quickly, the duration of the takes in fact. If I'm really ready for it, it's made in a few days. I've already done it once for "To Love": I recorded it very quickly in the memory of a very close friend, Jean Paul Fenneteau, who had died.

Q: In this album, you begin the "XMC" tune with a cover of Archie Shepp's "Le Matin des Noirs." Why?

CV: This record is also indirectly dedicated to Archie Shepp, and that's why I play drums only on this tune. I wanted to tell him something very personal, something dealing with Malcom X, and that's why the tune is named XMC. I also work very much on the musical modes of Alice Coltrane. And each time I listen to her or to John, I discover new things, new subtleties. For example, in "Everything We Say Goodbye," John exceptionally lets McCoy Tyner, Steve Davis and Elvin Jones finish the tunes, and I wondered myself why he did so. In fact, it's because this tune is a song and when the singer says goodbye he doesn't speak any longer. It's really logical! But here in France, the jazzmen always play after the "goodbye." Musicians have to know the lyrics if they want to play correctly the tunes correctly. In *HHAI*, I've taught the guitarist the lyrics so that he can play the song correctly. It's really easy, but only few musicians understood it. And in Coltrane, there are all these little tips that helped him achieve a more beautiful music. Each time I hear it, I understand something new.

(**Editors Note:** It seems hard to believe, but it is true, Magma finally made it to the USA (and Mexico) for a mini-tour. Along with a few selected dates in NY, Chicago and LA, they gave a stunning performance headlining the International Music Festival in San Francisco, and played two massive shows in Mexico City. As a witness to the SF show, I can say for a fact that listening to their music on album is a much inferior experience to the staggering spectacle of Magma live!)

Denis Desassis, Alexis Drion & Jérôme Schmidt
Translation: Jérôme Schmidt

Le Rock Francais
Europe's Best-Kept Musical Secret

Just like the rest of you, I got hooked. The realization that the Krautrock and German electronic music that suddenly emerged in 1971 had opened musical doors that most people never knew existed was staggering. It was only later on that, in many cases, the influences were spotted and at least some explanation as to its origins developed.

The French scene, however, was something very different. This article is not an historical document of that scene, but a personal overview of some of the players and the movement as an entire entity.

The German genre of Krautrock took hold in the UK, thanks largely to Melody Maker and NME press coverage, national radio play on John Peel's legendary "Top Gear" programs and "en masse" importation of the Krautrock albums by the shops. The French musical movement, however, which was also beginning to spread its arms far and wide throughout the home nation, remained a closely guarded musical secret to most of the potential music fans outside of France. Virtually all anyone knew of French homegrown music were Ange, Gong and Magma.

All three had emerged as front-runners in the area of proving that France could have its own musical scene and be taken seriously outside the UK. Ange had arisen in a similar manner to Genesis in the UK, in other words, a unique progressive music, the likes of which had not previously been heard in the country. They took hold because the musicians were talented, the vocals were in French, the group's stage shows were theatrical and some of the group's albums were.... gasp.... concept albums in the grand prog traditions. The compositions were original and intricate, always inspiring, and, you might have thought, perfect for all prog fans. However, all it did was illustrate how most English-speaking fans of the music couldn't get their heads around a group who played such great music and yet sang in a foreign language. Despite several attempts, admittedly somewhat half-heartedly, to promote them outside France, the group flopped dismally, and the French remained the sole and proud appreciators of what are still rightly viewed as one of the leading prog bands of the '70s.

Gong had it slightly luckier in that their leading light, Daevid Allen, wasn't actually French, but started out as the Australian lead guitarist for the seminal English band Soft Machine. He then went into exile in France, a wise choice in which to reside since this had been a core heartland of the Soft Machine's musical popularity. With a head full of ideas, he hooked up with one of the major players on the French psych music scene, by the name of Ame Son, and formed the outfit known as Banana Moon, evidence of whose music can be heard on the album *JE NE FUME PAS DES BANANES*. This paved the way for the outpourings into the real world of the musings and entire universe created, if you like, by Daevid, that encompassed everything from pothead pixies, flying teapots, Camembert, Octave Doctors and lots more. This all worked, thanks to the music that accompanied the lyrical flow, coming to full fruition, initially on the ground-breaking psychedelic album *CAMEMBERT ELECTRIQUE* and later covering the world on the remarkable *RADIO GNOME INVISIBLE* trilogy of albums. One of the fascinating things about Gong was the way that they used jazz, particularly in the flute and sax work of maestro musician Didier Malherbe, in a way that the audience never thought of it as jazz due to the context in which it was placed. The place of jazz in the history of French music is a much larger source of enjoyment than anywhere else in Europe. Right through their career, Gong have been viewed as a French band, which was not strictly the case, but close enough for rock 'n' roll. Either way, they spawned some fantastic musicians and remain a leading light in the history of French music.

Magma was the band from which legends are made and stories passed down from generation to generation about their concepts, playing, concerts, line-ups, offshoots, imitators and beyond. The brainchild of drummer and Coltrane fan Christian Vander, they were essentially from a jazz background, but the music that was revealed on their first "magnum opus" double LP, proved to be utterly innovative in every sense of the word. Not only was the line-up a mix of the electric and acoustic, but the brand of jazz-rock on offer was (a) more jazz than rock, (b) featured guitars, electric bass, drums, sax, trumpet, and electric piano as the musical core, (c) was predominantly vocal. The lyrics were made up of a language called Kobaian, sung in a phenomenally wide vocal range by Vander and the chief lead vocalist Klaus Blasquiz. And (d) the whole album was based on a self-created mythology, this time science fiction in nature and one quite breathtaking in its scope and execution. More than anything it was the sheer force and power of Magma's music that makes it such a force to be reckoned with, and when they came out with their first real "rock" album in the form of *MEKANIK DESTRUKTIW KOMMANDOH*, those who had caught on to the band had their musical lives turned completely upside down. They had a fair amount of press coverage in the UK, and to some extent the USA, and did quite a lot of concert dates in the UK, including the Reading Festival. They got signed to a major label for their two biggest albums; did an incredible hourlong John Peel session, which took up half the broadcast programme (which begs for a CD releases); and nearly cracked it in the UK. But their concept failed to win broad enough acceptance, the band's line-up changed yet again, and they were dropped by the label in the UK. They had a brief resurrection from snooker hero Steve Davis in the '80s, that again allowed UK fans to witness the Magma phenomenon.

France had begun its own music scene in the late '60s and the dawn of the '70s. Bands such as Komintern, Red Noise, Moving Gelatine Plates, Catharsis and Martin Triangle, to name but a few, turned a trickle into a flood, and a mass of talented home-grown groups and artists burst onto the scene, plugged in and let rip. The movement became known as "Le

Rock D'Ici," (the French equivalent of Krautrock), a term coined by the leading French journalist, musician and prime mover of the scene, Herve Picart. He wrote regular articles and interviews for the French magazine "Best." Thanks to all this coverage, alongside similar if not quite as extensive treatment in "Rock Et Folk," there was not only a healthy concert circuit established throughout France for most of the groups around, but sales for the LPs were also fairly healthy. In short, it looked as though the French finally had a music scene they could be proud of, one full to the brim with musical innovation and one which had the potential to be accepted outside the country, a vital factor if anything seriously big was going to happen.

Guess what... sure enough, it failed to take hold outside of France and remained lost to the unsuspecting musical world.

Picture the scene. It's about 1975, and I'm in London on one of my visits. I'm searching for new and unknown music, these were the days when there were a whole host of independent record shops who could stay in business without having to pander to commercial whims of the music industry and pay rents the size of the nearest star system. Somewhere around Paddington, I discover a small, in fact absolutely minute, shop with a few albums in the window, the likes of which I did not recognize at all. I wander in and playing over the shop stereo system was an album of electronic-based music that put the likes of the Kraut synth fraternity to shame. Here was a form of electronic/electric music that didn't so much space you out as batter you into a state of complete numbness and then steamroller over your lifeless corpse, taking no prisoners. I stood there for a full 20 minutes, open-mouthed in total awe of what I was hearing. The album turned out to be one side of a double album by a group called Heldon; the LP was titled *IT'S ALWAYS ROCK 'N' ROLL*. The sound of the synth, electronics, guitars, bass and drums remains absolutely mind-blowing to this day. It was on an obscure label called Disjuncta, and you had to struggle to decipher the sleeve notes and who was actually playing on which tracks. It was clearly of independent origin and began what became a personal and, later, professional addiction to the "cause celebre" of French music.

A short time later, armed with as many copies of "Best" as I could find, and thanks to a sister living in France, I discovered the delights of the Paris record shops. My search of them would reveal stacks of French albums which had never reached the UK, which no one in the UK knew anything about and which received no media exposure whatsoever. This remained the case, with only Archie Patterson's magazine EUROCK in the USA daring to cover the artists and groups of the French serious music scene. Later, Dave Elliott's excellent fanzine "Neu Musik" covered things for the UK.

Musically, there were five main categories into which, if you had to, you could place most of the best and, arguably, the most innovative music on the market. Most notably jazz-rock and fusion, progressive rock, electronic, New French music and avant-garde, with a few failing to be categorizable at all, such as the awesome Wapassou and the bizarre Urban Sax.

In the case of jazz-rock, in the light of the love affair that the nation has with jazz itself, it was absolutely inevitable that a massive and extraordinarily varied scene should arise in the fusion area of music. Begun by early pioneers such as Jean-Luc Ponty, it didn't really catch fire until after the mid-'70s, when a whole rush of groups and artists, many being legacies of the Magma school of music, pioneered a brand of jazz-rock music that put their UK and USA counterparts to shame. By 1976 we had witnessed the first fruits of careers by ZAO, Yochk'o Seffer, François Cahen, Richard Raux and Teddy Lasry out of the Magma camp, and Potemkine, Michel Ripoche and Edition Speciale from the more orthodox fusion world. ZAO was one of the most original of the bands, incorporating a variety of musical influences from jazz through ethnic and classical, combining it all in one musical melting pot and creating several albums that remain fresh and vibrant to this day. The genre of music explored by ex-ZAO and Magma musician Y. Seffer was even farther out. He used the generic heading of "Neffesh Music," and created a highly unorthodox mix of East European contemporary classical influences welded to a strong jazz background, all well-developed into a totally original set of compositions. Even a more "normal" band such as Potemkine would produce three albums of fusion music that was undeniably French, with a sense of adventure and exploration combining to keep the listener riveted with technique, atmosphere and emotion all on display.

Sadly, progressive rock was not faring all that well. In France, there were groups such as Atoll, Mona Lisa, Tai Phong and Tangerine all on the prog rock trail. They were song-based and singing in French. Denied outside acceptance because of this, it wouldn't have been so bad if they'd been really amazing, but out of the whole stack of groups that followed in their wake, such as Open Air, Artcane and others, only really Atoll climbed head and shoulders above the field. Their albums *L'ARIGNEE MAL* and *TERTIO* really caught fire and remain excellent examples of mid-'70s French prog. The one exception to this rule was Pulsar. Here was a group who, on the evidence of their first album *POLLEN*, revealed themselves to be a mainly instrumental band, their few French vocals actually fitting in with the music. They played compositions that were as close to early Pink Floyd as had been heard in a long while. It was this strength of composition, atmosphere, ensemble work and possible commercial sales that resulted, presumably, in their being signed up by a UK record label and the group actually being brought over to do English concerts. Their follow-up album, the last to get a UK release, was *STRANDS OF THE FUTURE* and was even more Floyd-like, its sidelong title track conjuring images of "Crazy Diamond"-era Floyd to this day. Subsequent albums were more proggy and less spacey, but still have had the potential for mega-sales if only some company would have had the foresight and belief to issue the things outside France.

Alongside the prog acts, there were a few groups who were mixing prog and fusion in largely instrumental settings. They were influenced to a great degree by groups ranging from Caravan and Camel to King Crimson and Genesis, but were in no way copyist or cliché-ridden. The best of these were Alpha Ralpha, Shylock and Carpe Diem, who played compositions that are intricate, smooth, hot and dynamic, a swell as melodic, powerful and never less than engaging.

In the area of New French Music, we have all sorts of styles, as it was a rule unto itself. The mid-'70s saw the emergence of Lard Free, ZNR, Pataphonie, Albert Marcœur and Art Zoyd. Lard Free's first release was a self-titled album that remains unique to this day, with its oddly hypnotic, angular and atmospheric mix of guitars, bass clarinet and drums, playing tracks that are essentially early examples of what is now termed "post-rock," only 24 years earlier. For the second album, *I'M AROUND MIDNIGHT*, they recruited the services of Heldon's Richard Pinhas on electric guitar and produced a fine, almost starkly biting album that lacked the jazzy influences of its predecessor, but made up for it in the power stakes. But if you thought the previous albums a bit strange, the third album positively left you standing with mouth open. Its two lengthy compositions were musical panoramas of urban landscapes and oppressive city life, the instrumental atmospheres and construction, in hindsight, seen to be a forerunner for the emergence, in 1977, of Gilbert Artman's massive musical project, Urban Sax. Still going, 20 years later, they are a group of anywhere between 20 and 30 sax players, plus bass, percussion and dancers. Today, they continuously perform a variety of live concerts in some of the most bizarre settings (a railway station, the Paris Metro, Central London, etc.) and play what amounts to live theatre with every concert treated as a real "event," one that will never be forgotten, once seen and heard. The music, sounding like some otherworldly giant electronic organism of erotic emotion, is equally amazing. The group is best represented on record by the awesome *FRACTION SUR LE TEMPS* album, although you really need a full-length video to appreciate this lot to the fullest extent.

Elsewhere, Albert Marcœur was trying to be a French Zappa, while Art Zoyd became the first in a long line of groups to play music that had been heavily influenced by the heady days of Magma. Unlike a lot of the others, however, Art Zoyd would use this as a springboard before shooting off into entirely new and uncharted waters that remained defiantly and definitely their own making. In the case of several of their albums, they created a brand of music that the world is still not ready for; examples include, *LE MARIAGE DE CIEL ET DU L'ENFER* and *BERLIN*.

In the case of orthodox (as opposed to the more avant-garde offerings from the INA-GRM school) electronic musicians, Richard Pinhas really started the ball rolling for home-grown talent by producing a debut album that many people said had been influenced by Fripp & Eno's first album and yet which was actually issued at the same time. Pinhas had taken influences from them, for sure, but also from other English areas of music, and gathered together a pool of musicians, including guitarist Alain Renaud, Georges Grunblatt and others, to form the cult electronic group Heldon and a label, Disjuncta, to put out the albums. Just before all that began, a series of independently played, financed and issued LPs had emerged on the Pole label. Artists included Pole, Philippe Grancher (an early French answer to Vangelis), Besombes and Rizet, and Fluence (on whose album Pinhas contributes some trademark guitar work). These early, and now rare, if poor-quality, vinyl pressings showed that French electronic music was hardly influenced by and in fact dwelt in a totally different universe from, the parallel German scene. It was much less "sweet," less aggressive, more daring, unafraid to substitute innovation for melody, more challenging, but ultimately more rewarding.

Pole didn't last long as a label. Disjuncta fared better, but eventually Pinhas decided it was too much to run both group and label, so he sold the label to allow more time for the group, on the understanding that the new label, Urus, would put out the Heldon music. The legacy of albums left by Heldon is, to this day, inestimably important in musical terms. A band of talented musicians, usually different combinations on each album, they produced a mixture of electronic and electric music that bore no resemblance to anything else around. They used drums like no other electronic band, not to mention all the synth/bass/electric guitar components that created the awesome instrumental compositions on those albums. Their supersonic sound culminated in the tremendous firepower of the cooking *STANDBY* album.

Pinhas went on to produce a set of solo LPs, from the chilling *ICELAND* to the brutal power of *L'ETHIQUE*, the more commercial (for Pinhas) *EAST WEST*, to the solo guitar textures of "De L'un Et L'autre." Other Heldon members fared equally well. Patrick Gauthier became the only musician to play for Heldon, Magma and Weidorje (a Magma offshoot formed by bassist Bernard Paganotti). Georges Grunblatt produced a Heldon-influenced LP called *K-PRISS* on which Pinhas played. Even journalist Herve Picard made an album under the name of Ose, on which Pinhas contributed. The story of guitarist Alain Renaud is less well known. He produced a debut album, *RENAUD*, featuring a sidelong track called "Back And In" that remains a magnificent melange of guitar and electronics to this day. John Peel actually played the whole track on a Top Gear programme, but sadly, Renaud never benefited from this because most of the shops in the UK had never heard of the label and couldn't get it even if they had. Therefore sales never materialized and the album vanished, still to this day begging for a CD issue. After two more albums, Renaud also vanished and has made no more music to this day.

Apart from Heldon, the French scene was alive with more melodic "traditional" offerings, from the Klaus Schulze-oriented space music of Didier Bocquet (particularly on the best-selling *VOYAGE CEREBRAL*). He went on to be signed, like Pinhas, by the UK Pulse label and put out two LPs which weren't a patch on *VOYAGE*, and, despite a support slot to Pinhas on his only UK concert, never capitalized on the success.

Then there was Frederic Mercier, whose music predated and was more interesting than Jean-Michel Jarre's by quite a way. The excellent Richard Vimal, whose *TRANSPARENCES* LP is widely acclaimed as something of a "lost classic" by synth fans all over the world. Synth artist Jean-Philippe Rykiel, whose debut album illustrated the idea that minimalism and melody could meet head on to produce one of the most beautiful synth LPs of the decade, using really just electric piano and synth. Conservatory-trained Cyrille Verdeaux, who led the group Clearlight, was signed by Virgin for 2 LPs, the first of which featured Gong musicians as well as guitarist Christian Boule and Lard Free's Gilbert Artman. Sadly it is still to see the light of day onto CD in its complete form. He then went off to the USA to join their "New Age Electronic" movement (at the time when it actually meant something). He produced a whole stack of seriously excellent synth releases, many of which are still not on CD, but that's another story. He also produced some spectacularly timeless cassette-only releases, culminating in the amazing 6-cassette, 6-hour epic *KUNDALINI OPERA* (on the EUROCK label). Other good musicians around at the time included Claude Perraudin (the French answer to Mike Oldfield, only more synth-oriented), Michel Magne, Patrick Vian (ex-Red Noise) and many more.

If Pinhas, Artman and others were important players on the French music scene, in terms of composer, performer and group leader/talent spotter, Christian Vander was the greatest, a sort of answer to Frank Zappa in terms of assembling talent and bringing the best out of it. He assembled, over the years, a staggering number of talented musicians, nearly all of whom would use their time with whatever line-up Vander had selected, to continue forward and produce solo or group context albums that could never have been made without the Vander influence. The list of just some of them read like a "who's who" of French music: Paganotti, Lockwood, Seffer, Cahen, Widemann, Chevalier, Bertram, Borghi, Lasry, Blasquiz, etc. Only bassist Jannik Top, who was the only one not to play at the individual 6-hour reunion series of 3 concerts in Paris by various Magma line-ups from the years, failed to pursue a solo/group career. He went instead into session/backing musician work, contributing some of his trademark gigantic bass guitar to unlikely but excellent things, including the Eurythmics' "Missionary Man."

So far, I've concentrated mostly on the '70s. In this decade French homegrown serious music was at its musical and popular height. Groups and artists could tour the country, sell albums and win over ever-larger audiences. However, due largely to the fact that, outside of the Gong-Magma-Ange trio, no major circulation magazines outside France were prepared to give this music any coverage, the hundreds of amazing groups and artists to emerge from France remained a closely guarded secret to most music fans. It's a shame because they missed a whole movement that has stood the test of time, overall, a lot better than much of its German counterparts.

Then God created punk...

...And the French "serious" music scene folded like a pack of cards as France embraced the punk-rock scene.

Touring stopped. The music remained but went underground, both in popularity and sales terms. Throughout Europe, the big players in the world of music chain stores had begun the long march on the independents, stomping over most of them in the process. They left few outlets behind to cater for the "uncommercial" music of the past, and, to a degree, the present, as it was then.

In the '80s, there began an extraordinary recovery for the French music scene, thanks largely to two people, neither of whom was a recognized musician. Bernard Gueffier and Francis Grosse took over the running of the French music magazine *Notes* in 1981; it had become the only media voice left in France for the style of music we have mentioned. From this, they went on to assemble the definitive book on the French "serious" music scene, "Le Discographie du Rock Francaise." A mighty work in English and French, it chronicled all the releases, including band and artist bios, line-ups, album covers and more, about all the albums released since the late '60s in these areas of music. The huge book was costly to put out, but financed through the sales of a tape that accompanied initial copies of the mag, featuring unreleased tracks by nine French artists and groups (including Atoll, Uppsala and Eskaton) who had donated these tracks free to help the book. It also marked the first tentative steps of a business partnership that led to the duo eventually forming the Musea label and retail outlet. It later came to act as the French "collecting house" for the release, promotion and distribution of new and reactivated French artists/groups. Later on from 1990, they re-issued, on new digital CD medium, many classics from the massive French musical archives of the '70s. With artistic packaging, most of these featured extra tracks and extensive sleeve notes. In fact it was their pioneering feats on the covers and musical output of these CDs that led to others following the idea of providing CD inserts with 20- to 24-page booklets, including unpublished photos, info, bios, etc.

Due to their efforts, the French scene was kept alive. Newer groups such as Eskaton (Magma-influenced, with two lead female vocalists), Asia Minor (neo-prog band influenced by Crimson and Tull), Uppsala (unique -- had to be heard to be believed), and many more, finally found a sales outlet for the music. They were creating, performing and, in many cases, independently financing their own productions. Musea's own label output went from one release in 1986 to the present levels of 20 to 30 annually.

Other major '80s players included Shub Niggurath (a harder, harsh, Magma-influenced band), plus Jean-Pascal Boffo, Elixir, Xalph, Minimum Vital, Raison de Plus and a stack of others. In the '80s, the main thing that set the French scene head and shoulders above its German counterparts was the large amount of bands continuing the musical growth begun and matured by many of the '70s bands, who by this time had largely disappeared, their next-door rivals only being able to offer shadows of their former selves.

The '90s saw the revival of Krautrock while the world still remained ignorant of the French scene over 20+ years of amazing music. One of the leading players on the current scene is Laurent Perrier, musician, label manager and retailer, whose Oddsize label is a new force in music. He praises new bands including Ulan Bator, Sister Iodine and Les Tetines Noires. He told me that the energy of the French scene so prevalent in the '70s is not as great in the '90s. Also, that it's very difficult to promote and play music in France in the late '90s, as there is not as much energy around you to be creative. Whereas, in England, there are 100s more shops and bands, while France just waits for the next English fashion. He mentions some techno bands such as Daft Punk, Dimitri From Paris and Laurent Garnier, who have a French style and are getting success in England. But for him, the new, good, talented musicians today come from Germany, and he thinks that people buying the music nowadays don't care as much about the origins of the artists.

Touring is better in France in the '90s as the bands have a minimum guaranteed fee. They also receive food and drink and a place to sleep, with most of the organizers/promoters being decent people. The down side is that the sound facilities are not always up to standard, and the level of organization is not very professional.

When asked for his comments on the scene in France in the '90s compared with the '70s, Bernard Gueffier of Musea stated that:

New bands to watch from France include Minimum Vital, Edhels, Jean-Pascal Boffo, Hecenia, XII Alfonso, etc. Most new good French music has very little connection with old bands such as Ange, Atoll, Magma and Pulsar. In the '70s in France there were 100s of places to play live. These places still exist, but are no longer interested in this sort of music. Most French prog rock bands play only two or three times a year in France, mostly financed by Musea (partially or totally), but with low audience attendance, it's not easy to make it pay. In the '70s there were about 3,000 record shops, mostly independent and ready to take risks when it came to stocking uncommercial music. Since then, FNAC (the French chain store) took most of the record market. With 25 big stores, they have killed 90% of the independent stores, which now number just 250. The big stores have a policy of decreasing the quantity of titles in stock, so they start by weeding out the uncommercial stuff, such as prog rock, and fewer of our releases appear in the shops. However, we are optimistic as the prog rock audience in France is slowly increasing with more people becoming bored with the standard music they hear on TV and radio, and are looking for a music which corresponds directly with their own personality.

It seems that things in France have turned, if not full circle, certainly a fair way round. All that is needed is some superstar like Julian Cope to extol the virtues of the French scene, and this would cause a vast renewed interest in the French scene.

With Heldon re-formed and a new CD due in '98, the French music scene could yet prove to be the most potentially successful, previously largely untouched, worldwide source of serious music archive works. There is also still a huge amount of excellent music that has not yet made it onto CD. This, along with the ever-increasing number of new bands coming along, offers hope that "Le Rock D'Ici" is far from dead and buried.

Andy Garibaldi

Manuel Gottsching Interview
Return of The Tempel

In the legends of the German Cosmic Music era, no name is more revered than Manuel Gottsching, the guiding light and musical spirit behind Ash Ra Tempel and Ashra.

Manuel began his musical life in the Steeplechase Blues Band, jamming for fun. When the late 1960s exploded and the first rays of the new age dawned on the horizon, Manuel and his mates, Hartmut Enke (bass) and Klaus Schulze (drums), transformed into Ash Ra Tempel and burst onto the German scene like the blazing solar fire of a cosmic comet.

Their name gave them a larger-than-life aura and set them apart from other groups at the time. Their music embodied the spirit of the times, with its free-flowing improvisations and instrumental excursions. The use of cosmological imagery and the German language for their song titles set them apart from the pack that only wanted to copy their Anglo heroes. These "normal" musicians created something of mythological proportions.

Now, some 25 years later, the group comes into the limelight once again with the release of *THE PRIVATE TAPES*, a 6 CD set that documents Manuel's musical career. Manuel has also done some recent live performances with a reconstituted A.R.T. The recorded results -- *SAUCE HOLLANDAISE*, a recording of a 1997 concert in Holland, and *@ASHRA* from a '97 show in Japan -- have both been released on CD to demonstrate that there is still plenty of musical life left in Manuel and friends. This interview offers a glimpse into the mind of one of the pioneers of the German scene and allows him to reminisce a bit about the good old days.

Q: What was the musical scene and cultural atmosphere like in Germany when you formed A.R.T.?

A: The late 1960s -- the student protests and hippie culture splashed over the ocean from the USA. Musically, most young Germans listened to and copied American and, more often, English rock and pop. It was the era of "Beat," "Rhythm and Blues" and a little "Soul."

But, there were a few bands in Germany trying to withstand the Anglo-American invasion. They were creating their own typically German style by turning their backs on common song structures. This was music made from scratch. Let the good times roll. Many years later, people described this music as "Teutonic Railroad Rock 'n' Roll."

The main bands came from basically three areas of Germany:

Cologne and Dusseldorf -- Can and Kraftwerk
Munich -- Amon Düül and Popol Vuh
Berlin -- Tangerine Dream, Agitation Free and Ash Ra Tempel

In addition, there were many more groups who appeared and disappeared.

Q: Was there a special meaning for the name?

A: My good friend and partner, bass player in Ash Ra Tempel Hartmut Enke always answered this beautiful question. He could expound for hours about the meaning and symbolism of those three words. In short:

Ash -- (an English word) the ash, the remains, the final curtain?

Ra -- the Egyptian Sun God, the energy, the source of our lives

Tempel -- a place for rest and contemplation (written in the German idiom)

Musically, we were just a three-man band in a traditional line-up: drums, bass, guitar and heads full of inspiration. I felt personally that, at least, no other band on earth would show up with a name as strange as that and music the same.

Q: The Ohr Records label released your first album. How did you get connected with that company?

A: Our concerts then were quite successful, if not legendary. Some of these performances are documented on the 6 CDs released as *THE PRIVATE TAPES*. Klaus Schulze played and recorded with Tangerine Dream on their first album *ELECTRONIC MEDITATION* for Ohr Records one year before, in 1970. So here we got our connection.

Q: What was the story of Ohr Records? Who founded it? Who decided about what groups to record? Who did the artwork? Was it a co-operative group of musical people, or more like a normal company where the artists only do what the owner tells them to do?

A: Even in a "normal company," no owner tells the artists what to do. At least, I don't know such a company. Also, I don't know any artist who only does what the owner of a company tells him to do. (A sentence by Klaus Mueller.)

Ohr Music was founded in 1970 by Rolf-

Ulrich Kaiser and a successful German "Schlager" publisher and producer Peter Meisel, as a label for new German rock music; such a label at this time was revolutionary. Today, we are used to hundreds of small labels for all kinds of music. In 1970, I repeat, this was a revolutionary task. The label lasted 4 or 5 years. During this time, all the major companies in Germany founded many other labels.

The daily business was done, in fact, by the driving force behind the label, Rolf-Ulrich Kaiser, whose genuine spirit explored the new trend a little earlier in time, when all of his "colleagues" within that branch were still snoozing. Peter Meisel gave the financial support and business structure.

Friends did artwork for our albums. The cover for *SEVEN UP* was painted by Walter Wegmuller, who later designed a new set of Gypsy Tarot cards for the release of a special album called *TAROT*. The cover of *JOIN INN* was made by a painter from Cologne. For the covers of the "Cosmic Couriers" series, Rolf-Ulrich Kaiser employed a designer of his choice.

Q: Later, Ohr Records turned into the Cosmic Music label, and the owners were reportedly very fond of Timothy Leary. How much did drugs have to do with the music in those days?

A: "Cosmic Music" was a branch of Ohr. "The drugs" had actually little to do with the music (nor with the label), but they were present, as they were present at this time in general. I speak of marihuana/hashish, which were very popular in those days. Everyone under 30 smoked this and that, the elders did so years ago, and still the rivers flow.......... Drugs have been and will be a part of life, not necessarily because one is a musician, a painter, an architect, or a psylocybinien?

They were around and took a great part of my time, but there was another drug that I fell in love with: *MUSIC*

Q: In the mid-1970s, A.R.T. dissolved, and you did a lot of solo work. The music became less rock and more electronic. How did your musical ideas change? What gave you the idea of doing solo electronic music featuring mainly guitar?

A: The influence of electronic equipment in producing music grew rapidly in those years. I was fascinated by these sounds, but even more, I was addicted to the idea of sequencing those sounds into continuous musical compositions.

I owned just my old Gibson guitar plus a few effects units. I asked my producer (Rolf-Ulrich Kaiser) to buy me a 4-track (TEAC) and 2-track (Revox) tape machines. I began to build my studio. I needed time, time for experiments, time for reflecting on the years that had passed, time to call for augurs.

What a trip it became. I created music with a minimum of equipment. The resulting music resembled the sound of sequencers and synthesizer, but was played with a single guitar. I recorded backwards, with the tape machines at double speed, half speed... I tuned the strings differently and fell in love with my dynamic pedals, which could, if you pluck a string, cut away the attack, and with the aid of lots of echo, I found my floating sound. Naturally, the echoes and delays were creating this "sequencing" effect (thus reflecting the trend of those days).

For sure, I am not the only musician at that time that knew about and played with these techniques. I only wanted to create music that was strong and profound enough to escort me into my future life.

Q: Not only the sound of your music

changed, but also the record company ceased to exist a short time later. What happened to the "Cosmic Couriers"?

A: From 1973 on, many groups like Tangerine Dream, Klaus Schulze, and Popol Vuh wanted to leave the company. Finally, this led to lawsuits that the company lost. Maybe this story deserves a better explanation, but "all good things must pass."

I still recorded *STARRING ROSI* and *INVENTIONS* for the label, and then I left in 1976. Rolf-Ulrich Kaiser, together with all of his labels, vanished, probably floating into the cosmic zones, as he never turned up again in music, or any other business.

Q: Did the music scene and overall social atmosphere in Germany change at that time?

A: The "Punk" era began around 1977. Virgin Records signed the Sex Pistols. Their influence was evident.

In Germany, at the turn of the decade, the atmosphere had changed completely. Now, the music was called "Neue Deutsche Welle" (NDW = New German Wave). But contrary to our first musical adventures 10 to 12 years back, this music was highly successful in a commercial sense.

Regarding electronic music, a new trend was the so-called "synthe-pop," mostly led by English bands like Human League or Orchestral Manoeuvers in the Dark. Of course, these new trends attracted the bigger record companies, and many new, small labels saw the light as well.

The hippie, cosmic days were gone. (Funny, but this spirit re-emerged some 10 years later -- although in a different costume -- with the rise of "techno," "house" or "rave" music.)

Q: After your solo album *INVENTIONS*, it was awhile before you did another album, and then you formed the group Ashra to do several records and perform live. Why/when did you decide to form another group and work with Harald Grosskopf and Lutz Ulbrich?

A: After the release of *INVENTIONS*, I wanted to re-form the band. Lutz Ulbrich joined me, and together we performed a beautiful concert in Paris in December 1974. We toured then as a duo in France and England during 1975. At the end of the year, Lutz quit to accompany Nico (the legendary "femme fatale" of the Velvet Underground) during her concerts of 1976.

I began recording a solo album again, *NEW AGE OF EARTH*, and did a tour as well in December 1976. These performances as a soloist were quite an experience for me. In the beginning of 1977, I signed a long-term contract with Virgin Records. When *NEW AGE OF EARTH* was released worldwide in summer '77, Virgin wanted a concert in London. I again asked Lutz Ulbrich and also Harald Grosskopf to join me. I had known Harald from the Cosmic Couriers sessions, and he had also played on the *STARRING ROSI* album in 1973.

Q: Your albums *NEW AGE OF EARTH* and *BLACKOUTS* are considered by many as the first electronic New Age albums. How did you come up with the particular concept or sound for those albums? Was there any other musician or style who perhaps influenced your musical ideas?

A: I started my musical career as a guitar player. After producing *INVENTIONS FOR ELECTRIC GUITAR*, I decided to expand my equipment in order to create compositions for keyboard and synthesizer. This was a new thing for me then.

A substantial influence in my style came about in 1974 with the discovery of so-called "minimal music" by composers like Steve Reich, Philip Glass and Terry Riley. Especially Steve Reich's music -- I have listened to it for many years. He is a genuine innovator in terms of creating music that combines the elements of improvisation with structured composition.

Q: In the 1980s, you seemed to disappear from the scene. What happened?

A: By the end of the '70s, the style and politics of Virgin Records, as I mentioned before, had changed. After *CORRELATIONS* in 1978/79, *BELLE ALLIANCE* in 1980 was the second recording with Lutz Ulbrich and Harald Grosskopf. I felt it showed the great variety of styles the band had to offer. I was rather disappointed with how little attention they gave to the release of the *BELLE ALLIANCE* album.

In 1981 I played a long tour as a guest with Klaus Schulze. Inspired by those daily live performances, in December 1981 I went into my studio and recorded the music of *E2-E4*. It took me exactly one hour, no overdubs, no editing. The only alteration I had to make was to cut the piece into two parts for the LP format, as there were no CDs in those days.

I half-heartedly offered *E2-E4* to Virgin Records in 1982, as I didn't trust them to promote it properly. I was lucky, when at the beginning of 1984 my old friend Schulze started a new label, "Inteam Records" and wanted to release it. This record gained a great deal of attention at the end of the '80s in the "house," "techno," "dance-floor" scene as dozens of re-mixes were made, and many parts were sampled (including the very successful "Sueno Latino" by an Italian group of musicians and DJs).

Q: Now in the 1990s, it seems you have re-emerged from retirement. You have had your entire catalog reissued by Spalax in France. Several albums of unreleased music have also come out, and now the *PRIVATE TAPES* Special Edition is about to be released. Does the music you made in the past still sound good to you today? Do you have any plans to record a new album to celebrate the coming millennium?

A: From 1985 on, I worked again with Lutz and Harald. During that year we played a concert in England and recorded the basic material for *TROPICAL HEAT*, which was finally released in 1991.

In between, in 1988, I had performed with Lutz Ulbrich at the Berlin Planetarium. The music was especially composed for the event and included lyrics as well. The four main themes of that composition (without the lyrics) were then released in 1989 as *WALKIN' THE DESERT*. In May 1991 I performed again with Lutz and Harald in Cologne. It was a nice open-air concert in the evening, in front of the Cologne Cathedral. The show also featured Klaus Schulze (we were only missing Tangerine Dream). A radio station and the City of Cologne, to honor a man whose weekly radio program had supported our music for more than 10 years, sponsored it.

In 1993 I began to work with Lutz on a new, guitar-based album. It should be in the style perhaps of *INVENTIONS*, but also incorporate the techniques of the '90s (reflecting the "German" atmosphere of today as well).

Yes, I like the reissues. That music directed my life. When I am sitting, thinking, wondering how all that came about, I choose an old tape and I begin to remember.

A new solo album? To celebrate the Millennium?

I just read that The Rolling Stones booked London's Wembley Stadium for December 31, 1999.

Well, I'm a king bee, baby.
Rollin' on and on and on... (like a German VW -- if you know what I mean).

Archie Patterson

Ashra in Japan

February 1997. It is 03:30 AM at night. The jet lag leaves no rest for me. After four hours, full of confused dreams, I lie totally awake in bed. After the 21-hour trip, I had a feeling that time had stood still. The red-orange striped horizon of an infinite sunset accompanied the 11-hour flight from Tokyo to Frankfurt by the northern route, seven hours solely over snow-covered Siberia. Infinite landscapes of frozen lakes and ice flows that wind through uninhabited landscape. Very impressing, like this whole trip! A strong need to inform somebody of my experiences during the last week pushes me in this early hour to my computer, to store all my impressions as best possible, before memory fades. Unfortunately, I can not yet call friends at this time in order to satisfy my communication urge.

This history begins exactly two months ago, on the 11th of December 1996. I have a flight ticket in my pocket for a six week trip to India, when my phone ring one late evening. Manuel (Gottsching), friend, guitarist, head of ASHRA, is on the line announcing himself with: "I am in the wax museum of Tokyo!" "You are not in Berlin?," I ask in a surprised manner. "Yes, but I am also in the wax museum of Tokyo at the same time," he replied, playing with my ignorance and bewilderment. Now I get the idea. He cannot be at two places at the same time. The lad is talking about his physical wax figure in a Tokyo wax museum. Not any wax museum, but the most popular wax museum in Tokyo. Mr. Gen Fujita -- owner of the Tokyo tower, one of Tokyo's landmarks, an orange-white painted steel tower that still surmounts "le tour Eifel" in Paris at 333 meters of height by 13 meters -- has been for years an ASHRA fan. He has put the good Manuel, immortalized at full size, as a wax figure, the red Gibson SG-Special on his chest, in the wax museum, between Queen Elisabeth, the Beatles, Frank Zappa, a Middle Ages torture scene depicting Jesus and his disciples' "Last Supper."

"Are you ready to appear in Japan?," is the next sentence which I hear. "Wow! Japan?! With ASHRA!? Sure man!," I answer without hesitation. "When does it begin? It is to be hoped not within the next six weeks. In two days I fly to Bombay!" He replies: "the beginning of February, for a week. Four gigs. Two festivals and two club gigs. Tokyo and Osaka." "It works!," I answer in a enthusiastic manner.

My objections: We can not play as we did in former times with the old ARP sequencer and for the unstable Minimoog. On stage in these times Manuel had, for every new piece, to adjust a new bass line, which caused sometimes, up to five minutes, feeble-minded doodling between songs. In addition, he was already then overloaded by the task of simply playing guitar, sequencer and keyboards simultaneously. I also fear that the good man will be so burdened with the organization of the Japanese gigs, that he would hardly be able to prepare at the musical machinery in such a short time. Former gigs, which we developed with backing tapes, I did not find overriding. Tapes remain too non-flexible. Every piece can sound differently. Sometimes the deep bass frequencies run out of control and the sets then do not sound as if they are created as one piece.

As a solution to this technical problem I suggest to Manuel that we take Steve (Baltes) along, my current young music partner, keyboardist, DJ and producer. Together we have produced N-TRIBE and HOLO SYNDROM, two electronic projects in the style of progressive house, tribal and trance/ambient. Steve is very musical, has great talent and masterful control technically. Since I met Oliver Lieb in 1993 at EYE Q Records in Frankfurt and observed his way of remixing and producing I feel great respect for the musical and technical abilities of the younger German scene. At the 1994 Montreux Jazz festival I had beaten the d-drums, along with three other drummer's for Oliver Lieb's AMBUSH project.

After Manuel's call, two days before my departure to India, it is uncertain whether Steve will travel with us. Also Lutz (Ulbrich) whom we all call Luel, guitarist and keyboardist with ASHRA must be contacted and invited along as well. Questions of cost must be clarified. A week later, after arriving in Goa, I faxed from a ramshackled building, between the palms of the village Benaulim, my first fax about this matter to Berlin. The answer comes on New Year's Eve. Steve is coming! I am pleased.

Nextly we need a certificate of eligibility for Japan. Certificate of eligibility = a visa. I instantaneously must send a copy of my passport to Germany and obtain passport photographs. I am almost seven thousand kilometers away from Germany.

Letters normally take three weeks to reach Europe and it often happens that the Indians like to remove stamps from the letters and throw away the mail. For a fifteen rupee stamp (quarter dollar), one can get two vegetarian Tali-meals here in India.

On January first I planned to travel from Goa to Hampi, a picturesque village that lies in a science-fiction lunar landscape, garnished with temple ruins. Hampi lies in the Indian state of Karnataka, 300 kilometers southeast of Goa. Twelve extremely dangerous, loud, dusty and lousy hours on a vehicle that should not be called a bus. Indians drive cars in a horrible manner.

I try at once to get a single photoprint in India! After the rough, infinite ride through overwhelmingly beautiful regions, I detect, as we turn into a bus station, swamped by waiting crowds and overloaded red and yellow busses, a small shop with the endorsement XEROX COPY. My chance! I jump off the bus, run, persecuted by hundreds of eyes, jumping over garbage, ox and cow shit, past carts, mopeds and fruit stands, back to that Xerox copy shop I just saw, put my passport under the lid, wait until the copy is ready, pay one rupee and run back. Wim, my Belgian trip companion, reserved my seat, watched my baggage and was, if needed, prepared to prevent the driver from setting off without me on board. That indeed occurs often here.

I read in my travel guide: No fax machines in Hampi. The next one will be in the Central Telegraph Building from Mysore, miles and days away from Hampi. After the incredible long trip we arrived there to find a building, designed and made last century, in the British colonial style. To fax there, means to face extremely unnerving Indian administrative methods. I will stay in the picturesque city Mysore for four days. To send a fax from India fortunately functions impeccably here. Manuel gets the passport photographs from me in Germany in time.

As I came back to Germany on 25th of January, Steve is already fully occupied with the musical and technical preparations. Sampling, hardware sequencer programming and so on. He is thrilled, that we will take him to Japan. We want to take along as little equipment as possible. The two of us load almost one hundred kilograms of baggage on to the scale of the JAL counter of the Frankfurt Rhine Main Airport. In the ten days up to the take-off I received the timetables from Manuel by fax. Those determine in detail when what happens with whom. The flight tickets come three days before take-off. I can fetch the visas for Steve and myself from the Japanese consulate in Dusseldorf just one day before take-off. I remain anxious up to departure. From Moenchengladbach via Cologne to Frankfurt we travel on the Federal Railroad. Upon arrival, from a distance I recognize Manuel, Luel and Sydow, our sound engeneer. The three arrived from Berlin by train. We are very pleased to meet again. They too have just arrived. We all are energized by thought of the adventure ahead of us.

I met the suntanned Kalle Becker, our German tour manager. He had just came back from Bali, where he managed a music project during the last weeks. A gamelan orchestra and Mani Neumeier (Guru Guru), who seems also be a bit of a star in Japan. Kalle immediately gets to work on our baggage with determination and make preparations for the flight.

We finally can be a bit more relaxed as we get onto the escalator to have a welcome beer, two hours before takeoff. We had not see each other for a long time, therefore have a lot of catching up to do. Gabbing with each other is an old ASHRA tradition. We'e always spent many happy hours talking with each other. At the beginning of the Eighties I had the funny idea to record and publish a conversation album with ASHRA instead of a music.

Japan Airlines (JAL) has extraordinarily good service. I can hardly sleep during the eleven hours on JAL 408, but time goes relatively fast with movies and good catering. The sun rises again at 3:00 PM MET. We land around 8:15 PM MET at Tokyo's Narita Airport. Here it is already afternoon. The day had already past before it began. Now in Japan it is Thursday, the 6th of February 1997.

Everything here is extremely clean. In that regard the Japanese are absolute world champions. As we go through customs control, we are welcomed by Colin, a young Englishman. He works for SMASH WEST. SMASH WEST is the greatest concert organization in Japan and works worldwide. Colin speaks fluent Japanese. I am impressed. We load our heavy baggage onto some trolleys again and climb aboard two waiting minibuses in a multistory car park. I detect Japanese car models which I've never seen before in my life. Everything shines here and seems to be freshly washed and carefully polished. Why does this fact strike me? Am I typically German? The Japanese characters, which do not mean anything to me make everything very surrealistic and somehow archaic. Left-hand traffic. Speed limits like in the Netherlands. Everything comes up, as move along as if we are moving in slow-motion. Bustling activity, but not frenetic. No one here pushes others, as in Germany. It is also winter here, but the snow-free landscape is dominated by grey and cyan colours. The skyline of Tokyo in dusk is overwhelming. Skyscrapers with these gigantic, bright Asiatic hieroglyphs. Strange, big architecture. Sixteen million live and work here like bees in a hive. Three-storyed motorways thirty metres high move through an ocean of houses. After almost two hours we reach the Roppongi quarter. "The bear quilts here," as we say in Germany. We are in the heart of Tokyo`s "pleasure mile." Bars and the "In" techno clubs are in Roppongi. In the middle, our hotel. The side streets are small and narrow. Colourful flashy illumination surrounds me. People are friendly and well dressed. I detect very beautiful, exotic women.

At the hotel foyer we are welcomed by the section chief of the wax tower museum, Mr. Takashi Fukushi and his assistant Mr. Keiji Oikawa, perfectly dressed in suits. There's the usual exchange of business-cards. Business-cards show the opposing person which business and social position the other holds. The name itself is of secondary importance. Mr. Takeshi would like to be referred to by us as Taka-san. They both presenting gifts to us, in form of a small parcel with Japanese picture postcards. The friendliness of the two gentlemen is accompanied by almost servile, fast bows, which we will often encounter in the next few days. A strange new behavior for me. My hotel room is relatively small, but has everything one needs. I turn on the TV and watch a few minutes of CNN-news, then an on-screen-display signals that there is a message for me. A small envelope is left on my table, containing a business-card of Mr. Gen Fujita, president of The International Leisure Corporation, that among other things, manages the Tokyo tower and it`s wax museum. I now detect a welcome present on the table. A bottle of the exquisite French champagne "Veuve Cliquot Ponsardin." An expensive drink, I think. What a reception. The wax museum has undertaken the financial assurances for our Japan tour.

Next I decide to take a bath in an ultra clean, light beige coloured bathroom of epoxy, that basically consists of two divisions -- one for toilet, the other a shower. Everything a bathroom needs. The seated bathtub is deep enough to cover me completely with water. I am nevertheless 1,90m large. The bathroom is refreshed daily with: toothbrush, toothpaste, manual electric shaver, shampoo, hair detergents, soap, cleaning pads, creme and eau de toilet. Every day a there is a new thin Japanese dressing gown (Kimono), ironed freshly, and a set of fresh bed linen. Glasses are packed in plastic bags. The toilet lid provides a paper stamp with the endorsement "sanitarized," that marks it cleanliness. What a waste, I think and I have this impression more often this week. What the reason for all that plastic material? Everything here is wrapped twice, or three times in plastic foil.

The tap water has a strong chlorine taste. Every time I take a bath or a shower, I get a strong feeling of being in a swimming pool. Our time schedule here will be quite tight and seems to be organized in the best possible manner. At the reception we meet the entire SYSTEM 7 crew. SYSTEM 7 is Steve Hillage`s band with which we will appear on the following evening in the "LIQUID ROOM" club. A technical meeting with ASHRA, SYSTEM 7, Colin, Nambo Hirukasu, boss of SMASH WEST/Tokyo, Sa-Sha from the Stage crew, John and Jonathan, and the SYSTEM 7 stage crew, is scheduled at 7:00 PM. Steve Hillage has in former times, with his partner Miquette Giraudy, a mercurial Frenchwoman that operates the SYSTEM 7 keyboards, performed with GONG, an English-French cult band of the seventies He has also done solo work and among other things, work with Alex Patterson and THE ORB. As we arrived in the "Cafe Paris," where the meeting would occur, Steve and Miquette are already present. Steve and Miquette know Manuel from both their earlier involvement with Virgin Records. Steve visited Manuel several times in Berlin and vice versa, the atmosphere is cheerful, relaxed and concentrated on the work that lies in front. Mobile phones chirping constantly. We all are very pleased to be in Japan and to be able to work here. The level of organization is perfect. Technical differences are clarified and end up on a printed sheet for everybody who is involved. The next day, Kalle Becker, our tour manager hands over notes of yesterday evening results. A comprehensive, several page document.

After the "Cafe Paris" meeting, we go to visit a typical Japanese restaurant for dinner. Servers place our orders into a conveniently small special handheld restaurant computer, that here apparently processes the meal orders in all restaurants. Colin orders our food. In an astoundingly short time, the two tables are bursting full with decoratively arranged delicacies. I love this kitchen, that does not only flatter the palate, but also the eyes. Steve (Baltes) has problems with sushi as it's small pieces of raw fish, but there are sufficient delicious things also for him. Around 11:30 PM I am wasted. It is, according to my body clock, already 7:30 AM on Friday morning.

Lots of prostitutes are passed on my way to the hotel, which is not very far from that restaurant. They stand about in small groups, talk to me and everybody who pass in a very friendly way, or may hand out a flyer with "delicate" information. Each of these small groups of prostitutes are dressed in the same way. Individually different only from one group to another. Fashionable! These charming whores appear to me to be dressed in some sort of uniform. Strange! In this clean, bright and flashing plastic styled environment, they seem so different from our whores. At this late time the night activity in Roppongi has just began. The streets are crowded with laughing, rattling and joking people.

No violence. Tokyo has the lowest violence crime rate on Earth. Cars accumulate. Above all, many colourful taxis. There are still construction workers in the subway. The construction sites also seem strangely clean and tidied up. A blue uniformed man, with helmet and a flashing stick in his hand, guarantees that nobody is endangered or hindered by the construction operations. When I arrive at the hotel I am dead, place my ears on the cushion and sleep until 9:30 AM the next morning. We have an appointment at ten o'clock for breakfast. Kalle Becker has a good knowledge of Roppongi and gets us to an Italian cafeteria with the name "Pronto." Just a couple of hundred meters away from the hotel, and again with hyper-friendly service. Sandwiches in plastic foil and coffee. We are now in the middle of Tokyo and I still can not believe it.

My back hurts because of sitting too long in the airplane. I decide to use the Shiatsu massage service which every Japanese hotel offers. At 1:00 PM there is a knock on my room door. Perfectly in time, as agreed. A small, purposeful old lady enters my room and starts talking Japanese to me, apparently without expecting answers of me. How could I? I should put on the dressing gown, she signals. One does not massage on naked skin here. We are in Japan, we are decent here. "Japanstyle" she says in broken English, pointing with her fingers to the dressing gown. The lady is very brash and works my muscles very effectively with her strong hands and thumbs for a whole hour. Sometimes quite painful. I feel myself newborn and pay her 5000 Yen (55 USD).

Oh yeah.., while I'm astonishing about this strange country and its unusual culture, it occurs to me that I am, above all here in order to work. Around 3:00 PM, we are fetched by Colin for the stage set up. The "LIQUID ROOM" is the (!) Techno underground club in Tokyo. Almost everybody who has a name in the world of raves has hung out here. In the most interesting graffiti covered dressing room, we find catered food of the highest quality. Masses of fruits, sandwiches and cold drinks. "Real dinner will be served later!" we hear. Wow...!

The line-up for the evening is: KEN ISHI, a well known Japanese DJ spins discs, SYSTEM 7 and ASHRA play live. HANADENSHA, a young Japanese psychedelic band plays. Our gig should go from 11:30 PM until 1:30 AM. We still have a lot of time. Manuel wants to go back into the hotel, for some relaxation. At first we wish to eat "real dinner." Ten minutes later, two gigantic plastic plates, stuffed with sushi and a big bowl, filled with a tasty noodle soup for each of us, appear out of nowhere. Again, everything is perfectly decorated and wrapped in plastic foil. We begin to eat. After a few minutes, Luel, who is somewhere outside, suddenly appears and shouts in a very exited state of mind: "Something has happened to Manuel!"

I run from the room and see, at the end of the walk, Colin and Luel bent over Manuel, who is lying at the ground. As I came closer, I recognize that he hurt himself badly. His nose is bleeding. Above his eyes is a laceration. The whole face is covered with blood. He has his eyes open, but doesn't react when I speak to him. We carry him into the elevator. The ambulance is already present. A hospital is located just around the corner. Luel and Colin accompany Manuel.

We are shocked and puzzled at what happened to him. Will he be all right before we perform? Will we be able to play this evening at all? I fear the worst case and see us depart Japan before the concerts even began. Kalle Becker, Sydow, Steve and I decide to leave it up to Manuel, whether we play at all, or get on stage with or without him. After two hours of uncertainty, Luel and Colin come back, accompanied by Manuel. Manuel has two white plaster strips on his nose, between the eyes and obviously feels embarrassed about this deformation. His nose did not break. He is still a bit dizzy, but it seems that he is fine again. All that stress during the last weeks. After the sleepless flight, and last night he just slept for two hours, that stress simply had knocked him down and out. While tipping over, he fell onto a tool case with his face. If that would not have happened, he would have been on his legs again ten minutes later.

Steve (Hillage) and Miquette are very symphatic and really concerned. Miquette told how the same thing happened to her after a Japan tour, back in the U.K., but then her nose was broken and she was in coma for two hours. The whole SYSTEM 7 crew is concerned about Manuel. Gabriel, our former French manager walks with Manuel each time he leaves the room and looks out for him. Jonathan who works the lighting for UNDERWORLD offers to take care of our lighting. John who has worked for GONG in the past wants to take care of our monitor mixing. The lads are unusual. They are incredibly friendly and very very helpful. Japan with its polite rituals has already influenced all of us.

Manuel wants to play. Nambo's Japanese announcement informs the audience about what had happened backstage with Manuel and a storm of applause bursts out. We are announced as ASH RA TEMPEL on the flyers. The press call our newer name: ASHRA. Japan does not advertise concert and gigs on posters like is customary in the rest of the world.

At 12:00 PM Steve (Baltes) goes on first to begin the set and is greeted by a stormy applause. He begins with soft string sounds and fades into light rhythmic guitar samples. After five minutes Luel enters the stage and is also greeted loudly. Then I go and start softly treating my hi-hat cymbals. The initial applause goes through me like electric energy. Manuel comes on stage a while after me, still with the white plaster in his face and a bit embarrassed. The 1,250 people who filled the "LIQUID ROOM" react frenetically. The tension drives us to record performance. As the Roland 808 of Steve, with the 4/4 bass drum line comes in, the atmosphere reaches a climax. I am glad that everything still runs so well and notice from the big smile on Luel`s and Steve`s face, that they are feeling like me. Kon-ban-wa Tokyo...! The show goes on very well and we must give multiple encores at the end.

Back in the dressing room I receive a kiss from Miquette. Most of the people present smile approvingly at us, or point upwards with their thumbs. Steve (Hillage) says we should come to England and play, our sound is absolutely in and would fit in perfectly with the British club- and rave-scene. Fo-Mi, a small Japanese woman, baked a sort of "highly colorful and flashy science fiction cake" for SYSTEM 7 and ASHRA. She loves our music, and it makes her totally happy that we like her cake art. Each of us gets a piece. Before the cake is cut, our autofocus-cameras take snapshots for reminiscence. The stage crews also react enthusiastically about the ASHRA concert. Wow....!! We are in Japan.

At 2:00 AM I am in bed. Long asleep? No way! Around 10:30 AM we have our breakfast appointment again in the "Pronto." Hotels in Japan do not offer breakfast. Sydow and Steve spent their night after the show on the street and in some clubs in Roppongi until the morning hours. Manuel has been awake since 8:00 AM, sightseeing and already had breakfast. I am quite kipped.

At 11:30 AM Colin comes and picks us with the bus, heading for the Tokyo Tower. Mr. Fujita has called a press conference. Employees beckon from a distance and signal the direction we're to move, as our bus enters the grounds of the tower area. At the ground floor we are met with politeness by Taka-san and Kenji. They accompany us to the elevators. What an effort! At two-hundred-fifty meters height the elevator stops. As the door opens, I can't believe my eyes. "WELCOME ASH RA TEMPEL TO THE TOKYO TOWER WAX MUSEUM," it reads in big German type. Then I detect a shop called "THE COSMIC JOKERS," named after an LP-record-title we recorded more than twenty-five years ago. A huge display displays all of our CDs. Recordings from our early era, but also later works. We are dumbfounded. In addition to diverse space knickknack, I detect a Japanese music magazine with the name *ARCH ANGEL* printed in bright lustre. The first forty pages are dedicated to ASH RA TEMPEL and Manuel Gottsching, with many photographs from the early 1970's, that I've never seen before. We are led into a big room where Mr. Fujita greets us with a friendly bow. We are served with coffee and other drinks. Taka-san, chief of the Tokyo Tower, had the task by M. Fujita, during their last Germany stay, to procure German snacks, pastry and drinks. Journalists are invited in, representatives of the four biggest Japanese music journals are present. *SOUND RECORDING, MARQUEE, THE DIG* and *ELEKING*. The English-printed *JAPAN TIMES* writes a very good review about our gig on the following day. All the journalists who saw our concert of are full of praise and cameras flash.

Colin translates questions into the English. According to the strict rules of Japanese hierarchy, Mr. ASH RA TEMPEL, Manuel Gottsching-san is questioned first.

The Japanese word san, used accordingly with the christian name or the first name, has two different meanings. I am from now on, called by close friends, Harald-san. For strangers and acquaintances I am, respectfully called Grosskopf-san. This is how I am called by Mr. Fujita and his men during all our meetings during the next few days.

After almost two hours, we are led into the wax museum. Photographs of us, in addition to the two made-out-of-wax heroes of the movie "Planet of the Apes." And there he is, our Manuel-san, made of wax, outfitted as he looked at the beginning of the 1970's. In addition to him is Klaus Schulze-san, who more or less looks like Bernd Kistenmacher, a musician and friend of ours. Vis-à-vis of Schulze, a very sinister staring GURU GURU, the good Mani Neumeier himself. Many famous people are represented there. From Ritchie Blackmore, Jimmy Page, Peter Gabriel, Jimi Hendrix, Elvis, the Beatles, Mahatma Ghandi, Marilyn Monroe, Albert Einstein to Jesus Christ. Everything is densely packed together. Taka-san and a another Japanese person accompany us onto the balcony of the top story of the tower. What a view! Tokyo in all directions extends up to the horizon. It is nearly dusk and the gigantic neon lights of the and all kinds of spotlights are already turned on.

Close to the "Cosmic Joker" shop is one of these typical Japanese amusement arcades. Computers control the mechanics of the games in real-time. You sit in front of a giant screen and control some flight machine and mercilessly combat very athletic terrorists. Photographic automats have greatest success here. You sit in front of a video screen and watch your portrait. If you like the pose you snap the picture. Then you may choose various frames and backgrounds and in the end you receive 16 tiny small pictures, which can be printed like stamps onto anything you like. The people stand in long lines to get to these apparatus. I receive a sample as a gift from Kalle Becker-san, our tour manager, and I decide to go to the hotel back on foot, a walk of 20 minutes. The air in Tokyo is clear and fresh, because of its proximity to the sea.

Two days later each of us receives as a reminder gift, an individually chosen photo album by Mr. Fujita of ASHRA in the Tokyo tower.

Back in the hotel I take a fast hot bath. I just have the time to change clothes and get to the foyer for another appointment at 8:00 PM. We are fetched by Colin again. Mr. Fujita invites us and the SMASH WEST crew for dinner. Being very punctual is a necessity in Japan, otherwise one offends the host, who never would bring his frustration directly to expression. In Japan you never show what you feel in front of people. We do not get there in time...... Sorry Mr. Fujita!

A restaurant of the superclass receives us, arranged with a lot of plants, Japanese interior designs and big fish ponds, which are admitted on the grounds. We are guided into a big, but narrow Separee where Mr. Fujita welcomes us. Table arrangement is predetermined. We sit next to Mr. Fujita. The managers at the side of us. The crews are placed at the other end of the long table. Sake is brought. "Kampai Kampai." The finest delicacies I've ever seen and tasted in my life are served in small portions. I love Japan! One sake after the other is brought. The food tastes excellent....... For desert, there is ice cream made of green tea.........

Mr. Fujita has been an enthusiastic supporter of our music for years and provides, among other things with his wax-museum, for its effective distribution in Japan. He often visits Germany on business. At 11:00 PM the table is closed. Mr. Fujita personally accompanies us to the hotel. His good night is a cordial "Arigato goseimash'ta." I am a little tipsy from the sake, but still feel myself quite fit. We decide to go into a club. It's named GAS PANIC and is not far from our hotel. The streets are full of people. The shops are partially still open and again one is constantly solicited by some of the whores. While passing by sex clubs, salaried black North Americans push flyers of pornographical contents into our hands.

We take an elevator to the seventh floor. A muscle-bound bodyguard scrutinizes us and lets us pass. GAS PANIC is full of high spirits. Hip Hop, Grunge, Techno. Loud, very loud! Many whites stay in the club. Some women dance on the bar. The atmosphere is great, everybody seems to have fun.

After two hours, Steve (Baltes) and I go back to the hotel. Next morning Kalle-san told us about a violent fight between Mexicans and Japanese. Our muscle man was involved. Tomorrow we go to Osaka. It's the 9th of February and at 3:30 AM I place myself into the hot bathtub and decide to write postcards. Then jet lag strikes me but I can only sleep only for two hours...

CNN reports about the Tamagotchi fever that broke out in Japan. A Tamagotchi is a colored, small chirping, electronic controlled plastic egg, with an LCD display that displays a small chicken. It performs some actions upon pressing the buttons, but if you make a mistake it perishes. It costs sixteen dollars, and because of strong demand has not been available for some weeks. Fanatics pay up to one hundred dollars for a one.

11:00 AM. Breakfast. This time French at the "CAFE DE PARIS," also situated just around the corner.

At 12 AM we check out of the hotel and leave in taxies for Shin-Tokyo (railway station). A railroad ride with the SHIN-KANSEN, one of the worlds fastest traveling trains awaits us. Again, everything here is spick-and-span. We take some souvenir pictures. Always Japanese background, in case nobody back home later believes us. Nambo, chief of SMASH WEST and tour manager bought tickets. In single file we follow him. Up the escalator up, down the escalator. Past a barrier. Past the controller in white gloves. Platform. No single cigarette butt on the railway tracks. The smoking zones on the platform are identified with a green line on the ground. On the opposite railway track, the coming in of a SHIN-KANSEN is expected. Pink dressed, well-behaved cleaning personnel, waits at the markings for the boarding doors. Those are positioned at the ground of the platform.

The white streamlined SHIN-KANSEN arrives and stops at the precise millimeter of the markers. We enter the air-conditioned chambers. Double lines of seats on the right, a row of three seats on the left side, adjustable seats, with ample room for leg freedom in front. An integrated, folding table in the backrest of the seat in front of me. Precisely on the minute the train rolls up. Six hundred kilometers distance will be traveled, the ride lasts somewhat less than three hours. The train rolls very softly and smoothly. An extremely friendly, feminine voice conveys messages in Japanese and English. We pass infinite suburbs. The entire route of a hundred kilometers appears as a single city to me. I doze off and am awaken by Gabriel, our former French manager and record company president (SPALAX), who offers me a glass of champagne. A panoramic view of Mount Fujijama is to be seen to the right side. Shit, I cannot switch off my camera's autofocus, nor put down the window pane.

The train rolls on past Nagoya and Kyoto. We arrive at Shin-Osaka (railway station) and are greeted by our guide Nambo who takes us in a taxi to check in at the hotel, which is clean, bright, classy. On the other side of Osaka lies Kobe, the city that was completely destroyed by the terrible earthquake of two years ago. It is only 20 kilometers away from Osaka, on the other side of the bay. Steve and I start paying attention for earthquake aftershocks.

Up to 1,000 small earthquakes occur here per year. That is on the average three per day. I do not notice it. It is 4:30 PM and we take a walk into the city centre's pedestrian arcade. Approximately 10 kilometers in length, it is like a colored science-fiction world. I think of a similar arcade in Duesseldorf. Steve separates himself and makes his way without us. Little by little we lose each other along the route. Manuel and I remain together and decide to eat odds and ends. We love sushi. Friendly service, delicious taste. On our return path, another ice cream. There is, in addition to the green tea ice cream, potato ice cream. Correctly heard, potato ice cream! We politely refuse and have the more familiar vanilla and walnut ice cream.

Not only cars receive police tickets here, but also bikes if they parked wrong. They will be towed away and only released again after paying a fine. I am so tired that I skip the announced supper with Nambo and his wife and sleep for a good 13 hours.

Luel disappeared. Our phone calls to his room are not answered. He doesn't appear the next morning for breakfast nor did he join us for that evening's dinner. Everything will be fine with him we hope.

Bright sunshine wakes me the morning of February 10th. After breakfast, in one of the numerous cafes, Steve and I take a walk for hours through the city. Everything is arranged in a square so finding out direction is easy here. We enter into one of these gaming halls, that sometimes are called ATARIATA and spend a couple of hundred yen on real time banging and karate games. The quality of screen solution is incredible. We then visit a music shop and check the new JP-8000 by ROLAND. It is already available here in Japan and priced lower than at home in Europe. We meet Luel on the way, he has slept through until this morning and did not hear his phone ring. No matter he is back again, healthy, alive, wonderful. The people of SYSTEM 7 were in Kyoto during the day and went sightseeing.

We have another three gigs coming up. We again meet up with Steve (Hillage) and Miquette at the soundcheck in the BAYSIDE JENNY club. There was great joy at meeting again. Miquette had her birthday yesterday. We present to her a Tarot-game designed Swatch watch that Walter Wegmüller, a Swiss painter, with whom we produced twenty-five years ago a long playing record (LP) titled "Tarot," designed for SWATCH.

At the soundcheck the equipment is huge, but does not have the same quality as at the LIQUID ROOM in Tokyo. SYSTEM 7 has problems with the monitors. Something is broken and needs to be repaired by John. We loaf about and wait for our soundcheck. On stage, ready to check the sound Steve's (Baltes) monitor blows up. He then tries a smaller one, on which the sound of the ROLAND 808-Bassdrum machine is not reproduced so well. He was afraid he would incur volume control problems because of bad monitors during the set.

Here in Osaka, we learn, that only a short

while ago the love for underground music just has begun. The audience in Tokyo might be considerably larger. On average, the people pay 5,500 yen for our shows, that is more than $40 US. We play on time at 12:00 AM for one hour. The club is full. On stage we cook instrumentally. In some parts we get quite aggressive and the audience at the end demands encores. Everything, except some limitations in the sound, worked out very well. Our stay in Tokyo, and the whole experience in Japan added excitement and gave us a lot of vigour playing-wise. The technical support facility of Sa-Sha and his stage crew was perfect, always friendly and very relaxed.

Steve (Hillage) and Miquette want to help us play in England, they say we definitely should play there. At the photo-session after the set we are interviewed by an American who lives here, speaks Japanese and writes for an English-speaking music magazine. He liked our show very much.

It is the last day in Japan for SYSTEM 7. The whole crew has to be at the Osaka Airport early in the morning. They have only four hours left. We say good-bye combined with the hope to meet again soon. It was a good thing to meet up with them here. Thanks to John for his support at the monitor and also a big thank for your terrific light Jonathan.

The 11th of February is a Japanese national holiday. One notices nothing from that. Shops are all open. The stupor of material consumption continues. We go to the seventh floor of a multi-story building, where SONY showrooms preview the latest electronic innovations. We are impressed with the high level of development here. Japan, science-fiction country. Products on the market here now will be available to us maybe in the next years.

The Japanese use modern technology very naïvely and totally without reservations. According to their Buddhist sense, everything, including inorganic matter, is, in their view, inspired with vital life. Consequently, things are not bad in principle provided that they are not abused. However painful some experiences may be due to the result of abuses, they can result in a positive outcome for the life of the individual and the masses because they drive evolution forward.

At 3:00 PM, Nambo fetches us from the hotel. The CLUB QUATTRO is only 10 minutes away from the hotel. We walk on foot and it snows briefly, as the wind is icy cold this afternoon.

We have super sound at the club. We play alone on stage this evening. Everything flows, we are all in a very good mood. Mr. Fujita has sent a gigantic bunch of flowers, a bottle of Napoleon champagne and number of the *TOKYO TIMES* and several other newspapers into our dressing room. The *TOKYO TIMES*, the biggest English-speaking daily paper in Japan, is full of praise for the gigs of ASHRA and SYSTEM 7 on our first day in Tokyo. The headline reads: LOST AND FOUND IN SPACE -- examples of old school-into-new school -- high on the energy, and so on. Taka-san and Keiji wear surprisingly very casual clothing today and film all of our movements on video. The show begins at 7:00 PM and goes on for over two hours. Everything works again in the best possible way. Our best gig up to now. The sound is extremely good. The Japanese engineer on the monitor mixer is a tough guy. Encores, autographs, interview. After the food buffet, we celebrate in my hotel room with Veuve Cliquot Ponsardin champagne. As a precaution, I had kept a bottle cool in my Frigidaire. Luel had the same idea and therefore the second bottle is also cooled well. Manuel detected a giant bowl with a choice of exotic fruit in his room that Mr. Fujita had sent, he drags it along. We celebrate very pleased with our success in Japan and enjoy the delicious fruits. The usual ASHRA gab. I fling the whole gang out of my room at 2:00 AM because I am, after three and a half half hours of drumming including soundcheck, pretty exhausted and in addition we must get up early tomorrow morning.

The next day Nambo fetches us from the hotel in the brightest sunshine at 9:30 AM. The SHINKANSEN back to Tokyo waits for us. Taka-san lent me his video camera so I film everything I see: entering the taxi by the band members, taxi ride, Shin-Osaka railway station from the inside, the ASHRA single file marching behind Nambo, the roll in of the SHIN-KANSEN into the railway station, the entering of the entire crew, the ride, infinite cities, snow-covered landscape, and Mount Fujijama. The sunshine after a vehement rain and snow showers cleared the air welcomed us at the Shin-Tokyo station.

The hotel and the club lie in the Shibuya quarter. This evening again we will have a single show, with just us playing. As I once again go back to the hotel, I almost get lost. That can easily cause huge problems here. Hardly anybody speaks English and in the external districts one only find indecipherable Japanese characters. After numerous cautious experiments searching in secondary lanes, I find the hotel and still have a little time to come back to the club to check the sound.

I have a monitor problem. However, I ignore every trouble that it has given me during the gig and the people rage their approval. Encores. Enthusiastic reactions backstage. That was it .....! We share the last two bottles of Veuve Cliquot Ponsardin champagne with the crew and say our thanks to every participant. Super work! `Til next time.

Kings Records, one of our Japanese record distributors, expects Gabriel Ibos and us for dinner after the show. We have to pack everything completely for the departure tomorrow before we can take them up on the invitation. The fans do not let us past on the street without us autographing a pile of their LPs and CDs. The food is superb again. Toby, a young, well-known Japanese DJ who calls himself Tobynation and who knows the German Techno scene, Oliver Lieb, and the people of EYE Q RECORDS from Frankfurt sit with us at the table. "Kampai, Kampai." I am impressed how many people know about ASHRA.

We then go into a club. However, it's not very interesting. In a pub next door we have a couple of beers and nice conversation about French existentialism, No-art, Kabuki and Butoh-dance with a strikingly attractive beauty. She speaks good English, is a poet that has accompanied Gabriel Ibos for days and struck me already on the first Tokyo gig in the "LIQUID ROOM." She is called Setsuko Chiba and has published a record with poetry and avant-garde music on Gabriel's French record label SPALAX. She introduced us at the "ON AIR WEST" club this evening. Setsuko, Luel, Gabriel and I philosophize further for a couple of hours in Gabriel's hotel room. At 3:00 AM I go to sleep. It is the last, but short night in Japan.

In the morning of the seventh day here in Japan, this amazingly, wonderful, exotic country, full of surprises and unique experiences for me, we at last managed it, to assemble the whole ASHRA crew precisely on the minute at the applied date, in the hotel foyer. Even Manuel is on time. Nambo and Colin fetch and bring us to the Narita Airport. The sun shines bright again. It is windy and spring-like mild. I feel wistful. A last photo of the group at the airport, a last "Sajonara" and a couple of "Arigato goseimash'ta" to Nambo and Colin. The next moment we sit in the Boeing 747, JAL 407. Kalle Becker-San put us in the "first floor" of that jumbo jet directly behind the cockpit.

Bye, bye Tokyo. Bye bye Japan. It was an outrageous experience. I would not mind if the trip would go on right now for a while longer. They want to see us here another time, we heard again and again. The aircraft lifts off at 2:00 PM. On time, of course. We have a drink called "Skytime," a yellow, fluorescent lemonade with a very strange taste. Not bad, from a visual point of view. Luel calls me Harald-Kiri. We all laugh about this funny joke.

Harald Grosskopf

Klaus Schulze
Electric-Music Maestro

As a founding father of electronic music, Klaus Schulze remains one of the genre's most important artists. Although he is commonly recognized as a very early member of Tangerine Dream (in 1969), his role in that group really wasn't one as a synthesist. It wasn't until he established a solo career several years later that the classic Schulze paradigm -- long, gently evolutionary and richly evocative pieces built around simple sequences and rhythms -- began to emerge.

Though several of his '70s-era albums are considered his most fundamental (particularly *TIMEWIND*, *MOONDAWN* and *X*), Schulze has remained prolific and artistically restless throughout the '80s and '90s, with a discography approaching 60 titles. A 50-CD retrospective of Schulze's recorded work will be released by Manikin Records on January 1 of next year. His work has been credited with laying the blueprint for several subgenres of contemporary electronic music (ambient, trance, etc.), but still Schulze's vision and integrity have remained vigorously untainted by the various pop-culture musical offspring that bear his influence.

Dave Kirby: It's been 30 years now since you first recorded with Tangerine Dream on *ELECTRONIC MEDITATION*. Would it be fair to say that at that time you were essentially a drummer who had discovered synthesizers and, along with Edgar Froese, were really just experimenting with sounds?

Klaus Schulze: "Fair" is not the right word. There were no synthesizers available at that time, at least not for us young musicians in Berlin, in Germany, in Europe. Yes, I did experiment with sounds, as some others in my hometown did. I cannot really say the same for Edgar Froese. He was an electric-guitar player who tried to sound like Jimi Hendrix. There's nothing wrong with that. I did like and still like Hendrix too. An often-told little story explains more the situation: At one of our Tangerine Dream concerts, I wanted to add some homemade experimental tapes (organ with echo, backwards -- something like that). Edgar forbid me that: "You are the drummer, so play your drums. Just the drums." He seemed not much impressed by new tryouts in that "electronic" direction, at this time. Only when I left TD, I could use and develop my strange ideas. Same happened with Conny Schnitzler; he also had some weird ideas. And he left TD soon after me.

DK: Was there ever a point that far back when you believed that the new synthesizer technology would have such a long lasting and profound impact on music? Or did this realization evolve gradually over time?

KS: I remember a conversation with my partner Klaus D. Mueller on a flight to London, 1974 or '75. We discussed the situation with all these upcoming new synthesizers, mainly pre-set keyboards. Many companies tried to get into that new market. We had the feeling (and the wishful thinking), if all those companies put so much energy, money and manpower into it... only for this reason there must be something big coming out... one day.

DK: You and Tangerine Dream parted company after *ELECTRONIC MEDITATION*, after which time you went on to form Ash Ra Tempel (1970), which you left only about a year later. Did you really decide then that you wanted to be a solo artist, or was it simply a matter of having artistic differences and never finding another full-time group situation you felt comfortable with?

KS: Yes, I wanted to do my own thing, wanted to do my solo stuff with my broken organ and freaky ideas. There were no huge "artistic differences" or any personal differences among us. We parted as friends. We still are friends. We were young, and the music was not yet a business for us. Many bands at that time were founded, closed down, and many musicians wandered from one band to another. I never searched for "another full-time group situation." I'm no rock-band musician looking for the warmth and the discussions in a "band," and I'm no orchestra member who urgently needs a conductor.

DK: Was it pleasing or difficult for you to watch as TD was "discovered" by John Peel, signed to Virgin and soon touring the world? Clearly, they were making more "commercial" music at that time (mid '70s) than you were, and yet somehow your recordings from those years seem less "dated" than TD's.

KS: It was neither of it. I just didn't care much what other bands did. TD did their thing; I did mine. Only journalists and fans compared both, TD and KS, and tried to find things that we have in common or that separate us. There was a time when Edgar was really sick of all these many questions about "KS" in interviews he actually gave for TD and TD's doings and new albums ... and the people were always asking for that f.... "Klaus Schulze." How he hated that!

DK: When I was first introduced to your music during 1976-1977, I learned that you played concerts regularly in cathedrals, and I suppose that became part of your "legend." How did that evolve? Was it a matter of acoustics, availability of space, "ambient" considerations? Do you still play cathedrals?

KS: What you call cathedrals were mostly "churches," to be accurate. Simply, to rent a church is cheaper than to rent a concert hall; concert promoters love that. And clergymen need the cash and a full house. Yes, I also like the acoustics in such buildings; it's perfect for my kind of music. Except for some rhythmic things: The echo sometimes is too heavy.

DK: One of your collaborative projects from those days was GO, the so-called all-star project assembled by Stomu Yamash'ta that also included Santana drummer Mike Shrieve, jazz fusion guitarist Al DiMeola and Steve Winwood. I read somewhere that Yamash'ta had planning sessions for the project, which included watching NASA films and so on. Do you have fond memories of that experience, including the live shows, and were you pleased with both the outcome and your role in it?

KS: We did rehearse for a month or so, in a studio north of London. Sometimes we sat together and talked, and also we went out for dinner once or twice. With Stomu, I visited the London Playboy (gamble) club, because Stomu liked to gamble. DiMeola only came into the recording studio for a few hours to record his parts and went back to America immediately after that.

I don't remember "watching NASA films," and I cannot imagine why we should, because these kinds of films are regularly shown on educational afternoon TV. We never watched any TV or films. Silly idea.

Yes, I did like the two concerts, especially the Paris one. The audience seemed to like me in particular; even the technicians -- who were unknown to me -- played one of my albums over the PA before the actual concert, when the crowd came in.

DK: Over the years, it seems that your live performances evolved from extensive European tours ('70s through mid '80s) to smaller, shorter tours (late '80s to early '90s) to only a handful of live appearances in select cities (currently). It seems ironic that as synthesizer technology has become more compact and portable, you seem to travel less now than 20 years ago. Is it a matter of time, a "travel fatigue" issue or other reasons you seem to play fewer and fewer live shows?

KS: After the tour in 1985, we decided: No annual tour anymore. It had various reasons, but nothing sensational. I announced it to the press then, to all fans, to special fanzines, etc. And recently we put it again in the regular "The KS Circle" newsletter because of a new generation of KS fans, and they ask for concerts. I only do exceptional events, maybe once a year.

DK: You were one of the first "Western" artists granted permission to play live shows across the Iron Curtain, in the early '80s. The *DZIEKUJE* double CD, recorded in Poland in 1983, is a great live document. You clearly sounded like you were relaxed and having great fun playing those shows. Later that year, Edgar Froese and Tangerine Dream also played a well-received concert in Warsaw. Were you pleased or surprised that your music was so well appreciated in Poland? Do you think there was something politically "safe" about your music (and Edgar's) that made it easier for the Polish communist authorities to let you come in and play?

KS: I doubt that I was the "first." Be it as it is. ... The year 1983 was the heyday of the Polish revolution, of martial law and of Solidarnosc. But in spite of all this turmoil, my '83 Polish concerts were even announced in the "normal" evening news on Polish TV.

The Polish audience was great. Not just in quantity. Their enthusiasm helped a lot to play great concerts for them. I do not know what's in the minds of Polish "authorities." I only could guess, but I won't.

DK: By the way, did you and Rainer Bloss have a percussionist on that tour, or is all the percussion synthesized/sequenced?

KS: No, I had no percussion player with me. All music was played electronically.

DK: In an interview I read with you somewhere (perhaps reproduced on your web site), it is noted that you have never played a concert in the United States, and your reasons had to do with what you believe is a "corrupting" influence of American culture on European (or any outside) art. Could you elaborate on that or, if I have mis-paraphrased you, please correct me? I know Edgar Froese has mentioned this point of contention between the two of you in a number of interviews he has given (although in the context of overall friendliness and warm personal relations between you two). As a professional musician -- and one of significant stature -- I find it quite amazing that you have never played in America. Personally, as a fan, I am disappointed that I will likely never see a live Klaus Schulze concert, at least not until I travel to Europe.

KS: Right, I never played a concert in the USA. And I don't see a chance that I will ever play there. Just listen to my albums and imagine the "typical" American's taste. The two just do not fit. I don't want to change, and I suppose the Americans won't change either. Their attitude to art is not mine. Not to mention the business side.

It's you who want to see me, so it's *you* who should come to me, to Europe. Why should I go to your place? I don't want anything from you. Isn't that logic? In "The KS Circle" was written once: "Beethoven never was in America, Bach never was in America, Mozart never was in America. So, why should Schulze go to America?"

It's nice to hear that Edgar Froese speaks well of me. There was a time not long ago when he said in interviews (and not just once) that he won't even sit down at a coffee table with any one of his ex-colleagues. Which I found a very strange statement because at the same time -- and before and after -- we had friendly meetings and conversations. Although not exactly at a "coffee" table.

DK: What were your impressions as you saw synthesizer technology gradually playing a more and more central role in pop music, especially in the '80s? It seemed for a few years that every young pop band had a synthesizer, and although much of what came out from those days was fairly insignificant, it *did* seem that some of the players were genuinely pushing the technology and expanding the boundaries of pop music. Would you agree with that?

KS: So what? "Every young pop band" has drum sets or guitars or singers, and what comes out is also often "fairly insignificant." That's the way the cookie crumbles. Not everyone can be top-notch all the time. There also must be the "humus soil." Although humus stinks, it's necessary.

DK: These days, it does seem as if electronic music has branched off into several roughly defined genres, such as Trance, Ambient, House, etc. Much of it is produced as dance music. Do you think there is something inherently inferior or shallow about dance-oriented electronica? Are you comfortable with those who would trace virtually all of this back to you and your early '70s recordings?

KS: There was and there is always a lot of inferior music; there is just very little excellent music, and the majority is mediocre music -- not just in electronic music but in all music, in all art, with all people, in all things of life.

It's not the question if I feel "comfortable" about it. It is like that, and I have and I can live with that. I do know -- in the beginning and for a long time -- it was just us three: Kraftwerk, TD and me.

DK: You have said that "it's the player, not the tools." Was there a point when you had to force yourself to concentrate more on your composing, or have you always considered yourself a composer first?

KS: No, I do not remember any such

point. I consider myself as a musician, and that includes a variety of crafts, among it: composer, producer, sound generator, studio technician, mixer.

DK: After running a couple of your own record labels over the years, do you think that the music industry in general is now better suited (than it was, say, 25 years ago) to appreciate artists for what they do instead of how much money they can make?

KS: The "couple of" were just two, IC and Inteam, from '79 to '83 and from '83 to '87, respectively. "The music industry" is not "better" or worse as before; it's different and the same. "Different" because the times have changed; they always change. I don't look back so often. Only for interviews. "The same" because people do not change as fast as their environment, the technique, the media. In fact, they don't change at all. For instance, musicians still want to be famous, want a lot of money and want many chicks. People in record companies still want to earn some cash for living too.

DK: Has the internet and your personal web site been very beneficial for you and your career?

KS: How should it? I do my music since 1972; the KS web site exists for three years. Most web surfers ask us in e-mails, "Where can I get CDs?" From a shoe shop, I suppose.

DK: What do you think about the advent of MP3s and the emerging ability of artists to bypass record labels altogether (to some extent at least), post their music on the internet and reach an audience directly?

KS: If it's not just a short-living fashion, it's dangerous for the whole music scene. The situation for the majority of serious artists is bad enough, and the common man's consciousness about music is already: It's for free. But music as we know it and love it exists only because musicians get paid for their work.

I am a musician, and I cannot pay the baker and the electricity, buy new trousers and socks just from my love for music. I must get paid for my work, by those who want to listen to it.

Some musicians put their music for "free" in the net. Some people always do what's possible and what's in vogue, without caring much what it could cause. Musicians are not automatically more clever-thinking people. They have the same share of idiots and shortsighteds among them as every other group of people.

The second (and that's the larger) group is those musicians that no one is interested in anyway; they offer their unwanted stuff for free in the wasted hope "to reach the audience" (and have the same in common: to get rich and famous, at least on their low level).

Before MP3, this existed already. For example, some of those many second- or third-class Schulze or TD copycats who record their revival music at weekends tried to bring their music to the audience by offering the homemade CDs for nearly free to specialized dealers. The same dealers then mourn and grumble when they should pay for a regular CD twice as much.

DK: I understand you are rebuilding your massive studio in Hamburen. How is that work coming along? Are you happy with the state of the technology these days, and is its greatest benefit musical flexibility or compactness? To what extent is the music you do today dependent on computers?

KS: This rebuilding was done over three

years ago(!) Yes, I am "happy with the state of the technology" and, a yes for both, the "flexibility and the compactness." Of course, I use the computer very much. I always used the most actual equipment as my tools. I think there's nothing remarkable with that.

DK: How much of your old equipment do you still have?

KS: Not much.

DK: It seems as though a disproportionate share of pioneering synthesizer music is produced by Germans -- you, Edgar, Chris Franke, Kraftwerk, Michael Hoenig, etc. Is this a misperception, in your view, or do you think there is a cultural basis for this phenomenon?

KS: It just happened this way. There were a few youngsters in Berlin with a love for Pink Floyd, and there were the Kraftwerk people in Dusseldorf. The "cultural basis" was many small things that happened. In Berlin, for instance, but that's too voluminous a story. A very good article about the Berlin situation in the late '60s was written and printed in a German book about me (from 1986, now deleted). The English translation was printed on eight pages in two 1996 issues of the newsletter "The KS Circle."

DK: You have a massive retrospective coming out in January: 50 CDs of music extending all the way back to the beginning of your career. Has the selection process for this offering been grueling and difficult for you, or have you enjoyed finding forgotten tracks, etc.? How much of the music will be remixed? Do you have a set idea of how many of these sets will be pressed?

KS: Actually, I have nothing to do with what you just described. I "only" did the music, once.

The "massive retrospective coming out" has a name: *THE ULTIMATE EDITION*. More info about it you can find on my web site (http://www.klaus-schulze.com). There will be no "remixes" -- one must not do everything that's possible (or just fashionable).

DK: Whose idea was it to have a wax likeness of you done in Tokyo?

KS: I don't know. Most certainly it was a Japanese fan. If you want, I can check for his name. But ...

Interview by Dave Kirby
Originally posted on www.radiospy.com

Hallucination on Sustain
25 Years of Amon Düül II

As an established trend of musical non-adventurism became the keynote of the early '70s, an alternative motif of sonic exploration became necessary and was provided in a most timely fashion by the German vanguard bands, Amon Düül II in particular. Unlike the other great Teutonic entities, Amon Düül II was slightly more accessible to Amerikana, if for no other reason than the fact that they had domestic releases, the first of which was the incredible *DANCE OF THE LEMMINGS*.

Upon hearing this landmark double album of sci-fi space rock, their two previous import albums became a necessity, as did those of Ash Ra Tempel, Guru Guru, Faust, Tangerine Dream, Can, Neu!, Cluster and Kraftwerk.

As the '70s gradually evolved, Amon Düül II progressed along with it, eventually replacing free-form acid jams and sci-fi manifestations with a more streamlined Indian-jazz influenced sound highlighted by an increasing political conscience. Fantasy was yielding to reality, and a whole new danger zone became their next excursion.

The transformation was smooth, as the hallucinations of "All the Years Round" juxtaposed nicely with the anti-secret police content of "CID in Uruk." The continuing endeavor became nonetheless risky as cosmic intermingling grounded in earthly woes were now the focus of Renate, the former flower child/solar princess, who was taking a much more prominent role as the group's most inspired and talented vocalist. Highlighted by Chris Karrer's weaving gypsy-like sound tapestries with his John Cale-like electric violin, the rest of the group contributed the remaining pieces of the sonic puzzle.

In the interim astral zone, an import only, titled *LIVE IN LONDON*, was released, destined to appeal greatly to their cosmic clients who weren't quite ready to succumb to the more earthly outputs.

By the time of their sixth studio album, *VIVA LA TRANCE*, the Amon Düül II spaceship had now landed, but not crashed. Their most melodramatic political statement yet came in the anti-racist "Mozambique." In her most heroic vocal to date, Renate makes the astute observation "...better to die as a free man than to live as a slave." Her sentiments veer toward unaccomplished yearnings in the tender "Jalousie," but venture into the opposite realm of the spectrum in "Trap," an angry escape-route manifesto.

What was to come next was confounding beyond belief to the diehard lysergic crowd who had locked into a sonic texture not likely to be abandoned. *HIJACK* was to these ears at least the only good disco album of the '70s. Taken at the face it reduced the rest of the genre to the lamentable muck history has proven it to be.

MADE IN GERMANY, a double LP overseas, was castrated into a single release domestically. The massive rock opera was left with little more than one good song sung by Renate, and unfortunately she and the majority of the group split afterwards. The two follow-up efforts had next to none of the original members, resulting in little more than disposable debris with only the name intact.

Now we are heading toward the late '70s, and signs of its demise were evident throughout the entire space rock contingent. Kraftwerk and Nektar each had AM radio hits. Can and Guru Guru had both become much more accessible to a wider audience. Klaus and Edgar were producing long suites of neo-symphonic electronic pomp that was already foreshadowed by Manuel's *NEW AGE OF EARTH*. Little did he know at the time how that title would become the musical and philosophical fad of the '80s. Don Robertson saw it coming, too.

To make matters worse, Cluster, Neu! and Faust all seemed dormant. It appeared that the best of "The Drone Zone" was now a lost art, like the "Free Your Mind" of the '60s. Befuddled and grief-stricken, I knew for me, at least, the time was ripe for a departure. To what, I did not know.

Ceaselessly grasping the desert dry lands, the lowlands, the rain forest wetlands and ultimately the highlands, I at last settled in at the high country, conducive to my whims of fulfillment via the "higher" elevation.

By the time of the early '80s, my interest in atmospheric treks was undergoing reactivation. It seemed as though groups influenced by Amon Düül II were arising everywhere. Tuxedo Moon played neo-psych gypsy mini-symphonies relying heavily on electric violin meandering. The Fibonaccis were excellent musicians that excelled in mutant funk that at times compared favorably with Renate. Seventeen Pygmies conjured up a vision of a stateside Amon Düül II, and their sister band, Savage Republic, brought to mind primal Amon Düül I remembrances.

Simultaneous with these developments was a growing curiosity as to what had transpired with EUROCK. Having entered into oblivion with only the void as hindsight, I had no idea until paging through the Sunday *LA Times*, stopping at an electronics review in the music section and picking up on a passing reference. Several years passed by and in the back pages of a monthly alternative source was a name I recognized at a new address. Sure enough I wrote and garnered a response and even contributed a small perspective piece for the 20th anniversary.

I was headed back toward the light, but the fact remained that I was leading a remote backwoods existence and was by now unfamiliar with nearly all the acts being lauded in the pages of EUROCK. To complicate matters further, I had no CD player or plans to acquire one, being a retro vinyl junkie. To the best of my limited knowledge, there either wasn't anything new I wanted to hear, or nothing of an older vintage (Krautrock) putting out anything now I needed to have. The last I knew, Kraftwerk was dabbling in high-tech dance rock, and Edgar was manufacturing soundtracks for sleep extravaganzas. It wasn't like there was an Amon Düül II regrouping in the works -- just yet.

Along about the summer of '96, a fellow record collector with a computer informed me that "Archie is on the internet selling 6 packs of Ash Ra Tempel CDs." By the time that pertinent info had sunk in, I'd finally come to grips that the time was now to get a CD player. Even if I heard next to nothing new, I could at least re-capture in recorded form some of the great cosmic treks of bygone eras. As winter of 1996-97 ever so slowly (up here) wound down, the guru of electronics once again contacted me, this time in regards to the 25th anniversary of EUROCK. He reassured me that I'd be delighted to hear all the old Amon Düül II and Ash Ra albums in the new sound format.

That brings us to what I perceived would never happen -- an Amon Düül II reunion. Renate, Lothar, Chris, Peter and Falk-U. Rogner (art and ambience) were combining their extraordinary resources for two astonishing mid-'90s releases, *LIVE IN TOKIO*, and the studio complexity, *NADA MOONSHINE #.*

Not knowing what to expect after some 20 years, I approached *NADA MOONSHINE #* with an open mind, which apparently some others did not have. Its aggressive hip-hop beats, mutant disco and techno pop all seemed to be a far cry from the intergalactic echoes of the archive ecstasy of two recently released retrospectives, *ETERNAL FLASHBACK* and *KOBE RECONSTRUCTIONS*. But let's face it -- 25 years later, it could hardly remain the same. Amon Düül II was always far too progressive and unpredictable to time-warp into yesteryear nostalgia like the latest 50 Foot Hose, which sounded like it got lost in a time vacuum.

In actuality, under closer scrutiny *NADA MOONSHINE #* is one supreme accomplishment. The lyrical content is so prolific you'd have thought they took off 20 years just to amass so much material. Fantasy and to a lesser extent politics still dominate the occasion, with some of the best musicianship attainable, especially Chris Karrer, who plays Spanish acoustic and waling siren electric guitar often in the same song. Renate no longer spews out childlike musings, instead personifying a much more mature expression with a few surprising Streisand-like nuances. We're older and wiser now, so it is just as well we sound like it. After all, we were fortunate indeed to have encountered and survived the first round of hallucinations.

In the words of Chris, off "Castaneda-da-Dream" from the grandeur of *LIVE IN TOKIO*: "Mercy for us, 'cause we conquered the world, we may conquer the universe too." Let's just hope that event can become a reality for their upcoming 30 year reunion!

(**Editor's note:** Alas, it seems the dream has come to an end for the mighty Düül. After smashing concerts and good reviews surrounding their visits to Japan and England, it seems the hydra of newborn success reared its head, and the band fell into a final bout of self-destructive musical battles. Rumors of Düül offshoots echo in the ether, but it's possible that Chris Karrer's solo endeavors may have to fortify the soul of diehards for the years to come. The band may be gone at last, but fortunately their music lives on.)

Scott Fischer

The Beat Has Gone
Thoughts and Opinions 'bout a Long Forgotten Scene

In 1968 a mutated kind of mindset emerged in then West Germany to form a scene that turned the tide of times, after the war in this dull, real square country, and set the general cultural directions for the next decade.

It was a spiritual elite of mostly unprivileged, non-academic, middle-class young people around 25 and 30 who consciously dropped out of mainstream society and stuffy jobs, eagerly exploring a brand-new way of living.

A life where no damned alarm clock rattled always at the same too early morning hour. Where one didn't have to go to work 40 hours a week just to live.

Where one wasn't glued to this out-spoken boring way for at least 40 years. Not held down by the burden of constant debt and/or family. Not settled down and hooked, hoping for the work bonus, or glorious pension.

These people had a lifestyle/way of thinking that knew what was just going on in England and America. Lived by cheap rent, a part-time job, a group of mutual friends and, most important, what was called a "thing," an activity one really liked to do and did believe in. They avoided early marriage, TV, alcohol, too much meat and didn't believe in money (the ground the "straights" stood on so heavily). They wanted freer relationships, liked discussion, used (at that time for a European an adventurous experiment) psychedelic drugs for mind-expanding trips, feeling experiences and de-conditioning from social norms, made food an important minor matter and did believe in freedom.

They were not dreaming hippies, not party-political fanatics, but people who had gotten the basic message (for them: turn on/tune in/drop out) directly on their personal antennas. They were aware that the system sucked, and that government just meant a bunch of lies. They let their hair grow not to go along with fashion, but they had no time and money to spend on a fashion. They didn't give a shit what the establishment thought of how they dressed or looked. They didn't consume for cake's sake, because they found real satisfaction in the few things that they had and did, and were interested more in life than in life insurance, more into making art then making money.

The medium for these people was not books or movies, it was mainly music. In particular, non-commercial, un-pop and out of the mainstream, psychedelic or experimental. The new electric music of Hendrix, Joplin, Dylan, The Doors, Jefferson Airplane, Grateful Dead, Velvet Underground, Pink Floyd, Cream and Soft Machine, who were erupting at that time.

Unlike surrounding European countries, the German musicians involved in that scene -- lacking the background of rock like their English or American counterparts -- were able to develop their own freak-out way of a chiefly instrumental music that -- judging from the very best of them -- was actually internationally outstanding. This music became the medium for the scene, since where the music was, there was the scene. It was the only way to meet and contact others, and the experiences made with music brought people closer and let them form a loose web on the fringe of and against the hostile square society.

(I'll never forget the time with Guru Guru when we went into a restaurant in Essen in 1968 trying to get some coffee. The owner muttered viciously, "For long-haired freaks there's nothing here to get but out of here," his buddies at the bar already getting ready to throw us out in case we didn't leave fast enough. It made me feel just like a white nigger.)

Then, musicians lived from month to month, playing -- since no official jazz or rock club generally took them -- mostly in underground clubs/dens that opened up, got closed and popped up again regularly. They appeared at small festivals organized by people from the scene, and weren't covered by the press. They lived a free, interesting, flowing life. It was basically a Cultural Revolution, where the people involved lived their beliefs, leading an existential life that made them strong. The natural impulse was to discover what turned you on. New ideas were discovered and discussed daily (there were hardly any books about such things then). The so-called New Age didn't get published, spread, summed up and finally exploited until 10 years later.

This all happened in a short time, from the germination of 1968 to its full blossoming in 1970. It spread like wildfire to nearly every part of countryside and nearly all the cities. Neglected by the culture industry, it grew stronger through its own momentum, increasing steadily, quadrupling in numbers. (I remember sitting 'round together then with Guru Guru being in another group's place -- I think it was with Xhol -- where we definitely had the feeling, if this continues, we will own the world in a few years, and we were all no fantasists).

This big rebellion against the old ways just couldn't last, like Spartacus & Co. Soon the state got wise about what was going on. The actual power of the movement was destroyed in '71. It happened through a concentrated collaboration between the government, mass media and the music industry.

The hard-core of the scene was criminalized. (Living near Heidelberg with Guru Guru then, the local hashish dealers told me that strange heavy guys coming from Frankfurt had broken suddenly into their business and ripped them off at gunpoint; there was the rumor it had been undercover agents of the CIA. Also the police was now much more aggressive about making arrests, and it became dangerous to smoke a joint on stage or in the streets too obviously. Guru Guru nearly got a ridiculous dope charge slapped on them when some clown reported us because he'd read in an interview with us that we'd stated that we had smoked shit and enjoyed it, too.)

The soft-core of the scene was then commercialized. (Due to the success of the Ohr label, a lot of German record companies quickly formed labels for progressive rock, as it was called at that time). With the steady rat-tail of air-play, magazines with feature articles, reviews and -- don't forget -- ads, they were able to slowly influence the listeners to strictly go for that which sells the most and also sounds the softest. The American music business, eager to get in full control again, after having safely packaged and corrupted the term "underground" -- produced a colored disk of the same title that featured on Side One the ultimately lame-tame song "Susanne" by Leonard Cohen, and put on Side Two, a moderate Hendrix, Joplin cut. Soon thereafter they spilled out the slogan: Let It Rock, headed by the Rolling Stones. That set the general direction for the future everywhere, also here in Germany.

The German leftists started to claim the movement a political one. This way they falsified the whole affair completely and since nobody contradicted them, it became quite fashionable to appear "engaged" then. They could go on and on with it to no end, thus turning a free and open cultural revolution into a rigid ideology. I dare to say a cultural revolution because I've been around and know the German political left of that time stood heavily against the sex, drugs and rock 'n' roll syndrome. They were into Lenin, Marx and Mao, not knowing Burroughs, Kerouac, Bukowski. Eventually they got into reading hippie stuff like Tolkien/Hesse, not listening to even normal rock, but acoustic guitar accompanied -- socialistic German Liedermachers, dreaming of a splendid socialism soon to come. But in the light of what was really going on, they were simply just dried-up wankers.

By 1972 the "original" scene was actually all finished. Now, no one from the scene could rent a hall again on easy terms and with the right band, have the house full with about 30 posters. No group could get a gig in three weeks' notice anymore, 'cause the underground clubs had all disappeared due to new high conditions on the sanitary level. (You had to have two real fine toilets now and an inspected safe emergency exit.) Now you were asked just like before, if the music was, what seemed to be the most important thing, "danceable." You had to submit a demo, things became straight again, and only the props had changed.

Most bands reacted to it by adapting. They let it rock much more and tried the one or other way to keep up with the market that had suddenly evolved. (I remember my surprise and anger when the first big widely read rock encyclopedia by German authors appeared in 1973. I beheld the names of Tangerine Dream and Amon Düül II -- but not Embryo and Guru Guru. There were also the likes of Triumvirat and Truck Stop -- the former a group that had not made the slightest influence on the scene, the latter an absolute commercial US rockabilly, country music band. Later I learned the qualification for a listing had been 30,000 copies sold of one LP at least.)

Others tried to piss against the wind, continuing their social outcast life and non-mainstream music, hoping for the best. But in 1974 the German record companies secretly decided not to take on any "Krautrock" anymore, and that was about the end, 'cause getting gigs was hard now if you weren't supporting a new LP. I set quite a record in 1974 by living in Berlin on 300 DM a month (everything included), but then there still was opportunity to earn the low rent with a one-night stand of dishwashing. That lingered on until the end of 1975, when the fading out began that continued until 'bout 1980. In this time span, the hashish became more and more diluted. LSD 25 disappeared completely, and cocaine was suddenly obtainable right on the street.

The mass media started to combine pot with terrorists/narcotics. Faded jeans and long hair became an ordinary fad. Rents went up amazingly, and jobs became much rarer. A creeping up of the inflation rate began to bite into the cost of just living. Many people's lives went back to "normal." There still existed people everywhere that lived a different lifestyle, but they were all dispersed and disconnected.

When I founded Spacebox, my first solo group, that gave me a real education about making honest music. I stood from the beginning on lost ground, seeing it becoming harder and harder to find an understanding for a music that was not molded after the official mainstream. It has to be understood that the first original musical wave of this scene, whose most important groups were Amon Düül II, Can, Guru Guru, Tangerine Dream and Embryo, used the normal instruments, but played them different in a really dynamic way (and naturally in combination with a special concept). When they came in conflict with the let-it-rock world that the music industry was heading for, and fell back in importance, the door was opened for electronic music, which dominated more and more the field. (Can's an exception: They never played much live, but found a lot of followers and fans with their well-edited records, being always near the static side of music.)

Headed by a very successful Kraftwerk, who established a new image, Tangerine Dream, who had went totally for synthesizers, and Klaus Schulze, too, led everyone to get the new equipment and try to do it, too. Labels developed solely for that kind of static music. With increasing interest from other foreign countries, a lot of people went into a special kind of electronic music, that became since 1975 the hallmark Teutonic creativity. It reached its commercial highlight in the

1980s, and is still going on today, while the dynamic instrumental war has nearly faded.

Today, everything's available, administrated and then pigeon-holed into a scene. But if everything is a scene, then there's no scene ('cause scene means something that's against the general trend of what's officially going on). So there's a situation now where one is able to read a hundred books 'bout virtually any topic. You can take/use nearly any way of therapy or method the times have washed ashore, or can participate in all kinds of strange or rare activities (just scan the ads in any city magazine). But it never really affects one's life. It's simply recreation. The crux is back: the separation between life and what one does for living. Also the times have gradually become much harder economically. There nearly are no cracks to hide in anymore, to just survive. The Left has vanished completely, and the music industry is long since in full control again. On the other hand, artistically, everything's allowed now, which means a lot of people, having no opposition, are doing things these days that are plainly not at all significant, but mainly just mediocre, superfluous seventh hand.

The kids who proclaim that they are the scene today (actually a quite conforming, materialistic bunch), change their lifestyle/interests whenever the industry tells them what is the newest fad. There's no spiritual consciousness, an amazing lack of sensitivity, a high conformity in outfit/language and the obviously strong wish to get zonked out with the hardest means that's possible. They never had to fight for certain things, are praised in all the media, take everything they get for granted, are on alcohol and speed, watch TV, eat lots of meat and do believe in money -- basically things have returned to the way they were before.

AFTERTHOUGHT

The kind of mentioned German Progressive music that treated things quite differently than the Anglo-Saxons did (mainly destroying song forms), disparagingly called Krautrock and actually neglected from the start, is presently being re-discovered internationally as the unique sound that it actually was. That's good to know, because this music is now finally heard and gets at least posthumous recognition, but on the other side, this interest is purely all historical, meaning that the movement is definitely finished.

But since I've always met and do meet young and older people with a mind tuned to the basic feelings and thinking that the '60s/'70s have brought into consciousness, it seems to be just a question of time before the minds meet again. It seems that every 40 years something spiritual happens (the '20s and the '60s are examples). The 30 years between assimilate, dilute, drench, trim, make popular and live off the earlier achievements. So a new scene could pop up in 2008, 'cause the spirit that had ruled those two decades is always there. It only needs some special focus lingering in the air (morphogenetic fields), to create the opportunity that will bring the diverse spiritually oriented concepts and people out of their isolation.

It may face the same fate of scenes that have passed before, but their larger achievement will be to create a ferment that breaks up rigid cultural, social forms and habits again. Let's hope for that and listen sometimes again to that 20-year-old turned-on music that was injected with a spirit inspired by the dedication to being true and free. The late '60s/early '70s were definitely a special time, and I'm real glad I could experience them to the hilt. My life has not been the same since then. For me, the beat's still going on stone strong.

AUTHOR'S NOTE: This article has been written not by a journalist or fan, but by a person who -- as a musician -- played in some important groups from the beginning -- and has been directly involved in building up the phenomenon which is here the theme. It therefore expresses a quite personal point of view, but being an artist, I must take my stand, and that's why there's also objectivity in, around, and in-between these very lines.

Uli Trepte

Old Times

Archie, whom I have been in touch with for 25 years now, asked me to write an article for him, with no limits in length and contents. Could I dare to say no? He wants to know something about my musical whereabouts, my taste, preferences... All this just because since nearly 25 years my name is connected with the more famous name of the other Klaus, the musician KLAUS SCHULZE.

My very first idea was to put together excerpts from the many letters that I sent to fans, my (partly very long) answers on their letters to Klaus Schulze (and me). When I checked my computer, there was not even one letter stored that included something about me and about what Archie had asked me. Therefore, I had to type something else, had to think anew...

It is indeed a great question: if the meaning of life and the fortunes of this world are founded either in the reflection and possession of a naked lady... or much more in a lasting and stubborn observation of some kind of art, of music, even "strange" music. A good deal speaks for the first, our classical education and some philosophical reasons speak for the latter. What the heck is "cosmic" or "spacey" music? There is no sound in space. And, what about the fact that Glenn Gould signed clearly (and always) as "Glen Gould" with just one "n"? What does all this mean? Is there a meaning?

Back to Klaus Schulze and his very special brand of music, and my role in the history of it. Yes, I remember the early years quite well... when we were almost alone with our crazy music and ideas. There was Kraftwerk and their more "popular" brand of rhythmic material. And Tangerine Dream under the helpful management of Richard Branson. And there was Klaus Schulze with his driving musical and personal energy, together with a persistent yet caring workaholic like me. If we all wouldn't have struggled for our crazy music for a quarter of a century, there would be no "Electronic Music" as we know it today. And the journalists? I remember that Archie was one of the rare few who reported about this music, who even seemed to understand and like it. At least I remember him as the only one outside Europe who publicly cared about these new crazy sounds as early as 1973.

It was 1973, too, when I began to work regularly for Klaus Schulze. From 1970 to 1973, I was hired as tour manager for various musical groups and artists. We made tours all over Europe with the great Duke Ellington Orchestra; with the moody but wonderful guitar player from Brazil, Baden Powell; with British art rockers Van der Graaf Generator; with the Lionel Hampton Band; the German all-around musician Klaus Doldinger; and even with the comedian Marty Feldman, who was not only a freak, but also a true hippie.

Quite by accident, my very first tour and my first job in the music business was a 10-day tour with the "Paul Bley Synthesizer(!) Show featuring Annette Peacock" in 1970. I had no idea what effect these new instruments would have on me in the coming decade, but also on the whole music scene worldwide.

Between these jobs I was the helpful hand for various rock groups in my hometown, Berlin. I also had a liking for Berlin avant-garde rock groups: Agitation Free, Os Mundi, Tangerine Dream, and Ash Ra Tempel. The work and the friendship with the members of the latter group changed my whole life. Also, I was a regular visitor of concerts and festivals of new music, be it free jazz, Eruption, John Cage, or plenty of exotic music from hidden corners of our world... I also worked for these people, concerts and festivals. The most important work was for Walter Bachauer's "Metamusik Festival" in 1974 and '76 in Berlin's "Nationalgalerie." Here, and for the very first time, avant-garde music and ethnological "world" music were brought to a wider public's eyes and ears. Great concept, great concerts. They were very successful and influential. Much later, fashions like "ethno" or "New Age" had an important starting point here at the "Metamusik Festival." We listened carefully to the music of Terry Riley, Steve Reich, Philip Glass, Henze (an unpleasant man), Prima Materia, Alvin Curran, Musica Elettronica Viva, Robert Laneri, Pauline Oliveros, Robert Moran, Peter Michael Hamel, Luc Ferrari, the brothers Kontarsky, Les Percussions de Strasbourg, to exotic music from Korea, Indonesia, Japan, Ghana, Senegal, India, Pakistan, Iraq, Tibet... During the concert free time in the morning and noon, we played for the normal visitors of the "Nationalgalerie" soft avant-garde and ethno music from our record collection; music of the type that was much later known as "ambient." Together with Michael Hoenig, I worked at (and enjoyed) these two 30-day events. A hard job, but plenty of interesting music. I am proud that I was part of it.

In early 1972, Hartmut, the bass player of Ash Ra Tempel, took me to pick up a Revox tape machine at a place in Berlin Steglitz, where their former drummer was living with his wife. We needed this first-class tape recorder for our preparations for the coming recordings with Timothy Leary, which later became the LP titled *SEVEN UP*. But this was not the first time I met KS, because he wasn't at home. His friendly wife Rita handed us the machine. I finally saw KS in the offices of the Ohr company. Klaus came into the office, and he had his homemade cover for *IRRLICHT*, a 12" x 12" piece of cardboard with blue velvet on it, and the wasted hope that Ohr would use the textile for the actual covers. Also, he showed one of his first promotion photos, a dreadful picture of his head full of dirt, mud, and water: very "progressive" at this time. It was the summer of '72.

Then our paths crossed again, when I did a removal for him. (I also made my living with this rather hard job. I remember that I did removals for Ax Genrich -- from Berlin to Highdelberg -- and Steve Reich.) After that, I visited Klaus a few times when he lived together with a resolute lady in Berlin Wilmersdorf (by that time he was divorced from his first wife Rita). KS then moved into what had been a small shop in Berlin's Schwäbische Straße. From now on this was his studio. We pasted over the huge shop windows with sticky blue plastic (which was still visible in 1996), and we made the front door almost burglar-proof. From then on KS lived there, in the adjacent two small rooms.

KS doesn't like -- or is even able -- to do such work as soldering, or similar non-musical necessities. I like to try out these small mechanical things, although I never studied it. Learning by doing. After awhile, I noticed that soldering wasn't the only work KS wouldn't do. I started to fix up what can be described as Klaus' office: set up files, answered letters, wrote letters and filed the copies, did the whole postage for him. From under his bed, I pulled various documents, contracts, clippings, put them into order, filed them, and this was the beginning of what became my huge KS archives. This nearly full-time job started in late '73 or in '74. Before this, there was an important event: KS' record company Ohr took the offer of the French magazine *ACTUEL* to do concerts in Paris with various exotic new German groups. As a result, on two days in February 1973 at the "Theatre de l'Ouest Parisienne," the sold-out auditorium saw and listened to Guru Guru and Kraftwerk on the first day, and to Tangerine Dream, Ash Ra Tempel (with KS), and Klaus Schulze as soloist on the second day. This was the first solo appearance of Klaus Schulze. On the way to Paris, we visited the Farfisa company near Cologne to talk them out of a new electric organ. When we reached Paris, we had a serious breakdown of our little truck, but the friendly Tangerine Dream people lent us their truck. We reloaded the instruments and got them to the concert hall in time. In the meantime, some friendly Frenchmen took our Ford Transit in for repair, and the next day we could use it again.

The concert was a triumph, and marked the beginning of the French success of the three "cosmic" groups Tangerine Dream, Ash Ra Tempel, and KS. Kraftwerk only became well-known one year later as a direct result of their (well-deserved) American success with "Autobahn." Guru Guru, the only non-electronic band, never really made it.

To this day, KS and Manuel Gottsching like to tell the story about the brand-new Farfisa organ, which was unpacked for the first time on stage in Paris. Klaus didn't even know how to switch it on. During his performance as the final "cosmic" attraction, Klaus managed this new tool very well. In addition he used only an echo (the Revox tape machine), and a pre-recorded tape with his own drumming. The 2,000 Frenchmen were enraptured.

Soon after, Hartmut the bass player completely stopped doing music, and Manuel and Klaus went different directions.

Then came the dissolution of Ohr, the dispute between some musicians and Rolf-Ulrich Kaiser, the boss of Ohr. Edgar Froese and KS were the only two who took the load and went to court against Kaiser, to free themselves from Kaiser's silly and harmful "cosmic" nonsense. All other Ohr musicians waited to see what would happen. Edgar and KS won their lawsuits, and were free to sign with other companies. The main reason for leaving Ohr was indeed the exaggerated promotion, which was in parts embarrassing, at least back then. Today, this somewhat ludicrous promotion is daily routine in rock- and other showbiz. In addition, Kaiser and especially his girlfriend (who some say was the main culprit) drifted away into fields of the paranormal. They believed what they were talking about, all that "cosmic" and drug nonsense...

The lawsuit against Kaiser was distinct: "It is very clear that the [producer's] boasting style is highly qualified to make fools out of his affiliated musicians...," and the judge meant in particular the "cosmic" nonsense. In an interview in April 1982, KS said: "The whole basis of the *COSMIC JOKERS* was LSD. That was the big influence of Timothy Leary and there was that producer who was totally influenced by Tim: Rolf-Ulrich Kaiser. We didn't really take these sessions seriously." Twenty years later, Kaiser's girlfriend still sent around ridiculous papers as a fortune teller (!) under the pseudonym "Star's Maiden." Absurd. Insane.

For the following 20 years, nobody was interested in these old "cosmic" recordings, neither the artists nor the public. The involved artists knew about the "quality" of these "cosmic" recordings and were happy that these LPs were off the market (even if you were deaf, the ugly covers tell it all!). Some crazy collectors liked these old platters, because they were not available and hard to get. Which has nothing to do with the actual music, but with the harmless hobby of collecting rare record albums. Which is OK, but not my cup of tea...

Back to the Schulze story: After he was freed from Ohr, Schulze signed with Metronome, who had already distributed the Ohr records. The first new LP was *BLACKDANCE* in 1974, then came *PICTURE MUSIC*, which was actually recorded before *BLACKDANCE*. Other bigger or smaller things happened then, among them was an international deal with Virgin.

I remember that during one of our flights from Berlin to London to visit Virgin Records, Klaus and I had a short discussion about the future possibilities of our music, this "electronic music." We didn't know what would happen, but we saw the hardware industry building more and more electronic keyboards of all kinds, and investing millions of DM or dollars for research in this direction. Our solution (and hope) was then that "electronic music" must take over, be it just because "the industry" invested so much manpower and money into the development and promotion of these new instruments (which was, in 1974 or '75, just a tinge of what they do today!).

Twenty years later, even the most reactionary or dull man must see it, and acknowledge that because of the huge "Techno" vogue, "Electronic Music" has succeeded.

Klaus D. Mueller, Berlin

Krautrock: A Personal Reflection

What to say about Krautrock, 25 to 30 years on? On the one hand, plenty, in that it's never really been taken seriously as an important and influential chapter in Western popular music. Sure, Can and Neu! get the odd reverential name check by the occasional enlightened journalist, but few have gone beyond that. On the other hand, isn't that what makes the whole Krautrock "era" (in reality only a few years) so enigmatic, innocent, precious? I'd be the first person to buy a book on it, but there's also something vaguely dissatisfying about turning it into so much cultural history. Music moves on, and there's plenty to get enthused about at any given time right across the globe. I've moved on so am kind of reluctant to wax nostalgically. Still, we're talking about real people here: musicians, artists, and organizers, so definitely credit where credit is due. Some of these guys (yes, Krautrock was as male a preserve as anything before or after) are still at it, to a greater or lesser degree. A bit of reappraisal might not be a bad thing; and those fans who have taken it upon themselves to re-release material are doing the right thing.

I was too young to make proper sense of it at the time, and didn't actually own any records until the fledgling UK Virgin label got involved in 1973, but you never forget your first love. It still informs my musical and cultural tastes. This is crass and hugely oversimplified, but I still prefer electronic instrumentation to a conventional rock line-up, instrumental to vocal, minimalism to intricacy, weird to pop. At the time I even made a decision to prefer German music to British/American but wised-up when comparing the likes of Jane to King Crimson.

I clearly remember the impact those first UK releases had on me: Tangerine Dream *PHAEDRA*, Can *TAGO MAGO*, Neu!'s reissued debut, Kraftwerk *RALF & FLORIAN*, Klaus Schulze *BLACKDANCE*, Faust *TAPES*. Each in its own way was an astounding affront to what was otherwise going on in Britain and the States. The fact that Tangerine Dream played only electronic instruments was like sticking two fingers up to rock. Can may have armed themselves with conventional rock instruments but through discipline, restraint and some unusual influences, turned rock into repetition into art form. Neu! went even further, precursors to punk's three-chord wonders. Kraftwerk somehow combined industry and romance, and later got people to dance to it. Schulze was the Lone Romantic following a Wagnerian muse. And Faust showed that Germans do have a sense of humor.

It took some searching, but from there I got into Ash Ra Tempel and -- to a lesser extent -- the whole Cosmic Courier vibe, Conrad Schnitzler, Cluster and Harmonia, the intensely mystical Popol Vuh, and others. And there were many: check out Steven & Alan Freeman's *"The Crack in the Cosmic Egg"* encyclopedia to find out how many. There was crap, too: bad imitators of the above, and conventional (in the British-American sense) rock bands masquerading as Krautrock. And try as I might, I couldn't get into Amon Düül in any of their incarnations. Sorry.

Krautrock is/was a paradox. It was both of its time and is timeless. I still play the stuff. It can take me back to a certain time and a place. I first played Ashra's "Nightdust" (from *NEW AGE OF EARTH*) immediately before and after watching a huge building ablaze in a local park on a hot summer night; it always reminds me of these families standing in the park in their dressing gowns and slippers, staring serenely, faces aglow. But the same record also sits quite happily amongst any number of recent purchases. Slip in a Schnitzler or early Cluster, and the clubgoers wouldn't miss a beat (in fact, DJ Mixmaster Morris does exactly that). Put Neu! on, and people ask, "Is this the new Stereolab?" And when you're in the chill-out room, is that The Orb or Tangerine Dream? It might even be both! (The former re-mixed the latter only this year).

Its time and place was/is pivotal. Indigenous culture was pretty much taboo after the war, and a new generation found itself growing up on a diet of the occupying forces' Popular Culture, essentially Rock 'n' Roll and Hollywood. It wasn't until the second half of the '60s -- when the Stones and Beatles went psychedelic, Pop turned Art on its head, and students took political matters into their own hands -- that young Germans felt able to think for themselves. By 1968, bands in Berlin, Munich and the industrialized Ruhrgebiet were taking the newest, best bits of British and American rock music (Pink Floyd, Zappa, Velvet Underground, etc.) and combining these with their own ideologies. From the outset, Krautrock was a political statement. While many chose English names, most chose not to sing in English (almost unthinkable then); others chose not to sing at all (equally provocative). Some were influenced by the electronic music of Stockhausen and involved themselves in galleries or avant-garde "happenings," often swapping band members and playing for free, before contemplating whether or not they were going to make records. Amon Düül, from Munich, formed a commune -- and to be honest it was a wonder they got anything down on vinyl.

Much happened by chance or through unorthodox channels. There was no rock industry to compare with the established corporations in the UK and US. Can, for example, were initially championed by a number of patrons, in the old artistic tradition. Organisation (who were to become Kraftwerk) recorded their *TONE FLOAT* album in a disused refinery, and via a series of chance connections, it actually appeared on the British RCA label, only available in Germany as an import. Kluster's *KLOPFZEICHEN* and *ZWEI OSTEREI* albums were commissioned by a progressive church! Otherwise, it was essentially United Artists and its subsidiary Liberty, and Metronome and its subsidiaries Brain, Ohr and Pilz. Perhaps the most amusing story of all was that of Polydor giving the music journalist Uwe Nettelbeck a large cash advance and told to form a group and produce "an epoch-making record." The group turned out to be Faust.

I have no idea how many people in (the then) West Germany -- let alone Britain and America -- were aware of what was going on. None of my schoolmates were into the scene, I was too young to see any (rare) concerts, and as far as I can remember, the music press couldn't really be bothered. And, of course, this was part of its appeal, its excitement: the notion that the scene was somehow a well-kept secret. When Brian Eno recorded with Cluster, I remember being almost disappointed that I would now have to "share" Moebius and Roedelius with a wider public. When Kraftwerk had a hit with *AUTOBAHN*, I was horrified -- not least because of their accessible new direction, though I quickly embraced that, too.

But apart from being a well-kept secret, what made Krautrock so special? For me, it was its idealism. I cannot think of one group who, up to the mid '70s, compromised their artistic vision in any seriously crass way, whatever trip they were on. They carried very little of the cultural baggage that weighed heavy on British and American groups. Most were quite unconcerned with the clichés of rock music, preferring instead to extend the boundaries of "music." Almost anything was possible. Can would play concerts lasting anything up to seven hours, with jugglers and acrobats. On one occasion, singer Malcolm Mooney set up an incessant scream of just two words, "Upstairs Downstairs," which started at the end of the first set, continued through the intermission and only stopped when he collapsed well into the second half. Side two of Neu!'s second album simply featured their single "Neuschnee/Super" at different speeds. A concert by Tangerine Dream in Reims Cathedral was enough to provoke the Pope to call for the building to be "resanctified." Faust took a pinball machine and road-drill on stage. Conrad Schnitzler would simply walk around Berlin with a megaphone welded on to a crash helmet.

Not many expected, nor made, the Big Time. The fact that Kraftwerk turned out to be so influential to dance music and so commercially successful would not have occurred to Hutter and Schneider as they dabbled in their abrasive, industrial kling and klang. By the late '70s, Krautrock had burnt out. Most bands succumbed to relative anonymity as native record companies went under or British ones withdrew their interest. A few labels, notably Sky, carried on with a mellow, middle-aged roster of artistes. Some musicians, like Klaus Schulze, set up their own labels; others returned underground (had they ever been overground?) or simply disappeared. Even Can went their separate ways. In the '80s, the term Krautrock was usually met with either derision or incomprehension. Tarred with the same brush that ridiculed Progressive Rock, it became -- for both lazy journalists and punters alike -- synonymous with long hair and druggy jams.

Now that long hair, druggy jams and even analog synths are back in fashion, it seems kind of inevitable that Krautrock is getting a second airing. Apart from the aforementioned Can/Neu!/ T.Dream name checks, people are delving deeper. The French label Spalax is re-releasing entire back catalogues on CD. Julian Cope must have turned on and tuned in hundreds (thousands?) with his love letter of a book, "Krautrocksampler." There have been encyclopedic tomes from the Freeman brothers and Dag Erik Asbjornsen, as well as books on Can, Kraftwerk and Tangerine Dream. Some are worthwhile, others simply cash-ins. Old favorites have reappeared, releasing new material or performing occasional concerts. Cluster -- who actually never really went away -- recently toured USA and Japan. Faust has played sporadically. Manuel Gottsching (a.k.a. Ashra) found his *E2-E4* on the receiving end of a hugely popular club remix and has literally ransacked his archives. Even Conrad Schnitzler -- who continued his guerilla life-as-art activities throughout the '80s and '90s -- has got himself a new manager. There was even an evening of Krautrock films at the National Film Theatre. But perhaps the image of people dancing to the stuff at the Kosmishe Club, run by ex-*SEVEN UP* casualty Brian Barritt, is the funniest or saddest of all, depending on your viewpoint.

And the point is that Krautrock will all be old hat again. And that's fine because then I won't feel I ought to be listening to it, only when the fancy takes me. I've had my dip in the nostalgia pool, and now I want to get out and listen to the new Massive Attack.

David Elliott

Fanzines

Fanzines offer that personal, unofficial and often highly subjective opinion on popular (and not so popular) culture. They rarely last more than a few clarion calls to this or that teen-age obsession. Some make it beyond this stage and into some sort of crusade. Before you know it, you're the editor of a "proper" magazine and part of the establishment you always (thought you'd) kicked against. The truth is, people start music fanzines 'cos they love music, overwhelmingly a certain type of music. Or a certain particular person. They are usually the product of one person or a group of friends, and are characterized by a fervor bordering on the religious. They generally do not concern themselves with the issues like revenue, deadlines and censorship. They are as much a part of music culture as the established publications.

Fanzines have been with us for as long as popular music. In the UK, they are usually associated with the punk rock explosion in 1976-77, which gave birth to hundreds of them. If bands could be formed in bedrooms having learned three chords, then "fanzines" were even easier. A typewriter, some pictures cut out of proper magazines, glue and an anarchic sense of "design" were all a rebellious but enterprising "publisher" needed. And, of course, a huge, lumbering photocopy machine in the basement of an office where your more sensible friend worked. You'd sneak in on a weekend and mercilessly run off as many copies as you dared or until the toner ran out. You'd then cart the stuff home and staple all the pages together, usually in the wrong order. It would be called *Puke* or *Ripped* or, more famously, *Sniffing Glue*. If you lived in a big city, then you might try selling them at gigs, or take them down to your newly opened independent record shop where there would be scores of the things, stuffed in racks, falling apart at the seams. But more often than not, you'd simply give them to your friends.

So punk was well catered for. But what of other musical sub-cultures? The alternative rock scene on mainland Europe was almost completely ignored in the UK. Essentially, the big weeklies were, in the '70s, concerned with the well-established and commercially successful British and American scene. Every once in a while you might have got the odd mention of Can, Focus or post-*AUTOBAHN* Kraftwerk. *ZigZag*, a decent alternative rock fanzine-cum-magazine, ran a few articles. The fledgling Virgin Records label kindled a cult interest in the likes of Tangerine Dream and Gong. There was a brief flirtation with Magma. It could be said that Punk actually made things worse. Eurorock was besmirched Progrock with a foreign accent. Synthesizer "boffins" such as Vangelis, Jean-Michel Jarre and Klaus Schulze were treated with the utmost disdain. It was only when Bowie and Eno started dropping names, Kraftwerk hit the charts, and New Wave spawned its largely electronic, experimental "Industrial" offshoot, that people started taking notice of what was happening sur le continent. John Peel, as ever, played a significant part, although in reality he had been playing the stuff -- such as was actually available -- throughout the '70s. It was Peel, after all, who made Tangerine Dream's *ATEM* his album of the year in 1973. Were there Euro-fanzines? Could the DIY spirit of punk apply to the Faust freak or Ashra aficionado?

Amazingly, yes, although ironically, it was an American one, EUROCK, which could justifiably claim to be the first of the genre. Founded in early 1973, before punk, you'll discover all about this influential publication elsewhere in this book.

The first UK-based fanzines on the Euro scene were *Face Out* and *Aura*, both appearing in, I think, early 1978. Editor Chris Furse introduced *Face Out* as "a rock fanzine, orientated towards the Science Fiction reader." I never really understood the Sci Fi angle, but no matter. The first issue consisted of album reviews of mainly German bands, before branching out into longer articles/interviews on French/other European bands, even on the odd occasion British ones. As each issue appeared, there would be new contributors, making it more of a forum of views. It was badly "designed" and terribly "printed" in best fanzine tradition. It was great.

Aura was more of a collaborative effort, even from Issue 1, although Phil Burford was the main man. Provocatively subtitled "The First UK Alternative Music Fanzine" (not quite true, actually), *Aura* was less specifically Euro and more about alternative music generally. Early issues featured Throbbing Gristle, Metabolist and the UK Industrialists alongside pieces on Magma, Embryo, Wigwam, French rock, etc. Both fanzines introduced contributors such as Steve Stapleton, Andy Garibaldi, Steve and Alan Freeman, Peter Harrison, and Denis and Jeanette Emsley, all of whom would play a major role in promoting Eurorock in Britain. *Aura* unfortunately lasted only four issues, although Phil cropped up as a contributor to *Face Out* -- which kept going 'til early 1981, producing eight issues.

Taking inspiration from the above, two new fanzines appeared in late 1979: *Mirage*, edited by Martin Reed in Bristol, and my own, *Neumusik*.

Although close in content to *Face Out*, *Mirage* introduced three new-ish concepts: decent printing, a cassette label and a distribution service. Mirage Tapes featured early releases by the likes of Mark Shreeve, Colin Potter and Steve Moore, while alongside these, Martin made available records, cassettes and fanzines from other sources.

While mail order was not a totally new concept -- EUROCK in America, Lotus Records in UK and *Atem* in France all offered extensive catalogues -- Martin's cassette label did much to foster young British synth talent. *Mirage*, the 'zine, lasted five issues, until Spring 1984.

I started *Neumusik* at university at the ripe old age of 18. Why? I guess it's a mix of things: "spreading the word" (there's all this great stuff out there, and it's a scandal that no one knows about it!), boredom/energy, egotism/control, the sheer spontaneous fun of it (which, if you're not careful, becomes deadline-driven and more like work). I had a fair amount of energy. I had a campus radio show, started a cassette label (YHR) and formed a group (MFH, later known as Pump). And crucially, I had the time. There was no wife, kids and office to distract. Instead there was Europe out there. At every opportunity, I'd board the ferry across the Channel and head for Paris, Berlin and all points in between. As part of my supposed studies, I spent a year in Strasbourg, chosen specifically because it was as near to the middle as you could get in (Iron Curtained) Europe. This was, I suppose, what made *Neumusik* a little different from the above three 'zines in that I was lucky enough to be in the thick of it, actually meeting all these musicians, seeing them play live, making lots of friends. It was an exhilarating time. Inevitably, each issue got bigger, the gaps between longer and my studies became more demanding. The sixth issue in the Spring of 1982 was the last. (I graduated, sold my soul to a national weekly, got a proper job in the cultural industry and remain on the periphery, so to speak -- but that's another story...)

As the '80s dawned, the UK was awash with Industrial music, cassettes and fanzines. *Flowmotion*, edited by Ian Dobson and Gordon Hope from Leeds, was mainly about the alternative UK scene but had extensive forays into Euro. In the finest tradition of fanzines, it was a complete mess: bits glued in, other bits falling out, a different size every issue, almost unreadable. I believe there were six issues, appearing intermittently from 1980-85. Even more anarchic was Gordon's one-off "solo" fanzine titled *Strange Sounds*, which was unreadable. *Stabmental*, edited by Geoff Rushton and Euan Craig, was predominantly Industrial and always had nice covers; Geoff went on to form Coil with TG's Peter Christopherson.

And in Europe itself? For sure, there were some, many even, but if they were in their own language (and why not?) then 99% would never make it over to the UK or USA. Of the better known 'zines, France surely had one of the best in *Atem*, edited by Gerard N'Guyen and Pascal Bussy. Covering everything from homegrown Heldon, Urban Sax and Magma to the German electronic scene, The Residents and Eno, *Atem* lasted an influential 16 issues from 1975-79. Then Gerard concentrated more on Atem Records and Pascal pursued an independent journalistic career (including the occasional *Tago Mago* cassette/zine and books on Can and Kraftwerk).

Also excellent was Dominique Grimaud's 2-volume *Un Certain Rock (?) Français* which charted, in anarchic style, the history of French rock from 1968-77.

The '80s saw two new fanzines: *Intra Musiques*, edited by Pierre Durr in Strasbourg (and distributed free), and *Notes*, founded by Bruno Chapoutot. By the late '80s, they were still going and may still be for all I know?

The Netherlands had the plush *Sonic Report*, edited by Wybo Goslinga, which unashamedly championed everything electronic. Jarl Hugo Lastad's *Agitasjon* was the main 'zine in Norway, and had close links with UK's *Mirage*. Italy had countless Industrial fanzines, more than the UK seemingly. In the early '80s there was not a week went by without receiving an unsolicited package of Xerox-collages, stickers, unmarked and un-listenable C60s and, well, porn. The fact that it was in English was a mixed blessing. However, there were some good ones, with Piero Bielli's *ADN (A Dull Note)* getting my top vote. A typical issue would include, badly photocopied on one side only, Soft Verdict, Pascal Comelade, Elliott Sharp, Ptose Productions and Pseudo Code.

But if your fanzine wasn't in English, then -- sadly -- it didn't get that much of an airing. Which brings me on to a quick mention of US 'zines. Although a long way from Europe, they were, as can be seen from EUROCK alone, as authoritative as any publication. John Loffink's *Surface Noise* and Thom Holmes' rather minimal *Recordings* were two such others, as well as the Canadian CLEM (Contact List of Electronic Music), which was less a fanzine and more, as the title suggests, a reference tool.

As the '80s settled in, so, too, did two new UK fanzines. *Inkeys* was a "cassette-zine" produced by Denis and Jeanette Emsley. Its big plus was that you could actually listen to this unfathomable music, as well as hear the artists speak in exclusive interviews. This was obviously great, but somehow I missed the critiques, the pictures and the mystery of buying something you'd not actually heard before. By the middle of the decade, most of the aforementioned fanzines (including those in Europe) had died a death.

And then along came *Audion*, edited by two of the most knowledgeable (and obsessive) Euro-rock fans ever: Steve and Alan Freeman. It was actually kind of inevitable; they'd written for most of the UK 'zines, started up a cassette label, Auricle, then a mail order business and finally (?) a record shop in Leicester called Ultima Thule. Renowned for their mind-boggling knowledge of the minutiae of Krautrock, the Freemans carried the crusade throughout the '80s and on into the '90s, covering not just alternative music from Germany, but also the rest of Europe, America and beyond. If I had a criticism, then I am a little mystified as to why *Audion* avoids the '90s alternative electronica/ambient scene that arose from club culture. Even Krautrock Granddaddy Klaus Schulze testifies to the "If you can't beat them, join them" axiom. That said, there are few 'zines to beat *Audion*.

Although it has to be said, there are few 'zines. Or maybe I'm just getting old. But it seems to me that, in this age of desktop publishing, internet, design-as-art-as-god and alternative culture ending up as simply another commodity, then the "innocent age" of personal, messy and anarchic fanzines is all but numbered. There are a few others: *Sound Projector* edited by Ed Pinsent in London debuted in 1996, covering everything from Krautrock revivalism and LaMonte Young to Stereolab and Keiji Haino.

Mention should finally be made of the plushly produced *Impetus* and *The Wire*. Essentially jazz magazines, they covered Europe extensively, particularly ECM, improvised music, Rock In Opposition, etc. Editor Kenneth Ansell ran *Impetus* from 1976 to the early '80s, after which *The Wire* carried on the jazz and improv crusade. Founded in 1982 by Anthony Wood, *The Wire* has since been through many changes and has now become the UK monthly magazine for new music in all its guises.

How big a role did fanzines play in opening up the European alternative music scene to UK and US listeners? I would say, initially at least, quite a considerable one. True, readership was never more than a few hundred each issue, but there undoubtedly was a knock-on awareness. Mail order companies, progressive-minded record labels and later the established rock press eventually started to take notice.

Other factors helped. As mentioned earlier, some Euro groups got name-checked so much that it began to seem obvious that it couldn't just be for show. Electronic instrumentation -- long an integral part of Krautrock -- gained acceptance in the UK scene, both with alternative artists (TG, Cabaret Voltaire) and pop (Depeche Mode, Human League). And not least the '80s realization that musics could intermix and be influenced by each other (globalization). Thatcherism, Reaganism and their attendant corporate cultures would deaden much of the spirit and sense of experimentation of the new disciples, the European "scene" itself would drift into artistic cul-de-sacs and somewhere amongst all this, fanzines, for me, lost much of their joie de vivre and raison d'être.

But there is cause for optimism. The future is almost certainly the internet. Reach out. This is the age of HTML. Start your own webzine.

David Elliott

2002

UK Electronica

When Tangerine Dream signed to Virgin in 1974 and released *PHAEDRA*, their first album on an international label, the world of "Cosmic Music" expanded exponentially. The ripple effect of that continues to this day, as a whole sub genre now exists on the commercial fringes, composed of people inspired by the electronic sound pioneered by TD way back when.

As a long time writer and promoter of that genre (which alternately at times feels like both a blessing and a curse) I've heard a lion's share of what's been produced by artists far and wide that contains elements of that original spirit. Upon consideration I'd have to say there are perhaps less than 10 neo-EM "groups" worldwide who truly nail the classic sound, and create something akin to the spirit of the golden age.

In the UK, two musicians can be considered the pioneers of electronica -- Adrian Wagner and David Voorhaus. Their original albums *DISTANCES BETWEEN* and *WHITE NOISE -- AN ELECTRIC STORM* were groundbreaking classics of the genre.

Mark Shreeve is one of the earliest UK synthesists to delve into the "Teutonic Electronic" realm, beginning with a series of cassettes he did in the early 1980s for the UK *Mirage* and Norwegian *Agitasjon* fanzines. These led to his first LP *THOUGHTS OF WAR*, released in Norway on the indie label Uniton. The scene was much different back then, mostly word of mouth, and EUROCK was one of the few outlets worldwide promoting/selling this sort of stuff.

Throughout his career he's done work for several labels, and had big selling titles, but never let his love for the glory days of analog electronics die as the albums of his latest group Red Shift demonstrate very well. Their three albums are rated by many as the best neo-Berlin School releases of the last decade.

Another of the top current UK bands making some of the best neo-Euro EM today is Radio Massacre International. They seem to have channeled the spirit of the golden age into a slightly more modern hybrid of sound. If listener response were used as any measure, they would have to be ranked up near the top of the current Euro EM scene.

They made a big splash on the scene in 1995 with the release of their debut double disc *FROZEN NORTH* on the Centaur label. Since then they have become perhaps the hottest selling indie electronic band from Europe. Their new album *PLANETS IN THE WIRES*, released by the group themselves, may well have surpassed their debut in terms of musical creativity.

This following interviews, done in the last month, sheds some light on the who, what and why of Mark and Redshift, as well as the RMI trio. More on the UK Electronica scene will be forthcoming in future.

Archie Patterson

Mark Shreeve Interview

Q: Let's begin at the beginning with some history. How did you first get into E.M. way back when?

M.S.: My first real experience of E.M. came when, as a child, I heard the theme music to "Dr. Who" (a cheap, but surreal show in the UK that started in the 60s). The sounds fascinated me (as well as the great theme). It was also the "atonal" qualities of some of the sounds that appealed to me too, the "otherworldliness" of their atmosphere.

As I became a teenager in the '70s I started listening to bands like ELP, Floyd, Zeppelin etc, the usual suspects. But I never quite got away from the weird stuff...obviously Pink Floyd at that time were a good supply of strangeness.

A friend's older sister played me TONTO's *ZERO TIME*...this was a major discovery for me...an all-electronic composition. A year or two after that, I was laying back in bed (after a spectacularly unsuccessful girl-hunting trip at a local rock disco), listening to John Peel on BBC radio... hoping for some Floyd.... and he played "Mysterious Semblance" from *PHAEDRA*. By chance, I had found heaven. To me, it was quite simply the most emotional and rather unsettling piece of music I had heard to date. From then on, I became hooked on German electronic music.

Eventually, it became clear to me that I needed to express myself as a musician rather than just as a listener. When I could afford it (not for the first time, I was bailed out financially by my girlfriend), I bought a Yamaha synth...in 78 I think. I have been searching for the lost chord ever since.

Q: Did you ever really feel an affinity for the so-called sound and philosophy of "cosmic music," or were you more oriented towards the more earthly plain (i/e scoring with the girls and making money, smile)?

M.S.: Hmmm..."cosmic music"... "girls"... "making money"... I've never been able to make that connection unfortunately. In fact, there seems to be no other form of music LESS likely to acquire those admirable goals than E.M.

I continue to do it because I feel a real "drive" to. I don't know why exactly, but the urge to create this music remains as strong as ever. On the other hand, I don't believe I have any deep philosophical agenda to pursue either. For me, music is about emotion, pure and simple. Most of the time I find creating music a very depressing experience, the only thing that keeps me doing it is, as I said, this strange self-destroying desire to hunt down that "perfect" piece... I know I shall never find it.

Q: What were the names of your early cassette only releases and what kind of equipment did you use back then? Did you tend to improvise like early TD, or work within more structured compositional structures?

M.S.: The first 2 cassettes released, simultaneously, by Martin Reed's *Mirage* label were *URSA MAJOR* and *EMBRYO*. Followed quickly by *PHANTOM*...they were all put out in 1980 I think (although recorded a year before).

The equipment for all 3 was basic... a Yamaha CS30 synth, Hohner K4 String Machine, phaser, flanger, all recorded onto a low speed Revox A77 which doubled up as tape delay machine.

Improvising was all I could do at that stage...everything was new to me then, the technology, music, composition, even the playing (I had only ever played guitar originally).

I would record a sequence line first, moving it, changing it constantly. Then I had to try and remember those changes while I added chords and/or top lines. The whole process was wonderfully organic, if a little primitive. When I listen to those pieces now they sound very raw, but they have heart... and the energy of youth.

Q: In retrospect I do think that *THOUGHTS OF WAR* stands up as a fine example of early, second generation EM. How did it come about that you got it released on a Norwegian label, as opposed to some UK outfit?

M.S.: Actually, Martin did release it as a cassette originally, but very soon after that Jarli Lastad, the mad Viking who ran *Agitasjon* in Norway contacted me saying there was a guy in Oslo who wanted to release *T. O. W* on vinyl and was prepared to pay for the pressings etc... so naturally I said yes. This was Tormod Opedal of Uniton Records.

Q: Do you have any idea how many copies it sold (I may be straining your old memory banks here)?

M.S.: I honestly have no idea...I would guess about 600 or so...based entirely on the number I've sold since of the CD re-release, but I may be wrong.

Q: The Uniton deal was for only that album, what happened after that one had come and gone? I think I lost track of you for a bit back then...

M.S.: Actually, Uniton released

ASSASSIN in '83 until Jive Electro signed me up in '84 and re-packaged it. My first "full" album for J/E was *LEGION*, released in '85. Then in '87 I put out *CRASH HEAD*, also on J/E. During this period I also got involved in writing songs for other artists, occasional soundtracks and some library music. In '95 I released *NOCTURNE* on the Sonic Images label... this was the last album I recorded as a solo artist (to date anyway).

Q: Since that time you've done a variety of releases for a couple different labels, major and indie. How would you compare the two types in terms of recording freedom, sales potential, business ethics and amount of money you have made for the various deals (that answer could well result in a doctoral thesis on the industry I realize, but maybe you can give it a go)?

M.S.: Hmmm. I think I'd rather talk about Jennifer Lopez...

Jive was actually considered a "major independent" at that time in the 1980s.

I've always found that I could record whatever I wanted really. The only constraint being studio time and equipment hire costs. The experience (a first for me) of working with other people, engineers, producers etc was a huge learning thing experience. Not the least of which I had to come to terms with the fact that other people can have equally good musical ideas as me. It was a shock I can tell you. Musician's egos are fragile at the best of times.

Once I had got round this (after, I am ashamed to confess, some legendary tantrums) I really began to learn more about music...both technically and artistically. I loved that period...the proverbial "kid-in-a-sweetshop" scenario. I never felt any corporate pressure to change my music in any way.

Obviously these kinds of record companies exist to make money...so by '89 when they decided that J/E wasn't doing this it was folded. So basically, TD, Michel Huygen and myself were label-less.

I never really felt bitter about it. They tried and failed... simple as that... E.M. never became the big seller they hoped.

I guess they never recouped the advances and studio costs that went into our albums... a common story. *LEGION* alone amounted to about £65,000 in studio costs, and I believe the maximum sales figures worldwide were about 20,000. Now I'm no mathematical prodigy, but even I can work out that those figures don't add up once you add promotion, advertising, packaging etc.

Since then I have effectively "worked for myself".... releasing albums as and when I feel like it. Clearly I can't put anything like the funding behind it as a major can... but as I said before, If I was motivated by money, I would have chosen a different form of music altogether.

My own experiences with record companies have generally been good... lucky for me I guess.

Q: Of all your previous releases, which ones still remain in print today?

M.S.: *T. O. W., EMBRYO, ETHER AND DOWN TIME*... all are on CD.

Q: What is the situation in terms of the rights to all these old albums?

M.S.: All the old cassettes are mine, as is *T. O. W.* The rights to *ASSASSIN*, *LEGION* and *CRASH HEAD* were bought up (at least the licenses were) by C + D Services. *NOCTURNE* is owned still by Sonic Images. *COLLIDE* is mine as are all

3 Redshift albums.

Q: A couple years back you formed the group Redshift. The overall response to them has been quite good. Was the intent with that band to "go back to your analog roots"?

M.S.: Not specifically. I think one of the many reasons was as a reaction to the tedium I felt with all the "normal" E.M. that had started to show up around the late '80s/early '90s.

There were bands and artists (particularly in the UK and Europe) who were creating shockingly bland music... you know... cheesy little ditties over badly programmed drum machines using horrid thin digital preset sounds. People were releasing 5th rate soundtracks, to 4th rate films, that already had 3rd rate soundtracks written for them. In short... The Sci-Fi Anorak had hijacked European E.M.

The "frontiers" style of E.M. had been suffocated by all this "easy-listening-for-midi-nerds-elevator-music." I was yearning to hear some darker, more unstable synthesizer music again, but no one seemed to be doing it.

Around that time I purchased a few old analogue synths (some I had already owned years before) and started to really fly. It was as if I had totally forgotten how inspirational these instruments really were. I started to record some of these sessions (initially it was a solo thing).

By chance I came into contact with Ed Buller who played me some earlier Node sessions on DAT. I was absolutely knocked out by what I heard... at last, someone was producing this huge, organic, threatening and above all, EMOTIONAL electronic music.

Ed (and also Martin Newcomb of the Museum of Synthesizer Technology) managed to track down a Moog 3C modular for me. Now obviously, I had heard many recordings that had used this instrument over the years... but nothing prepares you for what it sounds like in the same room. It is quite simply a stunning sound... so rich, so powerful, and yet capable of so much delicacy too.

I've been playing synths since the late '70s. I must have owned or hired dozens and dozens of different machines... and I'm telling you now... none of them even gets CLOSE to the beauty of a Moog Modular. It demands that you create music on it, there are no presets... keeping the same sound for any length of time is impossible... this for me is a virtue.

All these computer plug-ins that are released now, you know...the ones that claim to be replicas of old synths... they make me laugh... they are truly terrible... these companies should be sued for making those claims... they aren't even close to sounding like the real thing. I can only assume that it is hoped that the musicians who do use them have never heard a real analogue synth... or if they have, that they are tone deaf.

I played a gig at KLEM '95 in Holland (under my own name to promote the *NOCTURNE* album)... and because I needed 2 other guys to help out we thought it would be interesting if we dropped in a more free-flowing sequencer based piece half way through. The crowd reaction told us all we needed to know... they went crazy for it. Moreover, it was more satisfying for us as musicians to play. When we got home the other 2 said, "why don't we keep up with that style as a band?" (James and Julian by the way)... so effectively Redshift was born there and then. I had already finished most of the first Redshift album so the timing seemed right.

Q: You've done some live solo gigs over the years, as well as more recently shows with Redshift, how does the audience compare from one decade to the next in terms of size, gender types and occupation (OK, this is another higher education-type question, but for me these are very interesting things to ponder...)?

M.S.: I have a feeling it's the same audience basically. Therein lies the problem with E.M. I feel that the easy listening mafia has really put off any new blood being attracted as listeners. When I first got into E.M. in my early teens it sounded good to me because it was weird, dark, and yes..."cosmic" if you like. If I had been subjected to *TURN OF THE TIDES* or whatever as an introduction to E.M.. you would probably now be interviewing a Country and Western banjo player instead.

The hardcore E.M. audience are all getting older, some seem to have become rather jaded at a lot of the mindless pap being released and have left the scene (who can blame them?). Another strange anomaly is that the vast majority of E.M. fans are male. I have never really understood this. Good E.M. is surely amongst the most emotional music ever written. Maybe the lack of lyrics is the problem. It causes so much disappointment backstage after gigs too.

Q: You ultimately ended up starting your own label. Often musicians find it problematic to handle both the making of, and selling of their own music. What was your reason for this?

M.S.: Money. I had to be realistic about this. There was no way I could match the sales of *LEGION* and *CRASH HEAD* without a major company like Jive behind me. Some people did offer to release the Redshift albums, but the figures were ever so slightly in the rip-off area. It basically worked out that the label making the offer would rake in over 7 times the amount per CD than the artist would. It seemed totally unfair, and maybe another clue as to why E.M. is slowly dying. It simply can't afford those levels of individual greed.

Q: In terms of CD sales, how many copies did the Redshift releases sell?

M.S.: Not spectacular...the first Redshift has had a couple of re-presses, so it's around 2,000 in total, say 50 of those as complimentary copies. *ETHER* has done about 1,500, and *DOWN TIME* about 1,200. (Well I did say we weren't in it for the money!)

Q: How large of an actual audience do you think there is for this current 'neo-electronic space music' sound?

M.S.: Well, call me Mr. Overoptimistic if you like, but... I have always believed that if this music got more airplay, sales would definitely increase. As a rule people don't buy music they have never heard... so without airplay E.M. relies on "word-of-mouth" alone. This doesn't work. Tangerine Dream was regularly in the British album charts during the '70s. They were also on radio a fair amount. During the '80s, as their music became soulless and bland, the radio stations lost interest in them and their sales plummeted. Can you spot the connection?

I live in hope that an enterprising D.J. will hear Redshift by chance... get totally chilled by us and start a new craze. You never know... After all, that's how it happens for most forms of music.

Q: I've heard rumor now of a new Redshift release for ages. What's happening with that?

M.S.: There is a live album ready to go and a studio album half-way finished. All that is stopping us is... Yeah, you guessed... legal crap with an old publishing company. It's taking forever to sort out, but it will get sorted... eventually.

Q: As one of the "old masters" of E.M., do you now have a grand plan to explore the outer reaches of the cosmic, and conquer the pop charts in mind for that one (tongue firmly in cheek here), or perhaps some more humble plan for the future?

M.S.: A little less of the "old" please... In fact, just call me "master." In many ways I feel as if I have all I want from life, I'm with my partner of choice, and I do exactly what I want when I want. The quest for extreme riches has abated considerably, that sort of thing doesn't seem so important any more.

Musically I feel drawn to creating these strange concoctions even though the process is quite painful. The end result usually is a desire to start the next piece and make it better... a never-ending circle with an unattainable goal. And like so many musicians, I keep at it even though I don't understand why.

As I recall, back when I was a teenager, I only wanted to be a musician in the hope that I would meet the blonde girl from ABBA. There can be no finer reason for a life-quest such as this.

Archie Patterson

Radio Massacre International Interview

Q: Let's begin with some history. What was the intent behind the name, and how did you come up with it?

SD: The name came about several years before the band in its current form. Duncan and I would occasionally sit around with an electronic device each rammed into the mic sockets of my cassette deck and would basically attempt to take signal overload to its logical conclusion, for the duration of a C-90! One day the name just came to me as a good enough description of these tapes. There is therefore no intent or literal meaning but rather three words that just sounded good together and arrived from god knows where.

Q: Who exactly comprises the band RMI, and where did you all come from

musically in terms of previous musical experiences?
The band is in alphabetical order:
MR. STEVE DINSDALE - Keyboards, Drums
MR. DUNCAN GODDARD - Keyboards, Bass
MR. GARY HOUGHTON - Guitar, Synth

SD: We have known each other since we were 16 years old; therefore many of our previous musical experiences were collective. Even before we started in 6th Form College (6th Grade), Duncan and I had already managed to get talking to a guy called Mark Spybey a second year student whose job it was at the recruitment day to extol the virtues of the History course. He saw the band names painted on my haversack (the usual suspects) and said that the college had a synthesizer (Roland SH 1000), which we proceeded to borrow for about three years! We started a band with him, and through Mark met Gary shortly after.

Away from the band Duncan, Gary and I began to record in Duncan's room, which rapidly became our first studio. We called the group DAS, and made a cassette album *DAS 1 / EARTHDEATH* in 1980. We continued on this path and between 1980-7 DAS completed 12 albums none of which were ever released! (Mark Spybey eventually went on to join Sofornkontakt with the dearly departed Michael Karoli, and we had quite a reunion after 20 years at the Can Solo shows a couple of years ago!)

There then followed the inevitable life changes, day jobs and so on. I played drums in a couple of 'scene' bands after moving to London in 1988. Gary continued to play guitar, and Duncan continued to amass synthesizers at an alarming rate. He recorded lots of solo pieces during this time, and at this point we renamed the project Radio Massacre International. I eventually got disillusioned with the stupidity of the music business, as it became clear that the deeper you look into the abyss the less attractive and more like a job it becomes.

Duncan and I had remained close friends in London throughout and it was inevitable that when he found a space big enough for us to work in that we'd get going again. *STARTIDE* was recorded at one of the first sessions in 1993. It's an hour long and we couldn't have cared less if it had been two! It was a great feeling of freedom, and with enough equipment to record everything straight to tape with no need for overdubs. Gary came back on board shortly after in early 1994, he arrived with his guitar and in that day we made "Drown" (from *FROZEN NORTH*), "Diabolica" and "Upstairs Downstairs" (from *DIABOLICA*) in the time it would take my previous band to get a guitar sound they were happy with!

Q: Had you recorded anything previous to RMI? Outside of music what do you all do in the real world?

SD: See above for answer to if we had recorded anything previous to RMI. Those DAS albums were quite different to what we do now, but there is a definite path that can be traced. We're looking at ways of making this stuff available, but at an attractive price, as we believe it should be out there in some form. I also appeared on EPs by The Honey Smugglers and TV Eye as drummer.

In the real world I work as a studio manager for a Sports Media Group (TEAMtalk.com), Duncan is at MTV Europe as a Technical Manager, and Gary is in the big bad world of Corporate Finance.

Q: The main influence on your sound would seem obvious -- Tangerine Dream.

But when you first brainstormed forming RMI, was the central idea behind it to be 'the new TD' or something more?

SD: To be honest we never sat and discussed our aims, even the very first time we recorded. It was always Duncan saying, "I've got some gear, let's record." We just do it and see what happens. The idea behind RMI was purely as a creative outlet, to make music that we felt was missing from our collections. It wasn't even until a couple of years later that we actually found a deal and started putting it out. Obviously the TD thing comes up all the time, but in all honesty our influences are more universal than that. Electronic Music only makes up a very small percentage of our CD collections, and as far as our own music goes we simply see it as working with an established form the way you would if jazz or folk was your thing. As long as you come across with a strong personality of your own there's no more to be said. I think RMI are readily identifiable and distinguishable from everyone else.

DG: Not the main influence on the music, just the technology. The music we do has many influences besides other musicians.

GH: We're not the new anything! Our influences are from all sorts of areas, as Dunc says, not just musical. The only reason people continually refer to TD is because we use sequencers and Mellotron. It's a bit ridiculous really; it's like saying that all bands with bass, drums and guitars are copying Elvis.

Q: When it comes to EM, personally I am an 'old timer' from way back in the days when new albums were listened to by candlelight, with incense burning, and visions of sacred spaces were conjured up. You are younger, and I wonder do you have any affinity for the concept of 'cosmic music,' or does that seem outdated?

SD: "Visions of sacred spaces," I like that! We tend to make large spaces with our music, and add detail, foreground, background etc. It's a very good analogy. I'm not offended by the term 'Cosmic Music,' although I would say not as close as to Brian Eno's *ON LAND* approach in that a majority of our more descriptive efforts tend to refer to earthbound spaces like the *FROZEN NORTH* or *GULF*. Albums like *STARTIDE* and the album we made live at Jodrell Bank Radio Telescope could obviously be described as 'cosmic' which is fine, but it's not all we do. I would define Cosmic Music as "that which describes the wonder of space," and yes we certainly have.

GH: What you're describing is not unlike the experiences I used to have when I first started listening to some of the more spacey music. To be honest we just turn on plug in and play. What you hear on the CDs is the end result. Some of it is pretty cosmic though -- like *ZABRISKIE POINT* or "Blakey Ridge" (from *BORROWED ATOMS*).

Q: Everything today seems much more equipment-oriented and digitized. What equipment do you guys use, and do you prefer the old analogue sound, or?

DG: Whatever we feel like using. People will point at the Mellotron and say, "Why don't you use samples instead?" they don't sound the same, but that doesn't exclude them from the armory. Recent material has used the Mellotron less, but the analogue synths more. A few years ago, we weren't using analogue synth sounds at all for sequencing. As far as the recording process goes, we've always used a mixture of analogue and digital techniques and equipment. The basic philosophy with instruments and recording gear is to use whatever best meets the needs of the circumstances. We have the luxury of having a choice. Instruments or other studio gear that don't pull their weight or do their job to a satisfactory standard are quickly discarded.

We really just tend to mix and match and certainly don't stick to any one set up. We tend to prefer a small mobile and intelligent approach rather than looking like a synth museum. We use the Doepfer MAQ16 to drive two Moog Prodigy's for sequences on the fly, and we also have the superb Lactonic Notron which is a little less immediate to use but can provide some superb sequencer functions like triplets and allows for a huge frequency range. One person could physically carry both units under each arm and that's the way we like it.

GH: Strat, Marshall, Fender Twin, MXR Distortion, Jam Man, Line 6 Delay, Cry Baby Wah Wah, and sometimes a bit of flange can be nice ....oooooh matron!* (*English Humor SD)

Q: Much of your material is recorded live, is there a reason for this?

SD: Not sure if you mean live 'in concert' or live in the studio, but either way there is an immediacy that is captured when music is happening live in the here and now. Musicians behave differently when they are on the spot and improvising rather than playing through a rehearsed piece. This is exaggerated when there is an audience there too. We have become used to recording straight to two-track tape/DAT, and hence the mixing process happens as part of the improvising process. It may not always be perfect, but it eliminates the possibility of tinkering with the mix endlessly after the event! There's far too much time wasted in studios generally, (Again from previous personal experience!) and I would always point to the fact that *KIND OF BLUE* and *ASTRAL WEEKS* were each recorded in two 4-hour sessions! They are both in many people's all-time Top Tens and still sound incredible technically. Making records is a lot easier than many people would have us believe, just get in there and do it!

DG: Yes -- it's quicker and easier. We have a limited amount of time to capture this stuff, both because of our circumstances and because we're adept enough at improvisation to have escaped forever from the repetitious rigors of arrange/rehearse/record that, in other bands, detract from the creative flow.

Q: Do you compose pieces in advance, or perhaps follow the more improvised tradition?

DG: Both. After a while, we realized that live performances would be more satisfying if a) we had a "warm-up" period working through something we all knew the basic framework of, but that still allowed some improvisation and b) the audience would appreciate hearing live versions of familiar material. Not, surprisingly, such a great technical or musical challenge to reproduce improvised pieces on stage, but sometimes it takes a while to dismantle an older piece into its components for a live recital.

Most studio work is purely improvised, safe in the knowledge that we can edit out howling mistakes or bits that didn't work. The editing then becomes an element in the shaping of the finished piece. Live, we have tried every approach from 100% improv. to 50/50. Pure improv. tends to work best within a set also containing pre-written frameworks. Quite often it isn't particularly useful to hear one complete improvisation after another and this approach is rarely successful. If we are doing one concert a year then that hour on stage has to be good, and not an aimless wander in an electronic wasteland of our own making.

GH: Even our composed stuff is very loose. Generally we will have an idea for the feel of a piece and the key. That's all we really need.

Q: How many live concerts have you done, and what kind of attendances do you achieve?

SD: We tend to manage at least one concert a year, although we've clocked up about twelve to fifteen in about six years. The largest audience was 1,000 in Nijmegen at the Klemdag, and we played in Huizen at the Alfa Centauri Festival 2000 in front of about 300. Jodrell Bank planetarium is much more intimate (150), but we have played some good music there over the years, having done concerts there in 1996, 1997 and 2000. We had a series of pub/club gigs in London between about 1995-7 too, which were largely 'never again' experiences, but sort of fun in a masochistic way. It meant that we were sharing the bill with indie bands and were at least something of a curiosity.

Of course our largest audience would have been our MTV Europe live appearance in 1996, technically speaking!

Q: How large of an audience do you think there is for this 'neo-electronic space music' sound?

DG: Even if no one bought the stuff we'd still be doing it!

We couldn't really care less how large the audience is, but there's no denying that it isn't exactly expanding exponentially! The potential audience is a lot bigger, but people are just simply not aware that we're out there. They're too busy being spoon-fed by the Marketing Depts. of the major labels. We would be kidding ourselves if we pretended we were ever going to be suitable for mass consumption though.

Q: In terms of CD sales do you have any idea what was the most popular of the albums put out by the Centaur label? How many copies did it sell?

SD: Our two top sellers have been *FROZEN NORTH* and *BORROWED ATOMS*, the latter of which has been the most critically acclaimed. I guess we're talking about maybe 1,200-1,500 sales of *FROZEN NORTH* which doesn't seem much, but then imagining them all in a room together it does... especially if they each offered to buy us a drink! *FROZEN NORTH* might be enough RMI for some people, after all in old terms its 140-minute playing time is equivalent to 7 sides of vinyl! Similarly *BORROWED ATOMS* is also a double CD, and the one which perhaps comes closest to refining the 'classic' analogue sound.

We aim to make each release as good as the last and more importantly, to have an identity of its own. There's no telling what people will like, in fact signs are that *ZABRISKIE POINT* is proving to be very popular, which pleases us as it's truly on its own musically without even a sequencer in sight.

Q: Your sound has seemed to change a bit on recent releases, do you listen to much music outside the band and perhaps this has broadened your sonic palate?

SD: The music has evolved and changed completely naturally, we tend to view the making of music and the consumption of it separately, so there's no way one could influence the other. We just look for new approaches and new gear configurations, plus as improvisers we are always subject to the circumstances in the studio on that particular day. It's only when we look back that we realize that the sound has changed over time, and it's hard to pin-

Q: You also just started your own label. Often musicians find it problematic to handle both the making of and selling of their own music. What was the reason for this?

SD: Complete control over everything! We felt that maybe we were an established enough name to take a small risk and make our own product. We feel that we have made the most effort to promote and publicize the band ourselves, so we should reap the rewards. We have controlled all other aspects of production from day one. The only likely problem again might be the fact that we don't have a huge database of customers, however the internet has been an enormous help in allowing bands to sell their own music and long may it thrive. We also have a good relationship with a few outlets that can guarantee a certain level of sales, and have had invaluable help in those parts of the manufacturing process we are as yet unfamiliar with.

Q: It seems there is a ceiling on the genre that limits the level of success that a group can achieve. The only way to break through is with a product placement in a film or major media event. Do you have a future marketing 'master plan' or will you let the cosmos decide?

SD: We'll leave it in the lap of the gods! As Gary says, "It's not like we've just turned down Sony or something!" The people that buy our music are discerning and they have to actively seek out the CDs and discover the music for themselves... they buy the music they want to hear rather than being sold it. Many artists who I regard as being geniuses never broke through to the mainstream and they're not meant to. Most music is consumed on a very superficial level, which sounds snobbish but it happens to be true. We've been on Radio 1 (Major BBC national Music Station), the BBC World Service, BBC2 TV (Music featured in a documentary about Jodrell Bank) and MTV Europe and it has made very little difference to our sales. To really sell records you need a £300,000 promotional campaign, where you are shoved down people's throats on a continual and uncomfortable basis, or like you say to be prominently featured in a big movie. The whole thing is such a multimedia mass marketing exercise designed to maximize sales for conglomerates that probably own the film and the music on the soundtrack. Our music could work well as film soundtrack, but these days it's all about squeezing in all these has-been bands whose publishers are trying to rehabilitate their careers (he said, cynically).

The great thing about the seventies was that there was a genuine underground feeling and mystery to discovering your own band. We'd like to feel that a little of that spirit survives in what we do. Of course we'd like to sell lots, but we understand why that's not going to happen! It's important not to be financially reliant on the income we make from the music and therefore artistic freedom is maintained. We'll just keep on doing what we do!

Archie Patterson

RJ Stips Interview

Q: What was the first instrument you learned, and first band you played in?

RJS: I learned to play the piano from the moment (I was 4 or 5) my father had this budget -- (un)wise crazy idea -- to buy a wonderful grand piano. He played classical piano quite well himself and that was my inspiration: sitting underneath this 'cathedral of sound.' First I started finding out the keys and sounds myself and got lessons from when I was 8.

The first band was the school band called 'The Blubs' (!) which was the first seed out of which Supersister grew much later. Drummer Marco Vrolijk invited me for this school band in, I think it was, 1964; the other members followed later.

Q: How and when did Supersister originally come to be formed?

RJS: When the original school band (the Blubs beat group the Provocation) had been turned on by the revolutionary ideas of new-member Rob Douw, we called ourselves Sweet OK Supersister, very crazy, very hip, with an almost unlimited line-up, with poets, performers, musicians and so on.

In 1969 we decided to concentrate on the music with just the four of us.

Q: I remember many good groups from Holland back in the 1970s. Was there a very active rock scene then in terms of clubs where bands could play live, festivals and so forth; or was it more of a small scene with groups mostly recording and playing live only occasionally?

RJS: No, there was a band playing live on every suitable occasion, parties, festivals, and clubs; in the '60s in The Hague (pop. 300,000) there were about 4,000 bands! One could hear drum kits out of every other open window!

In the '70s it became more organized, club wise, mostly and bands expanding to abroad.

Q: Did Supersister and other such progressive bands actually sell many records?

RJS: Not really outrageously -- we are but a small country; an average maybe of 20,000, 30,000, not regarding the hit records, then.

Q: What was Supersister's biggest selling record?

RJS: Ask Polydor -- they don't know either! As a matter of fact we had a very steady selling curve, they didn't differ much from each release-to-release. To be honest (again and again) we were more interested in the effect and respect our music caused than the actual selling figures -- also the royalty percentage we had in our contract was as low as could be.

Q: What was your favorite Supersister record?

RJS: If there is one, it would be *PRESENT FROM NANCY*, because then we did everything for the first time, and as we all know: the first cut... We were so excited then to have the possibility of recording an album in a top (8-track...)

studio -- even though it had to be done in 4 nights between midnight and 6 o'clock in the morning, mixing included(!) I still remember some moments very strongly and often think back of how it felt and how much I want keep that mix of spontaneity, concentration, fun and seriousness alive while recording nowadays.

Q: Many, including myself find *PUDDING & GISTEREN* to be the most sophisticated album musically - perhaps the ultimate "progressive" album. It was done for a specific production I believe? Can you tell us about the conception of that album -- how long did it take you to write the music, rehearse, did you play it live along with the dance performances, etc...

RJS: We felt very honored to get an invitation from the Netherlands Dance Theatre, to write and perform the music for one of their productions. The NDT was then and still is now a high standard company, world famous for their approach and performances of modern ballet. Frans Vervenne, the whole ballet being 'the story of his life,' designed the actual choreography. He was also the one who came up with the title *PUDDING & GISTERN* for the ballet, which we adopted gladly for the music (it was weird enough to be a Supersister title...) as well. (The title is originally a typical joke from the '50s. Everyone who grew up in the Netherlands in that decade knows it and just by remembering the joke -- which was not a particular good one -- one remembers the atmosphere of their childhood or younger years.)

If I remember well Ron van Eck and I designed all the little pieces / scenes behind the piano and it took about half a year to get the whole production going from ground zero on. The original ballet contained some small pieces that were cut out when recording the album.

We did about 7 performances and even though it was a success in Holland, the tour that would follow (Australia was one of the countries mentioned) was cancelled, as we suspect mainly because of non-artistic, personal and very much ballet-world-like reasons... Helas!

Q: At one point I lost track of Supersister and nothing more was heard. You released a solo album or two, and then some time later I discovered you had joined the Nits. Was there a particular reason the band broke up, or was it merely atrophy?

RJS: The way you jump through the years in this question would take me too long too correct, but there was more between Supersister and Nits (one can find out on my site www.stips.net) The reason we broke up was that we all felt a little lost after discovering we had given the best of what we had in store. Where we felt so sure before, doubt was creeping in and we decided to stop working in this line up, which wasn't easy, breaking up with friends with whom you shared so many great experiences.

Q: Was being with the Nits different than Supersister -- did you compose music for them, or simply play?

RJS: The main way of working in the Nits was -- especially after *ADIEU SWEET BAHNHOF* -- writing while playing together. When there was an album to be made, most of the time we started out playing and recording almost everything on 2-track. After a week or two we mostly ended up with piles of tape from which we extracted the rough material and indications for the direction of the new album.

Besides that, Henk and I also wrote material at home and Henk wrote most of the lyrics parallel to the music coming together. This procedure was 'fruitful' until let's say *dA dA dA*, when Henk preferred to partly return to writing apart.

Q: You were on several Nits albums and did many tours with them I believe. Were they a commercially successful band?

RJS: Yes. But success was there mainly because of all the effort anyone involved with the band put into touring a lot. In the beginning we all invested years in playing, also when the record company wasn't too active. This paid off later and records slowly started to sell as well. The album and single *IN THE DUTCH MOUNTAINS* created one of the few break-outs caused by the 'record-side.' By then we already had created a large 'playing field' from Moscow to Canada and from Helsinki to Athens.

Q: The Nits experience was in another decade from that of Supersister. In terms of the Dutch music market (and business), how had it changed from the time of Supersister to the Nits -- was it larger, bigger sales, more clubs and festivals, or less?

RLS: It was all larger and more mature. Everybody had more experience and examples of how to, or how NOT to do things, while in Supersister times we all still had to find out.

Q: Why did you leave the Nits?

RJS: I felt the opportunities of working and creating together were getting smaller, while the balance in the group wasn't as natural and steady as it had been before.

Q: Tell us about the SOSS label. I believe you are one of the owners. What led you to form your own label and how hard is it to obtain distribution for an indie label in Holland, or Europe in general?

RJS: The reason for forming our own label is simple: I want to keep my material together instead of having it divided over several labels through the years.

Working together with record companies is fine, but when they change personnel -- and they often do, politics and 'artist-treatment' suddenly changes as well and that is sometimes hard to deal with.

Q: In the last year or so you reformed Supersister, why did you decide to do that?

RJS: It wasn't a decision, and certainly not mine alone: we happened to get together for a sad occasion, our former manager and friend Dick Zwikker had suddenly died and we all knew we had to play for him at his funeral. So we did -- together with Cesar Zuiderwijk (Golden Earring) who was also a close friend. We did a quick half an hour rehearsal the night before and everything felt so amazingly natural after almost 30 years that when we happened to receive the invitation for the LA ProgFest some months later, we were easily convinced to take the challenge.

Q: You amazingly finally played in America at the ProgFest in LA. How did that come about?

RJS: I simply got an (email) invitation of the organization.

Q: How was the ProgFest experience, was it your first trip to America?

RJS: For Supersister it was the first time ever. (I did several USA tours with Golden Earring.) The experience on the LA trip was overwhelming, we never expected so many people coming from such unexpected parts of the world like Japan, Mexico, Italy... to be at present there, also hearing the stories of fans after the concert about their 'way of life with

Supersister music...' really amazing.

Q: Has Supersister done other concerts since then?

RJS: After such a good experience we decided to not keep the Dutch fans out of this musical party, so in December 2000 we played the Paradiso in Amsterdam and in May we're doing 2 concerts in our hometown The Hague, back to where it all started.

Q: There was a "new" Supersister album released entitled *M.A.N.* that contained archive recordings. Do you have plans to record a new Supersister album, either live or in the studio?

RJS: There will be a live double album, recorded at the Paradiso.

So far we avoided the subject of a new studio album because this is quite a decision. Once we go for that, the innocence of this whole reunion project will be lost and new responsibilities will take its place (recording budgets and promotional obligations will be pressing our shoulders again, things that are still far from what we are thinking of now). The fun of playing without any stress whatsoever, is a luxury not many musicians can experience.

Q: In some ways I find the music of Supersister, just as it was back in the progressive golden age, still to be lively and different from most anything else being done now. How do you feel today about whether it holds up creatively, and how after all these years you seem to have come back to your beginnings musically?

RJS: Normally I am not the kind of person to look back too long, but this whole Supersister revival is a greater treat than I ever expected -- I am only too glad that the music we then made is more than worth to play again nowadays, with so much fun and appreciation. That makes it easy to push aside the need of working on new material, temporarily.

[**Editors Note:** Since this interview, I'm saddened to report that group member Sacha van Geest, whose flute, sax and vocal work added wonderful sonic spices to Supersister's magnificent music, has passed away. He will be greatly missed! May he R. I. P.]

Archie Patterson

Rock In Deutschland
Gerhard Augustin Interview

Throughout the history of music, as well as other forms of art, entertainment and business, there have always been celebrities. Behind the scenes are the managers who sometimes get attention as well (for better, and for worse). Occasionally there are those who served as a catalyst for something bigger. Whether a cultural shift, changes in musical style, or discovery of groundbreaking artists or bands, it's not uncommon for them to get little attention or recognition. Often their visionary ideas and groundwork are overlooked or written out of the public domain.

One such music lover is Gerhard Augustin. At a time in German culture when English was by and large an alien language, and "schlager" (German folk/pop music) was the norm, Gerhard began to groove to a different beat as a DJ in Bremen. As co-founder of the famous TV show The Beat Club, and A&R man who engineered the signing of Amon Düül II, Popol Vuh and Can to Liberty/United Artists Records in 1969-70, he helped lay the foundation for a cultural shift and musical revolution in Germany. He possessed the open mind, love of music and the business skills to act as a bridge between the underground and establishment. In effect he was the godfather of Krautrock, which still resonates musically in the world of pop music influencing many bands today.

His story is fascinating and it's past time for it to be told. I think you'll find the following interview, taken from a long video segment he did for EUROCK, offers a fascinating glimpse into the past and gives long overdue credit to one of Europe's literally unsung musical pioneers.

Q: Tell me, in the beginning how did you get German TV to allow you to produce "The Beat Club" music program? What year was the first program was broadcast?

GA: In 1963 I became the first German DJ in Bremen. There was a restaurant called The Gypsy Cellar that sometimes had live music in their basement. As I knew the owners I recommended to them that they turn it into a discothèque for dancing and they agreed. So we put in 2 turntables and it became one of the first youth clubs at that time -- called The Twen Club.

I had just come back to Germany after Kennedy was shot as I had been from living a while in the USA. I had seen Shindig there and Top of the Pops in England so around 1966 I started trying to promote doing a German version of those programs that turned into The Beat Club. It was produced by radio Bremen, directed by Michael Leckebusch and hosted by Uschi Nerke and myself. The first show was broadcast Sept. 23, 1966 on a Saturday afternoon at 4 PM.

Immediately reactions came in, letters, calls, etc. People from the older generation (old Nazis) hated it, young kids loved it and said things like "keep it going" and so on. It caused a real reaction between the generations.

Q: It became a sensation on the pop scene and helped start some of the most famous pop groups on their road to fame and fortune. Who was your favorite English pop group that appeared on the show?

GA: My favorite band in those days was The Who. We had become friends earlier when I had worked in England and our friendship continues today. I had met their manager, Kit Lambert, who gave me an acetate copy of their first single "Can't Explain" b/w "Bald Headed Woman." They were trying to get a label for it in the early days. I also liked very much The Kinks and the Stones who I met while in London around 1962. Everyone hung out at a pub near the Marquee Club back then.

Q: I've seen tapes of many of the English stars that appeared on the program. But at one point you started to feature also the newly emerging bands from the German space rock scene. How in the world did you get mainstream German TV station executives to allow that?

GA: The whole Beat Club thing was a result of the relationship I had with Mike Leckebusch over the years. When we created the show together we became great friends. However, slowly over time, he wanted to take more credit for the show and later some English managers recommended he should use a British DJ instead of me so the show might be of more interest to the English market. Larry Page and Robert Wace were the main ones behind this, they were part of a sort of 1960s UK music mafia of old business types who wanted to control pop music in Britain. Eventually they gave Mike some money to buy a big house, a Jaguar and all those things, so of course I was phased out and he went on to gain fame and fortune himself. It's an old story. He became very corrupt and there was lots of payola going on with the shows back then.

The English pop stars were often on the show because their songs were in the charts in Germany. Soon the record companies started helping with this as they realized that even though TV production was very primitive in those days – black and white, etc. – they saw it could influence sales greatly.

As for getting the more experimental bands on the show, I think Mike always had a bad conscience about pushing me out of The Beat Club. He knew I was the originator of the idea for the show and developed it after the other shows I'd seen on my trips overseas. So as a result of this, every time I came up with a new German progressive or experimental act I would bring it to him for exposure. I got groups like Amon Düül II and Popol Vuh on the show, but it took a lot of convincing. In the end because of his guilt he would put them on as sort of a favor to help me out.

Q: Around the same time you did The Beat Club I believe you also were head of A&R at Liberty/UA Records and involved in production of the first Amon Düül II and Popol Vuh records (around 1969-1970). Again I ask, how was it during that time that you were able to get those records made by a mainstream label? It must have seemed strange to do all this weird music and have a large corporation subsidize it?

GA: Well, not quite so. When I left The Beat Club, I went to America and lived in San Francisco. There I discovered bands like Santana and CCR for the German market. I also met Bill Graham and we became good friends. He introduced me to the Grateful Dead, Quicksilver, Sly & the Family Stone, Ike and Tina Turner, Tom Donahue (the original FM DJ playing undergound music) and Ralph Gleason who was one of the first journalists to write about the new underground music in the BAY area.. That was around 1968-'69. I was very fortunate to be at the right place, at the right time for all that was happening in SF then.

While I lived in SF I worked at KQED TV and was awarded a scholarship and got my diploma in Mass Communications at Stanford University. After graduation, I got a job in Los Angeles with United Artists Records and learned all about how the company worked. They then sent me to Germany to work for the company there. When I got over there they wanted to sign some domestic German bands to their roster. Sigi Loch, head of the famous Star Club record label, started a German flagship label for UA/Liberty Records, to be distributed at home and abroad. I got Amon Düül II, Popol Vuh and Can signed to contracts with them. The record company knew little about that type of music of course, so it was sometimes a rather strange situation as you might imagine.

Q: While doing The Beat Club and promoting Amon Düül II and Popol Vuh did you do the actual music/video production, or work have help from others like Olaf Kubler, etc?

GA: I was only involved in financing and management of the video production. We did one for "All the Years Round" by Amon Düül II. That was the first music video production in Germany. We paid a director and video company to do the filming. It was played, but there were very few media outlets for that type of thing in those days. We did several other videos as well, but that was the early days of TV and the experimental bands weren't really attractive to the mainstream media.

Q: As for Amon Düül, I believe they actually started as a political collective and the main members broke off to form a specific music group?

GA: Amon Düül did begin as a political commune in Berlin. It was formed by the coming together of politicos from Berlin like Rainer Langhans and Uschi Obermeier (who became a famous model later), with musicians from Munich -- Chris Karrer, Peter and Ulrich Leopold and Falk Rogner. Renate was not involved as she was living in England then working as an *au pair*. After a while there was a split into Amon Düül I (the political people), who recorded one big party/session before they descended into chaos. That resulted in several records having nothing to do with the real Amon Düül II. Amon Düül II (the musical side) moved back to Munich where the group was joined by John Weinzierl and Dave Anderson (who came over from England). The first album of Amon Düül II -- *PHALLUS DEI* -- was recorded in two days at Trixie Studios in Munich. It was the first space rock album and caused a sensation on the young scene.

Lothar Meid in the beginning was playing with Embryo, before he joined Amon Düül II later. He also played with Olaf Kubler (who was a jazz saxophonist). They played jazz and soul music on Sunday afternoons in a couple clubs around 1968-69. Olaf also produced and published the Amon Düül II, and many other albums. He was a real business Mafiosi type involved in the music business.

Q: What was the scene like back then? Did those record sell large numbers - for example do you remember how many copies *YETI* and *TANZ DER LEMMINGE* and *AFFENSTUNDE* sold?

GA: For the new underground groups without a hit single it was very hard. Some of the old Nazis were still in control of the media so they would never give exposure to new experimental rock music. Society in Germany was just about to start changing, so a few dared to promote this new music and ideas, but rock and roll was new to Germany. Here that sort of thing basically started 10 years later than in the USA. Most people still listened to Frank Sinatra, Sammy Davis Jr., Johnny Mathias and Peggy Lee. For the most part, English was not spoken much at all. Beat Music started to change this around 1965. Later a lot of German bands started to copy the English bands, covering their songs, and playing on The Beat Club as the most famous English bands became too big and expensive. Also payola started playing a large part in the music scene and it all started to change in many ways.

Q: During the heyday of the space rock scene in Germany was that type of music a significant market and did the albums produced by all those bands sell a great deal? Or perhaps has the myth always been bigger than the reality?

GA: Sales of these albums were actually very low. Amon Düül II was the first to start selling with *PHALLUS DEI*. Then Can had their song "Spoon" on a German TV crime show called "The Knife." That caused it to hit the charts and ultimately it went silver, which in Germany meant selling 250,000 copies. Later their album, *EGE BAMYASI*, with that song on it started selling as well. So Can made good money actually.

Over time Amon Düül II sold maybe 60,000 copies of *PHALLUS DEI*, their other albums sold between 20,000 - 50,000 worldwide sales over the years. They still sell today reissued on CD. Amon Düül II never had a hit single, though we tried with "Archangels Thunderbird," and a couple others, so their sales were smaller.

Q: In the last few years it seems there has been renewed interest in some of the original German bands. Amon Düül II reformed and did concerts in Japan and England. Is the band still together now? Who are the current members?

GA: There was actually some confusion surrounding the name and music of Amon Düül II as some albums came out in England that were not really connected to the band. So there was a court case in Germany where the members of Amon Düül II were actually certified. They are -- Renate Knaup-Krötenschwanz, Chris Karrer, Peter Leopold, Lothar Meid, Falk Rogner and John Weinzierl. A couple years back some of them reformed and we did some recording and live shows in Japan and the UK. But for something more permanent the chemical formula was not good...

Q: What about Florian Fricke, do you still have any contact or work with him?

GA: Florian Fricke was also from Munich. On the first Popol Vuh album, *AFFENSTUNDE*, he used the first Moog synthesizer in Germany. Along with Eberhard Schoener they pioneered the use of synthesizer in Germany. Later Florian sold his Moog to Klaus Schulze who became one of the leading electronic musicians in Germany even up to today.

[Florian Fricke]

Florian had perhaps more success than Amon Düül II because I arranged to have his music used in 5 of Werner Herzog's films, that helped them get more international exposure and better sales. In fact, right now one of his songs, originally in *AGUIRRE*, is being used in a successful American film that won a prize at the Cannes Film Festival; it's called *BEFORE NIGHT FALLS*. I produced most of the albums by Popol Vuh and I'm also the godfather of Florian's son, Johannes, who's now living in NYC. Florian himself is a little spaced out right now...

Q: What is your main area of work these days? You have a company called Gammarock Productions. Do you still do video production? How about consulting for record labels?

GA: Gammarock is my company formed in 1976 in LA with Patrick Gammon (who died in 1996). Now I handle all the music publishing, as well as the video and music production for the Gammarock material, which includes Amon Düül II, Popol Vuh and many more mainstream artists. We place artists with labels and get the music into films, etc.

I also now do a public radio show here in Bremen again. I've always loved being a DJ and still do today.

Q: After all these years what is the most memorable thing that music has brought into your life? A special concert, album or travel to some far away place? Could you imagine a life with no music in it?

GA: No, I don't want to imagine any life without music. Music has always been the most important thing for me – more important than sex, love or relationships. Music is essential to my life whether I sing it, play it, hear it, work with it, or make money with it. In my opinion as a publisher, producer, musician, artist and music lover, in the movies, music is more important than the actual pictures. It makes the film come alive. I'm what you call a music freak. I've survived with music, being a DJ, doing shows, and writing 8 books about different artists along with anthologies on pop, rock and beat music.

Some of the most memorable events in my life are associated with music. I traveled with Jimi Hendrix that last 3 weeks of his life. He was a very beautiful person and musical genius. Also with the Rolling Stones I had many breakfasts, trips, concerts, shows... I met John Lennon at the house of Jann Wenner (of *Rolling Stone*) in NYC, around the time of the recording and release of *IMAGINE*... I toured around the world with Ike and Tina Turner - Australia, Japan, Africa, at the height of their career and during their times of trouble and breakup.

Truly I cannot imagine a life without music. I don't want to even think about a life without music. I've met so many musicians, actors and great people; music has been a most wonderful life for me.

Archie Patterson

Giorgio Gomelsky Interview
"Le Souterrain Français"

If there ever was a man who lived and breathed music, it is the international vagabond Giorgio Gomelsky. Born in the former Soviet-Georgia, his parents fled Stalin and he grew up in France, Italy and Switzerland. As a teen he took off and hitched all over Europe soaking up the influences of boho "existentialist" culture and tuning in to the jazz vibe that was influencing the scene.

In 1955 he landed in London and with friends set up a little "Espresso Coffee Bar" where soon many of the future Anglo scene makers hung out, getting a caffeine buzz late into the night. This embryonic idea turned into the prototype early London beat club (1956-1961) featuring fledgling musicians and bands playing rock' n' roll and skiffle. He wrote articles for music magazines, made a series of documentaries about the British jazz and the budding blues scene, and got involved in promoting the latter by opening a blues club later known as The CrawDaddy.

During this period a young boho by the name of Brian Jones hyped Giorgio on his new band, lo and behold called The Rollin' Stones, got a residency at the club which started them on their way to fame.

The rock 'n' roll beat was growing louder and Giorgio was leading the charge. Over a span of time the Stones, the Paramounts (who became Procol Harum), the Muleskinners (who in part ended up as the Small Faces), Rod Stewart, Julie Driscoll, the Moody Blues, the Animals and the Yardbirds would all play there.

During this time as well Giorgio had made the acquaintance of another young and was kicking around ideas about making a film. As Bill Wyman recalls it, on April 14, 1963 he had a great surprise when Giorgio invited the Beatles to catch a Stones gig at The CrawDaddy and the two groups made their first contact. Ultimately the Stones signed with Andrew Loog Oldham and the Beatles with Brian Epstein, going on to produce their Dadaist music film classic *HARD DAY'S NIGHT* (hmmm, I wonder where that idea may have come from?). While secretly Giorgio must have been disappointed, to this day he carries nary a grudge, back then he barely skipped a beat.

In 1964 Giorgio produced his first Rhythm & Blues festival featuring the Yardbirds, Spencer Davis Group, Long John Baldry, and others. That led to his involvement with Mr. Relf, Clapton and the Yardbirds. Basically a blues band at that time, he recorded their very first album, and soon with Giorgio's help, they were making records with sitars, harpsichords and Gregorian chants as well as touring the States.

In 1967 he founded Paragon, a design, public relations and management company with a record label named Marmalade. London was swinging and Giorgio was making things happen, booking clubs, building a recording studio, recording and having great fun.

In December of 1969 he had a falling out with the Polydor Records and Deutsche Grammophon Companies who by and large had financed this adventure and he went off to France, his mother's country. Upon arrival there he reunited with old friend Daevid Allen who had been the Soft Machine's guitarist and had started Gong in Paris. He began to get involved in the French music scene, met up with Magma and decided to help them.

He first move was to form a talent agency, Rock Not Degenerated – Rock Pas Degeneré. It ultimately became the number one employer on the European progressive rock scene. In 1970 with the recording and release of the first Magma album, *LE SOUTERRAIN FRANÇAIS* – the French Underground – began to generate rumblings. From that impetus a new spirit and correlating burst of artistic and musical energy was born. Along with that a new cultural and musical hybrid emerged that replaced the "chanson" with a unique fusion of the European classics - American jazz and rock, plus the distinct character of French culture. Within 3 or 4 years, Magma ended up playing some 60 concerts a year to 2,000 or 3,000 people and selling 150,000 albums in France alone.

Living in NYC since 1978, for over 40 years Giorgio has been the ultimate instigator and promoter of avant music. He has always been ahead of the curve stylistically and constantly striving to stretch the boundaries of rock music in general. More importantly, for fans of "Euro Rock," he was at musical ground zero in France. The story he has to tell is fascinating, and Giorgio is a bard extraordinaire. So here we go...

Q: What was the music scene like in France when you first went over there after working in the UK for many years? What year did you go there?

GG: January 1970. I had spent 15 years in London and had enough of the "perfidious Albions" as Napoleon called them! My mother was French, so I spoke the lingo, had family and friends there and visited the country often. While living in London (from March 1955 to December 1969) many French (and other "continentals" or "frogs" as the British called us!) were relying on me to interpret for them what was going on and then to arrange interviews with UK artists for TV, radio and magazines. I guess I was probably also the first of the "managers" in London to set up early club dates, tours and promotional activities in continental Europe. I did believe that if the "prophet goes to the mountain" it would pay dividends for the artists down the road. Besides, the local pop music scenes on the Continent were very "pasteurized" poor copies (and translations!) of US commercial stuff. Imagine a French version of "Tutti-Frutti"! I felt an injection of the energy developed in the UK by young and more "authentic" artists could help bring about a change in those countries music scenes too. Furthermore, I liked touring there; the food was so much better!

Q: Who were the initial bands you heard?

GG: First of all, I had left England because after 15 years in London, I wanted some time to think about my life and my work, which was filmmaking. Although I managed to produce some documentaries in England, (all about music), I felt I now needed to concentrate on getting a feature film off the ground and get away from "managing" bands which I had taken up only because someone had to help the scene... *Rock & Folk,* a very respected French music magazine, ran a long interview with yours truly and during the interview played me a tape of a French band, which somehow seemed puzzling to them and asked for my opinion. I remember it well, even today. The music was original, with influences derived from non-anglo folk, classical, jazz and experimental music and, I said something like "very ambitious stuff, these guys seem to want to take on a lot, if they are really serious, it could be interesting." There must have been a conspiracy, because wherever I went in Paris, people were asking me if I had heard THAT tape! It turned out to be Magma!

I had rented a house in the country some 25 miles from Paris and started putting some order in my thoughts. I was living with a gorgeous French girl (Brigitte, later my wife), and my only ambition, after 15 years of intense work, was to do nothing at all for a while...

A few days after the interview was published, I got a phone call from Faton, Magma's pianist. They had read it and wished to ask me if I was interested in checking them out. I think they were playing one of their rare gigs a few days hence. No way, was my answer. No more taking on unknown (or any other) bands! I tried to explain to him I had gotten away from that scene and wished to sit under my tree and just watch nature and think. A few days later he called back. I got rather irritated and put him off as hard as I could. Brigitte however wanted to go to Paris to see her friends and, knowing me, suggested we should just go and have a good time, no strings attached.

So, a few days later we went, and the rest is history. I had never heard anything like it. I was very impressed by their "sources" and their musical skills. This was not run-of-the-mill stuff. It also wasn't "commercial" by any stretch of the imagination. But I'm a sucker for underdogs, so I was tempted to take on the challenge. At that time there wasn't any scene whatsoever for "independent," original music. The business in France consisted in descending order of the 3 great "auteurs-compositeurs," Georges Brassens first among them, a true pipe-smoking poet, accompanying himself on acoustic guitar and setting to music his immensely perceptive insights into the French psyche and the infinite variety of everyday events befalling humans. Than there was Jacques Brel, a Belgian by origin, with a beautifully crafted repertoire of tightly woven, somewhat sad and yet comic anecdotes of love and descriptions of "marginal" characters. The third was Leo Ferre, a lion-like, ferocious and fearless social-critic-anarchist. All 3 were also great performers. After them you had people like Charles Aznavour (known in the US for being in Truffaut's films), Gilbert Becaud who wrote a number of songs which often got covered by US crooners and made him and his publishers handsome profits. Down the line there were other "variete" singers, mostly manipulated by the French music publishers' fraternity, who hand in hand with the "major" record companies like Philips, Barclay, Vogue, etc., were really running the show. A French version of rock 'n' roll consisting of cover-versions of US (and later British) hits had been provided for the younger generation, mostly represented by Elvis imitators like Johnny Halliday (who is still going!), Eddie Mitchell, Dick Rivers and other such "anglicized" rather contrived "acts." They had originated in the late fifties from a small; more authentic rock scene based around the Golfe Drouot Club, but had soon been co-opted by the "business," keen to exploit the young public. By the mid '60s, based on the British model, a slew of rock bands were created by the "usual suspects" running the show. People like Les Variations, Les Chaussettes Noires, etc.. With a few exceptions, none of them were any good really. Even if they could actually play, French just didn't lend itself to rocking. The whole thing was a bit of a farce all over the Continent really. There were however some very good jazz musicians. Paris had been, still was to an extent, when I got there a center for jazz in Europe with a number of clubs, concerts, magazines and quite a few exiled Americans, like Kenny Clark and Bud Powell, and others.

Here I must mention Gong. As you probably know back in London I had tried to help Soft Machine get a recording deal, so I knew Daevid of course. I always felt bad for him because I was the one who in the summer of 1968 had sent them to St. Tropez (a holiday resort in the South of France) to play in a club and get their stuff together and when they came back to the UK, Daevid, an Australian citizen, was refused entrance, so he had to return to Paris where he started Gong!!

Q: Was there any sort of organized scene?

GG: Other than the commercial one? No.

Q: What was the cultural reference point of the French musicians? Were they as steeped in rock, jazz and other Western music styles as the British?

GG: As I said, after WW II Paris had been an important European jazz center. Unlike England where the Musicians Union did not allow foreign musicians to settle (!) Paris welcomed them and so many musicians from the States had settled there. First and foremost, Sidney Bechet in the late '40s, which opened up a New Orleans/Dixieland scene and later Bud Powell, Kenny Clark, Johnny Griffin and others who were "modern" jazzmen. They needed sidemen, so a local generation of jazz musicians sprung up. Mind you, Django Reinhardt's Hot Club de France had achieved international success before the war, so there was a sort of a jazz tradition. Matter of fact Christian's father Maurice Vander is a very respected jazz pianist and accompanied many US jazz greats.

Compared with England – or perhaps London – the big difference with regards to the development of "bands" was the lack of a local blues scene. However there was plenty of modern and avant-garde stuff. In 1968 by the way, while touring France with Julie Driscoll and Brian Auger, I had come across Aphrodite's Child from Greece, stranded there by the May '68 events and I became friends with Vangelis, with whom I worked later...

Q: After getting there, how did you meet up with Christian Vander and the various avant musicians in Paris? Was there a specific club or area that they hung out in?

GG: Regarding Christian, see above. There were jazz clubs and 2 or 3 rock clubs, but as described above, there wasn't a "progressive" scene as such.

Q: Both the UK and USA had local areas that served as catalysts for a larger scene sometime later – was it the same in France?

GG: No!

Q: When was the first time you saw Magma play live? How big was the audience?

GG: Around Easter 1970, there was an audience of around 300. They were about to release their first album.

Q: At some point the scene started to grow and I've heard you and Magma plus some others began to form a national circuit for concerts and promotion. How did the normal French music managers and club owners react to this?

GG: They just weren't interested in that kind of music and with very few exceptions we couldn't count on them. There were a few "Associations" (not-for-profit voluntary music lovers' groups), but mostly they aimed to become "big time" rock promoters! I had to invent something else...

Q: Who were the actual bands and people who instigated this circuit? Was it the bands themselves, their managers, agents, or?

GG: This is how it happened, literally! One afternoon I went to pick up Klaus Blasquiz, Magma's lead singer, to take him to a rehearsal. He was teaching comic strip drawing in a youth center outside Paris. I was early, so I walked around the place and, behold, discovered there was a small theatre at the back of the center. I guess it could hold around 200 people. I freaked out, sought out the center's director and asked him what kind of events they were holding there. "None," he answered, "we can't afford to book people..." Wow! I had a flash! It dawned on me there was a solution here, so I asked him if he would agree for Magma to play there, without guarantee or any money. We would promote the show ourselves, use his Xerox machine and the young kids to distribute fliers and give him 15% of the door and keep the rest. He thought that was a good deal and agreed to give us a date. This got my juices going, so I enquired how many of these "Youth Centers" (MJC - Maisons des Jeunes et de la Culture) there were and I found out there were some 200 around the country. Every political party seemed to have a "chain" of them, determined to recruit youth into their respective causes. Well, that was it! I got me a list of them and for a month I drove around Paris convincing them to go along with my plan. Just as in London with the blues in the early '60s I was determined to get the music out there one way or another. I found 25 of these MJC – some (mostly socialist or communist!) more receptive than others, some with theaters and some with access to "community" spaces. To cut a long story short, a couple of weeks later, Magma did their first MJC tour. Five weeks, 5 concerts a week, a total of 25 shows. You had better believe a band gets pretty good after that kind of experience, besides we were actually making some money too, enough for the musicians to consider giving up their day jobs...

From there I started to work on the rest of the country. Within a few months we had more than 120 venues, a complete circuit! Young people started getting interested in learning how to promote concerts, so we taught them how to form "associations," get permits, etc., You might not believe this, but today, the major music promoters in France started with us.

After our first tour I got Gong involved and then we formed an agency "Rock Pas Degeneré" and took in a whole bunch of groups which had sprung up, like Crium Delirium and many others. Later, we invited British, German, Dutch bands like Art Bears, Can, Supersister, etc. They in turn got the French bands gigs in their respective countries. Before long we had an international circuit... it was very cool!

Q: I've heard some say in effect this underground activity was in fact a virtual revolution in terms of normal French music culture. Would you agree?

GG: Indeed... Before I left France in 1977, Magma were playing some 100 or so regular concerts a year in France alone and making between $5,000 and $10,000 a show. The last tour I went on was a double bill with Leo Ferre – who loved Magma – held in circus tents holding 5,000 people!

Q: Can you explain how it actually worked - travel, logistics, booking, payments, etc?

GG: In the beginning we had to be very parsimonious, travel in old trucks/vans (I had a Mercedes and used to take 5 people with me) and stay with people, or in cheap (very cheap) hotels. France's territory is not as vast as the US, so most distances were between 100 and 200 or so miles. Payments had to be in cash of course, so we could eat, sleep and get to the next gig... Often, we just barely covered expenses. Later it got a lot better. But every time we played we were able to make friends and encourage the local scene. That really paid off!

Q: Were the bands able to make good money doing this or was it more like, "art for art's sake"?

GG: My view was that if the music was relevant we would succeed at building an audience, and, after a while, it would lead to our own little "market" and we could make a living at it, and so could many others. This happened.

Q: At some point Magma got a large

contract with the major label, Philips. How did that come about? Did they receive a large signing bonus in advance as is usual in the music business today?

GG: I wasn't involved in that, it was in 1969, before my time, but I know it wasn't a "large contract." Some of the musicians in that first edition of Magma were highly respected session men, like Claude Engel, the guitarist. He knew people in recording studios and at labels.

Q: What was the media and musical reaction like when they released their mammoth double LP in 1970?

GG: They had no idea. Some critics, the best ones, liked it very much. Magma always got good "press," such as it was, at the time. I guess that's the advantage of being active in a country where originality is respected...

Q: Was that in fact the first French underground rock album to come out?

GG: I think so...

Q: Did it open the door for more bands to make records?

GG: Magma was a trailblazer group for sure. With the addition of Gong the whole scene was spreading, so a lot of new energy came about. New magazines like *Actuel* helped a lot too and some radio and TV programs. People looked to Magma to fuel that energy, to be "taken aback," so to speak.

Q: Do you know how many copies of that first album were sold?

GG: No, but it's still around. When I appeared on the scene I worked out an independent production deal with Philips and later with A&M and RCA (for my Utopia label). The *LIVE AT THE OLYMPIA* double album sold 150,000 copies in France, that's like 300,000 "units," as they say in the industry.

Q: As an outsider I might guess that it in some way served to legitimized the scene. I say this because their second album received critical and cultural praise from more mainstream sources. So did the traditional French artistic tendency to encourage the avant-garde start to help the scene expand at that time?

GG: Well, good press didn't actually get you gigs - there weren't any in the mainstream - and anyway we had that under control. What really helped was the strategy of the "prophet going to the mountain" so many people all over the country were encouraged, enfranchised to start local scenes. Now and then we got big engagements, like at the Fête de L'Huma every year, the biggest open air event in France, and Christian got to write some film music, but above all we got credibility and people rallied around the cause, so to speak! This was during Pompidou's reign, there was quite a lot of subtle repression going on. For instance, every time we had to take a toll road our van would be searched for hours and we always got to gigs late... but then we played for 5 hours, so that upset the "authorities"!

Q: At its peak how successful was this idea of an underground circuit? Did the scene in France become highly profitable for record companies and artists alike?

GG: It completely transformed the scene by decentralizing it and by encouraging all sorts of local movements, like Alan Stivell in Brittany with his "Celtic" rock and the people in the southwest, with their "Occitan" poetry and music. Festivals sprung up everywhere.

As I said above, record companies were

just not interested in our stuff. We did everything a few independent labels and ourselves appeared and bands self-produced themselves. Towards the end of the '70s, some of the original bands in the circuit disappeared – others, like Can for instance, got very big indeed, relatively speaking. The "local" success allowed us to export our music to England, Germany, etc. Magma did very well in England. We took that country by storm! Unfortunately, the 25-day tour that was to establish the band permanently got cancelled because of internal struggles and the subsequent break up of the Vander - Jannick Top collaboration. That was when I left.

Q: At some point however things began to change internationally in the music scene and I'd imagine in France as well. Some say punk rock caused this change; in retrospect perhaps it was the inevitable and eternal creative cycle of events in the life of any social or cultural phenomenon. What happened to the underground scene in France?

GG: Punk rock was incorporated. The thing about Europe was, underground audiences were less divided and provided they liked what you were doing could support all manner of artists. The big event, in France at least, was that the socialists came to power and created a very strong Ministry Of Culture, which greatly encouraged native production. Had I stayed on I'm sure I could have gotten them to support "new music," they were very keen. I think that the underground went above ground and good things happened. But by that time I had come to New York got involved in the No Wave scene here, so I never benefited from that change of political and cultural direction! I believe that to this day the MOC is helping people. Magma told me recently that they got quite a bit of help from them.

Q: More particularly you stopped working with Magma after their double *LIVE* album I think it was? To me the original spirit of Vander and his music still lives on today, but it was not the same after that *LIVE* album musically or in terms of their overall evolution as a challenging, innovative group. What happened with the band?

GG: No, I produced *ÜDÜ WÜDÜ* and Magma was still under contract to Utopia, my then partner got them to record *ATTHAK*. Frankly speaking, I lost interest after the cancellation of the UK tour and the break with Jannick. Unfortunately, most of the time, when a band hits the "top" and there is real, substantial success, all kinds of conflicts appear. Most are rather childish and I just don't have any time for that. Christian had a lot of plans, Stella, his (ex) wife wanted to own a studio and play a bigger part in the band, my partners were goofing it. Offering was started, solo records, etc. For me, the spell was broken.

Q: Around 1978, some 10 years down the road from 1968, you came to the USA and staged the first progressive music festival in the USA - the legendary Zu Manifestival in NYC. Can you talk a bit about your reason for coming to the US and why you decided to promote a festival?

GG: I was involved with my Utopia Records project, which had been financed by RCA and must have been one of the best independent label deals ever. I had some New York partners who unfortunately absconded with the money (what else is new!) and I had to come to NY to sort it out. It took a lot longer than I thought, so I had all this time and spent days walking around the place, I sort of fell in love with it. After the partnership resolution, RCA retained me as a "consultant" and I had a great time checking out what was happening. I came across a lot of underground NY scenes and musicians, and slowly the idea of linking the local scene with what we had been doing in Europe, began to wink at me.

I got this house on West 24th Street and we began to put on experimental stuff. As you know some of the "Eurock"(!) bands had become fairly popular with some college radio people and I thought it might be challenging to see if we could build an "alternative" circuit for "NU music" here in the States, like we had done in Europe. The Zu-Manifestival was the result. I thought that if we could make enough noise in NY, it would carry us over to the rest of the country - or at least some parts of it. Man, I worked my guts out on that project. I put the whole thing together with $3,000 I got from Charly Records in London for a NY Gong album idea. The first thing I had to do was to find musicians who would constitute the basis of a "house band" that could deal among other things with the European repertoire and Gong's in particular since Daevid had agreed to come. This is where I found Bill Laswell, and it was the beginning of the Zu (house) Band, later Material, but that's yet another story.

The NY event got absolutely great reviews and I was very encouraged. Little did I know what was expecting me on the next step!!

Q: Who were some of the artists involved?

GG: Oh dear, mostly a combination of NY guys like Rhys Chatham, Glenn Branca, Theoretical Girls, and some 50 or so others, with Daevid, Chris Cutler, Fred Frith, Gilli Smyth, Yochk'o Seffer from Magma, etc. The show was sold out. It started on Sunday at 12 midday and ended at 4am on Monday. At that time, the police insisted the theater cut off the juice and I remember Daevid, in a totally darkened theater, leading some 70 musicians and 1,400 spectators in a rave acoustic jam...

Q: There was also another Manifestival a year later in Los Angeles. What was the idea behind this? Was it an attempt to form a bi-coastal music network in America, or?

GG: Well, as I said, the NY event was very encouraging, so for a follow-up some 4 months later I thought we take the show on the road and I started booking gigs across the country. I did lean a lot on college radio people whom, with a few exceptions, I had never met. To me they all sounded very together and enthusiastic. Used to European underground conditions and collaboration ideas, I took most of them at their word, trusting their good faith, and confident they represented their local situations honestly so we knew what to expect. Well, some did and some didn't and I found out how difficult it was to "do business" in this country. We ended up with about 33 gigs over a 3-month period, and if all went as it should we'd have established a "circuit," or so I thought. Around the middle of March I put some 24 musicians in an old school bus I had acquired, and off we went. To this day I regret that we didn't document that incredible adventure. I think there are a few photographs here and there, but nothing that could properly describe what befell us!

There isn't enough time to go into details now, but on the whole the 33 gigs turned out about one-third great, one-third middling and one-third disasters! Los Angeles belonged in the latter category. Early on when I was setting up the tour, I got a call from a fellow in LA who had some kind of a progressive label, can't remember the name (**Ed. Note:** it was Tony Harrington who had a label called All Ears Records). He was extremely keen to organize the LA venue and I was grateful to find someone who obviously had some experience – or so I was given to understand! Well, when we got there, I found there were all these bands on the bill he was producing/managing. Furthermore, the venue was a beautiful old theater, but on the wrong side of town. Very few people came and there was no money to pay us and he disappeared into the night! Having reasoned that LA should at least cover our expenses (about $1,000) we found ourselves stranded with no money whatsoever. Thank God, there was the school bus. My major concern (apart from feeding people) was to get the tour to the next stop, which was Phoenix, AZ, if I remember correctly. We didn't even have gas money! So I spent 2 days and 2 nights tracking down this guy. A proper nightmare! I had never ever experienced anything like this. Some of us were watching his house, others his wife's movements, others still his office. A real stake out. In the end we got about $100 out of him, enough to get to Phoenix. Alas, because of this guy, we got there late and the gig had been cancelled... Next...

Well, after some more adventures, like running out of gas in the middle of the desert, the radiator blowing up, the transmission falling off and other such mishaps, we made it back to NY. By that time, everybody hated everybody... That was the first and last attempt (on my part anyway) to try and set up an "alternative circuit." I think that a couple of years later, the people who ran The Kitchen and other such subsidized venues, did put together a "package" called "New Music USA," strangely resembling our earlier model, but without any European artists.

Q: Which do you consider the most successful festival in musical terms as well as environmentally? What I mean is, did NYC or LA seemed more tuned in to the progressive vibe you were trying to encourage?

GG: NY was a triumph compared to LA. The idea of "progressive" in LA had in fact nothing to do with what I thought the word defined. It appears to me it's gotten even worse now. I went to the ProgFest in SF last year, the one with Magma and Gong, and, seriously, I found very little of interest musically. I think it all stems from the mistake of considering ELP and other such derivatives as "progressive." Most of the music seemed to be inarticulate noodling, sometimes approaching the kind of emptiness of New Age stuff or multi-layered noise replacing a true lack of compositional ideas. I read that the guitarist Buckethead is now playing with Guns 'n' Roses... The major problem seems to be the lack of good composers, IMHO, but also one of true artistic endeavor and quality. But this is a large subject and perhaps merits another forum!

Q: With the dawning of 2001 we enter the new Millennium. How do you think the business of music today, and current social scene surrounding it has changed since the early 1960s when you went to London and were involved in the jazz and r&b scene there?

GG: When I got to London in the mid-fifties, the "pop" scene was just a pale imitation of white US commercial music. At least there was a local "do-it-yourself" music, "skiffle," (imported to the UK by British bandleader Chris Barber) derived from Lonnie Johnson and other blues/folksters, which allowed young people to take up instruments. The Beatles started out as "The Quarrymen" and were able to inject some freshness into music when they started to make it. The Stones and the other blues bands introduced a new generation to black music thereby rendering an invaluable service too. European musicians were practicing jazz, and although aesthetically more appreciated than in the US, it seemed less urgent, less "dramatic," less speaking to a new generation. So rock took over. Later the punks kicked everybody in the proverbial ---. This opportunity is still present, but bands/managers/labels are now so focused on making it in whatever category they and the "industry" define themselves to be, that a "major breakthrough" has become well nigh improbable. It's the old story yet again, the seemingly tragic-comic vicious circle between the true function and merit of art and that of commerce and politics. Ultimately, it's a question of education. I'm hopeful that the internet will allow the natural curiosity of those attracted to music to explore every nook and cranny of musical production and discover where the real values are and that bands will emerge who know what directions to pursue.

Q: Magma still continues making music and some think that the whole experimental and progressive music scene is in revival. Do you think it can ever be what it once was in terms of creative spirit, or sales?

GG: 6 months ago Magma had their 30-year reunion, quite an event, I believe. So did Gong a year earlier, right? Jeezes, it seems incredible! I didn't see these 30 years go by! But I also don't see young bands coming up with that dedication to truly progressive music and the will to survive whatever difficulties to establish themselves. Perhaps in the jazz scene, there might be the possibility of new synthesis between "local" scenes, say Indian, Chinese or other ethnic music-sources and modern rock and jazz traditions. It could be a sort of World Beat improvisational affair but within serious writing "envelopes," Harmolodic-Neo-Ethnic-Rock-Jazz-World Music!! I often ruminate about all this! Think globally and act locally is another element that I deem important. Music must resonate among the people, it must touch them because it describes them and their conditions, social, cultural and political, that allows for identification. In other words, it should be relevant to their lives.

Q: Do you feel that people in general and artists in particular are still as open to new ideas and forms of music as they were before? Or has the new dominance of limitless technology and the culture it's generated created a kind of short circuit between left-brain (technical / analytical) functions, and right-brain (musical / creativity) processes?

GG: I think people in general are always open to ideas. They expect the artist to provide them, and that's where the problem is. It's a question of imagination and vision. Today it's easier to use self-referential matrixes and templates. Machines are good at computing bits and pieces, sequencing, calculating. A hell of a lot of technology is truly amazing and timesaving – great for entertainment. But it still needs an overall design concept, a vision of the "bigger picture" so to speak, to create original art. From the printing press to the novel it took 200 or more years and it took the same amount of time to go from Mozart to Stockhausen. Things move faster now, but distances are still there, and the universe is expanding all the time as we speak. I like to think music will continue to be a measure of our experience on this planet. It's a relatively small place (!), where before we move into the wider perspective of space, we'll truly have to deal with additional dimensions!

Q: You surely still have a passion for music and provocation/promotion, what are you working on today that we will hear about tomorrow?

GG: Kepler said that "the only constant in the universe is change" and change is scary sometimes. I like to believe that the purpose of art is that of making change less fearful so we can face it with more joy than pain, with more information and less confusion, and celebrate this mysterious state of "being alive" to its fullest. Learning from the past seems important to me, so right now I've embarked on collecting on videotape the "oral history" of rock in New York. I've been interviewing some 30 people, artists, managers, club owners, writers, DJ's and just ordinary music lovers, who have witnessed key moments of the chronicle of rock in this city. I started a similar project in London and when I'm through with that, I'll tackle jazz and the avant-garde. It will end up on an interactive website, www.ohblabla.net (oh for oral history, blabla, well for ...talk!). The Internet is perfect for this kind of thing.

Q: If you could go back in time and do it all over again – the same way – or differently – would you?

GG: Good question! Going back has its advantages intellectually. You could correct errors you made, be forewarned, save a lot of time. Alas, it's not possible. Doing it differently? I think at times I should have insisted more on certain objective, practical aspects of life and perhaps less on subjective, aesthetic or moral issues, which made collective progress more difficult at times. Perhaps compromise a bit more? But I'm not sure even then; often compromise leads to a dilution of the original energy or vision. Who knows? Finally, we all have our tasks on this planet. Methinks, that all in all, I did the best I could. And I'm still here!

Archie Patterson

[KDM & KS]

Klaus D. Mueller Interview

Klaus D. Mueller has been one of EUROCK's best "friends" over the last 25 years in Germany. Over that time many phone calls; faxes and emails have been exchanged all in the service of information and support for each other's cause. Along the way we talked about many aspects of our life and love of music. It was both educational and fun

As friend, manager and publisher for Klaus Schulze since the beginning, KDM was been involved in the German music scene and has done every kind of work to help make the music happen over the years. He's set up equipment, promoted concerts, started labels, hustled record companies, done favors for fans, and ruffled a few feathers along the way as any outspoken, dedicated promoter and crusader will. He's grown up with music of some sort always in his life, and is one of the few who will always give me his good advice when I ask. Even when he was critical, there was a little smiley face next to his comment and I respect what he says.

As EUROCK began again to focus on netjournalism in the year 2001, I wanted to do interviews with the artists and people whom I respected and felt deserved perhaps long overdue recognition for their many years of making or supporting the music. KDM is high on the list of people who qualify. I hope you enjoy his story.

Q: Do you remember actually when and what was the very first record you heard, or bought, all those many years ago in your youth?

KDM: First it was the usual "Schlager" (hits) of the day, German "Schlager" of course; the names would mean nothing to you (later I learned: mostly cover versions of American hits). I was very young then. Then I remember hearing the shellac with "Rock Around the Clock" by guess who, over and over again. I loved it. Then it was (already my own) singles; I chose by song not by artist, then, in the mid to late fifties, American pop music of the time, 1957 to '60. We could hear the AFN here in Berlin, and especially the program "Frolic at Five" from five past five to six in the afternoon (hosted by a George Hudak; the opening music was always the same: "9:20 Special" by the Harry James Orchestra; but this I found out only much later), ...this program was not just my favorite, but all Berlin teens listed to it. Here we heard the hot music of the day and from God's Own Country that was never (never!) played on German radio (Eddie Cochran, The Drifters, Bobby Day, The Everly Brothers, Jerry Lee Lewis, Buddy Holly, Fats Domino, Paul Anka, Little Richard, Elvis Presley, Carl Perkins, Pat Boone, Brenda Lee, The Coasters, Ricky Nelson, Bobby Helms, Duane Eddy, Connie Francis, Wanda Jackson, The Kingston Trio, The Ventures, Don Gibson, Neil Sedaka, Johnny Cash, Marty Robbins, Johnny and the Hurricanes, Bobby Freeman, Freddy Cannon, Lloyd Price.

Mind you, there was no "youth culture" in Germany and in Europe, the teenagers were not seen yet as important customers. Blues jeans were just coming up (only one brand, the now classical Levis). "Black" music was not so often played on the AFN, as was white music; I don't remember hearing much of Chuck Berry or Bo Diddley then, on the AFN. Instead of Ivory Joe Hunter's originals they often played the white copies by Pat Boone etc. (But I realized that only very much later).

My first single that was of any importance to me had a black label, and it was "Just Walking in the Rain" by Johnny Ray.

Later, when I was 15 I discovered Dixieland music, cheap Dixieland I must confess (Dixie was then a short sensation in Europe). From here I heard Lonnie Donegan ("Rock Island Line" etc.) and for a short time some skiffle. Alexis Korner's first album was an eye-opener... and from there I went on to discover the originals: Big Bill Broonzy, Josh White, Leadbelly, and all the black singers, guitar pickers, harmonica and piano players of the thirties and forties, and finally from the fifties: Muddy Waters, Sonny Boy Williamson, Chuck Berry, Little Walter, Bo Diddley, Howlin' Wolf... I saw some of them in concert at those famous annual "American Blues Festivals." This was in the early to mid sixties. And I changed very quickly from cheap Dixieland to real historic jazz, up to "modern" jazz.

Q: When you were growing up what was your favorite type of music?

KDM: As just described: mostly it was the more "hot" hits of the day, the more rhythmic and wild stuff: rock 'n' roll. I could sing along with most of my singles, without knowing what I sang! Then it was blues and jazz from the past and present. I was very much into Charles Mingus and John Coltrane when they did their things. But I also loved the classic things from the twenties or thirties and forties, from King Oliver to Charlie Parker. Before I forget him: Ray Charles was always a favorite of mine.

At the end of the sixties I also had my listening experiences with Terry Riley and similar avant-garde musicians. Even worked for him at two huge and long 30-day-festivals in Berlin.

Q: You are a collector of information and music -- do you have still today a large collection of records and CDs?

KDM: Still a child, I gave away my "collection" (about 20 singles and EPs) of rock 'n' roll for the same amount of skiffle singles, around 1958 or '59. Soon I dropped also skiffle and started collecting jazz and blues, seriously for about ten years, buying at auctions etc. I was really into that scene. In 1970 I realized that I just collected, but rarely listened anymore to all the many LPs I had bought. As a result I sold the whole collection of albums, EPs, singles, and about 200 books (discographies etc.) to a Belgian collector. (A week later most of the money was stolen).

I started to collect again (only jazz and blues) in 1985. Ten years later I had the whole history of this lone genuine American artform on records again.

Q: During the beginnings of German rock in Berlin, what were the first bands you remember starting up in Berlin?

KDM: If I remember well, it was Agitation Free, their friends Os Mundi, and soon later: Ash Ra Tempel and Tangerine Dream. And I worked for a lesser-known band that played in American clubs on each weekend. I carried their equipment. With Agitation Free we had concert tours in France. But my main job in 1970 to '73 was being the tour manager for English or American artists, groups, even orchestras: Lionel Hampton, Duke Ellington, Paul Bley, Van der Graaf Generator, Baden Powell, Marty Feldman, ... etc.

Q: It seems to me that Berlin always had a tradition of avant-garde and artistic types living there. Am I right in this?

In the early days, were there places for the first bands to play and a scene of any sort there, in say 1966, '67, '68, '69?

KDM: Berlin is a large city and the cultural scene was and still is very much supported by the government, I mean money-wise. This brings a lot of "avant-garde" to the foreground; also a kind of avant-garde that is forgotten very fast (and justifiably). I remember the "Living Theater" visiting Berlin, they were a sensation. Also the concerts of free jazz musicians like Peter Brötzmann were great then -- young Brötzmann was really energetic. In the early seventies I did the furniture removal for a man called Steve Reich, who was a citizen of Berlin then (!). I did the same job for Ax Genrich when he left Berlin and moved to Heidelberg. Memories....

Of course, the government did NOT support rock music. Places to play were some small clubs that change names and owners every three months. All that started only after the "cultural revolution" in 1968 (a copy of what had happened at Berkeley a year before). Before that, we had "beat music," modern German groups sounded either like poor Beatles or like poor Stones. The music you are thinking of, Archie, started in circa 1969.

Q: When did you first start working with Klaus, Manuel and the others back in those days?

KDM: Must have been in 1972, with Agitation Free. Also in '72 and during one of my tours with international groups, I met Hartmut from Ash Ra Tempel in Frankfurt. He kindly invited me to visit him and A.R.T. when back in Berlin. I did so and became friends of Manuel, Rosi, and Hartmut, seeing them nearly daily. I helped them too with carrying speakers, amps, etc. to rehearsal rooms or concert venues. I was well known then for my "magic box," a simple toolbox that contained "everything" that was needed (so it seemed to the guys).

Klaus Schulze I met first in the old office of the Ohr label, when we (A.R.T.) asked for some cash to travel to Switzerland to do what became the *SEVEN UP* album. KS had left A.R.T. a year ago and discussed matters with an Ohr secretary about cover and photo for his first solo album. Later that year I also got to know him better and started to help him out, too. I even started to live at his flat, together with him and his girlfriend. In 1973 I worked regularly for A.R.T., TD, and KS (which means: on all their gigs).

Q: How did you get involved in the scene? There was very little business consciousness among musicians in those days (and maybe still today...); did you have some management, or personal business experience to help them?

KDM: With the exception of Edgar Froese, I was a bit older than all the Berlin musicians I worked for. In 1970 I had finished with a regular full time job that had lasted the previous 10 long years, and therefore I knew what work means. In opposition to all (!) those musicians my background is the "lower class." I had no such naïve ideas, I was a very realistic person and I still am. Also I had my European tour experience with sometimes quite difficult people from USA, Brazil, England... (even more difficult if you know that my English was sparse then.) Of course I had no knowledge about management or the music business. I was an accepted member of Agitation Free and A.R.T. except that my job in the group was the technique and transport. Only later -- and just with KS -- I started to look after business things too, and learned a thing or two.

Q: In America the birth of psychedelic music created an even larger social scene that ultimately changed society even up to today. Was it like that in Germany as well -- a social revolution caused by the music, or...?

KDM: West Germany copied and still copies everything that comes from the USA, including every silly fashion. In addition to the music from England, of course the German young bands also copied the (not-so-silly) music from America. At least, they tried. The San Francisco groups were highly regarded here, as much as British "Pink Floyd" and a lot of the many English blues rock groups. Sadly, their ability to do the same as the Anglo-Americans was not so prominent. Therefore, some believed that drugs were the necessary thing needed, what an error. What came out from the efforts by a few of the young and idealistic Germans lead finally to their own style. The huge majority of the German bands played the usual rock stuff, but with that stiff rhythm (Can and Kraftwerk were clever -- or courageous -- enough to take this as advantage.

Q: In fact was this new form of German rock music really such a big musical movement back then, or perhaps even in those days, the hype was bigger than the reality?

KDM: There was other music that was much bigger, which is a situation not very different from today. Only to the ears, eyes, mind and life of the interested people like you or me, this scene was important. The common man listened to other music. Probably Captain Beefheart's *TROUT MASK REPLICA* album sold more than TD of their first three LPs.

Q: From your perspective, what was the reaction of the German people in general to this new phenomenon called "Krautrock"?

KDM: No one in Germany called this music "Krautrock" then. Ash Ra Tempel or TD was called "Ash Ra Tempel" or "Tangerine Dream," or "those crazy people." The nationalistic British music press put the label "Kraut" or "Krautrock" on some of the bands, if they noticed them at all (after '73 and mostly because Virgin released some of them and paid for advertising). Of course, the Brits meant "Kraut" spitefully.

The Germans as a whole didn't react at all. Some journalists mentioned the names, some people bought the records. As said above, it was a minority. German rock music was not highly regarded. Apart from the albums I got for free from the people I worked for, I never bought a record by a German artist or group! It was just not cool. Pink Floyd WAS better than TD. Hawkwind WAS better than A.R.T. And the Stones WERE and ARE much better than all the hundreds of German copies. The exception was in 1973 when Kraftwerk hit it big with "Autobahn."

Let me take a parallel to the second wave of German bands, ten years later, called "New German Wave," in 1980 to '82. The better of those bands in the very early eighties sold hundreds of thousands of copies of albums and singles, played concerts in front of many thousands, had TV appearances, won awards, etc. (Ideal, Trio, Nina Hagen...). The first wave ten years earlier, Can, Amon Düül, TD, A.R.T., Klaus Schulze, they sold one or two, maybe five thousand copies. The eighties' German bands sold 100 times more. This is the reality. But, selling is not everything.

Q: Do you have any idea how much a percentage of the market sales of the new German rock bands accounted for overall - or did "normal" music still dominate the business even then?

KDM: If you speak about the early era: the latter. A successful album in Germany was then: 50,000 to 100,000 copies. 250,000 copies was Gold, 500,000 copies: Platinum. Every month there are lists published of Gold and Platinum albums. No Tangerine Dream, no Can, not one of the groups you think of, among the dozens of records. Same for radio play: nothing on the main stations at normal playing time. Nothing in the charts. Only exception was Kraftwerk after 1973. Oh, yes, and there was this Michael Rother, he had a huge success once with one of his records. But these two exceptions are not really part of the "new music scene" in Germany around 1970. These 2 had HITS with the wider public because they actually composed a song with a melody, a pop hit. That's still the key to success in music: a good melody. For instance, not one TD album contains such a catchy tune.

Q: In the early days what was the record industry's reaction to the music of KS? Over the years what was the largest selling KS album and how many copies did it sell?

KDM: Why and how should the record industry react? There was no such reaction.

Sales figures? Recently I discussed with KS if I could publish such figures in "The KS Circle," the monthly publication about Klaus. I have fascinating statistics that I made in the late seventies and in the early nineties. We agreed that these figures are still nothing for outsiders. Because, any statistic would be misinterpreted by most readers because they don't know, or forget, a record that is for 20 or 25 years available, sold of course more than one that is on the market for just the last six months. An album that is distributed worldwide by a huge label (for instance: *TIMEWIND, MIRAGE,* or *BABEL*), would sell automatically more than an album released only in Germany. This says nothing about the quality of an album. Readers would only see the figures... and not what's the reality behind them. Also people are used to (and seem to believe) exaggerated figures that other artists tell them. And IF I would print our figures, I would be honest. Therefore, we NEVER published sales figures of KS's albums.

Q: For a very long time now you have worked for Klaus Schulze. What exactly was the nature of your relationship with him?

KDM: I worked with him (notice the "with"), by doing the things he's not able or not willing to do: from bookkeeping, statistics and writing letters, to carrying and maintenance of the instruments. Also making photos, covers, tour management, the stage set-up, the stage lighting... Care of the instruments I dropped in the early eighties. Officially, and since 1978, I'm his publisher; I "publish" his compositions. And that's my only income. Except if I produce albums, then I get my share from this too.

I said in an older interview: "I try to bring order into the chaos." This explains in 8 words my job. If someone wants to know more details about my work then and now, this other interview is to find in the "Miscellaneous" section on the KS website: www.klaus-schulze.com.

Q: During the last 30 years together you and Klaus did 2 independent record labels (Innovative Communication and Inteam) to release his albums, and music by friends. Was there a specific reason for you to do this -- because of economics, desire for creative control, lack of interest by larger record companies, or...?

KDM: With both I had nothing much to do with them(!) I was against them from the beginning. KS is not the right person to lead a company. First, he had a good partner in IC, Michael Hajentes. Only when this partner left Klaus and later founded "Edel," I had to replace him, voluntarily without any payment (!). I still was "the publisher" only. Okay, I said to myself, if I finally accept to do this unwanted job, I'll do it right: I found a rock group here in Berlin, signed them for IC, produced them, and 18 month later we had a Platinum album.

Later, after I had left IC and Klaus had sold the company, he asked me to join his second effort "Inteam." I said no. I saw that the label would be soon bankrupt, for various reasons. Exactly this happened. A real musician should not try to manage a company, and vice versa.

Q: Today what is the situation like for new bands, and more experimental artists in Germany like KS since the market has become so dominated worldwide by the megacorps?

KDM: It's the same as it was 30 years ago. Good interesting new music has always a chance. It doesn't matter if the record companies are huge or small. And with "good interesting and new" I do not mean: "good" for a loony clientele, "interesting" to those with no taste, and "new" for those who don't know much music. Sorry for these harsh words, but during these many years I've had my experiences with bad taste, with naïve crazies, and with egocentricity.

Q: In America, the record stores have become like huge corporate supermarkets for the latest top pop products. The smaller indie stores have a real hard time and often exist only by selling used vinyl LPs. Is it the same in Germany, or does a strong independent spirit still exist there in the music field?

KDM: I don't know. This is -- if it does exist -- it's a part of the much younger generation. It's their game.

I haven't visited a record shop for ages; I buy only by mail order (because what I look for is rarely in the shops anyway.)

I remember my last CD shop visit: I ordered a six-CD set by Charlie Christian, on a Portuguese label. When after three weeks I collected and paid the CDs, the shop assistant asked me what kind of music is that? He actually had never heard about the man who invented and publicized the electric guitar (and its use) to the world! Millions of guitar players do what this black man offered, sixty years ago.... These are my little problems, far from thoughts if there are bigger or smaller shops. But maybe you're right and in smaller shops there would be shop assistants who know a bit more about music and its history?

When I look at all the many small labels that release new electronic music -- and I don't speak of those old-fashioned copycats, but of a new generation that's doing quite interesting new stuff -- it's rarely on a multinational big label, but mostly on small labels you never have heard before... Which is also very clever by the multis because of the risk involved. If it's a seller, the musicians involved come to them anyway (and voluntarily!) That's the way the cookie crumbles.

Q: What do you think of the current bit of renewed interest in the old Krautrock artists? Is it misplaced nostalgia by fans, or perhaps rediscovery of some good music that has been forgotten?

KDM: What "good music"? The few good ones from the past were always there, or their classic records were always available. The rest was luckily forgotten. I spoke to people who suddenly see their old, forgotten bands in the dim "Krautrock" limelight -- they wonder and laugh about the people who suddenly think that this music was and still is great. One of the greatest admirers and promoters of this mercifully forgotten music is a well-known drug addict and crazy man (This is not my description, but from a rock lexicon).

Q: How has your music taste changed over the years? Do you still like the music of your youth, or do you listen to different things?

KDM: Of course I listen to different music than I used to forty years ago. It's all kinds of music, except for pop or rock music, be it today's or yesterday's. For present pop I listen sometimes to the radio, during work, just to be up-to-date -- "Ah, another Beatles copy."

Privately it's mostly so-called "classical" music that I pull out of my shelves and put into my CD player. And here I go as much into detail as I did during the sixties with jazz and blues, until I was an expert. I'm now on the way to becoming an expert in classical music as well.

I feel nothing anymore when I listen to an old Pink Floyd album, but I have that special feeling if I listen to Gustav Mahler's 9th Symphony, the last part, the "Adagio," especially by the "Berlin Philharmoniker" under Sir John Barbirolli. Besides some nostalgic moments, the only "pop" music I still love to listen to and still buy, album for album, is: Van Morrison. My age.

Q: Now that you have passed the half-century mark age-wise, do you ever reflect about what things would have been like if you hadn't made music your love and your life?

KDM: "Now"? This mark I passed already six years ago. Yes I do reflect, mostly when and because people ask me about little or special parts from the past, and I like to give answers. But, sorry, Archie, I have no answer to the "what would have been" question. Literature is my other love.

Archie Patterson

The EUROCK CD-ROM
Reprinted from *Magnet Magazine*

Record collectors, start your hard drives: an unusually essential and downright user-friendly CD-ROM has just hit the market that's ready to scratch your data-greedy itch.

EUROCK: THE GOLDEN AGE is an outgrowth of music journalist Archie Patterson's long-running EUROCK 'zine, that much-respected journal of European progressive and psychedelic music. (Patterson also operates a similarly inclined Web mail order operation under the same name.) The ROM reproduces every issue going all the way back to its '73 debut, no mean feat at that, and loads in a wealth of extra goodies as well.

By way of personal testimony, I came across EUROCK a few years ago while trolling a studious internet mailing list devoted to Krautrock -- one of my personal obsessions dating back to my tender years -- and took note of the address as a likely source for records and CDs (I was right). Patterson also was one of the more astute posters to the list, which I duly noted as well.

According to Patterson, speaking of the impulse behind the ROM, "I felt books were old-fashioned and suggested we take it into the 21st century. I also had a lot of video material [among the video clips are performances by Krautrock heroes Amon Düül II and Popol Vuh] and liked the idea of incorporating that as well, thus making it a true multimedia representation." Additionally, the ROM contains a massive discography, complete with cross-referencing links and a search feature, making the disc a key reference work.

Easy to navigate, it sports crisp, uncluttered graphics; and a free version of QuickTime is included for playback of the videos. And as a bonus it includes a separate music section featuring 40 minutes of ethereal, stimulating prog by Japanese composer Hiro Kawahara. Worth noting too: if the project, which consumed over 3 years and numerous beta versions before the final incarnation, is successful, an updated DVD edition is likely.

Putting things into perspective, however, Patterson suggests there's a motivation simpler than wanting to go hi-tech: to keep spreading the word. As he puts it, "Music is the essence of life. It enriches beyond imagination. You can see, feel, touch, smell and fall in love to music."

What follows is the transcript of my interview with Patterson, which I initially conducted for *Magnet Magazine* for our music news item section. (Feel free to check *Magnet* out via our website at www.magnetmagazine.com). He was so forthcoming with his answers, and included so much excellent info about the ROM and EUROCK in general, that I felt I would be remiss if the entire thing were not made available to the general public.

Fred Mills: When/why did you decide to launch the project? Demand for the back issues as a prompt, or had you considered doing it all as a website at one stage, etc?

Archie Patterson: The project was initially brainstormed early in 1998, the 25th year of EUROCK's existence (it was started in 1973). I had amassed a virtual history of groups -- features, interviews and reviews -- from this particular music genre. A long-time friend Robert Carlberg suggested I digitize it all and do a book. I said, "Yikes, that'd kill me!" (laugh) He then said, "OK, I'll do it." We talked about it a bit. I felt books were a bit old-fashioned, and suggested we take EUROCK into the 21st century and do something for the computer, like a CD-ROM, that would have many more possibilities and be completely unique (at least for this type of journalism).

FM: How long did it take to get everything scanned in and/or reformatted? (How many pages total?) Were there any pitfalls along the way?

AP: It took Robert perhaps 4-6 months to scan everything in. He sent me diskettes, and I loaded them onto my computer and arranged the various parts into a coherent whole along the way. I actually never did a page count, but all the back issues combined make up a pile that is over a foot high. His incredibly hard work literally made it a reality.

The next big question was how to find a programmer who would do the actual ROM work. A friend of a friend put a notice on a local internet tech news group for me and I got several inquires. Out of them, one person named David Gillaspey was very interested, and a nice guy as well. We had a couple meetings, he suggested a modest fee, and took the project on. My oldest son Aaron (who is now in college and interns for Microsoft in the summers) had done some initial prep work for me on the project and sketched out a mock interface upon which David and myself built the "look" of the project. David did an extraordinary amount of work without complaint. Without him there would have been no finished product. From conception to finish overall, it took some 3½ years.

FM: Which of the added features posed the greatest, if any, obstacles? Was the discography easy enough to compile from your existing materials or was there additional research involved? How'd you go about getting the rights to include the videos?

AP: The discography was compiled from the original issues, with help from a few other people, as well as a few reference works listed in the credits section. Robert did much of that work, with me revising and checking things. Perhaps the index was the trickiest as it contained so many links cross-referencing the simple listings to multiple information sources. That was the last feature we decided to add in.

Fortunately it turned out less daunting than originally imagined programming-wise, or we (David particularly), might have died at that point. As we went along, many times we debated what to add in or delete from the final product. There were many obstacles, mainly trying to get all the components to work together as introducing a new feature often caused one of the others to need a change in terms of simple functionality. There were some 70-beta versions with various people on both Mac and PC testing several of them.

I've had a lot of video material sent to me over the years, and of course liked the idea of incorporating that and music as well into the project, thus making it a true multi-media representation of the genre. The addition of video gave the project a unique aspect; that has never been done before. I have always tried to take EUROCK into virgin territory. So I contacted the people who had originally sent me the video, and music, and asked them if I could include it. They were long-time friends and liked the idea. They said, sure you can use it, you've always helped promote the music, so let's go ahead and try this new way of journalism.

The project really was not looked upon as a commercial venture, but more as a cultural history of the music, the times, and my life's work. Over the years I was very lucky to meet some great people who helped me. Those people made my life very interesting and creative personally, and I helped them a little bit with their music. It was synchronicity. This whole project really -- art work, design, music, video and everything -- was done "with a little help from my friends" who worked like a sort of extended family to create something that I could have never been imagined at the outset. It was a very open process with everyone basically giving of themselves in an unselfish way to make it happen. I feel honored and blessed that they gave me their time and energy.

FM: What was your original intent or motivation with EUROCK, how has that extended into the present with your mail order operation, and do you foresee expanding things (such as updating stuff that's on the CD-ROM over time or going to DVD) or moving in other directions in the future?

AP: My original idea was simply to share the new, amazing music I had discovered with some new "friends." Inspired by Greg Shaw's great rock and roll fanzine, *Who Put the Bomp*, a friend, Scott Fischer and I, started writing and all else simply came to pass. One friend had access to a Xerox (at the office of the law firm where he was a gopher). Later another worked with an offset printing press (at the local public schools building). All the work was done "underground" at night (laugh). It was a wild and wonderful set of happenstance occurrences that could almost only have come about during those times.

As a result of the first couple issues of EUROCK, I was asked to run two of the original, pioneering, import music companies of the golden era of imports during the 1970s (Intergalactic Trading Company and Paradox Music, a part of Greenworld Imports). At the outset of the 1980s I decided to do EUROCK on my own and from there on things just kept growing. In a sense, the title The Golden Age (suggested by my 12 year old son Sky) was intended to reflect the particular spirit and nature of the music that was being produced during that time.

As for the future, there are now more interviews being done with new musicians, old music friends and fave groups from the past that keeps the spirit alive with musically today. They are incorporated into www.eurock.com periodically.

The next big project will be a book compiling the main articles from the CD-ROM and new ones that are now being done. Tentatively titled *Eurock - European Rock & the Second Culture*, it will reflect a bit different socio-political perspective than the CD-ROM, but nonetheless continue the concept that always underscored my work with EUROCK. After the CD-ROM came out I got many people asking for a book to curl up with and read in bed (hmmm, what can I say about that one, I might have a few other thoughts myself... laugh).

There could be DVD projects as well as that has been talked about and would be another step forward for EUROCK.

FM: Prog-rock, Krautrock, "Eurock" -- are labels useful?

AP: Labels can be good, but also meaningless. The Germans hate the name "Krautrock," considering it a derogatory word invented by English journalists. I read the very first articles on German space rock in the UK press however, and for the most part the writers were raving about how great the music was. So I think it's a sort of culture clash situation. As for "Eurock," of course that's a great name as I made it up (big laugh).

I do think labels can define a sound and style, but are often used to lump a lot of junk into a marketing category. Perhaps that's my (and others') big objection to the term Krautrock. Like everything else in life, both good and bad can flow from the same thing. What matters is whether you walk in a straight line and never speak with a forked tongue (laughing again).

FM: Record collectors: hopeless geeks, or passionate/enlightened freaks?

AP: Music is the essence of life and I think people who feel passionately about it understand that, which is great. Again, however, that can cut both ways (can't everything)? It can also inspire less than rational attitudes, and sometimes make people lose sight of the real value of music to their lives. I personally have been labeled as many things, and only occasionally do they seem to fit, in my estimation.

I do know that for myself music became a central part of my life very early on (10 years old in fact) and to this day enriches it beyond imagination. You can see, feel, touch, smell and fall in love to music. The great poets and musicians of the ages echo that, and from my own personal experience I can say it is definitely true.

Fred Mills
Magnet Magazine
http://www.magnetmagazine.com

Stephan Kaske - Mythos Interview

Q: Let us begin with a little ancient history. When you first conceived the group Mythos -- its name and musical sound -- what was your inspiration? It seems a very "cosmic" musical concept.

SK: We wanted to get on stage; we wanted to go on tour; we wanted to become famous and we wanted the girls! Honestly, we didn't think beyond that.

Q: What music had you listened to previously that influenced the early Mythos style?

SK: Mainly progressive and psychedelic stuff. Here is a listing of the live-set-list we performed at the end of the sixties before and while we composed our first own songs. Here is my calendar of summer '69. We played up to 5 songs of Pink Floyd, Jethro Tull, Iron Butterfly, The Doors, Steamhammer, Spooky Tooth or Ten Years After.

Q: I remember when I got the first album, saw the cover and heard it; I was astounded, as I'd never heard music like that. How did you come into contact with the Ohr label and convince them to release such non-commercial music?

SK: That has been rather simple. We had more than 100 concerts a year all over Germany in 1970 and '71. We also played several times in the legendary Beat Club Langelsheim. The boss was a real fan and a big supporter of Mythos and when he organized the Langelsheim Festival in summer '71 (the German Woodstock) with lots of rock world stars like Family, Ashton, Gardener and Dyke, Coliseum, Steamhammer, Golden Earring, Nektar and many others, he let us open the program on both days! So we had the full attention of the media and the people (the place was overcrowded with more than 14,000 enthusiasts) especially Mythos fans from all over Germany. It was an incredible experience and success in spite of our unique, but not very commercial music. That's why not only were lots of club and festival managers knocking at our door; Ohr convinced us to produce a record for them!

Q: Do you remember how many copies it sold?

SK: Still no need to remember! With time the first 4 albums developed into classics and are reissued periodically. More than a dozen companies worldwide paid and still pay for copies and copyrights of Mythos.

I know of at least of 3 labels offering the CDs today.

Q: Have you any idea what ever happened to Rolf-Ulrich Kaiser and Gille Letteman?

SK: Not really. After they had blown away their brains with dope they lost their credibility, reputation and at last their music and imperium. Dieter Dierks got all this in '78 or '79 as far as I know. Now his organizations (i.e. Venus Records) are managing the labels and pay my licenses. In 1980 "Starmaiden" wrote me a letter with extremely confused "cosmic" stuff. I answered her letter shortly to wish her good luck (honestly), but my letter returned unopened. "Sorry, Mr. Kaske. I cannot open this letter addressed to Gille Lettmann. Please send it again to >Starmaiden<!," she had written on the envelope. Anything left to say ?!?

Q: After Ohr you went to Sky Records and the Venus Records labels, your style changed somewhat. How would you describe this evolution in your sound? Perhaps you simply got older and better in terms of musicianship, or did your whole concept for the group change?

SK: You see, we've been in a special situation. Mythos had been a real performing live group all over for its first 10 years (contrary to many of the electronic musicians of that time). Remember, we played hundreds of concerts, festivals and especially Langelsheim. I did and financed absolutely everything in the group. I did booking gigs, telephone, mail, procuring posters, photos, press info., lighting, P.A., managing all media things, paying for the truck (and driving it), the rehearsal room, hotels, and so on. I did all this to find musicians to perform my music and to continue the Mythos-story. We simply needed lots of concerts to survive! And the only way to get those gigs and moreover a record company deal seemed to be to make more commercial music with more action. The times they are a-changin'; it was just not possible to get gigs and contracts with sitar, improvisations and 20 minute songs and "only" a certain portion of action.

All that led to the musical stuff of our LPs *STRANGE GUYS* and *CONCRETE CITY* (LPs no.s 3 and 4 released by Venus). At the end of the seventies, when the band "had troubles" again, there were new technical possibilities! The development of drum computers, software sequencers and certain studio equipment made it possible to create new musical ideas and sound without musicians and a thousand foul compromises! That's why and how I made my demos during '79 and contacted Sky to get a contract. All of that resulted in LPs no.s 5 and 6, *QUASAR* and *GRAND PRIX*.

Q: After this time (in the late 1970s, early 1980s if I remember right?) Mythos disappeared. I always wondered what happened, then I think it was in the early 1990s that a friend told me he had gotten a new production -- a double/triple (?) CD of classical music done electronically. Did you stop making music for some time, or take a hiatus form the music scene? What have you been doing these last 15-20 years?

SK: In fact up to the 1980s I worked with my music and became very successful. That's why in 1981 I founded my own studio -- Mythos Studio Berlin (MSB). Because I've been well known in the musicians' scene and had many press and radio appearances for the record release of the album *GRAND PRIX* ("Berlin boy recorded an LP in his own studio!!"). Within a few months I could order a professional 16-track-recording machine (in '82); 24 and 32 tracks followed later on. Also 32-channel-mixer (today 40-channel, computer mixer), digital stuff and effect-units I never heard of before. Remembering those early years I still smell the interior of my first new Jaguar. For years I lived in it, as well as in the studio except the few hours of sleep at home. Up to today more than 1000 groups, projects and musicians of all kind of styles have worked in the MSB. All my compositions and musical themes of that time were used for numerous TV- and radio-commercials or video- and film music.

Remember: after 4 LPs in a row ('78 to '81) I had been a little "fed up" with producing my own music. Moreover everything had been "bulldozed" by the stress and success of the MSB. But in all those studio-years I sampled ideas, tricks, effects, melodies, sounds and more in several, finally big folders. And in the end of '88 I began to produce new Mythos music. But then happened the "Big Hammer," like a "Cheap Shot"! I sent nearly 100 demos all over the world to get a contract, all in vain... Everybody refused to listen to the tapes (..."to be fair to our present artists..., ...currently not accepting unsolicited demo submissions...", etc.) or simply ignored them! Finally in 1989 I remembered an "old ally" (from the *STRANGE GUYS/CONCRETE CITY* years) and asked Jürgen Jacobsen who managed several companies in Switzerland. The following is part of Mythos history. He ordered and has published up to today 8 Mythos CDs and approximately 20 additional releases (i.e. *M.A.S.S.* and *CLASSIC ON SYNTH* productions).

Q: Perhaps you can make a listing of all the albums you have done over the years?

SK: OK, let's have a look at least at the Mythos discography:
MYTHOS (Ohr LP, 1972)
DREAMLAB (Cosmic Couriers LP, 1975)
STRANGE GUYS (Venus LP, 1978)
CONCRETE CITY (Venus LP, 1979)
QUASAR (Sky LP, 1980)
GRAND PRIX (Sky LP, 1981)
MYTHOS LIVE (Hits & Fun Maxi-Single + CD, 1989)
MYTHOSPHERE (Selected Sound Carrier CD, 1990)
SOUND OF SILENCE & HARMONY (Art & Music CD, 1995)
PURRR-SYMPHONY (Art & Music CD, 1997)
(W)INTERMEZZO (Art & Music CD, 1998)
LE PRINTEMPS MYSTIQUE (Art & Music CD, 2000)
THE DARK SIDE OF MYTHOS (Pastels CD, 2000)
FEUILLAGE (Art & Music CD, 2001)

Q: I've heard the latest releases and in some ways the sound is still the same, but with a more sophisticated approach. Would you say that the music and concept of Mythos has changed over the years? Or perhaps it's still motivated by the same concept?

SK: What a difficult question. You see, the world is changing dramatically and faster all the time. If you do not react to it and accommodate yourself to it you're simply going to disappear like the dinosaurs or the producers of wooden mail coaches. In the musical world you won't find concert venues, record companies and media feedback and thereby an audience. Musicians "die softly," imperceptibly! That's why a certain change in the music and concept has been a must. Otherwise Mythos would have disappeared in the early seventies like so many others before and after. On the other hand, the Mythos project is still inspired by the original motivation, the same spirit as in the very beginning! Search and find musical formats outside of the mainstream. If you can't avoid listening to other popular music -- do the contrary. If 140bpm stand for success and the charts -- my music's going to have 14 beats per minute! Try, experiment, provoke! But always stay on top of the tight rope. You are dancing between the realization of your dreams and the deep commercial fall!

Q: Materially your situation surely has changed. Now you produce and release your own music. Do you also work in other fields that complement this creative side, or have a more diverse occupation that allows more of a yin yang situation in regards to your musical creativity?

SK: Beside producing music I've got only some (hated) tasks to manage a certain property and some investments. But that's only a necessary kind of burden stealing my time. My real beloved alternative to the musical work is: active sports!

Since 1990 when I bought my first mountain bike I ride in the Berlin forests as often as possible, 1 to 3 times a week, all through the year. Additionally since 1996 my favorite passion is speed skating!

Approximately 5 to 7 times a year I skate in marathons (esp. the famous Berlin Marathon), half-marathons and city runs all over Germany. Ice-skating, indoor-cart-racing in winter and snooker and billiards complete the range of my interests outside of music.

But believe it or not: music's all around. Especially during the many hours out in the fresh air on the bike or speed skates, all alone in a wonderful environment, I sometimes get new musical ideas.

Q: We now truly enter the millennium period during 2001 and Mythos is 30 years old musically. If you had it all to do over again would you do anything differently?

SK: Contrary to what many people might say (...who did it MY WAY...), I would love to change and repair many things. I've made so many mistakes, unfortunate decisions, wrong moves and disappointed, or hurt some people in all periods of my life. I say, I'm sorry to everybody to whom it concerns!

From the musical point of view especially I should have finished the group-activities perhaps sooner, after the split of the Mythos I in 1973. It would have been probably more effective to invest all that time, energy and resources not in trucks, rehearsal rooms, P.A., light equipment and musicians, but in instruments, computers and recording equipment. But that is hypothetical. On the other hand, I would have never met my beloved wife. We have been together since the 1977 Germany tour and have a daughter since '92.

Q: Do you personally feel "cosmically" changed by the last 30 years, or have you become more down to earth?

SK: Actually, I think I always stayed the son of a merchant (Hi daddy, everything's alright in Heaven!?). That may sometimes reduce the cosmic range of ideas; but it's taking responsibility for a punctual and reliable delivery of work. I guess my partners enjoy it.

Q: What would you like to happen with Mythos in the next 30 years?

SK: There is a commercial spot on German TV -- somebody asking a woman what she would like to change: "Everything should stay like it is ...", she says. This corresponds to my feelings best today!

I love to produce 2 or 3 CDs for Jürgen Jacobsen a year, to work with those young guys in the Mythos Studio Berlin, and to race on blades and wheels through the forests, nature and cities!

Apart from this I would be seriously interested to have productions with some of the Big Guys of Electronic Music worldwide. Maybe exchanging song themes/fragments/parts/ideas via ADAT format, or via the internet. Then adding ideas, sending it to and fro' a few times and mixing it finally somewhere in the world, or at the MSB ?!?

Archie Patterson

Interview with Julien Ash of NLC

Q: When I first heard the music of NLC it seemed very different in concept and sound than any other music I had heard. What were the original rock or other musical artists that you listened to and liked in the beginning?

JA: My favorite musicians at the time I founded NLC were Chrome, Coil, Again, Schubert, Bach, Legendary Pink Dots, Pink Floyd, Nurse with Wound and Thomas Kenner. The only concept was freedom; the sound was what we were able to do with our old sampler and a four-track tape recorder.

Q: Did any of these early favorites influence the style of NLC directly in your opinion?

JA: Yes, I liked a lot Coil's moods and the melodic side of Pink Floyd and the Legendary Pink Dots. I think they influenced NLC's music directly, but as I said before, I didn't want to do any particular style of music, because I had not enough material to look like another real musician...

Q: When was the first production by NLC released?

JA: Our first release was the CD single *LOST SAND DIVINITIES* in May 1990. This release was quite a miracle, because we only wanted to record a tape, and as we had a friend running a label, he proposed to do a CD. It sold about 1,000 copies, that's the reason why I'm still doing music: not for money of course, but because some people seemed to like it.

Q: How did you decide on the name Nouvelles Lectures Cosmopolites?

JA: When NLC started, we were two (Angustére and myself). The name comes from a local company called "Nouvelles

Constructions Cosmopolites," that was quite a silly name we thought. So we called the "band" NLC, because of the NLCentrum, which was a great Dutch concert place, where a lot of our favorite bands played before.

Q: Can you translate that into English?

JA: The meaning is something like "new cosmopolitan readings," that's still silly indeed!

Q: Is NLC a "group project," or more specifically your own unique musical vision?

JA: Angustère left just after the double-tape boxed set *PÉRIODE TAOÏSTE*, in December 1990. I released a solo album called *INCANDESCENT*, because he didn't know about his relation with music and composition at this time, and after he said he wasn't interested anymore in music, so as the solo album had a little success too, I decided to go on and call my solo project NLC. But everyone interested may bring sounds and ideas, so it's not really my own vision of music. A lot of people have collaborated during all these years!

Q: The music seems a fusion of many different styles and ideas. Do you think there are any specific modern musicians who influenced the music of NLC?

JA: Sure, there are. A musician is like a medium: He just re-writes what he had felt or heard before. That's why I think the music of NLC is not mine, the best thing that may happen to this music is to be "stolen" again and again... And that's why I'm against copyrighting. If it were MY own music, nobody would have liked it.

Q: The music also seems to have gone through some changes over the years. Did you change your conceptual ideas for the music during this time?

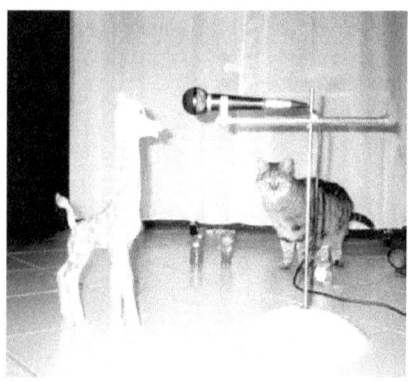

[NLC "Live in Concert"]

JA: No. My material has changed. I met different people. I had children... And I don't have any real concept about music!

Q: Can you give a list of all the productions done by NLC over the years?

JA:
Part I: Compact Discs
LOST SAND DIVINITIES (1990)
INCANDESCENT (J. Ash) (1991)
VESTIGES (1992)
ALLEGRO VIVACE (1993)
ANGELS OF OïKEMA (1993)
SPIRITUS REX (1994)
SECRET OF OïKEMA (1994)
CLEAN (1995)
UNCLEAN (1995)
UNIS (1996)
LE SANG DE LA LICORNE (1997)
LE SANCTUAIRE D'ïS (1997)
LE DOMAINE (1998)
LE LANGAGE DES AUTRES (1998)
ASD 002 - THE CEREAL KILLER (1999)
FRAGMENTS TAOÏSTES (1999)
UNIS (+ 3 bonus tracks) (1999)
OÏKEMA (2000)
HIDING IN TIME (2000)
MOON (2000)
LA CARPE MIROIR (Le Lieu Noir) (3 CDs) (2000)

Part II: Vinyl LPs
LA MER DES SARCASMES (1995)
LA MURE REINE (1995)
L'AMIRAL RAMIREZ (1995)
L'AMARRE-AILE (1996)
LA MORUE ENRHUMEE (1996)
VENUS DE MILLE EAUX (1996)

Part III: Cassette Tapes
PÉRIODE TAOÏSTE 1 (1991)
PÉRIODE TAOÏSTE 2 (1991)
ECMNESIA (MAELSTROM) (1992)
KRIEGSTRAUM (1992)
DIEU EST GROS (Triste Nuit Pour) (1992)
SCHIZOLITHE (1993)
NAKED (1995)
FRAGMENTS TAOÏSTES (1995)
LE LANGAGE DES AUTRES (1997)

Q: Do you make music full time, or do you have another career and do music as a purely an outlet for your artistic creativity?

JA: I'm an MD, I've just stopped working now to have more time with my family and on music too, but I don't live from music. In fact, I don't spend a lot of time really doing music. I'm also running the label, answering (often very interesting) questions (!!), working as sound engineer for other bands... I also enjoy a lot photography, painting, writing, cinema, nature, holidays... That's really too much, it was a real good idea not to work anymore! My work took all my time, and you can't really run such a job part-time, people always want you to be present night and day. And there is so much to do in a lifetime!

Q: What about future projects? Do you plan to try and be more commercially successful with NLC, or keep the music more as an artistic form of expression?

JA: Well, I do not plan anything special, and certainly not to have any commercial success, there would be the same troubles as when I worked: I want to be quiet!! Music is really something I need to do, it's compulsive. And the way I'm doing it is very pleasant, because I haven't got any imperatives. I don't care about art, but it's one of my favorite forms of expression!

Archie Patterson

Ole Lukkøye Interview

For obvious reasons the Cold War served as a major artistic blockade when it came to East/West cultural and music exchange. In the West society and music underwent a drastic change during the '50s, '60s and '70s. What was going on in the Eastern bloc was only know via word of mouth and subterranean commerce between free radical musical elements. Today all that has changed drastically as rock music has become not only more widely disseminated worldwide, but homogenized as well. Such is the way of the world.

In particular one of the most interesting developments has been the opening of the vaults of the Russian rock archives. Many of the bands that recorded back in the '70s and '80s, are now getting their material reissued today. Even more importantly, current musicians from Russia (and elsewhere in East Europe as well) are gaining exposure in the Western world. As the West has become a corporate spawning ground for formulaic music and overproduction, the emergence of these new Eastern bands has brought a new burst of creativity to the scene.

One of the best new Eastern bands today is Ole Lukkøye from St. Petersburg,

Russia. Their leader is Boris Bardash, who at one time was also a member of the legendary Russian band Rainy Season. Hans-Joachim Irmler of Faust produced the latest Ole Lukkøye album, and this collaboration would seem to bode well for the future of the band.

The following interview with Boris was done after the end of their most recent dates in Germany, Hungary and Croatia.

Q: As a Westerner, I'm quite interested to know at what age and year did you first hear rock music in the former Soviet Union, and what was the first band you liked?

BB: I was 11-12 years old (1976) when I became "ill" of rock music. In those times it was hard to find records from the west side of the world (they were just on the black market). Mostly we copied music from tapes to tapes (usually bad quality) ... Some names of bands: Beatles (of course), Rolling Stones, Led Zeppelin, Black Sabbath, Emerson Lake & Palmer, Deep Purple, Pink Floyd......

Q: When did you play in your first rock band, and what kind of music did they play?

BB: We formed our first school band -- Strangers -- in 1979. We played cover versions of underground, but popular Soviet bands like Time Machine, Aquarium and some western songs, but very soon we started to make our own music.

Q: Was there a scene back then for groups to play concerts, or in clubs, and make records?

BB: It was a very hard situation for this type of activity, mostly concerts were half legal or unofficial. Of course there was an "official" big scene of sweet 'n' stupid pop groups, but it was not really interesting for the more "progressive" young people.

That situation started to change in 1981 when the Leningrad Rock Club was founded. It gathered all best unofficial bands and made a real push to create a rock movement in USSR. But real changes came only with the start of the Gorbachev era in 1986.

Q: I know that you were formerly a member of Rainy Season. What Rainy Season albums did you play on?

BB: We recorded first "tape" album of Rainy Season in 1986 (unreleased), but the music we made in the following years was unfortunately was not recorded in a studio. There is just one live compilation CD *NOSTALGIE* with our participation. All another "real" albums the band made were done after Andrey and I had left the band in 1989.

Q: During that era was that type of space rock music or progressive music well known in Russia? Was that before Glasnost, or after?

BB: We had a lot of friends -- real music fans and collectors, so we could find any music for listening. It was like a special circle of people. But really popular were mostly hard rock and heavy metal (like everywhere, I think). OK, anyway the most well known names here were Pink

Floyd, King Crimson, Yes, Genesis, Brian Eno, Jethro Tull, Van der Graaf Generator, Frank Zappa, Grateful Dead... and it was before Glasnost...

Q: In what year did you first form Ole Lukkøye?

BB: Spring of 1989.

Q: Did you have any specific Western band that influenced the music you made with Ole Lukkøye?

BB: I was very influenced at that time by some solo works of Peter Gabriel (especially *PASSION*), Brian Eno, Jon Hassel, Dead Can Dance, Cocteau Twins...

Q: Does the name have an English translation?

BB: The name is actually translated to Russian and relates to Danish and Swedish mythology. He was a Scandinavian type of pagan god of dreams. Literally it means something like "Ole who closes eyes."

Q: In Russia today is there a good audience for music by bands like yours and other electronic or experimental rock music?

BB: Today the situation here is difficult for this music (not for Pink Floyd or such names of course). Mostly the scene consists of the big names of show business and the pop rock mainstream.

Q: Is there any media or radio that plays or promotes the sort of music Ole Lukkøye makes in Russia today?

BB: Not really. There are some small labels (for example Exotica in Moscow).

Q: Are there many other bands now in Russia playing this sort of "space rock" than there were originally, or is Ole Lukkøye the main one?

BB: I'm not sure that we play "space rock," but I don't know of any other bands here like Ole Lukkøye.

Q: How did you make contact with the people from Faust?

BB: After our concert at the Burg Herzberg Open Air Festival in Germany we got invited by the Think Progressive label to record a new album at Hans-Joachim Irmler's studio.

Q: I imagine the good people of Faust have helped you quite a bit to get recognition outside Russia. How is the reaction different during concerts in Germany as opposed to Russia?

BB: If you play in the right place there is no big difference in reaction... We played just now also in Croatia, it was great. The audience gets more excited than in Russia or Germany.

Q: I believe you just played in Hungary. I know a couple other bands there that do some sort of space rock - Korai Öröm and Galloping Coroners. Do you know these bands and perhaps do joint concerts together?

BB: Yes. KÖ are our friends and they always help us to organize concerts in Hungary. We also set up a concert for them in St. Petersburg.

Q: Is there an actual scene and good size audience in the various East Euro countries today for this type of music?

BB: Yes, I think so. We played several times in Hungary, in the Czech Republic, in Poland, in Slovakia, now (in April) in Croatia and found at every performance a very good reaction and new offers for more concerts.

Q: After the end of this tour when you return to Russia, what are your plans -- a new studio album, more touring or?

BB: We decided to spend this summer for our private lives and rest because we have not had a vacation for the 3 previous summers. Maybe we also will prepare something fresh in the studio...

Archie Patterson

Bernard Gueffier Interview
MUSEA Records

Q: Let's start at the beginning; what was the first record you ever bought? At what age?

Bernard Gueffier: My first ever record was the Moody Blues *ON THE THRESHOLD OF A DREAM* which I bought during a trip to England in 1969 when I was 15 years old. I had a chance to listen to previous Moody Blues tracks on radio in '67-'68 and their incredible sound blew up my mind. The discovery of Mellotron was a sound revolution for me. In fact, nobody was talking about progressive music at that time, but later, many journalists and music fans came to consider the Moody Blues the founders of Progressive Music.

Q: When did you start collecting progressive music? Was it during "The Golden Age" or later?

BG: Immediately after this discovery, my taste for original music developed and then listening to early Pink Floyd, King Crimson or Soft Machine turned me into a real progressive fan and record collector. I was living in a little town in France at that time, where it was impossible to find any of these albums. So, I started to buy from England by mail order. Most of the stuff from these catalogues was really outside of the commercial market.

Q: In the beginning, were you mostly interested in only French music, or perhaps other countries as well?

BG: So my first tastes were for British bands. But I rapidly discovered the French scene, starting with Gong and Magma, which were intensively touring at that time, even in small cities. They use to play in some kind of youth centers called MJC (for House for Youth & Culture), which existed in every French town. This opened the eyes of the progressive audience to see that this type of music was existing in several other countries. Rapidly, it became possible to find in French shops some German and Italian records as well. This allowed me to discover and collect LPs by Amon Düül, Agitation Free, Faust, Banco, PFM, etc.

Q: After the 1970s it seemed the progressive music scene died off somewhat, then experienced a bit of resurgence. In some ways the *French Discographie* book and Musea helped re-start that. Who had the original idea to start Musea? What year did you begin the original work on the book and start the Musea label?

BG: After a decade of masterpieces, it happened that progressive music was banned from all media at the end of the '70s. Most groups disappeared and the production was reduced to nothing. But of course, this was only the rules of the music market which led to this situation: music business had discovered other sources of easy profit in the form of punk music and later new wave, so why go on carrying those old fashion prog dinosaurs? This attitude was obviously neglecting many music lovers -- even if they were not as many as in the old days -- and not taking into consideration all the musicians who went on composing interesting works.

At that time, I was still trying to increase my knowledge of the progressive scene, trading LPs and live cassettes with other prog fans all over the world. This is how I met Francis Grosse, who had a special taste for the French scene. We rapidly decided in 1982 to gather our information and make it available for other prog fans. This took the form of *The French Rock Discography*, the first edition was published in 1984.

For several months, we gathered all possible information about past and existing French bands, meeting lots of musicians. The situation was the same for all of them: they had no label to release their work, so they had to self produce their albums, and no distributor to sell them. So they usually sold them to a few friends and kept the unsold copies in their cellar!

As soon as we started selling our book, the usual answer from our readers was: "Where can I find this record?" So we were in that special situation where we knew musicians without listeners, and music fans without records to listen to! What else can we do? We decided to be the missing link between them! We asked the musicians to give us some LPs on consignment, which we started selling to the *Discography* readers. And this was the real start of Musea. Needless to say that at that time, we had absolutely no plan for the future, no idea where this could lead us!

In 1985, while going to Paris to a music festival (with appearances by Shub Niggurath, Eskaton, Uppsala and others), Francis and I decided to found a record label and called it Musea, in reference to the Muses, Music and Museum.

In order to give our readers some musical elements, we asked several bands to record an original track to be included in a cassette given free with the book. This cassette was called *PRELUDE* and included unreleased tracks by Noco Music, Troll, Joël Dugrenot, Serge Bringolf/Strave, Pataphonie, Eskaton, Uppsala, Yog Xothoth and Datura. This cassette is the first ever Musea release! I think this request to bands for new material, with the guarantee to be distributed, even at a limited scale at that time, gave hope to many musicians and contributed to the re-birth of the French prog scene.

Q: I think there have been 3 versions of the book, how many copies have been sold up to today?

BG: First two versions were printed to 1,000 copies, the third one to 2,000 copies. This was not really a huge quantity, but it was clearly showing that the audience for this kind of music did not disappear completely. The second edition was published in 1988, a third one in 1994. The content was considerably improved with each edition.

Q: Will there be another *Discographie* released? If yes, when?

BG: Definitely yes ! We never gave up this work, and went on during all these years to gather all useful information for each new edition. We plan to release the fourth edition in 2001, probably in the form of a CD-ROM. This edition will include at least three times more bands and records than the previous one !

Q: In the beginning how did you obtain the money for the early albums?

BG: It was simple: we had absolutely no money for anything! This is the reason why in fact our first releases were totally financed by the bands themselves! As I told you, at that time, the ONLY existing solution for prog musicians was self production. At least with Musea they could let us do all the work regarding cover conception, pressing, legal declarations, and have the guarantee of a minimum distribution, which was real progress. But this made no difference on the bill: they still had to cover all costs. This was how our first 4 records were published: Jean Pascal Boffo *JEUX DE NAINS* (2001), Shub Niggurath *LES MORTS VONT VITE* (2002), Elixir *SABBAT* (2003) and Jean Pascal Boffo *CARILLON* (2004). With the profit we made on distributing these titles, we could afford to self-finance our next two releases: *ENNEADE* (2005) a compilation devoted to Magma-related bands and *ENCHANTEMENT* (2006), a compilation devoted to French progressive bands.

Q: How many labels does Musea publish today? Do they feature more than just progressive music?

BG: Today, Musea includes 11 different labels, each one devoted to a special musical style: Musea for Progressive Rock, Angular for Neo Progressive, Gazul for New Music, Rebel for Rock, Brennus for Hard Rock, Thundering for Metal, Ethnea for Folk, Dreaming for Electronic Music, Bluesy Mind for Blues, Musea Parallèle and Great Winds for Jazz and Fusion. Altogether, these labels have released almost 700 titles so far.

Q: Today MUSEA releases a very large number of productions -- it must be very expensive. How many do you release per year and how does the company raise the money for these?

BG: We usually release approx. 50 to 55 CDs per year (i.e. one new release every week). About half of them are financed by bands, the rest by Musea. The profit on previous releases allows us to finance the new ones.

Q: I'd be interested to hear a little about how the company works. I've heard it is a non-profit organization. Does that mean you cannot make any profits?

BG: Musea legally exists under a very special status defined by French laws, as a Non-Profit Association. This allows us to exist, to make a commercial business, even to make profit. The only limit is that this profit cannot be given to any private person or shared between investors. All profit has to be reinvested in our activity.

This is a very important aspect of our activity: we all knew, when starting this adventure, that there was no money to be made on this music. By choosing this Non-Profit status, we wanted to show to all our partners, musicians, music lovers, that our aim was not business or money, but just to share the music we love, to work in order to have it available for the largest possible audience. Our only motivation is musical passion.

Q: Does the company make a profit? What is done with the excess money you earn?

BG: Of course, we are aware of the economic reality and we manage our budget as best we can, not to make profit, but only to cover our costs, pay our bills and salaries and go on existing. If it sometimes happens to have a little money left, we invest it in promotion, productions or help financially our bands to tour in international festivals.

Q: Do people get paid a salary for their work?

BG: When we started Musea in 1985, it was only run by benevolent people. There was absolutely no money available to pay anybody. This happened for 10 years. But we reached a point where some tasks became too important to be done only on leisure time by benevolent members. In 1995, we hired an employee for logistics (shipments, stock keeping etc.). Then in 1998, two heads of Musea have been hired: Alain Robert as technical manager and myself as general manager. At that time, we spent all our evenings and nights, all weekends, all holidays for Musea, in addition to our regular jobs. It was too much for us and our families and we had to give up -- with regrets -- our benevolent status to become full time employees of Musea. Today, Musea has five employees and soon there will be seven. Of course lots of work is still done by benevolent members, approx. 15 persons.

Q: Who is currently the "Musea team" of workers?

BG: As said above, I'm the general manager, taking care of A&R matters, choosing bands and coordinating the whole thing. Alain Robert takes care of CD conception and pressing, as well as conceiving all printed matter (catalogues, promo documents etc.) and our web site and computers. Charles Wegner is responsible for commercial matters, sales and purchases. Alain Ricard is the head of the French distribution and Brennus label. Thiery Paya is in charge of logistics (shipments, warehouse etc.). Amongst benevolent members, we have Jean Claude Granjeon (Promotion), Alain Juliac (Musea Magazine), Bertrand Pourcheron (Japanese dept), Philippe Arnaud (Promotion Redaction), Jean Claude Hesse (Gazul label), Charles Zampol and Laurent Bocquet (Thundering label), Stefan Kost (Angular label), Ghislain Schmitt (catalogue), Jerome Mergen (catalogue), Yves Javier (catalogue), Albert Bergemont (Great Winds label), François Arnould (Author Rights dept), Philippe Gnana (Musea Magazine), Nicolas Juan (Promotion), Gilles Cador (Bluesy Mind label). We also have very active foreign representatives, running some Musea branches in several countries: Michael Suckow (USA), Enrique Gomez and Pascale Montiel (Mexico), Alexis Loppe Bello (Venezuela), John Bollenberg (Benelux), Jaume Pujol (Spain), Vitaly Menskikov (Russia) etc.

Q: How many countries does Musea have distribution in now?

BG: Musea is distributed in 90 countries: North and South America, all Europe from Scandinavia, EC, Eastern Europe, Russia, Middle East and Far East, Australia and

New Zealand. In some countries, we have only one exclusive distributor, taking care of one or several labels and providing all local shops with our titles. In some other countries, we deal with several importers or directly with shops and retailers. In the latter cases, we also sell directly to customers by mail order.

Q: What are the average sales for a new Musea title by a known artist? What about new artists?

BG: It is difficult to talk about an average quantity sold, as there are huge differences between our best sellers and our lesser ones: Prestigious reissues like *SANDROSE* or Pulsar *HALLOWEEN* reach quantities over 10,000 copies. For the lesser releases, we can go sometimes no higher than 300 copies! The average sales could be around 1,500 to 1,800 copies. There is no real difference between reissues and new artists: we have good sales for '70s reissues (Trace, Asia Minor, Kaipa, Neuschwanstein, Mona Lisa, Atoll, all between 4,000 and 5,000 sales) as well as for new artists (Änglagård, Now, Christian Decamps, Minimum Vital, Eris Pluvia, XII Alfonso, Galadriel).

Q: Does Musea promote concerts or have other musical activities in France, or elsewhere?

BG: We knew since the start of Musea that producing and distributing records is a completely different job than arranging concerts. So we always kept apart from this activity. It's really too much work and risk, and could cause some large loses of money that would be fatal to Musea's existence! We also know that music needs to exist on stage, not only on records. So our choice is to help financially concert arrangers who decide to include Musea bands in their programs. In that sense, being a large source of bands for concerts arrangers, we've cooperated with some famous events such as ProgFest, NEARFest, BajaProg, RIO Art Rock Festival, etc.

Q: Do you think the progressive scene is still growing now, or has it leveled off?

BG: Obviously, the progressive scene was bigger in terms of audience in the '70s. But after the dark period of the '80s when it was almost considered non-existent, it's slowly but regularly growing since the mid '80s. Today, the progressive scene is full of diversity and creativity, building bridges between different musical styles, and its audience is increasing every day. You know in the mainstream musical press in the '80s, it was kind of a shame to listen to prog! A prog lover belonged to another age, they were considered fossils! Today, the attitude of the official press is much different as after 30 years, progressive music has gained a kind of respectability, or at least the right to exist amongst other musical styles. Its a kind of peaceful co-existence!

Q: I feel that so many new labels and new releases swamp the scene, there is so much to choose from and only a certain audience. Do you think we are seeing "the law of diminishing returns" affect the marketplace today?

BG: You are right, it has become today so easy to record and manufacture a CD with the new technology that anybody can do it by himself. In the past, the investment to release a record was so high that any project had to go through the "filtration" of record companies, where professionals could select the most interesting ones. Of course, that caused a kind a market censure, but it mainly avoided the flooding of the market with music of little or no interest. Today's listeners have to make the selection themselves, they have to be more cautious. They have to be more active, to find the information by themselves in order to choose the really interesting music. This is also the responsibility of distributors to help them to make their choice. Apart from our own releases, our mail order catalogue MusiCDirect includes several thousands of independent or self-produced productions. In fact we receive from the whole world 10 times more submissions. It's our responsibility to select from this mass of music the few projects which we think are interesting for our audience, and avoid that the other ones come on the market.

Q: Does Musea have any special plans for the future to perhaps create wider interest in progressive music?

BG: Yes, we started a very special project in France these past few months in order to reach a wider audience. In the past, we had to go through distributors in order to have our CDs in retail shops. This was the weak point of the chain between us, the label and our audience. Due to the rather low quantity sold, and thus the low profit made, distributors were not really interested to invest their time on our releases. They would only satisfied the pre-existing demand, and had no real desire to increase the audience. For this reason, we started in 2000 our own distribution network in France. We have today 11 salesmen visiting over 500 record shops in France and offering directly to shop owners our releases. This offers us the ability to cut out any intermediary and thus increase our French sales. We hope to export this experience to more countries in the future.

Q: Personally I like all kinds of different musical styles. For your own enjoyment, do you listen to more than just progressive music yourself, or is that your exclusive interest?

BG: For several decades, I've opened my ears to lots of different musical styles, weird rock à la Zappa or Beefheart, New Music of all kinds, from Fred Frith to Urban Sax, recent classical or contemporary music (Stravinsky, Bartok, Varese, Boulez), jazz (Pat Metheney, Keith Jarrett, Chick Corea), folk music, etc. Progressive music has a special status in my mind as it was the music of my adolescence. I experienced some emotions connected with this music which I will never find with any other music, any time. But this is only my personal story, it has nothing to do with the music itself!

Q: What would be your 5 all time favorite progressive albums? And do you have 5 all time favorite non-progressive albums?

BG: Progressive:
1) Soft Machine - *FOURTH*
2) Magma - *M. D. K.*
3) Genesis - *FOXTROT*
4) Yes - *CLOSE TO THE EDGE*
5) King Crimson - *RED*
Non-progressive:
1) Zappa - *FREAK OUT*
2) Captain Beefheart - *LICK MY DECALS OFF, BABY*
3) Fred Frith - *GRAVITY*
4) Carla Bley - *MUSIQUE MECANIQUE*
5) Terry Riley - *A RAINBOW IN CURVED AIR*

Archie Patterson

Interview with Archie Patterson

JK: You started out covering the more Kosmische-oriented bands, and then moved on to include a wider scope of progressive rock, but typically the more avant-rock bands. Does this simply reflect the development of progressive rock in the 1970s, your own personal musical discoveries, or something more?

A: To some extent it reflects all of these. In the beginning there were few bands doing this new form of "weird" rock music. If not for Rolf-Ulrich Kaiser in Germany who started the Ohr label, who knows what would have happened? There is always a catalyst, and he was it! The normal record companies (as always) had no interest until something happened, then they stepped in to capitalize. Of course the artists had no problem leaving Kaiser behind for more money at first opportunity. I've heard he ended up with a broken heart, being sued in court and spending some time in a mental hospital in the end. As the Euro scene developed more indie labels came along and new experimental/progressive bands entered the scene in many countries. It was a rather miraculous flowering of music and culture that flowed naturally from pop music and the psychedelic revolution.

JK: A common thread throughout EUROCK's history, and certainly what seems to be the focus of your current catalog, is electronic music. Do you think electronic music has been the most consistently exciting over the years?

A: I'd have to say that the very first issue of EUROCK portrays pretty well my initial musical fascination as it features the holy trinity of Krautrock -- Amon Düül II, Can and Tangerine Dream. In the beginning there were more rock-oriented bands and fewer pure electronic artists. Over the years that ratio changed. I think that is mostly due to the fact that electronic music lends itself incredibly well to film soundtracks. For that reason it has withstood the test of time better than progressive rock on a creative level. In the beginning, it certainly conjured up imaginary movies for the mind. Now when used as a score for actual films it results in multi-media magic in the best of cases. It was also more unique stylistically in that it was a new development in terms of pop music and stood apart from the other rock hybrids from the outset. EUROCK as you say has continued to focus on that a bit more than prog rock. Part of that is simply taking what is submitted to me and picking out what I think is most interesting musically and then making arrangements to distribute it. I hear a lot, but hardly all that there is... Today everything sounds pretty derivative, but I find that electronic music, especially when cross pollinated with other musical forms (rock, acoustic, classical) can sometimes create quite an amazing new sound. The reality is that the entire spectrum of music has been changed by synthesizer technology -- for better and worse. Electronic music in the pop idiom led to a complete revolution in sound and style.

JK: Without the benefit of the internet or other publications like your own, how did you find out about all these bands when EUROCK started? (In my case it was either buying records strictly based on cool covers, or buying based on the descriptions in a 1976 JEM catalog I got at a local record store.)

A: In the beginning this music was not in the record stores. I began subscribing to the UK pop magazines *Melody Maker* and *New Musical Express* in the late 1960s (actually my grandfather bought me Xmas gift subscriptions in my teens). I then started buying Move and Zombies records and other singles/albums from the UK, spending my pittance of disposable income (while in college) on mail order from UK record stores. I think it was Ian McDonald (of King Crimson fame) who wrote some of the original small articles on "Euro rock" that I saw in those mags. Then one day I ran across an advert by the very first Virgin Records store in London's Notting Hill area (at that time a small hippie record store that marked the beginnings of the Branson empire, before the record label and airlines, etc.) They had a long list of strange new band names advertised under the label of "Krautrock." I immediately made a long distance call late one night (it was quite a different experience as I'd never called overseas before, and it cost a fortune in those days)!

I ask them to reserve 1 copy of each LP for me and emptied my bank account (a couple hundred $$$). Some weeks later a series of small packets arrived with 20 some albums by Can, Amon Düül, Guru Guru, Kraftwerk, and others. My mind was blown.

Later, a small record store/mail order called Moby Disc started up in LA and I struck up a friendship with this cat named Dana Madore who worked there. They imported direct from England and got in more of these cool new German platters. He kept me up on all the new arrivals and took lots of my money -- it was wonderful. Later one of the Moby Disc owners went on to open JEM West.

JEM East had started some time earlier, at first selling UK imports out of their car trunks, up and down the East coast. They were heavy anglophiles and not hip to the non-Kraut or other Euro stuff for some time. In fact, one of their earliest efforts promoting it came when they asked permission to reprint something from EUROCK that detailed the latest Cosmic Couriers releases. They then got into the groove and worked with Nektar, plus started distributing some other Euro bands.

JK: There was no internet then... how did you get the word out that EUROCK was available? I suppose you did this through Intergalactic Trading Company in 1975?

A: I did one initial classified advert in *Rolling Stone* in 1973 that attracted a bit of attention and then it just started to spread via the rock underground word of mouth. It took a long time, not like today where technology bombards us with new information every minute.

The founding of ITC certainly helped EUROCK and the Euro record scene here expand. We were the first to specialize in all the Euro experimental stuff and were the first ones to import Swedish, Finnish, French, Italian and many other obscure imports. There was also a company on the East coast, Peters International, which started bringing in some continental Euro imports at that time as well.

Around 1977 I moved to LA and helped start Paradox Music Mailorder, a branch of Greenworld (a company that went on to be one of the better and larger importers during that time before the bottom fell out of the marketplace in the 1980s). It was a conscious effort to expanded the ITC market further into the wholesale sphere and at its peak sold thousands of these strange albums to unsuspecting collectors across the country. As you say, the covers looked great, people experimented musically, and became converted to the cause. That was when the import scene exploded. Those years were totally amazing. I got some incredibly supportive feedback from customers and storeowners. They were astounded by what we were constantly discovering musically from all these far off countries by musicians who had never even registered on the music map in their own countries. Over the years I've gradually met many of the musicians I wrote about and they still talk fondly about how incredible it was when they read in a new issue of EUROCK that their next album was due for release in a couple months -- and in fact they were still in the studio recording it. I had very good sources in Europe at that time that helped me with music and information, but it took some time to communicate, as it was mostly all done via the post (long distance telephone calls cost a fortune back before the breakup of AT&T). It really was like a crusade for them, and me as well, because the music was so unique back then. It's very different now because music along with everything else has become basically just another commodity.

JK: As you got into the 1980s, the table of contents lists more and more bands I'm unfamiliar with, and many more formats in the reviews are listed as being cassettes. It seems like EUROCK was experiencing the emergence of the DIY (do-it-yourself) underground and global cassette networking?

A: To some extent that shift reflected the changing times in the music industry. The initial bloom was off the rose in terms of commercial record companies releasing and supporting that sort of music. The import scene in general went through a recession of sorts with JEM, Greenworld, Paradox MM, Peters International and ITC all being swept into the dustbin of history by the mid 1980s.

In 1981 I left Paradox/Greenworld and decided to make EUROCK itself an outlet for selling indie music. Due to the changing economic situation, the initial way musicians could self-produce their releases shifted to cassette. It was cheaper and easier. LPs were still being made of course, but they were more expensive to produce, they had to be made in larger quantities, and large-scale distribution was a problem. So the focus of the scene shifted to some extent and cassettes became an important part of it. The EUROCK cassette releases were among some of the first DIY productions. There were new labels springing up all around the world: DD Records in Japan, Marquee in Japan, Bain Total in France, Illusion Productions in France, Mirage in the UK, YHR in the UK, Transmitter in Germany and many others. Later as interest grew production moved more to the LP format. It was so different then as there was no precedent for doing such a thing, thus it was very hard. Then came the computer...

JK: Reading your editorials it sounds like you were/are involved in promoting progressive music well beyond the

EUROCK publication. You make references to being in charge of some record distribution companies, getting the chance to do a radio show, and you even mention giving a nine-week course on progressive music. I'd love as much detail about these as you'd care to share.

A: I've done many activities over the years related to music. The first was in 1971 when I lived in Fresno, California. It was right before the start of EUROCK when I did a weekly radio show for 3 years on the biggest commercial FM station in town (KFIG-FM). It was called "EUROCK" and on Wednesday night 9-11 PM. We played all the cosmic, German stuff at the beginning. A funny story -- Manfred Mann's Earthband was playing a concert in Fresno one time and Manfred was listening to the radio. He asked my friend, Ray Appleton, who was the station program manager, what the great music he was hearing was? My friend told him it was a show called "EUROCK," and the music being played was in fact Embryo's *ROCKSESSION* LP. I still have a couple reel-to-reel tapes of shows (in my garage so who knows what condition they are in)?

When I moved to Portland, Oregon I programmed a show for 2 years on the largest FM station there (KINK-FM). It was 3 hours of Euro and Anglo electronic and progressive music on prime-time Sunday nights, called "Other Worlds." It was incredible as we would play all this far out Euro music and the next week would sell hundreds of those albums in our local store Music Millennium (which was the parent company for ITC).

When I moved to LA I did a series of special shows on the local Pacifica public radio station there (KPFK-FM) that were quite popular with their audience. Also while in LA I got a call out of the blue from Michael Mann. He was looking for music to use as the score for his film "Thief." I made several sample tapes for him and went to Hollywood for a couple meetings that resulted in Tangerine Dream doing the film's music for him.

After I moved back to Portland, later in the 1990s, I taught classes at a local public high school. They were called "Roots of Rock." One dealt with the "rock revolution" of the 1950s and 1960s. Part of that was the 9-week series you mention that focused on "Euro Rock." It was an amazing experience talking to and sharing music and ideas with a new generation -- the classes were for grades 7-12. At one point the school decided they wouldn't offer the course any longer (it was an elective), so some 400+ of the schools students signed a petition asking that I be allowed to come back. The school reversed their decision and I taught it for 2 more years. I'd prepare sample music tapes and lectures that would illustrate a particular class topic. I actually recorded and released the Euro rock series as special limited set of EUROCK cassettes. People still today ask about them. Someday maybe I'll listen to the tapes again and see how they sound.

In June this year I'm going to start doing a column in *Progression Magazine* that will focus on other music from around the world that I don't think gets enough coverage in other publications today.

JK: In your editorial for issue #20, you introduce the Klaus Schulze interview and mention that it raises the question as to whether computers and art are compatible. How do you respond to that question now that computers are so much a part of our lives?

A: Computers and the development of CD technology have completely changed the music, the marketplace, and the entire way people function today. I'd definitely say that they have greatly enlarged the musical palette. On the other hand, today I'd pose the question somewhat differently: how come the music being made now that we have this incredible technology is not so creative? Personally I'm not sure what the answer is -- maybe it's simply a short circuit conflict between left and right brain functions? I will say however that there is very little music being released today that comes close to the creativity or emotional/cultural impact of say Elvis, the Beatles and Dylan to name just the most obvious (in terms of the mainstream). As far as the "second culture" is concerned, there is nothing nearly as innovative as Zappa, the original Magma, or the early Krautrock electronic experimentalists in Germany. Has the collective gene pool been drained, or has corporate control simply sapped us of our desire to do anything but replicate the past and become just another commodity in today's marketplace (the medium has become the message)? I think computer technology makes things in some instances perhaps too easy to do unfortunately. It becomes a struggle to escape the limitless pos-sibilities of technology and focus on the pure act of creativity. Maybe that's the Catch 22 for artists/humans today - "computers: can't live with them, can't live without them..."

JK: Affordable CDRs, web sites, MP3.com... Do you view the ease of virtually anyone making their music available as being a positive force? Do you think it's a true kick in the pants to the music-industrial complex?

A: Theoretically it makes the means of production more democratic and open to everyone as long as you follow the rules imposed on you by the software or provider. In a way the recent US election is an appropriate metaphor for this dichotomy. It illustrated the fallacy of "democracy" and "freedom" and what happens when rules and/or machinery breaks down. An arbitrary authority or system beyond rationality and reproach dictates the outcome. Here then may be the ultimate question: is music really about simply having access to better means of production, or is it more importantly about the search by creative minds for that elusive ultimate chord, tone or musical note?

I remember going to the first progressive music festival held in the USA in 1978. It was organized by Giorgio Gomelsky in NYC and called the Zu Manifestival. Some amazing Euro artists performed as well as early NY experimentalists. Also of prime importance was that the artists, journalists and fans from around the world all interacted in panel discussions and conversation. I remember one particular discussion with Chris Cutler. He said something to the effect that the problem of gaining exposure and promotion for good music was not that there was too much of it, but instead that there was too much music period, and most of it was bad; therefore it was incredibly hard to promote anything. That early invocation of the law of diminishing returns was prophetic and has become even truer now in light of the state of the music, and advanced economic systems of today. Your term "music-industrial complex" is absolutely appropriate now that control of the music business and much of the major media and consumer outlets are in the hands of a very few multi-national corps. They will end up basically controlling the major technological innovations you mention as well -- the net and its delivery systems. Soon 20 corporations (or less?) will own everything worth owning on the entire planet. Meanwhile the barbarians outside the gates (artists, musicians and those who've been left out of the post-Reagan new world order) will be left cannibalizing each other trying to get in on the action.

JK: Having been immersed in this music for so long, where do you see progressive music going in the new Millennium? Do you still hear music that is fresh and exciting, is it retro, or somewhere in the middle?

A: For the most part it is retro. Some of the original groundbreaking artists continue playing good music, but are hardly pioneers any longer. Being a creative genius at 30 years old is a rarity, being one at 50, highly improbable. Younger musicians today filter their musical and life influences through a very different cultural prism than was present during the "The Golden Age." Therefore the results are not the same. Some musicians have done this very well, but for most the level of creativity is not very high in my opinion. Others may disagree. Just because you create something (music), and make it available, does not mean that it's good. To some extent quality is a subjective question, but I always remember what one of my college philosophy professors told me -- be wary of people who say "that's only your opinion" -- that is the ultimate act of denying reality.

JK: What does EUROCK currently consist of? Of course you have the mail order catalog. Do you still do recordings released on the EUROCK label? Is EUROCK a full time endeavor?

A: The current incarnation of EUROCK consists of a printed catalog of recommended recordings consisting of the best music I've come across in the last 45-60 days. Over the span of a year there may be 4-6 of these, which form a cumulative catalog. I try to keep these items in stock as long as demand warrants it and/or I can get them, often they are limited editions. Once a year I print a complete stock catalog. To coincide with this eurock.com contains the same catalog, but with more things offered than in the print version due to the limitations of that medium. There are also many other features on the web site as it allows for much more freedom and creativity (that's a great advantage of technology and the net). I'm going to begin posting on the site new interviews with artists/music people I like, and who I think carry on the original creative spirit. There also exists the possibility (as my technological abilities increase) of adding more graphics and sound clips of each title offered and perhaps a "radio show" of the music reviewed as well. I might even do excerpts from the class cassettes perhaps. This is all contingent on technological improvements being made that are beyond me. My 20-year-old son Aaron is a genius at this and as we speak is revamping the entire site to improve the look and functionality. The main problem with the technological aspects is that he attends college in LA during the year and works for Microsoft in the summer so his time is limited. I'm always looking out for someone to become part of EUROCK in this regard.

The EUROCK Records label remains active, but only releases things that I believe in musically. I have national US distribution via DNA, but the sales-payment-returns equation is always problematic for a small label. EUROCK is my full time occupation and over the years I've developed a name for being a bit different from the rest of the pack. My main focus is on attempting to maintain a high level quality-wise. I'm quite proud of the fact that I started something from nothing, when few would even listen, and now almost 30 years later I've turned countless numbers of people on to great music made by some of the most creative musicians all around the world. My latest release is a multi-media project that I hope people can appreciate titled *THE GOLDEN AGE*. It is a CD-ROM that when taken as a whole is a rather remarkable musical and cultural history of those times. It has just been picked up for domestic release in Japan. I'd like to think that it allows those who were not around at the outset to experience that original vibe all over again; long after it has passed into history.

Jerry Kranitz
AURAL INNOVATIONS.COM

D.A.M.O. Interview

During the month of October Damo Suzuki and band made a short tour of the US in support of the excellent new album *ODYSSEY*. They played several dates along the West Coast. During their show in Portland on 10/07/00, Damo and I met up and arranged the following interview. It offers a glimpse into the past and current musical ideas of one of the original movers and shakers (literally) of "Krautrock." To see him live after all these years was a gas, and the fact that he has lost none of his energy or spontaneous creative juice was refreshing to say the least.

Q: In the last few years we've seen a rebirth of your musical activity. For some time before nothing was heard -- what did you do in the first years after Can?

D: I split from Can in the autumn of 1973, and then I joined the Jehovah's Witnesses religion. I got a normal job, at first working as a receptionist in a small business hotel.

Q: Have you been making music all this time?

D: No, not at all. From this time onward for about 11 years I never made music and had nothing to do with music scene.

Q: Your recent releases are all live recordings. Do you ever plan to do a studio album?

D: I'm not much interested in studio works. I love to play live, meet people and also interact with audiences. At the moment I'm not thinking of recording in the studio. I like the concept of INSTANT COMPOSING; so recording live is the best way I think. Living things are positive and have energy, I like to live in the moment and enjoy this moment. In front of an audience I can be natural and I feel energy coming from the people. Also DAMO'S NETWORK is not only about making music, we create a space you can enjoy AT THAT MOMENT, because it's a living creation.

Q: How does the overall vibe of the music scene today compare with the old days - in particular the concert atmosphere, business situation, etc.?

D: I can talk about this in terms of my own experiences at my shows because; I don't go to anyone else's concerts. I think the business situation has changed for the worse. But I don't worry about this so much as there's always a place to play. How much money I get is not important. The important thing is that there are people who still like to hear and see me, even if sometimes the audience is not so large. I'm really happy to meet the people coming, everywhere in the world. And if possible, I speak with them before, or after the show. That's why I began with the NETWORK group idea... I don't mean NETWORK in the computer sense. My meaning of NETWORK is a back to the roots thing. If you see the T-shirts with my logo, it says, "The Beginning was smoke - Established since the Stone Age." The first communication between people began with smoke giving someone a signal, to people on another hill who answered with smoke. That was also the beginning of music (communication with others). It all happened in the Stone Age (I think I'm getting away from your question, sorry!)

Q: What kind of audience do you get now -- mostly old fans, or younger experimentalists?

D: Oh, it is different from city to city, country to country. Last weekend we played in a very beautiful city called Schwerin, in the former GDR. There came older people, who were not able to see me in my time with Can for political reasons. No, I cannot say they are only old... mostly I'm the oldest in this situation. In 1998 I played a show in London, I saw only younger people between ages 18 and 24. I was like their father.

Q: You've played in many countries in the last years -- which has had the biggest audiences and best reaction?

D: I like every concert. When everyone is in the same space and time it can be very harmonious. For me it is a really great moment, sometimes even teardrops start falling because of my happiness. I feel very lucky to be in this moment with such an audience.

Q: To me it seemed to be sort of a "golden age" back in the beginnings of experimental and progressive rock. Does the scene seem different to you today -- less drugs, less political, less creative?

D: Fewer drugs would be not so bad. Less politics would also be OK, who can trust in politicians? On the other hand we're now living in a global family. Art should not mix with politics. I think today's generation is creative. They create in their own way. Also, it is impossible if you are living at the end of a year (now), to try and change for the better, things that have already happened earlier in the year (in the past).

Q: Do you have any special projects planned for the future?

D: Yes, I have. But, I won't tell you now. I'm just working it out, and then you will see. I don't want to talk about things before they happen. You know what I mean?

Q: Would you like to play again with the former members of Can and perhaps do a reunion concert or album?

D: Not really, maybe with Karoli? Reunion things are not for me. I'm not interested to see passed landscape again. I feel like I'm in a train traveling down the track... I'm anxious to get to the next station, and if this stop is not on map, it will be much more fun. I can paint with my music when I get there, as I like, a nice picture for the audience.

Archie Patterson

Electronic Music in Russia
Interviews with Edward & Artemiy Artemiev

The following interviews with Edward and Artemiy Artemiev were done in the latter part of 2001. They present a fascinating and rather comprehensive look at the careers of both musicians, and in addition the beginnings and history of Electronic Music in the USSR (now Russia).

I had certain preconceptions when I submitted the questions, and many of them proved to be correct, but many as well turned out to be quite mistaken. Artemiy was so kind as to do translation of much of these interviews, as well as provide me with much additional help and information. As the final form of the interviews came together I was rather astounded at how they portrayed a quite different way in which their own form of E-music came into being, and the dynamic of the society in which it emerged. In many ways their process of making music was/is quite different than the way music is made in the Western world. I was equally amazed as they described the ways in which they discovered, and formed a very personal bond with the newly discovered artists and sounds they were experiencing in the early years. Their experiences flashed me back to how that very same personal process unfolded for me, and others I know here in the West.

I have always felt that music was one of the strongest bonds that people all over the world could share with each other. It was an international language of sorts that could form cultural and social linkage no matter how disparate the countries and peoples might be. Now when reading this piece I see that I was indeed right. Artemiy, many others and myself have come to a similar place, by different routes perhaps, but ended up sharing a love for a certain sound, series of notes and colorful tone clusters. Music has brought us together, and every time we listen we are all one.

[Izolda, Artemiy & Edward Artemiev]

Interview with Edward Artemiev

Q: When did you first started making electronic music in the USSR?

EA: It was a long time ago in 1960, right after my graduation from Moscow Conservatoire, I met Evgeni Murzin, an

660, Eurock: European Rock & the Second Culture

outstanding inventor, creator of the unique photo-electronic synthesizer ANS (one of the first synthesizers in the world) and founder of the first experimental studio of electronic music in Moscow. This particular meeting predetermined my further creative destiny. A talented scientist and passionate music lover, E. Murzin became my teacher in electronics and acoustics; he introduced me to exact sciences, electronic technology, the practice of stereo sound recording. We can say, that the history of Russian electronic music began by putting into practice Murzin's electronic device – the ANS synthesizer, named after the famous Russian composer A. N. Scriabin. Eugene finished construction of his apparatus in 1955. Composer A. Volkonsky made the first creative experiments on ANS in 1958, and O. Buloshkin, A. Nemtin, S. Kreichi, S. Gubaidulina, A. Schnittke, E. Denisov, Sh. Kallosh and myself continued working a little bit later with the synthesizer.

E. Murzin called the ANS "a photo electronic optical synthesizer of sound." It is based on a photo-electronic device. The photo-electronic principle of synthesis, used by E. Murzin, implies the graphic imaging of soundings on a special plate, covered by a solid layer of black colour, which he has very exactly called "the score." Before the composer is a row of levers, on the end of each one of which is a chisel. In the necessary places the colour can be removed (with the chisels), and then one can create a system of breaks in a definite configuration: a richer sound requires drawing a line (instead of a point), and a chord required putting several points in different places. Working this way, breaks, points and lines serve to create a regulation of the brightness of light rays, directed onto photo elements through rotating discs – frequency modulators. Due to this effect of light there appears electric current, which was later transformed into real current. "The Score" also played a role as operative memory, letting the composer make various changes in the character of created sound signals, i.e. to correct the sound picture in accordance with the author's ideas.

The optical sound generators of the ANS synthesizer (there are 720 in number) make it possible to obtain 720 sinusoidal tones and compose from them oscillations having any level of complexity. The main sound range of an instrument is a division of the octave into 72 steps (144-step temperation was also possible). Practically having no temperation, ANS exceeds most commercial synthesizers of that time (for example, module synthesizers of the Moog type) by its unlimited polyphony, and possibility of strictly scientific synthesis (if you know the spectral composition of the timbre, it could be exactly reproduced on the keyboard of the device). A composer, working on the score of the synthesizer, is like a painter; he paints, retouches, erases and deposits coded pictures, immediately creating auditory control over the result. The sounds are completely unusual as a result of their spectra on the glass of the score. The device, which has a memory system, can remember these elaborations, so they can be used again later. Having no limitations in the timbres and their changes, ANS makes it possible to use artificial voices and noises of various constructions in the work.

The first thing I did when I started working on the ANS was record several of my compositions for piano on this grand apparatus and believe it or not, it was a real miracle when the graphics began playing sounds. My first piece composed especially for ANS and performed on this particular synthesizer was "Star Nocturne" (1961).

Q: At the time you began I think electronic music was not well known, even in the Western world. What were the early influences for you musically that led you to create this new form of music using some of the first electronic instruments?

EA: I would divide into three parts the nature of the music in its present state. There is a large, perhaps the main group of musicians, composers and artists, who have had traditional training, and experience in an academic school. There are a lesser number of musicians, who are making their creative search in a completely different area – electronic music; for the most part they do not come into contact with the academic school. The third part is rock-musicians.

So it happens, that the "academic" musicians are virtually unaware of the events taking place in the "electronic" area, for them it does not exist, they neglect it or are only making some timid attempts in this area. However – and this is already quite clear – during the last twenty years electronic music has become like an avalanche, and one cannot just ignore this fact. On the other hand, the musicians and more often technicians – engineers, who deal with new electronics in its extreme form – the avant-garde – do not look for contact with the traditional academic schools. It is like two opposite poles. As for rock-musicians, they use both approaches, but in a definite context.

I consider, that a true new music – perhaps the primary new one – will appear as a result of the combination of electronics (I mean not only the instruments, but also new acoustics, and all the other things which electronic technique will give us), and the academic school, traditional acoustic instruments. For me, this is the main direction, and it may absorb all the rest, depending upon the personality and conception of either, one or another author.

Creative work in the field of electronics is in many respects indebted to rock music due to the interest among the musicians, because of its energy, its lively sounding, and very emotional range.

I had a good academic school education. But upon experiencing the opera "Jesus Christ Superstar," that became a decisive factor for me (I consider this opera as one of significant phenomena of the 20th Century). I can say that I was formed as a composer in many respects thanks to rock music. There were practically no electronics in that opera, but there was a completely different vision embodied in its use of traditional Biblical themes, which were previously only embodied musically in academic ways, beginning with the works of Claudio Monteverdi, or maybe earlier, and concluding with Schoenberg's works ("Aaron and Moses"). I have always felt they lacked a certain sort of creativity, a more open emotional string, power and energy. All this I heard in rock music, and this really shook me. Rock music has taught me not to be ashamed of emotions – you do not need to hide them!

Rock musicians have created a principally new "sound" – a brighter one, with shining arrangements, like melted gold – this is my perception. Now it lives in my subconsciousness, which is very important for my creative work.

There were two turning points in my music career. The first one was in 1958 when I heard the composition "A Hammer Without Master" by Pierre Boulez. It impressed me greatly and created a desire in me to discover different sound spaces. The second was at the end of 1960s when I heard the music of such rock groups as Pink Floyd, King Crimson, Genesis, Yes, Gentle Giant, Led Zeppelin.

In general rock music influenced me

greatly. Under its influence I composed the cantata "Ode to Herald of Good," which was commissioned by the Olympic Committee for the opening ceremony of Olympic games in Moscow in 1980, also a cycle of instrumental-vocal poems "The White Dove," a symphonic picture "Ocean," and others…

In my compositions I often use instruments and a style of presenting sound material from the "arsenal" of rock music. Even more I use all this stuff for film music (soundtracks). If we add to this mixture my electroacoustic predilections then I can say that I exist in some three-dimensional musical space. I think that this helps me to work with such absolutely different film directors as Andrey Tarkovsky and Nikita Mikhalkov.

Q: How did you manage to get access to equipment and recording facilities back then?

EA: My familiarization with electronic music has coincided with the appearance of the first synthesizers and I have come rather a long way from "drawing" sounds on the ANS and exploring analog keyboards like the Moog to computer technologies, and it's impossible for me to prefer this or that period in my activity because the process of composing electronic music depends on the unique individual opportunities offered by the apparatus you're playing and working with. Two-dimensional fields of performance and synthesis of sound appear while you are working on the ANS and this particular field allows the author to see his composition wholly in its dynamic and spectral structure. All of this is united in performance macro graphics, and I must say that the opportunities of editing here are great. (Recently I visited a laboratory, where the ANS stands and became convinced that the possibilities of this machine are far from being exhausted.)

As for analog synthesizers, I can say that the attractive qualities of analog synthesizers are both the special qualities of the sound, and a very convenient, accessible and evident way of real time control. And, lastly, computer technologies step by step assimilate all achievements in the area of electronic music by uniting them in a system that controls the synthesis of sound, space and performance.

The shortcoming of this technology (I hope a temporary one) I consider to be the excessively complicated, multi-stage and labor-intensive programming access to all elements that form the nature of sound, its synthesis, editing, processing, etc.

The field of electronic music extends endlessly and this process is irreversible. It absorbs everything that is connected to a sound. Today, when we speak about the modern music environment, we mean thousands of schools, musicians, and currents, directions that are separated from each other and mostly disorganized. I think, that now the means and technology of electronics are capable again to unite them all in one powerful river – a river of music. As it was in Mozart's time, now there is the possibility for a truly new music, as music has always been born hand in hand with the developments in new technologies. Thus, for example, Bach's music became possible thanks to the tempered clavier.

Really, amazing changes have taken place in this sphere for more than 50 years. Having begun my involvement with laboratory research in the field of synthesis of sound, we now have such technology and tools that can allow us to solve any creative task. Moreover I think that the present level of technology and engineering outstrips the most courageous imaginations of musicians. So now a composer again has appeared as though before a clean sheet of a musical paper.

There is an infinite creative sphere that lies ahead. All you have to do is to create. Everything is possible here.

Q: What was the relationship between the government and arts/music scene in those days? It seems to me the Soviets might have considered music as a form of bourgeois entertainment and not liked it – was this true?

EA: Musical life in the former Soviet Union during the Brezhnev regime was supervised, but not as strictly as literature, painting, theatre and cinema. Musicians pretty much had access to the complete spectrum of information that occurred in other countries. We could order, via Soviet people working abroad, notes, LPs, books on music and the government didn't pay any real special attention. Even some so-called "home-clubs" of various music orientation (avant-garde, jazz, rock and classical music) appeared in Moscow at the end of 1960s. It happened because average people couldn't afford to buy highly quality equipment and LPs of foreign musicians. Such LPs cost 50 rubles per copy, which was practically a half of the average salary of the engineer of those years (the salary of the average Soviet citizen was 110-120 rubles.)

The Soviet government, management of the country, and its various institutes supported those musical directions and styles which are based only on classical traditions. That's why only certain kinds of music were played, broadcast and propagandized on radio, TV and in concert halls. In Soviet times, jazz and rock music were always associated with bourgeois culture and that idea is well illustrated in the quote from the well-known Communist writer Maxim Gorkiy: "Jazz is music for thick people," that was famous during the days of Soviet regime.

Q: Was there such thing as a "commercial" market for music produced in those days? Were there record stores? Did the music get played on the radio?

EA: Of course there were no "commercial" markets during Soviet era at all. Even the concept of "the commercial music market" didn't exist. The entire country worked and lived by "The Plan," and the government for every five-year period created this Plan. By the same Plan, Melodiya (our unique and only recording label in the country) could publish and release only a strictly supervised amount of LPs and MCs. The Ministry of Culture bought only a certain amount of compositions, etc. So the state dictated styles, genres and direction of all musical production in the spirit of Marxist aesthetics. The state was the unique and only customer during the days of Soviet regime.

Q: I believe the record label Melodiya was owned by the government. Was there any limits on what type of music could be released, or perhaps there was much more freedom of musical expression than I might imagine?

EA: Really, there was only one recording label in the country that published and issued music on LPs and MCs. Its name was "Melodiya," and the government owned it. The central office was in Moscow and it had branches in all Soviet republics. There was also a so-called "Arts Council" that gathered once a month to listen and select new compositions for publication on Melodiya. In those times mainly classical music both domestic and foreign was issued on this recording label. I can't say that they didn't publish modern music at all. Sure they did, but they issued strictly limited editions of jazz, pop and, very rarely rock music. Such modern genres of music were considered to be alien music that carried a certain harmful ideological influence to the hearts and souls of Soviet working people.

Q: After Glasnost, did the situation change radically in terms of more freedom for production, distribution and sale etc.?

EA: Two most important things happened during the period "Glasnost" – 1) The opening of the gates of information, and 2) The beginning of the opportunity to communicate freely in all areas of human activity. If "Perestroika" had never happened, then I'm sure that I would never have received an opportunity to work in Hollywood and to have lawyers and managers abroad. As for distribution and sales, I think that it's better to ask my son Artemiy about this. He is doing a great job with his label "Electroshock Records" and he is doing it very well.

Q: Do you still work on new music today, or do you leave that to your son Artemiy?

EA: "I'd Like to Return," was my last composition in the field of electro-acoustic music. I composed and recorded it in 1993. Then I took an almost 10 year break from working in this genre to devote all my heart and soul to finishing an opera entitled "Raskolnikov," based on ideas contained in the novel by F. Dostoyevsky's "Crime and Punishment" which I completed in 2000. I consider it to be the major product of my life. Besides during this break I scored several Russian, American and European feature films. But, perhaps, the main explanation of my temporary withdrawal from the electro-acoustic music scene was the necessity for me to make an assessment of my past methods of working musically and prepare for the new projects that I will undertake in the future in an area connected to audio-visual performances.

Interview with Artemiy Artemiev

Q: At what age did you get interested in your father's music?

AA: I was interested in my father's music since my birth. In 1966 (the year when I was born) we lived in a small one-bedroom apartment, my father, my mother, my grand mother, a concert Steinway grand piano and myself. As you know my father is a composer and my mother (I think you don't know this biographical fact) is a professional pianist. So I was listening to music all day long. I listen to my father's music and classical music of various composers performed by my mommy. My favorite place was under the Steinway. I made a playground there and liked to listen to the music under it. You know music sounds rather mystical if you listen to it under the piano. Have you ever tried this? To me I felt sometimes like "Alice in Wonderland." On the one hand you are listening to the music, but on the other hand it's not the music you are listening to, but the sounds under music. Yes, and maybe these sounds/timbres subconsciously appear in my compositions. We lived in this apartment until

1973 and then moved to a new three-bedroom flat, leaving this apartment to my granny. She died there in 1982 and the Soviet government took it together with the Steinway grand piano. Where is this old Steinway now? Nobody knows.

Q: Were you able to study the way he recorded and experimented with music and go to the studio with him?

AA: You know my childhood was a very interesting period of my life. At the age of 7–8 I started visiting the Moscow Experimental Studio of Electronic Music, the meeting place of very interesting composers – my father, Vladimir Martynov, Alexei Rybnikov, Edison Denisov, Alfred Schnittke, Stanislav Kreichi, Sofia Gubaidulina, Schandor Kallosh, Alexander Nemtin; musicians – Tatiyana Grindenko, Gidon Kremer, Alexei Lyubimov, brothers Sergei and Yuri Bogdanov; film directors – Andrei Tarkovsky, Andrei Konchalovsky (very young at those times) Nikita Mikhalkov; painters – Mikhail Romadin, Sergei Alimov, Vladimir Serebrovsky, Pavel Anosov and quite many people who are well-known now in Russia and abroad. I was also lucky to meet there two famous men – Italian and American film directors Michelangelo Antonioni and Francis Ford Coppola.

In that studio the world felt absolutely different. It was the 1973-79 period -- "the scent of Soviet flowers" and in there, in the dark of the small hemispheric room amazing happenings went on. The music of Herbert Eimert, Luciano Berio, Yes, King Crimson, Genesis, Klaus Schulze, Tangerine Dream, The Who, UK, Isao Tomita, Karlheinz Stockhausen, Luigi Nono, Pierre Schaeffer, Gyorgi Ligeti, Edgard Varese, Milton Babbit, Pierre Boulez, Francis Dhomont, John Cage, Pierre Henry, Earle Brown, York Holler, Takehisa Kosugi, Steve Reich, Henri Pousseur was played in this studio. And I must say that it was not just a simple listening to concerts played on the tape recorder with "son et lumiere" (sound and lights - which was very "cool" and avant-garde in those days). It was a detailed discussion of every musical composition.

There were also performances of my father's band "Boomerang," underground electronic music festivals and various informal art-rock events that also took place inside the building of the first Moscow Experimental Studio of Electronic music. A lot of people were coming and these gatherings were more like a Bolsheviks' meeting at one of the secret addresses that was just about to be busted by the Tzarist secret service than a cultural "underground" arrangement. I was more than intrigued by the atmosphere of the place, people, music and while listening to the music of the above-named composers and to the discussions after, naturally, I was inspired by it and started getting more seriously interested in genres of electronic, electro-acoustic and serious rock music.

Moscow Experimental Studio became my first school of music. I saw how my father worked with the ANS synthesizer, SYNTHI-100 and I was amazed. For me it was pure musical magic combining different twinkling lamps, buttons, levers, meters. My father, surrounded by huge apparatuses, two sound engineers always wearing black clothes and heaving beards and long hair, smoke that comes from their cigarettes. There was loud, very strange music in a dark basement where all these happenings frightened not only people who are used to this kind of music and atmosphere of the studios, but also local inhabitants and even policemen. There I first tried the ANS and SYNTHI-100 and made my first steps in the field of experimental-electronic music.

Q: Did you have any formal music

education?

AA: Yes, I graduated from Moscow High School of Music as a classical pianist. Of course the next step was the Conservatoire, but when one day I came to the concert of Sviatoslav Richter and saw him playing the piano I realized that I would never get to his level. So I went into rock music and played in various Moscow rock groups as a keyboard player. At the same time I entered Moscow Institute of Foreign Languages where I studied for five years and graduated with a Degree.

Q: What kind of music did you listen to while you were young? Did you have access to American rock and roll?

AA: As I stated, I started with British progressive and art-rock, German "Krautrock" music and experimental electro-acoustic music. You know it was difficult and dangerous during part of this period to get Western music into the former USSR. There was an Iron Curtain during this time and all Western cultural things were forbidden, but people tried to find a way out of this situation and practically every week someone would bring 8-10 new LPs to the Moscow Experimental Studio to listen and discuss the music. As I could remember there was no American rock and roll music among these LPs.

Q: Do you remember the first electronic music album you ever heard from the cosmic music scene?

AA: Yes, sure. It was the LP *PICTURE MUSIC* by Klaus Schulze. I liked it very much. It really impressed me, though I was only seven years old. By the way there were several LPs that impressed me greatly in my childhood and influenced my future activity as composer and musician. These are: *LIZARD, RED* and *IN THE COURT OF THE CRIMSON KING* by King Crimson, *PICTURE MUSIC, MIRAGE* and *X* by Klaus Schulze, *RELAYER* by Yes, *RUBICON, RICOCHET, STRATOSFEAR* and *FORCE MAJEURE* by Tangerine Dream, *ALBEDO 0.39* and *SPIRAL* by Vangelis, *QUADROPHENIA* by The Who, *SECONDS OUT* by Genesis. *UMMAGUMMA, DARK SIDE OF THE MOON* and *ANIMALS* by Pink Floyd and electro-acoustic compositions by Karlheinz Stockhausen, Luigi Nono, Pierre Schaeffer, Gyorgi Ligeti and Francis Dhomond.

Q: Do you think you were more influenced by the work of your father, or by the electronic pop music experimentalists from the West?

AA: It's rather difficult for me to give an answer to this question. I think that I collected and later assimilated into my style many different genres of music. I mixed them and created my own works based on these different music styles. I call it my "point of intersection." In 1997 I produced a CD under that name.

Q: Today I think the ways of production and music scene in general are much different in Russia than they were when your father worked. Where do you record your music, in a private studio or the same studio where your father used to?

AA: We have our own separate private studios where we work and record our compositions. I even have two studios – one for composing, recording and mixing, the other for mastering CDs.

Q: Do you own your own equipment, or use the some of the same equipment your father used?

AA: I have my own studio equipment and it differs from my father's. Of course it's not the best studio in the world, but it suits my needs.

Q: I know there is an underground scene of younger bands and musicians today making electronic music in Russia. They send me their own privately-made CDs. Do you ever play live performances, or have any connection to this scene?

AA: Unfortunately my music isn't suitable for live performances and that's why I never play live. What I do is tape concerts. I know about the existence of an underground scene in Moscow and many musicians send their tapes and CD-Rs to Electroshock Records for possible publication on our label. I even received tapes from Ukraine, Belarussia, Lithuania and Estonia. But unfortunately this music doesn't suit our label. They send us sweet "saccharine" New-Age tunes or Schulze-Tangerine Dream-like sequences, or something that they called "experimental-synthetic music" based on preset timbres of their synthesizers (mostly Roland and Korg). It's impossible for me to publish such kind of music on our label. Maybe it's good, maybe it's serious music by a new generation and I don't understand it? I don't know. I know only one thing – I must try and produce what I consider to be the best experimental, electro-acoustic and avant-garde music it on our Electroshock Records label.

Q: Does your music ever get played on the radio there?

AA: Yes, sure on radio and TV and quite a lot I must say. I also use a lot of music by the Electroshock Records artists in my radio-show, also called "Electroshock."

Q: What is the situation for promotion, sale and distribution of rock and electronic music today in Russia? Is it much different than it was for your father?

AA: I think that the situation with rock, electronic, experimental and serious music was much better during 1970-1990 and not only in Russia, but in the whole world. People could think, speak, write interesting books, shoot interesting films, and compose interesting music. They had inspiration; imagination and they were spiritually strong. Now it differs greatly as this is the time of a more modern-non-thinking-empty-soulless culture where everybody can do what he wants and no one tells them that they are wrong because thousands of people do the same things. The new generation has no authorities. All you can hear now is ugly modern popular music that blares out of every discotheque and nightclub, music that is aggressive, deconstructive and so faceless that the sound of every other musician seems like the continuation of a song by a previous one.

I also want to say some words about music scene in Russia and the Western countries. Now there's no difference between the music scenes in Russia and the Western countries. Here what is popular, is what's popular in the West – trance, hip-hop, rave, rap, house, etc. – in other words, non-thinking dancing styles of music. The mass media promotes only such types of music. It seems that the world has gone crazy. As for serious modern music I must say that the situation with electronic, electro-acoustic, contemporary, experimental and avant-garde music is very specific. People are interested in the above-mentioned genres of music. I can say this because of the positive reactions to my monthly lectures, radio and TV program on Moscow cable television (both programs have been very sporadic so far however because for my show I use only non-commercial serious music). Many people also complain that it's practically impossible to get music of this kind in our country. Really, it's very difficult to find CDs by Alejandro Vinao or Francis Dhomont, or Pierre Schaeffer for example.

Right now Electroshock is working on the possibility of opening a special CD store where we'll be distributing, selling and promoting only electronic, electro-acoustic, experimental and avant-garde music. If everything works out okay, then we'll open this particular CD store somewhere at the end of Autumn '01. As for various events devoted to the above-mentioned non-commercial genres of music in Moscow, I can say that once every three months the Russian Association for Electro-Acoustic Music stages concerts of serious electronic, electro-acoustic, experimental and avant-garde (EEE&A) music. Also we have the "Alternativa" festival devoted to EEE&A music, and besides that many interesting composers and musicians often visit Moscow for concerts and performances. Many people (by the way many young ones) attend these events. They're sick and tired of techno, pop, rap, hip-hop and other pieces of commercial shit. They're very interested in listening to and buying electro-acoustic, electronic, experimental and avant-garde music.

Now the cultural situation in the world is very sad (our countries are not the exception). Few people want to read serious books, watch serious films, and listen to serious music. The motto of the younger generation is "switch on rap and I'll cry." Yes! They call rap or techno "the highest level of art" and we can see tears of joy on their faces while they listen to 120 beats per minute. When we ask them who are Michelangelo or Leonardo da Vinci - they say, "Oh! I know! These are the names of the famous turtles, mutant heroes." My God, it's scary! And you're speaking about development. Development of what? Degradation? I think so. What is going on with our poor planet, do you know, I don't?

Q: Culturally is electronic music (and rock for that matter) still considered Western and a corrupted form of art?

AA: No of course not. You can listen to whatever you want.

Q: What is the life of a musician like now in Russia? In the Western press we hear stories all the time about how Russia is falling apart economically and the old Communist Party has now become the new criminal mafia that controls all trade and commerce. Is it better now for an artist, or was it better before (if you can remember those times)?

AA: Russia lives by its own laws that differ greatly from the laws of the other world. Unfortunately your press is right. Our economy is ruined after the crisis that we had in 1998, and of course we are economically falling apart. Now corruption and crime are everywhere. People even think that a new era of the KGB comes with Mr. Putin. The old Communist Party controls all trade and commerce since the end of Communist era and I think it'll control every sphere of economy and business until the old-age leaders die. Now Communists became so-called "Democrats." They changed their color, but the mentality remained the same. Unfortunately our country is heading toward a global catastrophe and very few people understand that fact. We have no new resources; we can't find money to repair the old equipment (we even don't dream about buying new things), our gas tubes are damaged (I think that you heard about the natural gas crises in our Far-Eastern region), the metro areas (practically in every Russian city) need to be repaired. People can survive only in big cities like Moscow or St. Petersburg. If you go to the country, then you see that life there differs greatly from life in Moscow. There is terrible poverty in the countryside. P-O-V-E-R-T-Y.

Imagine, the salary of the average man in

Russia is $100-150 a month, but you need at least $800-$1,000 per month to make both ends meet and to survive in the big city.

Of course we have a lot of pirate markets in Russia. For example, if you want to buy a CD or a video in the CD-store you must pay at least $20 per CD there and if you go to the pirate marketplaces you'll pay there $1-2, maximum $5 per CD. So it's again the question of the wages you make. If you receive $100 per month and want to buy a CD – where will you go, to the shop, or to the pirate market? I think the answer is clear. We have two official pirate markets in Moscow, "Gorbushka" and "Mitino." There you can buy whatever CD, video or software you want. The price is $1 - $5 per CD or CD-R.

When musicians from the Western countries come with to visit me I usually take them there and they are amazed with what they see and they rush to buy software CD-Rs. Imagine!

As for your question concerning when was "it was better for the artist," I can say that on one hand the life is obviously better now, but on the other hand, it's not. Living is better now for those who play "Russian pop-music," a certain style of "pop" that I'm afraid I can't find any comparisons for. I don't think you have such kind of genre in the West where people who play serious music are still trying to survive.

Q: You have released quite a few productions on your label. I would think that perhaps your father worked with the aid of government grants? Do you get support from government arts subsidies like other artists in European countries do, or do you finance it all with your own money?

AA: I must say that you are a little bit mistaken thinking that my father is working with the aid of government grants. His main work is scoring for films and he never got any aid from the government. I don't get support from government arts subsidies; I finance the production of CDs from my own pocket. I'd love to get support from he government or whatever (as it's very hard to work with non-commercial music), but nobody gives it to me though the government loves to say that they "have an official organization and recording label in Russia that promotes various forms of modern serious music and culture." That's not true.

Q: At one time in the West this type of electronic music was considered very revolutionary and "cosmic." Now it is much more a result of production techniques controlled by the nature of the highly advanced technology and the state-of-the-art studio equipment available. Do you have any conception of your music as spiritual, cosmic, and some kind of social expression? Or is it more a question of scientific sound exploration, based on the technology you have at your disposal?

AA: It's difficult for me to speak about my music, so I leave this to critics. All I can say is that I have no so-called system of composing music. I combine the use samples, sonic textures and rhythm. I can say that I like to create atmospheres, but I try to create a particular atmosphere for this or that composition, not with simple preset timbres of the synthesizer like when you put your finger on the key, hear the sound changing through the LFOs, ENVs, OSCs, DCAs, etc. and exclaim – Oh, what a great cosmic sound I made by only pressing on the key! No, it's not like this. I think that atmosphere is the combination of atoms of sounds created by you with the help of synthesizer, sampler, sound card of the computer and acoustic instrument, or human voice. You mix all the elements you need and begin working on it, creating your own specific sound to make people feel your composition with their mind and body. Technology only helps you to create the music you want. If your heart, soul and head are empty, then technology is useless.

Q: Do you sell a lot of CDs around the world and make your living by doing this or have some other job as well?

AA: I compose music, scoring films and theatre plays, producing and selling CDs around the world. I'm producing radio and very sporadically the TV-program "Electroshock," reading lectures, writing for the *Music Box* magazine (a big Russian music-magazine) where I'm heading the review department "Monitor" and making interviews with foreign electronic and electro-acoustic musicians and trying to survive in this country.

Q: What plans do you have for the future – an increasing number of productions, further collaboration with Western musicians, soundtracks? Anything special?

AA: In summer of 2002 I'm planning to produce for the Electroshock Records label 10-12 new CDs, and stage the "First Russian International Festival of Electronic, Electro-acoustic, Experimental and Avant-garde Music-Electroshock."

The CDs will be released to coincide with this. It is going to be a 10-day Festival of artists, musicians and media from all around the world scheduled for the end of July, early August 2002. Featured will be Edward Artemiev, Manuel Göttsching and Ash Ra Tempel, Art Zoyd, Hans-Joachim Roedelius, Tim Story, Michael Rother, Dieter Moebius, Mario Schönwälder and Detlef Keller, Jeff Greinke, Matthias Grassow, Iasos, Andrew Poppy, Michel Huygen to name only a few. There will also be MANY MORE…

The new CD productions scheduled as of now are - Artemiy Artemiev and Peter Frohmader: *TRANSFIGURATION*, Artemiy Artemiev and Phillip B. Klingler: *A MOMENT OF INFINITY*, Stanislav Kreichi: *VOICES & MOVEMENT*, Anatoly Pereselegin: *FASTGOD: E-PSALMS*, Antanas Jasenka: *DEUSEX-MASHINA*, Electroshock Presents: *ELECTROACOUSTIC MUSIC VOL. VII*, Oophoi: *BARDO*, Artemiy Artemiev and Christopher DeLaurenti: *57 MINUTES TO SILENCE*, Edward Artemiev: *THREE ODES* and Artemiy Artemiev and Karda Estra: *EQUILIBRIUM*.

Archie Patterson

[Photo © the Fricke Family]

Florian Fricke Interview

As the year 2001 came to a close Florian Fricke passed away. Thanks to Gerhard Augustin in Germany, Florian's good friend and mine, I was one of the first in the USA to hear Popol Vuh's music way back in 1970 when he sent me a copy of *AFFENSTÜNDE*. There's a story I like to tell about Popol Vuh from the days of EUROCK's initial incarnation as a FM radio program in Central California.

In late 1972 I aired a long 1-hour set of Popol Vuh music that featured one side each of *AFFENSTÜNDE, IN DEN GÄRTEN PHAROAS*, ending with *HOSIANNA MANTRA*. Near the conclusion there came a phone call from a woman who wanted to pass along a heartfelt thanks to the station for playing that music. She said her young daughter was teething and had been fussing all day, unable to nap, and in general miserable. As the show progressed and *HOSIANNA MANTRA* came on she said the baby calmed and drifted off by shows end. She was eternally grateful and asked that we please play it again in future.

That story illustrates the true power of great music, and Florian's magical musical talent in particular. When I passed along the news of his death, I got many people telling me of the special place some of his particular albums had played in their lives as well. They all had once again dug them out and were engaging in their own little personal memorials to the beauty and joy his music had brought them.

This interview done by Gerhard is incredibly rare. I had tried a couple times myself to arrange something, but have never seen any interviews with Florian. In fact, at times Popol Vuh was referred to as a "phantom band out of Munich" by people in the music business in Germany for Florian was a very private person. Therefore I consider it a wonderful gift to present here the first known English interview with him. Read it, listen to your favorite album of his, and remember him fondly.

His music will continue to eternally be an invocation of the Spirit of Peace for all who listen...

Gerhard Augustin: You have done a lot

of music for the films of Werner Herzog; do you know him personally very well?

Florian Fricke: Yes, I am a good friend with Werner Herzog for many, many years. We don't see each other too often anymore because he is very busy with his films and I am very busy with my music. And that is the reason why we see each other, or meet each other, only for our mutual work. There are some things that I do admire about Werner Herzog. The thing I admire most is his consequence in following through the things that he is planning to do, and he is actually doing them. Werner Herzog is one of my few friends that are very famous and have, regardless of their fame, not changed at all. Their personality has remained stable and he is in no way different from the way I knew him 25 years ago. He still drinks his beer from the bottle.

GA: By reading the old Mayan book *"Popol Vuh"* you must have gotten the idea of the band's name. What kind of inspiration, what kind of feelings did you have when you were reading the book?

FF: When I read the book for the first time, I got ideas all of a sudden by which I was able to define other old books. I found a key in the book of *"Popol Vuh."* I was able to understand the way people in the very early days described the creation of Earth. And the way of human evolution. I was touched like by a thunderstorm. In those days, in the late '60s, when musical groups were looking for names, they were usually looking for a name that was expressing their music within the name. Otherwise it doesn't have any particular meaning.

GA: But also, do you think that your feeling, or the inspiration that you got from the book *"Popol Vuh"* was also based on the counterculture movement on the '60s?

FF: In a certain way, yes. In those days the society was not only a political society, in Europe we had the '68 revolution which started in Paris, but also was part of the German change in culture and society, and music was a great part in this change. But there was also a spiritual revolution. We have discovered the Eastern part of this globe, of this world, over and over again. The culture of the old Maya, of the book "Popol Vuh," was one way for us to find ourselves, re-define our ideas in early days. So we were actually looking for these kinds of inspirations, where we could refer to holy books, whether it was The Bible or the "Popol Vuh" (the book of the Maya culture), or the Bhagavad-Gita, like this. Different sources of information were coming to us.

GA: Now, tell us about your gigantic Moog Synthesizer III, the system of the late '60s, which was only used by very few musicians. What sort of ideas did you try to express with the electronics of the Moog synthesizer?

FF: It was a great fascination to encounter sounds that were until those days not heard before from the outside. It was the possibility to express sounds that a composer was hearing from within himself, which in many cases are different from what a normal instrument could express. Therefore, this was a fantastic way into my inside consciousness, to express what I was hearing within myself.

GA: Why did you stop playing the synthesizer in '72?

FF: I always had this great desire to find an instrument that could express a human voice, of vocals or the singing of a girl for instance, by electronic means. When you listen to *IN DEN GÄRTEN PHAROAS* on the A-side you will find this voice. And all of a sudden this voice that I felt was in myself, really came into my life when Djong Yun appeared. I wanted to do something really new, in those days, and the synthesizer was part of what I wanted to do. You should know that over the last 25 years I have always tried to create new music and new styles of music. I think otherwise it would be too boring.

GA: Did the title *AFFENSTÜNDE* have a double meaning for you? Like a first step for the band's genesis of the book *"Popol Vuh"*?

FF: Yes, it had a double meaning. Each title has to be open for associations. That is a creative offer. What I, myself, really understand from *AFFENSTÜNDE*, is that it is the moment when the human being becomes a human being, where man becomes man. When a human being becomes a human being and is no longer an ape any longer. So that is my double meaning for *AFFENSTÜNDE*, that is the moment where the human being of a monkey turns into the human being of a human kind.

GA: I have thought that *AFFENSTÜNDE* could have been a kind of 'trip-music' for you, and you were inspired by your own drug experience. Is this right, or how do you feel about that?

FF: We were all, in one way or another, involved in some sort of excitement, which you may call drugs, whether it was taking LSD, or smoking hashish, grass or marijuana – minor experiences. But you know that the way electronic instruments could be used in those days offered such fantastic opportunities to express oneself. There's no doubt about it that my music has delighted a lot of people who were into drugs or smoking or taking trips or whatever, that was part of our musical culture in those days. And my music was especially geared towards this clientele. I did not make music for classical music lovers, but for people that were into contemporary, new music. But I did not make the music because of that.

GA: There are two songs in *IN DEN GÄRTEN PHAROAS*. Please tell me what idea did you have before making these tunes, and were these tunes improvised in the studio?

FF: One is a song that was recorded live in a church, "Vuh." And the A-side, "In Den Gärten Pharaos," Frank Fiedler and I, who had already worked on the *AFFENSTÜNDE* album, created this song actually in our home studio and later went into another studio to do the mastering for it. The last part of the song was recorded in the studio actually, like most of our music has been recorded in studios, this was the Fender piano in the end.

GA: It is said that *HOSIANNA MANTRA* is a musical Mass.

FF: Yes, in a way it was a Mass, a church Mass. But not for church! A conscious reflection upon religious origin is included in this music, but not in particular to any religious groups.

GA: In *HOSIANNA MANTRA* there are some new personnel, such as Conny Veit and Djong Yun. How did you meet them, and how did you come to play with them? Let's first talk about Conny Veit. How did you meet him?

FF: Actually, most of the musicians have always sort of found their way to me to play with me. I met Conny Veit at United Artists, my record label at the time, in the office of somebody I knew there [actually GA himself – Ed.]

GA: But this is how Conny started playing with you, he came to your house and you guys just sat down and played?

FF: Yes, and he has did this every day. And that is how we actually prepared for almost half a year to records the album *HOSIANNA MANTRA*.

GA: And then Djong Yun, how did she come into the picture?

FF: Djong Yun came to Munich; she is the daughter of a famous composer. She got the melodies, she was listening to what we were playing and she heard the melodies and started singing with us. Yeah, we called it rehearsal! [laughs]

GA: Did you, Conny Veit and Djong Yun ever perform as a band, publicly?

FF: Yes we did, actually, in Lieberkosen and Munich.

GA: Tell us, what was the theme and how did you get the ideas of recording *HOSIANNA MANTRA*? And then can you tell us something about the artwork?

FF: In creativity there are not always reasons. Some of the things are just flying straight through the window. But at that time I was especially interesting in using first the words, and then making music to the words, in other words there were existing lyrics that I wanted to add music to. I wanted to convey the depth of meaning contained in a word, and then transform this into musical sounds, a from of musical expression. That is one way of composing music for me. I don't always do it, but on and off I keep having an interest in composing in such way.

GA: The name *HOSIANNA MANTRA*, where does it come from?

FF: *HOSIANNA MANTRA* is actually a combination of two different cultures, two different languages, two different lives. It has a dual meaning, "Hosianna" which is a religious Christian word, and "Mantra" from the Indian religion of Hinduism. Behind all of that I was convinced that basically all religions are the same. You always find it in your own heart. And the music of *HOSIANNA MANTRA* is really touching your heart. It is made to touch your heart. That is why you can call it a Mass. A Mass for your own heart.

GA: Can you remember any episodes in making the album *HOSIANNA MANTRA?*

FF: I do remember when you ask me about episodes. One of the episodes was that Djong Yun was combing her hair more than she was taking time to rehearse our music. It was much more important to her personally to be pretty and beautiful for all of us. To look the way she felt comfortable in order to sing comfortably. We had absolutely nothing against that because she had very beautiful hair. Her hair is as beautiful as her voice. She was really a very nice, comfortable part of the group. Her behavior and everything was very soothing. But in general this production was no different from all the other productions. We'd go prepared into the studio having a certain amount of ideas and music available, and then improvise in addition to what we had already constructed. I've always looked for the fact that whenever we make music, or we were producing music, that whoever is part of the group playing, is responsible for their own playing within that formation. Groupies were not allowed. [laughs]

GA: How did you really get to meet Djong Yun, the very first time? Have you heard about her from other friends?

FF: In those days I was living in Munich in Halachein. Musicians from other towns and cities that came to town came to Munich, by recommendation or desire or whatever, came by my house, and we were just jamming. One day Djong Yun came there. I was playing with Andy Fix, the guitar player, and he was talking about this incredible girl from Berlin, this singer from Berlin, and he said that I had to meet he. That she was fantastic. I was working with Esther Ofarim in those days, but it didn't work out because she refused to sing Christian lyrics, being Jewish I guess, so she didn't want to interpret this kind of song. Which I did understand. In those days there was not this competitive feeling among musicians, and the contacts were loose and open. People were just visiting each other for the sake of music, and not to discuss their recording contracts. In a certain way we were all hippies in those days.

GA: I feel that this album *HOSIANNA MANTRA* is one of the greatest albums that German rock has produced in the '70s. What, in your opinion, does this album mean to you, and what position does this album take in the career of Popol Vuh for you?

FF: When *HOSIANNA MANTRA* was released we had a great feedback from the press and the public. There were these voices that said *HOSIANNA MANTRA* was certainly the most beautiful record that had been made until that day. Personally, I still consider this music as incredibly beautiful. But very rarely do I listen to music that I have made in the past. I'm always living with the music that I'm now realizing, or producing, or making, whatever. So I don't really dwell in the past, and I don't think too much of the past, I think more about tomorrow, the future, and what's happening right now.

GA: Why did Djong Yun not join *SELIGPREISUNG?*

FF: She was in America, and only returned for the record following *SELIGPREISUNG, EINSJAEGER & SIEBENJAEGER*. So actually it was because she was in America in the days when we made *SELIGPREISUNG*. I do regret that today, because I think I haven't really done a good service with my own voice to my record. So it would have been nice if Djong Yun had been there.

GA: Can you tell us the concept, or the theme, the basic ideas of the albums *EINSJAEGER & SIEBENJAEGER, DAS HOHELIED SALOMOS* and *LETZTE TAGE, LETZTE NACHT?*

FF: *EINSJAEGER & SIEBENJAEGER* is finishing, or closing of the cycle. *DAS HOHELIED SALOMOS* is the beginning of a new cycle. In addition to the guitar player Conny Veit, I invited Danny Fichelscher, the drummer and guitar player with Amon Düül, to play with me. And that was the beginning of an extremely fruitful collaboration. We have practically made music since then without interruption, we have been playing together since then. For example, the A-side of *EINSJAEGER & SIEBEN-JAEGER* was really played and recorded in the first try, in one piece in the studio, and that was it. We didn't change anything at all. Actually I was giving in so much on this album to the style of Danny Fichelscher, the music of Danny Fichelscher, that we have sort of stuck to this formula for the following seven years.

GA: I have a feeling that *EINSJAEGER & SIEBENJAEGER* and *DAS HOHELIED SALOMOS* were recorded in the same studio, and at the same time.

FF: No, they were not recorded at the same time. Quite to the contrary. I think we made *DAS HOHELIED SALOMOS* one year later, after *EINSJAEGER & SIEBENJAEGER*. In between there were studio dates and recording dates and tours. There were a lot of things happening. So it was not really at the same time.

GA: You often change a melody that you used before, and you use it again in a different tune. But the melodies in *EINSJAEGER...* seem to appear for the very first time there.

FF: This is what you could say about Mozart as well, because this is the individual style of an artist, that you identify the artist with a certain melody, sound, feeling or whatever it is. You are right insofar as that we have been using these melodies as sort of a trademark in the different works that we created. And we have been playing this in various ways, different ways. And sometimes we even like these new, different versions. Compared to the other albums, *SELIGPREISUNG* and *HOSIANNA MANTRA*, we felt that this music, with Danny and Djong in *EINSJAEGER...* was a more contemporary, modern sound and music. But whatever we were doing in those days was really hermeneutic music. It's one way of jubilation; it's our expression of jubilation.

GA: Please tell us, is *DAS HOHELIED SALOMOS* your homage to the Old Testament, or is it dedicated to Djong Yun?

FF: *DAS HOHELIED SALOMOS* was taken from the Bible, yes. It's a mystic love song. The whole album was dedicated to love, that's all.

GA: Around the period of *IN DEN GÄRTEN PHAROAS*, did you write the type of tune of *AGUIRRE*, and the album, why was it released in 1976, but the film was made in 1972?

FF: Don't ask me about those confusing facts about my musical record career. I'm not a part of that. The music industry has created these unfortunate circumstances. And if I would start talking about this in detail, I would have to mention names and persons and people, so I'm trying to avoid that. Insofar that some of these are not even living in our country anymore.

GA: Tell me something; are you actually playing on the album *YOGA?*

FF: This is part of the same chapter. *YOGA* is an unauthorized release. Some Indian musicians visited me in my studio, and somebody else took the tapes and sold them under the name of Popol Vuh, but it had nothing to do with Popol Vuh, really. I'm playing harmonium, and organ. I think it was released in Italy.

GA: I saw the film "Herz aus Glas" ("Coeur de Verre") and I found that not very much of your music was used. In the album with the same name of the film, *COEUR DE VERRE*, is Popol Vuh's original album to be the soundtrack for the movie?

FF: It was different. Sometimes they're produced for Werner Herzog's work. Sometimes he came to my house and he asked please open your box, where I have my tapes from my productions. When we are listening to music, sometimes he lifts his finger and says this part of your music would be great music for a film. Sometimes we have done in a very short day and night, time in studio at the end of production from his movies, chosen the music like this. The special music for *COEUR DE VERRE* ("Herz aus Glas") is Popol Vuh, but sometimes he needs music from Richard Wagner. But Richard Wagner never made film music for Werner Herzog.

GA: Now we come to a question about the French Egg release of *NOSFERATU*. This is a compilation of already-released materials, and unreleased old materials, with new songs. Did you choose the tracks?

FF: It actually was Part Two of the original soundtrack. The actual film music, the way it was composed for this movie, is on the record *BRUDER DES SCHATTENS, SOHNE DES LICHTS*. And when Werner was already almost finished with his film, he came to me and asked, "Florian, do you have music to be afraid by?" And I thought no, no, no, no. But I remembered some electronic pieces in my big, big, big, box of old material from the early years, and in this box I found 'angst music.' And so we made a second record, besides *BRUDER DES SCHATTENS*... we made 'music to be afraid by,' *NOSFERATU*, part two, released by a French company.

GA: Would you please tell us something about Maya Rose and Guido Hieronymus, who have played on recent Popol Vuh albums? What kind of background do they have, and what were they doing before they joined Popol Vuh? First Maya Rose, the singer.

FF: Maya lived in Yucatan in Mexico, and at different occasions she sent me some tapes where she was singing freely. I had listened to them and I had put it to the side, because in those days I was working with Renate, the Amon Düül singer, on the record *FOR YOU AND ME*. After many years I listened to these recordings again and I found the voice for an idea that I was working on which became the album *CITY RAGA*. To be precise, my son Johannes, he actually gave me this tip to do this kind of record. He said that this voice would please everybody.

GA: So this is how you met Maya, on tape. Did you ever see her personally?

FF: Yes, many years before in Köln. She was a member of the Breathing Therapy Society group, but moved to Yucatan and stayed in touch with me by sending these strange, wonderful cassettes, with her voice on there. When my son was hearing this voice he felt that it was really special.

GA: Guido Hieronymus, who has played on all the recent Popol Vuh Albums, what kind of background does he have?

FF: Guido is a bit younger than Frank and I are. He has studied music at the Conservatory in Munich. He is producing and playing with many different musicians in Munich, in the music scene. And when we started to work together, it was not clear from the beginning that Guido would eventually become a member of Popol Vuh. But by working with him over the last couple of years we have come to a point that Guido is very important to Popol Vuh. We are friends, we have a great understanding.

GA: Your work on *CITY RAGA* seems to be very different from your previous works. Do you feel that this is a drastic change, or a natural extension from your previous work?

FF: I have answered this question before; I always find new styles, different forms of playing, that I'm incorporating into the music of Popol Vuh. The essence of my music remains the same. The forms are changing, but the essence remains the same.

GA: Thank you very much for your interview.

FF: I want to tell you one more thing about what I feel to be the essence of my music. Popol Vuh is a Mass for the heart. It is Music for Love. Das ist alles (that is all)...

Gerhard Augustin
February 1996

Savage Rose Interview

One of my earliest Euro-rock discoveries was the Danish band Savage Rose. Their first album to be released in the USA was *IN THE PLAIN*, in 1970 (which was actually their second album proper, as they had an earlier Danish release simply entitled *SAVAGE ROSE*). *IN THE PLAIN* was stunning, with compositions and dual keyboards provided by the brothers Koppel that created an adventurous musical mix of idioms – pop, classical, jazz and blues. The group also possessed one of the most exotic and enchanting female vocal presences I've ever heard – Annisette.

Initially they gained wide critical acclaim in *Rolling Stone*. They had two other albums released domestically, *YOUR DAILY GIFT* and *REFUGEE*. These also garnered rave reviews, but a great band from Denmark had little chance for big time recognition in America back then. After their 15 minutes were up, they vanished into legendary status.

Over the years they have never stopped making music. As a "fan" and promoter of sorts, I did all I could to obtain their other very-hard-to-come-by releases. I found the later albums to be different in some ways, but equally compelling. Also thanks to friends who had relations in Denmark, I pieced together bits and pieces of their history, allowing me to publish an article and review or two.

Some years later I finally met with Thomas and Annisette after they re-located to Los Angeles. The personal stories they had to tell and their musical history were fascinating and inspiring. I discovered that not only were they great music artists, but two of the best human beings I'd met in my long years in the music business.

They now live in LA and have just released their 19th album - *FOR YOUR LOVE*. The entire Savage Rose catalog has been re-mastered and reissued as well. In November they did a showcase gig in LA, and have plans for other concerts in 2002. I think you'll find the following interview with Thomas and Annisette has some interesting history and insights in it – enjoy!

Q: Let's begin with a bit of personal history. I think you both have quite unique and very different beginnings for your careers. How and when did you each get started in music and performance?

Annisette: When I was 6 my older half-sister was a popular film child star in Denmark, and my mother arranged for both of us to perform at fun fairs and carnivals. My sister was blonde and Nordic, I was little and dark. Standing on the truck we were singing children's' songs and little pop songs in sunshine or rain. When my sister was to go to an actor's school, my mother told me I was not to perform anymore. That was the moment I found out I couldn't imagine a life without singing to an audience. I still see those faces as I saw then when I was 7, full of expectations and confidence, and I just had to be there with them. I talked to a girl friend that played the piano, and we put together a repertoire of pop songs and Italian songs, which I loved, and we continued performing on our own at family parties. Later on, I met a real rock band; they asked me to play the tambourine in the band. I was thrilled, a band with real electric guitars!! They then let me sing background vocals, and much later I was allowed to sing lead vocals as well. We played in discotheques; the weekends they had live bands - one British alternating with a Danish band, five hours each with 5 one-hour breaks in between! The discotheques were where I found out about Aretha, Tina Turner and the whole incredible R&B scene, and I knew that was what I wanted to do. My band and I did a single with a cover version of "River Deep Mountain High" and it went straight to the top of the charts. That's when I met Thomas...

Thomas: I, too, was focused on music since I could walk. My father was a classical composer and pianist, and when I was four I found his piles of blank music paper. I remember myself lying on my stomach, drawing millions of notes on the paper until the paper was almost black! I then went to my father's room and asked him to play what I had written, which was of course pretty much impossible, but I guess he didn't want to disappoint me, put the paper on the note stands of the grand piano and played the best he could what I had written. I was in another world. This was magic to me: you could write signs on a paper, and a big, dark, multitude of sounds would pour out of that big instrument and right into my own heart!! I knew that was going to be my life! They wanted me to have piano lessons, but I was screaming and impossible to drag to the piano. They left me alone, and I met with the magic instrument when nobody was looking, sat down and let the tones rise from its body. I improvised endless symphonies, which took shape over time, and suddenly I was able to write it down on that blank music paper and play it myself! Before I was 19, I had written string quartets, symphonies performed by major orchestras, and an opera performed for 2 years by the Royal Opera. But in '67 something started happening in the streets of Copenhagen: youngsters started occupying slum buildings and universities and new fantastic music was exploding across all borders, like Dylan, Jefferson Airplane, Jimi.... I just had to be where all that was happening and I wanted to create a band. That's when I met Annisette...

Q: I believe Savage Rose actually began as a band in 1968. What was "the scene" like at that time in Denmark? Were there a lot of experimental bands and political activities?

T: Yes, in '68 The Savage Rose had taken shape. Our orientation was primarily international. To us that was one of the incredible new things about the youth revolt. Denmark is a very small country and internationalism was like the doors and windows had been broken open and fresh air was pouring into our minds. That's why we created the songs with English lyrics...to become part of a worldwide movement. At that time a lot of the new movement in Denmark was pretty locally oriented. The hippies were mostly singing in Danish, they made new venues for music where they were singing hippie songs and jamming for days and weeks, and the air was thick with smoke. The intellectuals of the movement were not particularly fond of The Savage Rose, because we didn't really take part in all this. Honestly, to us it was slightly uninteresting, narcissistic, and unaware of the big perspective which to us meant a whole lot more than just getting stoned and being together: Social Revolt, Struggle for Freedom, breaking down borders, putting an end to a system that killed people everywhere including their own street corners in order to be able to continue feeding on the blood of human beings all over the planet. We began to socialize with the squatters and the sprouting anti-Vietnam-war movements and became inspired by the music they brought with them. "It's Alright Ma, I'm Only Bleeding..."

Q: A pop band from Denmark hardly seems of commercial interest for an American major label. How did it come about that you actually got your records released in America (luck or...)?

T: Our first albums were an explosion in Scandinavia where they opened a hole in the wall for creativity, Scandinavian music with an international message and potential. Our first albums got released in around 40 countries. We were at the Star Club in Hamburg one day, on French TV the next, in London for recordings with Giorgio Gomelsky on the third day. George Wein called us and suddenly we were on the stage of the Newport Jazz Festival between Sly And The Family Stone and James Brown. Two L.A. managers, George Greif and Sid Garris, knocked at the door of our rehearsal room outside Copenhagen and took us on a big tour of the US, an album recording in Rome (*YOUR DAILY GIFT*) and another one at Mick Jagger's mansion in the UK (*REFUGEE*) with Stones' producers Jimmy Miller and Joe Zagarino.

Q: Did you ever do any concerts or tours of the USA in those early days?

T: The US tour was a fantastic experience. It started out in Detroit at the Eastown Theatre with John Mayall and Taj Mahal... but the second show was interrupted because somebody in the audience (who were all stoned) had started a fire because the flames looked so beautiful or something, so the theatre burned. We made great friends with the US audience in Chicago at the Beaver's Club, as well as at several other larger huge venues across the country. The tour ended in L.A.

Q: Do you have any memory of how well those early releases sold over here?

T: In the meantime we got incredible reviews, including some by legendary rock critic Lester Bangs of *Rolling Stone*. And records started selling. Suddenly "Speak Softly" was #10 in Memphis, "My Family Was Gay" somewhere else. And we were *Billboard's* Hot Pick. The managers had this huge contract from RCA, but things went bananas when they wanted us to go to Vietnam to encourage the boys, and then have a picture taken shaking hands with President Johnson. That would be great promotion they said. "No way," said we, "we're not at war with any Vietnamese peasants; they never did us any harm." When I told George this, he was so furious he was about to punch my nose. He said we're going to downscale the RCA contract. We said okay, if that's what it takes. They kept our passports and sentenced us to 3 shows a day in their newly opened, extremely unsuccessful 'Gregar Club' in Hollywood. The sign said THE SAVAGE ROSE - DANISH ACT. Because at that time the term 'Danish Act' was often used to denote porn shows we had in the audience a lot of weird old men with big overcoats. But the waitresses became our beloved friends, they were all black and they took us home for food and R&B Sundays in South Central, and they were absolutely wonderful. We shall never forget these great Americans, so immensely different from the average Hollywood show-business guys. These warmhearted and hospitable people were so much bigger in a human perspective, and they started our deep love for the real American people, which has lasted for a lifetime now.

Q: For some years after the last US release I heard nothing and had assumed Savage Rose was no more. Then one day I read, in *Billboard Magazine* I think, that you had quit recording for major record labels, stopped singing in English, began living in a working class community in Copenhagen, started playing benefits and were recording only political records. This was a very interesting to me. Can you explain a bit about what actually happened at that time?

T: After returning to Denmark we wanted to give back some of the love we had received from black people in the US and recorded *BABYLON* - dedicated to the black freedom movement. The album starts with Annisette shouting "We dedicate this first song to Malcolm X"... who was murdered just when he took 'black nationalism' to a higher level, stressing race less and social revolution more. In other hands, he was becoming a whole lot more dangerous to society. Polydor didn't say a word when they heard what we were doing, but this was the first album they did not release internationally, and in Denmark it sold less then 2000 copies... But the Black Panthers had no objections to this music so we joined Huey P. Newton for numerous rallies around Europe, and we were invited to the mass rally they planned in Oakland when Bobby Seale was close to becoming Mayor of Oakland. We never got there, however, because only a week before the event the Panthers chose to cancel, because they had information the FBI was to mess up the rally and they didn't want the confrontation. After this, we kind of broke our ties to the music industry altogether. They didn't want us to get involved in anything that looked like real life, and we didn't want to submit. We wanted to preserve the heartbeat of the music and remain true human beings, and not be corrupted into frozen pop icons like so many of our colleagues. That was a great decision, because we stayed sane and close to our audience, while the icons tended to kill themselves with booze or junk, because they didn't like what they saw in the mirror. We then wanted to connect with the progressive movements of Denmark, and start exploring our own language. In short - we went underground. We had no money and moved to a rough working-class neighborhood, where everybody warmly accepted us. It was like coming home. We played for free whenever our music was needed for street parties, demonstrations, strikes, solidarity meetings, and funerals when somebody got hit on their heads by the cops. Our impact grew explosively and after a while we moved all over Europe from Greenland to the Palestinian refugee camps in Lebanon. Musically, we needed a simple set-up for all this and became a trio with Annisette, a drum (John Ravn), and my accordion or piano when there was one. We recorded a number of records without the 'assistance' of the record industry, and sales figures grew from album to album and were available from the Polar Circle to Spain.

Q: You have played some very provocative places, a wide variety of countries, venues and people; can you talk a bit about some of the more memorable ones? Here I mean in particular large pop festivals, Greenland, refugee camps, prisons, etc. You can talk in detail or only in short bits, but I found your stories about these experiences absolutely fascinating, so share what you like.

T: This period became the most important experience of our whole career. Music took on a hugely greater meaning – being just a direct instrument for true human communication of feelings, love, solidarity, mutual anger, humor. There were no 'filters' between the audience, and us we had rid ourselves from all the managers, agents, record guys, publishers and lawyers sitting on the shoulders of every successful artist and tying them up in a spindle of unwritten (or written) rules and limitations. The PLO invited us to Lebanon where we sang and played along with the Palestinian refugees who sang and played as well. Snipers were shooting at us, helicopters flew over at nighttime and kalashnikovs tore through the silence. We wrote 'Song Of Palestine' at Arnoun, the mountaintop in South Lebanon from where the Palestinians in the distance could see their homeland that they were separated from by a wall of death. We still play that song at our concerts this year, because the world still neglects this tragedy and permits a criminal and bloody occupation, which is actually a tragedy for the Palestinian people and the Israeli people alike. We played in the picket lines of the dock workers, in support of kindergartens in the slums, in the prisons, everywhere, - and because the industry saw we actually had a huge audience we started to get invited to the big festivals again.

There are so many more stories to tell as well…

Q: One of my favorite albums by Savage Rose is *DODENS TRIUMF*. That was music composed for a ballet performance. What is the story behind that musically, and the various performances?

T: The ballet *Dødens Triumf* ("Triumph Of Death") was created in 1970 by choreographer Flemming Flindt and me, Thomas. The Savage Rose performed the music. The story is a surrealistic one about a strange disease killing men, women, and children, eventually killing all of mankind. There's a lot of weird humor and drama in it. We made it for TV first, and it was broadcast in many countries. You can interpret the story in a number of ways; to me it was about the old dying colonial power of Europe desperately trying to revive herself through oppression and militarization. In '72 The Royal Ballet performed it at The Royal Theatre, and for the first time the theatre was invaded by older ballet lovers as well as barefoot youngsters of the streets. It became the greatest success ever for the Royal Ballet, with performances continually until only a couple of years ago, and a US tour as well which included the Metropolitan Opera in NYC. This October, it is being re-staged at another theatre in Copenhagen. For the first time the music will be performed live – in a re-arrangement by Catbird, the new band with our daughter Billie as the lead singer and talented producer/composer Frank Hasselstrom as arranger and director.

Q: In the 1990s you have once again begun to work with major labels and become very popular in your homeland. How did you come to a decision to get back into the "mainstream"?

T: We were contacted by the music business at several occasions – because we had proven that we had been able to generate a huge and faithful audience even without the business. We felt we would be able to mess with the industry because these underground years had strengthened us and we knew exactly what we were able to. We knew, that if it did not work cooperating with the business, it could never become a disaster - we had already tried to be on our own and that did not silence our music. We also felt that our music had a right to be distributed and supported like everybody else, and a right to be distributed worldwide through the mainstream organizations.

Q: To be successful at doing anything for over 30 years is miraculous. To be creative in the pop music realm for that long is also rare. It almost seems as if you are a Danish national cultural icon of sorts. Do you have any idea how Savage Rose could go from having hit singles, change musical orientation, then win Grammy awards and remain incredibly popular for decades in Denmark? Did you have a "master plan" (laugh), or...?

T: The greatest disaster to an artist we feel, is being separated from the lives and experiences of their audience. Those unfortunate artists find themselves alone with a mirror; they only have one story to repeat again and again: that of frustration and despair. If they have a story to tell at all, it's because a lot of artists living in their golden cages forget their story day by day. Money or Grammies can never make up for the loss of a real life. We took the conflict on ourselves and remained human. We know our path was risky – but life is risky, and if you don't want to take the risk of life you already got one foot in the grave.

Maybe it is just that – with all the injustice, suffering, and greed, we still love life and the humans. We love the Mexican families in downtown Los Angeles with their kids beautifully dressed up for the Feast of the Virgin Of Guadeloupe. We love that big fellow in the prison who was caught at the age of 17 stealing a few bucks from a gas station and then taken to the basement of the prison – where the guards sprayed him with cold water for a whole night – for the fun of it... still in prison after 25 years, but with a heart as innocent as a kid inside his huge body. We love the little lady down at the supermarket who always smiles so truly even if she is totally exhausted after 10 hours of work. We love the brave youngsters who dare to gather in the streets and tell the truth even when times are risky like now and gray shadows of fear rule the world. We love the ten million Spanish workers who did a general strike last week to let the world know they don't want war, racism and oppression for anyone. We love the 14-year old kids dancing right in front of the stage when we play at a beautiful Danish summer festival like the one we did yesterday, we love to look into their eyes and feel their expectations and hopes for the concert, for the future, for their lives.

Q: A few years back you came to the USA

to live – why did you choose to leave Denmark?

T: We came back because the waitresses of the Gregar Club were so kind to us back in 1970... Because we love the American people – the true American people that is – not the fabricated 'American Hero' icon the governments and some Hollywood films point to in order to excuse their own suspicious behavior. We're still very much at home in Denmark and don't feel we have really left our country. And this year we met a couple of hundred thousands of the Danish at our concerts. We have kids, friends – no, we never really left. We're Danish, American – citizens of the incredible Planet Earth!

Q: There was some question about your being able to stay here at one point. Has that been settled now?

T: We have had green cards for a couple of years now and we're OK!

Q: Is there a chance the new album will be released in the USA?

T: A lot of structural and financial problems within the Edel Record Company have effectively prevented releases outside of Denmark until now. We're working hard to get this disastrous problem solved as soon as possible. At least they are available from our website www.thesavagerose.com, and soon from EUROCK...

Q: I know you both have very strong moral positions about the issues of today. How do you think as artists you can best work in a positive way to help people understand the importance of being concerned about their fellow humans?

T: Of course our main language is music. True music opens little doors to secret chambers in the hearts, where all the unused human resources are hidden. That's what you can feel when a melody line or musical sound touches your heart and makes you feel sweet pain inside. That feeling means getting in touch with everything you really are, everything you are that isn't allowed out in the 'normal' life you're leading. At a concert, true music can make ten thousands of people feel that and make the event much more than just 'selling' some music. It becomes an important human event, a mutual promise for the future. A first picture of what life on this planet could become, when greed one day becomes an extinct dinosaur of the past. But also, we can't be exclusive and not participate in what we and our fellow humans feel is important. Now what's important is to stop the wars, stop the oppression of poor people around the planet, including inside the USA where millions of kids are suffering from poverty while a small group of paranoid speculators live in grotesque wealth. No amount of dollars can make anyone feel secure, and these people are the most afraid people on the planet. The only real security there is staying true to real humanism, love life however risky it is, and respect and share the riches of the planet. Music can be a peek into that future, which is actually no hippie dream but something very real, a vision shared by billions of humans. They will overcome all divisiveness, including racism and all the other obstacles, and find each other. When that happens, the Bush wars will seem as distant as the medieval burning of 50 million innocent people - the 'witches.' The magic of music is, that all that huge vision, the collective vision of all mankind, can fit into one simple little tune, which any street worker can whistle without even noticing.

Archie Patterson

eurock

Also Available!

The Golden Age (CD-ROM)

A History of Progressive Music from Germany, France, Spain, Italy, Eastern Europe, Japan, South America and points beyond!

In March 1973 *EUROCK Magazine* published its first issue pioneering the field of space rock journalism. To date 47 issues have published. In 1980 *EUROCK Records* released its initial production becoming one of the first independent labels Internationally specializing in electronic and progressive music. Over the next 20 years 40 albums were released. In 2000 *EUROCK* is releasing a totally unique new production. *THE GOLDEN AGE* is a Multimedia CD featuring 40 minutes of music, enhanced with CD-ROM technology - a complete Audio / Visual experience.

"EUROCK, one of the original alternative music magazines"...
 -Stephen Hill (Hearts of Space)

"EUROCK is a rare example of, I'd call it culture. The work of a man who not only had a definite idea and followed it, but also had the true spirit for the matter (that's rare)."
 -Uli Trepte (Guru Guru / Spacebox)

"Our music began shortly before Archie started to write about it. I have to point out that he was the very first to take E.M. seriously and who did a fanzine about it. This was some 4,000 miles away from where the music was happening -- in a pre-FAX era!"
 -Klaus D. Müller (manager Klaus Schulze)

The Music: Since 1980 Japanese master musician Hiro Kawahara has been exploring the realms of electronic and progressive music releasing albums as leader of the groups Osiris, Dr. Jekyll & Mr. Hyde, and more recently Heretic. His new album, featured on *THE GOLDEN AGE*, contains 40 minutes of music recorded between 1980 & 1999. A dense Zen electronic tone poem, it echoes the works of such luminaries as Kitaro, Steve Roach and Robert Fripp, yet has a distinct quality that puts it in a category all its own.

The Magazine: A Multimedia CD-ROM extravaganza, *THE GOLDEN AGE* contains 1,100 Articles, 300 rare Photos, 1,200 Reviews, 350 Discographies, a complete Index + 25 minutes of 16-bit, digitized audio / video by Amon Duul II, Popol Vuh and Urban Sax. In addition, there is a brand new issue of *EUROCK Magazine*. It contains recent articles and interviews featuring some of Europe's original journalists and musicians who created the scene.

$30
[+ $2 P/H US, $5 Foreign]

Multimedia CD-ROM
< MAC OS8 ~ WIN 95/98 ~ Audio CD Player >

Eurock Online: www.eurock.com - Email: apatters@eurock.com
P.O.B. 13718, Portland, OR 97213 USA - Tel / Fax (503) 281-0247

Appendix

Eurock Productions (to date):

Cassettes:
EDC01 **Plastic People** – *THE HUNDRED POINTS*
EDC02 **John Livengood** – *BALADJIN*
EDC03 **Fondation** – *SANS ETIQUETTE*
EDC04 **Ilitch** – *PTM WORKS*
EDC05 **Eskaton** – *4 VISIONS*
EDC06 **Pascal Comelade** – *SLOW MUSICS*
EDC07 **Cyrille Verdeaux** – *IMPOSSIBLE SYMPHONY*
EDC08 **Cyrille Verdeaux** – *CRYSTAL CITY*
EDC09 **Cyrille Verdeaux** – *WIND & FIRE*
EDC10 **Cyrille Verdeaux** – *HEART VISIONS*
EDC11 **Cyrille Verdeaux** – *SHAMBALA*
EDC12 **Cyrille Verdeaux** – *THIRD EAR*
EDC13 **Joël Dugrenot** – *SEE*
EDC14 Various Artists – *GERMAN ROOTS*
EDC15 Various Artists – *GERMAN ELECTRONICS*
EDC16 Various Artists – *FRENCH PIONEERS*
EDC17 Various Artists – *FRENCH UNDERGROUND*
EDC18 Various Artists – *ITALIAN RENAISSANCE*
EDC19 Various Artists – *EAST EUROPEAN PROGRESSIVES*
EDC20 Various Artists – *SOUTH AMERICAN PROGRESSIVES*
EDC21 Various Artists – *ZEN ELECTRONICS*
EDC22 **Don Robertson** – *DAWN*

LPs:
EURLP01 Various Artists – *THE AMERICAN MUSIC COMPILATION*

CDs:
ECD 2001 **Gandalf** – *MORE THAN JUST A SEAGULL*
ECD 2002 **Gandalf** – *& FRIENDS*
ECD 2003 **Robert Julian Horky** – *VOYAGER*
ECD 2004 **Gandalf** – *LABYRINTH*
ECD 2005 **Erik Wøllo** – *IMAGES OF LIGHT*
ECD 2006 **Green Isac** – *STRINGS & POTTERY*
ECD 2007 **Gandalf** – *REFLECTIONS*
ECD 2008 **Tim Story** – *THREADS*
ECD 2009 **Gandalf** – *GALLERY OF DREAMS*
ECD 2010 **Erik Wøllo** – *SOLSTICE*
ECD 2011 **Green Isac** – *HAPPY ENDINGS*
ECD 2012 **Tim Story** – *IN ANOTHER COUNTRY*

Appendix

CDs (Continued):
ECD 2013 **Dweller At The Threshold** – *NO BOUNDARY CONDITION*
ECD 2014 **Tim Story** – *3 FEET FROM THE MOON*
ECD 2015 **Dweller At The Threshold** – *GENERATION, TRANSMISSION, ILLUMINATION*
ECD 2016 **Dave Fulton** – *HARD PARTICLES*

CD-ROMs:
ECD 3001 *EUROCK – THE GOLDEN AGE*

Books:
EUROCK: EUROPEAN ROCK & THE SECOND CULTURE

Stay tuned to http://www.eurock.com for future developments....

Index

.019, Michael, 383
1980, 269
2 Bis, 217
3-D Sound, 149, 157
5th Ball Gang, 186
7th Records, 544
XII Alfonso, 553, 650
50 Foot Hose, 14, 579

A Barco Do Sol, 494
A&M Records, 114, 621
A.R. & Machines, 127
Aaltonen, Juhani "Junnu", 102, 302
Aaltonen, Vesa, 305
ABC Records, 172
Abraxas, 142
Abrial Stratageme Group, 189
Actuel, 537, 586, 621
Ad Majorem, 189
Adamis, Anna, 173
Adantacathar, 442
Aditus, 397
ADN, 593
Adorno, Theodor, 203
Adrian Marcator, 429
Adt, Daniel, 489
Aera, 160
Aerolit, 135
Ag Geige, 483
Agi, Yuzuru, 390
Agitasjon, 362, 593, 595, 597
Agitation Free, 27, 236, 244, 555, 585, 628, 647
Ahents, Princed, 381
Ahvenlahti, Olli, 302
Air Compagnie of Lyon, 452
Akita, Masami, 413
Aksak Maboul, 271
AKT Records, 543
Albrecht, Joey, 158
Albrighton, Roye, 37, 158
Alcatraz, 199
Alcazar, Louize, 233
Alimov, Sergei, 666
Alkatraz, 235
All Ears Records, 153, 197, 386, 624
Allegres, Los, 268
Allen, Daevid, 196, 199, 419, 546, 616
Alpes, 216

Alpha III, 494
Alpha Centauri, 454
Alpha Ralpha, 549
Alquinta, Eduardo "Gato", 470
Alta, Hans, 254
Alta, Rob, 254
Altaï, Armande, 424
Altman, Robert, 197
Alvarado, Carlos, 258, 269, 380
Amargos, Joan Albert, 200
Amazing Sounds, 525
Amboy Dukes, 39
Amenophis, 189
American Bandstand, 8, 196
Amiden, Jorge, 493
Amiga Records, 481
Amnesty International, 207
Amon Düül I, 1, 17, 34, 503, 514, 578, 588
Amon Düül II, 1, 14, 17, 41, 43, 64, 144, 155, 192, 235, 244, 269, 362, 502, 514, 515, 522, 555, 577, 582, 588, 611, 630, 647, 652, 676
Amplitude, 189
Anastesia, 510
Anderen, Die, 483
Anderson, Dave, 503, 613
Anderson, Julio, 471
Andre, Jean-Luc, 431
Andromede, 189
Andrst, Lubos, 140
Ange, 14, 81, 124, 189, 192, 323, 491, 546
Änglagård, 650
Angustére, 641
Anima, 425
Anosov, Pavel, 666
ANS synthesizer, 661
Ansell, Kenneth, 594
Antonioni, Michelangelo, 666
Apetrea, Coste, 269, 309, 366
Apostolis, Antymos, 135, 136
Apple computer, 438, 479
Appleton, Ray, 655
Apras, 189
April Records, 157, 221, 249
Aquapolis, 425
Aquarium, 644
Arachnoid, 189, 491
Arai, Manami, 386

Araujo, Marco Antonio, 495, 505
Arcane Records, The, 193
Arch Angel, 565
Archimedes Badkar, 212
Archipel, 189
Area, 81, 129, 184
Arista Records, 181
Arkham, 189
Armengol, Francesc, 377
Armstrong, Frankie, 179
Arnaud, Gérard, 404
Arnaud, Philippe, 649
Arnould, François, 489, 649
ARP synthesizers, 128, 258, 487, 527, 559
Ars Antigua Group, 485
Arsenic, 189
Art Bears, 395, 620
Art Zoyd, 189, 212, 228, 271, 394, 413, 473, 515, 549, 671
Art & Music Records, 639
Artcane, 549
Arte Moderno, 379
Artemiev, Artemiy, 660
Artemiev, Edward, 660
Artemiev, Izolda, 660
Arti e Mestieri, 81
Artificial Head system, 149, 158
Artman, Gilbert, 123, 149, 271, 280, 405, 452, 550
Arumekat Oiron, 389
Asanovic, Tihomir Pop, 223
Ascaris Megal, 189
Asfalto, 200, 376
Ash, Julien, 641
Ash Ra Tempel, 27, 34, 59, 67, 70, 237, 339, 442, 462, 498, 499, 514, 554, 572, 577, 585, 588, 628, 671
Ashra, 358, 554, 559, 588, 591
Asia Minor, 189, 491, 552, 650
Asphalt Jungle, 189
Asseline, Jean-Pol, 116
Assumpcao, Zeca, 496
Astarte, 463
Aste, Marcello, 281
Atem Magazine, 212, 243, 274, 302, 523, 592
Atenas, Jamie, 485
Atila, 461

Index

Atlantic Records, 157, 328
Atlantis, 75, 155
Atoll, 189, 192, 327, 491, 549, 650
Atom Cristal, 189
Atome, 189
Attrition, 442
Aubiat, Nicole, 219
Audat, Alain, 150
Audion, 593
Auger, François, 123, 326, 539
Augustin, Gerhard, 610, 672
Aura, 591
Auricle label, 593
Automatons, The, 288
Ayers, Kevin, 19, 321
Azahar, 199, 376
Aznavour, Charles, 618
Azobout, Jean Louis, 188
Azuma, Yoshitaka, 412

B-Team, 142
Baader-Meinhof Gang, 85, 123
Baah, Reebop Kwaku, 157, 295
Baar, Hans, 148
Babia, 378
Bacalov, Luis, 82, 184
Bacamarte, 496
Bacchus, 189
Bachauer, Walter, 585
Bachmann, Claus Henning, 311
Bacillus Records, 37, 237
Bailey, Derek, 177
Bailey, Jacqueline, 257
Bailleux, Jean-Marc, 451
Bain Total, 310, 654
Baines, Jeremy, 177
BajaProg, 650
Ballaud, Alain, 444
Balliet, Phillippe, 149
Baltes, Steve, 560
Balzer, Andre, 192
Banana Moon, 547
Banco, 81, 107, 183, 647
Bangs, Lester, 1, 284, 682
Baptista, Arnaldo Dias, 492
Baptista, Sergio Dias, 492
Barbarella, Poison, 442
Barclay Records, 260, 618
Bardash, Boris, 644
Bargeld, Blixa, 514
Barnes, Ken, 14
Barone, Bill, 65
Barrabas, 199
Barreca, Marc, 336
Barrett, Syd, 227, 379, 442

Barricade, 233
Barriere, Jean-Baptiste, 409, 527
Barritt, Brian, 590
Barros, Marconi, 496
Bartos, Karl, 73
Basset, Georges, 463
Batard, Didier, 326, 539
Battiato, Franco, 152
Bauer, Rainer, 17, 503
Baumann, Hans-Peter, 27, 220, 262, 349, 498
Bayashi, Yonin, 197
Bazaar, 287
Beat Club, The, 610, 637
Beatty, Cedric, 157
Becaud, Gilbert, 618
Becker, Kalle, 561
Bedjabetch, 189
Beefheart, Captain, 175, 208, 233, 630, 651
Begnagrad, 224
Bel Canto, 508
Belda, Juani, 379
Bellaiche, Alain, 539
Bellaphon Records, 37, 223
Belle Star, 189
Bello, Alexis Loppe, 649
Belzebuth, 189, 212
Benoit, 321
Benoit Blue Boy, 189
Berckmans, Michel, 215, 466
Bergemont, Albert, 649
Berger, Karl, 313
Berio, Luciano, 33, 666
Berkers, Jerry, 65
Bernardes, Marcelo, 494
Bernardi, Andre, 418
Bernas, Richard, 371
Berrocal, Jacques, 271, 281
Bert, Alain, 189
Bertram, Dominique, 329, 332, 551
Besombes, Philippe, 189, 550
Besser, Joachim, 66
Besset, Michel, 213
Best Magazine, 323, 548
Bestiole, 189
Between, 104, 313, 411
Beuys, Joseph, 259
Beya, Christian, 192
Bi Kyo Ran, 413
Bianchi, Maurizio, 311, 319
Biebl, Hansi, 482
Bielli, Piero, 593
Bijelo Dugme, 223
Bijou, 189

Bikialo, Gérard, 115, 543
Billboard, 682
Billingsgate Records, 80
Bin-Oral system, 158
Biriaco, Bruno, 171
Birth Control, 43, 75, 147, 156
Bischof, Ingo, 90
Bise De Buse, 271
Bixio Da Seda, 496
Bizot, Jean-François, 537
Bla Bla Records, 152
Black, Cottrell, 105
Black Panthers, 286, 682
Black Rat, 189
Blake, Karl, 289
Blasquiz, Klaus, 111, 325, 543, 547, 619
Blay Tritono, 376
Blegvad, Peter, 178, 196, 244
Blesing, Alain, 418
Bleu Profond, 189
Bley, Carla, 179, 651
Bley, Paul, 585, 628
Blitzkrieg, 65
Bloch, Klaus, 361, 393
Blom, Atte, 93, 310
Bloody Mary, 189
Bloque, 200, 376
Bloss, Rainer, 500, 573
Blubs, The, 607
Blue Effect Group, The, 140
Blues Section, 95, 269, 306
Bocquet, Didier, 189, 281, 551
Bocquet, Laurent, 649
Boeyen, Herman van, 267
Boffo, Jean Pascal, 489, 553, 648
Bogdanov, Sergei, 666
Bogdanov, Yuri, 666
Bohemia, 140
Bohn, Carsten, 144
Bohr, Manfred, 158
Bollenberg, John, 649
Bomis Prendin, 311
Bondage Fruit, 542
Bonnet-Maury, Marc, 424
Bonneville, 189
Boogaloo Band, 189
Boomerang, 666
Booz, Emmanuel, 424
Borgers, Bertus, 267
Borges, Jorge Luis, 495
Borghi, Emmanuel, 544, 551
Boris, 261
Born, Georgie, 179, 271
Bosch, Victor, 450

Boule, Christian, 551
Boulez, Pierre, 662
Bow Wow, 197
Boyle, Gary, 388
Bozi Mlyn Records, 250
Brabenec, Vratislav, 169
Bracos Band, 189
Brain Records, 42, 57, 157, 589
Branca, Glenn, 623
Brand X, 185
Brando, Ines, 505
Branson, Richard, 14, 245, 584, 653
Brassens, Georges, 618
Breakfast, 160
Breakout Blues Band, 134
Breathing Therapy Society, 678
Brel, Jacques, 125, 618
Brely, Denis, 366
Brenner, Vytas, 397
Bringolf, Serge, 647
Brockett, Mick, 37
Broek, Rein van den, 253
Broeselmaschine, 146, 157
Brötzmann, Peter, 628
Brown, Marion, 369
Brua, Freddy, 193
Bruce, Jack, 173
Bruchmann, Michael, 146
Bruehwarm, 221
Bruford, Bill, 423
Bruniusson, Hans, 365
Brunner, Helmut, 394, 445
Bryars, Gavin, 369
Bsme, Francesco, 265
Budd, Harold, 368
Buddy Odor Stop, 268
Budka Suflera, 134
Buldozer, 223
Buller, Ed, 599
Buloshkin, Oleg, 661
Bulteau, Michel, 189
Bunka, Roman, 41
Burchard, Christian, 41, 248
Burford, Phil, 591
Bursch, Peter, 146, 157
Bussy, Pascal, 592
Butzmann, Frieder, 394
Byrds, The, 39

C. Pickford, 311
Cabal, 117
Cabellera de Berenice, 378
Cador, Gilles, 649
Cage, John, 162, 228, 301, 312, 374, 585, 666

Cahen, François Faton, 111, 117, 188, 331, 333, 423, 549, 618
Cahen, Jacqueline, 334
Cai, 377
Cajo De Pandora, 380
Cake, 189
Cale, John, 313, 337, 371, 577
Cambouis, 189
Camizole, 189
Camona, Jesus, 378
Campos, Jorge, 485
Can, 2, 14, 32, 43, 75, 104, 144, 157, 187, 237, 244, 273, 293, 362, 383, 391, 442, 514, 515, 522, 555, 577, 582, 587, 591, 602, 611, 620, 630, 652, 658
Canabis, John Jean, 321
Canapolis, 425
Canarios, 81, 199, 376, 461
Cantemir, Dimitre, 242
Canterbury, 214, 378, 413
Cantuaria, Vinicius, 493
Cantusio Jr., Amir, 494
Canzani, "Pajarito", 471
Capiozzo, Giulio, 132
Cardew, Cornelius, 312
Cardon, Frank, 213
Carefully, 189
Carlucci, Bruno, 451
Carmina, 189
Carneiro, Nando, 494
Caroline Records, 70, 177, 246
Carpe Diem, 189, 549
Carrion, Alfredo, 199
Cartilier, Louis, 485
Casablanca Records, 388
Castelhemis, 189
Castelli, Richard, 476
Catalogue, 281
Cataract, 160
Catbird, 684
Catharsis, 547
Causse, François, 333
CBS Records, 136, 186, 221, 287, 376, 451, 469, 495
CCS, 448
Celeste, 507
Celestial Harmonies Records, 362
Centaur Records, 596, 605
Centre Kulture Kontrole Epidemia, 280
Centrifuge, 189
Cerf, Marty, 14

Certain Rock(?) Français, Un, 228, 231, 593, 647
Cervello, 181
Chac Mool, 270, 380, 478
Chale, Ilona, 466
Chant du Monde Records, 230
Chapa-Zafiro Records, 200, 376
Chapman, Michael, 129
Chapoutot, Bruno, 593
Charley, Alain "Paco", 111, 422
Charly Records, 623
Chatam Records, 278
Chatham, Rhys, 370, 623
Chats, Les, 322
Chaussettes Noires, Les, 618
Checkpoint Charlie, 221
Chemin Blanc, 189
Chenevier, Guigou, 271
Chevalier, Jean-Luc, 329, 544, 551
Chevrolet, Rik, 383
Chiba, Setsuko, 570
Chieftans, The, 81
Chien De Faience, 189
Chimere, 189
Christ, Jesus, 252
Christopherson, Peter, 592
Chrome, 194, 209, 248, 269, 641
Chronicle, 153, 197, 386
Chrysalis Idominee, 189
Chute Libre, 189
Cible, 189
Ciria, Jose Maria, 378
Citta Frontale, 181
Clark, Dick, 8, 196
Clarke, Robert, 318
Clearlight [Symphony], 150, 233, 423, 551
CLEM, 593
Clivage, 189
Clock DVA, 311
Cluster, 43, 77, 157, 219, 237, 262, 297, 389, 445, 514, 515, 577, 588
Coaquette, Ivan, 406
Cobra, 189
Cobra Records, 120, 123, 150
Cockelare, Laurent, 334
Coil, 592, 641
Coincidence, 189
Collectif Mu, 544
Collegium Musicum, 140
Columbia Records, 102, 134, 223, 439, 469

Index

Comedie Humaine, 189
Comelade, Pascal, 320, 593, 687
Compagnie de la Satire label, 451
Compania Electrica Dharma, 200, 376
Congresso, 483
Conrad, Tony, 246
Contact List of Electronic Music, 593
Cooper, Lindsay, 177, 271
Copenhagen Boys Choir, 283
Copostakowiz Ensemble, 81
Coppola, Francis Ford, 666
Corbeau Mort, 189
COS, 186, 466
Cosmic Couriers, 59, 160, 557, 588, 639, 653
Cosmic Jokers, The, 59, 70, 586
Cosmic Music, 59, 226, 556
Cosmic News Musik Verlag, 59
Cosmos Factory, 197
Cosmos Records, 79, 120
Costa, Marcelo, 494
Costa, Muri, 494
Coulaud, Franck, 444
Coulon, Pierre, 465
Coulonneux, Les, 465
Courlan Tromboson, 394
Cousins, Michael, 297
Couti, Christine, 334
Covaci, Nicolea, 242
Cowell, Henry, 177
Coxhill, Lol, 179
Craig, Euan, 592
Crawling Riders, 189
Creation, 197, 198
Creem, 2
Crek, Juan, 265
Crisis, 189
Crium Delirium, 620
Cromlech, 377
Cross, David, 423
Crumar Orchestron synthesizer, 258
Cryonic Records, 491
Crypto Records, 193
Cunningham, David, 321
Curved Air, 313
Cutler, Chris, 176, 196, 214, 623, 656
Cutler, Ivor, 177
Cutler, Peter, 200
Cyborg, 378
Cynthi Aum, 189

Czechoslovakia, 15, 137, 167, 250
Czukay, Holger, 33, 104, 293, 391

D'Andrea, Franco, 171
D'Anna, Elio, 80, 82, 180
DAF, 317, 362, 394
Daft Punk, 553
Dali, Salvador, 497, 532
Dallas Gang, 189
Dallio, Patricia, 475
Dammers, Roland, 294
Dandelion Records, 268
Dandy Swingers, 283
Daneliak, Stefan, 240
Dantec, Maurice, 538
Darren, Jenny, 223
DAS, 602
Datura, 647
Dauner, Wolfgang, 238
Davis, Steve, 547
Dax, Danielle, 289
Dayde, Joël, 422
Dayez, Michel, 465
DD Records, 385, 388, 414, 654
DDAA, 278, 350, 431
Dean, Elton, 267
Debris, 248
Debuchi, S., 389
DeCamps, Christian, 125, 650
DeCamps, Francis, 125
Decayes, The, 195
Dechained Company, 189
Decibel, 380, 478
Deficit Des Annes Anterieures, 278, 350, 431
DeGraaf, Huba, 267
Dei Rossi, Miki, 83
DeJong, Theo, 254
Dekadance, 483
Dekker, Cor, 254
Delachat, Jean-Claude, 463
DeLambra, Sergio, 381
DeLaurenti, Christopher, 671
DeLeeuwe, Peter, 254
Deleuze, Gilles, 161, 538
Deluxe, Liza, 192, 329
Demetrio, 120
Demokratischer Konsum, 483
Dendo Marrionett, 425
Denis, Daniel, 214, 475
Denisov, Edison, 661
DeNoyer, Jan, 458
Der Plan, 314, 362
Dernier Recors, 189

Descheemaeker, Dirk, 466
Desperados, 189
Détrée, Roberto, 105, 313
Deuter, Georg, 362, 393
Deutsch-Amerikanischen Freundschaft, 317, 362, 394
Deutsche-Grammophon Records, 616
Devo, 248, 291, 334
DG-307, 138, 168
Dhomont, Francis, 666
Dicap Records, 94
Die Anderen, 483
Die Firma, 483
Die Form, 310
Die Rundkopfe, 483
Dierks, Dieter, 66, 89, 147, 155, 228, 638
Diermaier, Werner, 52, 245
Diesel, 189
Diez, Frank, 159
Dig, The, 565
Digelius Music, 306
Dijk, Michel van, 254
DiMeola, Al, 572
Dimitri From Paris, 553
Din A Testbild, 394
Dinger, Klaus, 43, 48, 76, 78, 237, 362, 447
Dinger, Thomas, 448
Dinsdale, Steve, 602
Disjuncta Records, 118, 123, 193, 233, 325, 536, 548
Diskoton Records, 224
Divjak, R., 224
Divodorum, 189
Doa, 377
Dobson, Ian, 592
Doldinger, Klaus, 157, 584
Dollase, Jurgen, 65, 160
Dom, 142
Don't Die, 543
Donner, Otto, 93, 310
Doors, The, 2, 12, 39, 167, 448, 477, 580, 637
Dostal, Frank, 126
Dostoyevsky, Fyodor, 665
Douw, Rob, 607
Downbeat, 254
Dr. Space, 196
Dramms, 481
Dromm Records, 257
DRY Project, 425
Dublet, Daniel, 219
Duboc, Jane, 496
DuBois, Emile, 426

Dubuc, Xavier, 450
Dugan, Joan, 140
Dugrenot, Joël, 118, 422, 647, 687
Dungen, Jos Van Den, 508
Dupree, Champion Jack, 129
Duren, Wolfgang, 361
Durieu, Jacques, 485
Durman + Company, 142
Durr, Pierre, 593
Dutronc, Jacques, 422
Duvernot, Antoine, 150
Dwane, Mark, 509
Dwarf Records, 267
Dweller At The Threshold, 688

Earfood, 81
East Germany, 481
Eastern Works Records, 390
Eck, Ron van, 266, 608
Eckert, Alain, 213
Eclipse, 189
ECM Records, 151, 235, 493, 594
Edel Records, 631, 685
Edhels, 491, 553
Edition Speciale, 189, 491, 549
Edwards, Keith, 107
Egg, 176
Egg Records, 220, 259, 678
Ehrig, Joachim "Eroc", 239, 241
Eider Stellaire, 463
Eik, Jaap van, 255
Eimert, Herbert, 666
Einstürzende Neubauten, 514, 540
Ekseption, 226, 253
El Fulano, 485
El Queso Sagrado, 271
Electra, 483
Electric Callas, 189
Electric Light Orchestra, 226, 486
Electriquement Votre, 189
Electro Choc, 189
Electronic Delusion, 454
Electroshock Records, 665
Eleking, 565
Elektra/Nonesuch Records, 6
Elektrobus, 141
Eliscu, Robert, 64, 105, 313
Elixir, 491, 553, 648
Elliott, Dave, 548
ELO, 226, 486
Eloy, 155

Embryo, 14, 25, 41, 43, 144, 155, 221, 248, 411, 582, 591, 613, 655
EMI Records, 186, 358, 362, 469
Emile DuBois Group, 426
EMS synthesizers, 30, 135, 228, 260, 374, 411, 666
Emsley, Denis & Jeanette, 592
Enbor, 377
Energit, 140
Engle, Claude, 111, 422, 621
Enke, Hartmut, 67, 554, 585, 629
Eno, Brian, 78, 107, 122, 157, 161, 228, 264, 270, 292, 297, 321, 323, 334, 337, 360, 369, 395, 411, 456, 537, 550, 589, 593, 603, 645
Enossis, 189
Entrance, 429
Epic Records, 377
Epitaph, 155
Eppu Normaali, 269
Equinoxe, 189
Erdenklang Records, 528
Eriksen, Andreas, 508
Eriksson, Kalle, 366
Eris Pluvia, 650
Eroc, 239, 241
Errobi, 377
Eruption, 27, 220, 237, 259, 585
Es, Ruud Van, 508
Eskaton, 256, 271, 417, 552, 647, 687
Eskaton Kommandkestra, 189, 417
ESP Records, 370
Espindola, Edson, 496
Esposito, Toni, 186
Esprit De St. Louis, 189
Estra, Karda, 671
Estructura, 397
Etant Donnes, 311
Etat D'Urgence, 190
ETC, 141
Eterna Records, 481
Ethnic Trio, 333
Etron Fou Leloublan, 175, 190, 213, 231, 271, 368, 396, 515
EUROCK CD-ROM, 633
EUROCK Records, 16, 507, 687
Eurodisc Records, 192
Eurydice, 194

Everest, 190
Evers, Jorge, 41
Exit, 190
Exodo, 378
Exotica Records, 645
Experimental Quintet, 241
Eye Q Records, 560
Eyhani, Herve, 149

f., Frank, 314
Fab Two, 311
Face Out, 591
Factory, 190
Faes, Eric, 215
Fairfield Parlour, 442
Fall, The, 318, 515
Falsini, Franco, 107, 154
Family Fodder, 442
Far East Family Band, 154, 197, 385, 386, 412
Far Out, 385, 386, 412
Farfisa organ, 30, 586
Fargo, 160
Fariselli, Patrizio, 130
Fasoli, Claudio, 171
Faust, 14, 43, 51, 71, 144, 177, 238, 243, 381, 419, 442, 514, 515, 577, 588, 591, 644, 647
Federow, Gabrid, 116
Fee, Jean-Philippe, 431
Feeling B, 483
Fehl Farben, 318
Felicio, Claudio, 496
Fenneteau, Jean Paul, 545
Fermata, 140
Ferre, Leo, 618
Ferrer, Nino, 422
Ferry, Pascal, 489
Feza, Mongezi, 177
FFN, 241
Fiala, Eugen, 167
Fibonaccis, The, 578
Fichelscher, Daniel, 18, 64, 676
Fichot, Phillipe, 310
Fiedler, Frank, 63, 674
Fikejz, Daniel, 142
Filho, Arnolpho Lima, 492
Fine Automatic, 311
Finnforest, 151, 269
Finnish All-Stars, 97, 101
Fiori, Umberto, 200
Firma, Die, 483
Fischer, Ralph, 41
Fischer, Veronika, 482
Fischer, Wild Man, 57

Index

Fisher, Veetdharm Morgan, 425
FitzPatrick, Gregory Allan, 367
Fix, Andy, 676
Flamen Dialis, 190
Flaubert, Gustave, 194
Fleet, Ed Van, 435
Fleetwood Mac, 157
Flindt, Flemming, 286, 683
Floh de Cologne, 244
Flowmotion, 592
Fluence, 550
Flught, 381
Flür, Wolfgang, 73
Fobat, Luis, 265
Focus, 266, 591
Foetus, 190
Fondation, 406, 687
Fonit Records, 81
Fønix Records, 520
Fools Mate, 362, 385, 390, 523
Forgas, 190
Forum's Group, 190
Fowley, Kim, 95, 303
Foxy, 190
Franke, Christophe, 27, 260, 394, 498, 576
Frankfurt Music Fair, 401
Franta Hromada, 141
Franz K., 310
Free Sound, 450
Freeman, Allan "Taff", 37
Freeman, Steven & Alan, 588, 591
Freemasons Black Brain, 425
French, Peter, 159
Fricke, Florian, 63, 159, 614, 672
Fricke, Ron, 414
Fride, Jan, 90
Friedhof, 235
Friedkin, William, 498
Frightful Five, 190
Fripp, Robert, 81, 107, 112, 122, 150, 161, 228, 264, 270, 321, 323, 337, 413, 458, 537, 550
Frith, Fred, 176, 196, 247, 371, 390, 423, 623, 651
Fritz, Porky, 159
Fritz, Roger, 33
Froese, Edgar, 26, 219, 225, 236, 260, 361, 372, 497, 530, 571, 578, 629
Frohmader, Peter, 454, 539, 671
Fromy, Franck, 444
Frost, Peer, 286

Frumpy, 144
Fujimoto, Y., 389
Fukakusa, Akira, 386
Fukushima, Hirohito, 386
Fulano, El, 485
Fulton, Dave, 688
Fumio, 386, 412
Fur Fur Tapes, 289
Furan-Shitai, 425
Furse, Chris, 591
Fusion, 285
Fusion, 544
Fusioon, 199

Galadriel, 650
Galloping Coroners, 645
Gallota, Jean-Claude, 427
Galway, James, 105
Gammarock Productions, 614
Gammon, Patrick, 614
Ganafoul, 190
Gancev, J., 224
Gandalf, 467, 687
Gandil, Gilbert, 450
Garbarek, Jan, 493
Garber, Rene, 114, 542
Garcia, Jordi, 377
Garibaldi, Andy, 591
Garnier, Laurent, 553
Garret, Jac, 366
Garris, Sid, 681
Gascoyne, Brian, 388
Gasull, Feliu, 200
Gate, 157
Gaudi, 463
Gaurdon, 190
Gauthier, Patrick, 326, 533, 551
GBG, 377
Gee, Rosko, 157, 297
Geest, Sacha van, 266, 610
Gelas, Gerard, 219
Geller, Uri, 60
Genesis, 81, 125, 182, 380, 411, 418, 435, 458, 468, 492, 546, 645, 651, 662
Genocid, 190
Genrich, Ax, 54, 236, 585, 629
Gentle Giant, 81, 125, 148, 496, 662
Giddens, Bob, 314, 317
Giesler, Charlie, 394
Giger, H.R., 455, 544
Gila, 64, 87, 236
Gila Fuck, 236
Gillaspey, David, 634
Gillis, Jeannot, 465

Gilsanz, Tomas, 358, 463
Gimenez, Albert, 358
Gimenez, Josep, 378
Giraudy, Miquette, 562
Gismonti, Egberto, 493, 505
Glaser, Clemens, 394, 445
Glaser, Rudiger, 394, 445
Glass, Philip, 160, 264, 278, 320, 359, 369, 414, 508, 537, 558
Glass Records, 383
Glastonbury Fayre Festival, 176
Glugowski, Wlodek, 305
Gnana, Philippe, 649
Gnudmann, Ken, 286
GO, 197, 388, 572
Goddard, Duncan, 601
Godding, Brian, 115
Golden Earring, 79, 266, 609, 637
Golowin, Sergius, 59
Gomelsky, Giorgio, 114, 195, 284, 615, 656, 681
Gomez, Enrique, 649
Goncalves, Carlos, 496
Gong, 157, 196, 217, 378, 423, 515, 546, 562, 591, 616, 646
Gonzales, Fernando, 484
Gonzales, Patricio, 484
Gonzales, Sergio, 484
Good Medicine, 190
Good Time Charley, 190
Goomumbulaa, 265
Gorilla Music, 129
Goslinga, Wybo, 593
Gostnell, Irene, 527
Gotic, 199, 376
Gottsching, Manuel, 59, 67, 264, 349, 358, 401, 526, 554, 559, 578, 586, 590, 629, 671
Gotxi, Baxter & Guzman, 377
Goubert, Simon, 541
Goude, Jean-Philippe, 327
Goun, 190
Gozzo, Alain, 192
Graalo, 190
Graillier, Michel, 115, 543
Gramavision, 501
Granada, 199, 376, 461
Grancher, Philippe, 190, 550
Grand Rouge, 190
Granjeon, Jean-Claude, 489, 649
Grass Philosophy, 425
Grassow, Mathias, 671

Greaves, John, 177
Green Isac, 508, 687
Greenworld Imports, 516, 635, 654
Gregar Records, 285
Greif, George, 681
Greinke, Jeff, 671
Griek, Tim, 254
Grierson, John, 178
Griglak, Fero, 140
Grimaud, Dominique, 593
Grime, 190
Grimm, Chantal, 406
Grindenko, Tatiyana, 666
Grobschnitt, 157, 238
Grosse, Francis, 489, 552, 647
Grosse Catastrophe, 190
Grosskopf, Harald, 65, 358, 510, 557, 559
Groundstroem, Mans, 95, 102, 307
Group, The, 305
Groupa 220, 223
Grumbkow, Christian, 146, 155
Grumbkow, Jochen, 146
Grumbkow, Nanny, 146
Grunberg, Sven, 410
Grunblatt, Georges 327, 536, 550
Grupo Um, 495
Gruppo Sportivo, 268
Guadalquivir, 377
Gualberto, 199, 376
Guarino, Massimo, 82, 181
Guattari, Felix, 161, 535
Gubaidulina, Sofia, 661
Gueffier, Bernard, 489, 552, 646
Guerrero, Kiko, 377
Guillard brothers, 329
Guillaume, Eric, 418
Guimaraes, Marco Antonio, 505
Guirao, Carlos, 358, 379, 462
Gulgowski, Woldek, 81
Guru Guru, 14, 43, 52, 54, 81, 143, 155, 235, 244, 340, 419, 513, 514, 515, 561, 577, 580, 653
Guru Guru Groove, 54
Gustavson, Jukka, 94, 100, 268, 304, 306

Haapala, Eino, 365
Hackl, Tom, 394
Haden, Charlie, 493
Hagen, Nina, 482, 630
Haino, Keiji, 594

Hairy Chapter, 235
Haitokusha, 425
Hajentes, Michael, 631
Håkansson, Kenny, 211, 268
Hamel, Peter Michael, 84, 104, 311, 362, 585
Hammer, Jan, 136
Hammill, Peter, 125, 495
Hammoudi, Basil, 72
Hampel, Gunter, 4
Hanadensha, 564
Hanappier, Patrick, 215
Handke, Peter, 451
Hansen, Annisette, 282, 679
Hansen, Rudolf, 286
Hansson, Bo, 210, 268
Hansson, Vilgot, 366
Hansson & Karlsson, 211
Haouzi, Serge, 424
Happy Family, 542
Harada, Yujin, 386
Hard Pop, 483
Hardin, Tim, 296
Harlis, 157
Harmonia, 77, 158, 237, 588
Harmonix, Phil, 383, 441
Harrington, Anthony, 153, 387, 624
Harris, Don "Sugarcane", 6
Harrison, Peter, 591
Harry, Warren, 268
Harumi, 196
Haslinger, Paul, 498
Hasselstrom, Frank, 684
Hatfield and the North, 423
Hattler, Helmut, 90, 158
Hauf, Butch, 72
Hauru, Jukka, 81
Hausmann, Karl-Heinz, 3, 4
Hautes Reelles, 190
Hawkwind, 14, 19, 141, 340, 378
Head, Steve, 107
Hearts of Space, 421, 516
Hecenia, 553
Hecke, Denis Van, 466
Held, Zeus B., 147
Heldon, 120, 150, 161, 190, 321, 324, 535, 548, 592
Helidon Records, 224
Helwig, Oliver, 500
Hemenex, 142
Henri Roger, 190
Henry Cow, 175, 195, 202, 247, 273, 380, 389, 423, 483, 493

Hensel, Jennifer, 159
Heratius, 321
Herbert, Frank, 342
Herman, Lisa, 179
Herve, Jean-Luc, 444
Herzberg, Andre, 482
Herzog, Werner, 614, 673
Hess, Klaus, 89
Hesse, Herman, 106, 468, 528, 581
Hesse, Jean Claude, 649
Hesse, Martin, 90
Hiekkala, Jarmo, 151
Hieronymous, Guido, 678
Hietanen, Hessu, 99
Higelin, J. 190, 450
High Bass, The, 470
Hildebrandt, Herbert, 128
Hill, Stephen, 516
Hillage, Steve, 562
Hilozoizmo, 380
Him, 190
Himalaya, 268
Hinds, Sergio, 493
Hinten, P., 56, 420
Hitchcock, David, 157
Hits & Fun Records, 639
Hitweek, 266
Hladik, Radim, 140
Hlavea, Milan, 253
Hobo, 223
Hodgkinson, Tim, 176, 271
Hodicke, K.H., 259
Hoelderlin, 146, 156
Hoenig, Michael, 401, 414, 530, 576, 585
Hoffman, Edgar, 41, 249
Hofstede, Henk, 608
Hohmann, Andreas, 43, 237
Hollander, Marc, 187, 273
Hollmer, Lars, 365
Holmes, Thom, 593
Honey Dream, 190
Honey Smugglers, The, 602
Hope, Gordon, 592
Hopper, Hugh, 388
Horizon, 190
Horky, Robert Julian, 687
Horowitz, Richard, 527
Houghton, Gary, 602
Hourbette, Gerard, 213, 394, 476
Howden, Ron, 37
Hubaut, Joel, 280
Hubaut-Manou, Emanuel, 280
Hubble Bubble, 190

Eurock: European Rock & the Second Culture, 695

Index

Hulden, Mats, 94, 303, 306
Hurtado, Fernando, 484
Hutter, Ralf, 43, 72, 76, 158, 237, 448, 589
Huxley, Aldous, 393, 430
Huygen, Michel, 358, 377, 379, 461, 598, 671
Hybride, 190
Hyde, Paul, 364
Hydravion, 190
Hynding, Hans-Jurgen, 88

Iasos, 671
IBC Records, 187
Ibio, 199, 376
Ibos, Gabriel, 564
Iceberg, 200, 461
Ideal, 630
Iliffe, April, 441
Illitch, 264, 687
Illusion Production, 279, 431, 654
Image, 190
Imago, 378
Iman, 376, 461
Impetus, 594
Impulse Records, 370, 544
In Limbo, 508
In-Phaze Records, 442
Indexi, 223
Infra-Rouge, 190
Inkeys, 593
Innovative Communication Records, 345, 362, 393, 499, 575
Inteam Records, 499, 558, 575
Intence, 393, 445
Intercord Records, 149
Intergalactic Trading Co., 516, 635, 653
International Gypsy Co-op, The, 287
Intra Musiques, 593
IRCAM, 531
Iriondo, Alberto, 377
Irganon, Ericka, 321
Irmler, Hans-Joachim, 52, 245, 644
Iron Butterfly, 22, 39, 76, 486, 637
Iron Duke, 81
Ironic Afternoon Orchestra, 389
IRT Records, 471
Ishi, Ken, 564
Ishikawa, Kei, 386

Island Records, 26, 278, 325, 537
Isolation Intellectuelle, 322
Isotani, T., 389
Isotope, 388
It Viaie, 200
Ito, Akira, 386, 412
Itoiz, 377
Iz Records, 377

Ja-Ju-Ka, 425
Jackson, Jimmy, 25, 41, 249
Jacobsen, Jürgen, 639
Jacobson, Norbert, 147
Jade Warrior, 112, 515
Jadis, 190
Jäger, Wolfgang, 241
Jahsa, L., 224
Jaivas, Los, 470, 494
Jane, 89, 158, 588
Janko, Gottfried, 90
Japan Times, 565
Jaraka, 199
Jarre, Jean-Michel, 342, 363, 458, 467, 516, 551, 591
Jasenka, Antanas, 671
Jaubert, Miguel, 379
Javier, Yves, 649
Javis Single, 152
Jazz Fragment, 142
Jazz Q, 139
Jazz-Rock Workshop, 139
Jean, Laurie, 337
Jeanneau, François, 423
Jefferson Airplane, 2, 19, 38, 168, 267, 429, 448, 580, 680
JEM Imports, 136, 653
Jenkins, Mark, 536
Jenny-Clark, Jean-François, 493
Jeunes Musiciens de Champagne, Les, 271
Jirous, Ivan, 15, 168, 207, 251
Jive Electro Records, 598
Jofroy, 465
Johanna Records, 269, 310
Johnson, Barry, 181
Johnson, David, 295
Jokers, The, 253
Jolliffe, Steve, 26
Jones, Michael, 485
Jones, Percy, 185
Jordan, Jens, 87
Jouret, Christophe, 475
Juan, Nicolas, 649
Jugoton Records, 224

Juliac, Alain, 489, 649
Julian, Jo, 371
Julos, 465
Julverne, 465
Juma, 389
Jussi and the Boys, 303
Juul, Palle, 79

K Rock Mort, 190
K., Franz, 310
Ka-Spel, Edward, 382, 441
Kagerou Records, 425
Kahr, Volker, 241
Kainar, Josef, 141
Kaipa, 650
Kaiser, Rolf-Ulrich, 59, 87, 155, 226, 498, 556, 586, 638, 652
Kaleidoscope [Japan], 425
Kaleidoscope [UK], 442
Kalevala, 303
Kalfon Rockchaud, 190
Kallosh, Shandor, 661
Kalma, Ariel, 359
Kam And Bear, 190
Kamada, T., 388, 414
Kampen, Huib van, 254
Kanaan, 454
Kandahar, 186
Karasek, Svatopluk, 169
Karat, 483
Karoli, Michael, 33, 76, 293, 391, 602, 660
Karrer, Chris, 4, 17, 41, 503, 524, 577, 613
Karthago, 91, 158
Kaseberg, Joachim, 147
Kaseberg, Peter, 146
Kaske, Stephan, 637
Katapult, 142
Katka, Ismo, 305
Katoh, 198
Katra Turana, 425
Kayak, 256
Kebnekaise, 211
Keller, Detlef, 671
Kelley, John, 41
Kemner, Michael, 319
Kennedy, Jim, 236
Kenso, 413, 502
Kerlo, Eric, 190
Kerschowski, 482
Key, 482
Khalifa, Guy, 329
Kickbit Information, 144
Kin Ping Meh, 129

King, Dave, 41, 249
King, Simon, 48
King Crimson, 109, 125, 337, 379, 411, 413, 423, 435, 458, 468, 478, 491, 537, 549, 588, 645, 646, 653, 662
Kingdom Records, 450
Kissmer, Willi, 157
Kistenmacher, Bernd, 566
Kitajima, Osamu, 197, 413
Kitaro, 362, 386, 412, 530
Kleynnaert, Paule, 418
Klick, Roland, 33
Klick & Aus, 483
Klima, Ladislav, 252
Klinger, R., 209
Klingler, Phillip B., 671
Kluster, 219, 237, 259, 320, 589
Knaup-Krötenschwanz, Renate, 18, 503, 577, 613, 678
Kobaïa, 110, 542
Kobayashi, H., 389
Kobialka, Daniel, 527
Kochl, Edda, 245
Koivistoinen, Eero, 302
Kollaa Kestaa, 269
Kollektiv, 160
Kollen, Helmut, 159
Komintern, 453, 491, 533, 547
Kommers, Peter, 508
Konchalovsky, Andrei, 666
König, Gerard, 418
König, Hans 33
Koppel, Anders, 282, 679
Koppel, Billie, 684
Koppel, Maria, 282
Koppel, Thomas, 282, 679
Korai Öröm, 645
Korber, Gunter, 89
Korberg, Tommy, 305
Korg synthesizers, 258, 408, 486, 527, 668
Korgilov, Lt., 279, 351
Korn, David, 539
Korni Groupa, 223
Koshi, A., 389
Kosmischen Kuriere, 59
Kost, Stefan, 649
Kotilainen, Esa, 99
Koutev, Phillipe, 6
Kovach, Kornell, 223
Kovacs, Kati, 173
Koyaanisqatsi, 414
Kraan, 90, 147, 156

Kraftwerk, 43, 48, 72, 75, 149, 156, 237, 323, 337, 340, 347, 362, 445, 448, 514, 515, 537, 555, 576, 577, 582, 584, 588, 591, 653
Kramer, Jonathan, 527
Krantz, Wolfgang, 89
Kratochvil, Martin, 139
Krause, Dagmar, 177, 244
Kreichi, Stanislav, 661
Kremer, Gidon, 666
Krischke, Wolfgang, 24
Kruisman, Rob, 254
Krylon Hertz, 311
Kubler, Olaf, 613
Kuckuck Records, 362
Kühn, Gerd Otto, 241
Kukko, Sakari, 104, 132, 268
Kukuk, Hardy, 393
Kuramoto, T., 389
Kurkinen, Matti, 303

L'Autre Monde, 338
L'Orchestra, 205
La Dusseldorf, 237, 362, 448
La Souris Deglinguee-LSD, 190
La Tribu, 479
Labanda, 377
Lacrymosa, 425
Ladeira, Renato, 496
Laforet, Marie, 493
Laird, Rick, 136
Laizeau, François, 332
Lake, 156
Lakomy, Reinhard, 482
Lambert, Kit, 611
Lambiasi, Mauricio, 494
Lampe, Hans, 448
Lancaster, Jack, 256
Lane, Malcolm, 257
Langhans, Rainer, 613
Languirand, Pascal, 360
Lannhuel Manu, 190
Lansner, Maria, 283
Lard Free, 123, 149, 190, 405, 452, 549
Largounez, Bernard, 527
Larry Martin Factory, 190
Lasry, Teddy, 111, 549
Lastad, Jarl Hugo, 593, 597
Laswell, Bill, 623
Laurent, Jean Paul, 465
Laurent, Philippe, 537
Laux, Josef, 173
Lavilliers, Bernard, 190
Lawalree, Dominique, 438

Layos, Howard, 333
Le Bars, Michel, 463
Le Orme, 80, 81, 183
Leary, Timothy, 69, 339, 526, 556, 585
Leb i Sol, 223
Lebel, Jean-Jacques, 535
Leckebusch, Michael, 611
Ledo, Alberto, 471
Lee, Arthur, 34
Lee, Rita, 492
Lefebvre, Cyril, 190
Legendary Pink Dots, 383, 441, 513, 641
Legende II, 190
Leigh, Geoff, 177, 247, 271
Leimer, Kerry, 334
Leme, Mario, 496
Lemo, Ronaldo, 492
Lemon Kittens, 288
Leopold, Peter, 4, 17, 41, 503, 579, 613
Leopold, Ulrich, 503, 613
Les Chats, 322
Les Chaussettes Noires, 618
Les Coulonneux, 465
Les Tetines Noires, 553
Les Variations, 325, 618
Lessa, Marcos, 496
Lessa, Mimi, 496
Leton, Georges, 333
Lettman, Gille, 59, 587, 638
Liberty Records, 32, 63, 105, 589, 611
Libido, 425
Lichti, Jacques, 194
Lieb, Oliver, 560
Liebezeit, Jaki, 33, 76, 294, 391
Lietzau, Olaf, 87
Liffers, Dicter, 63
Lightning Records, 12
Limelight Records, 420
Linden, Pierre van der, 255
Linden, Rick van der, 253
Lindenberg, Udo, 156
Lindh, Bjorn J:son, 81
Linkola, Jukka, 151
Linn drums, 433
Lionel, 321
Little Bob Story, 190
Little Leaguers Elbow, 390
Livengood, John, 532, 687
Llanos, Alfredo, 379
LLE, 390, 425
Llosa, Mario Vargas, 472
Loach, Anton, 257

Index

Location, 425
Loch, Sigi, 612
Lockwood, Didier, 116, 120, 334, 543, 551
Lockwood, Sylvie, 334
Locomotiv GT, 142, 172
Loffink, John, 593
Lone Star, 199
Longo, Robert, 371
Loos, Charles, 466
Loose Heart, 190
Lopez, Ricardo, 378
Lopez, Vincente, 378
Lorenz, Rudiger, 393
Lorenzini, 491
Los Allegres, 268
Los Angeles Times, 578
Los Jaivas, 470, 494
Lotus Records, 592
Louize Alcazar, 233
Love Records, 93, 101, 133, 151, 269, 304
Lovecraft, H.P., 80, 124
LSD, 170, 235, 267, 339, 386, 419, 442, 498, 514, 577, 580, 586, 674
Lucas Trouble, 311
Lucifer's Friend, 43, 75, 158
Lumley, Robin, 185
Lund, Morten, 508
Lundsten, Ralph, 211, 511
Lux, Kaz, 256
Luz, Fuguett, 496
Lyons, Joseph, 196
Lyubimov, Alexei, 666

Ma Banlieue Flasque, 190
Machiavel, 186
Machin, 190
Machine Head, 190
Macintosh computer, 533
MacLaren, Malcolm, 315
Macromassa, 265, 271
Made In Sweden, 97, 305
Madore, Dana, 653
Madrigal, 190
Madrigal Records, 474
Madrigar, 190
Magdalena, 377
Magical Power Mako, 197, 385, 387
Magma, 14, 71, 109, 117, 123, 161, 187, 190, 192, 212, 244, 323, 329, 395, 422, 432, 442, 463, 491, 515,
540, 546, 591, 616, 646, 656
Magne, Michel, 551
Magnet Mazazine, 634
Magnetic Bleu, 311
Magnum, 190
Magrana, Pou, 265
Magus Optis, 190
Mahagon, 142
Mahavishnu Orchestra, 109, 137, 197, 200, 223, 313, 379
Mahjun, 190
Majest, Stret, 442
Malaena, 190
Malherbe, Didier, 547
Malicorne, 190
Mama Bea, 190, 424
Manchion, Olivier, 538
Manderlier, Jean-Luc, 114
Mandrake Memorial, 19
Mania D, 394
Manikin Records, 571
Mann, Manfred, 655
Mann, Michael, 498, 655
Mansson, Michel, 451
Manticore Records, 184
Mantler, Michael, 179
Marcator, Adrian, 429
Marcœur, Albert, 190, 365, 549
Mariano, Charlie, 41, 249, 267
Marie Et Les Garçons, 190
marijuana, 169, 366, 556, 674
Marlec, Yvan le, 334
Marmalade Records, 616
Marquand Quartet, 332
Marquee, 565
Marquee Moon, 385, 388, 390
Marquee Records, 654
Marquis de Sade, 327
Martin Circus, 422
Martin Triangle, 547
Martineau, Sylvie, 431
Marton, Vittorio, 84
Martynov, Vladimir, 666
Masal, 444
Massacre, 390
Masters, The, 484
Material, 623
Mathieu Donnard Street, 190
Mativet, François, 149
Maucher, Charly, 89
Mazed, May B. Irma, 383
Mazursky, Paul, 388
MB, 311, 319
McDonald, Ian, 653

Mega Hertz, 190
Meid, Lothar, 4, 24, 579, 613
Meier, Dieter, 66
Meifert, Arnulf, 245
Meisel, Peter, 59, 556
Meki Mark Men, 211
Mellotron, 32, 39, 66, 69, 80, 83, 89, 108, 125, 128, 134, 224, 387, 503, 603, 646
Melo, Carlos "Rosko", 471
Melodie, 139
Melodiya Records, 411, 664
Melody, 190
Melody Maker, 14, 28, 177, 522, 546, 653
Melos, 311
Memoriance, 190
Men Tan Pin, 197, 198
Mendes, Chico, 504
Menezes, Benito, 505
Menskikov, Vitaly, 649
Mephisto, 190
Mer' Grande, 190
Merces, Cesar das, 493
Mercier, Frederic, 551
Mercury Records, 420
Mergen, Jerome, 649
Mergenthaler, Andre, 474
Merzbow, 413, 513
Mess, 411
Message, 157
Metabolist, 257, 311, 591
Metamorphose, 425
Metal Urbain, 190
Meteors, The, 291
Metronome Records, 20, 42, 57, 158, 500, 587, 589
Metropolitan Opera, 684
Metternich, Count, 90
Meza, Arturo, 479
MFH, 592
MIDI, 487
Midnight Sun, 286
Midsummer Nights Dream, 168
Miekautsch, Dieter, 41
Migeot, Jean-Marie, 424
Mike Et Sa Clique, 190
Mikhalkov, Nikita, 663
Milladoiro, 377
Mille, Frank, 239
Miller, Daniel, 317
Miller, Jimmy, 285, 681
Millward, Simon, 257
Minimum Vital, 553, 650
Minton, Phil, 179, 271
Minuet Boulevard, 190

Mira Sound Studio, 284
Mirage, 362, 592, 595, 597
Mirage, 654
Miralles, Armand, 321
Mirasol, 199
Misik, Vladimir, 141
Missus Beastly, 160, 221
Mixed Media Company, 104
Miyashita, Fumio, 386, 412
Mladi Levi, 223
Mlinarec, Drago, 223
MNW Records, 210
Moby Disc, 653
Möbius, Ralph, 86
Modus, 142
Moebius, 190
Moebius, Dieter, 77, 157, 219, 261, 589, 671
Moerlen, Pierre, 304, 423
Moira, 221
Mollo, 241
Mona Lisa, 190, 549, 650
Monicks, Fred, 72
Monolith Records, 425
Monsieur Dupont, 190
Montiel, Pascale, 649
Moog synthesizer, 63, 103, 123, 134, 137, 139, 228, 461, 487, 494, 509, 536, 559, 599, 614, 661, 673
Mooney, Malcolm, 33, 76, 295, 391, 589
Moore, Anthony, 178, 244
Moore, Derek "Mo", 37
Moore, Gary, 80
Moore, Steve, 592
Moreau, Thierry, 489
Morelenbaum, Jacques, 494
Mori, A., 389
Morricone, Ennio, 370
Morris, Nigel, 388
Moscow Conservatoire, 660
Moscow Experimental Studio of Electronic Music, 666
Moshe-Naim Records, 332
Mosley, Ian, 255
Moss, David, 223
Mother Gong, 196
Mothers of Invention, 12, 141, 167, 208, 227, 267, 284
Moulin, Marc, 187
Moullet, Patrice, 216
Moura, Marcus, 496
MoviePlay Records, 199, 376
Moving Gelatine Plates, 547
Moziak, 190

Moze, Francis, 111
Mueller, Klaus D., 501, 517, 555, 572, 584, 626
Mueller, Rosi, 60, 69, 629
Muffins, The, 196
Mugen, 425
Muller, Thierry, 264
Muller, Wolfgang, 67
Mummert, Holger, 429
Munich Philharmonic Orchestra, 313
Munju, 160, 221
Murasaki, 197
Murdock, Alan, 158
Murray, William, 496
Murzin, Evgeni, 660
Musea Records, 489, 552, 646
Music Box, 671
Music Factory label, 104
Music Life, 390
Music Millennium, 655
Musica Dispersa, 199
Musica Electronica Viva, 405
Musica Urbana, 200, 376
MusiCDirect, 651
Musik Express, 237
Musikautomatika, 397
Musique Du Delta, 491
Musser, Michele, 458
Mutantes, Os, 492
Mute Records, 317
Mutis, Mario, 470
Muza Records, 137
Muzzle Blues & Jazz Orchestra, 483
Mythe Xero, 190
Mythos, 59, 637

N'Guyen, Gerard, 592
Nadolney, Werner, 89
Nadolski, Helmut, 135
Nakamura, T., 389
Nakano, Y., 425
Nakao, Michiko, 295
Napoli Centrale, 186
Narvaez, Jose Ignacio, 378
Nasal, 212
Nascimento, Milton, 505
Nath, Pandit Pran, 347
National Health, 273
National Philharmonic Orchestra, 255
Nautilus Records, 488
Nava, Miguel Angel, 258, 380
Navar, Jose Xavier, 271
Nazario, Lelo, 496

Nazario, Ze Eduardo, 496
NEARFest, 650
Nebbia, Litto, 381
Negasphere, 425
Nektar, 37, 75, 149, 155, 578, 637, 653
Nemtin, Alexander, 661
Nerke, Uschi, 611
Neruda, Pablo, 471
Neto, Mario, 496
Nettelbeck, Ewe, 51, 243, 589
Neu!, 34, 43, 48, 77, 159, 237, 246, 362, 419, 448, 514, 515, 577, 587
Neumeier, Mani, 54, 143, 236, 419, 561
Neumusik, 259, 548, 592
Neuronium, 358, 377, 379, 462
Neuschwanstein, 650
Nevergreens, 268
New Musical Express, 14, 515, 522, 546, 653
New Trolls, 81, 181
New York Dolls, 34
New York Gong, 196, 623
New York Shakespeare Festival, 281
Newcomb, Martin, 599
Next, 190
NHK, 425
Nich, Michael, 334
Nicholls, Maggie, 179, 271
Nickerl, Karin, 194
Nico, 19, 71, 358, 557
Nielsen, Rudi, 283
Niemen, Czeslaw, 134, 136
Nikamo, Vladimir, 94, 306
Nimrod, 190
Nine Inch Nails, 537
Nishikubo, Y., 389
Nits, The 268, 608
NLC, 641
Noco Music, 647
Nocturnal Emissions, 381
Node, 599
Noppeney, Cristoph "Nops", 147
Nordholt, Dick Schulte, 267
Norwid, Cyprian, 134
Nosferatu, 235
Notes, 394, 432, 463, 465, 473, 489, 552, 593
Nouvelles Lectures Cosmopolites, 641
Nova [Holland], 509
Nova [Italy], 180

Index

Novalis, 158
Now, 650
Nuberu, 377
Numan, Gary, 342
Numero Uno Records, 184
Nursery, 190
NY Gong, 196, 623
Nya Ljudbolaget, 366
NYL, 190

O Terco, 493
O'Reilly, Hot Thumbs, 99
Oberheim synthesizers, 437, 526
Obermeier, Uschi, 613
Occasional Orchestra, 179
Occasional Swing Combo, 253
Ocean, 190
Ocharinah, 190, 212
Octopus, 159
Oddsize Records, 553
Odeurs, 327, 536
Odyssey, 190
Oedipe, 190
Ofarim, Esther, 676
Offering, 432, 465, 540, 622
Officer, 442
Ohi, Y., 389
Ohr Records, 20, 27, 54, 59, 66, 237, 248, 259, 498, 555, 581, 585, 589, 629, 637, 652
Ohta, T., 389
Olaf, 190
Oldfield, Mike, 71, 177, 197, 239, 245, 304, 389, 411, 423, 551
Ole Lukkøye, 643
Olivares, Rene, 471
Olmos, Claude, 114, 424
OM, 199
Omega, 149, 172
Omega Red Star, 172
Omniena, 425
Ones, The, 26, 497
Ono, Yoko, 19
Oophoi, 671
Opaline Records, 230
Opedal, Tormod, 597
Open Air, 549
Opera of Firenze, 281
Opus III, 190
Opus Records, 140
Orb, The, 562, 588
Oregon, 313
Organisation, 72, 237, 320, 589
Organisation 2nd of June, 85

Origo Sound Records, 507
Ork, 190
Orkestra, The, 179
Orme, Le, 80, 81, 183
Orquestra Mirasol, 200
Orridge, Genesis P., 394
Os Mundi, 585, 628
Os Mutantes, 492
Osada, H., 389
Osamu, 197, 413
Osanna, 79, 180
Ose, 327, 551
Ostemann, Flemming, 283
Osterberg, Ronnie, 94, 306
Ottawa Music Co., 176
Otte, Hans, 314
Ougenweide, 159
Outatune Records, 317
Outeiro, 377
Outer Limits, 425
Oxomaxoma, 380
Oz, 197
Oziemski, Piotr, 135

Pacific Glory, 190
Paganini, Patrick Q., 442
Paganotti, Antoine, 533
Paganotti, Bernard, 116, 327, 535, 551
Page, Larry, 612
Pageant, 425
Pagliuca, Antonia, 83
Paisley, Laurie, 460
Palace of Lights Records, 336
Pallat, Nikkel, 87
Pandamonium, 406
Panka, Peter, 89
Pankow, 482
Panther, 88
Pantingruel, 190
Papa Speed, 190
Papathanassiou, Evangelos, 80
Papen, Rob, 508
Pappalardi, Felix, 197
Pappert, Johannes "Alto", 90
Paradox Music Mailorder, 271, 635, 654
Paragon, 616
Paragon Studio, 262
Parasites of the Western World, 195
Parnell, Ric, 181
Parra, Alejando, 471
Parra, Claudio, 470
Parra, Eduardo, 470
Parra, Gabriel, 470

Parra, Violeta, 472
Pascoal, Hermeto, 495
Pasolini, P.P., 281
Pasquier, Jacques, 15
Passport, 155
Passport Records, 91, 172
Pataphonie, 190, 271, 549, 647
Patterson, Alex, 562
Patterson, Archie, 8, 271, 513, 515, 517, 521, 633, 652
Pau Riba, 199
Paul, Mr., 496
Pauvros, Jean-François, 271, 281
Paya, Thiery, 649
PBK, 671
Peacock, Annette, 585
Pedersen, Niels-Henning Ørsted, 286
Peel, John, 266, 498, 546, 572, 591, 596
Pelican, 81
Pelloix, Frédéric, 532
Peltier, Michel, 536
Pembroke, Jim, 94, 304, 306, 515
Pems, The, 307
Pengon, Tomas, 223
Peracchi, Mirian, 496
Perea, Carlos Alvarado, 258
Pereselegin, Anatoly, 671
Perigeo, 171, 184
Peron, Jean-Herve, 52, 244
Perraudin, Claude, 551
Perrier, Laurent, 553
Pert, Morris, 388
Peru, 508
Peters, Steven, 336
Peters International, 79, 654
Petersen, Jurgen, 393
Petit, Roland, 474
PFM, 81, 107, 183, 495, 647
PGP RTB Records, 224
Phaidia, 425
Phew, 302
Philips Records, 83, 380, 479, 618
Phoenix, 241
Phonograph Record Magazine, 14
Phonogram Records, 118, 254
Picart, Herve, 547
Piel, Alex, 283
Pietton, Didier, 394
Piirpauke, 132, 268, 306
PIL, 302, 413, 483

Pilpoul, 190
Pilz Records, 59, 66, 147, 157, 237, 589
Pinaut, Jean Marc, 539
Pinhas, Richard, 120, 150, 160, 228, 270, 274, 321, 323, 409, 532, 549
Pink Fairies, 19
Pink Floyd, 2, 21, 28, 35, 39, 72, 197, 227, 267, 313, 340, 363, 370, 374, 381, 383, 386, 442, 450, 458, 468, 477, 486, 495, 509, 514, 519, 526, 549, 576, 580, 588, 596, 637, 641, 644, 646, 662
Pinkotecka Records, 391
Pinsent, Ed, 594
Piotrowski, Jerzy, 135, 136
Pirana, 81
Pirovic, Hugo, 485
Plan, Der, 314, 362
Plank, Conrad, 45, 48, 89, 147, 155, 228, 240, 261, 297, 448
Plastic People of the Universe, 15, 138, 167, 207, 250
Platon, Mauricia, 118, 423
Plesser, Andrew, 281
Poblete, Hernan "Piola", 471
Pohjola, Pekka, 95, 100, 101, 268, 302, 306
Poing, 190
Pole, 190, 550
Pole Records, 193, 320, 550
Polnareff, Michel, 422
Polydor Records, 51, 107, 158, 243, 267, 283, 326, 589, 607, 616, 682
Polygram Records, 478
Pond, 482
Ponsi Records, 269, 310
Ponty, Jean-Luc, 548
Pop Company, 389
Popol Ace, 81
Popol Vuh, 14, 43, 59, 63, 159, 360, 362, 498, 514, 555, 588, 611, 672
Poppy, Andrew, 671
Porta Westfalica, 222
Posseur, Henri, 33, 666
Potemkine, 190, 549
Potter, Colin, 592
Potter, Sally, 271
Pouin Final, 190
Pourcheron, Bertrand, 649

Povel, Ferdinand, 253
Powell, Baden, 359, 584, 628
Poyry, Pekka, 100
PPG synthesizers, 361, 526
Premiata Forneria Marconi, 81, 107, 183, 495, 647
Present, 395
Pressor, Gabor, 173
Primitives Group, The, 167
Prism, 197
Pritjatelji, 223
Private Music, 498
Prodisc Records, 193
ProgFest, 609, 624, 650
Progression Magazine, 655
Progressiv TM, 241
Prophesy Records, 4, 19
Provisorium, The, 141
Provocation, The, 607
Pseudo Code, 593
Psicodelics, 484
Ptose Production, 311, 321, 593
Public Image Ltd., 302, 413, 483
Puhdys, 483
Pujol, Jaume, 649
Pulsar, 190, 394, 449, 491, 549, 650
Pulse Records, 551
Pulst, Bernd, 89
Pump, 592
Purin, 190
Putti, Paul, 193
Pylchardd, Percii, 442
Pyrolator, 314, 362

Quatuor Vegh, 213
Queso Sagrado, El, 271

Ra, Sun, 109, 123, 369
Racaille, Joseph, 233, 273
Radar Favorites, 177
Radio Massacre International, 595, 601
Rae, Diana, 436
Rag Doll, 177
Rage Against The Machine, 537
Raghel, Anannka, 405
Ragnarök, 444
Rahmann, 191
Rahn, Eckart, 362
Rainbow, Jerry, 59
Rainbow, Peter, 52
Rainy Season, 644
Raison de Plus, 553
Raison Pure, 311
Raittnen, Eero, 101

Ramos, Decio Souza, 505
Ramses, 159
Ramses Records, 536
Random Radar Records, 177
Randy Pie, 159
Rather Ripped Records, 399, 515
Rattles, The, 126, 159
Raux, Richard, 111, 549
Ravn, John, 287, 683
Raymond, Xavier, 418
RCA Records, 72, 116, 164, 181, 285, 330, 589, 621, 682
RDM, 81
Real Axe Band, 160, 221
Rechardt, Pekka "Rekku", 95, 307
Recommended Records, 390, 396, 514
Recordings, 593
Red Balune, 177
Red Noise, 547
Red Shift, 595
Reed, Lou, 122, 157, 486
Reed, Martin, 592, 597
Reggio, Godfrey, 414
Reichel, Achim, 126, 159, 195
Reichstag, Eva Johanna, 310
Reil, Alex, 286
Reimar, Johnny, 284
Reininger, Gunther, 242
Release Music Orchestra, 147, 419
Remelink, Dick, 254
Renald, T., 452
Renaud, Alain, 536, 550
Rene Block Gallerie, 220, 259
Rennbahnband, 483
Renshaw, Phil, 318
Residents, The, 194, 195, 248, 483, 592
Reyes, Jorge, 270, 477
Rezende, Beto, 494
Rhino Records, 501
Ribeiro, Artur Andres, 505
Ribeiro, Catherine, 216, 219
Ricard, Alain, 649
Richard, Ferdinand, 271
Richard, Roland, 450
Rigaud, Jean-Yves, 118
Riley, Terry, 227, 246, 312, 340, 347, 359, 362, 401, 405, 516, 526, 558, 585, 651

Index

RIO, 174, 205, 258, 265, 271, 368, 395, 473, 483, 493, 594
RIO Art Rock Festival, 650
Ripoche, Michel, 549
Rizet, Jean Louis, 550
RMO, 147, 419
Robert, Alain, 489, 649
Robertson, Don, 420, 578, 687
Robinhood Records, 287
Robinson, Peter, 388
Robson, Frank, 102
Rock and Jokes Extempore Band, 141
Rock en Stock, 189
Rock et Folk, 7, 329, 332, 451, 548, 617
Rock In Opposition, 174, 205, 258, 265, 271, 368, 395, 473, 483, 493, 594
Rock Machine, 532
Rock Magazine, 385, 390
Rock Pas Degeneré, 616
Rock Station, 191
Rock'n Roller, 191
Rodriguez, Pepe, 378
Roedelius, Hans-Joachim, 77, 157, 219, 260, 268, 394, 589, 671
Roeder, Klaus, 73
Rogner, Falk U., 17, 503, 579, 613
Roland synthesizers, 487, 509, 565, 602, 668
Rolling Stone, 167, 266, 285, 522, 615, 653, 679
Roll's De Luxe, 191
Romadin, Mikhail, 666
Roman, Jacques, 450
Roman, Philippe, 450
Romby, Paul, 403
Romo, Arturo, 380
Rosas, Franco, 271
Rose, 191
Rose, David, 423
Rose, Maya, 678
Rosenbach, Ulricke, 259
Rosi, 60, 69, 629
Ross, Alyn, 388
Rosset, Renato, 181
Rota, Nino, 370, 466
Rother, Michael, 48, 77, 158, 237, 268, 448, 630, 671
Rough Trade Records, 318
Rousseau, 490
Rovescio Della Medaglia, Il, 81

Rowlatt, Mark, 257
Roxy Minette, 191
Royal Danish Ballet, 80, 286, 683
Royal Danish Theatre, 283, 683
Royal Philharmonic Orchestra, 254
Rozenberg, Gilles, 418
Rozenberg, Marc, 418
rrr, Moritz, 314
RTV Ljubljana Records, 224
Ruada Records, 377
Rugsted, Jens, 283
Ruins, 542
Rundkopfe, Die, 483
Rushton, Geoff, 592
Rustici, Corrado, 180
Rustici, Danilo, 80, 82, 184
Rybnikov, Alexei, 666
Rykiel, Jean-Philippe, 551
Rypdal, Terje, 81
Rzewski, Frederic, 312

S., Chihiro, 425
Sabates, Jordi, 200, 376
Sabina, Maria, 480
Sadistic Mika Band, 197, 198
Sadistics, 197
Sagrado Coracao Da Terra, 495
Sahara, 80
Saint D'Hondt, 191
Saint Exupéry, Antoine de, 254, 463
Salamandre, 191
Salmieri, Claude, 544
Sameyoshi, K., 425
Samla Mammas Manna, 175, 211, 365
Sandrose, 491, 650
Santiago Symphony Orchestra, 471
Santos, Paulo Sergio, 505
Sarasua, Jesus, 377
Sarkissian, "Loulou", 114
Sartori, Donato, 404
Satin Whale, 159
Sato, Osamu, 413
Savage Republic, 578
Savage Rose, The, 2, 282, 679
Sayu, Eiichi, 386
Sazo, Francisco, 484
SBB, 81, 135, 136
Schaab, Bruno, 55
Schaffer, Janne, 81
Schamoni, Thomas, 33
Scheisshouse Records, 237

Schell, Daniel, 186
Schenk, Josef, 318
Schicke-Fuhrs-Frohling, 159
Schittenhelm, Julius, 221
Schizo, 324
Schlotterer, Jorg, 87
Schmidt, Hildegaard, 362, 391
Schmidt, Irmin, 33, 296, 391
Schmidt, Walter, 380
Schmitt, Ghislain, 649
Schneeball Records, 221, 249
Schneider-Esleben, Florian, 43, 72, 76, 158, 237, 448, 589
Schnittke, Alfred, 661
Schnitzler, Konrad, 27, 219, 236, 259, 320, 361, 497, 571, 588
Schoener, Eberhard, 362, 363, 614
Schønning, Klaus, 518
Schönwälder, Mario, 671
Schoof, Manfred, 33
Schroeder, Barbet, 370
Schroyder, Steve, 27
Schulz, Klaus, 88
Schulze, Klaus, 14, 27, 43, 59, 67, 70, 81, 159, 197, 220, 228, 236, 239, 260, 270, 282, 292, 313, 323, 338, 347, 358, 360, 361, 363, 372, 386, 401, 421, 456, 460, 462, 467, 497, 499, 509, 514, 516, 518, 526, 530, 551, 554, 566, 571, 578, 582, 584, 588, 591, 614, 626, 655, 666
Schunke, Manfred, 158
Schwab, Sigi, 41, 249
Schwann Records, 219, 259
Schweizer, Irene, 54, 143, 419
Schwindt, Christian, 93
SCOPA Invisible Productions, 15, 207, 233
Scorpions, 43, 156
Scriabin, Alexander N., 661
SE, 269
Seagull Music, 469
Seale, Bobby, 286, 682
Search, Breakup & Build, 137
Second Culture, 251
Secret Oyster, 79, 287
Sectra Sonica, 200
Sedmina, 224
Seffer, Jeff "Yochk'o", 113, 117, 188, 191, 196, 332, 423, 549, 623

Segers, Guy, 215
Seguera, Javier, 379
Seidel, Wolfgang, 86
Seisme, 191
Selected Sound Carrier Records, 639
Semelka, Lesek, 140
Sensations Fix, 107, 154
September, 223
Serebrovsky, Vladimir, 666
Serfas, Dieter, 41, 503
Servi, 481
Seventeen Pygmies, 578
Sextant, 191
SFF, 159
Shakespeare, William, 474
Shakin Street, 191
Shapiro, Mickey, 20
Sharp, Elliott, 593
Shaw, Greg, 14, 522, 635
Shepp, Archie, 545
Shimizu, Yoshihisa, 413
Shocking Blue, 266
Showmen, 181
Shrat, 18, 503
Shreeve, Mark, 362, 592, 595, 596
Shrieve, Mike, 572
Shub Niggurath, 443, 553, 647
Shylock, 191, 491, 549
Sichtelmann, Kai, 86
Sidney, Tony, 171
Siebert, Jorg-Peter, 148
Silence Records, 210, 367
Silene, 191
Silent Types, 311
Silesian Blues Band, 136
Silly, 482
Silver Man, The, 441
Simas, Delto, 496
Sinfield, David, 336
Sinfield, Peter, 125
Singery, Patrick, 463
Sissi, 321
Sister Iodine, 553
Sivadier, Pierre-Michel, 544
Six Cylindres En V, 271
Size, 380
Skating Pears label, 413
Skrzek, Jozef, 135, 136
Skull's Crakers, 191
Sky Records, 157, 393, 445, 590, 638
Slamnik, 142
Slapp Happy, 52, 178, 196, 244
Sloan, P.F., 16

Sloane, 191
Smagus, 191
Smak, 223
Smash, 199
Smash, The, 447
Smiler, 191
Smyth, Gilli, 196, 623
Soarez, Jean Pierre, 213, 394
Socrates Drank The Conium, 79
Sofornkontakt, 602
Soft Machine, 121, 162, 227, 276, 273, 313, 340, 495, 546, 580, 616, 646
Soft Verdict, 593
Soft Weed Factor, 425
Soho, 191
Soler, Toti, 200
Solstice, 191
Som Nosso De Cada Dia, 493
Son, Ame, 547
Son, Pascal, 188
Soncna Pot, 224
Sonet Records, 287
Sonic Images Records, 598
Sonic Report, 593
Sony Music, 512, 518, 606
Sordid Sentimental, 322
Sosner, Rudolf, 52, 245
SOSS Records, 609
Sound Projector, 594
Sound Recording, 565
Sounds, 237, 442
Space Circus, 412
Spacebox, 144, 206, 221, 238, 419, 513, 582
Spacecraft, 405, 533
Spalax Records, 528, 558, 567, 590
Sparifankal, 221
Spector, Phil, 283
Speed Limit, 423
Spektar, 223
Spheroe, 191
Sphinx, 241
Sphinx Tush, 235
Spiegelei Records, 91, 147
Spielberg, Steven, 503
Spinrad, Norman, 328, 538
Spirit Free, 191
Spoon Records, 302, 362, 392
Sportouche, Thierry, 489
Spybey, Mark, 602
Stabmental, 592
Stachelhaus, Horst, 158
Stack Orientation, 391, 413
Staklene Perle, 224

Stapleton, Steve, 591
Stars of Faith, The, 286
Starshooter, 191
States, 191
Statos, Demetrio, 132
Steamhammer, 26
Steeplechase Blues Band, 554
Stehlik, 141, 170
Steitz, Ralph, 86
Stereolab, 588, 594
Sternenmadchen, 59, 587
Stewart, Ann, 444
Stewart, Dave, 176
Stinky Toys, 191
Stips, Robert-Jan, 266, 291, 606
Stivell, Alan, 81, 622
Stivin, Jiri, 139
Stockhausen, Karlheinz, 33, 52, 76, 152, 236, 260, 294, 344, 369, 374, 514, 589, 626, 666
Stooges, The, 2, 12, 34, 55
Stormy Six, 175, 200, 271, 396
Story, Tim, 671, 687
Strabach, Dominique, 471
Strange Sounds, 592
Strangers, 644
Stranz, Ulrich, 105
Strave, 647
Streetfighters, 191
Streetmark, 160
Streisfeld, Muriel, 115
Strobl, Heinz, 467
Strom, Pauline, 456
STS, 544
Stul, Marcos, 494
Stundher, 542
Suck Electronic, 358, 377, 461
Suck Electronic Encyclopedic, 377, 461
Suckow, Michael, 649
Suma, Kunio, 413
Sume, 81
Sune, Max, 200, 376
Suntreader, 388
Supersister, 266, 291, 442, 607, 620
Supraphone Records, 137
Surcosur Records, 377
Surface Noise, 593
Surplus Stock, 317
Surtel, Pierre, 219
Surya, 191, 424
Suzuki, Damo, 33, 77, 296, 515, 658

Index

Swedish National Symphony Orchestra, 255
Sweet, The, 156
Sweet d'Buster, 267
Sweet OK Supersister, 607
Symphonic Orchestra of Buenos Aires, 471
Synchestra, 435
Synex, 334
Syntasy Records, 528
Synthese, 191
Synthetic Pleasures, 460
System, 129
System 7, 562
Szajner, Bernard, 409

T99, 510
Tagliapietra, Aldo, 84
Tago Mago Magazine, 410, 593
Tahir, Amara, 418
Tai-Phong, 191, 549
Taillet, Michel, 192
Takahashi, Masaaki, 386
Takami, 425
Takasaki, Shizuo, 386
Takemitsu, Toro, 387
Takemura, N., 389
Tako, 223
Tamia, 444
Tamla Motown Records, 77
Tanaka, 198
Tangerine, 191, 549
Tangerine Dream, 14, 26, 43, 70, 73, 75, 81, 122, 144, 155, 196, 219, 225, 236, 259, 313, 320, 323, 339, 349, 360, 361, 363, 372, 389, 393, 456, 458, 460, 467, 486, 493, 497, 499, 509, 514, 522, 537, 555, 571, 577, 582, 584, 588, 591, 595, 602, 628, 652
Tango Luger, 311
Tangram Records, 537
Tapoica Records, 320
Taranis, 377
Tarkovsky, Andrei, 663
Tarot Band, The, 59
Tartempion, 213
Tasavallan Presidentii, 95, 101
Tavi, Liisa, 269
Tavolazzi, Ares, 132
Taxis, 191
Tazartes, Ghedalia, 271
Technical Space Composers Crew, 104

Teenage Head, 191
Teenage Lust, 191
Tegelman, Jussi, 151
Tegelman, Pekka, 151, 269
Teldec Records, 159
Telephone, 191, 323, 330
Tellah, 496
Tempano, 378, 397
Terpandre, 191, 491
Terreno Baldio, 496
Terrones, Gerard, 333
Test, 134
Tetines Noires, Les, 553
The End, 191
Theatre Du Chene Noir, 218
Theatre of Satire, 451
Theatro Municipal di Santiago, 471
Theoretical Girls, 195, 623
Thibault, Laurent, 112, 545
Thillaye, Marc, 486
Thillot, Jean Luc, 192
Think Progressive Records, 645
Third Ear Band, 313, 425
This Heat, 248, 271
Thomas, Chris, 198
Thompson, Robin, 388
Throbbing Gristle, 248, 273, 280, 394, 591
Tibet, Dave, 442
Time, 223
Time Machine, 644
Tinti, Richard, 359
Tloen, 142
Tobynation, 570
Toesca, Louis, 113
Tofani, Giampaolo, 132
Tojima, Toji, 425
Tokyo Times, 569
Tol, 377
Tolkien, J.R.R., 468, 581
Tolonen, Jukka, 95, 101, 302, 309
Tommaso, Giovanni, 171
Ton Steine Scherben, 85, 221
TONTO's Expanding Headband, 596
Tony, 379
Top, Jannick, 114, 123, 423, 543, 551, 622
Torgue, Henry-Skoff, 426
Torre, Denis, 496
Touch, 394
Toyoda, Takashi, 412
Trace, 255, 650
Traffic, 157, 297

Trance, 393, 429
Trands Jazz Rock, 191
Trans Europe Express, 191
Transform label, 429
Transister, 266, 291
Transmitter, 654
Treponem Pal, 191
Trepte, Uli, 52, 54, 143, 177, 206, 221, 236, 247, 362, 419, 513
Trettioåriga Kriget, 212
Tri Yann, 191
Triana, 199, 376
Triangle, 325, 422
Tribu, La, 479
Trigaux, Roger, 215
Trikont Publishing Company, 221
Trilobit, 142
Trio, 630
Triumvirat, 155, 582
Troll, 489, 647
Trombatro, 380
Trostel, Rolf, 361
Trova Records, 377
Truck Stop, 582
Truffaut, François, 618
Trülzsch, Holger, 63
Truong, Jean-My, 118, 424
Trust, 191, 323, 330
TSS, 85, 221
Tsurugi-no-mai, 425
Tucker, Maureen, 48, 67, 71
Turmel, Pierre, 322
Turuta, A., 389
Tuxedo Moon, 578
Tuxen, Neils, 284
TV Eye, 602
Twist, 282
Tyni, Pekka, 305
Tyni, Seppo, 305

Uakti, 504
Uber-Sakura, 425
Ueo, S., 389
Ulan Bator, 538, 553
Ulbrich, Lutz, 557, 560
Ultima Thule Records, 593
Ultimate Spinach, 14, 55
Un Certain Rock(?) Français, 228, 231, 593, 647
Un Die Spitzkopfe, 483
Unit 3, 425
United Artists Records, 5, 32, 40, 589, 611, 674
Uniton Records, 595, 597

Index

Univeria Zekt, 330
Univers Zero, 174, 186, 212, 271, 395, 466, 474, 493
Unnamables, The, 491
Uno, 80, 82, 180
Uppsala, 552, 647
Urban Sax, 191, 280, 403, 453, 548, 592, 651
Urbaniak, Michal, 81, 134
Urebe, John, 285
Urgence, 191
Uriah Heep, 40, 158, 173
Ursillo, Richard, 107
Ursini, Dezo, 141
Urus Records, 164, 550
Usami, K., 389
Ushioku, M., 389
Utopia, 25
Utopia Records, 116, 621

Vairetti, Lino, 80, 82, 181
Valdes, Juan Ignacio, 471
Valerie La Grange, 191
Vallicelli, Enzo, 82, 185
Vamp Records, 149
van Boeyen, Herman, 267
van den Broek, Rein, 253
Van Den Dungen, Jos, 508
van der Linden, Pierre, 255
van der Linden, Rick, 253
van Dijk, Michel, 254
van Eck, Ron, 266, 608
van Eik, Jaap, 255
Van Es, Ruud, 508
Van Fleet, Ed, 435
van Geest, Sacha, 266, 610
Van Hecke, Denis, 466
van Kampen, Huib, 254
Vanda & Younge, 81
Vander, Christian, 109, 117, 323, 329, 409, 432, 464, 533, 540, 547, 619
Vander, Maurice, 619
Vander, Stella, 114, 192, 329, 433, 622
Vander Trio, 544
Vangelis, 81, 323, 358, 360, 369, 378, 462, 467, 486, 493, 509, 516, 530, 550, 591, 619
Vanilla Fudge, 39, 429
Vanity Records, 390
Varga, Marian, 142
Variations, Les, 325, 618
Vartan, Sylvie, 422
VCO, 378

VCS3 synthesizer, 30, 228, 374, 536
VEB Deutsche Schallplaten, 481
Veit, Conny, 64, 87, 236, 674
Velvet Underground, 6, 12, 15, 20, 34, 52, 71, 168, 208, 244, 313, 448, 557, 580, 588
Venezuela, 397
Venturini, Flavio, 493
Venus Records, 638
Verdeaux, Cyrille, 233, 415, 527, 551, 687
Verdier, Veronique, 444
Vergsis, Eduardo, 485
Veronika Fischer Band, 482
Vertigo Records, 72, 105
Verve Records, 196
Vervenne, Frans, 608
Vesely, Oldrich, 140
Veuve Joyeuse, 191
Via Lactea, 258, 269, 380
Vian, Patrick, 551
Viana, Marcus, 495
Video Liszt, 327
Vienna Symphony, 33
Vigon et les Lemons, 422
Viklicky, Emil, 140
Villarim, Sergio, 496
Villaroel, Manuel, 424
Vimal, Richard, 551
Vinao, Alejandro, 668
Virgin Records, 14, 52, 100, 233, 244, 304, 373, 383, 423, 498, 551, 557, 562, 572, 587, 588, 591, 595, 653
Visa, 191
Visom Records, 506
Vivaldi, Renato, 484
Vivanco, Jaime, 485
Vivanco, Ricardo, 485
Vlotho, 222
Vocoder, 462
Vogue, 618
Voie Express, 191
Volcania, 191
Voldarepet, 381
Volkonsky, Andrey, 661
von Zamla, 365
Voorhaus, David, 595
Vortex, 191
Vos, Tony, 254
Vrolijk, Marco, 266, 607

Wace, Robert, 612

Wadenius, Georg, 305
Wagner, Adrian, 595
Wahnfried, 342
Walden, Narada Michael, 185
Waldron, Mal, 41, 249
Wallenstein, 59, 65, 69, 160
Walli, Hasse, 133, 268, 306
Walpurgis, 43
Walrus Records, 439
Wapassou, 191, 193, 548
Waring, Rob, 507
Warlliocks, 191
Warm Gun, 191
Warner Elektra Atlantic Records (WEA), 158, 424, 468, 478
Watt Records, 179
Waxtapers, 191
Webster, Ben, 286
Weeber, Pablo, 149
Weed, 235
Wegmuller, Walter, 59, 556
Wegner, Charles, 649
Wehler, Mathias, 69
Weidorje, 191, 212, 327, 551
Wein, George, 681
Weinzierl, John, 4, 23, 503, 613
Weise, Jan, 507
Weisse, Doudou, 329
Welfare State, 179
Wells Fargo, 191
Werneer, Rene Et L'Habit De Plumes, 191
Wes-Monzaemon Group, the, 425
Wesn, 191
Westbrook, Mike, 179
Westbrook Brass Band, 179
White Noise, 533, 595
Whitehead, Paul, 153
Who Put The Bomp, 14, 522, 635
Who, The, 10, 611, 666
Widemann, Benoit, 116, 327, 329, 539
Wiese, Klaus, 64
Wigwam, 94, 100, 268, 303, 306, 423, 515, 591
Wijtman, Henk, 267
Wild Horses, 191
Willems, Thierry, 394
Wilson, John, 435
Wintrup, 90
Wintrup Musik, 242
Winwood, Muff, 26, 326, 537
Winwood, Steve, 97, 537, 572
Wire, The, 594

Index

Wischnewski, Armin, 393, 429
Wishbone Ash, 156
Witthuser & Westrupp, 59, 146, 147
Wobble, Jah, 302
Wolbrandt, Peter, 90
Wøllo, Erik, 507, 687
Wonder, Stevie, 96
Wonderland, 126
Wood, Anthony, 594
Wood, Cher, 378
Work, The, 271, 390
Wumme, 245
Wustoff, Gunter, 52, 245
Wyatt, Robert, 120, 177

Xalph, 191, 553
Xhol, 144, 581
XII Alfonso, 553, 650
Xolotl, Bernard, 346, 399, 525
Xoxoa Records, 377

Yacoub, Gabriel, 191
Yakaa, 191
Yamaha synthesizers, 255, 437, 487, 526, 597
Yamash'ta, Stomu, 72, 197, 385, 388, 572
Yamashita, Tsutom, 388
Yamira-Micha, 389

Yasumura, F., 389
Yatha Sidhra, 129
Yes, 25, 45, 82, 140, 246, 411, 423, 435, 460, 492, 645, 651, 662
Yety, 461
YHR, 592, 654
YHVH, 378
Ym Stammen, 508
Yog Xothoth, 647
Yoshimatsu, K., 389
Young, LaMonte, 246, 313, 359, 526, 594
Young Flowers, 286
Youpi Trempoline, 191
Yu Groupa, 223
Yugoslavia, 223
Yun, Djong, 65, 674
Yvosky, Fernando, 397

Zaboitzeff, Thierry, 213, 394, 473
Zacher, Rolf, 25
Zackmoun, 191
Zagarino, Joe, 681
Zajicek, Pavel, 169
Zamla, von, 365
Zamla Mammaz Manna, 269, 271, 309, 365, 396
Zampol, Charles, 649

Zanov, 191
ZAO, 114, 117, 187, 191, 332, 423, 491, 549
Zappa, Frank, 6, 12, 52, 114, 227, 240, 244, 395, 550, 588, 645, 651, 656
Zardoz, 485
Zazou, Hector, 233, 273
Zed, 406
Zeleste Records, 200, 376
Zen, 377
Zepeda, Antonio, 479
Zeta Systems, 527
Zeuhl music, 542
Zig-Zag, 266, 317, 591
Znorko, W., 452
ZNR, 233, 271, 466, 549
Zodiak Club, 260, 497
Zoo, 192, 422
Zoom, 191
Zu Band, 623
Zu-Fest, 195, 622, 656
Zu Manifestival, 195, 622, 656
Zuiderwijk, Cesar, 267, 609
Zweistein, 237
Zwikker, Dick, 609
ZZ, 321

Book Credits

Editor..Archie Patterson

Associate Editor & Production Assistance.....................Robert Carlberg

Writers for the original EUROCK Magazine...
J.C. Allvin, Cyrille Amistani, Gerald Arneau, Art Zoyd, Julian Atkins, Jean-Marc Bailleux, Tom Bingham, Ivan Brantes, Harold Budd, Pascal Bussy, Dave Byers, Joe Carducci, Robert Carlberg, Pino Casale, Daniel Caux, Francisco Cruz, Janet Cucinotti, Peter Cutler, Denis Desassis, Dominique Diebold, Alexis Drion, Matthew Eastman, David Elliott, Wolfgang Fenchel, Scott Fisher, Dave Fuglewicz, Andy Garabaldi, Bob Giddens, Francis Grosse, Harald Grosskopf, Christian Grumbkow, Bernard Gueffier, Paul Hallaman, Peter Michael Hamel, Glenn Hammett, Russ Harrell, David Harrer, Robert Hay, Ollie Heima, William Hein, Stephen Hill, Steve Hitchcock, Milan Hlubucek, D. Houde, Alan Huotari, Georgette Johnson, Julie Johnson, Alain Juliac, Rolf-Urich Kaiser, Russ Ketter, Hazrat Inayat Khan, Doug Kroll, Reinhard Kunert, Michael Le Came, Legendary Pink Dots, Alex Lenard, Marvin Lewis, Dave Luhrssen, Dana Madore, Paul McHugh, Linda McLaughlin, Harald Mehl, Valdir Montanari, Manuel Montes, Peter Moser, Klaus D. Mueller, Jorge Munnshe, Gerard Nguyen, Nocturnal Emissions, Francisco Otegui, Neal Palmisano, Alan Pasternak, Archie Patterson, Jurgen Petersen, Herve Picart, Richard Pinhas, Patrick Plunier, Jeff Pollock, F.X. Projean, Mike Redmond, Jean-Michel Reusser, Jorge Reyes, Ferdinand Richard, Risiko, Don Robertson, Rock In Opposition, Angel R. Romero, John Saltzgiver, Mike Sary, Jerome Schmidt, Bill Sharp, Gregory Shepard, Robert Silverstein, George Spicer, Anne Steichen, Gorden Stewart, Neil Kempfer Stocker, Satoru Takazawa, Bruno Toneguzzi, Uli Trepte, Juan Villa, Paul Wilson, Bernard Xolotl, Henk Zweering

Translators for the original EUROCK Magazine....................................
Lois Bode, Charlie Miller, Susan Mollerskov, M. Nakafuji, Francisco Otegui, Kevin Shelton, Jocelyne Smith, Michelle Chantal Tuck, Jorge Wensing, Kevin Wilson

Cover Photo...Irmgard Pozorski
(Special Thanks Gilles Ypremain)

Cover Design & Layout..Wayne Stephens

Art & Photos for the original EUROCK magazine..................................
All Ears Music, Carlos Alvarado, Gerhard Augustin, Bain Total, Gordon Barbery, Vittore Baroni, Wilfried Bauer, Daniel Bernier, Paula Bethsebe, Tom Bingham, Brain Records, Buko, Dave Byers, Greg Cannone, P. Carre, Richard Castelli, Christophe Cheval, Cosmos Records, Sabine Crittall, Danielle Dax, Norm DeValliere, Gustav Dore, Egg Records, Pelle

Credits

Engman, EUROCK Archives, Margaret Fabrizio, Wolfgang Fenchel, Roland Fisher, Bob & Amy Francis, Bettina Fricke, Bruce Frauman, Marcel Fugere, Tomas Gilsanz, Harald Grosskopf, Christian Grumbkow, James Haley, Milan Hlubucek, Torger Houghen, Illusion Productions, Intercord Records, Tegan Javanka, Elfriede Johnson, Rolf-Ulrich Kaiser, T. Kamada, KDM and MG Archives, Ray Klinger, K. Leimer, Gille Lettman, Rudiger Lorenz, Love Records, Detlef Maugsch, Rick McMillen, T. Moreau, Peter Moser, Agnetta Nilson, Odile Pellissier, Irmgard Pozorski, Jimmy Pratt, RCA Records, Recommended Records, Michael Roden, Savage Rose, SCOPA International, Juri Soomagi, Bruce Sorenson, P. Thibault, Uli Trepte, Uniton Records, Wintrup Musik, Bernard Xolotl

Advice & Technical Consultation..........................Brian & Robin Romer

Special Thanks To..Linda, Aaron & Sky (Support and Encouragement for many years), Robert Carlberg (Making Dreams come true), Klaus D. Mueller (Long Years of music and information), Gerhard Augustin (Long Years of music and information), Gilles Ypremain (Long Years of music and information), Andy G. (Long Years of music and information), S. Flensing Hlanith (Help with PPU information),
And all of the subscribers who supported EUROCK since 1973

P.S..I must have forgotten someone, or made some errors or omissions, please forgive me!

www.ingramcontent.com/pod-product-compliance
Lightning Source LLC
Chambersburg PA
CBHW080401300426
44113CB00015B/2375